Minorities in American Society

Fifth Edition

Minorities in American Society

Fifth Edition

Charles F. Marden
Rutgers, The State University

Gladys Meyer
Bard College

 D. Van Nostrand Company

New York • Cincinnati • London • Toronto • Melbourne

D. Van Nostrand Company Regional Offices:
New York   Cincinnati

D. Van Nostrand Company International Offices:
London   Toronto   Melbourne

Copyright © 1978 by Litton Educational Publishing, Inc.
Library of Congress Catalog Card Number: 77-81809

ISBN: 0-442-23474-0

Published by D. Van Nostrand Company
135 West 50th Street, New York, N.Y. 10020
10 9 8 7 6 5 4 3 2 1

Preface

The situation of ethnic and racial minorities in American society is so fluid that textbooks rapidly become historical rather than contemporary. The Fifth Edition of *Minorities in American Society* is not only updated but also takes greater cognizance of the voices of minority spokesmen and attempts to convey the sense of their world.

Important recent trends include a revitalized neo-ethnic consciousness and identification and its politicization; the recurrence of black-white polarization and its potential spread; and the impact of the Third World consciousness on American minorities. New research, much of it done by scholars whose roots are in one or another minority experience, has helped correct formerly "dominant" assumptions and stereotypes.

The organization of this book has proven successful through four previous editions. Part 1 (Chapters 1 through 5) discusses major concepts under which dominant-minority interaction may be subsumed and analyzed. Part 2 (Chapters 6 through 17) considers the situation of specific minority groups. Part 3 (Chapters 18 and 19) examines social policy and social theory in key relevancies to dominant-minority relations. Each minority is discussed in the following thematic sequence: achievement of dominance, stabilization of dominance, decline of dominance.

We have, as in earlier editions, given much attention to the historical and contemporary situation of black Americans. We feel that this minority should receive disproportionate treatment in part because it is this nation's largest, still has a high proportion of members living in poverty, and has historically experienced the most severe and sustained discrimination. More importantly, however, we devote much attention to this group because the black challenge has led the way, stimulating other minorities to seek redress through the courts and to demand recognition for their dignity and abilities and an increasing role in making decisions affecting them. All Americans can learn a great deal from the black experience and especially from the era of protest that peaked in the 1960s.

We (and we are *all* ethnic) are facing new consciousnesses and new dilemmas that will challenge the creativity of all the peoples who make up our multi-ethnic society.

Acknowledgements

The authors wish to acknowledge the valuable help given them by the following persons in the preparation of this edition: Dr. Raymond B. Sakamoto, University of Hawaii; Dr. Rhoda J. Goldstein, Douglass College; and Karen Predmore Shell, Lecturer in Sociology, Rutgers, the State University.

Dr. Marden expresses his appreciation to his wife, Freda Wobber Marden, for her innumerable contributions in the preparation of this edition, ranging from creative suggestions to content, to editorial and secretarial assistance; and to his son, Dr. Philip W. Marden for his many contributions in the writing of the manuscript.

Dr. Meyer would like to acknowledge the stimulus and insight derived from discussions on identity by the participants in The Encampment for Citizenship, summer, 1976; and for the critical examination of the fourth edition prepared by her students at Bard College, autumn, 1976.

Introduction

This book was first conceived in the aftermath of World War II in response to a renewed interest in the situation of "minority peoples" of the United States. We had been through a war which heightened awareness of discrimination in American life. In fighting the Nazi ideology, America was forced to look at its own shortcomings. The labor necessities of war had seen the first national effort to eliminate discrimination in employment. The tragic and, to many, unneccessary internment of the Japanese had heightened awareness. The plight of the refugees and the greater involvements of blacks at a better level in the armed forces made it imperative that national attention be focused on minority issues so that the gains might be maintained and the mistakes rectified. In our first edition (1952), most minorities were still members of visible sub-communities with their own internal organization, leadership, and cultural roots. The first edition tried to present minorities primarily throught the focus of community.

The 1954 Supreme Court decision outlawing school segregation, together with the Court's other decisions making it clear that imposed segregation always meant inequality, began to undermine a long-institutionalized racial system of inequality. This legal decision was strongly resisted in the South. Thus our second edition (1962) perforce gave special attention to the conflicts this changed situation brought about: less attention was given to the minority communities, and at the time integration appeared to be the prospect for the future.

The postwar era led to a great development of interest in intergroup relations in the behavioral sciences, particularly those where ethnic or "racial" relations of a dominant-minority form were involved. Much research was undertaken in an attempt to provide a more extensive description and interpretation. Out of this also came suggested social policy by which change could be effected. In consequence, as we approached our third edition (1968) this broader base of available studies called for our giving greater attention to theories of intergroup relations and to the refinements of concepts. Of particular concern in this connection has been a developing challenge to previous theories of assimilation of the non-WASP (White Anglo-Saxon Protestant) ethnic and "racial" groups into American life.

During the 1960s the accelerating momentum of the black challenge to white dominance and the responses of white America to it became a major domestic phenomenon of the decade, and it continues to be of nationwide significance as migration of blacks to all the nation's large metropolitan districts continues apace. Even by the time our third edition (1968) appeared, the increasing militancy of the black challenge pointed to foreboding possibilities that required special attention. As we came to our fourth edition, the large-scale rioting of the sixties which had taken white America by surprise had diminished. But in urban communities with a large number, or a large proportion of blacks, polarization between blacks and whites had increased with frequent open inter-racial conflict.

In preparing a fifth edition we are responding to the growing impact of revitalization and politicization of ethnic identity. The response to the rapid development of a monolithic technological society with the trends toward increasing bureaucratization of all work, the geographic uprooting of people as centers of employment have shifted, have all contributed to a sense of unrootedness. Ethnicity has become one anchor for a deeper sense of identity and community.

This development has stimulated political action in the name of ethnic integrity. Much new publication and research is emerging as the nation confronts the reality of a pluralistic society. It is too soon to tell whether this emphasis will provide an evasion of the critical issue of "race" in American society. The common bond provided by ethnic consciousness, however, has brought into greater awareness the problems of some long-neglected minorities, both for the minorities themselves and for the larger body politic.

It is within this context that we shall approach the analysis of the situation of the major minority groups. Dominant-minority conflict arouses great anxiety in both the dominant group and the minority itself, and students of minority "problems" must recognize that conflict is one of the agents of social change. Conflict and competition of interest are part of the democratic process and channels have been established and must be expanded for the expression of conflicting interests and their viable and just resolution. Only when groups have been denied access to the structures of participation and power does conflict become violent.

Our concern is to write about the position of minorities within the social structure of the United States today. In a society as dynamic as that of America the situation of minorities is increasingly fluid. Therefore, where we can we will identify trends. Much conflict between dominants and minorities in the last two decades has been institutionally focused, as minorities have pressed for political and economic incorporation with equality of chances and equality of sanctions. Great gains have been made but the achievement is far from complete. In the end, however, the fundamental issues of dominant-minority relations will depend on how people in communities relate to one another, how they associate with one another, how they allow the dignity of difference.

The book is organized in three sections. After chapters that present the basic approaches to analyzing minorities in America, Part 2 discusses major minority situations today. A larger proportion of space is given to American blacks (1) because they are the largest minority in the United States; (2) because they have historically undergone the most severe discrimination, exploitation, and deculturization; (3) their situation, though improved, is for more than half of the group still severely deprived; and (4) the black movements of the twentieth century have served as a stimulus, and sometimes a model, for action on the part of other minorities. Part 3 examines the problems of ethnoracial politics, and provides an introduction to the way in which theory is built as it is related to a pluralistic society.

All writers have a point of view. Ours is that of the value of a democratic society; and that the welfare of the society as a whole, the nation or the local community, takes precedence over the special interests of any group; that a dynamic equilibrium in society depends on the consideration of the interests of all groups and their participation in decisions.

Contents

Part 1

Some Basic Approaches to Analyzing American Minorities

1

Minorities in the Modern World

> As linguistic, economic, social and cultural drives are integrated into philosophies of action by groups, it will become apparent that the . . . world is being submerged in tribalism and ethnic communities. . . . The crucial thing to note is that we have passed the point of no return, so that we cannot go home again. . . . By creating the most flexible situation we can, we may find the tools and techniques to survive the changes ahead. . . . There will be new tribes and new turf—in our lifetime.*

> By and large reality has been conceptualized in terms of the narrow point of view of the small minority of white men who live in Europe and North America. We must abandon [this] partial frame of reference of our oppressors and create new concepts which will release our reality, which is also the reality of the overwhelming majority of men and women on this globe.†

A generation ago, toward the close of a year's teaching in New York City, a distinguished British professor of sociology was asked his impressions of the United States. His first reply was a question: "What holds it together?" No doubt this comment was prompted by his observations of life in cosmopolitan New York City. His question reflected the assortment of different peoples he saw living in the city: white, black, brown, and yellow people; people of almost every nationality; Protestants, Catholics, Jews, and a long list of smaller religious groups, some native to this country, such as the Mormons, some originally foreign, such as the Amish. He would not have found such heterogeneity on Main Street, Northtown. But even then, and much more so now, far more people of the United States lived in cities than in towns and villages.

The nation has adjusted the relations of the different peoples so that most feel, to varying degrees, a common identification as Americans.[1] But this adjustment has not

---

*Vine Deloria, Jr., *We Talk, You Listen* (New York: The Macmillan Co., 1970).
†Lerone Bennett, Jr., "The Challenge of Blackness," *Black Paper Series,* Institute of Black World Publications, April, 1970.
[1]The term *Americans,* as used in this text, refers to citizens of the United States, exclusively. This common usage is an unfortunate example of this country's ethnocentrism because it excludes peoples living in the other Americas; however, we use it here to avoid repetition of the term "citizens of the United States."

been made without continuous tension and occasional overt intergroup conflict. As a part of this adjustment, a pattern of intergroup relations developed that ranks the various peoples on a scale of superordination and subordination. In sociological studies, those who rank as subordinate are called *minorities*. Those at the top of the scale, the superordinate people, are called *dominants*. Dominant-minority relations are conceived of as a status hierarchy based on differential power, not on population size. Turmoil exists today, for example, in Rhodesia, a nation where some 270,000 whites, mostly of English origin, control a society in which there is almost no participation in the polity and economy by over 6,000,000 black natives.

DOMINANT-MINORITY RELATIONS AROUND THE WORLD

The systematic study of intergroup relations, and especially the dominant-minority form, has been most extensively studied in the United States for several reasons. First of all, it has been in this country that the social science of Sociology has developed the farthest. Second, the heterogeneous racial and ethnic composition of the United States furnishes the widest field for exploration. But the dominance of a more powerful ethnic group over a less powerful group within the same territory has had an extensive history throughout much of the world since the fifteenth century. The search for a more general analysis and interpretation of dominant-minority relations as a logical consequence of the dynamics of the modern nationalistic world societies is attested to by the appearance of a number of comparative studies within recent years.

For the above reason, before preoccupying ourselves with minority peoples in the United States, we wish to provide a brief summary of similar phenomena in modern world history. Obviously, a brief analysis will have to omit many minor aspects of the areas we deal with and leave out some areas altogether.

Colonialism

The development of dominant-minority relations in modern history has resulted from two types of situations in which two or more peoples meet. One has been the invasion by persons from a more powerful nation of an area inhabited by less powerful peoples. This is known historically as colonialism. The other situation occurs when people dissatisfied with their condition in their homeland migrate to an established nation where they think they can improve their lot. The great non-English immigration to the United States is an example of this second situation and the resulting dominant-minority pattern is broadly the reverse of that resulting from the invader-colonial situation.

To a large degree, the establishment and maintenance of the dominant-minority pattern of interpeople relations derived from the invasion by European peoples of Africa, the Americas, and Southeast Asia from the early sixteenth century to well into the twentieth century. In the earlier years the main purpose of this invasion was primarily economic. Several of the areas invaded were either sparsely inhabited or occupied by peoples who were militarily or technologically less powerful than the invaders. Thus, the invaders were able to establish political control over such portions of these areas as they desired. In addition to seizing trade advantages, the Europeans began to exploit the agricultural and mineral potentials of the areas. For this they needed manual labor. Where the local inhabitants could efficiently be used for this purpose they were employed, and from this situation arose a colonial system with the relatively small number of Europeans in each area becoming administrators and rulers and, in terms of our study of relationships, a dominant group controlling the natives in subordinate status, using whatever force was necessary. Where the native population was either too small in number or culturally unable to efficiently be utilized, the dominant colonial Europeans imported slaves or sought out other, more sophisticated, immigrants.

The British, French, Portuguese, Spanish, and Dutch invaded coastal areas and islands of Sub-Saharan Africa, South America, and Southeast Asia. As Michael Banton writes, "By keeping the gulf between the races fairly marked and preserving white prestige, a relatively small group of people has been able to exercise close control."[2] According to Raymond Kennedy, the outstanding characteristics of this system have been the political and economic subordination of the native population; poor development of social services, especially education, for natives; and the color line with its rigid social barriers between the white ruling class and the subject people. Of these, the most important feature for the study of minorities is the last—the color line. Concerning this, Kennedy writes:

> The colonial code that dictates complete social segregation of the races is rationalized either by the commonplace assertion that natives are ignorant or unclean or uninteresting; or by the claim that they do not desire whites to become familiar with them; or by the argument that informality, camaraderie and, most of all, intermarriage would weaken the prestige of the ruling class in the estimation of their subjects. . . .
>
> The British colonial code draws the most rigid color line of all. Paradoxically, the greatest colonizers in the world are the most provincial in their attitudes toward strange groups and cultures. The British have been in contact for a longer time with more dark peoples than any other western nation, yet they hold aloof from their subjects to an unequalled degree. They refuse to associate freely or make friends with other races, and their exclusiveness had engendered a reciprocal feeling toward them on the part of their colonial peoples. The attitude of the latter varies from indifference to active dislike, but, except in isolated instances, it never approaches friendliness. Natives often express a grudging admiration for the moral rectitude, financial incorruptibility, and legalistic fairness of Britishers, especially government officials, in the colonies; but bonds of mutual friendship and affection are lacking. . . .[3]

Limited European acculturation of some natives took place, but aside from work contacts most natives retained their traditional way of life. Because of the small number and the frequently transient residence of the European administrators, miscegenation

[2]Michael Banton, "Africa South of the Sahara," in Melvin Tumin, *Comparative Perspectives on Race Relations* (Boston: Little, Brown & Co., 1969), p. 27.

[3]Raymond Kennedy, "The Colonial Crisis and the Future," in *The Science of Man in the World Crisis,* ed. Ralph Linton (New York: Columbia University Press, 1945), pp. 318, 320. By permission of the publisher, Columbia University Press.

was so limited that the number of "coloured" was small. Therefore, an essentially two-tiered stratification system based on race developed in these areas.[4]

Latin America

In South and Central America the ethnological picture was more complicated. In the highland and Andean areas, the Spanish, after defeating the Mayas, Incas, and the Aztecs, enslaved or peonized the native Indians and made them workers in the plantation system. In the lowland areas, especially Brazil, where they were unable to use the natives as workers, the Latins imported African slaves. As in North America, Indian lands were expropriated, the inhabitants were retired to the hinterlands and were highly decimated by disease and warfare. Two processes followed in Latin America that distinguish its ethnoracial history. The Latin Europeans tended to reside on a more permanent basis and continuous miscegenation produced a mixed racial population,—mestizo, in the Indian countries, mulatto, in Brazil and adjoining lowland areas. This mixed component formed an intermediary segment that, while still definitely a minority and economically only slightly better off than the pure blacks, was in a sense socially recognized as having higher status. However, after breaking their political ties with the home countries Latin American nations remained a two-class, essentially plantation society until the twentieth century.

The mixing of races over the centuries tended to prevent any such sharp distinction based on race as in colonial Africa and the South of the United States. The process went so far in Mexico that this nation became essentially a mestizo nation. Mexico's only "race" problem concerns the remaining rural pockets of Indians who still live apart from the main society in a traditional life style.

It is the areas where African genetic lineage is still prominent that degrees of color (black African genetic features) are one of several factors that influence the social status of a person in the general stratification system. But even here it is generally agreed that "money tends to whiten" and per contra "poverty tends to darken."

In the Caribbean areas, the general historic picture is that various European powers invaded and established colonial dominance. It is here that the small native Indian populations were essentially annihilated (bequeathing some genetic strains), and African slaves and their eventually freed descendants became the working class. Through the years miscegenation produced a proletariat of widely ranging degrees of colors. In Puerto Rico the skin color categories are recognized: white, mulatto, and black. But public opinion insists that while white skin color is preferred it plays a relatively insignificant role in social mobility and is not even important within class. There are, however, some evidences that preoccupation with color is not uncommon in the Islands.[5] (See Chapter 13.)

With the current political freedom of those areas where the socially dominant whites are few in numbers, there is a possible revival of "racism" between the "mulatto" and "black" portions of the population as a form of class struggle based on reputed race identifications.

---

[4]An ILO African labor survey including thirty-five states and territories south of the Sahara lists a quite small number of "coloureds" aside from the European "settled" states of Southwest Africa, Northern Rhodesia, and Angola. See Tumin, *Comparative Perspectives on Race Relations*, p. 26.
[5]Melvin Tumin with Arnold Feldman, "Social Class and Skin Color in Puerto Rico," in Tumin, *Comparative Perspectives on Race Relations*, p. 197.

Southeast Asia

In Southeast Asia the invading Europeans established political control to facilitate economic exploitation in their own interest and assumed the dominant-invader subordinate-native minority pattern: the English in Burma and Malaysia, the French in the Indo-China area, the Dutch in Indonesia, and the Spanish in the Philippines. In Southeast Asia, however, a new interracial situation emerged. Although native labor was used, immigrations also took place: Indians primarily entered Burma and Malaya and Chinese immigrated to all of Southeast Asia, but in large numbers to Malaysia (especially Singapore) and parts of Indonesia. Except for the Philippines these Southeast Asian societies became stratified tri-racially: the dominant Europeans, the immigrant races, and the natives. The intermediate rank position of the immigrant Indians and Chinese arose because they were in general more advanced than the natives in the knowledge and skills suited to technical and supervisory positions. For this reason their immigration was encouraged by the colonial rulers. In fact, Europeans favored and protected the immigrants from the animosity of the natives who resented their presence in the higher positions and the resulting favored status.

This situation is of considerable current interest because out of it has developed a "racial" problem which reached serious dimensions during the 1960s. While these former colonies were struggling independently to develop viable national sentiment, the position of the immigrant races, especially the Chinese, as numerical minorities became precarious. The most conspicuous example has been in Singapore. In 1948, the Malayan peninsula with Brunei and North Borneo became the Federation of Malaysia. But since 87 percent of the national population balance was Malay and 62 percent of the urban population balance was Chinese,[6] it is not surprising that the long-smoldering Malay hostility toward the Chinese engendered tensions resulting in serious rioting. As a result, Singapore, which had a roughly three-fourths Chinese population, seceded from the Federation. The fact that their ancestral homeland nation has become an increasingly powerful force in the world may, at least indirectly, eventually provide some reassurance to the Chinese in the other Southeast Asian nations, though most of the older generation is economically and ideologically deeply involved with Taiwan.

The British Commonwealth

As the period of colonialism came to a close, the former British colonies were, in general, better prepared for self-rule. This may well account in part for the goodly number of these new nations, the most important being India, who freely chose to become members of the British Commonwealth.

Further attention here is limited to the portions of this unique political federation where British people penetrated to the geographically temperate zones that became the new nations of Australia, New Zealand, and with earlier competition from France, our neighbor, Canada.

A major difference in the colonialism in these lands was that British people (as well as the French) settled permanently in these areas and actually worked their homesteads, as in our colonial New England. In both Australia and New Zealand, the British found preliterate peoples whom they were able to push out of the way.

---

[6]See Guy Hunter, *South-East Asia—Race, Culture, and Nation* (New York: Oxford University Press, 1966), p. 33.

New Zealand

The Maori in New Zealand fought the English invaders in the nineteenth century, finally losing to them in 1870. As in other similar situations, the native population declined, but after becoming essentially wards of New Zealand, the indigenous population began to increase again. Currently it comprises some 8 percent of New Zealand's about 3,000,000 people. Over 90 percent of the nation is of British descent. Auckland, the second largest city, with more than 70,000 Maoris, is considered to be the biggest Polynesian city in the world. Maoris are stereotyped by the white (pakeha) as inferior and are discriminated against, especially in employment and housing, but in recent years race relations have not been particularly antagonistic. While pakeha-Maori intermarriage is frowned upon by whites, in recent years it has nevertheless been substantial. Thompson in 1963 made the point that "the tendency for those of mixed Maori-pakeha parentage to opt for identification with the Maori group certainly suggests an absence of gross discrimination."[7] The urban-dwelling Maori are highly acculturated to Western society, and their former tribal culture is essentially dying out. The remaining vestiges are found in rural, essentially all-Maori, villages.

Australia

In Australia, the indigenous population proved no obstacle to British settlers. Many have been integrated into Australian society. Others have persisted in traditional life patterns in arid sections of the country. The Tasmanian natives, however, did put up a fight, which was settled eventually by the complete annihilation of the natives by the British. The policy of limiting immigration to Caucasians has only avoided any more "race" problems, but it has also limited the potential economic development of the nation because of the resultant inadequate labor manpower. Advertisements such as "Australia Wants You" were at one time placed in United States "want ads." However, the rising power of Communist China has caused Australia to reconsider its former superior attitude toward Asians. It has begun to admit small numbers of Japanese and to ally itself with the non-communist Asian nations politically.[8]

Canada

The ethnoracial history of Canada is more complicated. The history of Canadian-Indian relations broadly parallels that of the United States with about the same results in low status and welfare for Indians under the wardship of the federal government. While, in general, the national policy of Canada has been to keep it a white man's country, it did not prevent some migration of blacks so that in the larger eastern cities and in Nova Scotia there are conspicuous black population pockets. While integrated

---

[7]Richard Thompson, "Race Relations in New Zealand," in Tumin, *Comparative Perspectives on Race Relations*, pp. 186–187.
[8]The Southeast Asia Treaty Organization (SEATO) was framed (1955) to resist communist aggression. Members were Australia, France, Great Britain, New Zealand, Pakistan, Philippines, Thailand, and the United States. Disagreement over U.S. policy in Vietnam weakened its usefulness.

functionally into the Canadian economy, they occupy an alienated position in the national life.

Of greatest current interest, however, to the student of interpeople relations has been the development in Canada of what can be described as a "derived minority situation," specifically the relation of the French Canadians to their British fellow nationals. Here arises a minority situation—or at least so the French people think—derived from the eighteenth-century victory of one former dominant over the other. Up to this point, it is still true that in the distribution of wealth and class position, English Canadians clearly occupy the higher positions. How much of this is due to any strictly ethnic discrimination by the English sector and how much to the differences in cultural orientation remains an unsettled sociological question. The scientifically oriented cultural values of the largely Protestant English have been an advantage to them in the urban, success-oriented Western culture, in contrast to the rural, Catholic, humanistic-oriented cultural heritage of the French. It is clear that there is a strong feeling of superiority on the part of the English toward the French. Whether this biethnic division is a true dominant-minority situation, it has been and still continues to be a type of interpeople division that is a national problem periodically creating crises.

Following the increasing militancy of the French in recent years, the federal government is now officially bilingual. In 1976, the province of Quebec, where the French Canadians constitute a large majority but hold disproportionally lower economic positions, elected a French Provincial premier whose party platform was committed to independence. Since the federal government opposes this, Canada faces a serious political crisis.[9]

England: The Mother Country

During the nineteenth century and up to the end of World War II in Great Britain itself, interethnic relations were not a significant aspect of British society, in part because it was so highly homogeneous. While there were residing in London peoples from all parts of the world, the numbers of each ethnic group were small. As Banton put it, "in the past English society has been relatively successful in admitting small numbers of newcomers and making Englishmen of them."[10] Up to the current period, the non-British residents were looked upon as *culturally different immigrants* without much thought of color difference, even when clearly visible. But the substantial migration of Jamaican blacks as well as a stepped up immigration of Asian and African commonwealth citizens has caused, in Banton's words, "grounds for thinking that since the middle of the 1950s, the *immigration* perspective has become less appropriate to studies of the British scene and the *racial* one more so."[11]

While there is no official discrimination against any non-British group residing in England, there is no question that the colored peoples are discriminated against, especially in housing and occupation, as an official government survey has documented. Despite clear white disapproval there has been a substantial amount of West Indian-

---

[9]Rene Levesque, the Premier, in an address to the Economic Club of New York, made an eloquent espousal of Quebec's desire for independence. See James Reston, "Quebec's Challenge to the U.S.," *The New York Times*, Jan. 26, 1977, p. A 23.
[10]Michael Banton, *Race Relations* (New York: Basic Books, 1967), p. 373.
[11]*Ibid.*, p. 384. Italics ours.

white intermarriage. Faced with accelerating white concern at the mounting immigration, the Commonwealth Immigration Act came into effect in 1962 and has reduced immigration.

In the 1970s the colored population in England reached about one and a half million
people, nearly half of whom are of West Indian descent. Despite the limitations placed
on future immigration, the adjustment of English-colored immigrant relations remains
a serious problem.

The Decline of Political Colonialism

Political colonialism had virtually disappeared by 1976 as the colonial nations gave
up their control and each colony achieved political independence, became a nation, and
was usually recognized as such by the United Nations. However, the matter of what to
do about the many vested corporate interests from the former colonial nations
remained. Theoretically, they could be confiscated by the governments of the new nations. On the other hand, the native population generally lacked the professional and
managerial skills to operate economic enterprises. While many of the dominants fled to
their homelands, the new nations permitted, and in some cases encouraged, the former
colonial personnel to continue their administration and some amicable negotiations
concerning control and ownership took place.

In 1975 Portugal granted independence to Mozambique and Angola. Angolan independence was followed by bitter rivalry among native factions for political control. The
entrance of a Cuban military force (presumably engineered by the Soviet Union)
resulted in a victory for the leftist factions.

Three other critical situations where native opposition to white dominance became
violent in the 1970s occurred in Namibia (South-West Africa), Rhodesia, and the Union
of South Africa.

South Africa

Next to the United States the Republic of South Africa has the most complex interpeople composition of any nation in the world. Compared to the United States, however,
its current interracial pattern is far more specifically defined, and might be
characterized as relatively stable rather than in flux. The racially dominant position of
the slightly less than one-fifth of the Republic's white population over the four-fifths
who are nonwhite is firmly entrenched. The white population itself is divided about 6 to
4 between the Afrikaner (Dutch descended) and the English, along with a small Jewish
population. In a broad status ranking, the English, with higher economic level, rated
above the Afrikaners who have, however, since 1948 held political control. As van den
Berghe writes:

> The following basic aims and principles of "race policy" have been shared
> by all South African governments since Union:
> 1. The maintenance of paternalistic White domination.
> 2. Racial segregation and discrimination, wherever there was any threat
>   of equality or competition between Whites and non-Whites.

3. The perpetual subjugation of non-Europeans, and particularly Africans, as a politically powerless and economically exploitable group.[12]

Of the Republic's 25,470,000 population (1975), the 81 percent nonwhites include 3 percent Asians (Indians), 10 percent colored (mixed white-African), and 68 percent Africans (mostly Bantus). Since it is the Africans who prompt the rigid race-caste system, we shall pass over the other two groups except to point out that the operation of the official *apartheid* system did not improve the slight advantage they formerly had over the Bantus.

South Africa's racial policy, *apartheid* (apartness), has two main thrusts: (1) the native area reserve plan (homelands) and (2) maximum possible segregation of those nonwhites who live in white areas. The Bantu homestead areas comprise only 13 percent of South Africa's land and these areas do not have the rich natural resources of the white areas. Thus it is obvious that the larger part of the 18,600,000 natives will have to continue to reside in and earn their livelihood in white areas. In fact, they are needed to fill the requirements of menial labor below the level of skilled labor. Natives are not permitted to belong to unions and when of necessity they are employed in the same level of jobs as whites they are paid less. The small Bantu middle class gains its living providing professional and other services to the local black population.

Among the numerous practical hardships suffered by Bantus, those living in white areas are being increasingly forced to live in separate sections built on the outskirts of the cities from which they must travel long distances to their work. They are separated from their families when working in white areas. In addition, natives must have in their possession at all times a passbook in which their officially determined racial status is clearly indicated.

The enforcement of this system, probably the most ingenious, rigid racial subordination ever devised short of outright slavery, is an economic burden on the entire national economy. Despite this, South Africa is a relatively affluent nation with most of its income (beyond that needed to keep the Bantu alive and subordinated) going to the whites. In summarizing the situation in the mid-1960s, we draw upon van den Berghe.[13]

> South Africa is held together in a condition of "static equilibrium" through a grim mixture of political coercions and economic interdependence. However exploited the Africans are, they depend for sheer physical survival on Wage employment in the money economy. To withdraw one's labor is to face nearly immediate starvation. The price of survival at the minimum subsistence level is exploitation, oppression, and degradation. But 3,000,000 people cannot indefinitely repress the frustration and fury of 13,000,000 people living in their midst. A South Africa divided against itself awaits its impending doom.[14]

[12]From *South Africa: A Study in Conflict*, by Pierre L. van den Berghe. © 1965 Wesleyan University, Middletown, Conn. By permission of Wesleyan University Press.
[13]For a penetrating analysis of the implications of South Africa's racial policy on its economy, see Pierre van den Berghe, *South Africa: A Study in Conflict*, Ch. 8, "The Economic System and Its Dysfunction."
[14]From *Race and Racism*, by Pierre L. van den Berghe. Copyright © 1967 John Wiley & Sons, Inc. By permission of John Wiley & Sons, Inc. The population figures are as of 1960.

Until the 1970s, South African blacks engaged in comparatively few protests against white rule. Since 1914, Van den Berghe lists about six industrial disturbances, strikes, and a boycott climaxed by a nationwide African revolt leading to a police massacre of blacks at Sharpeville in 1960.[15] An escalation of black resistance began in 1976 when several riots occurred, the most serious in Soweto, the black compound for Johannesburg. *The New York Times* reported bombings of six black schools in Capetown, January 13, 1977. The blacks' grievance was a government order that Afrikaans, the language of the Afrikaners, be taught in the native schools. A boycott of black schools had been underway for six months. In response to resistance, the government withdrew the order and announced measures to improve black education—grants for black teachers to attend universities and free textbooks for high school students.

Another major demonstration occurred in Soweto, April 1977, after the South African government announced rent increases of 40 to 80 percent for the black township areas. In this instance the police acted in a restrained manner and those arrested were soon released. Furthermore, the government postponed the rent increases.[16]

But apartheid remained substantially unchanged, although there had been token concessions to the blacks. The first black homeland, the Transkei, was given statehood and "independence" with limitations. However, most nations of the world remained cynical about the actual freedom involved and refused to recognize the Republic of Transkei.[17]

The slight improvement in the atmosphere of race relations reverted to normal following the death in jail of Steven Biko in September 1977. Biko, the popular 30 year-old leader of the black consciousness movement, was the forty-fifth detainee to die in jail. His death was widely thought to be the result of police violence. The event shook South Africa more than any single event since the Sharpville massacre.[18] The widespread resentment manifested by blacks and sympathetic whites created such a tense situation that the government closed down newspapers and suppressed organizations that were considered critical of its policies, and arrested many thought to be involved.

This sweeping repressive action was severely criticized abroad as well as within the country and created strained international relations between the Republic and many nations, including the United States. The Security Council of the United Nations voted to boycott the sale of arms to South Africa, a compromise agreed to by the African nations who had first advocated economic sanctions as well. For the first time, the United Nations voted sanctions against a member country. Despite expressing anger at the external criticism of its race policy, South Africa reacted by making minor reforms in some of its restrictions, as in the matter of the hated "passbook" law, by altering, though not relinquishing, it.

Namibia

Namibia, a former German colony called South-West Africa, was mandated to the Republic of South Africa by the League of Nations at the close of World War I. In 1966 the United Nations General Assembly declared the mandate terminated. However, South Africa announced its intention to continue its administration and has done so

---

[15]*Ibid.*, p. 286.
[16]*The New York Times*, April 30, 1977, p. 3.
[17]See P. J. Cillie, *The New York Times Magazine*, Dec. 12, 1976, pp. 34 ff.
[18]John F. Burns, *The New York Times*, Sept. 20, 1977, p. C 5.

even after a ruling by the International Court of Justice that she give up the territory. With reference to the 900,000 indigenous blacks, the Republic applied essentially its own racial policy. However, in the crisis period that has developed it appears that South Africa, recognizing the inevitable, is open to negotiation of changes in the status of Namibia. Former Secretary of State Henry Kissinger committed American diplomacy in favor of independence for Namibia.

Rhodesia

Rhodesia, a former British self-governing colony, severed its commonwealth status in 1965 because the British government was pressing it to accord more voting rights to the blacks. It is a country of 275,000 whites, mostly English, and over 6.4 million blacks, constituting about 95 percent of the total population. During the recent period of white rule the race policy has been much the same as that of South Africa, although not so formally systematized.

Rhodesia accorded voting rights to blacks on an income basis, but on a level so high that only a very small number of blacks could qualify. This led to the election of a few blacks to the legislature but did not threaten white control. A most critical race problem developed in 1976. Native uprisings together with threats from surrounding black nations reached such a peak that Premier Ian Smith agreed to negotiate with native leaders over some procedure to transfer the rule of the country to the blacks and to include the best terms possible to protect the whites. These efforts started through the auspices of the United States and Great Britain. But at the Geneva Conference on Rhodesia divisions among the native leaders, the influence of five neighboring black African nations, and the intransigence of Premier Ian Smith complicated the process of reaching agreement. Smith's plan for a transition to black majority rule within two years proved unsatisfactory to many black nationalists. In the face of guerilla warfare, shuttle diplomacy conducted by the British chairman of the Geneva conference attempted to work out a peaceful and orderly transition to black majority rule in Rhodesia.

The government of Prime Minister Ian Smith faces mounting difficulties, not only because the small government force is "stretched thin by the guerrilla's widening war, leading to a breakdown of civil administration" in some areas, but also because economic strains are reaching the breaking point. "The economy which shrank by 1 percent in 1975 and 3.5 percent last year is likely to sag further. . . ." An even more serious problem is the loss of manpower. More than 1,500 whites left the country in the past months and the exodus is expected to quicken, even though many have considered Rhodesia their paradise. As of June, 1977, there was speculation that the white regime was close to collapse.[19]

MINORITIES IN OTHER COUNTRIES

Israel

The Jewish people for centuries, prior to the establishment of Israel, lived in scattered groups primarily in all Western-oriented, temperate-zone nations. In each locale despite their successful adjustment, Jews as a group have retained a distinctive com-

---

[19]See John F. Burns, *The New York Times,* June 9, 1977, pp. 1, A 14.

munal and cultural identity. Being also always a numerical minority, they have been at times in most places discriminated against. Discrimination has manifested itself in a wide range of persecution: residential segregation in ghettos, sporadic pogroms, particulately in Eastern Europe, climaxed by the Nazi practice of genocide. Thus, anti-Semitism has been a constant phenomenon in the Western world. Jews have often been described as the universal minority in the Western world. In broad outline the Diaspora phase of Gentile-Jewish relations is well illustrated in the United States and is treated in detail in Chapter 16.

The latest development concerning Jews of interest to the sociology of dominant-minority relations arises from the establishment of Israel (1948). Here we find a historic reversal, with Jews as the dominant people over an Arab minority of about 10 percent inside the State of Israel. Of further significance has been the development in the relations of the European immigrant Jews (Ashkenazim) and the Jewish immigrants from Arab countries of the Middle East and North Africa (Sephardim), especially from Morocco, in which the Europeanized Israelis behave as a nonformalized dominant over the "Arabized" Jews. While the superordinate status of the European over the non-European Israeli partakes of something of a class hierarchy, the cultural distinction together with the generally darker appearance of the latter give this intergroup relation a dominant-minority form. It is more like our native dominant-South European intergroup relations of earlier days.

Up to this point, this survey of ethnic and racial relations has referred to nations with capitalistic systems. We now proceed to consider the two most powerful communist nations, the U.S.S.R. and the People's Republic of China.

Soviet Russia

In Soviet Russia the virtual destruction of small tribal peoples in Asiatic Russia, the forced acculturation of non-Russian peoples within the Union, the annexation of contiguous Baltic nations against their will, and the indirect forcing of other adjoining nations to operate monolithic communist systems as the price of maintaining an outward form of independence, suggest that given somewhat different opportunities and adequately superior power, socialist nations are not different in subordination of ethnic groups.

The interpeople situation that has gained the most worldwide attention has been Soviet Russia's treatment of its several million Jews. A communist regime by its very nature cannot tolerate true ethnic pluralism. In the early decades of the regime it appeared that persons of Jewish ancestry would undergo no discrimination if they would give up being Jewish. But the U.S.S.R.'s inability to Sovietize all of its Jewish people has in recent years reopened the question. The most that can be said is that the Soviet government does not act as "racist" minded as most capitalistic nations. As long as a Soviet citizen is willing to refrain from voicing in any form whatsoever—even artistically—any opposition to the policies of the day, the color of the skin or their hair texture is less relevant. However, there is considerable indication that the attitudes of many European Russian persons toward their Asian compatriots is highly condescending and that the carryover of long-standing anti-Semitism is still present in the populace.

The recent change in official Soviet policy to permit limited immigration of its Jews to Israel has implications for sociological theory of intergroup relations. Despite the minority position of Jews in numerous democratic countries, world Jewry has exerted pressure on the governments where they resided to request Soviet Russia to permit Jews to emigrate. This the Kremlin has found it expedient not to ignore.

People's Republic of China

Within a year of its establishment, the Communist regime of China annexed the independent state of Tibet, whose culture was quite distinctive. In 1959 the Chinese military suppressed a revolution by the Tibetan people. In general, Communist China is racially and ethnically homogeneous. Ninety-four percent of its population is estimated to be Han Chinese, the rest made up of small minorities. The small number of non-Han Chinese, however, occupy 90 percent of China's border areas. Lucian Pye finds that the leaders of the "Republic" are concerned about this in terms of national security.[20] Traditionally, the Chinese had considerable differences in religion, mainly Confucianism, Buddhism, and Taoism, but high tolerance concerning religious differences has been common. While the Communist regime supposedly permits religious freedom, it tends to discourage religion per se.

The Third World

In this book in general we will be considering race or ethnic relations within any one nation (including noncontiguous areas over which a given nation has political control). In the past two decades, however, a new concept has emerged, which we shall also keep in mind: the idea of a Third World, composed of the underdeveloped nations in relation to the advanced industrial societies as a whole, which, if ever unified, may be fraught with racial overtones. Of this Daniel Bell writes ". . . while the divisions between advanced and developing or backward nations is nominally *economic,* the passions behind the attack on economic exploitation often disguise *color, ethnic,* and cultural interests as well as political and ideological purposes.[21]

The significance of this splintering of peoples has been well summarized by Harold Isaacs:

> This fragmentation of human society is a pervasive fact in human affairs and always has been. It persists and increases in our own time as part of an ironic, painful, and dangerous paradox: the more global our science and technology, the more tribal our politics; the more universal our system of communications, the less we know what to communicate; the closer we get to other planets, the less able we become to lead a tolerable existence on our own; the more it becomes apparent that human beings cannot decently survive with their separatenesses, the more separate they become. In the face of an ever more urgent need to pool the world's resources and its

[20]Lucian W. Pye "China: Ethnic Minorities and National Security," in *Ethnicity,* edited by and with introduction by Nathan Glazer and Daniel P. Moynihan (Cambridge: Harvard University Press, 1975), pp. 489–512.
[21]Daniel Bell, "Ethnicity and Social Change," in Glazer and Moynihan, *Ethnicity,* p. 152. Italics ours.

powers, human society is splitting itself into smaller and smaller frag-
ments.[22]

THE ESTABLISHMENT OF DOMINANCE

This brief survey of ethnoracial relations indicates that dominant-minority relations
under a common political authority have been a widespread phenomenon in the
modern world. Analysis of its frequency can be explored by asking, "What happens
when peoples meet?" In the literature it often has been argued that the primary stage is
one of positive reaction (friendly, curious, economically reciprocal), as with Indians
teaching Mayflower passengers how to survive in the wilderness or, as sometimes
claimed, in the spontaneous reaction of small children. Whereas such a utopian picture
may have been historically sporadically correct under conditions where both groups
were equally at the mercy of the environment, this can hardly be claimed for contemporary people or contemporary children in a world of mass communication and high
technology. Each individual brings to new contacts the imposed patterns of the society
in which he has lived. Therefore, in the meeting of peoples of different appearance or
behavior, whatever positive attitudes may be spontaneously present at some level, it is
inevitable that these will be modified or negated if confronted with unfriendly
avoidance, or competition, or aggression, with the resulting psychological correlates of
dislike or prejudice. Individuals are motivated to survive, minimize pain, and maximize
pleasure. In order to do this they must be in groups. They necessarily internalize group
identity and loyalty. In short each *peoples' self-interest and ethnocentrism* is basically
circumscribed to its own group. This inevitably means that some degree of conflict
between peoples will arise sooner or later. (We shall discuss this further in Chapter 2.)

The salience of the conflict and its earlier adjustment depend on two conditions: (1)
that the peoples in the contact situation differ sufficiently in either culture or
physiognomic appearance (genetically determined racial features) or both, and (2) that
one of the meeting peoples is sufficiently more powerful than the other to establish and
maintain dominance over the lesser.

Types of Conflict Situations

Dominant-Minority Conflict.   There are a number of different types of conflict
situations. Since *dominant-minority conflict* is the subject of our book, we need not
elaborate upon it here, but will consider briefly a few other types of conflict situations.

Interdominant Conflict.   Numerous instances of two (or more) invading peoples
who dominate various sections of an area and its native peoples result in conflict
between them. Out of this may arise an intermediary dominance of one of these over
the other. Some examples are the English vs. the French Canadians, the English vs.
the Afrikaner in South Africa, and Protestants vs. Catholics in North Ireland.

Interminority Conflict.   We have treated interminority relations as though only two
peoples meet in an area. In numerous instances, the United States being an obvious
example, there have been several different peoples interacting in the same areas. Out of

---

[22]Harold R. Isaacs, *Idols of the Tribe* (New York: Harper & Row, Publishers, 1975), p. 2. By permission of the publishers.

this situation often develops a hierarchy of minorities in which higher-ranking minorities deal with lower-ranking ones in the typical (if diluted) fashion. Japanese-Filipino relations in Hawaii would be an example.

Miscegenation. Miscegenation often creates a substantial mixed racial group, which in turn becomes an intermediary minority vis-à-vis dominant and subordinate pure racial groups, as with the mestizo population of Mexico and as was formerly true of Cape Coloreds. In some such situations the ethnoracial system is closely correlated with the class structure.

Alternate Results of Conflict

In the early phase of interpeople conflict, three broad types of adjustment may arise.

1. *Elimination of one people by the stronger.* One group may eliminate the other and retain or take the area for itself, ranging from annihilation to pushing the other into smaller and less valuable or desirable portions of the area. Probably complete annihila-tion did occur in prehistoric times. Close approximations have occurred in historic times, as with the Tasmanians and the American Indians, particularly in the Carribean area. (This does not preclude the survival of some genetic strains of the annihilated peo-ples through miscegenation). More commonly, aboriginal groups have been highly decimated by retiring to less desirable areas but nonetheless retaining their identity under difficulties.

2. *Accommodation and coordinate pluralism.* Interpeople conflict may be resolved by some political and economic arrangement that brings about some common political and economic unity (functional integration) but where each group retains much of its social and cultural identity. Usually, this has involved spatial separation, as with the French, German, and Italian sections of Switzerland.

3. *Superordinate-subordinate accommodation* (dominant-minority pattern). In the modern period the most frequent mode of accommodation developing in the *early* phases of interpeople conflict has been the establishment of dominance by one and subordination of the other. Since it is this pattern of interpeople relations as found in the United States that is the main subject of our book, further analysis of this pattern will be made below.

4. *Assimilation.* We shall see that in *later* phases of interpeople relations the total merging of the dominant and minority, ultimately including genetic amalgamation, frequently has taken place. This then ends the dominant-minority pattern as far as a particular pair of different peoples is concerned. From what has preceded, it should be clear that assimilation as an adjustment in the *earlier* phase of interpeople relations is not possible. Of all the European immigrant peoples coming to the United States after nationhood only the later British immigrants did not undergo a period of minority status.

Size of Minority Populations of the United States

A large portion of the population of the United States constitutes persons who either are or have descended from peoples that at some time were minority peoples in the status meaning of the term. The processes leading to assimilation have advanced many of these groups, especially those with European background, into the dominant cate-gory. However, there still remains a substantial number of peoples whose racial, ethnic, or religious identification carries with it minority status with varying degrees of discrimination.

Since our interest is in the percentage of the various minorities in the population of the United States, we use the 1970 Census figures for the racial minorities and for the nonracial groups, estimated figures from various sources near that date. Several points should be borne in mind concerning the Census figures. For the first time the Census racial designation was a self-identification given by respondents themselves. The high percentage growth of the Asian peoples is partly a statistical artifact due to the inclusion of Hawaii for the first time in 1970, after it became a state. Also there was substantial immigration from Asia itself facilitated by the change in the immigration law opening wider the doors to immigrants other than Europeans. We can be sure that the numbers of non-European groups are now greater than in 1970, a fact that will be documented in the 1980 Census. Knowledge of what changes have taken place in percentages of all the various groups in the total national population will have to await the next Census. We can note that one special Census interim report in 1975 showed the black population in the United States close to 12 percent.

In the second section of Table 1-1 are listed those people who are still generally considered "minorities" sociologically on bases other than race. Here the sources as indicated are only the best available estimates, and in Table 1-2 these are included in the

TABLE 1-1. Estimated Population of Minority Peoples in the United States in 1970 and Growth Percentage for the 1960–1970 Decade

Group	1970 Population rounded per 1000	Percentage of Total Population	Growth Percentage 1960–1970 decade
1 Negro	22,600 (a)	11.1 (a)	19.7
2 American Indian	793 (a)	.4 (a)	51.4
3 Japanese	591 (a)	.3 (a)	27.4
4 Chinese	435 (a)	.2 (a)	83.3
5 Filipino	343 (a)	.1 (a)	94.9
6 Other (Asians)	720 (ab)	.4 (a)	230.0
7 Jewish American	6.000 + (b)		
8 Mexican American	5,000 (1969) (c)		
9 Puerto Rican (Mainland)	1,500 +(c)		
10 Cuban	625 (d)		
11 Other Ethics	xxx		

(a) United States Census, 1970. P. C. (1) - 131, Table 60, p. 293.
(ab) The *Census* footnote includes here Koreans, Hawaiians (aboriginal), Aleuts, Eskimos, Malayans, and Polynesians.
(b) Population estimate for 1970, *American Jewish Yearbook* 1970, p. 354.
(c) U.S. Bureau of the Census, 1971.
(d) *New York Times Yearbook,* 1971, p. 287.

TABLE 1-2. Estimated Total of the Minority Population of the United States, 1970

Total Population of the United States 203,212,000
  Total Dominant "White" Population (a) 165,000,000
  Total Minority "White" Population (a) 13,500,000
  Total Minority Nonwhite Population (b) 24,500,000

(a) From Table 1 categories 7, 8, 9, 10 are subtracted from 178,000,000 white population as given by the 1970 U.S. Census.
(b) A rough and rounded total of categories 7 through 11 of Table 1-1, the so-called "racial" categories.

total white population by the Census. Because we are concerned with all categories treated by dominants as minorities, we have attempted a different approach as indicated in Table 1-2 by a process of adding and subtracting from the pertinent figures of Table 1-1.

Table 1-1 shows that Negroes currently comprise slightly over 90 percent of the total nonwhite population.[23] The basic tables of the Census fail to provide the numbers of "white" peoples who are generally considered minorities. Thus in Table 1-2 we have included four groups and subtracted this total from the Census "white" population figure to estimate the total proportion of the American population in minority status. Such a procedure, as indicated in Table 1-2, raises the minority total to nearly 20 percent.

Suggested Readings

Comparative Studies

Asaid, Abdul, and Simmons, Luiz R., eds. *Ethnicity in International Conflict: The Politics of Disassociation*. New Brunswick, N. J.: Transaction Books, 1976.
Main thesis is belief that ethnic conflict will replace class conflict as the twentieth century proceeds.
Banton, Michael. *Race Relations*. New York: Basic Books, 1967. Deals with theoretical conceptions with descriptive material drawn from many areas of the world.
Issacs, Harold R. *Idols of the Tribe: Group Identity and Social Change*. New York: Harper & Row, 1975.
A coherent perspective on the fragmenting of nations in America and around the world. Written in excellent literary style.
Schermerhorn, R. A. *Comparative Ethnic Relations: A Framework for Theory and Research*. New York: Random House, 1970.
Primarily theoretical, the book draws upon interpeople relations around the world.
van den Berghe, Pierre L. *Race and Racism*. New York: John Wiley & Sons, 1967.
Conceptualizing race relations in two models, Paternalistic and Competitive, the author provides a chapter each on Mexico, Brazil, the United States, and South Africa as bases for final comparative analysis and conclusions.

Specific Area Studies

Glazer, Nathan, and Moynihan, Daniel P., eds. *Ethnicity: Theory and Experience*. Cambridge, Mass.: Harvard University Press, 1975.
The experience section of this book includes single chapters on phases of ethnic relations in various areas of the world each written by a different author. Areas

---

[23]Prior to this Census the Negro portion of the total nonwhite population has been well over 90 percent. Thus many studies and reports used the white/nonwhite dichotomy as near enough to reflect black-white comparisons. If the relatively greater growth rate of the nonblack portion of the nonwhite population continues, data using the white/nonwhite division should be abandoned.

covered are The Subnations of Europe (William Petersen), Canada (John Porter), a Caribbean case study (Orlando Patterson), Peru (Francois Bourricaud), Southeast Asia (Milton Esman), Uganda (Ali A. Mazrui), the Soviet Union (Richard Pipes), India (Joytirindra Das Gupta), and China (Lucian W. Pye).

Hiro, Dilip. *Black British, White British*. New York: Monthly Review Press, 1973.
This study of blacks in England conveys the feeling that the British will never assimilate blacks into British society.

van den Berghe, Pierre L. *South Africa: A Nation in Conflict*. Middletown, Conn.: Wesleyan University Press 1965.
An outstanding history and analysis of South Africa's race relations from the beginning of white-black contact to the mid-'60s.

2

Introduction to the Sociology of Minorities

The interaction between dominant and minority peoples in America, or in any other complex society, is an area of selected focus within the general problems of sociological analysis. Before presenting the historical and contemporary situation of specific ethnic, religious, or racial minorities in the United States, as will be done in subsequent chapters, it is important to clarify some definitions and some key analytic concepts. These are the tools of sociology with which continuities and changes in social relations (and, in this instance specifically, dominant-minority relations) can be understood, discussed, and assessed.

DEFINITIONS

What Is "Dominant"?

In the discussion of minority problems the dominant group is one that shares a common history, a common value system, a common language, and that is able to control sufficient economic and political power to protect and advance its own group interest over that of other groups. Dominant values of what is "right," "desirable," "good," or "admirable" are historically derived; their preeminence is established and maintained by custom, law, influence, and potentially, ultimately, by coercion. Dominants, like other groups with common beliefs and common history, assume that the survival of the group and its society depends on the perpetuation of their values. This universal phenomenon is called *ethnocentrism*. Because of the power and influence of dominants, subgroups that do not fully share their traits and their values are restricted, formally or informally, to a greater or lesser degree, from full and equal participation in the full range of the life of the society.

Before the rise of national states, dominant-minority relations existed between kinship groups (tribes, clans, "peoples") or religious groups where varying patterns of subordination or of "tolerance" were to be found. In the modern world the secular state has the military and legal prerogative to determine the protection and participation of the people within its geographic borders, and in many instances, within its extended political hegemony. The state is distinguished from the other great institutions, such as the family and the church, by its "exclusive investment with the final power of coercion."[1]

In our discussion, then, we shall consider a dominant group *as one within a national state whose distinctive culture and/or physiognomy is established as superior in the society, and which treats differentially or unequally other groups in the society with other cultures or physiognomies in order to maximize its own group interest.*

What Is a Minority?

The anthropologists Charles Wagley and Marvin Harris, in presenting case studies in the Western Hemisphere from materials that, in part, were prepared for UNESCO by social scientists of five countries, have arrived at the following definition of a minority, which we have adopted as the fullest and most appropriate:

(1) Minorities are subordinate segments of complex state societies; (2) minorities have special physical or cultural traits which are held in low esteem by the dominant segments of the society; (3) minorities are self-conscious units bound together by the special traits which their members share and by the special disabilities which these bring; (4) membership in a minority is transmitted by a rule of descent which is capable of affiliating succeeding generations even in the absence of readily apparent physical or cultural traits; (5) minority peoples, by choice or necessity, tend to marry within the group.[2]

This statement gives us five criteria that can be applied to the designation of a group as a minority in a contemporary society. First, to be a member of a minority is not only to be part of a social group vis-à-vis another social group, but to be so *within a political unit*. Second, attitudes of members of the dominant group toward minorities are bound up with a system of values that hold in lower esteem certain *visible* physical and/or cultural traits. Third, minorities are conscious of themselves as groups. In some cases group consciousness stems from cherished values and historical roots that are, in varying degrees, different from those upheld by the dominants in society; sometimes, however, group consciousness rests primarily in the sense of historically shared discrimination. Fourth, one is a member of a minority by ascription, without choice. The chief limitation of the definition we have cited is its failure to stress *discrimination*. Minority status is an imposed status, except for some separatist groups, and has validity only as dominants possess the power to sustain it. Similarly, we should prefer to state Wagley and Harris's fifth criterion the other way around: Minority peoples tend by *necessity* or choice to marry within the group.

---

[1]Robert M. McIver and Charles H. Page, *Society* (New York: Rinehart and Company, 1937), p. 436.
[2]Charles Wagley and Marvin Harris, *Minorities in the New World: Six Case Studies* (New York: Columbia University Press, 1958), p. 10.

What Is Visibility?

For a differentiated ethnoracial structure to exist there must be some perceptible differences among groups in either appearance or behavior that identify them to other members of the society. "Race" and "ethnicity" are popular terms that indicate biological or cultural differences. The origin, tenuous stability, and purity of "racial" traits is discussed at length in Chapter 4. At this point we are concerned simply with the various ways people are identified on the basis of their appearance and behavior. *Ethnic* is a term that emphasizes the cultural ethos (values, expectations, symbols of a group). Dominants as well as minorities are members of an ethnic group. Unlike a "nationality group," an ethnic group is a population that has preserved visible elements of a tradition without primary reference to former loyalties to a nation-state. The French emigrés who who came to New Orleans after the French Revolution were a nationality group. The present French Canadians are an ethnic group. Minority status may strengthen ethnicity, just as ethnic identification by self and/or others may contribute to minority status.

Biological Visibility

Physical Type. The traits that have historically been highly valued in American society are the "Caucasoid" bodily features. The preference derives from the bone structure, texture and color of hair, mouth formation, shape and color of eyes, etc. of the early settlers who were of North European extraction. Where differences from this type are perceived, as in the physical features of Asians, we speak of biological visibility.

Lineage. Lineage is invisible visibility. We consider it an aspect of biological descent. In cases of severe devaluation of minorities even a small proportion of minority ancestry is enough to designate minority status. American "Negroes" who are so completely Caucasoid in their physical features that they cannot be identified by sight are identified by the general knowledge of their "Negro" lineage. In periods where dominant elements in a society strongly desire to exclude minorities from privileges and participation, and when biological visibility is tenuous, rules of descent have been made official, as was the case for Jews in Nazi Germany.

Cultural Visibility

Language and Nonverbal Communication. The practice of speaking another language in the family or among close associates may serve as a mode of identification in both a derogatory sense for the dominant group, or in a sense of cultural pride for the minority. The language of gesture, facial expression, posture, and emotional tone all express cultural learning and vary from culture to culture. Different societies allow different ways of expressing emotional reactions to joy or pain or trouble, and these reactive patterns also are used to identify minorities in a derogatory way. For example, one study by Zborowski[3] has shown that doctors and nurses with Anglo-Saxon norms of

[3]Mark Zborowski, "Cultural Components in Responses to Pain," in *Social Perspectives on Behavior*, eds. Herman D. Stein and Richard A. Cloward (Glencoe, Ill.: The Free Press, 1958).

reserve in emotional expression often fail to understand and are impatient with the reactions of patients from non-Anglo-Saxon societies (crying, complaining, etc.).

Dress.   Although there are only a few highly coherent minorities that maintain traditional modes of dress—for instance the Amish, Hassidic Jews, and Navahoes (on the reservation)—dress has in the past been a major symbol of cultural identity. Nationality societies whose members have long since adopted the dominant modes of dress for everyday living often still wear the traditional "costume" to celebrate patriotic or religious festivals. Modes of hair style and ornamentation may also indicate a particular cultural heritage. Sometimes an insecure group will adopt a mode of dress as part of a struggle for identification, as for example, the Zoot suits that were worn by young Mexican Americans in the early 1940s (see Chapter 12).

Institutional Behavior.   Different ways of behaving in family, economic, political, and religious life often make members of minorities conspicuous. For example, filial obligations and parental authority may make a young person different in his group participation from his schoolfellows. A minority member with different religious practices living in a highly coherent Protestant community may in this sense by visible to his neighbors.

Associations.   An aspect of visibility frequently ignored in the discussion of minorities is what we shall call *associational visibility*. An individual may have no visible traits that would designate him a member of a minority, but he identifies himself by the group with which he generally associates, particularly in his most intimate contacts. While as a means of identification associational visibility is derivative from other bases, it accquires significance through long practice.

Overlap of Traits.   A minority is sometimes identified only by physiognomic traits, but usually there is an overlap of physiognomic and cultural traits. Sometimes there are only cultural traits, which may occur in any of several combinations. Perhaps only two minority groups can easily be fitted into a simple visibility scheme: the immigrants from the north of Europe who differ in ethnic culture without basic religious difference and contemporary American Negroes, many of whom are distinguished almost solely by their physiognomic features.

A useful clue to arranging minorities in a classification based on visibility may be found by considering the ways in which the dominant-status group has reacted to the visibilities involved. Proceeding in this manner, it can be observed that the dominant groups in the United States have conceived of minority groups in three ways: as "foreigners," as "colored," and as nonbelievers in the faith of the dominant group. While in most specific situations the dominants look on the minority in some combination of these three ways, in each case it seems possible to accord priority to one. For example, although the great majority of Italians are known to be Catholics, it is that entire configuration of cultural elements which compose the Italian "ethos" that identifies them most prominently. Again, while the Japanese are often thought of as foreigners, it is their physiognomic visibility that first comes to the mind of a person of dominant status when the word "Japanese" is mentioned. The leading element in the consciousness of the dominant in his conception of the Japanese is appearance. In spite of the fact that "color" is one of the less accurate traits to employ in "racial" classifications of mankind, it is consciousness of color that has loomed largest in the white man's concept of the other peoples of the earth. Wherever color difference is associated with other differences in the United States, it has always taken precedence over other factors in retarding acceptance.

Numbers and Concentration as Related to Visibility

If there are only a few dispersed individuals or families, whatever their physical or cultural traits, they are less likely to be subject to all the disabilities of minority position. They may be viewed with curiosity, tolerated, or ignored. When there are large numbers of a particular minority in a community, however, there is more likely to be a consensus of differential treatment. This is all the more so if they are forced to cluster in a given area of the community, or if they do so from choice. They are then not only visible as individuals, but visible as a segment of the community as well.

What we are dealing with here, obviously, is peoples who, in one form or another, are perceived as different from one another. If they had encountered one another in the first days of exploration, they might have had only curiosity about each other's differences, but in today's world superordinate-subordinate relationships have been established and historically maintained, even if they are now being challenged. Thus there is a customary expected set of attitudes, approved ways of behaving, definitions of self, and differential access to opportunity that have been "structured" over time.

What Is Social Structure?

When we use terms such as "the structuring of a situation" we imply a *continuity* in attitudes, definitions of ourselves and others, and expectations of behavior that extend beyond any particular encounter. Social relations in any stable society take place within a complex fabric of such continuities. They are governed by a set of *beliefs* within each individual or group about themselves and about the way they must act in order to obtain benefits from their action. In sociological theory, we say that beliefs leading to action are *values*. For example, the dominant society in the United States has had a major "belief leading to action," (i.e., to policy) that *work* is good for the character. There are historical roots for this belief deriving from the struggle for power of middle-class merchants and artisans against feudal privilege. Early settlers of the United States had to work to survive. The conditions of settlement in an underdeveloped, underpopulated country reinforced, by experience, the necessity for work in order to have any security. Obviously, on the other hand, many blacks in slave gangs, who could have neither security nor reward from work, did not incorporate this value, whatever they may formerly have felt in their lost African culture.

Clearly not everyone shares the dominant values however much the attempt is made to instill them by education or enforce them by power. In any multigroup nation like the United States there are also *variant* values.[4] These are values that are integrated into a traditional culture other than that of the dominants. For example, Spanish Americans of the Southwestern United States are brought up to view the roles of men and women differently, to consider time more loosely than is necessary for Anglo industrial society, to place family loyalty in priority over job loyalty. Under these circumstances, an indi-

[4]Florence Rockwood Kluckhohn, "Dominant and Variant Value Orientations," Clyde Kluckhohn and Henry Murray with the collaboration of David M. Schneider, in *Personality in Nature, Society and Culture*, rev. ed. (New York: Alfred A. Knopf, 1953), pp. 342 ff.

vidual adhering to variant values may find himself disparaged, misunderstood, and discriminated against by the dominant society.

Both dominant and variant value systems are sets of *official values* designed to maintain continuity, and to give a form for expectations. They are acquired hierarchically: that is to say, from people commanding respect in the community (parents, teachers, textbook heroes, and so forth). *Unofficial values,*[5] on the other hand, are concerned with present interest rather than historical continuity. They are acquired and supported by present experiences, which lack hierarchical character. (From the point of view of dominants, these are usually called *deviant values*.) Unofficial values may be of many kinds, but they always contain some elements that are in conflict with official values. They may be values held by an artistic group, a political protest group, or a religious sect. They can even be obsolete values clung to by groups whose interests are suffering in the face of change. Members of minority groups are often attracted to groups that adhere to unofficial values because it may seem harmonious with their present interest to protest or deny official values. This is especially true where a minority person has felt the discriminatory character of the official value system. It may also be a way of minimizing the discomfort of minority identity to form associations with a group not necessarily of one's own heritage trying to escape from or to reform the society. On the one hand, they may try to set up a small society of their own, as with the many communal experiments today. On the other hand, they may unite around a political philosophy or a political party committed to the overthrow of the existing structure. Upholders of the official system have frequently linked *unofficial* values with "foreign" and sought to mobilize antiminority sentiment as a weapon against those professing unofficial values. Thus early miners' unions were described as "drunken fighting Irish."

In analyzing a stable continuous situation in society, in addition to talking about the values of the members of the society, we also use other terms to define expectations and differentiations.

Norms are the implicit rules of behavior—that is, the group, *according to its values,* defines what actions are approved, or "good," or "taken for granted" (normal). There are norms governing, for example, the conduct of family life, economic life, political behavior, religious participation, and education. When these norms have persisted across generations we speak of them as institutionalized, or a particular configuration establishing some segment of social behavior we call an *institution,* such as marriage as an institution of family life, a contract as an institution of economic life, the state as an institution of political life.

Within these institutionalized patterns individuals carry out their lives. The performance of their functions from day to day is a *role,* and there are expectations (norms) of how roles should be fulfilled: the "loving" mother, the "reliable" workman, the "efficient" secretary are rubrics expressing some aspect of role definition. Failure to carry out the institutional roles in the manner defined by the dominant culture is a major justification offered by dominants for devaluation of minorities: "They don't *do* right." The explicit or implicit definition of roles in the institutions of society ensures continuity and a reasonable degree of order. On the other hand, this very function of continuity often makes for a lag in appropriate or useful adaptation to change.

---

[5]Milton L. Barron, *The Juvenile in Delinquent Society* (New York: Alfred A. Knopf, 1954), p. 203.

Status defines the relative position of a person or a group with regard to other persons or groups in the hierarchy of prestige. Honored positions in the society usually go to those who best fulfill significant dominant institutional roles. The overall problems of status are linked with the problem of social class (access to the opportunity structure), or caste (absolute barriers to selective types of social participation). We are interested primarily in the relationships between dominants and minorities with regard to their *relative* status. Though this is, as we shall see, intertwined with questions of social class, it can be considered a separate matter. While some actions unite dominants and minorities on the basis of class interests (as in some labor unions, political parties, etc.), more common in the past, and to a considerable extent in the present, is the alliance of dominants across class lines to keep minorities in subordinate status.

What Is Social Process?

All groups interacting over time go through phases of relationship. Sometimes these phases are sequential; sometimes, to an extent at least, they may be simultaneous. Some writers, as we noted in Chapter 1, have claimed that initial contacts are dominated by curiosity, mutual assistance, and silent trade and barter, as, for example, the first contacts between Europeans and American Indians.[6] But it is equally true that some initial contacts have been hostile on the part of one or both groups. One of the first American sociologists to be concerned with contacts between races and cultures attempted to subsume these under three basic modes of interaction: *cooperation, competition,* and *conflict.*[7] Sometimes these modes have been treated as a basic sequence, occurring invariably in this order.

Another way of viewing social process is not in terms of patterns of interaction as if they were isolatable, but as dynamic aspects of social structure. These processes can then be seen as *sustaining* (of the established structure), *differentiating* (of its components—in the case of minorities, differential power and esteem), *disjunctive,* as with open conflict, or *integrative,* as new elements are incorporated in and/or modify the established structure. These are also sometimes treated as sequential.[8] These processes may take place not only in the larger multigroup national state, but within subgroups as well, both dominant and minority. In our discussions of historical and contemporary situations of specific minorities, these aspects of process will be implicit.

THE ESTABLISHMENT OF DOMINANCE

Differential Power

When peoples meet and occupy the same geographic terrain, the outcome might theoretically be a pattern of intergroup relations of coordinate status and multilingual communication. We can see that something of this sort appears to have happened,

---

[6]Franklin Frazier, *Race and Culture Contacts in the Modern World* (New York: Alfred A. Knopf, 1957).
[7]Robert E. Park, *Race and Culture* (Glencoe, Ill. The Free Press, 1950).
[8]See organization of material in Tamotan Shibutani and Kian M. Kuan, *Ethnic Stratification: A Comparative Approach* (New York: The Macmillan Co., 1955).

despite differences of language and religious practice, between peoples of German, French, and Italian descent in Switzerland. More generally, however, the outcome has assumed a superordinate-subordinate form. This has been achieved by military conquest, sometimes through economic hegemony based on superior technology and/or organization, sometimes through superior numbers. Whatever the means, the underlying component is the use of force or the threat of force, by which the dominant group succeeds in establishing its own values and institutions as normative.

By far the most important factor in the establishment of American dominant-minority relations, other than the forced displacement of American Indians, is that English-speaking people arrived early in the greatest numbers, became entrenched under the British government, with British values and institutions (despite minor variants), and in time edged out the French, Dutch, or Spanish attempts to hold part of the terrain. The American experience has been in large part the attempt of the entrenched White Anglo Saxon Protestants (WASPS)[9] to maintain the preeminence of their values and institutions, status and privilege, in the face of the transportation or voluntary migration to America of peoples whose values, language, customs, and often appearance have been different.

THE MAINTENANCE OF DOMINANT-MINORITY PATTERNS

Law and Custom

Law and custom replace force to sustain over time the achieved dominance, and the initial definition of subordinate group is expanded to apply to other visible groups that may be added to the population. Force, or the threat of force, however, remains the ultimate sanction for maintaining dominance. It may be legitimately used (law enforcement) to ensure the preservation of established relationships, or, in periods of tension, force may be used in defiance of law.

In stable periods the law has preeminence, with *authority* to enforce. Thus political control of the state by adherents to dominant norms will ensure laws upholding these norms. In the creation of policy toward minorities, the state may, for example, grant or deny citizenship, as in the United States, where for a long time it excluded Orientals and defined limited citizenship for the conquered American Indians. From time to time in American history there have also been legal restrictions on the right of movement and of assembly. These have applied primarily to Negroes, slave and free before the Civil War, and to white indentured servants as long as the indenture system controlled the labor supply. American-born Japanese were confined in internment camps along with their Japanese-born parents in World War II.

Custom governs the whole web of traditionally appropriate behavior. When dominance is maintained in a relatively unchanging society, custom ensures the continuance of previously defined appropriate ways of interacting. These may even be elaborated into a rigid etiquette that amplifies the fact of dominance in all spheres of life. Probably the extreme example of this is the pattern of relations between whites and

---

[9]The initials WASP have now become part of common usage. The term originally carried an edge of derogation. We find it germane to note that WASPS are also an ethnic group.

blacks in the more traditional sections of the South. The common understanding of what is expected and allowable between the two groups governs almost every phase of contact.

In the American legal system, resting as it does on English common law, there can never be too wide a gap between enforceable laws and accepted customs. The problem emerges most clearly in the tension between local and state laws and federal laws: while local and state laws cater to the needs and attitudes of the people of a particular region, federal laws legislate for a much broader and varied populace, including many who do not share the regional or local patterns. Thus federal and state laws may and often do come into direct conflict.

Furthermore, the state plays its role in the subjugation of minorities not only through law and policy, but through its system of education. It presents historical models of esteemed behavior: the founding fathers and other "great men." Conversely, only too often, idealized subordinate roles are also presented in the official education: Pocahontas and Uncle Tom become the faithful protectors and upholders of Anglo-Saxon dominance. Public rituals and symbols constantly stimulate or reinvoke sentiments of loyalty, affection, and commitment to dominant values.

Categorical Discrimination

Discrimination—differential and unequal treatment by the dominant of the minority—is an essential feature of the dominant-minority relationship. Discrimination is categorical when it is applied to all members of the minority. For example, Irish immigrants arriving in Boston in pre-Civil War days found signs at places of employment saying "No Irish need apply."

Discrimination may operate in hotels, jobs, social organizations, admissions to schools, colleges, and universities, and so forth, wherever there is categorical exclusion or categorical limitation of numbers. Discrimination may also operate to create unequal rewards for work that is done, in wage differentials, or in access to promotion. It may operate in the sphere of political rights, thus limiting access to the ultimate channel of power or redress. Provisions like the poll tax have effectively deprived many people from their share in the political decision-making process.

Political. Because our Constitution guarantees civil equality to all regardless of race, creed, or national origin, political institutions have become the major focus for efforts to reduce discrimination. On the whole, great strides have been made, and political discrimination persists only in localities and regions where state and local laws obtain. The several problems of political discrimination that remain are generally subsumed under the term "civil rights." Segregation in public education, rights for Indians, access to tax-supported facilities, such as recreation areas, and so forth, are also within the sphere of political discrimination.

Economic. The problem of economic discrimination is more complex, since attempts at regulation by law can in many instances be interpreted as unwarranted interference with the rights of private property. Types of economic discrimination include discrimination in employment, either by announced policy or by private agreement, and also the subtler problem of the promotions and privileges available in certain occupational channels. Another type of economic discrimination is residential discrimination, where informal agreements of property owners exclude some minorities from some residential sections.

The economic sphere has been increasingly invaded by state regulation in the twentieth century, and legislation has barred certain types of economic discrimination in some places. Economic pressure through threat of boycott or unfavorable publicity has lessened discrimination in those sectors of business most vulnerable to such mechanisms: transportation, hotels, and retail stores, for example. Discrimination in trade unions is another type of economic discrimination.

Social.   Discrimination in the private areas of life is not subject to control by law and will be the last to disappear. Most amenable to change, even in defiance of local sentiment on occasion, have been the religious institutions, though this is not occurring without struggle. Country clubs, fraternities, private schools, and other voluntary organizations may set their own rules and will maintain varying degrees of discrimination depending on how strong the in-group feeling of their membership is. The final area through which discrimination can continue to operate longer is in the family and its attitudes, from social invitations through the spectrum of private life to intermarriage: All practices, formal and informal, that limit admission to groups, or situations that are primarily sociable or prestige-defining, are what we shall in conformity with common practice refer to as *social discrimination,* without particular reference to their institutional base.

Segregation

Segregation is an enforced pattern of settlement, or a pattern in the use of facilities that has the effect of categorically defining inferior status. Formal and informal restrictions may operate to exert these limitations. The dislike on the part of many dominants for entering into close contact with various minorities leads to residential restrictions and/or to segregation in the use of public services. Local law and custom may require a member of a minority group to enter a public building by a separate entrance, to work in industry on a separate floor, to use separate waiting rooms and railroad cars, to attend separate schools. Segregation may be viewed as either ecological or institutional in character. It may be formally established, or formally demanded, but it is usually informally enforced.

Segregated communities almost always represent a poorer average level of living with respect to quality of housing, public services, health, and education. Thus, in the long run, segregation is a cost to the total community. Where formal and informal residential restriction has kept in inferior conditions of life those people who wished to move out, the situation is analogous to the medieval *ghetto* and is indeed often referred to as such in sociological writing and popular discussion of minorities.

The Class Structure as a Stabilizing Factor

The American colonies inherited the British class structure based on wealth and occupation, with the significant difference that at its apex there was no hereditary aristocracy. Until the first decade of the nineteenth century, class position was demarcated by customary dress, and since, apart from Massachusetts, there was no free public education until the 1830s (and even later in new states), modes of speech also characterized class levels.

The urgent need of the new continent was for unskilled and semiskilled labor. Immigrants were recruited under the indenture system and subsequently under contract labor and finally as free labor to supply this need in the North, while imported slaves provided the agricultural and domestic labor force for the agrarian South. The vast majority of migrants (voluntary or forced) therefore started low on the class scale. On the other hand, individual improvement in economic circumstances and social status is a historical norm in the American tradition. Discrimination gave "native" Americans a competitive advantage in the upward climb. A Senator from Massachusetts in 1852 described the mechanism clearly:

> That inefficiency of the pure Celtic race furnishes the answer to the question: How much use are the Irish to us in America: The Native American answer is, "none at all." And the Native American policy is to keep them away.
>
> A profound mistake, I believe. . . . We are here, well organized and well trained, masters of the soil, the very race before which they yielded everywhere besides. It must be, that when they come in among us, they come to lift us up. As sure as water and oil each finds its level, they will find theirs. So far as they are mere hand-workers, they must sustain the head-workers, or those who have any element of intellectual ability. Their inferiority as a race compels them to go to the bottom; and the consequence is that we are, all of us, the higher lifted because they are here. . . .[10]

As larger numbers of "different" peoples came, minorities were forced to seek improved positions within separate subcultural hierarchies. In the caste situation of the antebellum South, parallel class structures occurred even more dramatically. Differences of prestige became established between house servants, skilled workmen, and field hands on the plantation, and between Negro craftsmen and unskilled Negro workmen in the cities. Such a parallel hierarchy persisted in much of the South through custom and local ordinance even after the legal position of slaves and freedmen had changed.

The overall class position of minorities, then, from the mid-nineteenth century until after World War II could be described by the diagram in Figure 2-1.

A classic study of stratification in a New England small industrial city elaborates this. Taking ethnic as distinct from "racial" minorities, it was found that in 1933 in "Yankee City" members of an ethnic minority were distributed over several segments of the sixfold class structure. For example, some Italians were found as high as the lower-middle class. They were thought of, however, as Italians and reacted to accordingly. Within each class level to which they rose, the ethnics were thought of as somehow not quite the same as the native members of the same class—that is, until as individuals they became assimilated. If one examines the status of ethnic minorities in the United States, the conclusion seems inescapable that it represents a combination of the hori-

[10]Edward Everett, "Letters on Irish Emigration," in *Historical Aspects of the Immigration Problem, Select Documents*, ed. Edith Abbott (Chicago: University of Chicago Press, 1926), pp. 462–463.

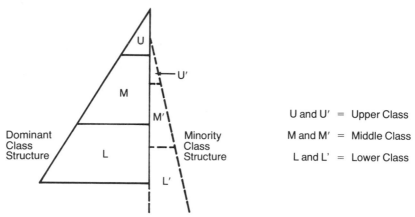

Figure 2-1   The Relation Between the Dominant-Minority Structure and the Class Structure

zontal and vertical principles of social differentiation. The test of the existence of a minority is to verify dominant behavior toward it within the same class.[11]

The Rationale of Dominance: Prejudice

As individuals, members of the dominant segment of the ethnoracial hierarchy are also members of numerous other social structures and possess other values—such as religious or ethical—that may conflict with their dominant behavior. To maintain a self-respecting image of themselves as human beings and to answer the criticism of outsiders (and maverick insiders) people of the dominant stratum need a psychological justification for their advantageous position. The rationale is accomplished by the development and perpetuation of prejudice. Whereas discrimination and segregation are actions within a system of institutional patterns, prejudice is an *attitude* unfavorable to or disparaging of a whole group, and to its individual members by virtue of their identification with the group. Prejudice may have cultural (value-related) and psychological (satisfaction-related) underpinnings, or both.

Prejudice as False Perception.   Sometimes prejudice is the result of a false perception of a minority as learned from the various socializing agents to which children and youth are exposed. It is probable that most dominant-status persons who consciously or unconsciously take advantage over minorities do so simply as a result of behaving in a customary way, without any personal or intentional hostility and often with limited experience of contact with the minority.

False perceptions are enhanced by *stereotypes*. A stereotype is an oversimplified generalization that emphasizes only selected traits of another group. It tends to evoke a

[11]See W. Lloyd Warner and Paul S. Lunt, *The Social Life of a Modern Community* (New Haven: Yale University Press, 1941), Ch. 5, "How The Several Classes Were Discovered," and p. 225, Table 7, "Class and Ethnic Groups."
Although it is now recognized, as theory of stratification has developed, that the "Yankee City" studies are classifications of "status" (prestige) rather than "class" (access to economic positions), we have retained the original terminology.

generalized reaction to any member of that group. To some extent stereotypes arise out of the tendency to save time and effort. As one author points out, "It is much easier to have a definite opinion as to the type of creatures women are, and behave accordingly, than to analyze and study each woman anew." What is significant in a stereotype of a minority group is that the selected traits tend to be those that emphasize difference from the dominant norm, and they tend to make up the whole image of an entire group, thus serving as an excuse for differential treatment. The assumption is that these traits are innate and hereditary and therefore that no change in the treatment of the stereotyped minority is warranted. Since newspapers and magazines and other forms of mass communication depend on popular approval for their sales, they often serve as reinforcing agents in the maintenance and continuance of such generalized popular stereotypes. They often help create a stereotype of the dominant groups as well. Minorities often have stereotypes regarding dominants, especially if they have a strong cultural tradition with different values from those of the dominants.

Prejudice as Personality Structure. Anthropology and psychiatry have called our attention to the fact that some personalities need to feel superior in order to have a secure self-image. In general, as far as we know from research, one can identify this need for dominance with an insecure person who has been brought up by very dominating adults. No community problems may occur if there are other outlets for his need to be superior—if, for example, the person may with cultural approval in turn dominate his children, or his servants, and if no major threat to his way of life occurs. When external circumstances challenge his way of functioning, his livelihood, his personal security, he may need to lay the blame for this at the door of members of the society whom he believes are of lesser worth—"aliens," "trouble-makers," "competitors." This is the person whose prejudices grow out of his *personality needs*. His prejudices develop with regard to any given important social stereotype that impinges on his environment. It may be a "native" in colonial Indonesia, an African in Afrikaner South Africa, a Japanese on the West Coast, a Jew in Nazi Germany. Some societies seem to produce fewer of this type of personality, while in other societies this type of personality seems to be more nearly the norm. No culture is composed *entirely* of one type of person or another.

It is these personalities that form the hard core of prejudiced citizens who resist change in the position of minorities and who refuse to surrender their stereotypes of minority groups. Persons who do not have such a personality structure may also have stereotypes that they acquired through learning in their environment, but they can relinquish them when given an opportunity for relearning. The personality type that needs prejudice to support its precarious self-esteem usually cannot modify it through learning.

Prejudice as Panic Reaction. A third type of prejudice may be brought into play in situations of generalized anxiety where persons are played upon by propaganda or mob psychology to share attitudes against a minority that they would not have imagined for themselves in a time free of stress and of which they are often later ashamed. The existence of dominant-minority patterns provides an outlet for frustrations that can under some circumstances be mobilized into temporary aggression against a minority.

Minority Responses to Dominance

When dominance has been established, dominants have in the past usually been able to define the appropriate responses to minorities in their positions of subordination.

Where differing traits have been very marked and the barriers to opportunity and self-determination have been very rigid, the pattern of stabilized accommodation has prevailed, as dominants have expected it and minorities have had no choice.

Stabilized Accommodation.   This mode of adaptation is one in which both superior and subordinate positions are taken for granted by the society. In situations of close personal contact a high degree of personal sympathy and understanding may in some instances develop between dominant and minority individuals, contingent, of course, upon *both* accepting the same rationalizations for the existing pattern.

The psychological costs of this system are high. For the minority person it may affect his perception of reality. Indeed, it was demonstrated testing to this effect by psychologists that was taken into account by the Supreme Court in the school desegregation issue. A stabilized subordinate position may create difficulty for a member of the subordinate group in handling inevitable resentment of prohibitions, with the threat of severe reprisal for any direct expression of it. Even in such a rigidly enforced system if occasional or repeated protest or revolt has occurred, this has been doomed to failure, not only because of the power and fear of reprisal, but because of the overwhelming difficulty of assessing the situation correctly for success. For members of the dominant group, too, there are greater psychic costs than are often recognized. The need to maintain such a closed system puts strains on the individual, especially in the period of childhood socialization, and often results in covert envy or sadistic exploitation of the subordinate group.

Acculturation.   Acculturation is one of the sustaining processes whereby minorities are incorporated into the dominant culture. The term, when used to define a process, refers to the changes in individuals (and, if sharing the same experiences, groups of individuals) whose primary learning has been in one culture and who take over traits from another culture. Dominants expect minorities to acculturate, at least to a degree. Since dominants, like all ethnic groups, assume *their* values and social system to be the best, and since some degree of familiarity with the dominant language is assumed essential to reciprocal communication, there is always some pressure for some acculturation even under severe restrictive patterns.

The process of acculturation takes place on two levels, often referred to as "external" and "internal." *External* acculturation is behavioral, in which material culture (refrigerators, cars, telephones, nylon stockings, etc.), everyday language, and secular (work, for example) roles are acquired. Key attitudes and behavior in the private spheres of life remain subcultural if acculturation is only external.

If the cultural element is paramount in differentiating the minority group, the degree of discrimination will vary directly with the degree of external acculturation. This is, however, often perceived with different priorities by dominants and by members of minorities.

While a substantial degree of acculturation is essential for a minority person to play his restricted functional role in the established dominance system, he is not always encouraged to be too ambitious in this respect. The purpose of the dominant system is to facilitate greater opportunity for dominants and lesser opportunity for members of the minority. While, of course, this to some extent applies to the class system (perhaps less so in the United States), the lower-class dominants have many advantages over the lower-class minorities.

The acculturation of many minorities to sufficiently assume their appropriate roles in the system often conflicts with the minority's own cultural system, as may be seen in their adaptation to occupational roles.

Occupational roles are key factors in the acculturation process. Improved occupational positions with the accompanying roles are much sought by minorities and are the point of interaction where much pressure and counterpressure is exerted. Conflict usually can be resolved only by minority members' learning new role behavior.

Although occupational roles are perhaps the most significant, other institutional roles are important also as focal points in dominant-minority relations. When the Irish entered politics the role of the political leader was defined by them in the light of their political heritage of protest and insurgence, the present necessity of vote-getting, and lack of access to the prerequisites of political leadership available to John Adams conservatives. The immigrant group created a new structure of urban politics and new roles in the ward boss and the local party boss, which brought bitter but not always successful opposition.

Family roles as defined by one group may be alien to the other. A Puerto Rican mother may quit her job and apply for public assistance because her daughter has reached puberty and in her cultural framework it is now the mother's duty to stay home and chaperone her daughter. A father, in many European societies, who sees his paternal role as providing for a good marriage for his daughter may be bewildered when a college scholarship committee tells him she is not eligible for scholarship aid as long as her dowry is in the bank.

For the dominants, fluent, unaccented language and performance of institutional roles according to dominant norms are the most important. The minority member may on the other hand view the material aspect of acculturation as paramount: the labor-saving device or the big car. Even under the condition of extreme barriers to minority participation in the full range of opportunity in the society, more recognition and respect has usually gone to the more acculturated.

Internal acculturation occurs where the cultural *attitudes* of the dominant culture have been acquired. If there is close congruence between the dominant and minority cultural values, internal acculturation may precede external, as with the North Europeans and to some extent the Japanese. On the whole, however, as our non-northern-European populations have come largely from pretechnological tribal or feudal societies, the other sequence has been more common. Behavior changes first, then dominant norms are internalized and become the assumption from which behavior emanates spontaneously.

The level of acculturation as a mode of adaptation in minority groups is typically generational—that is to say, the child of the immigrant becomes more acculturated than his immigrant parents and thus as a parent himself socializes his children to more of the dominant culture and less of the immigrant culture.

Minorities may, however, *choose stabilized acculturation and resist complete assimilation* as a mode of adaptation. This may be because they value a specific historic tradition of which they are part. Or they may feel that identity with a group that shares the same cultural tradition gives security. Or it may be their assessment that even with total acculturation all barriers to participation in the society will not be lifted for them.

In the past there has been great effort on the part of dominant "civic-minded" institutions and groups to aid acculturation. The dominant society has indeed largely succeeded in imposing cultural dominance despite the incorporation of some cultural products of minority peoples: jazz, spaghetti, canoes, etc. A current trend, however, is the revitalization of visible cultural symbols, rituals, and even speech patterns of minority peoples to proudly define for all others their cultural group identity. This is particularly true of groups who have suffered categorical discrimination on the basis of their "racial" appearance, where even complete acculturation has failed to remove all barriers to equal participation. Such groups—blacks, Indians, Asians, Spanish Americans—find unity in cultural pride and a rooted heritage out of which they seek power blocs to challenge the old stabilized pattern.

Assimilation. Throughout the period of the stabilization of dominance the expectation of the dominant culture is that "others" will either stay separate or subordinate or will be assimilable. Assimilation as viewed until nearly the close of the nineteenth century expected and allowed for *individuals* at all class levels to become part of the dominant society. At this time it meant that one must be "white," have acculturated externally and internally, speak English like a native (perhaps anglicize one's name), feel identity and loyalty as an American, and subscribe in behavior and feelings to the Protestant ethic. Indeed, in all but the very highest levels of society, the visible manifestation of Protestant affiliation was necessary. At the very top, men of wealth and talent might preserve a separate affiliation if their behavior and values were congruent with those of the dominants. This was more true of individual Jews than of Roman Catholics, except in local hierarchies (like Baltimore and New Orleans) where there had been old Catholic settlement.[12]

This was a possible adaptation for individuals, not for groups. As such it kept alive the expectation of mobility and success for the aspiring, and incorporated talents into the dominant structure. In this sense, *selective, individual assimilation* was a stabilizing factor in the society. The only *group* that was easily and almost totally assimilated in the nineteenth century was the British (not including the Irish).[13]

Attempts to assimilate sizable groups of "others" were first of all not possible in periods where sufficient continuing migration reinforced and kept alive old cultural attachments. In the second place, it would have aroused, as it eventually did (1880–1940), so much anxiety and apprehension on the part of segments of the dominant population that barriers which had not existed before would be erected against the complete acceptance of "others."

Nevertheless, although discrimination and prejudice increased for three-quarters of a century, the dominant society succeeded in imposing *cultural,* if not always institutional, dominance, despite the incorporation of some external, peripheral culture traits from the migrating groups.

The operating concept of assimilation has now largely changed in the second half of the twentieth century, as we shall discuss below; but this could not occur until large, sufficiently acculturated groups had brought great pressure to bear on the dominant segments of the society.

Marginality. In the theory of minority adjustment which assumed that minority groups moved through a series of steps to ultimate assimilation, certain groups were sometimes defined as being in a marginal *stage.* This referred to the fact that the direction of leadership and membership was toward the incorporation of dominant values and goals, emulating even if imperfectly dominant institutional roles, although "visible characteristics" of the minority and discrimination persisted. The group then took on a

---

[12]E. Digby Baltzell, *The Protestant Establishment: Aristocracy and Caste in America* (New York: Random House, 1964), p. 73.
[13]Rowland Tappan Berthoff, *British Immigrants in Industrial America, 1790–1950* (Cambridge, Mass.: Harvard University Press, 1953).

double identity illustrated by the self-designation of hyphenated status: "I am an Italian-American."[14]

Another way of discussing marginality is to see it as an *individual adaptation* to minority status. Robert K. Merton has defined the marginal person as one whose reference group (the group from which he takes his norms) is different from the group of which he is a member. That is to say, he emulates and strives to be accepted by a group of which he is not yet, or is only peripherally, a member.[15] Viewing marginality this way, it can be said to occur whenever an individual is abandoning the mode of adaptation that has prevailed in the group of which he is a member. This usually makes him, to a greater or lesser degree, an "outsider" to both groups.

Internally, the marginal person may suffer from conflict of values and conflict of loyalties. This may operate to make him anxious and to lower his efficiency in fulfilling the roles he is seeking to carry out. His anxiety may even keep him from perceiving the subtler aspects of role behavior in the group toward which he is striving. If he is able to rationalize his striving to the point where he suppresses or disciplines any conflicts in abandoning one group for the other, he risks being regarded as a renegade by the group he strives to leave and as an "operator" by the group he is moving toward.

His problem is often easier if he does not have to carry a double burden of class marginality along with race or culture marginality. Too often, however, there is this double burden as the minority member comes to accept the dominant American norm of class mobility. Since the institutional patterns of a culture are its guarantees of continuance, honored positions in the society go to those who best fulfill significant dominant institutional roles. People who have had prolonged subordination often have no opportunity to perceive or learn these roles, or feel they must reject them because they are impossible. Others cling to roles defined by variant value systems. Yet increasingly there is the rising aspiration for the benefits to be derived from improved positions, which leads to role relearning, role conflict, or role modification. This is where the real personal crises of dominant-minority relations occur.

For Baltzell, the marginal individual (as contrasted with the marginal culture) is the completely acculturated person who is still identified (sometimes by choice, though not necessarily) as a member by descent of a religious, ethnic, or "racial" minority. According to Baltzell's analysis, the top elite, nationally, can absorb a modest percentage of marginal men of high talent (bankers, federal judges, etc.) and does so, whereas the levels below, and to a large extent the *local* hierarchies of status, tend to persist in a parallel status structure.[16] The marginal *individual* challenges dominance by the successful competition for honorific occupational positions. This is possible in a technological or developing society so long as particular skills and/or abilities clearly contribute to the needs of the society at the decision-making level.

Where individual competition shows some degree of success, there has been in the past, and may persist, a tightening of *social* barriers against successful persons of minority identification or descent (however tenuous the minority tie). This may filter

---

[14]See Robert E. Park, *Race and Culture*. Baltzell refers to this (in *The Protestant Establishment*) as *marginal culture* without any implication of its being a stage in a sequence, pp. 62–70.

[15]Robert K. Merton, *Social Theory and Social Structure* (Glencoe, Ill.: The Free Press, 1968), pp. 290–291. In Merton's definition marginality may apply equally to movement between any contiguous groups, as for example, upward or downward mobility between social classes.

[16]Baltzell, *The Protestant Establishment*, pp. 62–70.

down from top levels and become not only social but more general discrimination for people lower on the status scale who fear that their opportunities for moving up are being jeopardized.

Marginal *groups* who have taken on enough aspects of the dominant culture to share its goals and have some frame for perceiving what means will help them achieve as a group rather than as individuals express their challenge to dominants in a struggle for legitimate or illegitimate power. This has been illustrated by the degree to which political organization depending on minority support and supporting minority interests in one period captured East Coast city politics and perhaps changed the character of large city politics throughout the nation. For a time city politics was linked with rackets and other nonlegitimate avenues to affluence, often attracting minority ability where legitimate channels were closed through discrimination.

Nonviolent civil rights efforts represent an innovating attempt to achieve legitimate power, in the sense that they exert pressure for the state to modify patterns of discrimination, for channels of economic opportunity to be opened, and for civil participation within the legitimate structure.

At another level people who have neither the confidence in nor knowledge of the legitimate channels will be vulnerable to spontaneous outbreaks of protest. If these become widespread (like riots spreading from city to city) it makes an impact on the Establishment. If this kind of protest is an isolated instance, it is usually ineffective. Sometimes it also retards the efforts of other modes of protest that seek to modify existing structures in a more sophisticated way. As a phenomenon of protest it is most often the weapon of the most depressed of the minorities, who are under the double pressure of severe discrimination and poverty, as with the Irish in the nineteenth century.

Nativism.   Any organized protest effort of any sizable minority group has the effect of creating *reactive* movements designed to legitimately or illegitimately restrain minorities. Conflict increases polarization of interest and *nativistic* movements on the part of dominants who seek to, and sometimes for a time are able to, increase discrimination and stimulate latent prejudice. The largest number of followers of such movements may themselves be (in the general sense) marginal, economically, socially, or even sometimes ethnically. This situation is likely to emerge and become even stronger if the total society is undergoing confusing changes, such as rapid industrialization, or urbanization, or war.

Dominant nativistic movements seek to maintain a particular historical value system and status as expressed in an idealized historical image. Polarization also gives rise to minority nativistic movements that reach for an idealized past as a locus of identification. The marginal character of adherents to such movements is clear as the image of the idealized past that they project is expected to include the benefits of the contemporary society, thus indicating the duality of reference groups. No Zionist, for example, sought a biblical society in Israel. Black Muslims have taken a great ethical, progressive, and "world" religion as the locus of their identity and combined it with a modern idea of power. The Garvey movement, which advocated the return of blacks to Africa, did not envisage return to a tribal society.

The processes of conflict and protest are of course *disjunctive processes:* they disrupt the ongoing social pattern. For those people who have adapted and conformed to the system, disruption in itself is anxiety producing. *Yet no social change occurs without disruption for some* (like the displacement of some people who are used to a neighborhood in order to build better housing for more people). Disjunctive processes are part of the ongoing social experience, and although they are often focal at a particular time, they do not preclude simultaneous sustaining processes, or integrative processes that grow out of the new demands on the society.

THE DECLINE OF DOMINANCE

The stabilization of dominance may become so embedded in the controls of beliefs, customs, and institutional roles that it can continue virtually unchanged for long periods of time, as with slavery in the South. When the whole society is adapting to general changes it may, for a time at least, undergo even more severe enforcement, as with South Africa today. The twentieth century in America, however, has witnessed the modification and gradual decline (not without struggle) of WASP dominance. This has been made possible through three broad processes: (1) general social changes, which, in our national history, have led to (2) modification of the structure of dominance as new needs had to be met, and this in turn has (3) made possible and effective the direct challenge and protest of minorities themselves.

General Trends Affecting Minorities

Industrialization. The transition from a predominantly agricultural and merchant to a predominantly industrial nation dominated in the second half of the nineteenth and first quarter of the twentieth century in the United States. This affected the recruitment of the growing industrial labor force, the status of workmen, and attitudes toward immigrants.

As industrialization grew and the factory system became the dominant pattern of production, the competition to cut labor costs brought a lower wage standard and a decline not only in the style of life of the industrial worker but in the prestige of his occupational group. Since immigrants contributed largely to this growing labor force, they shared and increased the lowered position of the American industrial workers. As more and more immigrants came, there was a tendency to identify all industrial labor as "foreign," all the more so when tensions grew up around the struggle to form labor unions. A study in the 1940s of a small industry in a midwest community showed that the industrial workers were referred to as "Poles," though in fact 50 percent of this group were of native American stock.[17]

For the minorities of European descent, in the period of national expansion, the expectation persisted *both* on the part of dominants and of minorities that the immigrants would assimilate and share the values and opportunities of the developing nation. The process, however, appeared to many as too selective and too slow, so that the turn of the century saw increasing protest and increasing organization of workers, and finally the successful political clout of the labor movement. Some employers attempted to support and strengthen the ethnic identity of various groups of workers. The effect of this, whatever the intent, was to "divide and rule."

Acculturation was successful enough, however, to instill in American labor the "racial" attitudes of the dominants. This was apparant in anti-Chinese sentiment on the

---

[17]August B. Hollingshead, *Elmtown's Youth* (New York: John Wiley & Sons, 1941).

West Coast in the 1880s and is present today in many working-class communities as black Americans move in larger numbers into the industrial labor force.

Urbanization.   The growth of our urban, multigroup society has had a significant effect on minority participation. Folk cultures, with their kinship patterns, language, and folk beliefs, have been brought in contact with other cultures, and subjected to the secularizing influence of dominant economic, educational, and legal systems. The institutional balance of folk cultures, where family and religion take precedence, is borne upon by the multigroup urban community, where the dominant institutions are economic and political.

Another aspect of urbanization has been that the size, density, and heterogeneity of cities have made possible segmentation of roles, so that public and private roles need not necessarily overlap. This has aided the acculturation process.

It is significant that three-quarters of the population of the United States now live in metropolitan areas—that is, in a big city or its suburbs. Although suburban patterns of dominant-minority relations vary from the patterns of the central city, the economic dependence of suburbs on the city, as well as other ideological influences emanating from the metropolitan core, has an impact that is being felt more and more.

The Welfare State.   The problems of an industrial society, the urban balance in national politics, the experiences of the great Depression of the 1930s and of world wars have led to an increasing centralization and extension of federal power. National responsibility has been accepted for at least a bare minimum guarantee of health and welfare. There has been a growing shift from the ideology of *laissez faire* to what is sometimes called "the reluctant welfare state." Federal legislation from the Social Security Act of 1935 to the civil rights and anti-poverty legislation of the 1960s has to a degree improved the situation of minorities, as ethnoracial/minority groups have had a proportionately higher percentage of "the poor," the "uneducated," the "untrained" (technologically). Federal legislation has made some important inroads on discriminatory ceilings of regional customary practices, whether it is Mississippi and blacks, Texas and Chicanos, California and Asians, or the whole nation and American Indians.

Such limited legislation, though helpful to segments of the minority populations, has not solved the problems of economic security, economic opportunity, or personal dignity of minorities. The response to a continuing devaluation has been, for many members of a minority, the reassessment and affirmation of their pre-American cultural heritage to establish their own self-worth, and the attempt to form ethnic political blocs to win access to more equal, rather than minimal or marginal security and opportunity.

International Pressures.   Dominant-minority relations in the United States must now, willy-nilly take cognizance of a world situation. We have had a public policy in this century of exerting our influence to preserve "democracy" and "private enterprise" throughout the world. We are facing the fact that we may have to deal with powerful segments of the world who are not ethnoracially North European, and whose economic organization is not ours. The Asian-African bloc is a wholly new dimension in the world balance and affects the hopes, identities, and aspirations of some minorities who find the barriers of American society too insurmountable. The ideal of a different organization of property attracts others who have seen in other nations more opportunity for the education of the able of whatever class, because a new economic organization has brought about a new and more future-oriented educational system. More opportunity for local participation in decision making, though encouraged by antipoverty legislation, is still viewed skeptically in this country by the vested interests of business or labor.

Some of the powerless turn toward Cuba, China, Algeria as one set of models; or the Soviet Union as a sophisticated, secular, technologically competitive model; or toward an emotional, rather than ideological, model of "homeland"—Israel, West Africa, Indian reservations (a sentiment stressing "peoplehood"). And the Third World has its strength of numbers if not at this point in time actual power.

Social Structural Changes Affecting Minorities

Overall adaptations to the needs of an urban industrial society have modified some structures, expanded others, and created new channels for members of minority groups to improve their status. The large-scale organization of business, labor, and government has brought together at work men and women of different ethnic backgrounds and reduced the "social distance" that many community residential patterns impose. Businesses are under pressure to be "equal opportunity employers." This has benefited minority individuals with competitive skills, reducing, if not eliminating, categorical discrimination. Labor unions have provided new avenues for minority members to improve their position as individuals and to achieve leadership roles; they have also improved the standard of living of organized industrial workers to the extent that many blue-collar workers can expect to see their children in middle-class positions.

By far the most significant increase in opportunity has come through public employment (including the military). The expansion of federal, state, and city bureaucracies, as has been needed with the growth of public services, has given members of minority groups access to employment at skill levels not earlier open to them. The larger body of the armed forces since World War II has brought young men and women into military training from all ethnic and racial backgrounds. The desegregation of the army in the Korean war opened army career channels to some, and studies of the military in World War II have shown that the associations in the armed services were effective in many instances in changing attitudes of both dominants and minorities in positive directions.

Education and communication have had their impact also. Historically, free compulsory education was probably the greatest single acculturative channel for minorities, however imperfectly it often fulfilled this function. At the present stage of dominant-minority relations possibly the most significant gains have been in the marked reduction of discrimination in higher education, the growth of community colleges, and extramural higher education programs for employed people. Mass communication has, to some degree, brought awareness of "others," some changed images, and some public issues affecting minorities to the diverse segments of the American population.

Stabilized Acculturation and Structural Pluralism

Association in work, in politics, and public life do much to break down the "social distance" between disparate groups. The public recognition of the achievement of minority individuals has enhanced the "respectability" of minority descent. As large segments of the ethnic minorities have moved into middle-class occupations and become acculturated to middle-class norms, ethnicity, at least in the large urban multigroup communities, becomes more and more a private matter or a symbolic appeal in some public or political situations. Blue-collar workers, too are more American than ethnic in their life styles. To some extent this process may be observed also with regard to "racial" minorities if housing patterns permit interracial community contact.

"Respectability" means, then, that at least in the secular spheres of life, to a considerable degree, acculturation, at whatever class level, has taken place. It means, furthermore, that minority institutional patterns have modified and become more coherent with dominant norms. Yet within this frame of acculturation there persists, it is argued, a preference for intimate associations with people whose cultural and/or religious and racial heritage is like one's own. We have called this mode of adaptation *stabilized acculturation*. Milton M. Gordon has used the term *structural pluralism:*[18]

> We have chosen to focus on the nature of group life itself in the United States as constituting the social setting in which relationships among persons of differing race, religion, and national origin take place. For these 190 million Americans are not just individuals with psychological characteristics. They belong to groups: primary groups and secondary groups, family groups, social cliques, associations or formal organizations, networks of associations, racial, religious, and national origins groups. And the nature of these groups and their interrelationships has a profound impact upon the way in which people of different ethnic backgrounds regard and relate to one another.
>
> In particular, we have called attention to the nature of the ethnic group itself as a large subsociety, crisscrossed by social class, and continuing in its own primary groups of families, cliques and associations—its own network of organizations and institutions—in other words as a highly structured community within the boundaries of which an individual may, if he wishes, carry out most of his more meaningful life activities from the cradle to the grave. We have pointed to the considerable body of evidence which suggests that the ethnic varieties of Americans, excepting the intellectuals, tend to remain within their own ethnic group and social class for most of their intimate, primary group relationships, interacting with other ethnic and class varieties of Americans largely in impersonal secondary group relationships. The United States, we have argued, is a multiple melting pot in which acculturation for all groups beyond the first generation of immigrants, without eliminating all value conflict, has been massive and decisive, but in which structural separation on the basis of race and religion—structural pluralism, as we have called it—emerges as the dominant sociological condition.

This is to say that the majority of the members of minority groups in urban America at the present time, if the primary differentiating characteristics have been religious and cultural, and if they are second or third generation, are assimilated at the appropriate class level in the spheres of work and political life and in their external life style. In the sphere of sentiment and intimate association, however, there are still strong religious and/or ethnic bonds. (This is equally true of WASPs as an ethnic group). Gordon makes an exception for the intellectuals as a true interethnic stratum. We pointed out earlier in this chapter Baltzell's observation that at one time, and perhaps reemerging

[18]Milton M. Gordon, *Assimilation in American Life* (New York: Oxford University Press, 1964), pp. 235–236.

today, the business and political elite associated as equals within the top echelons, despite differences of descent and affiliation. We might also add that protest movements in many instances create an interethnic associational base. Bohemias, the sections of metropolitan centers where the artists and their satellites congregate, have traditionally been exceptions to the pattern of structural pluralism.

The effect of the clustering of ethnic groups in the manner presented by Gordon has one dysfunction in that it may perpetuate some of the stereotypes of "others" among the different groups. Gans, in his study of an Italian working-class community, suggests that often this stereotyping of neighbors who are Irish, or bosses who are Jewish, is completely without malice.[19] Nevertheless there is always the risk, as Gordon points out, that stereotyping has a direct relation to prejudice and, as we have indicated, in times of general social stress can be used to mobilize insecure people to action against the stereotyped group.

We shall discuss in the chapter on religion and minorities the idea that there is no absolute reason why this kind of pluralism cannot be viable. In a certain sense the image of such a stabilized pattern is Utopian, because it assumes that, as in an ideal marriage, private sentiments never interfere with the common good. Indeed, however, there has been recognition increasingly that "respectable" differences are allowable. Even with regard to the most visible differences (physiognomic) there is no longer, as there once was, public, national, and academic argument that certain peoples are unassimilable.

Structural pluralism is a solution for a minority group in adjusting to the dominant society that may be held as ideal (and this ideal may be shared by some dominants). For others it may be seen not as ideal but as a transitional reality to be followed by complete incorporation of the dominant values and affiliations including the private spheres of behavior and sentiment.

To see any direction of movement one must relate the mode of adaptation to *possibilities* as well as to goals. Louis Wirth has posited four possible goals for minority groups: secession, pluralism, assimilation, and achievement of dominance.[20] As Wagley and Harris point out, at the present time only two of these alternatives have any significant place in minority aspirations in the Western Hemisphere: pluralism and assimilation.[21]

Integration

As we saw early in this chapter, when minorities have enough power (economic or political), cooperation has been through negotiation in the form of an implied contractual relationship between one group as a group and the other as a group. When individual cooperation between dominants and minorities *on the basis of equality* occurs, we have the phenomenon of integration. Thus children within an integrated school may be friends and equals. Neighbors in an integrated neighborhood may cooperate as equal members of a taxpayers group or a community committee or as members of a neighborhood parish. Integration occurs in the equal association of indi-

---

[19]Herbert J. Gans, *The Urban Villagers* (New York: The Free Press, 1962), p. 36.
[20]Louis Wirth, "The Problem of Minority Groups," in *The Science of Man in the World Crisis.* ed. Ralph Linton (New York: Columbia University Press, 1945), pp. 354–364.
[21]Wagley and Harris, *Minorities in the New World*, p. 286.

viduals when the minority still identifies itself as a minority. In this way it differs from assimilation.

Protest movements, despite their disjunctive effect on the previously existing social equilibrium, may be integrative factors in dominant-minority relations. This may be true *internally* through the opportunity they provide for committed members of both the dominant group and the minorities to come into frequent interaction as they work toward a common goal. They contribute *externally* to the degree that they have a successful impact on the social situation. The *internal* integrative effect will be minimized if the majority of the membership of a given movement is either dominant (as with the antislavery movement) or minority (as with the National Congress of American Indians). The *external* effect will be minimized if the movement fails to change institutional patterns, not merely to achieve official abrogation of discrimination. Another limitation to the integrative impact of protest movements is their contemporaneous focus. If in addition to their immediate demands they become ongoing organizations, they may lose flexibility in adapting to the changing needs of a new generation of membership.

Assimilation in a Pluralistic Society

The history of America has been that of absorbing many peoples. As long as the migration was predominantly northern European, it was assumed that all those of Caucasian stock would "disappear" as separate identities. For many this has been true. Coupled with this assumption was the designation of some peoples as "unassimilable." This was particularly a public argument regarding Asiatics on the West Coast, and was used as a platform for limitation of Asiatic migration. At one point, at the turn of the century, there was a variant of the older belief about assimilation: the *melting pot theory,* which claimed that from the merging of the many ethnic heritages a new type of person—the "American"—would evolve. At this time the public mind viewed people whose style of life was American and whose language was English as "assimilated," so long as there were no alien racial characteristics.

In contradistinction to the "melting pot" view was the concept of *cultural pluralism.* The heavy migration of the turn of the century with the resulting urban nationality subcommunities had an impact on political and social thinking within the urban milieu. Social workers, like those of Chicago's Hull House, were concerned with supporting the dignity of the cultural heritage of immigrants confused by the impact of the new American environment. Politicians were recognizing subcultural identity in their bids for the "Italian vote" or the "Polish vote." Ethnic groups often controlled one type of operation, one floor in an industry, or one local of a labor union.

The dangers to the state of really diverse value systems within it is real, for to preserve justice and public order there must be a common understanding of norms, of what is a "fair" way of dealing with others. Furthermore, the latent effect of a really established cultural pluralism can lead to the mechanism of "divide-and-rule." The maintenance of a total (or largely) separate cultural identity has often had the effect of increasing visibility and discrimination and deterring minorities from challenging their subordinate position. Effective challenge to dominance, as we have tried to show, can only come when at least some institutional acculturation has taken place.

What has happened in America has been that truly separatist communities, by choice, like the Amish, or by force, like the American Indians, have been small groups who kept their cultures intact by geographic and institutional separation. The rest of the groups, in interaction with others, acculturated to a greater or lesser degree as far as *secular* institutional participation was concerned (public schools, politics, jobs) and such pluralism as was retained was traditional religion, festival ritual, food and other aspects of the personal rather than the public world. Cultural pluralism in the visionary sense of the early decades of the twentieth century proved incongruent to the effective needs both of minorities and of the total society, however humanistically appealing it was as a philosophy.

If structural pluralism is a way station and assimilation a goal in dominant-minority relations, then to what must people assimilate? In view of changing beliefs and of changing power relations it is probably too late, and certainly would be too costly, to try to establish WASP tradition as an absolute norm. WASPS, as an ethnic group, will have to assimilate, too, to a multicultural heritage that is peculiarly American; to a society that has successfully eliminated categorical discrimination; to a nation less concerned with the past than with mobilizing all its human resources to meet the technological threats, the urban decay, the shocking rate of poverty, the destruction of natural resources, the plight of agriculture that will usher in the twenty-first century.

Suggested Readings

Gordon, Milton M. *Assimilation in American Life.* New York: Oxford University Press, 1964.
>   This provides the data out of which Gordon developed his theory of structural pluralism. It is useful to remember that his informants were members of the middle class.
Higham, John. *Strangers in the Land: Patterns of American Nativism, 1860-1925.* New York: Atheneum, 1965.
>   A history of social movements that were anti-foreign in sentiment and anti-immigration in policy.
LaGumina, Salvatore J., ed. *WOP: A Documentary History of Anti-Italian Discrimination in the United States.* San Francisco: Straight Arrow Books, 1973.
>   This is one of a series from this publisher on ethnic prejudice in America. This is a particularly good volume because it includes legislation, contemporary journalism, cartoons, and songs that give a picture of official and popular anti-Italian stereotyping. Others in the series include *Chink, Kike,* and *Mick* on, respectively, anti-Chinese, Jewish and Irish sentiment and action.
Selznick, Gertrude J. and Steinberg, Stephen. *The Tenacity of Prejudice: Anti-Semitism in Contemporary America.* New York: Harper Torchbooks, Harper and Row, 1971.
>   A national survey, of particular value because it indicates correlations with anti-black prejudice and anti-Catholic prejudice.
Williams, Robin. *Strangers Next Door: Ethnic Relations in American Communities.* Englewood Cliffs, N.J.: Prentice Hall, 1964.
>   A sample survey of how households feel about members of different ethnic or racial background as neighbors, as work associates, and as social associates, in four regions of the United States.

3

Religious Minorities

Religious minorities and nationality minority groups are *cultural* structures around central value systems that are to a greater or lesser degree at variance with the dominant value system. In any complex society there is potential intergroup conflict, and institutional conflict, where peoples have differing beliefs affecting specific issues of public policy. The conflict may be simply an adjustive mechanism if the groups have *equal status* and *equal protection*. In the sphere of religious difference this has largely been achieved, though not easily or to the exclusion of continuing potential vulnerability.

"SWEET LAND OF LIBERTY"

The Colonial Heritage of Religious Discrimination

The American colonies were settled in a period when Europe had not yet resolved the problem of separation of religious identity and national identity. The nations of Europe in consolidating the authority of the state against feudal interests had leaned on the support of religion by designating an "established" church. Countries whose powerful elites were anti-Roman Catholic developed national Protestant churches supported by state funds. European countries that remained Catholic incorporated powerful political roles for members of the Church hierarchy.

The established churches acted as a conservative force, upholding the prerogatives of the joint political religious power structure. They were effective in continuing traditional order. But with the growth of economic enterprise and the entry into economic power of groups not favored by the establishment, both religious and secular, there were further moves of disaffection. These were manifestly (that is, consciously expressed as) religious movements. People found new ways of expressing beliefs and then found themselves deprived of a voice in political affairs. The movements were therefore also latently political. These "dissenters" were eventually offered a solution in migration to the New World. William Penn wrote to his son in 1700 that "it was the Government (of the new colony) which engaged me and those that adventured with me. . . . for being Dissenters, we therefore came that we might enjoy that so far of which would not be allowed us any share at home."[1]

---

[1] *Papers Relating to Provincial Affairs,* Pennsylvania Archives of History and Biography, 2nd Series, VII. 11.

It is important to note that before independence the American colonies were subject to the religio-legal restrictions of the mother country, and there were instances of Catholics and Jews who were not by birth English, being denied citizenship because of religion.

The Principle of Disestablishment

The Crown colonies tended to be chiefly Anglican (Church of England) in the enfranchised population because of the position of the Governor and the military. Other colonies, however—Pennsylvania, Rhode Island, Maryland, Massachusetts— were "disestablishment" colonies. These latter controlled much of the commerce and had been the most restless with British rule. Thus in the formation of an independent nation the principle of disestablishment prevailed. This meant that there would be no *official* religion, and that no public funds would go for the support of any ecclesiastical body.

The American Constitution in its First Amendment guaranteed that there was to be no state religion, implying thereby no religious requirement for citizenship, franchise, or office holding; there was to be no meddling by the state in private religious practice. The statements were brief and general and have from time to time been annuled by state laws. The separation of church and state, as the principle has come to be called, differentiates between the claims of two bodies of authority.[2] It has been said that Thomas Jefferson was interested in the principle in order to protect the state from the church, and that Roger Williams was interested in it to protect the church from the state.[3]

Religion and the Social Structure

To understand the significant deepening and broadening of the guarantee of religious freedom and equality in America it is necessary to consider the nature of religious bodies within the larger social structure.

Religion is an internalized commitment to a *value system*. Certain central values are designated as *sacred*—that is not subject to utilitarian or empirical judgment. The "sacred" is something experienced, either by direct revelation or by repeated ritual. Freud sees it as man's confrontation with his powerlessness when he perceives himself in the hazardous crises of the life cycle, or of nature's scarcity, or of personal jeopardy and the struggle for survival. The particular content of religious belief is inevitably influenced by the social experience of a particular group in both the past and the present.[4]

Religious bodies differ from one another in their deeper felt orientations that both affect society and are affected by it. They also differ in their use of symbols, ritual, and

---

[2] A special note should be made of the distinctive position of Friends (Quakers). This body was so prestigious that it retained certain concessions won in colonial times: exemption from legal oaths and exemption from bearing arms. The military exemption has subsequently been extended to other sectarians, notably Mennonites and ultimately such contemporary groups as Jehovah's Witnesses and Black Muslims, but not without struggle.

[3] Earl Raab, *Religious Conflict in America* (Garden City, N.Y.: Doubleday & Co., Anchor Books, 1964), p. 7.

[4] Thomas F. O'Dea, *The Sociology of Religion* (Englewood Cliffs, N.J.: Prentice-Hall, 1966), Ch. 2.

liturgy, and it is usually these extrinsic features that make one group visible and "foreign" to another. A genuine religious movement that becomes institutionalized and persists over generations (as contrasted with a transitory cult or revitalization movement) has the problem of coming to terms with the secular society. It has the choice of becoming accommodated to the society and its other institutions with their expectations of economic, political, and familial behavior or of being critical of and rejecting secular societal norms. The former pattern is usually called a *church;* the latter a *sect.* A church attempts to be inclusive. Membership is by birth and theology is explicit. The sect is based on a principle of voluntary joining and is exclusive of all who have not shared its experience of regenerative commitment. A sect is apt to be austere and ascetic, at least initially. But persistence over time, especially if accompanied by prosperity, may lead to a lessening of its separatism from the secular world. At this point it becomes a denomination and a church.

The Rise of Religious Discrimination

The resurgence of religion as a rationalization for discrimination and the consolidation of WASP dominance is bound up with other struggles and social changes. Targets for religious discrimination have been Protestant sectarians, non-Protestants, and non-Christians whenever they have been conspicuous in numbers or had highly visible religious practices inimical to dominant mores.

Until about 1850 Protestant dominance was so sufficiently clear by virtue of numbers, early migration, and economic advantage that members of religious minorities could be incorporated in the secular life of the nation without having religion emerge as a categorical reason for discrimination.[5] The period was one of lively theological controversy, not unmixed with belief in Divine intervention, Divine mission, a modicum of superstition, and an upstanding conviction of human worth as more significant than doctrinal designation.[6] Popular evangelical, democratic, sectarian movements whose appeal was to farmers and workers contributed to the success of the Jacksonian revolution (eliminating, as it did, property qualifications for voting, imprisonment for debt, and advancing of free public education). Conflict in this period was within the framework of class and regional issues, with religious affiliation secondary. The "peculiar" people among native-born sectarians had the frontier to absorb them. A second factor of importance was that the largest body of non-Protestants did not migrate in great numbers until steamships were the common mode of trans-Atlantic travel.

The end of the nineteenth and the first decades of the twentieth century, however, saw the rise of real discrimination on religious grounds. On the part of the national elite it was first directed against the Jews. This temporarily successful effort to protect and consolidate WASP dominance was precipitated by several factors. The first and not the least of these was the displacement of the old commercial upper class by new wealth after the Civil War. First the transportation wealth and subsequently the industrial wealth pushed the old merchant families and their descendants into lesser positions of

---

[5]E. Digby Baltzell, *The Protestant Establishment: Aristrocracy and Caste in America* (New York: Random House, 1964), p. 73.
[6]Thomas F. O'Dea, *The Mormons* (Chicago: University of Chicago Press, 1957). See Ch. 1 for a summary of the religious ferment of the period.

power. Some of the newly rich validated their social position by intermarriage with the old families. Some old families were clever enough to seize on the new developments. But for most, they were left without economic or political power and retreated into creating structures of social exclusion. One must see this movement against the backdrop of very rapid economic development. (The national income quadrupled between 1870 and 1900, and doubled again by 1914). The displaced patricians were supported in their attempt to create exclusive enclaves in "society" (resorts, elite boarding schools, metropolitan clubs, and country clubs) by the new wealth that aped their parochialism in order to be "in." The result was "restriction" of membership where this had never occurred formally before.

The attitude leading to restriction filtered down to other segments of society. It was embraced by groups facing the heavy migration of Eastern European Jews whose folkways were conspicuously different. It affected provincial cities undergoing the pangs of industrialization, affording them a scapegoat offered by the national models.

A phenomenon of this period was the rise of "old stock" associations with their emphasis on descent and date of migration as the criteria for social status.[7]

The rise of the urban political machine, in a number of cities largely in the hands of the Irish, with its patronage system of dispensing jobs or other aid and its frequent collusion with enterprises unacceptable to old Protestant mores, led to the anti-Irish-Catholic syndrome. This was the more true as Irish clergy dominated the American Catholic Church at the time, and in some localities the church hierarchy had indirect controls on the local political machine. The response from many Protestants was the revival of the church-state issue.

Anti-Semitic and anti-Catholic feeling was at its height in the 1920s and even in the 1930s as World War I and the Depression made shockingly apparent the shift from a largely rural nation protected by two oceans to an industrial nation with international interdependence. The religious issue in dominant-minority relations has never been so widespread since, although there have been sporadic resurgences. (See Chapter 16 for a more extensive discussion of anti-Semitism.)

RELIGIOUS INTOLERANCE

The Sects—Protestant Revitalization Movements

Religious revitalization movements, with their strong sense of peoplehood and often with messianic hopes, have been prime targets for aggressive action against them in the name of religion. Below we present three examples, which in their sequence can illustrate the slow extension of the guarantee of religious freedom to religious movements outside established churches: the first involved unmitigated brutality; the second was solved by separatism and the flexibility of the religious body; the third by aggressive legal defense.

[7]Baltzell, *The Protestant Establishment,* p. 110 and pp. 90 ff, 114 ff.

The Ghost Dance[8]

> All Indians must dance, everywhere, keep on dancing. Pretty soon in next
> spring, Great Spirit come. He bring back all game of every kind . . . All
> dead Indians come back and live again . . . Whites can't hurt Indians then
> . . . send word to all Indians to keep dancing and the good time will come.
> (Wokoya, the Piute Messiah)

On October 9, 1890, about a year after the forced breakup of the great Sioux reservation, Kicking Bear told Sitting Bull of his visit to the Piute Messiah. Kicking Bear had always thought that Christ was a white man like the missionaries, but this man looked like an Indian. "I will teach you how to dance a dance, and I want you to dance it, and when it is over I will talk to you." They had danced late into the night and the next day he talked to them throughout the day. "In the beginning," he said, "God made the earth, and then sent Christ to earth to teach the people, but white men treated him badly, leaving scars on his body, and so he had gone back to heaven. Now he had returned as an Indian, and he was to renew everything as it had been and make it better." Sitting Bull was skeptical, but he was willing to let Kicking Bear teach the dance because many of his people had heard of it. Indeed on almost every Indian reservation the Ghost Dance was spreading like wildfire.

Indian Bureau inspectors and Army officers at Western stations were bewildered and frightened. "A more pernicious system of religion could not have been offered to a people who stood on the threshold of civilization," said Indian agent McLaughlin, a Roman Catholic. At McLaughlin's request Kicking Bear was arrested, but the Secretary of War refused to meet the request to arrest Sitting Bull also. As more arrests occurred on the reservations leaders took their followers to remote places where even as the wintry weather came they continued dancing. On November 20 the Indian Bureau telegraphed a list of "fomentors of disturbances" among the Ghost Dancers to Army headquarters in Chicago. Sitting Bull's name was on the list. Meanwhile troops had already been brought into the nearby Pine Ridge Reservation. A former agent of the Indian Bureau, asked to make recommendations, said "I should let the dance continue. The coming of the troops has frightened the Indians. If the Seventh Day Adventists prepare their ascension robes for the coming of the Savior, the United States Army is not put in motion to stop them. Why should not Indians have the same privilege?"

On December 15, an attempt was made to arrest Sitting Bull, but a crowd of Ghost Dancers intervened. In the scuffle between Ghost Dancers and military police a bullet struck and killed Sitting Bull.

One on the list of "fomenters" was Big Foot, who had a camp at Cherry Creek. Demoralized and fleeing Indians from Standing Rock reached him and told of Sitting Bull's death. Big Foot immediately gathered his people and set out for Pine Ridge to seek the protection of the last of the great chiefs, Red Cloud. On the way they were intercepted and taken to the cavalry camp at Wounded Knee. There were 120 men and 230 women and children. They were assigned a camping area and it was surrounded by mounted Hotchkiss guns (range, two miles). Big Foot lay in his tent hemorrhaging

[8]Adapted from Chapter 18 of *Bury My Heart at Wounded Knee,* by Dee Brown. Copyright © 1970 by Dee Brown. Reprinted by permission of Holt, Rinehart & Winston, Inc.

from tuberculosis. In the night a contingent of the 7th Regiment arrived and took charge (this was Custer's old regiment).

In the morning the Indians were assembled and disarmed. One Indian who was deaf did not understand and held on to his rifle. The Hotchkiss guns opened up. There were 153 known dead Indians, and doubtless more wounded who died that night in the dreadful blizzard that followed.

> I did not know then how much was ended. When I look back from this high hill of my old age, I can still see the butchered women and children lying heaped and scattered all along the crooked gulch as plain as I saw them with eyes still young. And I can see that something else died there in the bloody mud, and was buried in the blizzard. A people's dream died there. It was a beautiful dream . . . the nation's hoop is broken and scattered. There is no center any longer, and the sacred tree is dead. (Black Elk)

In dealing with American Indian religious manifestations it was not until 1961 that the "Native American Church" was recognized as a legitimate church in a Supreme Court ruling. This religious sect uses a hallucinatory drug in its ceremonies (peyote). Before 1965 there were some state laws against its use. In the 1966 scare about the widespread use of LSD, making its use a federal crime, an exception was made for hallucinogenics in the rituals of the Native American Church.[9]

Thus after more than seventy years the harmless expressions of religious hopes, enthusiasms, and visions have been protected. It is probably useful to recognize that even as late as 1960, with the decimation and demoralization of American Indians, the suit in their behalf was made by Anglos (the American Civil Liberties Union), the Indians themselves having had neither incentive nor opportunity to develop a legal cadre of their own. This is changing now.

The Church of Christ of the Latter Day Saints (Mormons)

> A man of near 60 years of age, living about 7 miles from this place, was taken from his house a few nights since, stripped of his clothing, and his back cut to pieces with a whip, for no other reason than because he was Mormon, and too old to make a successful resistance.[10]

Probably there is no instance of religious persecution in American history comparable in scope and severity to that inflicted on the Mormons. Originally a sect, now a worldwide church with two and a quarter million members, it was founded in 1830 in upper New York State. The original organization was created by six young men, the oldest thirty-one years of age. The theology, including the principle of continuing revelation, on which the sect was founded, is not germane to our discussion, though it

[9]Peter Nabokov, "The Peyote Road," *The New York Times,* Mar. 9, 1969, Sec. vi, pp. 30–31, 129–132, 134.
[10]News item in The *Quincy* (Illinois) *Whig,* May 30, 1864, cited in Frederick Hawkins Piercy, *Route from Liverpool to Great Salt Lake Valley* (Cambridge, Mass.: Harvard University Press, 1962), pp. 216–217.

undoubtedly agitated some in the beginning, in a period replete with religious controversy. Joseph Smith, the Mormon prophet, was arrested and imprisoned twice in the first year of the organized body's existence. The young sect was aggressive in missionary activity, attracted converts, sought to incorporate the Indians whom it defined as "the lost tribes of Israel," and projected an ideal community in the (then seen as) Far West near what became Independence, Missouri.

Between 1833 and 1839 some 1,500 Mormons moved to Missouri from New York and from a second settlement in Ohio. A temple was projected and they were initially welcomed by both Indians and white settlers. Shortly after their influx the U.S. Government forbade them to proselytize among Indians. Their economic pattern upset non-Mormon settlers; for Mormons, each man was to own and carry on his own enterprise (farm or business), retaining such part of his earnings necessary to maintain his family; the rest was to go to the church and there were to be no rich or poor. Finally, political issues arose. Mormons were antislavery and most of their neighbor settlers were pro-slavery. Pitched battles broke out between Mormon and non-Mormon settlers. The militia intervened. Several leaders, including Joseph Smith, were court-martialed and were to be executed. The soldier responsible for executing them refused. The entire community was ordered out of Missouri.

They chose a site on the Mississippi River in Illinois about 50 miles above Quincy and founded the town of Navoo (transliterated from the Hebrew, meaning "beautiful"). Here they built a prosperous town and, at last, their first temple (reputed to cost a million dollars). They offered religious freedom to all Navoo residents. The jailed Mormon leaders in Missouri escaped. There were repeated efforts to have them extradited. The Governor of Illinois defended them, but local vilification increased. There were clashes. Joseph Smith and two others, somewhat apprehensively, agreed to appear in court in Carthage to answer charges of incitement to riot. The judge continued the case to the next session; they were then charged with treason and put in jail, and on the 27th of June, 1839, a mob assassinated them. Joseph Smith was 39 years old.[11]

In the next years, as violent pressure increased against the Navoo community it was decided to move west. The first contingent of Mormons left for beyond the Rockies in February, 1846. In the next several years one of the great dramas of American migration took place as Mormons, some in their fourth migration (New York-Ohio; Ohio-Missouri; Missouri-Illinois; Illinois-Utah), as well as new Mormon converts from the docksides and mill centers of England, set out with ox teams or in bands of two or three hundred on foot, pushing handcarts, to "Zion."

Behind they left homes burned, and their temple in Navoo which had been fired by an incendiary. They came to the desert around the great Salt Lake and built a flowering city.

In 1896 Utah became a state. Coincidentally, or necessarily, the Mormons annulled their practice of polygamy (theologically, in an Old Testament-based religion polygamy is possible in "spiritual" and ritualistic marriages, with no relevance or implication for cohabitation, as women achieve salvation only through men—a patriarchal theology). Indeed there has always been some controversy within the Mormon Church about the intent or validity of social polygamy, and the practice began to die out naturally as a more settled life developed and the sex balance became more equal.

---

[11]Charles Samuel Braden, *These Also Believe* (New York: The Macmillan Co., 1949), pp. 421–431.

Mormons today are a strong antisecular body. They still require two years of "missionary" work (now, accepted by some as social service religiously motivated) from all young people. Able Mormons have given service to the nation in wartime and in peacetime in the same spirit that they give money and time to their church. Despite their world membership they are a particularly American kind of church with a great tradition of the virtues and manifest destiny of the American pioneer experience: the work ethic, social justice, personal responsibility, community mutuality. To some people today they appear conservative, and the risk for rank and file Mormons is that they may ally themselves with others who are conservative about individual property, work, etc., without the sense of communal responsibility that a religious commitment gives.

The Jehovah's Witnesses

A more recent militant sect, which has become increasingly urban, is the Jehovah's Witnesses. As we have seen, sectarianism arises out of social and emotional needs that are not met by the Establishment at any given time.

The Jehovah's Witnesses, now a rapidly growing religious movement, was founded in 1870 in Allegheny, Pennsylvania, and until 1931 was known by various names. It began as a Bible class. Followers in the United States and abroad now number nearly a million. Charles Taze Russell, its founder, was a member of the Congregational Church and of the YMCA. He was "converted" to the Adventist doctrine, which was fundamentalist and held to the literal interpretation of the prophecies of the book of Revelation that Christ would return to earth and reign for a thousand years. The central task for living men and women, then, in the belief of the Witnesses, is to convince others of the truth they hold, namely, the imminent violent end of this evil world. In order to be among those saved in the millennial reign one must bear witness to Christ in every act—that is all conduct is governed solely by religion. Every Witness is an ordained minister with a duty to preach. All free time must be spent spreading the gospel. The mode of proselytizing is chiefly through published tracts and the magazine *The Watch Tower,* which are distributed in house-to-house canvassing or on street corners, and engaging the recipients in persuasive discussion. The sect has survived the difficult problems of succession of leadership and is now a tightly knit organization controlled by three corporations, similar to an ecclesiastical autocracy.[12]

A Witness must refuse to obey any law that is contrary to God's law, as derived from fundamentalist theology. On the other hand, Witnesses must obey any laws that do not conflict and must never present the truth through lawless means. Witnesses are expected to bear action against them stoically and not to retaliate. Indeed, many rejoice in adversity, which they interpret as foreshadowing an imminent millennium. Witnesses are opposed to all organized religious bodies, as diverting people from the truth, and they are particularly anti-Catholic.

The Witnesses have experienced persecution and violence on the community level and have had many conflicts with the law. The violence against them either in direct outbreak or in illegal arrests was at a peak in 1940, with 335 incidents of mob vio-

[12]See Herbert Hewitt Stroup, *The Jehovah's Witnesses* (New York: Columbia University Press, 1945), p. 21, for a description of the corporate organization.

lence.[13] As they are opposed to military service, 4,300 served prison sentences for violation of the draft laws in World War II. It is estimated that about 6,000 to 10,000 Witnesses were sent to concentration camps in Nazi Germany, and other governments
abroad have taken action against them.[14]

The Flag Salute Controversy.   The Jehovah's Witnesses came into prominence over
their long battle to be exempt from saluting the American flag as a public-school requirement. The first flag salute statute was passed in 1898 in New York State. Thirty
states and various localities in the remaining states had enacted such statutes by 1938
when the American Civil Liberties Union undertook to survey the question. The requirement of the salute was pushed by patriotic organizations and reactionary nationalist groups. Manwaring cites the Ku Klux Klan (in 1925), the D.A.R. (1923), and
various fraternal groups.[15]

Before the issue became focused around the Jehovah's Witnesses there had already
been incidents of religious objection to the ritual from Mennonites and other sectarians.
On September 30, 1935, in a Lynn, Massachusetts high school, Carleton Nicholls, a
Witness, refused to salute the flag and was expelled from school. On October 6, Joseph
Franklin Rutherford, then President of the Witnesses, delivered a radio address uphold-
ing Nicholls' act. The Witnesses employed legal counsel and filed a petition with the
State Supreme Court for Nicholls' reinstatement. The court upheld the school.

It was decided not to appeal at the time. Nevertheless, the ground had been broken
for litigation. The Witnesses had no prohibition against using the courts; indeed,
Rutherford had been a practicing attorney for twenty-seven years before he became
president of his sect. Furthermore, as a small and unpopular body, the Witnesses could
not resort to political pressure for a change in the statute. The issue became increasingly serious to them as they equated the salute with the Hitler salute at a time when
their members were being persecuted in Germany. The first case to reach the Supreme
Court on the flag salute issue was that of *Minersville School District v. Gobitis* in 1940.
The Witnesses were defeated, Justice Frankfurter writing the majority opinion and Justice Stone presenting a dissenting opinion. This was a blow to the Witnesses, especially
as they had just before been upheld by the Court on an issue (*Cantwell v. Connecticut*)
involving distribution of literature and public proselytizing. The liberal press and the religious press (including two Catholic publications), much of the law press, as well as
much of the general press were adverse in their criticism of the decision. The decision
came just before the wave of violence against the Witnesses in the summer of 1940,
and the widespread nature of the outbreaks was generally attributed to the Court decision.[16]

In 1943 the Supreme Court heard the last of the flag salute cases (*West Virginia
State Board of Education v. Barnette.*) The decision this time was favorable to the Witnesses. Justice Jackson wrote the majority opinion. His central point distinguished
between state requirements of educational substance such as American history and requirements of ritual.

---

[13]See David R. Manwaring, *Render Unto Caesar: The Flag Salute Controversy* (Chicago:
University of Chicago Press, 1962), pp. 169–171, for charts of incidence of violence 1940–1943;
and Stroup. pp. 145–149.
[14]Manwaring, *Render Unto Caesar,* p. 30.
[15]*Ibid.,* pp. 4–5, 7, 8.
[16]For an analysis of the Supreme Court opinions and the reaction to the decision, see Manwaring,
Render Unto Caesar, Chs. 7 and 8.

The Jehovah's Witnesses are well equipped in organization, legal talent, and funds to carry on a long, hard, legal fight. Under present leadership, and since their success in the courts, some of the militancy has mitigated, though the dedicated spirit still dominates members. Jehovah's Witnesses have no racial barriers, as they see themselves obligated to save, by incorporation if possible, every man on earth.

Who Shall Shape Our Children?

The focal arena for testing religious freedom in the flag salute controversy was the secular public school. This key institution for American young people has often provided the occasion for conflict on grounds of belief. At one time there was great agitation over whether federal funds aiding education could be sought by Roman Catholic parochial schools. Since Catholic parents pay local taxes, even if their children do not attend public schools, and the considerable number of children attending parochial schools relieves the public school, it was argued that parochial schools should share benefits of transportation, equipment, and teaching aids provided through public moneys. Such moneys, so long as they are for enrichment and not for subsidy, are now available. Another controversy has centered around the former requirement for prayer at the opening of the school day. Since, by tradition, such prayers were Christian, some Jewish parents and those various agnostic groups have fought this practice with some success. The most clear-cut issue of a conflict of values involving a whole way of life has been the school issue among the Amish.

The Old-Order Amish. This long-established sect has sought the historic pattern of ecological separatism, with farming as a way of life, with strong communal bonds, ethnic affinity, and a social structure promoting a high level of personal responsibility and personal interaction.

The Amish belief system descends from the Anabaptists of sixteenth-century Bohemia. The religion emphasizes voluntary commitment to the community, represented by adult baptism, obedience to the literal teachings of the Bible, maintenance of communal congregational life like that of the early Christians as portrayed in the New Testament. The Amish renounce oaths, drinking, bearing of arms, and personal adornment. They are *visible* by their adherence to traditional dress and the fact that baptized males do not shave. These customs are symbols of their rejection of "worldly" values. They are, what one author has called, a "legalistic or objectivist sect"[17]—that is to say, they are rule oriented. They are opposed to modern technology, including electricity, automobiles, and farm machinery, as a central value is contact with the soil.

The Amish migrated to Pennsylvania in the eighteenth century. They have settlements now in Pennsylvania, Ohio, Indiana, Kansas, Illinois, Michigan, Iowa, North and South Dakota, Missouri, Nebraska, Oklahoma, and Oregon. Their communities are self maintaining, small, prosperous farming settlements. Overall they number somewhat more than 25,000 people.

The sect has been opposed to education beyond the eighth grade, although now they are developing some vocational programs. The preference is for a one-room school

---

[17]Elmer T. Clark, *The Small Sects in America,* rev. ed. (New York, Nashville: The Abingdon-Cokesbury Press, 1949), p. 147.

where children of different ages are taught family style by young men or women of the community who are seen to be good with children. They have shown strong resistance to state requirements that their children attend consolidated high schools where they will associate with worldly companions, become accustomed to technology, develop consumer rather than producer values.

Pennsylvania was the first state to try to enforce high-school attendance. Parents were summoned to the court and fined. They refused to pay the fines on the grounds of religious liberty and were jailed. After many confrontations and embarrassments a compromise was reached in the establishment of vocational schools. Amish lay leaders conduct the schools; the children perform farm and household tasks under the supervision of their parents; they keep a journal of their activities, and they meet in classes several hours a week. The schools are required to teach certain subjects and to file attendance reports, but teachers are not required to be certified. In 1967 Pennsylvania had twenty-five Amish vocational schools and Ohio had twenty-eight.[18]

An even more dramatic confrontation took place in Iowa in 1965 when Buchanon County school authorities invaded an Amish school in order to compel the children to board the bus to the consolidated town school. Frightened children ran for cover in cornfields and distressed parents were arrested. Fines, which parents refused to pay, amounted to thousands of dollars as the Amish continued to disregard the public-school attendance requirement. There were repercussions in the national press. The Governor of Iowa ordered a three-week "cooling off" period. This was extended to two years when a private foundation gave $15,000 to pay the salary of certified teachers in the two one-room schools for two years. In 1967, after a great deal of effort, the Iowa legislature amended its school code to permit a religious group to apply for exemption from compliance with the educational standards law. Proof of achievement in certain basic skills was made conditional. In the same year Maryland amended its school law so that the Amish were classified as a bona fide church organization and therefore not required to obtain approval of the Superintendant of Schools to continue to operate schools in that state.[19]

The little-known impact of these struggles on the Amish has been considerable. They have gradually organized on state and national levels to set up minimum standards for educating their children. Amish school boards are elected to raise funds, acquire equipment and books, and to hire and pay for teachers. Young people selected to be teachers are trained by other teachers in the classroom. There is a national magazine for Amish teachers.[20]

A process of "controlled acculturation" is taking place. Although Amish pupils show scores below the national level on achievement tests (though somewhat higher than all *rural* children), they show themselves strongly motivated toward the expectations and roles of the adults of their society, with a positive attitude toward work and a wide range of manual skills. They need a different type of schooling from the American middle-class child if they are to be effective within the values of an agrarian religious community.[21]

[18]John A. Hostetler, *Amish Society,* rev. ed. (Baltimore: The Johns Hopkins Press, 1968), p. 198.
[19]*Ibid.,* pp. 203–204.
[20]*Ibid.,* p. 207.
[21]*Ibid.,* p. 208.

It has been a long struggle to achieve coequal status for religious belief systems. The illustrations we have presented demonstrate the slow road we have taken to "protect the church from the state." Since sectarian movements are always to some degree critical of the secular society, they perforce arouse anxiety in some people. Often, too, antisectarian action has masked hidden economic motives: desire for Indian lands, or envy of Mormon prosperity, for example.

THE ESTABLISHED RELIGIONS AND THE DECLINE OF DOMINANCE

Since World War II there has been increasing sentiment that the religions that share the Judeo-Christian tradition are equally "respectable, American" institutions.[22] Whereas this optimistic outlook reflects the fact that an increasingly equal proportion of the "stable and respectable" middle class belongs to the three major religious bodies, historically both Catholics and Jews have experienced discrimination and aggressive action against them, not only in individual instances, but categorically as representatives of their religion.

The Roman Catholics

About 25 percent of the American population is Roman Catholic.[23] The problems of Catholics as a minority are bound up with, first, the historic factor that America was settled by Protestant groups that had a heritage of protest against the Church of Rome. Their own group solidarity was maintained, in part, by teaching to successive generations the nature of this protest.

There was both doctrinal and organizational foci for their opposition. All Protestants opposed the primacy and doctrinal authority of the Pope. Points of conflict were confession, penance, absolution, and indulgence. For most Protestants from the Reformation on, the Bible became the authority rather than "the Church." Initially, of course, for all, and still for some "fundamentalist" groups, this authority was accepted literally. But since the nineteenth-century development of documentary reexamination of the Bible and its sources, literalism has declined especially among the urban populations, though there is still the heritage of Biblical training (Protestant) versus Church Doctrinal training (Catholic). Some Protestant groups were also opposed to the centralized, bureaucratized structure of the Roman Catholic Church. Large denominations that elect their own leaders have seen the hierarchical appointments of Rome as antidemocratic. For antiliturgical Protestants the Catholic form of worship with its rituals, vestments, and symbolic participation has seemed pomp and splendor, or

---

[22]Will Herberg, *Protestant-Catholic-Jew* (Garden City, N.Y.: Doubleday & Co., 1955).

[23]Claims by religious bodies as to membership may vary depending on whether or not they count, in Christian churches, all baptized infants, or only adult church members in good standing. For non-Christian groups, also, there is the question of affiliation by descent or by present participation. The current estimates on the basis of present participation are about 36 percent for combined Protestant bodies including sectarians; about 25 percent for Roman Catholics; about 5 percent for Jews, about 2 percent for Eastern Orthodox, .03 percent for Buddhists, and the remainder nonaffiliated.

idolatry. To a young nation engaged in settlement, with early marriage patterns, the celibate clergy, and the monasteries of monks and nuns wearing strange traditional garments and living in enclosed communities, were objects of suspicion and mistrust. Thus in the problems of interreligious relations there were both doctrinal (intrinsic) and customary (extrinsic) areas of devaluation.[24]

The Catholic Church in the nineteenth century was ill equipped to interpret itself to non-Catholics. Many of the priests were foreign born and many foreign trained. They felt that their primary obligation was to minister to the migrating ethnic populations for whom they made a link with the Catholic heritage of the home country. The fact that the Irish were English-speaking gave them an advantage in achieving major influence in the Catholic Church in America, especially in the East.

There were then historical institutional roots for anti-Catholicism, which for many people provided an easy rationale on which to focus their distress about other uncertainties and change. The first large migration of the Irish in the 1850s coincided with the nativist Know-Nothing Movement, which was anti-immigration and anti-Catholic. Later class and labor issues as well as general "antiforeign" sentiment fanned mistrust of southern and eastern European Catholics as well as of the Irish. How much of nineteenth-century anti-Catholicism was primarily a religious issue is hard to estimate. But certainly as late as the first quarter of the twentieth century there were specific hostile acts categorically directed against Catholics by the Ku Klux Klan. Job discrimination at middle and upper levels continued till the 1950s. In the growing urban centers of the East and West Coast there was often a link between local Irish politicians and the Church hierarchy. Establishment Protestants, sectarians, and Jews took a dim view of this, and raised afresh the principle of separation of church and state, in this instance to "protect the state from the church."

Where the church, any church, is the focal center of a socioreligious community, recent research suggests that this tends to foster a provincial and authoritarian view of the world.[25] It is these enclaves that most often know the least about other groups, their values, and their customs. They are also probably most vulnerable to distress if general social change impinges on the security of their religious, cultural, and social unity.

One study has found that today status identification is in some instances more important than religious communality, but even in those circumstances where interreligious friendships occur within closed status groups, there may be little sense of the content of belief of religions other than one's own.[26]

The Jewish Religion

Throughout American history until this century Jews were viewed as a religious group and religiously tolerated, though often personally discriminated against in em-

---

[24]In the eighteenth century where there were occasions of Catholic political leadership in Maryland and briefly in New York, there was greater religious tolerance than under Protestants.
See John Tracy Ellis, *American Catholicism* (Chicago: University of Chicago Press, 1969), p. 19.
[25]Gerhart Lenski, *The Religious Factor* (Garden City, N.Y.: Doubleday & Co., rev. ed. for Anchor Books, 1963).
[26]W. Widick Schroeder and Victor A. Oberhaus, *Religion in American Culture: Unity and Diversity in a Midwestern County* (New York: The Free Press of Glencoe, 1964), p. 182.

ployment, education, and residence, and humiliated or injured. Anti-Semitism is such a complex problem that we discuss it elsewhere at length (Chapter 16). Whereas Catholic doctrine had until recently a specific definition of Jewish responsibility in the death of Christ, it is doubtful if this in itself had much to do with rank-and-file attitudes of Catholics toward their Jewish neighbors, which were, in urban settings, usually cordial. Protestants, as American Protestantism is so much more biblical than doctrinal, had little quarrel with Jewish religion, though often with what they perceived as Jewish competition. Only in the post-Nazi period have there been any significant acts of violence against synagogues or Jewish religious symbols.

Jews have been strong supporters of the separation of church and state, as indeed were colonial Roman Catholics when they were a small minority, though well placed in terms of social class.[27]

Religion and Black Americans

The Black Protestant Churches in their several forms and affiliations represent the most continuously independent institution of black Americans. Since 1816, when the African Methodist Episcopal Church was founded in Philadelphia, the black churches have given support to independent identity for black Americans: they provided an opportunity for leadership when it was denied in secular spheres; they gave a congregation experience in planning and budgeting money when the larger society offered no such opportunity.[28]

There has been no antireligious effort against the established black denominations (Methodist and Baptist), though there has been strong effort on the part of some white churches to integrate black Americans into white congregations. The established black denominational churches and integrated churches are chiefly a middle-class phenomenon. For the large mass of the black poor, sects and transitory cults have flourished as a means to affirm identity, to exercise a sense of social power, to preserve some key aspects of black folk culture. One black theologian claims

> The single element black church-, sect-, and cult-types hold in common and which is without parallel in white counterparts is the *cult* of power for black realization in the here and now . . . this is what abides in the religion of black folk after every other element finds white inspiration or nearly exact reduplication.[29]

There have been incidents against some black sects (Muslims, for example), but these have been basically racial and not religious.

---

[27]Ellis, *American Catholicism*, p. 31.
[28]E. Franklin Frazier, *The Negro Church in America* (Liverpool: The University of Liverpool, 1963; Schocken Paperback edition, 1966), p. 23.
[29]Joseph R. Washington, Jr., *Black Sects and Cults* (Garden City, N.Y.: Doubleday & Co., Anchor Books, 1972), p. 8.

RELIGIOUS FREEDOM, ECUMENISM, AND RELIGIOUS PLURALISM

Religious freedom seems to be accepted by present-day Americans and upheld by the final resources of secular power, as long as the position, or practice, is clearly defined as "religious." There will, of course, always be conflict of ideas and institutional policy, but if these are recognized as legitimate and reasonably coequal they are no different from the disagreements between Republicans and Democrats. They contribute to the creative ferment of an alive society.

Religious bodies themselves still face some dilemmas: their relation to their particular commitments and beliefs, the role of organized religion for an individual's sense of identity, and their relationship with other religions and secular society. Here we see two trends, as yet unresolved.

The ecumenical movement, initiated by Pope John XXIII, has stimulated much dialogue and attempted rapprochement between religious groups, as have the theological influences of the Jewish theologian Martin Buber and the Protestant theologian Paul Tillich. This effort has certainly made for greater understanding at some leadership and elite levels of coequal searches for the correct approaches to man, society, and God. Ecumenism may stimulate some community contacts between different religious groups, and some vague thinking that we are "all basically alike and respectable together within the Judeo-Christian ethics." This is a middle-class position, and there are counter movements.

Former "minority" religious institutions are at present less concerned with ecumenism than with the definition of differences. To a degree this constitutes a struggle by religious bodies to preserve their particular interpretation of God and man and in part a struggle to assure that ecumenism does not violate a church's identity. It is, in one way, an attempt to affirm one's own heritage of belief, which may be modified but not corrupted. Thus we have new affirmations of the historical bases on which Catholics assert their unique part in building America.[30] We have new statements of Jewish theology, pointing out some fundamental differences between Jewish and Christian religion.[31] We have the development now of black theology.[32] These appear to be attempts to make explicit the differences germane to a truly co-equal status, not based solely on legal tolerance.

Another problem confronting the established religions is the involvement of some of their adherents in civil protest against state policies. Black clergy took a major role in the early civil rights protests, especially Dr. Martin Luther King, Jr. There were the protest actions of Catholic activists, like the Berrigan brothers, against the Vietnam War. Neither of these efforts have been against *people;* the first was against customs and laws; the second was against symbols of the policy of the secular establishment. As we saw at the beginning of this chapter, the established churches face the problem of finding and maintaining an appropriate compromise with the secular social structure. Activism in the name of the church against specific state policies creates dilemmas for both the institution of the state and the church.

---

[30]Ellis, *American Catholicism,* p. 31.
[31]See, for example, Arthur A. Cohen, *The Myth of the Judeo-Christian Tradition* (New York: Schocken Books, 1971).
[32]James H. Cone, *Liberation, A Black Theology of Liberation* (Philadelphia: J. B. Lippincott Co., 1970).

What we see is, then, on the one hand both an official and popular acceptance of a plurality of religious values and rituals so long as they are "purely religious." The religious bodies, on the other hand, are trying to define themselves more specifically in terms of *coequal* pluralism. And on the issues of social change all are to one degree or another wrestling anew with the problems of the church and the world.

Suggested Readings

Baltzell, E. Digby. *The Protestant Establishment: Aristocracy and Caste in America.* New York: Random House, 1964.
   An account of the consolidation and beginning decline of WASP dominance.

Blau, Joseph L., ed. *Cornerstones of Religious Freedom in America: Selected Basic Documents, Court Decisions and Public Statements,* revised and enlarged edition. New York: Harper and Row, 1964.

Cohen, Arthur A. *The Myth of the Judeo-Christian Tradition.* New York: Schocken Paperback, 1971.
   A Jewish theologian challenges "fuzzy liberal" thought on Jewish-Christian similarities and differences of belief.

Cone, James A. *Liberation: A Black Theology of Liberation.* Philadelphia: J. B. Lippincott Co., 1970.
   A black Christian theologian defines the new black American theology.

Ellis, John Tracy. *American Catholicism,* 2nd rev. ed. Chicago: University of Chicago Press, 1969.
   A chronological account of the development of the Catholic church in America, integrated with the social and political history of critical periods.

Greeley, Andrew M. *The American Catholic: A Social Portrait.* New York: Basic Books, Inc., 1977.
   A presentation of wide sociological data on America's Catholics, showing the wide variations and effectively demolishing stereotypes.

Hostetler, John A. *Amish Society,* rev. ed. Baltimore and London: Johns Hopkins Press, 1968.
   Sectarian religion as a way of life.

Lantenari, Victor. *The Religions of the Oppressed: A Study of Messianic Cults,* trans. from the Italian by Lia Sergio. New York: Alfred A. Knopf, 1963; also available in Mentor Books ed., 1965.
   A cross cultural study of the meaning and types of contemporary religious movements that depend on prophecy and promise liberation.

Raab, Earl, ed. *Religious Conflict in America: Studies in Problems Beyond Bigotry.* Garden City, N.Y.: Anchor Books, Doubleday and Co., 1964.
   A symposium of leading sociologists and theologians on religious dilemmas in contemporary America.

Washington, Joseph R., Jr. *Black Sects and Cults.* Garden City, N.Y.: Anchor Press, Doubleday and Co., 1972.
   A review of leading black messianic movements in twentieth century America,

with emphasis on folk and African residues, the promises of charismatic leadership, and the deeper meaning of "liberation."

Weigel, Gustave, S. J. *Churches in North America*. New York, Schocken Books, 1965.
An excellent presentation of non-Roman Catholic religious bodies in America, written for Catholic students "as a bridge to understanding."

Zborowski, Mark and Herzog, Elizabeth. *Life Is With People*. New York: International Universities Press, 1952.
Two anthropologists reconstruct with great sensitivity and warmth the life of the Eastern European Jewish village of the pre-Nazi period and show the integration of culture and religion.

4

A Nation of Immigrants

Over forty-five million immigrants have come to the United States since 1820 when the first records were kept. Three-quarters of these came from various countries of Europe, and although some returned home, having made some money or been disappointed, most of them stayed. They represented a broad spectrum of differences in language and folkways. It was at first assumed that by at least the second or third generation they would be absorbed into the dominant American culture, and for many throughout the nineteenth century this occurred. In the first decade of the twentieth century America was called "the melting pot" where a fused brand of American was emerging from varying European lines of descent, molded by the American experience, but nevertheless fundamentally WASP. Today we hear a great deal about ethnic pride and witness the formation of ethnic protest groups and ethnic community organizations. America is facing in new terms the reality of an ethnic pluralistic society.

THE GREAT ATLANTIC MIGRATION

Immigration, as the United States of America has known it, has been a peculiarly American institution. One British author has described it as "the greatest folk migration in human history," and "the most persistent and pervasive influence" on the development of the United States.[1] The Great Atlantic Migration opened a continent, built an industrial nation, and was a demonstration of political democracy's capacity to survive religious, national, and racial heterogeneity. The survival of the political institutions on which identification as an American is so strongly based today did not occur without pressures and counterpressures in meeting the challenge of unity born of heterogeneity.

The European migration has traditionally been broken into three periods before the restrictive legislation of 1924: the colonial, the "old," and the "new" immigration. Although this classification has had an effect on public opinion and on policy, there is no valid reason for it. The reasons for which immigrants came at all periods were similar; the skills they brought and their ability to adapt to the American environment show great consistency, however much groups differed culturally. Some came earlier, some later. The *impact* of immigration, however, varied; and the attitudes toward immigrants varied at different periods of the nation's development.[2]

[1]Maldwyn Allen Jones, *American Immigration* (Chicago: University of Chicago Press, 1960), p. 1.
[2]*Ibid.*, pp. 4–5.

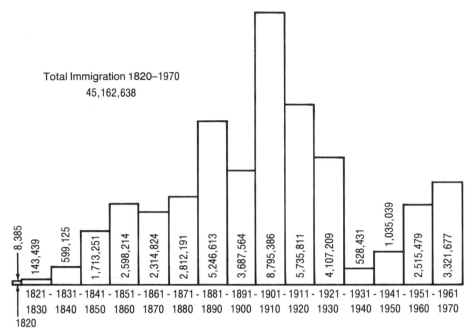

Total Immigration 1820–1970
45,162,638

| 8,385 | 143,439 | 599,125 | 1,713,251 | 2,598,214 | 2,314,824 | 2,812,191 | 5,246,613 | 3,687,564 | 8,795,386 | 5,735,811 | 4,107,209 | 528,431 | 1,035,039 | 2,515,479 | 3,321,677 |

1821 - 1831 - 1841 - 1851 - 1861 - 1871 - 1881 - 1891 - 1901 - 1911 - 1921 - 1931 - 1941 - 1951 - 1961
1830   1840   1850   1860   1870   1880   1890   1900   1910   1920   1930   1940   1950   1960   1970
1820

Source: *Statistical Abstract of the United States,* United States Department of Commerce, Bureau of the Census, 92 Ed., 1971, Table 130, p. 89.

Figure 4-1   Total Immigration to the United States by Decades.

Except for slaves and transported convicts, migration involved in most instances a *decision* and a risk, which to an extent may have strengthened self-reliance, adaptability, and enterprise. Despite lingering loyalties to distant lands, the experience of migration inevitably worked against traditional values.

Reception of the Immigrants

Public issues related to immigration in the American colonies before the Revolution involved immigrants who lacked visible means of support, those convicted of crimes abroad, and Catholics. The criteria for acceptance had to do with economics, religion, and "moral standing;" there was no nationality criterion, though from time to time the Scotch-Irish, the French, and the Germans briefly encountered hostile attitudes. The attitude toward immigrants could be summed up as "welcome tinged with misgiving."[3]

The power struggle of the Revolutionary and post-Revolutionary period assured the preeminence of English political institutions and the English language. The success of the War of Independence united diverse elements behind a leadership stemming from the predominance of Englishmen in the first two generations of settlement. Although only New England and the Tidewater areas of other colonies had a predominance of population of English descent, these were the entrenched and the powerful.

[3]*Ibid.,* p. 40.

The newcomers, of whatever origin, so far removed from Europe by the three-month voyage, were nevertheless sufficiently identified with the new world to be able to take individual positions—loyalist or revolutionary—without needing to form nationality blocs.[4]

The immediate post-Revolutionary period saw growing concern for the political influence of new migrants: political conservatives feared the growth-by-immigration of the antifederalists; the popular democratic front was suspicious of the acceptance of emigrés from toppling European aristocracies. The Alien and Sedition Acts of 1798 had "antiforeign" implications and were accompanied by "antiforeign" outbreaks. Attempts were made to lengthen the period of residence before enfranchisement from two, to five, to fourteen years, but the longer periods, though enacted, were evaded by states. The tension of establishing a new nation made itself felt. Both the American Revolution and the Civil War acted to improve the integration and the status of the immigrant groups. But the periods of tension preceding and during wars and accompanying economic depressions occasioned outbreaks against "foreigners."

The acculturation and assimilation of the nineteenth-century migrants depended on a number of factors. There was at the time a public policy against grants of land to ethnic groups, although several efforts were made to have such nationality enclaves established in the West. Dispersion greatly affected the rapidity of acculturation. Voluntary concentration on the part of the immigrants slowed their merging with the dominant Anglo-Saxon culture; but repeated nativistic movements also affected attitudes toward these new people. It is important here to distinguish between a passive dislike of foreigners based on ethnocentrism and the more violent mass xenophobia, marked by irrational hysteria, and often inspired by specific political interests.

Early nativism (pre-Civil War) had as its most prominent theme anti-"foreignism." Economic competition was not at this time a *manifest* issue. The Know-Nothing Party, which had its heyday in the two decades before the Civil War, revived the old Federalist efforts to limit office-holding to the native-born, to extend the period for naturalization, and to exclude criminals and paupers. Nativism reemerged after the unifying interim of the Civil War, particularly on the West Coast. The restrictive acts of 1882-1885 were not an integrated attempt to deal with immigration, but rather a series of unconnected measures favoring special interests. The role of organized labor in "anti-foreign" efforts began to be felt, in California and the Midwest, in mines, and in heavy industries, where new immigrants from Europe were used as strikebreakers or where other groups (such as Orientals) were willing to work for low wages. After the Haymarket bombing of 1886, the tendency to link the terms "foreign" and "radical" gained new impetus.

The nativistic movements of the nineteenth century reflected, in part, the struggles of the newly settled West to achieve a balance of power in federal policy; they reflected the unease of the agricultural sector, and of new industry, with the efforts to create a strong labor movement; and they reflected the problems of growing cities. All these factors contributed to the attempts to consolidate the dominance of the Anglo-Saxon Protestant segment of the population. With the 1890 census the frontier was declared closed, and soon thereafter the myth of the frontier as the basic American experience began to take shape. Since most of the post-1880 immigrants had little relation to the settling of the frontier, the myth helped to devalue latecomers.

---

[4]*Ibid.*, pp. 53 ff.

THE RESTRICTION OF IMMIGRATION

Immigration restriction is only one facet of the attempt, successful for a time, to ensure the dominance of one segment of the population, a population that bolstered its claim to legitimate privilege and leadership by descent, by language, and by having given, as it were, the *imprimatur* to "American" styles of thought and behavior. The heavy waves of immigration at the turn of the century were needed for growing industry. They were facilitated by better transport and encouraged by persecution or overpopulation in Europe. They precipitated a consolidation and articulation of the "Establishment" that manifested itself in social and political restrictive measures, despite the beginnings of reform movements and welfare efforts.

The Dillingham Commission

In 1907, when the nation was experiencing the greatest volume of immigration of all time, the Dillingham Commission was created to study the question of immigration and report to Congress. It was this Commission that coined the concept "old" and "new" immigration. The theme runs through the entire forty-one volumes of its report that the "old" immigration was of a different kind, had dispersed, and entered all phases of American life, whereas the "new" immigration had congregated together in such a way that assimilation was impeded. The implication was that these late arrivals constituted pockets of people without American standards, values, or loyalties. In comparing "old" and "new," the Dillingham Commission's report took no account of the longer period of settlement of the "old" immigrant group. Furthermore, it lumped all old and all new into two simple categories without taking into account the vast differences in skill, motivation, and social organization within each category.

The report came during a period of economic depression and gave support to a growing sentiment in favor of immigration restriction. Indeed, it provided the rationalizations on which the quota system subsequently was enacted. The anxieties of World War I, the increasing status of organized labor (won during the war), the fear of "radical" movements that appeared to be sweeping Europe at the close of the war, the psychological tests for the army that had shown low ratings for Southern Europeans from peasant cultures, all increased the pressure for restriction.

The movement to restrict immigration gained backing from three public groups. The first, and probably most influential, was organized labor. Labor's position was based primarily on the practical consideration that immigrant labor accepted low wages and was generally more tractable, thus retarding union efforts to improve the workers' economic position. A second public favoring restriction was composed of those various individuals scattered throughout the country who attributed many of the nation's ills to the presence of "too many ignorant foreigners." In examining the newspapers and magazines from 1900 to 1930, Woofter found that from 1907 to 1914 there occurred a marked change in public sentiment toward immigration. "The undesirability of certain racial elements" was becoming more persuasive than economic arguments against restriction.[5] Finally, there was a growing feeling that the nation could not go on in-

---

[5]T. J. Woofter, Jr., *Races and Ethnic Groups in American Life* (New York: McGraw-Hill Book Co., 1933), p. 31.

definitely trying to assimilate such large masses of people of different cultures. This point of view is reflected in the report of the United States Immigration Commission in 1911, which recommended restriction on economic, moral, and social grounds. The first congressional act to give expression to these pressures was the measure to bar as immigrants any aliens who were illiterate (a measure passed in 1917 over President Wilson's veto). This kind of test was aimed at curtailing southern and eastern European immigration. Actually, it failed to reduce materially the volume of immigration, and Congress turned to a system of numerical limitation.

The Quota System

Congress first passed the Immigration Act of 1921, the most important aspect of which was that it restricted immigration on a primarily numerical basis—the first time this principle had been applied. The act provided that the number of aliens of any nationality admissible to the United States in any one year be limited to 3 percent of the number of foreign-born persons of such nationality who were residents of the United States in 1910. The act did not apply to the Western Hemisphere or to countries otherwise regulated, such as China and Japan. The total yearly quota admissible under this act was 357,803. The effect, although not the wording, of this law was discriminatory against southern and eastern European nationalities. The quotas set up permitted about 200,000 immigrants from the northern and western countries and 155,000 from the others. Since from 1910 to 1914 the average annual immigration from the northern European countries had been less than the quotas allowed, in practice the law did not greatly limit immigration from these areas. But it did greatly restrict southern and eastern European immigration, which had averaged 738,000 annually during the 1910–1914 period.

The Immigration Act of 1921 at its expiration was supplanted by the Immigration Act of 1924. Two different systems of quota apportionment were then set up: one temporary, in order to give the Immigration Commission time to work out proper quotas for the other, the permanent quota allotment. The temporary quota, which was to operate for three years, provided that "the annual quota of any nationality shall be 2 per cent of the number of foreign-born individuals of such nationality resident in continental United States as determined by the United States Census of 1890, but the minimum quota of any nationality shall be 100;" The effect of this act was to reduce the number of yearly immigrants still further, to 164,667, and to discriminate even more strongly against the "newer" immigrant countries. Northern and western Europe were allotted 80 percent, whereas the southern and eastern nationalities had only 20 percent of the quota. The permanent provisions of the Act of 1924, which took effect in 1929, reduced the annual quota to 153,774. The law called for the apportionment of the total quota among the countries to which the act applied according to their relative contribution to the American population as enumerated in 1920. The actual immmigration at the time of the passing of the first restriction (1921) as compared with the quotas, for selected countries, demonstrates the effect of the quota system. In 1921 there were 652,364 immigrants from Germany; in 1929 there were 25,957. For Ireland there were 28,435 immigrants in 1921; the quota figure for 1929 was 17,853. For Italy there were 222,260 in 1921; the 1929 quota was 5,802. Several small modifications were made between 1929 and 1952 that represented the changed status of populations in the shifting of national borders or the creation of new nations.[6]

IMMIGRATION SINCE THE ESTABLISHMENT OF RESTRICTION

Although there have been amendments, and two special acts affecting immigration outside the quota system, there has been no fundamental change in the policy of restriction.

During the 1925–1930 period practically all European nations utilized their quotas to the full. The fact that total immigration exceeded the quotas is accounted for by the admission of nonquota immigrants as permitted by the act of 1924, the largest group of which were wives, husbands, or minor children of resident immigrants. Immigration dropped below the permissible limits from 1931 to 1935, reflecting the economic depression that made coming to America less attractive to Europeans. In addition, the federal government instructed its consulates abroad to apply rigidly the clauses in the legislation denying entry to persons likely to become public charges. World War II practically cut off all immigration, and because of the shortage of labor in a war economy the United States imported, on temporary visas, some 350,000 workers from Mexico, Canada, and the Caribbean.

Political changes in Europe began what has become a series of special provisions for refugees. The first large group was those people seeking asylum from persecution in the expanding Nazi Reich: about 243,000. After 1946 approximately 400,000 displaced persons were admitted. These were Europeans rendered homeless through the destruction of war or who for various reasons could not with safety return to their prewar communities.

The McCarran-Walter Act, 1952

The McCarran-Walter Act did not change the policy of the quota system but involved setting up preferences within the same system. Immigration officials were ordered to give first preferences to persons with skills currently in short supply, and second preference to relatives of persons already in this country. Other provisions of the act included codifying the entire series of immigration bills and allotting quotas for the first time to Asiatic nations, in most instances 100 per annum (185 for Japan). Immigration had been debated bitterly for the previous five years. The act was passed over President Truman's veto and reflects the continuance of "nativist" preferences and a fear of possible "subversive" infiltration. The failure to liberalize the approach to immigration on the one hand and the tiny concession to naturalization of Asiatics on the other represents the fundamental unease and inevitable compromises in democratic political action, with a changing world and America's new role within these changes.

The 1952 act made no real attack on the "national origins" bias of the quota system. It simplified the national origins formula of the 1924 act by basing the annual quota on

[6]Edmund Traverso, *Immigration: A Study in American Values* (Boston: D. C. Heath & Co., 1964), pp. 118–119.

a flat one-sixth of one percent of the population of that origin in the 1920 Census. The total quota was 154,657.

President Truman's veto message[7] sharply criticized the quota system as defined in the act, describing it as a "discriminatory policy." He cited the quota from Poland, for example: 6,500 as against 138,000 exiled Poles seeking to come here.

The Act of 1965

Sentiment against nationality quotas had been building up, and in the 1960 presidential campaign both Republicans and Democrats included some statement in their platforms urging modification. On October 3, 1965, further amendments to the immigration law were enacted, which, beginning December 1, 1965, were to eliminate over a five-year period of transition "national origins" as a basis for selective entry into the United States. Although only 10 percent of the total quota may be admitted from any one country in a single year, the principle of *preferential nationality* has been supplanted by one more equitable.

In the amended law the preference system of granting visas is retained from the 1952 revision with only minor modification to admit more professionals and to allow some adjustments in health requirements. The law defines different classes of immigrants: those eligible for preference visas (relatives, professionals, skilled or unskilled labor in short supply, refugees) who come within the total quota. There are additional places for nonpreference immigrants. These, like skilled and unskilled workers (category six) must have certification from the United States Department of Labor. Western Hemisphere immigrants enter freely, not as part of the quota, but also must have Labor Department certification. The 1965 amendment, in harmony with its relaxation of discrimination, adds free migration to Western Hemisphere colonials (largely Caribbean) on the same basis rather than as part of the applications of their mother country. The law still retains from the McCarran-Walter Act exclusion of members of "totalitarian" or "communist" political parties, a requirement often difficult to interpret justly.

Immigration in Perspective

The history of immigration legislation makes several issues apparant. When the United States needed a work force to develop natural resources, to provide manpower for its growing industries, immigrants were welcome and often recruited. There has always been, also, a humanistic as well as an economic motivation in immigration policy: political asylum, freedom of thought, family ties. When the great majority of immigrants were unskilled, semiskilled, or even skilled labor, they found their places within the class structure, in the lower ranks, and it was expected that as individuals they would improve their situation and rise, at least in exploiting opportunity for their children and grandchildren. Many succeeded in this pattern. On the other hand, it was as individuals moved up that discrimination became more apparant. In a class-structured society with a democratic ideology, "foreignness" became a convenient rationalization for resistance to sharing privilege.

---

[7]"House Document No. 520," *Congressional Record* (Washington, D.C.: Government Printing Office, 1952), 8225–8228.

The situation today is different. It is clear that no modern "welfare state" can absorb unlimited in-migration. The "developed" nations will continue to allow only limited and selective additions to the population. The establishment of preference quotas was a reflection of this selective process. In principle this policy tries to combine capacity for the economy to absorb into the labor force (based on labor department certification, skills in short supply, etc.) and concern for family unity (second preference) and refugees.

There are, however, many problems with our immigration laws as they now stand, since their additional amendation, special acts, and court decisions have created inconsistencies and confusion. Probably the most important tasks are (1) the clarification and refinement of the preference categories, with, it is recommended, assignment of a percentage to each category; (2) a review of the refugee situation to include it under the preference system and bring our policy in harmony with the United Nations protocol on refugees, which we signed; (3) some action to regularize the problem of the "undocumented alien." There are an estimated half million illegal entrants annually, about 100,000 of whom get caught and deported. It is recommended that employers be penalized, as the use of undocumented workers encourages substandard wages in labor intensive employment.[8]

The great pressure for entry into America brings an awareness of how the United States is affected by world poverty. The ultimate solution for the developed countries will have to lie in aid to the poor countries to hasten their own capacity to meet the basic needs of their own populations.

IMMIGRANT ADJUSTMENT: OLD STYLE

We have said that the emigration to America involved a decision and a risk. It also involved initial hardship for most, and culture shock. There is now a vast literature on the great century of migration, 1820 to 1920. Much of it was written by crusading journalists, reformers and social workers, sociologists and government agencies. Most of it was produced by dominants, however liberal and humanitarian many of them were. Only recently, with the ethnic revival are we learning more from the newcomers themselves, though some of their early advocates among dominant writers have quoted them trenchantly.

We know that it was a common pattern for the immigrants to come to, or subsequently send for relatives, to house them, and to make community linkages for them. Until the outlawing of contract labor in 1882, many came with commitments to jobs, however low paid. After 1882 agents of major industries waited at Ellis Island to meet the boats and select skills or brawn for America's industrial expansion. There was continually, also, a small flow of professionals and small-business men with some capital who could establish themselves more easily. A sizable proportion, of course, also settled in rural areas and engaged in farming occupations.

The Ethnic Subcommunity

Wherever immigrants settled in considerable numbers they at first clustered with people from home. Sometimes they even had little sub-subcommunities, where they

---

[8]The above discussion is derived from a conference on immigration held in May, 1977, by the American Immigration and Citizenship Conference, a voluntary organization.

had discovered neighbors and friends not only from the home country but from the home district, and they brought their district or regional rivalries with them. Then, as now with the Puerto Ricans, they settled in the sections of the city that were least desirable residentially, since this was what was available to them. Then as now, landlords discovered that exorbitant rents could be extracted for little space and poor quality of housing. Families were forced to crowd into single rooms or "old law" tenements, some of whose rooms had no windows. In the evenings, the people spilled out on the street, weather permitting, and gossiped, quarreled, exchanged news from home, shopped from the pushcarts, and insofar as possible recreated the life of the home village.

In the new environment, nationality groups developed traditional community structures for informal interaction: taverns, coffeehouses, sports clubs, a foreign language press, mutual aid socities. More formal organizations followed in the growth of nationality societies: Polish-American, Hungarian-American, etc. These larger more inclusive societies were in part a defense against their consciousness of minority status. To be an *Italian*-American was a defense against being treated as a Dago or a Wop. Although the nationality societies played some role in the preservation of traditional symbols (dress, festivals, etc.), they were primarily a channel for the expression of group interest and group dignity to the larger world beyond the subcommunity.

Dominants also developed, primarily in the cities, associations to aid immigrants: voluntary (secular) associations, settlement houses, religious groups, etc. Their intent was to ease adjustment. The majority of these efforts had "Americanization" and assimilation as their explicit or implicit goal; though it may be pointed out that early concepts of "cultural pluralism" emanated, at the turn of the century, from the settlement (house) movement. In the activities and services provided by settlement houses, immigrants encountered the resident Anglo staff as well as discovering other participants of other national backgrounds. It has been claimed that the settlements tended to reach the more ambitious individuals anxious to move out of the traditional subcommunity, and that later in the 1930s and 1940s, the gap between immigrant communities and middle-class WASP social workers widened to the point that the real needs of the subcommunities, and the real potentials for leadership, were ignored.[9]

Interaction In the American Institutional Structure

The urban political party, the lower ranks of the civil service, and the trade union were each major modes of involving the immigrant in American life.

The involvement of the immigrant in politics is as old as the nation and the early struggles between the propertied and the popular parties. The immigrant vote was marshaled for every election, often with the individual voter understanding the issues only very vaguely at best. The heavy concentration of the Irish in the port cities of the East let them very early play an active role in organizing local politics. As urban centers grew throughout the nineteenth century, "machine" politics developed, seeking local control and party influence in the state and national elections. In the East, and to some extent in other industrial areas, the machine was Democratic and the leadership initially was Irish. The political machine operated on a basis of patronage and personal favors, which aroused the criticism of the "good government" organizations. However, the machine was able to make politics more personal for the immigrant, and therefore

---

[9] William Foote Whyte, *Street Corner Society* (Chicago: University of Chicago Press, 1943).

more meaningful, than could forces whose approach to civil life was impersonalized and abstract.

Oscar Handlin describes machine politics as more characteristic of the second generation than of the immigrants themselves. Since the group that migrated often was too involved in other pressures, did not command the language, and had no history of political participation, it remained apathetic.[10]

During the nineteenth century, the lower civil service jobs in the cities became a channel for the establishment of immigrants and their children. The police force, the fire department, and the post office had their lower ranks filled from the new groups. The link between political patronage and the police allowed for a considerable amount of corruption, but it also kept the police of America free of the authoritarian and severe disciplinary attitude found in some of the immigrants' home countries.

The labor movement, too, involved the immigrant in an organizational structure that helped him adapt to the conditions of the new country. Throughout the nineteenth century, factories tended to deploy their labor force in a way that maintained ethnic solidarity, each department or shop having a particular ethnic character. Union locals therefore similarly were largely or exclusively composed of one ethnic group. But in the experience of a strike or in the conduct of union affairs above the shop level, native Americans, British, Irish, German, Welsh, Russian Jewish, Italian, and many others worked together. The major involvement of immigrant workers in unions came in the early twentieth century, but immigrants were prominent in the Workingmen's Party, a labor party before the Civil War, in the Knights of Labor, and in the formation of the American Federation of Labor.

While the school was a more important factor for the native-born children of immigrants, it played some role also for the immigrant generation. Many cities set up night schools, with curricula stressing English language and the civics necessary for naturalization. The main influence of the school on the adult immigrant, however, was indirectly mediated through the children. The children became the carriers of the English language and new ideas into traditional homes. While in the long run it was to be free education that opened opportunity to the descendants of immigrants, in the short run too often the school fell short of solving conflicts of feeling and identity. The elementary-school textbooks of the nineteenth and early twentieth century were based on the vocabulary and images of rural America, and were unreal to children of densely crowded urban low-income areas. Teachers, unknowingly, even if they were fond of the children they taught, patronized their "foreign" backgrounds and contributed to their sense of inferiority.

Generational Conflict and Marginality

What gave security to their elders created conflict for the children of the immigrant growing up in America. Like all other parents, immigrant parents conditioned their children to their accustomed social heritage. The children, as a result of their school experience and the other outside stimuli that their growing knowledge of the English language opened to them wanted to become "Americanized." The children began to perceive that the culture of their parents was not American as defined by the outside

[10]Oscar Handlin, *The Uprooted* (Boston: Little, Brown & Co., 1951), Ch. 8.

dominant native world. Furthermore, the immigrant children learned that the ways of their parents were defined as inferior and that they, too, were socially rejected because of their background. Handlin discusses the fact that a great deal of the generational problem was compounded by the insecurity of the immigrant parents in their own roles. In the new environment a confusion arose as to the old established rights and duties between husband and wife and parents and children. Without the protective cover of well-defined roles, father, mother, son, and daughter faced one another as individuals under the most trying conditions.[11]

Some of the second generation did become Americans in their incorporation of the American goal of achievement and success. The traditionally sanctioned means to business success were frequently closed to them, however, because of ethnic discrimination and low socioeconomic status. For many, achievement or monetary success could be found in politics or the rackets and, as Daniel Bell has pointed out, both politics and crime in the large urban areas have experienced successive invasions by ethnic groups.[12]

For some individuals who did correctly perceive the expectations and values of the dominant society, the situation in which they found themselves was often marginal. Taking the dominant group as their reference group and incorporating dominant norms and goals, they found themselves at a competitive disadvantage, and were often made to feel inferior. Such a person, Chick Morelli, is described by Whyte. He identified with the schools, his teachers, the settlement workers, saved his money, got an education, tried to organize an "improvement" program in his community of "Cornerville," but came to see politics as the only career open to him despite his associations with people outside his subcommunity. He even came to believe that Italians themselves were to blame for the discrimination they received, yet he did not successfully establish himself in "native" middle-class society.[13]

Making It: As an Individual, Old Style

> The first thing he did was anglicize his name: Paul Stanley. Through the aid of his athletic prowess he had graduated from college and gone to law school while supporting himself working in the law office of a local lawyer of upper middle-class (native) status.
>
> Paul's father and mother had come from Poland when they were children. They had both worked in the shoe factory and had gone to an "Americanization school" to improve their English. They were proud of their home, which they owned outright, kept well painted, and landscaped with cast-off tires, a border of half-buried beer cans, and well-tended garden and lawn. They looked down on their less ambitious neighbors and also the Riverbrookers (lower-lower class people with "native" status).

[11]*Ibid.*, p. 239.
[12]Daniel Bell, "Crime as an American Way of Life," *Antioch Review*, Summer, 1953. Also in Bell, *The End of Ideology* (Glencoe, Ill.: The Free Press, 1960).
See also for Robert K. Merton's analysis of the responses to available goals and means.
[13]Whyte, *Street Corner Society*, pp. 52–56.

Mr. Stanley was very fond and proud of his son, for whom education had opened the door to greater social heights. Their first serious rift came when Paul became interested in Annie Taylor, a Riverbrooker girl; Paul wanted to marry her and eventually did, much to the disappointment of his parents. Annie's family were a typical ne'er-do-well low-class family known to the truant officer. Annie herself was the most ambitious and respectable of the lot and had in school managed to be accepted in "better-class" cliques of girls. Because of all the in-law complications, Annie and Paul ran away to get married, causing a split in Annie's family, who said she had married a "damn foreigner" and a Catholic fellow. Following their marriage, the new Stanleys drew away from both sets of parents, who were not after all the kinds of parents they wanted their new friends to meet. Their new home was in a nonethnic neighborhood.

After graduating from law school Paul had been invited to join the Caribous, made up mostly of Yankees, with only a few Poles. Within a year after his marriage, Paul became a member of the Antlers (higher social rating then the Caribous) and played bridge there several nights a week. He began to neglect his Caribou contacts. The Stanleys were now in a social clique made up of Yankee lower-middle class folks but were not, of course, ever invited to dinner at the home of the still higher-class Antlers whom Paul knew at the club, or even called on by the nice ladies of Hill Street—upper class. "And anyway," they said, "we're going to see to it that our children have every advantage."[14]

Ethnic Succession

Throughout the century of free migration the newcomers who came earlier bolstered their status and compensated for their devaluation by the established society by devaluing the next group. As some of their members moved up and out of the subcommunities, their places were taken by the more newly arrived, often of different nationality and cultural roots. Caroline Ware, in her study of New York's Greenwich Village in the 1920s, found that for Italians the immediate consciousness of their subordinate position was in relation to the Irish rather than in regard to WASP society.[15] The authors of the study of Yankee City (Newburyport, Massachusetts) in the 1930s found a status hierarchy corresponding largely to the period of migration.[16] Where neighborhoods became interethnic often the cultural bond was reinforced for each group, at least for the migrating generation and for many of the second generation. Herbert J. Gans has studied one such urban neighborhood.[17] The largest ethnic group was Italian, although the neighborhood included Poles, Albanians, Ukrainians, Greeks, and a residue each of

---

[14]William Lloyd Warner and P. S. Lunt, *The Social Life of a Modern Community* (New Haven: Yale University Press, 1941). Condensed adaptation by Charles F. Marden of Warner and Lunt, pp. 188–193. By permission.
[15]Caroline F. Ware, *Greenwich Village* (Boston, Mass.: Houghton Mifflin Co., 1935), p. 131.
[16]William Lloyd Warner and Leo Srole, *The Social Systems of American Minority Groups* (New Haven, Conn.: Yale University Press, 1941).
[17]Herbert J. Gans, *The Urban Villagers: Group and Class in the Life of Italian-Americans* (New York: The Free Press, 1962).

elderly Irish and elderly Jews. There was also a scattering of middle-class professionals and students attached to the nearby teaching hospital, artists, gypsies, and groups of single men as well as some of the very poor, with the pattern of broken families and the mild pathologies of the psychologically disabled. Only 7 percent of the population was "American" in background.

Gans gives a picture of the second-generation Italians of today as a "peer group society" in which sociability centers around a gathering of family and friends, occurring several times a week. "One could almost say that the meetings of the group are at the vital center of . . . life, that they are the end for which other everyday activities are a means." The activities of such a group center largely around the exchange of news and gossip. This serves as a mechanism of social control, supplies information and advice, provides entertainment and drama about one's own group that are provided for others through the mass media. This translated "village" social behavior reinforces group identity and interprets selectively the "outside" world. It protects the group from disorganizing influences and substitutes for formal organizations.

Gans sees this tightly woven ethnic society threatened by larger social changes. In the specific instance, the neighborhood he studied had been designated for urban renewal, which would inevitably lead to the ecological dispersion of many of the families. The fact that the younger generation will stay in school longer will lead many of them out of the blue-collar occupational world of their parents. The discontinuance of arranged marriages will, despite the strong family controls, lead to increasing interethnic marriage.[18]

Ethnic succession not only affected neighborhoods, but the institutional hierarchies of employment and politics as well. There was a time up to the turn of the century when a worker could rise through the skill hierarchy, leaving entry-level jobs for newcomers. In many instances the ethnic control of a particular floor or operation succeeded in reserving entry-level jobs for new migrants of their own group, or relatives. Since World War II, however, Fair Employment legislation, national or state, has made this only informally possible.

The unions, also, have experienced succession in shop stewards, the union bureaucracy, the local Central Trades and Labor Councils, and, to an extent, in the top leadership. The persistent pattern of group solidarity, however, and the need to reserve hard-won gains for one's own kinship or group has affected apprenticeship policies, especially in the craft unions.

In local and state politics we also see succession. After the restriction of immigration, leadership passed from the Irish to other national groups, and by the 1948 national election the political pattern had changed so that the "ethnic vote" was held to be no longer a meaningful category.[19] There was an attempt in the 1972 election to revive a political

[18]Russo, in a study of three generations of Italian Americans in New York City, notes the increasing rate of outgroup marriage. Between the second and third generation there has been a decline in the number outmarrying other than Irish and an increase in Italian-Irish intermarriage, as both groups participate more in the general pattern of American Catholic religious and social organizations.

N. J. Russo, "Three Generations of Italians in New York City: Their Religious Acculturation," in S. M. Tomasi and M. H. Engel, *The Italian Experience in the United States* (Staten Island, N.Y.: Center for Migration Studies, 1970), pp. 195 ff.

[19]Samuel Lubell, *The Future of American Politics,* 2nd rev. ed. (New York: Doubleday & Co., Anchor Books, 1956). See index for analysis of nationality votes from 1929 to 1948.

base among white "ethnics." The Nixon strategy in both 1968 and 1972 was to identify black ethnicity with a life of crime, welfare cheating, and evasion of work. Formerly stigmatized ethnic groups like Jews, Irish, Italians, and Poles voted in one of the few times in forty years 40–60 percent Republican.[20]

Making It: As a Group

Although linguistically different, the Germans, Scandinavians, Swiss, and French Huguenots never suffered the categorical discriminations that most subsequent groups encountered. The more rapid acculturation and social acceptance of these northern Europeans was facilitated by many favorable circumstances. For one thing, they were less visibly different. Their cultures had more affinity to the dominant Anglo-Saxon culture. They were largely Protestant. They were more experienced in democratic political practices. And they possessed a heritage of independent agricultural occupation. The relatively small proportions that settled initially in cities were mainly skilled craftsmen or professionals. That they were "looked down on" and "poked fun at" is illustrated by the following jingle quoted by Smith, directed at members of an immigrant group in Minnesota:

> Swedie, Swedie, stuck in the straw,
> Can't say nuthin' but "Yaw, yaw, yaw,"[21]

But with the acquisition of the English language, without an accent in their children's cases, most north Europeans became accepted Americans. They intermarried (Germans and Scandinavians) in the second generation; in the third they outmarried and no longer spoke the language of their forefathers. They shared the Protestant ethic of hard work, improvement of self and land or enterprise, believed in education, and founded colleges. In the private spheres of life there was still some intragroup life in which they shared a sense of common heritage and nuances of communication. Like other American white Protestants of northern-European descent they maintained some sense of the country of their heritage, some interest in their traditional European roots, but the former "homeland" became, as one writer has called them "ghost nations," no longer experienced as real.[22]

The considerable number of Irish people who came to the colonies in the eighteenth century appear not to have been thought of as a people apart from the rest, except for a period when they arrived in large numbers. In the nineteenth century they were the first of the great ethnic migrations. They settled primarily in cities and stayed heavily concentrated in the North Atlantic states, except for those employed in mining and the construction of railways and canals. In the three decades before the Civil War they encountered much resistance and discrimination from the "native" population. For one

---

[20]Martin Kilson, "Blacks and Neo-ethnicity in American Political Life," in Nathan Glazer and Daniel P. Moynihan, *Ethnicity: Theory and Experience* (Cambridge, Mass.: Harvard University Press, 1975), pp. 242–243.

[21]W. C. Smith, *Americans in the Making* (New York: Appleton-Century-Crofts, 1939), p. 149, n. 28.

[22]Nathan Glazer, "Ethnic Groups in America: From National Culture to Ideology," in *Freedom and Control in Modern Society*, Monroe Berger, Theodore Abel, and Charles H. Page, eds. (New York: D. Van Nostrand Co., 1954), p. 179.

thing, they were Catholic and anti-British. They were rural people who had settled largely in cities and towns. They entered the lower occupational ranks of unskilled work, thus starting with lower-class status at a time when class distinction was becoming more important.

This was America's first confrontation with a peasant culture. The English, Scandinavians, or Germans who came to America in the nineteenth century came from towns or from freehold farming patterns. The Irish had been long exploited by the English landholding system. The unchallenged position of the Catholic Church cemented bonds of identity. A history of famine, a family and inheritance system that led to late marriage and many unmarried men and women, the ambivalent situation of being English-speaking but not part of English-derived institutions, and migration in large numbers put the Irish in a peculiar relationship to dominants. Some welcomed them as a necessary working-class contingent; others engaged in flagrant discrimination. This discrimination is memorialized in an American folksong popular in the music halls of the 1860s.[23]

> I'm a decent boy just landed from the town of Ballyfad;
> I want a situation, and I want it very bad.

> I seen employment advertised, "It's just the thing," says I
> But the dirty spalpeen ended with "No Irish need apply."

Prior to the great migration in the years 1846–1850, the Irish were distributed throughout the class structure. Glazer and Moynihan, writing on the Irish in New York today, find that this is once more true. In the interim period they were far outstripped by some of the other groups migrating at the same time. Glazer and Moynihan attribute this in part to their Catholicism, which did not impart a strong ethic of individual success, to their immediate involvement and ultimate success in politics, which strengthened attitudes of discrimination against them, and to their high rate of alcoholism.[24]

Father Andrew Greeley, a scholar long involved in ethnic studies, expresses in a popular article his regret that the Irish have opted to show WASPS that they can be "respectable," thereby losing their particular style and flavor, both as Catholics and as political pragmatists. He feels that in the light of their experience they should better have allied themselves with the political aspirations of black and Spanish-speaking Americans.[25]

Discrimination.   The degree to which there is still discrimination in entry to the job market is difficult to determine. Every ethnic group has had some historical experience of this though legal protections have been developed. It is access to training, and to jobs conveying greater prestige, that seems to be the focal point of concern about discrimination. Entrance to a grade A medical school, appointment to the staff of a prestigious

---

[23]Edith Fowke and Joe Glazer, *Songs of Work and Freedom* (Garden City, N.Y.: Doubleday & Co., 1961), p. 154.
[24]Nathan Glazer and Daniel Patrick Moynihan, *Beyond the Melting Pot: The Negroes, Puerto Ricans, Jews, Italians, and Irish of New York City,* rev. ed. (Cambridge, Mass.: M. I. T. Press), 1970.
[25]*The New York Times Magazine,* March 14, 1971, pp. 32 ff.

hospital, promotion within a corporation, etc., may in some regions only be open, exceptionally, to a few representatives of eastern or southern European background.

Social discrimination and personal devaluation are probably widespread, though these factors are hard to measure, and they are not as blatant as a reply once made by Senator Bilbo (Mississippi) to a letter by a Miss Josephine Piccolo urging support of the Fair Employment Practices Bill before the Senate. In answer he addressed her as "My dear "Dago."[26] Representative Marcantonio protested in a letter to Senator Bilbo, and his letter and the Senator's reply were written into the Congressional Record.

On the whole, in an era of mass communication and world awareness social discrimination has declined, though there are still those who view ambition and social mobility as admirable in Anglo-Saxons and as unsuitable, aggressive, even "impertinent," in an "ethnic" individual or group.

THE NEW ETHNICITY

The decade of the seventies has been called that of rising ethnic consciousness. There has been a flood of publication, a rise in "ethnic studies" in schools and universities, pressure for bilingual education, revival of the study of languages long neglected in the efforts of both dominants and minorites toward "Americanization."

Some see this upsurge of ethnic identity as a revolt against the alienation of a technological and bureaucratic society with its impersonal rewards, its standardized tasks, its materialistic status seeking. For these, "ethnic politics" is a cultural thrust, not an expression of economic interests.[27] It may be epitomized in a search for "roots" in a society changing so rapidly that the expectations of a generation ago seem no longer viable. In this dimension Harold R. Isaacs argues that there are basic essentials in any group identity: shared physical characteristics, language, name, history, and origins as they are transmitted explicitly or implicitly through the values and assumptions of the family and community, as they are institutionalized in religion and national origin.[28]

Another emphasis in viewing the rise of ethnicity is that of Daniel Bell, who sees social structural changes as precipitating (1) the need for smaller units of identity in a society that has created a great mingling of peoples, and large-scale organization of work, consumption, political power; (2) the need for an effective emotional attachment in the face of the changes in traditional authority structures such as nation and class as a locus for aspirations and loyalties; and (3) the politicization of decisions that affect communal lives of people. Ethnic politics becomes a ready means of "demanding group rights and providing defense against other groups."[29] Although Bell recognized the relevance of "rootedness," he is concerned in his discussion with "to what end," as well as "why now," has ethnicity emerged not only as self-definition but as a political thrust.

[26]Salvatore J. Lagumina, ed., *WOP: A Documentary History of Anti-Italian Discrimination in the United States* (San Francisco: Straight Arrow Books, 1973), p. 268.
[27]Michael Novak, *The Rise of the Unmeltable Ethnics* (New York: The Macmillan Co., 1971).
[28]Harold R. Isaacs, *Idols of the Tribe: Group Identity and Political Change* (New York: Harper & Row, 1975).
[29]Daniel Bell, "Ethnicity and Social Change," in Glazer and Moynihan, *Ethnicity: Theory and Experience,* p. 171.

He claims that ethnic politics is status politics, and is characteristic of periods of prosperity, in contrast with class politics, more relevant in periods of depression.[30]

Whether the new ethnicity rests on primordial common heritage and early childhood experience, or on status aspirations, both factors being real in some dimension, the factual problems of ethnic groups in urban settings are real. More than half of the "ethnics," "white" or otherwise, are workingmen: blue-collar, lower white-collar, or small business. In a time of high unemployment, rising inflation, declining central cities, shrinking real income, especially the fixed income of the retired, anxieties are acute. As one worker in an interethnic neighborhood put it: "For Christ's sake, poor is poor. Can't you understand?"[31] This economic stratum will also continue to pay the largest proportion of personal income of any group in the country to support the social security system.

Whereas middle-class ethnics may be concerned with residues of discrimination in higher rungs of the status ladder, may feel the need for roots and group support as they fight for greater equality in the brackets of their aspirations, there is real danger in splintering, in the "Balkanization" of ethnic groups. Without some interethnic unity, for all the pride of Yugoslavs, Greeks, Ukrainians, and others, there will be no adequate protest. These marginal poor, for example, lose the privilege of food stamps, and there is less money through inflation, higher taxes, and higher unemployment to maintain beloved cultural symbols: the communion dresses, the festival wines.

Against this climate of anxiety, as the worker's benefits fought for in the thirties have eroded, there has been the striking example of the progress achieved by American blacks, and the large amounts of public and foundation moneys that have contributed to this. Although there is still a higher proportion of blacks in poverty (according to federal poverty standards), there has been no comparable attention paid to deteriorating white urban neighborhoods (or Chinese, or the situation of urban Indians). This has made for some backlash, some stereotypic designations of blacks, and the charges that white "ethnics" are racist. One Polish American has pointed out, in reply,

> Liberals scapegoat us as racists. Yet there was no racial prejudice in our hearts when we came . . . The elitists who smugly call us racists are the ones who taught us the meaning of the word bigotry . . .
>
> Government is further polarizing people by the creation of myths that black needs are being met. Thus the ethnic worker is fooled into thinking that the blacks are getting everything.
>
> Old prejudices and new fears are ignited and the two groups end up fighting each other for the same jobs and competing so that new schools and recreation centers will be built in their respective communities. What results is angry confrontation for tokens, when there should be an alliance for a whole new Agenda for America. . . .[32]

---

[30]*Ibid.*, p. 173.

[31]Leonard Kriegel, "Last Stop on the D Train," in Stanley Feldstein and Lawrence Costello, eds., *The Ordeal of Assimilation: A Documentary History of the White Working Class* (Garden City, N.Y.: Doubleday & Co., Anchor Books, 1974), p. 431.

[32]Barbara Mikulski, "Who Speaks for Ethnic America," *The New York Times*, Sept. 29, 1970, pp. 33.

Immigrant Adjustment: New Style

In many ways the 386,194 immigrants (quota, nonquota, and refugee) who were admitted to the United States in 1975 will have similar adjustments to those of the earlier migration. Many will have to settle for entry-level jobs. Many will cluster with other immigrants from their home countries, and they will seek help and advice from relatives and neighbors more long established, and from community institutions. Like other immigrants they will find that the American reality is not congruent with their image of America. Many, perhaps most, will have to struggle with learning adequate English.

But there are some aspects of the migration and of America in the 1970s that are different. Father Joseph Fitzpatrick points out that they come to an America with diminished national and international prestige; to a society concerned with persistent poverty and with militant voices defining poverty as oppression; they come where there is not only a decline in traditional authority structures, but where there is a generational challenge to some fundamental historical values in our society. They come to a multi-ethnic, multi-"racial" environment, and it may be some generations before the stability of a common culture can evolve.[33]

ETHNIC POLITICS

Whether it is "cultural politics" or "interest politics" the concept of an ethnic minority has been legitimized, broadening the perception of inequality beyond the black-white issue that had such prominence in the 1960s. There have been some landmark gains, and there remain some current issues.

The passage by Congress of the Ethnic Heritage Studies Programs Act in 1972 has created a framework for ethnic studies in our schools; and such national legislation clearly affirms that we are a culturally pluralistic nation. Like most innovative legislation it has been slow in implementation and underfunded. Some states have passed similar provisions and developed innovative new curricula.

The Bilingual Educational Act of 1974 mandates instruction in English, "and to the extent necessary to allow a child to progress effectively through the educational system, the native language of the children of limited English speaking ability."[34] The National Council on Bilingual Education in its 1975 Report to the President and Congress defined bilingual education more broadly as "a process in which English and other languages and cultures that reflect the make up of the community are used in instruction." The Council uses the term "bilingual multicultural" to imply that students are not just learning a second language.[35]

The old ethnic politics was personalized. It was an important way of involving ethnic populations in the political process and there were individual rewards. This older pattern is no longer as viable, especially in large cities to the extent that ethnic neigh-

[33]Rev. Joseph K. Fitzpatrick, S.J., "Changing Responses of Newcomers to American Life," in William S. Bernard and Judith Herman, eds., *The New Immigration and the New Ethnicity: Social Policy and Social Theory in the 1970's* (New York: American Immigration and Citizenship Conference, 1974), pp. 5–11.
[34]Herbert Teitelbaum and Richard J. Hiller, "Bilingual Education: the Legal Mandate," in *Harvard Educational Review*, 47, 2, May, 1977.
[35]*Ibid.*, p. 139.

borhoods have declined and populations dispersed. There are interethnic counterpressures, too, for example, in the increasing role of organized labor in national
politics.

Some of the new ethnic politics has incorporated the techniques of confrontation
and demonstration, especially in local issues affecting the use of community resources
(schools, etc.) and access to occupational structures. Sometimes these techniques have
been effective, in restoring cuts in community services, or for hiring more ethnic
personnel in community institutions. Where mass communications have picked up the
story it has also helped to change the image of a particular group in the wider society.
The risks in this kind of strategy, however, are that sentiments may be polarized.
Leaders, to create solidarity in a constituency, may find it expedient to define a competing ethnic group as an enemy. Where there is real effort to unseat entrenched power
that is viewed as excluding or discriminatory, more and more it is being perceived that a
coalition is more effective than single-group solidarity.[36]

Ethnic politics is a movement for change. All change brings anxiety. Groups whose
entrenchment or whose gains are being challenged will be doubly anxious. There is the
risk that hostility will be the response; and that ethnic consciousness raising can get
trapped in the negativism of symbolically preserved focus on past injustices. The ethnic
revival should, it is hoped, rather contribute creative innovation in the political process,
with defined long- and short-term goals and carefully considered strategies.[37]

The voices of "ethnic" Americans are proof that they are deeply and actively part of
American life. Their assumptions are American assumptions, for good or ill, and their
creativity is at America's disposal, not just their wage-earning labor. The creation of a
stable and dynamic society that is religiously pluralistic has largely been achieved.
Whether a similar mosaic of peoples can be created depends on how much real respect
for variants can be engendered, and on fair and equal access to the opportunities that
American society offers. Americans respond easily to pleas of injustice, but many
Americans, of all the variant backgrounds, are uneasy with *differences*. The future of
America lies no longer in the hands of WASPS, but in the hands of all Americans who
may cherish, but must also transcend, their communalities.

Suggested Readings

On Immigration

The American Immigration Collection. New York: Arno Press, 1976.
> Under Oscar Handlin's editorship most of the classic studies of immigrant
> experience and adjustment have been reprinted and are available in individual
> volumes covering all ethnic groups. Catalogue for the 74 volumes is available from

[36]Richard Krikus, *Pursuing the American Dream: White Ethnics and the New Populism* (Garden
City, N.Y.: Doubleday & Co., Anchor Books, 1976), Ch. 8.
[37]See S. J. Makielski, Jr., *Beleaguered Minorities: Cultural Politics in America* (San Francisco: W.
H. Freeman & Co., 1973), Chs. 14–18, for an analysis of goals and strategies.

Arno Press, 330 Madison Ave., New York, N.Y.10017. Also available are the 41 volumes of the "Dillingham Commission" Report. Individual volumes may be ordered separately.

Coleman, Terry. *Going to America*. Garden City, N.Y.: Doubleday & Co., Anchor Books, 1973.

A lively account of immigrants from Great Britain and Ireland 1846–1855: why they left, the experience of the voyage, what they found.

Feldstein, Stanley, and Costello, Lawrence, eds. *The Ordeal of Assimilation: A Documentary History of the White Working Class*. Garden City, N.Y.: Doubleday & Co., Anchor Books, 1974.

Selections from classic accounts of immigrant experience, and a final section on the current situation.

Krikus, Richard. *Pursuing the American Dream: White Ethnics and the New Populism*. Garden City, N.Y.: Doubleday & Co., Anchor Books, 1976.

An excellent account of political trends and voting patterns, old- and new-style ethnic politics.

Makielski, S. J., Jr. *Beleaguered Minorities: Cultural Politics in America*. San Francisco: W. H. Freeman & Co., 1973.

Discussion of major minorities, but especially good in the analysis of strategies.

Novak, Michael. *The Rise of the Unmeltable Ethnics: Politics and Culture in the Seventies*. New York: The Macmillan Co., 1970, paperback, 1973.

A consciousness-raising statement and a challenge.

5

Race and Racism

In dominant-minority relations "race" is a basic category and provides the most obvious cue to visibility or identification. The term is placed here in quotation marks because its meaning and significance in the popular thinking and behavior of dominants are vastly at variance with current scientific thinking. That the beliefs about race which have become established in popular sentiment may well constitute "man's most dangerous myth" was anticipated in the 1880s by a French pro-Aryan writer, Vacher de Lapouge, when he wrote, "I am convinced that in the next century millions of men will cut each other's throats because of one or two degrees more or less of cephalic index."[1]

> In the long history of the world men have given many reasons for killing each other in war: envy of another people's good bottom land or of their herds, ambition of chiefs and kings, different religious beliefs, high spirits, revenge. But in all these wars the skulls of the victims on both sides were generally too similar to be distinguished. Nor had the war leaders incited their followers by referring to the shapes of their heads. They might call them the heathen, the barbarians, the heretics, the slayers of women and children, but never our enemy Cephalic Index 82.
> It was left for high European civilization to advance such a reason for war and persecution and to invoke it in practice. In other words, racism is a creation of our own time.[2]

The research of the last fifty years, in physical anthropology primarily but also in related fields, has given an entirely new perspective on the physiological groupings of man. There is now consensus in anthropology, biology, psychology, and sociology as to what races are and are not. In 1950, UNESCO published a series of research monographs that represent international scientific agreement on what is known about races. The understanding of the physiological phenomena of "race" has depended on the development of the sciences. In populations without basic scientific orientation the term "race" is connotive of social attitudes derived from historical social experience, the universal ethnocentrism of isolated peoples, or folk superstition. It is therefore important to know clearly what is fact about race as a correction for traditional usages.

[1]Vacher de Lapouge, cited by Ruth Benedict, in *Race: Science and Politics,* rev. ed. (New York: The Viking Press, 1945), p. 3. (The cephalic index is a ratio of skull measurements.)
[2]Benedict, *Race: Science and Politics,* pp. 3–4, by permission.

WHAT "RACE" IS

Origin of "Races"

To begin with, mankind apparently started out as one race. Since *Homo sapiens* evolved thousands of years before written history, it is not possible to know the racial features of prehistoric man with any exactitude. However, contemporary anthropology generally accepts on the basis of fossil evidence and the logic of evolutionary and genetic principles a monogenetic rather than a polygenetic theory of man's origin. Montagu has put it thus:

> Concerning the origin of the living varieties of man we can say little more than that there is every reason to believe that a single stock gave rise to all of them. All varieties of man belong to the same species and have the same remote ancestry. This is a conclusion to which all the relevant evidence of comparative anatomy, palaeontology, serology, and genetics points. On genetic grounds alone, it is virtually impossible to conceive of the varieties of man as having originated separately as distinct lines from different anthropoid ancestors.[3]

Differentiation of "Races"

Long before written history, the major differentiation of mankind into the main varieties occurred as a result of migration, and of natural selection as it affected the survival of certain variations in their environments. Ever since Linnaeus, the Swedish botanist, started the classification of plant and animal life in the eighteenth century, geneticists and physical anthropologists have been examining the differences in the physical characteristics of man. Linnaeus established four categories of man—*americanus, europaeus, asiaticus,* and *afer.* Since the eighteenth century these categories have been refined so that some discussions include seven major groups with many subgroups. The criteria for grouping depend on such factors as cephalic index, blood type, shape of facial features, degree of body hair, and so forth. Since no group is totally homogeneous in all of these indices, these older categories are now primarily of interest to researchers in the biological sciences and physical anthropology. What the groups of people represent in actuality are societies that through geographic isolation and barriers of social organization have intermarried for thousands of years, bringing into prominence selected dominant biological traits. These are sometimes referred to as "Mendelian populations," a term derived from the geneticist Mendel, who demonstrated the existence of dominant strains and recessive strains in inbreeding and crossbreeding. From this point of view the tall Watusi of Uganda, the pockets of blond Andalusians in Spain, and the Sherpas of Nepal are "Mendelian" populations.

> Such physical traits as the color of the eyes or hair and the pigmentation of the skin do pass through the genes from parents to children. The carriers

---

[3]M. F. Ashley Montagu, *Man's Most Dangerous Myth: The Fallacy of Race,* 4th ed., rev. and enl. (Cleveland: The World Publishing Co., 1965), p. 83. By permission.

have been identified and described. We know now that a group of individuals with common characteristics will procreate offspring with the same characteristics. Mankind is composed of a variety of populations which differ among themselves in the frequency of many genes. These Mendelian populations will reproduce themselves across time.[4]

Twentieth-century research has shown that physical type is not only the result of genetic transmission but is dependent on other factors as well. Selection affecting physical type can take place because of environment. Before the advent of modern medicine the physical type best suited to survival in geographic regions gradually emerged as dominant, and high infant mortality eliminated variations. Cultural factors such as language over time affect the mouth formation necessary to produce a selected sound. As a contemporary physical anthropologist writes, ". . . culture, which has affected other free-living animals too, has probably affected us more profoundly than it has any others because we created it, we cannot escape it, we have been constantly exposed to it as long as there have been men on earth, and we could not live without it."[5]

Since agreement on categories is basic to thinking and research, most scholars today work within the broad categories of Caucasoid, Mongoloid, and Negroid. These refer very generally to groups of people with visible physical traits. The designations, however, are matters more of convenience than of accuracy. As Ruth Benedict aptly writes:

> No one doubts that the groups called Caucasoid, Mongoloid, and Negroid each represent a long history of anatomical specialization in different areas of the world; but the greater numbers of individuals cannot be assigned to one or another of these races on the basis even of several . . . [physical] criteria. . . . There are Whites who are darker than some Negroids; dark hair and eyes are common among all races; the same cephalic index is found in groups of the most diverse races; similar hair form is found among ethnic groups as distinct as native Australians and Western Europeans.[6]

Instability of Racial Type

Throughout history great migrations alternating with long periods of endogamous mating created and recreated visible subtypes. The American Indian illustrates the process of subtype development. The ancestors of the Indians came from Asia and possessed general Mongoloid features. Natural selection and thousands of years of isolation, limiting the range or variability to that present in the original migrating groups, perfected a distinctive Indian type.

While throughout all history mixing occurred across main divisions, in the past few centuries the wandering and mixing of peoples has created many new subtypes, involving combinations of traits from the main racial divisions. We may cite the Pitcairn

---

[4]Oscar Handlin, *Race and Nationality in American Life* (Garden City, N.Y.: Doubleday & Co., Anchor Books, 1957), p. 151. (Reprinted by arrangement with Little, Brown & Co., Boston, Mass.)
[5]Carleton S. Coon, *The Living Races of Man* (New York: Alfred A. Knopf, 1965), p. 23.
[6]Ruth Benedict, *Race: Science and Politics,* pp. 45 ff.

Islanders, of *Mutiny on the Bounty* fame, and the American Negro. The present Hawaiian situation, where the various ethnic groups are intermarrying with increasing freedom, is a most interesting example of racial change going on today.

From the foregoing it can be seen that race is a highly unstable phenomenon. The racial variability of *Homo sapiens* has undergone more or less continuous modification. This changing nature of race makes the idea of a "pure" race meaningless. The greatest homogeneity in "racial" traits is found among small groups of people long isolated from the main currents of human travel and exchange.

All historical evidence makes us accept the inevitability of the crossing of strains wherever peoples come in contact with one another. But biological crossing is not the only modifying factor. In the early part of this century, Franz Boas, conducting an anthropological study of immigrants at the request of the United States Immigration Commission, was the first to show that a supposedly unchangeable index of physical type was mutable. He found that the cephalic indices of immigrants from south and eastern Europe, as compared with their children, altered according to the length of time spent in the American environment. Furthermore, they all altered toward a uniform type more nearly in accord with the measurements of older American stock. Japanese who emigrated to the United States are physically different from their siblings who stayed in Japan. During the last two centuries, Americans of British descent have grown three and a half inches taller than their Revolutionary ancestors, and proportionately heavier. The cephalic index may drop dramatically in a single generation among people who have abandoned cradling.[7]

Race and Physiology

Comparative studies of the physiology of samples of racial groups have shown in some cases significant differences, in others mutability over time, and in others no differences at all. There is much current research on how and why people are different from one another physiologically, and at the present time one can relatively accurately delineate how, but only hypothetically why; although Coon suggests that the "why" answers to the relationship between physical environment and physiological phenomena may not be far away.[8]

In the cluster of traits that make up visible differences the most relevant one to the American popular mind is *skin color*. According to contemporary research, skin color depends on the differences in melanin production in the body and on such secondary factors as disintegrated hemoglobin. That is, we know now the biological and physiological factors that make for darker or lighter skin. Coon thinks we are approaching the period where we will know why natural selection favors one or the other in different environments, for example, darker skins among people living in the wet tropics, or why the skin color of American Indians varies regionally. For Indians, skin color is darkest where radiation is at the peak, but in the tropical forests of South America (at high altitude) it is quite light, as is true of the inhabitants of rain forests in Borneo.

Another comparative dimension is immunity to disease. What seems to be apparent is that natural selection and adaptive mechanisms stabilize over time resistances to

[7]Coon, *The Living Races of Man*, Ch. 10.
[8]*Ibid.*, Chs. 8 and 9.

particular diseases in particular environments. Change in the environment may make people differentially susceptible to new diseases or may weaken resistance patterns to those endemic to their former environment. Coon suggests that malaria, so acutely debilitating to Europeans in Africa and Southeast Asia, and to which "native" populations have developed resistance, may actually have preserved these people from the onslaughts of technically superior and better organized Caucasians and Mongolians. He further cites the suggestion that malaria may have increased in these areas in the shift from a hunting-gathering economy to agriculture, which brought about cleared forests, pockets of still water in which mosquitos could breed, kept people anchored to specific places, and allowed human and animal excreta to accumulate.[9]

As a final illustration, we refer to "blood," about which so much popular superstition has developed. There are four types of human blood and each type is hereditary. But Caucasians, Mongols, and Negroes have all these blood types. Blood plasma derived from various racial groups was utilized for the wounded in World War II.

WHAT RACE IS NOT

Race and Culture

"Race" as it is used today only emerged as a concept in the late seventeenth and eighteenth centuries. Until this time for Europeans the definition of "others" was Christian vs. non-Christian. As European expansion and imperialism began to develop, peoples were encountered whose culture, values, and ways of life were different from the known and familiar. Since these people also looked different, there was the naïve assumption that their ways of behaving were related to the way they looked. Thus in the period of imperialist expansion for most people the concepts race and culture became inextricably intertwined. If one recognizes that culture is man's way of adapting to his environment, as we have indicated above, it is more likely that culture affected race than race, culture. The separation of physiognomic adaptations and cultural solutions did not become explicit until the development of the physical and social sciences. For almost three hundred years, then, from the seventeenth to the twentieth centuries, there was no factual basis for interpretation of differences, although always there were some sensitive individuals who appreciated other cultures without regard to visible physiognomic differences. As the fact or the spirit of imperialism grew, visible differences became the rationalization of what were really cultural conflicts. The technological superiority of the Europeans and European-descended peoples established dominance over less technologically developed societies and externally rationalized this on the basis of the confusion of race and culture. A European naïveté and ethnocentrism justified dominance in terms of "the white man's burden." As acculturation to the European dominance spread, the racial emphasis became more pronounced as the justification for subordination.

The institutionalization of dominant-subordinate relationships depends on the preservation of norms across generations. But norms are derived from values. Differences in the content and emphasis of values will give a different cast to patterns of subordination. For example, in Brazil, Catholic Christianity was sufficiently in control of the value

[9]*Ibid.*, pp. 277–278.

system in the early period of settlement that imported Negroes and indigenous Indians were accepted by Europeans and incorporated into the social system according to their education and "ability" if they were Catholic. It is true that as Brazil developed there was cruel exploitation of Indian labor, and Negro slaves coming in the later importations had less access to channels of opportunity. The result has been that lower classes tend to be darker. But in contrast to the North American traditional pattern, Negro or Indian descent has never been *per se* a barrier to entry into economic or social elites. In early Brazil intermarriage was frequent, manumission frequent, the family structure of slaves was protected, and tribal groups were often kept intact. In contrast in North America, the indigenous social structures of African peoples were shattered, sexual exploitation rather than Catholic marriage was more typical, and manumission, although it occurred, was less frequent than in Brazil. One factor in the North American situation was a less unified superordinate religious value system.

Race and Nationality

The tendency to identify race and nation is perhaps the most widely held of all beliefs relating race to culture. It is in Europe, the very region where racialist theories were most earnestly expounded, that the lack of correlation between racial subgroups and national culture is most clearly illustrated. This is notably true of Germany, France, and England, where Nordic, Alpine, and Mediterranean traits have been shown to be harmoniously blended in the citizenry of each nation. Dominian wrote "Northern France is perhaps more Teutonic than southern Germany, while eastern Germany is, in many places, more Slavic than Russia." Hankins points out that within Germany, "a relative purity of Germanic elements along the Baltic and North Seas (but mixed even there with Slavic Poles and Wends) gradually gives way to the southward to an increasing complexity in which Alpine and Mediterranean elements increase."[10]

Since the English were racially mongrelized within the broad Caucasian limits, it follows that the old American stock was correspondingly a mongrel mixture of European varieties. In a study of Americans descended from this English stock, Hrdlicka showed that they ranged widely in skin color, hair color, and eye color, with intermediates predominating over either the alleged Nordic type with fair skin, blue eyes, and blond hair, or the swarthy-complexioned, brunet, Mediterranean type. Altogether, the measurements indicate extensive hybridization in the old American stock.[11]

Social Race

From the foregoing discussion it is apparent that the term "race" as traditionally used has neither descriptive accuracy nor categorical validity. Nevertheless, this traditional concept persists in cultures as a mode, among others, of ranking people socially. This is what Wagley calls "social race."

---

[10]F. H. Hankins, *The Racial Basis of Civilization* (New York: Alfred A. Knopf, 1926), p. 286.
[11]Alec Hrdlicka, *Old Americans* (Baltimore: The Williams & Wilkins Co., 1925), Ch. 3.

"Social race" (i.e., the way in which the members of society classify each other by physical characteristics) is one of a series of values which give individuals rank and determine their social relations.[12]

In analyzing populations in rural Brazil, Wagley found he had to resort to the term "race" for the concept of "social race" because this was the common term not only in the popular vocabulary but also in the collection of census statistics.

Throughout this report, when the term "race" is used, the authors hold no brief for its validity as a physical or genetic classification. In one sense or another, the term is always used in this volume in a social and cultural sense. It is well known that colour or race data in population statistics reflect the social categories of the census takers, and it is interesting to reflect upon the variety of social definitions of "race" which would inevitably be involved in any census of Brazil. . . . Even our own observations as to the probable "racial" affiliation of an individual or group of people are by necessity "naked eye" judgements certainly coloured by our own social and cultural experiences. Throughout this report, then, we are interested in the social definitions of "race" . . . and in their effects upon the life of the people of the communities studied, while exact physical classification is of little interest for our purpose.[13]

In keeping with Wagley's position, we too shall have to discuss race with the understanding that we are referring only to popular social categories that affect the way in which individuals and groups behave toward one another.

Race and Intelligence

With the development of science in the nineteenth century and the infant social sciences toward the end of the century it was inevitable that "scientific" explanations should be offered for the visible differences between peoples. Biologists were still concerned with gross and simple aspects of genetics. Methodology in the social sciences was underdeveloped, largely merely some logical deduction from an unverified assumption with illustrative examples. The entire era was governed in biological and social science by a commitment to an evolutionary theory that saw evolution as a straight line from "lower" forms to "higher" forms. Evolution over millions of years in biological forms does show a direction of development from simpler to more complex organisms. Perhaps in the recorded years of human history from stone age to space age, societies have moved from simpler to more complex, but certainly in no straight line, as civilizations in Asia and Africa in times past surpassed the Europeans of the same period both in technology and in complexity of social organization.

The attempt to "scientifically" demonstrate that some peoples genetically have less ability than others emerged in a particular time when it was germane to the interests of

---

[12]Charles Wagley, ed. *Race and Class in Rural Brazil* (Paris: UNESCO, 1952), p. 14.
[13]*Ibid.*, p. 14. By permission.

particular established social patterns. It was not conscious or deliberate, but an aspect of the cultural assumptions of Europe and America. Since there has been a recent upsurge of the same kind of attempt to validate assumptions about *de facto* situations, the fallacies must be examined. As Baltzell points out in *The Protestant Establishment*,[14] scholarship is inevitably influenced by current ideologies; or as the Polish sociologist, Ossowski has said, "The relation of the state to the sociologist is that of a drunk to a lamppost, it wants support, not light."[15]

The Biological Fallacy

Arthur Jensen, a contemporary American, is the chief exponent of the primacy of genetic differences as an explanation of lower I.Q. scores for blacks as compared with whites.[16] Jensen has used wide comparative data, but in the first place his use of the genetic factor is simplistic. What are genetic, hereditary factors? John Hambley, a British biologist writing in criticism of Jensen and others, describes the biological process.[17]

Genes are the basic particles of heredity. They are located on the chromosomes found at the nucleus of each cell. They occur in pairs, one of each pair being transmitted from each parent. The pairs may contain identical or nonidentical genes. There is a very large number of genes in each organism.

The function of each gene is to produce protein (nutriment). Not all genes are active at any one time. From the moment of conception genes are being switched on and off. It is the interaction and integration of this switching on and off that constitutes development. The shuffling of these units in producing each egg and each sperm allows for tremendous scope for variation. Indeed, with the exception of identical twins, each individual is genetically unique.

Furthermore, genes are in continual interaction with the biological environment from conception on, both nourishing it and reacting to it; it is therefore impossible to predict from the initial gene pool what will be most active at any one time in development. Biology is only on the threshold of knowing what may affect gene activity (nutrition, for example, or hormone stimulation). Environment, biological and social, prenatal and postnatal, is so complex and the gene pool of an individual so large that variation is constantly taking place at all levels. This is what makes for individual adaptability.

What Is Intelligence?

Societies have usually recognized "intelligence" as a capacity to learn skills easily and to transfer and apply a specific piece of learning or observation to a new problem containing similarities and variations. This latter quality involves the ability to "concep-

[14]E. Digby Baltzell, *The Protestant Establishment* (New York: Random House, 1964), Ch. 4.
[15]Quoted in John Daniels and Vincent Houghton, "Jensen, Eysenick and the Eclipse of the Galton Paradigm," in Ken Richardson, David Spears, Martin Richards, eds., *Race and Intelligence,* (Baltimore: Penguin Books, 1972), pp. 71–72.
[16]Arthur R. Jensen, *Educability and Group Differences* (New York: Harper & Row, 1973).
[17]John Hambley, "Diversity: A Developmental Perspective," in Richardson *et al.*, eds. *Race and Intelligence,* pp. 114–127.

tualize"—to see relationships between objects, persons, or ideas apart from the individual properties of each. These folk understandings of intelligence are found in all societies, though not necessarily explicit, and not necessarily specifically rewarded.

In complex hierarchical societies, however, those people who can correctly assess object, personal, or idea relationships easily often have particular advantages. Even where there are barriers of class or caste and hereditary privilege, complex societies have to a greater or lesser degree had some channels of opportunity for the "intelligent" if this "intelligence" is channeled in the service of the established social system. In Imperial China the Imperial Civil Service was open to all who could pass the examinations, and often the extended kinship would aid the "brightest male" to have the tutoring necessary to compete. In medieval Europe the Church offered a career channel to the lesser privileged who had "ability."

This, though is a *social* definition of intelligence. There is also the possibility of a *biological* definition. The Swiss biologist Piaget, who has worked for half a century on the study of cognitive functions in children, emphasizes that "intelligence" is not a set of discrete capacities. Intelligence is an equilibrator in the organism that compensates for external disturbance. It has three functions: it organizes the organism into a whole entity in its interaction with environment; it assimilates and utilizes stimuli from the environment, incorporating them into the growing organism; it accommodates, that is, modifies, the internal structures of the organism to suit and make use of the input from the environment. Thus the growth of intelligence is the organization and adaptation of the total organism to the interaction with the environment. In this view, no separate skills, mathematical or manual, or any mechanistic combination of them is a measure of intelligence.[18]

I.Q. as a Measuring Instrument

Today intelligence is measured throughout Western society by comparative scores on standard examinations and/or psychometric tests. The two most widely used tests are the Stanford-Binet and the Wechsler (WISC) tests. These attempt to rate children on an achievement scale according to an average for their age group.

The first problem with these tests is the content. Children do not come from a standardized environment. Furthermore, as total organisms they have individual reactions to individual experiences that make them see relations differently from what may be expected. For example, an American Indian child of eight, in response to a multiple-choice vocabulary question: "This book belongs to me. . . . It is yours, mine, theirs, ours" underlined ours. She came from a common property culture. The Standard-Binet scales were standardized on whites only. Moreover, they have a middle-class bias (for example, "Why do we like books?" What will a shanty child from Appalachia do with this?)[19] Or consider the middle-class white child of six who, when asked in such a test "Are rocks like eggs?" replied "yes." The weekend before he had been at the seashore and he and his sister had collected smooth rocks that were egg shaped.

[18]John Redford and Andrew Burton, "Changing Intelligence," in *Race and Intelligence,* pp. 29–31.
[19]Joanna Ryan, "The Illusion of Objectivity," in *Race and Intelligence,* p. 53.

The second problem is the condition under which a person takes the test. Black children often do better if the tester is black. Children do better if they are told that they will probably do well. Minority children do better if they believe they are being measured against their own group rather than a national average.[20]

Standardized psychometric tests to a degree serve a social purpose. They are a mode of allocating individuals to slots in a particular social structure. Some experiments are being made to see if "culture-free" tests can be designed. In some places the effort is being made to test in small groups with a known and trusted tester. But these are few and far between. Aside from the fact that possibly no such test can measure intelligence, any gross data from them that compares the scores of different populations against a white, middle-class average is misleading. On the one hand, it may support the myth of biological inferiorities. On the other, it may agitate reformers to bend efforts to homogenize American society (forced or coaxed acculturation). Not only does such a policy destroy, for many, the equilibrium between the individual organism and the environment, but it also represents a social loss in that it reduces alternatives for the productive interaction of individual growth and social development. A standardized homogeneous society and a standardized measurement of "intelligence" may be an efficient and "fair" way to allocate position in the hierarchy of decision making—a meritocracy, but it may even more seriously impoverish both individuals and the society.

RACISM

The Ideological Dimension

The revival of the biological argument for "white" superiority is a measure of the crisis of our time. When the institutionalized pattern is threatened with change, additional supporting arguments are marshaled to uphold the existing structure. Thus the first arguments about the nature of "races" were based on biblical Old Testament "authority," and later the beginning of the scientific study of man, which, like all *beginning* scientific endeavor must deal with categories of phenomena and with differences, laid a base for a belief in biological determinism—that is, that ability and behavior are determined by physical type.

The popularity of pseudoscientific Nordic claims stimulated reactively vigorous research and writing that was ultimately to demolish, in intellectual circles, not only Nordic doctrine but all other expressions of racialism. From this exploration has emerged the scientific view of race presented earlier in this chapter. If the elimination of minority discrimination depended solely on "debunking" the racialist doctrine, such discrimination would disappear in a generation. But as the history of racial doctrine suggests, belief in its claims does not rest solely on inadequate knowledge of its objective error but partly in the desire of the dominant to believe it.[21]

---

[20]Peter Watson, "Can Racial Discrimination Affect I.Q.?" in *Race and Intelligence,* pp. 62–67.
[21]See Gerhart Saenger "The Effectiveness of the UNESCO Pamphlet Series on Race," *International Social Science Bulletin,* Vol. VI, No. 3. Dr. Saenger found many resistances to using the UNESCO material in schools and colleges.

The Ideological Factor

Ashley Montagu tells us that

> When we examine the scientific literature of the seventeenth century with a view to discovering what beliefs were held concerning the variety of man, we find that it was universally believed that mankind, was comprised of a single species and that it represented a unitary whole. . . . Physical differences were, of course, known to exist between groups of mankind, but what was unfamiliar was the notion that the differences exhibited by such peoples represented anything fundamental.[22]

In all modes of social conflict in the eighteenth and nineteenth centuries, "racism" became involved. It was invoked by the nobles of France to justify their superiority to the bourgeoisie, and later espoused by reactionary political theorists throughout nineteenth-century Europe.[23]

The potential power of racism in stimulating group conflict can be further illustrated by its application to two twentieth-century phenomena: the Japanese pan-Asiatic movement and the rise of the Hitler Reich. While it would be oversimplification to explain the aggressive policy pursued by Japan in the twentieth century wholly on the basis of their notion of race superiority, that this notion was prevalent and served a useful purpose in developing morale for aggressive political policies should not be overlooked. According to the Japanese scholar Hirata, "from the fact of the divine descent of the Japanese proceeds their unmeasurable superiority to the natives of other countries in courage and intelligence." While like all tribes and nations, the Japanese were always ethnocentric, the development of distinct "racial pride" as part of the cultural paraphernalia essential to whip up national enthusiasm for military, imperialistic expansion was a part of the great borrowing of Western ideas and knowledge that characterized modern Japan.[24]

In the West there was a group of writers representing the "Aryan" school. From philological research that revealed similarities in the languages of the Persians and Indians and those of the western Indo-Europeans, the Greeks, Romans, Teutons, Celts, and Slavs, they concluded that all languages derived from a common source, and they posited a primitive Aryan tribe from which all the later Aryans descended. Considering these languages superior and assuming without question that language and race are related, this school expounded the theory of the "superior Aryan race."

In the Nazi ideology, racism was a dominant theme. It was not, however, a new point of view, but rather the logical culmination of selected strains of political argument throughout the nineteenth century. As Barzun states, "the race-overtones are nothing new and the rearrangement of Tacitus's Nordic myth was peculiar to France only in its details. Hitler showed how readily it applies to the Third Reich."[25] Whereas French writers were debating the superiority of Franks to Romanized Celts and the English were dreaming of Anglo-Saxon encirclement and hegemony of the world, the Nazi's ap-

[22]*Man's Most Dangerous Myth: The Fallacy of Race*, 4th ed., rev. and enl., p. 16. By permission.
[23]See Jacques Barzun, *Race: A Study in Superstition*, rev. ed. (New York: Harper & Row, 1965), Ch. 2, "The Nordic Myth."
[24]Willard Price, "Japan's Divine Mission," *The New Republic*, Nov. 17, 1937.
[25]Barzun, *Race: A Study in Superstition*, p. 23.

plied the argument against the Jews, who in the century since the establishment of full civil rights for them in Germany had risen in status and made so many contributions to German enterprise and German thought. In the critical period of economic, political, and social reorganization after the defeat in World War I, the Nazi philosophers expounded the notion that the development of an "Aryan" state was the only bulwark against chaos, and that the German nation must be "purified" from the deteriorating "international" influence of the Jewish "race." In practice, the Nazis subjected Jews to persecution and extermination. Once the German Nordic "race" itself was thus purified, the rest of the "race" was to be incorporated into a pan-German state, and Germans in other parts of the world, notably the United States, were to be encouraged to retain their racial purity and to foster Nazi ideas.

Racial doctrine became the support of nationalist rivalries by adding to the cult of nationalism the idea that "our nation (or a dominant segment of it) is a superior race." But, most pertinent to our interest, racism became a strong support of slavery and imperialism.

> Racism did not get its currency in modern thought until it was applied to
> conflicts within Europe—first to class conflicts and then to national. But it
> is possible to wonder whether the doctrine would have been proposed at all
> as explaining these latter conflicts—where, as we have seen, the dogma is
> so inept—if the basis for it had not been laid in the violent experience of
> racial prejudice on the frontier.[26]

In the process of establishing their economic hegemony over most of the world and in developing less settled areas under this domination to their own greatest advantage, white Europeans, particularly the English—who passed on this tradition to the Americans—developed a caste-like relation to the "natives" of their colonies and, under an even more indisputably inferior status, to the forcefully imported slaves. In fact, it seems clear that in actual time sequence, the white men first exploited native labor and brought in slaves and then expounded a theory of the inferiority of the "colored" peoples to support their de facto status.

WHY DOES RACISM PERSIST?

The Psychological Dimension

Research has shown us that individuals who are unsure of their valuableness, their importance, or their sexuality are prey to a need to define someone else as inferior, or "less moral," or whatever. If the society offers them candidates in a minority as being either lesser or threatening, they can be rallied to vigorous antiminority sentiment.[27] Such a person has important needs that might be expressed simply by being derogatory to his children, his wife, or his associates. But it is much easier and less fraught with daily conflict if it can be projected on those the society defines as inferior.

---

[26]Benedict, *Race: Science and Politics*, p. 111. By permission.
[27]See Philip Mason, *Race Relations* (New York: Oxford University Press, 1970), Ch. 4, "Pressures from Within." For a theoretical discussion of this, see Ch. 19 of this text.

Groups of people, often when threatened with social or economic change over which they have no control, and which is inimical to their present assumptions or future aspirations, easily adopt racist attitudes. Sometimes these are focused on competitive access to scarce rewards. For example, a generation ago, under covert quota systems dominants had prime access to institutions of higher education and to professional schools, not to mention greater opportunity for financial aid. In the rectifying of this situation, segments of the dominant population today are expressing increased racial antagonism as their proportion of the anticipated reward is cut down. Declining neighborhoods on the one hand, or lily-white suburbs on the other, panic into group racism when visible minorities move into their neighborhoods and threaten to challenge their control of community life and leadership. Sometimes propagandists have deliberately offered a particular minority or several minorities as targets to channelize the unrest occasioned by widespread social stress. Thus in World War II there were organized anti-Semitic campaigns; there were riots against Mexican-Americans, as well as a predominant racial theme in sentiment and action about the Japanese.

Dr. James P. Comer, a black psychiatrist, describes racism as a low-level defense system and adjustment mechanism utilized by groups to deal with psychological and social insecurities. He points out that a given society may promote and reward racism to enable members of the group in control to maintain a sense of adequacy in the face of change at the expense of a group with less control. A racist society transmits racist attitudes from generation to generation as a value "similar to patriotism, religion and good manners."[28]

The Social Structural Dimension

Discrimination is structured inequality. It is maintained by customary (covert) or official (overt) barriers to jobs, to equal educational opportunity, to political participation. Legislative changes in the last two decades have removed many official barriers. But the implementation of legislation is still being fought on the community level throughout the nation. Powerful political interests, through patronage, and powerful economic interests, through, for example, apprentice programs, membership policies of organizations, and the like, still structure discrimination. This would be less possible if from the first grades on the content of education were changed to include and emphasize the whole American experience and the dignity of all Americans. A major bulwark of institutionalized racism is the educational system.[29]

"Race" has important social, cultural, and psychological ramifications, not because of "race" per se but because of historically rooted valuations of subordinate peoples who differed in appearance and behavior, both indigenous and adaptive, from their conquerors. Racism as it affects "whites" is a heritage from the colonial past of European conquest, long culturally incorporated so that its residues exist in inheritors of the culture who themselves had no participation in the original valuations. It is inevitable, then, that in such cultural anchoring the institutional structure is permeated with, often unconscious, racism.

---

[28]James P. Comer, "White Racism: Its Root, Form and Function," in *The American Journal of Psychiatry*, vol. 126, 1969, pp. 802–806.
[29]Michael B. Kane, *Minorities in Textbooks* (Chicago: Quadrangle Books, 1970).

This phenomenon is, of course, not only limited to the European experience, though that is the most germane to the American situation; imperial China and imperial Japan have in the past had racist attitudes, not only toward "westerners" but toward tribute peoples, as in Taiwan today, where the native Taiwanese are looked down on by the Chinese.

Racism does not become an *issue* as long as it is contained in a static *class* system with defined hereditary occupations. But this is no longer a possibility in a twentieth-century world with the great technological and communications advances that characterize our society.

RACE AND ETHNICITY

Ethnicity is related to identity and self-concept, in a cultural dimension: language (including dialect), customs, symbols, behavior with its positive and negative sanctions within primary groups, historical experience handed down. Where the myth of race with its presumption of naturally endowed inequality has been operative, an ethnic emphasis has been a means of creating a positive self-image for groups who have suffered from discrimination, cultural imperialism, and brainwashing by other "races." It also serves to defuse intergroup attitudes and contacts within the ideology of an intercultural world, for only a few traditional orthodoxies, revitalization movements, or isolated tribalisms believe behavior is defined by God.

Yet the intertwining of race and ethnicity is not simple, and in situations of extreme conflict the rationalization of race surfaces. Even in what is sometimes called "reverse racism" this is true. As James Baldwin said in a discussion of black anti-Semitism, "It is not anti-Semitic, it is anti-white."[30] The occasion was a strike by predominantly Jewish school teachers in New York City in 1968 against community control of schools.

The ethnic dilemma is also acute for people of mixed racial heritage. In colonial dependencies these have often had some greater privileges than "natives" and have culturally identified with though not been fully accepted by dominants. With the throwing off of colonialism these people have found themselves rejected by their new governments as well as by their former colonial masters, in many instances.[31] Faced with the necessity of a cultural choice some have opted to emigrate.[32] On the other hand,where a mixed population comes into dominance, as in Mexico, a variant of the dominant culture (Spanish) emerges. In the United States many descendents of mixed heritage have disappeared into the dominant population. Many others have opted for identification with their minority heritage, often achieving leadership positions, precariously bridging a culturally variant constituency and a middle-class dominant world. The older-status hierarchy that gave descendants of white-black unions status simply by virtue of lighter skin color or more Caucasian features seems to have disappeared.

[30]*Black Anti-Semitism,* with an introduction by Nat Hentoff, (New York: Schocken Books, 1970).
[31]Noel P. Gist and Anthony Gary Dworkin, eds., *The Blending of Races: Marginality and Identity in World Perspective* (New York: John Wiley & Sons, 1972).
[32]See, for example, Dennis Hilary Gouveia, "The Coloreds of Guyana," in Gist and Dworkin, eds. *The Blending of Races: Marginality and Identity in World Perspective*, pp. 103 ff.

RACISM IN WORLD PERSPECTIVE

It is important to point out, in conclusion, that racism is an international phenomenon, possibly so universal because it is so simplistic. Although scholarly knowledge of the differences and the essential equality of races as genetic types has existed for nearly half a century, it has probably been the horrifying spectacle of what destruction the racial myth can achieve as it did under the Nazis, and the independence movements that have brought an end to Western colonialism, that have caused the majority of people of good will to rethink their assumptions about race. The emergence of the "Third World" as a power bloc has been a stimulating influence to many members of minorities who have perceived themselves as "racially" devalued and powerless. Although the image has been a psychologically rewarding one for many, especially the young, the Third World of the developing Asian and African nations are beset with problems, which though different are as severe as those we face.

A racist appeal, whether it is used as an interim strategy by minorities to mobilize broad support, or reactively by dominants frightened or uneasy with social change, is retrogressive, with potentially high costs for individuals and the society.

Suggested Readings

Coon, Carleton S. *The Living Races of Man*. New York: Alfred A. Knopf, 1965.
    A review of what we now know about the genetic classification of "race," the instability of racial types, and the interaction of genetic type and culture.
Gist, Noel P., and Dworkin, Anthony Gary, eds. *The Blending of Races: Marginality and Identity in World Perspective*. New York: John Wiley & Sons, 1972.
    A collection of articles on the position and attitudes of people of mixed race in various social structures in the U.S. and in formerly colonial countries.
Kane, Michael B. *Minorities in Textbooks*. Chicago: Quadrangle Books, 1970.
    Forty-five secondary-school texts from major publishers are examined for their treatment of minorities.
Knowles, Louis L., and Prewitt, Kenneth, eds. *Institutional Racism in America*. Englewood Cliffs, N.J.: Prentice-Hall, 1969.
    An examination of the way racism is perpetuated politically, educationally, economically, ecologically, and in the administration of justice.
Richardson, Ken; Spears, David; and Richards, Martin, eds. *Race and Intelligence*. Baltimore, Md.: Penguin Books, 1972.
    Biologists, psychologists, and sociologists contribute to a review of recent research related to race difference. An invaluable book for exploding popular myth.

Part 2

Major Minority Situations in the United States Today

6

Negro (Black)-White Relations: Characteristics of Negro Americans and Slavery

The minority position of African-descended Americans occupies first place among America's minorities for many reasons, the most obvious being their large numbers, currently 25 million, far greater than any other minority. A perplexing problem in dealing with this minority situation at this particular time, as we noted in our introduction, is the appropriate name to use in describing the Afro-American component: the name "Negro" (or occasionally "colored") was universally used both in speech and writing up to World War II. But the designation "black" began to be used, and by the end of the 1960s in deference to the wishes of the young and more activist segments of this minority people, it became more general. According to Kilson, 19 percent of all Negroes favored the term "black" in 1969, but by 1972 nearly two-thirds preferred this term. Northern and middle-income Negroes were much more favorable to "black" than Southern and lower-income Negroes.[1] The matter of nomenclature has significance with reference to the current search for a unifying identity. There are those scholars who find "black" unsatisfactory. For example, recent outstanding research finds evidence that the currently popular "white" person-"black" person nomenclature promotes racial bias.[2] All these considerations led us to use "Negro" primarily for historical chapters and shift to "black" in the chapters dealing with more recent times in deference to what has apparently become, only recently, the preference of a majority of black Americans themselves.

In addition to being the largest minority group, Afro-Americans are the oldest, the first African slaves having been brought to Jamestown, Virginia, in 1619.[3] This minority, after all these years, still occupies the most caste-like position of all America's racial minorities. A large part of the Negro population has had a very low standard of liv-

[1]Martin Kilson, "Blacks and Neo-Ethnicity in America," in Nathan Glazer and Daniel P. Moynihan, eds., *Ethnicity: Theory and Experience* (Cambridge, Mass.: Harvard University Press, 1975), p. 246.
[2]John E. Williams, and J. Kenneth Moreland, *Race, Color, and the Young Child* (Chapel Hill, N.C.: The University of North Carolina Press, 1976). See Ch. 3, "Attitudes toward the Colors Black and White." The authors solve this problem by using the terms "Afros" and "Euros."
[3]Indian-white relations did not become dominant-minority relations in the true sense until the Indians became wards in 1871.

ing, although with the emergence of a middle class, its economic situation as a whole group has become highly variable. Differing from other minorities, the continuity from its original African heritage has to a large extent disappeared through the long years of servitude and caste conditions so that such, if any, cultural distinctiveness as blacks may now have is largely derived from the impact of slavery and caste.

The two basic factors that explain why Negroes have so long remained a minority are that (1) they are in varying degrees Negroid in physiognomic characteristics, or in their known lineage, and that (2) their ancestors were in the vast majority of cases slaves. In this chapter these two conditions will be discussed.

CHARACTERISTICS OF THE NEGRO AMERICAN PEOPLE

The minority status of Negroes in the United States has rested in large measure on the beliefs developed and sustained in the minds of the white population that being Negroid in racial ancestry means that Negroes are innately inferior in many ways. In our Chapter 5 on race, it was seen that contemporary social science seriously challenges this belief. In the first place, how actually Negroid is the population counted as such in the United States?

The Negro American: A New Genetic Type

The "visibility" of the Negro population is accounted for by the fact that all the members have some genetic lineage from Negro ancestry. In the United States a person is considered a Negro if he has any known Negro lineage, whether he can be identified by his appearance or not. There is no precise data indicating what distribution of the basic Negroid traits are now present in the population identified as Negro. The United States Census count in 1920—the last year a distinction between mulatto and black was made—gave the figure of 15.9 percent for mulattoes, which all students of the question consider a gross undercount. Pettigrew estimates that about one-fourth of the Negro gene pool consists of genes of Caucasian origin.[4]

Most Negroes in the United States show one or more of the basic Negroid traits: dark skin, thick lips, "wooly" hair, and prognathism; in a minor proportion, the evidence of these traits are so faint that one cannot be sure of identifying them; and in a relatively small percentage there is absolutely no somatic evidence of Negro lineage, but either the individuals themselves, or others who know them, vouch for some Negro ancestry. The American Negro population of today is, biologically speaking, quite different from that of the original slaves. The processes by which this change has come about will now be described.

Selective Mating Processes

Intertribal Mating.   While knowledge of the ancestry of American Negroes is not very precise, it is considered that most of the present Negro population traces the Negro part of its ancestry back to slaves who originally came from the West Coast of Africa.

[4]See Thomas Pettigrew, *A Profile of the Negro American* (New York: D. Van Nostrand Co., 1964), p. 71.

The first process to occur was the intermixing of the original tribal variations. This would have produced a new, but African, Negro type if it had not been for the crossing of slaves very early with both Indians and white people.

Negro-Indian Crossing.   Before the nineteenth century there was some intermingling between Indians and Negroes, with the result that some of the admixtures generally disappeared into the Indian and Negro population. Herskovits found 27 percent of a Negro sample to have some Indian lineage.[5] Additional Indian genetic strains resulted from the increasing importation, in the later periods, of slaves from the West Indies, where "crossing" with Indians had occurred. However, later studies suggest that the amount of Indian admixture in the Negro population is not as high as in Herskovits' sample.[6]

Negro-White Crossing.   The population from which the African slaves were recruited already had some admixture of Caucasian genes, as a result of miscegenation with the Portuguese who settled on the Guinea Coast for slave trading purposes and through contact in Europe, whence some slaves were brought to the West Indies.

In the Colonial period the first extensive Negro-white crossing took place between indentured white servants and Negro slaves. As the indentured service disappeared and the Negro slave system developed, mating between white and colored people continued through the access to Negro slave women that the system gave the white males.

The next stage came with the Civil War and its aftermath. "The Northern army left an unknown amount of Yankee genes in the Southern Negro people."[7] Under the caste system that supplanted slavery, interracial crossing continued in the same pattern of white male exploitation of Negro women, although the women had somewhat more freedom to reject advances than under slavery. While evidence is scarce, most writers agree that the amount of miscegenation declined throughout the twentieth century.

"Light" Selection Among Negroes.   It is generally acknowledged even by Negro students of race relations that mate selection within the Negro population itself favored those Negroes who were "whiter." Whites also favored lighter Negroes. Thus, in general, mulattoes had more economic and educational opportunity. This selective mating bias among Negroes had the effect of increasing the distribution of white genetic factors in the Negro population.[8] However, the current increasing pride among blacks in their black identity would be expected to decrease further white contribution to the future Negro gene pool.

Passing.   By "passing" is meant the successful assumption of "white" status by a person who knows he has Negro ancestry. In studying the African ancestry of the white population in the United States, Stuckert, using the method of genetic probability tables, estimated that during the years from 1941 to 1950 an average annual mean of 15,500 Negroes passed. There was an annual rate of 1.21 per 1,000 Negro population,

[5]Melville Herskovits, *The American Negro: A Study in Racial Crossing* (New York: Alfred A. Knopf, 1930).

[6]Pettigrew, *A Profile of the American Negro,* p. 68.

[7]Gunnar Myrdal, *An American Dilemma,* p. 127, Twentieth Anniversary Edition. Copyright © 1944, 1962 by Harper & Row, Publishers, Inc., New York. Quotes from this book are reprinted by permission of the publisher.

[8]For further discussion of this subject, see Otto Klineberg, ed. *Characteristics of the American Negro* (New York: Harper & Brothers, 1944), Pt. V, Ch. 9, "The Future of the Hybrid," by Louis Wirth and Herbert Goldhammer.

and the rate was found to be increasing.[9] This passing adds some Negroid admixture to the white population, but very little since the Negroes who pass have few Negroid genes to add, because "passers," when they marry, tend to select either white mates or equally white Negro mixtures.

The Negro American Genotype

The white racist myth has exaggerated the genetic differences between the races when in fact their similarities are far greater. Applied to the Negro American, Glass points out

> In all, it is unlikely that there are many more than six pairs of genes in which the white race differs characteristically, in the lay sense, from the black. Whites or blacks, however, differ among themselves by a larger number than this, a fact which reveals our racial prejudices as biologically absurd. It is only the consistency of the difference, not its magnitude which looms large in our eyes. . . . the chasm between human races and peoples where it exists, it is psychological and sociological; it is not genetic.[10]

Mental Capacity.   White racism has included the belief that Negroes are categorically inferior in mental capacity to white people. Our Chapter 5 points out that there is no adequate proof of differences in the intelligence of races. In studying Negro and white samples, behavioral scientists have relied on psychometric tests, especially intelligence quotient tests. Intelligence tests have some usefulness in distinguishing differences in mental capacity between individuals in a group where the respondents have been reared in a substantially homogeneous environment using test items related to their background. They are not of much use in comparing the differences between two components where the members of each were reared in such disparate cultural backgrounds as were white and non-white Americans. Furthermore if, despite the above, one uses the I.Q. tests as having some bearing on the mental ability question, even then the scores do not support the thesis. Usually, in such tests the median score of whites is somewhat higher than that of nonwhites, but there is a large overlapping in the distribution of the results of the two groups.[11] It is apparent then that one cannot gauge the intelligence of a person by observing his racial identity only.

Psychophysical Traits.   Dreger and Miller write concerning psychophysical traits as follows:

> In psychophysical and psychomotor functions, differences appear between whites and Negroes which may not be accounted for by differential envi-

[9]Robert P. Stuckert, "African Ancestry of the White American Population," in *The Ohio Journal of Science,* May, 1958, pp. 155–160. The main finding of this study was that 28 million "white" persons have some African ancestry.
[10]Bentley Glass, *Genes and the Man* (New York: Teachers College Press, 1943), pp. 173–174. By permission of the publisher.
[11]See Otto Klineberg, "Race and Psychology: The Problem of Genetic Differences," in *Race Science and Society,* rev. ed., Lee Kuper, ed. Paris: The UNESCO Press and New York: Columbia University Press, 1975).

ronment conditions. However, a tendency is prevalent in the literature to indicate that most differences of this nature may be leveled off when social and economic variables are controlled. . . . In temperament ("personality") studies, Rorschach, T.A.T., PAT., and P-F Studies, differences are found, but again there is insufficient evidence to determine the relative contributions of genetic constitution and experiences. At least in those reactions which indicate responses to a dominant group culture, experience seems to be the major, if not sole determinant. Overall likeness in psychodynamics appears more extensive than differences.[12]

Sociopathic Deviance. The white Americans' unfavorable view of Negroes was increased by the larger percentage of sociopathic behavior shown in comparative studies. Negroes are disproportionately found on police records, in penal institutions, and have higher recorded illegitimacy rates, intergroup violence, and homicide. While written with reference to crime, the following excerpt is also a good interpretation of the so-called Negro "pathology" in general.

White supremacists are quick to interpret these data as further evidence for their theories of the genetic inferiority of Negroes as a "race." There is, however, no scientific evidence to support such claims. But there are considerable data which indicate that a multiplicity of social factors produce these criminal patterns among Negroes.

One broad set of factors is socio-economic in character. When compared with white Americans, Negroes are concentrated in those social sectors which exhibit high crime rates regardless of race. Thus, Negroes are more often lower class and poor, slum residents of the nation's largest metropolitan areas, victims of severe family disorganization, Southern in origin, young, and unemployed. Note that each of these characteristics is an important social correlate of crime apart from race—and especially for those violations with the highest Negro rates.

The other, closely related set of factors involves the special type of discrimination inflicted upon Negroes. As with other minority groups who find discriminatory barriers blocking their path toward the mainstream of success-oriented America, many Negroes turn to crime. Crime may thus be utilized as a means of escape, ego-enhancement, expression of aggression, or upward mobility. The salient feature of Negro Americans is that they have accepted and internalized American culture, but are generally denied the chief rewards and privileges of that culture. High crime rates are but one consequence of this situation.[13]

[12]Ralph M. Dreger and Kent S. Miller, "Comparative Psychological Studies of Negroes and Whites in the United States," *Psychological Bulletin,* Sept., 1960, pp. 393–394. By permission.
[13]Pettigrew, *A Profile of the Negro American,* pp. 155–156.

Ashley Montagu has summarized the genotype of the American Negro as follows:

> . . . the American Negro represents an amalgam into which have entered the genes of African Negroes, whites of many races and social classes, and some American Indians, and that as far as his physical characteristics are concerned the American Negro represents a successful blending of these three elements into a unique biological type. All his characters are perfectly harmonic, and there is every reason to believe that he represents a perfectly satisfactory biological type. His biological future is definitely bright.[14]

Cultural Characteristics of Negro Americans

All the other minorities started out in this country with distinctive ethnic cultural differences that have been passed on to native-born generations in increasingly diluted form. The situation of Negroes in this respect is considerably different. The sharp impact of slavery went far to destroy the tribal cultures that the Africans brought with them. Scholarly controversy prevails among students of the history of the Negro in the New World concerning the extent to which African culture traits have survived, or to what extent Negro cultural adaptations in the New World were influenced by their aboriginal culture.[15]

A number of scattered, specific cultural traits have been found in specific Negro groups that can be directly traced to African origin. It is significant, however, that more of these have been found among Negro groups in the West Indies. For other, more, prevalent aspects of American Negro culture and behavior that did present a vague, general similarity to African cultural forms, the continuity of African heritage is highly debatable. For example, was the frequency of common-law marriage in Negro rural life derivative from African customs, or can it be explained by the highly destructive impact of slavery on the stability of Negro family life? Is the predilection of American Negroes for the Baptist denomination, which features total immersion, due to the surviving influence of West African "river cults," as Herskovits speculates, or is it more simply attributable, as Frazier suggests, to the vigorous proselytizing activities of the Baptist denomination.[16]

So far as African heritage is concerned, Elkins concludes that the cultural level and the social organization of various African societies from which the slaves were obtained "entitles one to argue that they must have had an institutional life at least as sophisticated as Anglo-Saxon England.[17] Thus if Elkins' conclusion is accepted it follows that most of any cultural distinctiveness of the Negro minority in America has developed out

---

[14]M. F. Ashley Montagu, *Man's Most Dangerous Myth: The Fallacy of Race* 4th ed., rev. and enl. (Cleveland: The World Publishing Co., 1965), p. 816. By permission of the author and publisher.

[15]A brief introduction to this historical problem is found in E. Franklin Frazier, *The Negro in the United States,* rev. ed. (New York: The Macmillan Company, 1957). Copyright © 1957 The Macmillan Company. See Ch. 1, "Significance of the African Background, "For further discussion of the topic, see Melville J. Herskovits, *The Myth of the Negro Past* (New York: Harper & Brothers, 1942).

[16]Frazier, *The Negro in the United States,* pp. 10–18.

[17]Stanley M. Elkins, *Slavery: A Problem in American Institutional and Intellectual Life* (Chicago: University of Chicago Press, 1959), p. 97. © 1959, 1968 by the University of Chicago, Reprinted by permission of the publisher.

of their experience in the United States. We will return to this topic again in Chapter 9 in connection with the goals of black activism. Here we note that in regard to significant aspects of culture, Negro Americans are Christian, predominantly Protestant, speak English, and their subcommunity social structure parallels that of the white community. Thus of all American minorities the Negro minority most resembles the WASP prototype.

PHASES IN NEGRO-WHITE RELATIONS

The centuries-old interaction between African-descended and white Americans in the United States has followed a more complicated course than that of other minority situations, requiring more adaptation of our general three-phase schema. Bearing in mind that any attempt to mark off the phases and to date them must be arbitrary since always there is overlap, the following outline will be followed: (1) Slavery: white dominance over Negroes as slaves, 1619–1863; (2) Early Reconstruction: decline in white dominance, 1866–1875; (3) Later Reconstruction: the reestablishment of white dominance, 1875 to circa 1900; (4) The maintenance of the dominant white Southern biracial system, circa 1900–1954; (5) The establishment and maintenance of white dominance in the North, from World War I to World War II; and (6) The sustained black challenge to white dominance following World War II on a nationwide basis.

Slavery: The Colonial Period

The dominance of white Americans over Negroes was established at the outset from the time the first twenty slaves were bought by Virginia settlers in 1619. However, since there was no precedent in English law at this time, it seems to have been assumed that the status of slaves was similar to that of white indentured servants, with stipulated ways of being manumitted. But early in colonial history, differential treatment of Negroes began. For example, when three bound servants, two white and one Negro, had been brought back to Virginia from Maryland after attempting escape from servitude, the court, having ordered thirty lashes for all three, further ordered that the white servants should serve three years in bondage, but that the Negro should serve his master for the rest of his life.[18] By court actions such as these, the differential status of Negroes evolved into a clear pattern of slavery, which eventually became established by more explicit law. In Virginia the slave status was fixed by a law making all non-Christians who came into the colony as servants from across the seas slaves for the rest of their lives. In 1682 this law was repealed and in its place another was substituted "making slaves of all persons of non-Christian nationalities thereafter coming into the colony, whether they came by sea or land and whether or not they had been converted to Christianity after capture."[19]

Although early developing into a fixed institution, Negro slavery grew indispensable only as the plantation system of agriculture became important and more widespread. This system involved the large-scale production of a staple crop for commercial exchange and required cheap labor. Thus Negro slaves filled the increasing manpower

[18]Frazier, *The Negro in the United States*, p. 24.
[19]*Ibid.*, p. 26. By permission of the publisher.

demand. The colony of Georgia, founded in 1735, first prohibited the importation of Negro slaves, but by 1750, as the plantation system began to spread into the new colony, the act was repealed. The number of Negroes in Georgia increased from a reported 349 in 1750 to 15,000 by 1773.[20] The nexus between the plantation economy and slavery is further illustrated by the difference between the two Carolinas. In North Carolina the plantation economy failed to develop on a large scale and so did slavery; in South Carolina, where the plantation system developed on a large scale, "the number of Negroes had become so numerous that it was felt necessary to encourage the importation of white servants to secure the safety of the colony."[21] Finally, in the North, where there was no plantation economy, no large-scale slavery developed.

The introduction of slavery into the colonies came as an extension of the institution already established in the West Indies. The slave trade was carried on largely by the British, although subsequently colonists themselves took a hand in it, especially New England port merchants.[22] This trade was a highly hazardous and adventuresome occupation. It was not easy to get the slaves or to deliver them since great mortality occurred from the usually overcrowded conditions in the "Middle Passage" journeys. However, when things went well, the profits were high. Franklin writes, "It was not unusual for a ship carrying 250 slaves to net as much as £7,000 on one voyage. Profits of 100 percent were not uncommon for Liverpool merchants."[23] Estimates of the number of slaves imported to the colonies and later to the states range from 500,000 to 700,000; and even though further importation was officially prohibited after 1808, Collins estimated that about 270,000 were imported between then and 1860.[24]

The National Period to the Civil War

In spite of the fixed position of slavery in the colonial economy during and for a short period following the Revolutionary War, there were signs that the slavery system might be abolished. Slavery was coming under increasing attack from a moral viewpoint, not only from Northerners but from enlightened slaveholders such as Washington and Jefferson. The first President desired to see a plan adopted for the abolition of slavery; and Jefferson wrote in his autobiography, "Nothing is more certainly written in the book of fate than that these people are to be free."[25]

The attitude of the public was affected by economic interests as well as moral idealism. Frazier indicates that opposition to slavery was expressed in Delaware, Maryland, and Virginia, where a diversified agriculture was supplanting the production of tobacco, whereas in the lower South, where the production of tobacco, rice, and indigo was still important, there was strong opposition either to suspending the slave trade or to the emancipation of the Negro.[26] In the midst of these conflicting attitudes toward

---

[20]*Ibid.*, pp. 32–33.
[21]*Ibid.*, p. 32. By permission of the publisher.
[22]Maurice R. Davie, *Negroes in American Society* (New York: McGraw-Hill Book Co., 1949), p. 18.
[23]John Hope Franklin, *From Slavery to Freedom* (New York: Alfred A. Knopf, 1947), p. 57.
[24]Winfield H. Collins, *The Domestic Slave Trade of the Southern States* (New York: Broadway Publishing Company, 1904), p. 20.
[25]Myrdal, *An American Dilemma*, p. 85.
[26]Frazier, *The Negro in the United States*, p. 35.

slavery, the Constitution of the new republic compromised on the issue by setting 1808 as the date after which the importation of slaves was to be abolished. The abolition of slavery in many state constitutions in the North and its declining economic significance led many people to share with Jefferson the belief that slavery was on its way out.

But the hopes of those opposed to slavery were dashed by the invention of the cotton gin. With this invention Southern cotton planters were able to meet the rapidly growing demand of the English market. The expansion of the cotton economy increased by leaps and bounds, especially from 1815 on. This development was accompanied by the growth of the slave system and the slave population. (See Table 6-1.)

From 1790 to 1803 the natural increase of the slave population was supplemented by foreign importation of over 100,000 slaves. Although, as Table 6-1 shows, the percentage of increase after 1810 declined, a substantial number of slaves was smuggled in to augment the natural increase. As the plantation system spread south and west away from Maryland, Virginia, and Kentucky, many slaves were bred for sale by their first owners in these states to work in the new areas.[27]

Having built not only its economy but a total society on the foundation of slavery, the South needed rationalizations to justify it. Thus there began to emerge in the pre-Civil War period learned treatises solemnly concluding that "the Negro" was naturally meant to be a slave and that he was obviously inferior to the white. Many of these treatises invoked biblical sanction and two of the most scholarly were written by Presbyterian ministers.[28] The growing intellectual support for the established system reached its climax in the words of Chief Justice Taney, who in his famous decision in the Dred Scott case declared, "A Negro has no rights which a white man need respect."[29] This decision involved a slave, Dred Scott, who sued for freedom because his master had taken him to Illinois for some time before returning with him to Missouri. Scott lost the case because the court ruled (1857) that the phrase in the Constitution "people of the United States" was not meant to apply to slaves.

TABLE 6-1 Growth of the Slave Population in the United States, 1790–1860*

Census Year	Slave Population	Percent of Decennial Increase
1790	697,624	—
1800	893,602	28.1
1810	1,191,362	33.3
1820	1,538,022	29.1
1830	2,009,043	30.6
1840	2,487,355	18.8
1850	3,204,313	28.8
1860	3,953,760	23.4

*U.S. Bureau of the Census, *Negro Population in the United States, 1790–1915* (Washington, D.C., 1918), p. 53.

SLAVERY: A PATERNALISTIC SYSTEM

In efforts to conceptualize the slave system of the Southern United States, recent writers have employed the term "paternalism."[30] Since this term carries with it some

[27]*Ibid.*, p. 39.
[28]*Ibid.*, 42–43.
[29]*Ibid.*, p. 43.
[30]Pierre van den Berghe, *Race and Racism* (New York: John Wiley & Sons), 1967.

benign connotations, it is well to keep in mind that slavery is fundamentally the most inhumane pattern of interpersonal relations. As Genovese puts it:

> Cruel, unjust, exploitative, oppressive, slavery bound two peoples together in bitter antagonism while creating an organic relationship so complex and ambivalent that neither could express the simplest feelings without reference to the other. Slavery rested on the principle of property in man— of one man's appropriation of another's person as well as of the fruits of his labor. By definition and in essence it was a system of class rule, in which some people lived off the labor of others.[31]

The paternal aspects of slavery gave complete control to the owner of the life of the slave and the right to punish the slave at will, whipping being the typical form. The consequence of this control was to make slaves completely dependent on the master for a living and also making the master responsible for their welfare. In order for the slave owner to maintain a self-respecting image of himself as a good Christian, rationalizations to justify the system were essential. The basic rationalization was that Negroes were inferior to whites and incapable of surviving without the master's care for their well-being. Genovese cites numerous examples of kindness by the master and of affection on the part of the master and his family toward the slave. Out of these instances arose the myth that in general slaves were contented and grateful. Informal mores did arise among whites that unnecessarily harsh treatment of slaves lowered the reputation of slaveholders among whites, but they were not otherwise penalized. On a different plane the self-interest of the slaveholder mitigated to a degree the potential harshness implicit in the system. A hungry or maimed slave was not an efficient worker. Thus not all overseers of slaves were "Simon Legrees."[32]

As a further rationalization for fatherly treatment of slaves there arose among white Southerners the Sambo image of the slave's personality, described by Elkins thus:

> Sambo . . . was docile but irresponsible, loyal, but lazy, humble but chronically given to lying and stealing; his behavior was full of infantile silliness. . . . His relationship with his master was one of utter dependence and childlike attachment; it was indeed this childlike quality that was the very key to his being. Although the merest hint of Sambo's manhood might fill the Southern breast with scorn, the child "in his place" could be both exasperating and lovable.[33]

While many slaves did behave with varying degrees like "Sambo," a large part of this behavior was role playing with tongue in cheek as a possible way to cope with the severe

---

[31]Eugene D. Genovese, *Roll Jordan Roll: The World the Slaves Made* (New York: Pantheon Books, a division of Random House, Inc., 1975), p. 3. Copyright © 1972, 1974 Eugene D. Genovese. Reprinted by permission of the publisher.

[32]The name of the slave overseer in Harriet Beecher Stowe's novel, *Uncle Tom's Cabin*, 1852, portrayed as a cruel taskmaster.

[33]Elkins, *Slavery: A Problem in American Institutional and Intellectual Life,* p. 97. Reprinted by permission of the publisher.

hardships of the system. Slaves developed ingenious ways to use this image to their advantage, for example, developing excuses for loafing on the job without too severe a penalty. All this tended to mislead the whites as to the slave's true personality. Elkins concluded that as far as the African heritage is concerned, "No true picture of African culture seems to throw any light at all on origins of what would emerge in American plantation society as the Sambo personality."[34]

The Work Ethic

Interpretations by one people of the behavior of another people are often a judgment based on a diverse value system. Taking the "laziness" of the slaves, Genovese suggests a conflict in value systems between the Puritan work ethic and the African work ethic. Of this Genovese credits Dr. W. E. B. Du Bois for suggesting that the "white worker brought to America the habit of regular toil as a great moral duty, and used it to make America *rich,* whereas the black worker brought the idea of work as a necessary evil and could, if allowed, use it to make America *happy.*[35] Genovese writes

> During Reconstruction the blacks sought their own land; worked it conscientiously . . . ; resisted being forced back into anything resembling gang labor for the white man; and had to be terrorized, swindled and murdered to prevent their working for themselves.[36]

Religion

Religious practices became one main focus of slave life. While most slaves embraced Christianity, some African practices were interwoven with their religious meetings and ritual. In general, religious services were highly expressive rather than formal and restrained, thus furnishing the slaves with a surcease from the anguishing frustrations of their slave existence. At first masters tended to oppose slave religious activity and conversion to Christianity for fear they might stimulate slave insurrection. But when they realized that the religious ritual served chiefly as an emotional outlet, the owners eventually encouraged it in order to deflect rebellious attitudes.[37]

The Slave Family

Earlier studies of the slave life tended to conclude that the slave system substantially destroyed family life. Indeed, it would be difficult to design a social system more calculated to destroy the family than the Southern slave system: the not infrequent selling of

---

[34]*Ibid.,* p. 152. By permission of the publisher.
[35]Genovese, *Roll Jordan Roll,* p. 310. Italics ours. Genovese questions whether the white European immigrant was enamored of hard work, but it was the Puritan ethic that became the white norm in the United States as a whole.
[36]*Ibid.,* p. 313. Reprinted by permission of Random House, Inc.
[37]*Ibid.,* pp. 161–284.

a mate, or of a slave child separately from a slave family, the many instances of sex violation of a slave's wife by a master or an overseer, and an economic setup in which the
father was not responsible (except as he chose otherwise) for his family's welfare—all
conspired to produce a high degree of family instability. Thus it is not surprising that
Genovese provides much evidence to show this situation. However, what is surprising
is that he records much evidence of slave effort to maintain a stable family life against
such odds. "I suggest only that the slaves created impressive norms of family life,
including as much of a nuclear family norm as conditions permitted, and that they
entered the postwar social system with a remarkably stable base."[38]

Active Slave Opposition

Vocally and in writing the white South expounded the belief that many slaves had
good, kindly, grateful feelings toward their masters. More recent research suggests that
all slaves hated white people generically, which their role playing behavior did not
show. Genovese cites the case of a house slave who, supposedly, had close and cordial
relations with the master's family, who left them after emancipation but returned
later to murder her former mistress. It is inevitable that under slavery intermittently
some frustrated Negro, throwing discretion to the wind, attacked a white person and
received punishment. There were "Kunta Kinte's" who stood up to their masters knowing that terrible punishment would follow.[39] Other bold slaves ran away hoping to escape to free areas. Despite the odds against them, "During the 1850's about a thousand
slaves a year ran away to the North, Canada, and Mexico."[40]

Organized revolts were obviously difficult. One unfavorable situation for success
was the scattering of slaves in relatively small numbers on different farms and plantations. Despite this, Aptheker documented about 250 slave insurrections, from which he
presumes among the South's slaves a tradition of revolution.[41] Genovese feels that
Aptheker overrated the significance of the revolts in comparison with the larger slave
revolts in Latin America. But there is enough in Aptheker's book to destroy forever the
myth of the contented slave.

Comparison of the Latin American slave system with that of the Southern United
States is instructive. In Latin America, law, religion, and a tolerant attitude toward
interracial miscegenation made the formal status of slaves markedly different from that
in the United States. Slaves had legal rights protecting them to a degree from severe
punishment and married slaves could not be separated from each other against their
will. The Latin system was more favorable to freeing slaves, and upon manumission the
ex-slave was accorded the privileges of citizenship.[42]

According to Tannenbaum, the differences in the Latin American system were accounted for by the presence of Spanish laws, which gave legal protection to slaves, and

---

[38]*Ibid.,* pp. 451–452. This thesis as to the strength of the black family is also developed by Herbert
G. Gutman, in *The Black Family in Slavery and Freedom, 1750–1925* (New York: Pantheon
Books), 1976.
[39]Kunta Kinte was the name of the first of Alex Haley's forbears to be enslaved in America, as portrayed in Alex Haley's *Roots.*
[40]Genovese, *Roll Jordan Roll,* p. 648.
[41]Herbert Aptheker, *American Slave Revolts* (New York: Columbia University Press, 1943),
p. 162.
[42]Tannenbaum, *Slave and Citizen* (New York: Alfred A. Knopf, 1947), pp. 53–54.

also by the influence of Catholic doctrine opposing slavery. However, many of the differences noted above, while legally stated on paper, to a considerable extent were not enforced. Harris[43] in particular is quite caustic in stating that the plantation owners living a long distance from the seats of authority paid little attention to these laws, and often were more cruel in dealing with slaves than those of the American South.

FREE NEGROES

In contrast to Latin America, the existence of a tiny Southern free Negro population was an anomaly to white Southerners. But the American Revolution "propelled large numbers of blacks from slavery into freedom,"[44] since the Revolutionary army needed all blacks it could persuade to fight with the promise of freedom. By 1810, there were over 100,000 free Negroes in the Southern states comprising 5 percent of the free population and about 9 percent of the black population.[45] The free Negroes had better jobs, owned property, and experienced a separate community life. They were a potential subversive influence over the slaves. Therefore, by every device possible white Southerners insisted that they conform to most of the pattern of "etiquette" (see pp. 120–121) governing slave-master relations. Initially, free Negroes had tended to look down on slaves, but this manner of treatment by whites developed a sense of unity with the slaves even though some owned slaves themselves.

Emancipation drastically changed the position of the free slaves, erasing the distinction between them and the former slaves. However, during the first Reconstruction period in the South, antebellum free Negroes became the "elite" of the black population. "Only 1 black person in 9 was free in 1860 but at least 10 of the 22 blacks who served in Congress between 1869 and 1900 were drawn from the old free Negro Caste."[46]

Reconstruction

The emancipation of slaves and the end of the Civil War were followed by a brief challenge to white dominance. But emancipation was forced upon the South against its will, of course, and the implementation of freedom could be carried through only by a costly, large-scale federal program and the application of considerable pressures on the South. The problem was twofold: how to guarantee the new political status of Negroes as free men and how to reconstruct the economy of the South in such a manner that Negroes would have a secure economic position.

The war had wrought enormous material property losses on Southern whites, as well as taking away their slaves. Many of the freed slaves who, both during the war and immediately after it, had flocked to the cities or to the vicinity of Northern army camps found no means of livelihood. In 1865 the Bureau of Refugees, Freedmen, and Abandoned Lands was established to aid in the economic rehabilitation of the freedmen, as well as the propertyless whites, and to promote an educational program for

---

[43]Marvin Harris, *Patterns of Race* (New York: Walker & Company, 1964).
[44]Ira Berlin, *Slaves Without Masters: The Free Negro in the Ante Bellum South* (New York: Pantheon Books, Random House, 1974), p. 16.
[45]*Ibid.*, p. 15.
[46]*Ibid.*, p. 385. A one-chapter account of the free Negroes is given by E. Franklin Frazier, *The Negro in the United States*, rev. ed., Ch. 4, pp. 59–79.

the Negroes. The general plan was to furnish land and tools with which the freedmen and landless whites might become self-sustaining farmers.

However, during the seven years of its existence (1865–1872), the Bureau was unable to accomplish its economic objectives. It had woefully inadequate funds for the size of the job. The amnesty granted former Confederates restored to them land that had already been leased to Negroes, who consequently became landless again. When efforts were made to resettle both white and Negro tenants on public lands in the Gulf areas, inability to raise enough capital and general discouragement with the whole program spelled failure. The desire of the more influential portion of the white South to retain the traditional system of agricultural production and to keep the Negro in his servile place did nothing to help. And the half-hearted support of Northerners contributed to the failure to carry through the program. The lukewarm support was due in part to the usual reluctance to appropriate the rather large funds needed for the task. Northerners, although believing in theoretical freedom for Negroes, were far from advocating that they be accorded full, equal status. The combination of proprietary interest in the South and the traditional white attitudes toward the proper status of Negroes, shared by many Northerners as well as nearly all the white South, conspired to defeat what appears in retrospect to have been a validly conceived plan for the economic rehabilitation of the South.

The same combination of interests and attitudes appeared in opposition to the fulfillment of the other objective in the Northern plan for reconstruction of the South: to make Negroes first-class citizens. Soon after the close of the war, eight Southern states instituted the so-called Black Codes. By various statutes affecting apprenticeship, labor contracts, debts, and vagrancy, these codes went far to reestablish the servile position of Negroes. Frazier cites the following example:

> The Florida code states that if any person of color failed to fulfill the stipulations of a contract into which he entered with a plantation owner or was impudent to the owner, he should be declared a vagrant and be subject to punishment for vagrancy.[47]

When the Republican government of the North realized that the South was in fact nullifying the Emancipation Proclamation, it exerted pressure to force acceptance. Through the Fourteenth Amendment to the Constitution (1866) abridgement of the full civic equality of all citizens was declared unlawful, and the supplementary Fifteenth Amendment (1870) specifically denied the right to abridgement of the voting privilege "on account of race, color, or previous condition of servitude." Still further, Congress passed in 1867 a series of reconstruction acts that called for the temporary governing of the South by military rule until such time as genuinely democratic elections could be held and governments so elected should get under way. In the governments that followed, many Negroes were elected to state assemblies, and twenty were sent to Congress. Some of these Negro officials demonstrated unusual ability.

In these turbulent years the majority of Southerners naturally resented the attempt of the "carpetbaggers" to reconstruct their society, aided by their own "scalawags," as the Southerners who cooperated with the Yankee officials were called. They made much of the point that complete civic equality for Negroes would give the colored population control over the South. Actually, in no state were Negroes ever the dominating

---

[47]Frazier, *The Negro in the United States,* p. 127. By permission of the publisher.

factor in the government, though in several states they constituted about half the population. The Southern attitude toward the Negro was not reconstructed, as the testimony of Carl Schurz indicates:

> Wherever I go . . . I hear the people talk in such a way as to indicate that they are yet unable to conceive of the Negro as possessing any rights at all. . . . The people boast that when they get freedmen's affairs in their own hands . . . "the niggers will catch hell."
>
> The reason of all this is simple and manifest. The whites esteem the blacks their property by natural right, and however much they admit that the individual relations of masters and slaves have been destroyed by the war and by the President's emancipation proclamation, they still have an ingrained feeling that the blacks at large belong to the whites at large.[48]

The next phase of the reconstruction drama opened as the Republican Congress began to weaken. In 1872, the disabilities imposed on the former Confederate leaders, which prevented their participation in political affairs, were removed. The Freedmen's Bureau was abolished, depriving many Negro laborers and tenants of much-needed economic support and moral aid. The climax came when the Civil Rights bill of 1875 was declared unconstitutional. This bill, as Myrdal puts it, "represented the culmination of the Federal reconstruction legislation, was explicit in declaring that all persons . . . should be entitled to the full and equal enjoyment of the accommodations, advantages, facilities, and privileges of inns, public conveyances on land and water, theaters, and other places of public amusement . . . applicable alike to citizens of every race and color, regardless of previous condition of servitude."[49] When the bill was declared unconstitutional, the North seems to have given up.

From 1875 on, the door was open for the unreconstructed white Southerners to carry out their own program of reconstruction. The result was the biracial pattern of race relations in which the dominance of white over colored was assured. This social system remained broadly intact down to the late 1950s. Reconstruction on this biracial basis involved the use of both legal and illegal procedures, since in the white Southern view Negroes had already advanced too far. The illegal phase of the reconstruction was spearheaded by a number of secret societies, of which the Ku Klux Klan is the most widely known. Extralegal activities by states were supplemented by further Black Code legislation, which segregated Negroes and otherwise accorded them unequal privileges. While it took some years to accomplish the task, the white South succeeded in establishing a color-caste system.

Reconstruction: An Object Lesson

What happened in the reconstruction period is an excellent object lesson in social science. It illustrates the consequences of attempting swift and radical social change without adequate social planning. In hindsight, it is clear that the federal government attempted to accomplish too sweeping objectives in too short a time against too strong a

---

[48]Report of Carl Schurz, Senate Executive Document, No. 2, 39th Congress, 1st Session, cited by W. E. B. Du Bois, *Black Reconstruction in America* (New York: Harcourt, Brace & Co., 1936).
[49]Myrdal, *An American Dilemma*, p. 579. By permission.

set of opposing forces and with too little public support from the North itself. For example, how could it have been expected that white Southerners, long steeped in the tradition of slavery, could change their complex attitudes and habits concerning Negroes overnight? Again, how could it have been expected that slaves, held to such a low level of literacy and molded into a servile, dependent personality pattern, could immediately become self-reliant and civically active? Furthermore, how could it have been expected that such a program could be carried on without a greater consensus of Northern opinion to support it? To raise such questions in hindsight and to leave the matter there is obviously unfair to the many intelligent and socially conscious white people, both North and South who set the objectives and tried to carry them out. Neither the theoretical knowledge of human nature and social processes nor the accumulated practice of social engineering had advanced to a point in 1865 to have made success possible. We cite the lesson for its value at the present time.

The United States since 1950 has been in an extraordinary period of disequilibrium in white-Negro relations, precipitated by the Supreme Court's school desegregation decision. We face this period with a considerably greater body of social theory, techniques, and practices in intergroup relations. In areas of the nation where the attitudes of the dominant group are not too intransigent, some of this knowledge has been usefully applied, as will be discussed in later chapters.

Suggested Readings

Aptheker, Herbert. *American Slave Revolts*. New York: Columbia University Press, 1943.
>An extensive history of the subject.
Bennett, Jr. Lerone. *Black Power, U. S. A. The Human Side of Reconstruction, 1867–1877*. Baltimore, Md.: Penguin Books, 1967.
>A full-length history of those ten years of the short period of Reconstruction when newly freed Negroes exercised extensive political power.
Berlin, Ira. *Slaves Without Masters: The Free Negro and the Ante-Bellum South*. New York: Pantheon Books, Random House, 1974.
>A full treatment of a neglected subject. The social position of free Negroes vis-à-vis slaves before and after Emancipation.
Davis, David Brian. *The Problem of Slavery in the Age of Revolution, 1770–1823*. Ithaca, New York: Cornell University Press, 1975.
>History and analysis of the debate both in America and England over the issue of abolition of slavery, pro and con, and the difference in the outcome.
Douglass, Frederick. *Life and Times of Frederick Douglass*. New York: Collier Books, 1969.
>The autobiography of this famous spokesman for the cause of Negro freedom whose life, 1817–1895, spanned the period of slavery and Reconstruction. Douglass was actively involved in the Negro cause in both periods.
Genovese, Eugene. *Roll, Jordan, Roll: The World the Slaves Made*. New York: Panthcon Books, Random House, 1974.

A brilliant treatment of slavery based on exhaustive research of documentary material. Objective treatment of the systems of slavery with fresh insights, especially
regarding the Afro-American slave community.

Gutman, Herbert G. *The Black Family in Slavery and Freedom, 1750–1925*. New York:
Pantheon Books, 1976.
Attacks the idea that slavery destroyed the Negro family. Research leads to conclu-
sion that slaves strove hard to keep their families together.

Kuper, Lee, ed. *Race, Science and Society*. Paris: UNESCO, 1975; New York:
Columbia University Press, 1975.
The latest findings of UNESCO's section on the study of race put together by
various authors in this volume, including material on Afro-Americans.

Miller, Floyd J. *The Search for a Black Nationality: Black Colonization and Immigration, 1787–1863*. Urbana: University of Illinois Press, 1975.
Main theme the belief of some antebellum free Negroes that even after abolition
America would never really accept Afro-Americans as equal citizens and the efforts
of some to plan for Negroes to emigrate outside the country.

Samuda, Ronald J. *Psychological Testing of American Minorities: Issues and Consequences*. New York: Dodd, Mead & Co., 1975.
Summarizes the debate concerning the use of I.Q. tests as measurements of
academic performance, primarily of blacks, and some material on tests scores and
occupational performances.

Tannenbaum, Frank. *Slave and Citizen*. New York: Alfred A. Knopf, 1947.
Compares the slave system of Latin America with the South of the United States,
relying largely on the formal pattern in legal and religious laws with less attention
to how much these formal rules were obeyed in practice.

Williams, John E., and Moreland, J. Kenneth. *Race, Color and the Young Child*. Chapel
Hill: University of North Carolina Press, 1976.
Research finds some evidence that the original fear of darkness plays some part in
the white child's antiblack attitudes, later strongly enforced by growing up in the
white Southern social environment.

7

Negro-White Relations: The Traditional Southern Pattern

The previous chapter briefly delineated the process by which the white South reestablished dominance in a new pattern of race relations after the abortive attempt to develop racial equality following emancipation and the Civil War. This chapter will describe that system and consider its implications for the South and the nation. By 1910 it had been crystallized and remained essentially intact until World War II. The strong resistance to change in the South is better understood by keeping in mind that many of today's adult white Southerners have been conditioned since birth to the biracial system here described.

The South includes seventeen states and the District of Columbia. The following states are considered border states: Delaware, Kentucky, Maryland, Missouri, Tennessee, Oklahoma, and West Virginia. The term "Deep South" is not so definite geographically. It certainly includes Alabama, Georgia, Louisiana, Mississippi, and South Carolina. Arkansas, Florida, North Carolina, Texas, Virginia, and the District of Columbia account for the rest of the South.[1]

CASTE SYSTEM

In common with many other, although not all, students of minorities, we shall designate the Southern interracial pattern as a caste system. In its ideology and in the institutions that governed race relations, the categorical segregation of the two races in a large number of social relations was clear. Intermarriage was flatly prohibited. While specific identification with a particular occupation, as was characteristic of the traditional Hindu caste system, was not so marked, nevertheless the Southern pattern did not generally permit the performance together of the same tasks by members of the two races. Furthermore, the rising middle class of Negroes in the South was in the main

[1]To Southerners "Deep South" meant the areas where the plantation economy earlier was extensive and vigorous.

118

segregated from the white middle class. It was the absence of explicit religious sanctions in support of its biracial system that mainly distinguished the Southern pattern from other caste systems.

The Southern caste system had two main features—segregation and the so-called caste etiquette. The former involved the physical separation of Negroes from whites; the latter included the rules to be followed when interaction must unavoidably take place between one or more members of each race. Both the patterns of segregation and the caste etiquette always symbolized the superordination of the white people and the subordination of the Negroes.

Segregation[2]

Residentially, in rural areas, Negroes were scattered but did not live close to whites except on plantations, where the mansion was separated conspicuously, though often not far, from the Negroes' shacks. In small towns there was a clustering of Negro homes on the edges of the community. In Southern cities there were various Negro residential patterns: the back-alley residence plan, as seen in Charleston; the isolated community, as in Tulsa; the one large Negro area with smaller scattered clusters found in many cities. Interestingly enough, Southern whites did not appear to object to having Negro families live near them, as Northern whites did. However, in the South when homes of Negro families were spatially proximate to those of white families, there was usually some outward manifestation of the superior-inferior status—for example, whites facing the streets and Negroes, the alleys.

A striking example of segregation was in hospitalization. In some places there were isolated wards for Negroes. But more often the hospitals would not admit Negroes, and there were few Negro hospitals. Instances occurred of Negroes in need of emergency operations dying because the nearest hospitals would not admit them.

Economic Segregation. Segregation in economic life had two main aspects: in employment, and in the role of the Negro as a customer. In regard to employment, the basic principle was that Negroes must not work alongside whites on equal functional terms. For instance, one restaurant might have all Negro waitresses and another across the street all white waitresses, but no restaurant would mix the two. This principle operated to limit Negro employment to occupations that whites did not care to enter. (The one important exception was tenant farming, in which both races engaged but in which they did not work together.) As a result, the most menial and the poorest-paid occupations were left for Negroes. When technological improvements made any particular occupation more rewarding, the whites tried to keep the Negroes out, as they did following the introduction of farm tractors and the mechanical cotton picker.

Until 1935 labor unions in the South excluded Negroes from membership, or at most permitted them to organize in separate auxiliary locals. Since the earlier days of the caste period, Negroes had become a majority in certain semiskilled or skilled trades; the development of unions had the effect of driving them from these occupations. The elimination of Negroes as engineers on railroad locomotives and the gradual decline in the number of Negro firemen and brakemen correlated with the rise of the railway workers' union.

[2]See Charles S. Johnson, *Patterns of Negro Segregation* (New York: Harper & Brothers, 1943), for the fullest single-volume discussion of segregation at the height of the development of the system.

The color line was less rigidly drawn against the Negro as a customer in commercial establishments. Two generalizations held largely true. The cheaper the price level of the goods to be sold, the more welcome was the Negro trade. Thus the five-and-ten-cent stores and the chain food stores generally welcomed Negro trade and provided reasonably courteous service, while the more exclusive stores either refused or discouraged Negro patronage through discourtesy. The other general rule was that the more intimate the personal relationship involved in a commercial transaction, the more likely the Negro was to be excluded. In beauty parlors and mortuary services the races were strictly separated. But when the services rendered, though involving considerable interpersonal relationships, were such that the position of the vendor was clearly superior to that of the buyer, as in the case of medical or legal counsel, white professional people often would take Negro clients.

Education.   Seventeen states had entirely separate school systems. No contact at all took place between the teachers or pupils of the two systems except the unavoidable contact of the white superintendent. This separation went far to root firmly in the attitudes and habits of children of both races the practice of race segregation. Negroes were not admitted generally into public libraries in the South, and a Negro had no access to library facilities unless he could get a white friend to take out a book for him. In a few large cities Negro branch libraries were established.

Public Segregation.   Public recreational facilities were generally scarce in the South outside the large cities, and whites did not share those that existed with the Negroes. Negroes were generally excluded from public parks, and only a few cities had parks for Negroes. Except where a special section of a public playground was set aside for them, the colored people were not permitted to use public playgrounds. At one time, a common sign in Southern parks was "Negroes, Soldiers, and Dogs Keep Out."

In hotels and restaurants, the segregation was absolute and complete. Outside the larger cities, where some Negro hotels and restaurants existed, it was impossible for Negroes who were traveling to get a meal or lodging unless some Negro family gave them hospitality. In public buildings, such as post offices and tax offices, Negroes usually waited in line until every white person appearing had been served. Separate toilets for each race was the general rule in public places where both races were admitted. The best-known device of the segregation system was "Jim Crow" transportation. In local transportation, where the vehicles were often not physically partitioned, Negroes had to go to the rear and whites to the front, the dividing line being set on each trip by the proportion of each race aboard. Of this Johnson wrote

> The operator is empowered to regulate the space occupied by each race in accordance with the respective number of passengers. This system is subject to abuse since it permits the attitude of the operator to become a factor in segregation.[3]

The Code of Race Etiquette

Since Negroes were an important part of the economic life of the South, they could not be totally segregated. To allow for some interpersonal relations there developed an

[3]*Ibid.*, p. 49.

elaborate pattern of racial etiquette,[4] the function of which was to make clear the superordinate caste positions. For example, a white man did not shake hands with a Negro when introduced to him. The white person did not address the Negro person as "Mr." or "Mrs.," but rather by his first name or by his last without the courtesy title; the Negro always addressed the white person as "Mister," "Marse," or "Missus," or better still by some such title as "Colonel," which often the white man did not actually possess. Professionally trained Negroes could be addressed as "Professor," "Doctor," or "Reverend." Negro women were never referred to as "ladies," but either as just "women," or, irrespective of age, as "girls." Negro men were expected to doff their hats when they spoke to white men, but the latter were not expected to reciprocate. When Negroes called at white men's homes, they came to the rear door. Whenever circumstances brought Negroes and white people together at mealtime or on recreational occasions, the races were not expected to sit together at the same table or play together. Thus when a white person visited a colored home, if the Negro hostess wished to provide food for her guest, etiquette prescribed that they not eat together. With the exception of young children, Negroes and whites did not ordinarily play together.

Endogamy is the primary principle of caste. Marriage across caste lines was not recognized and was forbidden by law in Southern states. Most adamant of all the taboos was the one against any sort of casual interpersonal relations between a white woman and a Negro man. No one thing was more dangerous to a Negro male than to be in a situation that could be even remotely construed as indicating personal interest in a white female. Negro men understood this and acted accordingly. Brought up to know that the rope awaited the Negro accused—falsely or otherwise—of "sexual" interest in a white woman, Negro men in the South, as a general rule, avoided white women.

The Interrelation of Class and Caste

In the South the class system was linked with the caste system in significant ways. In most Southern communities, particularly in cities, class differentiation developed within the Negro caste. Negroes performing higher-ranking functions—ministers, teachers, doctors, farm agents—had achieved a higher-class status within their racial group. The class position of such Negroes was generally recognized by white people, and they were accorded differential treatment from that accorded lower-class Negroes. Frequently upper-class whites came to the defense of higher-class Negroes who got into trouble with lower-class whites. Warner and Davis cite the case of a colored professional man who accidentally ran down and killed with his car a drunken lower-class white man. Local bankers offered money for the Negro's defense, and upper-class white women called at his place of business to indicate that they supported him in his difficulty.[5]

This class bond that cut across caste lines prompted upper-class whites on occasion to attend special functions conducted by upper-class Negroes, and at such occasions special courtesies not generally accorded Negroes by caste etiquette might be extended by the whites, such as addressing the Negro women as "Mrs."

---

[4]See Bertram W. Doyle, *The Etiquette of Race Relations in the South* (Chicago: University of Chicago Press, 1937), for a fuller description of the subject.

[5]W. Lloyd Warner and Allison Davis, "A Comparative Study of American Caste," in *Race Relations and the Race Problem,* Edgar T. Thompson, ed. (Durham: Duke University Press, 1939), p. 243.

This class-differentiated aspect of the caste system operated more to strengthen caste, however, than to undermine it. While it accorded upper-class Negroes some differential privileges, these always fell clearly short of equality; and to receive them upper-class Negroes had to accept caste, at least outwardly. This special relation also served practical purposes in the maintenance of the biracial system. While caste relations are fundamentally antagonistic, they cannot exist without some degree of cooperation. In their function as leaders, the middle- and upper-class Negroes were expected to exert their influence to control the Negro masses in order to preserve order.[6]

METHODS OF ENFORCING CASTE

The methods employed for sustaining this caste pattern of race relations in the South may be conveniently treated under the headings of legal methods, illegal force and intimidation, and custom. Bearing in mind that at many points these three methods of social control reinforce each other, let us discuss each in turn.

Legal Methods

Specific local and state laws required segregation of the two races in many of the categories of interaction noted above. Southern state supreme courts upheld these laws, and for a long time the Supreme Court of the United States upheld Southern segregation laws in the cases reaching it. However, in 1915, a Louisville, Kentucky, city ordinance forbidding Negroes to reside in certain areas was declared unconstitutional by the United States Supreme Court.[7] It further ruled that the segregated public facilities and services provided Negroes should be equal to those provided for whites. Every description of the facilities for Negroes in the South documented the fact that Negroes did not have equal public facilities, in spite of this interpretation of the Constitution. Segregation continued to be upheld by local law.

Denial of Voting.   Between 1890 and 1910, eleven Southern states adopted special requirements for voting designed to deny Negroes the franchise. One was the poll tax, requiring the citizen to pay a special tax of a dollar or two for the privilege of voting. While not a large sum, by various other devices it was made to serve its purpose. Sometimes the tax was retroactive—that is to say, in order to vote in any one year, poll tax receipts for a number of years had to be shown if asked for by the election official.

Negroes were barred from voting in the Democratic primary with the excuse that any political party may restrict its membership. Before 1941 the United States Supreme Court in decisions concerning these white primary regulations failed to overrule the specific laws in this connection. Other qualifications for voting left opportunity for discrimination through their administration. For example, educational tests were sometimes stipulated. By asking Negro applicants for registration questions concerning government that they could not possibly answer, officials could keep them off the list.

---

[6]These class-linked relations should not be confused with the intergroup relations that are in substance nonconformity to caste. There have been, of course, throughout the whole period considered, a few white people here and there, more particularly in cities, who did not believe in caste and who, with due deference to the personal costs of nonconformity, have participated in informal mixed gatherings on a plane of social equality.

[7]See Johnson, *Patterns of Negro Segregation*, p. 175.

Or such devices as giving the Negroes a day for registration when the white officials were not available were further employed.

Illegal Violence and Intimidation

Not all segregation and race etiquette, however, was upheld by law. The part of it not so covered was reinforced by intimidation and extralegal violence. The Negro who violated the customary etiquette found himself brought to order by whites through abusive language and warnings. If he persisted in violation or if the breach was considered particularly heinous from the dominant caste's viewpoint, he might be physically maltreated or even lynched. If the violations appeared to be in any sense en masse, a whole Negro street or area might be destroyed by white groups as a way of "teaching the nigger to keep his place." The authors of the book *Deep South* write:

> In fact, it is considered entirely correct for the white person to resort directly to physical attack upon the Negro. Thus, if a Negro curses a white, the white may knock the Negro down; and the failure to do so may even be considered as a failure in duty as a white. . . .
>
> It is a common belief of many whites that Negroes will respond only to violent methods. In accordance with the theory of the "animal-like" nature of the Negro, they believe that the formal punishments of fines and imprisonments fail to act as deterrents to crime.[8]

A planter puts the traditional Southern white viewpoint thus:

> The best thing is not to take these young bucks into the court house for some small crime but to give them a paddling. That does them more good than a jail sentence. If I catch a Negro stealing a hog or some chickens, what is the use of taking him into court? He would get a fine or a jail sentence and unless I pay him out he will lie up in jail, and when he gets out he will keep on stealing.[9]

As a result of this traditional support of intimidation and violence, law itself was caste-patterned, applying very unequally to the two races. When any altercation occurred involving a white and a Negro, the Negro was usually presumed to be wrong. The word of a white person was ordinarily taken against that of a Negro, even when many whites knew that the white person was lying. Furthermore, the law failed to protect the Negro against extralegal violence on the part of whites. It was generally impossible to get anybody to testify that he had any knowledge about illegal acts of violence perpetrated against Negroes. As a result, lynching after lynching occurred in the South. Even those reported in the national press, where the fact of lynching was incon-

---

[8]Allison Davis, Burleigh Gardner, and Mary R. Gardner, *Deep South* (Chicago: University of Chicago Press, 1941), pp. 45–46. Copyright © 1941 by the University of Chicago. Reprinted by permission of the publisher.
[9]*Ibid.*, p. 46. Reprinted by permission of the publisher.

trovertible, seldom resulted in indictments and trials. Negroes were carefully kept off juries in the South. However, Federal Supreme Court reversals of Negro convictions where the defense argued successfully that Negroes in the communities involved were purposely not called to jury duty began to break this caste practice to a degree.[10] For a long time the only chance for some measure of justice for the Negroes was if they had a white protector who would intercede for them. Frequently an employer would say a good word for his Negro employee and get the case dismissed or the sentence lightened.

White Southerners at times resorted to intimidation and violence for the purpose of preventing Negroes from voting. Davie furnishes the following example: "There are numerous instances of Negroes who attempted to register or vote being driven away, beaten up, or killed. More generally the opposition took the form of intimidation. For example, a Negro went to the registration booth in his county and asked if he could register. The white official replied: 'Oh, yes, you can register, but I want to tell you something. Some God-damn niggers are going to get killed about this voting business yet.'" In Dennison, Texas, in the fall of 1932, handbills were scattered throughout the town reading as follows:

NIGGER!
The white people do not want you to vote Saturday.
Do not make the Ku Klux Klan take a hand.
Do you remember what happened two years ago, May 9?
George Hughes was burned to death, the country courthouse destroyed
. . . . For good reason.

Riots on election day in which both whites and Negroes were killed occurred in various sections of the South.[11]

Custom

The casual traveler in the South would not have noticed the intimidation we have mentioned. He saw for the most part an orderly pattern of segregation and race etiquette. On the surface he saw no resentment. But, although indications of intimidation were not present each day, no Negro brought up in the South was unaware of the threat of violence. Negro children were taught by their earliest experience with white people to conform to the established pattern. Negro parents had to punish the rebellious inclinations of their children who naïvely approached white persons as equal human beings.[12] And the white children in the South were, of course, conditioned to assume all the appropriate attitudes and behavior patterns of the dominant caste. Any tendency to really like Negro children had to be sternly disciplined to make sure that they were not treated as equals. Thus the Southern caste pattern was supported by the conditioning and custom of the Southerners of both races to assume the reciprocal social roles required to keep it intact—the white to be arrogant, exploitative, superior; the Negro to be

[10]Myrdal, *An American Dilemma* (New York: Harper & Brothers, 1944), p. 549.
[11]By permission from *Negroes in American Society*, by M. R. Davie. Copyright © 1949. McGraw-Hill Book Co., p. 266.
[12]See Calvin C. Hernton, *Sex and Racism in America* (Garden City, N.Y.: Doubleday & Co., 1965), pp. 53–58, for personal testimony.

submissive, exploited, and inferior. Most of the time this combination of implicit intimidation and habituation worked quite successfully. The Negro who occasionally
threw caution to the wind and rebelled against the pattern was dealt with summarily.
The white person whose conscience occasionally pricked him submerged his inclination under the pressure of public sentiment.

EFFECTS OF THE CASTE SYSTEM

In discussing the effects of the race caste system as it operated in the South we will
consider its effect on personality and behavior, on the welfare of the Negro, on social organization in Southern communities, and on the political and economic development of
the region.

Effects on White Personality

The value of treating the social structure as an independent variable and the normative behavior of the people reared in it as the dependent variable is well illustrated by
considering how being reared in the Southern biracial system affected the personality
of the white Southerner. One of the earliest and best-known field studies of the
Southern racial system was that of John Dollard of a cotton community.[13] Dollard
analyzed the gains accruing to white people under the caste system that were in turn
"losses" to the Negroes. First was the economic gain, enabling white people to exploit
Negroes as workers and consumers. A typical year for the Negro tenant farmer ran as
follows: After the cotton had been sold and the Negro had paid his debts, he was broke.
The landlord advanced him "furnish" to carry him through the next harvest. The
charges for this "furnish" were not regulated and the accounting was typically in the
landlord's hands. It was difficult for the Negro to get justice if his accounting differed
from that of a landlord.

Second, Dollard mentions the "sexual gain." The system gave white men exploitative sexual opportunity with Negro women, while any sexual advances of Negro men
toward white women were absolutely tabooed and infractions often punished by death.
The white caste ideology considered Negro women sexually promiscuous and therefore
the numerous white males who took this advantage felt little guilt, whether they used
force or otherwise made it economically or socially advantageous for Negro women to
submit.

The third gain Dollard saw accruing to the white caste was "ego" gratification. The
daily expressions of superiority toward all Negroes that the whites could indulge in and
the responses of submissiveness by the Negroes bolstered the self-esteem of the whites,
especially those among the less-privileged ranks.

The normative white Southerner was a person who assumed the superordinate role
toward Negroes, which involved considerable ambivalence. The role called for "bully-
ing" and exploiting Negroes and for treating with patronizing kindness those Negroes
who acted in the appropriate subordinate role. It also called for unwavering defense of
the system—ideological and behavioral. There were two types of deviant white
Southerners: those who carried the superordinate role too far, who were overbullyish

---

[13]John Dollard, *Caste and Class in a Southern Town* (New Haven: Yale University Press, 1937).

and exploitative, lost repute but not status, and were not otherwise punished for such behavior, even though it was often illegal. The other deviant type of white Southerner was rare: one who openly called for and occasionally participated in some organized attempt to challenge the established system.

Lillian Smith depicts the effect of the system on white Southerners. In *Killers of the Dream* she describes her own childhood experience when her parents had taken into their family an apparently white child living with a Negro family only to return the child again to its adopted parents when it was discovered that in fact the child had Negro lineage. Miss Smith wrote as follows:

> Something was wrong with a world that tells you love is good and people are important and then forces you to deny love and to humiliate people. I knew, though I would not for years confess it aloud, that in trying to shut the Negro race away from us, we have shut ourselves away from so many good, creative, honest, deeply human things in life. I began to understand slowly at first but more clearly as the years passed, that the *warped, distorted frame we have put around every Negro child from birth is around every white child also*. Each is on a different side of the frame but each is pinioned there. And I knew that what cruelly shapes and cripples the personality of one is as cruelly shaping and crippling the personality of the other. I began to see that though we may, as we acquire new knowledge, live through new experiences, examine old memories, gain the strength to tear the frame from us, yet we are stunted and warped and *in our lifetime cannot grow straight again* any more than can a tree, put in a steel-like twisting frame when young, grow tall and straight when the frame is torn away at maturity.[14]

Effects on Negro Behavior and Personality

Dollard's study covers the range of possible adjustments of Negroes to the inevitable frustrations of being brought up in such a system.[15] However, in line with more recent theoretical analysis we distinguish between the normative type of adjustment and the more deviant adjustments. The normative adjustment was to accept the role assigned to a Negro under the system—to be docile, servile, and to adhere to the rules of etiquette and segregation. This type of behavior was sometimes accompanied by an internalization of the white stereotype of the Negro; and in other instances was merely *role playing* of necessity in order to get along better under the system. This tendency of most Southern Negroes most of the time to act normatively under the system furnished the basis for one of the major elements in the race ideology of the white Southerner, namely that on the whole "their" Negroes were content with the system. That Negroes seldom openly manifested hatred for white people should not be interpreted to indicate that they did not cherish such a feeling inwardly. Warner and Davis wrote that "Anyone who believes that the hostile statements uttered by Southern whites toward Negroes

---

[14]Reprinted from *Killers of the Dream* by Lillian Smith. By permission of W. W. Norton & Co., Inc. Copyright 1949, 1961 by Lillian Smith.
[15]See Dollard, *Caste and Class in a Southern Town*, Ch. 12.

are extreme should be allowed to hear those uttered by Negroes, even Negro children and adolescents toward whites."[16]

Deviant responses as adjustments to the frustrations of caste were numerous.[17] (1) *Ritualistic*. Certain Negroes whose circumstances and/or ability permitted strove to achieve higher status within the Negro community, for example as professionals or civil servants, through pursuing the goals of the white value system. Ironically, the very existence of the segregation system afforded this opportunity and their higher status was recognized by whites, as well as by Negroes, as long as they did not challenge the system. (2) *Retreatist*. Escape from the frustrations of caste took several forms. (a) *Hedonism*—enjoying as fully as possible those pleasures not denied by caste. Here one may distinguish those activities closer to the normal responses of all mankind, such as taking an unexcused day off from work to go fishing and losing a day's exploitative pay, or casual sexual activity, and those responses more personally disorganizing, such as drinking, drugs, and the other so-called vices.[18] (b) *Intragroup aggression*. Another way of coping with frustration is to fight other Negroes. There is much data on homicide among Negroes.[19] (3) *Rebellion*. Some (but, under the caste system, few) Negroes responded to systematic discrimination by attacking either white persons or the system. Some such acts were almost always impulsive, since all Southern-bred Negroes knew it would lead to violent reprisal. In other cases the action was deliberate, for example, participation in some planned activity usually by a group asking for some improvement in welfare. Sometimes if carried on with due deference such a response met with success.

While the life of Southern American Negroes under these established patterns of dominance was not a total vale of tears, there is ample empirical material to show that coping with the frustrations of caste left deep psychic scars.

Mark of Oppression

Many years ago Herbert A. Miller referred to the high prevalence among minorities of the attitudes of fear, hatred, resentment, jealousy, suspicion, and revenge—which he labeled the "oppression psychosis." The essential point made by Miller has been substantiated by research, even though the term "psychosis" may be applicable only to those more intensely affected by discrimination. Kardiner and Ovesey, after studying twenty-five Negro males by personality tests and psychoanalytic techniques, concluded as follows:

> On the whole we must be satisfied that the conclusions derived from the three different experimental approaches—the psychodynamic analysis, the

[16]Lloyd Warner and Allison Davis, "A Comparative Study of American Caste," in Edgar T. Thompson, ed., *Race Relations and the Race Problem*, p. 237.
[17]The terms used in our schema here are closely related to the meaning given them in Robert Merton's classic exposition in "Social Structure and Anomie," in *Social Theory and Social Structure* (Glencoe, Ill.: The Free Press, 1957), p. 130–160.
[18]See Harry Bredemeier and Jackson Toby, *Social Problems in America: Costs and Casualties in an Acquisitive Society* (New York: John Wiley & Sons, 1960), Chs. 7 and 8.
[19]While homicide is, of course, active in a sense, we place it under retreatism because it is taking out one's aggression on the wrong category of persons.

Rorschach test, and the T.A.T.—are essentially the same. The major features of the Negro personality emerge from each with remarkable consistency. These include the fear of relatedness, suspicion, mistrust, the enormous problem of the control of aggression, the denial mechanism, the tendency to dissipate the tension of a provocative situation by reducing it to something simpler, or to something entirely different. All these maneuvers are in the interest of not meeting reality head on. . . . The defects in adaptation are not of mysterious or racial origin but owe their existence entirely to the arduous emotional conditions under which the Negro in America is obliged to live.[20]

Karon studied a small but rigorously selected sample of Northern and Southern Negroes and Northern whites, employing the Tompkins-Horn Picture Arrangement Test. His findings were that caste sanctions have an effect on the personality structure of Negroes born and reared in the South in eleven characteristics, six of which are related to the problem of handling aggression. This research rejects the formerly oft-stated hypothesis that the Southern Negro, because he lives in a consistent interracial system, is not disturbed by caste sanctions, in contrast to the Northern Negro, who lives in a more ambiguous racial situation. Karon's findings show a consistent relationship between the severity of the caste sanctions and the appearance of these disturbed traits. Rural Southern Negroes are "worse off" than the urban Southern Negroes; Northern Negroes born in the South are worse off than those born in the North.[21]

Dreger and Miller in their review of studies up to 1960 conclude that "On the basis of the evidence available it does appear that Negroes more frequently (than whites) experience psychiatric difficulties, particularly of a severe nature."[22]

The Welfare of the Negroes in the South

In practically all indices of welfare, the Negro population continued through the first half of the twentieth century to rank well below that of the white population. Since this has been so amply demonstrated we will simply summarize the main points.[23]

Negroes were highly concentrated in the lowest occupational levels with a small percentage scattered in middle levels. Average family incomes were about one-third that of white families. Negroes were paid less for the same type of work at all levels. Negro housing was of poorer quality than that of whites. Comparative studies show markedly disparate health for Negroes and higher death rates. Associated with this was the lack of medical services, particularly hospitalization directly due to segregation.

[20]Abram Kardiner and Lionel Ovesey, *The Mark of Oppression* (New York: W. W. Norton & Company, 1951), pp. 337–338. Copyright © 1951 by Abram Kardiner and Lionel Ovesey. Reprinted by permission of Dr. A. Kardiner.
[21]Bertram A. Karon, *The Negro Personality* (New York: Springer Publishing Company, 1958), pp. 169–175.
[22]Ralph M. Dreger and Kent S. Miller, "Comparative Psychological Studies of Negroes and Whites in the United States," in *Psychological Bulletin,* Sept., 1960, p. 392. See Horace R. Cayton, *The Long Lonely Road* (New York: The Trident Press, 1963), for a dramatic personal illustration.
[23]See Gunnar Myrdal, *An American Dilemma,* Ch. 16; Maurice Davie, *Negroes in American Society,* Chs. 5, 6, 10, 11, and 12; and E. Franklin Frazier, *The Negro in the United States,* rev. ed. (New York: The Macmillan Co., 1957), Part 5.

Comparing the educational level of the Negro population in the South in 1930 with its level at the time of emancipation indicates tremendous strides. In 1870, 81.4 percent of Negroes were illiterate; in 1930, this figure had been reduced to 16.3 percent.[24] Comparing the educational facilities for Negroes with those of white persons in the South at any given time, however, reveals gross disparities. During 1939–1940 the Southern states spent $55.69 per white child in average daily attendance in schools as against only $18.82 for each Negro child.[25] At the higher educational levels the differential opportunity of Negroes was even more striking. In 1933–1934 only 19 percent of the Negro children of high-school age were in high schools, as compared with 55 percent of the white children of the same age.[26] Education of Negroes at the college level in the South before 1890 was exceptionally limited, and the schools available were supported largely by private contributions, chiefly from Northern religious denominational sources. In 1890 an amendment to the original Morrill Act adopted in 1862 required that federal funds be divided fairly between the white and the Negro institutions in states having the dual system. Subsequently, seventeen land-grant agricultural and mechanical colleges for Negroes were established. But wide disparities continued to exist in both the quantity and the quality of Negro higher educational institutions in the South.

THE IMPACT OF THE CASTE SYSTEM ON THE SOUTH

Tension and Violence

Despite the facade of a smoothly operating biracial system, racial tension was constantly present in the region in those local communities with sizable Negro populations. It is inevitable that where constant tension exists, violence will sporadically occur. Making some allowance for the tendency of novelists to dramatize, the writings of Southern novelists, such as Erskine Caldwell, for example, suggest that interpersonal violence in which individual white Southerners maltreated individual Negro people was more or less an everyday occurrence. More sporadically, two characteristic modes of expression of this violence have been lynchings and riots.

Lynching. In American history there were many lynchings of white people as well as blacks. From 1892 on, Negro lynchings greatly exceeded those of whites. With minor fluctuations, the numerical trend was sharply downward from the peak decade of 1892–1901, during which 1,124 Negro lynchings were recorded.[27] For the years 1952–1958 only four lynchings were recorded.

Lynchings occurred mostly in small towns in rural areas. The accusations made against persons lynched ranged widely from homicide to merely boastful remarks. A special study by Arthur Raper of nearly a hundred lynchings convinced the writer that a third of the victims were falsely accused.[28] Myrdal suggests that the conditions related

[24]Davie, *Negroes in American Society,* p. 139.
[25]See Frazier, *The Negro in the United States,* p. 437.
[26]*Ibid.,* p. 436.
[27]Tuskegee Institute started recording lynchings of both whites and blacks in 1892 and continued from then on.
[28]See Arthur Raper, *The Tragedy of Lynching* (Chapel Hill: University of North Carolina Press, 1933).

to lynching were poverty, the fear that the Negro was "getting out of place," and the general boredom of life in small communities in the South.[29] While in total volume of physical harm done to Negroes under the caste system, lynching looms small, Myrdal found it to have a "psychological importance out of all proportion to its small frequency." Of this Myrdal wrote

> The effects of lynchings are far reaching. In the locality where it has happened and in a wide region surrounding it, the relations between the two groups deteriorate. The Negroes are terror stricken and sullen. The whites are anxious and are likely to show the assertiveness and suspicion of persons with bad, but hardened consciences. Some whites are afraid of Negro retaliation or emigration. Every visitor to such a community must notice the antagonism and mutual lack of confidence between the two groups.[30]

Knowledge of a lynching had adverse effects throughout the nation, evoking brutalized feelings among some whites, twinging the consciences of others, and, for a time at least, raising the level of interracial tension in all racially mixed places.

This discussion of lynching should not be concluded without mentioning that many white Southerners deplored lynching, whatever their degree of commitment may have been to the caste system, in general. The organization of the Association of Southern Women for the Prevention of Lynching in Atlanta in 1930 is one example.

Racial Riots.   Under the Southern race system, racial rioting largely took the form of mob action by whites directed at defenseless Negro areas, stimulated usually by rumors of Negro assaults on whites. Franklin writes that "In the new century (1900) a veritable epidemic of race riots broke out and before the end of the first decade there had been at least half a dozen major racial upheavals."[31] While some of them took place in the North, they may be interpreted as one of numerous devices for sustaining the color line.

Political Effects

The South as a region has had a political development different from that in the rest of the country. (1) The proportion of people who participate in politics has been markedly smaller than in the rest of the nation. We have already referred to the virtual disfranchisement of Negroes. Bunche estimated that in eight Southern states, the so-called Deep South, never more than 80,000 to 90,000 Negro votes had been cast in general elections up to 1940, and only a handful in the primaries, the elections that really counted.[32] The proportion of the white electorate that participated in politics was also decidedly less than in the rest of the nation. In 1940 only 28 percent of the adult population of twelve Southern states went to the polls, in contrast with 53 percent for the rest of the country. (2) The South for all practical purposes has had a one-party

[29]See Myrdal, *An American Dilemma,* pp. 560–562, for a discussion of lynching.
[30]*Ibid.,* p. 564. By permission of the publishers, Harper & Row, Publishers.
[31]John Hope Franklin, and the Editors of Time-Life Books, *Black Americans: An Illustrated History* (New York, 1970), p. 92.
[32]Ralph J. Bunche, "The Negro in the Political Life in the United States" in *Journal of Negro Education,* July, 1941, pp. 567–584.

system, the Democratic Party. The primary contests in this party constituted in essence the final decision. (3) From this it followed that political opposition was more confined than elsewhere to rivalries between factions and personalities in which the basic issues contested in the nation as a whole were not debated. Since the Democratic Party in the South represented traditional and conservative influence in the national Congress, the liberal political pressures that had arisen elsewhere in the nation had not manifested themselves in any marked degree in the South. Since wide exercise of the franchise, a two- (or more) party system, and the vigorous debate of new ways to further the democratic ideal are signs of a healthy democracy, the democratic political process in the South may properly be regarded as having been retarded.

To what extent are these distinctive developments in Southern politics attributable to the effect of its system of race relations? Since we adhere to the general principle that the causal factors in such complex social phenomena are always multiple and interact with one another, we shall not suggest that the system of race relations is all determinative. Nevertheless, the interrelationship between the phenomena of race relations and these political developments is highly impressive. The elaborate devices to limit the electorate arose primarily as a way of preventing Negroes from exercising active citizenship. Once established, these political phenomena furthered the politicoeconomic interests of the middle and upper classes of the white South in opposition to those of the lower-class whites. The failure of the latter group to generate more effective political expression of its interests is in considerable measure related to its preoccupation with "keeping the Negro in his place."[33]

Effect on the Economy of the South

Rupert Vance, an outstanding student of the Southern region, described the South's position (1930) in the national economy in these terms: "the statistical indices of wealth, education, cultural achievement, health, law and order reduced to a per capita basis combine in every instance to give the Southern states the lowest rankings in the Union."[34] After a careful appraisal of the natural resources of the region, Vance concluded that it was not lack of adequate natural resources which accounted for the South's relative poverty. He found the chief explanation in the manner in which the Southern economy had been organized.

After the Civil War, as we have seen, Southern economic reconstruction called for carrying on the plantation agricultural economy, with chief emphasis on cotton production. Since this economy required cheap labor, the caste system developed in part as a means of guaranteeing the continued employment of Negroes in their accustomed role at subsistence wages. Furthermore, in order to hold its place competitively in a national economy generally more efficient than its own, the South was forced to exploit the soil to the point of diminishing returns. In this way, a cycle of reciprocal forces was established that operated to retard the economic development of the region. The relatively inefficient economy could provide only subsistence wages for the laborers involved. Their marginal income in turn retarded the regional demand for goods, which would have favored the development of industrial enterprise. Furthermore, the marginal

---

[33]See Lillian Smith, *Killers of the Dream,* pp. 154–168.
[34]Rupert B. Vance, *Human Geography of the South* (Chapel Hill: University of North Carolina Press, 1932), p. 442. By permission.

economy was unable to produce enough to furnish the capital needed for industrial development. This capital had to be furnished, therefore, from outside the region, which meant that part of the gains were drained from the region itself. In order to get this capital, the South offered the inducement primarily of cheap labor costs, which still further aggravated the low standard of living, extending it to a wider segment of its white population. While the expanding industrial economy offered some opportunity to transfer Negroes from farm work to city work, the caste system prevented their employment in other than the lowest-paying capacities.

Clearly, many factors are involved in interpreting the cycle just described. Nevertheless, the influence of the caste system is apparent at every turn. As Vance has written, "The South holds the Negro back; the Negro holds the South back; and both point in recrimination."[35]

Variation in the Southern Pattern

Rural-Urban.   The foregoing description has disregarded variations in order to indicate the general Southern pattern. Some significant rural-urban contrasts, however, should be noted. The city environment permitted some relief to Negroes from the omnipresent impact of caste through the opportunity it afforded to build a separate community structure. At least within this area, Negroes could live their own lives.[36] Compared with the smaller places, there was less actual personal interaction between the members of the two races in the city. Since traditionally the caste system carried with it much direct personal dependence of individual Negroes on particular white people, through which conformity to the mandates of caste could be closely scrutinized, the greater drawing apart of the two races in the Southern cities placed the control of caste on a more impersonal basis.

The Border States.   The major variation in the Southern pattern of race relations is seen by considering the border states. In none of these was the "white primary" to be found; among them, only Oklahoma had "Jim Crow" streetcars. In these states the code of etiquette was frequently less explicit and less binding. However, in all of them intermarriage between Negroes and whites was prohibited by law, and the segregation of Negroes in schools remained up to 1954.[37]

The pattern of race relations in Washington, D.C., is naturally of particular significance, not only because it is the capital but because it is visited by foreign officials of all other nations. On the one hand, Washington, as part of the Southern area, reflected in many ways the Southern attitude and behavior in Negro-white relations. On the other hand, the influence of the federal government imposed certain exceptions to the traditional Southern pattern. Thus Negroes were not "Jim Crowed" in District transportation; they had equal access to all institutions and services directly operated as federal government property. Before World War II, the national government employed a limited number of Negroes in higher-ranking occupations, qualified by the tendency to

[35]*Ibid.*, p. 43.
[36]One of the authors was told by a Negro physician in a Louisiana city that the members of his family went "down town" as seldom as possible because they so profoundly disliked the caste requirements.
[37]See Myrdal, *An American Dilemma*, p. 1072, Table 1, for a checklist of the various features of the caste system for each Southern state.

place them in special assignments dealing with Negro problems. But generally, Washington in the period before World War II presented substantially the same picture as other border cities. School segregation, for example, prevailed, and Negroes were denied the use of general restaurant and amusement facilities in the city.

Changes in the Southern Pattern

Between 1880 and World War II race relations in the South revealed changes that went rather rapidly in one direction and rather slowly in another. As we have seen, most of the gains made by Negroes following emancipation were lost by the establishment of the caste system. On the other hand, the welfare of Negroes improved somewhat along with the general national trend, even though at all times with wide discrepancies between that of the whites. Circumstances operating to improve Negro welfare were the opportunity presented by World War I for Negroes to find employment in the North, the tendency of the federal government to require more equitable use of federal funds for Negroes, especially during the Depression years of the 1930s. and the beginnings of some breakdown of segregation in labor unions in the mid-1930s.

The earnest efforts of a small group of Southern white liberals in behalf of Negroes deserve recognition as an influence in keeping the Southern pattern slightly unfrozen. The group comprised a few writers, journalists, educators, and some club women, whom Myrdal described as "mostly a fraternity of individuals with independent minds, usually living in, and adjusting to, an uncongenial social surrounding."[38] Because for the most part they possessed high social prestige either through their lineage from Southern aristocracy or through the national preeminence they had acquired in professional fields, their espousal of the Negro's cause was tolerated. Their first efforts were directed at striving for equal justice, particularly against lynching, and gaining for the Negro a fairer share of public monies spent for education, health, and other aspects of welfare. They were unable to challenge the system of segregation itself. The Southern liberals were not able to influence political life to any marked extent, and their influence was largely confined to the higher social and educational levels of Southern society. The main organization through which Southern liberalism found expression was the Commission on Interracial Cooperation, founded in 1919. In Myrdal's judgment its most far-reaching effect is *to have rendered interracial work socially respectable in the conservative South.*"[39]

Finally, we consider the effect of Negro leadership and organization on the course of Southern race relations during the caste period. Under slavery the organized activities of Negroes in their own behalf consisted, as we have seen, largely of abortive slave revolts. The outstanding leader among Negroes in the nineteenth century was Frederick Douglass. Following emancipation, which he had urged upon Lincoln, he worked to secure full equality for the Negroes, but saw the fight lost during the Southern reconstruction. Organized movements among Negroes subsequently divided into "protest" or "accommodative" patterns. The former, which Douglass espoused, aimed to secure full equality for Negroes; the latter aimed to secure the betterment of conditions without challenging the institution of caste itself. During the early twentieth century the protest type of activity was almost exclusively confined to Negroes in the

[38]*Ibid.*, p. 467.
[39]*Ibid.*, p. 847. Italics in original.

North, which we shall consider in Chapter 8. In the South a spokesman for the Negroes was Booker T. Washington, who was generally considered a leader of the accommodative type, though some of his biographers think the extent of his compromising has been overstressed, particularly in view of the circumstances he faced. Rose summarizes the role Washington played and the philosophy behind it:

> It is wrong to characterize Washington as an all-out accommodating leader. He never relinquished the right to full equality in all respects as the ultimate goal. But for the time being he was prepared to give up social and political equality, even to soft-pedal and protest against inequalities in justice. He was also willing to flatter the Southern whites and be harsh toward the Negroes—if the Negroes were allowed to work undisturbed with their white friends for education and business. But neither in education nor in business did he assault inequalities. In both fields he accepted the white doctrine of the Negroes "place." In education he pleaded mainly for vocational training. Through thrift, skill, and industry the Negroes were gradually to improve so much that later the discussion could again be taken up concerning their rights. This was Washington's philosophy.[40]

However one views the relative merits of the protest as against the accommodative program of action, beyond question Washington had the greatest influence of any single Negro on the development of Negro welfare during his time. His impact was most concretely evidenced in the development of Tuskegee Institute, over which he presided for many years.

Suggested Readings

Chalmers, David M. *Hooded Americanism: The First Century of the Ku Klux Klan.* New York: Doubleday & Co., 1965.
     A full-length and scholarly history of this well-known "nativistic" organization.
Davis, Allison, and Dollard, John. *Children of Bondage.* Washington, D.C.: American Council on Education, 1940.
     An intensive study of eight Negro adolescents in the Deep South indicating the effects of the Southern pattern on the Negro personality.
Dollard, John. *Caste and Class in a Southern Town.* New Haven: Yale University Press, 1937.
     A pioneer study in depth of a Mississippi plantation community.
Lewinson, Paul. *Race, Class and Party: A History of Negro Suffrage and White Politics.* New York: Grosset & Dunlap, Universal Library Edition, 1965.

---

[40]Arnold Rose, *The Negro in America* (New York: Harper & Brothers, 1948), p. 240. By permission.

A pioneer historical study of the interrelation of race and class in Southern political life from slave days to 1930.

Lewis, Hylan. *Blackways of Kent*. Chapel Hill: University of North Carolina Press, 1955.

A comprehensive and intimate account of the life of Negroes in a typical biracial community of the Piedmont area.

Meier, August. *Negro Thought in America 1880–1915*. Ann Arbor: The University of Michigan Press, 1966.

Analyzes the racial ideologies of Negro leaders in the age of Booker T. Washington.

Pettigrew, Thomas P. *A Profile of the Negro American*. New York: Van Nostrand Co., 1964.

Chapter 1, "The Role and Its Burdens," and Chapter 2, "Reactions to Oppression," examine the impact of white domination on the Negro personality.

Rohrer, John H., and Edmonson, Munro S. *The Eighth Generation: Cultures and Personalities of New Orleans Negroes*. New York: Harper & Brothers, 1960.

An intensive follow-up study of the subjects of Davis and Dollard's study of the children of bondage who as adults comprise the eighth generation of New Orleans Negroes.

Washington, Booker T. *Up From Slavery: An Autobiography*. New York: Doubleday & Co., 1901.

The self-written life story of a foremost Negro leader and longtime president of Tuskegee Institute, Alabama.

8

The Pattern of
Northern Dominance

While there were Negroes in the North from colonial days, the first great migration from the South and its metropolitan concentration lead us to focus this chapter on the pattern of Negro-white relations that developed in the North between the two world wars.

The main point is that in the North, Negroes were discriminated against substantially everywhere, but not in as many aspects of life nor so intensely as in the South.

A basic difference between the Northern and Southern situation was the absence in the North of such precise institutionalization of the minority position of Negroes as the Southern caste pattern involved. In the South, caste relations were well defined in law and in the regional mores; and control mechanisms for maintaining the system had become standardized through years of practice. In the North the discrimination and segregation that did exist lacked such explicit sanction in the mores; also lacking were such established control devices for holding the Negro in minority status. For Southern white people in general the attitudes and values of the caste system were an integral part of their personalities; and for Southern Negroes the reciprocal behavior patterns were deeply structured in their personalities. Caste was an intrinsic part of the Southern social structure and daily touched the lives of the people of both races. In the North the segregated position of Negroes was only a fragmentary aspect of Northern community life, and many white people, even in communities with sizable Negro populations, were scarcely aware of its presence.

The many contrasting circumstances in the two regional situations accounting for this basic difference can be stated only briefly in this overview. The North did not have the tradition of slavery, having abolished slavery decades before emancipation. And in no Northern community did the number of Negroes approach a majority. Thus, while Negroes were useful to the economy of the North, their labor was never considered essential to Northern economic life, as in the South, since European immigration furnished cheap labor. The concentration of Negroes in the larger cities of the North, where their residential segregation resembled that of other ethnic and racial minorities, made their position appear less sharply in contrast to the dominant white community than in the South, where Negroes were the only large minority.

136

THE ESTABLISHMENT AND MAINTENANCE OF DOMINANCE

The Pattern of Discrimination

A close-up view of the general pattern of Negro-white relations in the North may be obtained from the comprehensive study of Chicago made by Drake and Cayton. In essence their book, *Black Metropolis,* typified the Northern situation. Much of the material was gathered for this volume in the 1930s, though some of it refers to the impact of World War II.[1]

Residential Segregation. Negroes in Chicago were highly concentrated in residence; 337,000—90 percent of all—lived in the Black Belt. [174] The difference between this and other ethnic colonies in cities was that while the others tended to break up in time, the Negro area became increasingly concentrated in the lower South Side, considered by Chicago planning boards a "blighted area." The extent of congestion is indicated by the fact that Negroes were living 90,000 to the square mile, as compared with 20,000 in neighboring white apartment house areas. [204] This high degree of spatial segregation "is primarily the result of white people's attitudes toward having Negroes as neighbors. Because some white Chicagoans do not wish colored neighbors, formal and informal controls are used to isolate the latter within congested all-Negro neighborhoods." [174]

The real force of the measures to contain the Negro area began when the mass migration took place. "It was only after 1915, when 65,000 migrants came into the city within five years, that white resistance became organized." [177] Property-owners associations began to take active steps to forestall the sale and rent of property to Negroes outside the Black Belt. "A wave of violence flared up, and between July 1917 and March 1921 fifty-eight homes were bombed. . . . The victims of the bombings were Negro families that had moved into white neighborhoods, as well as Negro and white real-estate men who sold or rented property to them." [178] The major device for controlling the Negro community was the restrictive covenant—an agreement between property owners within a certain district not to rent or sell to Negroes. Attempts to upset restrictive covenants legally were for a long time unsuccessful. However, in 1917 the Supreme Court (245 U.S. 60) ruled that a municipal zoning ordinance that segregated Negroes and whites was unconstitutional, but it was not until 1948 that the highest tribunal declared that restrictive covenants in private housing transactions could not be upheld by law (334 U.S. 1–1948).

Occupational Discrimination. Discrimination in jobs was seen in the tendency to deny Negroes jobs when white people were out of work. Drake and Cayton state that in 1940, *"while Negroes made up only 8 per cent of the available workers, they constituted 22 per cent of the unemployed. . . .* Almost half of the Negro domestic servants, a third of the semiskilled workers, and a fourth of the unskilled were unemployed in 1935." [217] Negroes were substantially barred from numerous pursuits. "The job ceiling for Negroes . . . [tended] to be drawn just above the level of semiskilled jobs. . . . [262] Again Negroes had not consistently held their competitive position in certain occupa-

---

[1]Sections of this chapter are excerpted and abridged from *Black Metropolis,* Copyright © 1945 by St. Clair Drake and Horace R. Cayton. Renewed 1973 by St. Clair Drake and Susan C. Woodson. Reprinted by permission of Harcourt Brace Jovanovich, Inc., New York. Page numbers of future references to this work in this chapter will be bracketed and placed in the text.

tional fields. For example, during the Depression Negroes lost out to whites in restaurants and hotel jobs.

As small compensation for these inequities, Negroes had a substantial monopoly in
the two occupations of Pullman porter and redcap, where "the earnings and the prospects of advancement are dependent upon cheerful and, if necessary, ingratiating
service. . . . Even very well-educated Negroes did not scorn such jobs." [237]

The low economic position of Negroes was in part explainable by their relative lack
of skills and training for higher ranking jobs, and by the tendency of Southern Negroes
to flock to the North in numbers in excess of the job opportunities available to them.
But in considerable measure it was due to racial discrimination: to the tendency of
white workers to refuse to work alongside Negroes and to the tendency of white customers to resent being waited on by Negroes, except in the servile services.

Social Discrimination. In contrast to the South, Negroes in Chicago were not segregated in their use of many public facilities. Public parks, public transportation facilities,
stores, and public toilets were open to them. However, the more intimate the situation,
the more doubtful the acceptance of Negroes on equal terms. In theaters, restaurants,
and particularly swimming places, Negroes were discouraged by every possible means
from associating with whites. Bathing beaches and swimming pools were among the
primary tension points. The Negro press reported

POLICE OBJECT TO MIXING OF RACES
ON BEACH; ARREST 18.
SAY THEY ARE TRYING
TO PREVENT RACE RIOT. [105]

While the color line was seldom drawn in theaters or at large public gatherings, in
recreation situations that emphasized active mixing with whites Negroes were barred;
and in all situations where men and women participated together, there was a rigid line.
Whatever may have been their ultimate hope, Negroes themselves put less stress on the
desirability of achieving equality in this sphere than in others. This difference in the importance attached to social equality by the two races was favorable to facilitating adjustment in Negro-white relations in the North.

Civic "Equality". In marked contrast to the South was the civic "equality" accorded Northern Negroes. However, the term "equality" is here placed in quotes because what Negroes had in Chicago and elsewhere in the North was limited by the
framework of dominant-group attitudes toward them. It is hard to prove that a teacher
"looks down" on Negroes, or that a juror will not believe Negro testimony when it
contradicts that of a white person. But one cannot study such events without being convinced that equality was often qualified by prejudice.

Drake and Cayton wrote that "To Negro migrants, fresh from the South, Midwest
Metropolis presents a novel experience—a substantial measure of equality before the
law. Here, they can expect a reasonably fair trial in the courts, with a choice of colored
or white counsel. There are no lynchings." [108–109] Negroes had full political rights.
Even though they were thought of as a minority group, their right to vote and participate in political organization was not denied. What this opportunity to be a citizen
meant to Negroes is described as follows:

Politics became an important, perhaps the most important, method by
which the Negro sought to change his status. It was often the only avenue

open for struggle against caste tendencies. This struggle invested his political behavior, even when corrupt, with an importance and a dignity that similar behavior could not command in any other portion of the population. [343]

As a result of their political activities, Negroes made substantial gains in Chicago.

Within a decade after the Great Migration, Black Metropolis had elected two Negro aldermen, one State Senator, four State Representatives, a city judge, and a Congressman. . . . Wielding such political power, Negro politicians have been in a position to demand appointive positions for a few hundred individuals and equitable treatment in the courts for the masses (as well as dubious "benefits" from the great Chicago enterprise of "fixing" and "rigging" everything from traffic tickets to gambling dens). They have also been able to expose and check discrimination in the administration of the civil service laws and in the enforcement of the Civil Rights Law. They have created, among influential white politicians of all parties, an awareness of the Negro's desire for equal opportunity. [109–110]

The minority status of Negroes was reflected, however, in politics, as in all other phases of their lives. Of this Drake and Cayton write

The color line in politics is also reflected in the types of political plums that go to Negro politicians and their henchmen. The big contracts and the heavy graft are reserved for whites. Negroes get the petty "cuts" from gambling and vice protection. In fact, a tradition has developed that Negroes will not demand big political rewards. . . . Political leaders in Midwest Metropolis, balancing the pressures of ethnic, economic, and religious blocs, are forced to grant some of the demands of Negroes, and Negro politicians shrewdly demand all that they think the traffic will bear. [111]

Education. Curiously, in view of their exhaustive coverage of Negro life in Chicago, Drake and Cayton wrote very little about education. For this period we draw upon Myrdal's discussion.

For the North in general school segregation was not required by law. However some states and local communities did engage in segregation more often in elementary than in secondary schools. Much *de facto* segregation occurred in consequence of spacial concentration of the Negro areas abetted by frequent gerrymandering of school districts to keep schools segregated. Discrimination in the mixed schools was frequent in non-curricular activities where Negroes were kept out of swimming, dancing, and social clubs.[2]

[2]Myrdal, *An American Dilemma* (New York: Harper & Brothers, 1944), p. 633.

The opportunity for Negroes to acquire higher education in the North was less than for secondary schools. Northern state universities did not prohibit Negro enrollments, but the vast majority of the private institutions either did not accept Negroes or accepted only a "token" Negro or two. Myrdal concluded that there was no serious restriction on higher education of Negroes in the North, supporting his view by pointing out that only four Negro colleges, all established before the Civil War, were located in the North. However, it may be noted that before 1940 a large number of Northern Negroes had gone South to attend Negro colleges—3,000, for example, in 1938–1939.[3] They may have done this because these colleges were less expensive or because they received scholarships. However, it is also possible that they felt they would face unpleasant discriminations in Northern colleges. Caliver writes that Negro students "seldom lived on campus and in general, they seemed not to belong in the same way that white students felt themselves a part of the university."[4] Discrimination in higher education was likewise seen in the fact that before World War II not more than five white colleges had a Negro on their faculties.

Methods of Maintaining Dominance

Generally speaking, segregation outside the South was not supported by law. A few non-Southern states banned intermarriage; and certain local communities officially segregated Negroes in schools, but such laws were usually overridden by court decisions. In some communities the police attempted to keep Negroes out of certain public areas, such as beaches, but these actions were nowhere legally supported. Subterfuges, like making the commercial recreational place a "club," were sometimes successful. Law-enforcing agencies frequently supported segregation by refusing to arrest whites who molested Negroes.

Segregation was upheld by common practice—practices by whites to keep Negroes within the bounds of minority status and the reciprocal practices of Negroes to accept this status. While Negroes bitterly resented this, to have some peace of mind, they put up with discrimination most of the time. However, that these practices were of doubtful legality meant that Negroes could challenge civic discrimination on occasion, and by this means keep the pattern of relationships unfrozen. Generally, when Negroes pressed cases of discrimination involving civil rights they won them. But since legal vindication is a costly process, such cases were not numerous.

As in the South, the Northern pattern was supported by the prevalence of the "racial ideology" that looked upon Negroes in the mass as inferior. There was, however, a wider variation in racial attitudes and beliefs in the North. What in comparison appears clearest is that Northern attitudes were not crystallized into uniform public opinion. As Drake and Cayton wrote, "In the South, every white man feels impelled to protect every white family, clique, and church from 'Negro contamination.' In Midwest Metropolis, each person is concerned only with his own." [119]

---

[3]Ambrose Caliver, *United States Office of Education, National Survey of Higher Education of Negroes,* Vol. IV (Washington, D.C.: Government Printing Office, 1942–1943), p. 13.
[4]*Ibid.,* p. 13.

Variations in the Northern Pattern

In minor aspects the picture of Chicago's Negro community and its relation to the larger community is affected by its particular locale; but less extensive studies of other large cities indicate that *Black Metropolis* was typical of Negro-white relations in the metropolitan areas of the North, where the far larger proportion of the Northern Negro population lived.[5] Variations in the Northern pattern were in the main related to three situations.

Recency of Migration.   The status of Negroes in Northern cities varied with the extent to which a given city shared in the Great Migration. Generally the status of Negroes in the North as a whole declined in the years attending this migration. Furthermore, the occurrence of the Depression of the 1930s, during which so large a proportion of Negroes were on relief, retarded improvement in welfare. Even in New England, which did not greatly share in the Great Migration, the traditional tolerance toward Negroes declined. Frazier writes, "The increase in the Negro population [of Boston] during and following World War I accentuated race consciousness among Negroes as well as whites."[6]

The Smaller City Versus the Metropolis.   Since the major portion of the Northern migration went to the large cities, little attention had been given to Negroes in the smaller cities. In Muncie, Indiana, the Lynds found in 1929 that "the sense of racial separateness appears in widely diverse groups." Negroes were not permitted in the YMCA, for example. "News of the Negroes is given separately in the papers under the title 'In Colored Circles.' "[7] In 1935, in their post-Depression study of the same city, the authors found Negroes had better leadership and organization but that they "occupy a more exposed position . . . than before the depression."[8] In smaller communities, Negroes were further handicapped because their numbers were inadequate to make possible a complete, separate community life.

Influence of the Southern Pattern on the North.   It is pertinent to note two influences of the Southern pattern on the North and West. First, the migration of white Southern workers to the North, which, when recent and in substantial numbers, tended to disturb the pattern of toleration of Negroes in some Northern communities. This was notable as a factor in the tense Detroit situation of World War II. Second, in those Northern states bordering on a state with a Southern pattern, variation in race relations from south to north was noticeable. In New Jersey, for instance, before state government policies were inaugurated in the 1940s, school segregation was more pronounced in the southern than in the northern portion of the state. Southern Illinois illustrated the same point.

---

[5]See for example, Robert A. Warner, *New Haven Negroes* (New Haven: Yale University Press, 1940).
[6]E. Franklin Frazier, *The Negro in the United States,* rev. ed. (New York: The Macmillan Co., 1957), p. 254. Copyright © 1957 The Macmillan Company. Reprinted by permission of the publisher.
[7]Robert S. and Helen M. Lynd, *Middletown* (New York: Harcourt, Brace & Co., 1929), p. 479, footnote 1.
[8]Robert S. and Helen M. Lynd, *Middletown in Transition* (New York: Harcourt, Brace & Co., 1937), p. 465.

All these variations make it clear that throughout the North white Americans norma-tively were unwilling to accord Negroes real equality.[9]

THE IMPACT OF THE NORTHERN RACIAL PATTERN ON NORTHERN COMMUNITIES

The pattern of Negro-white relations just described affected the life of those Northern communities with any substantial Negro population in many ways.

The Negro Ghetto: A Blighted Area

The formation of separate subcommunities of Negroes fitted easily into the pattern of Northern city life where other ethnic subcommunities were no new phenomenon. But as time went on, the other ethnic colonies tended, first to move out of their original "slum" location, and later to disperse with a considerable assimilation of subsequent generations. However, the Negro subcommunity persisted and grew, creating serious problems in such cities. Resistance to admitting Negroes into new areas resulted in fantastic overcrowding. In Detroit in 1939 Negro rates for overcrowding were twice those of whites.[10] When finally the walls of the black ghetto burst, infiltration of Negroes into other dilapidated areas began. Moreover, when some Negroes did get a foothold, whites began to move out, more Negroes moved in, until the new section came to be generally Negro.

It has been demonstrated that all slum areas, regardless of who lives in them, al-though highly profitable to particular special interests, are an economic drain on the community at large and unvaryingly yield a disproportionate share of the social pathologies—delinquency, crime, high disease rates. Many studies show Northern Negro ghettos were no exception.[11]

Tension and Violence

The presence of segregated Negro areas became a source of interracial tension and sporadic interracial violence. In 1919 riots occurred in at least twenty-six American cities. Interracial violence tends to arise in non-work situations where whites and Negroes meet. One such circumstance occurs when Negroes begin to move into a new area, as in Detroit in 1942, where one of the worst riots (prior to the 60s) occurred. Of this Myrdal writes:

[9]A notable exception to the rigid line of discrimination in the North has appeared from a field study by George K. Hesslink, published as *Black Neighbors: Negroes in a Northern Rural Community* (Indianapolis: The Bobbs-Merrill Co., 1967). Hesslink uncovered a Michigan village in which Negro descendants of pre-Civil War fugitive slaves interacted with whites on a mutually equitable basis from the early years. The study is significant because it underscores the different pattern of interracial relations in a smaller community not steeped in traditions of interracial hostility but which then faced the potentially disruptive effects of migration and social change.

[10]Robert Weaver, *The Negro Ghetto* (New York: Harcourt, Brace and Co., 1948), p. 115.

[11]See Robert Weaver, *The Negro Ghetto*; E. Franklin Frazier, *The Negro in the United States*, Part IV; and Gunnar Myrdal, *The American Dilemma*, Ch. 14.

> . . . [I]n trying to move into a government defense housing project built for them in Detroit, Negroes were set upon by white civilians and police. The project was built at the border between Negro and white neighborhoods but had been planned for Negroes. Encouraged by the vacillation of the federal government and the friendliness of the Detroit police (many of whom are Southern born) and stimulated by the backing of a United States congressman and such organizations as the Ku Klux Klan, white residents of the neighborhood and other parts of the city staged protest demonstrations against the Negro housing project, which led to the riot.[12]

Public recreational areas are another stimulus to violence, as in the "Belle Isle Riot," also in Detroit near a recreational park.[13] Foreshadowing the 1960 riots was the Harlem Riot of 1935, where an outbreak of violence occurred in the Negro area itself. Some 10,000 slum dwellers smashed windows, hurled bricks, and looted stores, choosing those of white merchants.[14]

Ambiguity of the Northern Pattern

In contrast to the South, the Northern pattern was more ambiguous, creating additional problems for the Southern-born Negroes. The Negro was in many ways freer to do things he could not do in the South, but was frequently at a loss to know just how much freer. He could go to this restaurant, but that one refused him service. He could play on the school team, but he could not go to the dances. And, while treating him as a minority person, the Northern practice at the same time held the Negro more accountable to behave according to the general norms of the community. Petty thievery was almost expected of the Negro by the white Southerner, and was dealt with as one ordinarily deals with children. But the Northerners put him in jail for it. "Illegitimacy" in the South (often occurring within stable monogamic unions) was laughed off by Southern whites as "natural for darkies," but in the North it frequently brought investigation by a white welfare worker.

Finally, while the South held out no prospect to the Negro of ever rising above the confines of caste (allowing only for some upward class mobility within caste), the Northern situation, ill defined and perplexing as it was, was sufficiently fluid to encourage Negro aspirations. But since Northern white attitudes were by no means ready for the full step, Negroes' hopes were frequently raised too high, only to be dashed. The relatively better education offered the Negro in the North encouraged him to prepare himself for occupations, employment in which he would subsequently be denied. His desire for better housing, and often the means to pay for it, was raised, only to be frustrated by restrictive covenants. He was at the same time encouraged to develop higher cultural interests and refused a seat in a theater. Thus the uncertainties and fluidity characterizing relations with whites placed considerable strain on the Negro personality.

---

[12]Myrdal, *An American Dilemma,* p. 568. By permission of the publishers, Harper & Brothers.
[13]See Alfred M. Lee and Norman D. Humphrey, *Race Riot* (New York: Dryden Press, 1943), for a full account and analysis.
[14]Roi Ottley, *Black Odyssey* (New York: Charles Scribner's Sons, 1948), p. 258.

OPPORTUNITY TO CHALLENGE DOMINANCE

In spite of the disorganizing effect of the none-too-well-defined situation of the Negro and of the very considerable discrimination against him, compared with the South, the North afforded two advantages: the opportunity for individual Negroes to reach higher levels of success, and the greater opportunity to work effectively to advance the race.

The Rise of the Negro Middle Class

In the North the class structure was more elaborated than in the South. The social class structures of "Black Metropolis" is described as follows by Drake and Cayton:

> The process of differentiation among Negroes in Bronzeville has given rise to a loose system of social classes which allows for mobility upward and downward. This class structure operates as a system of social controls by which the higher-status groups "protect" their way of life, but admit "strainers" and "strivers" who can make the grade. Individuals and organizations on the higher-status levels become models for imitation and also serve as an incentive toward social mobility. . . . At the top are uppers, oriented predominantly around "Society" and Race Leadership, and with a small group of Gentlemen Racketeers who have gained some status as Race Leaders but who are not accepted socially. Below them is the middle class with four "centers of orientation"—church, social club, "racial advancement" (including *individual* advancement), and "policy." At the bottom is the lower class with a large "disorganized segment," but also with a "church-centered" group and a small group of "secular respectables" interested in "getting ahead." Underlying the whole structure is the "underworld" of the Black Ghetto. [710–712]

A few individual Negroes in the North had gained fame and fortune in areas competitive with white people: Joe Louis and, even earlier, Jack Johnson in prizefighting; Roland Hayes and Paul Robeson in concert singing; Paul Lawrence Dunbar, Countee Cullen, James Weldon Johnson in literature. The theme the artists emphasized was often related to Negro life and problems.

For many of the Negroes who achieved higher social and economic status, it was the very separation of the Negro community that provided most of this opportunity. It created a monopoly for those businesses that involved intimate contact with the person of the Negro, such as hairdressing, restaurants, and funeral service.

In professional service, however, where the relationship to the client is less personal, aspiring Negroes, when they managed to hurdle the difficulty of acquiring professional training, were in competition with white professionals for the trade of the Negro population while being generally barred from competition for the white trade. Negro physicians were handicapped by the lack of hospitals for their patients, and frequently were not permitted to treat their patients in general hospitals. Of the 1,063 Negro lawyers in the entire nation in 1940 two-thirds were in the North, with less than one-fourth of the Negro population. The ministry of Negro churches was the leading professional opportunity. Teaching offered much less opportunity since, contrary to the South where only Negro teachers could teach Negro children, white teachers taught schools of any racial composition.

Aside from these opportunities Negroes were conspicuously under represented in business, even compared with other racial minorities, such as Chinese and Japanese.[15]

One of the largest of all Negro businesses was insurance. "For the year 1945, the 44 member companies of the National Negro Insurance Association reported nearly 4,000,000 policies in force,"[16] largely health and accident policies. This opportunity arose because white-owned insurance companies were reluctant to underwrite Negro policies on the same actuarial basis as those of whites since there were such wide differentials in health and mortality rates between the two races.

Another higher occupational opportunity arose from the necessity of integrating Negroes somehow into the civic life of the whole community. Thus some Negroes held positions as liaison agents representing their people in communitywide activity. The not-too-active participation of Negroes in Northern politics offered some opportunity in party politics with occasional appointment to public positions, as a reward or through civil service.

Finally, it is inevitable that among a people so situated there should arise an "underworld," often abetted and patronized by whites, and affording opportunity for some Negroes to achieve financial, if not status, reward.

Thus the Northern scene afforded Negroes qualified opportunity for getting ahead and accounted for the growing upper and middle class in the Northern Negro communities. The values and modes of life among middle-class Negroes were similar to those in the white middle class. Drake and Cayton put it thus:

> The whole atmosphere of middle-class life is one of tension, particularly at upper-middle-class level, or among people on the way up, but not yet secure in their position. The drive to get ahead, to "lay a little something by," to prepare for the education of children, and at the same time keep up "front" by wearing the right kind of clothes, having a "nice home," and belonging to the proper organizations—the pursuit of these goals brings into being definite social types which Bronzeville calls "strivers," and "strainers." With limited incomes, the problem of striking a balance between the conspicuous consumption necessary to maintain status, and long-range goals like buying property and educating children, becomes a difficult one. During the depression years particularly, Bronzeville's middle-class families faced a continuous crisis. [667–668]

This opportunity for the more educated and ambitious Negroes in the North to rise to higher status presented something of a dilemma regarding their attitudes toward advancing the race. Frazier pointed out that segregation protects certain Negro professionals to some extent from competition with whites in corresponding occupations—a competition that was keener and that he felt many of the Negro professionals

---

[15]Ivan H. Light, *Business and Welfare Among Chinese, Japanese, and Blacks* (Berkeley: University of California Press, 1972).
[16]E. Franklin Frazier, *The Negro in the United States*, p. 401. Reprinted by permission of the publisher.

could not meet successfully.[17] It was clear that a rapid breakdown of the segregated pattern would create much insecurity for the Negro middle class, and it is reasonable to hypothesize that, unconsciously at least, this would temper the vigor of participation in desegregation movements.[18] On the other hand, esteem among Negroes was to be bestowed on those who championed the advancement of the race.

Organization of the Negro Protest

We have seen that even under slavery as well as under Southern caste, some Negroes actively protested against their minority status. In the North in the early twentieth century Negro efforts to advance the race embraced a wider range of activities.

Revitalization Movements. Of the movements aimed at revitalization most important despite its failure was the "Back to Africa" movement led by Marcus Garvey. A West Indian full-blooded Negro, Garvey arrived in Harlem in 1916 for the purpose of getting help in his efforts to improve the condition of Jamaican Negroes. Coming to the conclusion that Negroes in the United States could never become assimilated into the general white society, he organized the Universal Improvement Association, the broad aim of which was to establish an African Republic where American Negroes could live. Garvey was imprisoned in 1925, accused of using the mails to defraud in connection with the financing of his movement. Many white commentators felt that he had been ill-advised by associates, not realizing that he had broken the law. While the movement continued in various forms it had dwindled away by the time of his death in 1940.

Assessing Garvey's work, Cronon finds no tangible gain resulting from the movement, but, on the other hand, as he writes, "Garvey's work was important because more than any other single leader he helped to give Negroes everywhere reborn feeling and a new awareness of individual worth."[19] As such it foreshadowed the spirit of the current black challenge.[20]

"Glamor" Personalities. Highly successful blacks, such as Duke Ellington, Paul Robeson, and Marian Anderson, often functioned as Negro leaders, not so much because of their actual civil rights activities but because of the fame and fortune they achieved in the white man's world. Comparatively "glamorous" white people do not necessarily play a civic leadership role. In the case of Negroes, however, a sort of "race" leadership is thrust upon them by the barriers they broke in achieving recognition, whether or not they were inclined to achieve a leadership role.

---

[17]See E. Franklin Frazier, *The Black Bourgeoisie* (Glencoe, Ill.: The Free Press, 1957), for fuller treatment of the rise of the Negro middle class.

[18]This point is illustrated in the later school desegregation crisis. Many Negro teachers in the South viewed with anxiety the possible loss of jobs or demotion in administrative rank as a consequence of school integration.

[19]Edmund D. Cronon, *Black Moses: The Story of Marcus Garvey and the Universal Negro Improvement Association* (Madison, Wis.: The University of Wisconsin Press, 1955), p. 222.

[20]The other most publicized popular movement was a cult formed by Father Divine (George Baker). This charismatic leader established a cult practicing a doctrine of love among all people. Cultists who joined his "heaven" turned over their possessions and lived under his security. While it lasted he took care of his followers. See Hadley Cantril, *Psychology of Social Movements* (New York: John Wiley & Sons, 1941), Ch. 5, "The Kingdom of Father Divine," for an interpretation of this movement.

The Negro Intelligentsia. The 1920s saw the emergence of a group of Negro intellectuals whose purpose was to enhance the self-respect of Negroes by glorifying the great accomplishments of Negroes past and present. Prominent among these were W. E. B. Du Bois, editor of *The Crisis;* Charles S. Johnson, editor of *Opportunity;* Alain Locke, editor of the volume *The New Negro;* and Carter G. Woodson, who had organized The Association for the Study of Negro Life and History in 1915 and began the publication of *The Journal of Negro History.* This movement had much moral support and financial aid from liberal-minded white people.

Activist Organizations. The first effort to organize a movement among Negroes in active protest against their minority status was launched in 1905, when twenty-nine Negro intellectuals met at Niagara Falls and planned the formation of a national organization to challenge all forms of segregation and discrimination. Such a bold program was opposed by Booker T. Washington and thus in a way challenged his accommodative leadership. Although the organization itself ceased to be effective after 1915, it prepared the way for the formation of the National Association for the Advancement of Colored People (NAACP), through which the spirit of the Niagara movement lived on.

Following the Great Migration and World War I, some younger Negro leaders in the 1920s, of whom A. Philip Randolph, president of the Brotherhood of Sleeping Car Porters, was to become the most influential, saw the Negro's greatest hope in alignment with the postwar Socialist movements. It is clear, however, from the relative failure of urban radical movements that the majority of Negroes aligned themselves politically with the major parties. Generally, it appears that they merged with the New Deal element of the Democratic Party with only an occasional convert to Communism.[21] As we shall see in our account of the trends since 1940, the protest activity continued to gain ascendancy over the accommodative approach.

The first two organizations that have continued to be the most influential in working for the improvement of Negro welfare and status are the National Association for the Advancement of Colored People and the Urban League. These two organizations were not exclusively Negro but interracial, with substantial white membership. While they have operated in the South with considerable difficulty, they originated in the North and received greater support in this region.

The NAACP was formed in 1909 following a severe race riot in Springfield, Illinois, the previous year. The organization started on interracial initiative, but its active workers have usually been Negroes. The long-run objective of the Association has always been to win full equality for the Negro as an American citizen. Its specific activities have been in the field of civil liberties, fighting legal cases of discrimination, such as anti-lynching legislation, the abolition of poll taxes, and so on. The strategy of its approach has been practical and opportunistic. The Association did not conduct an omnibus legal campaign against the Southern caste pattern but selected strategically important cases in specific fields of discrimination. It saved many Negroes from unequal court treatment, prevented the extradition of Negroes from North to South for trial, and helped establish the precedents that led to inclusion of Negroes on juries—to select only a few of its many legal successes.

---

[21]See Wilson Record, *The Negro and the Communist Party* (Durham: University of North Carolina Press, 1951), for a full treatment of the topic. The author finds membership of American Negroes in the Communist Party to have been inconsequential and doubts that up to 1950 it ever exceeded 8,000.

The Urban League was founded in 1910 with financial support from white Americans. It arose primarily to help the recent Negro migrants adjust to Northern city life. In time it became a general social welfare agency performing various welfare services: health work, recreational work, delinquency prevention, and acting as an informal employment agency for Negroes. In contrast to the NAACP, the Urban League had used informal and educational methods in pursuing this goal rather than a legal approach.[22]

One great weakness of both these organizations was their lack of support from the Negro masses. This was a result in part of the generally low educational and economic status of the Negro masses and the widespread prevalence among Negroes of a resigned and hopeless attitude as far as cracking the color line was concerned. Lack of mass support was also due to the fact that, as in all class structures, the interests of the Negro middle class and the Negro lower class were not identical in all respects.

Black-White Relations: A National Issue

Before turning to consider the trend since World War II, when great changes in Negro-white relations have occurred, it is pertinent to emphasize that the very existence of regional attitudes and practices as disparate as those portrayed in the past two chapters had been a perennial source of regional controversy affecting the unity of the nation. The slavery issue threatened national unity until the close of the Civil War. From 1880 to World War I, the North in general tended to leave the Negro problem, as far as it was thought of as such, to the South. The Great Migration to the North brought the problem home. The discriminatory pattern that developed appeared at first to suggest a moving of the region closer to that of the South. However, more Northern people began to feel that the prevailing pattern of race relations could not permanently endure in a political democracy and began to work for change. In short, there emerged a definition of black-white relations as a *national* problem. This emerging new viewpoint of the race problem received considerable impetus from the New Deal. In the operation of large-scale relief and in other government-planned projects, the tendency was to provide Negroes a fairer share. Here and there Negroes were placed in new situations alongside whites.

While these new trends were developing in the North, there was no perceptible indication of the South's readiness to accept this redefinition of the race problem or to basically alter its traditional biracial system. Thus the approach of World War II found a long-standing regional issue assuming new dimensions, more sharply focused by the greater influence of the North—as the predominant center of national opinion-making—in the formation of national policy.

THE IMPACT OF WORLD WAR II

It is difficult to assess the effect of World War II on the patterns of Negro-white relations in both the North and the South. Such a major national crisis necessarily required some alteration in the established patterns. But in both regions, the broad trend immediately following the war was to resume the previous patterns. It was some ten or more years later that the Black Challenge to white dominance crystallized into a sus-

---

[22]Guichard Parris and Lester Brooks, *Blacks in the City: A History of the National Urban League* (Boston: Little Brown & Co., 1971).

tained movement. However, the carryover of new wartime experience in interracial contact for many persons both white and black reinforced other social forces that made the 1960s a ripe time for the Black Challenge.

Negro Job Opportunities

The main effect of the war grew out of the labor shortages that afforded Negro men and women new opportunities for employment, more steadily, and at higher wages with a consequent rise in the standard of living.[23] Some change in status occurred in the employment area. In some war jobs Negroes worked alongside whites on equal terms and were increasingly accepted into labor unions, to a limited extent even in the South, on an integrated basis.[24]

However, even under the urgency of war, acceptance of Negroes was not easy. Employers were reluctant to hire Negroes, and white workers showed resistance to accepting them as co-workers.[25] In order to overcome as much as possible of this resistance President Roosevelt issued an executive order in 1941 establishing the Fair Employment Practices Commission, which aimed to require all government agencies and all private firms with government contracts not to discriminate on the basis of race or national origin. While this commission had neither legislative sanction nor much real power of enforcement, substantial gains in the number of Negroes employed followed its establishment.[26]

Aside from these economic gains, the line of segregation held substantially the same. Even the National Capitol Housing Authority bowed to the prevailing housing pattern in building low-rent housing units.[27] In other more intimate areas of social relations, substantially no change took place.

The Armed Services

The armed services practiced a policy of segregation. In the Army, Negroes were assigned to colored units, most of which were in supply services where the tasks were largely menial labor. A few thousand Negro officers were trained and placed over Negro troops, frequently under the command of a white captain. In army posts, separate recreational rooms were maintained, and nearly all communities that any considerable number of soldiers frequented—North as well as South—restricted colored troops to the Negro areas and set up separate USO's. According to Rose, "In Europe there were some efforts made to keep Negroes from fraternizing with the civilian population, when no such bar was set up against the white troops."[28]

---

[23]See Robert C. Weaver, *Negro Labor a National Problem* (New York: Harcourt, Brace and Co., 1946).
[24]See Drake and Cayton, *Black Metropolis*, pp. 309–310, for the Chicago picture during World War II.
[25]See Herbert R. Northrup, *Organized Labor and the Negro* (New York: Harper & Brothers, 1944), for an account of this subject.
[26]See *Fair Employment Practices Commission, Final Report, June 28, 1946* (Washington, D.C., 1947).
[27]See *Segregation in Washington, A Report of the National Committee on Segregation in Washington* (Chicago, 1948).
[28]Arnold Rose, *The Negro in America* (New York: Harper & Brothers, 1948), p. 138. By permission of the publisher.

The policy of segregating Negro troops reflected the wishes of the white troops. A survey of the attitudes of servicemen made in March, 1943, revealed that about 80 percent of the white troops preferred to have the two groups separated in PX's, service clubs, and military units.[29] While over 90 percent of the Southern white respondents approved segregation, it is significant that over 70 percent of the Northern white troops likewise indicated approval. The Negro respondents showed far more opposition to being segregated, as would also be expected, but detailed findings provide significant indication of how Negroes viewed their situation generally. Of the Negro sample, 37 percent disapproved separation in military units, 36 percent approved, 17 percent thought it made no difference, and 10 percent were undecided. Comments by some of the antisegregation Negro soldiers emphasized primarily the democratic principle involved, for example: "Separate outfits shows that the Army continues segregation and discrimination. Is this the Democracy we are told we are fighting for?" The 36 percent of Negro soldiers who approved of segregation did so on the basis of expediency, on a realistic appraisal of white prejudice. Among the reasons given by Negroes for taking the prosegregation viewpoint were a fear of interracial friction—"A white soldier would call a colored soldier 'nigger' and it would be a fight"; a desire to withdraw from the situation of not being wanted—"so long as there are so many prejudiced white people, it would be too unpleasant"; a desire to prove that Negro groups can match the achievements of white groups; and finally, a desire to associate with those who understand one another—"I had rather be with my own color. Then I know where I stand."

Some experiments in desegregated units were conducted toward the war's end without any important difficulties—paving the way for the postwar integrated policy that was to come.[30]

In spite of segregation policy and practice, the total impact of experiences in the armed services had effects disturbing to the traditional pattern of caste relations. More objectively measurable was the introduction of colored servicemen to new standards of welfare—in diet, health, and sanitation; and the increased training in many new skills, some of which could be useful in peacetime. A measure of the Negro soldiers' feeling about the value of their army training is seen in their answers to the direct question on this, where 61 percent replied it would help them, compared with 39 percent among the whites.[31]

Less tangible but perhaps in the long run more significant was the impact of service experience on the attitudes of GI's of both races. Northern-born Negro servicemen trained in the South came face to face with the stricter Southern caste system. Southern Negro GI's stationed in the North experienced some measure of unaccustomed freedom. In Europe many Negro GI's found white people willing to accept them like any other American soldier. Equally disturbing to traditional attitudes and habits was the impact of war service on many white Southerners. This is most dramatically illustrated in Margaret Halsey's account of her experiences operating a servicemen's center in a large Northern city.[32]

---

[29]Samuel A. Stouffer et al., The American Soldier, Vol. I (Princeton: Princeton University Press, 1949), pp. 566–570.
[30]See John Dollard and Donald Young, "In the Armed Forces," in Survey Graphic, Jan., 1947, p. 68.
[31]Stouffer, The American Soldier, p. 537.
[32]Margaret Halsey, Color Blind (New York: Simon and Schuster, 1946).

BLACK IMMIGRANTS

Bryce-Laporte criticizes the failure of American scholars to give adequate attention to blacks who immigrated to the United States by their own choice. This may be due to their small numbers, which are, however, large enough to surprise most whites. Bryce-Laporte estimates that of the 45,162,120 total number of aliens entering the United States between 1820 and 1970, 1,000,000 were West Indians and 76,473 were Africans (not all of whom were blacks.). Of the 373,326 immigrants to the United States in 1970, 38,380 came from predominantly black countries including Jamaica, Trinidad, Haiti, and scattered islands in the West Indies. Others came from the Canal Zone and other Central American countries.

Concerning racism in these Latin American areas, Laporte, himself from Panama, writes as follows:

> The point is that racism exists in most of the countries from which black immigrants come to the United States. However, it often differs categorically, manifests itself differently, and may not be of the same order of magnitude or saliency as that practiced in the United States. While most all black immigrants have come from countries with some racist practices, the effect on them depends on the degree of institutionalization or personalization, blatancy or subtlety, permanence or transitoriness that characterized racism in the country (or part of it) from which they came. Of equal importance is the matter of how each immigrant would have been perceived and treated within the racial categories of his native land.
>
> In Panama (the land of my birth), for instance, both the institutionalized, blatant, and apparently permanent form of racism existed side by side, with the personalized, subtle, and apparently transitory form, and persons often shuttled from one to the other. In the American-administered Canal Zone, the first form predominated; but to the extent that blacks lived in homogeneous communities, had local institutions, could practice some forms of their own culture, and had access to a more relaxing situation in the Panamanian cities the personal levels were only felt during moments of formal unsymmetrical interaction, that is, at work, in prison, in hospitals, and so forth.[33]

In general, the class system presents the typical Latin American class-race system of European, mulatto, and black. The younger blacks could aspire to high positions, short of elite; for example, Panama has had two black vice-presidents. Despite the fact that the aspiring black immigrants had read about racism as applied to blacks in the United States, they found it difficult to adjust to being a black American even though they were in general accorded privileges. ". . . [T]he average black immigrant becomes an ardent practitioner of what Americans call the Protestant Ethic."[34]—if you work hard you can

---

[33]R. S. Bryce-Laporte, in Peter I. Rose, Stanley Rothman, and William J. Wilson, *Through Different Eyes: Black and White Perspectives on American Race Relations* (New York: Oxford University Press, 1973), p. 52. Copyright © 1973 by Oxford University Press Inc. Reprinted by permission of the publisher.
[34]*Ibid.*, p. 58. Reprinted by permission of the publisher.

make it. To some extent he looked askance at the native blacks, so many of whom had given up trying to get anywhere—probably with more reason than the immigrant realized. But for this attitude, the black foreigner was often envied and disliked by native-born black peers. However, having found that white racist discrimination applied to them, a number of second-generation black immigrants have been leaders in the recent black protest movements, for example, Stokely Carmichael, Harry Belafonte, Ossie Davis, and Shirley Chisholm.

DEMOGRAPHY OF NEGRO (BLACK) POPULATION

Growth

Table 8–1 shows that the number of Negroes in the United States has increased each decade since 1790. It also shows that broadly the proportion of Negroes to the total population declined from 1880 to 1930, primarily as the result of the great increase in the white population through immigration from Europe. From 1930 to 1970 the percentage of the national population counted as Negro increased slightly from 9.7 to 11.1 percent; and from 1950 to 1970 the percentage increase of the black population was about 8 percent greater than that of the white population. The fertility rates of Negro women have broadly followed the fluctuations in that of white women, although

TABLE 8-1   Growth of the Negro Population Since 1790*

Census Year	Number of Negroes	Percentage of Total Population	Percentage Increase of Negroes During Decade	Percentage Increase of Whites During Decade
1970	22,530,289	11.1	19.7	11.9
1960	18,871,831	10.5	25.4	17.5
1950	15,044,937	9.9	17.0	14.4
1940	12,865,518	9.8	8.2	7.2
1930	11,891,143	9.7	13.6	15.7
1920	10,463,131	9.9	6.5	15.7
1910	9,827,763	10.7	11.2	21.8
1900	8,333,940	11.6	18.0	21.2
1890	7,488,676	11.9	13.8	27.0
1880	6,580,793	13.1	34.9	29.2
1870	4,880,009	12.7	9.9	24.8
1860	4,441,830	14.1	22.1	37.7
1850	3,638,808	15.7	26.6	37.7
1840	2,873,648	16.8	23.4	34.7
1830	2,328,642	18.1	31.4	33.9
1820	1,771,656	18.4	28.6	34.2
1810	1,377,808	19.0	37.5	36.1
1800	1,002,037	18.9	32.3	35.8
1790	757,208	19.3		

*U.S. Bureau of Census, *Negroes in the United States, 1920–1932*, pp. 1–2; *Sixteenth Census of United States, Population*, Vol. II, p. 19. 1960 Census, P. C. (A2)–1, p. 4. 1970 Census P. C. (1) 3, p. 262.

at a substantially higher level than that of whites.[35] But death rates retard their proportional increase.

The black population was estimated at 24.0 million April 1, 1974, an increase of 1.4 million over 1970.[36] The average rate of growth between 1970–1974 was 1.6 percent, a drop from 1.8 percent in the 1960–1970 period. The lower rate of population growth was due to the declining birth rate among blacks, although it was still higher than that of the total population. The Census Bureau has long been aware that they undercount some minorities; especially the various Hispanics and the blacks are low. The Bureau estimates that in 1970 the undercount of whites was about 1.9 percent and for blacks 7.7 percent.

Regional Distribution

Through the entire national period up to 1910 the Negro population was highly concentrated in the South—over 90 percent. However, the Southern and Southwestern expansion of the plantation economy from the upper South was paralleled by a corresponding expansion of the Negro population in these areas. In spite of the freedom for Negroes to move where they desired after the Civil War, very few migrated to the North, and almost none to the West. From 1910 there was a marked migration out of the region (slowed down somewhat by the Depression decade), so that by 1970 the proportion of the total Negro population in the South had dropped to 53 percent. Until 1940 this exodus from the South was to the Northeast and the North Central regions. A small but hitherto unprecedented trend toward the West began in consequence of the labor demands in that region created by World War II. Most of this migration was to California, which led all the other states in the percentage rise in Negro population during the 1951–1960 decade—90 percent. By 1970 the state had 1,400,143 Negroes. A prime factor accounting for this trend out of the South has been increasing job opportunities outside the region. In their studies the Taubers did not find any clear support for the thesis that among the "push" factors was the desire to escape the southern discriminatory pattern of race relations.[37] However, autobiographies of Negroes do show that this desire was a compelling motive in some instances.[38]

The most striking change in black migration in the early '70s was movement back to the South. The Census survey finds evidence that such movement was greater than migration to the North. The blacks moving South are not exclusively those who were born in the Southern region. Substantially all are moving to cities and many are professional blacks. Some corporations have assigned Northern blacks to the South and some Northern black physicians have located in rural areas of the South where federal funding has furnished financial aid.

---

[35]Reynolds Farley, *Growth of the Black Population* (Chicago: Markham Publishing Company, 1970), p. 244.
[36]U.S. Bureau of the Census, *The Social and Economic Status of the Black Population,* 1974. It is in this decade that the Bureau changed the name from Negro to Black.
[37]Karl E. and Alma F. Tauber, "The Negro Population in the United States," Ch. 2 of John Davis, ed., *The Negro Reference Book* (Englewood Cliffs, N.J.: Prentice-Hall, 1966), p. 111.
[38]See, for example, Richard Wright, *Native Son* (New York: Harper & Brothers, 1940); and Horace Cayton, *Long Lonely Road* (New York: The Trident Press, 1965).

During the early 1970s the black suburban migration increased at a higher annual rate but by 1974 it represented still only 4.4 percent of the total national suburban population. To a considerable extent this movement created black clusters rather than a random distribution of black families among white suburbanites.

Urban Trend: Metropolitan Concentration

The most significant change in the distribution of the Negro population since 1910 has been the shift from rural to urban, more marked than that of the white population and also strikingly concentrated in the larger metropolitan areas as indicated in Table 8–2. As examples, Chicago had a sixteenfold increase in its percent Negro from 1910 to 1970; and New York had a tenfold increase. Washington, D.C., with over 70 percent Negro, approaches being a "Black City." In 1970, of the larger cities, in Newark, New Jersey, and Atlanta, Georgia, the population reached over 50 percent black; and several smaller cities were more than half black: Gary, Indiana (52.8 percent), and Compton, California (71 percent). It is probable that other cities have since 1970 passed the 50 percent mark.

The list of leading cities does not provide an adequate picture of the degree of concentration. In many places, the Negro areas have pushed out to an adjacent municipality: for example Newark's main Negro area has extended into adjacent East Orange,

TABLE 8-2   The Twenty-five Leading Cities in Negro Population in 1970 and Their Percent Negro, 1910, 1950, 1960, and 1970

City	Negro Population, 1970 (In Thousands)	Percent Negro Of Total Population			
		1970 (.00)	1960 (.00)	1950 (.00)	1910 (.00)
New York City	1,667	21	14	10	02
Chicago	1,103	33	23	14	02
Detroit	660	44	29	16	*
Philadelphia	654	34	26	18	06
Washington, D.C.	538	71	54	35	29
Los Angeles	504	18	14	9	*
Baltimore	420	46	35	24	15
Houston	317	26	23	21	30
Cleveland	288	38	29	16	*
New Orleans	267	45	37	32	26
Atlanta	255	51	38	37	34
St. Louis	254	41	29	18	06
Memphis	243	39	37	37	40
Dallas	210	25	19	13	*
Newark	207	54	34	17	*
Indianapolis	134	18	21	15	10
Birmingham	126	42	40	40	40
Cincinnati	125	28	22	16	05
Oakland	125	35	23	12	*
Jacksonville	118	22	23	27	51
Kansas City, Mo.	112	22	18	12	10
Milwaukee	105	15	9	3	*
Pittsburgh	105	20	17	12	05
Richmond	105	42	42	32	37
Boston	105	16	10	5	*

All data except the 1910 column taken from the U.S. Census, 1970, P.C. (S1)2, *Negro Population in Selected Places and Counties,* Table 1, Cities with a Negro Population of 50,000 or more by rank 1970, 1960, 1950. 1910 data: U.S. Bureau of Census, *Negro Population, 1790–1915.*
*Leading 1970 cities that had few Negroes in 1910.

N.J., which also has a majority Negro population. This process is further illustrated by the growth of the Negro population of Oakland, California, in the San Francisco metropolitan area, from less than 10 percent Negro in 1910 to 35 percent in 1970, totaling 125,000 Negroes. The extent of concentration can be carried further. Smaller suburban satellite industrial cities near metropolises often have large proportions of black people; for example, New Brunswick, New Jersey, 35 miles from New York City, had a 24 percent Negro population.

In general, the leading Southern cities listed in Table 8–2 have had substantial Negro populations for some time. Thus it is not surprising that the percentage of their Negro population does not show much increase and in some cases drops.

The implications of these striking changes in the distribution of the Negro population will be discussed in later chapters. In conclusion here we point out that the national Negro population is expected to increase a little more proportionally than the white population but to remain a definite numerical minority, one important factor in power vulnerability. On the other hand, the exceptionally high urban concentration already has had two effects: (1) providing in some local areas such a substantial number as to give blacks considerable political power; and (2) markedly accentuating interracial tension in such areas.

Suggested Readings

Brotz, Howard. *Negro Social and Political Thought, 1850–1925*. New York: Basic Books, 1966.
   Well-selected readings from outstanding leaders such as Frederick Douglass, Booker T. Washington, and Marcus Garvey.
Du Bois, W. E. Burghardt. *The Souls of Black Folks*. Greenwich, Conn.: Fawcett Publications, 1961.
   A story of Black Americans in an "alien world" as they struggle for human rights. Written by a leading black writer of the first half of the twentieth century.
Frazier, E. Franklin. *The Black Bourgeoisie*. Glencoe, Ill.: The Free Press, 1957.
   The eminent Negro sociologist describes the Black Bourgeoisie with criticism of their role in the Negro movement.
Grant, Robert R. *The Black Man Comes to the City*. Chicago: Nelson Hall, 1974.
   A documentary account of the great migration of blacks from the South to Northern cities, 1915–1930.
Lee, Frank F. *Negro and White in Connecticut Town*. New York: Bookman Associates, 1961.
   A study of race relations in a small town emphasizing the techniques of social control.
Osofsky, Gilbert. *Harlem: The Making of the Ghetto*. New York: Harper & Row, Publishers, 1966.
   An outstanding history of Negro New York, 1890–1930.
Waskow, Arthur I. *From Race Riot to Sit-In: 1919 and the 1960's;* Garden City, N.Y.: Doubleday & Co., Anchor Books, 1966.
   The first half of this volume describes and analyzes the major race riots of 1919 in the light of their origins, the riot process, and how they were dealt with.

9

Changing Black-White Relations:
a National Crisis

The Southern and Northern patterns of black-white relations were dealt with as essentially stable interracial systems. As we turn from the end of World War II to the present the predominant focus is on change. Furthermore, the reciprocal roles of the two races underwent a change. While prior to 1950, blacks had made protests and occasional riots took place, in general blacks took relatively little vigorous initiative toward change, adjusting themselves to white requirements and accepting minor concessions at the local levels. However, in the post-World War II period the racial interactive process changed with the blacks taking the initiative and whites finding it necessary to make significant adjustments to a mounting black challenge that ultimately brought the nation to a racial crisis. In this chapter the main changes in black welfare and status through the 1960 decade will be presented, leaving analysis of the Black Challenge as a movement and the white response to it to the following chapter.

PROLOGUE TO THE BLACK CHALLENGE

Following World War II the pattern of black-white relations tended to resume much of its prewar character. In the South little change occurred until the crisis that was precipitated by the Supreme Court's school desegregation mandate in 1954, which, in the Deep South, was successfully resisted until the 1960s. The tempo of interracial tension and violence rose as Southern blacks sought to have successive court rulings outlawing local public accommodations enforced.

The North approved of the courts' rulings on school desegregation and other public forms of discrimination, and was generally critical of the South's resistance. But it should not be overlooked that much of what the South was being ordered to do was what had long been practiced in the North. However, because of the flexibility of the Northern racial pattern, other forms of Northern discrimination were being challenged by individual blacks or local groups, sometimes successfully and sometimes not. This sort of piecemeal process was whittling away at discrimination in public and civic discrimination in the absence of any broad challenge. The separation of the races spatially and socially remained intact. But the increasing flow of Southern blacks to the great metropolitan centers created problems in housing, employment, and welfare, and aggravated racial tensions.

As background for analyzing the Black Challenge, attention is directed to broad social forces in the society that bore on this new black-white situation.

The Effect of Social Forces

Economic, Technological, and Ecological Trends.   The expanding economy offered some new jobs for blacks and some at higher levels for those who qualified. This was considerably offset by a decrease in demand for unskilled workers brought about by technological changes leading to large-scale black unemployment. The nation in general became increasingly more affluent. In this blacks shared but disproportionally to whites. Their concentration in larger cities gave them increased localized political power, but aggravated slum conditions, and increased racial tension. Theoretically, "rationalization" of the economic system favors job placement on the basis of achieved qualifications rather than ascribed status, and competition for profit turns attention to the rising purchasing power of the black population. But long-standing racial mores impeded these trends.

Political and Governmental Trends.   The traditional basis of democratic governmental institutions pressed for more equality for blacks as reflected in court decisions, civil rights legislation, and governmental administration, particularly at the federal level and, outside the South, at some state and local levels. The growing black vote influenced office-seekers to promise improvements and prompted office-holders to pay some attention to black requests. The general trend toward the "welfare state" helped to sustain the welfare of the many poorly paid and unemployed blacks. Provision of this aid, however, reinforced a traditional concept among whites that blacks won't work and were glad to live on relief.

Cultural Trends.   The general increase in educational facilities was shared by blacks if unevenly and spottily, aside from the matter of desegregation. The increasing dissemination of social science findings was creating a younger generation of white adults who at the intellectual level were more aware of the errors of the doctrine of racism and more conscious of its damaging consequences to American society. All these influences favoring the decline in discrimination prompted some of the leading organized religions to reassess the implications of their practices in regard to the race question.

The Elaboration of Mass Media.   In the postwar period there was an elaboration of the mass media. American newspapers and magazines gave racial news wide coverage and tended to editorialize in favor of the American Creed. Television, however, was the medium that had the most powerful influence on both blacks and whites. Witnessing the jeering faces of white mothers as black students entered hitherto white schools may have been a stimulus for the cause of racial justice. Likewise, the televising of civil rights activities aroused in many witnessing blacks the desire to participate in the movement themselves, as indicated by Seymour Spilerman.[1]

Since the net effect of the operation of these social forces was to improve the welfare of blacks and to a limited extent their status, it tended to raise their aspirations still further and to spur more concerted direct action by blacks and some whites committed to the black cause.

World Opinion.   Increasing sensitivity to adverse world opinion concerning racial discrimination in the United States influenced government and some voluntary action

---

[1]Seymour Spilerman, "Structural Characteristics of Cities and the Severity of Racial Disorders," in *American Sociological Review*, 41, 5, Oct., 1976, pp. 771–793. Spilerman considered the televising of riots was an important factor in causing so many riots in so short a time.

groups to work against American racism. Not well recognized by the public was the incubating conception of the Third World, to be composed of nonwhite peoples as against the two white worlds of communism and the capitalist West.[2]

THE CHANGING SOUTH

Before 1954

In the South following World War II the prewar pattern of race relations was continued with some minor exceptions.

In the area of civil rights, the following developments may be noted: an increase in black voting—595,000 blacks were on the voting rolls in 1947 and 1,008,614 in 1953[3]; some increase in black jury service prompted by a growing disposition of the federal courts to overturn convictions where the failure to call blacks into service was attested; some beginnings of arresting and trying white people for crimes of violence against blacks; the appointment of some black police officers to cover black areas. No precipitate rise in violence toward blacks was apparent, although the virtual disappearance of lynching was somewhat offset by a rise in the bombing of black homes—more than forty were reported for a year and a half period during 1951 to 1952.[4] While there was some reactivation of racist organizations, such as the Ku Klux Klan, white public opinion against such extremists was evidenced by the outlawing of masked gatherings in some Southern cities.

In education, two significant developments in the postwar years were (1) a partial breach in the pattern of segregation in higher education at the graduate level, and (2) a trend toward greater improvement of the segregated black school system, prompted in the hope that they might influence the impending Supreme Court decision not to order desegregation.[5]

Thus on the surface the Southern biracial system remained intact. Then came the Supreme Court decision outlawing school segregation.

The Supreme Court School Desegregation Decision: May 17, 1954

This decision concerned five separate cases, which the court consolidated since the same legal question was involved in each of them. In each case Negro children through their legal representatives had sought admission to white public schools, had been denied this right by local courts, and eventually had appealed the unfavorable decisions to the Supreme Court of the United States. The National Association for the Advancement of Colored People took charge of the case, directed by Thurgood Marshall, later to

---

[2]Current chaotic political conditions between and within the supposedly Third World nations do not auger well for their unity. See Ronald Segal, *The Race War* (New York: The Viking Press, 1967), Ch. 1.
[3]Margaret Price, *The Negro and the Ballot* (Atlanta: The Southern Regional Council, 1959), p. 9.
[4]"Blight, Bigotry, and Bombs," *The New South* (Atlanta: The Southern Regional Council, July, 1952).
[5]Truman M. Pierce *et al., White and Negro Schools in the South* (Englewood Cliffs, N.J.: Prentice-Hall, 1955), p. 292. See pp. 291–292 for summary.

become a Supreme Court justice himself. The core of the decision is found in the following excerpts:

> We conclude that in the field of public education the doctrine of "separate but equal" has no place. Separate educational facilities are inherently unequal. Therefore, we hold that the plaintiffs and others similarly situated for whom the actions have been brought are, by reason of the segregation complained of, deprived of the equal protection of the laws guaranteed by the Fourteenth Amendment. . . .
>
> Segregation of white and colored children in public schools has a detrimental effect upon the colored children. The impact is greater when it has the sanction of law; for the policy of separating the races is usually interpreted as denoting the inferiority of the Negro group. A sense of inferiority affects the motivation of the child to learn. Segregation, with the sanction of the law, therefore has a tendency to retard the educational and mental development of Negro children and to deprive them of some of the benefits they would receive in a racially integrated school system. . . .
>
> Whatever may have been the extent of psychological knowledge at the time of Plessy vs. Ferguson, this finding is amply supported by modern authority. Any language in Plessy vs. Ferguson contrary to this finding is rejected.[6]

The way the Supreme Court handled these cases indicated awareness of strong negative reactions and that enforcement would be beset with considerable difficulties. The decision in the school case was unanimous and read by Chief Justice Earl Warren. The Court postponed its implementing order until May 31, 1955, when it ordered compliance "with all deliberate speed." This phraseology indicated that the Court did not expect affected states to integrate all schools at once, but that some reasonable plan for eventual complete integration should be made and a beginning announced. It was left to district federal courts to decide whether a particular plan presented in its area was designed to accomplish complete integration in a reasonable time.

The implications of the school decision went far beyond the matter of schools alone. The reasoning presented in supporting the decision appeared to have general application—in effect the court was saying that all state-imposed racial segregation was unconstitutional. By stating it was reversing *Plessy v. Ferguson* (1896), which held that segregation in public transportation was legal provided the facilities were equal, the Court seemed to imply this general application. Subsequent decisions by various courts within the federal system in divergent fields further supported this interpretation. In short, the school desegregation decision appeared to undermine the entire legal, or *de jure*, basis of *public* racial discrimination throughout the United States. Obviously, for the South this legal situation was bound to create a crisis of a profoundly critical nature. Since we wish to discuss the Southern crisis in these broader terms, we will at this point

---

[6]347 U.S. 483. The number 1 case was *Brown et al. v. Board of Education of Topeka, Kansas.* Three other cases were linked together with *Brown et al.*: *Briggs v. Elliott* (South Carolina); *Davis v. County School Board of Prince Edward County, Virginia; Gebhart v. Belton* (Delaware). A separate decision in *Bolling v. Sharpe,* 347 U.S. 497, to the same effect was read following *Brown et al.* This case concerned segregation of public schools in the District of Columbia and therefore involved the federal government directly.

summarize the main facts concerning school desegregation and later discuss the crisis period and its broader implications.

School Desegregation in the Southern Region

The most striking fact was the slow pace of desegregation. The District of Columbia integrated the September following the decision. The border states began integrating next so that by 1960–1961 49 percent of their black pupils were in schools with whites. Seven of the eleven Southern states desegregated largely in "token" form—selecting a few blacks—and by 1965 only five percent of the black pupils attended schools with whites.[7] Before 1960, no public school desegregation at all had taken place in Louisiana, Georgia, Alabama, and Mississippi. The first break in these states came in New Orleans, where in November, 1960, under federal court order the Orleans Parish School Board admitted three pupils to one elementary school and one to another. The first sharp increase in the Deep South came as a result of pressure brought by the U.S. Department of Health, Education, and Welfare requiring all school districts to submit "affidavits of compliance" with court orders as a requirement for receiving federal funds. Despite this, by 1967 only 15.9 percent of all black pupils were in school with whites.

It was not until the school years 1970–1972 that the South began in earnest to desegregate on a widespread scale, and in some cases even to use busing for this purpose.

School desegregation in the South had other difficulties. "Tokenism" slowed up integration since the few black students, if not openly abused—as some of the first to enter were—were not socially accepted and therefore often black students selected hesitated to enter and those who did sometimes withdrew. Moreover, where desegregation took place with considerable black enrollment, resegregation, or decided imbalance, occurred through the withdrawal of white students.[8] The housing segregation, especially in cities, plus the flight to the suburbs by whites, made the distinction between *de facto* and *de jure* significant in the South as it later became in the North. A large number of new *private* schools for whites only appeared, housed in all sorts of available buildings generally not adequately equipped. Finally, the desegregation process caused many black teachers to lose their jobs and black school administrators to be demoted in rank when assigned to desegregated schools.[9]

The Southern Crisis

Thus, the school case decision of 1954 precipitated a crisis for the South, especially the Deep South. Since the implications of the decision were, from the Southern point of view, revolutionary, it is not surprising that what followed was a bitter struggle between

---

[7]These seven states listed in order of first district desegregation were Texas, Arkansas, Tennessee, North Carolina, Florida, South Carolina, and Virginia.

[8]In 1960 in Orchard Villa School, Dade County, Florida, the admission of even a few Negro students brought white student withdrawals. At the end of the school year the school was all Negro.

[9]"Statistical Summary of School Segregation-Desegregation in Southern and Border States, 1966–1967," *Southern Education Reporting Service,* April, 1967, p. 2.

those committed to traditional continuity and those intent on basic change in the Southern interracial system.

Following the school desegregation decision, tension and conflict between the races rose sharply. Biracial relations in most communities were polarized between active black groups and reactionary white groups, pitted against each other on the desegregation issue. Moderate white leadership was unable to exert influence; white liberals faced extraordinary reprisals. Effective communication between the white and black communities broke down. The issue had become the abolition or survival of the segregation system itself.

The interracial struggle followed a course of this sort: (1) Southern whites viewed the situation as a crisis and the prevailing segment reacted accordingly with strong resistance. (2) Negroes challenged further areas of segregation with considerable success. (3) Further extraregional pressures were brought upon the South: from Congress in the form of Civil Rights legislation, which led to increasing intervention by the federal government, and from voluntary groups, such as the "Freedom Riders." (4) Under the impact of all these pressures, the resistance movement began to weaken and reluctant compliance with desegregation orders was increased.

White Resistance. A measure of the unreadiness of the white South to accept desegregation can be gained from public opinion polls. On the school issue itself, the extent of Southern white disapproval was indicated by a Gallup Poll in 1954 that found 71 percent of its Southern white sample disapproving the school decision, as compared with 30 percent outside the South.[10] As to segregation in general, nearly three-fourths of the Southern white respondents were for segregation, while only about one-sixth favored integration.

In such an attitudinal climate it is not surprising that tension increased. A report found 530 cases of violence, reprisal, and intimidation from 1955 to 1958.[11]

White Citizens Councils. Of the various groups opposing desegregation, the most prominent was the White Citizens Council movement. Originating in Mississippi, it spread to other states. Members included people of high status and power, which may explain why its activities were less violent. Besides influencing state legislation, the Council's chief activity was to apply economic pressure on both blacks and whites who participated openly in the desegregation. One effect of this was illustrated by the eviction by white landlords of Negro tenants from their farms in two counties of Tennessee (1960). The reason given for this action was that because of mechanical improvements they were no longer needed. But the evicted tenants included blacks who had been active in attempting to register to vote. A federal district court order stopped these evictions.

Success of White Resistance. In addition to its success in delaying public-school desegregation, the white resistance movement was effective in two other areas: (1) a pre-1954 trend toward integration of blacks in college was slowed down[12] and (2) ef-

---

[10]Data furnished by American Institute of Public Opinion, Princeton, N.J., which has conducted polls on the question of desegregation since 1954.

[11]"Intimidations, Reprisal, and Violence in the South's Racial Crisis," published by the Southeastern Office, American Friends Service Committee, Department of Racial and Cultural Relations, National Council of Churches of Christ in the United States of America; and the Southern Regional Council, 1959.

[12]United States Commission on Civil Rights, *Report on Racial Discrimination in Higher Education,* 1961, as reported in *The New York Times,* Jan. 16, 1961, p. 1; p. 14.

forts to limit further extension of the voting franchise to blacks were made. A Florida study showed that most of the postwar black registration occurred by 1950. The author commented that "Increasing tension over the segregation issue is making it more difficult for officials and candidates in the South to maintain a moderate position on the [voting] issue or to seek Negro support on other issues."[13]

On March 12, 1956, 101 Congressmen almost all from Southern states, denounced the desegregation of schools ruling in a manifesto, called a "Declaration of Constitutional Principles," which was presented to Congress. They argued that it was unconstitutional and urged the Southern states to disobey it.[14]

Black Reaction to the Crisis.   To many white Americans the most surprising consequence of the Southern situation was the reaction of blacks. This arose because of the wide discrepancy between the way the white people thought the black people felt and the way the blacks actually felt. As a consequence of the social distance between the two groups, whites seldom learned much of the blacks' feelings. This was further aggravated by the tendency of blacks in conversation with white people to conceal their real feelings. Finally the misinterpretation on the part of whites was largely a matter of wishful thinking. Many believed what they wanted to believe, helping to justify the situation.

It is easily understandable that induration to minority status prevented many blacks from active participation in the desegregation movement. Fighting for their rights was fraught with danger and the experience of integration itself was often uncomfortable. But this was not the prevailing mood in black response.

The Supreme Court's decision in the school cases raised the level of aspiration of American blacks to new heights. For the first time since the Southern Reconstruction, younger blacks began to feel that first-class citizenship was a possibility within their own lifetime. For an increasing number of American Negroes, "Uncle Tom" was now dead.[15] This prevailing mood was demonstrated in various protest movements.

The Montgomery Bus Protest.   "Jim Crow" laws as applied to public transportation had always been a major source of irritation to the colored minority. Aside from the principle involved, they were a practical inconvenience, heightened by the fact that blacks used public transportation more than whites. The practice promoted inefficiency and was costly. It is therefore not surprising that a black challenge on this point should be one of the next steps.

As is often the case in such a situation, the precise time and the particular place resulted from a fortuitous incident, in this instance in Montgomery, Alabama, in 1955.[16]

On December 1, 1955, a black woman, Mrs. Rosa Parks, refused to "move back" on a crowded bus so that a white woman could have her seat. For this the bus driver had her arrested. The black community of Montgomery reacted by organizing a boycott of the

---

[13]H. D. Price, *The Negro and Southern Politics: A Chapter of Florida History* (New York: New York University Press, 1957), p. 106.

[14]*The Congressional Record,* 84 Congress, 2nd Session, pp. 4515–4516.

[15]The name "Uncle Tom" was used among Negroes to designate those Negro leaders who placated whites by not challenging the segregation system, thus strengthening the accommodative relationship while hindering attempts at social change.

[16]See L. D. Reddick, *Crusader Without Violence: A Biography of Martin Luther King, Jr.* (New York: Harper & Brothers, 1959). Chs. 8, 9, and 10 give an account of the Montgomery bus protest movement.

buses. The blacks walked or arranged car pools. The movement was led by the Montgomery Improvement Association, formed for the purpose. The leader was the Reverend Martin Luther King, Jr., who, as a result of his role in the protest movement, emerged as a nationally recognized black leader. A remarkable development in this affair was the practically unanimous and well-disciplined cooperation of the blacks of the city.

The bus boycott continued for many months at great loss to the local bus companies, while a legal case was carried finally to the United States Supreme Court. On November 14, 1956, this Court upheld a previous district court decision declaring the transportation segregation laws of the State of Alabama unconstitutional. On December 21, 1956, integrated buses rolled down the streets of Montgomery for the first time, with Dr. King and other M.I.A. leaders sitting up front.

"Sit-Ins." Other challenges involved "sit-ins" directed at the taboo against blacks eating in public restaurants with whites. In 1960 black students in Rock Hill, South Carolina, sat down at a local store lunch counter and were refused service. This form of protest activity spread despite much abuse from white Southerners and frequent arrests. Moreover, it led to rioting. Within a year most Southern branch stores of national corporations served black customers on the same basis as whites.

"Freedom Riders." In May, 1961, a group of Northerners of both races decided to test the extent of Southern compliance with the court ruling that segregation in public facilities involving interstate commerce was illegal. As the riders proceeded farther South they met increasing resistance, culminating in a riot in Montgomery that led Attorney General Robert F. Kennedy to send in federal marshals to abate the tension. Despite a federal request to let matters "cool off," similar rides took place, meeting with varying degrees of resistance.

The striking aspects of these protest activities were the use of nonviolent techniques by the protesters and their discipline in this regard. News and television portrayals of incidents involved usually showed the whites in a most unfavorable light as compared with the protesters.[17]

Further Federal Pressures: The Courts and Administration

Federal Action on Voting.   While the federal courts were continuing to issue orders of desegregation, the Congress of the United States made no supplementary moves to further the desegregation process until 1957, when the first Civil Rights Act for many years was passed.[18] Its main provisions were (1) to authorize the establishment of a Commission of Civil Rights, whose duties were to study the entire problem, including specifically denials of the right to vote; to collect information concerning legal developments denying equal protection of the laws; and to appraise the laws and policies of the federal government with respect to equal protection, (2) to empower the Attorney General to seek court injunctions against interference with the voting rights of any indi-

[17]The Congress of Racial Equality (CORE) had trained some student protesters in nonviolent activity.
[18]Students of the realities of politics and government in the United States will know that the Southern Congressional representation has special means at its command to block any legislation dealing with racial discrimination—for example, chairmanships of key congressional committees acquired through seniority.

vidual, and (3) to establish a Civil Rights Division in the Department of Justice. But, as the long effective resistance to school desegregation shows, court rulings and laws depend on their administrative implementation. State governments of the Deep South did little to implement them. Only Southern federal district courts and efforts of the federal government to intervene were effective, although at times these attempts were hampered by Southern Congressman as well as by the varying attitudes of the presidents.

Voter Registration. The Commission found that in 1956 only about 25 percent of the nearly five million Negroes of voting age as the 1950 Census were registered, in contrast to 60 percent of voting-age whites. Five months elapsed after this report appeared before any complaints were filed, first from Alabama and Louisiana. In the hearings held, ample proof of discrimination was found despite the refusal of local authorities to testify. But the Commission found that the federal government faced difficulties in prosecuting violations. "The history of voting in the United States shows, and the experience of this commission has confirmed, that where there is a will and opportunity to discriminate against certain potential voters, ways to discriminate will be found."[19]

Reluctant Compliance

From roughly 1960 on, Southern white reaction took the form of reluctant minimum compliance to federal law, delaying as long as possible. Gradually, the threat by a black organization to take cases to court or of federal intervention spurred some white authorities to institute "voluntary" desegregation.

Certain consequences of the increased tension and conflict, which affected the region adversely strengthened the trend toward compliance:[20] (1) Unfavorable economic effects were felt. The South lost national conventions because the cities were unable to guarantee nondiscriminatory treatment of black members. Certain businesses otherwise disposed to locate in the South were waiting until the racial atmosphere cleared. (2) The education of whites as well as blacks became seriously disturbed. Southern universities lost many faculty members and found difficulty recruiting new ones. (3) Southern politicians with aspirations for public office found that the segregationist label, necessary for election in the South, is often a disqualifying mark at the national level.

Southern Black Reaction to Limited Gains

The Gains. Along with the nation, the welfare of Southern blacks improved during the fifties, but wide disparities between their welfare and that of whites remained. Some illustrations are these:

---

[19]"With Liberty and Justice for All," an abridgement of the *Report of the United States Civil Rights Commission,* 1959, p. 88.
[20]See *The Price We Pay,* prepared by Barbara Patterson and other staff members of the Southern Regional Council and the Anti-Defamation League, for extensive examples of the various costs of discrimination, particularly to the South.

"Poverty among Negroes in the South is about three times more prevalent than in the rest of the country."[21]

Health had improved but the seven- to eight-year lower life expectancy as compared with whites still remained.[22]

There were far more blacks attending the formerly all-white state universities.[23]

Against subtle discrimination practices by unions, some upward mobility had occurred in industry but not in the clerical fields.[24]

In public accommodations, blacks gained formal equality but customary habituation tended to cause blacks often not to assert their rights.

Considerable gains occurred in the administration of equal justice. The white man pleading guilty of shooting James Meredith in June, 1966, while Meredith was making a protest march, was sentenced to three years in prison, the highest sentence given a white assailant of blacks up to that time.

A landmark in the history of Mississippi justice occurred in October, 1967, when an all-white Neshoba County jury presided over by a Mississippi-born federal judge, found seven out of fifteen white Mississippians guilty of participating in a plot that had resulted in the death of three civil rights workers in 1964. One of the convicted defendants was the chief deputy sheriff of the county. At first the jury reported itself deadlocked but were "persuaded" by the judge to try again to reach a verdict of guilty.

Political Participation. In its long-run implications, perhaps the most significant gain for Southern blacks was, and continues to be, increasing participation in the political arena.

> During the 1960s black Americans in the South made remarkable gains in their struggle for the right to participate meaningfully in the political process. Registration of blacks has more than doubled (reaching about 4 million in 1972). The number of black elected officials increased six-fold. [But] there are still more than two million Southern blacks not registered.[25]

In the year 1970, the number of Southern black elected officials had reached over 650, including fifteen members of the Georgia Legislature, one of whom, Julian Bond— who when first elected was refused seating until a court ordered his admission—has acquired a national reputation. One indication of the effect of this black political participation has been the tendency for Southern white candidates for office to ignore the race issue.

Interracial Tension and Violence. It is inevitable that in a period of heightened tension, violence would increase. Despite the efforts of Dr. Martin Luther King, Jr., to lead the protest movements with the nonviolent technique, from 1955 through June, 1966,

---

[21]Andrew R. Brimmer, "The Negro in the National Economy," Ch. 5 in John P. Davis, *The Negro American Reference Book* (Englewood Cliffs, N.J.: Prentice-Hall, 1966), p. 263.
[22]See William Payne, "There Is Hunger Here," *U. S. Civil Rights Digest,* 1969, pp. 34–40.
[23]In 1971 the percent of black enrollment in the University of Mississippi was 3.2; in the University of Alabama, 3.7; and in the University of South Carolina, 5.1.
[24]See Herbert Hill, "The Pattern of Job Discrimination Against Negroes," in *Minority Problems,* Arnold M. Rose and Caroline B. Rose, eds. (New York: Harper & Row, 1965), pp. 153–55.
[25]Data supplied by the Voter Education Project, Atlanta, Georgia, as of early summer, 1972.

108 persons were known to have been killed in race-related incidents.[26] Six of the thirty-one riots reported up to mid-August for the year 1967 were in Southern cities.[27]

Assessment of the Southern Situation: 1965

Now that black-white relations had become a national problem, focused in metropolitan areas, there were increasing similarities in all regions. Since the pace of change resulting from the Black Challenge had slowed down, it appears that the assessment of the Southern situation made by Blumer in the mid-1960s, with some qualifications, was still broadly applicable in the early 1970s.

> It is a serious mistake, however, to regard the achievement by Negroes of civil rights, as presently defined, as equivalent to removing the color line. . . . The contested area of civil rights is . . . but the outer band of the color line. Inside of it lies the crucial area of economic subordination and opportunity restriction—an area of debarment of Negroes which is exceedingly tough because it is highly complicated by private and quasiprivate property rights, managerial rights, and organizational rights. Still further inside of the color line are the varied circles of private association from which the Negro is grossly excluded. Thus, the successful achievement of civil rights merely peels off, so to speak, the outer layer of the color line. By itself, it does not alter significantly the social positions of the two racial groups. It raises somewhat the position of the Negro on the dominance-subordination axis but leaves this axis of relationship essentially intact.[28]

The main qualifications stem from the increasing political power of Southern blacks. As we have noted, Southern politicians already play down the race issue. But more broadly, in the past few years, the moderate and liberal white Southerners have been able to challenge the power of the traditional white Southern racists, for example in the election of Reuben Askew as Governor of Florida. In short, in the urban areas of the South, white Southerners are becoming adjusted to accepting the civil rights of blacks and to interact with blacks on a formally equal basis in regard to public matters.[29]

In conclusion, it is essential not to overrate black progress obtained via the political route. Registration to vote does not mean that all registrants will vote, as was indicated by the over-whelming defeat of Charles Evers, the black mayor of Fayette, Mississippi,

---

[26]"Violence," *New South*, Nov., 1965, and a 1966 supplement, The Southern Regional Council, Atlanta, Georgia.

[27]"Riot Toll: 1967 and Before," *Time*, Aug. 11, 1967, p. 11.

[28]Herbert Blumer, "The Future of the Color Line," Ch. 15 in John C. McKinney and Edgar T. Thompson, eds., *The South in Continuity and Change* (Durham, N.C.: Duke University Press, 1965), pp. 329–330. Copyright © 1965 by Duke University Press. Reprinted by permission of the publisher.

[29]Even so die-hard a segregationist as George Wallace, who made a symbolic gesture of defiance of federal law by confronting the federal marshal escorting the first black student to be admitted into Alabama State University, no longer talks about "Segregation Forever." In his brief 1972 campaign for the Democratic nomination for president, his main race-related issue was opposition to busing school children, which had considerable appeal nationwide.

in his recent campaign for governor of that state. As with American voters in general, apathy plays a part; but also the long-ingrained fear of reprisals affects black participation, particularly in smaller communities.

THE CRISIS IN THE NORTH

The presence of sizable black communities in the major cities of the North up to World War I presented no serious situations for the white North. And even the substantial influx of blacks to the North during and following this war, as seen in "Black Metropolis," was not viewed by the general white public as a major problem. For blacks their situation was in many ways more satisfactory than in the South, but the failure to break the caste barrier prevented the majority of blacks from economic improvement relative to the non-blacks, and coping with the humiliation of being second-class Americans was a constant frustration. It was the period following the greater migration from the South to the North during and after World War II that black-white relations developed into a major crisis.

The Ecological Pattern

In a study of Pittsburgh in the mid 1950s Grodzins found Negroes to be highly concentrated and made the following prediction, which is still broadly accurate: "The picture for the future is clear enough: Large non-white concentrations (in a few cases numerical majorities) in the principal cities; large white majorities, with scattered Negro enclaves in their suburbs."[30]

In large cities with substantial black populations, the residential distribution of black people tends to follow this pattern: (1) A main black area—Harlem, for example—is located not far from the central business district, where a large part of the population dwells and major businesses and recreational enterprises cater to blacks. (2) Some mixed black-white neighborhoods are found in the inner core of the metropolitan area where both whites and blacks are very poor. (3) Population growth forces black movement in two ways. The first is simply an extension of the ghetto beyond its present borders as vacancies occur when upwardly mobile white families begin to move out. Or black families "jump" to some other area growing less desirable to whites, but which often represents better housing for the blacks than they had before. (4) Both of the outward processes are first resisted by whites, but when some blacks happen to get homes, whites panic and move out, more blacks move in, and the section becomes all black.[31] (5) The same process is noted when blacks move to the suburbs.

The Social Organization of the Black Ghettos

A large portion of the population of the black ghettos consists of migrants from the South and their children. Whatever elements of stable social organization or cultural norms the migrants may have brought with them were less adaptable to city life, espe-

---

[30]Morton Grodzins, *The Metropolitan Area as a Racial Problem* (Pittsburgh: University of Pittsburgh Press, 1958), p. 4.
[31]See "Where Shall We Live?" *Report of the Commission on Race and Housing* (Berkeley: University of California Press, 1958), Ch. 2.

cially in the case of Southern rural migrants. Thus adjustments had to be made *ad hoc,* which understandably resulted in weak social organization, reflected most extremely in the life of black youths.

Viewed from the normative white standards, the black ghetto family life deteriorated. The main statistical indices for this are stated by Levitan *et al.* as follows:

> Marital and family patterns are the only social dimension in which the balance of change was clearly for the worse. The extent of [family] deterioration is sometimes exaggerated, but the directions of change are unmistakable: blacks are now less likely to marry; their marriages more frequently end up in separation or divorce; and their children more often grow up in split homes. Birth rates have declined among blacks as among whites, but the drop has been greater among married than unmarried women. More than a third of black births each year are illegitimate, and the incidence of illegitimacy among black women in their young teens has not declined.[32]

The ghetto area generally had weak community organization. Liebow, on the basis of his in-depth study of a small sample of young adults in Washington, D.C., finds that "this streetcorner world does not at all fit the traditional characterization of the lower-class neighborhood as a tightly knit community whose members share the feeling 'we are all in this together' "[33] As to a distinctive culture, the same author writes "[N]or does it seem profitable . . . to look at it [streetcorner society] as a self-supporting on-going social system with its own distinctive 'design for living,' principles of organization, and system of values." Following up the same theme the author writes

> No doubt, each generation does provide role models for each succeeding one. Of much greater importance for the possibilities of change, however, is the fact that many similarities between the lower class Negro father and son (or mother and daughter) do not result from "cultural transmission" but from the fact that the son goes out and independently experiences the same failures, in the same areas, and for much the same reasons as his father. What appears as a dynamic self-sustaining cultural process is, in part at least, a relatively simple piece of social machinery which turns out, in rather mechanical fashion, independently produced look-alikes."[34]

---

[32]Sar A. Levitan, William B. Johnston, Robert Taggart, *Still a Dream: The Changing Status of Blacks Since 1960* (Cambridge, Mass: Harvard University Press, 1975), pp. 338–339. © 1975 by the President and Fellows of Harvard College. Reprinted by permission of the publisher. Illegitimacy is disapproved of by blacks generally but is considered more sympathetically than among whites. Premarital intercourse by whites less often results in childbirth because whites are generally more knowledgeable about birth control and are better able to afford the techniques to prevent or to cover up the prospect of or fact of illegitimacy.
[33]Elliot Liebow, *Tally's Corner: A Study of Negro Streetcorner Men* (Boston: Little, Brown & Co., 1967), p. 219.
[34]*Ibid.,* p. 223.

Economic Welfare

Major problems for blacks have been inadequate income, occupations limited to menial jobs, and high rates of unemployment. But during the 1960s considerable progress was made in all of these matters. Levitan *et al.* summarize as follows:

> 1. The black occupational distribution moved closer to that of whites as blacks progressed at a much faster rate out of the lowest paying categories and penetrated into higher paying occupations. . . .
> 2. The mean annual earnings of black males increased from 53 to 66 percent of those for whites between 1959 and 1971, and average black female earnings moved very close to equality with the earnings of white females.
> 3. The job gains were widespread and affected broad categories of black workers. The percent of black males earning less than $3,000 annually (in 1969 dollars) dropped from 40 to 22 percent between 1959 and 1969, while for females the decline was from 75 to 52 percent. The proportion earning over $10,000 (in 1969 dollars) rose from 3 to 9 percent for black males and from 1 to 5 percent for black females. . . .
> 4. Blacks received 6.4 percent of all wages and salaries at the beginning of the 1960's, but 8.1 percent at the end.
> 5. The severe employment problems of blacks persisted, but improvement can be noted. Black teenage unemployment rates rose throughout the decade, absolutely and relatively, but the critically important unemployment rate—that of adult black males—declined. Labor force participation rates fell among black males of all ages, but the pull of alternatives to work such as school, retirement, and more readily available disability benefits were the major contributing factors.[35]

The number of blacks dependent on some public assistance rose from 8 percent in 1961 to 21 percent in 1971.[36] A large part of the welfare cases are however poor black women with children and no available husband.

Class Stratification in the Black Community

Up to this point we have broadly dealt with blacks as a homogeneous group. This is far from the case. In fact, as Figure 9–1 suggests the black community now has an elaborate class structure.[37] But the image of the black that most white Americans hold is suggested by Levison, as follows:

---

[35]Sar A. Levitan, William B. Johnston, Robert Taggart, *Still a Dream: The Changing Status of Blacks Since 1960.* pp. 76, 78. © 1975 by the President and Fellows of Harvard College. Reprinted by permission of the publisher.
[36]*Ibid.,* p. 198.
[37]James E. Blackwell, *The Black Community: Diversity and Unity* (New York: Harper & Row, Publishers, formerly published by Dodd, Mead & Co., 1975), p. 74.

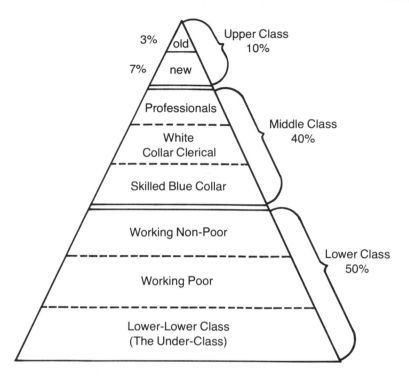

(Solid lines denote relatively stable divisions between classes whereas broken lines indicate that demarcations between substrata are often blurred.)

Figure 9-1   The Social Structure of the Black Community

NOTE: The above figure is taken from James E. Blackwell, *The Black Community: Diversity and Unity* (New York: Harper & Row, 1975), p. 74, Figure 3-1. Copyright © 1975 by Harper & Row, Publishers, Inc. Reprinted by permission of the publisher. The lowerclass section of this pyramid is based on the model presented by Andrew Billingsley, *Black Families in White America*, Copyright © 1968 by Prentice-Hall, Inc., Englewood Cliffs, N.J.

. . . [T]he undeniable injustices of unemployment and welfare have often led to a visual image of the black community as entirely composed of unemployed ghetto youths and welfare mothers. This, along with the social crises of bad housing and medical facilities, narcotics, and crime results in a liberal vision of the black community as some unique "underclass" or "culture of poverty."[38]

A full-chapter discussion of the social structure of the Black Community is provided by Blackwell, including Figure 9–1. An abbreviated adaptation of this characterization of these classes follows.[39]

---

[38]Andrew Levison, *The Working-Class Majority* (New York: Coward, McCann & Geoghegan, Inc., 1974), pp. 44–45. Copyright © 1974 Andrew Levison. Reprinted by permission of the publisher.
[39]James E. Blackwell, *The Black Community: Diversity and Unity*, pp. 75–92.

Upper Class.   The old upper class are descendents of upper-class parents, well-to-do (enough to maintain the style of the elite), socially reject the new upper class, conventional, proper, but not ostentatious.

The new upper class have risen high on the income scale, and are often richer than the old upper class. Many are entertainers and athletes. Ostentatious, flashy dress, lavish parties, yet they feel insecure. This group also includes more stable people born into the middle class who were usually successful in their profession

Middle Class Professional.   Have most stable marriages, few children, conventional life style. Are highly educated, but their occupation and income are inadequate for upper class.

White collar.   Clerical and kindred workers whose life style is similar to middle class in general.

Blue collar.   Skilled workers with steady employment. While not very well educated, aspire to higher education for their children. Income provides living but not much saving, stress family stability.[40]

Lower Class Working Non-poor.   Semiskilled, steadily employed and industrial workers. Also include more poorly paid craftsmen and mechanics, not unionized because of exclusionary practices. Wives usually work. Group is prone to join black activists, and some become Black Muslims.

Working poor.   Borderline poverty, unskilled occupations include farm laborers, janitors, domestics. Disenchanted, alienated Americans. Day-to-day existence. This is the largest single subgroup in the black stratification system.

Lower-lower (or underclass) poor.   Earn less than $3,000, a year (in the 1960s), have little education, work at odd jobs, waitresses. Have evolved a unique culture adjustment to status as non-person. The segment consitutes the bulk of black welfare recipients. Most single parent, female-headed families are in this class.

Subterranean.   This group has been little studied.[41] These are blacks participating in the illegitimate system who are distinguished at all class levels, the counterpart of the white illegitimate class system. Theoretically, operating underground, they have some control, but not as much as whites, over organized vice and often receive police protection. Range from big-time vice-lords to bookies, pimps, call girls, and finally down-and-out junkies and prostitutes.

Perusal of the preceding classification should dispel many myths about the American black population. The image that many whites hold of black persons is that of the roughly 20 percent of the lower class and possibly the subterraneans. Clearly the substantial percentage of blacks comprising the middle and upper class is not a problem to the white community, even though the white community may cause humiliating frustration for *all* blacks (except occasional black individuals) by their discriminatory attitude and practices toward them.

Housing

During the 1960–1970 decade, the housing of blacks improved, but at a lesser rate than that of whites. The percentage of black households classified as substandard

---

[40]Earlier white class divisions usually included this skilled blue-collar group as the top of the lower class even though their incomes frequently exceed the lower white-collar middle. Their inclusion in the black middle class may account for the 50 percent above the lower class.

[41]See Frances A. J. Ianni, *Black Mafia Ethnic Succession in Organized Crime* (New York: Simon and Schuster, 1974).

declined; the number of rooms per person increased; and black homes were better equipped. But in regard to all of these absolute gains, the relative gains of whites were greater. Black ownership of homes also gained, but only slightly relative to white home ownership.[42]

Government efforts to provide multiple-unit housing for the poor have not worked out well. Planned as open housing, these units generally became all black tenanted. While or when low-income housing was inhabited by a majority of whites, it was better equipped and maintained than when blacks were the majority. Some low-income housing had been deliberately planned in white areas to encourage integration. But some of these projects, called "scatter-site" housing, have been either abandoned or reduced in size because of the strong resistance of whites living in the neighborhoods chosen, as in Forest Hills, Queens, New York. In the latter case, after confrontations for a considerable period of time between city officials and residents of the areas, the matter was settled by reducing the original number planned for the project by almost 50 percent.[43]

The summary statement of the serious inadequacy of black housing by Levitan *et al.* reads as follows:

> A fourth of all blacks still live in homes which are severely deteriorated or lack adequate plumbing. A fifth contain more than one person per room. Blacks at all income levels are less likely to own their homes; when they do, the value is much lower and probably less secure than for homes owned by whites. Black homes are older and have fewer amenities on the average, yet they may cost more than those occupied by whites. Worst of all, blacks do not have equal opportunity to choose where and how they want to live.[44]

Housing Discrimination. While polls through the 1960s show that a majority of Northern whites say they would not object to blacks as neighbors, there are many indications that when faced with the actual situation, most whites do not behave accordingly. Through the 1960s little change occurred in breaking down racial residential segregation of blacks.[45] Much of the concentration of ghetto blacks in less desirable housing occurred because of their low income and because few whites sought such areas. Attempts by public housing authorities to furnish new housing, or to subsidize in part private business outside the black areas—"scatter-site housing"—met with strong resistance because according to federal law, such housing must be "open housing" (racially).[46]

White Beliefs: Myth or Fact. What are the main reasons—beliefs, fears, rationalizations—given by white people for rejecting blacks as neighbors?

---

[42]Sar A. Levitan, William B. Johnston, Robert Taggart, *Still a Dream: The Changing Status of Blacks Since 1960,* p. 161. Reprinted by permission of the publisher.
[43]See Blackwell, *The Black Community: Diversity and Unity,* Ch. 5, "The Ghettoization of Blacks," for fuller discussion.
[44]Levitan *et al., Still a Dream: The Changing Status of Blacks Since 1960,* p. 161.
[45]"Crisis of Color, '66," *Newsweek,* Aug. 22, 1966, p. 28.
[46]A recent attempt by New York City to locate a high-rise apartment complex on a "run down" section of otherwise high-class Forest Hills was a continuing source of local community dispute in 1971 and 1972.

(1) *Deteriorating Property Values*   The belief is widespread that entrance of blacks into an area inevitably causes property values to decline.

(2) *Black "Bad" Housekeeping and Disorderly Behavior*   These two closely related beliefs held by whites are part of the long-held stereotype of blacks as inferior people. Whites who hold these beliefs fear deterioration of the physical appearance and moral climate of their neighborhood.

(3) *Interracial Conflict*   Whites express the fear that there will be interracial conflict in which their own safety will be endangered.

(4) *Fear of Inundation*   It is commonly believed that once any black family moves into their block, others will follow and the neighborhood will become all black. As we shall see, it is this belief that stands as the last barrier to developing racially mixed residential areas.

(5) *Fear of Loss of Status*   A revealing illustration of this feeling is seen in this incident:

> A white woman, commenting on a Negro family's purchase of a house a few doors away, observed that it was a "fine" family, the husband was a surgeon, and she had no personal objection to them whatever. But, she added, people driving by see the little boy playing on the sidewalk. "How are they to know he is a doctor's son?"[47]

From various studies of race and housing during the 1960s the following conclusions emerged: (1) Where whites do not move out en masse, there is often little effect on property values, aside from those that might have taken place because of the changing situation of the area as a whole. (2) It is after the area begins to reach a point of all-black occupancy that the less desirable consequences of overcrowding and downgrading of the area begin to set in. The first blacks to take advantage of a vacancy in the white area tend to be similar in income, education, habits, and manners to their white neighbors. (3) Interracial conflict is more frequent on the borders of black-white areas and at the beginning of the entrance of blacks in new neighborhoods.[48]

While there are numerous other variables affecting minority housing, Glazer and McEntire state that it is likely that color alone plays a dynamic role in the situation.[49]

Methods of Segregating Blacks in Housing.   The direct process by which blacks were kept from moving into white areas involved the real estate and financial businesses. Some realtors would not handle such a transaction, or there was the reverse phenomenon, "block busting": when one or two Negro families managed to move into a white neighborhood, realtors were known to have encouraged whites to sell and move quickly before the "inevitable decline in property values" began, and from then on they showed the properties for sale to Negroes only. For realtors this was a highly profitable business.[50]

---

[47]*Report of the Commission on Race and Housing*, p. 18.

[48]See these studies all published by the University of California Press (Berkeley and Los Angeles), Nathan Glazer and Davis McEntire, *Studies in Housing and Minority Groups*, 1959; Davis McEntire, *Residence and Race*, 1960; and Luigi Laurenti, *Property Values and Race*, 1960.

[49]Glazer and McEntire, *Studies in Housing and Minority Groups*, p. 10.

[50]See George and Eunice Grier, *Equality and Beyond: Housing Segregation and the Goals of the Great Society* (Chicago: Quadrangle Books, 1966), pp. 34–35.

In general, mortgage-lending institutions were unwilling for a long time to finance black home purchasing, and even as increasing legal pressures were brought to bear, still showed considerable reluctance.[51]

Even those whites who claim to be willing to live in an integrated neighborhood do not mean one that is largely black. The crucial point in planning mixed racial areas is to avoid the "tipping" point, which should be well below 50 percent black. Since to set "quotas" is now illegal, "benign quotas" must be voluntary. Often black residents themselves try to discourage further black purchases in the area.[52]

The Extent of Black-White "Neighborhoods". For the first time, a systematic study of "neighborhoods" including both blacks and whites was completed, in 1974.[53] The general conclusion of this study is as follows:

> Thus, 81 percent of the nation's households remain in segregated neighborhoods, while roughly 10 percent are in integrated neighborhoods where Negroes represent only 3 percent or less of the neighborhood population. To put it another way, *only 4 percent of the households in the United States are located in integrated neighborhoods that are more than 10 percent Negro.*
>
> It is probable that a substantial number of white residents in the integrated neighborhoods we studied, because they are in the overwhelming majority, have no social or community-based contact with the few Negroes who live in their neighborhoods. It is even possible that most white residents in some of our integrated neighborhoods are unaware of the presence of any Negroes.[54]

We added the italics in the above summary to emphasize that as of 1967 the "tipping point" following which resegregation may be expected is indeed quite low. The report is based in fact on "mixed" neighborhoods in which there is apparent movement of some families of both races into the area, thus eliminating neighborhoods where black resegregation is on the way.

Future Prospects. The Bradburn team made the following prediction as to the future:

> The proportion of Negro households in open and moderately integrated neighborhoods will rise slowly with little fuss being made. In northern and western substantially integrated neighborhoods, there will be a more rapid increase in the Negro population, but some of these neighborhoods will become resegregated. More white segregated neighborhoods will get their first Negro families, and in most cases there will be no major reactions. Where there are strong reactions, the neighborhood will probably become a

[51]*Ibid.*, p. 34–35.
[52]Dan W. Dodson, "Can Intergroup Quotas Be Benign?" *Journal of Intergroup Relations,* Autumn, 1960. Reprinted in Earl Raab, *American Race Relations Today* (Garden City, N.Y.: Doubleday & Co., 1962), pp. 125–134.
[53]Norman Bradburn, Seymour Sudman, and Galen L. Gockel with the assistance of Joseph R. Noel, *Side by Side: Integrated Neighborhoods in America* (Chicago: Quadrangle Book Co., 1971). Copyright © 1971 by Norman M. Bradburn, Seymour Sudman, and Galen L. Gockel. Based on a national opinion research monograph, *Racial Integration in American Neighborhoods: A Comparative Survey* (NORC Report No. 111-B). The data were acquired in 1967.
[54]*Side by Side.* p. 62. Italics ours. By permission of Quadrangle/The New York Times Book Co.

changing or Negro segregated one. Most white segregated neighborhoods, however, will remain segregated for the foreseeable future.[55]

In interpreting their prediction of a quite modest increase in *mixed neighborhoods,* it should be clearly understood that this term refers solely to the fact that a few black *households* are found there. The accounts that are provided in their in-depth study of six communities out of their sample show that the first black entrants met with serious opposition, and that after the area settled down to stable integration (of less than 5 percent black), the blacks were treated with indifference or cooly and in no sense socially integrated. From their admittedly (and now regretted) limited probing of black respondents the authors can only predict without the important variable of what blacks themselves are likely to do. Such limited information as they acquired indicated that blacks who moved into white neighborhoods did so in order to have a more desirable place to live, not to "mix with whites."[56]

Education

Blacks made significant gains in education, at least quantitatively. Among the data pertinent to black educational progress are the following: The proportion of black high-school graduates, aged between 25 and 29, leaped from two-fifths in 1960 to two-thirds in 1972. The median years of black education rose from 8.2 in 1960 to 10.3 in 1972. The dropout rate for blacks in the 19- to 24-year range declined from 22.8 in 1967 to 17.5 in 1972. Enrollment of blacks in college increased between 1960 and 1973 by 540,000, a gain of 370 percent. The gap between black and whites attending college was closing, with the ratio of blacks to whites over the same period changing from 1 in 20 to 1 in 12.[57]

Despite quantitative gains in black exposure to education it is more difficult to evaluate the quality of education achieved. Black schools have generally been inferior, as was reflected by the lower extent of achievement of black students at various age levels. The U.S. Bureau of the Census reports that by age 17, more than half of black males are behind their modal class, and 30 percent are back two grades or more. Much depends on the extent of desegregation and on the capacity of school integration to improve the educational achievement of blacks.[58]

Northern Schools and Desegregation.   The Supreme Court school decision had less immediate impact on the North because with some few exceptions segregated schooling for blacks as an *official* policy had been abandoned wherever it existed. Nevertheless, the decision prompted review of school districting and assignment practices. Since there was much *de facto* school segregation arising out of housing segregation, many smaller Northern communities made changes in pupil assignments to correct "racial imbalance." However, many local school boards gerrymandered district school lines to promote segregation. From time to time as such cases were taken to court, school boards involved were usually ordered to redraw the lines to provide more desegregation. Some of these changes required busing some students of both races out of their neigh-

---

[55]*Ibid.,* p. 192. By permission of Quadrangle/New York Times Book Co.
[56]*Ibid.,* Ch. 2, "Neighborhood Profiles."
[57]Levitan *et al., Still a Dream: The Changing Status of Blacks Since 1960,* pp. 79–84.
[58]*Ibid.,* p. 85.

borhoods, with considerable opposition from parents of both races, as in the widely publicized South Boston controversy.

The growth of the central-city black population in large metropolitan areas reached a
point where efforts were made to allow the busing of black students to adjoining
suburbs. A further problem arose when some smaller communities that had been sending their high-school students, mostly white, to adjoining larger communities, began to
withdraw their students from these schools as they became increasingly black.[59] The
issue of busing became increasingly a political issue in many areas, and was raised to
the national level when in 1972 President Nixon called for a moratorium on further busing, at least for the time being.

From the viewpoint of social policy, the main objective of school desegregation was
to provide equal educational opportunity for blacks. The tentative conclusion of social
science is that for blacks to attend a predominantly white middle-class school improves
their educational achievement through the more ambitious learning climate set by the
white students.[60] For the beneficial effect to be maintained, the black ratio should be
relatively small. Black students in classrooms less than half white achieve no more than
those in all black classrooms.[61]

Another value of desegregation, depending on one's philosophy, is the opportunity
for blacks and whites to interact as peers. Yet there are many indications that while
blacks and whites may enter the school through the same door and attend mixed
classes, in most of the informal aspects of school life the races stay apart. Sports are an
exception. But in the more socially related aspects, not only separation but also discrimination is found.

> When the black students at Plains High School attend a basketball game,
> the contrast they experience as they watch five black athletes on the court
> while seven white girls lead the cheering on the side lines, is a constant
> reminder of white prejudice and white exploitation.[62]

Discrimination in Law Enforcement and Justice

In the American society, it has long been clear that law and justice have been differentially enforced and administered with some degree of inequality related to class
status and power. This was systematically documented by Edwin H. Sutherland in
White Collar Crime thirty years ago. This being true with respect to class, it is bound to
be the case with reference to minorities who lack power. In the South we have seen that
it was openly institutionalized. Outside that region it simply became recognized
practice, focused more around police action than in the courts.

---

[59]In 1972 the U.S. Supreme Court denied a Virginia community the right to remove their students
from the consolidated school.
[60]J. S. Coleman *et al., Equality of Educational Opportunity* (Washington, D.C., U.S. Government,
1967). Actually Coleman concludes that for lower-class students, irrespective of race, to attend
schools where middle-class students set the academic climate is beneficial, but it is even more so
for blacks.
[61]Thomas Pettigrew, *Racially Separate or Together* (New York: McGraw-Hill Book Co., 1971),
p. 63.
[62]Frank A. Petroni and Ernest A. Hirsch, with C. Lillian Petroni, *Two, Four, Six, Eight, When You
Gonna Integrate?* (New York: Behavioral Publications, 1971), p. 252.

Given the total situation in black-white relations it is inevitable that the police will to some extent discriminate against blacks. This total situation includes these factors: (1) White people discriminate against blacks generally. (2) While in democratic theory the administration of justice is equal, in practice it is differentially administered with some degree of inequality related to status. This being generally true even in regard to class status, it is even more bound to be the case where dominant-minority status prevails. Dominant-status people are not apt to be deeply concerned about discriminatory police treatment of minority people, and police practice reflects in the long run the attitudes of the dominants. (3) Generally, white police not only share white prejudice but are, because of recruitment from lower-ranking status levels, apt to be drawn from the segments of the white population where the salience of white prejudice is highest. (4) Black policemen, as blacks, are less secure and under pressure to conform to white police practice.[63]

The black slum dweller's image of the policeman is not that of a protector but of a punisher. Representing white law in which most blacks have experienced or witnessed discrimination, the policeman is viewed with hostility. The police and blacks hold reciprocal hostile images of each other: the police look upon the black masses as inclined to be lawbreakers; the black masses view white police as prejudiced. Thus it is inevitable that mutual distrust will continue to exist as long as the white community generally treats blacks as a minority.

The foregoing can stand without special reference to the Black Challenge. But the revolt has given it increasing significance for at least two reasons. The revolt inevitably heightens the salience of the conflict and the increasing polarization of white versus black as "enemies." It is not too difficult to understand that many blacks in such a conflict situation view *any* arrest of a black as a discriminatory act even when the arrest is obviously valid. Furthermore, the revolt situation increases the occasion for police-black conflict. Both from a strictly legal view and from a police administrative view the boundary line between a legally proper "protest" activity and an illegal one is not always easy to draw. To this may be added the tendency of court interpretations to be currently more fluid and unpredictable, which adds to the perplexity of police authorities.

The continuation of police and military brutality is still widely alleged by black people, particularly the more militant black groups, with varying degrees of factual support. There are, however, many communities where special efforts have been made to train policemen to deal with individual black persons with more understanding and to act with more restraint in dealing with black protests and confrontations. Also juries, even when all-white, have shown a tendency to acquit black defendants when their guilt is not established. In this process of change, the failure of the social control system to be completely just and fair is understandable, although not forgiveable. Cases of serious and tragic miscarriage of justice against blacks in the South have continued to occur up to at least 1977, especially in small communities, as attested by the Poverty Law Center, Atlanta, Georgia.[64]

---

[63]See Nicholas Alex, *Black in Blue: A Study of the Negro Policeman* (New York: Appleton-Century-Crofts, 1969). Also Robert F. Wintersmith, *Police and the Black Community* (Lexington, Mass.: Lexington Books, 1974).

[64]It is not overlooked by blacks that the killing of white students by national guardsmen at Kent State in 1972 evoked more unfavorable public criticism than did the killings of black students by White Militia at Jackson State in the same year.

Integration in Government and in the Armed Services

Government at both the federal and local levels has been a major factor in attempting to improve the economic welfare of ghetto blacks and in fostering integration in employment for all blacks, some in high status positions. While at first this started by appointing to many government agencies a black liaison officer between the agency and the black community, it began to go beyond this. For example, Thurgood Marshall was named to the United States Supreme Court by President Lyndon Johnson. The concentration of blacks in metropolitan areas accounted for there being twelve black Congressmen in 1972. Edward Brooke's election as Senator from Massachusetts could not have occurred without substantial white votes.

The Armed Services.   The order of President Harry Truman in 1948 to integrate the Armed Services was completed well before the Vietnam fighting. This integration was ordered against the advice of most military authorities and against the wishes of a majority of white soldiers. Experience has shown its functional value from the viewpoint of military efficiency.

Integration in the armed services has also had significant consequences in the interracial field. The earlier opposition of white soldiers to military integration showed a marked drop between 1943 and 1951.[65] It is most interesting that attitudes of white soldiers in mixed units consistently reveal more approval of desegregation than white troops in all-white units. "Yet the fact remains that the general pattern of day-to-day relationships *off the job* is usually one of mutual racial exclusiveness."[66] Comradeship in the "foxhole" did not carry over when white soldiers returned to civilian life.

The attitudes of blacks in the armed services was mixed, but in general it was favorable. Blacks were drafted proportionately in excess of whites, probably due to the greater legitimate reasons for deferment on the part of white young men. On the other hand, the reenlistment rate of blacks was high. Obviously, the military offers the blacks a secure job; their first experience of equal association with whites; and in cases of promotions provide the experience of "commanding" whites. In Vietnam a larger proportion of blacks were in combat units.[67] Moskos considers it "probable that military experience contributes to an activist posture on the part of Negro servicemen returning to civilian life."[68] He also finds it more than coincidence that the founders of the Deacons for Defense, a paramilitary group organized in 1964 to counter Ku Klux Klan terrorism, were all veterans of Korea or World War II. While there have been numerous incidences of physical conflict between black and white troops off-duty, in this respect they mirror the currently normative situation between young black and young white males since the onset of the Black Challenge to dominance.

The shift to an all-volunteer, professional military force has had somewhat favorable economic benefits for blacks in general, but only slight improvement in race relations as against these relations in civil life. Census data indicate 298,000 black men and women in the armed forces in June, 1974, about the same number as in 1970, even though the total armed forces had declined during this period. Thus blacks comprised a large pro-

---

[65]Samuel A. Stouffer *et al.*, "The Negro Soldier" in *The American Soldier,* (Princeton: Princeton University Press, 1949), p. 586.
[66]Charles C. Moskos, Jr., "Racial Integration in the Armed Services," *American Journal of Sociology,* 72, Sept., 1966. The entire article covers pp. 132–148.
[67]Some black leaders view this as a part of a subtle genocidal effort on the part of whites.
[68]Moskos, p. 146.

portion of the military personnel—14 percent in 1974 as compared with 10 percent in 1970.[69] We shall discuss this further in our next chapter.

Suggested Readings

Blackwell, James E. *The Black Community: Diversity and Unity*. New York: Harper & Row, 1975.
    A thorough generalized description of the black community of the '70s. Viewed as a diverse group of people within a wide range of social classes, life styles, and attitudes, its unity arises in response to the racism of the larger community.
Gould, William B. *Black Workers in White Unions: Job Discrimination in the United States*. Ithaca, N.Y.: Cornell University Press, 1976.
    A full-length historical treatment of the topic from the beginning to the mid-'70s.
Ianni, Francis A. J. *Black Mafia: Ethnic Succession in Organized Crime*. New York: Simon and Schuster, 1974.
    Discusses the beginnings of organized crime among some blacks as a possible succession to earlier ethnic groups in organized crime syndicates.
Ladner, Joyce. *Tomorrow's Tomorrow: The Black Woman*. Garden City, N.Y.: Doubleday & Co., Anchor Books, 1972.
    Finds the black woman in general and her family made healthy adjustments despite adverse conditions and white discrimination.
Levitan, Sar A.; Johnson, William B.; and Taggart, Robert. *Still A Dream: The Changing Status of Blacks Since 1960*. Cambridge, Mass.: Harvard University Press, 1975.
    Presents a wealth of data on the favorable changes in material welfare, education, occupations, and income from 1960 to early the 1970s, but finds the overall gap between blacks and whites still far from closed.
Mack, Raymond, ed. *The Changing South*. New Brunswick, N.J.: Transaction Books, 1970.
    Assessment of South's response to the Civil Rights legislation finds favorable economic change for blacks but little change in political and legal structures.
Mitchell, George. *I'm Somebody Important: Young Black Voices from Rural Georgia*. Urbana: University of Illinois Press, 1973.
    The life stories of six teen-aged blacks living in rural Georgia as told to the author in many interviews for each child. A minimum of editing of the young people's own words.
Molotch, Harvey L. *Managed Integration: Dilemmas of Doing Good in the City*. Berkeley: University of California Press, 1972.
    The story of an attempt to develop a black-white community on the south shore of Chicago.
Nelson, Hart M., and Nelson, Anna Kusena. *Black Church in the Sixties*. Lexington: University of Kentucky Press, 1975.

[69] U.S. Census, *The Social and Economic Status of the Black Population,* 1974.

Study of thirty sets of data (1954–1969) leads authors to conclude the black church was an instrument of protest and change, debunking the theory of it as an opiate for frustrations.

Report of the National Advisory Commission on Civil Disorders. New York: Bantam Books, 1968.
This edition includes a special introduction by Tom Wicker of *The New York Times*.

Rose, Peter I.; Rothman, Stanley; and Wilson, William J., eds. *Through Different Eyes: Black and White Perspectives on American Race Relations*. London: Oxford University Press, 1973.
Twenty different writers, about half black and half white, express their perspectives on a wide number of different sectors of society regarding black-white relations.

Rosengarten, Theodore. *All God's Dangers: The Life of Nate Shaw*. New York: Alfred A. Knopf, 1974.
Taped life story of an Alabaman sharecropper from 1885 to 1970, illustrative of the black man in Southern agriculture.

10

The Black Challenge

The Black Challenge to white domination as a sustained movement began following World War II. The movement was a large mixture of individual and collective black actions. Some were unorganized, sporadic and spontaneous; some planned and organized. It was highly diffuse with no centralized command; and the various challenging entities differed as to the exact definition of the goal, and correlatively, differed as to the methods to be pursued. Perhaps one may say that the unifying theme was the subjective mood of nearly all black Americans as expressed by the oft-repeated "We shall overcome" and "Black Power."

THE THRUST FOR CHANGE

Civil Rights Legislation

The first thrust was to strike at the most vulnerable point in white American racism—the inconsistency between its written constitution, particularly in the Bill of Rights, and the flagrant failure to apply it to blacks. Beginning with the courts, followed considerably later by legislation in some states and by congressional action, one by one all forms of public discrimination were outlawed on paper, culminating in the outlawing of discrimination in housing in 1968.[1] But, as grossly illustrated in the South, court edicts and legislative acts are only effective to the degree that the administrative agencies enforce them. As indicated in the Southern resistance to school desegregation and other court decisions, effective administration at the local level and the reluctance of the federal government to bring pressure made blacks realize that other more aggressive action was needed.

Protests and Demonstrations

Nonviolent Resistance. The first forms of confrontation were protest and demonstrations using passive resistance as in the Montgomery bus boycott, the sit-ins, Freedom Riders, and James Meredith's March in Mississippi. This phase grew out of the influence of Dr. Martin Luther King, Jr.'s philosophy. The first step away from this technique was deliberate civil disobedience as illustrated by Dr. King's defying a court order in Birmingham which resulted in his arrest and the repression by white officials

[1]Law H.R. 2516, PL 90-2-84. See *Congressional Quarterly Almanac,* Vol. XXIV, 1968.

of protest activities. Dr. King's efforts to spread the nonviolent protest movement to wider areas were not successful and were tragically terminated in Memphis by his assassination. The organization that had grown out of Dr. King's Montgomery triumph, the Southern Christian Leadership Conference, continues and still represents the non-violent approach, but as an organization it now has less influence. Its leaders, Dr. Ralph Abernathy and Coretta S. King, still have considerable personal influence in the 1970s.[2]

Two other organizations using nonviolent techniques were The Congress of Racial Equality (CORE) and The Student Non-Violent Coordinating Committee (SNCC).

The Congress of Racial Equality. CORE antedates the Negro Revolt, having been founded in 1942 in Chicago by people who felt that direct action and demonstrations were needed to supplement the previous sorts of challenge to white dominance. It used the "sit-in" technique in a Chicago restaurant in 1943 and in Palisades Amusement Park, New Jersey, in 1947–1948, successfully effecting desegregation. But it was not until the Negro Revolt began in earnest that CORE became a major civil rights organi-zation. We have previously cited its Freedom Riders action in the South; the organiza-tion has continued direct action. CORE was not always able to control its more militant chapters, as in the case of the somewhat unsuccessful "stall-in" to keep people from the New York World's Fair in April, 1964.[3] It was the most interracial in membership but changed to all black during the "black power" phase. Currently CORE focuses on cooperation with the Third World movement.

The Student Non-violent Coordinating Committee. SNCC, or "Snick," as it is often referred to, was organized in 1960 to coordinate the activities of numerous college student groups of both races on behalf of civil rights. Its direct action protests, sit-ins, and demonstrations were successful in desegregating hundreds of segregated facilities in Southern cities.[4] SNCC carried on more sustained activities of education and voter registration. It identified more successfully with the rank and file of Southern Negroes than the other organizations. Many of its members, white and black, were jailed.

As we pass to a new mood in the Black Movement, assessment of passive resistance is in order. In the past at particular times and places, it had considerable value. Any more militant technique used prior to the 1960s in the South would have been severely repressed, as the suppression of a Birmingham riot showed. But passive resistance is more effective when the minority, as in India, is overwhelming in numbers. When used by small groups, it requires special training to keep the protestors nonviolent against official rough handling. Furthermore, such a technique runs counter to American culture, in which aggressive individual and collective competition to get ahead with the least interference of the state to limit this competitive drive has been a dominant theme. American history is replete with instances where conflict arising from the pursuit of this cultural norm has transcended the legal rules of the game, from the lawless frontier through strife in labor's struggle to unionize, and in other sporadic uprisings.[5]

[2]Both were listed among the 100 most influential black Americans by *Ebony.* See Issue of May, 1972, pp. 77–84.
[3]Kenneth Clark, *The Negro American* (Boston: Houghton Mifflin Co., 1966), p. 609.
[4]C. Eric Lincoln, "The American Protest Movement for Negro Rights," in *The American Negro Reference Book* (Englewood Cliffs, N.J.: Prentice-Hall, 1966), p. 42.
[5]See Ovid Demarius, *America the Violent* (New York: Cowles Book Co., 1970), for an account of violence in American history.

A highly dramatic event, the March on Washington, took place on August 28, 1963. Initiated by A. Philip Randolph and organized by Bayard Rustin, some 250,000 Americans held a day-long protest before the Lincoln Memorial, perhaps the largest single demonstration in the nation's history, highlighted by the immortal speech by Dr. Martin Luther King, Jr., "I have a dream." All black organizations, aside from the separatist groups, were represented, as well as whites in interracial groups and other white sympathizers. Despite the fears of many Washingtonians, the occasion was extremely orderly. The March was a symbolic culmination and zenith of Dr. King's phase of brotherhood.

The following years the failure of the Freedom Democratic Party to get their Mississippi delegation seated at the Democratic Convention in Chicago caused many blacks to turn away from the possibility of working through the system. This event may mark the turning point away from the integration movement through peaceful means toward a more militant stance.

Unorganized Violence

Given the ghetto conditions, the changing mood of black Americans, and the sharper polarization of the black-white relations as a conflict situation, it would be expected that increasing interracial violence would occur. Vandalism and robbery, accompanied often by physical violence on the part of ghetto youth, became a normal aspect of inner-city life. Interracial conflict was also quite common between young male groups of both races in situations where they met, for example, in integrated schools or in public recreational areas. While such violent episodes were not part of the organized black action, they heightened the tension in race relations and increased white backlash.

Riots. The most destructive and publicized form of unorganized violence was rioting within the ghettos themselves. Riots with interracial implications were no new phenomenon. Grimshaw identified thirty-three major interracial disturbances in the United States between 1900–1949.[6] But the '60s witnessed an unparalleled number of riots with a substantial number of deaths and injuries, and enormous property losses. From 1964 to midsummer of 1967 there were fifty-eight cities in which large-scale rioting occurred in ghettos. There were 141 people killed, close to 5,000 reported injured, and vast property damage.[7]

The Kerner Commission report on "Civil Disorders" (a conservative term for riots) found the basic cause of rioting in racism. But the riots occurred in so many different types of situations that no generalized riot pattern could be seen. The House Commission on Civil Disorders made note of disadvantaged conditions, intensive pervasive grievances, and a series of tension-heightening conditions, all culminating in the eruption of disorders at the hands of youthful, politically aware activists.[8]

In general, the riots were unpremeditated, set off by some specific incident, such as an arrest of a black, the assassination of Martin Luther King, Jr., or the suggestive in-

[6]Allen D. Grimshaw, "A Study in Violence" (Doctoral Dissertation, University of Pennsylvania, 1959), pp. 178–180. For a fuller treatment and analysis, see Grimshaw, *Racial Violence in the United States* (Chicago: Aldine Publishing Co., 1969).
[7]See *Time*, August 11, 1967, p. 11.
[8]*Report of the National Advisory Commission on Civil Disorders*, New York Times ed., 1968, p. 10.

fluence of watching rioting in other cities on television programs.[9] But since the Cleveland shoot-out in 1968, "many observers have suggested that civil disorders are beginning to take a new form, characterized by some degree of planning, organization, and leadership." One new form, it was alleged, was the planned and organized sniping at police.[10] The riots did not involve confrontation with other whites, except the police, although white-owned property was vandalized; they did not occur in the most disadvantaged black communities, or in the most depressed areas. The participants were a cross section of the ghetto areas, except that they tended to be young and male, not the most disorderly persons in the communities.[11]

As a result, riots were followed in many cases by some improvements in ghetto conditions by city governments; better training of police in dealing with blacks; and the granting of permanent status to the U.S. Civil Rights Commission. It is of interest to note that, in general, mass rioting has not often been repeated in the same cities, reflecting a feeling that more of the same would not serve a useful purpose. In a negative sense, riots increased black-white polarization and stimulated white backlash among some elements of the white population. Overlapping with the Civil Rights achievements and the rioting, different practices and conflicting goals were developing within the movement.

Relative Deprivation

The Black Challenge of the nature just described took most Americans by surprise. As we saw in Chapter 9, black Americans as a group made substantial gains in civil rights and moderate gains in welfare—income, health, and education—although the gap between black and white had not been closed. In the 1950s and 1960s blacks mounted a challenge to their position with varying degrees of aggressive action. Aside from the continuous frustrations at their normative caste position with its constant prejudice and discrimination, an explanation of this situation is provided by a sociological proposition set forth some thirty years ago:

> Militancy, except for sporadic and short-lived uprising, is not characteristic of the most deprived and oppressed groups, but rather of those who have gained considerable rights so that they are able realistically to hope for more.
>   A militant reaction from a minority group is most likely when (a) the group's position is rapidly improving, or (b) when it is rapidly deteriorating, especially if this follows a period of improvement.[12]

[9]Seymour Spilerman, "Structural Characteristics of Cities and the Severity of Racial Disorders," *American Sociological Review,* 41,5, Oct., 1976, pp. 771–793.
[10]Terry Ann Knopf, "Sniping . . . A New Pattern of Violence?" in Peter H. Rossi, ed., *Ghetto Revolts,* 2nd ed., (New Brunswick, N.J.: Transaction Books, 1973), pp. 153–174.
[11]See Peter H. Rossi, ed., *Ghetto Revolts,* pp. 1–20, for a description of particular riots and analyses of ghetto revolts in general. Also see Gary T. Marx, "Two Cheers for the National Riot Commission," in *Black America,* John F. Szwed, ed. (New York: Basic Books, 1970), pp. 78–96.
[12]Robin M. Williams, Jr., *The Reduction of Intergroup Tensions* (New York: Social Science Research Council, Bulletin 57, 1947), p. 61. By permission of the publisher.

These propositions have been amplified in later sociological theory by the concept "relative deprivation." This concept means that the person's sense of frustration is relative to the welfare and status of others about him. A further distinction was noted by Runciman between "egoist" and "fraternalistic" relative deprivation—that is, whether one compares his own personal situation with others belonging to his group or whether he compares the position of his group with others in the society. This distinction is especially pertinent to dominant-minority relations.[13] The individual black college graduate with a white-collar job may feel less deprived than his unemployed brother, but when he finds it impossible to locate a home in a neighborhood commensurate with his socioeconomic position, he becomes aware of the deprived position of his group. This distinction contributes to understanding why the Black Challenge, as with other popular uprisings, is not generally led by the most objectively deprived members of their group.[14]

Revolutionary Activists

It is axiomatic that among oppressed groups in the modern world some will reach the conclusion that their oppression will never be removed under the existing politicoeconomic system and that the solution of their problems lies in bringing about a new system. Several short-lived movements among blacks with this revolutionary orientation arose, such as the Revolutionary Action Movement (RAMS).[15]

A crucial dilemma among black revolutionaries was whether to work for a separate Black Revolution or to join forces with whites who also had a revolutionary orientation. Considering the numerical minority position of blacks, the former course seemed unlikely to make much headway.[16]

The Black Panthers. The Black Panther Party was organized in 1966 by Huey Newton and Bobby Seale.[17] Much of its activity was in the California region but it had a limited spread to other parts of the country. While the organization adopted a socialist orientation, looking on the black situation as a class problem as well as one of race, many of its demands were similar to those of the NAACP, but they were more militant in pressing for them. Starting as a black nationalist group, the party gradually allied itself with other oppressed peoples and their needs, in line with its Marxist ideological orientation. The Panthers disagreed generally with the black groups interested in the revitalization of Afro-American culture, although they were sympathetic with the student tendencies in this direction in the 1960s. The Panthers concerned themselves mostly with the needs of the more underprivileged segments of the black population—

[13]W. G. Runciman, *Relative Deprivation and Social Justice* (London: Routledge and Kegan Paul, 1966).
[14]See Thomas Pettigrew, *Racially Separate or Together* (New York: McGraw-Hill Book Co., 1967), Ch. 7, "Why Black Unrest in the 1960's," for extensive discussion of this topic.
[15]See "Revolutionary Nationalism," in John H. Bracey, Jr., August Meier, and Elliott Rudwick, eds., *Black Nationalism in America* (Indianapolis: The Bobbs-Merrill Co., 1970), pp. 504–556.
[16]See Lewis M. Killian, *The Negro Revolution: Possible or Impossible?* (New York: Random House, 1968), for an extensive treatment of the black revolutionary dilemma.
[17]Alphonso Pinkney, *Red, Black, and Green: Black Nationalism in the United States* (London: Cambridge University Press, 1976), Ch. 6, "Revolutionary Nationalism: The Black Panther Party and Other Groups," pp. 98–126. Much of our discussion of this movement is derived from this source.

poverty and its related consequences and legal justice—but acquired admiration from many middle-class blacks.

The militant activity together with its known revolutionary aims led to harsh repression by government agencies. "In its short history, the Black Panther party became one of the major targets of the repressive machinery of the American judicial system."[18] In pressing its demands, many confrontations occurred leading to violence between the police and Panthers in which dozens of Panthers were killed and thousands arrested on charges of "attempted murder" and "resisting arrest." Bobby Seale was arrested on a murder charge in New Haven, Connecticut, in 1969. After a long trial, the case was dismissed because of a deadlocked jury.

This severe repressive activity, together with internal division within the party itself, changed the activities of the Panthers. Of necessity it has subsequently maintained a low profile on militant activity but provided news in the *Intercommunal News Service* about the liberation struggles and revolutionary activity around the world.

In the 1970s the Black Panthers have continued the community service started during the active militant period, including free breakfast programs, health clinics, free clothing distribution, and they have opened one free shoe factory.[19] For the time being at least, the Panther Party is working within the legitimate political system through voter registration. Seale himself has subsequently run for mayor of Oakland, California, receiving a substantial vote but not winning.[20]

Separatists

By separatists is meant those black activists who have concluded that white Americans will never accept blacks as equals, and therefore see no hope but to try to maximize the degree of their separation from whites. The theme of separation has a long history among blacks in the United States.[21]

The Black Muslims. Among contemporary black activist organizations, the Black Muslims is the most clearly separatist of all black American organizations. While founded in Detroit in 1930, its continuity and development dates from 1934, when Elijah Muhammad (born in Georgia as Elijah Poole) became head. He remained its leader until his death in 1975. Being a highly secretive group, the size of the membership is not known. While in the mid-1970s it had some eighty temples located in cities with large black ghettos, its membership countrywide embraced only a small proportion of even the ghetto-residing blacks.

The movement began as a racial-religious sect. Its membership was recruited from the poorest and most disorganized elements of the black ghettos. They developed a strong personal discipline and devoted much time to the cause. The philosophy was completely racist, proclaiming the superiority of the black man over the white. It stereotyped the white race generally as devils, and believed that there was no such thing as a "good" white man. To Muslims, Christianity was anathema. To quote Elijah

[18]*Ibid.*, p. 108.
[19]*Ibid.*, p. 114.
[20]See Lewis M. Killian *The Impossible Revolution: Phase 2, Black Power and the American Dream* (New York: Random House, 1975).
[21]See Bracey, Meier, and Rudwick, eds., *Black Nationalism in America.*

Muhammad, "The white man have 'given you Jesus' while he has robbed you blind."[22] The movement itself was organized as a religion, "The Nation of Islam in the West," and carried on religious meetings and rituals resembling Mohammedanism, but it had no formal association with Islam.

The Muslim position on violence was ambivalent. On the one hand, its philosophy was based on total hatred of the white man. On the other hand, having to live in a white society, the members were enjoined to obey white laws and work diligently when employed by whites, and were commanded not to be aggressive toward whites unless attacked.[23] This ambivalence toward the use of violence may serve, as Lincoln observed, the function of "providing outlets, short of physical violence, for the aggressive feelings roused in its members" toward whites.[24] In their policy statement, the Muslims asked that some area in the United States be given over to them as a short of binational section of America.[25] More realistically, the movement became the wealthiest black organization by means of the tithing practice among its members and shrewdly investing its capital, making possible the operation of many small business enterprises, all black operated, with considerable success.

The Black Muslims remained aloof and, until recently, unrelated to the other black activist organizations. However, they provided continuity to the concept of Black Nationalism and in many particular parts of their program, such as the "Black Capitalism" effort, they maintained an activist orientation. Recently, the Muslims have cooperated with other separatist groups.

Wallace Muhammad, Elijah's son, succeeded him as leader and initiated changes. The name of the news weekly became the *Bilalian News* and perusal of its contents indicates much more news of activity by other black organizations, with less emphasis on the diabolical nature of all whites.[26]

The new leader relaxed some of the strict rules of personal conduct for members under his father's regime. Whether the movement is growing or not is not clear. The October 29, 1976, copy of *Bilalian News* lists some 125 local mosques widely spread throughout the United States in cities with substantial black population, including cities in the Southern states, and also including eight mosques in the Caribbean areas.

AIMS OF THE BLACK CHALLENGE

As we saw in Chapter 9, the postwar period was in a sense "ripe" for blacks to mount a sustained challenge. But, as will later be indicated, white America was not prepared for it. In a broad sense the ultimate aim of most black Americans was to achieve a position individually and/or collectively in which they would have *complete equality of op-*

---

[22]*Mr. Muhammad Speaks,* May 2, 1959. (A newspaper published by the movement.)
[23]The killing of a New York policeman who entered a mosque on police business in the summer of 1972 is illustrative. It has been a standing practice that all persons entering a mosque are routinely "frisked."
[24]C. Eric Lincoln, *The Black Muslims in America* (Boston: Beacon Press, 1961). See pp. 248–253 for a fuller discussion of the functions and dysfunctions of this movement for American society.
[25]See Elijah Muhammad, "What Do the Muslims Want?" in *Black Nationalism in America*, pp. 404–408.
[26]Malcolm X, an astute minister under Elijah Muhammad, broke with the Black Muslims over this point and founded a new organization, which ceased with his assassination in 1965.

portunity and *exactly the same freedom as all other Americans.*[27] The main differences among them focused around the integrationist-separatist axis. These may be labeled Integrationist Assimilation, Pluralistic Assimilation, and Separatism.

Integrationist Assimilation

In its purest form integration ultimately involves the complete assimilation of blacks into the entire social structure of American society—both at the primary and secondary institutional levels. In theory it would ultimately reach a point where former identification as Negroid would disappear. There would be no more black community. This is approximately what occurred, as we saw in Chapter 4, with the descendants of the European immigrants, especially those from northern countries. Discrimination would be impossible because NEgroid visibility would have no greater salience in such a society than Americans. In fact, however, such integration as has occurred among black Americans has been limited to specific public segments of American life, for example, in schools and in hotel accommodations.

Remaining closest to the idea of direct assimilation of blacks into main American society were the earlier established agencies. The NAACP, besides continuing its legal efforts to gain enforcement of laws, assisted in the political registration of blacks and in helping to get more blacks educated for law, much needed in the South. The Urban League, while Whitney Young was its director, carried out as one of its main projects the operation of a "job bank" for employers to use for filling new openings with qualified blacks. This project is credited with placing some 60,000 blacks in suitable positions in mostly white-controlled enterprises. The A. Philip Randolph Institute, directed by Bayard Rustin, focuses on black poverty as the central issue and works toward the integration of blacks in American unions. These organizations have made many pragmatic contributions to the direct integration of blacks into the mainstream of American society.

Pluralistic Assimilation: Ethnicity

Pluralistic assimilation, which has in recent years become known as ethnicity, or as Kilson considers it, neo-ethnicity, is defined as "the revitalization of weak collectivities (for example, Negro Americans) or the rehabilitation of dwindling ethnic cohesiveness (for example, Irish Catholics, Jews, Italians)."[28] In fact, it was black Americans who initiated the current flurry of neo-ethnicity in American social life among other ethnics, particularly those more discriminated against, ironically just at a time when the traditional pattern of ethnicity was attenuating.[29] Black Americans developed a new ethnicity because "the salient factor in Negro behavior is rather the historical refusal by white supremacists in American society to accord Negroes a quality of ethnic characterization comparable to that accorded white ethnic groups. The new ethnicity is then initially an effort to redress this inferior characterization."[30]

[27]See Whitney Young, *To Be Equal* (New York: McGraw-Hill Co., 1964.
[28]Martin Kilson, "Blacks and Neo-ethnicity in American Political Life," in Nathan Glazer and Patrick Moynihan, eds., *Ethnicity: Theory and Experience* (Cambridge, Mass.: Harvard University Press, 1976), p. 236.
[29]*Ibid.*, p. 236.
[30]*Ibid.*, p. 237.

Pluralism takes two forms, structural and/or cultural. Structural pluralism refers only to the organizational structure of the ethnic community. In practice, pluralistic groups usually manifest some of both of these forms but tend to stress one more than the other, as we shall see. But in any case, all pluralists agree that to achieve ethnic pluralistic status requires strengthening the sense of black unity, pride in their ethnic identity, and mobilizing their collective power to promote their chances for equality and an end to discrimination. Cultural pluralism implies that black people have values, a style of life, and an approach to the problems of existence distinct from that of white Americans. In practice, pluralistic groups usually manifest some of both of these forms but tend to stress one more than the other, as will be illustrated later.

Cultural Pluralism

There are a number of possibilities on which black American culture is, or may be, based: (1) on African cultural heritage; (2) on creative developments from 350 years of American white dominance; (3) or the development of a new subculture, possibly related to twentieth-century Pan Africanism.

The African Heritage.   The black American Pluralists have pressed for a more accurate teaching of the history of the Negro throughout time, including the great African civilizations of the past.[31] But from the sixteenth century on much of the history of Africa is tragic, including slave exportation and colonialism. Essentially what this fact of the great empires demonstrates is the myth of innate genetic superiority of Causasians, as we saw in Chapter 5. The pulverization of tribal heritages was so thorough under slavery that the continuity of American Negroes with African culture had been virtually lost. Thus, while it may develop some sense of race pride to recall the glorious empires, certainly any subculture of the American Negroes living in twentieth-century urban-industrial society is not to be based on adaptive survivals of either the empires or tribalism.

On the other hand, more recent research has indicated much evidence of African cultural survival through slavery, especially in the realm of the arts. Ivan Vansertima finds in the way many Afro-Americans speak the influence of the linguistic and mythological structures of Africa.[32] Hendricks writes that "the traditions of African art below the Sahara span several thousand years and are as relevant to the black American as European art, from classical Greece to Picasso, is to the white American."[33] Kinney states that "Rhythm is the most striking aspect of African music with drumming displaying it in its most complex form. African dance responds to this rhythm and makes visible its complexities."[34] Kinney maintains that the complexities have not necessarily diminished even in the United States, where the degree of hybridization is at its

---

[31]See Daniel Chou and Elliot Skinner, *A Glorious Age in Africa* (Garden City, N.Y.: Doubleday & Co., 1960), who state that "at the heights of their power, the great earlier kingdoms of West Africa, Ghana, Mali, and Senegal compared favorably with their contemporary counterparts in Europe and Asia." (p. 116)

[32]Ivan Vansertima, "African Linguistic and Mythological Structures in the New World," in *Black Life and Culture in the United States*, Rhoda L. Goldstein, ed. (New York: Thomas Y. Crowell, 1971), pp. 12–35.

[33]Geoffrey Hendricks, "African Art," in *Black Life and Culture in the United States*, pp. 36–48.

[34]Esi Sylvia Kinney, "Africanisms in Music and Dance of the Americans," in *Black Life and Culture in the United States*, pp. 51–52.

greatest. A number of African folksongs and stories transmitted orally through the generations have now been printed.[35]

The Unique Experience of Black Americans. The distinctive position of slaves produced a distinctive slave culture, as we saw in Chapter 6. This culture embodied different purposes. To survive, slaves showed considerable ingenuity in developing ways to cope with the dominant white requirements. "Black folk were forced into the position of a self-conscious outgroup; and out of the inevitable social isolation of such a status they had to create cultural, institutional and psychological patterns of coping and surviving."[36] Another contribution of the slave culture was to adapt elements of their original way of life into a new Afro-American culture as circumstances permitted. These were in the expressive area of life of which religion and music played a large part.[37]

A "New" Afro-American Black Culture. Another cultural pluralistic possibility is the development of a "new" black culture, much of which might be built in part from the preceding one. There is little likelihood of a distinctively black culture with reference to such public matters as economics and government. However, there is a greater chance for a distinctive black culture in other areas of life, as indicated by the concept "soul." During the '60's the term "soul" came into usage as a key word to denote black culture, particularly among the lower classes. Hannerz in studying the Washington, D.C., ghetto area indicates that soul is not easy to define. But in part he writes

> Black people are soul brothers and soul sisters. There is soul music and soul food, by black people, for black people. To have soul is to know and appreciate the ways of walking and talking by which white people only feel confounded and threatened, to have a feeling for soul food, the fashions, and the music, to know how to clap your hands correctly in church or at the rock-and-roll concert, to have the background understandings which make it possible to enjoy the jokes about the battle of the sexes. . . .[38]

In the 1960s among young black intellectuals, especially students and those preferring the name Afro-American for their race, such things as Afro hair styles, and learning Swahili were popular but appear to have declined. The most creative aspects of a new black culture are in the arts. Pinkney writes that "Within the last few years black theatre groups have emerged in cities and towns throughout the country."[39] A main objective of black artists is to equal, surpass, or repudiate white art. There is not much acknowledgment by blacks of the favorable attitudes manifested by many whites toward this creative movement in the black arts. In fact, many whites recognize that some of these black artistic creations have become part of the national culture, such as jazz and gospel music.

---

[35]Bessie Jones and Bess Lomax Hawes, *Step It Down: Games, Plays, Songs, from the Afro-American Heritage* (New York: Harper & Row, 1972).
[36]W. M. Phillips, Jr., "Survival Techniques of Black Americans," in *Black Life and Culture in the United States*, pp. 153–164.
[37]See Erika E. Bourguignon, "Afro-American Religions: Traditions and Transformations," in *Black America*, ed., John F. Szwed (New York: Basic Books, 1970), Ch. 16.
[38]Ulf Hannerz, "Soul," in *Black America*, ed., John F. Szwed, p. 104. Copyright © 1970 by Basic Books, Inc.,Publishers, New York. Reprinted by permission of the publisher.
[39]Alphonso Pinkney, *Red, Black, and Green: Black Nationalism in the United States*, p. 79.

To what extent a new black American culture may emerge out of this orientation is a question that should by no means be dismissed. There is ample latitude in American society to develop "designs for living" that place greater emphasis on how to live rather than on how to make a living.

Black Students. It would be expected that black students who were increasingly being admitted to predominantly white colleges and universities would play a significant role in the black movement and begin cultivating a more distinctive new black American subculture. While the exact proportion of black students who came to be considered activists is not known, this segment assumed leadership on the campus. According to Edwards, 1966 marked a turning point among black activist students.[40] Before this they had engaged in the general civil rights movement and earlier protest activities in the outside community; since then they have been turning attention inward to the college and campus, promoting black liberation. Their main demands centered around the establishment of black studies as a major curriculum and gaining separate facilities for black students, in housing and centers for social and cultural activities, in order to intensify their sense of black identity.

In a narrower sense, the desire for maximum separation within the campus was due to a need for time to get adjusted to the new experience of associating with whites in an equal "peer" situation. It was also related to the prejudiced reactions from many white students. In a broader sense, promoting both campus separation and black studies programs were forms of "laboratory" training for leadership roles in the liberation movement in the black community. In this activity, confrontations rather than protest became a usual technique. These confrontations have involved forceful methods, such as occupying buildings and closing them for use, and holding college administrators hostage in order to force acceptance of black demands.

The campus proved to be a safer place for these activities than the outside community. In general, outside the South, college administrators as well as many faculty members attempted to be understanding and sympathetic toward black students; also, in general, the colleges preferred to deal with these confrontations by themselves without the aid of outside law enforcement agencies. There was considerable outside criticism of the college authorities for acting, as many whites felt, in too lenient a manner. But, as would be expected, such confrontations were occasionally in white eyes, so unruly, that outside security forces were called in to restore order, and they were likely to deal with the "confronters" in a more rough-handed manner.

Black Studies. Black studies courses treated black-white history in terms of white oppression; in the social sciences, emphasis was on communicative skills and techniques to foster black liberation, and the study of black cultures in Africa and other areas. Their purpose was clearly not directed toward promoting integration. The curriculum was designed to prepare black students for leadership in the black community. While some white students did take individual courses in the black studies curriculum, they were not particularly wanted and, therefore, the courses functioned less effectively to stimulate white interest in cooperating with blacks in the common national interest than would have been the case had their participation been desired by blacks. However, in colleges where whites were a numerical majority, a substantial number of white students enrolled in black studies courses.

[40]Harry Edwards, *Black Students* (New York: The Free Press, 1970), p. 61.

Structural Pluralism: Black Power

A new ideology arose which placed less emphasis on black culture and more on uniting blacks more fully to exercise their power especially in areas where their numbers were substantial. As a slogan to symbolize the ideological emphasis the term Black Power came into use.

This term has been so widely and ambiguously used both by its proponents and the white media that some interpreters consider it as a symbolic term to unify the maximum number of all black activists—an "umbrella" term. It can be viewed as the dynamic part of the structural-pluralistic approach that is suggested by the following from Stokely Carmichael and Charles V. Hamilton, leading proponents:

> It is a call for black people in this country to unite, to recognize their heritage, to build a sense of community. It is a call for black people to begin to define their own goals, to lead their own organizations, and to support those organizations. It is a call to reject institutions and values of this society.
>
> The concept of Black Power rests on a fundamental premise: *Before a group can enter the open society, it must first close ranks.* By this we mean that group solidarity is necessary before a group can operate effectively from a bargaining position of strength in a pluralistic society.[41]

In attempting to crystallize the Black Movement under the banner of Black Power and to reach agreement on specific goals to promote it, the first National Conference was held in Newark, New Jersey, in July, 1967. Alphonso Pinkney reported as follows:

> This conference was attended by more than 1,000 black delegates from 42 cities in 36 states. They represented a broad cross section of black leaders, ranging from the militant black nationalists to employees of government agencies. One of the most significant aspects of the conference was its bringing together for the first time a wide assembly of black people who met in workshop sessions to define the concept of Black Power and who agreed to implement its components. When the conference ended, a series of resolutions had been passed, including the following: (1) the establishment of black financial institutions such as credit unions and nonprofit cooperatives, (2) the establishment of black universities. (3) selective purchasing and boycotting of white merchants in black communities, (4) the demand for a guaranteed annual income for all people, (5) a boycott by black athletes of international Olympic competition and professional boxing, in response to the stripping of the world heavyweight boxing title from Muhammad Ali, (6) boycotts of Negro churches which are not committed to the "black revolution," (7) boycotts of Negro publications accepting advertisements for hair straighteners and bleaching creams.[42]

---

[41]Stokely Carmichael and Charles V. Hamilton. Reprinted by permission of Random House, Inc. (New York: Vintage Books, a division of Random House, Inc., 1967), p. 44. Copyright © 1967 by Stokely Carmichael and Charles Hamilton. Reprinted by permission of Random House, Inc.
[42]Alphonso Pinkney, *Black Americans* © 1969, p. 200. Reprinted by permission of Prentice-Hall, Inc., Englewood Cliffs, New Jersey.

Except for the proposal for a guaranteed income for all Americans, the above program led away from integration. In fact, pressure was exerted on black integrationists to act in accordance with the Black Power point of view.

Two of the most concrete manifestations flowing from the Black Power movement are "black capitalism" and black politics.

Black Capitalism

Black Capitalism is a movement to encourage the maximum development of separate economic enterprises owned and controlled by black people and serving mainly black people.

From the economic viewpoint, Black Capitalism has dubious merit. Dr. Andrew Brimmer, the single black governor on the Federal Reserve Board, argued strongly against it. Among the reasons he advanced is that "the attempt to expend small scale, Negro owned business is running against a strong national trend."[43] This is seen particularly in the great increase in supermarket branches that outsell small neighborhood food stores and that offer lower prices. Brimmer observed that in 1968 "a self-employed male in retail trade earned only 63.8 per cent of the earnings of a salaried manager."[44]

Ironically, the limited integration of blacks into white business at a higher level decreased the number of black enterprises by opening the opportunity for blacks to be accommodated in the general (and white-owned) public facilities.

While the federal government, and some financial institutions, gave this idea limited support, black business operations to date have not shown much promise, as Seder and Burrell have indicated.

> The vast majority of black enterprises are still small retail and personal-service establishments—grocery stores, barbershops, luncheonettes, dry-cleaning stores, gas stations. Only a handful of black entrepreneurs have managed to make their way in finance, manufacturing, contracting or wholesaling. And even in the retail and service fields, there are very few establishments of any size. A study published in 1969 in New York City purported to show that more than half of the stores in Harlem were black-owned. However, the survey was taken on sections of Seventh and Eighth Avenues, where only small stores are located. The important shopping areas in New York's black community are 116th Street, 125th Street and 135th Street in Harlem, and Fulton Street, Broadway and Nostrand and Pitkin Avenues in Brooklyn. Practically all of the larger stores and theatres on these major shopping thoroughfares are white-owned.[45]

Brimmer and Terrill assert that the potential for economic improvement through black capitalism is not very great. It might indeed be harmful if it discouraged black

---

[43]Andrew F. Brimmer, as quoted by George R. Metcalf in *Up from Within: Today's New Black Leaders* (New York: McGraw-Hill Book Co., 1971), p. 282.

[44]*Ibid.*, p. 283.

[45]John Seder and Berkeley Burrell, *Getting It Together: Black Business Men in America* (New York: Harcourt Brace Jovanovich, 1971), p. 213. By permission.

participation in the larger national economy, where opportunities for advancement are substantially greater.[46]

Increasing ownership and control of business enterprise would no doubt bolster black pride. But there are other ways in which their low economic condition can be raised by the use of black economic power. One is selective boycotting of stores that fail to hire blacks and to upgrade them in functional position. This technique was employed with considerable success by the Reverend Frank Sullivan in Philadelphia in 1967. Picketing in orderly fashion is a use of black economic power; such devices have the important advantage of being completely in line with procedures now recognized as legitimate for all Americans.

Black Political Power

A highly significant—possibly the most significant—development to advance the position of black Americans has been the rapid rise in the number of blacks who hold public office. In 1967 there were about 650 blacks who had been elected to public office. By 1971 there were over 1,600 distributed in forty-one states.[47] The elective offices ranged in prestige and influence from Sheriff Lucius Amerson of Macon County, Alabama,[48] to United States Senator Edward Brooke of Massachusetts.

Analysis of the types of situations in which blacks hold public office are most easily related to the numbers and percentages of blacks in the various electoral subdivisions: where blacks comprise a substantial majority of the political units' population, and where they total a substantial numerical minority.

Black Majority Electorates.   In the United States at present, black majority political electorates have been found in a few large cities and, in the South, in small towns where the flow of population toward cities has left a black majority.

Of large cities, Gary, Indiana's black Mayor Richard Hatcher is an example. The spreading by blacks out from large city ghettos into adjacent suburban municipalities until they reach substantial majorities is illustrated in New Jersey. In 1972 there were five black mayors of relatively small cities located in suburban sections of Newark and of the Philadelphia-Camden metropolitan area. In contrast in the South was the election of Charles Evers as Mayor of Fayette, Mississippi, in 1969, carrying with him an all-black board of aldermen.

Another type of substantial black majority electorate comprises districts within large cities of sufficient size to be allotted representatives to Congress, and in more instances representatives to state legislatures. In 1972 there were twelve black Congressmen in the House of Representatives and a number of state legislators, generally representing electoral districts in the large metropolitan areas, for example, New York, Chicago, Philadelphia, and Cleveland. Andrew Young of Atlanta, presently Ambassador to the United Nations, was the first black to be elected Congressman from the South since the Reconstruction period.

[46]Andrew F. Brimmer and Henry S. Terrill, *"The Economic Potential of Black Capitalism,"* in *Public Policy,* 19, 2, 1971.
[47]See Mervyn M. Dymally, ed. *The Black Politician: His Struggle for Power* (Belmont, Calif.: Duxbury Press, 1971), Preface.
[48]See a printing of a speech delivered by Mr. Amerson at Tuskegee, Alabama, January 1, 1969, in *The Black Politician,* pp. 6–10.

Large Black Minority Electorates. City politics is sometimes non-partisan, but even when partisan there are frequently more independent parties or candidates competing for office.[49] Also there are often special circumstances that make a particular incumbent running for reelection especially weak as the election approaches. Such situations open up the possibility for minority-status candidates to win.

The election of Carl Stokes in 1967 as Mayor of Cleveland was the first major city election of a black mayor. It could not have taken place without a substantial number of white votes. His opponent, Seth Taft, had high WASP status. While Cleveland was at least two-thirds white, it had a Democratic majority, and Stokes had won his party's nomination with considerable difficulty. But as contrasted with Newark's Mayor Kenneth Gibson and Gary's Mayor Richard Hatcher, Stokes was less clearly identified with the grass roots of the black community, and, therefore, was more palatable to whites.[50]

From his observations as a journalist after studying a number of the important black politicians, Whittemore reached the conclusion that the more acceptable a black politician is to whites the less effective he can be in using his office to help blacks; and that the less black-identified the black politician is, the better his chances are for high political office.[51]

The election of Kenneth Gibson as black mayor of Newark is a borderline instance. At the time, Newark's black population was just around the 50 percent mark (with Puerto Ricans comprising around 10 percent of the 50 percent white population). But his opponent, a well-entrenched incumbent, was at the time on trial on corruption charges (subsequently found guilty) and under his administration the city's political image was extremely low. Thus, about one-sixth of Newark's whites voted for Gibson, a black, who was a professional man of apparent integrity. Unlike former Mayor Stokes and Senator Brooke who, as Whittemore puts it, "overcame" their blackness, Gibson expressed pride concerning his racial membership and visibility and maintained his grass roots connections.[52]

Significance of Black Political Power. The increasing political acceptance of black Americans by other Americans is an example of functional, or instrumental, integration and does not involve social integration. However, associating with whites on a social basis has never been a matter of high priority for the majority of blacks and, with the current pluralistic orientation, may well have still lower priority.

This greater integration of black Americans in the political arena has occurred simultaneously with increasing tension, conflict, and polarization in this interracial sphere, which lends support to the militant "Black Power" approach. In terms of common national interest, it is an approach that may be, and on the whole has been, pursued without resort to violence.

The use of Black Power in politics has turned out to be, in many ways, a promising avenue for blacks to move toward equality, and a means of providing a limited measure of black-white cooperation in the midst of an otherwise highly divisive situation.

For blacks, these political gains give an increasing role in the decision-making area of politics as well as in government. The selection of black State Senator Basil Paterson

---

[49]Mayor John Lindsay of New York was reelected as an independent candidate against Republican and Democratic opponents by less than 40 percent of the vote cast.
[50]L. H. Whittemore, *Together* (New York: William Morrow & Co., 1971). pp. 305–306.
[51]*Ibid.*, p. 307.
[52]*Ibid.*, pp. 306–308, 311.

of New York as vice-chairman of George McGovern's campaign for president, following soon after his own candidacy for Lieutenant Governor of New York State on the Democratic ticket, is an example. Even though a small minority in the state legislatures, where either of the two white parties need a few extra votes, black legislators are in a position to bargain for something they want. This leads to a larger generalization: *the use of group power in this way is neither white nor black but thoroughly American.*

The use of Black Power in politics has had a more unifying effect on the wide range of factions in the Black Movement than any other activist effort. Julian Bond, black member of the Georgia legislature, maintains that only those who openly identify with the black community will succeed in holding its support. Since it is unfeasible for blacks to form a separate political party, except at the local level, black legislators in either party can act in accordance with their party *except* on race-related issues. There Bond insists they must always vote "black."

The gains made by blacks in politics, however, presented problems. The cities where they gained political control were in a process of decay. However much this exercise of power may enhance black pride, the cities cannot by themselves embark on the extensive urban renewal programs requiring large amounts of money, currently available only from the federal government.[53]

Reaction of the Black Population to the Black Movement

This review of the Black Movement has concentrated on those actively engaged in it, which does not necessarily indicate how the total black population feels about the issues involved. Gary Marx provided the most extensive review of studies of black opinions as of 1967. While there was considerable variation in the numbers responding to similar questions in various cities, Marx's discussion permits the following generalizations: (1) Greater support for moderate organization and leaders than the opposite. (2) Disapproval of violence as a means to their goals, although some of this disapproval was on the basis of strategy rather than principle. (3) Approval of protest activities of the sort least likely to provoke violence, such as picketing. (4) A majority opinion that blacks had made substantial gains in the past decade or so, but that the progress has been too slow. (5) A majority favoring integration as distinct from pluralism, but also believing in strengthening black institutions and developing pride in blackness. (6) Concern over inadequate police protection in their areas and of police brutality in handling black arrests.[54]

WHITE RESPONSES TO THE BLACK CHALLENGE

How has white America responded to the Black Challenge? As a base from which to start we will use Paul B. Sheatsley's assessment of white sentiment as of the early sixties after the challenge had started but before it had reached its peak in mass rioting

---

[53]See Fred J. Cooke, *The New York Times Magazine,* July 25, 1971, p. 7, for an article on the plight of Newark, N.J.
[54]See Gary Marx, *Protest and Prejudice* (New York: Harper Torch Books, Harper & Row, 1967), Ch. 8, "Civil Rights and Tolerance." The generalized statements are our own, drawn from his review of the data.

and violence accompanying confrontations. Sheatsley's assessment is based on analyzing the findings of polls taken up to this time.

> Certainly there is no evidence that the majority of American whites eagerly look forward to integration. Most are more comfortable in a segregated society, and they would prefer that the demonstrators slow down or go away while things are worked out gradually. But most of them know also that racial discrimination is morally wrong and recognize the legitimacy of the Negro protest. Our survey data persuasively argue that where there is little or no protest against segregation and discrimination, or where these have the sanction of law, racial attitudes conform to the existing situation. But when attention is kept focused on racial injustice and when acts of discrimination become contrary to the law of the land, racial attitudes change. Conversely, there is no persuasive evidence thus far that either demonstration and other forms of direct action, or legal sanctions applied by government, create a backlash effect and foster segregationist sentiment. On the contrary, they may simply demonstrate, ever more conclusively, that it is more costly to oppose integration than to bring it about. The mass of white Americans have shown in many ways that they do not want a racist government and that they will not follow racist leaders. Rather, they are engaged in the painful task of adjusting to an integrated society. It will not be easy for most, but one cannot at this late date doubt the basic commitment. In their hearts they know that the American Negro is right.[55]

Analysis of white reactions to the accelerated Black Challenge will be treated under the following headings: repression, token concession, acceptance, and cooperation. It must be kept in mind that any typology cannot account for the many individual shadings in between each category. Furthermore, there is the assumption that those falling into each type act consistently with reference to the race issue. However, most white Americans have a generalized attitudinal and behavioral orientation toward blacks and how the white-controlled system should deal with it.

Repression

In a broad and historical sense, it may be said the white-controlled system is repressive, and that in this sense all white Americans, except those actively cooperating to change it, share personal responsibility. Here, however, we limit the term to that segment of whites who still act to suppress any further advance in the status of blacks and for whom this belief has high priority.

Most students of American racism agree that in the nation as a whole not more than 10 percent believe in actively repressing by all legal (and sometimes illegal) means any further equality of opportunity for blacks, although the percentage is higher in the South. Indications of their relatively small proportions are found in voting patterns.

[55]Paul B. Sheatsley, "White Attitudes Toward the Negro," in *The Negro American*, Talcott Parsons and Kenneth B. Clark, eds. (Boston: Houghton Mifflin Co., 1966), pp. 322–323. Reprinted by permission of *Daedalus*, Journal of the American Academy of Arts and Sciences, Boston, Massachusetts.

Perhaps the clearest is the vote for George Wallace in the 1968 presidential election. Outside the South, where repression had so long been normative, Wallace received 8 percent of the votes. Pettigrew's analysis of the Wallace supporters indicates that those elements of the white population who felt relatively deprived voted for him, and they showed strong anti-black sentiments. It was also found that those classified as anti-black in the sample were found to be two-and-a-half times more likely to agree that the "police should shoot to kill" to prevent looting during a riot.[56]

That repression of blacks in a far more violent form may eventually be America's way of solving its racial crisis has been cogently argued with extensive documentation by Samuel F. Yette in a book with the subtitle *The Issue of Black Survival in America.* The gist of his case is found in this paragraph:

> The obsolescence of Blacks in America and their will to survive nobly—demand and fight for their rights—provide some with an adequate rationale for black extinction. Legal sanctions for the systematic invasions of black sanctuaries—homes, schools, and establishments—were signed into law before Congress adjourned for the fall, 1970, elections. But, in America, as in Asia, these essentially military measures bespoke the failure of insincere or basically unsound efforts to help black people.[57]

By obsolescence of blacks Yette refers to the fact that large numbers of the black masses are not now needed as workers as a result of technological changes that make obsolete the only sort of jobs many of them are prepared to take.[58] But though not needed, the increased determination of the black masses to fight to survive and their increasing militancy, Yette argues, may precipitate uprisings that will require legal sanctions for more repressive acts. Yette considers the laws passed by Congress since 1968 giving stronger powers to law enforcement agencies a sign of a trend in the repressive direction.[59] He further refers to plans proposed by some Congressmen and the military to cope with possible larger-scale uprisings using martial law, and for such procedures as internment camps.

Yette further refers to indirect forms of repression. While he does give considerable credit to President Johnson for pushing through civil rights legislation and setting up the Office of Economic Opportunity (OEO) and to Sargent Shriver for trying hard to make it work, he found that by 1970 these efforts had been slowed down due to lack of local community support and cooperation. Similarly, the various anti-poverty programs were bogged down by lack of adequate financing and by local white resentment of the cost. Such behavior, he argues, indicates that there is strong sentiment not to reduce the poverty and disease, which cuts down the size of the black population (the black population is, in fact, increasing at a higher rate than the white population). Yette even

---

[56]Thomas F. Pettigrew, *Racially Separate or Together,* p. 243. An extensive analysis based on a sample of voters in Boston, Cleveland, and Gary, Indiana. A more intensive analysis was made in Gary.

[57]Samuel F. Yette, *The Choice: The Issue of Black Survival in America* (New York: G. P. Putnam's Sons, 1971), p. 31. © 1971 Samuel F. Yette. Reprinted by permission of the publisher.

[58]Sidney M. Wilhelm, *Who Needs the Negro?* (Cambridge, Mass.: Schenkman Publishing Co., 1970), Wilhelm makes much the same point.

[59]See Ch. 6, "The Laws: A Legal Police State," in Yette, *The Choice,* for an extensive discussion.

further construes efforts to encourage blacks to use birth control and sterilization as a means of controlling the growth of the black population.[60]

Token Concession

Illustrations of token concession are found among whites who do not want blacks to achieve full equality but face in a practical sense the need to appease the black by some concessions in order to limit interracial disorders. The term "tokenism" arose first during the Southern resistance to school desegregation, in that instance not only to appease militant blacks but to satisfy pressures from the federal government to comply. By accepting a few blacks into some white schools, those in opposition could for a while maintain that they had complied with the government ruling. The overt manifestations of token concessions more often come from those in authoritative positions, not only in government but in the economic sphere. This is illustrated by businesses and unions that, in order to comply with nondiscriminatory laws or to avoid the threat of a black confrontation, hire or admit a black or two as a concession. Currently, there are more signs of a broader nondiscriminatory policy to hire blacks, to train them, and to place them in higher ranking positions.

Passive Acceptance

A large portion of white Americans fall into a category indicating no strong prejudice against blacks achieving more equality. They do not act to place obstacles in the way of either governmental promotion of programs designed to aid blacks or resent having a black employed to work alongside them. There are limits to passive acceptance. Such whites will voice criticism of violent activity and support police action to deal with it. They are probably not well enough informed to know that the authorities may act in a discriminatory manner. They also resent confrontations that cause them great inconvenience. In general, they do not want to associate with blacks socially, nor to have them as neighbors. Included in this category are those who move when it appears that their neighborhood is due to receive any substantial number of black residents. Passive acceptors are not greatly disturbed if one "respectable" black family moves in near them, nor are they likely to lend support to those white neighbors who try to harass this "intruding" black family. These white Americans do not view the rising gain of blacks as a matter of great concern to them personally, and they do not view the black problem as a major domestic issue.

An aspect of white reaction to the disorder produced by the present racial tensions appears not to have been widely considered—namely, the factor of white fear. Many white Americans who would not have been classified among the more prejudiced, or anti-black, may become so as a result of increasing black pressures on their community. Even whites sympathetic with the Black Challenge often hesitate to send their children to integrated schools where interracial conflict is frequent.

---

[60]Yette does not indicate that such measures are part of a general trend in the entire American society and are therefore not discriminatory. Nor does he indicate that although the black fertility rates are declining, those of whites are declining more.

Cooperation

White Liberals.   Our conception of the category of cooperation is broader than that acceptable to the black activist. We conceive this to include those whites who believe in the total equality of all blacks. In mildest form here are the "liberals" (much despised by black activists). In action, liberals have expounded their views in public—orally and in writings; have joined interracial organizations; and have attempted to treat blacks as equal human beings, not as "blacks." Unconsciously, their efforts may seem to have patronizing undertones to blacks. Since they are total liberals, not just on the race issue, they do not condone violence, although they are more understanding of why black activists find this necessary in self-defense. Like all human beings liberals have personal problems—their own and their families' interests—which they are often unwilling to jeopardize to promote the black cause. More of them are found in the higher educational brackets and in academic circles, especially the behavioral scientists. Politically, it appears they are more frequently found among Democrats than among Republicans in the North.[61]

The opportunity for liberals to be useful in aiding the black cause is affected by the broad racial atmosphere at any given time and place. We have seen the Southern liberals' inability to be helpful during the strong Southern resistance period of 1954–1960; increasingly during the 1960s they showed more influence in that region. In the North, they could get a better hearing during the Kennedy-Johnson Administration than in the Nixon Administration, which found it politically expedient to woo the South and the antischool busing sentiment in the North. But the white liberal finds that the strong current tendency for blacks to push their cause on their own tends to limit his usefulness. While the black activists do not disdain liberal support, they make it clear that it is to be on the sidelines and not involved in decision-making policy.

White Radicals.   In using the term "white radicals" we refer here to those whites who feel that the total social structure, particularly in its economic aspects, should be basically changed—usually to socialism. The small number of Americans who hold this view also want it accomplished by nonforceful means—usually distinguished from communism by the term "democratic socialism." Of all the black movements, the Black Panthers in their philosophy, at least, hold the same view (see p. 185), which furnishes a basis for white radical cooperation with the Panthers.

White Positivism.   "White positivism" refers to that small number of white Americans who not only think that blacks should gain complete equality for their own sake but believe that it is essential for liberating whites, morally and ethically. The idea is represented by our earlier quotation from Lillian Smith (see p. 126). Specific illustrations are white parents who desire to have their children have black children not only as schoolmates but also as playmates, and by Lois Stalvey's efforts to associate with blacks as equals, not only to help blacks, but to help herself achieve a self-respecting image.[62]

ASSESSMENT OF THE BLACK CHALLENGE TO THE EARLY 1970S

From 1954 to the early 1970s, black Americans made more advances toward equality than in the entire twentieth century preceding 1954. The greatest gain was in the de-

---

[61]See Thomas Pettigrew, *Racially Separate or Together,* Ch. 10, "The Social Psychology of the Wallace Phenomenon."
[62]Lois Stalvey, *The Education of a WASP* (New York: William Morrow & Co., 1970).

cline of discrimination in political and economic areas and in publicly operated facilities. But the degree of decline in discrimination was limited by various forms of white resistance and inadequate law enforcement; blacks were disillusioned and black activist groups mounted a challenge that led to dangerous racial conflict.

The black movements aimed at developing a greater sense of unity and a positive image of their black identity. The development of this distinctive subethnicity sharpened the polarization between black and white as opposing segments in the national population. The main division within the black movement concerns whether the aim of the movement should be toward total integration or toward consolidating a distinctive subcommunity and culture—frequently considered "nationalistic" by some.[63] The more militant black activists insist on the right to defend themselves by whatever means necessary against discriminatory treatment. There has been a noticeable development of more hostile anti-white attitudes among black American youth, a more critical attitude toward the values and institutions of white American society, and a greater desire to associate primarily with blacks even in instances where the choice to associate with whites as equals is presented. In an assessment of recent developments in race relations Barron, quoting Goldman, states that "The two Americans were separate and alien when the decade of the 1960's began. They were farther apart still when it ended."[64]

BLACK-WHITE RELATIONS IN THE SEVENTIES

At the turn of the 1970 decade, the momentum of the Black Challenge slowed down. We have seen that there was a severe repression of the more militant groups in the early '70s, for example, when Black Panther leader Fred Hampton was shot in bed by raiding law-enforcement officials. A marked change occurred in the Nixon era, as Kilson writes:

> The War on Poverty was treated as a carry-over from the Kennedy-Johnson era, not as a policy of intrinsic value. It was killed outright after the 1972 election. The Nixon administration formulated policies which attacked violence and riots as such, regardless of their social causes and other roots in the racist patterns of the black-white relations.[65]

However, of equal or more importance in muting the black challenge was the onset of the recession in the early 1970s. Whereas in the '60s race relations was considered a main domestic issue, the recession unavoidably changed national attention and governmental concern to the problems of the national economy. In consequence, race relations, as well as numerous other social problems, received far less attention. In a *Newsweek* poll (Dec. 10, 1973) on the question "What are the biggest problems?" the respondents ranked race relations twelfth among fourteen items; education ranked ninth and housing fourteenth.

---

[63]See Charles V. Hamilton, "The Nationalist vs. the Integrationist," *New York Times Magazine*, Oct. 1, 1972, for a discussion of this issue among black leaders.
[64]Milton L. Barron, "Recent Developments in Minority and Race Relations," in *Annals of the American Academy of Political and Social Sciences*, 420, 1975, pp. 149–150.
[65]Martin Kilson, "Blacks and Neo-Ethnicity in American Political Life," in Nathan Glazer and Patrick Moynihan, *Ethnicity: Theory and Experience*, p. 239.

The most dramatic race-related incident of the 1970s was the nationwide reception given to the televising of the book *Roots: The Saga of an American Family*.[66] It is estimated that upwards of 70 million people viewed the program. Whatever the final judgment as to the detailed accuracy of the book itself or its television version, they both vividly portrayed the essential features of American slavery. The book gives a better picture of the African society from which Haley's African ancestors came than the television version does, and helps to dispel the widely held myth that this and other African societies consisted of savages. Whether reading or viewing *Roots* will have any permanent effects on furthering the Black American cause is questionable. Many comments indicated unawareness and insensitivity to this inglorious period of American history. Among white viewers, the carryover effect may be greatest on children.

The drastic slowdown of the Black Challenge in the 1970s does not mean that the overall gains made by blacks in the previous decade were lost or that no new gains were being made. Like other Americans, blacks suffered economically from the Depression, but it appears that they did not lose ground relative to the situation of whites.

Farley found that the racial differences in education, occupation, and income that declined in the 1960s, continued to decline in the 1970s.[67] However, the gap between the races was still far from closed. In regard to education, between 1968 and 1976 blacks had "narrowed the gap" with whites in the proportion completing twelve years of education. "Among those in their early twenties today, 85 percent of the whites and 78 percent of the blacks completed high school . . . Between 1969 and 1975 college enrollment rates of blacks increased more than those of whites."[68]

In the economic sphere "Racial differences in the occupations of employed workers continued to decline."[69] The income gap separating black and white families has remained constant. However, in regard to unemployment, the picture is mixed. Black men were severely limited in employment opportunities, and the young men about to enter the labor market were especially handicapped. Joining the armed services was one opportunity for young black men in the 16–24 age category. The reduction in employment opportunities of black males was partly offset by the gains of black women, seen in the 1960s, who have maintained their employment position relative to that of white women even during the recession. The upgrading of blacks into higher-status positions, for example, as managers and in sales, in the 1970s appears to exceed that of the 1960s.[70]

In conclusion, Farley writes that

> the occupational upgrading of blacks and their growing representation in politics (U.S. Bureau of Census 1975 A: Table 99) imply that they are more represented in the American decision making process than they were at the start of World War II . . . [and] even during a pervasive recession, blacks did not lose the gains they previously experienced. On the other hand reductions in inequality are small when compared to the remaining

[66]Alex Haley, *Roots: The Saga of an American Family* (Garden City, New York: Doubleday & Co., 1976).
[67]Reynolds Farley, "Trends in Racial Inequalities: Have the Gains of the 1960's Disappeared in the 1970's?" in *American Sociological Review*, 42, 2, April, 1977, pp.189–207.
[68]*Ibid.*, p. 192. By permission of the American Sociological Association.
[69]*Ibid.*, p. 206. By permission.
[70]*Ibid.*, p. 193, p. 198.

differences on many indicators. A continuation of the trends of the 1960's and 70's offers no hope that racial differences will be eliminated soon.[71]

The later '70s show American blacks taking a moderate course concerning the integrationist-separatist axis, a moderate pluralism. The polarization of the two races continues. The black community is increasingly geographically separated into different areas, especially in the larger cities. Structural pluralism continues to exist; how far the interest in, and development of, cultural pluralism continues is in question. Black studies courses are still taught in schools and the larger colleges and universities have Afro-American departments. Several American universities have set up exchange programs involving students and faculty in Third World areas.

The black organizations, greatly handicapped by the absence of unifying charismatic leadership and by inadequate funds since the recession, carry on their customary activities as well as they can. There is more cooperation among them. The Black Muslims, for example, are no longer a "separatist" group. The Southern Poverty Law Center was developed recently in Montgomery, Alabama, under the leadership of Julian Bond. The Center works to defend poor blacks in cases where it feels guilty verdicts, some with death sentences, are unwarranted and reflect race bias, especially in smaller Southern communities. The most serious setback among black organizations involves a legal suit brought against the NAACP.[72]

In 1966 a local branch of the National Association for the Advancement of Colored People, with cooperation by the national organization, organized a boycott against the white merchants of Port Gibson, Mississippi, protesting discrimination against blacks. In 1969 the white merchants brought suit against the organization based on a 1968 state statute that allowed an injured party to receive damages if two or more parties conspired to harm a third party. The law was applied retroactively to the 1966 boycott and a local judge awarded $1,200,000 to the merchants against the NAACP. He also ordered the posting of a $1,600,000-bond to appeal the case, which would probably have forced the organization into bankruptcy. Fortunately, in 1976 a federal judge reduced the bond obligation to $100,000. But the original award of $1,200,000 still has to be litigated, which will take some years and severely handicap other activity. Contributions from several unions were made to the NAACP funds to appeal the case because such a judgment, if upheld, might affect the types of protest employed by unions themselves. The United States Supreme Court agreed to consider the case in the 1977 term.

Political Gains of Blacks

In politics in the mid-70s, blacks continued to make gains, the number of elected officials surpassing 3,500 in 1975. Most of these were elected in black majority population districts, many in rural areas of the South where the migration of whites to cities left a black majority electorate. The main change in this period has been an increasing number of blacks elected to public office in black minority electorates. Los Angeles, with a black population less than 25 percent (17.9 in 1970), elected Thomas Bradley as

[71]*Ibid.*, p. 206. By permission.
[72]Data furnished by official reports of the NAACP.

its first black mayor. Other blacks were elected to statewide office: Mervyn M. Dymally, as Lieutenant Governor of California, and C. Dolores Tucker, as Pennsylvania's Secretary of State. Most of the incumbent black Congressmen and women were reelected in 1976.[73]

After the indifference of the Nixon-Ford administrations, blacks looked forward to the election of Jimmy Carter and gave him an overwhelming vote on the basis of his apparent problack attitudes, atypical of Southern white politicians in the past. As we write, Carter's actions as to black problems have been largely limited to his appointments. The selection of Griffin Bell of Georgia as Attorney General was a disappointment because of some of Bell's earlier judgments, viewed as antiblack by some. This was partly offset by the naming of a black, Drew S. Days, as Assistant Attorney General. The new president also named two blacks at the cabinet level, Andrew J. Young, as Ambassador to the United Nations, and Patricia Harris, head of the Department of Housing and Urban Development.

The marked rise of blacks in politics has given blacks a greater sense of group power. Black area concentration works in opposite ways. In large black districts they can elect one of their own as Congressman or City Council member. For the same reason they are gaining responsibility and some control over local affairs, such as local schools. On the other hand, they have little chance of election to office in political units where they do not constitute close to half of the population.

Cross-Racial Contacts and Black-White Attitudes

A preliminary report of a survey of black-white relations between 1964–74 indicates cross-racial contacts increased during the period.[74] Members of both races reported increasing cross-racial contacts in their neighborhoods, work places, schools, and among friends. White attitudes grew more favorable toward blacks over this period. Between 1964 and 1974, the proportion of whites favoring "strict segregation" declined from approximately one-quarter to one-tenth. While the trend of response of blacks was the same as whites, it was in the'60s that blacks expressed a strong feeling of favorable change in conventional racial patterns. But this appeared to have diminished somewhat in the seventies. In particular, in the 1972–74 period black people began to sense no further improvement, although at no time did blacks feel that the situation was getting worse. The frequent inadequacy of responses to attitude questions as an indication of how people will act is revealed in the white response to mixed racial housing. There was a small gain between 1972–74 in the proportion of whites who said they would be willing to live in a mixed neighborhood, but they meant by this a "mostly white" neighborhood.

Differences in opinion between blacks and whites were found, with blacks supporting federal intervention on behalf of fair treatment in employment and of school in-

---

[73]Most of the blacks holding high government posts were listed in *Ebony,* May, 1977, among the magazine's list of "The 100 Most Influential Black Americans." The list also includes mayors of major cities with substantial, if not majority black electorates. Also named are some six federal judges,in addition to Thurgood Marshall, Justice of the United States Supreme Court, and one Vice Admiral in the Navy, S. L. Gravely.
[74]"Cross-Racial Contacts Increases in Seventies, Attitude Gap Narrows for Blacks and Whites," *Institute for Social Research Newsletter* (Ann Arbor: University of Michigan), Vol. 3., No. 4, Autumn, 1975.

tegration to a greater extent than whites, although the feeling was less widespread in 1974 than in previous years.

In regional differences, cross-racial contact increased most in the South, where in 1974 respondents were less likely than people in other parts of the country to describe their schools, work places, and shopping areas as all-white. Southern whites are far more accustomed to having black people in their midst than whites in other sections of the country, but the places indicated in the newsletter where interaction takes place do not necessarily call for "peer" status interaction. White people in the North Central States who reported one of the strongest patterns of segregation in 1964 maintained that position in 1974, particularly with respect to schools and neighborhoods. Chicago, Illinois, has had a most unsatisfactory record for compliance with school desegregation since 1964, when the federal law requiring cutting off federal funds to agencies practicing discrimination was passed. Another legal effort was made recently to force the Board of Education to increase integration.[75]

Increasing cross-racial contacts in mixed work groups or in shopping centers are not the best tests of a real break in the color line—acceptance as equals in a primary-group situation. Our random observations lead to the conclusion that generally mixed associations that bring black people into white homes, or vice versa, are limited to situations where civic interests are involved.

The South in the 1970s

Despite the shift of black-white racial problems from the South to the nation as a whole, there still remained differences in the South, some of which were related to the traditional regional pattern and some to changing conditions. Ecological changes played a part. We noted earlier the trend of black movement from the North to the South roughly balancing the South-North population mobility.[76] In general the South adjusted formally to the requirements of the civil rights legislation. But the carryover of the heritage of the caste-race line manifested itself in Southern white behavior designed to maintain the color line informally, well illustrated in the school situation.

Education. While a large percentage of school districts in the South were officially desegregated, many white parents circumvented desegregation by sending their children to private schools recently established for whites. (There were about 3,500 such schools in 1976.) Despite a 1976 United States Supreme Court decision making it illegal to ban Negro students from these schools also, it is unlikely that many blacks will apply, for both economic and traditional reasons.[77]

Economic Welfare. Historically, the South has had more poverty than the other regions of the country, even though, along with the nation as a whole, progress in economic status has improved in recent decades. Levitan *et al.,* drawing on Census Bureau materials, show both the decline in poverty in the South by both blacks and whites and

---

[74]"Cross-Racial Contacts Increases in Seventies, Attitude Gap Narrows for Blacks and Whites," *Institute for Social Research Newsletter* (Ann Arbor: University of Michigan), Vol. 3., No. 4, Autumn, 1975.

[75]Editorial "Bypass for a Segregation Impasse," *The New York Times,* April 20, 1977, p. A 24.

[76]This is a general trend, involving whites as well, brought about by the increasing industrialization of the South.

[77]See B. Drummond Ayers, Jr., "South's 'Seg' Schools Are Now Part of the System," *The New York Times,* June 27, 1977, Sec. 4, p. 1.

the racial and regional gaps that remain. In 1959 the incidence of poverty in the South was 26.6 percent for whites and 67.4 percent for blacks. Comparable figures for the North and West (combined) were 14.6 percent for whites and 33.4 percent for blacks. In 1972 the incidence of poverty was 11.5 percent for Southern whites and 39.8 percent for Southern blacks. In comparison, the figures for the North and West were 8.0 percent for whites and 26.2 percent for blacks.[78] Anderson notes that in 1974 the South was still the poorest region of the country. In the eleven states of the South, 12 percent of white families were poor as against 41 percent of black families (note the comparability with the Levitan *et al,* figures for 1972). Anderson adds that the Southern states had a poor record in providing public assistance: only 6 percent of Southern families received basic public assistance, while 17 percent of all families were poor by federal definition. With a quarter of the country's population, the South contained 38 percent of its poor and 44 percent of its working poor.[79]

Politics in the South. Increased participation of Southern whites, as well as blacks, in politics is noted in the increase in voter registration and voting. In a recent research project exploring the reasons for the increased Southern interest in politics, the researcher found one cause to be the belief of many whites that the major political parties now take a sufficiently different stand on the race issues to warrant their voting. The final conclusion is that the increased salience of racial issues will remain important in Southern politics despite a growing tendency on the part of Southern politicians to play down or ignore the race issue in campaigning, at least openly.[80]

Reaction to Roots. One sign of a more favorable racial atmosphere in the South was the successful showing of *Roots* in 1977 over the main networks throughout the region. According to a *New York Times* report, "as recently as 1973, a syndicated series featuring Barbara McNair ceased production when the distributor despaired of being able to sell it to a single station in the South."[81] In contrast *Roots* dominated conversations and was discussed in schools and in church sermons, according to a survey by Southern broadcasters. There was some hate mail and reports of racial tension in schools, but in general the reactions reflected a measure of progress in the South.

Selected National Problems in the 1970s

During this period of relative calm in black-white relations in the nation, many difficulties have arisen in implementing the gains called for in the civil rights laws of the 1960s. We will deal briefly with four particular areas: welfare, "redlining" as related to housing, the highly controversial topic of affirmative action, and continued difficulties with school desegregation.

[78]Sar A. Levitan, William B. Johnston, and Robert Taggart, *Still a Dream: The Changing Status of Blacks Since 1960* (Cambridge, Mass.: Harvard University Press, 1975), p. 34.
[79]Robert E. Anderson, Jr., "10 Million Southerners Are Still in Poverty," in *Southern Voices,* Vol. 1, No. 3, August/September, 1974.
[80]John L. Hammond, "Race and Electoral Mobilization?" in *The Public Opinion Quarterly,* Vol. 41, No. 1, Spring, 1977, pp. 13–27.
[81]Les Brown, "*Roots* Success in South Held a Sign of Change," *The New York Times,* Feb. 10, 1977, p. 18.

The Welfare Problem.   The welfare problem has become a highly controversial issue in the past two decades, with its focus on the black recipients whose income is below the amount necessary for adequate existence. The welfare administration is criticized as inefficiently operated. A wide discrepancy exists in the qualification for welfare from state to state. This convinces many people that the welfare system should be operated exclusively by the federal government. Another issue arises out of beliefs held extensively by many Americans that most families on welfare should not be there. The newly elected Carter government realized that the handling of welfare needed extensive reforms. When the officials of the Department of Health, Education, and Welfare started to plan reforms, the Department's secretary, Joseph A. Califano, concluded, as social scientists and social workers have long known, that "past debates about welfare have too often focused on myths about the poor in America . . . . We must center the welfare debate around blunt talks about real facts."[82]

It is widely believed that the majority of people on welfare are able bodied, shiftless people who do not wish to work and prefer loafing and procreating illegitimate children on welfare assistance. The actual facts reveal this belief to be a myth![83] Around 1970, 25 million Americans were officially below the poverty level. Of these, 15 million received some form of public welfare. About half of the recipients were blacks, although blacks were only 12 percent of the national population. A high percentage of all welfare of both races went to children and their mothers. News articles in 1977 reported that more than half of the heads of poor families were working, but were so poorly paid that they needed partial benefits. The evidence available showed that less than 150,000 able-bodied men were on welfare and many of them were enrolled in government-sponsored training programs. Nearly three-fifths of the children of black welfare families were legitimate children. Seventy-three percent of welfare recipients have fewer than four children per family; and 30 percent have only one child.[84] Black women tended to have fewer children in the early and middle 1970s.[85] Whatever plans for the reorganization of welfare administration are formulated, the biggest problem will be to convince the American public of the facts as distinguished from myths.

Affirmative Action.   The policy of Affirmative Action became a cause celebre in 1977, as attested by *The New York Times* devoting an entire editorial page to it.[86] This extensive coverage was prompted by the *Regents of California v. Bakke* case, scheduled as of the present writing to be decided by the U.S. Supreme Court in the 1977–1978 term. The case is considered by many to be the most important race relations case since the 1954 *Brown v. Board of Education* decision on school desegregation. Affirmative Action has also become a topic of stormy controversy among sociologists as well as among employers and college administrators, as reflected by an extensive debate on the subject in *The American Sociologist.*[87]

---

[82]David E. Rosenbaum, "Officials Are Up Against the Myths of Welfare," *The New York Times,* May 22, 1977, p. 1, 3.
[83]See James E. Blackwell, *The Black Community: Diversity and Unity* (New York: Harper & Row, Publishers, 1975), pp. 54–57.
[84]*Ibid.,* p. 56.
[85]U.S. Bureau of the Census, *The Social and Economic Status of the Black Population, 1974,* Introduction, p. 4.
[86]*The New York Times,* July 3, 1977, Sec. 4, p. 12. Also see Sheila Rush, "Race and Legal Doctrine," *The New York Times,* June 16, 1977, Op. Ed.
[87]See *The American Sociologist* for "Debates: Affirmative Action-Reverse Discrimination?" Vol. 11, No. 2, May, 1976.

The object of Affirmative Action is to increase equality of opportunity for members of various minority groups in occupational and educational fields. The pursuit of this goal arose from the Civil Rights Act of 1964, which made it unlawful to "deprive any individual of employment opportunities or otherwise adversely effect his status because . . . of race, color, religion, sex, or national origin (Title VII).[88] To implement this law, President Lyndon Johnson issued an executive order to all employers calling for a public statement of their adherence to the law. The order also required employers to take affirmative action to seek out minority persons. In practice this meant that in many cases preference was given by employers and administrators to minority applicants over perhaps better-qualified nonminority applicants. Minority applicants unqualified by the standards set up by majority officials were often given special training to help them become prepared.

Proponents of Affirmative Action persuaded some institutions to set minority quotas (contrary to the provisions of the 1964 act). However, H.E.W. Secretary Joseph A. Califano felt that quotas were necessary to reduce hiring bias and racial imbalance in work places and schools. [89] The main argument for Affirmative Action is a moral one representing a just compensation for the long-standing discrimination that denied minorities equal opportunities. Opponents argue that acceptances based on race or ethnic identification is reverse discrimination, and that it is not only illegal but unjust, and in practice, impossible to administer fairly.[90]

Opponents also believe a strict choice on the basis of merit as determined by white standards should be used for admission to college, graduate schools, and jobs. In practice, there is less problem in connection with the lower levels of occupations, such as skilled workers, since most blacks can be trained for such positions. The main obstacle on this level is the limited resistance of white skilled workers to admitting blacks. At the professional level it has been almost impossible to get black applicants proportionate to the total black population.

A 1977 report on the enrollment of minority students in medical schools showed that even though there has been a fivefold increase in enrollment of minority students, the number is far from their percentage in the general population.[91] The report further shows that there is one white physician to 538 white persons in the country in contrast to one black doctor to 4,100 blacks.

The issue of affirmative action involves a conflict in values. For example, which should have priority: the training of more white specialists reared in privileged backgrounds or more well-trained blacks, who, the report suggests, are more likely to be headed for primary-care roles in family practice in black communities? In the *Regents of California v. Bakke* case, Allan Bakke, a California white man, was rejected for admission to the University of California Medical School at Davis. When he learned that his grade point average was superior to that of some blacks who were admitted, he sued the Regents of the University of the State of California. Having lost his case at two court levels in the State of California, he appealed to the United States Supreme Court.

---

[88]*Ibid.*, p. 69.
[89]Nancy Hicks, "Califano Says Quotas Are Necessary to Reduce Bias in Jobs and Schools," *The New York Times,* March 18, 1977, pp. A-1, 16.
[90]See Nathan Glazer, *Affirmative Discrimination: Ethnic Inequality and Public Policy* (New York: Basic Books, 1975).
[91]Charles E. Odegaard, "Minorities in Medicine: From Receptive Passivity to Positive Action, 1966–1976," 1977, Josiah Macy, Jr. Foundation, 1 Rockefeller Plaza, New York.

"Redlining"—A Housing Problem.   The opportunity for ghetto blacks to improve their living conditions by purchasing homes and to rehabilitate them has been handicapped by banks refusing to finance mortgage money. The practice of "redlining" developed, involving marking off certain areas, in the slums and working-class neighborhoods, as categorically out of consideration for loans irrespective of the soundness of some buildings or the creditworthiness of the applicants. The procedure has been increasing to such an extent that several states have taken steps to alter this situation.[92] The Connecticut legislature passed a bill making it illegal for a bank to refuse home loans arbitrarily on the basis of its location. New Jersey announced a program to lend mortgage money to be used in areas rejected by lending institutions. As we write, the New York State legislature is considering a bill somewhat similar to the Connecticut bill. A California regulation provides that a person whose mortgage request is denied may appeal to a special board of inquiry.

Continued Problems in School Desegregation.   The problem of school desegregation continued to be acute in metropolitan areas with large black populations. Clearly, a large percentage of the white American people agree in principle that the Supreme Court's decision outlawing school desegregation is the only decision consistent with democratic ideals. But it should be kept in mind that a substantial proportion of the white American public at any given time is not personally faced with the problem of having children of school age subject to the mixed racial situation. Many of these object to having their children in racially mixed schools under the present urban interracial climate fraught with considerable tension in general.

Critical situations arose in two ways. The movement of the black population outward from the inner areas where increasingly black children were assigned to previously white schools was disliked by many white parents. Numerous white families moved out to the suburbs, an ecological trend well in process independent of the school situation. But the new school policy increased "white flight" and thus made the objective of improving racial balance more difficult. Bullock noted that in Atlanta some whites moved away from areas that had some of the best schools in the city to avoid having black neighbors as well as integrated schools.[93]

In other situations black children were assigned to predominantly white schools out of their own areas which required additional busing, sometimes to schools in white ethnic enclaves, as in South Boston. Often whites opposed to accepting black students in their neighborhood schools seized upon busing as a plausible excuse for preventing integration. But as Willie put it, "Thirty thousand kids were being bused in Boston before there was any desegregation plan . . . The estimated number of students to be bused in the final court order was . . . still less than the number that used transportation before court ordered desegregation."[94]

Some cities, where feasible, developed an "open enrollment" plan that permitted students to transfer from their neighborhood schools to others they preferred, space be-

[92]See Joseph Fried, "The Struggle Over Redlining By Banks Is Increasing," *The New York Times,* May 1, 1977, p. E-7.
[93]Charles S. Bullock III, "Desegregating Urban Areas: Is It Worth It? Can It Be Done?" in *School Desegregation: Shadow and Substance,* Florence Hamlish Levinsohn and Benjamin Drake Wright, eds. (Chicago: University of Chicago Press, 1976), p. 133.
[94]Charles V. Willie, "Racial Balance or Quality Education?" in Levinsohn and Wright, p. 9.

ing available. However, a 1973 survey concluded that this plan had not at that time accounted for a significant amount of desegregation.[95]

In response to local opposition to mixed racial schools, some school boards were pressured into redrawing district lines on various pretexts intended to avoid or decrease the extent of desegregation. In one suit brought by a black group against a school board it was alleged that the board drew discriminatory district lines. Here the court ruled against the plaintiffs on the ground of inadequate evidence that the school board had been "motivated" by intention to discriminate by race. One device used by some communities with a small number of black students was to contract with neighboring communities with a larger black population to accommodate their own black students. Another difficulty in building an effective program was the division within some school boards between those for and against desegregation, precipitating frequent clashes among members.[96]

The foregoing discussion suggests that being a member of a school board or a school administrator was not altogether enviable where interracial problems were involved. It should not be overlooked, as Gottlieb reminds us, that "De facto school desegregation is the result of racially segregated housing and residential patterns."[97] This in turn is basically rooted in white racism. Therefore, governments—national, state, city and school boards—should not always be criticized for all the shortcomings in the school desegregation process when the fundamental difficulties lie elsewhere.

Problems with school desegregation in metropolitan areas have resulted in questioning some of its anticipated values. The supposition that desegregation would improve the quality of education for blacks has been challenged because results differed under variable conditions. Again, the expectation that desegregation would improve relations between black and white students has not been universally the case. As we have seen, formal school integration of the two races has often been accompanied by informal segregation and discrimination inside the school, sometimes by school administrators and often in the extracurricular life of the school. Interracial confrontation and skirmishes between white and black male students occurred frequently. As one classroom teacher put it, "Black children not only endured the hostility of white children and teachers who opposed integration of schools but also generated hostility for the same reason."[98] On the other hand, black students' sense of worth and pride was enhanced when a black student outdid a white in studies. The increased self-esteem of many black students and the increased motivation to succeed constituted extremely important values related to the desegregation issue, noted in an appendix of the original Supreme Court decision in 1954.

Working out reasonably racially balanced schools within the city lines of metropolises has become more of a problem where black sections have spread close to

[95]George Richard Meadows, "Open Enrollment and Fiscal Incentives," in Levinsohn and Wright, p. 143.
[96]See Lillian B. Rubin, *Busing and Backlash: White Against White in an Urban School District* (Berkeley: University of California Press, 1972).
[97]Harry N. Gottlieb, "The Ultimate Solution: Desegregated Housing," in Levinsohn and Wright, p. 157. Reprinted by permission of the publisher.
[98]"The Way I See It: Reflections on School Desegregation by Teachers from Four Cities," in Levinsohn and Wright, pp. 173–205. In general, other teachers' comments indicated much disharmony in race relations.

county lines. In some instances black children were living much closer to schools just over the county line than to a school in their own city. In such cases, assigning students of each race to the other county school is a logical move. Such a case gained much attention in 1977 when a suit was brought to assign black students from Andrew Jackson High School, in Queens, New York City, an essentially all black school, to the predominantly white Elmont High School, Nassau County, and white students from Elmont to Jackson High School. Crossing county lines has not been an obstacle for performing many public services, but to cross them for the purpose of school integration was met with much resistance.[99] Various zoning requirements, such as prohibiting multiple dwellings or requiring lot sizes for residences so large that few blacks could afford them, were often adopted as barriers to mixed neighborhoods.

The above difficulties in accomplishing mixed racial schooling, as well as interracial problems in general, led the United States Commission on Civil Rights to report as follows:

> The migration of blacks and minorities to the cities in search of opportunities and the suburbanization of whites has left the nation with a new racial separation, not merely of segregated schools but segregated school systems coexisting within the same metropolitan area . . . Increasingly, the boundaries between cities and suburbs have become not merely political dividing lines but barriers that separate people by race and economic class. Accordingly, the future of school desegregation in these large urban areas hinges upon whether the obligation to provide a remedy ends at the city line.[100]

Some Black Views in the Mid-1970s

An appraisal of how black Americans view their situation in the late seventies can be gained from some conclusions reported in polls conducted by ACRA in 1976. Our selection from the findings is based on our judgment of their relative importance and whether the proportion of the responses was sufficiently large to be adequately meaningful.[101] The sampling was nationwide. Interviews were conducted by telephone using a random digital dialing technique.

> The basic orientation is toward "traditional" political involvement, i.e. "working within the system," which is seen as the most promising avenue of change by most black Americans. (p. 6). Regarding discrimination in general, the results were not encouraging. Over half felt there was either more (24 percent) or about the same amount (32 percent) of discrimination as there was five years ago. Thirty-nine percent felt there had been a decrease in the amount of discrimination faced by blacks (p. 9).

[99]See Iver Peterson, *The New York Times*, "Testing the City-Suburban Barriers," July 31, 1977, Sec. E6.
[100]U.S. Commission on Civil Rights Report, Feb. 1977.
[101]Associate Control, Research Analysis, Inc. (ACRA), *ACRA Black Opinion Survey*, Vol. 1 (Washington, D.C., 1977).

Blacks felt that racial discrimination is still a significant fact in the world of work. Three-fourths agreed that to get equal recognition, "a black person has to do a better job than a white person"(p. 8).

A slight majority (55 percent) disagree with the statement "Black workers are better off working with black supervisors than under white supervisors." Black people picked the government as the best place to work (38 percent), "big companies" next (32 percent), and "small companies" third (11 percent)(p. 10).

A majority (52 percent) believe that trade unions discriminate against blacks (p. 10).

Blacks do not feel there are significant differences between the North and the South in the opportunities available to them. "The North is long past being the promised land for blacks" (p. 9).

Confidence in the ability of the public schools to meet the needs of black children is low (p. 14). Slightly over half feel that black children receive better education in integrated schools and they approve busing to achieve this goal (p. 4).

Three-fourths of the respondents felt that supermarkets in black neighborhoods charged inflated prices and offered inferior quality goods (p. 12).

Slightly over half felt that they can rely on the police to be helpful if called. However, 56 percent agreed that a black person can't get a fair trial in most American courts (p. 16).

A majority (52 percent) were dissatisfied with the way blacks were portrayed on T. V. (p. 13).

Confidence in news media reporting of African affairs was low (p. 13).

An Assessment of the 1970s

The Black Challenge of the 1960s slowed down in the '70s as a result of two main circumstances: (1) the repression of the radical leaders and militant activity, and the failure of government (at least through 1977) to implement the social policies and programs designed to make the civil rights laws a reality; (2) the recession, diverting national attention away from race relations to the problems of unemployment and inflation. Despite these conditions it appears that blacks did not lose their gains vis-à-vis the white population in the 1970s. As a carryover from the previous decade the increased education of blacks, accelerated by the policy of affirmative action, led to more blacks being employed at higher occupational levels. This gain together with their continued political advances provided blacks a beginning role in the decision-making process both within and outside the black community.

Blacks in general followed a moderate course in the use of black power to gain more equality within the economic and political life of the nation. However, just as white people appeared to be ready for more integration, blacks elected to take the pluralistic road. Structural pluralism was strengthened with the development of more pride in black identity. A corollary cultural neoethnicity, related to their past heritage, increased, even though the extent to which this affected the entire black population is open to question. In addition to the use of political power to gain improvements and more local control in their own area, black groups protested discrimination with firmness but without violence. In borderline residential areas and around mixed recreational areas and schools, groups of young blacks and whites frequently engaged in confrontations, sometimes belligerent.

The reaction of white people to increasing black equality was mixed. Whites accepted it in public life with various degrees of tolerance, South as well as North. The results of polls and publicly expressed attitudes showed whites more willing to accept further equality for blacks, but when actually faced with the possibility of blacks becoming neighbors they were more resistant. Open hostility against blacks was more often found in close-knit white ethnic neighborhoods, where whites felt threatened by the possibility of having black neighbors and of receiving ghetto black children in their schools.

The higher-status whites outwardly manifested more liberal attitudes toward blacks in general, but when blacks encroached on their own interests, they subtly discriminated. Increasing unionization of blacks interfered with the split racial labor market to the advantage of blacks. Negative reactions to social interaction with blacks by the higher social classes were expressed by moving farther out in suburbs or by making suburban zoning laws that would indirectly preclude black incursion.

The color line between blacks and whites remains essentially in tact. Occasionally, cracks have broken the segregated line in housing. Friendships on the basis of equality are found intermittently. It is doubtful, however, that school or college interracial friendships carry over after graduation. It is in the ultimate test of equality, namely, intermarriage, that the persistence of the color line is most clearly demonstrated. While any racial intermarriage is legal, relatively few such marriages take place, although the rate is increasing, particularly in white-Asian intermarriage. The significant difference is in the social attitudes of the white population toward racial marriages. In this respect blacks are singled out from other nonwhite races. Marriages between Amerindians or Asians and whites incur far less disapproval than black-white marriage. In such marriages, the nonwhite partner is accepted as a social peer in white social circles, whereas the black partner is not.

Black Americans are unlikely to stop trying to erase the color line with its attendant discrimination; and thus its continuance is an ever-present portent for renewal of militant behavior. The final outcome lies in the hands of the more powerful dominant whites. It will be a serious mistake for white America to assume that because the 1970s have not been fraught with the black militancy of the '60s, the process of providing genuine equality for Americans of African heritage should not be speeded up. As Killian put it,

> To subscribe to the general principle of racial equality is one thing; to pay the personal price in terms of sharing traditionally white-held advantages is quite another. It is this sort of segmental, foot-dragging resistance that may

again change the mood of blacks from one of conditional faith in gradualism and assimilation to one of impatience and angry rejection of whites. Angry black ideologists stand on the edge of the fray ready to exploit such a shift in mood and to precipitate a resumption of the "impossible revolution."[102]

Suggested Readings

ACRA Black Opinion Survey, Vol. 1. Washington, D.C.: Associate Control, Research and Analysis, 1977.
   Results of a poll survey of black opinions on race issues conducted in 1976. A brief narrative overview of the poll results followed by methods used and demographic tables.
Althauser, Robert P., and Spivak, Sidney S. *The Unequal Elites.* New York: John Wiley & Sons, 1975.
   A sample of white and black college students indicates that higher educational attainments for blacks did not result in rewards and benefits comparable with whites.
Baron, Harold M. "Black Powerlessness in Chicago," in Yetman, Norman R., and Steele, C. Hoy. *Majority and Minority,* 2nd ed. Boston: Allyn & Bacon, 1975, pp. 381–389.
   Finds that the actual power vested in black policy makers is about one-third as great as the percentage of posts they hold.
Barron, Milton, L. "Recent Developments in Minority and Race Relations," *The Annals, AAPSS,* 420, July, 1975.
   The periodic account of the subject for 1968 to 1973. Wide coverage of these five years, behaviorally and ideologically, with footnotes that list a large part of the scientific literature over this span of years.
Farley, Reynolds. "Trends in Racial Inequalities: Have the Gains of the 1960's Disappeared in the 1970's?" *American Sociological Review,* 42, No. 2, April, 1977.
   In general, the economic gains relative to whites held up, but showed no significant overall relative gains.
Glazer, Nathan, *Affirmative Discrimination: Ethnic Inequality and Public Policy.* New York: Basic Books, 1975.
   Argues that the policy of affirmative action violates the rights of the individual and is unjust as well as illegal.
Hammond, John L. "Race and Electoral Mobilization: White Southerners, 1952–68" in *Public Opinion Quarterly,* Vol. 41, No. 1., Spring, 1977, pp. 13–27.
   Analyzes why white Southerners are now voting more.
Killian, Lewis M. *The Impossible Revolution: Phase II Black Power and the American Dream.* New York: Random House, 1975.

---

[102]Lewis M. Killian, *The Impossible Revolution: Phase 2, Black Power and the American Dream* (New York: Random House, Inc., 1975), p. 175. Copyright © 1968, 1975 Random House, Inc. Reprinted by permission of the publisher.

The pessimistic outlook for blacks in America voiced in his 1968 volume has somewhat mellowed in the 1975 edition, but the author remains doubtful about continued progress by totally peaceful means.

Levinsohn, Florence Hamlish, and Wright, Benjamin Drake, eds. *School Desegregation: Shadow and Substance*. Chicago: University of Chicago Press, 1976.
A series of articles by various writers present the 1970 problems in school desegregation. In general, the backlash developing in the '70s promotes a pessimistic tone to the book as a whole.

Malcolm X, with Alex Haley. *The Autobiography of Malcolm X*. New York: Grove Press, 1965. A gripping life story of a slum black who rose to leadership in the Black Muslims but broke with the organization before his assassination.

Pinkney, Alphonso. *Red, Black and Green: Black Nationalism in the United States*. London: Cambridge University Press, 1976.
A comprehensive coverage of the black nationalist movement. The "Green" in the title refers to the Third World.

Rubin, Lillian. *Busing and Backlash: White Against White in an Urban School District*. Berkeley: University of California Press, 1972.
A case study of conflict within a particular city between the pro and anti-busing members of the school board.

Szwed, John F., ed. *Black America*. New York: Basic Books, 1970.
An eclectic set of readings. Two parts deal with black culture and black action.

U.S. Bureau of Census. *The Social and Economic Structure of the Black Population in 1974*.
An Introduction summarizes the main findings.

11

American Indians

The American Indians, or Native Americans, as many now prefer to be called, are a classic case of colonial subjugation: the appropriation of geographic space and resources, and the destruction of the cultural and social integrity of technologically weaker peoples.

For nearly three hundred years as the tide of Europeans spread across the continent, white-Indian relations were frought with recurring conflict. Settlers spread, reduced the forest cover, preempted the prairie. The great buffalo herds were exterminated. The sacred Black Hills of South Dakota fell prey to gold prospectors and U.S. military power. The Governor of Colorado, in 1880, succeeded in sweeping the state clean of Indians— Cheyenne, Arapaho, Kiowa, Comanche, Jacarilla, and Ute—to be resettled in arid areas of Utah that Mormons didn't want.[1]

> If one prepares charts showing comparative population statistics for the various colonies, it is possible to see that white success in arms occurred most conspicuously when the white population curve going up crossed that of the Indian going down. This point was reached in the seventeenth century in New England and Virginia, and progressively later in the other colonies and in the later states of the Federal Union. It is well to remember that the U.S. Army was subduing the last vestiges of Indian power late in the nineteenth century only shortly before being called upon to deal with Spain and later Germany.[2]

In addition to expropriating land and resources Euro-Americans sought to engraft upon Indians a new religion, a different kind of property arrangement, a new language, and a standardized educational system. Furthermore, with little or no recognition of the cultural diversity of the native Americans of different tribes and regions, they succeeded in creating a generalized concept "Indian," which in policy and practice became a reality.

The result of a relationship based on warfare isolated Indians and after 1870, when most of the military conquest had been completed and Indians confined to reservations, they became for most whites generalized objects rather than people, and created for most Indians a self-image based on powerlessness.

[1]Dee Brown, *Bury My Heart at Wounded Knee* (New York: Holt, Rinehart & Winston, 1970), p. 380.
[2]Wilcomb E. Washburn, ed., *The Indian and the White Man* (Garden City, N.Y.: Doubleday & Co., Anchor Books, 1964), p. 220.

White America has shown an ideological ambivalence about Indians. On the one hand there is romanticization of Pocahontas, and of Uncas, "the last of the Mohicans" in Cooper's novel. An Indian head in war bonnet has graced our coinage. Of all minorities, Indians have had the longest established government bureau, charged with aiding Indians. Indian "blood" in the genetic heritage of whites has not been devalued as with other "racial" minorities. But until very recently these native Americans have been severely devalued by contiguous white populations; myths of their former "savagery" and their present laziness and drunkenness have persisted, and they have been allowed to become the most economically and educationally handicapped segment of the American population.[3]

THE INDIANS OF THE UNITED STATES

Numbers and Concentration

Estimates of the number of Indians in 1492 in the area that is now the United States range from 700,000 to 1,000,000. By the time Indians became wards of the government in 1871, the population had been reduced to less than half a million. It is generally agreed that under the early reservation system the population declined still further, reaching its lowest around 1900. Table 11-1 records the Indian population of the United States from 1890 to the present.

TABLE 11-1.   Indian Population of the United States*

1890	248,253
1920	244,437
1940	333,369
1960	523,591
1970	792,730

*U.S. Census data for the specified years.

Census figures are often considered an underestimate, due in part to inadequate recording, and also due to differences in identifying persons of mixed descent: Indian-white and Indian-Negro. Nevertheless, the figures in Table 11-1 suggest to some extent an improvement in conditions for Indians, picking up by 1940. Although Indians are still rated the poorest minority in the United States, changes in policy and in the extension of health services have at least reversed the genocidal trend of the turn the century.

Distribution of the Indian Population

There are people classified by the census as Indian in nearly every state in the Union. Regionally the largest concentration of Indian population is in the Southwest—

---

[3]In 1949 the American Council on Education in a study of textbook presentations of American Indians found only two themes: cruel, bloodthirsty savages, or noble high-minded sons of nature. There was no presentation of Indians as people, no discussion of the cultural characteristics of the wide variety of Indian life past or present. See Michael B. Kane, *Minorities in Textbooks* (Chicago: Quadrangle Books, 1970), p. 112; and also Chris Cavender, *An Unbalanced Perspective: Two Minnesotan Textbooks Examined by an American Indian* (Minneapolis: University of Minnesota Press, 1970).

mainly in Arizona and New Mexico—where about one-fifth of all Indians live. The next largest concentration is in Oklahoma, a former Indian territory now containing about 10 percent of the Indians of the United States. In the South there are scattered groups in Texas, Louisiana, Mississippi, Alabama, Florida, South Carolina, and Virginia; the Cherokee tribes of North Carolina outnumber all other groups combined in the Southern region. In the Northeast the largest numbers are in upper New York State, but there are scattered groups in Maine, Massachusetts, Connecticut, New Jersey, Pennsylvania, Delaware, and Maryland. In the North Central states there are substantial reservations in Minnesota, South Dakota, and North Dakota, with smaller groups in Nebraska, Wisconsin, and Michigan. There is an intermittent scattering throughout California and the Northwestern states.

Half or more American Indians live on reservations. Others, who as a result of one period of government policy sold subdivided land, have moved to city slums or shantytowns.[4] Some, like the Mohawk steelworkers of Brooklyn, have lived clustered in the city that gives these high structural-steel workers their specialized employment, but they return annually to their reservation and all are buried there.[5] The trend of movement to the cities has accelerated in the last two decades, partly through government policy, partly through voluntary migration, though this migration is often not viewed by the migrants as permanent. There are sizable Indian populations in New York (including Brooklyn), Cleveland, Detroit, St. Louis, Minneapolis, Omaha, Denver, Phoenix, Los Angeles, San Francisco, and Seattle.[6]

Biological and Cultural Characteristics

Anthropologists believe that the Indian peoples migrated to the Western Hemisphere from Asia, but in the 18,000 years that they have inhabited North and South America they have developed a physiognomic type distinguishable from Asiatic peoples. They are brown in skin color, have straight black hair, little facial or body hair. Head shape and nasal index vary widely. Pure-bred Indians are usually distinguishable in their physical appearance even when acculturated to the dominant society.

Indigenous Indian cultures, including language, vary widely and are either highly discrete, or loosely related according to the geographic location and historical economic base. Notwithstanding the difficulties of generalizing about such widely varying cultures, certain broad characteristics of Indian societies may be noted, with some reference to their contrast with the cultures of the white invaders. The characteristic features we shall discuss here apply to the Indian people before 1871, when they became wards of the government.

1. The Indian cultures were all preliterate. Thus knowledge and mores were inculcated through the spoken word and the teaching of youth by the elders.

2. While all preliterate societies appear small in contrast with modern societies, Indian societies north of the Rio Grande tended to be small even in the perspective of pretechnological societies. Tribal relationships were almost entirely personal, and the Indians lacked experience with those secondary, impersonal, formalized relationships characteristic of large-scale complex societies.

---

[4]Stan Steiner, *The New Indians* (New York: Dell Publishing Co., 1968), pp. 175 ff.
[5]*Ibid.*, pp. 160–161.
[6]*Ibid.*, p. 177.

3. The Indian economies were primarily hunting and gathering, with fishing in certain areas. In what is now the United States, hoe agriculture was practiced among the Eastern tribes and the Southwest, where maize growing was prevalent. When hoe agriculture was practiced, it was usual for the women to perform the gardening tasks.[7]

4. While individuals sometimes owned items of personal adornment and had property rights to certain songs and crests, property with economic value usually belonged to extended kin or tribal groups. It was inconceivable that any individual member of the group should lack necessities as long as they were available to anyone else.

5. Class distinctions were generally less marked than in preliterate societies in other areas, and where they did exist the material standard of living did not vary greatly from commoner to noble. Too, individual power was greatly limited. Thus in comparing the position of chief among four widely contrasting North American tribes, Goldenweiser writes, "in no case is he [the chief] permitted to exercise actual control over the actions of his people—barring such drastic situations as war or other temporary exploits—and . . . in his daily life he is scarcely distinguishable from any of his subjects.[8]

One of today's most articulate spokesmen for Indians has pinpointed essential differences:

> The vital differences between Indians in their individualism and the traditional individualism of Anglo-Saxon America is that the two understandings of man are built on entirely different premises. White America speaks of individualism on an economic basis. Indians speak of individualism on a social basis. While the rest of America is devoted to private property, Indians prefer to hold their lands in tribal estate, sharing resources in common with each other. Where Americans conform to social norms of behavior and set up strata for social recognition, Indians have a freeflowing concept of social prestige that acts as a leveling device against the building of social pyramids.[9]

The Indian Concept of Land and Resources

Like all subsistence societies the Indians were concerned with the conservation of the resources that were their life. Before the coming of white settlers they thought of the land as boundless, with enough for all. Indeed, the colonists initially thought the same. Benjamin Franklin testified before Parliament in 1765 about "those vast forests beyond the Alleghenies not likely to be inhabited in any time to come." Parts of their accustomed terrain had religious and sacred significance to the Indians. The sacred Blue Lake has been restored to the Taos Indians of New Mexico (1972). The sacred Black Hills of South Dakota were lost to the ten Sioux nations forever. To nonagricultural Indians the common heritage of mankind—the earth—was to be held inviolate.

Indian voices have spoken this way:[10]

---

[7]Robert H. Lowie, *Primitive Society* (New York: Liveright Publishing Corp., 1947), p. 75.
[8]Alexander Goldenweiser, *Early Civilization* (New York: Alfred A. Knopf, 1922), p. 120.
[9]Vine Deloria, Jr., *We Talk, You Listen* (New York: The Macmillan Co., 1970), p. 170.
[10]From *Bury My Heart at Wounded Knee* by Dee Brown. Copyright © 1970 by Dee Brown. Reprinted by permission of Holt, Rinehart & Winston, Inc., pp. 265, 269, 241, 316, 273.

In 1625 some of the colonists asked Samoset to give them 12,000 additional acres of land. Samoset knew that land came from the Great Spirit and is as endless as the sky and belonged to no man.

Of the 3,700,000 buffalo destroyed between 1872 through 1874, only 150,000 were killed by Indians.

The Indians killed only enough animals to supply their needs for winter— stripping the meat carefully to dry in the sun, storing marrow and fat on skins, treating the sinews for bow strings and thread, making spoons and cups of the horns, weaving the hair into ropes and belts, curing the hides for tepee covers, clothing and mocassins.

I have heard that you intend to settle us on a reservation near the mountains. I don't want to settle. I love to roam over the prairies. There I feel free and happy, but when we settle down we grow pale and die. . . . Has the white man become a child that he should recklessly kill and not eat? When the red men slay game they do so that they may eat and not starve. (Santana, Chief of the Kiowas)

The earth was created by the assistance of the sun, and it should be left as it was. . . . The country was made without lines of demarkation, and it is no man's business to divide it. . . . The earth and myself are of one mind. . . . I never said the land was mine to do with as I chose. (Chief Joseph of the Nez Perces)

One does not sell the earth upon which the people walk. (Tashunka Kiko, "Crazy Horse")

You ask me to plow the ground. . . . Shall I take a knife and tear my mother's bosom? Then when I die she will not take me to her bosom to rest. You ask me to cut grass and make hay and sell it, and be rich like white men but how dare I cut my mother's hair? (Wowoka, the Piute Messiah)

Indians had basically a nonexploitive relationship with the natural environment. They lived in an approximate equilibrium with their world. The coming of whites destroyed this balance. The situation was exacerbated by the difference of property systems: individual, temporary, and transferable ownership in the white system, and collective and perpetual use in the Indian system.

THE ESTABLISHMENT OF DOMINANCE

Period of Community Diplomacy: 1607–1778

During the colonial period each local English or Dutch settlement dealt with the Indians by whatever means seemed best to it.[11]

---

[11]The Dutch established the policy of buying land from the Indians, as in the famous purchase of Manhattan Island for a purported $24. The Quakers in Pennsylvania developed a friendly policy toward the Indians and tended, in the early days at least, to fulfill with scrupulous honesty the bargains they made.

In Virginia the first settlement, which was founded in 1607, lay within the territory of the Powhatan Confederacy, whose chieftain, Waukunsenecaw, left the small white group in peace. When a new wave of settlers appeared, however, his successor, Opechancanough, fought to drive them out. But in 1644 he was decisively beaten. In Massachusetts, peace prevailed between the Indians and the white men for more than ten years, in part because of an illness that heavily depopulated the tribes nearest the shores. Again, however, as the white settlers became more numerous and began to press westward, many tribes grew hostile. While in some cases Indian resistance was temporarily successful, the ultimate outcome was always white victory. The technological superiority of Europeans acted here, as elsewhere throughout the era of colonial expansion, to subjugate indigenous peoples. There was friendly trade and barter when whites needed Indians. When whites "needed" Indian lands there was conflict. For most Europeans this was their first encounter with a preliterate culture and they had no orientation that would enable them to understand the customs and social structure Indians had developed as their adaptation to environment. During the French and Indian Wars the French made alliance with Indians in their common goal of driving out the English settlers, and this increased fear and antagonism in the colonial era.

In 1754 the British Crown formulated a policy for dealing with the Indians that took jurisdiction away from the individual colonies or border groups. Under this policy, "the tribes were independent nations, under the protection of the Crown; Indian lands were inalienable except through voluntary surrender to the Crown; and any attempt by an individual or group, subject to the Crown, or by a foreign state, to buy or seize lands from Indians, was illegal.[12] The attempt of the British Government to carry out this policy amidst innumerable local violations increased the antagonism of the colonists, especially those in the border area, toward the Crown. Thus the Indians indirectly contributed to the final issue of the American Revolution.

Period of Control by Treaties: 1778–1871

The policy of the British Crown was in essence taken over by the new American Government. For the first hundred years the relation of the Indian tribes to the federal government was characterized by treaties, nominally negotiated by the government with so-called sovereign Indian nations. Yet whenever the Indians failed to agree with what the government wanted, they were met with military force. Frequently, special local groups moved against the Indians quite independently of the national government, as when the Georgia Legislature passed an act confiscating all Cherokee land and declaring Cherokee tribal laws invalid within the state. Persistently, when the white people rode roughshod over their own treaties, the Indians fought back, and a number of Indian wars of considerable dimension took place east of the Mississippi. The Seminole War in Florida and the Black Hawk War in the Illinois Territory, in which Lincoln fought, were among the more famous. The final outcome east of the Mississippi was that most of the Indian tribes were forced into the newly established Indian Territory (now the state of Oklahoma). The exceptions were a few small, relatively harmless bands in Maine, New York, Virginia, and Florida, and a considerable number of Chero-

---

[12]John Collier, *Indians of the Americas* (New York: Mentor Books, The New American Library of World Literature, 1947), pp. 116–117.

kees in North Carolina, who put up so much resistance that they were let alone in the wilds of the Smoky Mountain region.

West of the Mississippi, much of the story of Indian-white relations centers around, first, the situation in California following the Gold Rush and, second, the subjugation of the Plains Indians throughout the vast Midwest. In California the white men in search of gold forced the Indians out of any area they wanted. From 1851 on, the federal government negotiated treaties with many local tribes by which the Indians agreed to surrender more than half of California. These treaties, because of frontier political pressure, were never ratified by the Senate, and the government subsequently sold to white people much of the land pledged to the Indians.

The subjugation of the Plains Indians beginning about 1870 is described by Collier:

> First there was military assault, on slight pretexts or no pretexts at all, and the government exploited tribal rivalries in order that Indians should kill Indians. The limited and disciplinary war customs of the Plains turned into total warfare, aimed at annihilation, with the United States Army as the driving power. The tribes were finally beaten, however, not through overwhelming numbers or superior armament (though these existed) but through starvation after the whites had destroyed the buffalo. . . . That revelry of slaughter, which had no sportsmanship in it, was recognized as a war measure against the Indians and was deliberately encouraged.[13]

The great Indian wars west of the Mississippi were in large measure resistance to reservation life. People were being removed from the land they loved, their freedom of movement restricted, and usually the reservation land was arid terrain that whites did not want.

> If the Texans had kept out of my country there might have been peace. But that which you say we must live on is too small. The Texans have taken away the places where the grass grew thickest and the timber was best. Had we kept that we might have done the things you ask. But it is too late. (Ten Bears of the Yamaparika Comanches)[14]

It was not until 1915, with the Ute War, that the last of Indian conflict subsided. But the symbolic end was the massacre at Wounded Knee nineteen years—a generation— after the passing of the Reservation Act (see Chapter 3 for an account of Wounded Knee). The tribes had been decimated by war and starvation, and now a half century of demoralization and alienation was about to begin.

MAINTAINING DOMINANCE

Reservation Period: First Phase—Forced Assimilation

In 1871, Congress decreed that no Indian tribe "shall be acknowledged or recognized as an independent nation, tribe or power, with whom the United States may

---

[13]John Collier, *Indians of the Americas,* p. 133, by permission.
[14]Dee Brown, *Bury My Heart at Wounded Knee,* p. 242.

contract by treaty,"[15] thus marking the beginning of a definitely new phase in Indian-white relations. The Indians were now wards of the federal government, a unique status for any minority group in the United States. The policy and practices of the Indian Office from this time on were aimed at weakening the tribal organization of the Indians, destroying their culture, and forcing the assimilation of Indians as individuals into the normative American way of life. After several years of public and Congressional debate, a new land policy was adopted with the passage of the famous Dawes Act in 1887. This legislation empowered the President to divide the lands of any tribe by giving allotted individual portions to family heads or other individuals. But the plots so allotted were to be held in trust for twenty-five years, after which they were to become the unrestricted property of each owner. In the meantime they could not be sold. The object of this program was to force each Indian breadwinner to become a self-supporting individual by working his own land. In the meantime the Indians were to be supported directly by the government.

The Dawes Act was the result of crusading efforts on the part of aroused public opinion about the extreme exploitation and decimation of the Indians. It represented a move of the American conscience, but an extremely naïve move, within the ideology of its period. Understanding nothing of Indian social organization, nor recognizing the problems of a nontechnological people, despite the good intentions of crusaders[16] and Congressmen, the land allotment policy was disastrous to the Indians. They lacked the technical knowledge needed to make their holdings pay. They lacked credit to acquire materials (seed and tools) to operate the land. The division of land through inheritance was inimical to most tribes, who held land as common property. Under these circumstances they were prey to whites who leased land allotments at below value (ranchers, for example, would lease contiguous allotments for grazing beef cattle for the urban market), and to squatters who impinged on Indian property that was not fenced or cultivated. Over the entire period in which the allotment policy was in effect (1887–1914), the lands held by the Indians were reduced (largely by squatter occupation) from 138 million acres to the present estimate of 56 million acres.[17]

Another phase of the policy of forced assimilation concerned the educational program. Indian children at school age were taken out of their tribal homes and placed in boarding schools, where the use of Indian languages and the practice of Indian ways, such as dress and hair styles, were forbidden. The curricula of the schools were largely that of the white schools, without any adaptation to the particular needs of the Indians. In Macgregor's opinion, whatever practical training the Indian children obtained either for making a living or making better homes was gained from the labor they performed to help support the school.[18]

[15]Ray Allen Billington, *Westward Expansion* (New York: The Macmillan Co., 1949), p. 668. Ch. 32, "The Indian Barrier," pp. 651–670, describes the history of Indian-white relations from 1860 to 1887.
[16]See Helen Hunt Jackson, *A Century of Dishonor*, which first appeared in 1881 (New York: Harper & Brothers). It has now been reissued by Harper & Row as a Harper Torchbook (1965). Mrs. Jackson is also known for her novel *Ramona*, which deals with the sad fate of California Indians. She has been sometimes called the Harriet Beecher Stowe of the Indian cause. In her view wardship and the Allotment Act were great steps forward for the protection and integration of Indians.
[17]Steiner, *The New Indians*, Ch. 13.
[18]Gordon Macgregor, "Indian Education in Relation to the Social and Economic Background of the Reservation," in *The Changing Indian*, Oliver LaFarge, ed. (Norman: University of Oklahoma Press, 1942), pp. 116–127.

The first period of reservation policy, until the Reorganization Act of 1934, not only failed to understand cultural differences, and the slow rate of cultural change, especially for segregated groups as was *per se* characteristic of reservations, it further fell short of its objective because of inefficient administration. The Indian Service, particularly in its earlier years, was not conspicuous for the high standards of its personnel. Nor was a particular interest in Indians and their welfare a prerequisite for employment in the Service. Furthermore, the appropriations granted it were inadequate. Even when well-intentioned officials attempted to carry out some sort of policy, they were beset with powerful pressures from special interests to twist the policy to the latter's advantage.

During the 1920s constant pressures were brought to bear by certain vested white interests to enact legislation that would have expropriated further the rights of Indians to their resources. These efforts were defeated and as one result of the publicity attending the hearings in this connection, a comprehensive study of the problems of the administration of Indian affairs was undertaken (1927) by a private agency, the Institute for Government Research, at the request of Secretary of the Interior, Hubert Work. The findings of this study, usually known as the Merriam Survey, went far to create a more favorable government attitude toward the Indians.[19]

But lasting damage had already been done. Perhaps the demoralization was the greatest for the Plains Indians, who fought so long and bitterly against confinement to reservations. The Sioux were relegated to reservations (Rosebud in South Dakota, Standing Rock in North Dakota, and Pine Ridge in Nebraska.) They had been a mobile, hunting culture ranging over a wide terrain. They did not have the social organization or patterns of childhood training to adapt to village life. Everett Hagan, who visited the Dakota (the indigenous name for the Sioux) reservations as late as 1961, attested to the enduring despair of these peoples.[20] Hagen stated that "at first the reservations were essentially concentration camps." In the case of the Sioux the aggressiveness fostered in children and the strict self-control necessary to survival in a hunting culture was symbolized and compensated for in a central tribal ceremony: the Sun Dance. Since this ceremony involved self-inflicted pain, on the one hand, and orgiastic release, on the other, it was forbidden by the new masters. "The whites, moved by their own values, unwittingly removed the last vestige of meaning from lives whose external base had already been destroyed." The result was demoralization, cultism, and eventually apathy. The inhabitants of the reservation seemed to be suffering from a malaise "more pervasive than malnutrition and more pentrating than cold . . . [They were] as ghosts walking about, withdrawn, passive, lifeless. . . ."[21]

Reservation Period: Second Phase—the "New Deal"

The phrase, "New Deal," coined to characterize the early years of Franklin D. Roosevelt's administration, was peculiarly apt with reference to Indian affairs. While the time was ripe in 1933 for reorganization of Indian policy, the sweeping character of

---

[19]Institute for Government Research, *The Problem of Indian Administration* (Baltimore: The Johns Hopkins Press, 1928).
[20]Everett E. Hagen, *On the Theory of Social Change* (Homewood, Ill.: The Dorsey Press, 1962), pp. 481–484. See Ch. 19 for a case study of the Sioux on the reservations.
[21]*Ibid.*, p. 484.

the changes undertaken at this time was in considerable measure due to a long-standing sympathetic interest in Indians of the new Secretary of the Interior, Harold I. Ickes, and to the appointment of John Collier as Commissioner of the Bureau of Indian Affairs.

Behind the efforts that culminated in the passage of the Indian Reorganization Act, sponsored by Senator Burton Wheeler of Montana, was a new philosophy concerning Indians held by the new Commissioner and strongly supported by the new federal administration. In essence, this philosophy aimed at integrating Indians into the national life as Indians, making Indian groups self-sustaining while also retaining as much of their tribal culture and group identification as was consistent with life in a modern civilized nation. Collier not only admired the Indians as persons but felt that much of their culture should be preserved, that there was a place for Indians in a multigroup democratic society. He expressed his philosophy thus:

> The new Indian policy . . . seeks to reinstate the Indians as normally functioning units, individual and group, into the life of the world. It makes them equal in the management of their own affairs and the direction of their own lives.
>
> On the purely cultural side, only sheer fanaticism would decide the further destruction of Indian languages, crafts, poetry, music, ritual, philosophy, and religion. These possessions have a significance and a beauty which grew patiently through endless generations of a people immersed in the life of nature, filled with imaginative and ethical insight into the core of being. . . .[22]

The point of view of the new commissioner was reflected in the Indian Reorganization Act passed by Congress in 1934, the chief provisions of which are as follows:

1. With certain qualifications, Indian societies were to be empowered to undertake political, economic, and administrative self-government.
2. Land allotment was to be stopped, and under certain conditions, additional lands could be added to current holdings.
3. A system of agricultural and industrial credit was to be established, and the needed funds were authorized.
4. An Indian Civil Service was to be established and provisions for the training of Indians themselves in administration and the professions were called for.

The Reorganization Act called for the acceptance of its provisions by each tribe individually, determined on the basis of a referendum using secret ballot. Those who voted to accept could organize under it for self-government and could organize themselves as a federal corporation to conduct economic enterprise.

The Indian Reorganization Act was a major shift in government philosophy and policy. Its implementation was slower than hoped, in part due to the enormous

[22]From Report of House of Representatives Subcommittee on Appropriations for the Interior Department, 1934.

pressures on the government occasioned by World War II. It was not until the end of the 1940s that achievements anticipated for a decade earlier began to emerge.

The task envisioned at the passage of the act was enormous. Memories, preserved in oral tradition, were long. Retreatism, apathy, and the devaluing attitude of whites in the regions surrounding the reservations had taken a high toll. In a study published in 1947, the anthropologists Kluckhohn and Leighton described the dilemmas of the Navaho:

> Different sets of Navahos (depending partly upon age, schooling, location of residence with respect to non-Navaho contacts, and other factors) have shown different major responses to the insecurities, deprivations and frustrations of the immediate past and especially to the "between two worlds" problem. . . . Some focus their energies upon trying to be as like whites as possible. Some find relief in becoming followers of vocal leaders. Others dissipate much hostility in factional quarrels or scatter their aggression in family fights, in phantasies about witchcraft or in attacking "witches," in verbal and other indirect hostilities toward whites, or they turn their aggression inward with resultant fits of depression. The culturally patterned releases in humor and in "joking relationships" with certain relatives continue to play some part. The central response of certain individuals is in flight—either in actual physical withdrawal or in the escape of narcotics, alcohol, and sex. Still others turn to intensified participation in rites of the native religion and to new cults (e.g., peyote). Partial solutions are achieved by a few individuals by rigid compartmentalization of their lives and by various rationalizations.
>
> Those who have set themselves to follow the white man's trail find themselves—as have representatives of other minority groups—in a (rationally) odd dilemma. While as youngsters they are rewarded by school teachers and others for behaving like whites, as adults they are punished for having acquired skills that make them competitors of their white contemporaries. The more intelligent ones had, by early maturity, realized that their education would bring them into conflict with or isolation from their own unschooled relatives. But the experience of being turned on by their white mentors comes as a painful surprise. They find they are seldom received on terms of social equality, even by those whose standards of living, dress, and manners they have succeeded in copying almost perfectly. They learn that they must always (save within the Indian Service) expect to work for a salary at least one grade lower than that which a white person of comparable training and experience receives. They overhear remarks by those same groups of whites who had goaded them to give up "those ignorant Indian ways." "You can never trust these school boys." "Give me a 'long hair' every time. They may be dumb but they are honest and they work hard." "Educated Indians are neither fish nor fowl. They give me the creeps." Rejected by the white world they have made so many emotional sacrifices to enter, some attempt a bitter retreat to the Navaho world. Others, in sour disillusionment, abandon all moral codes. Still others achieve a working (but flat and empty) adjustment.

Navahos are well aware of the difficulty of their situation. Surrounded by powerful pressures to change, they know that indifference and withdrawal can no longer serve as effective responses. They are conscious of the need to develop some compromise with white civilization. But doubt as to the best form of compromise makes them angry and anxious. Thus suspicion and hostility are becoming a major emotional tone of their relationships with whites.[23]

Progress Under the Indian Reorganization Act

The new deal for the Indians nevertheless meant considerable strides in economic rehabilitation, increasing tribal self-government, and a slow rise in the welfare of Indians as a whole. By 1948 a total of seventy-three tribes had received charters of incorporation, which meant that with the economic assistance of the government and the technical advice and approval of the Indian Service these groups improved their economic welfare and gained experience in helping themselves. Some tribes through loans were able to purchase additional lands or to put hitherto unused acreage into effective use. One problem was, in view of pressures from whites, to prevent too great a depletion of Indian land resources because of the desire of many Indians to sell their land to non-Indians or to lease it without adequate safeguards against deterioration. Marked increases in the requests by Indians, some with individual holdings, to sell their lands were reported by the Bureau in 1948 and 1949.

By 1948 a total of ninety-three tribes had adopted written constitutions and had begun to assume larger political self-government. Typically there is a Tribal Council which theoretically can suggest measures of administration, and approve or reject proposals of the Agency staff. It has considerable control of the tribal finances and appoints a Tribal Court of Indian Judges, which tries all cases of criminal law except those involving the ten most serious offenses, over which the federal court retains jurisdiction. Nevertheless, the great gap between tribal legal and political practices and those of the white democracy could not be closed at once. For example, it was the practice of both the Navaho and the Papago to decide important matters by face-to-face meetings of all concerned in which the issues were discussed until unanimity was reached, in contrast with the system of majority decision under white democracy.

Although Congress enacted a law in 1924 making all Indians citizens, seven states barred Indians from voting until about 1940, either by discriminatory laws or interpretations of laws. Following 1940, five of these states began to allow Indians to vote by not enforcing these statutes. Court decisions in Arizona and New Mexico in 1948 opened the door to full voting privileges for Indians.

Education for Indian children improved. From 1950 to 1960 the number of Indian children enrolled in schools increased from 26,716 to 133,316; over the same period the percentage of Indian children attending public schools, rather than the federally operated schools for Indian pupils alone, increased from 50 percent to 63.5 percent. It is

---

[23]Clyde Kluckhohn and Dorothea Leighton, *The Navaho* (Cambridge: Harvard University Press, 1947), pp. 113–115. By permission.

The above analysis is a classic illustration of Robert K. Merton's paradigm of possible adaptations to competitive goals and means. For a discussion of this theorem, see Ch. 19.

of special interest to discover that in 1959 some twenty-five tribes themselves provided scholarships in higher education totaling about $500,000.[24]

Later Trends in Official Policy

A considerable reversal in the Indian policy and program occurred in the 1950s. Efforts to speed up the process of liquidating the government's responsibility to the Indians took forms that may be designated as "relocation" and "termination."

Termination. The termination policy stemmed from a resolution by Congress passed on August 1, 1953, which stated in part:

> . . . [I]t is the policy of Congress, as rapidly as possible, to make the Indians within the territorial limits of the United States subject to the same laws and entitled to the same privileges and responsibilities as are applicable to other citizens of the United States, to end their status as wards of the United States, and to grant them all the rights and prerogatives pertaining to American citizenship. . .[25]

Following passage of this resolution, efforts were made to order or to persuade tribes to request termination of their relation to the federal government. This would have meant in many instances dissolution of tribal organizations and the devision of tribal assets among the several members. In view of the lack of acculturation of most Indians to the normative American way of life, especially to the norms of economic self-reliance, termination might well have resulted in the demoralization and pauperization of the Indians of many tribes. Alarmed at this prospect, friends of the Indians protested the policy and it was revised. Indian groups were not to be pressured to terminate unless they themselves wanted it. Thus, in fact only a few tribes were actually terminated, the most important being the Klamaths of Oregon and the Menomines of Wisconsin, both owners of large tracts of valuable timber.

Termination as a policy created many problems both for the Indians and for the government, and has now been abandoned. Termination costs the government nearly $3 million for each case. When wholesale termination was anticipated a special federal agency, the Indian Claims Commission, was set up to clear up unpaid Indian treaty claims and claims of past fraudulence. This proved to be a Pandora's box and opened the way for continuing claims and litigation.

The shift from a common-property culture to individual ownership; common enterprises now subject to corporate rules of the Anglo culture; liability for state taxes from which the reservations had been exempt; county politics—all worked to the disadvantage of the Indians. James Ridgeway, writing of the Menomines in 1965, predicted that "the tribe is likely to be slowly extinguished, the Indians either moving down to the cities or dying in the woods. The old reservation seems fated to become a State Park."[26] Brandon sees the effort to force termination as an aspect of "McCarthyism" and quotes the late Felix S. Cohen, the principal government expert on Indian legal affairs: "Like

---

[24]Annual Report of the Secretary of the Interior, 1960.
[25]House Concurrent Resolution 108, 83rd Congress, 1st Session.
[26]James Ridgeway, "The Lost Indians," *The New Republic,* Dec. 4, 1965, p. 20.

the miner's canary, the Indian marks the shift from fresh air to poison gas in our political atmosphere; and our treatment of Indians, even more than our treatment of other minorities, reflects the rise and fall of our democratic faith."[27]

Relocation. In 1952 the Bureau of Indian Affairs started what was called the Voluntary Relocation Program, under which reservation Indians, either individually or in family groups, who desired to move to industrial centers for permanent employment and settlement were offered financial and other assistance to enable them to relocate. One argument for adopting this program was the fact that most Indian tribal lands were inadequate to permit viable economies with a rapidly growing population.

The early days of the relocation program were not very successful and worked great hardship; expenses were paid to move from the reservation, but there was no aid for the Indian to return if he found the urban experience unsuitable or unbearable. One-fourth to one-third of relocated Indians had returned to the reservations by 1965.

Life in the city has often been difficult and puzzling for relocatees who moved from wardship status on the reservation to the hazards and monetary pitfalls of urban society. Accustomed to depend on government for commodities, health services, and the like, many have been ill-prepared for the confusion of alternatives available in an individualistic money economy. Those who remained in the city are those who have most successfully conformed to white standards, at least in the economic sphere.[28]

To assist migration the Bureau of Indian Affairs offered two programs: a direct employment program and an adult vocational trainee program. Between 1952–1968 over 100,000 Indians participated in these programs. A study made by the Bureau of a sampling of these participants to determine success in adjusting to life off the reservation found that successful migration was closely related to higher educational level. Indians who had participated in the Bureau training programs earned more than migrating Indians who had not. Nevertheless, budget limitations have prevented these programs from assisting enough applicants to markedly reduce the level of surplus labor on the reservations.[29]

A University of Minnesota report on Indians in Minneapolis stresses housing as a principle problem, due to lack of income and overcrowding. It also emphasizes the lack of coordination of all agencies, public and private, offering services to Indians.[30] Another report from the same Center emphasizes the helplessness felt by agency personnel in dealing with cross-cultural difficulties between Indians and whites. There is a lack of in-depth understanding by agency personnel, an inadequate understanding of agencies by Indians themselves, and structural rigidities in agencies that are frustrating and impeding to employees attempting to provide adequate service. This paper finds agency personnel to have predominantly positive attitudes toward Indian youth and predominantly negative attitudes toward older Indians.[31]

---

[27]William Brandon, *The American Heritage Book of the Indians* (New York: Simon and Schuster, 1961), p. 369.

[28]Joan Ablon, "American Indian Relocation: Problems of Dependency and Management in the City," in *Phylon,* Winter, 1965, pp. 362–371.

[29]Alan Sorkin, "Some Aspects of American Indian Migration," in *Social Forces,* Dec., 1969 pp. 243–250.

[30]Fred Berger, *The Minnesota Indian in Minneapolis,* Training Center for Community Programs, University of Minnesota, Sept., 1970.

[31]Arthur M. Harkins and Richard G. Woods, *Attitudes of Minneapolis Agency Personnel toward Urban Indians,* Training Center for Community Programs, University of Minnesota, Dec., 1968.

In a comparison of Samoans and American Indians settling in West Coast cities, it was found that the Samoans' positive self-image was a factor in successful adaptation.[32]

The success of urban adjustment, then, seems to depend on educational level, degree of preparation for migration, the historical social organization of the particular tribe, and the Indians' own self-image. Cities absorbing an Indian labor force need agency personnel more acquainted with Indian values and customs, more housing, more job training, and job-upgrading programs.

As with any program of this sort, the results vary with the attitudes and efficiency of the officials operating the program at local levels. Many Indian leaders, as well as such friends of the Indians as The Association on American Indian Affairs, favor this program in principle. This latter organization feels that the program could be improved by (1) making it clear that relocation opportunities are available to those Indians who really want it without any undue pressures being exerted; (2) improving liaison with local community agencies in the cities of relocation in order to facilitate the adjustment of the resettled Indians; and (3) not stressing the point of permanence of relocation.

Reservation Development

Early in the Kennedy Administration, Congress adopted the Area Redevelopment Act, which was to be administered by the Department of Commerce. It provided for loans, grants, and technical assistance to areas designated as depressed and underdeveloped. Various Indian reservations were classified as eligible for assistance under the act.

One of the first proposals submitted was by the Navajo.[33] In October 1961 participation in the Area Redevelopment program was authorized by the Tribal Council "at a duly called meeting, at Window Rock, Arizona, at which a quorum was present, and . . . [the proposal] was passed by a vote of 56 in favor and 0 opposed. . . ."[34] An overall development program was designed jointly by Indian Bureau advisers and Tribal representatives. This document is a little case study in development since the bleak picture of the Navajos presented by Kluckhohn and Leighton in the 1940s.

> The Navajo Indian Country, including the Reservation and adjacent lands used and occupied by Navajos, embraces nearly 16 million acres. . . . The topography varies from mountains 11,000 feet high with clear streams and stands of timber, to semi-desert lands at 4,500 feet elevation. The climate for the most part is semi-arid and suited primarily for grazing. The land is used principally for grazing small subsistence flocks of sheep and goats under herd, as well as cattle and horses.
>
> Individual income is very low on a per capita basis.[35] Major sources of in-

[32]Joan Ablon, "Retention of Cultural Values and Differential Urban Adaptation," in *Social Forces*, March, 1971, pp. 385–392.

[33]Navajo is the name given to the Dinetah people by the Spaniards. The tribe itself still retains the Spanish spelling, but most Anglos write it as it sounds: Navaho.

[34]*Looking Forward: Navajo Overall Economic Development Program*, Transmitted January 4, 1962.

[35]Average (mean) annual income for 1970 is given as $700. John Upton Terrell, *The Navajos* (New York: Harper & Row, 1970), p. 316.

come are: *off reservation:* railroad work, farm labor, seasonal harvesting; *on reservation:* State, Federal and Tribal payrolls, welfare and surplus commodities, livestock, agriculture, Tribal public works programs.

There are (1961) approximately 90,000 Navajos in the area, with an estimated labor force of 15,000 to 20,000.

The Navajo Tribe is a distinct political entity, having territorial boundaries within which it exercises a dependent sovereignty subject only to treaty provisions and to the plenary power of the Congress, and within this sphere has and exercises the power of regulating its internal and social relations. The Navajo Tribal Council is the governing body. . . . The Chairman and Vice Chairman are the Executive Branch. . . . The Council, the Chairman, and the Vice Chairman are elected for four-year terms by the vote of the people.

The main income to the tribe, to date, has come from bonuses and royalties accruing from uranium, oil, gas and construction materials such as sand and gravel. With the exception of surface use for farming, grazing, and individual business purposes, all income from Tribal lands reverts directly to the Tribal treasury and not to individual Navajo people. This income, though it aggregates many millions of dollars has never been sufficient to warrant individual distribution. Consequently, the Navajo Tribe has utilized tribal funds for the support of programs which benefit members of the tribe in common.

The proposal then lists sixteen categories of projects undertaken by the Tribal Council. The proposal itself is for the collection of critical data for planning: Population Census, including skill, aptitude, income, education, etc.; potential for development of recreation areas; utilities studies; forest development; occupational training and retraining; mineral potential.

Each one of the above points rests not only on development of the *physical* resources, but equally important, on comprehensive knowledge of the *human* resource, its aptitudes and its aspirations. Every proposed Overall Economic Development project is spiced with the salt and pepper of physical and human resource amalgamation.

Reservation development has proceeded considerably since this early Navajo proposal. Today, Navajos operate a number of new enterprises including their own telephone system. The Pine Ridge Sioux have set up their own construction company so that off-reservation white contractors are no longer needed to build reservation housing, roads, and public works. The Standing Rock Sioux have submitted a plan for fifteen enterprises including a bank, a motel, a shopping center, and a cattle ranching operation. Some small industry has been developed in some reservations, both by outside companies and by Indians themselves. These have been small enterprises, as Indians have resisted large-scale development and work routines that would corrupt their culture and environment.[36] Tourism and movie location have been another develop-

---

[36]Steiner, *The New Indians,* Ch. 10.

ment for those reservations with spectacular scenery. Navajos have leased rights for uranium mining. More recently there has been controversy about coal mining leasing in Wyoming and Montana, where Indians have held out for soil restoration after strip mining.

The Costs of Conquest

Of the 2.9 percent of the land area of the United States that is left to the Indians the Bureau of Indian Affairs division of soil conservation estimates that 14 million acres are critically eroded, 17 million "severely" eroded, and 25 million slightly eroded. That is to say none of it is prime *arable* land. As the humorist Will Rogers commented. "In wars, the slogan is Honor, but the object is land. . . . They are always fighting for independence, but at the finish they always seem to use quite a snatch of the defeated opponent's land to be independent on."[37]

Will Rogers was a Cherokee. He was born in the free Cherokee nation before the Curtis Act of 1898 terminated Cherokee treaty status. Accommodation and negotiation had preserved this independence for Cherokees through two removals, but under the wave of forced assimilation inspired by the Dawes Act their tribal lands were subject made to allotment and their government terminated.[38]

With all the good intentions of the Kennedy and Johnson Administrations and the efforts stemming from the Indian Reorganization Act, Indians have remained the poorest segment of the United States population. There has been improvement, but not very much. In the 1960s the adolescent suicide rate was still 100 times that of the general population; the death rate from tuberculosis 400 times that of the general United States population.[39]

The most recent data on Indian health[40] and welfare have been prepared by the Department of Health, Education, and Welfare based on 1970 figures.[41] Their findings show some improvement, despite persistent poverty: 64 percent of rural Indian heads of household (male or female) have incomes of less than $4,000 a year. Indians have the lowest median income and larger families than the national average (5 or more children for rural families and for 32 percent of urban families). The unemployment rate for rural males is 3.6 times the national rate, and for urban Indians the rate is 10 percent. Only 9 percent of Indians have incomes of $10,000 or over.

Educationally there has been advance. In 1960 48 percent of rural Indians and 26 percent of urban Indians had eight years or less of schooling. In 1970 high-school graduation had risen to 42 percent for urban Indians and 23 percent for rural Indians. In 1970, 86 percent of urban Indians and 87 percent of rural Indians (of the appropriate age) were enrolled in high school.

[37]*Ibid.*, p. 162.
[38]See account in Vine Deloria, Jr., *Behind the Trail of Broken Treaties* (New York: Dell Publishing Co., 1974), pp. 133–134.
[39]See Steiner, *The New Indian,* Ch. 15, for 1960s data on poverty and Indians' response to being designated "poverty areas."
[40]In 1955 the Indian health service was transferred to the Department of Health, Education, and Welfare.
[41]*A Study of Socio-economic Characteristics of Ethnic Minorities Based on the 1970 Census.* Vol. III, American Indians. HEW Publication N (OS) 75–122, July, 1974.

Life expectancy has risen to 63-64 years; twenty years longer than in 1955. There has been a 56 percent decrease in the infant death rate, a 50 percent decrease in maternal deaths, a 57 percent decrease in death from influenza and pneumonia, and an 86 percent decrease in death from tuberculosis.

INDIAN ORGANIZATIONS

There have been Anglo organizations concerned with protecting and aiding Indians, especially the long-established American Association of Indian Affairs with headquarters in New York. It is, however, only since the Indian Reorganization Act that a national, intertribal Indian organization has developed, large enough and with a large enough treasury to maintain a lobby in Washington: The National Congress of American Indians. This is made up of elected representatives of tribal governments. Until recently it has been a cautious and a conservative group. The National Indian Youth Council has represented a more activist position. It is made up of younger Indians and has focused on reservation development. The urban Indians have a nationwide organization, American Indian Movement (AIM), which, to a large extent initially, modeled its tactics on the Civil Rights Movement.

It has always been argued that Indians were too splintered and lacked organizational skills to be able to effectively challenge government policy. Yet after World War II, regional Indian organizations and Indian centers in cities and on campuses brought together Indians from different tribes and different parts of the country. It was inevitable that in a decade like the '60s Indians should become concerned about their identity as Indians and to demonstrate and protest past and present issues in which the government held "stacked cards" against their peoples.[42]

INDIAN PROTEST

One of the first widely publicized protests, beginning in 1963, was that of Indians of northwest Washington over fishing rights. These had been assured by the treaty of Medicine Creek in 1854. Since then these rights had been eroded: by the building of dams that ruined traditional fishing grounds; by public law, which, in the Eisenhower campaign to end federal services to Indians, had given states the right to assume jurisdiction and enforcement on any reservation without the consent of the tribe; by the sportsmen's state lobby and that of the commercial canneries. Some of the small tribes found they had the right to fish and nowhere to fish, as they were arrested when they fished in other than the traditional sites. These are small tribes whose livelihood is fishing (for consumption, not for market). Protest "fish-ins" were the first step, initiated by the newly formed Survival of American Indians Association. The National Indian Youth Council took up the cause and organized a demonstration at the state capitol in Olympia, Washington. Actor Marlon Brando (who is part Indian) came to lend his support, and was arrested, but released. The demonstration had national media coverage.

The following year Dick Gregory participated in a series of protest fish-ins on behalf of the Survival of American Indians Association. He was arrested, convicted, and served

[42]Alvin M. Josephy, Jr., *Red Power: The American Indians Fight for Freedom* (New York: McGraw-Hill Book Co., 1971), p. 185.

a jail sentence. Demonstrations continued. The American Civil Liberties Union entered
the case, and shortly thereafter the Department of Justice announced that at the
request of a tribe it would defend Indian fishermen. On May 27, 1968, the United
States Supreme Court upheld the rights of two of the tribes (Nisquallys and
Puyallups.)[43]

A second event to gain national publicity was the occupation of Alcatraz, the
abandoned island prison in San Francisco Bay. On November 20, 1969, a landing party
of seventy-eight Indians, calling themselves Indians of All Tribes, took over the island
and held it for nineteen months. Their announced intention was to establish a national
Indian culture center.

> We realize . . . that we are not getting anywhere fast by working alone as
> individual tribes. If we can gather together as brothers and come to a com-
> mon agreement, we feel that we can be more effective, doing things for
> ourselves, instead of having someone else doing it, telling us what is good
> for us.
>   So we must start somewhere. We feel that if we are going to succeed, we
> must hold on to the old ways. This is the first and most important reason we
> went to Alcatraz Island.[44]

Vine Deloria, Jr., in assessing the nineteen-month occupation implies that the group
was too impatient to wait out the long negotiation and legal case that would (hopefully)
establish their claim to the island under an old provision that Indian land taken for
government use would revert to Indians when the government no longer used it.
Rather, some of the leadership became entranced with the prospect of occupying other
government-abandoned property.[45] This occurred with success in the occupation and
negotiation for permanent use of an abandoned Coast Guard station on Lake Michigan,
but other attempts were not so successful.

In 1972 several activist groups, perhaps inspired by the Poor People's March on
Washington, designed a similar march and demonstration: The Trail of Broken
Treaties. Although it was charged that this was representative of only urban activists,
according to Deloria, 80 percent of the participants were reservation Indians of all
ages.[46] The caravan stopped in St. Paul, Minnesota, and worked out a twenty-point
program to submit to the Bureau of Indian Affairs. The Bureau opposed the march; the
Indian representatives commissioned with arranging housing and meeting places in
Washington did not do their job; the result was that the Indians occupied the Bureau
after they felt they had been "pushed around" by guards at the building when they
sought aid from the Bureau. Five days later the Bureau paid to send the participants
home; but there had been great wreckage and defacement inside the building. Deloria

---

[43]American Friends Service Committee, *Uncommon Controversy: Fishing Rights of the Muckleshoot, Puyallup and Nisqually Indians* (Seattle, University of Washington Press, 1970), Ch. 5.
[44]Josephy *Red Power*, p. 188. From a letter of December 16,1969.
[45]Deloria, *Behind the Trial of Broken Treaties*, p. 37.
[46]*Ibid.*, p. 47.

claims there were agents provocateurs among the most militant and destructive of the protesters.[47]

The last of the dramatic confrontations, beginning in March of 1973 and lasting for seventy-two days, was the occupation of Wounded Knee, South Dakota. The place was symbolically important to Indians. Many people from many tribes participated, including revered medicine men. The demand was for the right of the Oglala Sioux to determine their own borders as negotiated in the treaty of 1868, and that the issue be considered by the Senate Foreign Relations Committee. Thus the *treaty issue* became the focal point. Furthermore, it became a shooting war. A settlement was negotiated finally by executive intervention, although when a White House task force was sent to the reservation after the Indians' withdrawal, it was pointed out with regard to Indian demands that the matter was one for Congressional action and that the executive branch had no authority. The morale effect on the Indians was high, however. More than a thousand Indians were involved, including many traditionalists. Deloria feels that the support of the traditionalists in both the march to Washington and at Wounded Knee was a fortunate alliance. It is at least in part responsible for stimulating young Indians to become more interested and more knowledgeable about their Indian heritage.

Indians and the Bureau of Indian Affairs

The Bureau of Indian Affairs was established in 1824 within the War Department. In 1849 it was transferred to the Department of the Interior, where it remains. As Josephy writes,

> An untrusting, sometimes corrupt, and often incompetent white man's bureaucracy, accountable in practise to Congress and the Bureau of the Budget rather than to the Indians, it exercised autocratic veto power over all aspects of Indian life.[48]

The BIA had in 1970 over 16,000 full-time employees at three levels: Washington (500 employees), regional, and reservation. As in other large bureaucracies, each function at each level is compartmentalized. Decisions must move up and down through the three layers and also move sideways to coordinate on each level. The result is inevitable slowness and frustration. Professor Ovsiew, in analyzing the structure of the Bureau in 1968, notes," The BIA's philosophy of organization derogates the grass roots Indians, specialists, and coordinating administrator [on the reservation] in favor of echelons of administrators and absentee specialists higher up."[49] Although the BIA has had dedicated people working for it at various times and various places the problems remain complex. The weight of the structure has operated against innovation. It has been consistently against the activists, designating them all as "urban Indians" (for whom it has no responsibility within its assigned trust), "communist inspired." It has in the past been willing to deal only with individual tribes, opening up a charge of "divide and rule." Since World War II more Indians have been employed by the BIA. The activists

[47]*Ibid.*, p. 57.
[48]Josephy, *Red Power,* pp. 5–6.
[49]*Ibid.*, p. 117.

have compared this to the European colonial pattern of "native civil servants." They have been called "Uncle Tomahawks," as administrators of a paternalistic program. On some reservations Bureau personnel live comfortably in good housing apart from the rural poverty of the Indians they serve. Some have patronage at their disposal.[50]

There have been conflicts both at the reservation level between progressives and upholders of the Bureau tradition and at the top level. In 1971 there was an attempt to downgrade Commissioner Louis R. Bruce, a Mohawk-Sioux, and a group of progressives who surrounded him, by transfer to regional offices. This precipitated a revolt. A group of Indians, led by Peter MacDonald, the then chairman of the Navajo Tribal Council, occupied the Bureau's Washington offices and had to be forcibly ejected by the police. The publicity forced a shake-up and a reinstatement of Commisioner Bruce.[51]

Indian Conferences and Policy Statements

While the '60s and early '70s produced a climate of confrontation, nevertheless, during the same period there were a number of conferences in which Indians from various tribes met together to clarify their position vis-à-vis the United States government. In 1961 Indians from sixty-seven tribes met in Chicago and drafted a "Statement of Purpose." This lengthy document, which deals with resources, economic development, health, education, intertribal relations, relations to state and federal government, and taxation, contains two key affirmations:

> We believe in the inherent right of all people to retain spiritual and cultural values, and that the free exercise of these values is necessary to the normal development of any people.

> We most urgently recommend that the present organization of the Bureau of Indian Affairs be reviewed. . . . The basic principle involves the desire on the part of Indians to participate in developing their own programs.[52]

In 1964 several hundred Indians gathered in Washington for the American Indian Capital Conference on Poverty to insure that Indians be included in programs of the Office of Economic Opportunity. At this time the policy of termination had not been abandoned. Toward the close of the conference the chairman of the National Indian Youth Council spoke for the "young Indians." A few excerpts from his speech carry the same note of self-determination:

> We have got to take a good look at what approach we are going to use to be rid of poverty. The young people of the Indian tribes are going to be the ones to live with this, and sometime the Indian people are going to have to make a great effort . . to remove poverty and other conditions that have held back the Indians. . . .

> We do not wish to be pushed into the mainstream of American life. . . .

[50]Steiner, *The New Indians,* p. 257; Deloria, *Behind the Trail of Broken Treaties,* p. 70.
[51]*The New York Times,* Jan. 9, 1972, pp. 1, 56.
[52]Josephy, *Red Power,* pp. 37, 39.

> For any program to work we must be involved at the grass roots level. The responsibility to make decisions must be placed in Indian hands. Any real help for Indian people must take Indian cultural values into consideration. Programs set up to help people must fit into the cultural framework. . . .[53]

Reservations were included in the OEO programs, and, however short-lived they eventually were, they provided new opportunities for many Indians to participate in planning and developing programs, through the OEO requirement that proposals must include "maximum feasible participation of the poor."

In February, 1967, the Department of the Interior prepared a bill on Indian Resources Development. The Commissioner of Indian Affairs, Robert Bennett (an Oneida, and the first Indian to be commissioner in the twentieth century), was sent to the reservations to discover reactions to the bill. There was almost unanimous opposition. A large group of Indians met in Washington, protesting that Indians had not been consulted before the drafting of the bill. One aspect of the bill that aroused fear and bitterness was the failure to abrogate the 1953 Congressional resolution on termination. The group addressed a sharp letter of opposition to the President and the so-called Omnibus Bill died.

Other conferences and other statements occurred in this period. The continuing conferencing bridged a gap between urban and reservation Indians; it developed a considerable consensus of demands by Indians as a whole; it stimulated greater participation in politics whereby Indian voting has, in some places increased 150 percent.[54] Indian voting is concerned with issues affecting Indians and is nonpartisan in terms of national political parties. Indians in some western states can control the swing vote.

The Republican campaign preceding the 1968 election capitalized on the ethnic issue, including promises to Indians. On taking office, President Nixon requested a report with recommendations on Indians and the Bureau of Indian Affairs. This was prepared by Alvin M. Josephy, Jr., and presented February 11, 1969.[55] It offered criticisms of the Bureau and recommendations, with some alternatives. One of these raised the possibility of removing the Bureau from the Department of the Interior. The report clearly articulated the distresses of Indians and some of the structural problems of the administration of Indian affairs. The President then created a Council on Indian Opportunity with six (later expanded to eight) Indian members, under the chairmanship of the Vice-President of the United States. This was the first time that Indians had been included in equal status in a policy conference affecting Indians. The Indian members, although some of them were skeptical that this would be no more than another attempt to "rubber stamp" decisions already made, prepared a precise enumeration of Indian needs and recommendations for solutions. This was submitted to the President, January 26, 1970.[56]

---

[53]*Ibid.,* pp. 54–56.
[54]Steiner, *The New Indian,* Ch. 7, pp. 231 ff.
[55]See Josephy, *Red Power,* pp. 95–127, for excerpts of this report.
[56]*Ibid.,* pp. 192–210. The Indian members of the Council were Roger Jourdain, Chairman of the Red Lake Chippewa Tribal Council; William Hensley, an Eskimo and member of the Alaska State Legislature; Wendell Chino, Chairman of the Mescalinero Apache Tribal Council; Cato Valandra of the Rosebud Sioux Tribe of South Dakota; Mrs. LaDonna Harris, Comanche Indian of Oklahoma and wife of Senator Fred Harris; and Raymond Nakai, Chairman of the Navajo Tribal Council.

On July 8, 1970, President Nixon sent a Presidential Message to Congress on Indian Affairs that was historic in tone and intent. Although it did not halt abruptly the tradition of paternalism in government, it pointed federal policy in a new direction. It abandoned the concept of and pressure towards termination of tribal status; it upheld "self determination"; it restored some "sacred" lands; it recommended tripling the revolving loan fund for reservation projects; it recommended federal support for centers for urban Indians; it called for the establishment of a Trust Counsel Authority to represent Indians in legal issues regarding rights to natural resources.[57]

At the same time the Council on Indian Opportunity conducted two series of meetings with Indians across the country to discuss pending bills and to allow them to make recommendations and suggest new measures. Finally, in late November the Bureau of Indian Affairs announced changes in the Bureau, formulated with the help of Indians, in both structure and procedures to accelerate achievement of self-determination.[58]

THE DECLINE OF DOMINANCE?

The climate has changed. There is a nucleus now of educated Indians who are concerned with tribal integrity. More young people from the reservations are going to college in the expectation that they will be needed to advance reservation development. Decisions that formerly rested with regional offices of the BIA are now the responsibility of the reservation officer (no longer called "superintendent" but "field administrator") in cooperation with the tribal council. There is more coordination in Washington between various agencies with responsibility for Indian projects (Commerce, HEW, HUD, etc.).

There are, however, many problems and a long way to go.

The Cultural Problem. Indians wish to retain the symbolic aspects of their heritage. This includes retaining their languages, religion, ceremonials, architectural style, use of space, and the like, all of which are different from Anglo patterns. They wish to retain council decisions by consensus rather than majority vote. They wish to hold their property in common. Surrounded as they are by a totally different culture, and of necessity having to an extent deal with these differences, implies the development of a viable and valuable educational system that bridges two cultures. The creative challenge in Indian education must also be met by Anglo education in an emphasis on respect for differences.

The Economic Problem. No sustained reservation development can take place at this stage without outside capital. This must come from the U.S. government or from the lease of resources to private corporations. Indians point out that the capital made available by the government to the developing nations of Asia, Africa, and Latin America far exceeds help for Indians. Tribal leaders are cautious about private corporations, particularly any that will introduce values and behavior patterns of the secular technological world, or that will permanently impair resources.

The Social Problem. There is an increasing mood of separatism. Long memories of white encroachment, derogation by contiguous white settlements, insensitive tourists—all have made many reservation Indians anxious to keep to themselves. In

[57]*Ibid.,* pp. 213–230.
[58]*Ibid.,* p. 212.

1949, Felix S. Cohen, then head of the Indian Claims Commission, wrote

> Professed believers in self-government continually turn, when concrete
> cases arise, [to] the vocabulary that talks about "a state within a state".
> . . . There is nothing wrong about having a state within a state; that, in
> fact is the whole substance of American federalism and tolerance.[59]

The Legal Problem.   Indian rights in the use of resources, and title to lands that
have been occupied by whites or infringed upon by technological developments without
Indian consent, are legal issues of long standing and great complexity. Indians have
sought redress through several structures: the United States Court of Claims, the Indian Claims Commission, the state and federal civil courts, and now there is the new
Trust Council Authority. Although there have been some successful cases and settlements of claims, many cases have undergone long delays. There have been exhorbitant
legal fees; there has been interference by reservation "superintendents" in the choice of
lawyers; there have been inconsistent rulings in the separate structures. Nevertheless,
litigation will probably continue as a preferable or perhaps only alternative to resigna-
tion.[60]

The younger generation of Indians has demonstrated that it will not settle for apathy
and paternalism. It has proved itself capable of working intertribally in order to influence policy. The task now is to safeguard, and possibly extend, the degree of self-
determination it has won and to move toward economic rehabilitation of the Indian
people. This will depend most critically on consistency in government policy; on a bureaucracy in the Bureau of Indian affairs that sees itself as representing, not managing,
Indian interests; on offering technical assistance; and on a Congress willing to give
capital assistance either through negotiated restoration and indemnity or through long-
term, low-interest loans or both. Some Indian leaders envisage a wider role as models
for patterns of development for Indians throughout the Western Hemisphere, and for
other poverty-stricken tribal societies in Asia and Africa.

Suggested Readings

American Friends' Service Committee. *Uncommon Controversy: Fishing Rights of the
    Muckleshoot, Puyallup and Nisqually Indians.* Seattle: The University of Wash-
    ington Press, 1970.
    A full and careful analysis of the fishing rights issue in the Puget Sound area and
    the Indian protest efforts.
Brown, Dee. *Bury My Heart at Wounded Knee: An Indian History of the American
    West.* New York: Holt, Rinehart & Winston, 1970.

---

[59]Josephy, *Red Power*, p. 21.
[60]See statement by Felix S. Cohen in Josephy, *Red Power*, p. 24, and Deloria, *Behind the Trail of
Broken Treaties,* Ch. 10, for a discussion of legal channels for claims.

This eloquent documentary collection of Indian views of the coming of the white man is now a classic.

Cahn, Edgar S. *Our Brother's Keeper: The Indians in White America*. Washington, D.C.: The New Community Press, 1969.

An outstanding report on the condition and sentiments of Indians prepared by the Citizen's Advocate Center of Washington, D.C.

Deloria, Vine, Jr. *We Talk, You Listen*. New York: The Macmillan Co., 1970.

An impassioned statement of the new pluralism by a leading Indian spokesman.

————. *Behind the Trail of Broken Treaties: An Indian Declaration of Independence*. New York: Dell Publishing Co., 1974.

The author who has a law degree, presents legal arguments and precedents for the reestablishment of treaty relations between Indian tribes and the United States government.

Driver, Harold E. *Indians of North America*. Chicago: University of Chicago Press, 1961.

A comprehensive comparative description of Native American cultures.

Josephy, Alvin M., Jr. *Red Power: The American Indians' Fight for Freedom*. New York: McGraw-Hill Book Co., 1971; paperback, 1972.

An invaluable documentary collection of the gathering strength of Indian protest from 1961 to 1970.

Steiner, Stan. *The New Indians*. New York: Dell Publishing Co., 1968.

A popular, readable, and vivid account of rising activism and of issues among American Indians, prepared with the cooperation of Indian groups and individual informants. Excellent appendices: chronology, documentary statements, bibliography.

Terrell, John Upton. *The Navajos: The Past and Present of a Great People*. New York: Harper & Row, 1970.

A good account of the largest of the Indian nations, especially illustrating the effects of vascillating government policy.

12

Mexican Americans—*La Raza*

There were approximately 9 million persons of Spanish-speaking origin in the United States in 1970, including over 5 million who were of Mexican descent. The largest concentrations are in the five southwestern states of California, Arizona, New Mexico, Colorado, and Texas, though there has been some steady spread to the northern Midwest: Illinois, Minnesota, Iowa, Wisconsin, Ohio. Today 80 percent of the Mexican American population live in urban communities (though given the pattern of urban sprawl in western cities, this does not necessarily mean the slums of central cities), 85 percent are native born, and 50 percent are third generation.[1]

PATTERNS OF MIGRATION

The greatest proportion of Mexican Americans have migrated since the annexation of the territories of the Southwest. Trends in immigration have largely been affected by the "pull" of employment opportunities, and the "push" of adverse economic or political conditions in Mexico. As with other groups, immigration declined sharply during the Depression. Then the great demands for manpower during World War II precipitated a rise which reached a peak about 1953. Until the enforcement of immigration restriction after 1929, Mexicans crossed the border freely. The majority came from the rural folk culture of Mexico, to some extent deviants from a feudal social system that viewed economic advancement of the individual as unworthy.[2] A minority came from more sophisticated strata in the hope of improving their financial position. Still others came as refugees from the political upheavals of Mexico.

---

[1] The precise figures for this rapidly growing population are difficult to arrive at. The 1930 Census attempted to enumerate the Spanish-speaking people of the Southwest under the heading "Mexican," defining this group as people born in Mexico or children of people born in Mexico. This eliminated the older hispano population of the Southwest. In 1940 the census dropped this category, but attempted to determine the size of the Spanish-speaking and other foreign-language groups by a 5 percent sample of "what language other than English was spoken in your home." This sample was relatively accurate for large cities, but not for small cities and rural areas. In 1960 a sample was taken in five states of people with a Spanish surname, but this of course failed to include those who had anglicized their names or women who had intermarried. The current population reports asked the respondents to identify their ethnic descent. Since the actual count is slightly lower for people of Mexican descent than in the 1960 Census, we may possibly assume that there has been an increase in assimilation. Nevertheless, the Latin Americans—Mexican, Puerto Rican, Cuban, and Central American together—make up the second largest minority in the United States.
[2] William Madsen, *The Mexican-Americans of South Texas* (New York: Holt, Rinehart & Winston, 1964), p. 24.

241

Undocumented Aliens

The enforcement of immigration restriction led to the growth of illegal migration. The 2,000-mile border between Mexico and the United States offers opportunities to evade patrols. Many swam the Rio Grande, and were popularly designated "wetbacks." More recently, they have slipped in in the vicinity of border towns, often paying high prices to guides. The Immigration Service and the border patrol returned thousands, often to have them immediately try again.

> Alfredo is a tall, handsome man in his fifties who proudly calls himself a Texan. He freely admits to his friends that he entered the United States as a wetback. "My determination to stay was great," he said, "fourteen times they caught me and threw me out but here I am." [3]

Braceros

Braceros came legally to the United States as agricultural labor under contract with the Mexican government. Many of them liked the United States and decided to stay. The statute admitting this type of seasonal labor was allowed to expire at the end of 1964 and braceros are no longer admitted to the country. [4]

THE ESTABLISHMENT OF DOMINANCE

Spanish-speaking people have been in the Southwest for over 350 years. Some of the villages north of Santa Fe, New Mexico, were founded in 1598. A century later Spanish settlements were made in Texas, and almost two centuries later, in California. In each of these three areas, distinctive Spanish cultures developed. Another influence was the relation of the Spanish to the many different Indian groups with which they came in contact. Until about the middle of the nineteenth century, the *californios,* the *nuevo mexicanos,* and the *texanos* went their separate cultural ways, held together only slightly by, at first, the slender ties of Spain, and later, briefly, by the uncertain and flimsy bonds of independent Mexico.

From the turn of the eighteenth century to the Mexican-American War, intergroup relations ranged from individual friendships to competition, antagonism, and, in many instances, violent conflict rising out of ethnic and racial distinctions. The Mexican society was sharply divided between upper-class property owners and peons. The invader-immigrant Anglos as individuals often competed and sometimes came in conflict with the upper-class Mexicans for economic gain; however, there were many who cooperated with the ruling Mexican elements and through intermarriage became part of Mexican society. Both upper-class Mexicans and Americans considered the peons an inferior, servile class. With the increasing infiltration of Americans, however, relations between Mexican and American became more antagonistic. In Texas, where by 1836 Americans far outnumbered Mexicans, this antagonism expressed itself in a successful revolution resulting in the formation of the Republic of Texas.

---

[3]*Ibid.,* p. 25.
[4]See Celia S. Heller, *Mexican American Youth: Forgotten Youth At the Crossroads* (New York: Random House, 1966), p. 11, for analysis of this statute, public law 78, and its termination.

By the Treaty of Guadalupe Hidalgo, terminating the Mexican-American War, all the Mexican territory north of the Rio Grande became part of the United States. From this point on, American influence became dominant over Spanish-Mexican; some upper-class Mexicans attempted to join American society; the poorer and illiterate Mexicans became a distinct ethnic minority, notwithstanding the fact that they had become citizens of the United States. The antagonistic character of Anglo-Mexican relations is reflected in the terms "gringo" and "greaser," which each group came to apply to the members of the other, with contemptuous implications. In popular usage before the conquest, "gringo" referred to any foreigner who spoke Spanish with an accent. The term "greaser" referred to a native Mexican or a native Spanish American, and was originally applied disdainfully by the Americans of the southwestern United States to Mexicans.

Given this situation against the setting of the "trigger-fingered" frontier, it was not surprising that violence should frequently arise. Paul S. Taylor in his study of a border community testified to many instances of violence from both groups. He cites the comment of a local official: "Undoubtedly robberies and murders by Mexicans have continually been perpetrated in Texas, but in retaliation Americans have committed terrible outrages upon citizens of Mexican origin."[5]

In 1914, when diplomatic relations between Mexico and the United States were temporarily severed, the Mexican Americans of South Texas were frequently identified with "the enemy." As Madsen reports

> A wall of fear grew between Anglo and Latin communities. Recalling this period, a Mexican-American said, "All our people were afraid. And here we were in our own country but the Anglos thought we were not from here."[6]

Dominance was achieved by military aggression and by Anglo-American astuteness in seizing economic advantage. After the annexation of Texas, land speculators were able to buy up land confiscated for unpaid taxes. In 1877, a 3,027-acre original Mexican land grant whose Mexican American owner was in tax arrears was sold by the sheriff to an Anglo for fifteen dollars. The boom in land speculation continued until 1930.[7]

Visibility

Physical. The "racial" composition of the population of Mexico has been in this century approximately 10 percent white, 60 percent mestizo (mixed Indian and white), and 30 percent Indian. Since the immigrants to the United States have been more numerous from the latter two population elements, especially the mestizo, it is not surprising that the results of the United States Census of 1930, enumerating the Mexican stock by racial designation as "white" and "colored" for the first and only time, showed less than 5 percent as "white," 65,968 out of 1,422,533 total Mexican stock listed.[8] More recently Dworkin has estimated that well over 80 percent are mestizos but points

---

[5]Paul S. Taylor, *An American Mexican Frontier* (Chapel Hill: University of North Carolina Press, 1934), p. 65.
[6]Madsen, *The Mexican-Americans of South Texas*, p. 9.
[7]*Ibid.*, p. 56.
[8]Maurice R. Davie, *World Immigration* (New York: The Macmillan Co., 1936), p. 215.

out the difficulty in having any precise figures. He quotes Moore and Cuellar: "The paradox comes to the surface when a hazel-eyed, pale skinned man talks about his 'Indianness' and a dark skinned, Indian-featured man talks about his 'whiteness.' "[9]

Thus Mexican Americans are not a homogeneous group in appearance, but are often identifiable. To the extent that they are predominantly now American born, they are also showing some physical changes, as have the children of other immigrants to the United States: increase in stature, hand length, and nasal index.[10]

Madsen quotes an uneducated Anglo (about 1960) as saying "The Meskin's not a white man, but he's a hell of a lot whiter than a nigger."[11] A study of a California city of about the same date finds similar comparative attitudes on the part of dominants toward Mexican Americans and Negroes.[12] Madsen also points out that the South Texans whom he studied will only let the term "white" be used for an Anglo. He quotes one anglicized Mexican American as follows:

> I think like an Anglo and I act like an Anglo but I'll never look like an Anglo. Just looking at me, no one could tell if I am an American or one of those blasted Mexicans from across the river. It's hell to look like a foreigner in your own country.[13]

Cultural. The value system of the Mexican Americans has been traditionally associated with the concept of *La Raza* (the race). In the sense this term is used it is nineteenth-century and has no relation to the racialism of North Europeans and American WASPS. Just as the French speak of themselves as a race, so *La Raza* is a cultural concept. It applies to all Latin Americans who are united by cultural and spiritual bonds. It implies that God has planned a great destiny for this people, though it never may be attained because of the individual sins of its members. In other words, it is a concept of peoplehood and of destiny, creating deep psychic bonds. One can see the same phenomenon among Jews and, in the early periods of American history, nordic Americans. The central character of the value system of *La Raza,* however, reflects in the Mexican Americans the long history of feudalism from Spain, oppression in Mexico, and discrimination in the United States. For most of the older generation it is a Catholicized fatalism.

Acceptance and appreciation of things as they are, says Madsen, constitute the primary values of traditionalist members of *La Raza.* He quotes an expression of the world view of the Mexican American:

> We are not very important in the universe. We are here because God sent us and we must leave when God calls us. God has given us a good way to live and we should try to see the beauty of His commands. We often fail for

[9]Anthony Gary Dworkin, "The Peoples of La Raza: The Mexican-Americans of Los Angeles," in Noel P. Gist and Anthony Gary Dworkin, *The Blending of Races: Marginality and Identity in World Perspective* (New York: John Wiley & Sons, 1972), p. 168.

[10]Marcus S. Goldstein, *Demographic and Bodily Changes in Descendants of Mexican Immigrants* (Austin: University of Texas, Institute of Latin American Studies, 1943).

[11]Madsen, *The Mexican-Americans of South Texas,* p. 11.

[12]Alphonso Pinkney, "Prejudice Toward Mexican and Negro Americans: A Comparison," in *Phylon,* First Quarter, 1963, pp. 355 ff.

[13]Madsen, *The Mexican-Americans of South Texas,* p. 8.

many are weak but we should try. There is much suffering but we should accept it for it comes from God. Life is sad but beautiful.[14]

Because God controls events the Anglo orientation to and planning for the future is alien to the true member of *La Raza*. For him, honor, to behave like "a whole man," to maintain dignity and courtesy, to show respect, and to fulfill his obligations to the family of his birth as to the one he founds, these are the core values.

Religion. Religion and culture are closely intertwined in the average Mexican American household. The presence of a family altar in the house symbolizes the family-centeredness of the culture as much as it does the religious faith.[15] However, as Ruth Tuck points out, Mexican Catholicism is not church-centered and she found in *Descanso* that men rarely went to church.[16] Conservative Mexican Americans may still name their sons Jesus, which seems peculiar and even sacriligious to Anglo Protestants. "We live with God while the Anglos lock Him in to Heaven."[17]

Language. The principal language for Mexican Americans, whether first, second, or third generation, is some variant of Spanish. This is often a local dialect intermixed with hispanisized English words, and there is considerable variation: from "Tex-Mex" to the Spanish spoken by the Hispanos of New Mexico to that of the largely generational dialect, *Pachuco,* spoken by Mexican American urban youth.[18]

The greatest deficiency in the English of Mexican Americans is in informal English. Often they hesitate to speak English at all if they do not know it well, as to do so might be discourteous. They do not encourage Anglos to speak Spanish to them. Heller suggests that they may perceive the imperfect Spanish of an Anglo as "talking down" to them. Also, they seem to be embarrassed for the Anglo for his poor Spanish.

Spanish is spoken in the home as long as one identifies with the Mexican American community. Some parents speak some English to their children "so that it won't be so hard for them in school," and upper-class Mexican Americans pride themselves on perfect Spanish and English.

Institutional Roles. Next to family roles, "manliness," (*machismo*) is the most important community ideal. To be a "whole man" involves a high degree of individuality, yet this is within the family framework as every Mexican American male is expected to represent his family with honor at all times. The manly role makes him sensitive to any authority or competition that would darken his public image with threat of devaluation or failure. According to Madsen, "ideally the Latin male acknowledges only the authority of his father and God. In case of conflict between these two sources of authority he should side with his father. No proper father, however, would act counter to God's will, for such behavior would make him less of a man."[19]

This sensitive pride leads the Mexican American to avoid associations that threaten him: to be punctilious about indebtedness, to avoid accepting charity, to occasionally

---

[14]*Ibid.,* p. 17.

[15]Madsen seems to indicate that the family altar is less conspicuous as one goes up the status scale of Mexican American society. It ceases to be in the living room and may rather be in the mother's bedroom. *Ibid.,* pp. 35–41.

[16]Ruth D. Tuck, *Not With the Fist* (New York: Harcourt, Brace & Co., 1946), p. 153.

[17]Madsen, *The Mexican-Americans of South Texas,* p. 7.

[18]Celia S. Heller, *Mexican American Youth,* pp. 29–30, 59–62.

[19]Madsen, p. 18.

seek personal revenge, to feel that the obligations of affiliation with formal organizations weakens his independence.

Great value is put on male sexual virility with the resulting double standard of sexual morality. Girls are carefully guarded by their mothers and brothers, and wives by their husbands. The approved roles for women are within the household and the family. The Mexican American wife is expected to show her husband absolute respect. Her fulfilment is in helping her husband achieve his goals as he sees fit.

Father and mother alike share the task of teaching children how to conduct themselves. Proper relations to others in Mexican American society involve patterns of respect and formal courtesy. An "educated" person is one who has been well trained as a social being.

> As long as a Latin conforms to the rules of proper conduct, he is entitled to his own beliefs. One may resent another's actions but not another's opinions or interpretations. The view is expressed in the Mexican American saying, *Cada cabeza es un mundo* (Each head is a world unto itself). A person may think as he pleases but he should not try to impose his ideas on anybody else. These concepts of propriety are a major factor in the hostility felt toward missionaries and public health workers who are trying to change Mexican American beliefs. A distinguished Latin citizen voiced his opinion on what he called "brain washing." "Americans have abandoned geographic imperialism, but to them mental imperialism is a wide open field."[20]

The cultural profile as drawn above must not be taken as a stereotype. It is useful for people who do not share the traditional Spanish culture in its North American variant to see some of the core historical attitudes. But it is important to remember that today these attitudes may be held flexibly. Catholicized fatalism has been an adaptation of exploited peasantry of more than one European cultural tradition. It will only persist—the fatalism—if similar situations of closed opportunity and devaluation persist in the environment. That there is more hope and that for many this is changing to a different kind of ethnic pride will be apparent in the subsequent discussion in this chapter. Nevertheless, core elements remain.

In a recent study of children's attitudes in a low-income Mexican American neighborhood ("barrio") in Houston, Texas, the authors concluded that

> Training in helping, in discipline, and in respect for others all occur early. Most children have numerous relatives who take active interest in them. . . . Most Barrio fathers do command respect, and most Barrio households where there are school age children do have fathers, both legally and functionally. . . .
>
> In the larger study of which this child study is a part, our research group has learned that the mood of the Mexican American community of Houston tends to be expansive and optimistic. Anglo prejudice is lessening, the

---

[20]*Ibid.*, p. 21.

Spanish language is more accepted, things Mexican are gaining popularity. . . . Certainly the Mexican Americans now take considerable pride in their ethnic heritage.

It is our impression that the values of the Barrio children are on the whole conducive to modest success in contemporary urban society. It seems likely that their life chances are better in this respect than those of the Negro children we interviewed.[21]

MINORITY ADAPTATION: EARLY PERIOD

In towns and cities with any sizable Mexican American population there are still today the residential enclaves where the majority of this ethnic group are concentrated. Mexican Americans refer to them as "colonia" and dominants call them "Mextown" or "little Mexico." In 1954 John J. Burma estimated that about three-fourths of all the Mexican Americans in the United States lived in *colonia*.[22]

Mexican immigrants in the Southwest found employment in unskilled occupations, chiefly as agricultural laborers. Their wages, in common with agricultural labor generally, were low—usually lower than that paid any Anglos employed in the same work. Employers often maintained that this differential was justified because Anglo laborers were more productive than Mexicans. These Mexican laborers were slow to become unionized. Earlier efforts at organization, opposed strongly by the agricultural employers, were generally unsuccessful. While by the late 1920s an increasing number of the Mexicans were buying or building homes of their own, they did not buy farm land for themselves, and they showed little interest in sharecropping. Few opportunities existed for Mexicans in higher-ranking occupations, both because they were not equipped to fill them and because of the discrimination against their employment in occupations involving Anglo fellow workers or serving Anglo trade. Some Mexican clerks were employed in low-priced stores for the purpose of encouraging Mexican trade.

For the initial period, the studies of Paul Taylor[23] in four different areas of the Southwest are the most extensive. The housing of the more settled Mexicans was found to be of the lowest standard; and that of Mexicans employed in agriculture of a nondescript variety, sometimes haymows or improvised shelters in the woods. In spite of these poor economic conditions, Mexicans were not often on relief rolls, partly because of their tradition of mutual aid. Nor did Taylor find their criminal arrests more than proportionate.

---

[21]Mary Ellen Goodman and Alma Beman, "Child's-Eye-Views of Life in an Urban Barrio," in Nathaniel L. Wagner and Marsha J. Haug, eds., *Chicanos: Social and Psychological Perspectives* (St. Louis: The C. V. Mosby Co., 1971), pp. 118–119.
[22]John H. Burma, *Spanish-Speaking Groups in the United States* (Durham: The Duke University Press, 1954), p. 88.
[23]Paul S. Taylor, *Mexican Labor in the United States* (Berkeley: University of California Press, Publication in Economics, Vol. 6, 1928). In this volume are included three monographs: No. 1 on Imperial Valley, California; No. 2 on the Valley of South Platte, Colorado; and No. 5 on Dimmit County, South Texas. While Taylor, an economist, was primarily interested in the labor situations of the Mexicans, his field of inquiry embraced the general pattern of social relations between the Anglos and Mexicans.

Discrimination

Whereas there were few legal restrictions against Mexican Americans except in some counties, in subtle ways they were "kept in their place." The pattern of discrimination was summed up in an extensive study of Texas communities conducted during the war years.

> *Economic Discrimination.* (1) Unfair employment practices forcing low economic status upon the majority of Latin Americans. (2) Discrimination exercised by both management and Labor unions in the admission and upgrading of Latin Americans. (3) Exploitation in agriculture. (4) Demand of growers for cheap labor carried to the extreme of favoring illegal seasonal influx workers.

> *Social and Civic Inequalities.* (1) Refusal of service in some public places of business and amusement. (2) Denial of the right to vote in some counties. (3) Denial of the right to rent or own real estate in many cities. (4) Denial of the right to serve on juries in some counties. (5) Terrorism on the part of law-enforcement officers and others.[24]

Many Mexican Americans were formerly discouraged from contemplating political action because of discrimination in various places through the poll tax and the disqualification of Mexican Americans for voting in Democratic primaries. In the 1940s Ernesto Galarza complained that

> Mexicans are a political non-entity in the U.S. . . . They keep clear of political obligations and therefore do not take advantage of political opportunities. . . . Therefore all pleas to the state governor, the President of the United States, the legislature or Congress must be based on considerations of high human sentiment. In the American political system, however, such sentiments have always been found to fare much better when supported by precinct organization and votes in the ballot box.[25]

As is characteristic of dominant groups, southwestern Anglos tended to play down the extent of their discrimination and to rationalize what could not be denied by invoking an unfavorable stereotype of the Mexican American. Tuck put it thus:

> There is nothing Descanso [Anglos] will deny more stoutly than any intention of keeping its Mexican-Americans disadvantaged in order to derive an economic gain from their position. That is why it resents the words caste or semicaste being applied to its practices. Descanso argues, rather, that the bulk of its Mexican-Americans are so low in type that they could not profit by advantage. It seems rather odd to prove this point by making sure that they have continued inferior advantage, but Descanso sees no hint of a vi-

---

[24]Pauline R. Kibbe, *Latin-Americans in Texas* (Albuquerque: University of New Mexico Press, 1946), pp. 271–272.
[25]Ernesto Galarza, "The Mexican American: A National Concern," in *Common Ground*, 9, Summer, 1949, pp. 27–38.

cious circle in this procedure. The "low type" of Mexican, says Descanso, is getting about what he deserves. If he encounters segregated schooling, segregation in use of public facilities, unequal employment opportunities, unequal pay for equal work, or prejudiced law enforcement and justice— what of it?

. . . .

You have to recognize, argues Descanso, that some people are just born inferior, generation after generation. As the leader of a church study group put it, "there are always hewers of wood and drawers of water."[26]

The "Zoot Suit" Riot of 1943

One of the severest outbreaks against Mexican Americans occurred during the Second World War at a time when Mexico was our ally. It was the first of a series of riots that summer which in part reflected the tension of a country at war.

The anti-Mexican riots in Los Angeles ranged from June 3, 1943, until June 9. This was wartime; a nearby naval base made Los Angeles the mecca for sailors' leaves. The riots were touched off on June 3 by two incidents. Some servicemen walking through a deteriorated street in a Mexican section of the city were beaten up by a gang of Mexican boys. In a nearby precinct on the same evening some Mexican boys returning from a "club" conference at the police station on how to avoid gang strife were beaten up by a gang of non-Mexican boys. It does not seem as if the two incidents were connected. The police took no immediate action, but then after their regular duty was over, a so-called "vengeance squad" set out to clean up the gang that had attacked the sailors. They found no one to arrest, but great newspaper publicity was given to the incidents and to the policemen who had made the fruitless raid.

The following night about 200 sailors hired a fleet of 20 taxicabs and cruised the Mexican quarter. The Mexican adolescent boys had a fad of wearing long, draped jackets (zoot suits). Four times the taxicab brigade stopped when it sighted a Mexican boy in a zoot suit and beat up the boys, leaving them lying on the pavement. There was no mobilization of police. One police car did intercept the caravan, and nine sailors were taken into custody, but no charges were preferred against them. In the morning papers the war news was pushed off the front page with stories of the night before on a triumphal note of the sailor's move to clean up "zoot-suited roughnecks." The third night, June 5, scores of sailors, soldiers, and marines marched through the Mexican quarter, four abreast, stopping and threatening anyone wearing zoot suits. No sailors were arrested, either by the police, the shore patrol, or the Military Police, although twenty-seven Mexican boys were arrested. In various bars Mexicans were beaten up or their jackets torn off and ripped up. The police announced that any Mexicans involved in rioting would be arrested.

---

[26]Ruth D. Tuck, *Not With the Fist*, pp. 54–55; By permission.

On the night of June 6 six carloads of sailors cruised through the area, beating up teenage Mexicans and wrecking establishments. The police came after them in mopping-up operations and arrested the boys who had been beaten up. In the morning forty-four severely beaten Mexican boys were under arrest.

Whipped up by the press, which warned that the Mexicans were about to riot with broken bottles as weapons and would beat sailors' brains out with hammers, the excitement erupted and two days of really serious rioting occurred, involving soldiers, sailors, and civilians, who invaded motion picture houses, stopped trolley cars, and beat up the Mexicans they found, as well as a few Filipinos and Negroes. At midnight on June 7 the military authorities declared Los Angeles out of bounds for military personnel. The order immediately slowed down the riot. On June 8 the mayor stated that "sooner or later it will blow over," and the chief of police announced the situation "cleared up." However, rioting went on for two more days. Editorials and statements to the press lamented the fact that the servicemen were called off before they were able to complete the job. The district attorney of an outlying county stated that "zoot suits are an open indication of subversive character." And the Los Angeles City Council adopted a resolution making the wearing of zoot suits a misdemeanor.[27]

The role of the police is to be understood only if one presumes that their refraining from interference was deliberate and related to an entirely different matter. At the time of the riots a police officer was on trial in the courts for charges of brutality. Shortly after the riots, according to Carey McWilliams, a Hollywood police captain told a motion picture director that the police had touched off the riots to give a break to their colleague in demonstrating the necessity for harsh police methods. As a matter of fact, the charges against the officer were dismissed a month later.

The use of the stereotyped image of the zoot suit appeared in all the publicity and what was simply an adolescent fad was linked in the minds of the readers with the characterizations "gang," "roughneck," "subversive," and so forth. The press and the radio leaped on the bandwagon and were largely responsible in their unanimity for inflaming the population.

The tone of the press clearly reflects the war psychology and the support of servicemen. The servicemen themselves were young men away from home, uprooted from the normal community controls in the anonymous and sex-segregated climate of military life. Many of them engaged in actions that would have been unthinkable in their home environment.

Writing of the problem of Mexican American youth gangs in Los Angeles just after the riots, George I. Sanchez commented that

> The seed for the pachucos was sown a decade or more ago by unintelligent educational measures, by discriminatory social and economic practices, by provincial smugness and self-assigned "racial" superiority. . . .

[27]Carey McWilliams, *North From Mexico* (Philadelphia: J. B. Lippincott, 1949), pp. 244–253. Adapted by the authors.

When the pachuco "crime wave" broke last year, I communicated with the Office of War Information: "I understand that a grand jury is looking into the Mexican American problem in Los Angeles and that there seems to be considerable misunderstanding as to the causes of gang activities of Mexican youth in that area. I hear also that much ado is being made about "Aztec forebears," "blood lust" and similar claptrap in interpreting the behavior of these citizens. It would be indeed unfortunate if this grand jury investigation were to go off on a tangent, witchhunting in anthropological antecedents for causes which, in reality, lie right under the noses of the public service agencies in Los Angeles.[28]

Organizational Patterns

Before World War II, Mexican Americans were weak in organizational structure. Tuck describes the situation in Descanso:

The proliferation of societies, clubs, and associations which distinguishes American life has not yet intruded on the *colonia*. The number of kin of each family is extensive enough to provide a wide circle of friends. There is one large men's organization, the Confederation of Mexican Societies, a council of four mutual insurance groups, whose chief activity is to celebrate two Mexican national holidays. It rather vaguely acts for the "economic, moral, and cultural improvement of the Mexican people." Its constitution specifically restricts any civic activity which is political in nature. From time to time, other organizations had arisen which were more definitely political; however, "most of them have had brief, fitful lives."[29]

MINORITY ADAPTATIONS: SECOND PHASE

Immediately following World War II, many veterans began to take active roles in community leadership. Some were able to buy better homes, continue education under the G.I. bill, and often obtain better employment. Some were able to be elected or appointed to public office. In Los Angeles four years after the zoot suit riots the first Mexican American since 1881 was elected to a municipal office.[30]

One of the oldest "civic" organizations, LULAC, the League of United Latin-American Citizens, founded in 1929, began in the fifties and sixties to shift from a "betterment" type of organization to a more specifically politically oriented organization. It

---

[28]George I. Sancnez, "Pachucos in the Making," in Wayne Moquin and Charles Van Doren, eds. *A Documentary History of the Mexican Americans* (New York: Praeger Publishers, 1971; Bantam edition, 1972), pp. 410–411. The original article was published in *Common Ground,* Autumn, 1943.

Pachuco is a youth dialect and a self-designation given by these young people to themselves. The word probably stems from a place name in Mexico, possibly associated with place of origin of leaders or members.

[29]Tuck, *Not With the First,* p. 160.

[30]See Beatrice W. Griffith, "Viva Roybal—Viva America," in *Common Ground,* Autumn, 1949, for a description of the candidate and of the mobilization of the Mexican American community for the election in which 15,000 new voters were registered.

is moderate, as might be expected of a membership made up of older and more es-tablished segments of the Mexican American community, but it has been active in pressing for reforms and bringing grievances before state and federal officials. MAPA, the Mexican American Political Association, and the Political Association of Spanish-speaking Organizations, PASO, have been more directly political, concerned with equal employment, voter registration, and the election of Mexican Americans to office.

Mexican Americans Go to Court

Of what is probably the greatest significance, overt segregation of Mexican children in the public schools has been eliminated to all intents and pur-poses. The federal court cases in California, Arizona, and Texas—both those that came to trial and those which did not—have made it abundantly clear that American children of Mexican descent cannot be segregated in the public schools. Even where school authorities have sought to use pseu-dopedagogical reasons for separating "Anglos" from "Latins" the courts have either condemned the practices or have made it patent that the proof of the pudding would be in the eating, thus discouraging the use of sub-terfuges to cover up "racial" segregation. This break-through in school cases has served as precedent for the attack on segregation in other public services, with widespread success. In all areas there still remain many fronts on which the civil liberties battle will have to be fought. Recalcitrant communities (rather, recalcitrant government boards) will seek "legal" ways to perpetuate segregation—in education the devices will include "neighborhood schools," "free choice" in the selection of a school, "ability grouping," "special" provision for migrant children, and the like. Most of these subterfuges will be the subject not of court action but of political ac-tion, as has been demonstrated already in a number of communities.

In the area of civil liberties, the *Pete Hernández Case* (Supreme Court of the United States, No. 406, October Term, 1953) has not drawn the atten-tion it deserves, for it is significant not only for Spanish-Mexicans in the United States but for all groups that are treated as a class apart. This case, about a "Mexican" who was tried and sentenced by a jury in a county where "Mexicans" had never served on juries, was carried on up to the Supreme Court of the United States by lawyers of Mexican descent who were financed entirely by funds raised by people of Mexican descent. The unanimous judgment of the Court, written by the Chief Justice, finding for the plaintiff, included the following:

> Throughout our history differences in race and color have defined easily identifiable groups which have at times required the aid of the courts in securing equal treatment under the laws. But community prejudices are not static, and from time to time other differences from the community norm may define other groups which need the same protection. Whether such a group exists within a community is a ques-tion of fact. When the existence of a distinct class is demonstrated, and it is further shown that the laws, as written or as applied, single out that class for different treatment not based on some reasonable classifi-

cation, the guarantees of the Constitution have been violated. The Fourteenth Amendment is not directed solely against discrimination due to a "two-class theory"—that is, based upon differences between "white" and Negro.

This far-reaching decision, handed down two weeks before the *Brown v. Board of Education* (segregation of Negroes) case, laid down a principle on which the Americans of Mexican descent (as well as others) can rely for protection against discrimination and the mistreatment of their class in every area of official public endeavor. The Hernandez case served another cause of equal importance: it gave heart to the "Mexican" leadership, a leadership whose sights had been raised with their victory in the previous Mendez and Delgado (school segregation) cases.[31]

Union Organization

In the 1940s and '50s there were sporadic attempts to organize by Mexican Americans. In 1944 the CIO International Union of Mine, Mill and Smelter Workers succeeded before the War Labor Board in eliminating discriminatory wage rates. But the critical problem for many Mexican Americans is that of low wages for agricultural labor. Although there had been an attempt to organize grape pickers in California in the 1930s these efforts were defeated.

Efforts to organize 1,500 farm workers, seeking a $1.25 minimum wage, in the lower Rio Grande Valley in the '60s received national attention and created conflict with the Roman Catholic Bishop of Texas, who disciplined a priest active in organization efforts.

Poverty and Protest

In 1970, 29.4 percent of Mexican American families had incomes below the poverty line: 1,283,000 persons; and for individuals not living in families the percentage was 34.5 percent: 53,000 individuals.[32]

In 1974 unemployment averaged 8.1 percent for all workers of Spanish origin (8.1 for Mexicans, 8.5 for Puerto Ricans, and 6.2 for Cubans).[33] Data on subemployment is spotty, but it is enough to give some indicators. Subemployment, according to the "Wirtz index" (Wirtz was at the time—mid-1960s—Secretary of Labor) as used in ten selected urban poverty areas (November, 1966), showed the highest rate for San Antonio. The unemployment rate was 8.1; the subemployment 47.7, the highest of all the 10 study sites; the third highest was Phoenix, Arizona, 41.7 (with only New Orleans higher: 45.3 percent).[34] San Antonio and Phoenix have high concentrations of Mexican Americans. The report points out that "the subemployment survey had gone to the core

[31]From an unpublished summary prepared for the authors by George I. Sanchez, University of Texas.
[32]U.S. Bureau of the Census, "Characteristics of the Low-Income Population," 1971.
[33]Helen Ginsburg, *Unemployment, Subemployment and Public Policy* (New York University School of Social Work, Center for Studies in Income Maintenance Policy, 1975), Appendix, Table 4B.
[34]*Ibid.*, pp. 94–95.

of the urban crisis: unemployment and the inability of many workers from slums to earn a decent living."

Dworkin, in a study of Mexican Americans in Los Angeles, points out that Los Angeles spreads over 410 miles and lacks a rapid transit system. People on welfare, he states, are often forbidden to buy automobiles. This makes barrio residents dependent on local employment; and for consumers barrio stores charge more for given items.[35]

In agriculture nearly 50 percent of Mexican Americans are farm laborers and a 1970 study of the border economy diclosed that 72 percent of illegal entrants were employed in agriculture.[36] Briggs examines the status of state laws regarding farm workers in the five states of California, New Mexico, Arizona, Colorado, and Texas. California, New Mexico, and Texas, as of 1970, had minimum wage requirements (California $1.65; New Mexico, $1.30; Texas, $1.10), whereas Colorado and Arizona had none. None required payment for overtime; none except California had workers covered by unemployment insurance and workman's compensation. All except Texas had mandatory standards for housing field crews.[37]

Briggs concludes his study by pointing out that by denying coverage by social legislation to workers on farms and allowing "green card commuters"[38] and illegal entrants to depress wage standards, Chicanos are victims of "institutionally imposed poverty."[39]

Cesar Chavez: A Nonviolent Militant[40]

The entire nation now knows the name of this gentle, diminutive man. All know he is a profound Christian, a follower of Ghandi in his deep commitment to nonviolence and in his use of fasts and boycotts as well as strikes as tactics in the struggle for benefits for Mexican American agricultural workers. Sometimes he is called "the Chicano Messiah."

Chavez' first major thrust was to organize grape pickers on ranches supplying the corporate wine industries. In Delano, California, he cooperated with a striking Filipino organization and together, by June 1966, after the longest farm strike in California history, they had won a contract with Shenley giving a minimum wage of $1.75 an hour.

Chavez had attempted to keep his union independent, but when threatened by another grower's invitation to the Teamsters Union, Chavez and the Filipino organization merged (August 1966), becoming the United Farm Workers Organizing Committee, AFLCIO. The big wineries were a logical first target, as they were nationally advertised and vulnerable to adverse publicity. By September 1968, nearly all the *name* brands had signed contracts (Gallo, Christian Brothers, Almaden, Paul Masson).

---

[35]Anthony Gary Dworkin, "The Peoples of La Raza: The Mexican-Americans of Los Angeles," in Gist and Dworkin, *The Blending of Races*, p. 196.
[36]Vernon M. Briggs, Jr., *Chicanos and Rural Poverty* (Baltimore: The Johns Hopkins Press, 1973). pp. 26, 44.
[37]*Ibid.*, p. 51.
[38]Holders of "green cards" have permanent resident status, though not citizenship. For many Mexicans green cards were obtained (before this became impossible under the 1965 revisions of the immigration law requiring Labor Department certification of employment) and they became a commuter labor force moving between Mexico and the U.S.).
[39]*Ibid.*, p. 74.
[40]Peter Matthiessen, *Sal Si Puedes: Cesar Chavez and the New American Revolution* (New York: Dell Publishing Co., 1969).

Apart from the rival Teamsters, the major threat to California pickers were "green card" workers. These were Mexicans with permanent visas as resident aliens—a measure to circumvent the discontinuance of the bracero program and to meet farm labor shortages. Green card holders were not supposed to work in fields where a strike had been called, but enforcement was lax.

Table grapes became a target when a subsidiary of one corporation that had a union contract permitted nonunion growers to use its label. This led to first a statewide boycott on table grapes in support of striking grape pickers. Then, as California grapes appeared in Eastern markets labeled "Arizona grapes," the boycott became nationwide.

The Defense Department in 1967 bought six times as many grapes to send to Vietnam as it had bought before the strike began. Green card labor was imported and temporary injunctions were obtained permitting use of green card workers on the grounds that the labor clause was unconstitutional.

Chavez' workers then dispersed across the country in a massive effort to spread the boycott. By January 1969, only one chain in New York still sold grapes; stevedores in England, Sweden, Norway, and Finland refused to unload California grapes. By July 1970, the big growers signed. One issue that delayed contract agreement was the union's firm stand against the use of DDT.

Fruit is a large (usually corporate) farm industry in California. Seven percent of the growers employ 75 percent of the workers. Wages have averaged $1,500 a year. The UFWOC contracts contain no-strike clauses for the duration of the contract, with stringent immediate binding mediation and court action in the event of violation. They also provide better wages, establish grievance and arbitration procedures, make provision for job security, overtime pay, rest periods, jointly administered health benefit plans, certain holidays and vacations with pay, health and safety protections on the job (including field toilets), etc. Dues to UFWOC are $3.50 per month.

Efforts to obtain contracts with the big lettuce growers again used the tactic of boycott. Senator Edward Kennedy, addressing the Democratic National Convention in 1972, opened his speech to nominate candidate George McGovern with the words "Fellow lettuce boycotters."

In a dispute in the mid-1970s where the Teamsters Union was seeking control of the farm workers and offering, it was claimed, "sweetheart contracts" to employers, California appointed a special commission to investigate and make recommendations in the dispute. The commission dragged its feet, but under pressure from Governor Brown a resolution was finally arrived at granting the United Farm Workers jurisdiction in all organizing in the fields. The UFWOC has recently been active on the East Coast among the vegetable and fruit growers of New York, New Jersey, and Pennsylvania.

The Chicano Movement

The Chicanos began as young urban militants, speaking, they felt, for the poorer stratum of Mexican Americans, and emphasizing pride in their Indian heritage. Like most other movements, they have gone through several phases. In the beginning there was some violence; and there was the usual struggle to clarify identity and goals. One thing they were clear about was that they rejected the image of the passive "Catholicized fatalism" of Anglo researchers.

The term *Chicano* is usually explained as a shortening of *Mexicano*, using an obsolete pronunciation of the x as a *ch*. Lydia Aguirre describes a Chicano as "a

Mexican American with a non-Anglo image of himself."[41] The movement has numerous roots and embraces great variation. One contributing factor was the Vietnam veterans. Overrepresented in the armed forces and on the casualty lists,[42] many of the survivors were ripe for protest. Students inspired by the Civil Rights movement, educators frustrated by Anglo school boards unwilling to consider the difficulties of Spanish-speaking children,[43] Roman Catholic priests defying their bishops, and the young Mexican Americans seeking pride and identity, all contributed to the rapidly spreading movement that gave them a sense of peoplehood.

Not all Mexican Americans have supported the movement. One Mexican American Congressman denounced the Chicanos in the House of Representatives.[44] A Mexican American priest, writing to the Los Angeles *Times* in 1970, objects to the word "Chicano" and assigns to it a Castilian root meaning "tricky" or "cheat" (from the same root as the English word "chicanery").[45] As with all large populations, there are those who seek change less militantly. But most of the young and some of the older people are impatient and mistrustful of "gradualism." The most severe split is generational, although all wish to retain their language, at least in private life.

Another division has seemed to be in the mistrust of the Church, which was perceived as, perhaps unwittingly, at the service of an Anglo-dominated hierarchy, and an upholder of "internal colonialism." One response to this has been the formation of a national organization of Chicano priests. P.A.D.R.E.S., which has as part of its program leadership development workshops, advocacy within institutions for structural change, training for selected priests and sisters in the theology of liberation.[46]

After a period of upsurge of vague nationalistic (and for some, separatist) rhetoric and goals, the Chicano movement has been developing with more pragmatic focus. The "liberation" party, La Raza Unida, has been concentrating on regional and local issues, as in Crystal City, Texas, where it pushed out of office old-line Mexican American Democrats. The focus on the region has been aided by the proliferation of newspapers espousing a Chicano point of view: about education, changing women's roles, the administration of justice and discrimination by police, job discrimination, the politics of access and the politics of inclusion.

INDIGENOUS HISPANOS: A VARIANT

As we have noted, included in the population of the Southwest are those Spanish-speaking people who are descended from Spanish-Mexican lineage indigenous to the area at the time of the annexation, some of whose ancestry goes back to the sixteenth century. In view of the general statistical confusion concerning Americans of Latin

[41]Lydia Agirre, "The Meaning of the Chicano Movement," in Phillip D. Ortéga, ed., *We Are Chicanos* (New York: Pocket Books, 1973), p. 122.
[42]Ralph Guzmán, "Mexican American Casualties in Vietnam," in Carlos E. Cortés, Arlin I. Ginsburg, Alan W. F. Green, and James A. Joseph, *Three Perspectives on Ethnicity in America* (New York: G. P. Putnam's Sons, 1976), pp. 282–288, tables and discussion.
[43]Dennis H. Mangers, "Education in the Grapes of Wrath," *Ibid.,* pp. 289 ff.
[44]Mouquin and Van Doren, eds. *A Documentary History of the Mexican Americans,* pp. 463–470.
[45]Julian Nava, *Viva La Raza: Readings on Mexican Americans* (New York: D. Van Nostrand Co., 1973), p. 156.
[46]Fr. Juan Romero, "Chicano Liberation and the Church," in Cortés *et al., Three Perspectives on Ethnicity in America,* pp. 360 ff.

ancestry, their numbers and proportion are difficult to establish. It is clear, however, that in New Mexico and southern Colorado a large proportion of the Spanish-speaking people derive from this Hispano lineage as distinct from migrant Mexican lineage; in Texas and Southern California the situation is roughly reversed.

Hispanos in New Mexico

Hispanos comprise about half the population of New Mexico. There are several counties where they number more than 80 percent of the population. Both Spanish and English are official languages in the state. Compared with the obvious minority status of immigrant Mexicans in other Southwestern states, Hispanos do not appear at first to be a minority at all. They are all citizens, and no efforts are made by Anglos to deny them civic privileges. All over New Mexico there are Hispanos who participate actively in politics, and in counties where they predominate heavily they frequently run the government. Free and equal access to all public places is accorded all ethnic and racial elements—the Indians and the relatively few immigrant Mexicans, as well as the his-panos. In the entire Southwest region, New Mexico exhibits the least "racial" in-tolerance. The reason for New Mexico's distinctiveness in this connection appears to lie in the fact that through a long part of the state's history as a United States territory, Anglos were a distinct numerical minority, and that, therefore, a pattern of racial tolerance was developed at the outset of Anglo-Hispano contact which has been strengthened by tradition. But beneath the surface of this substantial intergroup harmony lie subtle discriminations against the Spanish-speaking people of middle-class status and until recently the pitifully low welfare status of the lower-class Hispanos.

The Hispanos of Rimrock[47]

Spanish *conquistadores* and other travelers, officials, and priests passed through western New Mexico from 1540 to the annexation. The present hispano settlement, however, descends from migrants from eastern New Mexico who settled in the region in the 1860s. They were scattered and relatively prosperous ranchers. Their largest village, Atrisco, was founded in 1882. Since the 1920s Atrisco's population has declined so that in 1950 it had only 89 residents. The other cultural groups in Rimrock are Indians (Zuni and Navaho), Mormons who came in the 1870s, and Texans who came in three small waves beginning at the turn of the century and ending the '30s.

Anglo-Hispano relations in Rimrock have been characterized by the acquisition of dominance by the Texans, not without conflict and abrasion of feeling at various times. Before migration the Texans had known Spanish Americans only in the depressed position of field labor. Mexicans were considered as Negroes. The migrants were distressed to discover that their children would have to attend school in a Hispano village, and that many county officials were "Mex." On the other hand, the Hispanos were initially tolerant of the newcomers, many of whom they pitied because they were so poor.

Friction began when Texans began to fence land and acquire title to acreage that had been traditionally open range. The first outbreak of hostility occurred in 1934,

---

[47]Evan Z. Vogt and Ethel M. Albert, *People of Rimrock: A Study of Values in Five Cultures* (Cambridge, Mass.: Harvard University Press, 1966).

when a Spanish American teacher, the son of one of the most respected families in Atrisco, was assigned to the newly constructed Homestead school in the Texan village. In the first weeks of school the windows were broken at night and signs appeared: "We Don't Want Any Chile Pickers for Teachers." Finally, the schoolhouse was burned down. It is now the consensus of both groups that the fire was started by a Texan extremist.

By 1938 the high school was shifted from Atrisco to Homestead and a few years later the grade school in Atrisco was closed so that hispano children had to go to school in Homestead.

Another serious conflict occurred in 1947. It started with a fight between a Texan and a Hispano at a dance; the fighting spread and continued for several days. This outbreak (nicknamed "The Spanish American War") has not been forgotten by either group. The antagonism between the groups remains, and such relations as there are between them are sustained by the pattern of employee-employer relations (Hispanos always employed by Texans, never the reverse), pupil-teacher, storekeeper, and the tenuous associations at public dance places. Three couples in the Rimrock area represent Anglo-Hispano intermarriage. One couple moved away. Both groups talk a great deal about the other two couples (two daughters of the former *patrón* of Atrisco each married a Texan). Texans tend to call the children half-breeds; hispanos refer to them as coyotes, meaning unpredictable—that is, impossible to say how they will turn out. The children are being raised as Catholics and one Texan husband has converted to Catholicism.

Rural Hispanos of Northern New Mexico

Relatively isolated for generations, rural Hispanos preserve a folk culture and community life based on subsistence agriculture. They have not so much been discriminated against in the usual dominant-minority sense as neglected.

From an account of a county superintendent of schools we get a picture of these people as they seemed in 1931 before the impact of change.

> Here is a typical mountain community, entirely occupied by Spanish-Americans, a gentle, industrious, and intelligent people, brown eyed and sun-tanned. The houses are flat roofed, and are plastered with adobe of warm brown color which conforms to the earth around. Wherever possible, space has been cleared for gardens and little farms. . . . The men and women work together . . . children have been working at the side of the father since they were old enough to work. . . . I have been lenient about school attendance in the fall of the year since they must bring their children into the work in order to save their crops. . . . I mention this in an effort to get across a vital point. . . . If we could, for example, in New Mexico include in our rural school curriculum the old arts such as dyeing, blanket weaving, tin work, needle work and wood carving, employing experts in these lines from the community, and give credits in the schools for this work . . . we might perpetuate something of lasting educational value for the people.[48]

[48]Adelina Otero, in Moquin and Van Doren, eds., *A Documentary History of the Mexican Americans,* pp. 368–370. Original article in *Survey Graphic,* May 1, 1931.

But changes have come about to a degree. Military service during and since World War II has drawn off young men, and many have subsequently sought a future in the colonia of towns and cities, where they often start at the bottom as newcomers replacing those that have moved up and out. State and federal programs in health and agriculture have planted slow germinating seeds of change.

> Rural hispanos, while helped considerably by job opportunities opened through federal spending for defense projects (especially in central New Mexico—up and down the Rio Grande Valley), and by the rising level of prosperity of the nation in recent years, remain a somewhat disadvantaged population in terms of welfare status. Their incomes are lower, their health status less good, their education less complete than those of their urban counterparts. Selective migration has resulted in high proportions of the very young and the very old in some rural areas with the consequent need for institutionalized Anglo-type educational, health, and welfare services. The old hispano culture has proved remarkably resistant—Spanish is still the preferred language in the homes of many rural families—but it is gradually being eroded by the intrusions of Anglo technologies and Anglo institutions. The discovery of uranium and other new and valuable minerals and the increased exploitation of oil and gas resources have brought boom conditions and urban-type employment to some rural areas; but in the core area of hispano culture, the upper Rio Grande Valley, the rate of change, though steady, is slow, and there is much in the life of the area now that would be familiar to one who knew the area a quarter of a century ago.[49]

Tijerina's Republic of San Joaquin del Rio de Chama

A symptom of the circumstances of these northern depressed, rural Hispanos is the revitalization or nativist movement of the Federal Alliance of Land Grants, which claimed millions of acres to which titles are held from original Mexican land grants valid before annexation. This group, led by Reies Tijerina ("king tiger") wished to establish a separate Hispano state. To dramatize their cause members of this group marched to Santa Fe in the summer of 1966. In October they held a great rally in the National Forest in the foothills of the Rockies. The membership is estimated to be about 20,000.

The governor of New Mexico met with leaders of the movement and felt there was little threat to stability and order from the group. The Santa Fe District Attorney, however (who has a Spanish surname, but it is not clear whether he is Hispano or Mexican American), is an active member of the American Legion and saw the movement as "communist," "subversive," and believed it had a great cache in the mountains of rifles and machine guns. Therefore in 1967 when an annual meeting of the Alliance was scheduled, again in the northern picnic preserves of the National Forest, he arrested several of the leaders and confiscated the membership lists. In retaliation fifteen

---

[49]Lyle Saunders made these observations for the authors. See also Lyle Saunders, *Cultural Difference and Medical Care: The Case of the Spanish Speaking People of the Southwest* (New York: Russell Sage Foundation, 1954), pp. 285–288.

Alliance members swept down on the hamlet of Tierra Amarilla and attempted to present a warrant for a citizen's arrest of the District Attorney. A fight ensued in which two policemen were wounded and a reporter taken as hostage by the Alliance members. The governor, who was out of state and may have been misinformed, panicked and called the National Guard. Two tanks were sent up into the hills, and after a five-day search in which fifty people, including women and children, were held for two days without food, water, or sanitary facilities, Tijerina was arrested. He was acquitted, but subsequently arrested again and sentenced to two years in prison on charges of assault stemming from the original incident.

Tijerina has sometimes been called the Chicano Don Quixote. His movement promised a "return" to justice, faith, and salvation as expressed in the traditional pastoral life of the past.[50] The publicity surrounding the Alliance brought support and eventually competition from the national Chicano movement. In 1969 Tijerina broke with the Alliance and with the national movement. He has remained a heroic symbol to Mexican American activists, but in northern New Mexico it is now the voice of the Chicano paper *El Grito de Norte* that has become the spokesman.

SUMMARY APPRAISAL

It seems evident that the more aggressive approach of Mexican Americans has promoted change and faster action on the part of the dominant society. There are more voters, more office holders, more college students, more universities offering courses or programs in Mexican American studies, some innovation in elementary- and high-school education. But severe problems remain. It will take time and much more effort to reduce the high-school dropout rate. This is a *local* problem dependent on local Boards of Education, school personnel, and curriculum.[51]

The economic problem is the more severe one, and in part is bound up with the problem of undocumented aliens. Estimates run to a million jobs held by people (not all Spanish-speaking) who have come here illegally, the jobs chiefly in agriculture and the service industries (hotels and restaurants, primarily).[52]

President Carter has proposed amnesty for undocumented aliens who have been here seven years, temporary five-year legal residence status for those who came later, but before January 1, 1977, and penalties for employers. The Spanish-speaking organizations are pleased that something is being done, though some are dubious about employer penalties for fear it will create across-the-board prejudice in hiring Latins.[53]

Probably more important in the long run for the Mexican Americans of the United States is how America faces and tackles the whole problem of poverty in the face of ethnic stereotypes and fears of change. The Mexican Americans, however, have found a voice and will not let the issues rest.

---

[50]Peter Nabokov, *Tijerina and the Courthouse Raid* (Albuquerque: The University of New Mexico Press, 1969).
[51]See interview with Professor Julian Samora, in Phillip D. Ortega, ed., *We Are Chicanos*, pp. 112–121.
[52]*The New York Times*, May 1, 1977, Sec. E, p. 3.
[53]*Ibid.*, Aug. 12, 1977, Sec. B, p. 2.

Suggested Readings

Briggs, Vernon M., Jr. *Chicanos and Rural Poverty*. Baltimore: The Johns Hopkins
    Press, 1973.
    A clear, short discussion of the situation of Mexican American agricultural laborers
    and the policies affecting them.
Castro, Tony. *Chicano Power*. New York: Saturday Review Press/E. P. Dutton & Co.,
    1974.
    The first half is background and history, the second a full account of the growth of
    the Chicano movement.
Cortés, Carlos E.; Ginsburg, Arlin I.; Green, Alan W. F.; and Joseph, James A. *Three
    Perspectives on Ethnicity in America: Blacks, Chicanos and Native Americans*.
    New York: G. P. Putnam's Sons, 1976.
    This comparative reader is well arranged to show similarities and differences, both
    historically and contemporaneously between three minorities. Some good material
    not brought together elsewhere.
Duran, Livie Isauro, and Bernard, H. Russell. *Introduction to Chicano Studies*. New
    York: The Macmillan Co., 1973.
    The most comprehensive reader on the past and present situation of Mexican
    Americans.
Galarza, Ernesto. *Barrio Boy*. Notre Dame: University of Notre Dame Press, 1971.
    Professor Galarza's autobiographical account of migration from a mountain village
    and survival in a California barrio. Delightful and illuminating.
Ortega, Phillip D., ed. *We Are Chicanos*. New York: Pocket Books (Simon and
    Schuster), 1973.
    An anthology of Chicano writing, political and creative.

13

Puerto Ricans on the Mainland

The island of Borinquén, which the Spanish renamed Puerto Rico, has a population, social structure, and culture influenced by vestiges of the Tainos Indian heritage, 500 years of Spanish colonialism, and three-quarters of a century of American permeation and exploitation.

Apart from genetic heritage little is left of the Indian's values, way of life, or language. Spanish dominance, on the other hand, established and maintained to the end of the nineteenth century the Spanish language, a feudal agricultural system, the Roman Catholic church, and a civil and military administration. The result was a predominantly rural population, largely illiterate, speaking a Spanish variant; a feudal hierarchy of respect; a strong male-dominated family system; and a population of genetically mixed Spanish, Indian, and some African heritage. The small (by contemporary standards) cities were centers of civil and military administration and a merchant class involved in exchange of goods with Spain. Much of the urban population was Creole (Spanish-Indian). There was never a large African slave population, but some were imported for work on the sugar and coffee plantations. Slavery was abolished in 1873.[1]

PUERTO RICO AND THE UNITED STATES

When in October 1898 Puerto Rico became an American possession a new economic frontier was opened for American capital. The old hacienda owners were gradually displaced as a class by large American corporate enterprise through its representatives. Before 1932 the federal government assumed a laissez-faire attitude toward the island's economy, with the result that American investment in the development of Puerto Rico came from mainland private capital. The extent of absentee interest in the Puerto Rican economy was summarized in 1930 as follows:

> . . . Sugar is 60 percent absentee-controlled; fruit is 31 percent, or more; public utilities, 50 percent; and steamship lines, approximately 100

[1]For background on pre-American Puerto Rico see Adalberto Lopez and James Petras, *Puerto Rico and the Puerto Ricans* (New York: John Wiley & Sons, 1974), pp. 12–86.

percent. There is no important source of wealth that is not partially in the hands of outsiders, and in some instances, such as steamships, outsiders control the entire business. Any estimate of Porto Rico dependence on absentees which places the total at less than 60 percent of the island's wealth is certainly too low. Not all of the industries belong to absentees, but those which do not are so indebted to continental banks as to be virtually in their possession. Not all of the good land is in the hands of outsiders, but a large portion of it is, and much of the remainder is heavily mortgaged. And finally, there is that type of dependence on absentees which Porto Rico suffers, because of her long dependence on a monopolizing mother country, the necessity of importing vast quantities of food, clothing, machinery, chemicals and drugs. The control of the absentee is all but complete and with the aid of the Coastwise Shipping Act and the American Tariff bids fair to absorb all of the profitable enterprise.[2]

Under Franklin D. Roosevelt's early administrations, governmental effort at reorienting the Puerto Rican economy with more regard for the welfare of the islanders themselves was undertaken. The Puerto Rican Relief Administration was succeeded by the Puerto Rican Reconstruction Administration, which undertook irrigation projects, new highways, new schools, new houses, and other development efforts. In 1942 Pattee said "There is little doubt that the present administration . . . postpones, at least, a collapse in Puerto Rican economy."[3]

The Puerto Rico Reconstruction Administration "made definite progress but did not achieve that complete reform that was so desperately needed."[4] An indigenous reform program developed from the emergence of a new political party on the island, the Partido Popular Democrato. By somewhat faltering steps, democratic political institutions were established, with increasing degrees of self-government permitted. On November 2, 1948, Puerto Rico elected its own governor for the first time. Except for the Presidential appointment of the auditor and Supreme Court justices, and for the power of the United States Congress to annul any law passed by the Insular Legislature (something which has not yet been done), the island is self governing.

Despite aid from the federal government, conditions had not markedly improved. Although the death rate dropped, the birth rate remained one of the highest in the world. In 1898, 83 percent of the population was illiterate. By 1940 it was only 31 percent, but policies had shifted back and forth as to which language, English or Spanish, was to be taught at what levels. This wavering led to a reduced effectiveness of education. Neither English nor the Spanish cultural heritage were adequately transmitted. The island suffered heavily during the Depression because of the major dependence on the cash crop of sugar.[5]

[2]W. Bailey Diffie and Justine Whitfield Diffie, *Porto Rico: A Broken Pledge* (New York: Vanguard Press, 1931), pp. 135–136. By permission.
[3]Richard Pattee, "The Puerto Ricans," in *Annals of the American Academy of Political and Social Sciences,* Sept. 1942, 223: 52.
[4]*Ibid.,* p. 52.
[5]Nathan Glazer and Daniel Patrick Moynihan, *Beyond the Melting Pot: The Negroes, Puerto Ricans, Jews, Italians, and Irish of New York City* (Cambridge, Mass.: M.I.T. Press, 1963), pp. 87, 88.

Operation Bootstrap

Under self-government Puerto Rico launched "Operation Bootstrap," a development program to raise the levels of living on the island. In twenty years these efforts of the Puerto Rican government raised the per capita income on the island 307 percent. The program concentrated on two areas of economic improvement. The first was diversification of agriculture. Many of the large sugar areas were made available for smaller landowners under the "500 acre law," which had been on the books since 1900 but was not enforced. Many new crops were introduced.

The second effort was to encourage industry. By February, 1960, some 600 new factories had been established, creating jobs for 45,000 people. The government aided in the training of personnel, by building factories for rent at reasonable rates, and by other measures. In 1956 the income from manufacturing surpassed the income from agriculture for the first time. Puerto Rico has surpassed every Latin American country in increase in per capita income. The social aspects of Operation Bootstrap included a major public health effort and marked achievements in education. Although Spanish is the primary language, English is a required subject from the first grade on. Now almost the only illiterates are older people. The number of schoolrooms, teachers, and pupils has more than doubled; higher education has tripled; extension services in education have been developed; and the Division of Community Education has become a focus of interest and training for workers from many countries engaged in development programs.

Although Operation Bootstrap seemed to promise great advances in the well-being of the island, the result in the long run has been more nearly a further economic penetration of the island and, through capital-intensive enterprise, wage differentials as compared with continental United States, tax exemptions, and other government incentives, the greatest beneficiaries in the post-1940 policy of industrialization have been the corporations based outside the island: chiefly American, but with some Canadian and Japanese investment also.[6] Nearly 2,000 foreign enterprises through an investment of over $2 billion, have set up businesses in Puerto Rico since 1940.[7]

Puerto Ricans have benefited from the government moneys invested in roads, housing, education, health, and welfare. Companies have also needed this infrastructure to make enterprises viable. In 1972 per capita income stood at $1,713, thirty years after "Operation Bootstrap" had promised a per capita income of $2,000.[8] The distribution of income became increasingly skewed. An urban, consumer-oriented middle class has developed, and has had enough political strength to successfully oppose continental minimum wage standards.[9]

In 1940 nearly 50 percent of the labor force was employed in agriculture. By 1972 only 4.4 percent were employed in this sector of the economy. The result has been an urban migration. In 1971 the Puerto Rican planning board agreed that unemployment was 30 percent of the labor force.[10]

These are the factors behind the heavy Puerto Rican migration to the continental United States: economic and cultural penetration; displacements in traditional occupa-

[6]Morris Morley, "Dependence and Development in Puerto Rico," in Adalberto Lopez and James Petras, *Puerto Rico and the Puerto Ricans*, pp. 224–228.
[7]*Ibid.*, p. 225.
[8]*Ibid.*, p. 229.
[9]*Ibid.*, pp. 231–232.

tional securities; the creation of an urban underclass as a result of the decline of agriculture and capital-intensive, rather than labor-intensive development; some romanticization from U.S. media and experience in the armed forces.

To a degree Puerto Ricans have been welcomed in the United States as a new "immigrant group" to fill in the lowest-level jobs that earlier migrants are retiring from, and whose children are elsewhere in the status structure.[11]

THE MIGRATION TO THE MAINLAND

There was a trickle of Puerto Rican migration between annexation and World War II, rising sharply after the restriction of European immigration. By 1910 a little over 1,500 had settled here; nearly 12,000 by 1920; by 1930, 52,004; by 1940, though the migration had slowed because of the Depression, still it did not wither altogether, and there were 69,967 reported living in the continental United States for that year.[12]

We can see this migration in this period as a response to the creation of a sugar-dominated economy on the island, the potential for small merchants to be squeezed in the process and hopefully to find better opportunity on the mainland, the need for replacement in the urban labor force on the mainland as European migration was reduced.

Most of the early migration was to New York, as it was the port for ships carrying island traffic. Most of this group spoke English, were townsmen where English was the required language for school.

The major migration, however, has been since World War II. In the years since the war unemployment has risen on the island, and population has risen, as is always true of developing countries as health services penetrate. There has been a public policy of family planning and birth control, but it is difficult to estimate its effect in a Catholic country where children are highly valued within the family.

The Post-World War II Migration

The Puerto Rican migration has been the heaviest foreign language migration to the Atlantic states since World War I. Up to 1947 and 1948, a large proportion of the Puerto Ricans who came to the continent were contracted for agricultural and domestic labor. There was much unethical traffic in human beings until the island legislature enacted legislation to control and correct the situation. Offices of the Commonwealth of Puerto Rico, set up to assist migrants, were established in New York and Chicago. At present the Migration Division of the Department of Labor of the Commonwealth of Puerto Rico maintains offices in San Juan and in twelve mainland cities. The division's personnel work in approximately one hundred mainland towns and cities each year. Cooperation has also been established between the Puerto Rico Employment Service and the United States Employment Service. Since Puerto Ricans are citizens, job orders from American industry pass through the United States Employment Service to the Puerto

[10]*Ibid.*, p. 233.
[11]Glazer and Moynihan, *Beyond The Melting Pot*, p. 98. The authors point out that Puerto Rico supplied 65,000 G.I.'s in World War II, and 43,000 in the Korean War.
[12]Adalberto Lopez, "The Puerto Rican Diaspora: A Survey," in Adalberto Lopez and James Petras, *Puerto Rico and the Puerto Ricans,* p. 318.

Rico Employment Service when qualified local workers are not available. Employers may recruit labor in Puerto Rico directly only with the approval of the Puerto Rican government, and only when a legitimate order is cleared through regular United States Employment Service channels.

In 1948 the Columbia University study[13] of Puerto Ricans in New York City found that 85 percent of the immigrants had quit jobs in Puerto Rico to come to the United States. What they sought was not so much any job but a *better* job. The data on age of immigrants also suggest that the principal motive for migration has been economic.

Nevertheless, this study found that motivations and expectations did not always cohere. The authors present a table of the direction of mobility: last job in Puerto Rico and New York job at time of interview.[14]

Direction of Mobility	Males	Females
Upward	21%	17%
Stable	39%	43%
Downward	40%	40%

Furthermore the upward mobility was largely restricted to the climb from unskilled to semiskilled wage work. Money wages were higher in continental U.S., whatever the job category, though it is questionable whether real wages were, in view of cost of living differentials, and all the more so when later there was an inflationary economy.[15] Senior and Watkins believe there has been real advantage, as costs of living in San Juan have followed continental levels, and this would hold true if migrants all came from urban areas. But with the decline of agriculture more rural[16] migrants are coming to the continent.

Emigration has been a policy solution, as has been true of other governments in the past where industrialization and "development" have brought rising populations, urban crowding, and unemployment. The Migration Division of the Office of the Commonwealth of Puerto Rico works both on the island and in its offices in mainland cities to aid adjustment through "preparatory" radio programs on the island and other mass media, giving information about climate, clothing, documents needed for schools, driver's license information, and warnings about installment buying; and on the continent programs urging night school for English competency, and vocational training.

By 1970 there were 1,429,604 first- and second-generation Puerto Ricans in the continental U.S.[17] Although New York still receives a large influx, as relatives and friends are here, the Puerto Ricans have spread now to other parts of the country. Lopez lists urban concentrations in 1970 in New York, Chicago, Philadelphia, Jersey City,

[13]C. Wright Mills, Clarence Senior, and Rose Kohn Goldsen, *The Puerto Rican Journey* (New York: Harper & Brothers, 1950).

[14]*Ibid.*, pp. 69–71.

[15]Clarence Senior and Donald O. Watkins, "Toward a Balance Sheet of Puerto Rican Migration," in Francesco Cordasco and Eugene Bucchioni, *The Puerto Rican Experience: A Sociological Sourcebook* (Totowa, N.J.: Littlefield, Adams & Co., 1975), pp. 157 ff.

[16]U.S. Dept. of Labor, *The New York Puerto Rican, Patterns of Work* Experience (Poverty Area Profiles No. 19, Washington, D.C., 1974), Table 15.

[17]*The New York Times*, March 5, 1973.

Newark, Los Angeles, Miami, Paterson, N.J., San Francisco, and Boston.[18] The growing spread is indicated in the following table:

TABLE 13-1. Heaviest Population by State*

State	1970	1960
New York	872,471	642,622
New Jersey	135,676	55,351
Illinois	87,515	36,081
California	46,078	28,108
Pennsylvania	44,535	21,206
Connecticut	38,144	15,247
Massachusetts	24,394	5,217
Ohio	20,918	13,940

*State-by-State census figures reported in *The New York Times,* July 9, 1972, p. 49.

ADJUSTMENT ON THE MAINLAND

"Racial" Visibility

The Puerto Ricans at the time of annexation by the United States, had adopted and adapted Spanish institutions and Spanish culture to form their own variant of Latin American civilization. Into the composition of the population had gone white, Negro, and Indian strains. The social structure was that of a plantation economy in which a small upper class, chiefly of landed proprietors, was distinguished from a peasantry, some of it on plantations, some in mountain villages.

Since the abolition of slavery in the island there has been no civic and public discrimination in Puerto Rico because of race. None of the forms of interracial conflict or violence that have been found on the mainland has occurred. This formal absence of discrimination is similar to other patterns in Latin cultures in the Western Hemisphere. Furthermore, the population of Puerto Rico presents so wide a range of combinations of physiognomic features that a pattern of dominant-minority relations based on "race" would be difficult to maintain.

Although Puerto Rico has been often cited for its absence of prejudice based on "color" visibility, and intermarriage between people of different racial heritages has long been recognized, there is some consciousness of differences. Taken together with the factors of wealth and education, color may affect status. This has become all the more true as continental influence has permeated more widely, and as the Creole population has become a more affluent urban middle class.

But for many migrating Puerto Ricans who have had little sense of "color" as compared with status according to economic position, continental U.S. "racial" attitudes come as a shock and cause confusion.

Padilla has made a chart that shows the differences in the way in which biological visibility is perceived by mainlanders, by other Puerto Ricans, and by individuals with regard to themselves.[19]

---

[18]*Ibid.,* p. 323.
[19]Elena Padilla, *Up From Puerto Rico* (New York: Columbia University Press, 1958), pp. 47–48.

References (Mainlanders)	References of Ingroup (Hispanos)	References of Individuals Describing Self
White	White Trigueno Hispano Grifo *Intermediates**	White Hispano Trigueno
Puerto Rican or Mixed	Negro Trigueno Indio Grifo Hispano	De Color (of color) Trigueno Hispano Indio
Negro	Negro Trigueno Indio Grifo Hispano	De Color Trigueno Hispano Indio

*A category to include the numerous racial terms used by Puerto Ricans, used by C. Wright Mills, Clarence Senior, and Rose Kohn Goldsen, in *The Puerto Rican Journey.*

This chart shows us that no individual in the group of migrants studied designates himself a Negro. Neither will he call himself Grifo. The hispano group, however, may call him either of these, with implied derogation. When appearance is predominantly "white," the outgroup, mainlanders, may accept the individual as white where both hispano individuals and the hispano group will make some differentiation. Nevertheless, in our racist society, teachers, police, and other officials are apt to qualify "white" by saying "white Puerto Ricans."

Color is clearly a problem for mainland Puerto Ricans. Mainland attitudes have produced ambivalent attitudes. On the island the greater differential was class rather than color. Furthermore when the earlier migration of Puerto Ricans came there were better relations with blacks than with the Italians who were contiguous to *El Barrio.* Italian youth were hostile to Puerto Rican youth and black youth more accepting. There is the memory of the fact that during World War II, army camps on the island segregated Puerto Rican troops, and the Navy would not take Puerto Ricans. Puerto Ricans, unless very dark and with Negroid features are listed as white in New York City. The proportion of "colored" in the Puerto Rican population drops from census to census (4 percent in 1960). Father Fitzpatrick, Professor of Sociology at Fordham University, made a study of Puerto Rican marriages in six Catholic parishes. He found, in the late 1950s, that 25 percent of the marriages of Puerto Ricans in these widely varying parishes involved people of different color.[20]

Culture and Identity

It is difficult to make holistic statements about Puerto Rican culture within the variants of rural vs. urban populations and the different social classes. Furthermore, Puerto Rican society on the island is undergoing change, and the impact of migration is affecting mainland Puerto Ricans.[21]

[20]Joseph P. Fitzpatrick, *Puerto Rican Americans: The Meaning of Migration to the Mainland* (Englewood Cliffs, N.J.: Prentice-Hall, 1971), p. 111.
[21]For a review of the studies and the dilemmas of this problem, see Sidney W. Mintz, "Puerto Rico: An Essay in the Definition of National Culture," in Francesco Cordasco and Eugene Bucchioni, *The Puerto Rican Experience: A Sociological Sourcebook,* pp. 26–90.

Culture has historical roots, and in many aspects Puerto Ricans share the heritage of Spanish tradition in their interaction: retention of the Spanish language; a fundamental Catholic ideology, regardless of degree of religiosity; acceptance of a class-structured society with *respect* as the linkage between segments of a hierarchical structure; a strong sense of the worth of the individual and the concept of "dignidad," both as an ideal and as a defense; a double standard of sexual morality with a value on "machismo"; the need for interaction with others (not a great need for privacy); hospitality; emphasis on spiritual and human values rather than the commercial and practical.[22]

The problem of identity is difficult for the younger Puerto Ricans who either have migrated as young adults or who have grown up in the low-income Puerto Rican urban communities of the mainland. Very few have been exposed holistically to the traditional culture, or if so in a "united family," have had the counterinfluences of the environment outside the home. All second-generation immigrants have had some culture conflict. But for the Puerto Rican child American cultural norms are perceived through school, which often devalues him;[23] through the media, which give selective emphasis; and through consumer items, which attract him, often futilely. In addition, there is the "racial" ambiguity to which he is exposed.

Part of the thrust of young Puerto Ricans today, as we shall discuss later in this chapter, is to revive cultural roots, to press for bilingual education, to support a Puerto Rican nationalism, to avoid the deculturizing effects of the slums of New York or of San Juan.[24]

PATTERNS OF DOMINANCE

Spatial Distribution

In New York City, where more than half of the Puerto Ricans on the mainland live, the old subcommunity, *El Barrio,* south and east of Harlem has overflowed to many other parts of the city. There are concentrations of Puerto Ricans in Brooklyn and the South Bronx, but they still make up about a third of the population of Manhattan, creating different patterns of neighborhood relationships in different situations. Thus on Manhattan's West Side the avenues have large middle-class and upper middle-class apartment houses occupied by "continental whites," while the side streets are filled with Puerto Rican families crowded into converted former private residences that have been abandoned as single-family dwellings in the changing pattern of city and suburban living. Here social class as well as cultural barriers create social distance, and often tension, between mainlanders and migrants.

In New York's Lower East Side, housing conditions are often not as bad for the migrants because of extensive urban renewal in this district. Furthermore, because of its

---

[22]*Ibid.,* pp. 78–81.

[23]Paulette Cooper, ed., *Growing Up Puerto Rican,* (New York: Mentor Books, The New American Library, 1972). This is a collection of life histories of young Puerto Ricans, with some bitter comments on their school experience.

[24]See Morris Morley in Adalberto Lopez and James Petras, *Puerto Rico and the Puerto Ricans,* pp. 238–239, for a discussion of the development of a "subproletariat" in the urban slums of Puerto Rico as a result of development policy.

historic role as an immigrant neighborhood, the Lower East Side is one of the best-ser-
viced and most intercultural subcommunities in New York City.

Many of the longer-established Puerto Rican families are, like other New Yorkers,
going to the suburbs, and to the less crowded boroughs of the city.

Raymond A. Glazier of the Community Council of Greater New York has said that
the Puerto Rican population in nearby New York suburban counties more than doubled
in the 1960–1970 decade.[25] (See Table 13–2.)

TABLE 13-2.   Population Increase 1960–1970, New York Suburban Areas

		Increase from 1960	
Area	1970	Number	Per Cent
New York City	811,843	199,269	32.5
Nassau	7,224	3,025	72.0
Suffolk	17,179	9,839	134.0
Westchester	5,715	2,610	84.1
Rockland	3,814	1,602	72.4

Income and Poverty

Whereas median income for *all* Puerto Rican families in New York rose from 1959 to
1970, from $3,811 to $5,575, the gap between median for all New York families and
Puerto Rican families was $4,107: twice the size of the gap for all families and blacks.
The Puerto Ricans are the poorest and most deprived segment of metropolitan New
York.[26] A U.S. Department of Labor report of a 1959 survey of New York poverty areas[27]
(Harlem, East Harlem, South Bronx, and Bedford-Stuyvesant) found among Puerto Ricans one-fifth of all two-person families, one-fourth of four-person families, and one-
half of families with six or more persons had incomes below the poverty threshold as defined by the Social Security Administration. The unemployment rate was 9.6, two and a
half times the citywide rate; and the subemployment rate for East Harlem ("El Barrio")
was 36.9. Subemployment refers to those under 65 years of age who are heads of
households and earn less than $60 a week. The report points out that there is a very real
possibility of undercount. It also emphasizes the effect of such poverty on the numbers
of children in these families.[28]

Discrimination

No other place in the United States, probably, gives as much lip service to the ideal
of nondiscrimination against religious, ethnic, or racial minorities as does New York.
Nevertheless, there is much discrimination through evasion of laws and in the areas of
daily living not covered by special codes against it.

[25]*The New York Times,* July 9, 1972, p. 49.
[26]*The New York Times,* July 9, 1972, p. 41.
[27]U.S. Department of Labor, "The New York Puerto Rican: Patterns of Work Experience," in
Adalberto Lopez and James Petras, *Puerto Rico and the Puerto Ricans,* p. 380.
[28]*Ibid.,* p. 363, 382.

Since Puerto Ricans form such a large part of New York's unskilled labor force, they have found employment readily in the lowest-paying jobs. Discrimination at the lower levels of the occupational structure seems to be linked with the factors of the language handicap, union policies, and traditional "corners" on certain types of employment that have been held by some other ethnic group. Union control of a shop's choice of workers through hiring halls has sometimes been used to break the hold of a particular ethnic group on a shop by forcing mixed crews on the employers. In the white-collar field, public employment is, for Puerto Ricans as for earlier immigrant groups, a channel of access.

There have been issues both in education and in health about licensing professionals trained in Puerto Rico for positions in schools or hospitals. The Department of Welfare in New York City has accepted training at the University of Puerto Rico for its Spanish-speaking workers, but the Department of Health and the Board of Education have resisted. This might be considered a very mild aspect of discrimination but it does express a rigidity in the face of generic competence in needed areas.

Political discrimination is primarily linked with the question of English-language literacy. Some Puerto Ricans feel there is discrimination in the courts, since the procedure of American courts deprives them of a chance to plead their cause with emotion, gesture, and Latin eloquence.

Discrimination in good housing continues in many parts of the city. Eagle, in a study of the housing of Puerto Ricans in New York City, was surprised to find so few Puerto Ricans feeling themselves discriminated against. To the question, "Do you think you can live anywhere in the city if you have the money to pay the rent, 87 percent answered "Yes," and only 5 percent stated that they felt they had actually experienced discrimination in seeking housing. A partial clue to this apparent unawareness of discrimination lies in the fact that the great majority of Puerto Ricans can afford to seek housing only in the less desirable dwellings. The same study found that while only 3 percent of those who had lived in the city three years or less complained of discrimination, 10 percent of those who had lived in New York longer voiced such a complaint.[29]

Migrants to metropolitan centers in America today, although there are some older subcommunities that are predominantly one nationality, more and more are finding themselves in interethnic urban areas. One such settlement of Puerto Ricans has been studied by Elena Padilla:[30]

"Eastville"

"Eastville" is not "El Barrio Latino." It is an interethnic slum, not a homogeneous nationality subcommunity.

Regardless of how long they have been melting in the pot, the people of Eastville are seldom identified as just plain Americans. They are designated "Hungarians," "Puerto Ricans," "American Negroes," "American Indians," "East Indians," "Russians," "Italians," "Chinese"—and all of these group

[29]Morris Eagle, "The Puerto Ricans in New York City," in *Studies in Housing and Minority Groups,* Nathan Glazer and Davis McEntire, eds. (Berkeley: The University of California Press, 1959), pp. 166–167.
[30]Elena Padilla, *Up From Puerto Rico,* pp. 1–2, 11–12. by permission.

labels are conceived as indicating something about the personal, social and biological traits of various group members. It makes little difference in this categorizing whether the individuals were born or have lived all their lives in this country if they still possess characteristics—real or assumed—in physical appearance, in styles of wearing apparel, in knowledge of another language than English, and in their names, that allow them to be distinguished from "real Americans." The term "American" is used, as a rule, with reference to outsiders who do not live in the neighborhood and who, although they may themselves be members of ethnic groups, do not meet the criteria that suggest to Eastvillers membership in any particular group with which they are familiar.

In "Eastville" there are ties of neighborhood that cut across ethnic lines and other identifications that are ethnic.

Among Eastvillers there are levels on which feelings of neighborhood solidarity bind members of all ethnic groups together. By the process of discrimination and dislike people get involved in relationships of conflict, and by common understandings and participation in common activities sentiments of solidarity develop. Both the positive feelings and the negative ones work together to shape the social body that is the neighborhood. The idea that the neighborhood is a bad place in which to live is a shared one among Eastvillers. So, too, is their attitude toward discrimination by outsiders against them. . . .

On the other hand, it is difficult to organize programs of social action in Eastville when ethnic group barriers are ignored or when the sources of loyalty within an ethnic group are not recognized. Beneath the intergroup tensions and conflicts among ethnic groups are working interpersonal relationships among individuals, which override ethnic affiliation.

Although there is neighborliness and often mutual helpfulness, the urban slum neighborhood lacks the homogeneity and long residence of the village.

First and last names are seldom known or recognized in Eastville. People are identified according to whatever characteristic they are best known by in the neighborhood—the man from Italy, the lady who owns the candy store, the woman from Ponce. . . .

Housing is a problem in "Eastville," although the overcrowding is not comparable to that in some districts where there are whole families in one room. The 1950 census reported an average of three persons per room for "Eastville." Apartments are self-contained units that include a bathroom (sometimes with the tub in the kitchen). Some are "old law" (pre-1911) tenements with windows only in the front and back rooms and airshafts for the intervening rooms. Rents in the middle 1950s, at the time of Padilla's study, ranged from $14 to $80 a month, with "under the table" fees from $800 to $1,500 "for the key." Utilities are extra. The entire area is rat-infested; repairs in electric installations, plumbing, and plaster must usually be undertaken by tenants themselves, as complaints are consistently ignored by the absentee landlords. When weather permits, much of the life of the neighborhood goes on on the street.

> Strewn with garbage though they are, the streets and alleys are notable for the number of people of every conceivable ethnic group who spend a considerable part of their time there to get away from their apartments. Day and night the juke boxes in the candy stores deluge the streets with the tunes of the latest records of the season, and it is not strange to see youngsters or young adults dancing by themselves inside the stores or on the sidewalks to rock 'n' roll rhythms by the Velvets or to Xavier Cugat's mambos and meringues. Others watch and then try the ones they like under the tutelage of those who know the steps and proper motions for the dances. Noise of music and of words in Yiddish, Spanish, Italian and English, barking dogs, movement of people, cars' horns, are interwoven in a polyphonic soundtrack which records the pace of the neighborhood. Only very cold weather or news echoed through the grapevine that gang fights are scheduled, keep people off the streets. Otherwise the streets, the sidewalks, the stores, and the bars are filled with people meeting, chatting, and relaxing.[31]

Living in the midst of people who have conscious ties to ethnic groups, hispanos have continued the pattern of vesting individuals with ethnic identity. The principal ethnic groups recognized by hispanos in "Eastville" are Cubans, Americans, American Negroes, Italians, and Jews. Of these, Americans and Italians are the most highly rated. Jews, Cubans, and American Negroes are, as a rule, less favored, especially the two latter groups.

> An undisputed American, or someone who is American and nothing else, is conceived as having a name that cannot be identified with or traced to a foreign origin; as being reddish and white in complexion, tall, blond, and blue eyed; as doing professional work; and as not knowing Spanish or having an accent when speaking it. He does not understand the Hispano people. Americans are nice, honest, beautiful and funny. Should one or more of these traits be missing, the individual is suspected of not being a "real American," but something else instead.[32]

Barriers to Adjustment

There are a number of areas that become focal points of attention in adjustments between traditional acceptable ways of the island and the dominant norms of the mainland. Adjustment has been eased to some extent by the fact that the people of the older urban migration were familiar with public education, wage systems, large hospitals, mass communication, and the electoral process. New migrants have increasingly had experience with these forms as a result of the development of the island. Rand mentions an informant in Chicago in the 1950s who felt that the Puerto Ricans had an ad-

[31]*Ibid.*, p. 9. By permission.
[32]*Ibid.*, p. 90. By permission.

vantage over the Mexicans in that city because of the longer exposure, in the island, to certain key structures of mainland society, as well as to entrepreneurial values.[33]

The most obvious problem of acculturation is language. Employers complain of a labor force with which they can communicate only through one or two bilingual members, and they are not sure whether or not directions are being communicated accurately. The Employment Service finds trouble placing workers with little English. The problem for the schools is acute, since hundreds of children enter the public school system with little or no English. A random sample of 213 Puerto Rican households in New York's Lower East Side in 1972 found that three out of four respondents spoke no or very little English. About half the children were reported as knowing no English when they entered school.[34]

The problem of punctuality is acute for the migrants from rural background, who have not had the experience of industrial society, and for women, who have been confined to a limited sphere of activity.

Since the family is the dominant institution in the island culture, it is in family patterns and roles that many adjustments are required. Consensual marriage is not recognized in New York State, which outlawed, by statute, common-law marriage nearly half a century ago. Thus the mother of children born in a consensual marriage is ineligible for benefits that might accrue to her on the disability, death, or desertion of a husband in a registered marriage. The custom of early marriage comes in conflict with the New York State age of consent, which is sixteen with parents' permission and eighteen without. The role of women in traditional hispano culture is often at variance with the expectations for women in institutional structures. Independent participation in church and school activities may be denied a Puerto Rican woman by a conservative husband or by the extended kinship group. One finds the phenomenon of a husband having to take a leave of absence from his work to take his wife and children to the clinic, "since she could not go alone." Yet, because New York City is the center for the needle trades, and needlwork has been a traditional skill among the women, many Puerto Ricans have found employment in the factories of the garment district and in the sewing rooms of custom dress shops. Often a woman in the garment industry can earn more money than the men of her family, a fact which creates conflict of roles within the family.

The American ideal of the nuclear family, if adhered to, often can neither provide security nor assure authority. Roles of parents and children become confused without the support of kinship and hispano community approval. Nevertheless, Puerto Ricans are criticized by mainlanders for kinship obligations that take precedence over work or school commitments.

The school system, where it is practicable, has attempted to draw zone lines so that the ethnic balance of a school's population will not exceed one-third Puerto Rican. The problem is aggravated, however, by the principle of homogeneous grouping, which syphons off the better students into separate classes. Since the number of Puerto Ricans who have qualified for these classes is still not large, the other classes have disproportionately more Puerto Ricans.

[33]Christopher Rand, *The Puerto Ricans* (New York: Oxford University Press, 1958), p. 144.
[34]Valle Consultants, Ltd., *What Holds Sami Back? A Study of Service Delivery in a Puerto Rican Community* (Flushing, N.Y.: Valle Consultants, Ltd., 1973), p. 6.

The public welfare agencies, the private nonsectarian welfare agencies, various Protestant denominations, and Catholic parishes and religious orders have given thought and effort to meeting the needs of the new migrant group.

Padilla gives an account of one "welfare" family in "Eastville":

> Mr. Rios was injured in an industrial accident in 1953. This later involved orthopedic surgery. Workmen's Compensation was paid for a short period and for the subsequent surgery, but after the discontinuance Mr. Rios continued to suffer pain, and with his injured arm could not find a job. A visiting nurse suggested the family should seek help from the Department of Public Welfare—"go on welfare," and she herself made the contact for the family. The case with the Compensation Board was reopened and Mr. Rios now receives $18 a week from this agency. Mrs. Rios and the three children have supplemental aid from the Department of Welfare. Mr. Rios has been attending night school, has finished grammar school and is now in junior high school. He still has pain and receives treatment from both public and private clinics. He still consults lawyers in the hope of getting indemnification for his injury. In the last seven years the rent has been doubled.
>
> The Rios family have been in New York for twenty years. They belong to a store front church, and the children have been to the church camp summers, although when the daughter reached puberty, her parents no longer allowed her to go to camp. The children are not allowed to play on the streets, though the boys are often "given permission" to go to the park. The children are doing well in school. Mrs. Rios earns a little money by caring for the children of working mothers in her home. Mr. Rios hopes when he "has completed his education" to be able to get a job so they can get off welfare. He is 45 years old.[35]

Mr. Rios represents the kind of need for which the welfare system was devised: the possibility of maintaining the thin line between despair and self-respect. On the other hand, the welfare system, being nationwide and bureaucratic, cannot change flexibly, and it is significant that the landlord can raise the rent without the delays and counterpressure of a city administration or Congress. Furthermore, Mr. Rios lives in "Eastville," which is not as isolated or neglected as *El Barrio.*

Joseph P. Fitzpatrick sees the major adjustment problems for Puerto Ricans as first the shift in roles between husband and wife, as women have opportunities for economic independence and are brought into greater involvement in social, political, and community patterns than was true of the poorer classes on the island. Even more difficult is the changing role of the child in relation to his parents and his peers: for boys the street culture, for girls unchaperoned associations of girls and boys in the neighborhoods and schools.

[35]Elena Padilla, *Up From Puerto Rico,* pp. 134–141, adapted by the authors.

The second difficult shift is from the kinship network of support and the personalist values to the formal structures of assistance, reflected in preparation and competition for employment and advancement in impersonal bureaucratic structures.[36]

Such demands for adaptations are not new, but because of free migration and the constant inflow they are likely to persist for a long time.

The Puerto Rican Underclass

"Underclass" is a term now common for the very poor in cities. For the Puerto Ricans of New York, these are mostly found in the tenements of East Harlem. As the mobile move out, the poorest newcomers come in. Much of the housing is still "old law" (pre-1911): half a floor of an old private residence or a four- or five-story tenement, with the toilet in the outside hall for the use of the whole floor, a tub in the kitchen, two of the rooms with air shafts instead of windows, and rats. Garbage collection in these poor districts of New York is twice a week, whereas in middle-class residential sections it is every day.[37]

The anthropologist Oscar Lewis has given us a vivid portrait of a migrant to *El Barrio*.[38] Soledad, whose mother migrated to San Juan from rural poverty in Puerto Rico, brought her children up in a San Juan slum. Soledad came to the continental United States because one of her brothers had come. She came with her children and worked briefly as an agricultural laborer in New Jersey. She then wound up in *El Barrio*, where she knew some people from San Juan. A woman not without strength and primitive intelligence, Soledad is a true product of "the culture of poverty."[39] She is confused, full of antagonism when confronted with the bureaucracy of the welfare department, the health clinic, the school system. Her colorful argot, her unstable relations to men, her overprotective yet harsh dealings with her children, her general personal disorganization (by any middle-class standard) still show a woman struggling against odds: some private clinging to bastardized religious beliefs, some great strength in enduring and fighting.

Lewis's *La Vida* has offended many Puerto Ricans, as they fear it will contribute to a derogatory stereotype of them as a group. But Soledad (the name means solitude—"alienation") does not represent traditional national culture. She is of the culture of the most depressed of the urban poor. Without understanding Soledad one cannot understand why the only riot in New York City in 1967—that summer of desperate riots across the country—was in *El Barrio*. As one writer expressed it, "Some of the nation's most intensive community project work had been insufficient to counter the feeling of separation and rejection that had so long afflicted the Spanish-speaking ghetto."[40]

Organizations Among the Puerto Ricans

Puerto Ricans have been active in forming organizations. As with other minorities, some of these represent the more established segments of the Puerto Rican community

---

[36]Joseph P. Fitzpatrick, *The Puerto Rican Americans,* pp. 95–98.
[37]Professor Meyer found this to be true when working as a field supervisor for a study for the U.S. Dept. of Health, Education, and Welfare in 1965.
[38]Oscar Lewis, *La Vida: A Puerto Rican Family in the Culture of Poverty —San Juan and New York* (New York: Random House, 1965), pp. 127–245.
[39]For a discussion of the concept "the culture of poverty," see *La Vida,* pp. xlv-lii.
[40]*The New Yorker,* Aug. 5, 1967, pp. 29–33.

in the United States. On the other hand, there is also the emergence of a militant anti-establishment group.

There is one Spanish daily newspaper in New York City. In addition to carrying the usual type of copy it offers itself now as the informant about night classes, the PTA, presents itself as the champion of the Spanish-speaking population against the police and other agents of authority who "do not understand the Spanish people." The paper was not founded by Puerto Ricans, but certainly the present journal acts as a force to unify the sense of identity of all the Latin American community.

Labor unions, some with locals almost 100 percent Puerto Rican, serve also as adaptive institutions. A 1959 survey found that 63 percent of the New York Spanish-speaking households surveyed had one or more union members. These may not have been all Puerto Rican households, as Glazer and Moynihan point out that Mexicans and Cubans appear on the executive board of a major union, along with two Puerto Ricans, though the majority of the labor force in this local was Puerto Rican. The authors imply that Puerto Ricans have not yet achieved competitive leadership positions in proportion to their numbers.[41]

In Manhattan there has been an ongoing struggle for political leadership among the Puerto Ricans. In the Bronx a borough leader has clearly emerged. The Puerto Rican vote has risen to nearly a quarter of a million registered voters in New York City.

A number of indigenous organizations have developed. The Spanish Merchants Association has 200 Puerto Rican members. The Puerto Rican Civil Service Employees Association is thirty-five years old, owns its own building, and has established a successful credit union. The Spanish Club of the New York City Police Department has 250 members, mostly Puerto Rican. The Association of Puerto Rican Social Workers has more than 1,000 members. There are organizations of lawyers, ministers, teachers, nurses, electricians, barbers, bar owners, taxi owners and drivers, and baseball umpires. The Council of Puerto Rican and Spanish-American Organizations of Greater New York now includes fifty-four civic, social, cultural, religious, and fraternal organizations. The Federation of Puerto Rican Organizations of New Jersey has thirty member groups. Aspira is an organization for community development, and is vigorously concerned with raising educational and vocational aspirations.

The Young Lords Party

Puerto Ricans also have had their young militants, who were organized in the Young Lords Party. This group was initiated by students and members of a gang that had turned political under the influence of militant youth movements among other minorities. It was organized in 1969 and was Third World in orientation. It was primarily interested in Barrio improvement: cleaning up streets, demonstrating for better services; and in the development of identity.[42] In its account of Puerto Rican history it stressed the admixture of the black slave population brought to Puerto Rico by the Spaniards, chiefly from the Yoruba tribe. In this emphasis it attempted to counteract lower-status feelings of dark Puerto Ricans, as well as to declare its alliance with other Third World movements. There have been branches of the Young Lords Party in New York, Philadelphia, Bridgeport, and Chicago. It was active in involving women, and

[41]Glazer and Moynihan, *Beyond The Melting Pot,* p. 102.
[42]Young Lords, *Palente* (New York: McGraw-Hill Book Co., 1971.)

had some nationwide attention in regard to a breakfast program for school children. Four years after it formed, and somewhat older, the group moved politically left and merged scatteredly with various political groups, especially the Puerto Rican Socialist Party, which espouses the cause of island independence.[43]

THE DECLINE OF DOMINANCE?

One can hardly speak of the decline of dominance as long as Puerto Rico remains a colony. The ultimate policy for the island will have an effect on mainland Puerto Ricans. Island politics has been stabilized by the development of a strong middle class and the only viable issues for it are continuance of the status quo (which brings tax advantages to citizens as well as enterprises) or statehood, as has been the solution for Alaska and Hawaii. The first elected governor, Luis Muñoz Marín, advocated independence, and was the initiator of Operation Bootstrap. But after the influx of mainland capital in the postwar period, he saw advantages in the prolongation, though not interminably, of the status quo. The advocates of independence are probably stronger on the mainland, and their identification is both ethnic and class oriented in concern for a different pattern of development and for some better solutions to the poverty and blight that so grindingly besets their people on the island, and in the cities or migratory labor force of the continent.

Fitzpatrick has defined the alternatives for Puerto Rican individuals and families as (1) those who seek to become as much like the established mainland culture as possible and seek to dissociate themselves from the ethnic tie and to merge into the dominant society, (2) those who withdraw into the traditional island culture and lock themselves into an old way of life, and (3) those who seek to build a cultural bridge between the two cultures.[44]

Many of the earlier migration have successfully moved into the larger society, as has also a proportion of those who came later. Some have gone back, or dream of a home village where "we were poor, but we were happy." Some, like Mr. Rios of "Eastville," will be able to hold to their value system and "dignitad" with the aid of some of the structures of the larger society: the night school, the evangelical congregation, the social security system. Others, like Soledad, or some dropout addicts, will be lost in the survival struggle of the streets.[45]

It will be for the students, the professionals, the organizational leaders to build the cultural bridges. To an extent this has been taking place and gains have been made. One of the most important is in education. The number of Puerto Rican students in high school has risen to 85 percent; this represents a reduction of the dropout rate. Probably the most talked of issue has been that of bilingual education. The Yarborough amendment to the Elementary and Secondary School Act of 1967 provides federal funds for bilingual education. The arguments for bilingual education for children where a language other than English is spoken at home have been demonstrated in a summary of experiment and research in this area.[46] Students in a special bilingual program, for example, did as well in English classroom achievement as those not in the

---

[43]Stan Steiner, *The Islands: The Worlds of Puerto Ricans* (New York, Harper & Row, 1975), Ch. 30.
[44]Joseph P. Fitzpatrick, *Puerto Rican Americans,* p. 98.
[45]See Steiner, *The Islands,* Chs. 25 and 26, for a discussion of addiction and prostitution.
[46]Hernan LaFontaine, "Bilingual Education," in Cordasco and Bucchioni, *The Puerto Rican Experience,* pp. 325 ff.

program, and better than the control group in English reading ability; there were definite decreases in anxiety; the students in the bilingual program were superior to the control group in effort and reliablity, though no better or worse in conduct; bilingually taught children retain more of the parental culture than did those in the control group.[47] Wider implementation of this potential depends on curriculum experiment, innovative and competent personnel, and the flexibility of the system. How fast can the school system move? "Institutional change" has been the battle cry of ethnic and poverty reformers, but the great bureacracies such as the New York City Board of Education and the Teachers Union, have strong vested interests in the status quo.

The issue of bilingual education, initiated in Congress by Senator Yarborough from Texas, was a response to the concerns of the Spanish-speaking minority of the Southwest. At the invitation of Aspira, however, a National Conference of Puerto Ricans, Mexican Americans, and educators was called on the special needs of Puerto Rican Youth.[48] This is an indication of a developing coalition of the bridge builders of the two principal Spanish-speaking minority groups.

Education and cultural identity will release creativity in young Puerto Ricans, but this alone is not enough. The critical issues of the future are employment, housing, day care, medical care. Education, and local community development initiative and leadership may enable people to effectively use scarce resources, but the provision of adequate resources cannot rest on the minority alone.

Suggested Readings

Cooper, Paulette, ed. *Growing Up Puerto Rican*, New York: The New American Library (A Mentor Book), 1972.
    Seventeen autobiographical statements by a variety of young Puerto Ricans.
Cordasco, Francesco, and Bucchioni, Eugene. *The Puerto Rican Experience: A Sociological Sourcebook*. Totowa, N.J.: Littlefield, Adams & Co., 1973.
    This sourcebook has an excellent section (IV) on education on the mainland.
Fitzpatrick, Joseph P. *Puerto Rican Americans: The Meaning of Migration to the Mainland,* Englewood Cliffs, N.J.: Prentice-Hall, 1971.
    This sensitive summary analysis of the mainland Puerto Rican situation, dilemmas and challenges, is classic.
Lopez, Adalberto, and Petras, James. *Puerto Rico and the Puerto Ricans*. New York: John Wiley & Sons, 1974.
    An excellent documentary collection. Especially good on Puerto Rico–U.S. relations.
Padilla, Elena. *Up From Puerto Rico*. New York: Columbia University Press, 1958.
    A social anthropologist presents the daily living of Puerto Ricans in one New York neighborhood.
Steiner, Stan. *The Islands: The Worlds of the Puerto Ricans*. New York: Harper & Row (Harper Colophon Book), 1974.
    A rich, lively book in the best tradition of crusading journalism.

---

[47]*Ibid.,* p. 336.
[48]The report of this conference, "Hemos Trabajado Bien," is included in Cordasco and Bucchioni, *The Puerto Rican Experience,* pp. 301–304.

14

Chinese Americans

China's is one of the oldest cultures in recorded history. It is indeed timeless, for the Chinese language has no tenses, so that one only knows from the context of a statement whether it refers to the past or the present. For centuries China was a feudal, hierarchical society bound by reciprocal oblications within the extended kinship, according to age, sex, and birth order, and between classes according to traditional roles and responsibilities.

THE CHINESE IN THE UNITED STATES

When the first Chinese came to the United States early in the nineteenth century they were more culturally visible than "racially," though they were early defined as a racial group in harmony with the racial attitudes of European-descended people.

The real migration began after 1850, when Chinese labor was sought for mines and railroads. Most stayed west of the Rockies in this period. Immigration increased until 1882, when the first of a series of exclusion acts barred any further heavy migration. In 1924 the Chinese were categoricaly excluded for a generation. Many who came in the nineteenth century did not expect to stay permanently. Others obtained citizenship before the first exclusion act. Still others, of course, eventually were American born, so that there are some fourth-generation families today.

The Chinese Exclusion Act drastically curtailed, though it did not completely eliminate, further immigration after 1882. During several decades the number of Chinese returning to China exceeded the number of arrivals. "From 1908, when records of departures began, to 1930, while 48,482 Chinese immigrant aliens were admitted, 72,796 departed, thus showing a net loss."[1] Normal natural increase was prevented by the disproportion of the sexes. In 1910 there were 1,430 males to every 100 Chinese females; in 1920, 695.5; and in 1940, 258.3. Finally, because of exclusion there had been an undue proportion of elderly Chinese in the population, which accounted for a relatively high death rate for the group. Thus the Chinese population declined from a peak of 107,488 in 1890 to a low of 61,639 in 1920. From 1921 to 1940 the Chinese in America increased but slightly, to a 77,504 total in 1940.

The 1940–1950 decade showed an increase of 51.8 percent in the Chinese population. Part of this may reflect a more accurate census count gained through the use of Chinese recorders for the first time. But there is doubt if even this measure succeeded

[1]Maurice R. Davie, *World Immigration* (New York: The Macmillan Co., 1936), pp. 315–316.

in getting all the resident aliens counted, since many avoid official contacts because of illegalities in their status—fraudulent claims to derivative citizenship, "jumping ship" by seamen, crossing borders without detection, and "smuggling." Much of the increase actually occurred in the postwar years, when an unprecedented number of female immigrants admitted under the War Brides Act helped bring the sex ratio of this population to 1.89. (In 1890 there had been 27 Chinese males to every 1 Chinese female.)

The "Slot Racket"

Unique to the Chinese in the United States has been the so-called slot racket. A section of the 1870 citizenship law passed by Congress recognized the right to confer citizenship on Americans born abroad. Chinese residents in this country have made much use of this law to secure entry of others, especially relations with the same surnames. As we have seen, many male Chinese immigrants returned to China from time to time for protracted visits to their families abroad and conceived children there. In countless instances, "sons never born" were reported, thus creating a "slot" on the family tree. Those "slots" enabled people to claim derivative citizenship and enter the United States. Persons claiming derivative citizenship, if born before 1934, were eligible for admission to this country if they could prove that their fathers or grandfathers resided in the United States at one time. The "racket" aspect has been in the selling of these "slots" by legitimate claimants. Arrangements were made to sell the "slots" through Hong Kong brokers for prices ranging from $2,500 to $6,000.[2]

Most of the Chinese who came in the nineteenth century were poor villagers. Within the pattern of the Chinese family system the men came, leaving their wives and children, if they had them, within the shelter of the kinship circle in China. Many of them came as contract laborers, especially for railroad construction. They made no particular effort to settle in agriculture, perhaps because American agriculture was alien to their patterns of cultivation at home. Some returned to China for a time, or several times, to invest their earnings in a strip of land in the home village, to pay the bride price for a wife, or to contribute to the joint family purse.

Probably a very high proportion of them came and stayed as "sojourners." This term has been applied to the Chinese who have lived in this country with the idea of making enough money to return to the homeland to live. Siu describes this category thus. "The Chinese sojourners maintain a psychological and social separateness from the larger society and insulate themselves against the full impact of the dominant societies' values, norms, attitudes, and behavior patterns." With this attitude, the sojourner lives a dual existence "which contributes to his sense of non-belongingness in both societies, a fact that is seldom admitted by the sojourner." It is this psychological orientation that marks a Chinese as a sojourner whether foreign or native-born, irrespective of his class position, or whether the time ever comes that he feels affluent enough to return to his homeland.[3]

Others saw as their goal small entrepreneurial enterprises in America, where they were free from the "squeeze" of officialdom or the limitations of the class system. Obviously, as the Chinese population increased, merchants came also to the principal centers to maintain the supply of familiar Chinese goods. Many of these merchant

[2]*Time,* Jan. 20, 1958, p. 17.
[3]Paul C. Siu, "The Sojourner," in *American Journal of Sociology,* July, 1952, pp. 34–44.

families were related through organizations of merchants or through family ties to others in other cities of America. They became the power structure of the Chinese sub-communities of the large cities.[4]

Students and Intellectuals

From 1847, when an American missionary brought three Chinese boys to study at an American academy, there has been a steady stream of students and intellectuals coming to American schools and universities, at first channeled through American schools and colleges in China, subsequently promoted by the government. Many of these returned to eminent positions in the government, especially of the Republic of China, and in science, commerce, and banking. During the Japanese invasion of China in the late 1930s many well-to-do families sent their young people to study here and wait out the long period of war: with the Japanese, World War II, and civil war in China. With the change of government in China in 1948 they have remained. Until very recently they have had little interest in the older immigrants clustered in Chinatowns. An influx of similar young people from well-placed families still comes annually from Taiwan.

Changes in the immigration law opened possibilities for citizenship. The first was during World War II, when in 1943 the Exclusion Act was repealed and Chinese were given an annual quota of 105.[5] After 1946 the numbers rose somewhat, because under the War Brides Act wives and children of American citizens could be admitted as nonquota immigrants. Other than dependent women and children, under the preference quotas of the MacCarran-Walter Act the largest number admitted were professional and technical personnel, many already here under permanent residence status.

With the 1965 revision of the immigration laws, abolishing nationality quotas (though retaining the preference system) there was an enormous upswing in Chinese migration: 13,736 whose place of birth was China and 3,872 from Hong Kong in 1966, as compared with 4,769 from both places for the preceding year. (Immigrants born in Hong Kong may come in under the visas available to Great Britain.)[6] This heavy migration has continued, as well as a large number who came first under refugee status, and have applied for a change of status from permanent residence to immigration visa status.

Undocumented Aliens

Since the Chinese had no recourse against the exclusion laws, they used their wits to circumvent them. There was no strength in the Chinese government at the time of the exclusion laws to back them; their testimony was not allowed in U.S. courts. In addition to border smuggling, ship smuggling, and the slot racket, other stratagems were

---

[4]For a good brief summary of the early migration, see Betty Lee Sung, *Mountain of Gold* (New York: The Macmillan Co., 1967), Ch. 3, pp. 21–36.
[5]*Ibid.*, Ch. 6, pp. 77 ff., a discussion of migration in the period in which this quota was operative.
[6]*Ibid.*, p. 94.

used. When the San Francisco earthquake of 1907 leveled the old Chinatown, destroying all records, many Chinese emerged as American born.[7]

From time to time immigration personnel have made raids to find illegal entrants. This has created a climate of fear; the Chinese community has usually protected them, but also, using the threat of reporting and deportation, has exploited them. When the possibility of regularizing status was offered after the 1965 immigration amendments, many of the older Chinese were afraid to take advantage of it.

Immigration figures are not necessarily a true reflection of the American population of Chinese ancestry because those who entered illegally took care not to be counted, and an accurate census count has been difficult in a closed subcommunity. The 1970 census, however, again used Chinese interviewers and there were efforts in major Chinatowns to urge people to respond openly to the census takers. (See Table 14–1.)

TABLE 14-1 Chinese Immigration to the United States and Population of Chinese Ancestry as Recorded by Census

Year	Total Admitted*	Total Recorded**	Per Cent Increase or Decrease
1820 to 1830	3	——	—
1831 to 1840	8	——	—
1841 to 1850	35	758	—
1851 to 1860	41,397	34,933	—
1861 to 1870	64,301	63,199	80.9
1871 to 1880	123,201	105,465	66.9
1881 to 1890	61,711	107,488	1.9
1891 to 1900	14,799	88,869	−16.4
1901 to 1910	20,605	71,531	−20.4
1911 to 1920	21,278	61,639	−13.8
1921 to 1930	29,907	74,594	21.6
1931 to 1940	4,928	77,504	3.4
1941 to 1950	16,709	117,140† (150,005††)	51.8
1951 to 1960	9,657	190,095† (237,292††)	62.3 (58.2††)
1961 to 1970	96,062	(435,062††)	(54.5††)
TOTAL	504,601		

*Annual Report of Immigration and Naturalization Service, Washington.
**United States Census for each decade.
†Includes mainland United States without Hawaii.
††Includes Hawaii.

Population Distribution

The American Chinese population is highly urbanized. By 1950, as many as 94 percent were officially counted in cities of various sizes, and according to Lee only 1 percent could be said to have really rural residence.[8] The trend has been toward concentration in a few large cities. In addition to San Francisco, with the largest Chinatown in the nation, enough Chinese to form a local "colony" are found in Chicago,

[7]Ibid., p. 98.
[8]Rose Hum Lee, The Chinese in the United States (Hong Kong: Hong Kong University Press, 1960), p. 38. Distributed in the United States by the Oxford University Press.

Detroit, Los Angeles, Brooklyn, New York, Boston, Washington, D.C., Dallas, Houston, and Philadelphia. The most interesting recent change in the geographical distribution of the American Chinese population has been the southward movement. In 1950 there were 10,432 in the South. While this was still a small percentage of the then 117,629 national total, it represented an increase over 1940 of 112.5 percent. Of this Lee writes

> The southern movement gathered momentum during the depression, when the South surpassed all other regions in attracting families who owned and operated general merchandise, food, and service establishments. The Chinese function as middlemen in a multi-racial society where the social relations between the whites and Negroes are strained and hostile. They also play this role in the Southwest, where Mexicans and American Indians are numerous and the Chinese cater to all groups. This is similar to the position the Chinese occupy in South-East Asia, the Caribbean, and elsewhere.[9]

It is of interest to find that in 1940, a hundred years after the Chinese immigration started, for the first time the American-born Chinese exceeded the foreign-born Chinese population. The exceptional tendency for Chinese immigrants to return to their homeland and the long period in which the group had had an excessively high male preponderance account for the delay.

THE ESTABLISHMENT OF DOMINANCE

Visibility

To the Westerners settling the Pacific Coast and the Rocky Mountain area, the Chinese appeared particularly alien. Although the China trade had been active for some decades, few of these "pioneers" had ever seen an Asiatic. The Chinese were immediately subject to derogating attitudes as a "race."

Actually, however, what struck Anglo-Americans were cultural characteristics, more than racial. The peculiarities of the Chinese language, with its high sing-song intonation and its ideographic writing, bore no relation to any spoken or written language they had known. The men, who were in preponderance and hence most visible, still dressed according to the old-style Chinese custom: long queues, felt slippers, cotton blouses, and little round hats. They were also ridiculed because they accepted domestic work at a time when there were few women available to do it. This did not fit American ideas of a masculine role.

Religiously, almost none of the nineteenth-century migrants were Christian, although soon the Protestants and subsequently in the twentieth century, the Catholics, began to proselytize among the new migrants.

Discrimination

The discovery of gold in California was a magnet for the first Chinese as it was for many Americans. The Chinese have developed mining all over Southeast Asia, and the

[9]*Ibid.*, p. 29.

pattern for overseas enterprise for the son of a joint family is centuries old. Perhaps much of the peculiarly violent and rough treatment accorded these first Chinese immigrants can be understood when it is remembered that Chinese-native-white interaction first took place in the especially lawless setting of the frontier. Opposition arose to the Chinese as gold miners because they were industrious and persevering, often taking on mining locations that whites considered worthless and making them pay. Thus began the cry that the Chinese depressed the wages and the standard of living of whites, an allegation that was to dog the Chinese as they subsequently became laborers in all the occupations available—as railroad construction workers, as farm laborers, and in various kinds of service for households. In the initial settlement of the Pacific Coast among the settlers going West men far outnumbered women, and the Chinese seized opportunities as cooks, launderers, and other household servants. They filled an acute labor need for a time, but even then were ridiculed for their foreign dress, accents, and customs. They were systematically excluded from white-collar and professional occupations. This persisted until World War II. Although there were some merchants engaged in large international trade, the chief activity of the entrepreneurs was confined to supplying the needs of the resident Chinese.

State legislation and local ordinances discriminating against the Chinese were passed throughout the thirty years (1850–1880) before the national exclusion Acts following 1882. Although much of the basic motivation was economic—to eliminate competition of Chinese labor—the rhetoric and racial assumptions of legislators and courts operated to institutionalize prejudice, and validate as well as create popular anti-Chinese attitudes and stereotypes. There were immigrant taxes, taxes on foreign miners, an ordinance making it a misdemeanor to carry baskets suspended from a pole across the shoulders (a Chinese custom for delivery of goods), a laundry tax: $2 quarterly for those using one-horse vehicles and $15 for those using no vehicle. Chinese witnesses were excluded from testimony in California courts in 1854 and this was reaffirmed in the State Court of Appeals in 1871.[10]

Frequently, the Chinese were exposed to violence, especially in periods of hard times. As a result of the panic of 1873, riots occurred during which the Chinese were robbed, beaten, and murdered by hoodlums who made the Chinese the scapegoats for the ills of the times. Eyewitness accounts report that "it was a common sight in San Francisco and other cities to see the Chinese pelted with stones or mud, beaten or kicked, having vegetables or laundry stolen from their baskets, and even having the queues cut." It was also reported that their washhouses were set afire, and when they tried to escape from burning houses they were beaten and sometimes compelled to die in the flames. The police afforded little protection against these outrageous attacks and the victims did not retaliate. The Chinese government, however, demanded an indemnity, which was paid by the United States government.

Agitation for the exclusion of the Chinese rose throughout the 1870s. At first, there was little support in Congress as most people east of the Rockies had not encountered many Chinese, if any, and the Southern states were watching to see whether, after Emancipation, they might not need to replace Negro labor with Chinese. With the collapse of Reconstruction, the Southerners in Congress supported the Californians, and the Chinese Exclusion Act was passed in 1882, suspending all Chinese immigra-

[10]Cheng Tsu Wu, ed., "Chink" (New York: The World Publishing Co., 1972), pp. 11–103, includes the texts of many of these ordinances, judicial rulings, and the Exclusion Act.

tion for ten years. This was repeated for another ten years in 1892; and in 1902 suspension of Chinese immigration was extended indefinitely. This remained the status of Chinese until 1943, when, under the pressure of the war situation, as we have seen, China was added to the quota immigrant nations and allotted 105 annual entries.

The exclusion of the Chinese by federal legislation is a clear illustration of Congress yielding to the specific will of one of its individual states in the absence of any general national demand. McWilliams has noted the following factors: (1) all but one of some eight anti-Chinese measures passed by Congress were passed on the eve of national elections and for avowed political purposes; (2) the interrelationship of the Southern attitude toward the Negro and the California attitude toward the Oriental prompted Southern representatives to side with California on a *quid pro quo* basis; (3) there was no real knowledge of the Chinese on the part of white Americans throughout the nation, and they failed to recognize the issue as related to national interest.[11]

MINORITY ADAPTATIONS TO DOMINANCE

The Chinese reaction to conflict with dominants was one of passivity and withdrawal. They sought niches in which they would be inconspicuously tolerated.

Occupations

With the decline of surface mining and the use of heavy machinery in the mines, Chinese moved out of primarily rural areas, and except for seasonal labor as harvesters, did not become part of the agricultural sector of the economy. Neither, after the decline of mining and railroad construction, did they become part of the industrial sector, probably because of discrimination. They concentrated in small merchant enterprise and the service occupations.

Residence

Like other minorities, the Chinese, where there was any considerable number, clustered in ethnic subcommunities. This was, in part, natural and voluntary because of cultural and language ties, but the persistence and closed quality of these communities was a result of discrimination and fear.[12] Chinatowns have spread to all the major cities in the United States wherever there is a sizable Chinese population.[13] Until the last decade, and to some extent still, Chinatowns have largely been worlds of their own with their own system of organization.

[11]See Carey McWilliams, *Brothers Under the Skin* (Boston: Little, Brown & Co., 1943), pp. 87–96, for an extensive account and interpretation of the legislation against the Chinese.
[12]Chia-ling Kuo, *Social and Political Change in New York's Chinatown: The Role of Voluntary Associations* (New York: Praeger Publishers, 1976).
[13]There are no Chinatowns in cities under 50,000, nor in states with very small Chinese populations. D. Y. Yuan, "Voluntary Segregation: A Study of New York Chinatown," in *Phylon*, Autumn, 1963.

Chinatown: The Stereotype

The Chinese, especially when clustered, seemed very strange to the average westerner: clothing, the singsong intonation of the language, the characters of the written language in street signs or menus, the shopkeepers with their abacuses for accounting, the exotic goods in shops. For the police, the do-gooders, and reformers the image was of nefarious activities. Three major commercial operations (at one time on a considerable scale) were illegal, and inimical: the opium trade, prostitution, and gambling. Opium had always been smoked in China since the British introduced it in the nineteenth century. It is not surprising therefore that the Chinese became middlemen for narcotics smuggling. In former times large fortunes were made by this trade, which was at its height in the 1880s.[14] It has largely declined since then and drug traffic is in the hands of other syndicates. Prostitution was inevitable in a social situation where the sex ratio is in such severe imbalance. Laborers migrated without their families, and at its peak in 1890, as we have seen, the imbalance was extreme.[15] Gambling was common in China, and in the western frontier, but it was not only illegal but immoral in the eyes of the upholders of the Protestant Ethic.

Chinatown: The Reality[16]

Chinatown serves social, economic, cultural, and political functions. Socially, Chinatown is indispensable for Chinese, as still a high proportion have no nuclear family life. (There are many single males, living alone, scattered through the metropolitan areas and having no social contact with their local neighborhoods.) Economically, Chinatown is an entrepot for the redistribution of Chinese goods, especially foods for the great Chinese restaurant industry. Culturally, it supports Chinese newspapers, Chinese schools, bookstores, printing houses, and Chinese movie theaters. Politically, it houses the headquarters of all political and social organizations.

The social organizations of Chinatown make up an inner government, capable of controlling social behavior.[17]

Family Associations. The basic form of organization in Chinatown is the family (clan) association. These are societies of people bearing the same surname. They do not need to be blood relations. Generally, there will be two or three family associations in each Chinatown that are the most powerful. Not all family names have enough people to support an organization, in which case a few of the weaker families will make a combined group. However, these combinations are not at random. They find some justification for association in Chinese history or literature. The family association is subdivided into a smaller group called a *fong,* which is organized according to the village from which the immigrants came. The family associations have social and economic functions. They find jobs, provide capital, finance education, adjudicate disputes among members, provide housing, contacts, and so on. The social functions (mostly held on Sundays) are also important for the dispersed, isolated members of the family group.

[14]Leong Gor Yun, *Chinatown Inside Out* (New York: Barrows, Mussey, Inc., 1936), p. 216.
[15]Sung, *Mountain of Gold,* Table A-3, p. 320.
[16]We are using the term Chinatown, here, as a generic model, as all Chinese subcommunities in cities are organized in the same pattern.
[17]Chia-ling Kuo, *Social and Political Change in New York's Chinatown,* p. 17.

Territorial (District) Associations.   There are organizations of people from the same district in China who speak the same dialect. Most of the Chinese have come from four counties of the province of Canton, and the largest proportion of these from the plateau and mountain region of Toishan, a land-locked area, whose nearest port, however, is Hong Kong.[18] There are also Hakka-speaking people (originally from north China who settled generations ago in Canton province); smaller groups from other provinces of eastern, and more recently, western China; and northern Mandarin-speaking Chinese. These associations form the intermediate stratum of the local power structure.

The Merchant Associations (Tongs).   Tongs were originally formed to assist new migrants,[19] to allocate territory for Chinese enterprise, controlling competition so that each businessman had a reasonable opportunity to earn a living. Inevitably, given the history of Chinese economic enterprise in the United States, they have controlled the illegal activities, and sometimes come into conflict, with violence, over control. In the 1920s newspaper headlines played up "tong wars." The more powerful associations have national and international linkage to their members in other cities and other countries.

The Consolidation of Power.   At the apex of the power structure in Chinatown is the Consolidated Benevolent Association (its equivalent for San Francisco is called the Six Companies). This consolidation has gone through a developmental process. Originally, this structure was responsible to the great clans of China for the behavior of its overseas members. It is made up of the heads of the family associations of each Chinatown. Initially, the structure of the various organizations (family, district, merchant) provided for diffuse leadership and clearly demarcated jurisdictions. But in a climate of fear and withdrawal, interlocking emerged. The Benevolent Association represented the sub-community to the "outside," policed its own community, and presented the image of a crime-free sober community going its own way. In her study of New York Chinatown in 1976, Dr. Kuo found that there was a "directorship of a small elite." There were nineteen powerful traditional leaders. They were the leaders of their own family associations, district associations, merchant associations, and the Benevolent Society.[20] They have been a strong force for resisting change. In 1972 the then chairman of the Benevolent Association in New York did not speak English.

Beginnings of Change

The structure of New York's Chinatown was first challenged with the organization of the Hand Laundry Alliance in 1933. Until this time the Chinatown power structure controlled the lives of the little people with the pattern of gentlemanly "face" and power structure "favor" and a considerable amount of official "squeeze," in the best style of Chinese officialdom. It is probable that the laundrymen would never have had the boldness to organize—so humble was their position in the hierarchy—had not outside circumstances threatened their very existence. The large American laundries instituted a systematic campaign against the Chinese laundries, displaying placards showing Chinese laundrymen spitting on white shirts. The Chinese Consul-General protested

[18]Sung, *Mountain of Gold*, p. 14.
[19]*Ibid.*, pp. 24–25.
[20]Chia-ling Kuo, *Social and Political Change in New York's Chinatown*, pp. 22–23.

and with the aid of city police succeeded in having most of the placards removed. The Chinese Consolidated Benevolent Association assessed each laundryman a dollar as an "anti-placard" fee. In March of 1933 there was a proposed city ordinance to license public laundries, with a $25 fee and a $1,000 security bond required. The liberal *Chinese Journal* took up the cause of the laundrymen. The CCB, through the editor's prodding, had to take some action, but it was concerned with keeping control. However, an able leader, Louis Wing, emerged from among the laundrymen, and with the help of the editor of the *Chinese Journal,* in space rented from the Roman Catholic Church on Mott Street, an organization was formed that became an independent, self-determining body. There were many struggles to bypass the Chinatown power structure, and at one point the *Chinese Journal* was boycotted, but both the Alliance and the *Journal* survived. The organization grew, it cooperated with the efforts for improved conditions of other organizations of service trades, and by 1935 moved its headquarters outside Chinatown.[21] Its trucks may be seen all over New York today.

During the 1930s and 1940s there was a considerable exodus from Chinatown. The younger, the better educated, in the better occupational positions tended to go to newer sections of cities. Chinatown in the early 1950s was left with an older, poorer, less well-educated general population, which for the oldest generation contained a sharp cleavage between the power elite and stranded sojourners. Many of the American-born second generation are more conservative than the newest immigrants, as Chinatown managed to preserve a pattern of behavior that began to modify in China decades ago. The teenagers of the third generation are often in open conflict as they seek to emulate American behavior patterns.

The Suburban Chinese: The Chinese of Long Island[22]

Dr. Kuo studied two social clubs: *The Circle* and *The Center on Long Island.* These serve a dispersed membership in various suburbs within commuting distance of New York City. The families live in Anglo neighborhoods and represent the same socioeconomic status as their neighbors. The informants report no incidents of hostility. Kuo attributes this in part to the fact that they are dispersed rather than heavily concentrated. Furthermore, she emphasizes three other factors that gain them acceptance: they maintain an appropriate style of life consistent with their neighbors; their children are well behaved and often achieve high academic status in school; they are courteous in their attitudes and behavior toward their neighbors.

The Circle is a women's club of about seventy members. It is composed of a young group (average age thirty) of American-born Chinese who are teachers, social workers, and white-collar workers. Their husbands have occupations that are skilled, professional, or business. Kuo estimated their average annual income for the family to be about $10,000 (1970). Some of these women are college educated. This club has a typical American cast. It provides social events for adults, teenagers, and children; it raises scholarship funds for able young Chinese Americans.

Most of the members of *The Circle* did not grow up in Chinatown. English is the first language for them, though many can speak Chinese to elders or relatives in Chinatown.

[21]Leong, *Chinatown Inside Out,* Ch. 5, pp. 85–106.
[22]Chia-ling Kuo, "The Chinese of Long Island: A Pilot Study," in *Phylon,* Autumn, 1970. By permission of the author.

Most of their parents were skilled workers. In their homes, only English is spoken. They share the American dream of mobility, have aspirations for their children, and have frequent contacts and some friendships with other Americans.

We see this group of American Chinese, then, to be like any other mobile descendants of immigrants in their values and their behavior. Their need to form a "circle," however, suggests that they are aware of themselves as a distinct minority and find pleasure and security in associations with people of their own ethnic background and similar socioeconomic level.

The Center has about a hundred members, men and their wives, of a more successful stratum. They are a more recent migration, persons who came from China to the United States for advanced training and could not return after the fall of the Nationalist government. They are of upper-middle-class and upper-class origin in China and have maintained or improved their status in America. (This organization does not include the most elite of the New York Chinese, such as Pei, the architect, or Tsai, the eminent member of the New York Stock Exchange.) Nevertheless, they are engineers, professors, managers and owners of small factories, consultants, and accountants.

The Center consciously works to further Chinese-American cultural relations. The programs are designed on the one hand to widen the membership's knowledge and appreciation of American culture, and on the other hand, to acquaint the American-born children and the non-Chinese community with Chinese art, philosophy, drama, and the classical Chinese language.

According to Kuo this group is unevenly acculturated. Those who were upper class in origin, or who were raised in the large coastal cities of China, or who were raised in Christian high schools and universities, are the most acculturated because of early and constant exposure to Western culture in China. Those who belong to only one or none of these categories are still in the process of acculturation. Most of the men associate with non-Chinese at work. They are active in local civic organizations. Eighty percent of the women are active in church groups. In their daily life they live like other Americans of similar economic status. Since they are a more highly trained group than the young members of *The Circle,* they are in a higher income bracket, have larger and better furnished homes, celebrate the American New Year with open house for their neighbors, take up tennis, swimming, dancing. They feel they have not encountered prejudice, but they are more ethnocentric in their attempts to preserve for their children and communicate to the non-Chinese community their regard for scholastic achievement, filial piety, harmony, and compromise in human relations as presented in Confucian ethics. Although these families speak English at home, and their children, who go to private schools and Ivy League colleges do not speak Chinese, their children are more familiar with Chinese history and culture than the children of the American-born group studied.

In the years since these pilot studies the distinction between these two groups has narrowed and there is now some overlap in membership. This may be attributed to the rising economic status of American-born Chinese in the suburbs, and to the rising ethnic consciousness that is concerned with preserving cultural roots.

Living Conditions

Rose Hum Lee, publishing in 1960, felt that as the older generations died, Chinatowns would disappear. This has not happened, chiefly because since 1966 they have been repopulated by an influx of new immigrants.

Cattell describes many barriers that aggravate the situation of many Chinatown families. There is unfamiliarity with and cultural resistance to using the health and welfare services available. Yet there is a high incidence of illness and of mental illness. In a sample study of 105 cases (1958–1960), the highest percentages were infective diseases and nutritional diseases.[23] These reflect some of the principal problems of Chinatown: low income and bad housing.

Of the 2,323 Chinese families living in New York Chinatown in 1950, 37 percent had incomes of less than $3,000, and 55 percent had less than $4,000. The New York State Housing Survey of 1950 reported that more than 30 percent of the dwelling units did not contain flush toilets; 48 percent had no bathtub or shower; 40 percent lacked hot water; 71 percent did not have central heating.[24]

Although some improvements in housing have been made, the 1970 Census reports that for the four census tracts that include the old heart of New York Chinatown, and where the proportion of Chinese residents is highest, there are still 1,100 dwelling units lacking some or all plumbing. There are 471 dwelling units without kitchens. In 35 blocks occupied by dwellings live 26,755 persons; 1,678 of these are children under five, over 1,000 are over seventy-five, and two-thirds of these men. The average size of dwelling units is three rooms (median 3.1; mode 3).[25]

Chinatown suffers from the deterioration of all old urban neighborhoods. Behind the facade of its shops and restaurants that are so attractive to tourists is a poverty ridden, overcrowded ethnic slum.

As for income, figures for five selected states of Chinese with income less than poverty level in 1970 indicate, for families, 9.9 percent for California, 13.8 percent for New York, 5.5 percent for Hawaii, 10.3 percent for Illinois, 12.7 percent for Massachusetts. The national average (for Chinese) is 10.3 percent. For unrelated individuals (Chinese) in poverty, the national figure is 40.3 percent for those over 14 years of age, and 24.1 percent for those over 65.[26]

One of the effects of the new immigration has been the growth of new industries in Chinatown, particularly the clothing industry. This has also brought more women into the labor force. Many of the new migrants came with high hopes and great myths. But if their English was inadequate they perforce had to settle in some Chinatown. There has been a considerable dispersion East. At one point San Francisco was claiming that it was receiving 8,000 annually (visa immigrants and refugees), though subsequent research placed the number at 2,500 to 3,000. The occasion for the exaggerated claim was, of course, the pressure of new population on already inadequate resources. For the new immigrants it meant crowded, substandard housing, entry-level employment, the dilemmas of schools unprepared to deal with non-English speaking children. Language was, of course also a barrier to adults seeking employment outside Chinese enterprises. A phenomenon of earlier European migrations emerged: the exploitation of newcomers by their own ethnic group. For a time and still, to some extent, employers took ad-

[23]Stuart H. Cattell, *Health, Welfare and Social Organization in Chinatown, New York City*. A Report Prepared for the Chinatown Public Health Nursing Demonstration of the Department of Public Affairs, Community Service Society of New York, August, 1962, p. 52. (Mimeographed)
[24]D. Y. Yuan, "Chinatown and Beyond: The Chinese Population in Metropolitan New York," in *Phylon*. Fourth Quarter, Winter, 1966, pp. 324–325.
[25]U.S. Census, 1970. New York County. Table P-1, General Characteristics of the Population and Table H-1, Occupancy, Utilization, Financial Characteristics of Housing Units.
[26]Betty Lee Sung, *Chinese Americans: Manpower and Employment* (New York: Praeger Publishers, 1976).

vantage of the language handicap and unfamiliarity with America to pay seriously substandard wages. Government action has brought considerable improvement.[27]

There have also been difficulties for youth, particularly the older unattached youth. Gangs have formed. For a time most of the gang fights were between overseas-born and American-born youths. In New York in 1972 more trouble arose on the interethnic front as Chinese and Puerto Rican youths crowded each other. Chinese culture is age-graded and when these youths fail to show respect and good behavior, their sponsors, and even their parents if they have them, wash their hands of them.[28]

CHINATOWN FACES THE FUTURE

The older leadership in America's Chinatowns have been confused and anxious at the changes that confront them. They have no tradition of public service, though on occasion they have sponsored short-term service to new migrants supported by public moneys and staffed by Anglo agencies. They are ill equipped, culturally and psychologically, to meet the problems emerging, and they fear change, as one informant reported: "because it is not in their interest: they see it coming, but hope it will be slow."

Russell D. Lee sees some indication of a transfer of "legitimate" leadership to second-generation Chinese who have formed, in some places, civic associations on the Anglo model. Whereas he finds that most of the membership is suburban Chinese, nevertheless they understand and can assist in planning and funding proposals.[29] Lee indicates a third generation of Chinese-American youth that have formed dissident groups which neither the traditional power elite or the civic associations have been willing to include in decision making. The result is a disunited front that certainly affects funding for community development from both public and private sources. Ernest D. Chu points out in an article the difficulty of knowing "Who speaks for Chinatown?"[30]

Nevertheless small gains are being made. In San Francisco there have been excellent planning studies and hearings before the State Labor Department on minimum wage violations. In New York there is greater voter registration. The International Ladies Garment Workers Union is teaching English to workers in the unionized shops of Chinatown's expanding garment industry. In New York a youth group has set up an information center, is developing programs in the arts, and is taping the history of Chinatown as remembered by the older residents. Some of the newer approaches to community problems are beginning to be developed with increasing participation of Chinese as paraprofessionals or as volunteers.

The youth gangs that a decade or so ago were members of petty criminal organizations, often supported by the tongs, and warring with each other as between the native born and the Hong Kong born, have at least developed some new models. Russell Lee describes the Leways (legitimate way) of San Francisco, who, however, were forced to

[27]Bay Area Social Planning Council, "Chinese Newcomers in San Francisco," February 1971, p. 63. (offset)
[28]For a comparison see Pei-Ngor Chen, "The Chinese Community in Los Angeles," in *Social Casework,* Vol. 51, No. 10, Dec., 1970.
[29]Russell D. Lee, "Patterns of Community Power: Tradition and Social Change in American Chinatowns," in Donald E. Gelfand and Russell D. Lee, *Ethnic Conflicts and Power: A Cross National Perspective* (New York: John Wiley & Sons, 1973), p. 352.
[30]Ernest D. Chu, "The Two Faces of Chinatown," *The Journal of Philanthropy,* 18, 2, March-April, 1977, pp. 18–26.

disband in 1969 under harassment from the local power structure and the police.[31] Chia-ling Kuo speaks of the Ghost Shadows of New York turning legitimate under the influence of a "reformed" Puerto Rican gang.[32]

The problems on the local level will persist, however, in the face of the continuing in-migration unless there is modification of the old power structure; a larger involvement in Chinatown of the better-established American born; for the time being, at least, a considerably larger infusion of funds and professional and technical assistance from the outside; and this may depend on the outcome of the present struggles for leadership and control.

On the national front there are the Organization of Chinese Americans, Inc., with headquarters in Rockville, Md., and the Chinese American Citizens Alliance, based in San Francisco, as well as various coalitions of Asian-Pacific Americans hoping to carve a place in the ethnic politics of the nation.

Suggested Readings

Barth, Gunther. *Bitter Strength: A History of the Chinese in the United States, 1850–1870.* Cambridge, Mass.: Harvard University Press, 1964.
> A vivid account of the life conditions and work conditions of Chinese in the period of the heaviest migration. Excellent source materials.

Lee, Rose Hum. *The Chinese in the United States of America.* Hong Kong: Hong Kong University Press, 1960 (Distributed in the U.S. by Oxford University Press, New York).
> The most comprehensive and informative single volume on the Chinese in the United States.

Sung, Betty Lee. *Chinese Americans: Manpower and Employment.* New York: Praeger Publishers, 1976.
> An analysis of 1970 data on income, employment, education. This data is also available for Chinese, state by state, in Sung, Betty Lee. *Statistical Profile of the Chinese in the United States.* U.S. Department of Labor: Manpower Administration.

———. *Mountain of Gold: The Story of the Chinese in America.* New York: The Macmillan Co., 1967.
> A lively, popular account, with colorful bits of information not found elsewhere.

Wu, Cheng-Tsu. *"Chink": A Documentary History of Anti-Chinese Prejudice in America.* New York: The World Publishing Co., 1972. Here are the documents, with a good introduction and editorial comment by Professor Wu; and also an added insight in the autobiographical foreword by Ben Fong-Torres.

[31]Russell D. Lee, "Patterns of Community Power," p. 352.
[32]Chia-ling Kuo, *Social and Political Change in New York's Chinatown,* p. 51.

15

The Japanese in the United States Mainland[1]

In recent years, most writing about Japanese Americans describes their position in terms of a "success story" and with a substantial basis in fact, as this chapter will show. As an introduction, it is instructive to compare their experience in mainland United States with the Chinese. Like the Chinese on the mainland, the Japanese settled on the West Coast, but in a more stable period in that region's history. Thus, disregarding for the moment the special indignities they suffered as racially kin to an enemy nation in World War II, they were spared much of the physical violence perpetrated on the Chinese in more lawless frontier days.

Although most of the Chinese remained on the West Coast, a considerable number scattered in cities throughout the northern part of the country. But up to the time of their relocation the Japanese remained more highly concentrated in the Pacific Coast states. While the Chinese reacted to native opposition with extreme passivity, the Japanese were less tractable. They held their ground, refusing to disperse like the Chinese, and made ingenious adaptations to the various economic discriminations inflicted on them, such as having an alien father buy land in the name of his native-born son. Consequently, while the native population came to think of the Chinese in terms of stereotype A—the inferior, humble, and ignorant, who could be condescendingly tolerated—the Japanese came to be treated according to stereotype B—the ambitious, cunning, and conspiratorial, requiring other means by dominants to keep them "in their place."

While the Japanese, like the Chinese, retained a relatively great interest in their homeland, they were not as "sojourner" oriented as the Chinese. Most of the Japanese immigrants expected to stay. This is one reason why the Japanese population in the United States (see Table 15-2) shows an almost steady rise, while up to 1930, as we have seen, that of the Chinese showed years of decline. Finally, both groups suffered from the humiliation of severe legislative discrimination, culminating in drastic restrictive immigration. The manner, however, of handling the federal restrictions was noticeably more diplomatic in the case of the Japanese, a contrast attributable to the greater power of the Japanese government, able to protest more effectively against discriminatory treatment of their nationals in this country than the Chinese.

---

[1]We confine this chapter to the mainland Japanese and disregard the Japanese in Hawaii because there are too many differences in the situation to deal with them both in the same chapter.

JAPANESE POPULATION TRENDS

For over 200 years, from 1638 to 1868, Japanese citizens were forbidden to go abroad, and foreigners, with few exceptions, were forbidden to enter Japan. The first to go out from the Land of the Rising Sun were students sent to gain knowledge from the rest of the world. Soon after, a limited number of laborers were permitted to leave. But it was the agreement signed by the Japanese government and certain Hawaiian sugar plantation owners in 1885 by which Japanese contract laborers were permitted to go to Hawaii that set emigration into momentum. From then until 1924 there was considerable Japanese migration to Asiatic Russia (302,946), to Hawaii (238,758), to the United States (196,543), and to China (105,258); and, in more limited numbers, to Canada, Brazil, the Philippines, Peru, Korea, and Australia. Considering the enormous rate of population growth in Japan during these decades and the consequent population pressure, this modest amount of emigration is surprising. Failure to emigrate in larger numbers to areas of the world settled by Europeans was due in part to the unfriendly manner with which the Japanese were received and to legal restrictions imposed. The special circumstances leading to substantial Japanese immigration to Hawaii are discussed in Chapter 16.

A comparison of Table 14-1 in Chapter 14 with Table 15-1 shows that Japanese immigration "picks up" at the same time that Chinese immigration "falls off" (especially in the 1891–1900 decade). Tables 15-1 and 15-2 show the number of Japanese immigrants admitted from 1861 to 1975 and the total population at the decennial years.

The increase in the Japanese population from 1880 to 1910 was due largely to immigration itself, since the great preponderance of the newcomers were male. After the agitation on the West Coast for restricting Japanese immigration, President Theodore Roosevelt negotiated directly with the Japanese government, and the so-called Gentleman's Agreement was made in 1907. It provided that Japan would not issue passports for the continental United States unless the persons were coming to resume a formerly acquired domicile, to join a parent, husband, or child, or to resume control of a farming enterprise that they had left. After 1907 immigration continued, but on a greatly diminished level. Immigration from Japan virtually came to a halt in 1924. The Oriental Exclusion Act, passed in that year, stated that no alien ineligible for citizenship shall be admitted to the United States. It is significant, however, that in the two decades prior to this act, many Japanese immigrants were women, often "picture brides." By 1930 the sex ratio among the Japanese on the mainland had declined to 143 males for every 100 females—much more normal than that of the Chinese. The more equitable sex ratio set the stage for greater "natural increase" (defined as excess of births over deaths) than occurred among the Chinese. Natural increase accelerated at the same time that immigration decreased. The only decennial decline in Japanese population oc-

TABLE 15-1.   Japanese Immigration to the United States*

1861–1870	186	1921–1930	33,462
1871–1880	149	1931–1940	1,948
1881–1890	2,270	1941–1950	1,555
1891–1900	25,942	1951–1960	46,250
1901–1910	129,797	1961–1970	39,988
1911–1920	83,837	1971–1975	26,005
Total, 1861–1975	391,389		

*Based on the *1975 Annual Report: Immigration and Naturalization Service:* Immigration by Country for Decades 1820–1975, Table 13, pp. 62–64.

TABLE 15-2.   **Japanese Population in Mainland United States***

Census Year	Number	Decade	Percentage Rate of Increase
1970	373,983*	1960–70	43.4*
1960	260,887*	1950–60	83.3*
1950	141,768	1940–50	11.6
1940	126,947	1930–40	– 13.1
1930	138,834	1920–30	25.1
1920	111,010	1910–20	53.8
1910	72,157	1900–10	196.6
1900	24,326	1890–00	1,093.0
1890	2,039	1880–90	1,277.7
1880	148	1870–80	169.1
1870	55	1860–70	
1860	0		

*U.S. Bureau of the Census, *Population Characteristics By Race of Non-White Population.* Based on mainland figures subtracting Hawaii. Including Hawaii, the Japanese population was 591,290 in 1970 and 464,332 in 1960. Before 1950 the Hawaiian population was not included in the total but listed under a separate table of the population of the territories. The percentage rates of increase for the total U.S. Japanese population including Hawaii for the 1960–1970 decade was 27.4 percent; for the 1950–1960 decade, 27.2 percent.

curred in the 1930–1940 decade, when the number of Japanese returning to the homeland (approximately 8,000) exceeded the new immigrants (approximately 2,000). This trend apparently continued up to the time of Pearl Harbor, since the estimated population in 1942 was only 122,000.

As Table 15-2 shows, the population of Americans of Japanese descent on the mainland has continued to increase, reaching 373,983 in 1970.[2] The surprising mainland increase in the 1950–1970 decades cannot be accounted for by births or by the allocation to Japan of an annual quota of 185 for the first time under the McCarran-Walter Immigration Act in 1952. It is largely due to the admission of wives of male American citizens, Oriental or Caucasian. From 1961 to 1965, of the 19,126 Japanese immigrants admitted to the country, 13,601, or 68 percent, were wives of American citizens.[3] The mainland population was further raised by substantial migration from Hawaii to the mainland.

The high concentration on the West Coast has remained only slightly diminished up to the present. In 1940, 88 percent of the then 127,000 mainland Japanese resided in this region. California alone had 83 percent, and most of these were in the Los Angeles area. Outside the West Coast, only New York and Chicago had substantial Japanese subcommunities. The New York subcommunity had, at the outbreak of World War II, declined from an earlier peak of 5,000 to 2,000.[4]

In 1970, 64 percent of the mainland population was still on the West Coast. Adding Hawaii's Japanese, only 20 percent of the total national Japanese population is outside the West. Chicago was the main non-Western city where the Japanese community permanently gained in size from the relocation of internees.

[2]Figure obtained by subtracting the Japanese in Hawaii in 1970 (217,307) from the total Japanese population of the United States (591,290). See note in Table 15-2.
[3]Annual Reports of Immigration and Naturalization Service.
[4]Bradford Smith, *Americans from Japan* (Philadelphia: J. B. Lippincott Co., 1948), p. 336.

THE ESTABLISHMENT OF DOMINANCE

The Characteristics of the Immigrant Japanese

The Japanese immigrants were Mongoloid in "racial type" and therefore easily identifiable as different by white Americans, even though not always distinguishable physiognomically from other Asians.

The culture in which the Japanese immigrants had been reared differed more markedly from that of America than the culture of the European immigrants. In some respects, however, it prepared the Japanese for more successful adjustment to life in this country. Before the period of Japanese immigration, Japan had begun transforming itself from a semifeudal into a modern industrial nation. The ferment of rapid change had begun in earnest at the beginning of the Meiji Era (1868–1912). The conscious policy of the ruling elite was to transform Japan into an industrial nation with Western technological methods under a centralized government. To the already great skill in farming, necessitated by population pressure and little tillable acreage, new scientific agricultural methods were added. Public education was brought to a high level. The development of scientific medicine and programs of public health were encouraged. These changes apparently had a marked effect on Japanese culture and social character.

The culture of Japan was a mixture of the traditional and the new. Basic in its traditional culture was the intricate set of mores that defined the strong obligation of the individual to the group, to the family, to those of superior class, and to the state. The authoritarian nature of Japanese social organization produced markedly obedient and self-effacing personality traits. The strong sense of subordination of the individual to the welfare of the group was reflected in the solidarity of Japanese subcommunities in this country. Deriving also from long tradition was the intricate pattern of etiquette and ritual that prescribed the proper way of behaving in every situation. To conform punctiliously to these elaborate social rituals was a major drive in the Japanese personality, accounting for the reputation for courtesy and good manners acquired by the Japanese.

The tradition-oriented character traits facilitated acceptance of the Japanese in America, primarily because they made the immigrants appear to be "nonthreatening." These traits included group loyalty and obedience (the *samurai*, or Japanese upper-class, values); avoidance of embarrassing situations; modesty, humility, and respect in the presence of superiors (*enryo*); general courtesy; emotional self-restraint, endurance, and absence of complaining in the face of hardships (*gaman*).[5]

Superimposed on these traditional traits were "modern" ones fostered by the industrial revolution in Japan, the "merchant values": risk-taking, tolerance for insecurity, rationalism, a common-sense approach to problem-solving, and the value of

---

[5]For a discussion of *gaman,* see Amy Iwasaki Mass, "Asians as Individuals: The Japanese Community," in *Social Casework,* 57, March, 1976, p. 161. In regard to the *enryo* concept, see Gerald M. Meredith, "Interpersonal Needs of Japanese-American and Caucasian-American College Students in Hawaii," in *The Journal of Social Psychology,* 99, Second Half, August, 1976, p. 157. The *samurai* values are discussed by Joe Yamamoto and Mamoru Iga, "Japanese Enterprise and American Middle-Class Values," in *The American Journal of Psychiatry,* 131, May, 1974, p. 578.

education as a goal in itself as well as a means to occupational success.[6] The work ethic of the immigrant Japanese seemed to involve the same drive and dedication as the Protestant work ethic of white Americans. However, whereas the latter was highly individualistic, the Japanese work ethic was collectivistic, intended to bring honor to family, community, and Japanese nation. The drive to succeed was probably as strong, if not stronger, than that of European immigrant groups motivated by the Protestant Ethic. Furthermore, in willingness to learn and to experiment in technological and economic matters, the Japanese surpassed not only all other Asians but many European immigrant groups as well.

In summary, the unique constellation of traditional and modern character traits, resulting from the rapid industrialization of an authoritarian semifeudal society, greatly facilitated the adjustment of the immigrants to life in the United States, and would eventually propel the Japanese, through the success of the immigrants' children, into the position of "model Americans."

Native Reaction to the Japanese

The West Coast region to which the Japanese first came was, in comparison with the East Coast, relatively undersettled and provided economic opportunity for population growth and economic development with many menial jobs to be filled. The Japanese were therefore welcomed by the natives in the capacity of laborers. At first, Japanese were employed in domestic service. As their numbers increased, some engaged in a wide variety of menial jobs and others began to operate small shops. Since their numbers were small and the jobs they took did not affect the employment opportunities of white American workers, little opposition was felt. Beginning about 1890, however, antagonism began to be displayed by members of labor unions. In that year Japanese cobblers were attacked by members of the shoemakers' union. In 1892, a Japanese restaurant in San Francisco was attacked by members of the local cooks' and waiters' union.[7] From then on, anti-Japanese activity grew steadily in California, rising to a climax in the famous School Board Affair in 1906, when the San Francisco Board of Education passed a resolution requiring the segregation of all Oriental children in one school. At the time there were ninety-three Japanese attending twenty-three different public schools of San Francisco. The resolution brought protest from the Japanese government and precipitated a crisis between the Imperial Government and that of the United States, which led to the signing of the Gentleman's Agreement in 1907.

The rising antagonism toward the Japanese in the cities led them to turn to agriculture.[8] They started out as farm laborers and by the late 1890s outnumbered the Chinese laborers. By 1909 they constituted a large part of the farm labor force in the Western states. It was natural for the Japanese to turn to agriculture. They brought with them knowledge of intensive cultivation of the soil superior to that of many American native farmers. It was likewise natural that more and more of them should aspire to operate

---

[6]Yamamoto and Iga, "Japanese Enterprise and American Middle-Class Values," p. 578. By and large the immigrants were not merchants but lower-class farmers. Nevertheless, they were strongly influenced by these values.

[7]Yamato Ichihashi, *Japanese in the United States* (Stanford:Stanford University Press, 1932), pp. 229–230.

[8]*Ibid.*, see Chs. 11, 12, 13, for an account of the progress of the Japanese in American agriculture.

farms themselves. By 1909 there were 6,000 Japanese operating farms, the greater number by far as tenants.[9] They experimented with small-scale farming, finally concentrating on fruits and vegetables. They were adaptable, thrifty, and industrious, and the number of Japanese-operated farms increased until 1920.[10]

The success of the Japanese in moving from laborer to entrepreneur, even though on a small scale and usually involving the payment of rent to white owners, led to opposition from white farmers, culminating in the passage in California of the first alien landholding act in 1913. Under this legislation, aliens ineligible for citizenship could lease agricultural land for periods not to exceed three years but could not own it. When it was discovered that the Japanese were buying stock in land-owning corporations and acquiring land in the name of their native-born children, further pressure resulted in a new act, which in substance prohibited the leasing of land by any method by Japanese foreign-born. Similar laws were passed by other Western states, and their constitutionality was upheld by the United States Supreme Court in a test case in 1923. From then on the role of the Japanese in agriculture declined, and the return to the cities increased. Nevertheless, at the time of Pearl Harbor they controlled large segments of California's berry and vegetable crops.

THE STABILIZATION OF DOMINANCE

Adjustment of the Japanese as a Minority: The Issei[11]

As with all immigrant groups, the Japanese reacted to minority status by forming separate subcommunities that were a mixture of Old World traits and accommodative institutions. On the West Coast the main little Tokyo's were in San Francisco, Los Angeles, and Seattle. For the latter, Miyamoto made an extensive study at the end of the 1930s, from which we draw.[12]

> The traditional heritage was most clearly seen in continuance of the patriarchal Japanese family, with its extreme emphasis on male authority and filial obligations. In recreation likewise, their play life tended "to revolve about activities that are essentially Japanese in character." The two Japanese

[9]*Ibid.*, p. 178.
[10]*Ibid.*, p. 193.
[11]Japanese Americans, according to Stanford Lyman, are the only immigrant group to specify by a linguistic term and characterize with a unique personality each generation of descendants from the original immigrants. The distinctions are much more refined than the usual terms of "foreign-born" and "native-born." The foreign-born are labeled *Issei;* the second-generation, *Nisei;* third-generation, *Sansei;* fourth-generation, *Yonsei;* fifth-generation, *Gosei*. In addition, the term *Kibei* is used for those American-born who were sent to Japan for a substantial portion of their formative years. The term *Nikkei* refers to the Japanese as a whole, rather than to a particular generational category. Hereafter these terms will not be italicized. See Stanford M. Lyman, "Japanese-American Generation Gap," in *Society*, 10, Jan/Feb 1973, p. 56.
[12]Shataro Frank Miyamoto, *Social Solidarity among the Japanese in Seattle,* University of Washington Publications in the Social Sciences, Vol. 11, No. 2 (Dec., 1939), pp. 57–130.

daily newspapers in Seattle in 1935 were heavily devoted to activities of the homeland, and few of the foreign-born Japanese read American papers.

Among the accommodative institutions were the economic "pools," the *Tanamoshi*. While 31 percent of the Japanese were in domestic service and 45 percent in the trades, there were a substantial number operating small mercantile establishments of their own. But few could accumulate enough capital for these ventures; it required the help of friends and relatives for the start. Often kinfolk formed pools from which various members could draw in initiating new enterprises. Seattle's Japanese had a local branch of the Japanese Chamber of Commerce *(Ken-Jin)* which served social and charitable functions, as well as acting as an agency of social control throughout the Japanese community and representing it in its relations to the larger community.

The high value which Japanese placed on education served to accelerate acculteration. While most of the immigrants themselves lacked higher education, they encouraged their children not only to continue school but also to excel in their studies. Strong parental discipline reinforced the authority of the school. Between 1930 and 1937 in the nine Seattle high schools fifteen Japanese students were either valedictorians or salutatorians of their classes.

In religion, it is somewhat striking to note that 1,200 Seattle Japanese belonged to Christian churches in 1936, more than belonged to all the Japanese religious groups combined. Miyamoto suggests that the many practical services rendered by the mission churches encouraged Japanese membership.

In one very important respect the Issei differed from their Chinese counterparts. Within a relatively short period of time (usually between ten and twenty years), the Issei men brought over Issei women, reflecting their lesser "sojourner" orientation. The practice of marrying "picture brides" was widespread, and often spared the Issei male the expense of his own round-trip fare to Japan.[13] As a result, the sex ratio plummeted from 2,370 (2,370 males per 100 females) in 1900 to 190 in 1920,[14] and the Japanese American family institution was firmly established. The result was a large contingent (large in comparison with Chinese Americans) of second-generation Japanese Americans, highly motivated by both the Japanese culture of their parents and white middle-class Protestant culture of their peers to succeed in American society.

[13]"Picture brides" usually came from the Issei male's community in Japan. They were generally known to his relatives or friends, who acted as "go-betweens." The Japanese Government, under pressure from the American Government, ceased to issue passports to "picture brides" in 1920. This act, along with the U.S. Immigration Act of 1924, left 42.5 percent of the adult Japanese males virtually no hope of marriage in the New World.
[14]Stanford M. Lyman, *The Asian in the West* (Reno and Las Vegas, Nevada: Social Science and Humanities Publication No. 4, Western Studies Center, Desert Research Institute, University of Nevada System, 1970), p. 79. Comparable figures for Chinese Americans are 1,887 (in 1900) and 696 (in 1920).

The American-Born Japanese: The Nisei

An unbalanced sex ratio among the Issei resulted in a large proportion of them remaining unmarried. The sex ratio declined slowly, reaching 131 males per 100 females in 1940, and the increase in the proportionate numbers of Nisei was correspondingly quite gradual. As late as 1940, only 27,000 of the 80,000 Nisei were over age 21.[15]

The Nisei grew up in communities dominated by Issei males. Constituting a proportionately small group, they were more vulnerable to influence by parents and elders, such as the staff members of the Japanese language schools and cultural and recreational centers, than would have been the case had their numbers been larger. The family structure was patriarchal, and discipline often severe. Nisei experienced a somewhat lonely, harsh, and isolated childhood.[16] They were taught to suppress emotions, to conform to etiquette patterns rigidly, to avoid spontaneous expression of any kind, and to develop self-control to the point where composure and equanimity were maintained even under the most stressful circumstances. They were taught, furthermore, that they were "worthless" until they attained maturity, maturity being defined in terms of educational and occupational success and independent living, and also in terms of fulfilling the ideal of *samurai* stoicism.

Punishment was often swift and severe for Nisei children who cried, were loud or boisterous, expressed anger or fear, or who were recalcitrant or obstreperous. The primary mechanism of social control was ridicule. There was little escape from this strict home environment. The indulgent grandmother, offering a refuge from the harsh authoritarianism of parents and typical of the extended family in Japan, was absent in the New World, with its two-generation family. There was no escape to a sympathetic peer group: at adolescence the peer group shared authority over the individual with parents and reinforced Issei values and norms. As a result, Nisei social character embodied the idealized traits of self-control, affective neutrality, stoicism, and educational and occupational achievement.

The authoritarian and patriarchal family pattern was probably most prevalent among those residing in large Japanese communities. The Nisei resisted the efforts of the Issei to discipline them. Because the Nisei wanted to dress and act like other American youth, intergenerational conflict was inevitable. The conflict was mitigated for some Nisei, perhaps, by the practice of sending children to Japan to be educated. In 1942 it was estimated that at least 25,000 United States citizens of Japanese ancestry had been educated in schools in Japan. Among these Kibei, as they were designated, were the Japanese considered most probably disloyal in sentiment at the time of Pearl Harbor.

Thus, as in the case of the Chinese, the conflict of the generations had a different sequel from that of the European nationalities. Anxious as the Nisei were to become Americans and forget Japan, they found that, despite their acculturation, the native community looked upon them as "Japs" because of their "racial" visibility. They continued to be discriminated against in three areas—employment, public places, and social contacts.

In employment the educated Nisei had three choices. He could accept prejudice for what it was, and assume the inferior tasks of houseboy, dishwasher, migratory laborer, cannery hand—just what the dominant group expected of him as an inferior. He could

---

[15]Smith, *Americans from Japan,* p. 245.
[16]See Lyman, *The Asian in the West,* pp. 81–97.

go to Japan and forsake America. Or, if he tried, he could sometimes get a job at a higher level, though far below his actual qualifications.

Many barbershops, restaurants, and hotels refused service to Orientals. Several large coastal cities had restrictive covenants that kept the Japanese out of attractive neighborhoods. And there was discrimination in the social sphere.

> The fear of rebuffs, the constant horror of being humiliated in public, made the Nisei draw together in a tight circle, even at college. . . . [Such] organizations only perpetuated their difficulties. They formed noticeable groups on campus. "There's a barrier between Nisei and the other students," said one. "You can feel it. They never feel easy with each other."
>
> Hostility in the social sphere did not as a rule become noticeable until adolescence. The fear of "miscegenation," the old superstitions about racial "hybrids," the fear that friendship might be construed as having a sexual intent introduced at the courting age, a stiffening of attitudes, yet the Nisei were quite as set against intermarriage as the Caucasians, their own fears and superstitions as deeply rooted.[17]

EVACUATION AND RELOCATION: A CASE HISTORY IN WHITE AMERICAN DOMINANT BEHAVIOR

The stabilized accommodation of the Issei-Nisei generations was rudely shattered by Pearl Harbor. On February 19, 1942, the Army was given authority to establish military zones from which any persons, citizens or aliens, might be evacuated and excluded. All Japanese people were ordered to leave the West Coast. This action was the most unprecedented single national action against a large group of people in American history. Analysis of its causes provides insight into the dynamics of dominant-minority relations in the United States. (We shall return to this after carrying forward an account of what happened to the Japanese after February 19.)

At first the Japanese were given time to remove themselves. A few did leave, but soon discovered that they were not wanted elsewhere. A report from the *Los Angeles Times,* March 24, 1942, reads, "Japanese evacuees moving inland from California in a great mass migration will be put in concentration camps if they enter Nevada, Governor E. P. Carville warned tonight." Therefore the Japanese were ordered to stay where they were pending their mass evacuation under military supervision. A new federal agency, The War Relocation Authority, was established to plan for the supervision of the Japanese under detention. Between February and August 8, all West Coast Japanese (over 110,000) were transferred to ten hastily built centers in the Rocky Mountain states and in Arkansas.

In addition to the shocklike psychological effect and the bitterness that evacuation engendered, the Japanese faced enormous economic losses. While the government took steps to protect the material property owned by the Japanese, the guarantees appeared so uncertain that many sold their effects—under the circumstances, of course, at a loss.

---

[17]Bradford Smith, *Americans from Japan,* p. 250. Copyright © 1948 by Bradford Smith. Reprinted by permission of J. B. Lippincott Company.

A business enterprise and a crop in the field could not be "frozen." They had to be disposed of for whatever they would bring at hurried sale or lease, or be abandoned. Real estate brokers, furniture dealers, and other businessmen made considerable profits from these hurried sales. Japanese home-owners and owners of businesses were enraged; little hostility, however, was displayed overtly.

Life in the Settlement Centers

The most severe damage to Japanese Americans was not physical but psychological and social. The policy of "mess-hall dining," with its separation of parents from their children, fostered family disintegration. The humiliation, shame, fear, and resentment resulted in such behavioral manifestations as withdrawal, listlessness, and problem drinking. The "cultural contradictions" involved may have been more difficult to cope with than the injustice and brutality of being forcefully uprooted and relocated in concentration camps:

> There was the very American school yearbook, with a barbed wire design on the cover. There were dancing classes and criminally inadequate medical facilities. There were, eventually, lush gardens and orchards, where men like Jeanne's father squatted in alcoholic despair.[18]

The War Relocation Authority faced a unique problem in American history. The policy of the WRA was to organize the community life with maximum self-control by the Japanese. All the evidence indicates that the personnel were highly sympathetic to the Japanese, an attitude criticized by the same elements of the white population that had clamored for evacuation. As was almost inevitable under such circumstances, a number of rebellious activities followed. Of these the most serious was a strike by some evacuees at Poston Center, Arizona, arising out of a feeling that two alleged attackers of a white official had been unfairly punished. In consequence of incidents of this nature, Tule Lake Center, California, became a segregation camp where active malcontents from all other centers were placed and controlled under strict discipline.

The recent pilgrimages of Japanese Americans to the relocation centers are disconcerting to some white Americans. Perhaps such pilgrimages are an index of the degree of hurt and harm done a people whose only "real crime" was the color of their skin.[19]

Resettlement

The WRA was assigned also the task of finding employment and residence for the inmates outside of the relocation centers. In addition, the agency assumed responsibility for helping the resettler adjust to his new community and new job. Finding a place for the resettler to live became one of the most difficult tasks of the Authority. Its activities beginning in the spring of 1943 included the resettlement of a few Japanese particularly in the Midwest and the Mountain States. Lack of extensive resettlement in

---

[18]Dorothy Bryant, review of *Farewell to Manzanar,* in *The Nation,* 219, Nov. 9, 1974, p. 469. See Jeanne Wakatsuki Houston and James D. Houston, *Farewell to Manzanar* (Boston: Houghton Mifflin Co., 1973).
[19]See "Tule Lake 30 Years Later," *Time,* 103, June 10, 1974, p. 31.

the East was due to Army opposition. Most of those leaving the camps were young adult Nisei who, when they became successfully resettled, often sent for relatives to join them. In the large metropolitan centers it was fairly easy to place Japanese in a wide range of menial and semitechnical jobs. It was difficult to place them in industries with war contracts or in positions calling for contact with the public. Frequent opposition from unions arose. Among the reasons often given for not hiring the Japanese were distrust of their loyalty, the fact that other employers would resent it, that customers would resent it, and that "my son is in the Pacific." Many of the resettlers left their jobs because of their interest in finding work where they could acquire new skills.[20]

Up to January 1, 1945, the date after which evacuees were permitted to return to the West Coast, the WRA had resettled 31,625 Japanese in other parts of the country. Interestingly enough, when the opportunity came, the vast majority of the evacuees returned to their former communities. The evacuees were under pressure to decide where to move, because the date for terminating the WRA had been set, and the agency no longer would be able to give individual assistance. In spite of this, whether because of fear, shame, resentment, or demoralization, fully 43,000 (more than one-third) Japanese remained in the camps until September, 1945, when the war was officially ended.[21]

Analysis

As we have noted, the evacuation of all persons of Japanese ancestry from the West Coast and their subsequent internment was a government action without precedent in American history, involving constitutional issues of grave significance. The Supreme Court of the United States upheld the constitutionality of evacuation in wartime,[22] although strong dissents were written by a minority of the justices. However, in retrospect, the whole incident appears to have been a serious error in judgment. For this reason some analysis of the circumstances that led to the steps taken is highly pertinent to the study of dominant-minority relations. The central question is this: To what extent was the decision for evacuation and internment of the Japanese arrived at as a logical necessity for national security, and to what extent was the decision made in response to regional pressures unrelated to security?

The Military's Judgment. The Western Defense Command of the U.S. Army prepared a report that provided the basis for that section of Executive Order No. 9066 which required the evacuation of the Japanese from the West Coast.[23] The report mentioned a few acts of espionage and illegal shore to sea signaling, but presented no evidence that Japanese Americans or Japanese aliens were involved. The report mentioned one spot raid by the FBI on Japanese homes in which 60,000 rounds of ammunition and a substantial number of rifles, shotguns, and maps were found. Such articles had been declared contraband for enemy aliens.

---

[20]The authors are indebted to Gordon Berryman, a former employee of the WRA, for sharing these insights into the resettlement process.
[21]Yamamoto and Iga, "Japanese Enterprise and American Middle-Class Values," p. 578.
[22]*Koramatsu* v. *United States,* 323, U.S. 214. The decision came after the internment was over.
[23]"Need for Military Control and for Evacuation," *Final Report, Japanese Evacuation from the West Coast* (Washington D.C.: Government Printing Office, 1943), pp. 7–19.

Perhaps realizing that such information was insufficient evidence for an evacuation decision, the Army made use of sociological research, selecting those findings that supported their position and omitting those findings that would indicate loyalty of the Japanese to the United States. Included were statistics on the number of American-born Japanese who had been educated in Japan and subsequently returned to live in the U.S. Also included were facts about the activities of Japanese associations, which naturally reflected an interest in the ancestral homeland, and in some instances involved contributions on behalf of Japan's war with China.

Perhaps the most shrewd use of sociological materials was the reference to "ties of race," reflected in the residential patterns (which also seemed too close to strategic locations) and in-group solidarity of Japanese communities. The implication was that the "ties of race" were so strong that loyalty to Japan would exceed loyalty to the United States. Alternative explanations for such residential patterns and group cohesion (such as geographic accessibility, job opportunities, discrimination, pride in ancestral homeland, and the like) were not given.

While conceding that many Japanese Americans were loyal to the United States, no sociological evidence to support this position was presented. Although many social scientists had studied Japanese Americans intensively for many years, the military did not capitalize on their knowledge and advice.[24] The military had already decided: The task of separating the loyal from the disloyal was too great. The only "safe" course was to evacuate everyone of Japanese ancestry from the West Coast.

The Justice Department disagreed with the military. As late as January 12, 1942, Attorney General Biddle stated that a policy of wholesale internment would not only demoralize guiltless aliens, it would also deprive the nation of a valuable source of labor supply at a time when it was badly needed.[25]

The case submitted in the Army report was unimpressive as justification for such drastic action as mass evacuation. To explain why this action occurred we must examine other factors in the situation.

Pressure Groups.   Grodzins stresses the influence of pressure groups: "The most active proponents of mass evacuation were certain agricultural and business groups, chambers of commerce, the American Legion, the California Joint Immigration Committee, and the Native Sons and Daughters of the Golden West."[26] The list of pressure groups can be divided into those with economic motivation for getting rid of the Japanese and those with a nativist, antiforeign orientation. The following excerpt from a resolution adopted by an Oregon American Legion Post illustrates the sort of pressure that was exerted:

> [that] this is no time for namby-pamby pussyfooting. . . . that it is not the
> time for consideration of minute constitutional rights of those enemies but
> that it is time for vigorous, whole-hearted, and concerted action . . . toward

[24]Grodzins writes, "as later research has shown military officers did not in a single instance rely on the large mass of scientific materials that had been gathered about American Japanese by such men as Steiner, Park, Strong, Bogardus, and Bailey." See Morton Grodzins, *Americans Betrayed: Politics and the Japanese Evacuation* (Chicago: University of Chicago Press, 1949), p. 305. Reprinted by permission of the publisher.
[25]Alexander H. Leighton, *The Governing of Men* (Princeton: Princeton University Press, 1945), p. 17.
[26]Grodzins, *Americans Betrayed,* p. 17. Reprinted by permission of the publisher.

the removal of all enemy aliens and citizens of enemy alien extraction from all areas along the coast and that only those be permitted to return that are able to secure special permit for that purpose.[27]

Ten Broeck and his associates[28] place greater responsibility on the commanding officer and his superiors, and on the people of the West Coast generally, among whom there was widespread fear caused by the war and Japan's early military successes.

In summary, we suggest that the evacuation resulted from the interaction of a series of factors: (1) the well-established pattern of dominant-minority relations, long nurtured throughout the history of the relations between native Americans and the Japanese on the West Coast; (2) the crisis of war, engendering fear of those racially identified with an enemy nation, a fear capitalized upon the exacerbated by the press, notably the Hearst Press, in its "Yellow Peril" campaign; (3) a situation ripe for special groups antagonistic to the Japanese to exploit; (4) the failure of liberal West Coast native Americans to bring sufficient counterpressure; (5) the position of authority of a commanding officer with unsophisticated sociological judgment; and (6) the fact that higher federal officials had to make a decision while beset with the enormous burdens of conducting a war.

The Hawaiian Contrast.   It is instructive to conclude the discussion of the evacuation episode with a brief account of a contrasting situation in Hawaii.

At the outbreak of war with Japan, persons of Japanese ancestry comprised about a third of Hawaii's population. Following Pearl Harbor, rumors arose of espionage activities on the part of some island Japanese. Both the military and the insular authorities, failing to find specific evidence, placed their official weight on the side of allaying the rumors and indicating their confidence in the loyalty of the Hawaiian Japanese as a group. Limited restrictions were imposed on the alien Japanese, and a few Japanese whose records before the war rendered them suspicious were interned. But some elements of the insular population who, fearful of the possible dangers from the Japanese, called for firmer action. As Lind indicates, there was an increase in public demonstrations against Japanese persons, apparently more from the Filipinos in Hawaii than from the white or other ethnic elements.[29] Nevertheless, the authorities held firm to their policy of vigilance over the Japanese and arrest of only those who acted in a suspicious manner. Fear of the Japanese subsided, and their relations to the rest of the archipelago's population resumed, in the main, their prewar character. The soundness of the official judgment that the Japanese in general constituted no serious security threat to Hawaii was borne out by future events. Subsequent hearings on the charges of subversive activity by local Japanese brought forth emphatic denials from the War Department, the Federal Bureau of Investigation, and from various insular authorities.[30]

On the whole, it can be said that the Japanese were cooperative in accepting the mild restrictions, continued their economic role in Hawaiian production, and ultimately made contributions to the armed services. "The final count of Hawaiian war casualties revealed that 80 percent of those killed and 88 percent of those wounded throughout

---

[27]*Ibid.*, p. 42. By permission.
[28]Jacobus Ten Broeck, Edward N. Barnhart, and Floyd W. Matson, *Prejudice, War, and the Constitution* (Berkeley: University of California Press, 1954).
[29]Andrew Lind, *Hawaii's Japanese* (Princeton: Princeton University Press, 1948), pp. 56–61.
[30]*Ibid.*, pp. 38–47.

the war were of Japanese ancestry."[31] The military record of Hawaiian Japanese was impressive. The 442nd Regimental Combat Team, composed of Japanese Americans from Hawaii, was the most highly decorated military unit in American history.[32]

How can we account for the strikingly different policies adopted in Hawaii and on the West Coast? Contrary to what one might at first think, the much greater proportion of Japanese in the islands operated against a policy of internment. To have interned one-third of the population would have been a costly process. Furthermore, the removal of the Japanese from the labor force would have drastically reduced the productive capacity of Hawaii just when a maximum increase in production was essential to the war effort.

Underlying the more favorable treatment of the Japanese were certain facets of the general pattern of intergroup relations in Hawaii, which are discussed in more detail in Chapter 16. Here we briefly call attention to two factors that stand in sharp contrast to the West Coast situation. First, a less discriminatory pattern of intergroup relations prevailed in Hawaii. Tradition frowned on any public or explicit color discrimination. Second, the relatively subordinate economic position of the Japanese may have worked in their favor. While by 1940 the Japanese as a group had moved far from their earlier role as plantation workers toward various city occupations, this transition had not yet brought them into much direct competition for jobs with the dominant white population.

The Effects of Evacuation

The short-range effects of the evacuation and temporary resettlement on the national welfare were costly indeed. Particular segments of the West Coast population, as we have seen, made substantial gains out of removal of the Japanese. For these gains, the nation paid a heavy price. The removal of the Japanese retarded the war effort. While eventually many Japanese did find useful work during the war, they would have contributed more if they had remained where they were. In fact, there were so many high-paying opportunities in California created by the manpower shortage that many Mexicans and Negroes migrated there. The whole process of evacuation, the operation of the centers, and the effort of the WRA to relocate the evacuees cost time, money, and energy that could have been used to more constructive purpose.

Furthermore, the Executive Order and the subsequent action of the Supreme Court had a damaging effect on the legal structure of the country. Professor Eugene V. Rostow, of Yale Law School, has noted that when the High Court upheld the constitutionality of the order, it "converted a piece of wartime folly into political doctrine and a permanent part of the law."[33] Soon after the order was issued, then Secretary of War Henry L. Stimson expressed privately that "a tremendous hole in our constitutional system" would be made. Publicly, however, he went along with it, yielding to Army panic and the largely press-induced public hysteria. Earl Warren, then Attorney General of California (from 1953 to 1969 Chief Justice of the U.S. Supreme Court), later called his support of this action the greatest mistake of his public career. Finally, in 1976, President Gerald Ford rescinded Executive Order No. 9066, and resolved that

---

[31]*Ibid.*, p. 126.
[32]Yamamoto and Iga, "Japanese Enterprise and American Middle-Class Values," p. 578.
[33]Editorial in *The Nation*, 222, March 6, 1976, pp. 259–260.

this kind of governmental error shall never be made again. Professor Rostow commented that the dangerous precedent was not erased by Ford's cancellation order and "comes nowhere near to atoning for the crime."[34]

The effect of the evacuation on the prestige of the United States in world opinion is difficult to appraise. Because of their imperialist activities in Asia, the Japanese abroad were much hated by many other Asian peoples. Nevertheless, the fact that no comparable treatment was given the German-Americans and Italian-Americans was evidence of strong color-based prejudice, and cannot have raised our moral standing with nonwhite people at home and throughout the world.

U.S. Senator S. I. Hayakawa (Republican, California) feels that the relocation program had long-term beneficial effects. By removing Japanese Americans from their close-knit ethnic neighborhoods, he believes, the policy facilitated, after the war, their integration into American life.[35]

Later in this chapter the thesis is presented that the Sansei may be in a position of "delayed assimilation." The evacuation program may have had a concomitant and contradictory effect to the one discussed by Hayakawa: strengthening the "hold" of the Nisei over the Sansei, and delaying their full assimilation into American life.

THE DECLINE OF DOMINANCE

Following the end of the evacuation order on January 1, 1945, the Japanese were free to go where they wanted. As we have seen, many returned to the West Coast. By 1970, the number of Japanese in the states of California (213,277), Washington (20, 188), and Oregon (6,213) accounted for 65 percent of the mainland Japanese population. Since in 1940 as many as 88 percent were concentrated on the West Coast, the difference reflects the dispersive effect of evacuation. There was a tendency to move toward the Northeast, Midwest, and Mountain states, as opposed to the South and the Plains region.[36] Nevertheless, the majority remained on the West Coast, the largest settlement being in the Los Angeles-Long Beach area (with approximately one-third of the mainland Japanese population).

Economic Readjustment

Bloom and Riemer estimated the economic loss of the Japanese at $367,500,000, if income losses were added to all other losses: forced sale of their assets, loss of business goodwill, and other losses attendant on their rapid removal.[37] A sample survey of 206 Japanese American families found the median loss per family to be $9,870 at the 1941 value of the dollar.[38]

---

[34]*Ibid.*
[35]Thomas M. Brown and Martin Smith, "For the Senate . . . And the Main Event West," *New York Times Magazine*, Oct. 31, 1976, p. 24.
[36]In 1970, there were sizable numbers of Japanese in the following states: New York (19,794), Illinois (17,645), Colorado (7,861), New Jersey (6,344), and Texas (6,216). These U.S. Census figures are given in Harry H. L. Kitano, *Japanese Americans: The Evolution of a Subculture*, 2nd ed. (Englewood Cliffs, N.J.: Prentice-Hall, 1976), pp. 210–211.
[37]Leonard Bloom and Ruth Riemer, *Removal and Return* (Berkeley: University of California Press, 1949), pp. 202–204.
[38]*Ibid.*, p. 144.

Some small part of this loss was compensated under an Act of Congress in July, 1948 (Public Law, 886, H. R. 2999), which empowered the Attorney General to reimburse any person not to exceed $2,500 for "damage to or loss of real or personal property . . . that is a reasonable and natural consequence of the evacuation." Claims had to be filed within eighteen months, and any claims for loss of anticipated profits or earnings were excluded. Evacuees filed 24,064 claims. By March 1, 1956, all but 1,936 had been adjusted and paid. Delayed settlements involved claims in excess of the original $2,500 limit. In 1956, Congress amended the act to permit settlement up to $100,000. Settling these claims involved the difficulty of proving the losses and few Japanese had obtained documentary proof of sale in anticipation of such indemnity. The last claim was settled in November, 1965; two of the original plaintiffs had died.[39]

The evacuation undermined the occupational position of the Japanese and forced readjustment upon return at lower socioeconomic levels. Few farmers could reestablish themselves, and produce dealers were far fewer than before the war. Many went into contract gardening, which provided a measure of the independence they formerly enjoyed. The great shortage of housing available for the Japanese increased the number of boarding and rooming houses where the Japanese who did have homes added to their income by charging high prices to fellow Japanese. The housing shortage also increased the number of returnees who went into domestic service, which often provided housing. In general, the pattern of employment for the returnees involved a shift from being either independently employed or working for other Japanese to working for non-Japanese employers.

Reaction of Dominant Americans

On the West Coast, knowledge that the Japanese were coming back evoked reaction from racist-minded groups that had been instrumental in causing their evacuation. The American Legion, Veterans of the Foreign Wars, Native Sons of the Golden West, the California Farm Bureau all protested. New "Ban the Jap" committees sprang up. A number of newspapers ran scare headlines that made many Californians uneasy. "Hood River had jumped the gun by erasing the names of its sixteen Nisei soldiers from the honor roll" [subsequently restored].[40] In the first half of 1945 more than thirty serious incidents occurred throughout California.

This time, however, there was a second set of reactions, which had been missing before. Many individuals and groups demanded that the Japanese be given fair play and became active in insisting that they get it. The Fresno Fair Play Committee organized to file eviction suits on behalf of those Japanese unable to move back into their former homes. When machinists of the San Francisco Municipal Railway threatened to strike in protest against the employment of a Nisei, Mayor Roger Lapham averted the strike by going to the shop in person and explaining to the men why the Nisei was entitled to the job. Churches up and down the Coast were focal points of support for the Nisei. This second reaction finally won out.

[39]William Petersen, "Success Story: Japanese-American Style," *New York Times Magazine,* Jan. 9, 1966, p. 33.
[40]Smith, *Americans from Japan,* p. 346. By permission.

The pressure of public opinion all over the country put California on the defensive. It came to a point where the civic pride of the several communities was challenged and race baiting lost favor. At the beginning of 1945 the West Coast papers had been four to one against the Japanese. A year later they were four to one in favor of fair and equal treatment.[41]

The Challenge to Dominance

The American Japanese have as a group made little active challenge to the minority status accorded them. As we have seen, as individuals the majority have been diligent and alert to take the opportunities not denied them to improve their welfare and to rise in class status. While evacuation came as a shock, as a whole, they put up with it with unusual grace.[42] Mainland Japanese Americans have not been as active in politics as some other minorities and thus have not made maximum use of political pressure to improve their status, although a few Japanese have been elected to state offices in California from areas of heavy ethnic concentration.[43] The election of S. I. Hayakawa to the U.S. Senate in 1976 may not be taken as an indicator of political activism on the part of Japanese Americans in general. However, his election is an indication that the war-associated negative feelings toward the Japanese are over, and the general prejudice toward Oriental-Americans on the mainland has lessened substantially.

Various court decisions invalidating laws and practices that had discriminated against both the Japanese and the Chinese were handed down from 1948 to 1950. These included a California law that had prohibited fishing licenses to persons ineligible for citizenship and a California Supreme Court decision revoking the law against interracial marriage.[44]

The one important organization that acted in part to defend the interests of the Japanese against discrimination was the Japanese American Citizens League formed by the Nisei (succeeding the Issei Japanese Association). As time solved many of their ethnic group's problems JACL broadened its interests to include general community affairs, much like the Anti-Defamation League of Jewish Americans. This change facilitated the acculturative process.

Japanese American Citizens League.   The JACL was organized in 1930 to facilitate Nisei occupational success, and to promote their integration and assimilation into American life.[45] Before World War II the organization lobbied on behalf of citizenship rights for Nisei (and Caucasians as well) who had lost them due to marriage to Japanese aliens. The League also fought for citizenship rights for Issei, often with success.[46] During the war, the League represented the interned Japanese before various govern-

---

[41]*Ibid.*, p. 349. By permission.
[42]See Dorothy S. Thomas and Richard S. Nishimoto, *The Spoilage: Japanese American Evacuation and Resettlement* (Berkeley: University of California Press, 1946).
[43]Kitano, *Japanese Americans*, p. 191. The first Japanese American, Norman Y. Mineta, to be elected mayor of a major mainland city, San Jose, California, took office in 1970. His election apparently had no connection with his race, as only 3 percent of San Jose's population was Japanese. *The New York Times*, Oct. 19, 1971.
[44]Later a decision of the United States Supreme Court declared any state laws against racial intermarriage illegal.
[45]Bill Hosokawa, *Nisei: The Quiet Americans* (New York: William Morrow & Co., 1969), p. 197.
[46]*Ibid.*, p. 199.

mental agencies in Washington, and kept the dispersed Japanese in touch with one another. During these trying times, the JACL and its national secretary, Mike M. Masoaka, performed an important function in maintaining the morale of the Japanese.[47] After the war, the League fought to regain land-owning rights for Japanese Californians,[48] to obtain compensation for financial losses sustained because of the evacuation program,[49] on behalf of more liberal immigration and naturalization laws regarding Asians,[50] and to repeal Title II of the 1950 Internal Security Act, which permitted the kind of detention the Japanese had experienced during the war.[51] More recently, the JACL passed a resolution in 1974 in support of Iva Toguri D'Aguino ("Tokyo Rose").[52] The California state legislature unanimously asked for a Presidential pardon in 1976, and in January, 1977, she received a pardon from President Gerald Ford.[53]

Soon after World War II, the JACL recognized that it could not defend the civil rights of Japanese without working for a political climate in the United States favorable to just treatment of all minority groups.[54] The League, accordingly, has joined other civil rights organizations in fighting racially restrictive housing covenants and in supporting the desegregation of schools and other public facilities.[55]

[47]*Ibid.*, pp. 381–382.

[48]*Ibid.*, p. 450. The League successfully fought to have the discriminatory alien land law of California declared unconstitutional. The law denied land-owning rights to aliens and prohibited them from buying land in the names of their children, who were citizens. The JACL also worked to defeat Proposition 15, a further effort to deprive California's Japanese of land-owning rights. This proposed state constitutional amendment was defeated by a wide margin.

[49]*Ibid.*, p. 447. The Japanese American Evacuation Claims Act of 1948 resulted in the eventual recovery of only 5 to 10 percent of the losses. The real significance of the act, however, was that it implied an admission by Congress that the evacuation program had been a mistake.

[50]*Ibid.*, pp. 451–455. The 1952 Walter-McCarran Immigration and Naturalization Act overrode the Oriental Exclusion Act of 1924 and permitted Asians to immigrate to the United States. It also eliminated race as a barrier to naturalization, giving Japanese aliens the right to become citizens. The JACL also lobbied on behalf of the 1965 Immigration Law, which eliminated discrimination on the basis of nationality and color, and emphasized occupational skills and being a relative of people living in the United States as the important criteria for permission to immigrate.

[51]*Ibid.*, p. 453. Title II permitted the detention of persons on reasonable suspicion of espionage or sabotage during times of war or insurrection. It provided additional legal justification for the kind of evacuation and internment program the Japanese experienced during the war. Title II was repealed in 1971. See *The New York Times*, "Aid to Tokyo Rose and Miss Yoshimura Reflects Japanese-Americans' New Confidence," Feb. 7, 1977, p. 15.

[52]*The New York Times*, "Aid to Tokyo Rose. . . ."

[53]David Bird, "Ford Pardons 'Tokyo Rose' in One of Last Official Acts as President," *The New York Times*, Jan. 20, 1977, p. 8. Mrs. D'Aguino was a Japanese American who was trapped in Japan by World War II and who was required by the Japanese Government to participate in radio broadcasts designed to lower the morale of American servicemen. Convicted in 1949, Mrs. D'Aguino was sentenced to ten years in prison and was fined $10,000. She served six and a half years before being paroled, and finished paying her fine in 1975.

[54]Japanese evacuees in Arkansas during the internment years were astonished to find that they were regarded as white by whites and as colored by blacks. While on the one hand, the whites insisted that they sit in the front of buses, drink from the whites' fountains, and use white rest rooms, on the other hand the blacks told them, "Us colored folks has got to stick together." Such wartime experiences provided greater insight for the Japanese into American racism and may have helped to set the stage for this change of emphasis of the JACL. See Hosokawa, *Nisei: The Quiet Americans*, p. 473.

[55]*Ibid.*, p. 450.

As late as 1967 the 30,000-member JACL still felt very much on the defensive, and with good reason. A poll taken in that year found that almost half (48 percent) of Californians still approved of the evacuation program.[56] Japanese Americans, quite understandably, fear that they might serve once again as a scapegoat should a crisis of any kind develop between Japan and the U.S. One Nisei stated, ". . . the destiny of the Nisei . . . is tied in perpetuity to the land of his ancestors because of white America's racism."[57]

THE RISE OF THE JAPANESE

Accompanying the rapid change in attitude of dominants toward the Japanese, from hostility to friendly acceptance, was an equally rapid rise in the status of Japanese Americans. The abrupt break in the previous accommodation pattern, due to the war-time internment, may indeed have accelerated the process. Leadership was transferred to the Nisei, who during the internment years often earned more money than the Issei working in the vicinity of the camps. The relocation of Japanese outside of the West hastened their acculturation to American life. For example, a postwar government survey reported that the Nisei were no longer amenable to the traditional practice of "arranged marriages." Community-managed schools were not reopened. And the number of Japanese language newspapers was fewer than before the war.

In the evacuation centers a wide range of occupations was open to the Nisei, who were able to fill every job a community requires (except administrative).[58] Although camp jobs were low-paying, the experience and training helped many to obtain higher status jobs (such as teaching) after the war than would have been the case had internment not occurred. More importantly, educational and occupational aspirations and expectations were raised. Despite all of the damaging aspects of the internment program, these were some of its positive, though unplanned, effects. The combination of early socialization and the experience during internment contributed to the development of a highly motivated, upwardly mobile generational category.

A Record of Success

In the postwar period Japanese Americans have achieved success in almost every sense of the word. The high mean family income (Kitano, p. 90),[59] low percentages of members who are poverty cases or receiving public assistance (Kitano, p. 214), low rates of unemployment,[60] high percentage of high school graduates (Kitano, p. 110),[61] low morbidity rates (including very low rates of mental illness ([Kitano, p. 150]) and

---

[56]A poll taken in 1942 found that 80 percent of Californians approved of this program. See Hosokawa, p. 497.

[57]*Ibid.*

[58]Harry H. L. Kitano, *Japanese Americans: The Evolution of a Subculture,* 2nd ed., © 1976, p. 91. We shall use this reference extensively in the section on the rise of the Japanese. Accordingly, we shall immediately cite the author and the pages in parentheses rather than footnote. Quotes from this book are reprinted by permission of Prentice-Hall, Inc., Englewood Cliffs, New Jersey.

[59]U.S. Bureau of the Census, *Statistical Abstract of the United States: 1976,* p. 412.

[60]William Petersen, *Japanese Americans: Oppression and Success* (New York: Random House, 1971), p. 132.

[61]c.f. U.S. Bureau of the Census, *Statistical Abstract of the United States: 1976,* p. 123.

long life expectancy,[62] and low rates of crime and juvenile delinquency (Kitano, pp. 144–148) all point to the Japanese as being, like the Jews, "model American citizens."

Although the full range of occupations is still not fully available to the Japanese, the major occupations are definitely middle or upper class, and include the professions (medicine, law, teaching, engineering), farming (in the roles of owner or manager), family gardening, and federal civil service. However, jobs connected with "real estate, insurance, specialty shops, banks, savings and loan associations, law, and medicine" are still primarily dependent upon the ethnic community (Kitano, p. 104).

Model Minority or Middleman Minority?

Based on the success record of the Japanese the label "model American minority" has been applied to them. This judgment, however, is made from the point of view of dominants. "Japanese Americans are good because they conform—they don't 'make waves'—they work hard and are quiet and docile." (Kitano, p. 204) Kitano contends that the Japanese should share in an evaluation of the efficacy of their adjustment. It may be a disservice to the Japanese to impose a definition of hard work, conformity, and goodness upon them and to reward them for fulfilling the stereotype. During World War II, it was conformity and goodness that led them to accept docilely the evacuation program. After World War II the stereotype was an important factor in the success of the Nisei, who "drove themselves" so hard that health problems eventually occurred.[63] In contemporary times, introjection of the stereotype by the Sansei and Yonsei may preclude "self-discovery"—a major goal in American society. There is evidence that the Nisei are projecting their own intense desire to succeed onto the Sansei, and putting great pressure on them to succeed in school.[64] Perhaps the growing drug problem among Japanese youth is, in part, a reaction to the excessive pressure to succeed.

Indeed, based on the record of educational and occupational success and of relatively low rates of social problems, Japanese Americans, like Jewish Americans, have been a "model American minority." The personal and social costs, however, have been high.

A second term applied to Japanese Americans is that of "the middleman minority."[65] This is a minority that, because of some competitive advantage (perhaps in an occupation, such as business or agriculture), rises above other minority groups, which remain on the lower stratum of a society. Discrimination, however, imposes a ceiling to their mobility, so that they remain "caught in the middle," often playing a buffer role between competing power groups. Such a minority "must placate the power elite for protection and approval, but they must also contend with the wrath and frustration of those lower in the system," and they serve as a convenient scapegoat in times of crisis (Kitano, p. 199).

Japanese Americans are in this position, Kitano continues, between blacks and whites, and between Japan and the United States. However, he notes that the mid-

[62]Petersen, *Japanese Americans*, pp. 145–148. Also see H. H. Hechter and N. O. Borhani, "Longevity in Racial Groups Differs," *California's Health*, 22, Feb. 1, 1965, pp. 121–122.
[63]Amy Iwasaki Mass, "Asians as Individuals: The Japanese Community," p. 163.
[64]*Ibid.*, pp. 160–164.
[65]Harry H. L. Kitano, "Japanese Americans: The Development of a Middleman Minority," in *Pacific Historical Review*, 43, Nov. 1974, pp. 500–519. See also Edna Bonacich, "A Theory of Middleman Minorities," in Norman R. Yetman and C. Hoy Steele, eds., *Majority and Minority: The Dynamics of Racial and Ethnic Relations*, 2nd ed. (Boston: Allyn & Bacon, 1975), pp. 77–89.

dleman status of the Japanese may be a temporary one, and that their adaptation to the United States is similar to that of many European groups (p. 199). One obstacle to the assimilation and integration of the Japanese may be voluntary segregation and retention of traditional values (Kitano, p. 200). There is evidence of a revival of ethnic and pan-Asian identity and of a desire to maintain structural pluralism, by means of continued residence in Japanese communities, joining Japanese associations and churches, and marrying endogamously.

Decline in Discrimination

It is unquestionably clear that discrimination against Japanese Americans has markedly declined ever since World War II. Petersen finds it difficult to find data on discrimination other than that based on personal anecdotes.[66]

In the areas of housing, education, and politics, discrimination has posed little or no problem for the Japanese in the 1970s. In the occupational area, opportunities for positions commensurate with training and experience "appear to be better away from California" (Kitano, p. 191). The quota system appears to be in operation. Kitano notes, "it would be unusual to see more than one person of Japanese ancestry in an executive position in the same American business, even on the East Coast" (p. 191). He adds that ". . . positions below the executive level remain plentiful for the Japanese American." The conclusion seems to be that there may be slight occupational discrimination.

Concerning intermarriage, the barriers are not based on discrimination, but to marital pressures of the Japanese themselves. Historically, in-group pressures for endogamy have been strong. Recently, however, along with the decline in the barriers against intermarriage erected by the dominant society, such as the declaring of laws against miscegenation unconstitutional, there has been a concomitant increase in tolerance for outmarriage among the Japanese (Kitano, p. 107).

THE JAPANESE AMERICAN FAMILY AND COMMUNITY IN RECENT TIMES

The Family Institution.   Despite the disruptive and dispersive influence of evacuation and relocation on the Japanese family and community, in the postwar period both families and communities remained quite cohesive. One major change since World War II was that the patriarchal family of the Issei was replaced by a more equalitarian one among the Nisei, with greater emphasis on the American middle-class norms of companionship, equality, sharing, and affection between the Nisei parents and their Sansei children. However, the traditional respect and affection for, and loyalty to, aging parents remained strong. One study found over 50 percent of the Issei seeing their children and grandchildren daily, and 46 percent actually living with their children.[67] Such findings should not obscure the fact that there are many poor, single Issei living isolated lives in substandard rooming houses. These men find themselves old and alone in a country where the elderly are not respected. Rates of alcoholism and mental illness

---

[66]William Petersen, *Japanese Americans*, pp. 116–117.
[67]John W. Connor, "Acculturation and Family Continuities in Three Generations of Japanese Americans," in *Journal of Marriage and the Family*, 36, Feb., 1974, p. 161.

are higher than the public realizes among this segment of the Japanese population. Furthermore, there is a tendency to avoid seeking help from agencies because of a sense of shame for bringing such "dishonor" to the Japanese community, and for not being able to endure hardships without complaining.[68]

A second major change in Japanese family structure since the war is the development of the three-generation family. The third generation, the Sansei, are less vulnerable to parental influence and control partly because they have emotional support from grandparents, something lacking in the upbringing of the Nisei. Despite the development of the three-generation family, the average size of the Japanese family in 1970 was 2.67, having declined from 4.0 in 1960 (Kitano, p. 107). In the early and middle 1970s the surviving Issei were retired and facing the problems of old age (Kitano, p. 105). The typical Nisei were well into middle-age, and the Sansei were beginning to raise the fourth generation, the Yonsei. (The Sansei are discussed later in a separate section.) The prewar practice of sending children to Japan for upbringing (the Kibei) has now disappeared, however substitute patterns of tourism, longer visits, and some schooling in Japan have emerged (Kitano, p. 109).

Japanese-Caucasian intermarriage rates received an enormous boost in the decade after the end of World War II through the marriages of American servicemen to the Japanese "war brides" (Japanese women who married American servicemen during the Allied occupation of Japan from 1945–1951). It is estimated that in 1960 there were 25,000 such brides in the United States (Kitano, p. 161). Many of these marriages ended in divorce.[69]

Rates of outmarriage (Japanese Americans marrying outside of their ethnic group) have been increasing. For example, in Los Angeles County the percentage of outmarriage was 12 percent in 1948. By 1972 it had reached 49 percent. In Fresno, California, the rates were below 20 percent through 1963, while in 1969 they had reached 58 percent, the same figure as for San Francisco in 1971 (Kitano, pp. 106–107). The majority of outmarriages were to Caucasians, with Chinese next.

Japanese American Communities.   "Japanese towns" ("J-towns") are still visible in West Coast cities, "but now they serve primarily as places of business, and the proprietors retreat to the suburbs after hours" (Kitano, p. 112). Outside of the J-town main business area, Japanese tend to reside together in small clusters of homes. The great majority (88 percent) of Japanese-American families lived in cities in 1970 (Kitano, pp. 96–97).

Structural pluralism characterizes organizational life, and the organizations are modeled after American ones, often with American-like names, programs, and values (Kitano, p. 113). Japanese have their own men's social and service clubs, Y's, Boy and Girl Scouts, and Junior Chambers of Commerce. Structural pluralism is present also on college campuses; all-Asian sororities (mainly Japanese), for example, are quite popular (Kitano, p. 114). Such organizations have largely replaced the Japanese language schools and cultural and recreational associations of the prewar communities (Kitano, p. 110). In one sense, perhaps, the Japanese outdo dominants on "being American."

---

[68]Amy Iwasaki Mass, "Asians as Individuals," pp. 160–161.
[69]*Ibid.*, pp. 160–161. Many of these women were unable or too ashamed to return to Japan. They remained in the United States, saddled with the responsibility of raising racially mixed children who were rejected by the Japanese community and who could not fully identify with the dominant society.

They tend to be more equalitarian with less emphasis on social class distinctions (Kitano, p. 195).

The financial solidarity, new buildings, and impressive social programs of Japanese Protestant churches has made them appealing to the non-Japanese neighbors, especially Caucasians. While established along the pattern of structural pluralism, they are becoming increasingly integrated (Kitano, p. 115).

In summary, structural pluralism in combination with assimilation seems to be characteristic of Japanese communities on the West Coast; integration and assimilation seem characteristic of Japanese living elsewhere in the nation. Acculturation, rather than assimilation, seems characteristic of Japanese family life, as the evidence suggests that traditional "familism" is still strong in the 1970s, although not as strong as in previous times. Marriage patterns show a definite and rapid change, away from the pluralistic model and toward integration (intermarriage).

The Sansei: Japanese Americans or American Japanese?

In the early and middle 1970s the Sansei were typically in their teens, 20s, and 30s. It is possible to argue for or against the proposition that they are fully assimilated. First, on the negative side, there is evidence of "delayed acculturation" among the Sansei. Studies show that they score higher than non-Japanese youth on such psychological traits as need for affiliation, need for order, deference, abasement, and submission. These psychological needs are based in Japanese traditions, and the suggestion is that the Nisei socialized their children in "old world" ways. Indeed, Connor notes that even Sansei mothers themselves are socializing their children in a traditional manner, specifically, emphasizing vocal lulling, breast and bottle feeding, and playing with baby to a greater extent than do white middle-class mothers.[70] As a result, Japanese children are more dependent on others, more vulnerable to influence, more "other-directed" than non-Japanese children. The traditional norm of respect for elders is further evidence of the maintenance of socialization patterns practiced by the Issei. When Nisei parents were asked what behavior of the Sansei would be most likely to upset them, the most frequent reply was "lack of respect to parents and elders."[71]

Kitano notes that the Sansei may still be in the "transitional" stage. Sansei college students are still somewhat subdued and conforming; their education is job-oriented; they enter "secure" professions; they have a fierce desire for upward mobility; they prefer to marry other Sansei. Kitano believes that these are signs "of an aspiring rather than a fully acculturated middle-class American" (Kitano, p. 196).

Ambivalence about the culture of the ancestral homeland versus American culture was typical of second-generation European immigrant groups. In the case of Japanese Americans, such role conflict has apparently continued in the lives of the third generation, exacerbated, perhaps, by the popular trend to rediscover one's ethnic roots, to revive and practice ethnic cultural traditions, and to prize one's ethnic identity. Lyman contends that the Sansei want to rediscover and practice traditional Japanese culture but find that their own Americanization has proceeded too far to permit effective

---

[70]Connor, "Acculturation and Family Continuities in Three Generations of Japanese Americans," p. 164.
[71]*Ibid.*, p. 163.

recovery.[72] Some Sansei try to discover their identity by going to Japan. However, they find that they are not fully accepted there and may even face rejection, "since they have 'Asian faces' but do not speak or behave in a manner expected by the Japanese" (Kitano, p. 133). Ironically, they also find life in Japan's large cities to be more "American" than life in the "Japanese towns" in which they grew up.

In summary, there appears to be some evidence of delayed acculturation among the Sansei. Possible factors include prejudice and discrimination based on race, the burden of having a "positive stereotype" (conformity, hard work, quietness) imposed on them by the dominant society, maintenance of traditional Japanese patterns of socialization by the Nisei, and the internment program of the war years, which may have strengthened the "hold" of the Nisei over their children and in-group solidarity as a whole.

On the "pro" side of the proposition that the Sansei are fully acculturated, their test results, achievement and interest preferences, and social values are typically American (Kitano, p. 196). As we have noted, they have participated in "American-like" organizations. Like American youth, they tend to be inactive in churches (Kitano, p. 115). Furthermore, they have had increasing tendencies to join non-Japanese social organizations, to date and marry outside of their ethnic group, and to engage in such "American" practices as "living together" (Kitano, p. 109). They are no less likely to go on to college and graduate school than are dominant children. Like other third-generation Americans, their knowledge of the language and culture of their ancestral homeland is minimal (Kitano, p. 133). The Issei and Nisei see the Sansei as completely acculturated, and the Sansei tend to share this picture of themselves.[73]

It is true that the Sansei are products of a freer and more open world (Kitano, p. 197). They were not as trapped by the racial stereotypes of dominants or by the rigid social controls of their elders as were the Nisei. Accordingly, they have a wide span of expectations, life styles, and behavior. Their expectations are too varied and too individualistic to be met within Japanese communities, and hence they are propelled by their own aspirations into an integrated society (Kitano, p. 197).

Ironically, it may be that further acculturation of the Sansei will involve moving not *up* in society, but *down,* toward more typical norms of dominant society, including their share of deviance and disorganization. Mass finds rates of drug addiction, problem pregnancies and unwed motherhood, and maladjustment in school are rising among Japanese American youth.[74] Petersen also states that the delinquency rate among Japanese youth is probably rising.[75] Possible explanations for the increase in use of drugs and other types of deviance are the excessive pressure put on the Sansei to succeed in school, and the tendency of Japanese parents to foster dependency needs in their children, which may make them more easily "led astray" by their peers.[76]

Higher rates of deviance may be one of the prices that have to be paid not only for assimilation, but also for freedom of the Sansei (and their children, the Yonsei) to be original, experimental, and creative as are other young Americans. Historically, Japanese Americans have been "overconformists," for example, working "as if they

[72]Stanford M. Lyman, "Japanese-American Generation Gap," in *Society,* 10, Jan/Feb 1973, p. 63.
[73]Connor, "Acculturation and Family Continuities in Three Generations of Japanese Americans," p. 163.
[74]Amy Iwasaki Mass, "Asians as Individuals," p. 161.
[75]Petersen, *Japanese Americans,* p. 208.
[76]Lyman, "Japanese-American Generation Gap," p. 63.

were addicted to it" (Kitano, p. 131). The recent increase in deviant behavior suggests that the Japanese are "loosening up" and becoming less ritualistic. Future studies may show a concomitant increase in creativity (perhaps in art, music, or literature) among the Sansei and Yonsei.

The young Japanese of the early and mid-1970s may have used Wendy Yoshimura as a role model. Miss Yoshimura, a Berkeley artist, active in the anti-Vietnam war movement, and ardent feminist, was arrested in 1975 along with Patricia Hearst.[77] Convicted on three counts of illegal possession of weapons, she was sentenced in March, 1977, to between one and fifteen years in prison.[78] Her case is of interest here partly because of her background. She was born in a detention camp during World War II. Her parents renounced their American citizenship after the war and moved to Japan. There Wendy witnessed the damaging effects of the atomic bomb. The family subsequently returned to the United States. She told authorities that it was her family's suffering in the concentration camp that had helped to turn her against United States involvement in the Vietnam War.[79] She saw both the war and the internment program as directed against Asian peoples. The Japanese community rallied to her support, providing her bail (in cash) and paying for her legal defense. The fund-raising campaign united liberal and conservative segments in the Japanese community in California and even elicited support from Chinese Americans.[80]

The case of Wendy Yoshimura suggests that future generations of Japanese Americans may not be as docile and conforming as were the Nisei and Issei. Instead they may follow the lead of black Americans and become increasingly active in political and civic affairs, identifying not only with the Japanese American community but with all Asian peoples and the "Third World."

Kitano hopes that "the next generation of Japanese Americans will integrate the best of the Japanese and the American cultures, and their lives will reflect the richness of both" (p. 204).

Japanese Americans and Racism

The most important contribution of the saga of mainland Japanese to a theory of intergroup relations concerns the concept of race and racism. The long-held idea that race difference is an insurmountable barrier to assimilation has been substantially refuted by the Japanese in the United States. But "racism" is as much based on a syndrome of mythical beliefs in the minds of most dominants as it is founded upon measurable physical difference. That it can either be manufactured or developed to high salience when it suits the purpose of a powerful dominant has, ironically, been demonstrated in this century at the expense of the most "successful" minorities: mainland Japanese Americans and Jewish-Germans during World War II.

---

[77]Eve Pell, "Detention Camp to Hearst Hideout," in *Ms.*, 5, July, 1976, pp. 19–20.
[78]The defense made an interesting motion: To apply the three years she spent in the relocation camp (as an infant and young child) to her time served. The judge denied this unusual request. However, as of the present writing, there is reason to believe that her sentence will be reduced to between sixteen months and three years. See *The New York Times*, March 18, 1977, p. 12.
[79]*The New York Times*, "Aid to Tokyo Rose . . . ," Feb. 7, 1977, p. 15.
[80]Eve Pell, "Detention Camp to Hearst Hideout."

Suggested Readings

Caudhill, William, and George De Vos. "Achievement, Culture, and Personality: The Case of Japanese Americans," in *American Anthropologist*, 1956, 1102–1126.
An outstanding study of the Chicago Japanese in the 1950s.

Connor, John W. "Acculturation and Family Continuities in Three Generations of Japanese Americans," in *Journal of Marriage and the Family*, 36, February, 1974, pp. 159–165.
Discussion of Japanese child-rearing methods and the continuity of familistic values across the generations.

———. "Jōge Kankei: A Key Concept for an Understanding of Japanese-American Achievement," in *Psychiatry*, 39, August, 1976, pp. 266–279.
Discussion of the roles of social ranking and sensitivity to opinions of others in the success of the Japanese.

Daniels, Roger. *The Politics of Prejudice: The Anti-Japanese Movement in California and the Struggle for Japanese Exclusion*. New York: Atheneum, 1970.
A historical study of the anti-Japanese movement from 1861 to the Japanese restrictive provisions of the Immigration Act of 1924.

Gee, Emma. "Issei: The First Women," in *Civil Rights Digest*, 6, Spring, 1974, pp. 48–53.
Hardships experienced by Issei women in adjusting to life in America.

Houston, Jeanne Wakatsuki, and Houston, James D. *Farewell to Manzanar*. Boston: Houghton Mifflin Co., 1973.
A Nisei woman relates her experiences as a child and the suffering of her family at Manzanar Camp during the internment years.

Kitano, Harry H. L. "Japanese Americans: The Development of a Middleman Minority," in *Pacific Historical Review*, 43, November, 1974, pp. 500–519.
Comparison of Hawaiian Japanese with Japanese on the mainland.

Kitagawa, Daisuke. *Issei and Nisei: The Internment Years*. New York: The Seabury Press, 1967.
A hard-hitting study of the internment years by a former Christian Japanese clergyman.

Lyman, Stanford M. "Japanese-American Generation Gap," in *Society*, 10, Jan/Feb 1973, pp. 55–63.
Description of personality and character traits of Nisei and Sansei.

Mass, Amy Iwasaki. "Asians as Individuals: The Japanese Community," *Social Casework*, 57, March, 1976, pp. 160–164.
Discussion of the social problems in the Japanese American community and some of their subcultural sources.

Ten Broeck, Jacobus; Barnhart, Edward N.; and Matson, Floyd W. *Prejudice, War and the Constitution*. Berkeley: University of California Press, 1954.
A scholarly account of the Japanese evacuation during World War II with special emphasis on legal aspects.

Thomas, Dorothy S. *The Salvage*. Berkeley: The University of California Press, 1962.
A scholarly account of the internment and restoration of the internees to normal community life.

Thomas, Dorothy S., and Nishimoto, Richard S. *The Spoilage: Japanese-American Evacuation and Resettlement*. Berkeley: University of California Press, 1946.
    An intensive study of those Japanese who became bitter enough about evacuation to renounce their citizenship.

16

The Peoples of Hawaii

Intergroup relations in Hawaii are so very different from any other state that to follow our usual format for treating American minority situations is difficult. With less than a million total population, Hawaii has the most heterogeneous ethnoracial composition of any state. Although the dominant status of the white people of Euro-American background over the peoples of Oriental origin was well established when Hawaii became American territory, intergroup relations have continuously been distinguished by the absence of any legal or public discrimination. Nonofficial discrimination, however, by the white residents against both the native Hawaiians and the successive immigrant groups has been evident. The absence of formal discrimination has led many writers and students to picture Hawaii as a paradise of interracial relations; the informal discrimination has led others to view it less favorably.

ETHNORACIAL COMPOSITION OF HAWAII

Table 16-1 presents the official differentiation of Hawaii's population by ethnoracial components. However, the extensive interracial marriage that has taken place over the years makes the official tables highly artificial. Recognition of this was made in the 1970 Census when the distinction between Hawaiians and part-Hawaiians was finally given up. A large portion of the 9.2 percent of the state's population listed in the 1970 Census as "Hawaiian" had been formerly designated as part-Hawaiian (see page 322). The difficulty of ethnoracial classification was further reflected in the 1970 Census by the use of the category "Ethnic Stock" and the notation that persons of mixed ancestry are classified by race of father. A considerable portion of the citizens of Hawaii either identify themselves or are labeled by others as belonging in one of the ethnoracial groups listed in Table 16-1. But one is well-advised to look upon them as distinctively identifiable culturally, with an indeterminable amount of genetic lineage traceable to the ethnoracial group for which the labels originally stood.

Throughout the chapter, we will use the term *haole* (how-lee). The native meaning of this word is "stranger" and it was first applied to the Euro-American invaders. It is now used to mean any "white" or Caucasian person.

The actual figures given in Table 16-1 by decades are not strictly comparable since changes in the basis of classification have occurred over the years. The changes in ethnic composition are reasonably clear, however. (1) Between the time of the first white contact in 1778 to about 1850, there were only small numbers of haoles residing in the Islands, with an essentially homogeneous native Hawaiian population. (2) From about 1850 to 1930, successive waves of immigrant peoples—Chinese, Japanese, Filipinos—came to the territory. At various times other ethnics entered Hawaii in

TABLE 16-1 Population of Hawaii by Ethnic Components at Specified Intervals and by Percent of Total, 1853, 1900, 1950, and 1970

	1853[1]	1853 %of Total	1884[1]	1900[1]	1900 %of Total	1920[1]	1950[1]	1950 %of Total	1960[2]	1970[4]	1970 %of Total	1976[7]
Hawaiian	70,036	95.8	40,414	29,799	19.3	23,723	12,245	2.5	11,294	71,375[6]	9.2	98,177
Part Hawaiian	983	1.3	4,218	9,857	6.4	18,027	73,845	14.8	91,169			
Caucasian	1,687	2.3	16,579	26,819	17.4	49,140	114,793	23.0	202,230	298,160	38.7	279,128
Portuguese	87		9,967	18,272		27,002						
Other Caucasian	1,600		6,612	8,547		19,708						
Chinese	364	0.5	18,254	25,767	16.7	23,507	32,376	6.5	38,197	52,039	6.7	47,482
Japanese			116	61,111	39.6	109,274	184,598	36.9	203,455	217,307	28.2	235,257
Korean						4,950	7,030	1.4		8,656	1.1	13,048
Filipino						21,031	61,062	12.2	69,070	93,915	12.2	109,127
Puerto Rican						5,602	9,551	1.9				
Negro	5	0.0		233	0.2	348	2,651	0.5	4,953	7,573	0.9	9,416
All Other	62	0.1	1,397	648	0.4	310	1,618	0.3	12,305[3]	18,410[5]	2.4	45,764
Total	73,137	100.0	80,578	154,234	100.0	255,912	499,769	100.0	632,772	768,561	100.0	827,399

[1]See Andrew Lind, *Hawaii's People* (Honolulu: University of Hawaii Press, 1967), p. 28, for the data through 1950.
[2]U.S. Census, 1960, for 1960 *Population by Race, Final Report* (P C 2)—C, p. 254.
[3]The Negro component is subtracted from the above U.S. Census table "All Other" category, leaving the "All Other" largely Korean.
[4]"Population Summary for Hawaii, 1972," Statistical Report 87, Department of Planning and Economic Development, State of Hawaii.
[5]"All Other" for 1970 include Aleut, Eskimo, Malayan, Micronesian, Polynesian, etc.
[6]In the 1970 Census, for the first time, no differentiation was made between Hawaiian and Part Hawaiian.
[7]The 1976 figures are based on a sample of 38,818 persons. Source: *The Population of Hawaii: 1976: Statistical Report 119*, State of Hawaii Department of Planning and Economic Development, April 2, 1977.

response to the demand for plantation labor. Portuguese, Puerto Ricans, and Koreans arrived in sufficient numbers to be classified as separate groups in earlier population tables. There have been, in addition, Spaniards,.Germans, Islanders from scattered areas of the Pacific, and Russians.[1] (3) During this period the native Hawaiian population declined. Out-marriage of Hawaiians with other ethnics was so extensive that by 1930 the "Part-Hawaiian" began to exceed the pure-Hawaiian category. (4) During this period also the Japanese came to a position of numerical predominance among all the ethnics. (5) By 1940 the proportions of the ethnic components were showing a tendency to stabilize. (6) Since World War II the proportion of the Caucasian population has been increasing. Whereas in 1950 the Japanese comprised about 37 percent and the Caucasians 25, by 1970 the latter had jumped to 39 percent and the Japanese made up only 28. However, a substantial part of the haole population growth is accounted for by military dependents (not counting military personnel itself), and thus haole influence on Hawaiian civic life became somewhat less than that of the Japanese. Contributing to the reduction of the Japanese population has been a net loss in their island and mainland interchange.[2]

The story of ethnic intergroup relations in Hawaii will be divided into three periods: (1) the period of European invasion and the decline of the aboriginal Hawaiian civilization, from 1778 to about 1850, when the immigration of Asiatic people began; (2) the period of haole dominance over both the Hawaiians and the other subsequent immigrant peoples from 1850 to World War II; (3) the period of declining haole dominance, which characterizes the years since World War II.

THE ESTABLISHMENT OF HAOLE DOMINANCE

The Decline of the Hawaiians

At the time of the first white contact with Hawaii in 1778, the Islands were inhabited by a people of Polynesian origin and physiognomic features, who had brown skin, black hair, and were considered handsome by Caucasians.

Their society, though preliterate, was highly elaborated. Early estimates of the native population in 1778 placed the number at about 300,000 but contemporary scholars believe it to have been far less. The early explorers saw only the settlements near the coast and based their estimates of the total population on the assumption that the interior was just as densely populated. It became known that the island of Hawaii, for example, partly covered by bare lava, was quite sparsely populated. The Hawaiians had developed a distinctive way of life suitable to themselves and with sufficient resources available to sustain them. Within a century after the coming of the white man, this civilization was virtually destroyed. The population declined almost to the point of extinction and the small group of white newcomers supplanted the natives as the controlling element in this insular community.

Except for missionaries, the few Euro-Americans who came to Hawaii before the middle of the nineteenth century were motivated almost entirely by economic interests.

[1]See Andrew Lind, *An Island Community* (Chicago: University of Chicago Press, 1938), p. 194.
[2]*Components of Change in the Civilian Population by Ethnic Group and Military Dependency, for Hawaii 1950–1960.* Estimated by the Department of Planning and Research of Hawaii.

First confining themselves to trading, the whites gradually became interested in cattle raising and rice growing—introduced first by the Chinese—and finally in sugar growing, destined to become the economic foundation of the future Hawaii. Thus the haoles sought and gained permanent tenure of more and more valuable lands.

The reactions of the Hawaiians to the haoles were compounded chiefly of awe and friendliness, which aided the haoles in gaining their immediate ends. Their technological superiority evoked native admiration and helped establish haole prestige. As Burrows writes, "They [the natives] seem to have made the generalization that because the foreigners were superior to them in certain points of technology, they were superior in everything."[3] Although some native groups did oppose the haoles as they encroached on their land, in general, encroachment was accomplished peacefully. In 1845 an act was passed by the native Hawaiian government prohibiting aliens from acquiring title to land.[4] Like the Indians on the mainland, however, when this act was repealed in 1850, native Hawaiians often sold their land for ready cash. The native Hawaiian population declined at a staggering rate. In 1950 only about 12,000 pure Hawaiians were recorded.

Adams has summarized the causes for this phenomenal population decline: (1) the sanguinary wars that continued for seventeen years after Captain Cook's first visit; (2) the introduction by foreigners of diseases new and highly fatal to the natives; (3) the hardship and exposure incident to new relations with foreigners, such as cutting and carrying candlewood, service on whaling ships, and the contributions of foodstuffs required for trade; (4) the serious disorganization of production due to trade and contacts with foreigners; (5) the disruption of the old moral order; and (6) the inability of a primitive people to meet the requirements of the new situation promptly.[5] In short, it is clear that this rapid decimation of the Hawaiian population was influenced by haole infiltration, even though haoles as a group or as individuals did not directly contribute to it or desire it.

In this early period a pattern of interracial relations began to emerge quite contrary to those established by north Euro-Americans in their imperialist expansion elsewhere. The number of white people in Hawaii was quite small. They came from various nations and no one nation had gained ascendancy. Hawaiian political autonomy, although influenced by white intrigue, was maintained. The power situation called for treating Hawaiians with due respect and with at least formal equality. Furthermore, the white population was predominantly male, and thus many of those who remained married Hawaiian women. Intermarriage was further facilitated by the freedom regarding marriage within the loosely organized native Hawaiian system.[6] Thus many conditions in the early situation conspired against the drawing of a color line by the white people. Haole prestige, obvious even in the early days, was based more on social-economic power than on race consciousness. For the study of dominant-minority relations, this is the most significant development in the early period.

In the latter half of the nineteenth century, white people established a firm control over Hawaiian society. Nationalistic rivalries among the whites from imperialist nations

[3]Edwin G. Burrows, *Hawaiian Americans* (New Haven: Yale University Press, 1947), p. 17. Copyright ©, 1947, by Yale University Press. Reprinted by permission of the publisher.
[4]*Ibid.*, p. 40. At that time, land was owned by the king. In 1848, a division of the land gave some of it to the people.
[5]Romanzo Adams, *Interracial Marriage in Hawaii* (New York: The Macmillan Co., 1939), p. 7.
[6]*Ibid.*, pp. 46–48.

were resolved in favor of the Americans. Agitation in the islands for annexation to the United States then arose, ultimately producing a revolution and formation of a provisional government favorable to annexation. Official transfer of sovereignty from the Republic of Hawaii to the United States occurred on August 12, 1898.

Economic Dominance

Control over the Hawaiian economy by haoles had been substantially accomplished through the concentration of control over the elaborated plantation system and its auxiliary financial and shipping enterprises. This control was vested substantially in five corporations. Called the "Big Five," these corporations controlled 96 percent of the islands' sugar production and had holdings in other enterprises such as pineapple production, public utilities, docks, shipping companies, banks, hotels, and department stores.[7]

This great economic development in Hawaii under Euro-American corporate direction would not have been possible without an additional labor supply. Because of native population decline there were not enough Hawaiians. Furthermore, the natives did not make good plantation workers. Burrows writes, "The whole idea of steady work for wages was so foreign to their old culture that it had no value to appeal to them. . . . When an Hawaiian was hired to work on the plantations, he would work, as a rule, only until he had enough money to buy what he wanted at the moment, and to give his friends a good time."[8] The labor problem was solved by the importation, either under contract or by active persuasion, of a succession of immigrants from various parts of Asia and elsewhere. The order of succession of these ethnic groups is seen in Table 16-1—the Chinese, the Portuguese, the Japanese, and considerably later, the Puerto Ricans and Filipinos.

This process of immigration developed into a pattern. The need was for cheap and tractable labor. Each new ethnic group would at first serve as plantation workers. As its members became better adjusted to island life, some, growing discontented with their menial lot, would desert the fields for the city or return home. Thus the planters needed replacements. As the numbers of any one ethnic group increased, characteristic antagonism arose, first showing itself among competing workers. The planters' strategy was to import new ethnic labor sources to allay public antagonism against any one group. Furthering this course of action was the fact that the longer any group of workers stayed in Hawaii, the less tractable they became.

While the growth of a strong labor movement in Hawaii is a recent development, there was some organization among workers and some attempted strikes in the early twentieth century. An ethnically divided working group, however, was not likely to develop strong labor solidarity.

> Early in the century, the policy of denying to Orientals membership in the skilled trades unions smashed all hopes for effective organization, for a "one-nationality" union arouses prejudice and may be crippled by compet-

---

[7]Ralph S. Kuykendall and A. Grove Day, *Hawaii: A History* (Englewood Cliffs, N.J.: Prentice-Hall, 1948), pp. 271–272.
[8]Burrows, *Hawaiian Americans*, pp. 41–43. By permission of the publishers, Yale University Press.

ing workers from another national or racial group, who will work for lower wages or even act as strike-breakers. Discrimination has been charged; it was once a common saying in Hawaii that there are three kinds of payment for the same kind of work—what *haoles* pay *haoles,* what *haoles* pay Orientals, and what Orientals pay Orientals. Racial loyalties have conflicted with labor-group loyalties, although racial antagonism in Hawaii has never been acute. Language difficulties and differences in culture and outlook have further divided allegiances to working-class ideals.[9]

Although after annexation contract labor became illegal, the planters still managed to locate and control the inflow of the additional labor supply needed.

Political Dominance

Wherever the economic control of an area is highly concentrated in relatively few hands, the same economic interests in large measure control the politics and government. While it is true that under American rule all the formal democratic institutions of the American governmental system were established, most students of Hawaii agree that the Big Five controlled the political life of the Islands from annexation to World War II. Illustrative are the remarks of Barber:

> Moreover, they [the Big Five] are represented indirectly in the political affairs of the Territory, members of the legislature being linked with the Big Five, either through former association (or as in the case of the Speaker of the lower House, through being legal counsel for the sugar industry), or through the bonds of kinship.[10]

The non-haole groups combined constituted a numerical majority. However, until about 1930 they did not begin to challenge haole political domination. Although the Japanese were by far the largest of the ethnic groups, "it was not until 1930 that a number of Japanese-American candidates appeared in the primaries."[11] At that time federal law made foreign-born Orientals ineligible for citizenship.

Intergroup Relations

The pattern of intergroup relations in Hawaii before World War II involved haole social dominance over and discrimination against the non-haole ethnic groups. However, the reality of the formal, institutionalized pattern of racial equality in Hawaii is attested by practically all writers on Hawaii. From the start there were no Jim Crow

---

[9]Ralph S. Kuykendall and A. Grove Day, *Hawaii: A History* (Englewood Cliffs, N.J.: Prentice-Hall, Inc., 1948), p. 275. Copyright © 1976 Gloria H. Kuykendall, Delman L. Kuykendall, and A. Grove Day. Reprinted by permission of Prentice-Hall, Inc.

[10]From *Hawaii, Restless Ramparts,* by Joseph Barber, Jr., copyright 1941, used by special permission of the publishers, The Bobbs-Merrill Company, Inc., p. 46.

[11]Bradford Smith, *Americans from Japan* (Philadelphia and New York: J. B. Lippincott Company, 1948), p. 166. Copyright © 1948 by Bradford Smith. Reprinted by permission of J. B. Lippincott Company.

laws, no segregation in schooling, no laws against intermarriage. However, beneath the surface there was evidence of prejudice and discrimination in which race consciousness was a predominant factor. Burrows writes:

> . . . throughout their school years the Hawaiian born of Oriental stock have become more and more American. The process was favored by an atmosphere kindlier toward their race, and more tolerant of racial and cultural differences, than that of the American mainland. But when they got out of school, and set out to win their way toward prosperity, as good Americans are expected to do, they met with a rude shock. They found that the tolerance and friendliness among races, for which Hawaii has been justly celebrated, prevailed only within limits, and at a price. The price demanded by the dominant haoles—never in so many words, but nevertheless insistent—has been cheerful acceptance by other peoples of a subordinate place.[12]

Referring to haole relations with the Japanese, Bradford Smith cites instances of occupational and social discrimination.

> Discrimination appears in social life as well as in business. . . . The principal of a Honolulu school told me that in sixteen years as a teacher . . . he had come to know only three or four haoles well enough to enter their homes, and all of them were from the mainland. Even in the faculty lunch rooms racial lines hold in the table groups.
> Social considerations also affect advancement in jobs. A plantation manager wanted to appoint a Nisei chief electrician. If he did, the Nisei and his family would move into a house in the supervisor's area and his wife would have to be invited to social affairs with the other supervisors' wives. The ladies refused to do this. So the man was not appointed.[13]

The dominance of the haoles was in considerable measure a function of their class position. The upper class was composed almost entirely of haoles. Most other haoles were in the middle class. The smaller number of lower-class haoles were, or were descended from, sailors or other occasional travelers who decided to stay, some of whom belonged in the "beachcomber" category. In occupational upgrading and in wage rates within the same job levels, non-haoles were discriminated against. How much this discrimination was based on "race consciousness" is a difficult question. Judged by comparison with Euro-Americans on the mainland United States, the haoles certainly showed less negative reaction to "color," as the frequency of haole out-marriage indicates (see Table 16-2). Before annexation, Hawaii classified its residents on the basis of nationality rather than race. After annexation the territorial government did classify Euro-Americans as Caucasian, and the offspring of a mixed marriage was classified as belonging to the non-Caucasian parent's group. In a plantation community where the differentiation of haoles as the upper class was strongly marked, Norbeck found the dis-

---

[12]Burrows, *Hawaiian Americans,* p. 85. By permission of the publishers, Yale University Press.
[13]Smith, *Americans from Japan,* p. 166. Reprinted by permission of the publisher.

tinction between the haoles and the Japanese and the Filipinos to be more often thought of as cultural rather than racial.[14]

Status distinctions developed among the non-haole groups themselves. The main Hawaiian gradient was haole-Chinese-Japanese-Filipinos. Native Hawaiians were interspersed but generally toward the bottom. Puerto Ricans and Portuguese also had a generally low status. In a study of the race preference of the Japanese in Hawaii, Matsuoka found the first preference to be their own kind, followed by Caucasians, Chinese, White-Hawaiians, Koreans, Hawaiians, Portuguese, Filipinos, Puerto Ricans in that order. "In general, preference depends not on physiognomy but on socioeconomic status."[15] Within the non-haole groups, status differences had significance. Among the Hawaiians, the families descended from chiefs were superior to the commoners; among the Chinese, the Punti were superior to the Hakka; and the "regular" Japanese considered themselves above the Okinawans.

Non-Haole Reaction to Haole Dominance

How did non-haoles react to haole dominance? Burrows analyzed three types of reaction by the minorities to the stress and frustration engendered by minority status: aggressiveness, withdrawal, and cooperation.[16]

Aggression. This had not been characteristic of any of the groups except the Hawaiians at the two periods of their maximum stress: around 1830, when the haoles were rapidly assuming dominance, and in the period of the 1880s, when haoles assumed control of the government. The only form of aggression at all common among the minorities was the mildest one of grumbling.

Withdrawal. The extreme forms of withdrawal were more frequent among Hawaiians than among Orientals: reactions manifested in happy-go-lucky apathy, drinking extensively, and taking life easy—going fishing and strumming the ukulele. Extreme withdrawal was manifested in religious reversion, either in the revival of traditional Hawaiian rites and practices or the embracing of new cults.

According to Burrows, "recreation reversion" gained ground during the last generation [circa 1947] in pronounced forms. This mildest form of withdrawal was illustrated by revival of interest in the traditional culture of the non-haoles' native lands: among the Hawaiians, the revival of ancient pageantry, the hula, and folklore; among the Chinese, the revival of Chinese drama and music; among the Japanese, the revival of Japanese art. While the withdrawal response was more common than aggression, it was still confined to a minority of the persons involved.

Cooperation. Cooperation was the main reaction to haole dominance. For the most part, it involved passive conformity to the demands placed on the non-haoles by the haoles. Less often it took the form of asceticism, where the individual meticulously avoids all that is forbidden and drives himself to do his full duty.[17]

---

[14]Edward Norbeck, *Pineapple Town* (Berkeley: University of California Press, 1959), p. 118.
[15]Jitsuichi Matsuoka, "Race Preference in Hawaii," in *American Journal of Sociology,* 1935–1936, pp. 635–641.
[16]Burrows, *Hawaiian Americans,* Part II.
[17]*Ibid.,* pp. 167–198.

Acculturation of the Non-Haole Peoples Prior to World War II

Despite these reactions, acculturation of the minority ethnic groups went on. The children of immigrant Orientals were being acculturated rapidly to the haole way of life. All the native-born were educated in public schools of the American type. "By 1940, approximately 65 percent of the American citizens of Japanese ancestry over the age of twenty-five had completed eight or more years of American schooling as compared with only 30 percent in the entire population of the Territory."[18] The public-school system encouraged all its pupils to conceive of themselves as full-fledged members of a free and democratic society. As the native-born came of age, which did not occur before 1920 in any considerable number except for the Chinese and Hawaiians, they began to participate more actively in political life. Illustrative of the American orientation of the native-born Japanese, is Bradford Smith's comment on Nisei reaction to Issei attitudes toward Japan's informal war against China after 1931. "The Nisei resented the partisanship of their parents. They resented anything which set them apart from other young Americans. They resented the contributions to Japanese militarism. Family arguments grew bitter, family relations more strained."[19]

Like the Chinese earlier, the enterprising Japanese moved from agricultural work into the cities, and began upward occupational mobility. "By 1930 the Japanese were operating 49 percent of the retail stores in Hawaii and provided 43 percent of the salesmen. . . . Fifteen percent of the Japanese gainfully employed in 1940 were in preferred professional, proprietary, and managerial occupations as compared with 13.7 percent of the total population."[20]

Let us conclude our examination of Hawaii's ethnic relations marked by haole dominance by noting those developments that generated social forces leading to the period marked by the rise of the non-haoles.

In the relatively short span of less than 200 years, Hawaii changed from an aboriginal, self-sustaining, isolated, stone-age culture to a modern, urbanized, commercial, industrial community linked closely to international trade. In the early part of this process there was a dichotomized, semifeudalistic type of society, with an upper-class haole component and the natives (with due deference to the native rulers) and the immigrants as lower class. In the dominant haole value system, capitalism, political democracy, and Christianity was basic. These values generated social forces that resulted in the rise in status and power of the Asian ethnic groups. Among the noneconomic developments that contributed to this change were (1) the maintenance of political control by native Hawaiians for over a century following discovery, (2) the development of a free and integrated public-school system, (3) the introduction of American political concepts with constitutional guarantees of equality of all before the law, and (4) the missionary influence.[21]

[18]Andrew Lind, *Hawaii's Japanese: An Experiment in Democracy* (Princeton, N.J.: Princeton University Press, 1946), p. 18. Copyright 1946 © 1974 by Princeton University Press. Published in cooperation with the American Council Institute of Pacific Relations, Inc. Reprinted by permission of the publisher.
[19]Smith, *Americans from Japan,* p. 147. By permission of the publisher, J. B. Lippincott Company.
[20]Lind, *Hawaii's Japanese,* pp. 17–18. By permission of the publishers, Princeton University Press.
[21]Based on correspondence with Douglas S. Yamamura, University of Hawaii.

HAWAII'S CHANGING ETHNIC PATTERN

Since 1940 certain broad trends in the development of Hawaii have produced changes in the relations of Hawaii's ethnoracial peoples. (1) World War II had a marked impact on Hawaii and its people. (2) Agriculture continued to operate on the large-scale plantation system and the ownership of agricultural land is still concentrated in a few hands—largely in the "Big Five." [22] (3) The decline in the needed manpower in agriculture led to urbanization, which has been highly concentrated in one area. In 1970, about 82 percent of the state's population resided in the city and county of Honolulu. (4) Political control, long Republican and haole, in the early 1950s changed to Democratic party control in which the Japanese played a major role. (5) The changed political picture together with the increased military expenditures and statehood (1958) greatly increased the proportion of people employed by the federal and state government. (6) The population has grown about 50 percent since 1950, affected by the increase in military dependents and migration from the mainland of more haoles. For the first time in the Island's history the haole component is about 40 percent of the population. (7) The state has become increasingly affluent, with the phenomenal rise of tourism playing a large part in addition to factors mentioned above.

World War II

World War II marked a turning point in Hawaiian intergroup relations. The circumstances of war introduced new tensions, which were of a temporary nature. However, the war further accelerated certain trends that had begun in the period of haole dominance. The exigencies of war brought to the islands an influx of mainland civilian workers and military personnel not accustomed to Hawaii's pattern of race relations. Lind points out that

> As early as 1940 the mounting tide of defense workers, which was to more than double the size of the civilian population of Caucasian ancestry in Hawaii within six years, had begun to make its impact upon the sensitive balance of race relations within the territory. Despite the fairly frequent instances of "shacking up" with local girls, the defense workers generally were highly critical of the free and easy association of the various racial groups in the Islands. Most of them came with fixed ideas, derived from experience with the Negro in the South or with the Oriental and the Filipino on the West Coast. Although living in Hawaii, the psychological barriers they brought with them, along with the limitations imposed by their occupations and their segregated residence, prevented most of them from really becoming "at home" in Hawaii. [23]

[22]Frederick Simpich, *The Anatomy of Hawaii* (New York: Coward, McCann & Geoghegan, 1971), Ch. 4, "The Land."
[23]Andrew W. Lind, "Recent Trends in Hawaiian Race Relations," in *Race Relations*, Vol. V, Numbers 3 and 4 (Dec., 1947, Jan., 1948), p. 60. By permission of the publishers, Fisk University.

Acculturation of the Non-Haole Peoples After World War II

In 1970, approximately 90 percent of Hawaii's citizens were native American born. Having all been educated in American schools they were literate in the English language and 75 percent considered English their "mother tongue."

Economic Acculturation

Occupational Distribution.   Each immigrant group started out as plantation laborers and then gradually moved urbanward, first into menial occupations. By mid-century, all immigrant groups were present in the higher occupational strata roughly in proportion to the time order of their arrival—Chinese, Portuguese, Japanese, and Filipinos. This process continued so that the distribution of the non-haole occupational levels got closer to that of the haoles. For example in 1960 the percentage of the first comers, the Chinese, in professional occupations was almost equal to that of the haoles.[24] At the same time some of the latecomer Filipinos had just begun to enter the professions. Simpich states that in the 1960s they were advancing rapidly.[25]

Income.   A 1964–1966 sample survey on Oahu indicated that the annual median family income by ethnic stock of the father was $9,372 for the Chinese, $8,777 for the Japanese, and $7,246 for the Haole. When the incomes of the military groups were eliminated from the haole total, the haole civilian groups dropped to $5,287 per family, which was lower than that of the pure Hawaiians who had a median family income of $5,593.[26] In short, it is clear that taken as groups in general the various ethnic groups were approaching similarity with two exceptions—the Hawaiians (part or "pure") and the Portuguese. While the Filipinos remained lower, they were catching up. Since the upper-level haoles were among the wealthiest, it appears that the range of distribution of income among the haoles was wider than among other groups.

Unionization.   Further economic acculturation was seen in the great success of the unionization of labor. As "latecomers" more concentrated in the lower-occupational ranks, the Filipinos played a considerable role in unionization. But in any case the "divide and rule" technique of business ownership no longer worked. The greater proportion of the Chinese in civil service jobs came because, as first comers, they could qualify on examinations.

Political Acculturation: The Case of the Japanese

The largely Republican, haole control of territorial politics was first lost in 1954 when the Democrats gained control of the legislature and the Japanese became its largest single ethnic component. After World War II a Democratic coalition of Hawaii's minority groups and labor organizations was organized by Jack Burns, who subsequently became Governor. The Japanese played a significant role in the new coalition. Hawaii's admission to statehood in 1958 gave the Japanese the chance to elect representatives to Congress. By 1965, three of the state's four members of Congress

[24]Andrew Lind, *Hawaii: The Last of the Magic Isles* (London and New York: Oxford University Press, 1969), © 1969 the Institute of Race Relations, London.
[25]Simpich, *The Anatomy of Hawaii,* p. 46.
[26]Lind, *Hawaii,* p. 64. Survey conducted by the Hawaiian Department of Health.

were Japanese Democrats: Daniel Inouye (elected to the Senate in 1962), Spark Matsunaga (elected to the House of Representatives in 1962), and Patsy Mink (elected to the House in 1964). Senator Hiram Fong, Republican of Chinese lineage, completed Hawaii's roster. In the 1977 Congress, Matsunaga joined Inouye in the Senate, and the two members of the House of Representatives were Democrat Daniel Akaka, of native Hawaiian lineage, and Democrat Cecil Heftel, a wealthy white. In 1974, another Japanese, George Ariyoshi, became Governor. The Japanese-backed Democrats have remained politically strong despite the population gain of the whites. The prediction of Sakumoto in 1967 has been largely substantiated: "The role of the other ethnic factors in the future, we suspect, will revolve around the Japanese/Democratic—Caucasian/Republican axis."[27]

Summary

The acculturation process of the immigrant-descended Asians advanced rapidly after World War II. They share the major values of American culture: ambition to improve their individual material wealth, desire for higher educational achievement, belief in the democratic process. In short, they became thoroughly American, illustrated by the fact that of those who moved away from Hawaii, most migrated to the American mainland.

ASSIMILATION: INTEGRATED OR PLURALISTIC?

Whether the current trends in Hawaii's ethnic relations are leading toward stabilization on a multiethnic basis of Hawaii's "peoples" or toward a common neo-Hawaiian identity of an integrated "people" is problemmatic. There are trends leading in both directions. Favoring an integrated development are the exceptionally high rate of intermarriage, the wide range of social class differentials among the major ethnic groups, the steady decline in the dominance of haoles, and the historic tendency for discrimination to be based on social class or cultural factors rather than on race.

Operating against a neo-Hawaiian integration are the continued strength of structural pluralism among the major ethnic groups (reinforced by the revival of ethnic consciousness on the mainland), a revitalization of cultural as well as structural pluralism on the part of native Hawaiians or those identifying themselves as such, and the recent influx of immigrants from Samoa and Asian countries. In fact, the last factor alone may "set Hawaii back" several decades on progress toward integration and assimilation.

Two other special factors in Hawaiian social organization, the presence of the military and large-scale tourism, important as they are for the island's economy, are not likely to have a substantial effect on the trends in interethnic relations.

Interracial Marriage

Table 16-2 shows the steadily rising rates of interracial marriage from 1913 to 1974. Since 1965 the intermarriage rates have tended to "level off." The table also shows that

[27]Raymond E. Sakumoto, "Voting Preferences in a Multi-Ethnic Electorate." Paper prepared for the Pacific Sociological Association Conference, March 31, 1967, at Long Beach, California, p. 9.

TABLE 16-2 Interracial Marriages as Percentage of All Marriages, 1912–1974

		1912–1916*	1920–1930*	1930–1940	1940–1949†	1950–1959††	1960–1964††	1965–1969††	1970–1974††
					% Out-Marriages				
Hawaiian	Grooms	19.4	33.3	55.2	66.3	78.9	85.9	85.7	85.5
	Brides	39.9	52.1	62.7	77.2	81.5	85.4	92.7	90.8
Part-Hawaiian	Grooms	52.1	38.8	41.0	36.9	41.3	47.0	56.4	58.6
	Brides	66.2	57.7	57.9	64.2	58.4	56.8	56.5	57.2
Caucasian	Grooms	17.3	24.3	22.4	33.8	37.4	35.1	24.3	26.2
	Brides	11.7	13.8	10.7	10.2	16.4	21.1	19.3	21.3
Chinese	Grooms	41.7	24.8	28.0	31.2	43.6	54.8	61.1	60.3
	Brides	5.7	15.7	28.5	38.0	45.2	56.6	65.4	64.6
Japanese	Grooms	0.5	2.7	4.3	4.3	8.7	15.7	28.0	29.8
	Brides	0.2	3.1	6.3	16.9	19.1	25.4	30.3	38.2
Korean	Grooms	26.4	17.6	23.5	49.0	70.3	77.1	73.0	68.4
	Brides	0.0	4.9	39.0	66.7	74.5	80.1	83.6	84.4
Filipino	Grooms	21.8	25.6	37.5	42.0	44.5	51.2	50.0	46.7
	Brides	2.8	1.0	4.0	21.0	35.8	47.5	51.1	47.6
Puerto Rican	Grooms	24.4	18.6	29.8	39.5	51.3	65.0	74.0	77.2
	Brides	26.4	39.7	42.8	50.3	60.5	67.2	73.5	76.7
Total		11.5	19.2	22.8	28.6	32.8	37.6	35.0	38.3

*Derived from Romanzo Adams, *Interracial Marriage in Hawaii*, pp. 336–9.
†Bureau of Vital Statistics, 1 July 1940–30, June 1948 and calendar year 1949.
††Bureau of Health Statistics, calendar years 1950–74.
Source: Romanzo Adams, *Interracial Marriage in Hawaii* (New York, The Macmillan Co., 1937), pp. 336–9; *Annual Reports of the Bureau of Vital Statistics* (Honolulu, 1943–9); *Annual Reports, Department of Health Statistical Supplements* (Honolulu, 1950–74).

the smaller and more recent immigrant groups, such as the Koreans and Puerto Ricans, tend to outmarry more than the larger, more established groups. This is partly due to their high ratios of males to females. It is obvious that just as the official ethnic population figures are highly artificial so also are the official outmarriage rates. Substantial numbers of the brides and grooms listed under specific categories are themselves from mixed marriages. Lind illustrated the point by quoting a university coed in 1966 who wrote of herself:

> Just who should I tell you that I am. . . . Two of my grandparents were immigrant laborers from Japan, one of whose sons most unfilially married the daughter of a Chinese wedded to a part-Hawaiian lass of God-only-knows-how-many sailor strains. According to your census enumerators I am part-Hawaiian. . . .[28]

This indicates that ethnoracial designation is in part a matter of which ethnic group the couple chooses to identify with, probably in most cases that of the father. The one exception seems to be an official designation of anyone admitting or suspected of having a Polynesian ancestor to be labeled part-Hawaiian. As for mixtures that do not involve any native Hawaiian ancestry, the majority of offspring are absorbed into one or the other parental ethnic group. Some, however, actually identify themselves as "mixed" or as "cosmopolitan," and they do so with considerable pride. This mixed category may constitute a new Hawaiian ethnoracial variant.[29]

Ethnic Group Identity

It is no longer the case, as in earlier days, that the class and racial stratification system tend to fuse. The educational, income, and occupational range of all the main ethnoracial components indicate what Gordon called "eth-class" system.[30] Second, there is little racial residential segregation. Of this Lind writes "It is possible, for example, to designate areas of Honolulu where each of the five largest ethnic groups—Japanese, Caucasian, Hawaiian, Chinese, and Filipinos . . . is more heavily represented than any other. . . . However, all five of these groups had some residents in all but one of the census tracts in 1960."[31] As a specific illustration, Lind further refers to a former upper-middle-class and exclusively haole residential area that now has owner occupants distributed as follows: five of Japanese ancestry, five haoles, two Portuguese, one Chinese, one Filipino, and four racially mixed.[32]

Ethnoracial Organizations.   There are racially oriented (not necessarily exclusively so) clubs, a major function of which is to celebrate their traditional holidays and ceremonials, much like the mainland Irish St. Patrick's Day parade. There are recreational

[28]Lind: *Hawaii,* p. 120. By permission of the publisher.
[29]Bernhard L. Hormann, "Hawaii's Mixing People," in Noel P. Gist and Anthony Gary Dworkin, *The Blending of Races: Marginality and Identity in World Perspective* (New York: John Wiley & Sons, 1972), pp. 229–230.
[30]Milton Gordon, *Assimilation in American Life* (New York: Oxford University Press, 1964), p. 51. Defined as "a subsociety created by the interaction of the vertical stratification of ethnicity with the horizontal stratification of social class."
[31]Lind, *Hawaii,* pp. 108–109. By permission of the publisher.
[32]*Ibid.,* p. 109.

and civic clubs based somewhat on ethnic descent. Furthermore, there are ethnic religious congregations, some based on Buddhism, and many of various Christian denominations. "But Buddhism has changed in the Hawaiian atmosphere, more often
adopting English hymns similar to those of Christianity, and introducing pews, candles,
and pulpits."[33]

Decline in Discrimination

Ethnoracial discrimination has been formally illegal, and tradition has long made it
bad manners to express racial slurs publicly. Historically, both discrimination and
prejudice were revealed most markedly when one by one, the immigrant groups, after
having moved from plantation to city, began to push upward occupationally and outward from their "ghettos." The earlier-arriving immigrant groups, which achieved
higher status, manifested prejudice toward the next-comers; furthermore, the more
successful members of large ethnic minorities showed prejudice toward the lower-
status subgroups of their own ethnic lineage. Racial discrimination, in such areas as
housing, business, religion, and relationships with the Armed Forces, has been much
more subtle than that practiced on the mainland, and much more easily "broken"
through economic pressure.[34] The upward socioeconomic mobility of the immigrant
Asians, the residential dispersion, and the extensive intermarriage all support the
overall claim that Hawaii's racial situation is one of the "best" in the world.

Our discussion of the rise of the non-haoles indicates that in the main, Hawaii has
now reached assimilation on the basis of structural ethnoracial pluralism. This broad
generalization, however, applies most accurately to the adjustment of the larger,
earlier-arriving immigrant minorities such as the Chinese and Japanese, rather than to
that of the smaller, later-arriving minorities such as the Filipinos and Puerto Ricans.

Recent In-Migration from Asian Areas and Samoa[35]

Hawaii had substantial in-migration from various Asian areas and Samoa from 1965
to 1975, creating additional health and financial problems and also some degree of
interethnic conflict. During this ten-year period, immigrants included 30,651 Filipinos,
4,748 Koreans, and 3,338 Chinese. A substantial number of Samoan American nationals also in-migrated. The state conducted a special study in order to assist in
developing plans for coping with the influx. Concerning health, most of the new cases
of tuberculosis during the 1965–1974 period occurred among immigrants from the
Philippines, Korea, Taiwan, and Hong Kong.[36] Most of the new leprosy cases during the
1969–1973 period occurred among those from the Philippines and Samoa.[37] In regard
to welfare, the study found that applicants for public assistance increased between July,

[33]Walter Kolarz, "The Melting Pot in the Pacific," in Social Process in Hawaii, 19, 1955, pp.
23–26.
[34]"Our Race Relations," Honolulu Advertiser (Sept. 16, 1967).
[35]Discussion of this topic is based on An Analysis of Impact of Immigration on State Services,
University of Hawaii Center for Governmental Development, Honolulu, Hawaii, Oct. 1975. We
use the term "in-migration" rather than "immigration" because Samoan migrants had the status of
American nationals.
[36]Ibid., pp. 19–20.
[37]Ibid., pp. 19–21.

1971, and January, 1973, as follows: Filipinos, 2,169 percent; Samoans, 555 percent; Chinese, Japanese, and Koreans, 304 percent. By contrast, Hawaiian-born relief applicants over the same period dropped by one-third.[38] Aside from these practical problems, there were broader sociological implications. The new immigration upset the stable adjustment that Hawaii's ethnoracial groups had made to each other. For example, "Altercations have occurred between immigrant students and local born students in the schools . . ."[39] The influx may postpone the possibility of the "neo-Hawaiianization" of the islands' peoples.

Blacks in Hawaii

The presence of a small number of blacks in Hawaii might serve as a further test of the society's racial tolerance. A few hundred blacks lived in the territory before World War II. They were often referred to as *Haol-ellele*—black haoles. The 9,416 blacks in Hawaii in 1976 included former servicemen who chose to remain there after their military service. Hawaii's blacks moved more or less directly into occupations above the lowest levels. While Smith Street in Honolulu was considered a black area, the blacks were scattered in other areas appropriate to their economic status. Soon after World War II there were some indications that blacks were thought of as less desirable neighbors by other Hawaiian ethnics. For example, a study of ethnic preferences of landlords found more prejudice against blacks as tenants than against any other ethnic group.[40] In the final test of racial tolerance—intermarriage—it is noteworthy that in the 1970–1974 period out of 1,065 black grooms 631 (59.2 percent) outmarried, as did 77 (15.1 percent) of 511 black brides.[41] For both black men and black women, the largest share of outmarriages was to whites (for men, 226, or 35.8 percent of the outmarriages; for women, 49, or 63.6 percent), followed by Hawaiians or part-Hawaiians. There was a tendency for blacks to marry members of more recent immigrant groups, such as Samoans or Filipinos, rather than members of the more established Asian groups, such as the Chinese or Japanese.[42]

To sum up, it appears that "mild" manifestations of prejudice against blacks by both white and yellow Hawaiians has existed, but not enough to greatly affect the Islands' reputation for racial tolerance. However, the black component has been small, and there are no indications that it will increase greatly in size in the future. A better test of Hawaii's racial tolerance would be provided if blacks substantially increased their migration to the state.

The Changing Position of the Haoles

The rise of the Asian-descended peoples of Hawaii has qualified the power position of the haoles particularly in politics and government. This raises the question as to

[38]*Ibid.*, p. 125.
[39]*Ibid.*, p. 13.
[40]Harry V. Ball and Douglas S. Yamamura, "Ethnic Discrimination and the Market Place: A Study of Landlords Preferences in a Polyethnic Community," *American Sociological Review,* Vol. 25, 1950, No. 5 pp. 687–694.
[41]State of Hawaii Department of Health Annual Report, 1976, Tables 45, 46, 50, 52, and 59.
[42]*Ibid.* For a comparison of black-white intermarriage rates in Hawaii and on the mainland, we give the Hawaiian figures here: 21.2 percent of black grooms in 1970–1974 married whites, as did 9.6 percent of black brides.

whether haoles are any longer a dominant group as they clearly were up to World War II. To assess their position requires examining the internal structure of the haole component. Greatest prestige accrues to descendants of the nineteenth-century Euro-Americans—the *Kamaainas*—some of whose forebears were members of the earlier Hawaiian aristocracy. Control of much of the land and the larger businesses was held by some of this group together with other haoles. In Simpich's discussion of the ownership and control of land, agriculture, and other economic enterprises, the names mentioned were almost exclusively Euro-American.[43]

However, in more recent years control has been more widely shared. Financiers and other businessmen on the mainland and those belonging to Hawaii's various "minority groups" have had increasing influence in Hawaiian economic affairs. For example, the Board of Trustees of the Bishop Estate, which in 1970 owned about 10 percent of all the land of the islands, has included a Chinese, a Japanese, and native Hawaiians (part-Hawaiians), as well as haoles. Estate income was willed by Mrs. Bernice Pauahi Bishop, a Hawaiian princess, for the purpose of educating native Hawaiian children. The Trustees are appointed by the Hawaiian Supreme Court. The failure to appoint more people of native Hawaiian ancestry to the Board has given impetus to the new nativistic movement among Hawaiians.[44]

The decreasing influence of the haoles in Hawaiian economic life combined with the increasing numbers of white lower status and "beachcomber" segments has had the effect of lowering the prestigious image of the haoles as a whole. Many of the more successful and conventional non-haoles looked down upon, and showed prejudice toward, less successful haoles. While a small number of upper-class haoles still share in the domination of the economy, white visibility as such no longer automatically carries with it superior status.

The impact of the current haole influence upon politics will depend on the extent to which the now widely class-ranging haoles tend to act politically as an ethnic block or incline to identify with their actual class interest.

The presence in Hawaii at any given time of the two large aggregates of mainland people—the tourists and the military personnel and their descendents—requires assessment.

The Military.   Hawaii has had a military establishment ever since annexation in 1898, the size of which was overwhelming during the World War II years, and which has remained at substantial numbers in the years since. In 1976 there were 56,000 military personnel and 67,000 military dependents, together constituting 14 percent of the resident population of Hawaii.[45] Most of the military personnel and their dependents living there have been mainlanders. Romanzo Adams regarded this as a serious threat to the benign race mores of the territory even before Pearl Harbor.[46] Military establishments generally are isolated from the larger community about them, and at the officer level, status conscious. As everywhere, homeless enlisted men seek

[43]Simpich, *The Anatomy of Hawaii*, Chs. 4 and 5.

[44]We gratefully acknowledge reports from several meetings where Hawaiian nativist groups have voiced a militant stance in connection with the Bishop Estate matter, sent to us by Professor Raymond E. Sakumoto of the University of Hawaii. Discussion of the Bishop Estate is also based on Simpich, *The Anatomy of Hawaii*, pp. 127–132.

[45]*The Population of Hawaii, 1976: Statistical Report 119*, State of Hawaii, Department of Planning and Economic Development, April 2, 1977.

[46]Romanzo Adams, "The Unorthodox Race Doctrine of Hawaii," in *Race and Culture Contacts*, E. B. Reuter, ed. (New York: McGraw-Hill Book Co., 1934), p. 159.

association with local girls and some intergroup tension emerges. Lind's appraisal of this phenomenon in Hawaii is that on the one hand, bearing in mind the economic gain that the military brings to the Islands, "Islanders have sometimes compromised with their local code of racial equality," and on the other hand, service personnel have often adjusted to local mores—even to the point of marrying non-haoles and permanently residing in Hawaii.[47] Simpich maintains that the military authorities remain aloof from Hawaiian affairs other than those directly involving their work.[48]

Tourists. It is estimated that there was an average of 78,500 tourists in 1976.[49] The tourist influx each year inevitably has some influence on the Islands' race relations. The tourist, like the military personnel, often holds mainland racial attitudes; but, contrary to the military, can better afford to express these attitudes freely. As Lind writes, "Theoretically, therefore, the tourists afford a sort of pipeline for the introduction of mainland conceptions of race relations, and the Islanders economically dependent on their patronage, notably taxi drivers and hotel operators, tend to 'play up' these imported ideas."[50] He further observes that the tourist in search of new experience and in an uninhibited vacation mood often discards his usual prejudices for the time being at least.

> One of the paradoxical aspects of tourism is that the individuals who are most careful to preserve the conventionally defined distances between themselves and other ethnic or racial groups at home frequently become most enamoured with persons of these same or other out-groups in the permissive atmosphere of Hawaii.[51]

The Hawaiians

Ending the discussion of ethnic-racial peoples in Hawaii with a consideration of the group that in terms of pure native lineage is nearly extinct may seem unusual. But two considerations suggest it.[52] First, it is vestiges of native culture that give Hawaii its main cultural flavor, however genuine or superficial these vestiges may be, symbolized by the word "Aloha." Second, within the Hawaiian group has developed one of the newest manifestations of ethnic "nativism," with organized efforts to revive pride in ancestry and to protect and improve the position of the Hawaiians (mostly mixed bloods) who personally identify with the Hawaiian subgroup.

More superficial aspects of the native culture—dances, native foods, and the like—are exploited by the tourist business, which employs extensively persons of Hawaiian ancestry as "entertainers and tour guides, presumably because of the 'spontaneity of their aloha' and their cheerful dispositions for the deception of gullible tourists. . . ."[53]

---

[47]A. W. Lind, in Jitsuichi Matsuoka and Preston Valien, *Race Relations: Problems and Theory* (Chapel Hill, N.C.: University of North Carolina Press, 1961), p. 76.

[48]Simpich, *The Anatomy of Hawaii,* p. 270.

[49]*The Population of Hawaii, 1976: Statistical Report 119,* State of Hawaii, Department of Planning and Economic Development, April 2, 1977.

[50]Lind, in Matsuoka and Valien, *Race Relations,* pp. 73–74.

[51]Lind, *Hawaii,* pp. 36–37. By permission of the publisher.

[52]It is of interest to note that the only ethnic subgroup to which Lind in *Hawaii* devotes a separate chapter is the Hawaiians, Ch. 4, "Folk People in an Industrialized World."

[53]Lind, *Hawaii,* p. 77. By permission of the publisher.

However, a more general Hawaiian Renaissance has developed in the 1970s having several purposes: to revitalize interest in native Hawaiian culture through such means as research, Hawaiian studies programs, and publishing a Hawaiian dictionary; to upgrade the generally low image of the Hawaiians by calling public attention to the increasing number achieving higher educational levels in other areas than the arts with which Hawaiians have usually been identified; to improve the political position of the native Hawaiians.[54] Dr. George Kanahele reported that members of other ethnic groups have shown considerable interest in this Renaissance movement, especially university students.

Summary

From annexation as a territory by the United States to 1940, intergroup relations assumed a form of polyethnic stratification in which haoles were dominant and the other ethnics were minorities. The ethnic stratification system was considerably fused with the class system. Since World War II, Hawaii has moved toward a coordinate ethnoracial pluralistic form of assimilation. The composition of the subethnic group is based on some degree of option on the part of the legion of persons who have mixed racial lineage. This ethnic pluralism is, however, more structural than cultural. Identification with and association with members of the same ethnic groups in primary (personal) as distinct from secondary (impersonal) relations, rather than behavior and attitude related to their ancestral heritage, are what provides their subethnic unity. The current "nativistic" revival among a segment of the 10 percent or less of the state's population that is considered Hawaiian does not appear likely to disturb Hawaii's general ethnoracial pattern. Hawaii's *peoples* may not for a considerable time become Hawaii's *people* in the *ethnoracial* sense, but they are already "all American" in the *nationality* sense.

The major current factor that has potential for altering interpeople relations is the recent greater proportion of the haole population. However, the long-established and institutionalized democracy in which "racism" has low salience and the continuing intermarriage of haoles with non-white Hawaiians, even if at a somewhat lower rate, points toward the continuance of Hawaii's reputation for intergroup tolerance.

Suggested Readings

Adams, Romanzo. *Interracial Marriage in Hawaii.* New York: The Macmillan Co., 1937.
    While primarily concerned with intermarriage, the book contains much material on intergroup relations in Hawaii from the beginning of Euro-American contact to the mid-1930s.

[54]George Kanahele, "Hawaiian Renaissance," *Star-Bulletin and Advertiser,* Honolulu, April 17, 1977, pp. 1-1, 1-3. Dr. Kanahele is president of the Hawaiian Music Foundation and author of books on Hawaiian matters.

Chaplin, George, and Paige, Glenn D., eds. *Hawaii 2000: Continuing Experiment in Anticipatory Democracy*. Honolulu: The University Press of Hawaii, 1973.

Extensive report of an advisory committee appointed by Governor Burns in 1969 to plan for the future of the state in such areas as the economy, housing and transportation, science and technology, education, the arts, and the quality of personal life.

Gallimore, Ronald; Boggs, Joan Whitehorn; and Jordan, Cathie. *Culture, Behavior, and Education: A Study of Hawaiian-Americans*. Beverly Hills, California: Sage Publications, 1974.

A study of the socialization of Hawaiian-American youth in a village community in Oahu.

Hormann, Bernhard L. "Hawaii's Mixing People," in Gist, Noel P., and Dworkin, Anthony Gary. *The Blending of Races: Marginality and Identity in World Perspective*. New York: Wiley-Interscience, 1972, Ch. 11.

Discussion of racially and ethnically mixed people in Hawaii and their search for identity.

Kinloch, Graham C. "Race, Socio-Economic Status, and Social Distance in Hawaii," in *Sociology and Social Research,* 57, January, 1973, pp. 156–167.

Studies the social distance or prejudice between Hawaiian ethnic groups using socioeconomic status and cultural viability as independent variables.

Lind, Andrew. *Hawaii's Japanese*. Princeton: Princeton University Press, 1948.

Useful for comparing the Japanese experience in Hawaii during World War II and its aftermath with the Japanese American experience on the mainland.

Norbeck, Edward. *Pineapple Town*. Berkeley: University of California Press, 1959.

An anthropological study of a pineapple plantation community in Hawaii.

Simpich, Frederick, Jr. *Anatomy of Hawaii*. New York: Coward, McCann & Geoghegan, 1971.

Describes the "establishment" in Hawaii, the business community, mass media, and political parties, and the increasing roles of ethnic minorities within the power structure. Include chapters on tourists and the military presence in Hawaii.

Wright, Theon. *The Disenchanted Isles*. New York: Dial Press, 1972.

Discussion of how a coalition of ethnic minorities achieved political power in Hawaii after World War II.

Young, Nancy F. "Changes in Values and Strategies among Chinese in Hawaii," in *Sociology and Social Research,* 56, January, 1972, pp. 228–241.

Assesses the extent to which Chinese Hawaiians retain traditional Chinese values as opposed to being assimilated into dominant American culture.

The Jews in the United States

The situation of the Jews in various times and places has encompassed every aspect of dominant-minority relations. The history of the Jews in the ancient world included the experience of being a colonially conquered people. Early in the Christian era they were driven out of their homeland. In this period, usually referred to as the Diaspora, or "Dispersion," and in the succeeding eighteen centuries, they were dispersed throughout the whole civilized world. The persistence of segregated colonies of Jews created a pattern of cultural minorities.

The particular historical developments of the twentieth century have added other dimensions to the position of Jews as a minority. When the National Socialist Party undid for Germany all the gains made in western European social thought since the Age of Enlightenment and exterminated six million Jews, the bonds of identity of Jews throughout the world, which had loosened under two centuries of improved civil status, were reestablished and intensified. The founding of the state of Israel has given many Jews a Jewish political identity and affected the feelings of Jews in other countries.

One cannot consider Jewish-Gentile relations without this historical perspective. It accounts for the fact that Jews have been identified, and have identified themselves at various times and in various places, as a religious minority, an ethnic minority, and a "racial" minority.

The rationale for devoting a special chapter to the Jews as a minority, rather than seeing them simply as members of an established religious group in American society, is this very complexity of identity. Jews have a long history of stabilized minority status throughout the world, in which they performed important functions in the dominant societies surrounding them. Except in conditions of enforced segregation, as in Russia in the late nineteenth century, Jews have incorporated the secular goals of dominant societies, and often major components of the culture. Jews have attenuated visibility, if any (except for some sectarian religious Jews who maintain traditional modes of dress and hairstyle). Yet Jews think of themselves as Jews, and they have, however loose, bonds with other Jews.

THE PROBLEM OF JEWISH IDENTITY

American Jews in the twentieth century have been concerned with the question "Who is a Jew?" Barron cites the frequency with which this has been discussed in general and in Jewish periodicals and other publications, as well as how difficult the problem of definition has been for the Israeli government.[1]

---

[1] Milton L. Barron, "Ethnic Anomie," in Milton L. Barron, ed., *Minorities in a Changing World* (New York: Alfred A. Knopf, 1967), p. 26, and note 14.

Are the Jews a Race?

In Chapter 5 we discussed the fact that "race" as used popularly is a social and not a scientific category. We pointed out that present genetic theory accepts only the fact that certain genetic traits are reinforced by isolation and inmarriage. There seems to be little evidence that Jews were ever totally biologically separated from the surrounding peoples. Even initially in the ancient world it is probable that the strong prohibitions against out-marriage were a defense against a considerable intermixture. The goal was preserving the religion, not purity of descent, except as this is characteristic of all tribal peoples.

As the Jews dispersed, the people with whom intermixture occurred became progressively more differentiated in physiognomic features. The Ashkenazim, especially, who were dispersed through northern Europe and from whom most American Jews are descended, are a blending of Nordic and Alpine with eastern Mediterranean traits.[2] The other main branch of Jews, the Sephardim lived long in Spain and the Mediterranean region and through in-marriage tended to develop a degree of physical distinctiveness from other Jews. People of this appearance are often, however, indistinguishable from other Mediterranean peoples. "The wide range of variation between Jewish populations in their physical characteristics and the diversity of the gene frequencies in their blood groups render any unified racial classification for them a contradiction in terms."[3]

Shapiro, who has examined all the research, anthropological and medical, on the biological traits of Jews, makes the following comment:

> I suppose that one of the reasons, aside from political and cultural ones, that incline many people to accept readily the notion that the Jews are a distinct race, is the fact that some Jews are recognizably different in appearance from the surrounding population. That some are not to be identified in this way is overlooked and the tendency, naturally enough, is to extend to all the stereotype of a part. This process occurs in so many other situations it is scarcely surprising that it does here too.[4]

Are American Jews an Ethnic Group?

It is the fashion today to define any minority as an "ethnic group." As we pointed out in Chapter 2, the term *ethnic* refers to shared culture patterns that are a primary focus of group identification. Many Latin Americans, for example, have a strong sense of cultural foci that are different from those of the United States. There is no overall cultural ethos that distinguishes American Jews from other Americans. To examine this question for American Jews one must consider country of origin, status of Jews in the country from which they migrated, degree of open opportunity in the United States at the time and place of immigration, size and clustering of the migrating group.

In the seventeenth century, Sephardic Jews came to the American colonies. These

[2]Carleton S. Coon, "Have the Jews a Racial Identity?" in Isacque Graeber and Steuart Henderson Britt, eds., *Jews in a Gentile World* (New York: The Macmillan Co., 1942), p. 33.
[3]Harry L. Shapiro, *The Jewish People: A Biological History* (Paris: UNESCO, 1960), pp. 74–75.
[4]*Ibid.*

were Dutch citizens, descendants of Spanish and Portuguese Jews who had settled in Holland after the expulsion of the Jews from Spain in 1492. Their descendants in America formed an essentially closed elite society. They have been secularly assimilated for generations; so much so, that when a migration of village Sephardim from Greece and the Balkans took place in the first decades of the twentieth century, they established an assistance program for these "oriental Jews," but initially did not allow them to join their congregations. Throughout their history in America, despite their sense of tradition and separatism, there has been some intermarriage with American Protestants and today increasing intermarriage with the descendants of Ashkenazim.[5] The Balkan Sephardim followed the adaptive patterns of other twentieth-century immigrants, clustering, frequenting their coffee houses, reading their weekly newspaper (in Ladino, the Hebrew-Latin vernacular of their tradition). There are no longer Ladino newspapers and the young third generation in their Long Island suburbs meet their Ashkenazim neighbors at the Jewish Center with little, if any sense of distinctiveness.

The eighteenth and nineteenth centuries saw a considerable migration of Western European Jews, who came at a time of open opportunity, and many of whom had been considerably assimilated into the national cultures of Western Europe from which they migrated. Until the last two decades of the nineteenth century there was real opportunity in rapidly developing America, with little overt discrimination in the large cities, although there were anti-Semitic incidents in the South and the West. The successful German Jewish families maintained close relations with one another, however, intermarried with one another, spoke German at home, and established their pattern of life on the model of the stable, cultured merchant wealth of Europe.[6] These families were, on the whole, strongly behind the movement for Reform Judaism; some were involved in the founding of the Ethical Culture Society, were members of social clubs, felt themselves a true part of American life by the third generation, and were traumatized by the anti-Semitism of the end of the century. They could not in any sense be called an "ethnic" group, although they were forced into a stronger sense of Jewish identity just at the point where they were becoming most American (as contrasted with European).

The largest migration of Jews came between 1880 and 1924. These were primarily from Eastern Europe, where they had largely lived in segregated villages or ghettoes of small cities. Most of them were poor and started life in America as skilled and semi-skilled workers or small entrepreneurs. Because of the enforced segregation under which most of them had lived in Europe, they maintained a folk orthodoxy in religion which so dominated the daily lives of the villages that it gave this group a cultural uniqueness.[7] Glazer and Moynihan point out that as this was the largest migration of Jews to America it has colored Jewish behavior in many parts of the United States and contributed to the larger culture some of its culturally idiomatic language usages, food, etc.[8] This group of Eastern Jews, like the first and second-generation Balkan Sephardim, might have been correctly defined as an ethnic group at one time. They

[5]Steven Birmingham, *The Grandees* (New York: Harper & Row, 1971).
[6]Stephen Birmingham, *"Our Crowd": The Great Jewish Families of New York* (New York: Harper & Row, 1967).
[7]See Mark Zborowski and Elizabeth Herzog, *Life Is With People* (New York: International Universities Press, 1952). Two anthropologists have sensitively reconstructed the life of these Jewish villages: a way of life that was destroyed totally by the Nazi conquest of Eastern Europe.
[8]Glazer and Moynihan, *Beyond the Melting Pot*, (Cambridge, Mass.: M.I.T. Press, 1963), pp. 141–142.

have been, however, economically and geographically mobile, and like other ambitious Americans are concerned with secular status symbols and relatively oblivious to discrimination, either actual or potential within American society.[9]

Jews as a Religious Group

Jews are divided by their religious affiliation into three groups: Orthodox, Reform, and Conservative. Orthodox Jews keep as closely as possible to the Mosaic Law and its Talmudic elaboration. This means that they observe their Sabbath (Saturday) as a day of absolute abstention from the work of the other six days. For example, they refrain on the Sabbath from using transportation, from cooking, and from secular reading. Orthodox Jews keep the traditional dietary laws, which include prohibitions of particular kinds of foods and ritualistic regulations concerning the preparation of food. Within Orthodoxy there are some sects, the largest of which is the Hassidic, that are distinguished by their dress, hair style, and the character of worship. Orthodoxy is characteristic chiefly of the Spanish-Portuguese elite and the older generations of the Eastern European immigrants. In recent decades it has had a revival among Jewish intellectuals.

Reform Judaism is an outgrowth of the philosophy of Enlightenment as it affected Jews primarily in Germany. The Reform movement attempted to adapt Jewish religious life to the dominant Protestant model without losing the essential characteristics of Judaism. This means that it is altered legally and ritualistically, leaving theology unchanged. Some Reform Jews adapted to the dominant culture in observance of Sunday as the Sabbath, and incorporated in their temple services such modifications as organ music, mixed choirs, and the unsegregated seating of women. The Reform movement in the United States has its main center in Cincinnati and has grown among the German Jewish population. Despite some inroads from Conservative Judaism, it is still the dominant pattern for Midwestern and Southern Jews.

Conservative Judaism represents a compromise and is in part a protest against the extreme modification initiated by the Reform Jewish movement. Less rigid than Orthodox Judaism, it has nevertheless retained much of the liturgical emphasis of Orthodoxy and some of the social practices that preserve the distinctiveness of the Jewish community. Conservative Judaism has often been the comfortable solution for the second and third-generation descendants of Orthodox Jews in America.

As with other groups in the United States, Jews have a large segment who are secularized, some to the degree of being completely nonreligious, while others retain a tenuous formal relationship to religion. This is probably most characteristic of metropolitan areas, where religious affiliation is not visible, and among salaried professionals where the career provides out-group contacts and a secular focus on the task to be performed (business bureaucracies, academic bureaucracies, civil service, etc.). Glazer and Moynihan believe that only a minority of New York City Jews belong to synagogues.[10] The rate of conversion to Christianity is claimed to be small, and probably this is correct with regard to baptism and formal affiliation with Christian churches. But it would be difficult to assess how many have sought anonymity in

---

[9]Judith R. Kramer and Seymour Levantman, *Children of the Gilded Ghetto* (New Haven: Yale University Press, 1961).
[10]Glazer and Moynihan, *Beyond the Melting Pot,* p. 142.

membership in sectarian religious groups (Quakers, Christian Scientists, etc.) where baptism is not required and therefore does not symbolically constitute a betrayal of one's heritage.

The Jews Are a Minority

As we have seen, the Jews are not a "race," nor can American Jews be subsumed as an ethnic group. Neither are all people who designate themselves as Jewish members of one or another of the denominations of Judaism. Yet the interplay of historic forces has created a centripetal bond that both operates against total assimilation and creates security and varying degrees of mutuality for its members. To be a minority that does not have its sense of identity rooted in strong subcultural values, or in religion, and that competes successfully and seeks admission to full participation in the larger secular society, puts the group in a particularly vulnerable position. Throughout the history of the Jews, economic success and the acceleration of social integration have been followed by policies and actions against Jews.[11]

THE AMERICAN JEWS

Size and Distribution of the Population

About 3 percent of the American population is Jewish. The five and a half million Jews are about the same number as a decade ago. Their proportion to the rest of the population is gradually declining as the higher reproduction rate of other segments, such as the Spanish-speaking populations, increases.

Approximately 75 percent of the American Jewish population live in large metropolitan areas: Baltimore, Boston, Chicago, Cincinnati, Cleveland, Detroit, Los Angeles, Miami, New York City, Newark, Philadelphia, Pittsburgh, St. Louis, and San Francisco. Nearly half of the Jews in the United States live in the New York metropolitan area (the city and its suburbs). About one-third of the white, non-Puerto Rican population of New York City proper is Jewish.

One stereotype of the Jews has described them as an urban people, and indeed since the decline of feudalism in Europe this has largely been true for Western European Jews. But such a stereotype has implied that they had no roots in the feudal agricultural world. Contemporary research is beginning to discover that there have been a variety of historical ecological *loci* for Jews: they have been landowners, village craftsmen, administrators for feudal estates, and so on. Jews suffered as scapegoats in the transition and uprooting that characterized the collapse of feudalism and the beginning of the modern era. Many of them sought the cities free of feudal control. In this country, however, relatively few moved into agricultural life until the twentieth century, when intensive farming (poultry and dairy farming) opened a channel of opportunity more coherent with the European agricultural practices they had known than the isolated open-country farming of the American expanding West.

---

[11]See for example Merton's discussion of in-group virtues that become out-group vices in Robert K. Merton, "The Self-fulfilling Prophecy," *Social Theory and Social Structure,* rev. ed. (Glencoe, Ill.: The Free Press, 1957), p. 426.

There was greater opportunity for Jews in the larger cities as the migration on the whole coincided with urban growth in the United States; there was also the possibility of association with other Jews, which provided a sense of community, made available marriage partners for sons and daughters, and allowed them to fulfill the historic obligation of a good Jew: community responsibility. For second- and third-generation Jews, and indeed for some first-generation migrants, this sense of obligation has extended beyond the "Jewish community" to a responsibility for the welfare of the larger community of which they were a part.

For the majority of Jews in America who are urban and middle class, there has been positive interaction with dominants, and any differences are differences of nuance and of opportunity. It is true that there are some Jews who can and do live out their lives in an ecological cluster that allows them association only with their own "eth-class."[12] Higher education, and work experience in the open employment market are changing the pattern for young people. We would hypothesize that the degree of definable difference in behavior varies with one or more of the following factors: age as related to recency of migration, socioeconomic status, degree of Jewish traditional religious identification, and ecological clustering.

Jewish Institutional and Organizational Patterns

The Jewish Family.   The cohesiveness of the family is one of the strongest characteristics of the Jewish group. This derives in part from the emphasis in Jewish religion on marriage and family life, as well as adaptations of this tradition in such a practice as early (and, in former times, arranged) marriage, and in part from the mutual aid and protection of the extended kinship. Jewish families on the whole live in the nuclear pattern, keeping in closer touch with their relatives, visiting more frequently, and being more willing to aid a promising relative than is characteristic of the dominant pattern.[13] Among the older generation of eastern European Jews, there is the beloved stereotype of the Jewish mother who will sacrifice everything for her family.

Male and female roles are sharply defined, even though American Jews encourage the education of women and their participation in community affairs. Authority in the family is in the hands of the men. For religious Jews, it is important to have sons, since certain rituals can be carried out only by males. Even where this religious emphasis is no longer stressed, the high valuation of sons seems to persist.

The family not only has had important traditional religious functions to fulfill, it has also been a bulwark for joint economic endeavor. Glazer and Moynihan point out how often Jewish enterprises involve fathers and sons or groups of brothers.[14] There are many such business partnerships, and there are family associations that form investment pools. (This latter is characteristic of the traditional Chinese family system, of

---

[12]The term is one coined by Milton Gordon in *Assimilation in American Life: The Role of Race, Religion and National Origins* (New York: Oxford University Press, 1964).

[13]Stanley R. Brav, *Jewish Family Solidarity: Myth or Fact?* (Vicksburg, Miss.: Nogales Press, 1940).

[14]Glazer and Moynihan, *Beyond the Melting Pot,* p. 154. See also Birmingham, *Our Crowd,* for the involvement of brothers, sons, and sons-in-law in the founding of the great German Jewish fortunes of nineteenth-century America. (Family trees showing descendants and intermarriages are on the end papers of this volume.)

many European bourgeois families, but has not been a characteristic of WASP families in America except at the top financial levels since the imposition of income taxes.)

One of the indices in the past of complete assimilation has been intermarriage between members of the minority and dominants. Because Jews have been with each generation more acculturated to American attitudes and mores there has been an increase of intermarriage. In the past where Jews were sharing the nineteenth-century rewards of the country's rapid development there was a modest degree of intermarriage perhaps in part because there were insufficient marriage partners for Jewish young people, and perhaps in part because the climate was one of euphoria with regard to lack of discrimination against Jews.

A recent study summarized the facts that Jews who intermarry compared with those who in-marry.[15]

1. Jews who intermarry are more likely to have a history of broken homes and lack of contact with the extended family. Jewish men are more favorably disposed toward intermarriage. Intermarrying Jews marry later. Oldest children are least likely to intermarry and youngest children and only children the most likely.

2. Jews living in rural areas and small towns are more likely to intermarry than Jews living in cities. Children of recent residents are more likely to intermarry than children of long-established residents. Jews living in new communities are more likely to intermarry than Jews living in older communities. Reform and unaffiliated Jews are more likely to intermarry than Conservative and Orthodox Jews.

3. Intermarriage seems to appeal to Jews whose socioeconomic positions place them at the periphery of the Jewish community, or outside it. Intermarriage, therefore, is more frequent among the highly upward-mobile members of the salaried professions; Jewish professors and government experts are more likely to intermarry than physicians, dentists, lawyers, business owners. Intermarriage also is more frequent with downward mobility. Small-town Jewish craftsmen, foremen, or other blue-collar workers are more likely to intermarry.

The preponderance of intermarriage is Jewish husbands and Gentile wives (the reverse of the nineteenth-century pattern). Intermarriage rates vary enormously from community to community and little is accomplished in discussing an average national rate. Factors such as size and length of establishment of the Jewish community, comparative opportunity for status, economic success, and freedom of association between the Jewish community and the Gentile world must be considered.

In a study of "Lakeville," an upper-middle-class midwestern suburb, only 50 percent of the sample said they would feel *very unhappy* if their child were to marry a non-Jew. This score is for families who also rate low on a scale favoring integration. In other words, people with a strong group consciousness are the most opposed to intermarriage.

> I want her to stay within our group, just as I did and my husband did. It's a different culture, and a lot of things are involved.[16]

However, when presented with the choice for their children of a loved Gentile as compared with an unloved Jew, 85 percent chose a Gentile. For the generations close to

---

[15]Lewis A. Berman, *Jews and Intermarriage: A Study in Personality and Culture* (New York: Thomas Yoseloff, 1968), Ch. 14, pp. 547–560.
[16]Marshall Sklare and Joseph Greenblum, *Jewish Identity on the Suburban Frontier* (New York: Basic Books, 1967), pp. 308–309.

migration preference for a Jewish marriage is strong enough to choose a lower-occupational status in preference to an equal- or upper-status out-marriage. However, only 1 percent of the families interviewed said they would reject their child if the child out-married. Ninety-three percent said they would try to build a meaningful relationship with the Gentile person.[17]

Occupations. Accurate estimates of the occupational distribution of Jews are difficult to make, since they must be compiled from studies of different localities, where the job classifications are often not comparable. Some data, however, can give an indication of the character of the Jewish labor force.

According to Seligman, it appears that a smaller proportion of the total Jewish population is part of the labor force than is true of the general population. It is suggested that this may be related to such factors as the longer period of schooling for Jewish children, or to the emphasis on the domestic role of women.[18]

The Jewish male labor force in most of the communities for which we have data appears to be higher in proportion to the general population in the employer and self-employed class. Classifications by industry indicate a concentration in the wholesale and retail trades. Although it is a popular belief that Jews are found most frequently in the professions, community studies that provide occupational information show the manufacturing (proprietary and managerial) group greater than the professional in most cases. If we consider the nationwide pattern of Jewish occupations, the exclusive occupational emphasis of Jews on the professions seems to be less than has been generally believed. "In more recent years proprietorship has been of first rank in virtually all the Jewish population studies included here, with clerical occupations second and professional work in third position."[19]

Jews as a group have a higher average age than the rest of the population. Since the older age groups in this country have a higher proportion of professionals, semi-professionals, proprietors, managers, and officials, this is a factor that must be taken into account in considering the proportions of the Jewish labor force in these categories. In the female labor force by 1950 the Jewish urban population approached the proportions found in the general labor force.

Although in the nineteenth and early twentieth century there were prominent Jewish families in finance and industry, there has since been a dispersion. Jewish business fortunes have come from clothing manufacture, merchandizing, and the entertainment field. Since the late 1930s an even wider diversification has taken place to include a range of light manufacturing, real estate, and building.[20]

The Jewish businessman, from the small storekeeper to the newer manufacturer in electronics, has had to find those sectors of the economy that were not preempted by white Protestants. As a historic minority Jews have been alert to these opportunities. The strong family system has enabled them to mobilize capital (even if in small sums).[21] Even in the culture market of publishing, movies, television, theatre, music,

---

[17]*Ibid.,* p. 315.
[18]Ben B. Seligman, *et al.,* "Some Aspects of Jewish Demography," in Marshall Sklare, ed., *The Jews: Social Patterns of an American Group* (Glencoe, Ill.: The Free Press, 1958), pp. 70–78.
[19]*Ibid.,* p. 73.
[20]Glazer and Moynihan, *Beyond the Melting Pot,* p. 151.
[21]*Ibid.,* p. 154.

and architecture, both as producers and consumers they have been interested more in the new than in the old and traditional.[22]

The proportion of working-class Jews is declining, although the institutions within the labor world that they created survive. There is, as is to be expected, a higher proportion of Jews in working-class and lower-middle-class occupations in cities like New York, where there is such a large Jewish population. In cities where they are perhaps 5 percent of the population they are more apt to be in middle- and upper-middle-class occupations.

A study by Herbert Bienstock, Regional Director of the Bureau of Labor Statistics, based on 1967 data, showed 74.9 percent of Jewish high-school students hoping to enter professional and technical jobs, whereas only 20 percent of their fathers had such jobs in 1964. Because of a projected slow rise in professional and technical jobs, the federal analyst urged Jewish organizations to counsel Jewish youths to consider craft skills where the demand and consequent security may be greater. He also suggested that Jewish organizations might provide capital to enable young Jews to develop a trend toward self-employment in accounting, contract services, law, etc.[23]

The Jews in American Politics.   Throughout the nineteenth century Jews could and did participate in any political organization to which their interests inclined them. During the Civil War, Jews were among the partisans of both the North and the South, and within both major parties. The number of Jews before 1880 was so small that they were viewed and viewed themselves as individual voters rather than as group representatives. Western European Jews who participated in European politics at all after restrictions on political participation were removed adhered chiefly to the moderate democratic movements of the times. Much of the same spirit permeated Jewish political positions, whatever the party affiliation, in the United States. In this period they tended to recoil from all extreme movements, such as the radical Abolitionist movement or the Know-Nothing Party.[24]

After 1880, however, the immigrants from eastern Europe were strongly influenced by radical intellectuals, and for a period Jewish workers and their leaders formed the backbone of the anarchist and socialist movements in this country. Partly this was due to an overreaction after the suppression of political liberty they had experienced under the czarist government. "When the Jewish intellectual came to the United States, he was suddenly given an opportunity to theorize openly and to his heart's content. He took full advantage of it: for many years, the Lower East Side [in New York City] was one big radical debating society."[25]

Jews have not only been a voting bloc whose liberal voting pattern has been of great persistence, but, where as in New York City there have been large numbers of Jews, there have been the usual urban political careers. Glazer and Moynihan think the Jewish vote is largely ideological and rarely is influenced by whether or not the candidate is Jewish. They give a series of examples where the Jews of New York have preferred a liberal Catholic or Protestant over a conservative or "party machine" Jew.[26]

---

[22]*Ibid.*, p. 174.
[23]*The New York Times*, June 25, 1972, p. 27.
[24]Werner Cohn, "The Politics of American Jews," in Sklare, ed., *The Jews: Social Patterns of an American Group*, pp. 619–620.
[25]*Ibid.*, p. 629.
[26]Glazer and Moynihan, *Beyond the Melting Pot*, pp. 166–171.

Jewish Organizations. Possibly the Jewish minority is the most highly organized of any group in the United States. The organizations fall into four categories: welfare, fraternal, aid to Israel, antidiscrimination.

The welfare organizations are the oldest. Within the tradition that Jews are responsible for their own people, there were by the beginning of this century agencies to aid migration and agencies in each community to aid families in need, children in trouble, educational foundations, hospitals, and clinics. Jewish welfare agencies have been in the forefront in developing high professional levels of practice and in pioneering new services in health and welfare. Today, although still supported by Jewish funds in a national federation, many agencies have become nonsectarian as far as the clients whom they serve.

The fraternal organizations have mobilized volunteer services of men and women to help meet local community needs, though the organizations are national, with local chapters.

Aid to Israel is carried on by a number of groups with different ideologies and different degrees of commitment to Israel, though a very high percentage of Jews at least buy Israel bonds to help provide capital for development of the country.

In the 1960s "Lakeville" Jews were interviewed as to their degree of support for Israel. Ninety-one percent approved of raising money for Israel, 63 percent thought Jews should influence U.S. foreign policy with regard to Israel. Less than a third (31 percent) belonged to Zionist organizations. Only 14 percent would give Israeli financial need priority over local Jewish causes. Only 1 percent would encourage their children to emigrate to Israel or consider emigrating themselves. On the other hand, nearly 15 percent of Lakeville's Jewish families said they would feel no personal sense of loss if Israel were to be destroyed, and a little over a fourth, however they felt about Israel's survival, thought that the existence of Israel has had a harmful effect on Jewish status and security in the United States.[27]

The antidiscrimination efforts of Jewish organizations have included data gathering and research, publication, and participation in public hearings from grassroots to the Congressional level. Here, too, the data gathering is not limited to Jews, but is concerned with broader aspects of discrimination as it affects all minorities.

Sklare and Greenblum found in "Lakeville" that the highest rate of activity in Jewish organizations was among those who had some degree of religious commitment, though they found no significant difference between strongly observant and mildly religious individuals in the support of Jewish organizations. Furthermore, they suggest that for some who are nonreligious, organizational participation provides a secular alternative mode of identification with the Jewish community.[28]

THE JEWISH COMMUNITY

Wherever any considerable number of Jewish people reside in an American community there has developed a separate Jewish substructure, usually called the "Jewish community," which has a characteristic relation to the larger Gentile community. Sometimes these are actual ecological communities that have developed through

---

[27]Sklare and Greenblum, *Jewish Identity,* pp. 226–228.
[28]*Ibid.,* p. 261.

residential discrimination or self-clustering; in other cases residence is dispersed, and the network of social and organizational relationships constitutes the Jewish community. There have been many studies of Jewish communities in different parts of the United States. Over 200 communities are affiliated with the Council of Jewish Federations and Welfare Funds, many of which have been studied from one point of view or another.[29]

A large percentage of American Jews have middle-class status and, like the rest of the American urban middle class, Jews are moving to the suburbs. Let us study briefly the origin and growth of a typical suburban Jewish community.[30]

The Jewish Community of Park Forest

Park Forest is a post-World War II planned community south of Chicago. The men of the community were earning from $4,000 to $10,000 a year in 1949, when the study was made. Among 1,800 families, about 25 percent of them Catholic, the Jewish community numbered just under 150 families. Of these, about twenty (fifteen of them mixed marriages) rejected all relationships with the formal Jewish community. The Jewish group was made up of young, highly educated, second-generation Jews of Eastern European parentage, most of whom had achieved or were likely to achieve with continued prosperity middle-class income status. Park Forest Jews lived like other Park Foresters. They wore the same fashions, ate the same food except on special occasions, and participated with other Park Foresters in the culture of the "young moderns." The Jewish families were scattered, with rarely two Jewish families in adjacent houses.

Soon after these young Jewish families arrived they aligned themselves in a number of cliques, which in a remarkably short time formed a network through which news and gossip could be communicated. Gans points out that "The Jews form a cohesive in-group and tend to behave differently toward a member of the in-group than toward a non-Jew, in many cases reserving the intimacy of friendship for the former."[31] He then describes the process by which Jews attempted to recognize other Jews. They were aided in this by a Protestant minister who conducted a religious survey and informed interested Jews who the other Jews in their neighborhood were. Although there was no automatic progression from recognition to acquaintance to friendship, in many cases the desire to associate with other Jews was implied from the first. In general, it was a matter of only four to eight weeks before people said they had friends whom they saw regularly.

Sociability patterns did not become exclusively Jewish, but in about half the cases it was pointed out that "best friends" were Jewish. This was defended on the ground that sociability as a primary leisure activity should permit relaxation and self-expression, which was more likely when Jews associated with Jews.

The development of the formal community began with the organization of a B'nai B'rith lodge and a chapter of the National Council of Jewish Women. Attendance and active participation in the Council of Jewish Women was soon greater than in B'nai

[29]See Sklare, *The Jews: Social Patterns of an American Group,* for articles based on the reports of many of these studies.
[30]Herbert J. Gans, "The Origin and Growth of a Jewish Community in the Suburbs: A Study of the Jews of Park Forest," in Sklare, pp. 205 ff.
[31]*Ibid.,* p. 210.

B'rith, reflecting, according to Gans, the women's greater desire for Jewish companion-ship.[32] Nearly a year after the new suburb of Park Forest had been occupied, some of the leaders in B'nai B'rith met one evening to discuss setting up a Sunday school, which was to be part of a synagogue, either Reform or Conservative. The women in the Council, however, refused to help form a congregation and insisted that all they needed at the time was a Sunday school. Thus began four months of discussion, argument, and conflict.

> In other groups such conflicts can often be explained in terms of power struggles between two socio-economic strata or ideological factions. In the Jewish community, however, they may signify conflicts between groups representing different stages in the ethnic adjustment to American life. .
> . . In Park Forest, where almost everyone is native born and acculturated to a large and similar extent, the history of the conflict over the Sunday school may be explained as the ascendency of a new type of formal Jewish community, the *child-oriented* one. This contrasts with the traditional Jewish community, which may be described as adult-oriented.[33]

The child-oriented group was successful in creating a school with a historical ap-proach to Judaism rather than a liturgical and theological one. The Sunday school thus became an institution through which to transmit norms of ethnic culture and symbols of identification, whereas the home and family were regulated according to secular, middle-class behavior patterns. Some parents, in expressing their reasons for choosing this kind of Sunday school, pointed out that a Jewish child should know how to identify himself in relation to his Catholic and Protestant playmates. A number wanted their children to know the Jewish tradition so that they could later make a choice as to whether or not they wished to remain Jewish. Others saw Sunday school as providing a defense against later psychological hardships arising out of the minority position of Jews. And some parents were concerned about the fact that, although they selected their intimate friends from among the Jewish group, their children chose playmates without regard to ethnic or religious origin. Although a synagogue was not yet es-tablished at the time of Gans' study, there was already considerable discussion of one. The reasons for wanting a synagogue were not entirely religious. For many it was to be a symbol of group respectability or of Jewish solidarity.[34]

This suburban community of young Americans reveals facets of Jewish accultura-tion that contrast with the Jewish subcommunities of a generation earlier. Perhaps this is best shown in the adaptations made in the Park Forest congregation finally es-tablished in 1951. The congregation was designated as "Eastern European Reform." It combined a permissive attitude toward practices in the home that involve the sacrifice of secular pleasures (food restrictions and so forth), Conservative ceremonies, Hebrew reading, and responsive singing. The temple kitchen was not kosher but did not serve pork. The rabbi, who was from Eastern European background, had been trained as an Orthodox rabbi but later had changed to Reform. A lecture series on secular Jewish

[32]*Ibid.*, p. 213. However, it should be pointed out that this greater organizational activity of women is a general suburban pattern.
[33]*Ibid.*, p. 215.
[34]*Ibid.*, pp. 224–225.

topics attracted good attendance. Otherwise, large attendance occurred mainly on the high holy days.

The example of Park Forest shows that there is a reality to the concept of "the Jewish community" which is bound up with sentiment, preferences, feelings of security, and also with organizational patterns.

The status structure within the Jewish community once was marked by sharp divisions of prestige, paralleling the nineteenth-century criteria of prestige in the dominant society: date of migration, wealth, country of origin. Status differentiation has become more blurred today: this is partially due to the mobility of the descendants of the later migrants, partially due to greater Jewish solidarity evoked by the anti-Semitism of the twentieth century in Europe and America.

GENTILE ATTITUDES TOWARD JEWS

The history of Jewish-Gentile relations is so old, has been so fluctuating, and has been clouded by so much dramatic, desperate, and barbaric action against Jews, even in our own time, that we have little real data about ordinary contacts. Nevertheless, some research can contribute preliminary insights.

Robin Williams and associates, of Cornell University, studied attitudes toward minorities in small cities in four regions of the United States. He and his team asked WASPS whether they had reservations about having various minority members as neighbors, work associates, members of organizations they belonged to. Those objecting to Jews were very small percentages.[35] (See Table 17-1.)

TABLE 17-1   Regional Attitudes Toward Jews

Those Objecting	Northeast	High Ethnic Industrial Town	Small Southern City
As neighbors	2%	6%	3%
As work associates	3%	- 4%	5%
As organizational members	2%	- 4%	8%

There are only two important figures in this: high ethnic communities don't want "outsiders" as neighbors, though they are more than willing to have them as work associates and in organizations (assumedly secular, i.e., labor or civic). The small Southern city doesn't mind neighbors as much as it minds work associates and organizational membership. Is it afraid of competitive leadership and strength? The study hazards no explanation.

Williams found Jews in small cities bicultural, rather than marginal, having strong feelings of Jewish identity and high levels of activity in both formal and informal community activities. Overwhelmingly, he says, Jews feel themselves accepted without dis-

[35]Robin Williams, Jr., *Strangers Next Door* © 1969. Table 17-1 reprinted by permission of Prentice-Hall, Inc., Englewood Cliffs, N.J.

crimination. This self-image, however, is not fully in accord with the conceptions held by Gentile *leaders* in the small communities. About 80 percent of these subscribe to prejudicial stereotypes of Jews. "Those who had close Jewish acquaintances regarded them as 'different'; 'not the Brooklyn type.'" Nevertheless, he found that those who had repeated close contact and personal association often altered their image and evaluation of Jews more generally.[36]

Williams broke down his WASP informant sample according to a model of stereotyped attitudes to separate bigots from tolerants. In a sample of those classified as bigots the question was asked, "Which of the following groups are most threatening: Jews, Negroes, foreign born, Catholics, labor unions, big business?" Forty-five percent of the sample ranked Jews as the most threatening. (The next highest ranking was labor unions, and the lowest was Catholics).[37] It seems obvious from this finding that the fear and resentment here is that of threat to an established set of assumptions on which status rests in the face of new competitors. Whether individual Jews were in fact competing is irrelevant—they were seen as a risingly successful "other."

The real upsurge in feeling against Jews as economic competitors appears to have started after 1900, reaching a high peak in the decades following World War I. In Severson's study of discriminatory want ads, one finds that beginning in 1911 "ads requesting 'Christians only' or 'Gentiles only' appeared at the rate of 0.3 per 1,000, rose to 4 percent in 1921, to 8.8 in 1923, to 13.3 in 1926; averaged 11 percent from 1927 to 1931; dropped to 4.8 percent in 1931, and then rose to 9.4 percent in 1937.[38] Severson's thesis is that it was not immigration per se, or cultural conflict, that developed this latent prejudice but rather that the particular exigency of the occasion was the coming into the clerical labor market, particularly of girls into typing and stenography, of second-generation East European immigrants.

ANTI-SEMITISM IN THE UNITED STATES

Anti-Semitism as a public issue in the United States is usually dated from 1887. There had been hostile incidents against Jews in various localities from time to time but these were brief local affairs. But in 1877 when the New York banker Joseph Seligman wrote for reservations at the Grand Union Hotel in Saratoga Springs, New York—a fashionable resort hotel where he and his family had often stayed before—he was informed that the hotel had adopted a new policy and "did not accept Israelites." Seligman's had been one of the banking houses that had floated the United States government bond issue of 1870–1871, which, in the words of President Grant, "established American credit abroad,"[39] after the financial drain of the Civil War. Joseph Seligman was on the platform at President Grant's inauguration, attended the inaugural ball, and was a frequent guest at the White House. He was one of the earliest members of the Union League Club of New York. His refusal at the Grand Union made the national press from coast to coast.[40]

---

[36]*Ibid.*, p. 304.
[37]*Ibid.*, p. 106.
[38]A. L. Severson, "Nationality and Religion in Newspaper Ads," in *American Journal of Sociology,* Jan., 1939, p. 545.
[39]Birmingham, *Our Crowd,* p. 104.
[40]*Ibid.*, Ch. 18, pp. 141–150.

There were many factors in this incident. One was the personal and political animosity between Seligman and the new owner of the Hotel, Judge Hilton. Another was that this hotel was no longer the favorite of the most elite families who had been fellow guests in earlier days with the Seligmans, and the question has been raised as to whether or not Hilton was attempting to recruit a new clientele that was less secure, more *arriviste,* and therefore more anxious to prove their exclusiveness. Whatever the weight of these various factors, the incident and its publicity precipitated a polarization and brought to the surface much latent anti-Semitism. Birmingham thinks the results of the Saratoga Springs incident, in bringing into the open anti-Jewish attitudes, broke Joseph Seligman's spirit. He died within a year.[41]

Anti-Semitism rose in the ensuing decades, probably reaching its peak in the first half of the 1920s, but persisting in organized efforts until World War II. Baltzell, in *The Protestant Establishment,* has traced the role of intellectual and social forces in its development. He delineates the anti-Semitism of the aging Henry Adams, who saw the Jews as epitomizing all the evil of industrial America, in which people of his own stratum (the old Protestant leadership of the New England merchant and scholarly occupations) had lost power and took refuge in caste-like exclusiveness. Early American social scientists at the beginning of the twentieth century reflected both the influence of European racist thought and the mistrust of growing urbanism and "business ethic," which they linked to industrialization and immigration.[42]

The Populist movement, extolling the virtues of homogeneous rural life, viewed the declining importance of the rural segment of America as due to the manipulations of urban financial power, and the stereotype of the Jewish international financier, involving a conspiracy of power (and usury), emerged. Anti-Semitism was a factor in many pressures to restrict immigration. The fact that anti-Semitism increased concurrently with the large migration of Eastern European Jews after 1880 led many people, Gentiles and established Jews, to see the migration as the *cause* of anti-Semitism. Whereas this rationalization may have been important in the minds of some who saw the Eastern Jews as more strange and even "unassimilable," as we have seen, anti-Semitism had emerged before this migration began and was rooted in other problems and anxieties associated with social change.

Perhaps the most dramatic example of this is the mob hysteria stirred up by a Southern Populist leader against Leo Frank, a young Jewish factory manager in Georgia, which culminated in his being lynched (August 17, 1915).[43] Mr. Frank came from New York City. He was a graduate of Cornell University. He married into an established circle of Jewish business and banking in Atlanta, and symbolized the alien world of big business and big city.

It is a commonplace that when antiminority feeling is running high, sexual charges are part of the picture. (This was true of anti-Catholic charges of the immorality of priests and nuns.) Leo Frank was charged with the murder of a very young girl who was employed in his factory. The evidence was of the flimsiest and the trial was conducted with a mob milling about outside. Frank was convicted. His case was

---

[41]*Ibid.,* p. 148.
[42]E. Digby Baltzell, *The Protestant Establishment: Aristocracy and Caste in America* (New York: Random House, 1964), pp. 87–93.
[43]Harry Golden, *A Little Girl Is Dead* (New York: Alfred A. Knopf, 1965). See also "Why Frank was Lynched," *Forum Magazine,* Dec., 1916, p. 678.

brought to the Supreme Court, where the conviction was upheld, Mr. Justice Holmes writing the dissenting opinion. The Governor of Georgia ruined his political career by commuting the sentence. A day later a mob broke into the jail and transported Frank to another part of the state where he was lynched. Oscar and Mary Handlin feel that the commutation of the sentence appeared to the anti-Semites as proof of the influence on the governor of big business and money.[44] Not the least interesting aspect of the whole case was the cautious attitude of many Jews. On the whole, initially, the Jewish community of Atlanta was frightened. There were five prominent Jews on the grand jury that indicted Frank. Only after the case became a national issue were more Atlanta Jews willing to come forward in his defense. The fear was there that the national attention would create anti-Semitism where there had been none. The Georgia Chamber of Commerce, in a letter to the *New York Times*, denied any anti-Semitism in Atlanta or any prejudice against industrial employers. The *Times,* in an editorial, pointed out that Atlanta was no different from any other American city.[45]

In considering the Leo Frank case it is important to compare the caution of established Jews of Atlanta (and to a degree elsewhere) with the fact that the great Negro leader of the same period, Booker T. Washington, refused to join the newly created NAACP, for he feared for the ultimate result of a militant Negro organization.

Anti-Semitism similar to that known in Europe, political in its implications, more organized, and more vitriolic in its propaganda, began to arise about 1917. In the few years following the close of World War I, large quantities of anti-Semitic literature identifying Jews with the rising European revolutionary ideology appeared; the new Ku Klux Klan arose in the North, with its generally antiforeign orientation including anti-Semitism; the Fellowship Forum widely distributed copies of the forged Protocols of the Elders of Zion; and Henry Ford commenced his anti-Semitic campaign through the publication of the *Dearborn Independent.*[46]

That these new anti-Semitic activities had an effect is indicated by an increase in various incidents, of which the following are illustrative:

> The board of directors of a Milwaukee golf club asked eight Jewish charter members to resign.
>
> The secretary of the Chamber of Commerce in St. Petersburg, Florida, announced that the time had come to make St. Petersburg "a 100 per cent American gentile city."
>
> Several large real estate concerns in New Jersey, New York, Georgia, and Florida were found to have restricted new subdivisions against Jewish occupancy.
>
> Of more than passing interest in this period was President Lowell's graduation address at Harvard in June 1922, in which he advocated quotas against Jews. While the trustees of Harvard later rejected this suggestion, it was painfully apparent that the quota system was spreading.[47]

---

[44]Oscar and Mary F. Handlin, *Danger in Discord: Origins of Anti-Semitism in the United States* (New York: Anti-Defamation League of B'nai B'rith, 1959).
[45]*The New York Times,* March 5, 1914, p. 10.
[46]Donald S. Strong, *Organized Anti-Semitism in America* (Washington, D.C.: American Council on Public Affairs, 1941), p. 15.
[47]Carey McWilliams, *A Mask for Privilege,* pp. 38–39. By permission of the publisher Little, Brown & Co.

Abating somewhat during the late 1920s, anti-Semitism rose again in the early 1930s as the Depression intensified. Strong has indicated that there were 121 organizations actively spreading anti-Semitic propaganda in the 1933–1940 period.[48] In the late 1930s anti-Semitism began to be used for the first time openly in political campaigns. The manager of the nativist third party in the 1936 Presidential election is quoted by McWilliams as stating, "the trouble with this country now is due to the money powers and Jewish politicians."[49]

While the sweeping victory of Franklin D. Roosevelt in 1936 temporarily set back the agitation, it resumed with new intensity in the late 1930s and continued until Pearl Harbor. Involved in this activity were the Christian Front, led by Father Charles Coughlin, and the Silver Shirts, directed by William Pelley. In a period of nineteen months before July 31, 1938, Pelley mailed approximately three and a half tons of anti-Semitic propaganda from his headquarters. All of this organization and propaganda obviously cost a good deal of money, and though the program was conducted by relatively unimportant people, it occasionally received support in high places. For example, McWilliams quotes Congressman John Rankin as stating to Congress that "Wall Street and a little group of our international Jewish brethren are still attempting to harass the President and Congress into plunging us into the European War."[50]

During World War II overt manifestations of anti-Semitism disappeared. They were considered inimical to the war effort and were discouraged by the government. Furthermore, the ideological inconsistency of supporting anti-Semitism while fighting the arch Jew-hater, Adolph Hitler, had some deterrent effect. In the few months following the end of World War II, however, the Fair Employment Practices Committee noted an increase in discrimination against Jews in employment.

Two decades later in a nationwide study it was found that there was a marked decline in support for discrimination in the public, secular sphere:[51] 90 percent of the respondents felt people should be employed who were the most capable of doing the job, without discrimination (against Jews, in this instance); 86 percent did not object to having Jewish neighbors, and 80 percent would not object to a Jewish president of the United States. This data, collected in 1964, did not portray such a clear picture in areas of more subtle attitudes toward Jewish participation and attitudes. More than a quarter of the sample defended exclusion of Jews from private clubs; and over 80 percent felt that Christmas carols should be taught in public school even where there were Jewish children in the school. Both of these latter issues have created some public attention.

In this same study the authors examined acceptance of some common Jewish stereotypes. They found that these are interrelated to create a portrait of a "mythical" Jew, and that such simplistic anti-Semitism is closely correlated with level of education achieved.[52]

Although structured anti-Semitism declined, the social changes and the protests of the '60s created a climate of anxiety for many and inevitably some hostility was directed

---

[48]Strong, *Organized Anti-Semitism in America*, pp. 146–147.
[49]Carey McWilliams, *A Mask for Privilege*, p. 42.
[50]*Ibid.*, p. 46.
[51]Gertrude J. Selznick and Stephen Steinberg, *The Tenacity of Prejudice: Anti-Semitism in Contemporary America* (Anti-Defamation League of B'nai B'rith, Harper & Row, Torchbook edition, 1971), Ch. 3.
[52]*Ibid.*, Ch. 8.

against Jews. We have noted that some anger of ghetto black Americans was directed against Jews as part of the general emergence and mobilization of black pride. But other sporadic occurrences, some spreading with contagion, seem to reflect a helplessness and anger in the face of the tensions, both overt and subtle, of modern living. Beginning on December 24, 1959, with an incident in Cologne, Germany, a wave of vandalism and defacement swept through the United States for nine weeks. There were 643 incidents, two-thirds of which only involved painting swastikas on buildings. About 60 percent of the incidents occurred in cities of more than 100,000 inhabitants. Not all the acts were directed toward specific Jewish targets. For example, schools and churches were in some instances also defaced. The larger the community, the higher the proportion of Jewish targets. The pattern was not consistent throughout the United States; Arizona had an unusually high number of incidents in proportion to its population and its Jewish population, whereas some large cities, such as St. Louis, Newark, New Orleans, Buffalo, and Indianapolis, had hardly any. In the South, states that had made some token effort of desegregation had more incidents than those that had not integrated at all or had made considerable progress in integration.[53]

This pattern of anti-Semitism continued as an attempt to damage property and especially symbolic property of the Jewish communities. The Anti-Defamation League tabulated 12 dynamite explosions, 2 other explosions, 9 fire bombings, 4 attempted bombings, and 47 bomb threats for the 1960–1970 period. These occurred in Maryland, Louisiana, New Jersey, New York, Massachusetts, and Washington, D.C. A number of these occurred on High Holy Days, or at Jewish schools. Vandalism and desecration in 1969–1970 occurred in Louisiana, New York, New Jersey, Connecticut, Massachusetts, Indiana, Maine, and California.[54] These are acts of anger, terrorization, and contempt by frightened, confused and therefore angry people—probably most of them young. They *do* terrorize many Jews who can remember by reading or experience the November night in 1938 when almost all the synagogues in Germany were burned and from then on Jews had to wear yellow arm bands to identify themselves. Many of these perished in concentration camps along with the Jews of the conquered countries—6 million altogether. The Jews are neither a major political force or a major economic threat in the society as a whole. On the contrary, they have contributed beyond their numbers to the development (and perhaps the civilization) of this country.

Why Does Anti-Semitism Persist?

There are different degrees of intensity of anti-Semitism, different rationalizations for it, and social science is discovering different levels of motivation. Before we indicate these different levels, it is important to point out that the problem of Jewish-Gentile relations can probably never be divorced entirely from the historical tradition. In our opinion, and contemporary evidence seems to bear this out with regard to the Soviet Union, even a revolutionary reorganization of society will not automatically solve the problem. A literate tradition, unlike the oral tradition of a folk society, can never entirely

---

[53]David Caplovitz and Candace Rogers, *Swastika 1960* (New York: Anti-Defamation League of B'nai B'rith), pp. 28–30, pp. 51–52.
[54]Testimony before the Permanent Subcommittee on Investigations of the Committee on Government Operations. U.S. Senate, Aug. 4, 1970.

lose historical attitudes and the awareness of historic problems. This affects Gentile and Jewish thinking alike.

We have already discussed some of the forms in which anti-Semitism expresses itself. We are here interested in the psychological dimension that leads people either spontaneously to express anti-Semitic sentiments or to be receptive to organized anti-Semitic efforts.

Much of what are popularly considered individual psychological reactions really constitute appropriate behavior within given social-structural situations. All groups with a highly developed sense of identity perceive other groups as different from themselves (ingroup, outgroup relations). Thus, many spontaneous sentiments are construed as anti-Semitic, though they do not necessarily carry with them any inner commitment or virulence. They may, however, lay the base for mobilizable sentiments if a stable situation is in the throes of change.

Another type of anti-Semitism is related to the larger minority problem of competition between those whom the dominant culture favors and the able members of any minority. It is obvious that many less able people are retained in occupational positions by the practice of discrimination. Occupational discrimination furthermore has social concomitants, involving choice of mate, club membership, social admission, and so forth. The local community power structure is reinforced by this web of relationships. The end product is to create an effect on general public policy.

A popular interpretation of anti-Semitism derives from the so-called "scapegoat" theory, which attributes the need to project blame for personal and social difficulties on somebody else. Here the historic position of the Jews make them particularly vulnerable to being used as scapegoats, although a comparable attitude was not unknown toward the Japanese through World War II among people on the West Coast. There are different levels of insecurity in which this operates, one of which is insecurity of status, such as the threatened loss of middle-class occupation and style of life, where the individuals feel, correctly or incorrectly, that a competitive threat comes from the minority members. Paul Massing has analyzed this factor with regard to the growth of anti-Semitism before the Nazis took over in Germany and in the subsequent support given the Nazi leadership.[55] A 1956 study of the Nazi leaders demonstrated that in one way or another these were all marginal men in their societies.[56] What we see from this is that organized anti-Semitism can be aroused in a threatened stratum of the society, and that leaders emerge from those who are less well integrated in the society than the general population of their age group.

The prejudiced personality has been studied from the viewpoint of both sociology and psychiatry. The study of the authoritarian personality which we present in Chapter 19 suggests that certain types of upbringing create this personality need, and that children in authoritative situations where they feel helpless are more apt to be prejudiced than children given freedom to express themselves, to be inventive and exploratory. A person brought up in this manner, it appears, attempts to repress fear, weakness, sex impulses, and aggressive feelings in order to be approved of by the punishing parents. He then compensates by attributing these "bad" repressed impulses to others whom society holds in less esteem, whether or not there is any basis for it in their be-

[55]Paul Massing, *Rehearsal for Destruction* (New York: Harper & Brothers, 1949).
[56]Ithiel daSola Poole and Daniel K. Lerner, *The Nazi Elite* (Stanford: The Stanford University Press, 1956).

havior. Wherever the social situation provides a target for derogation, the repressed wishes will be assigned to the derogated person.

As was pointed out in the study by Selznick and Steinberg, people with a high index of anti-Semitism are apt to be anti-black also. The prejudiced personality will seize on any object that there is traditional sanction for devaluing. Anti-Semitism, like racism is endemic to Western European society. Institutional anti-Semitism has declined. Consciousness raising, legislative protection, and accurate information have reduced the number of those who in the past passively followed a pattern of discrimination.

Jews and the New Ethnicity

There has been a revival of Jewish tradition in many households; a demand for respect for Jewish holidays; the development of Jewish Centers to provide a locus for social activities for Jewish young people; an increase in Jewish parochial schools. All these developments counteract the self-image that many Jews had of themselves as a despised people. In this connection, also, the state of Israel has provided a model of Jews as builders and developers. So important has this image been that many Jews view failure to support Israel in the present Israel-Arab conflict as anti-Semitism.

Yet the position on Israel is not unanimous. The Orthodox rabbinate defines being Jewish in religious terms and is distressed by Jewish identity being linked to a secular state. Others, as was seen in the study of Lakeville, especially older and more integrated people, are uneasy about Israel and fear Israel's aspirations will revive anti-Semitism in America, or contribute to polarization between those who have an ideological commitment to the "Third World" (which, by definition includes the Arab nations) and those supporting Israel.

Jews and Other Minorities

When Jews were in America in relatively small numbers in the nineteenth century with their belief that, after Europe, here really was an open society in which they could take their place, they did not think of other minorities, but followed the established patterns of dominants. It embarrasses some Jews today, if they know, that some of those early Sephardim who helped build the first synagogue in America made a fortune in the slave trade. Jews from Western Europe shared the attitudes of Western Europe, and there were always many "establishment" Jews.

Equally there are Jews who have empathized with others against whom discrimination, injustice, and violence have been directed. Jews were active, financially and personally, in the Black Civil Rights movement.

Other minorities often don't like Jews, either out of their own imitation of what they "think" is a dominant attitude, or because, as Mario Puzo has said of the Italians, they envy the elder brother who has been more successful. In today's climate, many blacks are anti-Semitic. Part of this stems from the fact that Jews have been merchants to the black community when blacks hadn't the business skills, tradition, and capital, and WASPS didn't seek black business. For some blacks, Jews become the only direct contact they have had with whites and are therefore the target for outbreaks of generalized hostility, or for the specific efforts to have blacks control business in the ghettoes.

Middle-class Jews like other middle-class families have fled the central cities as the proportion of blacks in schools and neighborhoods increased. Sometimes the migration to the suburbs has created what are in effect all-Jewish suburbs, strengthening a pluralistic relationship to the larger society. Though the attitudes of individuals in the Jewish group present a wide spectrum, it is well to remember that no other group, with the exception of Quakers, has so clearly and consistently worked to reduce discrimination for all minorities and to increase intergroup understanding.

Suggested Readings

Birmingham, Stephen. *The Grandees: The Story of America's Sephardic Elite*. New York: Harper & Row, 1971 (Dell paperback, 1972).
    A very readable account of the Spanish-Portuguese Jews before and after migration to America, based on some newly available family archive materials.
———. *Our Crowd: The Great Jewish Families of New York*. New York: Harper & Row, 1967.
    A popular book about the great German Jewish families of nineteenth-century New York, their descendants, and their impact on business, the arts, and welfare.
Howe, Irving. *World of Our Fathers: The Journey of the East European Jews to America and the Life They Found and Made*. New York: Simon and Schuster, 1976.
    A rich, exhaustive account of the culture and adaptation of the Eastern European Jews in America.
Sklare, Marshall, and Gerenblum, Joseph. *Jewish Identity on the Suburban Frontier: A Study in Group Survival in the Open Society*. New York: Basic Books, 1967.
    A superb study of an interethnic prestigious suburb of a midwestern city.
Teller, Judd L. *Strangers and Natives: The Evolution of the American Jew from 1921 to the Present*. New York: Delacorte Press, 1968 (Dell paperback, 1970);
    Rich and readable presentation of main currents and crosscurrents in twentieth-century American Jewish life.

Part 3

Some Problems of Policy and Theory

18

Looking Ahead: A Summary Overview

The decade of the 1970s is already being referred to as the decade of the ethnic revival. The great struggle in dominant-minority relations of the '50s and the '60s was that of black Americans to reduce institutionalized discrimination: in voting, in job opportunities, in education, in housing, in use of public facilities. The movement represented "the politics of access." It inevitably began with black Americans. In the national arena they were the largest minority; they were subject to the severest categorical discrimination, had been kept the poorest segment of the population, and were the most powerless. The black challenge developed social techniques, many adapted from the struggles of organized labor to legitimize collective bargaining: the sit-in, picketing, demonstration, and confrontation.

The decade of the '70s saw other segments of the population finding a sense of group identity based on common cultural values and a history of discrimination, some gross, some subtle, and all implying devaluation. Adopting, in many instances, the techniques of the black movement, they demanded the right to share in the decisions affecting them. This has been called "the politics of inclusion."

In this chapter we shall examine these overall trends of the revitalization of ethnic identity: the demand for access, the demand for inclusion, and the problems, prospects, and policy issues that now confront the nation as a pluralistic society.

The American dominant-minority pattern is, in broad terms, similar to that of inter-people relations throughout the modern world, as we found from the comparative section of Chapter 1. To briefly restate, the factors involved are group self-interest, ethnocentrism, superior power, and a situation in which their self-interest can best be pursued by establishing dominance. Given these elements, the more powerful establish institutional arrangements that are favorable to them and unfavorable to the other.

The society established by the original WASP dominants was focused around four main value orientations: (1) the democratic ethos with its stress on equality, freedom, individualism; (2) the belief in private economic enterprise, with the associated traits of activity and work, achievement and success, and material comfort; (3) Judeo-Christian beliefs (with Protestantism dominating), which have developed in the United States, as Williams views them, a somewhat distinctive "moral orientation" not as strongly present in other Western nations; and (4) secularism with emphasis on rationality, progress, and scientific achievement.[1]

---

[1] Robin Williams, Jr., *American Society: A Sociological Interpretation* (New York: Alfred A. Knopf, 1951), Ch. 11, "Value Orientation in American Society."

Institutional arrangements are ideally the way in which continuity is insured in perpetuating cherished values. But values are not the only element in a given institutional pattern. Another factor is the necessity of adaptation to the particular environment, both physical and social. Mediating between avowed values and the demands of environment are the cultural symbols: language, ritual, images, sacred places, which influence the perception of reality and give a selective emphasis to one or another aspect of the values.

Minorities may have a different emphasis in values, a different experience, as contrasted with dominants, of the physical and social environment, and a different perception of "reality." As Lerone Bennett declares in the quotation cited at the beginning of Chapter 1, "By and large, reality has been conceptualized in terms of the narrow point of view of the small minority of white men who live in Europe and North America. We must abandon [this] partial frame of reference. . . ." Or as Vine Deloria, Jr., has said, speaking from another tradition of the relation of man to his environment, "This country was a lot better off when the Indians were running it."[2]

WASP institutional development took place within the following perceptions of reality: In the country from which the majority of the early settlers had migrated they had been without access to political voice or economic improvement, either because of religious discrimination or the limitations of an inflexible class system; they came in a period of advancing colonialism and it took them nearly two centuries not to take colonialism for granted; the struggles of Britain, France, and Spain for control of the Western Hemisphere heightened, as is always true in periods of conflict, the normal ethnocentrism of people who were essentially ethnically homogeneous; there were both theological and early scientific (in the first development of genetics) concepts available to rationalize the superiority-inferiority syndrome. Today the genetic argument is usually only found in relation to peoples of non-European lineage: "blacks, browns, and yellows," but this was not always so. The Irish, Jews, south and east Europeans have also in various periods been categorically defined as genetically inferior. Myrdal makes the observation that "the race dogma is nearly the only way out for a people so moralistically equalitarian, if it is not prepared to live up to its faith."[3]

It is often stated that racism is the main factor in perpetuating dominance. This has much validity if one makes sure to include the *behavioral* aspects of racism, i.e., discrimination, and not define racism solely in terms of prejudiced attitudes and feelings. Once racist beliefs become well established, and continue to be reconditioned in children with a substantial core of prejudice, it becomes the *normative* way of life of dominants. Not to be racist—that is; comforming—is to be a deviant and looked at askance by one's associates, or to suffer greater penalties. It is not surprising, therefore, that the pressures for immigrants to assimilate included taking on dominant attitudes toward the more visible minorities, and this was, of course, reinforced by the public education system. As Barbara Mikulski pointed out in the passage cited in Chapter 4, "The elitists who smugly call us [white ethnics] racists are the ones who taught us the meaning of the word bigotry."[4]

[2]See page 1, Chapter 1.
[3]Gunnar Myrdal, *An American Dilemma* (New York: Harper & Brothers, 1944), Vol. 1, p. 89.
[4]Barbara Mikulski, "Who Speaks for Ethnic America," *The New York Times,* Sept. 29, 1970, p. 33.

   Discrimination cannot take place without a broad base of conviction in innate inequality: that is, prejudice. Although prejudice is a personal attitude about which one cannot legislate, not all people who discriminate against another ethnic category, or who support such discrimination, hold uniform attitudes. This is important to understand. In conflict situations the "prejudiced" are apt to be stereotyped, seen as a united opposition front, or as a single symbolic entity: a bogey, or a devil. Robert K. Merton has, however, developed a typology more nearly coherent with the facts.[5]

   Type I. *The Unprejudiced Nondiscriminator, or All-Weather Liberal.* Since this type of person believes unequivocally in the Democratic Creed, he practices what he believes consistently. Obviously, such people are logical leaders for social action in the same direction. However, Merton considers the all-weather liberal prone to accept three fallacies. The first, the fallacy of group soliloquy, refers to the tendency for such like-minded people to gather in small groups and reinforce each other's attitudes and convictions rather than joining other groups and influencing them in the desired direction. Growing closely out of this is the second fallacy, called the fallacy of unanimity, which is the tendency to exaggerate the extent to which the rest of the community shares their own viewpoint. A third limitation to effective action by all-weather liberals is their addiction to the fallacy of private solutions to social problems. Since he himself has solved the problem, this liberal may not feel compelled to do anything more. Rightly, he feels no guilt for himself.

   Type II. *The Unprejudiced Discriminator, or Fair-Weather Liberal.* This is the type of man who has no prejudices against ethnic groups and on the whole believes in the American Creed. But he is primarily a man of expediency, who tends to support discriminatory practices when it is the easier or more profitable course. He does, however, feel guilty about his discrimination. He is therefore capable of cure, because he really wants to be cured.

   Type III. *The Prejudiced Nondiscriminator, or Fair-Weather Illiberal.* This type of man does not believe in ethnic equality. Being, however, also a man of expediency, he conforms in situations in which the group sanctions are against discrimination through fear of the penalties that might otherwise ensue. But whenever the pressure against it is removed, he discriminates.

   Type IV. *The Prejudiced Discriminator, or the All-Weather Illiberal.* This type is the true bigot. Since he believes firmly that certain minorities ought to be discriminated against, he can be counted on to discriminate as thoroughly as is permitted by the customs and institutions of the community. This type is obviously hardest to change, although the situation varies in relation to the prevailing mores of the area where he lives. When the mores support his position, he is a conformist, and change means making himself open to community criticism. When the mores in general are against him, he is a social deviant, and here change on his part would draw him closer into the general community structure.

   The Merton typology reminds us that institutional conformists are not necessarily incapable of change. Some of the timid, cautious, or vulnerable may welcome change, though they would not fight to initiate it; some will accept it when it has been achieved, as this becomes the new pattern of conformity.

[5]Robert K. Merton, "Discrimination and the American Creed," in Robert M. MacIver, ed., *Discrimination and National Welfare* (New York: Harper & Brothers, 1949), pp. 99–126.

"Institutional change" has been a slogan of protest efforts since the Civil Rights movement and the antipoverty programs of the Johnson administration. And indeed institutional change has occurred in dominant and minority relations. One cannot legislate away prejudice, but legislation, if implemented, can to some extent quarantine its effects, so that over time people adjust and take the changed situation for granted.

Institutional Change

The outstanding characteristic of dominant-minority relations in America in the third quarter of this century has been the politicization of minority demands. All people make demands on society, though not consciously and overtly if the society is such that they may on the whole fulfill their expectations. Individuals who make claims on the society for recognition or riches or justice or survival may do so with greater or less success, but claims must be aggregated if they are to have any impact.[6]

Before World War II it was common for employment agencies to state "no Catholics" in advertising white-collar jobs. Jewish young men and young women had an even more difficult access in the general employment market. Chinese college graduates had to settle for jobs as waiters in restaurants. Unions discriminated against blacks. A first major break in the pattern developed out of the exigencies of war and the associated labor shortage. As we have seen, as a war measure in World War II the federal government enacted the Fair Employment Practices Act outlawing discrimination against minority workers employed in any industry producing under government contract. Although this was a temporary measure, after the war a number of states set up even broader legislation. But it took the thrust of the Civil Rights movement to achieve a national statute.

These were the decades of the politics of access, and it is not surprising that they were years of tension. Makielski points out that since dominants have allowed minorities, by definition, limited claims on the society, they are affronted when these "outsiders" make claims, especially if these are made in the name of minority status rather than as individual "exceptions."[7] Furthermore, even those dominants who tolerate or support minority claims are often dismayed by successful results, for the amelioration of deprivation requires some transfer of resources. This may mean higher taxes; it may mean invasion of homogeneous neighborhoods; it may mean new competition for scarce places in preferred colleges and professional schools; and it widens the competitive pool in the job market.

Dominants, whether specifically and intentionally or not, have benefited from minority deprivation, economically, socially, and psychologically; and change in established status of minorities impinges in all these dimensions and creates anxiety. "In short, friction comes from a clash of pragmatic interests or perceptions of the world."[8]

The politics of access is particularly important in the economic institutions. It operates not only against old patterns of categorical discrimination at entry level, but more significantly, for all minorities, at the successively higher levels. Kirkus argues that ethnic solidarity is the critical factor in breaking barriers, but sees the greatest

---

[6]For this discussion see S. J. Makielski, Jr., *Beleaguered Minorities: Cultural Politics in America,* (San Francisco: W. H. Freeman & Co., 1973) pp. 38–39.
[7]*Ibid.*, p. 39.
[8]*Ibid.*, p. 39.

strength in large-scale organization that involves coalition between ethnic groups: either as members of national, industrywide labor unions, or as Catholics, or as residents of a central city, for example.[9] He cites Chicano solidarity in a Texas strike against a national clothing manufacturer for recognition of Amalgamated Clothing Workers; and of similar success in a North Carolina textile strike involving black workers; or a new generation of college-educated Poles and Italians and other third-generation white ethnics who are abjuring the old-line Democratic Party ethnic politics, are opposing the old ethnic societies with their parades and their concentration on the cold war in East Europe or the civil war in Ireland, and are concerned with bringing services to the neglected ethnic communities of cities or of Appalachia under the sponsorship of one or another organization such as the National Center for Urban Ethnic Affairs or one of the community development programs of the Catholic church.

The politics of access flows naturally into the politics of inclusion. The politics of access has been a thrust toward the economic and the concomitant social opportunity structure. The politics of inclusion is toward decision-making power.

At its most generalized and simplest level this began with voter registration, bringing back into the political arena those who were disenfranchised by deviousness or neglect. This has had an effect on the established parties. More blacks have supported the Democratic Party than was traditionally so. As we saw in Chapter 11 in some states Indians have the swing vote. In the 1972 election the Republicans vigorously wooed the ethnic vote. Some, disaffected with the old-style political leadership, have formed independent parties, like La Raza Unida, which have had some local success. Others have fled to the antiestablishment rhetoric of someone like George Wallace. In other instances in local politics minority coalitions have unseated established "bosses." This has resulted in considerable ferment, increasing experience in the political process with its imperatives of clarifying goals and overcoming factionalism.

At a more complex level there has been in the large urban centers with their ethnoracial subcommunities the demand for "community control of our own institutions." This is, of course, coherent with the principle of federalism that permeates the American system. This development is still so new that it is beset with problems. It is not entirely clear which institutions a subcommunity can or should control, since it is not economically self-sufficient and must lean on the larger units of government, city, state, and federal, for the support of many services. Community boards in some instances still have not been able to clarify and compromise on long-term versus short-term goals, strategies, and tactics, and have become a focal structure for competing political careerists. The one traditionally defined jurisdiction open to community boards is that of the local schools and it is in this sphere of public education that the problems and controversies of control in the urban ethnic subcommunity are at present located. In New York City, on the positive side, the community boards have brought in many more teachers and teacher aides of the same ethnic background as their pupils. In Spanish-speaking subcommunities there has been the beginning of a thrust at bilingual education and auxiliary personnel to work with parents. Promotion within the school system of blacks and Puerto Ricans has increased. On the negative side, there is a chasm, wider or narrower depending on the school, between the teachers who are not of the same background as the community and those who are. Neither the members of

---

[9]Richard Krikus, *Pursuing the American Dream: White Ethnics and the New Populism* (Garden City, N.Y.: Doubleday & Co., Anchor Books, 1976), Ch. 8.

the community boards or the teachers are yet clear about how to use ethnoracial heritage as a frame for acquiring the basic skills for a technological society, although there has been some isolated creative experimentation. The community board is constantly under the pressure of the Teachers Union and the City Board of Education. These bodies are not primarily interested in creative teaching, but in job security and in standards as defined by the schools of education of a generation ago.

We have been discussing the impact of the minorities ethnoracial self-affirmation with regard to the principal secular institutional structures of society. But there has also been an impact on the more personal institutional structures as well: the family and religion. The fact that the new ethnicity, although preserving cherished aspects of tradition, is not narrowly traditional can be illustrated in two aspects of family living; the first is the increase in outmarriage. This has been going on for a long time, but within special limits. Second- and third-generation descendants of immigrants married interethnically but within the same religion. In the pre-World War II period in the southern states Chinese men married black women, as no Chinese women were available and whites were prohibited. We have had a generation of Asian war brides. In the postwar period there was a rise in black/white marriages, and today one sees an increase in Chinese/Hispanic marriages. Perhaps the same factor holds true for these trends in outmarriage that Berman found for Jews: that highly upwardly mobile members are more likely to outmarry;[10] or it may be that *minority* identity is a stronger bond than ethnicity, creating mutuality, common goals, and respect for differences.

A clearer example of the impact on the family of the new ethnicity is the changing role of women. More minority women are entering the work force, are making use of day care in new institutional patterns (day care centers) rather than the traditional kinship and neighborhood resources, are active in community roles, and participate in social movements.

The religious bodies have also been challenged, and are changing. For the Catholic church one could cite the increasing role of laymen in the church, the Mass in the language of the parish, the greater community activities of priests and nuns, especially in those religious orders devoted to education or social services. In the Protestant churches there has been some move toward integration, and a decline in "home missionary" activity. Where there has been any successful integration it is usually in urban congregations where all members, whatever ethnic or racial background, are established middle class. Religious motivation can be an impelling force for change toward a more just, more humane, more honest society. Minorities have recognized this and have appealed for support in the name of religious belief and ethic. Too often the response has been occasional, niggardly, and subtly patronizing; resulting in condemnation by minorities of the institutionalized religion of dominants,[11] and a withdrawal into ethnic religious group expression, which, whatever else the content of the belief system, is definitely within "the theology of liberation."

Ethnicity and Class

The United States is an example of an "open-class" society. It is argued that class position in an open-class society is fluid, is not hereditary, and that an individual with

---

[10]Lewis A. Berman, *Jews and Intermarriage* (New York: Thomas Yoseloff, 1968), Ch. 14.
[11]See Carlos E. Cortés *et al.*, *Three Perspectives on Ethnicity in America* (New York: G. P. Putnam's Sons, 1976), pp. 344–368, for minority challenges of dominant religious institutions.

ability or talent and the discipline of hard work may change his class position. This has been the core of the American Dream for most voluntary migrants to America. From this point of view it may be said that there is in America a class system closely related to recency of migration, and that there is an "ethnic succession" in gaining access to better positions in the economic structure. For example, in the New York City school system in the first decade of this century most New York City school personnel (both teaching and administrative) were WASPS; twenty years later the majority were Irish; then after World War II a larger number of them were Jewish; and today there is an increasing number of blacks and Puerto Ricans.

On the other hand, prejudice and discrimination have operated more in the direction of creating a fixed class system; allowing only the exceptional individual to move to upper levels involving power. Those who defend the, acknowledgedly imperfect, justice of the system and point to ethnic succession, which has indeed occurred to a degree, forget the generations of black, Mexican American, and American Indian deprivation and poverty. De facto and de jure segregation kept them out of sight, and if they thought about it such defenders of the system might join Edward Everett in his comment on the Irish, "They are here that we may all be lifted up." Racism, institutionalized and perpetuated, has made possible the "Dream" for much of white America.

It is in those segments of the population who have experienced the most severe discrimination, limitation of opportunity, conquest and internal colonialism that there is a call for *basic* change in the system, or for separation. Separation has been proposed from time to time within the black movements of the past and the present; it is true today of one small segment of the Chicano movement; and some Indians are advocating a return to treaty status in relation to the United States government. But this is not the majority. The ethnic revitalization is aimed at removing categorical barriers erected against a *group,* and presses for *group* opportunity, within an American environment that is its home. It is the group pressure, as we pointed out, that arouses resistance and anxiety.

Ethnic Politics

The future of the new-style ethnic politics is not yet clear, and will have several sets of problems if it is to have continued impact.

The first of these is clarification of goals, both long term and interim. "Access" and "inclusion" are "vestibule" thrusts. When the doors open, what then? Are the goals, primarily cultural, a movement for the recognition and appreciation of variant values and life styles within the common demands of an urbanized technological society? Are they demands of an urbanized technological society? Are they demands primarily for a return to some base of community? Are they demands for modification of the bureaucratized work process on which the technological society rests? Are there inherent contradictions in pursuit of all of these goals, all at once? serially? Are the goals for some the abandonment of the technological society, including its consumer benefits, and can enclaves for such variants be negotiated, as have the Amish? Much of the rhetoric is still vague and confusing, but a social movement, to be successful, needs concrete goals and planned strategies.

The second problem is that of strategies, the crux of which lies in assessing correctly the opposition, not merely the opponent as confronted, but the supportive reference groups of the opponent. Successful strategies, of course, rest not only on the opponent's strength and collateral support, but on the movement's own organized reliability and collateral support.

The third problem is the choice of tactics, whether at any particular stage high visibility or low visibility is more likely to be effective. Flexibility in tactics is important. Confrontation and negotiation are not mutually exclusive. Coalition, for a specific effort, or for longer-term goals is another consideration.[12]

A different kind of problem is that of competing ethnic groups seeking the limited available resources of government, foundations, business donations for the development programs sponsored by their group. There is at present, of course, not only interethnic competition, but competition between factions in the same ethnic group.

Communication with the members of a movement must go beyond rhetoric if the movement is to have sustaining strength. The continual communication of goals, strategies, and tactics for a specific effort, is essential to building a self-disciplined organization.

Ethnic politics seems to some to be revitalizing the American political scene, and it is probable that the issues it raises will be with us for a considerable time to come. There are the beginnings of several major blocs: Blacks, Chicano-Puerto Rican-Indian, and Asian-Pacific. Should these mature they may change the complexion of the political scene still more.

Social Trends and Ethnic Power

Implicit in this summary discussion of the current situation in dominant-minority relations is the basic underlying fact of prejudice and discrimination and how to control it and diminish it. In all the talk about ethnic consciousness, ethnic identity, and actual or potential alliances, the issue is that of power: who has it and how is it being used. The task before the nation on the local, state, and national level is an equitable and rational redistribution of power. Discrimination has been a major device for maintaining the power of one ethnic group.

We are, however, facing some profound changes in the allocation of political power. Federal revenue sharing, a policy moving toward decentralization, is swinging the balance of power away from the central cities to the suburbs. Here white ethnics are emerging as a major population force. The suburbs are no longer the refuge of homogeneous affluents. There are working-class populations and pockets of poverty. How will these suburban groups use an increase in power? Will they support socially progressive ideas? Or will they be defensive of their own prerogatives and find the old racist rationalization? Can we build bridges and policy alliances between the ethnic demands of central cities and the suburbs?[13]

Another kind of political development is also possible. Kirkus sees a politicization of the working class and of the labor movement in the near future as the major thrust for

---

[12]For a more developed discussion of the above problems, see Michael Lipsky, "Protest As a Political Resource," in Donald Gelfand and Russell Lee, *Ethnic Conflicts and Power: A Cross National Perspective,* (New York: John Wiley & Sons, 1973), pp. 266 ff.; and S. J. Makielski, Jr., *Beleaguered Minorities,* Chs. 14, 15, 16.

[13]These questions were raised in an address by Irving M. Levine, "Social Policy and Multi-Ethnicity in the 1970's," available from the Institute on Pluralism and Group Identity of the American Jewish Committee.

"a more equal distribution of wealth and income and the decentralization of power to insure citizen participation".[14] He foresees, not a homogeneous, but a united, organized working class in which ethnoracial interests and working-class interests supplement each to achieve the two stated goals. The danger, of course, lies in an ethnic consciousness that becomes an end in itself, and would splinter any such united effort. Since there are class divisions within each ethnic group, some ethnic leaders would be made anxious by such a coalition of forces. It furthermore would be to the advantage of people resisting change to employ a strategy of supportive recognition of cultural pride and multicultural contributions to American life. This in itself would be good, but as a substitute for improving the socioeconomic situation of ethnic poor and working-class communities it would be diversionary

Whereas the problems of prejudice must be solved in the childhood surroundings of home, school, and community, and the control of discrimination through the mechanisms of public policy, we cannot overlook the fact that the rise of ethnic identity and its embrace goes beyond national boundaries. This is not to raise a bogey of "foreign agitators." It is inevitable that given the degree of neglect, Indian political and cultural consciousness should ally itself to some extent with the exploited Indians of the rest of the Western Hemisphere, that black Americans should feel some identity with the struggles for liberation or political stability in black Africa and that the concept of the Third World should be part of their reality, that our people of Latin American heritage should have some emotional alliance with other neglected populations in Central and South America.

The dominant power bloc is also caught in a world situation as this nation competes for markets, resources, and technological superiority. It is the hope that if we will *listen,* and commit our resources and best intelligence we can pioneer in the creation of a participatory democracy that is pluralistic, just, flexible, and perhaps unique.

Suggested Readings

Gelfand, Donald, and Lee, Russell. *Ethnic Conflicts and Power: A Cross National Perspective.* New York: John Wiley & Sons, 1973.
   An excellent collection of papers on ethnic conflict in the U.S. and other parts of the world.
Krikus, Richard. *Pursuing the American Dream: White Ethnics and the New Populism.* Garden City, N.Y.: Doubleday & Co., Anchor Books, 1976.
   A rich analysis of rising political consciousness in white ethnic groups and a platform for a labor-ethnic political coalition.
Makielski, S. J., Jr. *Beleaguered Minorities: Cultural Politics in America.* San Francisco: W. H. Freeman and Co., 1973.

[14]Krikus, *Pursuing the American Dream: The New Populism and White Ethnics,* p. 351.

The second half of this book is a good analysis of the tasks of building a political movement: goals, strategies, tactics.

Publications of the Institute on Pluralism and Group Identity of the American Jewish Committee, 165 East 65 Street, New York, N.Y. 10022.

Pamphlets for group discussion, especially *Moving Up: Ethnic Succession in America, The Schools and Group Identity: Educating for A New Pluralism, Practical Guide to Coalition Building.*

19

Sociological Theory and Dominant–Minority Relations

WHAT IS THEORY?

Throughout this book there have been references to various theoretical propositions. Indeed, Chapters 10 through 17 roughly examine the validity of the proposition with which we concluded Chapter 2: that dominant-minority relations in the United States are taking the form of structural pluralism rather than the "melting pot" or assimilation expectations of half a century ago. In a sense, therefore, the student has been examining data to test a hypothesis, which is the theoretic task. Students may even be ready to ask pertinent questions which will stimulate further exploration that may refine, correct, or develop the original statement. For example: Is structural pluralism chosen as a mode of adaptation more by young people or by older age groups? Is it more characteristic of affluent or poorer members of a minority? To what extent is it imposed by dominant patterns of exclusion or freely chosen by a minority group? Answering these questions will be theory building.

The social sciences are still very young compared to the natural sciences. There is much more refinement still to come both of theory and of research methods. The Romans developed a crude theory of physical stress that was sufficient for them to be able to build bridges and aqueducts, but they were not advanced to the point of putting a man on the moon. Social science is still largely in the bridge and aqueduct stage.

THE INTERDISCIPLINARY NATURE OF SOCIAL SCIENCE

The "social" or "behavioral" sciences have all been concerned, though with different emphases, with man's interaction with other men and with his physical environment. Psychology, psychiatry, anthropology, sociology, and history have all contributed to our understanding of dominant-minority relations. Usually, psychology and psychiatry have been concerned with problems of learning and perceiving as they are related to people's motivation, attitudes toward others, adaptability in the face of change, and reactions to stresses of the environment or the life cycle. Anthropologists have seen man as a "culture building animal" and have focused on culture (values, beliefs, language, and other symbols as well as social organization) as man's instrument of adapta-

375

tion to the physical environment. Much of anthropology has concentrated on small societies that can be studied whole through the careful recording of a researcher who has lived, often at recurring intervals, among the people he or she is describing. Sociologists have increasingly concentrated on studying the stabilized forms of social organization and have developed increasingly sophisticated mathematical methods for analyzing large bodies of data. History, of course, gives a comparative dimension essential to the analysis of social change. Today, large interdisciplinary teams may work together, each contributing their specific skill, just as in medicine, biology, or astrophysics most research is team research involving people from different but related fields.

In the studies we have cited in this book we have leaned heavily on the related behavioral sciences, though the focus of our analysis has been *sociological*. Minorities exist within the larger social structure and share in the broader social processes. Therefore there is no separate body of theory of dominant-minority relations, though minority groups may be a special focus for research and for the formulation of special segments of theory. In this chapter we will not attempt to review all the theoretical contributions to our understanding of minority situations. Nor are we writing any new integrated theoretical statement of our own. The purpose of the chapter is to show what theory is about, how it grows, and to give students a chance to speculate on and to challenge the illustrations we have selected. It is the nature of science that it is never complete; one theoretical insight builds upon another or is corrected by another and raises new questions to be explored.

In examining theory the proper questions to be asked are, Does it take into account all the facts that are relevant to its theme? Are the assumptions underlying the initial formulation acceptable? What verifying evidence has been submitted, or should be undertaken as research?

The sources of insight that lead to theory building occur in several ways. Some may be arrived at from concern about problems demanding action. Sometimes theory evolves out of the accidental observations of a person thinking about the general relationships that the particular incident makes vivid. It is part of the folklore of science, for example, that the observation of an apple falling from a tree crystallized Newton's formulation of the theory of gravity. Much of the advanced development of science is derived from logical, abstract thought, which must then be validated by appropriate testing procedures. Application can be an end product, as well as an initial stimulus of theory building.

Action and theory are not a dichotomy. As action inevitably stimulates speculation, in a scientifically oriented society theory sooner or later must be tested if it is to survive in the accepted system of knowledge. Part of the task of the behavioral sciences in the twentieth century has been to develop increasingly reliable methods of testing propositions. That great gains have been made in reliability and acceptance of scientific investigation in the behavioral fields is attested by the use of an "expert brief," prepared by social psychologists, sociologists, and anthropologists in the United States Supreme Court Decision (*Brown* v. the *Board of Education*) on school desegregation.

Theory building occurs on several levels. There is the search for more refined and therefore more precise definition of terms on which all researchers may agree. This, in the jargon of professional research, is call "conceptual clarification." It is essential that this process take place so that there can be a common understanding of what terms mean in order to have different studies comparable, widening the range of information from which generalizations can be made. A single study will formulate its conclusions, and this allows for a simple, preliminary level of generalization or leads to new hypotheses. Comparable studies can lead to some even more abstract (therefore more widely applicable) propositions. This has been called "middle range theory." Finally, there are those scholars who by temperament and endowment have concerned themselves with attempts to analyze complex societies as a whole. These writers of "grand theory" rely on the researches of others and segments of their analyses provide hypotheses for new research.

Some theory will be ahead of what is now testable or applicable. Astronomy advanced far beyond its known applications, and much could not be experimentally verified until technology based on other sciences provided the empirical tools. So it is with the social sciences. For a long time to come we will be improving empirical tools and "getting the bugs out" of applied efforts as we are finding must also be done in aerospace efforts or in virus control. This should not detract from the excitement of the theoretical adventure.

THEORY BUILDING: GENERALIZATIONS AND RESEARCH

To open our discussion of theory—how it comes about, and how trustworthy it is— we have chosen two specific "classical" studies that have influenced a generation of research and theory about dominant-minority relations. These illustrate also the relation of research to theory. An important question is, Does some theoretical formulation precede a research investigation, or should one go in cold and just accurately record? Each illustration shows one way of proceeding.

We are more critical of one than of the other. This is a decision made with regard to how much the study's conclusions are still a valid guide to dominant-minority relations today. To an extent the two studies should not be measured against each other as the method of research in each was different: one sought to explore a generalized problem while the other sought to describe a community reality. Nevertheless, they are both great pioneer studies that raise important questions.

The Authoritarian Personality[1]

For the last several decades there has been a growing literature bringing together psychological and sociological concepts about personality structure. One of the postulates on which such conceptual integration rests is that the individual's early experiences exert a lasting effect on his personality, what he learns as norms (sociology) and how he reacts emotionally to this learning (psychiatry). There is now a wide range of material to document the different modes of child-rearing in different cultures.[2] Looking toward a crosscultural typology in the field of social structure and personality, one major step has been taken in the formulation of a type: the authoritarian personality. This was first described in the early 1930s by the German philosopher and

[1]T. W. Adorno, Else Frankel-Brunswik, Daniel J. Levinson, R. Nevitt Sanford, *The Authoritarian Personality* (New York: Harper & Brothers, 1950).
[2]For examples see Margaret Mead, *Childhood in Contemporary Culture* (New York: Columbia University Press, 1958).

sociologist Max Horkheimer.[3] The authoritarian personality is one that has been molded by a fear of authority, as, for instance, in the relationship to a strict patriarchal father whose decisions are binding and often arbitrary, and who punishes for lack of respect. Some cultures, including the Puritan strain in our own, have valued this type of family structure. The child trained in this way responds to all authority as he did to his father, submissively, and as an adult becomes authoritarian in turn. Deeper study of such personalities has shown that obeying arbitrary authority in childhood results in bottled-up fear and resentment. The child who successfully weathers the discipline develops into a man who is frightened by and morally indignant about (and perhaps covertly envious of) people whose behavior is different from the conduct that he has bitterly achieved. His residue of fear and suppressed wish to retaliate can all too easily be mobilized wherever and whenever an appropriate rationalization is supplied.

This is one example of an analytic concept in the social sciences that has been tested, in at least one dimension, by a major field study. Under the auspices of the American Jewish Committee, T. W. Adorno, a colleague of Horkheimer, and several associates set out to test the relationship between authoritarian versus nonauthoritarian upbringing and degree of anti-Semitic prejudice. They derived from their empirical work a summary profile of the prejudiced and the nonprejudiced personality. The prejudiced personality tries to repress from his consciousness unacceptable tendencies or impulses in himself; the unprejudiced person shows more awareness of his faults and is more willing to face up to them. The prejudiced person particularly attempts to repress fear, weakness, sex impulses, and aggressive feelings toward those in authority—for example, his parents. He shows also a tendency to compensate for this overrepression by manifesting a drive for power and success along conventional lines. The prejudiced seem to gain less pleasure from emotional experience—companionship, art, or music—than the unprejudiced. Outward conformance to conventions is a marked characteristic of the prejudiced; the unprejudiced are more genuinely concerned with discovering a valid ethical value system for themselves. The prejudiced are more interested in achieving power; the less prejudiced seek love and affection as satisfactory ends in themselves. The high scorers on the prejudice scale are extremely rigid in their standards of behavior, intolerant of any deviation from the conventional codes of morals or manners; in contrast, the low scorers are more flexible in their own adjustments to the mores, more appreciative of the complexities of human behavior, and more sympathetic with those who err.

The basis for these two contrasting personality types was found by these research workers to have been established in the contrasting patterns of family life to which the subjects were exposed in childhood. The prejudiced report rigid discipline, with affection made conditional on the child's approved behavior. In the families of the prejudiced there were clearly defined roles of dominance by parents and submission by children, in contrast with families where equalitarian practices prevailed.

The study we have just presented is an example of an insightful idea in an essay on family structure. This idea was adopted as the hypothesis for a field study. Since this pioneer study, the hypothesis has been further refined and scales of degree of prejudice as related to authoritarianism have been further developed for use in community

---

[3]Max Horkheimer, "Authority and the Family," in Bernard Stern, *The Family, Past and Present* (New York: D. Appleton-Century, 1938), p. 428.

studies.[4] The deep-rooted nature of prejudice that serves a personality need has, of course, implications for public and educational policy.

Theory is related to research in another way: undertaking research about "a problem" and then proceeding to find out all about the problem without any preliminary hypotheses. Theoretical statements may then emerge in the end from the relationships that the data show. This was the case with Gunnar Myrdal's study of the American Negro that we have cited in Chapters 7 and 8.

As an example of this kind of emergence of theory we are presenting a summary (in our words) of some propositions that were distilled out of a large community study of a New England industrial small city. This study was conducted by a team of Harvard anthropologists. Of its five volumes, Volume 3 deals with interethnic relations.

"Yankee City"[5]

A major systematic attempt to delineate the variables in assimilation was made by Warner and Srole. Their criteria of assimilation were the amount and kind of participation permitted the minority ethnic group by the dominant group, as measured by residential mobility, occupational mobility, social class mobility, and membership in formal associations. On the basis of their research they suggest certain variables as determining the rate of assimiliation. In each case the variable mentioned should be read as if preceded with the phrase "other things being equal." They may be summarized as follows:

The Recency Factor. The more recently the ethnic group has come into the community, the slower the degree of assimilation.

The Cultural Similarity Factor. The more divergent the culture of the ethnic group from the normative culture of the dominant status group, the slower the degree of assimilation.

The Concentration Factor. The larger the numerical proportion of the ethnic group in relation to the total population of the area, the slower the degree of assimilation.

The Physiognomic Factor. The "darker" the general physical appearance of the group, the slower the degree of assimilation.

The Permanency Factor. The more temporary the ethnic group conceives its residency in the host society, the slower the degree of assimilation.

These variables lend themselves to the following proposition regarding the assimilation of ethnic groups.

> The greater the difference between the host and the immigrant cultures, the greater will be the subordination, the greater the strength of the ethnic social systems, and the longer the period necessary for the assimilation of the ethnic group.[6]

Whereas this early study was full of rich data, and the theoretical propositions were good descriptive generalizations of what the team found, at least two criticisms can be

[4]See Robin Williams, Jr., *Strangers Next Door* (Englewood Cliffs. N.J.: Prentice-Hall, 1969), pp. 82–110.
[5]W. Lloyd Warner and Leo Srole, *The Social Systems of American Ethnic Groups,* Vol. 3 of the Yankee City Series (New Haven: Yale University Press, 1945).
[6]*Ibid.,* p. 285.

made of the study, and to a degree these criticisms reveal the hazard of not clearly defining assumptions and hypotheses at the beginning of research. The first assumption was that all groups seek assimilation in the four areas they defined. *Indeed this may have been true* for this community, but it is an inadequate assumption for any *inclusive* theory of minorities. Second, the researchers reflect the dominant WASP ethnic group's expectation that the burden of change is on the minorities—therefore assimilation is easiest for those most like dominants in values and behavior (provided they aren't dark complected). No cognizance is taken of discrimination as a factor. In the Yankee City analysis, dominant attitudes of acceptance or enforced subordination and distance *depend* upon minority behavior and appearance (these dominant attitudes then constitute the *dependent variable*). Independent variables can vary. Dependent variables can only respond. The Civil Rights movement showed that many dominants can be reckoned with the statistical group that are the independent variable. This is one of the dangers of not only entering the research task without carefully considered hypotheses, but also of the field technique of living in a community long enough to study it widely and richly without taking on its assumptions and values.

THEORY BUILDING: THE REFINEMENT OF CONCEPTS

If we are to analyze dominant-minority relations, sociology must come to some accepted understanding of the meaning of terms describing the ways in which dominants and minorities relate to one another within a structured situation. (This entails understanding the way in which people pitch their expectations of each other—"structure"—as compared with the way in which they might interact as individual persons.)

We are here presenting three illustrations of critical terms that have changed and expanded in their usage from a very simple reference to a more complex one: acculturation, role, marginality.

Acculturation

All contemporary writing on acculturation takes cognizance of the two levels on which cultural characteristics must be acquired when an individual is divesting himself of one culture and accepting another. These have been described by the terms "manifest" versus "intangible," or "behavioral" versus "attitudinal," or "external" and "internal." Whereas these distinctions are commonplace, little attention has been given to the selectivity involved in taking on new cultural traits, whether external or internal. There is very little known about the resistances that may arise at the introduction of a new culture trait or about specific conditions affecting the traits that are accepted or rejected. For example, there will be a difference of behavioral and/or attitudinal acceptance or resistance according to whether culture traits are forced upon a people or are received voluntarily by them. It will make a difference whether or not there is social or political inequality between groups. The analysis of acculturation must be refined to take cognizance of the situations within which acculturation occurs.[7]

---

[7]Melville J. Herskovits, *Acculturation: The Study of Culture Contact* (Gloucester, Mass.: Peter Smith, 1958). Appendix, "Outline for the Study of Acculturation," by Robert Redfield, Ralph Linton, and Melville J. Herskovits, p. 133.

Warner and others have claimed that acculturation is apt to occur more quickly when two cultures are similar. Here the differentiation between behavioral and attitudinal needs also to be made, as is pointed out by Broom and Kitsuse.[8] They call attention to the fact that the obvious, external culture traits of a minority may be markedly different from those of the host society, but this does not mean that the attitudinal ones are necessarily different. They cite the example of the Japanese, and account in this way for the relatively rapid acculturation of Japanese Americans despite many different external modes of behavior in Japanese culture.

Broom and Kitsuse also point out that the person who is taking on a new culture must "validate" his acculturation by having *qualified* and been *accepted* in the major institutional patterns of the dominant society.[9] In order to do this he must also give up any privileged protection or immunities he has enjoyed by virtue of being a member of a minority. This has been recognized by Frazier and others who have described as "vested interests" the resistances to assimilation of certain status groups within the minority, where incorporation into equal competition with dominants might diminish their advantages. Dominants can equally shut out minorities by patterns of overprotection, by making pets of individual minority members to whom they have some personal tie, or granting disproportionate privilege to those toward whom they feel guilty. In this connection, Margaret Mead, as anthropologist consultant to the Israel Ministry of Health, cautions with regard to the Arab minority:

> . . . There seemed to be a tendency to demand for the Arab health services far less local contribution than Jewish communities would make and to treat some Arab nomadic groups with a considerable amount of patronage. I fully realize the delicacy of the problem . . . but I think the only safe course of action is to accord the Arab population the same type of expectation, privilege, and responsibility accorded other Israeli citizens, for over-privilege can be as discriminatory as under-privilege, even though there are fewer immediate ill effects.[10]

Validation is the point at which the move to ultimate assimilation will or will not be made. If minority members reject participation in some but not all the major institutional forms of the dominant culture, they have made a choice for stabilized pluralism, with the ensuing development of particular established patterns of interaction with dominants.

Roles

There is an increasing interest in sociological theory in role behavior. A role, as we have seen, is the appropriate behavior associated with a given position in the society.

[8]Leonard Broom and John Kitsuse, "The Validation of Acculturation," in *American Anthropologist,* 57, Feb., 1955, pp. 44 ff.
[9]*Ibid.*
[10]Margaret Mead, "Problems of Cultural Accommodations," in *Assignment in Israel,* Bernard Mandelbaum, ed. (New York: The Jewish Theological Seminary of America, Harper & Brothers, 1958), p. 113.

There are socially expected ways of behaving in each society—a father, a student, a priest, a teacher, a chairman, and so on.

The problem of roles in the older theoretical tradition regarding dominant-minority relations was perceived as part of the problem of culture conflict. Handlin has written eloquently on the threatened patriarchal role of the immigrant father, which did not fit the role definition of an "American" father.[11] The first concern with roles, then, was with conflicts in definition of institutional roles between the dominant groups and subcultural groups. Often this may involve the necessity for *role relearning*.

Other writing on minorities has dealt with a second problem of roles: that of *learning new roles,* which are associated with structures and positions that do not exist in the society in which the individual grew up, so that he has had no opportunity to acquire this kind of role behavior in his general social learning. Individuals from folk societies have had to learn the roles appropriate to large-scale technological societies, such as behavior in formal organizations.

Role theory has pointed out that many dilemmas for the individual are contained in the *conflict of roles* he must assume in a complex society. Conflict may occur between the roles of citizen (cooperative in emphasis), entrepreneur (competitive in emphasis), and member of a family (authoritative, or supportive, or subordinate).[12]

Role theory is concerned with analyzing roles characteristic of situations found recurrently in comparable situations. Thus Yankee traders invading the Reconstruction South played roles associated with marginal business and were stereotyped with traits similar to the stereotype some Gentiles have of Jews. This passing insight of Lipset's was picked up and expanded by Rinder, who suggested crosscultural similarities in the role of the stranger-trader.[13] Stryker has carried the delineation further in an article that explores the circumstances under which prejudice will develop against these middlemen traders. He compares attitudes toward three groups of these peoples in the nineteenth century: Jews in Germany, Christian Armenians in Turkey, and Parsis in India. Prejudice developed against Jews and Armenians, but the variable within these two societies, which was absent in the case of the Parsis, was emergent militant nationalism.[14]

This discussion of the minority trader and the way his role is perceived by the dominant society not only shows the value of a wider conceptual frame in making evaluations of particular social behavior, but the sequence of the discussion from Lipset to Rinder to Stryker is an excellent example of how theory is developed.

Marginality

Park was the first sociologist to be concerned with the concept of marginality. He and his students emphasized the role of culture conflict affecting the marginal individual. Thus marginality, in Park's terms, refers to the situation in which an individual finds himself when he still retains values and behavior from the culture group in which

---

[11] Oscar Handlin, *The Uprooted* (Boston: Little, Brown & Co., 1951).
[12] Robert K. Merton, *Social Theory and Social Structure* (Glencoe, Ill.: The Free Press, 1968), p. 369.
[13] Seymour Martin Lipset, "Changing Social Status and Prejudice: The Race Theories of a Pioneering American Sociologist," *Commentary,* May, 1950, pp. 475–479. p. 477; Irwin D. Rinder. "Strangers in the Land," in *Social Problems,* Winter, 1958–1959, 6:253 ff.
[14] Sheldon Stryker, "Social Structure and Prejudice," in *Social Problems,* Spring, 1959, 6:340 ff.

he had his early childhood training and subsequently attempts to incorporate other values and ways of behaving derived from experience outside his own group. Stonequist expanded Park's concept of marginality to show alternative individual modes of adaptation to this conflict.[15] The emphasis of these earlier writers was on the conflict engendered in the personality by the attempt to internalize two differing sets of values.

Merton sees marginality as behavior "in which the individual seeks to abandon one membership group for another to which he is socially forbidden access." For Merton the concept of marginality is a special instance of reference group theory.[16]

The term *reference group* was introduced by Herbert Hyman, and has been expanded by Merton and his associates. In his initial article, Hyman pointed out that many individuals tend to identify themselves with a group to which they do not in fact belong but to whom they accord prestige. This group is their point of reference, whose behavior and attitudes they attempt to adopt.[17] Frazier states that in the post-Civil War South there was an invasion of "New England School marms" setting up schools for Negroes, who were able to create a generation of Negroes with the best culture of New England.[18] These teachers were a reference group for their students. But, as Merton comments, such reference group behavior may be dysfunctional to the person's best interests. If his reference group is a closed group to which he can never belong—that is, if he is marginal—his newly adopted behavior may initially lead to confusion.[19] However, if positions in the social structure are open to the person, he will be able to use the new behavior he has learned.

The rigidity or fluidity of the society as a whole will affect how the person is received. If the society has rigid barriers against movement from one group to another, the person adapting to modes of a group other than his own will be rejected and ridiculed by the outside group, as some Southerners at times speak of educated Negroes as "uppity." If the society is less rigid, a Negro who achieves a good job, good manners, and good speech may, in New York for example, be respected by whites and Negroes alike.

Park and Stonequist's approach to marginality supplied sociological dimensions for the explanation of behavior that had previously been viewed as individual deviance and evaluated in moral terms. They wrote at a time when American society was incorporating large groups of migrants of diverse cultural origins. Under Merton the concept of marginality is enlarged, so that it applies not only to individuals of ethnic or racial subgroups but to any individual who seeks entrance to and is denied admission to a group, a stratum, or a community. Merton stresses the role of the excluding group as a new dimension of Park's original formulation.

THEORY BUILDING: MIDDLE-RANGE THEORY

Robert K. Merton, who coined the term "middle-range theory," has stated that ". . . theory must advance on . . . interconnected planes: through special theories adequate

---

[15]E. V. Stonequist, *The Marginal Man* (New York: Charles Scribner's Sons, 1937).
[16]Robert K. Merton and Alice Rossi, "Contributions to the Theory of Reference Group Behavior," in Robert K. Merton, *Social Theory and Social Structure,* p. 266.
[17]Herbert H. Hyman, "The Psychology of Status," in *Archives of Psychology,* No. 269, 1942.
[18]E. Franklin Frazier, *Race and Culture Contacts in the Modern World* (New York: Alfred A. Knopf, 1957), p. 309.
[19]Robert K. Merton, *Social Theory and Social Structure,* pp. 266 ff.

to limited ranges of social data, and the evolution of a more general conceptual scheme adequate to consolidated groups of special theories."[20] We have just dealt with an array of generalizations based on a limited range of data, and in some instances seen how they have modified or amplified one another. Middle-range theory seeks a consolidation of related insights at a more abstract level than those we have considered thus far in the framework of theory building.

Merton envisages theory growing out of empirical data and an inductive process of reasoning, though he himself has largely worked deductively. Middle-range theory thus far has not stated a relationship to one or another "grand theory," but many of the assumptions underlying it are so derived. In Merton's own work, with its emphasis on structure and function, one may see his heritage, though modified and made his own, from Parsons.

Middle-range theory has made significant contributions to problems of dominant-minority relations. It now awaits increased testing on comparative material to define accurately which variables are generic to minority situations. To illustrate this level of theory we present two of Merton's theoretical formulations that are now a recognized part of all thinking about minority situations, and a third illustration.

"The Self-Fulfilling Prophecy"[21]

In this classic essay Merton explores the phenomenon of the *vicious cycle* created by discrimination. He is concerned with analyzing how it gets started and what is inherent in its control. Merton's theory has broader applications than just the vicious cycle, and lends itself equally well to an analysis of, for example, outbreaks of violence.

Starting with the theorem of W. I. Thomas, "If men define situations as real, they are real in their consequences," Merton points out that the trouble begins with an incomplete or false definition of the situation. If this false definition is acted on, it brings about a situation that fits the definition. His first illustration is of how a bank can be caused to fail when a rumor starts that it is shaky. The rumor (false definition) brings about a run on the bank (behavior) that precipitates its failure. His second illustration is of unions excluding Negroes because Negroes have been strike breakers; then since they cannot join unions they will obviously have no union loyalty that would keep them from accepting employment in a shop whose workers are on strike. Merton's theory illuminates the nature of stereotypes. The dominant group's beliefs (definitions of situations) result in discriminatory actions that so structure the interacting of dominants and minorities that they force the minority to intensify the derogated behavior and thus give the stereotype validity.

Furthermore, Merton points out that when a minority has been enclaved in a stereotype—that is to say, a false definition of character and behavior—the minority individual who behaves in the approved mode of the dominant group is criticized for so doing. The same behavior is defined differently by the dominant group, depending on whether it is displayed by one of their own group or a member of the minority group. What is virtue for the dominant group becomes vice in the eyes of the majority for the

[20]*Ibid.,* Introduction, pp. 9–10.
[21]*Ibid.,* pp. 421–436.

stereotyped minority. If, as Merton cites, a Presbyterian rises from rags to riches, he is held up as a model. If a Jew does the same he is condemned as being too acquisitive and too ambitious.

In considering how the circle of self-fulfilling prophesies can be broken, Merton posits that, logically and ideally, one should begin with a redefinition of the situation. This, however, is not a simple act of will or good will, for deep-seated beliefs are themselves the products of social forces. He notes, furthermore, the hopelessness of trying to persuade the psychologically disturbed. Similarly, he is less than optimistic about education as the way out. The fact that the educational system is itself part of the normative institutional structure of the dominant society makes it subject to the, at best, "incomplete" definitions that dominants make of minorities.

For this reason, Merton sets his hope for remedy in the deliberate enactment of institutional change. Returning to his initial illustrations of the failure of a bank and action against Negroes, he points out that banking legislation, or the statutory creation of interracial public housing have been effective enacted institutional controls. The original proposition then may be restated in this way: "The self-fulfilling prophecy, whereby fears are translated into reality, operates only in the absence of deliberate institutional controls."[22]

"Social Structure and Anomie"[23]

In this essay Merton shows how the social structure poses problems of adaptation for individuals in the competitive opportunities offered the members of society. He points out that the person who achieves an honored place in the society is expected to pursue goals which society values, using the means of which the society approves. But other patterns of adjustment occur depending on opportunity within the society. Some people have incorporated the approved goals into their thinking very early and have been trained appropriately at successive stages in how to pursue them. The boy who goes to a good school, a college of standing, and a recognized school for business or professional training, or becomes associated with a reputable firm, may expect, according to his talents, to achieve desirable goals by legitimate means. But the boy who goes to an overcrowded, understaffed school and cannot get into a good college, or any college, will be at a competitive disadvantage in achieving those same goals. He may lower his aspirations but retain the approved means of pursuing such goals as he can attain. He will be good, conscientious, but not so successful. He may on the other hand, retain the goals and abandon the approved means. He may then become a racketeer or robber baron or a canny politician. He may make a fortune, and perhaps his descendants will endow a college or a church. Or if the barriers are too great or too confusing, he may reject both goals and means. He may retreat into reactive movements, cults, daydreams perhaps stimulated by television or other mass escape mechanisms, or opiates.

The final alternative offered in Merton's paradigm is that of rebellion: the attempt to change both the goals and means. This alternative suggests the association with groups supporting "unofficial values" or counter ideologies. (See Chapter 2.)

---

[22]*Ibid.*, p. 436.
[23]*Ibid.*, pp. 131–160. *Anomie* is a term used to describe a condition characterized by lack of norms.

Merton has prepared a now well-known paradigm that summarizes the choices of adaptation to goals and means.[24]

Modes of Adaptation	Culture Goals	Institutional Means
I. Conformity	+	+
II. Innovation	+	−
III. Ritualism	−	+
IV. Retreatism	−	−
V. Rebellion	±	±

The contribution of this theory is not in labeling the behavior as rebellion or innovation but in providing an explanation of why one might expect to find such behavior more frequently in minority groups than in the dominant group. The explanation, according to Merton, lies in the differential access to the means (education, capital, and so on) for achieving the goals of the dominant culture. According to this theory, as these minorities achieve equality of opportunity, one would expect a decline in such types of deviant behavior.

In Kluckhohn's description of the Navaho as quoted in Chapter 11, p. 226, we can see an almost perfect application of this paradigm. It is interesting that in the first version of Merton's essay he did not include the dimension of rebellion. When it was pointed out that there was a fifth alternative Merton revised his essay, as may be seen from the comparison of his first edition and his revised edition of *Social Theory and Social Structure*. Indeed the whole revised edition includes continuities of former ideas, reflecting not only further research, but also the stimulus of discussion and debate with other critical minds. The productive intellectual life can only flourish in intellectual interaction. Theory building depends on this as well as on valid research.

Revitalization Movements

Movements that are organized efforts to revitalize "native" culture and sentiments are now generally recognized to be a special phenomenon of social change. The term "nativist" may apply to a movement within any group, dominant or minority.

A special characteristic of a nativist movement is that it seeks to solve the discomforts which its adherents feel by eliminating what is perceived as alien: persons, artifacts, customs, values.[25] As long as there are visible minorities, they are in a vulnerable position as the target of organized nativist sentiment and action from the dominant group.

Some nativist movements seek to revive and reinstate customs, values, and even beliefs that were thought to be part of the culture complex of earlier generations but are not now present. The Nazis did this with their appeal to *Blut and Boden* (blood—German "Aryan"; and soil—homeland).

The definable stages of the growth of nativist movements have been analyzed by Wallace. At the beginning of the movement the emphasis on excluding alien elements

[24]*Ibid.*, p. 140. By permission.
[25]Anthony F. C. Wallace, "Revitalization Movements," in *American Anthropologist,* 59, 1956, pp. 264 ff.

is commonly very low, subordinate to other emphases. Over a number of years the movement grows where individuals or some population group (class, religious, or other definable social group) is experiencing stress. There is a continued lessening of the culture's efficiency in satisfying the needs of this group. The type of leader who reformulates a desirable social system for the group tends to be of the charismatic leadership type, the man with strong personal appeal.

After the movement is conceived and leadership established, it must deal with the establishment of communication and with organization. If it is successful through these initial stages, its success or failure rests on the adequate prediction of the outcome of conflict situations. If it is "unrealistic" about the amount of resistance it will engender, about the consequences of its own and its opponent's moves in a power struggle, it will run the risk of early collapse. Whether its ideology or organization will be viable for long beyond its demise in the power struggle will depend on whether its formulations and structure lead to actions that maintain a low level of stress. This would account for the collapse of defeated political nativistic movements that maximize stress, in contrast with the persistence of religious revivalist or sectarian movements that lower the threshold of stress.

We have cited revitalization movements in Chapters 4 and 12, but it might be interesting to take this theoretical schema and examine antiminority nativist movements in the United States as presented by the historian John Higham.[26]

THEORY BUILDING: A TASTE OF "GRAND THEORY"

We have chosen four examples of general, overall theoretical positions by sociologists of this century in America who have sought to analyze society as a whole. The first two emphasize interaction as the critical focus of the study of society. The last two emphasize social structure, that is to say, the persistent patterns that ensure stability and continuity.

It is impossible to summarize briefly the rich contributions of these four men. We have selected just enough to demonstrate approaches, and how these approaches can be related to understanding dominant-minority relations.

Robert E. Park

Robert E. Park's systematic analysis of society revolved around three postulated basic modes of human *interaction:* cooperation, competition, and conflict. Race and culture contacts were subsumed under this system.[27] He attempted to explore the diversity in race and culture contacts, from those of accommodative peace to those of open conflict. His assumptions were the evolutionary beliefs that were the critical intellectual issues of his period—the early part of this century. With this orientation, Park saw relations between dominants and minorities as moving through a definite cycle, with one outcome, the assimilation of the minority into the dominant society. The se-

[26]John Higham, *Strangers in the Land: Patterns of American Nativism,* (New Brunswick, N.J.: Rutgers University Press), 1955.
[27]Robert E. Park, *Race and Culture* (Glencoe, Ill.: The Free Press, 1950).

quence of competition, conflict, cooperation was a dynamic process in which Park ignored any volitional elements. This makes him the most deterministic of the theorists we are presenting and the least concerned with psychological and motivational dimensions.

Park's work, together with that of his colleague, Louis Wirth, made the first major impact on theory of dominant-minority relations. The work of these two men and others associated with them as colleagues or students comprise what has been called the Park-Wirth school of thought about "race relations." Several of Park's formulations have been incorporated into all subsequent thinking about minorities and have been validated or expanded by subsequent theory and research. One of the most significant of these is the concept of the marginal man. Park also saw that prejudice is to be separated from discrimination, that it cannot be dispelled by knowledge alone, that it rises in periods of social change as individuals and vested interests resist change in the status of minorities, or, otherwise threatened, vent hostility on a vulnerable minority. Park took cognizance of conflict of interest in the dynamics of social interaction, a dimension neglected by some contemporary theorists. He was also interested in the effect of urbanization on conflict between races and nationality groups. He felt that urbanization increased tension between dominants and minorities. Contemporary research in urban patterns of interaction suggests this may not always be so, depending on other variables.[28]

George C. Homans

A contemporary sociologist whose analysis is on the basis of *interaction* is George C. Homans. The fundamental unit in society, for Homans, is the group as a social system. The elements of group behavior are activities, interaction, and sentiment. These three elements in their various interrelations and priorities constitute the social system.[29]

Homans distinguishes between an "external system" of relationships of these elements that relate primarily to survival in the environment and an "internal system" that is related to liking and preferences. External and internal systems are never wholly independent of one another, but a different order of precedence of the three basic factors governs each system. Essentially, what Homans is accounting for is the type of interaction related to survival in the larger society as contrasted with the type of interaction that allows the persistence of widely differentiated subgroups within the society.

Homans derives his three basic elements of behavior from a series of empirical case studies of group behavior, ranging from kinship to occupation. He develops some specific propositions, several of which can be applied to dominant-minority relations.

> Proposition 1
> . . . persons who interact with one another frequently are more like one another in their activities than they are like other persons with whom they interact less frequently.

---

[28]For a reevaluation of Park by a contemporary sociologist, see Lipset, "Changing Social Status and Prejudice: The Race Theories of a Pioneering American Sociologist," pp. 475–479.
[29]George C. Homans, *The Human Group* (New York: Harcourt, Brace & Co., 1950).

Thus, in line with this proposition, which establishes in Homans' scheme the basis for group coherence, one would expect that individuals in a minority group or in the dominant group who associate frequently would develop similarities of activities that would identify them both subjectively and objectively with their group. This might serve as a base for the development of stereotypes, but, equally, if group barriers disappear to permit frequent interaction, the differences of activity should disappear also.

Proposition 2
. . . the more frequently persons interact with one another, the stronger their sentiments of friendship for one another are apt to be.

This proposition would be basic to the reduction of intergroup diffidence or antagonism. Antagonism can be dispelled if there is a structured situation within which dominants and minorities can interact as equals. Out of interaction sentiments of friendship will develop, as, ideally, with school integration.

Proposition 3
. . . to the degree that the activities of the other individual in a reciprocal role relationship conform to the norms of one's own group, one will like him.

One might interpret this proposition to suggest that where minority group individuals and dominants carry out their roles in relation to one another with the same standards (for example, two civil servants), they are more likely to conceive of each other as individuals to whom one assigns liking and respect, rather than as representatives of their group.

It is hardly necessary to point out that many efforts at improved intergroup relations operate on one or another of these propositions, whether or not the organizers of programs have ever heard of Homans. Homans' analysis has also stimulated a large development in small group research. His concern is with the dynamics of relationship and he gives greater weight to effective sentiments in his basic schema than do many sociologists. Homans' later work moves even closer to psychology.

Robert M. MacIver

Robert M. MacIver must be included in any discussion of general theory particularly relevant to dominant-minority relations for a number of reasons. Perhaps the least significant but most obvious of these is that he has, in addition to general theory, written specifically on dominant-minority relations.[30]

MacIver's contributions to general theory are largely those of precision and emphasis. He is in the tradition of the classical sociologists of continental Europe, England, and America. Like Park, his assumptions are evolutionary; unlike Park, he avoids the value judgment of "progress," nor is he as deterministic as Park in his view of social

---

[30]Robert M. MacIver, *The More Perfect Union* (New York: The Macmillan Co., 1948). For MacIver's general analysis of social structure and change, see Robert M. MacIver and Charles H. Page, *Society* (New York: Holt, Rinehart & Winston, 1949).

change. For MacIver, for good or ill, societies evolve from the simple to the complex. Within the broad limits of evolutionary development, however, there is room for voluntaristic action to determine directions of change and solutions to problems created by change.

The complexity of the evolving modern social world intrigues MacIver. His main concerns are with the analysis of social structure as a mechanism for sustaining an appropriate balance of necessary controls and optimum individual creativity. He has coined the term "the multi-group society." MacIver sees the State in a preeminent role in modern society (he is also distinguished for his writings in political science). Nevertheless, he is convinced of the limited effectiveness of the State if it intrudes beyond its proper sphere, which is adjudicator of competing interests.

MacIver makes a distinction between like (competing) interests and common interests. The function of the State is to regulate *like* interests. *Common* (cultural) interests, where the pursuit of the interest by some members of the society does not detract from the total available to others, is a sphere in which the State is ill-suited or incapable of functioning.

MacIver, concerned as he is with the institutional regulatory patterns of society, still emphasizes that the social reality is groups and associations of people. For him culture is the vehicle for creative and spontaneous expression. All compulsion in the cultural sphere is deadening. MacIver, in his insistence on the independence of the cultural sphere, opens the way to a redefinition of the question of cultural pluralism more in harmony with what currect research is finding to be the reality.

Talcott Parsons[31]

The most ambitious attempt at overall formulation of an inclusive theory of society is that of Parsons, and no discussion of theory could omit mention of his work. Here we can only present his basic approach and discuss briefly one of his theoretical contributions that has become a useful tool for analysis. Parsons seeks for as abstract formulations as possible and he often links words in a complicated way to indicate a specific concept as an expression of various related dimensions. He has, therefore a rather special and difficult vocabulary.

Parsons begins with emphasizing three dimensions of human behavior: the social, the cultural, and the motivational. These are not just randomly part of a person's relations to others, but each dimension shows recurring regularities—in short, it is a system of behavior. There are motivational systems, cultural systems, and social systems. Consider for example the motivations of Anglo sportsmen and Indian fishers in the controversy described in Chapter 11. Their difference in motivation changes the way they fish, so that net fishing by Indians concerned with preserving their food supply is not as depleting as net fishing might be for sportsmen interested in a competitive size of catch; yet the sportsman responds to a motivation that is part of his personality and that of others who have been brought up in a competitive society. It is not individual greed that motivates him, but an accepted way of being—a system of behavior. In the same way cultural behavior occurs within a systematic set of symbols: "We speak English," "We are a church-going family" are expressions of symbolic behavior.

---

[31]Talcott Parsons, *The Social System* (Glencoe, Ill.: The Free Press, 1950).

The social system is made up of the patterns that insure the survival and continuity of the society: kinship, occupation, etc. These three dimensions—motivation, culture, and society—are held together and made coherent by a consensus of central values. Values, as we pointed out in Chapter 2, are defined by Parsons as "beliefs leading to action." Historically in America we have held as values that man should attempt to overcome and control the hazards of the natural environment; that competition and private property are appropriate values on which to build our economic life; that the nuclear family of father, mother, and children has priority over the extended kinship of aunts, uncles, and grandparents. The survival of a particular society with its values makes necessary the creation of specific positions that represent the distribution of functions in the society. These might be occupational positions, such as banker, machinist, farmer, private secretary, and so forth; or within the kinship patterns, father, aunt, stepmother. These positions are statuses, ranked higher or lower in community evaluation according to how central they are to the preservation of the core values and how limited they are in replaceability. East status demands the carrying out of a function in a socially defined way. This is role.

Parsons' chief focus thus far has been on the *social* system. He sees its institutional structure as regulative, defining the legitimate limits of action, and as relational in its establishment of reciprocal role expectations. Institutions for Parsons translate the private acceptance of values into public commitment, through the carrying out of institutionally defined roles. He sees such problems as negative stereotyping as *deviance by the dominant* from his own institutional norms for the entire society. So long as discrimination is accepted and reinforced within the dominant society, no *single individual has to pay the price for deviance of this kind,* as in other circumstances he would through various kinds of social punishments.[32]

Critics of Parsons have charged that he is too limited in his emphasis on institutional integration and socially induced personality stress. It is felt that he overlooks real conflict of interest in his concern for the stabilizing regulative mechanisms of society and individual acceptance of or reaction formation against these structures.

In Parsons' own view his most significant theoretical contribution has been in the development of what are generally called "pattern variables." These are five pairs of alternatives that the individual may choose as a way of relating to others. Clearly the individual does not choose deliberately, but as a person socialized within a culture and within a given social situation with its expectations of role and status behavior. On a very simple level the pattern variables can delineate dichotomies in expectations as between one culture and another, or a village society and a cosmopolitan society. Some of the variables in their original formulation[33] were

(1) Particularism versus universalism—that is, in a particularistic pattern a person or object is significant, whereas in universalism a precept is significant. For example, Puerto Ricans today, like older ethnic groups in the past, may see employment in terms of getting a relative a job (if they have one and know of another in the same shop). This is particularism. The union, however, is interested in general hiring policies, and seniority privileges regardless of personal or ethnic ties (ideally). This is universalism.

(2) The second pair of variables is affect positive versus affect neutrality. Affect positive means the willingness to risk the expression of feeling in the expectation of a re-

[32]*Ibid.*, p. 290.
[33]*Ibid.*, p. 67.

warding response. This is characteristic of small groups with frequent interaction of the members, or with very stable small subsocieties. In urban society, with its many daily contacts and its multigroup character, it is impossible to risk the psychic burden of affective relationships in all contacts, and a pattern of viable choice develops in which the individual is restrained, cautious, and uninvolved (affect neutral).

Others of the variables need not be elaborated: they are self-interest (individualism) versus collective interest; achievement versus ascription (performance as contrasted with known quality); specificity versus diffuseness (specialization of roles and/or contractually defined limits of obligation versus commitment beyond any defined limit, or roles so loosely defined that they encompass many diverse interactions with varying obligation and response patterns depending on the interaction and not on the role definition).

Parsons has somewhat revised this earliest formulation to make the variables more abstractly stated in the hope of making them more flexible tools for many levels of analysis. In this earliest formulation, however, they already add a considerable dimension for our view of areas of conflict in behavioral expectations as between dominants and cultural minorities, or as between rural and urban patterns of living and evaluating. For example: A small homogeneous village society will not be able to offer wide choices of roles, therefore role specialization is not a realistic choice; or collective interest may be made by the pressure of social norms to take priority over individual self-interest. The student might attempt to apply these to the five communities of Rimrock as discussed in Chapter 12.

The three contemporary theorists we have just presented have taken cognizance, by their respective designations of "like," "external," and "social," of the separation of the secular systems of relationship and the cultural systems of relations. These latter allow, in MacIver's terms, more creative spontaneity; in Homan's terms, more sentiment-engendered interaction; in Parsons' terms, more particularistic values; and in keeping with all three, the possibility of great variety of group life. The cultural sphere is, as it were, terrain for abundant variant flowering, flourishing from a root of common interest, common norms, and established position in the secular order. All three theorists recognize the interdependence of the social and cultural, but all recognize that the spheres are of a different order. Thus the base is laid for the role of culture in our pluralistic society.

Only the experience of America could produce such a theory. Heretofore, cultural pluralism has been discussed as if whole cultures, with their sacred and secular systems intact, were to be incorporated in a quasi-federal fashion. The risks of fragmentation, separation, loss of benefit, and eventual instability of the nation-state have been apparent in this older theory,and aroused grave doubts about the support of that kind of pluralistic society. The solution here presented suggests the appropriateness of separating those functions that are uniquely cultural from the totality, allowing their voluntary development in a variety of patterns and strengthening unity in areas of secular public interest. MacIver feels strongly that such a possibility is inherent in the democratic state. It is in the light of these theories that we can then understand Frazier's vision of cosmopolitan urban societies of the future, in which the interaction of people of varying racial and ethnic identification on the basis of equality will lead to a new flow of human creativity.[34]

---

[34]E. Franklin Frazier, *Race and Culture Contacts in the Modern World* (New York: Alfred A. Knopf, 1957).

Suggested Readings

Dahlke, H. Otto. "Race and Minority Riots—A Study in the Typology of Violence," in *Social Forces,* May, 1952.

In this article Dahlke extrapolates the common elements in disparate situations in which riots have occurred. It is a good example of how theoretical hypotheses are developed.

Hughes, Everett C. "Social Change and Status Protest," in *Phylon,* Vol. X, First Quarter, 1949.

The author, who has richly contributed to the literature on minorities, anticipates here by nearly three decades some of the phenomena we are now witnessing in the Negro revolt.

(This article is available in a Bobbs-Merrill reprint.)

MacIver, Robert M. *The Web of Government.* New York: The Macmillan Co., 1947.

The entire argument is an elaboration of MacIver's theory of the state, and the last chapter on the "multi-group" society is especially relevant.

Merton, Robert K. *Social Theory and Social Structure,* rev. ed. Glencoe, Ill.: The Free Press, 1957.

Merton's principal contributions to middle-range theory, including elaborations and further thoughts on the self-fulfilling prophecy, social structure and anomie, and reference groups.

Parsons, Talcott. *The Social System.* Glencoe, Ill.: The Free Press, 1950.

Parsons' elaboration of the structure of the social system. Chapter 3 discusses the various combinations of particularistic and universalistic values found in different cultures.

Index of Authors

Index of Subjects

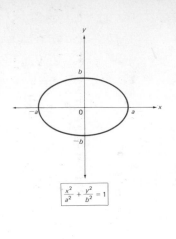

$$\frac{x^2}{a^2} + \frac{y^2}{b^2} = 1$$

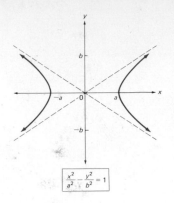

$$\frac{x^2}{a^2} - \frac{y^2}{b^2} = 1$$

$y = \sin x$

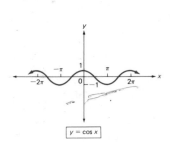

$y = \cos x$

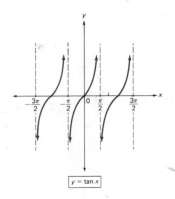

$y = \tan x$

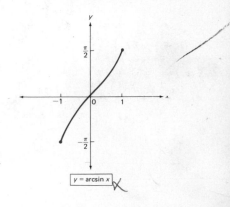

$y = \arcsin x$

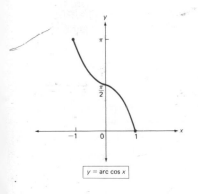

$y = \text{arc cos } x$

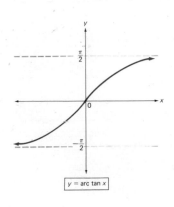

$y = \text{arc tan } x$

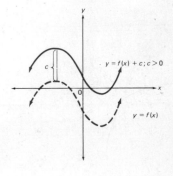

$y = f(x) + c\,;\,c > 0$

$y = f(x)$

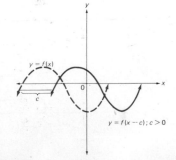

$y = f(x)$

$y = f(x - c)\,;\,c > 0$

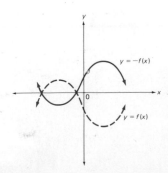

$y = -f(x)$

$y = f(x)$

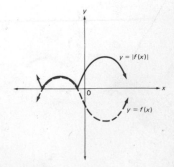

$y = |f(x)|$

$y = f(x)$

ALGEBRA AND

PRENTICE-HALL, INC., ENGLEWOOD CLIFFS, NEW JERSEY   07632

ALGEBRA AND TRIGONOMETRY
A PRE-CALCULUS APPROACH

TRIGONOMETRY

A PRE-CALCULUS APPROACH

SECOND EDITION

Max A. Sobel

Montclair State College

Norbert Lerner

State University of New York at Cortland

Library of Congress Cataloging in Publication Data

Sobel, Max A.
    Algebra and trigonometry.

    Includes index.
      1. Algebra. 2. Trigonometry. I. Lerner, Norbert.
II. Title.
QA154.2.S59 1983   512′.13   82-13346
ISBN 0-13-021634-8

**ALGEBRA AND TRIGONOMETRY:
A PRE-CALCULUS APPROACH
Second Edition**
Max A. Sobel/Norbert Lerner

10 9 8 7 6 5 4 3 2 1

Editorial/production supervision: Kathleen M. Lafferty and Paula Martinac
Interior and cover designs: Walter A. Behnke
Editorial assistant: Susan Pintner
Manufacturing buyer: John B. Hall
Cover illustration: Vitalia Hodgetts

ISBN 0-13-021634-8

PRENTICE-HALL INTERNATIONAL, INC., *London*
PRENTICE-HALL OF AUSTRALIA PTY. LIMITED, *Sydney*
EDITORA PRENTICE-HALL DO BRASIL, LTDA., *Rio de Janeiro*
PRENTICE-HALL CANADA INC., *Toronto*
PRENTICE-HALL OF INDIA PRIVATE LIMITED, *New Delhi*
PRENTICE-HALL OF JAPAN, INC., *Tokyo*
PRENTICE-HALL OF SOUTHEAST ASIA PTE. LTD., *Singapore*
WHITEHALL BOOKS LIMITED, *Wellington, New Zealand*

CONTENTS

1

Real numbers, equations, inequalities
page 1

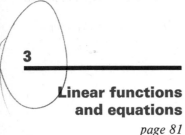

2

**Fundamentals
of algebra**
page 35

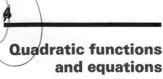

3

**Linear functions
and equations**
page 81

4

**Quadratic functions
and equations**
page 133

PREFACE

Algebra and Trigonometry: A Pre-Calculus Approach has been written to provide the essential concepts and skills of algebra and trigonometry that are needed for further study in mathematics, with special emphasis given to direct preparation for the study of calculus. Thus a major objective of this book is to provide a text that will help students make a more comfortable transition from elementary mathematics to calculus. Many users of the first edition of this text found this pre-calculus approach to be extremely helpful, and this approach has been expanded in this revised second edition.

All too often students are unable to adapt their knowledge of basic mathematics to calculus. In an effort to solve this complex problem of transition, the authors have included exercises and material that can best be described as being *directly supportive* of topics in calculus. Some examples of these *supportive* items follow. Note that the calculus topics themselves are *not* included in the text.

Simplifying derivatives.   *Calculus topic*

Procedures needed to simplify derivatives are included using the   *Pre-calculus support*
same algebraic forms as will be encountered later in calculus. For

$$\frac{1}{x^{\frac{2}{3}}} = \frac{4(x-2)}{3}$$

example, the students learn to convert $x^{1/3} + \dfrac{x-8}{3x^{2/3}}$ (the derivative of $x^{1/3}(x-8)$) into the form $\dfrac{4(x-2)}{3x^{2/3}}$.

Calculus topic	The concept of a derivative.
Pre-calculus support	Work with difference quotients is introduced early and reinforced throughout as new functions are studied.
Calculus topic	Using the signs of derivatives.
Pre-calculus support	Inequalities are considered early in the book. These concepts are applied later to determine the signs of a variety of functions. A convenient tabular format is used throughout that can easily be extended for working with signs of derivatives when the students get to calculus.
Calculus topic	The chain rule for derivatives.
Pre-calculus support	In addition to the usual work in forming composites of given functions, special material is included that shows how to reverse this process. For example, the student learns how to view a *given* function, such as $f(x) = \sqrt{(2x-1)^5}$, as the composition of other functions. Much of the difficulty students have later with the chain rule appears to be related to the inability to do this type of decomposition.
Calculus topic	Applied or verbal problems.
Pre-calculus support	A major difficulty that many students have throughout calculus with such problems deals with setting up functions related to practical or geometric situations. Students are introduced to this type of thinking in Section 3.8 (a new section for this edition), and this experience is reinforced later via follow-up exercises as the course progresses.

There is an extensive review of the fundamentals of algebra in Chapter 2. However, much of the work with solving equations is delayed until the appropriate functions are studied. Thus, for example, quadratic equations are studied in the setting of quadratic functions. This allows for further building on algebraic skills as the course progresses while simultaneously showing how solutions to equations can be viewed as intercepts of related curves.

The text also contains a strong emphasis on graphing throughout. The objective is to have students become familiar with basic graphs and learn how to obtain new curves from these by using translations and reflections.

Improving the students' ability to read mathematics should be a major goal of a pre-calculus course. To assist students in this direction, the exposition here is presented in a relaxed style that avoids unnecessary mathematical jargon without sacrificing mathematical accuracy. Also, a number of highly successful pedagogical features that were commended in the first edition have been maintained and expanded. Included in this text are the following features that are designed to assist the students in using the book for self-study and to reinforce classroom instruction:

TEST YOUR UNDERSTANDING:

These are short sets of exercises (in addition to the regular exercises) that are found within most sections of the text so that students can test knowledge of new material just developed. Answers to these are given at the end of each chapter.

CAUTION ITEMS:

Where appropriate, students are alerted to the typical kind of errors that they should avoid.

ILLUSTRATIVE EXAMPLES AND EXERCISES:

The text contains numerous illustrative examples with detailed solutions. There are approximately 4500 exercises for the students to try, with answers to the odd-numbered exercises given at the back of the book.

REVIEW EXERCISES:

Each chapter has a set of review exercises that are keyed directly to the illustrative examples developed in the text. Students can use these as a review of the work of the chapter and compare results with the worked-out solutions that can be found in the body of the chapter.

MARGINAL NOTES:

Marginal notes are a new pedagogical feature of this second edition designed to assist the students' understanding throughout the text.

SAMPLE TEST QUESTIONS:

Sample test questions are given at the end of each chapter, with answers provided in the back of the book.

In preparing this second edition, the authors have expanded the number of exercises, review exercises, and sample chapter test questions. In addition, several new sections have been added to increase the emphasis on both graphing and applications. A new Chapter 11, Complex Numbers and Polar Coordinates, has also been added. The two optional sections on complex numbers from the first edition have been incorporated into this new chapter.

COURSE STRUCTURE

The text allows for considerable flexibility in the selection and ordering of topics. The first five chapters should be done in sequence. Thereafter the dependency of the chapters is displayed in the diagram.

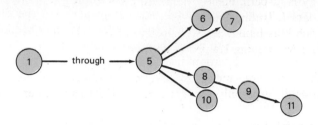

Note: Section 11.1, Complex Numbers, can be incorporated into the work of Chapter 4 on quadratics so that imaginary numbers are available as roots of quadratic equations.

If the students' background is adequate, much of Chapters 1 and 2 can be assigned as self-study or covered quickly. Also, the first few sections of Chapter 3 can be covered quickly in such classes. This would allow for substantial coverage of much of the remaining chapters.

■ This symbol is used to identify exercises that are more *directly* supportive of topics in calculus than the other exercises. Also, when this symbol appears next to a section heading it means that the section and its exercises fall into this support category. For such sections the exercises are not separately labeled with this symbol.

The subject matter labeled with ■ may be treated as optional. It is not prerequisite to the subsequent developments.

✳ This symbol is used to identify exercises of a more challenging nature.

There are different points of view at this time as to the role that calculators should play in a mathematics course. The authors feel this is a choice that must be left to the judgment and discretion of the individual instructor. In this text students are advised occasionally to make use of a calculator to enhance the pedagogical development, as well as to complete certain exercises that involve cumbersome computations. However, use of a calculator is neither a prerequisite nor a requirement for the completion of the course.

Additional comments regarding course content are given in the Instructor's Manual, which is available upon adoption.

ACKNOWLEDGMENTS

The preparation of this second edition was significantly influenced by many individuals. We sincerely thank the many students who used the first edition of *Algebra and Trigonometry: A Pre-Calculus Approach* and who contributed their comments and suggestions. For their detailed reviews, constructive criticisms, and suggestions as we prepared this revision we thank the following professors:

Frank Battles, Massachusetts Maritime Academy
Joe W. Fisher, University of Cincinnati
James Hall, University of Wisconsin, Madison

Louise Hasty, Austin Community College
Kay Hudspeth, Pennsylvania State University
Adam J. Hulin, University of New Orleans
Erich Nussbaum, State University of New York, Albany
Paul M. Young, Kansas State University

For their encouragement, support, and assistance we thank the staff at Prentice-Hall, especially Robert Sickles, Kathleen Lafferty, and Paula Martinac.

For his careful proofreading of the manuscript at all stages, as well as for his many valuable suggestions, we thank George Feissner of the State University of New York at Cortland.

Finally, we thank Karin Lerner for her excellent typing of the manuscript as well as the accompanying Instructor's Manual.

The authors sincerely hope that you will find this book teachable and enjoyable, and welcome your comments, criticisms, and suggestions.

Max A. Sobel
Norbert Lerner

SUGGESTIONS FOR THE STUDENT

You probably are taking this course to prepare for some future course in mathematics, such as calculus. The study of calculus is not easy. One of the major problems that students encounter involves a lack of skill with topics that should have been mastered in advance. It is this necessary preparation that we shall deal with throughout this course.

There will probably be many topics covered in this book that you have seen before in one form or another. Be careful! Don't allow yourself to become complacent because of such familiarity. All too often students will relax their efforts because of such assumed familiarity and fail to recognize that the development of skill in these prerequisite topics is the major objective of preparatory courses such as this. They then come to the calculus or other advanced courses no better prepared than if they had never taken a pre-calculus course in the first place!

How does one succeed in a mathematics course? Unfortunately, there is no universal prescription guaranteed to work. However, the experience that the authors have had with many students throughout their teaching careers provides some guidelines that seem to help. We suggest that you make an effort to follow these suggestions that have been useful to other students who have taken similar courses in the past:

1 Read the text! We recognize that mathematics is not always easy to read, but we have made every effort to make this book as readable as possible. Don't look upon the textbook merely as a source of exercises. Rather, read each section thoroughly to reinforce classroom instruction.

2 Try to complete the illustrative examples that appear within each section before studying the solutions provided. Mathematics is not "a spectator sport"; study the book with paper and pencil at hand.

3 Attempt each "Test Your Understanding" exercise and check your results with the answers given at the back of each chapter. Re-read the section if you have difficulty with these exercises.

4 Try to complete as many of the exercises as possible at the end of each section. Complete the odd-numbered ones first and check your answers with those given at the back of the book. At times your answers may be in a different form than that given in the book; if so, try to show that the two results are equivalent. Considerable efforts have been made to assure that the answers are correct. However, if you happen to find an occasional incorrect answer, please write to let us know about it.

5 Prior to a test you should make use of the review exercises that appear at the end of each chapter. These are collections of representative examples from within each chapter. You can check your results by referring back to the designated section from which they are taken where you will find the completely worked-out solution for each one.

6 Each chapter ends with sample test questions that will help tell you whether or not you have understood the work of that chapter. Check your work with the answers that are given at the back of the book.

7 If you find yourself making a careless error in completing a problem, it would be wise to attempt another similar problem. If you make the same mistake again, it is best to go back and review, since a serious misunderstanding of basic concepts may be involved.

8 If convenient, find time to solve problems with a classmate. Such cooperative efforts can be quite beneficial as you attempt to explain ideas to each other.

We hope that you will have a profitable semester studying from this book. Good luck!

Max A. Sobel
Norbert Lerner

ALGEBRA AND TRIGONOMETRY
A PRE-CALCULUS APPROACH

REAL NUMBERS, EQUATIONS, INEQUALITIES

Real numbers and their properties

Throughout this course we will be concerned with the set of **real numbers**. Here are some examples of such numbers:

$$7 \qquad -5 \qquad \tfrac{2}{3} \qquad \sqrt{13} \qquad 0.25 \qquad 0.333\ldots \qquad \sqrt[3]{17} \qquad \pi$$

We can represent these numbers on a **real number line** and find that each point on the number line may be named by a real number, and each real number is the *coordinate* of a point on the number line. We say that there is a *one-to-one correspondence* between the set of real numbers and the set of points on the number line. Here is a number line with some of its points labeled by real numbers.

WATCH THE MARGINS!
We will use these for special notes, explanations, and hints.

You are undoubtedly familiar with many of the basic properties of the real numbers, although you may not know their specific names. Here is a list of some of these important properties that you may use for reference. In each case letters, called *variables*, are used to represent real numbers.

Closure properties The sum and product of two real numbers is a real number. That is, for any real numbers a and b,

$$a + b \text{ is a real number}$$
$$a \times b \text{ is a real number}$$

The product $a \times b$ may be written in a number of other ways, such as $a \cdot b$, $(a)(b)$, $a(b)$, $(a)b$, or just ab.

Commutative properties The sum and product of two real numbers is not affected by the <u>order in which</u> <u>they are combined</u>. That is, for any real numbers a and b,

$$a + b = b + a$$
$$a \times b = b \times a$$

For example, $12 + 17 = 17 + 12$. Also, $12 \times 17 = 17 \times 12$.

Associative properties The sum and product of three real numbers is the same when the <u>third is</u> combined with the first two or when the first is combined with the last two. That is, for real numbers a, b, and c,

$$(a + b) + c = a + (b + c)$$
$$(a \times b) \times c = a \times (b \times c)$$

For example, $(15 + 23) + 18 = 15 + (23 + 18)$.

Also, $(15 \times 23) \times 18 = 15 \times (23 \times 18)$. The order in which three real numbers are added or multiplied does not affect the result.

Before proceeding with some additional properties of the real numbers, let us pause to be sure that the preceding properties are understood.

TEST YOUR UNDERSTANDING

Throughout this book we shall occasionally pause for you to test your understanding of the ideas just presented. If you have difficulty with these brief sets of exercises, you should reread the material of the section before going ahead. Answers are given at the end of the chapter.

In Exercises 1–6, name the property of real numbers being illustrated.

1 $3 + (\frac{1}{2} + 5) = (3 + \frac{1}{2}) + 5$ 2 $3 + (\frac{1}{2} + 5) = (\frac{1}{2} + 5) + 3$

3 $6 + 4(2) = 4(2) + 6$ 4 $8\pi = \pi 8$

5 $(17 \cdot 23)59 = (23 \cdot 17)59$ 6 $(17 \cdot 23)59 = 17(23 \cdot 59)$

7 Does $3 - 5 = 5 - 3$? Is there a commutative property for subtraction?

8 Give a *counterexample* to show that the set of real numbers is not commutative with respect to division. (That is, use a specific example to show that $a \div b \neq b \div a$.)

9 Does $(8 - 5) - 2 = 8 - (5 - 2)$? Is there an associative property for subtraction?

10 Give a counterexample to show that the set of real numbers is not associative with respect to division.

11 Are $3 + \sqrt{7}$ and $3\sqrt{7}$ real numbers? Explain.

Counterexamples are important in mathematics. To disprove a statement, we need only find *one* case where the statement does not hold.

There is a very important property of the set of real numbers that combines the two operations of addition and multiplication. To introduce this property let us evaluate the expression $5(3 + 9)$ in two different ways.

(a) Add first, then multiply.

$$5(3 + 9) = 5(12)$$
$$= 60$$

(b) Multiply first, then add.

$$5(3 + 9) = (5)(3) + (5)(9)$$
$$= 15 + 45$$
$$= 60$$

The same result is obtained either way. This example illustrates the use of the **distributive property of multiplication over addition**.

The product of a real number times the sum of two others is the same as the sum of the products of the first number times each of the others. That is, for real numbers a, b, and c,

Distributive property

$$a(b + c) = ab + ac$$
$$(b + c)a = ba + ca$$

Verify, by example, that $a(b - c) = ab - ac$.

EXAMPLE 1 Use the distributive property to find the product 7×61.

Solution Think of 61 as $60 + 1$.

$$7 \times 61 = 7 \times (60 + 1)$$
$$= (7 \times 60) + (7 \times 1)$$
$$= 420 + 7 = 427$$

This shows how the distributive property can be used to do mental arithmetic.

The sum of any real number a and zero is the given real number, a.

Identity properties

$$0 + a = a + 0 = a$$

We call zero the *additive identity*.

The product of any real number a and 1 is the given real number, a.

$$1 \cdot a = a \cdot 1 = a$$

We call 1 the *multiplicative identity*.

Inverse properties For each real number a there exists another real number, $-a$, called the negative of a, such that the sum of a and $-a$ is zero.

$$a + (-a) = (-a) + a = 0$$

We also call $-a$ the *additive inverse* or *opposite* of a.

For each real number a different from zero there exists another real number, $\dfrac{1}{a}$, such that the product of a and $\dfrac{1}{a}$ is 1.

$$a \cdot \frac{1}{a} = \frac{1}{a} \cdot a = 1 \qquad a \neq 0$$

We call $\dfrac{1}{a}$ the *multiplicative inverse* or *reciprocal* of a.

EXAMPLE 2 What basic property of the real numbers is illustrated by each of the following?
(a) $6 + (17 + 4) = (17 + 4) + 6$
(b) $\frac{3}{4} + (-\frac{3}{4}) = 0$
(c) $57 \times 1 = 57$
(d) $\frac{2}{3}(12 + 36) = \frac{2}{3}(12) + \frac{2}{3}(36)$
(e) $(-43)\left(\dfrac{1}{-43}\right) = 1$

Solution **(a)** Commutative, for addition **(b)** inverse, for addition **(c)** identity, for multiplication **(d)** distributive **(e)** inverse, for multiplication

Properties of zero The product of a real number a and zero is zero.

$$0 \cdot a = a \cdot 0 = 0$$

This is often referred to as the *multiplication property of zero*.

If the product of two (or more) real numbers is zero, then at least one of the numbers is zero. That is, for real numbers a and b:

If $ab = 0$, then $a = 0$ or $b = 0$, or both $a = 0$ and $b = 0$.

The opposite of the opposite of a real number a is the number a.

$$-(-a) = a$$

The opposite of a sum is the sum of the opposites. That is, for real numbers a and b,

$$-(a + b) = (-a) + (-b)$$

The opposite of a product of two real numbers is the product of one number times the opposite of the other. That is, for real numbers a and b,

$$-(ab) = (-a)b = a(-b)$$

The preceding properties have been described primarily in terms of addition and multiplication. The basic operations of subtraction and division are defined now in terms of addition and multiplication, respectively.

The difference $a - b$ of two real numbers a and b is defined as

$$a - b = a + (-b)$$

For example, $5 - 8 = 5 + (-8)$. Alternatively, we say

$$a - b = c \text{ if and only if } c + b = a$$

Thus $5 - 8 = -3$ because $-3 + (8) = 5$.

When we say "statement p *if and only if* statement q" it means that if either statement is true, then so is the other. Here we say that $a - b = c$ if and only if $c + b = a$ and thus imply these two results:

Whenever $a - b = c$ is true, then so is $c + b = a$.
Whenever $c + b = a$ is true, then so is $a - b = c$.

These statements may also be written in the following briefer "if–then" form.

If $a - b = c$, then $c + b = a$.
If $c + b = a$, then $a - b = c$.

The quotient $a \div b$ of two real numbers a and b is defined as

$$a \div b = a \cdot \frac{1}{b} \qquad b \neq 0$$

For example, $8 \div 2 = 8 \times \frac{1}{2} = 4$. Alternatively, we say

$$a \div b = c \text{ if and only if } c \times b = a \qquad b \neq 0$$

Thus $8 \div 2 = 4$ because $2 \times 4 = 8$.

The statement $a \div b = c$ if and only if $c \times b - a$ means:

If $a \div b = c$, then $c \times b = a$.
If $c \times b = a$, then $a \div b = c$.

This is very important: DIVISION BY ZERO IS NOT POSSIBLE.

Using this definition of division we can see why division by zero is not possible. Suppose we assume that division by zero is possible. Assume, for example, that $2 \div 0 = x$, where x is some real number. Then, by the definition of division, $0 \cdot x = 2$. But $0 \cdot x = 0$, leading to the false statement $2 = 0$. This argument can be duplicated where 2 is replaced by any nonzero number. Can you explain why $0 \div 0$ must also remain undefined? (See Exercise 39.)

EXERCISES 1.1

Name the property illustrated by each of the following.

1 $5 + 7$ is a real number.
2 $8 + \sqrt{7} = \sqrt{7} + 8$
3 $5 + (-5) = 0$
4 $9 + (7 + 6) = (9 + 7) + 6$
5 $(5 \times 7) \times 8 = (7 \times 5) \times 8$
6 $(5 \times 7) \times 8 = 5 \times (7 \times 8)$
7 $\frac{1}{4} + \frac{1}{2} = \frac{1}{2} + \frac{1}{4}$
8 $(4 \times 5) + (4 \times 8) = 4(5 + 8)$
9 $-13 + 0 = -13$
10 $1 \times \frac{1}{9} = \frac{1}{9}$
11 $\frac{1}{2} + (-\frac{1}{2}) = 0$
12 $3 - 7 = 3 + (-7)$
13 $0(\sqrt{2} + \sqrt{3}) = 0$
14 $\sqrt{2} \times \pi$ is a real number.
15 $(3 + 9)(7) = (3)(7) + (9)(7)$
16 $\dfrac{1}{\sqrt{2}} \cdot \sqrt{2} = 1$

Replace the variable n by a real number to make each statement true.

17 $7 + n = 3 + 7$
18 $\sqrt{5} \times 6 = 6 \times n$
19 $(3 + 7) + n = 3 + (7 + 5)$
20 $6 \times (5 \times 4) = (6 \times n) \times 4$
21 $5(8 + n) = (5 \times 8) + (5 \times 7)$

22 $(3 \times 7) + (3 \times n) = 3(7 + 5)$
23 If $5(x - 2) = 0$, then $x = 2$. Explain this statement using an appropriate property of zero.
24 (a) Convert $14 + 3 = 17$ into a subtraction statement.
  (b) Convert $(-6)12 = -72$ into a division statement.
25 Give a basic property that justifies each of the numbered steps.

$$
\begin{aligned}
(5 \div 6)(-3) &= -[(5 \div 6)3] & \text{(i)} \\
&= -[(5 \cdot \tfrac{1}{6})3] & \text{(ii)} \\
&= -[5(\tfrac{1}{6} \cdot 3)] & \text{(iii)} \\
&= -[5(\tfrac{1}{2})] \\
&= -\tfrac{5}{2}
\end{aligned}
$$

26 Give a basic property that justifies each of the numbered steps.

$$
\begin{aligned}
(3)[(-4) - (-9)] &= 3[(-4) - (-9)] & \text{(i)} \\
&= 3[(-4) + (-(-9))] & \text{(ii)} \\
&= 3[(-4) + 9] & \text{(iii)} \\
&= 3(-4) + 3(9) & \text{(iv)} \\
&= -(3 \cdot 4) + 3(9) & \text{(v)} \\
&= 15
\end{aligned}
$$

27 Give the basic property that justifies each step.

$$d[(a + b) + c] = d(a + b) + dc \qquad \text{(i)}$$

$$= (da + db) + dc \qquad \text{(ii)}$$
$$= da + (db + dc) \qquad \text{(iii)}$$
$$= da + (bd + cd) \qquad \text{(iv)}$$
$$= (bd + cd) + da \qquad \text{(v)}$$
$$= (b + c)d + da \qquad \text{(vi)}$$
$$= da + (b + c)d \qquad \text{(vii)}$$

28 Give the reasons for the following proof that multiplication distributes over subtraction.

$$a(b - c) = a[b + (-c)] \qquad \text{(i)}$$
$$= ab + a(-c) \qquad \text{(ii)}$$
$$= ab + [-(ac)] \qquad \text{(iii)}$$
$$= ab - ac \qquad \text{(iv)}$$

29 Note that $2^4 = 4^2$. Is the operation of raising a number to a power a commutative operation? Justify your answer.

30 Give an example showing that addition does *not* distribute over multiplication; that is, $a + (b \cdot c) \neq (a + b) \cdot (a + c)$.

Give two statements that can be made in place of each of the following "if and only if" statements.

31 $10 - x = 7$ if and only if $7 + x = 10$.

32 $12 \div x = 4$ if and only if $4 \times x = 12$.

33 n is an even integer if and only if n^2 is an even integer.

34 n is an odd integer if and only if n^2 is an odd integer.

35 Triangle ABC is congruent to triangle DEF if and only if the three sides of one triangle are congruent to the three sides of the other triangle.

36 A triangle is a right triangle if and only if the sum of the squares of two sides is equal to the square of the third side.

Replace each pair of statements by an "if and only if" statement.

37 If n is a multiple of 3, then n^2 is a multiple of 3. If n^2 is a multiple of 3, then n is a multiple of 3.

38 If n is an odd integer, then $n + 1$ is an even integer. If $n + 1$ is an even integer, then n is an odd integer.

*39 Explain why $\frac{0}{0}$ must remain undefined. (*Hint:* If $\frac{0}{0}$ is to be some value, then it must be a unique value.)

*40 Explain why the real numbers have the closure property for both subtraction and division, excluding division by 0.

Sets of numbers

Within the set of real numbers, there are other collections of numbers that we will have occasion to consider. One such set is the set of **whole numbers**:

$$\{0, 1, 2, 3, 4, 5, \ldots\}$$

This is an example of an **infinite set**; there is no last member. The three dots are used to indicate that this set of numbers continues on without end. By contrast, some of the sets of numbers that we will use will be **finite sets**. The members of a finite set can be listed and counted, and there is an end to this counting. For example, the set of whole numbers that are less than 5 is an example of a finite set:

$$\{0, 1, 2, 3, 4\}$$

At times a set can be classified as finite even though it has so many elements that no one would really want to list them all. Thus the set of counting numbers from 1 through 1,000,000 is a large set, but nevertheless finite inasmuch as it does eventually have a last member. We adopt the convention of using three dots to indicate that some members of a set are not listed and can write this as

$$\{1, 2, 3, \ldots, 1,000,000\}$$

The set consisting of the whole numbers greater than 0, $\{1, 2, 3, 4, 5, \ldots\}$, is often referred to as the set of *natural numbers* or *counting numbers*.

How long do you think it would take you to count to 1,000,000 at the rate of one number per second? (Don't use 1 million seconds as your answer!) First guess. Then use a calculator to help find the answer.

*Throughout the text, an asterisk will be used to indicate that an exercise is more difficult than usual or involves some unusual aspect.

Another set of numbers that we will refer to frequently is the set of **integers**:

$$\{\ldots, -3, -2, -1, 0, 1, 2, 3, \ldots\}$$

We can represent the integers on a number line by locating the whole numbers and their opposites. For example, the opposite of 3 is located three units to the left of 0 on the number line and is named -3 (negative three). The opposite of 2 is -2, the opposite of 1 is -1, and the opposite of 0 is 0.

Observe that the *positive integers* are located to the right of 0 and that the *negative integers* are located to the left of 0. The number 0 is an integer, but is neither positive nor negative. We see that every integer is the coordinate of some point on the number line. Can every point on the line be named by an integer?

TEST YOUR UNDERSTANDING

The word "list" here means that you are either to show all the members of a set or to indicate the members through the use of three dots.

List the elements in each of the following sets.

1 The set of whole numbers less than 5.

2 The set of whole numbers greater than 10.

3 The set of whole numbers *between* 1 and 10. (*Note:* The word "between" means that 1 and 10 are not included.)

4 The set of integers between -3 and 4.

5 The set of negative integers greater than -5.

6 The set of integers less than 2.

7 Which of the preceding sets are finite?

As you can see, there are many points between the integers. Some of these points can be identified by introducing all the numbers that can be written in the form $\frac{a}{b}$, where a and b are integers, with $b \neq 0$. The set of numbers that can be represented in this way is called the set of **rational numbers**.

A **rational number** is one that can be written in the form $\frac{a}{b}$, where a and b are integers, $b \neq 0$.

Every integer is a rational number because it can be written as the quotient of integers. For example, $5 = \frac{5}{1}$. However, not every rational number is an integer. Thus $\frac{2}{3}$ and $-\frac{3}{4}$ are examples of rational numbers (*fractions*) that are not integers.

Every rational number can be written in decimal form. Sometimes the result will be a terminating decimal, as in the following examples:

$$\tfrac{3}{4} = 0.75 \qquad \tfrac{7}{8} = 0.875 \qquad \tfrac{23}{10} = 2.3$$

Other rational numbers will produce a repeating decimal:

$$\tfrac{2}{3} = 0.666\ldots \qquad \tfrac{19}{22} = 0.86363\ldots \qquad \tfrac{3}{7} = 0.428571428571\ldots$$

Usually, a bar is placed over the set of digits that repeat, so that the preceding illustrations can be written in this way:

$$\tfrac{2}{3} = 0.\overline{6} \qquad \tfrac{19}{22} = 0.8\overline{63} \qquad \tfrac{3}{7} = 0.\overline{428571}$$

Some decimals neither terminate nor repeat. You are probably familiar with the number π from your earlier study of geometry. This number is *not* a rational number; it cannot be expressed as the quotient of two integers. The decimal representation for π goes on endlessly without repetition. In fact, one computer recently computed π as a decimal to 100,000 places. Here are the first 100 places:

> A method for converting a repeating decimal into fraction form is considered in Exercises 45 and 46.

$$\pi = 3.14159\ \ 26535\ \ 89793\ \ 23846\ \ 26433\ \ 83279\ \ 50288\ \ 41971\ \ 69399$$
$$37510\ \ 58209\ \ 74944\ \ 59230\ \ 78164\ \ 06286\ \ 20899\ \ 86280\ \ 34825$$
$$34211\ \ 70679\ \ldots$$

It is true that every rational number is the **coordinate** of some point on the number line. However, not every point on the number line can be labeled by a rational number. For example, here is a construction that can be used to locate a point on the number line whose coordinate is $\sqrt{2}$, the *square root* of 2.

At the point with coordinate 1 construct a one-unit segment perpendicular to the number line. Connect the endpoint of this segment to the point labeled 0. This becomes the hypotenuse of a right triangle, and by the Pythagorean theorem can be shown to be the square root of 2, written as $\sqrt{2}$. Using a compass, this length can then be transferred to the number line, thus locating a point with coordinate $\sqrt{2}$.

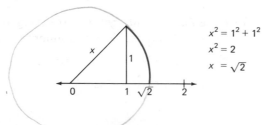

$$x^2 = 1^2 + 1^2$$
$$x^2 = 2$$
$$x = \sqrt{2}$$

It can be proved that $\sqrt{2}$ cannot be expressed as the quotient $\dfrac{a}{b}$ of two integers, and thus is *not* a rational number. We call such a number an **irrational number**. Some other examples of irrational numbers are $\sqrt{5}$, $\sqrt{12}$, $\sqrt[3]{4}$, and π. The term "irrational" is chosen to indicate that such a number cannot be expressed as the ratio of two integers.

When the set of rational numbers and the set of irrational numbers, are combined we have the collection of *real numbers* which will suffice for most of our work in this text. Every real number can be represented by a

PYTHAGOREAN THEOREM

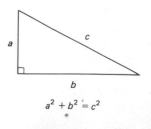

$$a^2 + b^2 = c^2$$

decimal. If the decimal terminates or repeats, the number is a rational number; otherwise, it is an irrational number.

EXAMPLE Classify each number into as many different sets as possible:
(a) 5 **(b)** $\frac{2}{3}$ **(c)** $\sqrt{7}$ **(d)** -14

Solution
(a) 5 is a whole number, an integer, a rational number, and a real number.
(b) $\frac{2}{3}$ is a rational number and a real number.
(c) $\sqrt{7}$ is an irrational number and a real number.
(d) -14 is an integer, a rational number, and a real number.

EXERCISES 1.2

List the elements in each of the sets described in Exercises 1–10.

1 The set of whole numbers less than 3.

2 The set of whole numbers greater than 100.

3 The set of whole numbers between 2 and 7.

4 The set of integers greater than -3.

5 The set of negative integers greater than -3.

6 The set of positive integers less than 5.

7 The set of integers less than 1.

8 The set of integers that are not whole numbers.

9 The set of whole numbers that are not integers.

10 The set of integers that are also rational numbers.

In Exercises 11–20, answer true or false.

11 Every whole number is an integer.

12 Every integer is a whole number.

13 Every integer is a rational number.

14 Every rational number is an integer.

15 Every real number is a rational number.

16 Every irrational number is a real number.

17 Every point on the number line can be associated with a rational number.

18 Every point on the number line can be associated with a real number.

19 Every rational number is the coordinate of some point on the number line.

20 Every real number is a rational or an irrational number.

Classify each number as being a member of one or more of these sets: (a) whole numbers; (b) integers; (c) rational numbers; (d) irrational numbers; (e) real numbers.

21 -15

22 72

23 $\sqrt{5}$

24 $-\frac{3}{4}$

25 $\frac{16}{2}$

26 0.01

27 $\sqrt{49}$

28 1000

29 $\sqrt{12}$

30 $\sqrt{\dfrac{9}{16}}$

31 $\dfrac{-5}{\sqrt{100}}$

32 Draw a number line and locate a point with coordinate $\sqrt{2}$, as shown in this section. At this point construct a perpendicular segment of length 1. Now construct a right triangle with hypotenuse of length $\sqrt{3}$ and use this construction to locate a point on the number line with coordinate $\sqrt{3}$.

*33 Locate a point on the number line with coordinate $\sqrt{5}$.

*34 Locate a point on the number line with coordinate $-\sqrt{2}$.

*35 Take a circular object (like a tin can) and let the diameter be 1 unit. Use this as a unit on a number line. Mark a point on the circular object with a dot and place the circle so that the dot coincides with zero on the number line. Roll the circle to the right and mark the point where the dot coincides with the number line after one revolution. What number corresponds to this position? Why?

*36 From a mathematical point of view, it is common practice to introduce the integers after the counting numbers have been discussed and then develop the rational numbers. Historically, however, the positive rational numbers were developed before the negative integers.

(a) Think of some everyday situations where the negative integers are not usually used but could easily be introduced.

(b) Speculate on the historical necessity for the development of the positive rational numbers.

Use division to convert each fraction into a terminating or repeating decimal.

37 $\frac{4}{5}$ **38** $\frac{257}{100}$

39 $\frac{2}{7}$ **40** $\frac{25}{8}$

41 $\frac{45}{13}$ **42** $\frac{18}{7}$

43 $\frac{13}{900}$ **44** $\frac{279}{55}$

45 Every repeating decimal can be expressed as a rational number in the form a/b. Consider, for example, the decimal 0.727272 ... and the following process:

Let $n = 0.727272 \ldots$ Then $100n = 72.727272 \ldots$

$$100n = 72.727272 \ldots$$

Subtract: $\quad n = .727272 \ldots$

$$99n = 72$$

Solve for n: $\quad n = \frac{72}{99} = \frac{8}{11}$

Use this method to express each decimal as the quotient of integers and check by division.

(a) 0.454545 ... $(0.\overline{45})$ (b) 0.373737 ... $(0.\overline{37})$

(c) 0.234234 ... $(0.\overline{234})$

(*Hint:* Let $n = 0.234$; multiply by 1000.)

*46 Study the given illustration for $n = 0.2737373 \ldots$ and then convert each repeating decimal into a quotient of integers.

Multiply n
by 1000: $1000n = 273.\overline{73}$ The decimal point is *behind* the first cycle.

Multiply n
by 10: $10n = 2.\overline{73}$ The decimal point is in *front* of the first cycle.

Subtract: $\quad 990n = 271$

Divide: $\quad n = \dfrac{271}{990}$

(a) 0.4585858 ...   (b) 3.21444 ...

(c) $2.0\overline{146}$ (d) $0.00\overline{123}$

A statement such as $2x - 3 = 7$ is said to be a **conditional equation**. It is true for some replacements of the variable x, but not true for others. For example, $2x - 3 = 7$ is a true statement for $x = 5$ but is false for $x = 7$. On the other hand, an equation such as $3(x + 2) = 3x + 6$ is called an **identity** because it is true for *all* real numbers x.

To *solve* an equation means to find the real numbers x for which the given equation is true; these are called the **solutions** or **roots** of the given equation. Let us solve the equation $2x - 3 = 7$, showing the important steps.

$2x - 3 = 7 \qquad$ Add 3 to each side of the equation.

$(2x - 3) + 3 = 7 + 3$

$2x = 10 \qquad$ Now multiply each side by $\frac{1}{2}$.

$\frac{1}{2}(2x) = \frac{1}{2}(10)$

$x = 5$

We can check this solution by substituting 5 for x in the original equation.

$2(5) - 3 = 10 - 3 = 7$

In the preceding solution we made use of the following two basic *properties of equality.*

1.3

Introduction to equations and problem solving

A flowchart can be used to illustrate an equation.

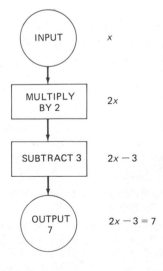

The strength of these two properties is that they produce equivalent equations, equations having the same roots. Thus the addition property converts $2x - 3 = 7$ into the equivalent form $2x = 10$.

ADDITION PROPERTY OF EQUALITY:
For all real numbers a, b, c, if $a = b$, then $a + c = b + c$.

MULTIPLICATION PROPERTY OF EQUALITY:
For all real numbers a, b, c, if $a = b$, then $ac = bc$.

The properties of equality can also be used to solve more complicated equations. The procedure is to *collect all terms with the variable on one side of the equation and all constants on the other side.* Although most of the steps shown can be done mentally, the next two examples will include the essential details that comprise a formal solution.

You should practice showing all steps in the solution of an equation. With experience, however, you will be able to complete many of the details mentally.

EXAMPLE 1 Solve for x: $6x + 9 = 2x + 1$.

Solution

$$6x + 9 = 2x + 1$$
$$6x + 9 + (-9) = 2x + 1 + (-9) \qquad \text{(addition property)}$$
$$6x = 2x - 8$$
$$6x + (-2x) = 2x - 8 + (-2x) \qquad \text{(addition property)}$$
$$4x = -8$$
$$\tfrac{1}{4}(4x) = \tfrac{1}{4}(-8) \qquad \text{(multiplication property)}$$
$$x = -2$$

Check: $6(-2) + 9 = -3$; $\ 2(-2) + 1 = -3$.

EXAMPLE 2 Solve for x: $2(x + 3) = x + 5$.

Solution Here we have an additional step because of the parentheses, which can be eliminated by applying the distributive property. Try to give a reason for each step in the solution that follows.

$$2(x + 3) = x + 5$$
$$2x + 6 = x + 5$$
$$2x + 6 + (-6) = x + 5 + (-6)$$
$$2x = x + (-1)$$
$$2x + (-x) = x + (-1) + (-x)$$
$$x = -1$$

Each of the equations in Examples 1 and 2 is an example of a *linear equation* because the variable x appears only to the first power.

Check this solution. Does $2[(-1) + 3] = (-1) + 5$?

TEST YOUR UNDERSTANDING

Solve each linear equation for x.

1 $x + 3 = 9$ **2** $x - 3 = 12$ **3** $x - 3 = -7$

4 $2x + 5 = x + 11$ **5** $3x - 7 = 2x + 6$ **6** $3(x - 1) = 2x + 7$

7 $3x + 2 = 5x + 6$ **8** $5x - 3 = 3x + 4$ **9** $x + 3 = 13 - x$

10 $2(x + 2) = x - 5$ **11** $2x - 7 = 5x + 2$ **12** $4(x + 2) = 3(x - 1)$

The properties of equality can be used to solve equations having more than one variable. The next example shows the use of properties of equality to solve a formula for one of the variables in terms of the others.

EXAMPLE 3   The formula relating degrees Fahrenheit and degrees Celsius is $\dfrac{5F - 160}{9} = C$. Solve for F in terms of C.

Solution   Try to explain each step shown.

$$\frac{5F - 160}{9} = C$$

$$5F - 160 = 9C$$

$$5F = 9C + 160$$

$$F = (\tfrac{1}{5})(9C + 160)$$

$$F = \tfrac{9}{5}C + 32$$

Here is an example of the use of this formula:
When $C = 20$, then $F = \tfrac{9}{5}(20) + 32 = 36 + 32 = 68$. Thus $20°$ Celsius $= 68°$ Fahrenheit.

Let us now explore the solution of problems that are expressed in words. Our task will be to translate the English sentences of a problem into suitable mathematical lanugage, and develop an equation that we can solve. To illustrate this process let us explore a "think of a number" type of puzzle. The directions to this puzzle are given below at the left. Follow these instructions first with a specific number and verify that your result is 5. Then study the mathematical explanation given at the right as to why the result will always be 5, regardless of the number with which you start.

Instruction	*Example*	*Algebraic representation*
Think of a number.	Let $n = 7$	n
Add 2.	$7 + 2 = 9$	$n + 2$
Multiply by 3.	$3 \times 9 = 27$	$3(n + 2) = 3n + 6$
Add 9.	$27 + 9 = 36$	$(3n + 6) + 9 = 3n + 15$
Multiply by 2.	$2 \times 36 = 72$	$2(3n + 15) = 6n + 30$
Divide by 6.	$72 \div 6 = 12$	$\dfrac{6n + 30}{6} = \dfrac{1}{6}(6n + 30) = n + 5$
Subtract the number with which you started.	$12 - 7 = 5$	$(n + 5) - n = 5$
The result is 5.		

Try to make up a similar puzzle of your own and explain why it works.

Solving verbal problems often creates difficulties for many students. To become a good problem solver you need some patience and much practice. Study the solution to the following problem in detail, as well as the examples that follow. Then try to solve as many of those problems as possible given in the exercises.

Problem: The length of a rectangle is 1 centimeter less than twice the width. The perimeter is 28 centimeters. Find the dimensions of the rectangle.

1 *Reread the problem and try to picture the situation given. Make note of all the information stated in the problem.*
The length is one less than twice the width.
The perimeter is 28.

2 *Determine what it is you are asked to find. Introduce a suitable variable, usually to represent the quantity to be found. When appropriate, draw a figure.*
Let x represent the width.
Then $2x - 1$ represents the length.

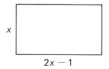

$$x$$
$$2x - 1$$

3 *Use the available information to compose an equation that involves the variable.*
The perimeter is the distance around the rectangle. This provides the necessary information to write an equation.
$$x + (2x - 1) + x + (2x - 1) = 28$$

4 *Solve the equation.*
$$x + (2x - 1) + x + (2x - 1) = 28$$
$$6x - 2 = 28$$
$$6x = 30$$
$$x = 5$$

5 *Return to the original problem to see whether the answer obtained makes sense. Does it appear to be a reasonable solution? Have you answered the question posed in the problem?*
The original problem asked for both dimensions. If the width x is 5 centimeters, then the length $2x - 1$ must be 9 centimeters.

6 *Check the solution by direct substitution of the answer into the original statement of the problem.*
As a check, note that the length of the rectangle, 9 centimeters, is 1

centimeter less than twice the width, 5, as given in the problem. Also, the perimeter is 28 centimeters.

7 *Finally, state the solution in terms of the appropriate units of measure.* The dimensions are 5 centimeters by 9 centimeters.

EXAMPLE 4 A car leaves a certain town at noon, traveling due east at 40 miles per hour. At 1:00 P.M. a second car leaves the town traveling in the same direction at a rate of 50 miles per hour. In how many hours will the second car overtake the first car?

Solution Problems of motion of this type often prove difficult to students of algebra, but need not be. The basic relationship to remember is that rate multiplied by time equals distance ($r \times t = d$). For example, a car traveling at a rate of 60 miles per hour for 5 hours will travel 60×5 or 300 miles.

Now we need to explore the problem to see what part of the information given will help form an equation. The two cars travel at different rates, and for different amounts of time, but both travel the same distance from the point of departure until they meet. This is the clue: Represent the distance each travels and equate these quantities.

Let us use x to represent the number of hours it will take the second car to overtake the first. Then the first car, having started an hour earlier, travels $x + 1$ hours until they meet. You may find it helpful to summarize this information in tabular form.

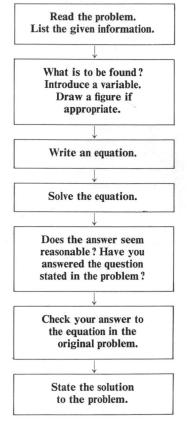

Guidelines for problem solving:

Read the problem.
List the given information.

What is to be found?
Introduce a variable.
Draw a figure if appropriate.

Write an equation.

Solve the equation.

Does the answer seem reasonable? Have you answered the question stated in the problem?

Check your answer to the equation in the original problem.

State the solution to the problem.

	Rate	Time	Distance
First car	40	$x + 1$	$40(x + 1)$
Second car	50	x	$50x$

Equating the distances, we have an equation that can be solved for x:

$$50x = 40(x + 1)$$
$$50x = 40x + 40$$
$$10x = 40$$
$$x = 4$$

The second car overtakes the first in 4 hours. Does this solution seem reasonable? Let us check the solution. The first car travels 5 hours at 40 miles per hour for a total of 200 miles. The second car travels 4 hours at 50 miles per hour for the same total of 200 miles.
Solution: The second car takes 4 hours to overtake the first.

EXAMPLE 5 David has a total of $4.10 in nickels, dimes, and quarters. He has twice as many nickels as dimes, and two more quarters than dimes. How many dimes does he have?

Solution Begin by letting x represent the number of dimes. Then from the statement of the problem we can let $2x$ represent the number of nickels, and $x + 2$ the number of quarters.

Next, observe that whenever you have a certain number of a particular coin, then the total value is the number of coins times the value of that coin. For example, if you have 8 dimes, then you have 10×8 or 80¢. If you have 9 nickels, then you have 5×9 or 45¢. For our problem:

Let $10x$ represent the value of the dimes, in cents.
Let $5(2x)$ represent the value of the nickels, in cents.
Let $25(x + 2)$ represent the value of the quarters, in cents.

Since the total value of these coins is \$4.10, or 410¢, we write and solve the following equation:

$$10x + 5(2x) + 25(x + 2) = 410$$
$$10x + 10x + 25x + 50 = 410$$
$$45x + 50 = 410$$
$$45x = 360$$
$$x = 8$$

Check: If David has 8 dimes, then he must have $2x$ or 16 nickels, and $x + 2$ or 10 quarters. The total amount is

$$8(10) + 16(5) + 10(25) = 80 + 80 + 250 = 410, \text{ that is, } \$4.10$$

Solution: David has 8 dimes.

Now it's your turn! For Exercises 38–50, use the guidelines suggested earlier in this section, and try to solve as many of the problems as you can. Don't become discouraged; be assured that most mathematics students have trouble with verbal problems. Time and practice will most certainly help you develop your skill at problem solving.

EXERCISES 1.3

Solve for x and check each result.

1 $3x - 2 = 10$

2 $5x + 1 = 21$

3 $-2x + 1 = 9$

4 $-3x - 2 = 10$

5 $-3x - 5 = 7$

6 $3x + 2 = -13$

7 $2x - 1 = -17$

8 $-2x + 3 = -12$

9 $2(x + 1) = 11$

10 $3(x - 2) = 15$

11 $3x + 7 = 2x - 2$

12 $2.5x - 8 = x + 3$

13 $\frac{1}{2}x + 7 = 2x - 3$

14 $\frac{5}{2}x - 5 = 3x + 7$

15 $\frac{4}{3}x - 7 = \frac{1}{3}x + 8$

16 $5x - 1 = 5x + 1$

17 $\frac{3}{5}(x - 5) = x + 1$

18 $5(x + 4) = \frac{5}{2}x - 5$

19 $\frac{7}{2}x + 5 + \frac{1}{2}x = \frac{5}{2}x - 6$

20 $2(x + 3) - x = 2x + 8$

21 $-3(x + 2) + 1 = x - 25$

22 $\frac{4}{3}(x + 8) = \frac{3}{4}(2x + 12)$

23 $1 - 12x = 7(1 - 2x)$

24 $2(3x - 7) - 4x = -2$

25 $x + 2(\frac{1}{6}x + 2) = \frac{6}{5}x + 16$

Solve for the indicated variable.

26 $P = 4s$ for s

27 $P = 2l + 2w$ for w

28 $F = \frac{9}{5}C + 32$ for C

29 $N = 10t + u$ for t

30 $7a - 3b = c$ for b

31 $C = 2\pi r$ for r

32 $2(r - 3s) = 6t$ for s

33 $6 + 4v = w - 1$ for v

Use the formulas in Example 3 to make these conversions.

34 $0°$ Celsius to Fahrenheit

35 $10°$ Celsius to Fahrenheit

36 $-4°$ Fahrenheit to Celsius

37 $32°$ Fahrenheit to Celsius

38 Find a number such that two-thirds of the number increased by one is 13.

39 Find the dimensions of a rectangle whose perimeter is 56 inches if the length is three times the width.

40 Each of the two equal sides of an isosceles triangle is 3 inches longer than the base of the triangle. The perimeter is 21 inches. Find the length of each side.

41 Carlos spent $4.50 on stamps, in denominations of 10¢, 18¢, and 20¢. He bought one-half as many 18¢ stamps as 10¢ stamps, and three more 20¢ stamps than 10¢ stamps. How many of each type did he buy?

42 Maria has $169 in ones, fives, and tens. She has twice as many one-dollar bills as she has five-dollar bills, and five more ten-dollar bills than five-dollar bills. How many of each type bill does she have?

43 Two cars leave a town at the same time and travel in opposite directions. One car travels at the rate of 40 miles per hour, and the other at 60 miles per hour. In how many hours will the two cars be 350 miles apart?

44 Robert goes for a walk at a speed of 3 miles per hour. Two hours later Roger attempts to overtake him by jogging at the rate of 7 miles per hour. How long will it take him to reach Robert?

45 Prove that the measures of the angles of a triangle cannot be represented by consecutive odd integers. (*Hint:* The sum of the measures is 180.)

46 The width of a painting is 4 inches less than the length. The frame that surrounds the painting is 2 inches wide and has an area of 240 square inches. What are the dimensions of the painting? (*Hint:* The total area minus the area of the painting alone is equal to the area of the frame.)

*47 The length of a rectangle is 1 inch less than three times the width. If the length is increased by 6 inches and the width is increased by 5 inches, then the length will be twice the width. Find the dimensions of the rectangle.

*48 The units' digit of a two-digit number is three more than the tens' digit. The number is equal to four times the sum of the digits. Find the number. (*Hint:* We can represent a two-digit number as $10t + u$.)

*49 Find three consecutive odd integers such that their sum is 237.

*50 The length of a rectangle is 1 inch less than twice the width. If the length is increased by 11 inches and the width is increased by 5 inches, then the length will be twice the width. What can you conclude about the data for this problem?

Properties of order

As you continue your study of mathematics you will find a great deal of attention given to *inequalities*. We begin our discussion of this topic by considering the ordering of the real numbers on the number line. In the following figure we say that *a is less than b* because *a* lies to the left of *b*. In symbols, we write $a < b$.

Also note that *b* lies to the right of *a*. That is, $b > a$; this is read "*b is greater than a.*" Two inequalities, one using the symbol $<$ and the other $>$, are said to have the *opposite sense*.

The fundamental property behind the study of inequalities is known as the **trichotomy law**. This law states that for any two real numbers a and b exactly one of the following must be true:

$$a < b \qquad a = b \qquad a > b$$

There are a number of important properties of order that are fundamental for later work. We list them in terms of the following rules.

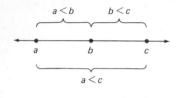

RULE 1. **If $a < b$ and $b < c$, then $a < c$.**
This is known as the **transitive property of order**. Geometrically, it says that if a is to the left of b, and b is to the left of c, then a must be to the left of c on a number line.

RULE 2. **If $a < b$, then $a + c < b + c$ for any real number c.**
Since $5 < 7$, then $5 + 10 < 7 + 10$; that is, $15 < 17$.
Since $5 < 7$, then $5 + (-10) < 7 + (-10)$, or $5 - 10 < 7 - 10$; that is, $-5 < -3$.

CAUTION: Rules 3 and 4 often cause trouble! If you multiply both sides of an inequality by a positive number, the sense of the resulting inequality is the same as the sense of the original inequality. Multiplying by a negative number changes the sense of the inequality.

RULE 3. **If $a < b$ and $c > 0$, then $ac < bc$.**
Since $5 < 10$, then $5(3) < 10(3)$; that is, $15 < 30$.
Since $-4 < 6$, then $-4(\frac{1}{2}) < 6(\frac{1}{2})$; that is, $-2 < 3$.

RULE 4. **If $a < b$ and $c < 0$, then $ac > bc$.**
Since $5 < 10$, then $5(-3) > 10(-3)$; that is, $-15 > -30$.
Since $-4 < 6$, then $-4(-\frac{1}{2}) > 6(-\frac{1}{2})$; that is, $2 > -3$.

RULE 5. **If $a < b$ and $c < d$, then $a + c < b + d$.**
Since $5 < 10$ and $-15 < -4$, then $5 + (-15) < 10 + (-4)$; that is, $-10 < 6$.

RULE 6. **If $0 < a < b$ and $0 < c < d$, then $ac < bd$.**
Since $3 < 7$ and $5 < 9$, then $(3)(5) < (7)(9)$; that is, $15 < 63$.

These rules can also be restated by reversing the sense. For instance, Rule 5 would read as: If $a > b$ and $c > d$, then $a + c > b + d$.

RULE 7. **If $a < b$ and $ab > 0$, then $\dfrac{1}{a} > \dfrac{1}{b}$.**
Since $5 < 10$, then $\frac{1}{5} > \frac{1}{10}$.
Since $-3 < -2$, then $-\frac{1}{3} > -\frac{1}{2}$.

We have developed the concept of $a < b$ by saying that a is to the left of b on a number line. It is often useful to state this relationship in terms of this algebraic definition:

For any two real numbers a and b, $a < b$ (and $b > a$) if and only if $b - a$ is a positive number, that is, if and only if $b - a > 0$.

For example, $2 < 5$ because $5 - 2 = 3$, a positive number; $5 - 2 > 0$. Also, since $-2 - (-7) = 5 > 0$, then $-2 > -7$.
With this definition of order, we can prove the rules discussed earlier. The next example shows how this can be done.

EXAMPLE 1 Prove Rule 1: If $a < b$ and $b < c$, then $a < c$.

Solution We note that $a < b$ and $b < c$ means that $b - a$ and $c - b$ are positive numbers by definition. Since the sum of two positive numbers is also positive, it follows that

$$(b - a) + (c - b) > 0$$

But

$$(b - a) + (c - b) = c - a$$

Hence $c - a$ is positive, and the definition implies that $a < c$.

These additional symbols of inequality are also used:

$a \leq b$ means *a is less than or is equal to b;* that is, $a < b$ or $a = b$.
$a \geq b$ means *a is greater than or is equal to b;* that is, $a > b$ or $a = b$.

We may use these symbols in the rules of order previously listed. Thus Rule 1 may be stated in these forms:

If $a \leq b$ and $b \leq c$, then $a \leq c$.
If $a \geq b$ and $b \geq c$, then $a \geq c$.

The two inequalities $a < b$ and $b < c$ may be written as $a < b < c$. Also, if $a \leq b$ and $b \leq c$, then $a \leq b \leq c$. A similar statement may be made for the $\geq$ relationship.

EXAMPLE 2 Translate each verbal statement into a statement of inequality.
(a) x is to the right of zero.
(b) x is between 2 and 3.
(c) x is greater than or equal to -1.
(d) x is at least 10 but less than 100.

Solution (a) $x > 0$ (b) $2 < x < 3$ (c) $x \geq -1$ (d) $10 \leq x < 100$

We can use inequalities to define *bounded intervals* on the number line. This is shown in the next figure, together with specific examples of each.

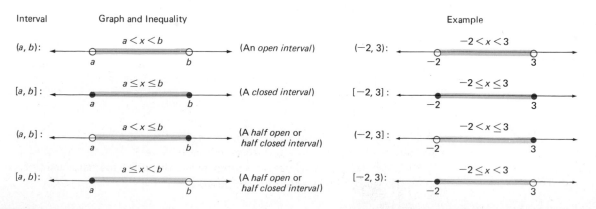

Note that the parenthesis in $(a, b]$ means that the number a is not included in the interval, and that the bracket means that b is included. Also, regardless of the parentheses or brackets, the numbers a and b are boundaries for all of the values x in the interval.

There are also *unbounded intervals*. For example, the set of all $x > 5$ is denoted by $(5, \infty)$. Similarly, $(-\infty, 5]$ represents all $x \le 5$. The symbols ∞ and $-\infty$ are read "plus infinity" and "minus infinity" but do *not* represent numbers. They are symbolic devices used to indicate that *all* x in a given direction, without end, are included, as in the following figure.

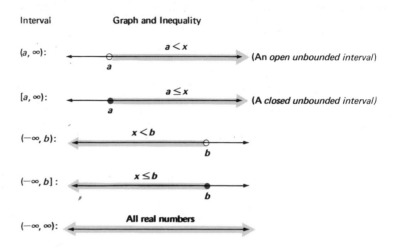

TEST YOUR UNDERSTANDING

Show each of the following intervals as a graph on a number line.

1 $(-4, 1]$ **2** $[0, 3]$ **3** $[-1, 2)$ **4** $(-2, \infty)$

Express each inequality in interval notation.

5 $-1 \le x \le 2$ **6** $0 < x < 3$ **7** $x \le 0$
8 $1 \le x < 4$ **9** $-3 \le x$ **10** $-5 < x < -2$

EXERCISES 1.4

In Exercises 1–8, insert the appropriate symbol, $<$, $=$, or $>$, between the given pair of real numbers.

1 -100____2

2 $\frac{1}{2}$____$\frac{1}{3}$

3 $-\frac{4}{5}$____$-\frac{2}{3}$

4 2.619____2.621

5 0.7____$\frac{7}{9}$

6 $-\frac{13}{14}$____$-\frac{20}{21}$

7 $\frac{1}{2}(4.02)$____2.01

8 $\frac{1}{9}$____0.111

In Exercises 9 and 10, translate each verbal statement into a statement of inequality.

9 (a) x is to the left of 1.
  (b) x is to the right of $-\frac{2}{3}$.
  (c) x is at least as large as 5.
  (d) x is more than -10 but less than or equal to 7.

10 (a) x is between -1 and 4.

(b) x is no more than 6.

(c) x is to the right of 12.

(d) x is a positive number less than 40.

In Exercises 11–18, classify each statement as true or false. If it is false, give a specific example to explain your answer.

11 If $x > 1$ and $y > 2$, then $x + y > 3$.

12 If $x < 2$, then x is negative.

13 If $x < 5$ and $y < 6$, then $xy < 30$.

14 If $0 < x$, then $-x < 0$.

15 If $x < y < -2$, then $\dfrac{1}{x} > \dfrac{1}{y}$.

16 If $0 < x$, then $x < x^2$.

17 If $x \leq y$ and $y < z$, then $x < z$.

18 If $x \leq -5$, then $x - 2 \leq -7$.

Show each of the following intervals as a graph on a number line.

19 $(-3, -1)$ 20 $(-3, -1]$

21 $[-3, -1)$ 22 $[-3, -1]$

23 $[0, 5]$ 24 $(-1, 3)$

25 $(-\infty, 0]$ 26 $[2, \infty)$

Express each inequality in interval notation.

27 $-5 \leq x \leq 2$ 28 $0 < x < 7$

29 $-6 \leq x < 0$ 30 $-2 < x \leq 4$

31 $-10 < x < 10$ 32 $3 \leq x \leq 7$

33 $x < 5$ 34 $x \leq -2$

35 $-2 \leq x$ 36 $2 < x$

37 $x \leq -1$ 38 $x < 3$

39 Complete the following proof of Rule 3: If $a < b$ and $c > 0$, then $ac < bc$.

(a) $a < b$ implies _____, by the definition of $<$.

(b) Since $c > 0$, the product _____ is also positive.

(c) But $(b - a)c =$ _____.

(d) Therefore, _____ is positive.

(e) Thus _____ < _____ by the definition of $<$.

*40 Use Rule 3 to prove that if $0 < a < 1$, then $a^2 < a$.

*41 Use Rule 3 to prove that if $1 < a$, then $a < a^2$.

*42 Prove: If $a < b < 0$ and $c < d < 0$, then $ac > bd$.

Conditional inequalities

The inequality $3x - 4 > 11$ is true for some values for x, such as 10, and false for others, such as 3. Inequalities that are not true for all allowable values of the variable are called **conditional inequalities**. Solving such an inequality means finding the set of all x for which it is true. Our basic rules of Section 1.4 will be helpful in this work, as in the following example.

$$3x - 4 > 11$$

$3x - 4 + 4 > 11 + 4$ By Rule 2 we may add 4 to both sides.

$$3x > 15$$

$\tfrac{1}{3}(3x) > \tfrac{1}{3}(15)$ By Rule 3 we may multiply each side by $\tfrac{1}{3}$, or divide each side by 3.

$$x > 5$$

Because we are multiplying (or dividing) by a positive number, we do not change the sense of the inequality.

The answer then consists of all real numbers x such that $x > 5$. This answer may also be displayed graphically on a number line.

$(5, \infty)$: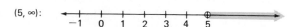

The heavily shaded arrow is used to show that all points in the indicated direction are included. The open circle indicates that 5 is *not* included in the solution. Why not? When the open circle is replaced by a solid dot we have the following graph, which represents the solution of the conditional inequality $3x - 4 \geq 11$. In this case 5 is a solution of the inequality.

$[5, \infty)$:

EXAMPLE 1   Solve for x and graph: $5(3 - 2x) \geq 10$.

Solution   Multiply each side by $\frac{1}{5}$ (or divide by 5).

$$\tfrac{1}{5} \cdot 5(3 - 2x) \geq \tfrac{1}{5}(10) \qquad \text{(Rule 3)}$$
$$3 - 2x \geq 2$$

Add -3 to each side.

$$3 - 2x + (-3) \geq 2 + (-3) \qquad \text{(Rule 2)}$$
$$-2x \geq -1$$

Multiply by $-\frac{1}{2}$ (or divide by -2).

Note the change in the sense of the resulting inequality because we are multiplying (or dividing) by a negative number.

$$-\tfrac{1}{2}(-2x) \leq -\tfrac{1}{2}(-1) \qquad \text{(Rule 4)}$$
$$x \leq \tfrac{1}{2}$$

$(-\infty, \tfrac{1}{2}]$:

In Example 2, note that $x \neq -4$. Why not?

EXAMPLE 2   Solve: $\dfrac{2}{x + 4} < 0$.

Solution   Since the numerator of the fraction is positive, the fraction will be less than zero if and only if the denominator is negative. Thus

$$x + 4 < 0$$
$$x < -4$$

EXAMPLE 3   If $x < 2$, is $x - 5$ positive or negative?

Solution
$$x < 2$$
$$x - 5 < 2 - 5 \qquad \text{subtract 5}$$
$$x - 5 < -3$$

Therefore $x - 5$ is negative.

Example 3 can also be solved by selecting one convenient test value from the interval $(-\infty, 2)$. Thus if $x = 1$, then $x - 5 = 1 - 5 = -4$. From this we can conclude that $x - 5 < 0$ for *all* $x < 2$. You can see that this process makes sense by studying this figure.

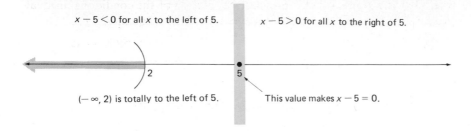

$x - 5 < 0$ for all x to the left of 5.

$x - 5 > 0$ for all x to the right of 5.

$(-\infty, 2)$ is totally to the left of 5.

This value makes $x - 5 = 0$.

Since $(-\infty, 2)$ is completely to the left of 5, all x in $(-\infty, 2)$ satisfies $x - 5 < 0$. Therefore any specific value of x in that interval may be used as a test value.

TEST YOUR UNDERSTANDING

Solve each inequality for x. Graph the solution for Exercises 1 and 2.

1 $x - 3 < 0$ **2** $x + 5 > 0$ **3** $x + 1 < -3$

4 $x - 2 \geq \frac{1}{2}$ **5** $2x + 7 < 11$ **6** $3x + 1 \leq x - 4$

Solve for x.

7 $-2(x + 6) < 0$ **8** $-2(x + 6) \geq 0$ **9** $-\dfrac{1}{x} < 0$

10 $\dfrac{5}{3 - x} < 0$

11 Assume that $x < -1$. Classify as positive or negative: **(a)** $x + 1$; **(b)** $x - 3$.

12 Assume that $4 < x < 5$. Classify as positive or negative: **(a)** $x - 4$; **(b)** $x - 5$.

Let us explore in detail the solution to a more complicated inequality:

$$(x - 2)(x - 5) < 0$$

Since $(x - 2)(x - 5) = 0$ if and only if $x = 2$ or $x = 5$, we need to consider the other possible values of x. First observe that the numbers 2 and 5 determine three intervals.

Recall that
$(x - 2)(x - 5) = 0$
if and only if either
$x - 2 = 0$ or $x - 5 = 0$.
That is, if $ab = 0$, **then** $a = 0$
or $b = 0$.

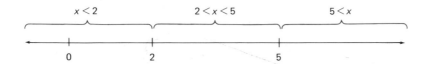

$x < 2$ $2 < x < 5$ $5 < x$

These three intervals are listed left to right at the top of the next table. Now select a value in the first interval $(-\infty, 2)$, such as $x = 0$, and use it as a test value to determine the signs of the factors $x - 2$ and $x - 5$. The minus signs next to the factors $x - 2$ and $x - 5$ under the heading $x < 2$ indicate that these factors are negative for this interval. Furthermore, since the product of two negative factors is positive, a plus sign is written next to $(x - 2)(x - 5)$ for this interval.

Note that 2 and 5 are not
within any of the intervals listed
at the top of the table.

Interval	$x < 2$	$2 < x < 5$	$5 < x$
Sign of $x - 2$	$-$	$+$	$+$
Sign of $x - 5$	$-$	$-$	$+$
Sign of $(x - 2)(x - 5)$	$+$	$-$	$+$

Using a test value such as $x = 3$ in the interval $(2, 5)$ shows that $x - 2$ is positive, $x - 5$ is negative, and consequently that $(x - 2)(x - 5)$ is negative. This explains the signs in the column under $2 < x < 5$.

The entries for the last column can be checked using $x = 6$ as a specific example. The results in the last row of the table show that $(x - 2)(x - 5) < 0$ only for the interval $(2, 5)$, which is the solution to the given inequality.

EXAMPLE 4 Graph on a number line: $\dfrac{1 - 2x}{x - 3} \leq 0$.

Solution First find the values of x for which the numerator or the denominator is zero.

$$1 - 2x = 0 \qquad x - 3 = 0$$
$$-2x = -1 \qquad x = 3$$
$$x = \tfrac{1}{2}$$

Now locate the three intervals determined by these two points.

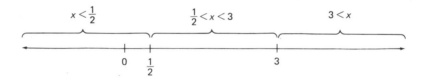

Next, select a specific value to test in each interval and record the results in a table as follows.

Interval	$x < \tfrac{1}{2}$	$\tfrac{1}{2} < x < 3$	$3 < x$
Sign of $1 - 2x$	$+$	$-$	$-$
Sign of $x - 3$	$-$	$-$	$+$
Sign of $\dfrac{1 - 2x}{x - 3}$	$-$	$+$	$-$

The table shows that the fraction will be negative when $x < \tfrac{1}{2}$ or when $x > 3$. Also note that $x = \tfrac{1}{2}$ satisfies the given inequality but that $x = 3$

is excluded from the solution. Can you explain why this is so? The solution consists of all x such that $x \leq \frac{1}{2}$ or $x > 3$.

This solution cannot be described easily using a single inequality. For example, it makes no sense to write $3 < x < \frac{1}{2}$ since this implies the false result $3 < \frac{1}{2}$.

Solve for x and graph.

1 $x + 4 < 0$ 2 $2x - 3 \geq 1$

3 $5 - x \leq 0$ 4 $5x - 10 > 10$

5 $-3x + 4 \geq 0$ 6 $3x - 4 \leq 0$

7 $2x + 7 \leq 5 - 6x$ 8 $3x - 2 > x + 5$

9 $-5x + 5 < -3x + 1$

10 $3(x - 1) \geq 2(x - 1)$

11 $2(x + 1) < x - 1$ 12 $\frac{1}{3}(x + 4) > 2$

13 $\frac{2 - x}{5} \geq 0$ 14 $\frac{1}{x} < 0$

15 $-\frac{2}{x + 1} > 0$

16 Assume that $-2 < x$. Classify as positive or negative: **(a)** $x + 2$; **(b)** $x + 4$.

17 Assume that $x < \frac{1}{2}$. Classify as positive or negative: **(a)** $x - \frac{1}{2}$; **(b)** $x - 1$.

18 Assume that $-1 < x < 3$. Classify as positive or negative:
   (a) $x + 1$ **(b)** $x + 4$
   (c) $x - 3$ **(d)** $x - 6$

19 Assume that $-\frac{3}{2} < x < -\frac{1}{2}$. Classify as positive or negative:
   (a) $x + \frac{3}{2}$ **(b)** $x + 2$
   (c) $x + \frac{1}{2}$ **(d)** $x - 1$

Solve for x and graph.

20 $3x + 5 \neq 8$ (The symbol $\neq$ is read "is not equal to.")

21 $2x + 1 \not> 5$ (The symbol $\not>$ is read "is not greater than.")

22 $3x - 2 \not< 1$ (The symbol $\not<$ is read "is not less than.")

23 $12x + 9 \neq 15(x - 2)$

24 $3(x - 1) \not> 5(x + 2)$

25 $2(x + 3) \not< 3(x + 1)$

26 $\frac{5}{3}x \not< 2x - 1$

27 $x + 2 \not> \frac{3}{4}x$

*28 $\frac{2}{9}(3x + 7) \not\geq 1 - \frac{4}{3}x$

■ *Construct a table to solve each inequality.*

29 $(x + 1)(x - 1) < 0$ 30 $(x + 3)(x + 2) > 0$

31 $(x + 5)(2x - 1) \leq 0$ 32 $(2x - 1)(3x + 1) > 0$

33 $\frac{x}{x + 1} > 0$ 34 $\frac{x - 2}{x + 3} < 0$

35 $\frac{x + 5}{2 - x} < 0$ 36 $\frac{1}{x} \geq 2$

37 $(x + 3)(x - 1)(x - 2) \geq 0$

38 $(x + 5)(x + 1)(x - 3) \leq 0$

*39 Here is an alternative (graphic) method for solving conditional inequalities like $(x - 2)(x - 5) < 0$. On the top number line, the bold (dark) half represents those x for which $x - 2$ is positive $(x > 2)$, and the other half gives those x for which $x - 2$ is negative $(x < 2)$. The bottom line has the same information for the factor $x - 5$.

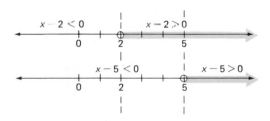

Since $(x - 2)(x - 5) < 0$ when $x - 2$ and $x - 5$ have *opposite* signs, the set of x for which this is the case are those between the vertical lines at 2 and 5. Thus the solution is $2 < x < 5$. Find the solution of $(x - 2)(x - 5) > 0$ from the preceding graph.

*40 Solve Exercise 30 by the method of Exercise 39.

■ Throughout this text, this symbol will be used to identify exercises or groups of exercises that are of special value with respect to the later study of calculus. See the preface for further discussion.

Absolute value   What do the numbers −5 and +5 have in common? Obviously, they are different numbers and are the coordinates of two distinct points on the number line. However, they are both the same distance from 0, the **origin**, on the number line.

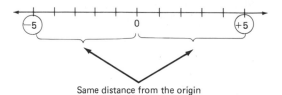

Same distance from the origin

In other words, −5 is as far to the left of 0 as +5 is to the right of 0. We show this fact by using **absolute value notation** as follows:

$|-5| = 5$ read as "The *absolute value* of −5 is 5."
$|+5| = 5$ read as "The *absolute value* of +5 is 5."

Geometrically, for any real number $x, |x|$ is the distance (without regard to direction) that x is from the origin. Note that for a positive number, $|x| = x; |+6| = 6$. For a negative number, $|x| = -x; |-6| = -(-6) = 6$. Also, since 0 is the origin, it is natural to have $|0| = 0$.
We can summarize this with the following definition.

In words, if x is positive or zero, the absolute value of x is x. If x is negative, the absolute value is the opposite of x.

·DEFINITION OF ABSOLUTE VALUE

For any real number x,
$$|x| = \begin{cases} x & \text{if } x \geq 0 \\ -x & \text{if } x < 0 \end{cases}$$

Some useful properties of absolute value follow, presented with illustrations but without formal proof. The variables represent any real numbers.

PROPERTY 1.   If $|a| = k$, then $a = k$ or $-a = k$, that is, $a = k$ or $a = -k$; $|0| = 0$.

This property follows immediately from the definition of absolute value. For example, an equation such as $|x| = 2$ is just another way of saying that $x = 2$ or $x = -2$. The graph consists of the two points with coordinates 2 and −2; each of these points is 2 units from the origin.

EXAMPLE 1   Solve: $|5 - x| = 7$.

We use Property 1 for this solution, noting that $5 - x$ plays the role of a.

$$+(5 - x) = 7 \quad \text{or} \quad -(5 - x) = 7$$
$$5 - x = 7 \qquad\qquad -5 + x = 7$$
$$-x = 2 \qquad\qquad x = 12$$
$$x = -2$$

These two solutions, -2 and 12, can be checked by substitution into the original equation.

Check: $|5 - (-2)| = |7| = 7; |5 - 12| = |-7| = 7.$

Now consider the inequality $|x| < 2$. Here we are asked to find all the real numbers whose absolute value is less than 2. On the number line, we can think of the solution as consisting of all the points whose distance from the origin is less than 2 units, that is, all of the real numbers between -2 and 2. The solution of this inequality can be written in either of these two forms:

$$x < 2 \quad \text{and} \quad x > -2 \qquad -2 < x < 2$$

The graph of $|x| < 2$ is the interval $(-2, 2)$.

Conversely, the graph also shows that if $-2 < x < 2$, then $|x| < 2$. If the endpoints are included, then we would have $-2 \le x \le 2$; that is, $|x| \le 2$.

We can now generalize by means of the following property.

PROPERTY 2. $|a| < k$ if *and* only if $-k < a < k$.

Note that $-k < a < k$ is the same as saying that $a < k$ *and* $a > -k$.

EXAMPLE 2 Solve: $|x - 2| < 3$.

Solution Let $x - 2$ play the role of a in Property 2. Consequently, $|x - 2| < 3$ is equivalent to $-3 < x - 2 < 3$. Now add 2 to each member to isolate x in the middle.

$$-3 < x - 2 < 3$$
$$\underline{+2 \phantom{<} + 2 \phantom{<} +2}$$
$$-1 < x + 0 < 5 \qquad \text{Thus } -1 < x < 5$$

In Example 2 we could also have solved the inequality by writing and solving two separate inequalities in this way:

$$|x - 2| < 3 \quad \text{means} \quad x - 2 < 3 \quad \text{and} \quad x - 2 > -3$$

Thus $x < 5$ and $x > -1$. The word "and" indicates that we are to consider the values for x that satisfy *both* conditions. Therefore, the solution consists

of those numbers that are both greater than -1 and less than 5; that is, $-1 < x < 5$.

The quantity $|a - b|$ also represents the distance between the points a and b on the number line. For example, the distance between 8 and 3 on the number line is $5 = |8 - 3| = |3 - 8|$. The idea of distance between points on a number line can be used to give an alternative way to solve Example 2. Think of the expression $|x - 2|$ as the distance between x and 2 on the number line, and then consider all the points x whose distance from 2 is less than 3 units.

Think: $|x - 2| < 3$ means that x is within 3 units of 2.

Observe that the *midpoint* or *center* of the interval in the preceding discussion has coordinate 2. This value can be found by taking the average of the numbers -1 and 5; $\dfrac{-1 + 5}{2} = 2$. In general, we have the following result.

MIDPOINT FORMULA FOR A LINE SEGMENT

If x_1 and x_2 are the endpoints of an interval, then the coordinate of the midpoint is

$$\frac{x_1 + x_2}{2}$$

EXAMPLE 3 Find the coordinate of the midpoint M of each line segment AB.

(a)

-4	0	6
A	M	B

(b)

-10	-2	0
A	M	B

Solution   (a) $\dfrac{-4 + 6}{2} = 1$ (b) $\dfrac{-10 + (-2)}{2} = -6$

Throughout the text you will find sets of CAUTION items. These illustrate errors that are often made by students. Study these carefully so that you understand the errors shown and can avoid such mistakes.

CAUTION: LEARN TO AVOID MISTAKES LIKE THESE

WRONG	RIGHT
$\left|\frac{3}{4} - 2\right| = \frac{3}{4} - 2 = -\frac{5}{4}$	$\left|\frac{3}{4} - 2\right| = \left|-\frac{5}{4}\right| = \frac{5}{4}$
$|5 - 7| = |5| - |7| = -2$	$|5 - 7| = |-2| = 2$

WRONG	RIGHT
If $\lvert x \rvert = -2$, then $x = -2$.	There is no solution; the absolute value of a number can never be negative.
If $\lvert x - 1 \rvert < 3$, then $x < 4$.	If $\lvert x - 1 \rvert < 3$, then $-3 < x - 1 < 3$; that is, $-2 < x < 4$

Next, consider the inequality $\lvert x \rvert > 3$. We know that $\lvert x \rvert < 3$ implies that $-3 < x < 3$. Therefore, $\lvert x \rvert > 3$ consists of those values of x for which $x < -3$ or $x > 3$. The graph of this set may be drawn as follows.

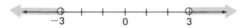

This graph shows the set of points whose distance from 0 is more than 3 units. The property involved is summarized in this way.

PROPERTY 3. $\lvert a \rvert > k$ if and only if $a < -k$ or $a > k$.

Also, $\lvert a \rvert \geq k$ if and only if $a \leq -k$ or $a \geq k$.

EXAMPLE 4   Graph: $\lvert x + 1 \rvert > 2$.

Solution   Think of $\lvert x + 1 \rvert$ as $\lvert x - (-1) \rvert$ so as to have it in the form $\lvert a - b \rvert$. This represents the distance between x and -1, and we wish to find all the points that are more than 2 units away from the point -1.

CAUTION: A common error that students make is to write the solution for Example 4 as $1 < x < -3$. Explain why this is *not* correct.

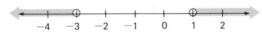

The solution is $x < -3$ or $x > 1$.

In Example 4 we could have solved the inequality by using Property 3.
$$\lvert x + 1 \rvert > 2 \quad \text{means} \quad x + 1 < -2 \quad \text{or} \quad x + 1 > 2$$
Thus $x < -3$ or $x > 1$. The word "or" indicates that we are to consider the values for x that satisfy either one of these two conditions; that is, x may be less than -3 or x may be greater than 1.

TEST YOUR UNDERSTANDING

Solve for x.

1 $\lvert x + 3 \rvert = 5$ **2** $\lvert x - 2 \rvert = 3$ **3** $\lvert 4 - x \rvert = 1$

4 $\lvert 2x - 1 \rvert = 3$ **5** $\lvert 3x + 2 \rvert = 5$ **6** $\lvert 1 - 2x \rvert = 2$

Solve and graph.

7 $\lvert x - 3 \rvert < 1$ **8** $\lvert x + 3 \rvert > 1$ **9** $\lvert 2 - x \rvert \leq 3$

The absolute value of a real number is the same as the absolute value of its negative.

PROPERTY 4. $|a| = |-a|$

For example, $|2| = |-2| = 2$. A useful application of this property is the result that for any real numbers x and y, $|x - y| = |y - x|$. Note that $x - y$ and $y - x$ are negatives of one another; for example, $|2 - \pi| = |\pi - 2| = \pi - 2$ because $\pi - 2 > 0$.

A real number is always between its absolute value and the negative of its absolute value.

PROPERTY 5. $-|a| \le a \le |a|$

For example, verify that each of the following is correct:

$$-|7| \le 7 \le |7| \qquad -|-7| \le -7 \le |-7|$$

The absolute value of a product is the product of the absolute values.

PROPERTY 6. $|ab| = |a| \cdot |b|$

For example:

$$|(-3)(5)| = |-15| = 15 \quad \text{and} \quad |-3| \cdot |5| = 3 \cdot 5 = 15$$

The absolute value of a quotient is the quotient of the absolute values.

PROPERTY 7. $\left|\dfrac{a}{b}\right| = \dfrac{|a|}{|b|}; \; b \ne 0$

For example:

$$\left|\frac{-9}{3}\right| = \left|-\frac{9}{3}\right| = |-3| = 3 \qquad \text{and} \qquad \frac{|-9|}{|3|} = \frac{9}{3} = 3$$

The absolute value of a sum is less than or equal to the sum of the absolute values.

PROPERTY 8. $|a + b| \le |a| + |b|$ (the triangle inequality)

Verify that each of the following examples is correct.

$$|2 + 7| \le |2| + |7| \qquad |(-2) + (-7)| \le |-2| + |-7|$$
$$|(-2) + 7| \le |-2| + |7| \qquad |2 + (-7)| \le |2| + |-7|$$

EXERCISES 1.6

Classify each statement as true or false.

1 $-|-\frac{1}{3}| = \frac{1}{3}$ **2** $|-1000| < 0$

3 $|-\frac{1}{2}| = 2$

4 $|\sqrt{2} - 5| = 5 - \sqrt{2}$

5 $\left|\dfrac{x}{y}\right| = |x| \cdot \dfrac{1}{|y|}$ **6** $2 \cdot |0| = 0$

7 $\|x\| = |x|$ **8** $|-(-1)| = -1$

9 $|a| - |b| = a - b$ **10** $|a - b| = b - a$

Solve for x.

11 $|x| = \frac{1}{2}$ **12** $|3x| = 3$

13 $|x - 1| = 3$ **14** $|3x - 4| = 0$

15 $|2x - 3| = 7$ **16** $|6 - 2x| = 4$

17 $|4 - x| = 3$ **18** $|3x - 2| = 1$

19 $|3x + 4| = 16$ **20** $\left|\dfrac{1}{x - 1}\right| = 2$

21 $\dfrac{|x|}{x} = 1$ **22** $\dfrac{|x|}{x} = -1$

Solve for x and graph.

23 $|x + 1| = 3$ **24** $|x - 1| \le 3$

25 $|x - 1| \ge 3$ **26** $|x + 2| = 3$

27 $|x + 2| \le 3$ **28** $|x + 2| \ge 3$

29 $|-x| = 5$ **30** $|x| \le 5$

31 $|x| \ge 5$ **32** $|x - 5| \ne 3$

33 $|x - 5| \le 3$ **34** $|x - 5| \ge 3$

35 $|x - 3| < 0.1$ **36** $|2 - x| < 3$

37 $|2x - 1| < 7$ **38** $|3x - 6| < 9$

39 $|4 - x| < 2$ **40** $|1 + 5x| < 1$

41 $|x - 4| \not> 1$ **42** $|x - 2| \not\ge 0$

43 $\dfrac{1}{|x - 3|} > 0$

Find the coordinate of the midpoint of a line segment with endpoints as given.

44 3 and 9   **45** −8 and −2

46 −12 and 0   **47** 0 and 11

48 −5 and 8   **49** −7 and 7

*50 Prove Property 5 of this section. (*Hint:* Consider the two cases $x \geq 0$ and $x < 0$.)

*51 Cite at least four different examples to confirm this inequality: $|x - y| \geq ||x| - |y||$.

*52 (a) Prove that $|xy| = |x| \cdot |y|$ for the case $x < 0$ and $y > 0$.

  (b) Prove this product rule when $x < 0$ and $y < 0$.

*53 Prove $\left|\dfrac{x}{y}\right| = \dfrac{|x|}{|y|}$ for the case $x < 0$, $y > 0$. ·

*54 Prove that if x is a real number, then $x^2 = |x^2| = |x|^2$.

55 Write in absolute value notation.

  (a) $-3 < x < 3$ (b) $-\frac{1}{2} < 2x < \frac{1}{2}$

  (c) $-1 < x < 5$ (d) $-\frac{1}{2} < x < \frac{3}{2}$

56 Write an equivalent inequality without absolute values for $|x - a| < c$.

▬ 57 Prove: $|x - 1| < \frac{1}{10}$ implies that $|y - 8| < \frac{3}{10}$, where $y = 3x + 5$, by completing the following steps.

  (a) $|x - 1| < \frac{1}{10}$ implies that $-\frac{1}{10} < x - 1 < \frac{1}{10}$. Add 1 throughout to obtain:

  _____ $< x <$ _____

  (b) Multiply each member by 3:

  _____ $< 3x <$ _____

  (c) Add −3: _____ $< 3x - 3 <$ _____

  (d) Now note that if $y = 3x + 5$, then $y - 8 = 3x - 3$. Therefore:

  _____ $< y - 8 <$ _____

  (e) Convert the last statement to absolute value form.

58 One endpoint of a line segment is located at −7. The midpoint is located at 3. What is the coordinate of the other endpoint of the line segment?

REVIEW EXERCISES FOR CHAPTER 1

The solutions to the following exercises can be found within the text of Chapter 1. Try to answer each question without referring to the text.

Section 1.1

1 Given two real numbers a and b, write in symbols the commutative property for addition and for multiplication.

2 Repeat Exercise 1 for the associative property.

3 Use the distributive property to find the product 7×61.

4 What basic property of the real numbers is illustrated by each of the following?

  (a) $6 + (17 + 4) = (17 + 4) + 6$

  (b) $\frac{3}{4} + (-\frac{3}{4}) = 0$

  (c) $57 \times 1 = 57$

  (d) $\frac{2}{3}(12 + 36) = \frac{2}{3}(12) + \frac{2}{3}(36)$

5 If $ab = 0$, what do you know about the numbers a and b?

6 State the definition of subtraction in terms of addition.

7 State the definition of division in terms of multiplication.

8 Explain what the phrase "if and only if" means.

9 Why is division by zero not possible?

Section 1.2

10 What is meant by the set of whole numbers?

11 Write the decimal form of $\frac{19}{22}$.

12 State the definition of a rational number.

13 Using straightedge and compass, locate the irrational number $\sqrt{2}$ on a number line.

14 State the relationship between the real numbers and their decimal representations.

15 Classify each number into as many different sets as possible:

  (a) 5   (b) $\frac{2}{3}$

  (c) $\sqrt{7}$ (d) −14

16 True or false: Every rational number is the coordinate of some point on the number line.

Section 1.3

17 State the addition property of equality.

18 State the multiplication property of equality.

19 Solve for x: $6x + 9 = 2x + 1$.

20 Solve for x: $2(x + 3) = x + 5$.

21 The formula relating degrees Fahrenheit and degrees Celsius is $\dfrac{5F - 160}{9} = C$. Solve for F in terms of C.

22 The length of a rectangle is 1 centimeter less than

twice the width. The perimeter is 28 centimeters. Find the dimensions of the rectangle.

23 A car leaves a certain town at noon, traveling due east at 40 miles per hour. At 1:00 P.M. a second car leaves the town traveling in the same direction at a rate of 50 miles per hour. In how many hours will the second car overtake the first car?

24 David has a total of $4.10 in nickels, dimes, and quarters. He has twice as many nickels as dimes, and two more quarters than dimes. How many dimes does he have?

Section 1.4

25 State the transitive property of order for real numbers a, b, and c.

26 True or false: If $a < b$ and $c < 0$, then $ac < bc$.

27 True or false: If $a < b$ and $ab > 0$, then $\dfrac{1}{a} > \dfrac{1}{b}$.

28 Prove: If $a < b$ and $b < c$, then $a < c$.

29 Translate each verbal statement into a statement of inequality.
  (a) x is to the right of zero.
  (b) x is between 2 and 3.
  (c) x is greater than or equal to -1.

(d) x is at least 10 but less than 100.

30 Show each interval as a graph on a number line.
  (a) $(-2, 3)$ (b) $[-2, 3]$
  (c) $(-2, 3]$ (d) $[-2, 3)$

Section 1.5

31 Solve for x: $3x - 4 > 11$.

32 Solve for x and graph: $5(3 - 2x) \geq 10$.

33 Solve: $\dfrac{2}{x + 4} < 0$.

34 Graph on a number line: $\dfrac{1 - 2x}{x - 3} \leq 0$.

Section 1.6

35 State the definition of the absolute value of a number.

36 Solve: $|5 - x| = 7$.

37 Solve: $|x - 2| < 3$.

38 What does $|a - b|$ represent with respect to points a and b on a number line? Illustrate with two specific values.

39 Graph: $|x + 1| > 2$.

40 What is the coordinate of the midpoint of a line segment with endpoints x_1 and x_2?

SAMPLE TEST QUESTIONS FOR CHAPTER 1

Use these questions to test your knowledge of the basic skills and concepts of Chapter 1. Then check your answers with those given at the end of the book.

1 Check the boxes in the table to indicate the set to which each number belongs.

	Whole numbers	Integers	Rational numbers	Irrational numbers	Negative integers
$\dfrac{-6}{3}$					
0.231					
$\sqrt{12}$					
$\sqrt{\dfrac{9}{4}}$					
1983					

2 Explain how to locate $\sqrt{10}$ on a number line by using straightedge and compass.

3 Classify each statement as true or false.
  (a) Negative irrational numbers are not real numbers.
  (b) Every integer is a rational number.
  (c) Some irrational numbers are integers.
  (d) Zero is a rational number.
  (e) If $x < y$, then $x - 5 > y - 5$.
  (f) The absolute value of a sum equals the sum of the absolute values.
  (g) If $-5x < -5y$, then $x > y$.
  (h) $|x - 2| < 3$ means that x is within 2 units of 3 on the number line.

4 Name the property or definition illustrated by each statement.
  (a) $3[(4 + 5) + 6] = 3(4 + 5) + 3(6)$
  (b) $0 + 7 = 7$
  (c) $-6 \cdot 1 = -6$
  (d) $-5 - (-2) = -5 + (2)$

(e) $(8 \times 3) \times \sqrt{2} = 8 \times (3 \times \sqrt{2})$

(f) $-10 < -3$ since $-3 - (-10) > 0$

5 State, in symbols, each property:

(a) addition property of equality

(b) multiplication property of equality

6 (a) Find the coordinate of the midpoint of the line segment with endpoints at -4 and 6.

(b) One endpoint of a line segment is located at -7. The midpoint is located at -2. What is the coordinate of the other endpoint of the line segment?

Solve for x.

7 $\frac{3}{4}x - 1 = 11$ **8** $4x + 20 = 2x - 2$

9 $3(x + 2) = x - 3$

10 Find the dimensions of a rectangle whose perimeter is 52 inches if the length is 5 inches more than twice the width.

11 A car leaves from point B at noon traveling at the rate of 55 miles an hour. One hour later a second car leaves from the same point, traveling in the opposite direction at 45 miles per hour. At what time will they be 200 miles apart?

Show each interval on a number line.

12 $(-2, 2]$ **13** $[-3, 1)$

14 $(-2, 0)$ **15** $[-1, 1]$

Solve for x.

16 $|3 - 4x| = 2$ **17** $\dfrac{|x + 2|}{x + 2} = -1$

18 $\dfrac{|x - 2|}{x - 2} = 1$

Solve and graph each inequality.

19 $2(5x - 1) < x$ **20** $|2x - 1| \geq 3$

21 $\dfrac{3}{x - 2} > 0$ **22** $(2x - 1)(x + 5) < 0$

ANSWERS TO THE TEST YOUR UNDERSTANDING EXERCISES

Page 2

1 Associative property for addition.

2 Commutative property for addition.

3 Commutative property for addition.

4 Commutative property for multiplication.

5 Commutative property for multiplication.

6 Associative property for multiplication.

7 No; no.   **8** $12 \div 3 \neq 3 \div 12$ **9** No; no.

10 $(8 \div 4) \div 2 \neq 8 \div (4 \div 2)$

11 Yes; the closure properties for addition and multiplication of real numbers, respectively.

Page 8

1 $\{0, 1, 2, 3, 4\}$ **2** $\{11, 12, 13, \ldots\}$ **3** $\{2, 3, 4, 5, 6, 7, 8, 9\}$

4 $\{-2, -1, 0, 1, 2, 3\}$ **5** $\{-4, -3, -2, -1\}$ **6** $\{\ldots, -2, -1, 0, 1\}$

7 The sets in Exercises 1, 3, 4, 5.

Page 13

1 6   **2** 17   **3** -4 **4** 6   **5** 13   **6** 10

7 1   **8** 2   **9** 5   **10** -9 **11** -3 **12** -11

Page 20

1

2

3

4

5 $[-1, 2]$ **6** $(0, 3)$ **7** $(-\infty, 0]$ **8** $[-1, 4)$ **9** $[-3, \infty)$ **10** $(-5, -2)$

Page 23

1 $x < 3$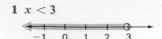

2 $x > -5$

3 $x < -4$

4 $x \geq \frac{5}{2}$

5 $x < 2$

6 $x \leq -\frac{5}{2}$

7 $x > -6$

8 $x \leq -6$

9 $x > 0$

10 $x > 3$

11 (a) Negative; **(b)** negative.

12 (a) Positive; **(b)** negative.

Page 29

1 $-8, 2$

2 $-1, 5$

3 $3, 5$

4 $-1, 2$

5 $-\frac{7}{3}, 1$

6 $-\frac{1}{2}, \frac{3}{2}$

7 $2 < x < 4$

8 $x < -4$ or $x > -2$

9 $-1 \leq x \leq 5$

FUNDAMENTALS OF ALGEBRA

Integral exponents

Much of mathematical notation can be viewed as efficient abbreviations of lengthier statements. For example:

$$4^9 = 4 \times 4 \times 4 \times 4 \times 4 \times 4 \times 4 \times 4 \times 4$$

This illustration is a specific example of the fundamental definition of a *positive integral exponent*.

DEFINITION OF POSITIVE INTEGRAL EXPONENT

If n is a positive integer and b is any real number, then

$$b^n = \underbrace{b \cdot b \cdot \cdots \cdot b}_{n \text{ factors}}$$

The number b is called the **base** and n is called the **exponent**.

Here are some illustrations of the definition:

$$b^1 = b$$

$$(a + b)^2 = (a + b)(a + b)$$

The most common ways of referring to b^n are "b to the nth power," "b to the nth," or "the nth power of b."

"Raising to a power" is not commutative or associative. Verify this by showing that $2^3 \neq 3^2$ and $(2^3)^4 \neq 2^{(3^4)}$.

$$(-2)^3 = (-2)(-2)(-2) = -8$$
$$(\tfrac{1}{3})^4 = \tfrac{1}{3} \cdot \tfrac{1}{3} \cdot \tfrac{1}{3} \cdot \tfrac{1}{3} = \tfrac{1}{81}$$
$$(-1)^5 = (-1)(-1)(-1)(-1)(-1) = -1$$
$$10^6 = 10 \cdot 10 \cdot 10 \cdot 10 \cdot 10 \cdot 10 = 1{,}000{,}000$$

A number of important rules concerning positive integral exponents are easily established on the basis of the preceding definition. Here is a list of these rules in which m and n are any positive integers, a and b are any real numbers, and with the usual understanding that denominators cannot be zero.

RULE 1. $b^m b^n = b^{m+n}$

Illustrations:

$$2^3 \cdot 2^4 = 2^{3+4} = 2^7$$
$$x^3 \cdot x^4 = x^7$$

RULE 2. $\dfrac{b^m}{b^n} = \begin{cases} b^{m-n} & \text{if } m > n \\ 1 & \text{if } m = n \\ \dfrac{1}{b^{n-m}} & \text{if } m < n \end{cases}$

Illustrations:

$(m > n)$ $\dfrac{2^5}{2^2} = 2^{5-2} = 2^3$ $(m = n)$ $\dfrac{5^2}{5^2} = 1$

$\dfrac{x^5}{x^2} = x^{5-2} = x^3$ $\dfrac{x^2}{x^2} = 1$

$(m < n)$ $\dfrac{2^2}{2^5} = \dfrac{1}{2^{5-2}} = \dfrac{1}{2^3}$

$\dfrac{x^2}{x^5} = \dfrac{1}{x^{5-2}} = \dfrac{1}{x^3}$

RULE 3. $(b^m)^n = b^{mn}$

Illustrations:

$$(2^3)^2 = 2^{3 \cdot 2} = 2^6$$
$$(x^3)^2 = x^{3 \cdot 2} = x^6$$

RULE 4. $(ab)^m = a^m b^m$

Illustrations:

$$(2 \cdot 3)^5 = 2^5 \cdot 3^5$$
$$(xy)^5 = x^5 y^5$$

Eventually, the rules for exponents will be extended to include all the real numbers (not just positive integers) as exponents. We will find that all the rules stated here will still apply.

RULE 5. $\left(\dfrac{a}{b}\right)^m = \dfrac{a^m}{b^m}$

Illustrations:

$$\left(\frac{3}{2}\right)^5 = \frac{3^5}{2^5}$$
$$\left(\frac{x}{y}\right)^5 = \frac{x^5}{y^5}$$

The proper use of these rules can simplify computations, as in the following example.

EXAMPLE 1 Evaluate: $12^3(\frac{1}{6})^3$.

Solution This expression can be evaluated without use of any of the rules of exponents.

$$12^3(\tfrac{1}{6})^3 = 1728(\tfrac{1}{216})$$
$$= \tfrac{1728}{216}$$
$$= 8$$

Using Rule 4, the work proves to be much easier.

$$12^3(\tfrac{1}{6})^3 = (12 \cdot \tfrac{1}{6})^3$$
$$= 2^3$$
$$= 8$$

Here is a proof of Rule 4. You can try proving the other rules by using similar arguments.

$$(ab)^m = (ab)(ab) \cdots (ab) \qquad \text{(by definition)}$$

$$= (a \cdot a \cdot \cdots \cdot a)(b \cdot b \cdot \cdots \cdot b) \qquad \begin{cases}\text{(by repeated use of the} \\ \text{commutative and associative} \\ \text{laws for multiplication)}\end{cases}$$

$$= a^m b^m \qquad \text{(by definition)}$$

EXAMPLE 2 Simplify: **(a)** $2x^3 \cdot x^4$ **(b)** $\dfrac{(x^3y)^2y^3}{x^4y^6}$

Solution

(a) $2x^3 \cdot x^4 = 2x^{3+4} = 2x^7$

(b) $\dfrac{(x^3y)^2y^3}{x^4y^6} = \dfrac{(x^3)^2y^2y^3}{x^4y^6} = \dfrac{x^6y^5}{x^4y^6} = \dfrac{x^2}{y}$

TEST YOUR UNDERSTANDING

Evaluate each of the following.

1 5^3 　　　　　　 **2** $(-\frac{1}{2})^5$ 　　　　　　 **3** $(-\frac{2}{3})^3 + \frac{8}{27}$

4 $(10^3)^2$ 　　　　　 **5** $2^3(-2)^3$ 　　　　　 **6** $(\frac{1}{2})^3 8^3$

7 $\dfrac{17^8}{17^9}$ 　　　　　 **8** $\dfrac{(-2)^3 + 3^2}{3^3 - 2^2}$ 　　　　 **9** $\dfrac{(-12)^4}{4^4}$

10 $(ab^2)^3(a^2b)^4$ 　　 **11** $\dfrac{2^2 \cdot 16^3}{(-2)^8}$ 　　 **12** $\dfrac{(2x^3)^2(3x)^2}{6x^4}$

Our discussion of exponents has been restricted to the use of positive integers only. Now let us consider the meaning of 0 as an exponent. In particular, what is the meaning of 5^0? We know that 5^3 means that we are to

This discussion provides meaning for the use of 0 as an exponent. That is, an expression like 5^0 will now be defined.

use 5 three times as a factor. But certainly it makes no sense to use 5 zero times. The rules of exponents will help to resolve this dilemma.

We would like these laws for exponents to hold even if one of the exponents happens to be zero. That is, we would *like* Rule 2 to give

$$\frac{5^2}{5^2} = 5^{2-2} = 5^0$$

But it is already known that

$$\frac{5^2}{5^2} = \frac{25}{25} = 1$$

Thus 5^0 ought to be assigned the value 1. Consequently, in order to *preserve* the rules of exponents, we decide to let $5^0 = 1$. And, from now on, we agree to the following:

Notice that the definition calls for b to be a real number different from 0. That is, we do not define an expression such as 0^0; this is said to be undefined. (See Exercise 68.)

DEFINITION OF ZERO EXPONENT

If b is a real number different from 0, then

$$b^0 = 1$$

Let us explore the first part of Rule 2 for exponents in greater detail.

$$\frac{b^m}{b^n} = b^{m-n}, \qquad m > n, \qquad b \neq 0$$

Suppose that we try an example where $m < n$, and apply the same rule:

$$\frac{x^2}{x^5} = x^{2-5} = x^{-3}$$

What meaning should be assigned to x^{-3}? To answer this question we can return to the original meaning of an exponent, in this way:

This discussion provides the motivation for the definition of a negative exponent.

$$\frac{x^2}{x^5} = \frac{x \cdot x}{x \cdot x \cdot x \cdot x \cdot x} = \frac{x \cdot x}{x \cdot x} \cdot \frac{1}{x \cdot x \cdot x}$$

$$= \frac{x^2}{x^2} \cdot \frac{1}{x^3}$$

$$= 1 \cdot \frac{1}{x^3}$$

$$= \frac{1}{x^3}$$

It thus seems to make sense to *define* x^{-3} as $\frac{1}{x^3}$. Furthermore, this is consistent with Rule 1 for multiplication and the definition of x^0:

$$(x^3)(x^{-3}) = x^{3+(-3)} = x^0 = 1$$

Since $(x^3)(x^{-3}) = 1$, it also follows that $x^3 = \frac{1}{x^{-3}}$. In general, we make the following definition:

If n is an integer and $b \neq 0$, then

$$b^{-n} = \frac{1}{b^n}$$

Note that in making definitions for b^0 and b^{-n}, the major guideline is to *preserve* our earlier rules for exponents. That is, we want those rules to hold regardless of the kind of integers m and n represent.

It follows from this definition that $\left(\frac{a}{b}\right)^{-1} = \frac{b}{a}$, since $\left(\frac{a}{b}\right)^{-1} = \frac{1}{\frac{a}{b}} = \frac{b}{a}$.

In other words, a fraction to the -1 power is the reciprocal of the fraction. Can you show that $\left(\frac{a}{b}\right)^{-2} = \left(\frac{b}{a}\right)^{2}$?

EXAMPLE 3 Evaluate:

(a) $(\frac{1}{7})^{-2}$ (b) $(\frac{1}{2})^3(2)^{-3}$ (c) $\frac{5^{-2}}{15^{-2}}$ (d) $\left(\frac{400 - 10^4}{80^2}\right)^0$

Solution

(a) $(\frac{1}{7})^{-2} = \frac{1}{(\frac{1}{7})^2} = \frac{1}{\frac{1}{49}} = 49$ or $(\frac{1}{7})^{-2} = (7^{-1})^{-2} = 7^2 = 49$

As in Example 3(a), more than one correct procedure is often possible. Finding the most efficient procedure depends largely on experience.

(b) $\left(\frac{1}{2}\right)^3(2)^{-3} = \left(\frac{1}{2}\right)^3 \frac{1}{2^3} = \left(\frac{1}{2}\right)^3\left(\frac{1}{2}\right)^3 = \left(\frac{1}{2}\right)^6 = \frac{1}{64}$

(c) $\frac{5^{-2}}{15^{-2}} = \left(\frac{5}{15}\right)^{-2} = \left(\frac{1}{3}\right)^{-2} = (3^{-1})^{-2} = 3^2 = 9$

(d) $\left(\frac{400 - 10^4}{80^2}\right)^0 = 1$

It should be noted that the three cases of Rule 2 can now be condensed into this single form.

RULE 2. (revised): $\frac{b^m}{b^n} = b^{m-n}$

Illustrations:

$$\frac{3^4}{3^2} = 3^2 \qquad \frac{3^2}{3^4} = 3^{-2} \qquad \frac{3^2}{3^2} = 3^0 = 1$$

$$\frac{x^8}{x^2} = x^6 \qquad \frac{x^2}{x^8} = x^{-6} \qquad \frac{x^2}{x^2} = x^0 = 1$$

EXAMPLE 4 Simplify $\left(\frac{a^{-2}b^3}{a^3b^{-2}}\right)^5$ and express the answer using positive exponents only.

Solution There are several ways to proceed; here are two.

(a) $\left(\frac{a^{-2}b^3}{a^3b^{-2}}\right)^5 = (a^{-5}b^5)^5 = (a^{-5})^5(b^5)^5 = a^{-25}b^{25} = \frac{b^{25}}{a^{25}}$

(b) $\left(\dfrac{a^{-2}b^3}{a^3b^{-2}}\right)^5 = \left(\dfrac{b^5}{a^5}\right)^5 = \dfrac{(b^5)^5}{(a^5)^5} = \dfrac{b^{25}}{a^{25}}$

It can be shown that the rules presented in this section apply for all integral exponents. Here is a proof of Rule 4, for zero and negative integral exponents. The remaining rules can be proved in a similar manner.

If $m = 0$, then $(ab)^0 = 1$. Also, $a^0b^0 = 1 \cdot 1 = 1$. Thus $(ab)^0 = 1 = a^0b^0$. If $m < 0$, let $m = -k$, where k is the appropriate positive integer. Thus

$$(ab)^m = (ab)^{-k} \qquad \text{(substitution)}$$

$$= \frac{1}{(ab)^k} \qquad \text{(definition)}$$

$$= \frac{1}{a^kb^k} \qquad \text{(Rule 4 since } k \text{ is a positive integer)}$$

$$= \frac{1}{a^k} \cdot \frac{1}{b^k} \qquad \text{(property of fractions)}$$

$$= a^{-k}b^{-k} \qquad \text{(definition)}$$

$$= a^mb^m \qquad \text{(substitution; } m = -k)$$

CAUTION: LEARN TO AVOID MISTAKES LIKE THESE

Many errors are made when working with exponents because of misuses of the basic rules and definitions. This list shows some of the common errors that you should try to avoid.

WRONG	RIGHT
$5^2 \cdot 5^4 = 5^8$ (Do not multiply exponents.) $5^2 \cdot 5^4 = 25^6$ (Do not multiply the base numbers.)	$5^2 \cdot 5^4 = 5^6$ (Rule 1)
$\dfrac{5^6}{5^2} = 5^3$ (Do not divide the exponents.) $\dfrac{5^6}{5^2} = 1^4$ (Do not divide the base numbers.)	$\dfrac{5^6}{5^2} = 5^4$ (Rule 2)
$(5^2)^6 = 5^8$ (Do not add the exponents.)	$(5^2)^6 = 5^{12}$ (Rule 3)
$(-2)^4 = -2^4$ (Misreading the parentheses)	$(-2)^4 = (-1)^42^4 = 2^4$ (Rule 4 or definition)
$(-5)^0 = -1$ (Misreading definition of b^0)	$(-5)^0 = 1$ (Definition of b^0)

WRONG	RIGHT
$2^{-3} = -\dfrac{1}{2^3}$ (Misreading definition of b^{-n})	$2^{-3} = \dfrac{1}{2^3}$ (Definition of b^{-n})
$\dfrac{2^3}{2^{-4}} = 2^{3-4} = 2^{-1}$ (Carelessness in subtracting exponents)	$\dfrac{2^3}{2^{-4}} = 2^{3-(-4)} = 2^7$ (Rule 2)
$5^3 + 5^3 = 5^6$ (Adding exponents does not apply because of plus sign.)	$5^3 + 5^3 = (1+1)5^3 = 2 \cdot 5^3$ (Distributive)
$(a+b)^{-1} = a^{-1} + b^{-1}$ (Wrong use of definition)	$(a+b)^{-1} = \dfrac{1}{a+b}$ (Definition)

EXERCISES 2.1

Classify each statement as true or false. If it is false, correct the right side of the equality to obtain a true statement.

1 $3^4 \cdot 3^2 = 3^8$

2 $(2^2)^3 = 2^8$

3 $2^5 \cdot 2^2 = 4^7$

4 $\dfrac{9^3}{9^3} = 1$

5 $\dfrac{10^4}{5^4} = 2^4$

6 $\left(\dfrac{2}{3}\right)^4 = \dfrac{2^4}{3}$

7 $(-27)^0 = 1$

8 $(2^0)^3 = 2^3$

9 $3^4 + 3^4 = 3^8$

10 $(a^2 b)^3 = a^2 b^3$

11 $(a+b)^0 = a+1$

12 $a^2 + a^2 = 2a^2$

13 $\dfrac{1}{2^{-3}} = -2^3$

14 $(2+\pi)^{-2} = \dfrac{1}{4} + \dfrac{1}{\pi^2}$

15 $\dfrac{2^{-5}}{2^3} = 2^{-2}$

Evaluate.

16 10^5

17 $2^0 + 2^1 + 2^2$

18 $(-3)^2(-2)^3$

19 $\left(\dfrac{2}{3}\right)^0 + \left(\dfrac{2}{3}\right)^1$

20 $[(\tfrac{1}{2})^3]^2$

21 $(\tfrac{1}{2})^4(-2)^4$

22 $\dfrac{3^2}{3^0}$

23 $\dfrac{(-2)^5}{(-2)^3}$

24 $\left(-\dfrac{3}{4}\right)^3$

25 $\dfrac{2^3 \cdot 3^4 \cdot 4^5}{2^2 \cdot 3^3 \cdot 4^4}$

26 $\dfrac{8^3}{16^2}$

27 $\dfrac{2^{10}}{2^5 \cdot 2^3}$

28 $\dfrac{3^{-3}}{4^{-3}}$

29 $(\tfrac{2}{3})^{-2} + (\tfrac{2}{3})^{-1}$

30 $[(-7)^2(-3)^2]^{-1}$

Express each answer using positive exponents only.

31 $(x^{-3})^2$

32 $(x^3)^{-2}$

33 $x^3 \cdot x^9$

34 $\dfrac{x^9}{x^3}$

35 $(2a)^3(3a)^2$

36 $(-2x^3 y)^2(-3x^2 y^2)^3$

37 $(-2a^2 b^0)^4$

38 $(2x^3 y^2)^0$

39 $\dfrac{(x^2 y)^4}{(xy)^2}$

40 $\left(\dfrac{3a^2}{b^3}\right)^2 \left(\dfrac{-2a}{3b}\right)^2$

41 $\left(\dfrac{x^3}{y^2}\right)^4 \left(\dfrac{-y}{x^2}\right)^2$

42 $\dfrac{(x-2y)^6}{(x-2y)^2}$

43 $\dfrac{x^{-2} y^3}{x^3 y^{-4}}$

44 $\dfrac{(x^{-2} y^2)^3}{(x^3 y^{-2})^2}$

45 $\dfrac{5x^0 y^{-2}}{x^{-1} y^{-2}}$

46 $\dfrac{(2x^3 y^{-2})^2}{8x^{-3} y^2}$

47 $\dfrac{(-3a)^{-2}}{a^{-2} b^{-2}}$

48 $\dfrac{3a^{-3} b^2}{2^{-1} c^2 d^{-4}}$

49 $\dfrac{(a+b)^{-2}}{(a+b)^{-8}}$

50 $\dfrac{8x^{-8} y^{-12}}{2x^{-2} y^{-6}}$

51 $\dfrac{-12x^{-9}y^{10}}{4x^{-12}y^7}$

52 $\dfrac{(2x^2y^{-1})^6}{(4x^{-6}y^{-5})^2}$

53 $\dfrac{(a+3b)^{-12}}{(a+3b)^{10}}$

54 $\dfrac{(-a^{-5}b^6)^3}{(a^8b^4)^2}$

55 $x^{-2}+y^{-2}$

56 $(a^{-2}b^3)^{-1}$

57 $\left(\dfrac{x^{-2}}{y^3}\right)^{-1}$

■ **58** $-2(1+x^2)^{-3}(2x)$

■ **59** $-2(4-5x)^{-3}(-5)$

■ **60** $-7(x^2-3x)^{-8}(2x-3)$

Find a value of x to made each statement true.

61 $2^x \cdot 2^3 = 2^{12}$

62 $2^{-3} \cdot 2^x = 2^6$

63 $2^x \cdot 2^x = 2^{16}$

64 $2^x \cdot 2^{x-1} = 2^7$

■ Recall that this symbol is used to identify exercises that are of special value with respect to the later study of calculus.

65 $\dfrac{2^x}{2^2} = 2^{-5}$

66 $\dfrac{2^{-3}}{2^x} = 2^4$

**67 Express as a single fraction using only positive exponents: $\dfrac{1}{a^{-1}+b^{-1}}$.

**68 We have said that 0^0 is undefined. The following shows why we have not defined this to be equal to 1. *Suppose* that $0^0 = 1$. Then

$$1 = \frac{1}{1} = \frac{1^0}{0^0}$$
$$= \left(\frac{1}{0}\right)^0$$

(a) What rule for exponents is being used in the last step? (b) What went wrong?

**69 Use the definition of a^{-n} to prove that $\dfrac{1}{a^{-n}} = a^n$.

2.2

Radicals and rational exponents

You may recall using radicals in the past as you worked with square roots. For example, $\sqrt{25}$ is called a *radical* and denotes the positive number whose square is 25. Now it is true that $5^2 = 25$ and $(-5)^2 = 25$, but the **radical sign** $\sqrt{}$ implies the positive or *principal square root of a number*. Thus we say that $\sqrt{25} = 5$. We denote the negative square root as $-\sqrt{25} = -5$.

In general, the *principal nth root* of a real number a is denoted by $\sqrt[n]{a}$, as in these illustrations:

In the preceding section b^n was defined only for integers n. The next stage is to extend this concept to include fractional exponents—that is, to give meaning to such expressions as $4^{1/2}$ and $(-8)^{2/3}$.

$$\sqrt[3]{64} = 4 \quad \text{because} \quad 4^3 = 64$$
$$\sqrt[5]{32} = 2 \quad \text{because} \quad 2^5 = 32$$
$$\sqrt[3]{-8} = -2 \quad \text{because} \quad (-2)^3 = -8$$

The expression $\sqrt[n]{a}$ does not always have meaning. For example, let us try to evaluate $\sqrt[4]{-16}$:

$$2^4 = 16 \qquad (-2)^4 = 16$$

It appears that there is no real number x such that $x^4 = -16$. In general, *there is no real number that is the even root of a negative number*. However, it is a fundamental property of real numbers that every positive real number a has exactly one positive nth root. Furthermore, every negative real number has a negative nth root provided that n is odd.

DEFINITION OF $\sqrt[n]{a}$; THE PRINCIPAL nTH ROOT OF a

Let a be a real number and n a positive integer, $n \geq 2$.
(i) If $a > 0$, then $\sqrt[n]{a}$ is the positive number x such that $x^n = a$.
(ii) $\sqrt[n]{0} = 0$

(iii) If $a < 0$ and n is odd, then $\sqrt[n]{a}$ is the negative number x such that $x^n = a$.

(iv) If $a < 0$ and n is even, then $\sqrt[n]{a}$ is not a real number.

The symbol $\sqrt[n]{a}$ is also said to be a *radical*; $\sqrt{}$ is the radical sign, n is the *index* or *root*, and a is called the *radicand*.

EXAMPLE 1 Evaluate: **(a)** $\sqrt[3]{\tfrac{1}{8}}$ **(b)** $\sqrt[5]{-32}$ **(c)** $\sqrt{0.09}$

Solution

(a) $\sqrt[3]{\tfrac{1}{8}} = \tfrac{1}{2}$ since $(\tfrac{1}{2})^3 = \tfrac{1}{8}$

(b) $\sqrt[5]{-32} = -2$ since $(-2)^5 = -32$.

(c) $\sqrt{0.09} = 0.3$ since $(0.3)^2 = 0.09$

In order to multiply or divide radicals, the index must be the same. Here are illustrations that motivate Rules 2 and 3 stated below.

$$\left.\begin{array}{l} \sqrt[3]{8}\,\sqrt[3]{-27} = 2(-3) = -6 \\ \sqrt[3]{8(-27)} = \sqrt[3]{-216} = -6 \end{array}\right\} \quad \text{so } \sqrt[3]{8} \cdot \sqrt[3]{-27} = \sqrt[3]{8(-27)}$$

$$\left.\begin{array}{l} \dfrac{\sqrt{36}}{\sqrt{4}} = \dfrac{6}{2} = 3 \\[2mm] \sqrt{\dfrac{36}{4}} = \sqrt{9} = 3 \end{array}\right\} \quad \text{so } \dfrac{\sqrt{36}}{\sqrt{4}} = \sqrt{\dfrac{36}{4}}$$

In the following rules it is assumed that all radicals exist according to the definition of $\sqrt[n]{a}$ and, as usual, denominators are not zero.

RULES FOR RADICALS

1. $(\sqrt[n]{a})^n = \sqrt[n]{a^n} = a$

2. $\sqrt[n]{a} \cdot \sqrt[n]{b} = \sqrt[n]{ab}$

3. $\dfrac{\sqrt[n]{a}}{\sqrt[n]{b}} = \sqrt[n]{\dfrac{a}{b}}$

4. $\sqrt[m]{\sqrt[n]{a}} = \sqrt[mn]{a}$

The proofs of Rules 2 and 3 are called for in Exercises 70 and 71.

EXAMPLE 2 Simplify: **(a)** $(\sqrt[4]{7})^4$ **(b)** $\sqrt{9 \cdot 25}$ **(c)** $\sqrt[4]{\tfrac{16}{81}}$ **(d)** $\sqrt[2]{\sqrt[3]{64}}$ **(e)** $\sqrt{72}\sqrt{\tfrac{1}{2}}$

Solution

(a) $(\sqrt[4]{7})^4 = 7$ by Rule 1.

(b) $\sqrt{9 \cdot 25} = \sqrt{9} \cdot \sqrt{25} = 3 \cdot 5 = 15$ by Rule 2.

(c) $\sqrt[4]{\dfrac{16}{81}} = \dfrac{\sqrt[4]{16}}{\sqrt[4]{81}} = \dfrac{2}{3}$ by Rule 3. (*Note:* $2^4 = 16$ and $3^4 = 81$.)

(d) $\sqrt[2]{\sqrt[3]{64}} = \sqrt[6]{64} = 2$ by Rule 4. (*Note:* $2^6 = 64$.)

(e) $\sqrt{72} \cdot \sqrt{\frac{1}{2}} = \sqrt{(72)(\frac{1}{2})} = \sqrt{36} = 6$ by Rule 2.

In applying the rules for radicals, care must be taken to avoid the type of error that results from the incorrect assumption of the existence of an nth root. For example, $\sqrt[2]{-4}$ is *not* a real number, but if this is not noticed, then *false* results such as the following occur:

CAUTION: Here is a common error you must avoid.

$$4 = \sqrt{16} = \sqrt{(-4)(-4)} = \sqrt{-4} \cdot \sqrt{-4} = (\sqrt{-4})^2 = -4$$

TEST YOUR UNDERSTANDING

Evaluate each of the following.

1 $\sqrt{121}$ **2** $\sqrt[3]{-64}$ **3** $\sqrt[5]{32}$

4 $\sqrt{\sqrt{81}}$ **5** $\sqrt{(25)(49)}$ **6** $\sqrt[3]{\frac{27}{125}}$

7 $(\sqrt[4]{2})^4$ **8** $\sqrt[3]{(-1000)(343)}$ **9** $\sqrt[4]{\frac{256}{81}}$

10 $\sqrt{(9)(144)(225)}$ **11** $\sqrt[3]{\frac{(-8)(125)}{27}}$ **12** $\sqrt{\frac{144}{49}} \cdot \sqrt{\frac{196}{36}}$

13 $\sqrt[3]{-8} \cdot \sqrt[3]{-27}$ **14** $\sqrt[3]{\frac{81}{-3}}$ **15** $\sqrt[3]{\frac{1}{24}} \cdot \sqrt[3]{-81}$

We are now ready to make the promised extension of the exponential concept to include fractional exponents. Once again our guideline will be to preserve the earlier rules for integer exponents.

First let us consider exponents of the form $\frac{1}{n}$, where n is a positive integer. (Assume that $n \geq 2$ since the case $n = 1$ is trivial.) That is, we wish to give meaning to the expression $b^{1/n}$. If Rule 3 for exponents is to work, then

$$(b^{1/n})^n = b^{(1/n)(n)} = b$$

Thus $b^{1/n}$ is the nth root of b (provided that such a root exists). This leads us to the following definition for $b^{1/n}$.

Since $\sqrt{-1}$ is not a real number, $(-1)^{1/2}$ is not defined. In general, $b^{1/n}$ is not defined within the set of real numbers when $b < 0$ and n is even.

DEFINITION OF $b^{1/n}$

For a real number b and a positive integer n ($n \geq 2$),
$$b^{1/n} = \sqrt[n]{b}$$
provided that $\sqrt[n]{b}$ exists.

Illustrations:

$$\sqrt{15} = 15^{1/2} \qquad\qquad \sqrt[3]{-6} = (-6)^{1/3}$$

$$9^{-1/2} = \frac{1}{9^{1/2}} = \frac{1}{\sqrt{9}} = \frac{1}{3} \qquad (-27)^{1/3} = \sqrt[3]{-27} = -3$$

$$(-16)^{1/4} \text{ is not defined}$$

We now wish to give meaning to an expression such as $b^{m/n}$. To do so, we note that squaring $8^{1/3} = \sqrt[3]{8}$ produces $(8^{1/3})^2 = (\sqrt[3]{8})^2$. But to preserve the rules for exponents we write $(8^{1/3})^2 = 8^{2/3}$. Thus it is reasonable to let $8^{2/3} = (\sqrt[3]{8})^2$. Similarly, $8^{2/3} = (8^2)^{1/3} = \sqrt[3]{8^2}$. These observations lead to this definition:

DEFINITION OF $b^{m/n}$

If m/n is a rational number in lowest terms with $n > 0$, then

$$b^{m/n} = (\sqrt[n]{b})^m = \sqrt[n]{b^m}$$

provided that $\sqrt[n]{b}$ exists.

Note that a rational number can always be expressed with a positive denominator; for example, $\dfrac{2}{-3} = \dfrac{-2}{3}$.

Using only fractional exponents, we may also write

$$b^{m/n} = (b^{1/n})^m = (b^m)^{1/n}$$

EXAMPLE 3   Evaluate: $(-64)^{2/3}$.

Solution   Using $b^{m/n} = (\sqrt[n]{b})^m$, we get

$$(-64)^{2/3} = (\sqrt[3]{-64})^2 = (-4)^2 = 16$$

Using $b^{m/n} = \sqrt[n]{b^m}$, we get

$$(-64)^{2/3} = \sqrt[3]{(-64)^2} = \sqrt[3]{4096} = 16$$

Obviously, the first approach is less work. For most such problems it is easier to first take the nth root and then raise to the mth power, rather than the reverse.

EXAMPLE 4   Evaluate: $8^{-2/3}$.

Solution   First rewrite the example using positive exponents; then apply the definition.

Note: $8^{-2/3} = 8^{2/{-3}} = 8^{-(2/3)}$.

$$8^{-2/3} = \frac{1}{8^{2/3}} = \frac{1}{(\sqrt[3]{8})^2} = \frac{1}{4}$$

TEST YOUR UNDERSTANDING

Write each of the following as a radical.

1 $5^{1/2}$ **2** $(-9)^{1/3}$ **3** $10^{1/4}$ **4** $5^{2/3}$ **5** $2^{3/4}$

Write each of the following using fractional exponents.

6 $\sqrt{7}$ **7** $\sqrt[3]{-10}$ **8** $\sqrt[4]{7}$ **9** $\sqrt[3]{7^2}$ **10** $(\sqrt[4]{5})^3$

Evaluate.

11 $25^{1/2}$ **12** $64^{1/3}$ **13** $(\frac{1}{36})^{1/2}$ **14** $(\frac{1}{125})^{1/3}$ **15** $(\frac{9}{25})^{1/2}$

16 $49^{-1/2}$ **17** $4^{3/2}$ **18** $4^{-3/2}$ **19** $(-8)^{2/3}$ **20** $(-8)^{-2/3}$

The definition for $b^{m/n}$ calls for the fractional exponent to be in lowest terms so as to avoid situations as in Example 5.

EXAMPLE 5   Find what is wrong in the following "proof" that $2 = -2$.
$$-2 = \sqrt[3]{-8} = (-8)^{1/3} = (-8)^{2/6} = \sqrt[6]{(-8)^2} = \sqrt[6]{64} = 2$$
Solution   Since $\frac{2}{6}$ is not in lowest terms, we are *not* permitted to write
$$(-8)^{2/6} = \sqrt[6]{(-8)^2}$$
If we restrict ourselves to the roots of only *positive* numbers, then the requirement that the exponent $\frac{m}{n}$ must be in lowest terms can be relaxed. For example:
$$2 = 8^{1/3} = 8^{2/6} = \sqrt[6]{8^2} = \sqrt[6]{64} = 2$$

Since the definition of fractional exponents was made on the basis of preserving the rules for integral exponents, it should come as no surprise that these rules apply. This is illustrated in the examples that follow.

EXAMPLE 6   Evaluate: $27^{2/3} - 16^{-1/4}$.

Solution

$$27^{2/3} - 16^{-1/4} = (\sqrt[3]{27})^2 - \frac{1}{16^{1/4}}$$
$$= 3^2 - \frac{1}{\sqrt[4]{16}}$$
$$= 9 - \tfrac{1}{2}$$
$$= \frac{17}{2}$$

EXAMPLE 7   Simplify, and express the result with positive exponents only.
$$\frac{x^{2/3}y^{-2}z^2}{x^{1/2}y^{1/2}z^{-1}}$$

In Example 7 you might find it easier to first rewrite the original problem using positive exponents only.

Solution

$$\frac{x^{2/3}y^{-2}z^2}{x^{1/2}y^{1/2}z^{-1}} = x^{2/3-1/2}y^{-2-1/2}z^{2-(-1)}$$
$$= x^{1/6}y^{-5/2}z^3$$
$$= \frac{x^{1/6}z^3}{y^{5/2}}$$

CAUTION: LEARN TO AVOID MISTAKES LIKE THESE

WRONG	RIGHT
$\sqrt{25} = \pm 5$ (Misuse of the definition of $\sqrt{a}$)	$\sqrt{25} = 5$

WRONG	RIGHT
$16^{3/4} = (\sqrt[3]{16})^4$ (Misuse of the definition of $b^{m/n}$)	$16^{3/4} = (\sqrt[4]{16})^3$ or $\sqrt[4]{16^3}$
$(-2)^{-1/3} = 2^{1/3}$	$(-2)^{-1/3} = \dfrac{1}{(-2)^{1/3}} = \dfrac{1}{\sqrt[3]{-2}}$
$a^{-1/2} + b^{-1/2} = \dfrac{1}{\sqrt{a+b}}$	$a^{-1/2} + b^{-1/2} = \dfrac{1}{\sqrt{a}} + \dfrac{1}{\sqrt{b}}$

Write with a fractional exponent.

1 $\sqrt{11}$ 2 $\sqrt[3]{21}$

3 $\sqrt[4]{9}$ 4 $\sqrt[3]{-10}$

5 $\sqrt[3]{6^2}$ 6 $(\sqrt[3]{-7})^2$

7 $(\sqrt[5]{-\frac{1}{5}})^3$ 8 $\dfrac{1}{\sqrt[3]{4^2}}$

Write in radical form.

9 $3^{1/2}$ 10 $7^{1/3}$

11 $(-19)^{1/3}$ 12 $6^{2/3}$

13 $2^{-1/2}$ 14 $7^{-3/2}$

15 $(\frac{3}{4})^{-1/4}$ 16 $(-\frac{1}{3})^{-2/3}$

Classify each statement as true or false. If it is false, correct the right side of the equality to obtain a true statement.

17 $\sqrt[3]{-27} = -3$ 18 $4^{1/2} = -2$

19 $(-8)^{2/3} = 4$ 20 $64^{3/4} = (\sqrt[3]{64})^4$

21 $(-\frac{1}{8})^{-1/3} = 2$ 22 $(\sqrt{100})^{-1} = -10$

23 $\sqrt{1.44} = 0.12$ 24 $(0.25)^{3/2} = \frac{1}{8}$

25 $\sqrt{\frac{49}{9}} = \frac{7}{3}$

Evaluate.

26 $121^{1/2}$ 27 $125^{1/3}$

28 $\sqrt[3]{-64}$ 29 $81^{-1/2}$

30 $(-64)^{1/3}$ 31 $(64)^{-2/3}$

32 $\sqrt{5} \cdot \sqrt{20}$ 33 $\sqrt[3]{9} \cdot \sqrt[3]{-3}$

34 $\dfrac{\sqrt{75}}{\sqrt{3}}$ 35 $\dfrac{\sqrt[3]{-3}}{\sqrt[3]{-24}}$

36 $\dfrac{9^{1/2}}{\sqrt[3]{27}}$ 37 $\dfrac{\sqrt{9}}{27^{-1/3}}$

38 $\sqrt[4]{\dfrac{16}{81}}$ 39 $\sqrt[3]{(-125)(-1000)}$

40 $\sqrt{(4)(9)(49)(100)}$ 41 $\left(\frac{1}{4}\right)^{3/2} \cdot \left(-\frac{1}{8}\right)^{2/3}$

42 $\sqrt{\dfrac{2}{3}} \cdot \sqrt{\dfrac{75}{98}}$ 43 $\sqrt{\sqrt{\sqrt{625}}}$

44 $\sqrt[5]{(-243)^2} \cdot (49)^{-1/2}$ 45 $\sqrt{144 + 25}$

46 $\sqrt{144} + \sqrt{25}$ 47 $\left(\frac{1}{8} + \frac{1}{27}\right)^{1/3}$

48 $\left(\frac{1}{8}\right)^{1/3} + \left(\frac{1}{27}\right)^{1/3}$ 49 $\left(\frac{16}{81}\right)^{3/4} + \left(\frac{256}{625}\right)^{1/4}$

50 $\left(\frac{8}{27}\right)^{2/3} + \left(-\frac{32}{243}\right)^{2/5}$ 51 $\left(-\frac{125}{8}\right)^{1/3} - \left(\frac{1}{64}\right)^{1/3}$

52 $\left(-\frac{125}{8} - \frac{1}{64}\right)^{1/3}$

Simplify, and express all answers with positive exponents. (Assume that all letters represent positive numbers.)

53 $(8a^3b^{-9})^{2/3}$ 54 $(27a^{-3}b^9)^{-2/3}$

55 $(a^{-4}b^{-8})^{3/4}$ 56 $(a^{2/3}b^{1/2})(a^{1/3}b^{-1/2})$

57 $(a^{-1/2}b^{1/3})(a^{1/2}b^{-1/3})$ 58 $\dfrac{a^2b^{-1/2}c^{1/3}}{a^{-3}b^0c^{-1/3}}$

59 $\left(\dfrac{64a^6}{b^{-9}}\right)^{2/3}$ 60 $\dfrac{(49a^{-4})^{-1/2}}{(81b^6)^{-1/2}}$

61 $\left(\dfrac{a^{-2}b^3}{a^4b^{-3}}\right)^{-1/2}\left(\dfrac{a^4b^{-5}}{ab}\right)^{-1/3}$ ▬ 62 $\frac{2}{3}(3x-1)^{-1/3} \cdot 3$

▬ 63 $\frac{1}{2}(3x^2 + 2)^{-1/2} \cdot 6x$ ▬ 64 $\frac{1}{3}(x^3 + 2)^{-2/3} \cdot 3x^2$

▬ 65 $\frac{1}{2}(x^2 + 4x)^{-1/2}(2x + 4)$

▬ 66 $\frac{2}{3}(x^3 - 6x^2)^{-1/3}(3x^2 - 12x)$

Simplify, and express the answers without radicals, using only positive exponents. (Assume that n is a positive integer and that all other letters represent positive numbers.)

*67 $\sqrt{\dfrac{x^n}{x^{n-2}}}$

*68 $\left(\dfrac{x^n}{x^{n-2}}\right)^{-1/2}$

*69 $\sqrt[3]{\dfrac{x^{3n+1}\,y^n}{x^{3n+4}\,y^{4n}}}$

*70 Prove: $\sqrt[n]{a}\cdot\sqrt[n]{b}=\sqrt[n]{ab}$.
(*Hint:* Let $\sqrt[n]{a}=x$ and $\sqrt[n]{b}=y$. Then $x^n=a$ and $y^n=b$.)

*71 Prove: $\dfrac{\sqrt[n]{a}}{\sqrt[n]{b}}=\sqrt[n]{\dfrac{a}{b}}$.

2.3

Simplifying radicals

Computations with radicals cause no difficulty when the radicals represent rational numbers, as in the following.

$$\sqrt{36}+\sqrt[3]{-27}=6+(-3)=3$$

When the radicals involve irrational numbers, however, special methods are needed. To *simplify* an expression such as $\sqrt{24}$ means that we are to rewrite the radical so that no perfect square appears as a factor under the radical sign. Thus

> **Note that the fundamental idea used here is that** $\sqrt[n]{ab}=\sqrt[n]{a}\cdot\sqrt[n]{b}.$

$$\sqrt{24}=\sqrt{4\cdot6}=\sqrt{4}\cdot\sqrt{6}=2\sqrt{6}$$

We say that $2\sqrt{6}$ is the *simplified form* of $\sqrt{24}$.

EXAMPLE 1 Simplify: **(a)** $\sqrt{50}$ **(b)** $\sqrt[3]{16}$ **(c)** $\sqrt[3]{-54}$

Solution
(a) $\sqrt{50}=\sqrt{25\cdot2}=\sqrt{25}\cdot\sqrt{2}=5\sqrt{2}$
(b) Here we search for a perfect cube as a factor under the radical sign:

$$\sqrt[3]{16}=\sqrt[3]{8\cdot2}=\sqrt[3]{8}\cdot\sqrt[3]{2}=2\sqrt[3]{2}$$

(c) $\sqrt[3]{-54}=\sqrt[3]{(-27)(2)}=\sqrt[3]{-27}\cdot\sqrt[3]{2}=-3\sqrt[3]{2}$

The rule for multiplication of radicals provides a way to find the product of any two radicals having the same index. For example,

$$\sqrt{4}\cdot\sqrt{9}=\sqrt{4\cdot9}=\sqrt{36}=6$$

Does a similar pattern work for the addition of radicals? That is, is the sum of the square roots of two numbers equal to the square root of their sum? Does $\sqrt{4}+\sqrt{9}=\sqrt{4+9}$? This can easily be checked as follows:

$$\sqrt{4}+\sqrt{9}=2+3=5$$

But $\sqrt{4+9}=\sqrt{13}$. Therefore, $\sqrt{4}+\sqrt{9}\neq\sqrt{4+9}$.

In general, $\sqrt{a}+\sqrt{b}\neq\sqrt{a+b}$.

> **This discussion tells you the conditions under which radicals can be combined.**

Addition and subtraction of radicals is possible, under certain conditions, and is achieved through the use of the distributive property. Consider, for example, this sum:

$$3\sqrt{5}+4\sqrt{5}$$

Although we will usually perform the computation mentally, we can complete this example by thinking of x to replace $\sqrt{5}$.

$$3x + 4x = (3 + 4)x = 7x$$
$$3\sqrt{5} + 4\sqrt{5} = (3 + 4)\sqrt{5} = 7\sqrt{5}$$

That is,

$$3\sqrt{5} + 4\sqrt{5} = 7\sqrt{5}$$

In order to be able to add or subtract radicals, they must have the same index and the same radicand.

At times a fraction can be simplified by a process known as **rationalizing the denominator**. This consists of eliminating a radical from the denominator of a fraction. For example, consider the fraction $4/\sqrt{2}$. To rationalize the denominator, multiply the numerator and denominator by $\sqrt{2}$.

$$\frac{4}{\sqrt{2}} = \frac{4}{\sqrt{2}} \cdot \frac{\sqrt{2}}{\sqrt{2}} \qquad \left(\frac{\sqrt{2}}{\sqrt{2}} = 1\right)$$
$$= \frac{4\sqrt{2}}{2}$$
$$= 2\sqrt{2}$$

One reason for rationalizing denominators is to make computations easier. For example, suppose that we wish to evaluate $\dfrac{4}{\sqrt{2}}$ ($\sqrt{2} = 1.414$) to three decimal places. It certainly is easier to multiply 1.414 by 2 than to divide 4 by 1.414. Another reason for rationalizing denominators is to achieve a standard form for radical expressions in which they are more easily combined or compared.

If a calculator is to be used, $\dfrac{4}{\sqrt{2}}$ is just as easy to evaluate as $2\sqrt{2}$ and would therefore be an acceptable form.

EXAMPLE 2   Combine: $\dfrac{6}{\sqrt{3}} + 2\sqrt{75} - \sqrt{3}$.

Solution   Rationalize the denominator in the first term:

$$\frac{6}{\sqrt{3}} = \frac{6}{\sqrt{3}} \cdot \frac{\sqrt{3}}{\sqrt{3}} = \frac{6\sqrt{3}}{3} = 2\sqrt{3}$$

Simplify the second term:

$$2\sqrt{75} = 2\sqrt{25 \cdot 3} = 10\sqrt{3}$$

Now combine:

$$\frac{6}{\sqrt{3}} + 2\sqrt{75} - \sqrt{3} = 2\sqrt{3} + 10\sqrt{3} - 1\sqrt{3} = 11\sqrt{3}$$

TEST YOUR UNDERSTANDING

Simplify each expression, if possible.

1 $\sqrt{8} + \sqrt{32}$ **2** $\sqrt{12} + \sqrt{48}$ **3** $\sqrt{45} - \sqrt{20}$

4 $2\sqrt{9} - \sqrt{18}$ **5** $\sqrt[3]{16} + \sqrt[3]{54}$ **6** $\sqrt[3]{128} + \sqrt[3]{125}$

7 $\dfrac{8}{\sqrt{2}} + \sqrt{98}$ **8** $\dfrac{9}{\sqrt{3}} + \sqrt{300}$ **9** $2\sqrt{20} - \dfrac{5}{\sqrt{5}}$

10 $3\sqrt{63} - \dfrac{14}{\sqrt{7}}$ **11** $\dfrac{2}{\sqrt{2}} - \sqrt{2}$ **12** $\dfrac{1}{\sqrt{2}} + \dfrac{1}{\sqrt{8}}$

Do you think that $\sqrt{x^2} = x$? This is *not* always so. Study this explanation carefully; it is important for future work in mathematics.

Sometimes it is necessary to simplify a radical that contains a variable, such as $\sqrt{x^2}$. In this example, the usual reaction is to claim that $\sqrt{x^2} = x$. But suppose that x were negative, such as $x = -5$:

$$\text{If } \sqrt{x^2} = x, \quad \text{then } \sqrt{(-5)^2} = -5$$
$$\text{But } \sqrt{(-5)^2} = \sqrt{25} = 5$$

It was stated earlier that the radical sign, $\sqrt{}$, means the *positive* square root of a number. Therefore, it is necessary that $\sqrt{(-5)^2}$ be equal to 5, and not -5. That is, we must have each of the following:

$$\sqrt{5^2} = 5$$
$$\sqrt{(-5)^2} = 5$$

This leads to the following important result:

For all real numbers a, $\sqrt{a^2} = |a|$

EXAMPLE 3   Simplify: $\sqrt{75x^2}$.

Solution

$$\sqrt{75x^2} = \sqrt{25 \cdot 3}\sqrt{x^2}$$
$$= 5\sqrt{3}\,|x|$$

EXAMPLE 4   Simplify: $2\sqrt{8x^3} + 3x\sqrt{32x} - x\sqrt{18x}$.

Solution   For this problem, $x \geq 0$. Thus we need not make use of absolute-value notation.

Note that the expressions under the radicals would be negative for $x < 0$. Since the index is even, we must assume that $x \geq 0$ in order for these to have meaning.

$$2\sqrt{8x^3} = 2\sqrt{4 \cdot 2 \cdot x^2 \cdot x} = 4x\sqrt{2x}$$
$$3x\sqrt{32x} = 3x\sqrt{16 \cdot 2x} = 12x\sqrt{2x}$$
$$x\sqrt{18x} = x\sqrt{9 \cdot 2x} = 3x\sqrt{2x}$$

In each case the radicand and the index are the same, so that the distributive property can be used to simplify.

$$4x\sqrt{2x} + 12x\sqrt{2x} - 3x\sqrt{2x} = (4x + 12x - 3x)\sqrt{2x}$$
$$= 13x\sqrt{2x}$$

CAUTION: LEARN TO AVOID MISTAKES LIKE THESE

WRONG	RIGHT
$\sqrt{9 + 16} = \sqrt{9} + \sqrt{16}$	$\sqrt{9 + 16} = \sqrt{25}$
$(a + b)^{1/3} = a^{1/3} + b^{1/3}$	$(a + b)^{1/3} = \sqrt[3]{a + b}$

WRONG	RIGHT
$\sqrt[3]{8} \cdot \sqrt[2]{8} = \sqrt[6]{64}$	$\sqrt[3]{8} \cdot \sqrt[2]{8} = 2 \cdot 2\sqrt{2} = 4\sqrt{2}$
$2\sqrt{x+1} = \sqrt{2x+1}$	$2\sqrt{x+1} = \sqrt{4(x+1)} = \sqrt{4x+4}$
$2 - \dfrac{1}{\sqrt{2}} = \dfrac{2-1}{\sqrt{2}}$	$2 - \dfrac{1}{\sqrt{2}} = 2 - \dfrac{\sqrt{2}}{2} = \dfrac{4-\sqrt{2}}{2}$
$\sqrt{(x-1)^2} = x - 1$	$\sqrt{(x-1)^2} = |x-1|$

Simplify.

1 $\sqrt{2} + \sqrt{18}$

2 $\sqrt{48} - \sqrt{3}$

3 $\sqrt{25} + \sqrt{49}$

4 $\sqrt{64} - \sqrt{16}$

5 $\sqrt{12} - \sqrt{27}$

6 $\sqrt{32} + \sqrt{72}$

7 $\sqrt{6} \cdot \sqrt{12}$

8 $\sqrt[3]{4} \cdot \sqrt[3]{12}$

9 $2\sqrt{5} + 3\sqrt{125}$

10 $-5\sqrt{24} - 2\sqrt{54}$

11 $2\sqrt{200} - 5\sqrt{8}$

12 $3\sqrt{45} - 2\sqrt{20}$

13 $\sqrt[3]{128} + \sqrt[3]{16}$

14 $\sqrt[3]{24} + \sqrt[3]{81}$

15 $\sqrt{50} + \sqrt{32} - \sqrt{8}$

16 $\sqrt{12} - \sqrt{3} + \sqrt{108}$

17 $\dfrac{8}{\sqrt{2}} + 2\sqrt{50}$

18 $\dfrac{12}{\sqrt{3}} - \sqrt{12}$

19 $\sqrt[3]{56x} + \sqrt[3]{7x}$

20 $\sqrt[3]{54x} + \sqrt[3]{250x}$

21 $3\sqrt{8x^2} - \sqrt{50x^2}$

22 $5\sqrt{75x^2} - 2\sqrt{12x^2}$

23 $\sqrt[4]{32} + \sqrt[4]{162}$

24 $\sqrt[5]{32} + \sqrt[5]{64}$

25 $3\sqrt{10} + 4\sqrt{90} - 5\sqrt{40}$

26 $3\sqrt{24} - \sqrt{54} + 2\sqrt{150}$

27 $\dfrac{1}{\sqrt{2}} + 3\sqrt{72} - 2\sqrt{2}$

28 $\dfrac{2}{\sqrt{3}} + 10\sqrt{3} - 2\sqrt{12}$

29 $\sqrt{24} + \sqrt{54} - \sqrt{18}$

30 $\sqrt{36} + \sqrt{28} + \sqrt{63}$

31 $\sqrt{18x} + \sqrt{50x} - \sqrt{2x}$

32 $10\sqrt{3x} - 2\sqrt{75x} + 3\sqrt{243x}$

33 $3\sqrt{9x^2} + 2\sqrt{16x^2} - \sqrt{25x^2}$

34 $\sqrt{2x^2} + 5\sqrt{32x^2} - 2\sqrt{98x^2}$

35 $\sqrt{x^2y} + \sqrt{8x^2y} + \sqrt{200x^2y}$

36 $\sqrt{72xy} + 2\sqrt{2xy} + \sqrt{128xy}$

37 $\sqrt{20a^3} + a\sqrt{5a} + \sqrt{80a^3}$

38 $\sqrt{12b^3} + \sqrt{27b^3} + 2b\sqrt{3b}$

Rationalize the denominators and simplify.

39 $\dfrac{20}{\sqrt{5}}$

40 $\dfrac{24}{\sqrt{6}}$

41 $\dfrac{8x}{\sqrt{2}}$

42 $\dfrac{9y}{\sqrt{3}}$

43 $\dfrac{4}{\sqrt{2}} + \dfrac{6}{\sqrt{3}}$

44 $\dfrac{10}{\sqrt{5}} + \dfrac{8}{\sqrt{4}}$

45 $\dfrac{1}{\sqrt{18}}$

46 $\dfrac{1}{\sqrt{27}}$

47 $\dfrac{24}{\sqrt{3x^2}}$

48 $\dfrac{20x}{\sqrt{5x^3}}$

49 $\dfrac{8}{\sqrt[3]{2}}$

50 $\dfrac{12}{\sqrt[3]{-3}}$

*51 Use the result $\sqrt{a^2} = |a|$ and the rules for radicals to prove that $|xy| = |x| \cdot |y|$, where x and y are real numbers.

2.4

Fundamental operations with polynomials

The expression $5x^3 - 7x^2 + 4x - 12$ is called a **polynomial in the variable** x. Its *degree* is 3, because 3 is the largest power of the variable x. The *terms* of this polynomial are $5x^3$, $-7x^2$, $4x$ and -12. The *coefficients* are 5, -7, 4, and -12.

All the exponents of the variable of a polynomial must be nonnegative integers. Therefore, $x^3 + x^{1/2}$ and $x^{-2} + 3x + 1$ are *not* polynomials because of the fractional and negative exponents.

A nonzero constant, like 7, is classified as a polynomial of degree zero, since $7 = 7x^0$. The number zero is also referred to as a constant polynomial, but it is not assigned any degree.

A polynomial is in *standard form* if its terms are arranged so that the powers of the variable are in descending or ascending order. Here are some illustrations.

Polynomial	Degree	Standard form
$x^2 - 3x + 12$	2	Yes
$\frac{2}{3}x^{10} - 4x^2 + \sqrt{2}\,x^4$	10	No
$32 - y^5 + 2y^3$	5	No
$6 + 2x - x^2 + x^3$	3	Yes

Some of the preceding polynomials have "missing" terms. For example, $x^3 - 3x + 12$ has no x^2 term, but it is still a third-degree polynomial. The highest power of x determines the degree, and any or all lesser powers may be missing.

In general, an nth-degree polynomial in the variable x may be written in either one of these standard forms:

$$a_n x^n + a_{n-1} x^{n-1} + \cdots + a_2 x^2 + a_1 x + a_0$$

$$a_0 + a_1 x + a_2 x^2 + \cdots + a_{n-1} x^{n-1} + a_n x^n$$

You should become familiar with this notation, as you will encounter it frequently in future mathematics courses.

The coefficients $a_n, a_{n-1}, \ldots, a_0$ are real numbers. The *leading coefficient* is $a_n \neq 0$, and a_0 is called the *constant term*.

In a polynomial like $3x^2 - x + 4$ the variable x represents a real number. Therefore, when a specific real value is substituted for x, the result will be a real number. For instance, using $x = -3$ in this polynomial gives

$$3(-3)^2 - (-3) + 4 = 34$$

Note that polynomials represent real numbers regardless of the specific choice of the variable. Thus computations with polynomials are based on the fundamental properties for real numbers.

Adding or subtracting polynomials involves the combining of **like terms** (those having the same exponent on the variable). This can be accomplished by first rearranging and regrouping the terms (associative and commutative properties) and then combining by using the distributive property.

EXAMPLE 1

(a) Add: $(4x^3 - 10x^2 + 5x + 8) + (12x^2 - 9x - 1)$.

(b) Subtract: $(4t^3 - 10t^2 + 5t + 8) - (12t^2 - 9t - 1)$.

Solution

(a) $(4x^3 - 10x^2 + 5x + 8) + (12x^2 - 9x - 1)$
$$= 4x^3 + (12x^2 - 10x^2) + (5x - 9x) + (8 - 1)$$
$$= 4x^3 + (12 - 10)x^2 + (5 - 9)x + 7$$
$$= 4x^3 + 2x^2 - 4x + 7$$

(b) $(4t^3 - 10t^2 + 5t + 8) - (12t^2 - 9t - 1)$
$$= 4t^3 - 10t^2 + 5t + 8 - 12t^2 + 9t + 1$$
$$= 4t^3 - 10t^2 - 12t^2 + 5t + 9t + 8 + 1$$
$$= 4t^3 - 22t^2 + 14t + 9$$

In Example 1(b), think of $a - b$ as $a - 1 \cdot b$ and use the distributive property to simplify.

An alternative method for Example 1 is to list the polynomials in column form, putting like terms in the same columns.

Add: $4x^3 - 10x^2 + 5x + 8$ Subtract: $4t^3 - 10t^2 + 5t + 8$

$$12x^2 - 9x - 1 \qquad\qquad 12t^2 - 9t - 1$$

$$\overline{4x^3 + 2x^2 - 4x + 7} \qquad \overline{4t^3 - 22t^2 + 14t + 9}$$

The use of the distributive property is fundamental when multiplying polynomials. Perhaps the simplest situation calls for the product of a **monomial** (a polynomial having only one term) times a "lengthier" polynomial, as follows.

$$3x^2(4x^7 - 3x^4 - x^2 + 15) = 3x^2(4x^7) - 3x^2(3x^4) - 3x^2(x^2) + 3x^2(15)$$
$$= 12x^9 - 9x^6 - 3x^4 + 45x^2$$

In the first line we used an extended version of the distributive property, namely,

$$a(b - c - d + e) = ab - ac - ad + ae$$

Next, observe how the distributive property is used to multiply two **binomials** (polynomials having two terms).

$$(2x + 3)(4x + 5) = (2x + 3)4x + (2x + 3)5$$
$$= (2x)(4x) + (3)(4x) + (2x)(5) + (3)(5)$$
$$= 8x^2 + 12x + 10x + 15$$
$$= 8x^2 + 22x + 15$$

Here is a shortcut that can be used to multiply two binomials.

$$(2x + 3)(4x + 5): \qquad (2x + 3)(4x + 5) = 8x^2 + 22x + 15$$

$8x^2$ is the product of the *first* terms in the binomials.

$10x$ and $12x$ are the products of the *outer* and *inner* terms;
$$10x + 12x = 22x.$$

15 is the product of the *last* terms in the binomials.

EXAMPLE 2 Find the product: $(5x - 9)(6x + 2)$.

Solution

$$(5x - 9)(6x + 2) = 30x^2 + (10x - 54x) - 18$$
$$= 30x^2 - 44x - 18$$

In general, we may write the product $(a + b)(c + d)$ in this way:

Keep this diagram in mind as an aid to finding the product of two binomials mentally.

$$(a + b)(c + d) = ac + ad + bc + bd$$

The distributive property can be extended to multiply polynomials with three terms, **trinomials**, as in Example 3.

EXAMPLE 3 Multiply $3x^3 - 8x + 4$ by $2x^2 + 5x - 1$.

Solution

Note that the column method is a convenient way to organize your work. Be certain to keep like terms in the same column. Let $x = 2$ and check the solution.

$$3x^3 - 8x + 4$$
$$2x^2 + 5x - 1$$

(add) $\begin{cases} \qquad\qquad - 3x^3 \qquad\qquad + 8x - 4 & (-1 \text{ times } 3x^3 - 8x + 4) \\ \qquad 15x^4 \qquad - 40x^2 + 20x & (5x \text{ times } 3x^3 - 8x + 4) \\ 6x^5 \qquad\quad - 16x^3 + 8x^2 & (2x^2 \text{ times } 3x^3 - 8x + 4) \end{cases}$

$$6x^5 + 15x^4 - 19x^3 - 32x^2 + 28x - 4$$

TEST YOUR UNDERSTANDING

Combine.

1. $(x^2 + 2x - 6) + (-2x + 7)$
2. $(x^2 + 2x - 6) - (-2x + 7)$
3. $(5x^4 - 4x^3 + 3x^2 - 2x + 1) + (-5x^4 + 6x^3 + 10x)$
4. $(x^2 + x + 1) + (-3x - 4) + (6x - 5) - (x^3 + x^2)$

Find the products.

5. $(-3x)(x^3 + 2x^2 - 1)$ 6. $-4x(\frac{1}{8} - \frac{1}{2}x - x^2)$

7 $(2x + 3)(3x + 2)$

9 $(4x + 7)(4x - 7)$

11 $(x^3 + 7x^2 - 4)(x + 2)$

8 $(6x - 1)(2x + 5)$

10 $(2x - 3)(2x - 3)$

12 $(x^2 - 3x + 5)(2x^3 + x^2 - 3x)$

More than two polynomials may be involved in a product. For example, here is a product of three polynomials:

$$(x + 2)(x + 3)(x + 4) = [(x + 2)(x + 3)](x + 4)$$
$$= (x^2 + 5x + 6)(x + 4)$$
$$= x^3 + 9x^2 + 26x + 24$$

Sometimes more than one operation is involved, as demonstrated in the next example.

EXAMPLE 4 Simplify by performing the indicated operations:

$$(x^2 - 5x)(3x^2) + (x^3 - 1)(2x - 5)$$

Solution Multiply first and then combine like terms.

$$(x^2 - 5x)(3x^2) + (x^3 - 1)(2x - 5)$$
$$= (3x^4 - 15x^3) + (2x^4 - 5x^3 - 2x + 5)$$
$$= 5x^4 - 20x^3 - 2x + 5$$

Compare the areas of the two congruent squares in terms of the segments a and b.

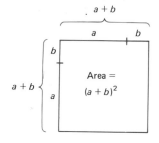

The product of $a + b$ times itself is given by

$$(a + b)(a + b) = a^2 + 2ab + b^2$$

Using exponents, we have

$$(a + b)(a + b) = (a + b)^2$$

Thus

$$(a + b)^2 = a^2 + 2ab + b^2$$

We say that $a^2 + 2ab + b^2$ is the *expansion*, or expanded form, of $(a + b)^2$.

Caution: $(a + b)^2 \neq a^2 + b^2$.

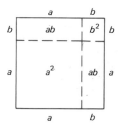

Explain how these figures provide a geometric interpretation for the expansion of $(a + b)^2$.

EXAMPLE 5 Expand: $(a + b)^3$.

Solution First write

$$(a + b)^3 = (a + b)(a + b)^2$$

Then, use the expansion of $(a + b)^2$:

$$(a + b)^3 = (a + b)(a^2 + 2ab + b^2)$$
$$= a^3 + 2a^2b + ab^2 + a^2b + 2ab^2 + b^3$$
$$= a^3 + 3a^2b + 3ab^2 + b^3$$

The result of Example 5 provides a formula for the cube of a binomial, that is, for all expansions of the form $(a + b)^3$.

Can you find the product 38×42 mentally? Think of this as $(40 - 2)(40 + 2)$ and use this fact to multiply.

The next example makes use of $(a - b)(a + b) = a^2 - b^2$ to rationalize denominators. Each of the factors $a - b$ and $a + b$ is called the *conjugate* of the other.

EXAMPLE 6   Rationalize the denominators:

(a) $\dfrac{5}{\sqrt{10} - 3}$ (b) $\dfrac{x}{\sqrt{x} + \sqrt{y}}$.

Solution

$\sqrt{10} + 3$ is the conjugate of $\sqrt{10} - 3$.

(a) $\dfrac{5}{\sqrt{10} - 3} = \dfrac{5}{\sqrt{10} - 3} \cdot \dfrac{\sqrt{10} + 3}{\sqrt{10} + 3}$

$= \dfrac{5(\sqrt{10} + 3)}{10 - 9}$

$= 5(\sqrt{10} + 3)$

$\sqrt{x} - \sqrt{y}$ is the conjugate of $\sqrt{x} + \sqrt{y}$.

(b) $\dfrac{x}{\sqrt{x} + \sqrt{y}} = \dfrac{x}{\sqrt{x} + \sqrt{y}} \cdot \dfrac{\sqrt{x} - \sqrt{y}}{\sqrt{x} - \sqrt{y}}$

$= \dfrac{x(\sqrt{x} - \sqrt{y})}{x - y}$

EXERCISES 2.4

Add.

1 $3x^2 + 5x - 2$
   $5x^2 - 7x + 9$

2 $5x^2 - 9x - 1$
   $2x^2 + 2x + 7$

3 $3x^3 - 7x^2 - 8x + 12$
   $x^3 - 2x^2 + 8x - 9$

4 $x^3 - 3x^2 + 2x - 5$
        $5x^2 - x + 9$

5        $4x^2 + 9x - 17$
   $2x^3 - 3x^2 + 2x - 11$

6 $2x^3 + x^2 - 7x + 1$
       $- 2x^2 - x + 8$

Subtract.

7 $3x^3 - 2x^2 - 8x + 9$
   $2x^3 + 5x^2 + 2x + 1$

8 $x^3 - 2x^2 + 6x + 1$
       $- x^2 - 6x - 1$

9 $4x^3 + x^2 - 2x - 13$
       $2x^2 + 3x + 9$

Simplify by performing the indicated operations.

10 $(3x + 5) + (3x - 2)$

11 $5x + (1 - 2x)$

12 $(7x + 5) - (2x + 3)$

13 $(y + 2) + (2y + 1) + (3y + 3)$

14 $h - (h + 2)$

15 $(x^3 + 3x^2 + 3x + 1) - (x^2 + 2x + 1)$

16 $7x - (3 - x) - 2x$

17 $5y - [y - (3y + 8)]$

18 $(x + 3) + (2x - 2) - (6x + 10)$

19 $(x^2 - 3x + 4) - (5x^2 + 2x + 1)$

20 $x(3x^2 - 2x + 5)$

21 $2x^2(2x + 1 - 10x^2)$

22 $-4t(t^4 - \frac{1}{4}t^3 + 4t^2 - \frac{1}{16}t + 1)$

23 $(x + 1)(x + 1)$

24 $(2x + 1)(2x - 1)$

25 $(4x - 2)(x + 7)$

26 $(5x + 3)(4x + 6)$

27 $(5x - 3)(4x - 6)$

28 $(5x + 3)(4x - 6)$

29 $(x + \frac{1}{2})(x - \frac{1}{4})$

30 $(12x - 8)(7x + 4)$

31 $(-2x + 3)(3x + 6)$

32 $(-2x - 3)(3x + 6)$

33 $(-2x - 3)(3x - 6)$

34 $(\frac{1}{2}x + 4)(\frac{1}{2}x - 4)$

35 $(\frac{2}{3}x + 6)(\frac{2}{3}x + 6)$

36 $(7 + 3x)(9 - 4x)$

37 $(7 - 3x)(4x - 9)$

38 $(15a + 30)(15a - 30)$

39 $(ax + b)(ax - b)$

40 $(ax - b)(ax - b)$

41 $(x - 0.1)(x + 0.1)$

42 $(x + \frac{3}{4})(x + \frac{3}{4})$

43 $(\frac{1}{5}x - \frac{1}{4})(\frac{1}{5}x - \frac{1}{4})$

44 $(x - \sqrt{3})(x + \sqrt{3})$

45 $(\sqrt{x} - 10)(\sqrt{x} + 10)$

46 $(\frac{1}{10}x - \frac{1}{100})(\frac{1}{10}x - \frac{1}{100})$

47 $(\sqrt{x} + \sqrt{2})(\sqrt{x} - \sqrt{2})$

48 $(x^2 - 3)(x^2 + 3)$

49 $(\sqrt{3} - \sqrt{2})(\sqrt{3} + \sqrt{2})$

50 $(5 - 3x)(x^4 + x^3 + x^2 + x + 1)$

51 $(x^2 + x + 9)(x^2 - 3x - 4)$

52 $(x^2 + 5x - 1)(36x^2 - 30x + 25)$

53 $(2x^2 - 3)(4x^2 + 6x + 9)$

54 $(x^{1/3} - 2)(x^{2/3} + 2x^{1/3} + 4)$

55 $(x - 2)(x^2 + 2x + 4)$

56 $(x - 2)(x^3 + 2x^2 + 4x + 8)$

57 $(x - 2)(x^4 + 2x^3 + 4x^2 + 8x + 16)$

58 $(x^n - 4)(x^n + 4)$

59 $(x^{2n} + 1)(x^{2n} - 2)$

60 $5(x + 5)(x - 5)$

61 $3x(1 - x)(1 - x)$

62 $(x + 3)(x + 1)(x - 4)$

63 $(2x + 1)(3x - 2)(3 - x)$

■ 64 $(2x^2 + 3)(9x^2) + (3x^3 - 2)(4x)$

■ 65 $(x^3 - 2x + 1)(2x) + (x^2 - 2)(3x^2 - 2)$

■ 66 $(2x^3 - x^2)(6x - 5) + (3x^2 - 5x)(6x^2 - 2x)$

■ 67 $(x^4 - 3x^2 + 5)(2x + 3) + (x^2 + 3x)(4x^3 - 6x)$

Expand each of the following and combine like terms.

68 $(a - b)^2$

69 $(x - 1)^3$

70 $(x + 1)^4$

71 $(a + b)^4$

72 $(a - b)^4$

73 $(2x + 3)^3$

74 $(\frac{1}{2}x - 4)^2$

75 $(\frac{1}{3}x + 3)^3$

76 $(\frac{1}{2}x - 1)^3$

Rationalize the denominator and simplify.

77 $\dfrac{12}{\sqrt{5} - \sqrt{3}}$

78 $\dfrac{20}{3 - \sqrt{2}}$

79 $\dfrac{14}{\sqrt{2} - 3}$

80 $\dfrac{\sqrt{x}}{\sqrt{x} + \sqrt{y}}$

*81 $\dfrac{\sqrt{x} + \sqrt{y}}{\sqrt{x} - \sqrt{y}}$

82 $\dfrac{1}{\sqrt{x} + 2}$

Rationalize the numerator in Exercises 83–85.

*83 $\dfrac{\sqrt{5} + 3}{\sqrt{5}}$

*84 $\dfrac{\sqrt{5} + \sqrt{3}}{\sqrt{2}}$

*85 $\dfrac{\sqrt{x} + \sqrt{y}}{\sqrt{x} - \sqrt{y}}$

■ *In Exercises 86 and 87, show how to convert the first fraction given into the form of the second one.*

86 $\dfrac{\sqrt{x} - 2}{x - 4}$; $\dfrac{1}{\sqrt{x} + 2}$

87 $\dfrac{\sqrt{4 + h} - 2}{h}$; $\dfrac{1}{\sqrt{4 + h} + 2}$

*88 Find a geometric interpretation for the formula $(a - b)^2 = a^2 - 2ab + b^2$.

Factoring polynomials

Can you solve this equation: $x^3 - 3x^2 - 4x + 12 = 0$? This may not be an easy question to answer at first. The solution is not difficult, however, once you rewrite the equation in this form:

$$x^3 - 3x^2 - 4x + 12 = (x + 2)(x - 2)(x - 3) = 0$$

Therefore, $x^3 - 3x^2 - 4x + 12 = 0$ when $x + 2 = 0$ or when $x - 2 = 0$ or when $x - 3 = 0$. Consequently, $-2, 2, 3$ are the solutions to the original equation.

Recall that the product of two or more factors is zero whenever any one of the factors is zero.

The key to the preceding solution was the conversion of the polynomial $x^3 - 3x^2 - 4x + 12$ into the *factored form* $(x + 2)(x - 2)(x - 3)$. As you have just seen, it is precisely this conversion that made it possible to solve the original equation. And since solving equations is of vital importance throughout mathematics, it will be worthwhile to become familiar with some methods of factoring. In the preceding section, we multiplied polynomials like this:

$$(x + 2)(x - 2)(x - 3) = [(x + 2)(x - 2)](x - 3)$$
$$= (x^2 - 4)(x - 3)$$
$$= x^3 - 3x^2 - 4x + 12$$

In a sense, factoring is "unmultiplying."

Now we want to *begin* with $x^3 - 3x^2 - 4x + 12$ and factor (unmultiply) it into the form $(x + 2)(x - 2)(x - 3)$.

One of the basic methods of factoring is the reverse of multiplying by a monomial. Consider this multiplication problem:

$$6x^2(4x^7 - 3x^4 - x^2 + 15) = 24x^9 - 18x^6 - 6x^4 + 90x^2$$

As you read this equation from left to right it involves multiplication by $6x^2$. Reading from right to left, it involves "factoring out" the *common monomial factor* $6x^2$. These are the details of this factoring process:

Note the use of the distributive property in this illustration.

$$24x^9 - 18x^6 - 6x^4 + 90x^2 = 6x^2(4x^7) - 6x^2(3x^4) - 6x^2(x^2) + 6x^2(15)$$
$$= 6x^2(4x^7 - 3x^4 - x^2 + 15)$$

Suppose that in the preceding illustration we were to use $3x$ as the common factor:

$$24x^9 - 18x^6 - 6x^4 + 90x^2 = 3x(8x^8 - 6x^5 - 2x^3 + 30x)$$

This is a correct factorization but it is not considered the *complete factored form* because $2x$ can still be factored out of the expression in the parentheses. In general, the instruction to factor calls for arriving at the complete factored form. We can extend factoring techniques to polynomials with more than one variable as in the example that follows.

EXAMPLE 1 Factor:

(a) $21x^4y - 14x^5y^2 - 63x^8y^3 + 91x^{11}y^4$

(b) $8x^2(x - 1) + 4x(x - 1) + 2(x - 1)$

Solution

(a) $21x^4y - 14x^5y^2 - 63x^8y^3 + 91x^{11}y^4$
$$= 7x^4y(3 - 2xy - 9x^4y^2 + 13x^7y^3)$$

(b) $8x^2(x - 1) + 4x(x - 1) + 2(x - 1) = 2(x - 1)(4x^2 + 2x + 1)$

Note: If you have trouble seeing this, then think of $x - 1$ as a single value and use $x - 1 = a$. Then

$$8x^2(x - 1) + 4x(x - 1) + 2(x - 1) = 8x^2a + 4xa + 2a$$
$$= 2a(4x^2 + 2x + 1)$$
$$= 2(x - 1)(4x^2 + 2x + 1)$$

We will now consider several basic procedures for factoring polynomials. You should check each of these by multiplication. These forms are very useful and you need to learn to recognize and apply each one.

THE DIFFERENCE OF TWO SQUARES

$$a^2 - b^2 = (a - b)(a + b)$$

Illustrations:

$$x^2 - 9 = x^2 - 3^2 = (x - 3)(x + 3)$$
$$49t^2 - 100 = (7t)^2 - 10^2 = (7t - 10)(7t + 10)$$
$$(x + 1)^2 - 4 = (x + 1)^2 - 2^2 = (x + 1 - 2)(x + 1 + 2)$$
$$= (x - 1)(x + 3)$$

In the second illustration, the second step may be omitted if you recognize that $a = 7t$ and $b = 10$.

Can $3x^2 - 75$ be factored by using the difference of two squares? It becomes possible if we first factor out the common factor 3.

$$3x^2 - 75 = 3(x^2 - 25) = 3(x - 5)(x + 5)$$

The trick is to look for a common factor first in each of the given terms. This step will not only save you work in some problems, but it may well be the difference between success and failure.

It is strongly recommended that whenever you attempt to factor, you *first look for common factors* in the given terms.

THE DIFFERENCE (SUM) OF TWO CUBES

$$a^3 - b^3 = (a - b)(a^2 + ab + b^2)$$
$$a^3 + b^3 = (a + b)(a^2 - ab + b^2)$$

Be sure to check each of these facts by multiplication.

Illustrations:

$$8x^3 - 27 = (2x)^3 - 3^3$$
$$= (2x - 3)(4x^2 + 6x + 9)$$
$$2x^3 + 128y^3 = 2(x^3 + 64y^3)$$
$$= 2[x^3 + (4y)^3]$$
$$= 2(x + 4y)(x^2 - 4xy + 16y^2)$$

TEST YOUR UNDERSTANDING

Factor out the common monomial.

1 $3x - 9$ 2 $-5x + 15$ 3 $5xy + 25y^2 + 10y^5$

Factor as the difference of squares.

4 $x^2 - 36$ 5 $4x^2 - 49$ 6 $(a + 2)^2 - 25b^2$

It is not possible to factor $x^2 - 5$ as the difference of two squares by using integral coefficients. There are times, however, when it is desirable to allow coefficients other than integers. Consider, for example, these factorizations:

$$x^2 - 5 = x^2 - (\sqrt{5})^2 = (x + \sqrt{5})(x - \sqrt{5})$$
$$x^3 - 5 = x^3 - (\sqrt[3]{5})^3 = (x - \sqrt[3]{5})[x^2 + \sqrt[3]{5}\,x + (\sqrt[3]{5})^2]$$

When other than polynomial factors are allowed, it becomes possible to factor $x - 8$ as the difference of two squares as well as the difference of two cubes.

$$x - 8 = (\sqrt{x})^2 - (\sqrt{8})^2 = (\sqrt{x} + \sqrt{8})(\sqrt{x} - \sqrt{8})$$
$$x - 8 = (\sqrt[3]{x})^3 - 2^3 = (\sqrt[3]{x} - 2)[(\sqrt[3]{x})^2 + 2\sqrt[3]{x} + 4]$$

Using fractional exponents, this last line becomes

$$x - 8 = (x^{1/3})^3 - 2^3 = (x^{1/3} - 2)(x^{2/3} + 2x^{1/3} + 4)$$

In general, we follow this rule when factoring:

Unless otherwise indicated, use the same type of numerical coefficients and exponents in the factors as appear in the given unfactored form.

TEST YOUR UNDERSTANDING

Factor the following as the difference of two squares. Irrational numbers as well as radical expressions may be used.

1 $x^2 - 2$ **2** $7 - x^2$ **3** $x - 9$

Factor the following as the difference (sum) of two cubes. Irrational numbers and radical expressions may be used.

4 $x^3 - 4$ **5** $1 - h$ **6** $x + 27$

Just as we learned how to factor the difference of two squares or cubes, we can also learn how to factor the difference of two fourth powers, two fifth powers, and so on. All these situations can be collected into the single general form that gives the factorization of the difference of two nth powers, where n is an integer greater than 1.

The factorization of $a^n - b^n$ is one of the most useful in mathematics; it will be needed in calculus. Study it carefully here so that in later work you will be able to recall it with minimal effort.

THE DIFFERENCE OF TWO nTH POWERS

$$a^n - b^n = (a - b)(a^{n-1} + a^{n-2}b + a^{n-3}b^2 + \cdots + ab^{n-2} + b^{n-1})$$

To help describe the second factor, we may rewrite it like this:

$$a^{n-1}b^0 + a^{n-2}b^1 + a^{n-3}b^2 + \cdots + a^1b^{n-2} + a^0b^{n-1}$$

You can see that the exponents for a begin with $n-1$ and decrease to 0, whereas for b they begin with 0 and increase to $n-1$. Note also that the sum of the exponents for a and b, for each term, is $n-1$.

EXAMPLE 2   Factor: $a^5 - b^5$.

Solution   Use the general form for $a^n - b^n$ with $n = 5$.

$$a^5 - b^5 = (a - b)(a^4 + a^3b + a^2b^2 + ab^3 + b^4)$$

EXAMPLE 3   Use the result of Example 2 to factor $3y^5 - 96$.

Solution

$$\begin{aligned}
3y^5 - 96 &= 3(y^5 - 32) \\
&= 3(y^5 - 2^5) \\
&= 3(y - 2)(y^4 + 2y^3 + 4y^2 + 8y + 16)
\end{aligned}$$

EXAMPLE 4   Factor $x^4 - 81$ as the difference of two fourth powers and also as the difference of two squares.

Solution

$$\begin{aligned}
x^4 - 81 &= x^4 - 3^4 = (x - 3)(x^3 + 3x^2 + 9x + 27) \\
x^4 - 81 &= (x^2)^2 - (9)^2 = (x^2 + 9)(x^2 - 9) \\
&= (x^2 + 9)(x + 3)(x - 3)
\end{aligned}$$

Note: The second answer in Example 4 is the complete factored form of $x^4 - 81$ since none of its factors can be factored further (allowing only polynomials with integral coefficients). Unless otherwise directed, always try to arrive at the complete factored form.

The two answers in Example 4 imply that

$$(x - 3)(x^3 + 3x^2 + 9x + 27) = (x^2 + 9)(x + 3)(x - 3)$$

Divide each side by $x - 3$ to obtain

$$x^3 + 3x^2 + 9x + 27 = (x^2 + 9)(x + 3)$$

How can this factorization of $x^3 + 3x^2 + 9x + 27$ be found directly? The answer is to *group* the terms first and then factor, as follows.

$$\begin{aligned}
x^3 + 3x^2 + 9x + 27 &= (x^3 + 3x^2) + (9x + 27) \\
&= x^2(x + 3) + 9(x + 3) \\
&= (x^2 + 9)(x + 3)
\end{aligned}$$

CAUTION: $x^2(x + 3) + 9(x + 3)$ is *not* a factored form of the given expression.

Here are alternative groupings that lead to the same answer.

$$\begin{aligned}
x^3 + 3x^2 + 9x + 27 &= (x^3 + 9x) + (3x^2 + 27) \\
&= x(x^2 + 9) + 3(x^2 + 9) \\
&= (x + 3)(x^2 + 9) \\
x^3 + 3x^2 + 9x + 27 &= (x^3 + 27) + (3x^2 + 9x)
\end{aligned}$$

$$= (x + 3)(x^2 - 3x + 9) + (x + 3)(3x)$$
$$= (x + 3)(x^2 - 3x + 9 + 3x)$$
$$= (x + 3)(x^2 + 9)$$

EXAMPLE 5 Factor $ax^2 - 15 - 5ax + 3x$ by grouping.

Solution

Not all groupings are productive. Thus in Example 5 the grouping $(ax^2 - 15) + (3x - 5ax)$ does not lead to a solution.

$$ax^2 - 15 - 5ax + 3x = (ax^2 - 5ax) + (3x - 15)$$
$$= ax(x - 5) + 3(x - 5)$$
$$= (ax + 3)(x - 5)$$

EXERCISES 2.5

Factor out the common monomial.

1 $5x - 5$

2 $3x^2 + 12x - 6$

3 $16x^4 + 8x^3 + 4x^2 + 2x$

4 $4a^2b - 6$

5 $4a^2b - 6ab$

6 $(a + b)x^2 + (a + b)y^2$

7 $2xy + 4x^2 + 8x^4$

8 $-12x^3y + 9x^2y^2 - 6xy^3$

9 $10x(a - b) + 5y(a - b)$

Factor as the difference of two squares.

10 $x^2 - 9$　　　　　**11** $81 - x^2$

12 $x^2 - 10,000$　　**13** $4x^2 - 9$

14 $25x^2 - 144y^2$　 **15** $a^2 - 121b^2$

Factor as the difference (sum) of two cubes.

16 $x^3 - 8$　　　　　**17** $x^3 + 64$

18 $8x^3 + 1$　　　　 **19** $125x^3 - 64$

20 $8 - 27a^3$　　　　**21** $8x^3 + 343y^3$

Factor as the difference of two squares, allowing irrational numbers as well as radical expressions. (All letters represent positive numbers.)

22 $a^2 - 15$　　　　　**23** $3 - 4x^2$

24 $x - 1$　　　　　　**25** $x - 36$

26 $2x - 9$　　　　　 **27** $8 - 3x$

Factor as the difference (sum) of two cubes, allowing irrational numbers as well as radical expressions.

28 $x^3 - 2$　　　　　**29** $7 + a^3$

30 $1 - h$　　　　　　**31** $27x + 1$

32 $27x - 64$　　　　 **33** $3x - 4$

Factor by grouping.

34 $a^2 - 2b + 2a - ab$　　**35** $x^2 - y - x + xy$

36 $x + 1 + y + xy$　　　 **37** $-y - x + 1 + xy$

38 $ax + by + ay + bx$　　 **39** $2 - y^2 + 2x - xy^2$

Factor completely.

40 $8a^2 - 2b^2$　　　　**41** $7x^3 + 7h^3$

42 $81x^3 - 3y^3$　　　 **43** $x^3y - xy^3$

44 $5 - 80x^4$　　　　　**45** $x^4 - y^4$

46 $81x^4 - 256y^4$　　 **47** $a^8 - b^8$

48 $40ab^3 - 5a^4$　　　**49** $a^5 - 32$

50 $3x^5 - 96y^5$　　　 **51** $1 - h^7$

52 $(2a + b)a^2 - (2a + b)b^2$

53 $3(a + 1)x^3 + 24(a + 1)$

54 $x^6 + x^2y^4 - x^4y^2 - y^6$

55 $a^3x - b^3y + b^3x - a^3y$

56 $7a^2 - 35b + 35a - 7ab$

57 $x^5 - 16xy^4 - 2x^4y + 32y^5$

■ *Simplify by factoring.*

58 $(1 + x)^2(-1) + (1 - x)(2)(1 + x)$

59 $(x + 2)^3(2) + (2x + 1)(3)(x + 2)^2$

60 $(x^2 + 2)^2(3) + (3x - 1)(2)(x^2 + 2)(2x)$

61 $(x^3 + 1)^3(2x) + (x^2 - 1)(3)(x^3 + 1)^2(3x^2)$

62 Find these products.

(a) $(a + b)(a^2 - ab + b^2)$

(b) $(a + b)(a^4 - a^3b + a^2b^2 - ab^3 + b^4)$

(c) $(a + b)(a^6 - a^5b + a^4b^2 - a^3b^3 + a^2b^4$
$\qquad\qquad\qquad - ab^5 + b^6)$

63 Use the results of Exercise 62 to factor the following:

(a) $x^5 + 32$ **(b)** $128x^8 + xy^7$

*64 Write the factored form of $a^n + b^n$, where n is an odd positive integer greater than 1.

Factoring trinomials

By multiplication we can establish the following products:

$$(a + b)^2 = (a + b)(a + b) = a^2 + 2ab + b^2$$
$$(a - b)^2 = (a - b)(a - b) = a^2 - 2ab + b^2$$

Each product is called a *perfect trinomial square*. In each case the first and last terms are squares of a and b, respectively, and the middle term is twice their product. Reversing the procedure gives us two more general factoring forms.

PERFECT TRINOMIAL SQUARES

$$a^2 + 2ab + b^2 = (a + b)^2$$
$$a^2 - 2ab + b^2 = (a - b)^2$$

Observe that in $a^2 \pm 2ab + b^2$ the middle term (ignoring signs) is twice the product of the square roots of the end terms. Hence the factored form is the square of the sum (or difference) of these square roots.

Illustrations:

$$x^2 + 10x + 25 = x^2 + 2(x \cdot 5) + 5^2$$
$$= (x + 5)^2$$
$$25t^2 - 30t + 9 = (5t)^2 - 2(5t \cdot 3) + 3^2$$
$$= (5t - 3)^2$$

EXAMPLE 1   Factor: $1 + 18b + 81b^2$.

Solution

$$1 + 18b + 81b^2 = (1 + 9b)^2$$

EXAMPLE 2   Factor: $9x^3 - 42x^2 + 49x$.

Solution

$$9x^3 - 42x^2 + 49x = x(9x^2 - 42x + 49)$$
$$= x[(3x)^2 - 2(3x)(7) + 7^2]$$
$$= x(3x - 7)^2$$

Always remember, as in Example 2, to search first for a common monomial factor.

Another factoring technique that we will consider deals with trinomials that are not necessarily perfect squares. Let us factor $x^2 + 7x + 12$.

From our experience with multiplying binomials we can anticipate that the factors will be of this form:

$$(x + \underline{?})(x + \underline{?})$$

We need to fill in the blanks with two integers whose product is 12. Furthermore, the middle term of the product must be $+7x$. The possible choices for the two integers are

$$12 \text{ and } 1 \qquad 6 \text{ and } 2 \qquad 4 \text{ and } 3$$

To find the correct pair is now a matter of trial and error. These are the possible factorizations:

$$(x + 12)(x + 1)$$
$$(x + 6)(x + 2)$$
$$(x + 4)(x + 3)$$

With a little luck, and much more experience, you can often avoid exhausting all the possibilities before finding the correct factors. You will then find that such work can often be shortened significantly.

Only the last form gives the correct middle term of $7x$. Therefore, we conclude that $x^2 + 7x + 12 = (x + 4)(x + 3)$.

EXAMPLE 3   Factor: $x^2 - 10x + 24$.

Solution   The final term, $+24$, must be the product of two positive numbers or two negative numbers. (Why?) Since the middle term, $-10x$, has a minus sign, the factorization must be of this form:

$$(x - \underline{?})(x - \underline{?})$$

Now try all the pairs of integers whose product is 24: 24 and 1, 12 and 2, 8 and 3, 6 and 4. Only the last of these gives $-10x$ as the middle term. Thus

$$x^2 - 10x + 24 = (x - 6)(x - 4)$$

Let us now consider a more complicated factoring problem. If we wish to factor the trinomial $15x^2 + 43x + 8$, we need to consider possible factors both of 15 and of 8. Because of the "$+$" signs in the trinomial, the factorization will be of this form:

$$(\underline{?}\,x + \underline{?})(\underline{?}\,x + \underline{?})$$

Here are the different possibilities for factoring 15 and 8:

$$15 = 15 \cdot 1 \qquad 15 = 5 \cdot 3$$
$$8 = 8 \cdot 1 \qquad\;\; 8 = 4 \cdot 2$$

Using $15 \cdot 1$, write the form

$$(15x + \underline{?})(x + \underline{?})$$

Try 8 and 1 in the blanks, *both ways*, namely:

$$(15x + 8)(x + 1)$$
$$(15x + 1)(x + 8)$$

Neither gives a middle term of $43x$; so now try 4 and 2 in the blanks both ways. Again you see that neither case works. Next consider the form

$$(5x + \underline{?})(3x + \underline{?})$$

Once again try 4 with 2 both ways, and 8 with 1 both ways. Here is the correct answer:

$$15x^2 + 43x + 8 = (5x + 1)(3x + 8)$$

Factoring $15x^2 - 43x + 8$ is very similar to factoring $15x^2 + 43x + 8$. The only difference is that the binomial factors have minus signs instead of plus signs; that is,

$$15x^2 - 43x + 8 = (5x - 1)(3x - 8)$$

EXAMPLE 4 Factor: $12x^2 - 9x + 2$.

Example 4 shows us that not every trinomial can be factored.

Solution Consider the forms

$$(12x - \underline{?})(x - \underline{?})$$
$$(6x - \underline{?})(2x - \underline{?})$$
$$(4x - \underline{?})(3x - \underline{?})$$

In each form try 2 with 1 both ways. None of these produces a middle term of $-9x$; hence we say that $12x^2 - 9x + 2$ is *not factorable* with integral coefficients.

TEST YOUR UNDERSTANDING

Factor the following trinomial squares.

1 $a^2 + 6a + 9$ **2** $x^2 - 10x + 25$ **3** $4x^2 + 12xy + 9y^2$

Factor each trinomial if possible.

4 $x^2 + 8x + 15$ **5** $a^2 - 12a + 20$ **6** $x^2 + 3x + 4$
7 $10x^2 - 39x + 14$ **8** $6x^2 - 11x - 10$ **9** $6x^2 + 6x - 5$

In some problems you may find it easier to leave out the signs in the two binomial forms as you try various cases. Thus, to factor $6x^2 - 7x - 20$ consider the forms

$$(6x \ \underline{?})(x \ \underline{?}) \qquad (3x \ \underline{?})(2x \ \underline{?})$$

Then as you try a pair, like 5 with 4, keep in mind that the signs must be opposite. As soon as you see that the difference of the two partial products is $\pm 7x$, then insert the signs to produce the desired term $-7x$. In this problem the answer is $(3x + 4)(2x - 5)$.

EXAMPLE 5 Factor: $15x^2 + 7x - 8$.

Solution Try these forms:

$$(5x \ \underline{?})(3x \ \underline{?})$$
$$(15x \ \underline{?})(x \ \underline{?})$$

In each form try 4 with 2 and 8 with 1 both ways. The factored form is $(15x - 8)(x + 1)$.

All the trinomials we have considered were of degree 2. The same methods can be modified to factor certain trinomials of higher degree, as in Example 6.

EXAMPLE 6   Factor each trinomial:
(a) $x^4 + x^2 - 12$ **(b)** $a^6 - 3a^3b - 18b^2$

Solution

(a) Note that $x^4 = (x^2)^2$ and let $u = x^2$. Then

$$x^4 + x^2 - 12 = u^2 + u - 12$$
$$= (u + 4)(u - 3)$$
$$= (x^2 + 4)(x^2 - 3)$$

(b) $a^6 - 3a^3b - 18b^2 = (a^3 - 6b)(a^3 + 3b)$

The substitution step in Example 6(a) is a very useful one to learn for future use.

CAUTION: LEARN TO AVOID MISTAKES LIKE THESE	
WRONG	RIGHT
$(x + 2)3 + (x + 2)y = (x + 2)3y$	$(x+2)3+(x+2)y=(x+2)(3+y)$
$3x + 1 = 3(x + 1)$	$3x + 1$ is not factorable by using integers.
$x^3 - y^3 = (x - y)(x^2 + y^2)$	$x^3 - y^3 = (x - y)(x^2 + xy + y^2)$
$x^3 + 8$ is not factorable.	$x^3 + 8 = (x + 2)(x^2 - 2x + 4)$
$x^2 + y^2 = (x + y)(x + y)$	$x^2 + y^2$ is not factorable by using real numbers.
$4x^2 - 6xy + 9y^2 = (2x - 3y)^2$	$4x^2 - 6xy + 9y^2$ is not a perfect trinomial square and cannot be factored using real numbers.

EXERCISES 2.6

Factor each of the following perfect trinomial squares.

1 $x^2 + 4x + 4$

2 $x^2 - 8x + 16$

3 $a^2 - 14a + 49$

4 $r^2 - 2r + 1$

5 $1 + 2b + b^2$

6 $100 - 20x + x^2$

7 $4a^2 + 8a + 4$

8 $4a^2 - 8a + 4$

9 $9x^2 - 18xy + 9y^2$

10 $64a^2 + 64a + 16$

11 $9x^2 + 12xy + 4y^2$ **12** $4x^2 - 12xy + 9y^2$

Factor each trinomial.

13 $x^2 + 5x + 6$ **14** $x^2 - 7x + 10$

15 $x^2 + 20x + 51$ **16** $12a^2 - 13a + 1$

17 $20a^2 - 9a + 1$ **18** $4 - 5b + b^2$

19 $x^2 + 20x + 36$ **20** $a^2 - 24a + 63$

21 $9x^2 + 6x + 1$ **22** $x^2 - 20x + 64$

23 $25a^2 - 10a + 1$ **24** $8x^2 + 14x + 3$

25 $3x^2 + 20x + 12$ **26** $5x^2 + 31x + 6$

27 $14x^2 + 37x + 5$ **28** $9x^2 - 18x + 5$

29 $8x^2 - 9x + 1$ **30** $30a^2 - 17a + 1$

31 $4a^2 + 20a + 25$ **32** $a^2 - 9a + 18$

33 $b^2 + 18b + 45$ **34** $6x^2 + 12x + 6$

35 $8x^2 - 16x + 6$ **36** $12x^2 + 92x + 15$

37 $12a^2 - 25a + 12$ **38** $18t^2 - 67t + 14$

39 $15x^2 - 7x - 2$ **40** $15x^2 + 7x - 2$

41 $6a^2 + 5a - 21$ **42** $6a^2 - 5a - 21$

43 $4x^2 + 4x - 3$ **44** $15x^2 + 19x - 56$

45 $24a^2 + 25ab + 6b^2$

Factor each trinomial when possible. When appropriate, first factor out the common monomial.

46 $3a^2 + 6a + 3$ **47** $5x^2 + 25x + 20$

48 $18x^2 - 24x + 8$ **49** $4ax^2 + 4ax + a$

50 $x^2 + x + 1$ **51** $a^2 - 2a + 2$

52 $49r^2s - 42rs + 9s$ **53** $6x^2 + 2x - 20$

54 $50a^2 - 440a - 90$ **55** $6a^2 + 4a - 9$

56 $36x^2 - 96x + 64$ **57** $2x^2 - 2x - 112$

58 $15 + 5y - 10y^2$ **59** $2b^2 + 12b + 16$

60 $4a^2x^2 - 4abx^2 + b^2x^2$

61 $a^3b - 2a^2b^2 + ab^3$

62 $12x^2y + 22xy^2 - 60y^3$

63 $16x^2 - 24x + 8$

64 $16x^2 - 24x - 8$

65 $25a^2 + 50ab + 25b^2$

66 $x^4 - 2x^2 + 1$

67 $a^6 - 2a^3 + 1$

68 $2x^4 + 8x^2 - 42$

69 $6x^5y - 3x^3y^2 - 30xy^3$

70 $3x^4 + 6x^2 + 3$

71 $a^6 - 2a^3b^3 + b^6$

■ **72** Factor completely: $3(x^2 - 2x + 1)^2(2x - 2)$

Fundamental operations with rational expressions

A **rational expression** is a ratio of polynomials. Rational expressions are the "algebraic extensions" of rational numbers, so that the fundamental rules for operating with rational numbers extend to rational expressions.

The important rules for operating with rational expressions, also referred to as *algebraic fractions*, will now be considered. In each case we shall give an example of the rule under discussion in terms of work with arithmetic fractions so that you can compare the procedures being used. Also, in each case, we exclude values of the variable for which the denominator is equal to zero.

RULE 1. $-\dfrac{a}{b} = \dfrac{-a}{b} = \dfrac{a}{-b}$ $\left[-\dfrac{2}{3} = \dfrac{-2}{3} = \dfrac{2}{-3}\right]$

Negative of a fraction.

The negative of a fraction is the same as the fraction obtained by taking the negative of the numerator or of the denominator.

Illustration:

$$-\frac{2 - x}{x^2 - 5} = \frac{-(2 - x)}{x^2 - 5} = \frac{2 - x}{-(x^2 - 5)}$$

Note that since $-(2 - x) = x - 2$, each of these fractions is also equal to $\dfrac{x - 2}{x^2 - 5}$.

Reducing fractions.   RULE 2. $\dfrac{ac}{bc} = \dfrac{a}{b}$ $\left[\dfrac{2 \cdot 3}{5 \cdot 3} = \dfrac{2}{5}\right]$

Reading this formula from left to right, it shows how to reduce a fraction to *lowest terms* so that the numerator and denominator of the resulting fraction have no common polynomial factors.

Illustration:

Any nonzero number divided by itself is equal to 1.

$$\frac{x^2 + 5x - 6}{x^2 + 6x} = \frac{(x-1)(x + 6)}{x(x + 6)} \qquad\qquad \frac{x+6}{x+6} = 1$$

$$= \frac{x-1}{x} \qquad \text{(Rule 2)}$$

Multiplication of fractions.   RULE 3. $\dfrac{a}{b} \cdot \dfrac{c}{d} = \dfrac{ac}{bd}$ $\left[\dfrac{2}{3} \cdot \dfrac{4}{5} = \dfrac{2 \cdot 4}{3 \cdot 5} = \dfrac{8}{15}\right]$

Illustration:

Whenever we are working with rational expressions it is taken for granted that final answers have been reduced to lowest terms.

$$\frac{x-1}{x+1} \cdot \frac{x^2 - x - 2}{5x} = \frac{(x-1)(x^2 - x - 2)}{(x+1)5x} \qquad \text{(Rule 3)}$$

$$= \frac{(x-1)(x + 1)(x - 2)}{(x + 1)5x} \qquad \text{(factoring)}$$

$$= \frac{(x-1)(x - 2)}{5x} \qquad \text{(Rule 2)}$$

This work can be shortened.

$$\frac{x-1}{x+1} \cdot \frac{x^2 - x - 2}{5x} = \frac{x-1}{x+1} \cdot \frac{(x + 1)(x - 2)}{5x} = \frac{(x-1)(x - 2)}{5x}$$

Note that $\dfrac{x^2 - 3x + 2}{5x}$ is an alternative form of the answer.

Division of fractions.   RULE 4. $\dfrac{a}{b} \div \dfrac{c}{d} = \dfrac{a}{b} \cdot \dfrac{d}{c} = \dfrac{ad}{bc}$ $\left[\dfrac{3}{5} \div \dfrac{2}{3} = \dfrac{3}{5} \cdot \dfrac{3}{2} = \dfrac{3 \cdot 3}{5 \cdot 2} = \dfrac{9}{10}\right]$

Illustration:

There are a number of alternative forms for Rule 4. For example:

$$\dfrac{\dfrac{a}{b}}{\dfrac{c}{d}} = \dfrac{a}{b} \div \dfrac{c}{d} = \dfrac{ad}{bc}$$

$$\dfrac{\dfrac{a}{b}}{c} = \dfrac{a}{b} \div \dfrac{c}{1} = \dfrac{a}{bc}$$

$$\dfrac{a}{\dfrac{b}{c}} = \dfrac{a}{1} \div \dfrac{b}{c} = \dfrac{ac}{b}$$

$$\frac{(x+1)^2}{x^2 - 6x + 9} \div \frac{3x + 3}{x - 3} = \frac{(x+1)^2}{x^2 - 6x + 9} \cdot \frac{x - 3}{3x + 3} \qquad \text{(Rule 4)}$$

$$= \frac{(x+1)^2}{(x - 3)^2} \cdot \frac{x - 3}{3(x + 1)} \qquad \text{(factoring)}$$

$$= \frac{(x+1)^2(x - 3)}{(x - 3)^2 3(x + 1)} \qquad \text{(Rule 3)}$$

$$= \frac{(x+1)(x + 1)(x - 3)}{3(x - 3)(x + 1)(x - 3)} \qquad \text{(rewriting)}$$

$$= \frac{x + 1}{3(x - 3)} \qquad \text{(Rule 2)}$$

The preceding example can be shortened as follows:

$$\frac{(x+1)^2}{x^2 - 6x + 9} \div \frac{3x + 3}{x - 3} = \frac{(x+1)^2}{(x - 3)^2} \cdot \frac{x - 3}{3(x + 1)} = \frac{x + 1}{3(x - 3)}$$

Simplify each expression by reducing to lowest terms.

1 $\dfrac{x^2 + 2x}{x}$

2 $\dfrac{x^2}{x^2 + 2x}$

3 $\dfrac{x^2 - 9}{x^2 - 5x + 6}$

4 $\dfrac{x^2 + 6x + 5}{x^2 - x - 2}$

5 $\dfrac{x^2 - 4}{x^4 - 16}$

6 $\dfrac{3x^2 + x - 10}{5x - 3x^2}$

Perform the indicated operation and simplify.

7 $\dfrac{2x - 4}{2} \cdot \dfrac{x + 2}{x^2 - 4}$

8 $\dfrac{x - 2}{3(x + 1)} \div \dfrac{x^2 + 2x}{x + 2}$

9 $\dfrac{a}{b} \div \dfrac{a^2 - ab}{ab + b^2}$

10 $\dfrac{x + y}{x - y} \cdot \dfrac{x^2 - 2xy + y^2}{x^2 - y^2}$

RULE 5. $\quad \dfrac{a}{d} + \dfrac{c}{d} = \dfrac{a + c}{d} \qquad \left[\dfrac{3}{7} + \dfrac{2}{7} = \dfrac{3 + 2}{7} = \dfrac{5}{7}\right]$

Addition and subtraction of fractions—same denominators.

RULE 6. $\quad \dfrac{a}{d} - \dfrac{c}{d} = \dfrac{a - c}{d} \qquad \left[\dfrac{7}{9} - \dfrac{2}{9} = \dfrac{7 - 2}{9} = \dfrac{5}{9}\right]$

Illustration:

$$\dfrac{6x^2}{2x^2 - x - 10} + \dfrac{-15x}{2x^2 - x - 10} = \dfrac{6x^2 + (-15x)}{2x^2 - x - 10} \qquad \text{(Rule 5)}$$

$$= \dfrac{6x^2 - 15x}{2x^2 - x - 10}$$

$$= \dfrac{3x(2x - 5)}{(x + 2)(2x - 5)} \qquad \text{(factoring)}$$

$$= \dfrac{3x}{x + 2} \qquad \text{(Rule 2)}$$

RULE 7. $\quad \dfrac{a}{b} + \dfrac{c}{d} = \dfrac{ad + bc}{bd} \qquad \left[\dfrac{2}{3} + \dfrac{3}{4} = \dfrac{2 \cdot 4 + 3 \cdot 3}{3 \cdot 4} = \dfrac{8 + 9}{12} = \dfrac{17}{12}\right]$

Addition and subtraction of fractions—different denominators.

RULE 8. $\quad \dfrac{a}{b} - \dfrac{c}{d} = \dfrac{ad - bc}{bd} \qquad \left[\dfrac{4}{5} - \dfrac{2}{3} = \dfrac{4 \cdot 3 - 5 \cdot 2}{5 \cdot 3} = \dfrac{12 - 10}{15} = \dfrac{2}{15}\right]$

Illustration:

$$\dfrac{3}{x^2 + x} + \dfrac{2}{x^2 - 1} = \dfrac{3(x^2 - 1) + 2(x^2 + x)}{(x^2 + x)(x^2 - 1)} \qquad \text{(Rule 7)}$$

$$= \dfrac{5x^2 + 2x - 3}{(x^2 + x)(x^2 - 1)} \qquad \text{(combining terms)}$$

$$= \dfrac{(5x - 3)(x + 1)}{x(x + 1)(x^2 - 1)} \qquad \text{(factoring)}$$

$$= \dfrac{5x - 3}{x(x^2 - 1)} \qquad \text{(Rule 2)}$$

Here is an alternative method for the preceding example. It makes use of the **least common denominator (LCD)** of the two fractions.

$$\frac{3}{x^2 + x} + \frac{2}{x^2 - 1} = \frac{3}{x(x + 1)} + \frac{2}{(x + 1)(x - 1)}$$

The LCD of the two fractions is $x(x + 1)(x - 1)$. We express each fraction using this common denominator and then add the numerators.

$$= \frac{3(x - 1)}{x(x + 1)(x - 1)} + \frac{2x}{(x + 1)(x - 1)x} \qquad \text{(Rule 2)}$$

$$= \frac{3(x - 1) + 2x}{x(x + 1)(x - 1)} \qquad \text{(Rule 5)}$$

$$= \frac{5x - 3}{x(x^2 - 1)}$$

EXAMPLE 1 Find the LCD of the fractions whose denominators are the following:

(a) $x^2 + x$, $x^2 - 1$ (b) $x^4 - x$, $x^2 - 2x + 1$, $x^4 + 2x^3$

To find the LCD, take *each* factor that appears in the factored forms of the denominators the *maximum* number of times it appears in any *one* of the factored forms.

Solution

(a) $x^2 + x = x(x + 1)$
$x^2 - 1 = (x + 1)(x - 1)$
$\text{LCD} = x(x + 1)(x - 1)$

(b) $x^4 - x = x(x^3 - 1) = x(x - 1)(x^2 + x + 1)$
$x^2 - 2x + 1 = (x - 1)^2$
$x^4 + 2x^3 = x^3(x + 2)$
$\text{LCD} = x^3(x - 1)^2(x + 2)(x^2 + x + 1)$

EXAMPLE 2 Combine and simplify: $\dfrac{3}{2} - \dfrac{4}{3x(x + 1)} - \dfrac{x - 5}{3x^2}$.

Solution The least common denominator of the fractions is $6x^2(x + 1)$.

$$\frac{3}{2} - \frac{4}{3x(x + 1)} - \frac{x - 5}{3x^2} = \frac{3 \cdot 3x^2(x + 1)}{2 \cdot 3x^2(x + 1)} - \frac{4 \cdot 2x}{3x(x + 1) \cdot 2x} - \frac{(x - 5) \cdot 2(x + 1)}{3x^2 \cdot 2(x + 1)}$$

$$= \frac{(9x^3 + 9x^2) - 8x - (2x^2 - 8x - 10)}{6x^2(x + 1)}$$

$$= \frac{9x^3 + 7x^2 + 10}{6x^2(x + 1)}$$

TEST YOUR UNDERSTANDING

Combine and simplify.

1. $\dfrac{x}{5} + \dfrac{2x}{3}$

2. $\dfrac{4x}{3} - \dfrac{x}{2}$

3. $\dfrac{2}{3x^2} - \dfrac{1}{2x}$

4. $\dfrac{3}{2x} + \dfrac{5}{3x} + \dfrac{1}{x}$

5. $\dfrac{7}{x - 2} + \dfrac{3}{x + 2}$

6. $\dfrac{9}{x - 3} + \dfrac{7}{x^2 - 9}$

7. $\dfrac{5}{(x - 1)(x + 2)} - \dfrac{8}{x^2 - 4}$

8. $\dfrac{5x}{(2x + 5)^2} + \dfrac{3x - 2}{4x^2 - 25}$

The fundamental properties of fractions can be used to simplify rational expressions whose numerators and denominators may themselves also contain fractions.

EXAMPLE 3 Simplify: $\dfrac{\dfrac{1}{5+h} - \dfrac{1}{5}}{h}$.

Solution Combine the fractions in the numerator and then divide.

$$\frac{\dfrac{1}{5+h} - \dfrac{1}{5}}{h} = \frac{\dfrac{5 - (5+h)}{5(5+h)}}{h} = \frac{\dfrac{-h}{5(5+h)}}{h}$$

$$= \frac{-h}{5(5+h)} \cdot \frac{1}{h}$$

$$= \frac{-h}{5h(5+h)} = -\frac{1}{5(5+h)}$$

The expression in Example 3 is a type that you will encounter in calculus. Be certain that you understand each step in the solution.

EXAMPLE 4 Simplify: $\dfrac{x^{-2} - y^{-2}}{\dfrac{1}{x} - \dfrac{1}{y}}$.

Solution

$$\frac{x^{-2} - y^{-2}}{\dfrac{1}{x} - \dfrac{1}{y}} = \frac{\dfrac{1}{x^2} - \dfrac{1}{y^2}}{\dfrac{1}{x} - \dfrac{1}{y}}$$

$$= \frac{\left(\dfrac{1}{x^2} - \dfrac{1}{y^2}\right)(x^2 y^2)}{\left(\dfrac{1}{x} - \dfrac{1}{y}\right)(x^2 y^2)} \qquad \text{(Rule 2)}$$

$$= \frac{y^2 - x^2}{xy^2 - x^2 y}$$

$$= \frac{(y - x)(y + x)}{xy(y - x)}$$

$$= \frac{y + x}{xy}$$

Note that we multiplied both the numerator and denominator by $x^2 y^2$ to simplify. Can you simplify this fraction in an alternative way without this step?

CAUTION: LEARN TO AVOID MISTAKES LIKE THESE	
WRONG	RIGHT
$\dfrac{2}{3} + \dfrac{x}{5} = \dfrac{2 + x}{3 + 5}$	$\dfrac{2}{3} + \dfrac{x}{5} = \dfrac{2 \cdot 5 + 3 \cdot x}{3 \cdot 5} = \dfrac{10 + 3x}{15}$

Working with fractions often creates difficulties for many students. Study this list; it may help you avoid some common pitfalls.

WRONG	RIGHT
$\dfrac{1}{a} + \dfrac{1}{b} = \dfrac{1}{a+b}$	$\dfrac{1}{a} + \dfrac{1}{b} = \dfrac{b+a}{ab}$
$\dfrac{2x+5}{4} = \dfrac{x+5}{2}$	$\dfrac{2x+5}{4} = \dfrac{2x}{4} + \dfrac{5}{4} = \dfrac{x}{2} + \dfrac{5}{4}$
$2 + \dfrac{x}{y} = \dfrac{2+x}{y}$	$2 + \dfrac{x}{y} = \dfrac{2y+x}{y}$
$3\left(\dfrac{x+1}{x-1}\right) = \dfrac{3(x+1)}{3(x+1)}$	$3\left(\dfrac{x+1}{x-1}\right) = \dfrac{3(x+1)}{x-1}$
$a \div \dfrac{b}{c} = \dfrac{1}{a} \cdot \dfrac{b}{c}$	$a \div \dfrac{b}{c} = a \cdot \dfrac{c}{b} = \dfrac{ac}{b}$
$\dfrac{1}{a^{-1} + b^{-1}} = a + b$	$\dfrac{1}{a^{-1} + b^{-1}} = \dfrac{1}{\dfrac{1}{a} + \dfrac{1}{b}} = \dfrac{ab}{b+a}$

EXERCISES 2.7

Classify each statement as true or false. If it is false, correct the right side to get a correct equality.

1 $\dfrac{5}{7} - \dfrac{2}{3} = \dfrac{3}{4}$

2 $\dfrac{2x+y}{y-2x} = -2\left(\dfrac{x+y}{x-y}\right)$

3 $\dfrac{3ax - 5b}{6} = \dfrac{ax - 5b}{2}$

4 $\dfrac{x + x^{-1}}{xy} = \dfrac{x+1}{x^2 y}$

5 $x^{-1} + y^{-1} = \dfrac{y+x}{xy}$

6 $\dfrac{2}{\frac{3}{4}} = \dfrac{8}{3}$

Simplify, if possible.

7 $\dfrac{8xy}{12yz}$

8 $\dfrac{24abc^2}{36bc^2 d}$

9 $\dfrac{x^2 - 5x}{5 - x}$

10 $\dfrac{n-1}{n^2 - 1}$

11 $\dfrac{n+1}{n^2 + 1}$

12 $\dfrac{(x+1)^2}{x^2 - 1}$

13 $\dfrac{3x^2 + 3x - 6}{2x^2 + 6x + 4}$

14 $\dfrac{x^3 - x}{x^3 - 2x^2 + x}$

15 $\dfrac{4x^2 + 12x + 9}{4x^2 - 9}$

16 $\dfrac{x^2 + 2x + xy + 2y}{x^2 + 4x + 4}$

17 $\dfrac{a^2 - 16b^2}{a^3 + 64b^3}$

18 $\dfrac{a^2 - b^2}{a^2 - 6b - ab + 6a}$

Perform the indicated operations and simplify.

19 $\dfrac{2x^2}{y} \cdot \dfrac{y^2}{x^3}$

20 $\dfrac{3x^2}{2y^2} \div \dfrac{3x^3}{y}$

21 $\dfrac{2a}{3} \cdot \dfrac{3}{a^2} \cdot \dfrac{1}{a}$

22 $\left(\dfrac{a^2}{b^2} \cdot \dfrac{b}{c^2}\right) \div a$

23 $\dfrac{3x}{2y} - \dfrac{x}{2y}$

24 $\dfrac{a + 2b}{a} + \dfrac{3a + b}{a}$

25 $\dfrac{a - 2b}{2} - \dfrac{3a + b}{3}$

26 $\dfrac{7}{5x} - \dfrac{2}{x} + \dfrac{1}{2x}$

27 $\dfrac{x-1}{3} \cdot \dfrac{x^2 + 1}{x^2 - 1}$

28 $\dfrac{x^2 - x - 6}{x^2 - 3x} \cdot \dfrac{x^3 + x^2}{x + 2}$

29 $\dfrac{x-1}{x+2} \div \dfrac{x^2 - x}{x^2 + 2x}$

30 $\dfrac{x^2 + 3x}{x^2 + 4x + 3} \div \dfrac{x^2 - 2x}{x + 1}$

31 $\dfrac{2}{x} - y$

32 $\dfrac{x^2}{x-1} - \dfrac{1}{x-1}$

33 $\dfrac{3y}{y+1} + \dfrac{2y}{y-1}$

34 $\dfrac{2a}{a^2-1} - \dfrac{a}{a+1}$

35 $\dfrac{2x^2}{x^2+x} + \dfrac{x}{x+1}$

36 $\dfrac{3x+3}{2x^2-x-1} + \dfrac{1}{2x+1}$

37 $\dfrac{5}{x^2-4} - \dfrac{3-x}{4-x^2}$

38 $\dfrac{1}{a^2-4} + \dfrac{3}{a-2} - \dfrac{2}{a+2}$

39 $\dfrac{2x}{x^2-9} + \dfrac{x}{x^2+6x+9} - \dfrac{3}{x+3}$

40 $\dfrac{a^2+2ab+b^2}{a^2-b^2} \div \dfrac{a^2+3ab+2b^2}{a^2-3ab+2b^2}$

41 $\dfrac{x^3+x^2-12x}{x^2-3x} \cdot \dfrac{3x^2-10x+3}{3x^2+11x-4}$

42 $\dfrac{n^2+n}{2n^2+7n-4} \cdot \dfrac{4n^2-4n+1}{2n^2-n-3} \cdot \dfrac{2n^2+5n-12}{2n^3-n^2}$

43 $\dfrac{n^3-8}{n+2} \cdot \dfrac{2n^2+8}{n^3-4n} \cdot \dfrac{n^3+2n^2}{n^3+2n^2+4n}$

44 $\dfrac{a^3-27}{a^2-9} \div \left(\dfrac{a^2+2ab+b^2}{a^3+b^3} \cdot \dfrac{a^3-a^2b+ab^2}{a^2+ab} \right)$

Simplify.

45 $\dfrac{\dfrac{5}{x^2-4}}{\dfrac{10}{x-2}}$

46 $\dfrac{x+\dfrac{3}{2}}{x-\dfrac{1}{2}}$

47 $\dfrac{\dfrac{1}{x}-\dfrac{1}{4}}{x-4}$

48 $\dfrac{\dfrac{1}{x}+\dfrac{1}{5}}{x+5}$

49 $\dfrac{\dfrac{1}{4+h}-\dfrac{1}{4}}{h}$

50 $\dfrac{\dfrac{1}{x^2}-\dfrac{1}{9}}{x-3}$

51 $\dfrac{\dfrac{1}{x+3}-\dfrac{1}{3}}{x}$

52 $\dfrac{\dfrac{1}{4}-\dfrac{1}{x^2}}{x-2}$

53 $\dfrac{\dfrac{1}{x^2}-\dfrac{1}{16}}{x+4}$

54 $\dfrac{\dfrac{1}{x^2}-\dfrac{1}{4}}{\dfrac{1}{x}-\dfrac{1}{2}}$

55 $\dfrac{\dfrac{1}{x}-\dfrac{1}{y}}{\dfrac{1}{x^2}-\dfrac{1}{y^2}}$

56 $\dfrac{\dfrac{4}{x^2}-\dfrac{1}{y^2}}{\dfrac{2}{x}-\dfrac{1}{y}}$

◼ 57 $\dfrac{(1+x^2)(-2x)-(1-x^2)(2x)}{(1+x^2)^2}$

◼ 58 $\dfrac{(x^2-9)(2x)-x^2(2x)}{(x^2-9)^2}$

◼ 59 $\dfrac{x^2(4-2x)-(4x-x^2)(2x)}{x^4}$

◼ 60 $\dfrac{(x+1)^2(2x)-(x^2-1)(2)(x+1)}{(x+1)^4}$

Simplify, and express as a single fraction without negative exponents.

*61 $\dfrac{a^{-1}-b^{-1}}{a-b}$

*62 $\dfrac{(a+b)^{-1}}{a^{-1}+b^{-1}}$

*63 $\dfrac{x^{-2}-y^{-2}}{xy}$

*64 There are three tests and a final examination given in a mathematics course. Let a, b, and c be the numerical grades of the tests, and let d represent the examination grade.

(a) If the final grade is computed by allowing the average of the three tests and the exam to count the same, show that the final average is given by the expression $\dfrac{a+b+c+3d}{6}$.

(b) Assume that the average of the three tests accounts for 60% of the final grade, and that the examination accounts for 40%. Show that the final average is given by the expression $\dfrac{a+b+c+2d}{5}$.

*65 Some calculators require that certain calculations be performed in a different manner to accommodate the machine. Show that in each case the expression on the left can be computed by using the equivalent expression on the right.

(a) $\dfrac{A}{B} + \dfrac{C}{D} = \dfrac{\dfrac{A \cdot D}{B} + C}{D}$

(b) $A \cdot B + C \cdot D + E \cdot F$
$$= \left[\dfrac{\left(\dfrac{A \cdot B}{D}+C\right) \cdot D}{F} + E \right] \cdot F$$

◼ 66 If $x^2+y^2=4$, show that $\dfrac{-y-x\left(-\dfrac{x}{y}\right)}{y^2} = -\dfrac{4}{y^3}$.

◼ 67 If $y^3-x^3=8$,

show that $\dfrac{2xy^2-2x^2y\left(\dfrac{x^2}{y^2}\right)}{y^4} = \dfrac{16x}{y^5}$.

The binomial expansion

The factored form of the trinomial square $a^2 + 2ab + b^2$ is $(a + b)^2$. Turning this around, we say that the *expanded form* of $(a + b)^2$ is $a^2 + 2ab + b^2$. And if $(a + b)^2$ is multiplied by $a + b$, we get the expansion of $(a + b)^3$. Here is a list of the expansions of the first five powers of the binomial $a + b$.

$$(a + b)^1 = a + b$$

$$(a + b)^2 = a^2 + 2ab + b^2$$

$$(a + b)^3 = a^3 + 3a^2b + 3ab^2 + b^3$$

$$(a + b)^4 = a^4 + 4a^3b + 6a^2b^2 + 4ab^3 + b^4$$

$$(a + b)^5 = a^5 + 5a^4b + 10a^3b^2 + 10a^2b^3 + 5ab^4 + b^5$$

You can verify these results by multiplying the expansion in each row by $a + b$ to get the expansion in the next row.

Our objective here is to learn how to find such expansions directly without having to multiply. That is, we want to be able to expand $(a + b)^n$, especially for larger values of n, without having to multiply $a + b$ by itself repeatedly.

Let n represent a positive integer. As seen in the display, each expansion begins with a^n and ends with b^n. Moreover, each expansion has $n + 1$ terms that are all preceded by plus signs. Now look at the case for $n = 5$. Replace the first term a^5 by a^5b^0 and use a^0b^5 in place of b^5. Then

$$(a + b)^5 = a^5b^0 + 5a^4b + 10a^3b^2 + 10a^2b^3 + 5ab^4 + a^0b^5$$

In this form it becomes clear that (from left to right) the exponents for a successively decrease by 1, beginning with 5 and ending with zero. At the same time, the exponents for b increase from zero to 5. Also note that the sum of the exponents for each term is 5. Verify that similar patterns also hold for the other cases shown.

Using the preceding observations, we would *expect* the expansion of $(a + b)^6$ to have seven terms that, except for the unknown coefficients, look like this:

$$a^6 + \underline{}a^5b + \underline{}a^4b^2 + \underline{}a^3b^3 + \underline{}a^2b^4 + \underline{}ab^5 + b^6$$

Our list of expansions reveals that the second coefficient, as well as the coefficient of the next to the last term, is the number n. Filling in these coefficients for the case $n = 6$ gives

$$a^6 + 6a^5b + \underline{}a^4b^2 + \underline{}a^3b^3 + \underline{}a^2b^4 + 6ab^5 + b^6$$

To get the remaining coefficients we return to the case $n = 5$ and learn how such coefficients can be generated. Look at the second and third terms.

$$\underbrace{\boxed{5}a^{\boxed{4}}b}_{\text{2nd term}} \qquad \underbrace{10a^3b^{\boxed{2}}}_{\text{3rd term}}$$

If the exponent 4 of a in the *second* term is multiplied by the coefficient 5 of the *second* term and then divided by the exponent 2 of b in the *third* term, the result is 10, the coefficient of the third term.

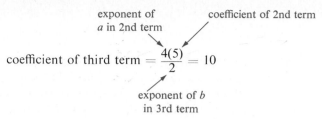

coefficient of third term $= \dfrac{4(5)}{2} = 10$

exponent of
a in 2nd term

coefficient of 2nd term

exponent of b
in 3rd term

Verify that this procedure works for the next coefficient.

On the basis of the evidence we expect the missing coefficients for the case $n = 6$ to be obtainable in the same way. Here are the computations:

Use $⑥a^⑤b + \boxed{15}a^4b^②$:   3rd coefficient $= \dfrac{5(6)}{2} = 15$

Use $⑮a^④b^2 + \boxed{20}a^3b^③$:   4th coefficient $= \dfrac{4(15)}{3} = 20$

Use $⑳a^③b^3 + \boxed{15}a^2b^④$:   5th coefficient $= \dfrac{3(20)}{4} = 15$

Finally, we may write the following expansion:

$$(a + b)^6 = a^6 + 6a^5b + 15a^4b^2 + 20a^3b^3 + 15a^2b^4 + 6ab^5 + b^6$$

You can verify that this equality is correct by multiplying the expansion for $(a + b)^5$ by $a + b$.

More labor can be saved by observing the symmetry in the expansions of $(a + b)^n$. For instance, when $n = 6$ the coefficients around the middle term are symmetric. Similarly, when $n = 5$ the coefficients around the two middle terms are symmetric.

EXAMPLE 1   Write the expansion of $(x + 2)^7$.

Solution   Let x and 2 play the role of a and b, respectively, in $(a + b)^7$.

$$(x + 2)^7 = x^7 + 7x^62 + \underline{\quad}x^52^2 + \underline{\quad}x^42^3$$
$$+ \underline{\quad}x^32^4 + \underline{\quad}x^22^5 + 7x2^6 + 2^7$$

Now find the missing coefficients as follows:

$$3\text{rd coefficient} = \frac{6(7)}{2} = 21 = 6\text{th coefficient}$$

$$4\text{th coefficient} = \frac{5(21)}{3} = 35 = 5\text{th coefficient}$$

The completed expansion may now be given as follows:

$$(x + 2)^7 = x^7 + 7x^62 + 21x^52^2 + 35x^42^3 + 35x^32^4 + 21x^22^5 + 7x2^6 + 2^7$$
$$= x^7 + 14x^6 + 84x^5 + 280x^4 + 560x^3 + 672x^2 + 448x + 128$$

After some experience with these computations you should be able to write the expansion for the general case $(a + b)^n$, the **binomial formula**:

$$(a + b)^n = a^n + \frac{n}{1}a^{n-1}b + \frac{n(n-1)}{1 \cdot 2}a^{n-2}b^2$$
$$+ \frac{n(n-1)(n-2)}{1 \cdot 2 \cdot 3}a^{n-3}b^3 + \cdots + \frac{n}{1}ab^{n-1} + b^n$$

EXAMPLE 2 Use the binomial formula to write the expansion of $(x + 2y)^4$.

Solution Use the formula with $a = x$, $b = 2y$, and $n = 4$. Then simplify.

$$(x + 2y)^4 = x^4 + \frac{4}{1}x^3(2y) + \frac{4 \cdot 3}{1 \cdot 2}x^2(2y)^2 + \frac{4 \cdot 3 \cdot 2}{1 \cdot 2 \cdot 3}x(2y)^3 + (2y)^4$$

$$= x^4 + 8x^3y + 24x^2y^2 + 32xy^3 + 16y^4$$

To get an expansion of the binomial $a - b$, write $a - b = a + (-b)$ and substitute into the previous form. For example, with $n = 6$,

$$(a - b)^6 = [a + (-b)]^6 = a^6 + 6a^5(-b) + 15a^4(-b)^2 + 20a^3(-b)^3$$

$$+ 15a^2(-b)^4 + 6a(-b)^5 + (-b)^6$$

$$= a^6 - 6a^5b + 15a^4b^2 - 20a^3b^3$$

$$+ 15a^2b^4 - 6ab^5 + b^6$$

Be certain that you recognize the difference between the expansion of $(a - b)^n$ and the factorization of $a^n - b^n$.

This result indicates that the expansion of $(a - b)^n$ is the same as the expansion of $(a + b)^n$ except that the signs alternate, beginning with plus.

EXAMPLE 3 Expand: $(x - 1)^7$.

Solution Use the coefficients found in Example 1, with alternating signs.

$$(x - 1)^7 = x^7 - 7x^61^1 + 21x^51^2 - 35x^41^3 + 35x^31^4$$

$$- 21x^21^5 + 7x^11^6 - 1^7$$

$$= x^7 - 7x^6 + 21x^5 - 35x^4 + 35x^3 - 21x^2 + 7x - 1$$

EXERCISES 2.8

Expand and simplify.

1 $(x + 1)^5$

2 $(x - 1)^6$

3 $(x + 1)^7$

4 $(x - 1)^8$

5 $(a - b)^4$

6 $(3x - 2)^4$

7 $(3x - y)^5$

8 $(x + y)^8$

9 $(a^2 + 1)^5$

10 $(2 + h)^9$

11 $(1 - h)^{10}$

12 $(x - 2)^7$

■ *Simplify.*

13 $\dfrac{(1 + h)^3 - 1}{h}$

14 $\dfrac{(3 + h)^4 - 81}{h}$

15 $\dfrac{(c + h)^3 - c^3}{h}$

16 $\dfrac{(x + h)^6 - x^6}{h}$

17 $\dfrac{2(x + h)^5 - 2x^5}{h}$

18 $\dfrac{\dfrac{1}{(2 + h)^2} - \dfrac{1}{4}}{h}$

19 Evaluate 2^{10} by expanding $(1 + 1)^{10}$.

20 Write the first five terms in the expansion of $(x + 1)^{15}$. What are the last five terms?

21 Write the first five terms and the last five terms in the expansion of $(c + h)^{20}$.

22 Write the first four terms and the last four terms in the expansion of $(a - 1)^{30}$.

23 Study this triangular array of numbers and discover the connection with the expansions of $(a + b)^n$, where $n = 1, 2, 3, 4, 5, 6$.

```
        1   1
      1   2   1
    1   3   3   1
  1   4   6   4   1
1   5  10  10   5   1
1  6  15  20  15   6   1
```

This triangular array of numbers, called **Pascal's triangle**, is named after the French mathematician Blaise Pascal (1623–1662).

24 Discover how the 6th row of the triangle in Exercise 23 can be obtained from the 5th row by studying the connection between the 4th and 5th rows indicated by this scheme.

$$\underbrace{1 \quad 4 \quad 6 \quad 4 \quad 1}$$
$$\quad + \quad + \quad + \quad +$$
$$1 \quad 5 \quad 10 \quad 10 \quad 5 \quad 1$$

The solutions to the following exercises can be found within the text of Chapter 2. Try to answer each question without referring to the text.

Section 2.1

Simplify.

1 $12^3(\frac{1}{6})^3$

2 $2x^3 \cdot x^4$

3 $\dfrac{(x^3 y)^2 y^3}{x^4 y^6}$

4 $(\frac{1}{2})^3 (2)^{-3}$

5 Simplify and write without negative exponents: $\left(\dfrac{a^{-2} b^3}{a^3 b^{-2}}\right)^5$.

6 Prove that $(ab)^m = a^m b^m$, where m is a negative integer. (*Hint:* Let $m = -k$ and apply the rules for positive integral exponents.)

7 What is the motivation behind the definition $b^0 = 1$?

Section 2.2

8 What is the definition of $\sqrt[n]{a}$, where $a > 0$ and n is a positive integer ≥ 2?

Evaluate.

9 $\sqrt[3]{\frac{1}{8}}$

10 $\sqrt[5]{32}$

11 $\sqrt{0.09}$

12 $(\sqrt[4]{7})^4$

13 $\sqrt{9 \cdot 25}$

14 $\sqrt[4]{\frac{16}{81}}$

15 $\sqrt[2]{\sqrt[3]{64}}$

16 $\sqrt{72} \cdot \sqrt{\frac{1}{2}}$

17 $(-27)^{1/3}$

18 $(-64)^{2/3}$

19 $8^{-2/3}$

20 $27^{2/3} - 16^{-1/4}$

21 Simplify, and express the result with positive exponents only: $\dfrac{x^{2/3} y^{-2} z^2}{x^{1/2} y^{1/2} z^{-1}}$.

Section 2.3

Simplify.

22 $\sqrt{50}$

23 $\sqrt[3]{16}$

24 $\sqrt[3]{-54}$

25 $3\sqrt{5} + 4\sqrt{5}$

26 $\dfrac{6}{\sqrt{3}} + 2\sqrt{75} - \sqrt{3}$

27 $\sqrt{75x^2}$

28 $2\sqrt{8x^3} + 3x\sqrt{32x} - x\sqrt{18x}$

Section 2.4

29 Add: $(4x^3 - 10x^2 + 5x + 8) + (12x^2 - 9x - 1)$.

30 Subtract:
$(4t^3 - 10t^2 + 5t + 8) - (12t^2 - 9t - 1)$.

Multiply.

31 $3x^2(4x^7 - 3x^4 - x^2 + 15)$

32 $(5x - 9)(6x + 2)$

33 $(a + b)(c + d)$

34 Multiply: $3x^3 - 8x + 4$ by $2x^2 + 5x - 1$.

35 Simplify by performing the indicated operations: $(x^2 - 5x)(3x^2) + (x^3 - 1)(2x - 5)$.

36 Expand: (a) $(a + b)^2$ (b) $(a + b)^3$

37 Rationalize the denominators:

(a) $\dfrac{5}{\sqrt{10} - 3}$

(b) $\dfrac{x}{\sqrt{x} + \sqrt{y}}$

Section 2.5

Factor.

38 $24x^9 - 18x^6 - 6x^4 + 90x^2$

39 $8x^2(x - 1) + 4x(x - 1) + 2(x - 1)$

40 $3x^2 - 75$

41 $8x^3 - 27$

42 $(x + 1)^2 - 4$

43 $2x^3 + 128y^3$

44 $a^5 - b^5$

45 $3y^5 - 96$

46 $x^4 - 81$

47 $ax^2 - 15 - 5ax + 3x$

48 Factor as the difference of squares using irrational numbers: $x^2 - 5$.

49 Factor as the difference of cubes using irrational numbers: $x - 8$.

Section 2.6

Factor.

50 $a^2 + 2ab + b^2$

51 $a^2 - 2ab + b^2$

52 $1 + 18b + 81b^2$

53 $9x^3 - 42x^2 + 49x$

54 $x^2 - 10x + 24$

55 $15x^2 + 43x + 8$

56 $15x^2 - 43x + 8$

57 $15x^2 + 7x - 8$

58 $x^4 + x^2 - 12$

59 $a^6 - 3a^3b - 18b^2$

Section 2.7

60 Reduce to lowest terms: $\dfrac{x^2 + 5x - 6}{x^2 + 6x}$.

61 Multiply: $\dfrac{x-1}{x+1} \cdot \dfrac{x^2 - x - 2}{5x}$.

62 Divide: $\dfrac{(x+1)^2}{x^2 - 6x + 9} \div \dfrac{3x+3}{x-3}$.

63 Add: $\dfrac{3}{x^2 + x} + \dfrac{2}{x^2 - 1}$.

64 Combine: $\dfrac{3}{2} - \dfrac{4}{3x(x+1)} - \dfrac{x-5}{3x^2}$.

65 Simplify: $\dfrac{\dfrac{1}{5+h} - \dfrac{1}{5}}{h}$.

66 Simplify: $\dfrac{x^{-2} - y^{-2}}{\dfrac{1}{x} - \dfrac{1}{y}}$.

Section 2.8

Expand.

67 $(a+b)^5$

68 $(x+2y)^4$

69 $(x-1)^7$

SAMPLE TEST QUESTIONS FOR CHAPTER 2

Use these questions to test your knowledge of the basic skills and concepts of Chapter 2. Then check your answers with those given at the end of the book.

Classify each statement as true or false.

1 $\dfrac{x^3(-x)^2}{x^5} = x$

2 $\left(\dfrac{3}{2+a}\right)^{-1} = \dfrac{2}{3} + \dfrac{a}{3}$

3 $(-27)^{-1/3} = 3$

4 $(x+y)^{3/5} = (\sqrt[3]{x+y})^5$

5 $\sqrt{9x^2} = 3|x|$

6 $(8+a^3)^{1/3} = 2 + a$

In Exercises 7–9, find the correct choice. There is only one correct answer in each case.

7 $\dfrac{4^2(-3)^3 2^0}{6^3(12^2)} =$

   (a) $-\dfrac{1}{216}$ (b) $-\dfrac{1}{72}$

   (c) $-\dfrac{1}{36}$ (d) $\left(-\dfrac{1}{6}\right)^5$

   (e) $\dfrac{1}{6^3}$

8 $\left(\dfrac{27a^6b^{-3}}{c^{-2}}\right)^{-2/3} =$

   (a) $\dfrac{b^2}{9a^4c^{4/3}}$ (b) $\dfrac{b^2}{3a^4\sqrt[3]{c}}$

   (c) $\dfrac{c^2}{18ab}$ (d) $-\dfrac{9c^3b^2}{a^4}$

   (e) $\dfrac{-3b^2}{a^4c^{4/3}}$

9 $\dfrac{30}{\sqrt{20}} - 2\sqrt{45} =$

   (a) $\dfrac{15 - 3\sqrt{5}}{\sqrt{5}}$ (b) $-3\sqrt{5}$

   (c) $-15\sqrt{45}$ (d) $\dfrac{3\sqrt{2}}{2} - 6\sqrt{5}$

   (e) $-\dfrac{5}{2}$

Simplify.

10 $(ab^2 + 5cd) - (3ab^2 - 2cd + a^2) + (2ab^2 - 5a^2)$

11 $(5x+3)(2x-4) - (3-x)(3+x)$

12 $(x^2 + 3x)(3x^2) + (x^3 - 1)(2x + 3)$

Factor completely.

13 $64 - 27b^3$

14 $3x^5 - 48x$

15 $6x^2 - 7x - 3$

16 $x^5 - 32$

17 $2x^2 - 6xy - 3y^3 + xy^2$

18 $ax^2 - 2x + 3ax - 6$

Perform the indicated operations and simplify.

19 $\dfrac{x^2 - 9}{x^3 + 4x^2 + 4x} \cdot \dfrac{2x^2 + 4x}{x^2 + 2x - 15}$

20 $\dfrac{x^3 + 8}{x^2 - 4x - 12} \div \dfrac{x^3 - 2x^2 + 4x}{x^3 - 6x^2}$

21 $\dfrac{\dfrac{1}{x^2} - \dfrac{1}{49}}{x - 7}$

22 $\dfrac{4x - 1}{2x^2 - x - 3} + \dfrac{2}{3 - 2x}$

23 Combine and simplify:
$$\dfrac{1}{x+3} - \dfrac{2}{x^2 - 9} + \dfrac{x}{2x^2 + x - 15}.$$

24 Write the first four terms in the expansion of $(a-2)^{20}$.

25 Expand and simplify: $(x - 3y)^4$.

Page 37

1 125   2 $-\frac{1}{32}$ 3 0   4 1,000,000   5 -64 6 64

7 $\frac{1}{17}$ 8 $\frac{1}{23}$ 9 81   10 $a^{11}b^{10}$ 11 64   12 $6x^4$

Page 44

1 11   2 -4 3 2   4 3   5 35   6 $\frac{3}{5}$

7 2   8 -70 9 $\frac{4}{3}$ 10 540   11 $-\frac{10}{3}$ 12 4

13 6   14 -3 15 $-\frac{3}{2}$

Page 45

1 $\sqrt{5}$ 2 $\sqrt[3]{-9}$ 3 $\sqrt[4]{10}$ 4 $\sqrt[3]{25}$ 5 $\sqrt[4]{8}$ 6 $7^{1/2}$

7 $(-10)^{1/3}$ 8 $7^{1/4}$ 9 $7^{2/3}$ 10 $5^{3/4}$ 11 5   12 4

13 $\frac{1}{6}$ 14 $\frac{1}{5}$ 15 $\frac{3}{5}$ 16 $\frac{1}{7}$ 17 8   18 $\frac{1}{8}$

19 4   20 $\frac{1}{4}$

Page 49

1 $6\sqrt{2}$ 2 $6\sqrt{3}$ 3 $\sqrt{5}$ 4 $6-3\sqrt{2}$ 5 $5\sqrt[3]{2}$ 6 $4\sqrt[3]{2}+5$

7 $11\sqrt{2}$ 8 $13\sqrt{3}$ 9 $3\sqrt{5}$ 10 $7\sqrt{7}$ 11 0   12 $\frac{3\sqrt{2}}{4}$

Page 54

1 $x^2 + 1$ 2 $x^2 + 4x - 13$

3 $2x^3 + 3x^2 + 8x + 1$ 4 $-x^3 + 4x - 8$

5 $-3x^4 - 6x^3 + 3x$ 6 $-\frac{1}{2}x + 2x^2 + 4x^3$

7 $6x^2 + 13x + 6$ 8 $12x^2 + 28x - 5$

9 $16x^2 - 49$ 10 $4x^2 - 12x + 9$

11 $x^4 + 9x^3 + 14x^2 - 4x - 8$ 12 $2x^5 - 5x^4 + 4x^3 + 14x^2 - 15x$

Page 59

1 $3(x - 3)$ 2 $-5(x - 3)$ 3 $5y(x + 5y + 2y^4)$

4 $(x + 6)(x - 6)$ 5 $(2x + 7)(2x - 7)$ 6 $(a + 2 + 5b)(a + 2 - 5b)$

7 $(x - 3)(x^2 + 3x + 9)$ 8 $(x + 3)(x^2 - 3x + 9)$ 9 $(2a - 5)(4a^2 + 10a + 25)$

10 $3(x + 4)(x - 4)$ 11 $a(x + y)(x^2 - xy + y^2)$ 12 $2h(x + 2h)(x - 2h)$

Page 60

1 $(x + \sqrt{2})(x - \sqrt{2})$ 2 $(\sqrt{7} + x)(\sqrt{7} - x)$

3 $(\sqrt{x} + 3)(\sqrt{x} - 3)$ 4 $(x - \sqrt[3]{4})(x^2 + \sqrt[3]{4}\,x + (\sqrt[3]{4})^2)$

5 $(1 - \sqrt[3]{h})(1 + \sqrt[3]{h} + (\sqrt[3]{h})^2)$ 6 $(\sqrt[3]{x} + 3)[(\sqrt[3]{x})^2 - 3\sqrt[3]{x} + 9]$

Page 65

1 $(a + 3)^2$ 2 $(x - 5)^2$ 3 $(2x + 3y)^2$

4 $(x + 3)(x + 5)$ 5 $(a - 10)(a - 2)$ 6 Not factorable.

7 $(5x - 2)(2x - 7)$ 8 $(3x + 2)(2x - 5)$ 9 Not factorable.

1 $x + 2$

2 $\dfrac{x}{x + 2}$

3 $\dfrac{x + 3}{x - 2}$

4 $\dfrac{x + 5}{x - 2}$

5 $\dfrac{1}{x^2 + 4}$

6 $-\dfrac{x + 2}{x}$

7 1

8 $\dfrac{x - 2}{3x(x + 1)}$

9 $\dfrac{a + b}{a - b}$

10 1

Page 70

1 $\dfrac{13x}{15}$

2 $\dfrac{5x}{6}$

3 $\dfrac{4 - 3x}{6x^2}$

4 $\dfrac{25}{6x}$

5 $\dfrac{2(5x + 4)}{(x - 2)(x + 2)}$

6 $\dfrac{9x + 34}{x^2 - 9}$

7 $-\dfrac{3x + 2}{(x - 1)(x^2 - 4)}$

8 $\dfrac{2(8x^2 - 7x - 5)}{(2x + 5)^2(2x - 5)}$

LINEAR FUNCTIONS AND EQUATIONS

Introduction to the function concept

Suppose that you are riding in a car that is averaging 40 miles per hour. Then the distance traveled is determined by the time traveled.

$$\text{distance} = \text{rate} \times \text{time}$$

Symbolically, this relationship can be expressed by the equation

$$s = 40t$$

where s is the distance traveled in time t (measured in hours). For $t = 2$ hours, the distance traveled is

$$s = 40(2) = 80 \text{ miles}$$

Similarly, for each specific value of $t \geq 0$ the equation produces *exactly one* value for s. This correspondence between the distance s and the time t is an example of a *functional relationship*. More specifically, we say that the equation $s = 40t$ defines s as a *function* of t.

We say that $s = 40t$ defines s as a function of t because for *each* choice of t there corresponds *exactly one* value for s. We first choose a value of t. Then there is a corresponding value of s that depends on t; s is the *dependent variable* and t is the *independent variable* of the function defined by $s = 40t$.

In contrast, the equation $y^2 = 12x$ does *not* define y as a function of x; for a given value of x there is *more than one* corresponding value for y. If $x = 3$, for example, then $y^2 = 36$ and $y = 6$ or $y = -6$.

Because the variable t represents time in the equation $s = 40t$, it is reasonable to say that $t \geq 0$. This set of allowable values for the independent variable is called the **domain** of the function. The set of corresponding values for the dependent variable is called the **range** of the function.

DEFINITION OF FUNCTION

A **function** is a correspondence between two sets, the domain and the range, such that for each value in the domain there corresponds exactly one value in the range.

This is an important definition. Much of the work in calculus deals with the study of functions.

The specific letters used for the independent and dependent variables are of no consequence. Usually, we will use x for the independent variable and y for the dependent variable. Thus the equation $y = 40x$ can be used to define the same function as $s = 40t$. However, letters that are suggestive, such as t for time, can prove to be helpful.

Most of the expressions we encountered earlier in this text can be used to define functions. Here are some illustrations. Note that in each case *the domain of the function is taken as the largest set of real numbers for which the defining expression in x leads to a real value.* Unless otherwise indicated, this will be our policy throughout this text.

Function given by	Domain
$y = 6x^4 - 3x^2 + 7x + 1$	All real numbers
$y = \dfrac{2x}{x^2 - 4}$	All reals except 2 and -2
$y = |x|$	All real numbers
$y = \sqrt{x}$	All real $x \geq 0$

Explain why x cannot equal 2 or -2.

Explain why x cannot be negative.

EXAMPLE 1 Explain why the following equation defines y as a function of x and find the domain: $y = \dfrac{1}{\sqrt{x - 1}}$.

Solution For each allowable x the expression $\dfrac{1}{\sqrt{x - 1}}$ produces just one y-value. Therefore, the given equation defines a function. To find the domain observe that $x - 1$ cannot be negative because the even root of a negative value is not a real number. Thus $x - 1 \geq 0$, or $x \geq 1$. But $x = 1$ produces division by zero, so we must exclude it as well. Hence the domain consists of all $x > 1$.

EXAMPLE 2 Find the domain of the function given by $y = \sqrt{1 - x^2}$.

See Section 1.5 for methods to solve such inequalities.

Solution To avoid square roots of negative numbers we must have $1 - x^2 \geq 0$, or $x^2 - 1 \leq 0$. Now factor $x^2 - 1$ and solve the inequality

$(x + 1)(x - 1) \leq 0$. The domain consists of all values of x from -1 through 1; that is, $-1 \leq x \leq 1$.

TEST YOUR UNDERSTANDING

Decide whether the given equation defines y to be a function of x. For each function, find the domain.

1 $y = (x + 2)^2$

2 $y = \dfrac{1}{(x + 2)^2}$

3 $y = \dfrac{1}{x^2 + 2}$

4 $y = \pm 3x$

5 $y = \sqrt{x^2 + x - 6}$

6 $y^2 = x^2$

7 $y = \dfrac{x}{|x|}$

8 $y = \dfrac{1}{\sqrt{x^2 + 2x + 1}}$

Thus far only equations have been used to define functions. One could gain the impression that equations are the only way to state functions. This impression is *not* correct. Since a function defined by an equation is the *correspondence* between the variables, such correspondences can be stated in many ways. Here, for example, is a *table of values*. The table defines y to be a function of x because for each domain value there corresponds *exactly one* value for y.

Sometimes we say that an equation, such as $y = 40x$, is a function. Such informal language is commonly used and should not cause difficulty.

x	1	2	5	-7	23	$\sqrt{2}$
y	6	-6	6	-4	0	5

Instead of using a single equation to define a function, there will be times when a function is defined in terms of more than one equation. For instance, the following three equations define a function whose domain is the set of all real numbers.

$$y = \begin{cases} 1 & \text{for } x \leq -6 \\ x^2 & \text{for } -6 < x < 0 \\ 2x + 1 & \text{for } x \geq 0 \end{cases}$$

Note that if $x = 5$ the corresponding y-value comes from $y = 2x + 1$, namely 11; if $x = -5$, $y = (-5)^2 = 25$; and if $x = -7$, $y = 1$.

EXAMPLE 3 Decide whether these two equations define y to be a function of x.

$$y = \begin{cases} 3x - 1 & \text{if } x \leq 1 \\ 2x + 1 & \text{if } x \geq 1 \end{cases}$$

Solution If $x = 1$, the first equation gives $y = 3(1) - 1 = 2$. For $x = 1$ the second equation gives $y = 2(1) + 1 = 3$. Since we have two different y-values for the same x-value, the equations do *not* define a function.

EXAMPLE 4 Use the definition of absolute value (Section 1.6) to explain why the equation $y = |x|$ defines a function whose domain consists of all real numbers x.

Solution The definition of absolute value says that $|x| = x$ for $x \geq 0$ and $|x| = -x$ for $x < 0$. Thus $y = |x|$ defines a function because each real value x produces just one corresponding y-value.

A useful way to refer to a function is to name it by using a specific letter, such as f, g, F, and the like. For example, the function given by $y = \dfrac{1}{x - 3}$ may be referred to as f. The domain of f is the set of all real numbers not equal to 3; that is, $x \neq 3$. We write

$$f(x) = \frac{1}{x - 3}$$

to mean the value of the function f at x is $\dfrac{1}{x-3}$. For example:

$$f(4) = 1 \text{ means that when } x = 4, \ y = 1$$
$$f(4) = 1 \text{ is read as ``} f \text{ of 4 is 1'' or ``} f \text{ at 4 is 1''}$$

CAUTION: Note that $f(x)$ does *not* mean that we are to multiply f by x; f does not stand for a number.

We use $f(x)$ to represent the range value for the specific value of x given in the parentheses. In this illustration f stands for the function that is given by $y = \dfrac{1}{x - 3}$. For $x \neq 3$, $f(x) = \dfrac{1}{x - 3}$. Then

Note that $f(3)$ is undefined. Can you explain why?

$$f(0) = \frac{1}{0 - 3} = -\frac{1}{3} \text{ and}$$
$$f(9) = \frac{1}{9 - 3} = \frac{1}{6} \leftarrow \begin{cases} 9 \text{ is the } input \\ \frac{1}{6} \text{ is the } output \end{cases}$$

Let us explore the function notation with another example. Let g be the function defined by $y = g(x) = x^2$. Then we have

$$g(1) = 1^2 = 1$$
$$g(2) = 2^2 = 4$$
$$g(3) = 3^2 = 9$$

Note that $g(1) + g(2) \neq g(3)$. To write $g(1) + g(2) = g(1 + 2)$ would be to assume, *incorrectly*, that the distributive property holds for the functional notation. This is not true in general, which comes as no great surprise since g is not a number.

Keep in mind that the variable x in $g(x) = x^2$ is only a *placeholder*. Any letter could serve the same purpose. For example, $g(t) = t^2$ and $g(z) = z^2$ both define the same function with domain all real numbers.

EXAMPLE 5 For the function g defined by $g(x) = \dfrac{1}{x}$, find: **(a)** $3g(x)$
(b) $g(3x)$ **(c)** $3 + g(x)$ **(d)** $g(3) + g(x)$ **(e)** $g(3 + x)$ **(f)** $g\left(\dfrac{1}{x}\right)$

Solution (a) $3g(x) = 3 \cdot \dfrac{1}{x} = \dfrac{3}{x}$ (b) $g(3x) = \dfrac{1}{3x}$ (c) $3 + g(x) =$

$3 + \dfrac{1}{x}$ (d) $g(3) + g(x) = \dfrac{1}{3} + \dfrac{1}{x}$ (e) $g(3 + x) = \dfrac{1}{3 + x}$

(f) $g\left(\dfrac{1}{x}\right) = \dfrac{1}{\frac{1}{x}} = x$

EXAMPLE 6   Let $g(x) = x^2$. Evaluate and simplify the *difference quotient*:
$\dfrac{g(x) - g(4)}{x - 4}$; $x \neq 4$.

Difference quotients will be used in the study of calculus.

Solution $g(x) = x^2$ and $g(4) = 16$

$$\frac{g(x) - g(4)}{x - 4} = \frac{x^2 - 16}{x - 4}$$

$$= \frac{(x - 4)(x + 4)}{x - 4}$$

$$= x + 4$$

EXAMPLE 7   Let $g(x) = \dfrac{1}{x}$. Evaluate and simplify the *difference quotient*:
$\dfrac{g(4 + h) - g(4)}{h}$; $h \neq 0$.

Solution $g(4 + h) = \dfrac{1}{4 + h}$ and $g(4) = \dfrac{1}{4}$

$$\frac{g(4 + h) - g(4)}{h} = \frac{\dfrac{1}{4 + h} - \dfrac{1}{4}}{h}$$

$$= \frac{\dfrac{4 - (4 + h)}{4(4 + h)}}{h}$$

$$= \frac{-h}{4h(4 + h)}$$

$$= -\frac{1}{4(4 + h)}$$

CAUTION: LEARN TO AVOID MISTAKES LIKE THESE

In each of the following, the function f is defined by $f(x) = 3x^2 - 4$.

WRONG	RIGHT
$f(0) = 0$	$f(0) = 3(0)^2 - 4 = -4$
$f(-2) = -f(2)$	$f(-2) = 3(-2)^2 - 4 = 8$ $-f(2) = -[3(2)^2 - 4] = -8$

In each case $f(x) = 3x^2 - 4$.

	WRONG	RIGHT
	$f\left(\dfrac{1}{2}\right) = \dfrac{1}{f(2)}$	$f\left(\dfrac{1}{2}\right) = 3\left(\dfrac{1}{2}\right)^2 - 4 = -\dfrac{13}{4}$ $\dfrac{1}{f(2)} = \dfrac{1}{8}$
	$[f(2)]^2 = f(4)$	$[f(2)]^2 = 8^2 = 64$ $f(4) = 3(4)^2 - 4 = 44$
	$2 \cdot f(5) = f(10)$	$2 \cdot f(5) = 2[3(5)^2 - 4] = 142$ $f(10) = 3(10)^2 - 4 = 296$
	$f(5) + f(2) = f(7)$	$f(5) + f(2) = 3(5)^2 - 4$ $\qquad\qquad + 3(2)^2 - 4 = 79$ $f(7) = 3(7)^2 - 4 = 143$

EXERCISES 3.1

Decide whether the given equation defines y to be a function of x. For each function, find the domain.

1 $y = x^3$ **2** $y = \sqrt[3]{x}$

3 $y = \dfrac{1}{\sqrt{x}}$ **4** $y = |2x|$

5 $y^2 = 2x$ **6** $y = x \pm 3$

7 $y = \dfrac{1}{x + 1}$ **8** $y = \dfrac{x - 2}{x^2 + 1}$

9 $y = \dfrac{1}{1 \pm x}$ **10** $y = \sqrt{x^2 - 4}$

11 $y = \dfrac{1}{\sqrt{x^2 - 4}}$ **12** $y = \dfrac{1}{\sqrt[3]{x^2 - 4}}$

Decide whether the given table defines a function with domain x and range y. If it does not define a function, give a reason.

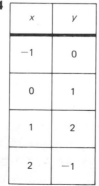

13

x	y
3	4
2	3
1	2
3	1

14

x	y
−1	0
0	1
1	2
2	−1

Classify each statement as true or false. If it is false, correct the right side to get a correct equation. For each of these statements, use $f(x) = -x^2 + 3$.

15 $f(3) = -6$ **16** $f(2)f(3) = -33$

17 $3f(2) = -33$ **18** $f(3) + f(-2) = 2$

19 $f(3) - f(2) = -5$ **20** $f(2) - f(3) = 11$

21 $f(x) - f(4) = -(x - 4)^2 + 3$

22 $f(x) - f(4) = x^2 + 19$

23 $f(4 + h) = -h^2 - 8h - 13$

24 $f(4 + h) = -h^2 - 10$

In Exercises 25–36, find (a) $f(-1)$;   (b) $f(0)$;   and (c) $f(\frac{1}{2})$, if they exist.

25 $f(x) = 2x - 1$ **26** $f(x) = -5x + 6$

27 $f(x) = x^2$ **28** $f(x) = x^2 - 5x + 6$

29 $f(x) = x^3 - 1$ **30** $f(x) = (x - 1)^2$

31 $f(x) = x^4 + x^2$

32 $f(x) = -3x^3 + \frac{1}{2}x^2 - 4x$

33 $f(x) = \dfrac{1}{x - 1}$ **34** $f(x) = \sqrt{x}$

35 $f(x) = \dfrac{1}{\sqrt[3]{x}}$ **36** $f(x) = \dfrac{1}{3|x|}$

37 For $g(x) = x^2 - 2x + 1$, find:
(a) $g(10)$ (b) $5g(2)$ (c) $g(\frac{1}{2}) + g(\frac{1}{3})$ (d) $g(\frac{1}{2} + \frac{1}{3})$.

38 Let h be given by $h(x) = x^2 + 2x$. Find $h(3)$ and $h(1) + h(2)$ and compare.

39 Let h be given by $h(x) = x^2 + 2x$. Find $3h(2)$ and $h(6)$ and compare.

40 Let h be given by $h(x) = x^2 + 2x$. Find **(a)** $h(2x)$

  (b) $h(2 + x)$ **(c)** $h\left(\dfrac{1}{x}\right)$ **(d)** $h(x^2)$.

■ *In Exercises 41–46, find the difference quotient* $\dfrac{f(x) - f(3)}{x - 3}$ *and simplify for the given function f.*

41 $f(x) = x^2$ **42** $f(x) = x^2 - 1$

43 $f(x) = \dfrac{1}{x}$ **44** $f(x) = \sqrt{x}$

45 $f(x) = 2x + 1$ **46** $f(x) = -x^3 + 1$

■ *In Exercises 47–52, find the difference quotient* $\dfrac{f(2 + h) - f(2)}{h}$ *and simplify.*

47 $f(x) = x$ **48** $f(x) = -x + 3$

49 $f(x) = -x^2$ ***50** $f(x) = \sqrt{x + 2}$

*51 $f(x) = \dfrac{1}{x^2}$ ***52** $f(x) = \dfrac{1}{x - 1}$

The rectangular coordinate system

A great deal of information can be learned about a functional relationship by studying its graph. A fundamental objective of this course is to acquaint you with the graphs of some important functions, as well as to develop basic graphing procedures. First we need to review the structure of a **rectangular coordinate system**.

    In a plane take any two lines that intersect at right angles and call their point of intersection the **origin**. Let each of these lines be a number line with the origin corresponding to zero for each line. Unless otherwise specified, the unit length is the same on both lines. On the horizontal line the positive direction is taken to be to the right of the origin, and on the vertical line it is taken to be above the origin. Each of these two lines will be referred to as an **axis** of the system (plural: **axes**).

The union of algebra and geometry, credited to French mathematician René Descartes (1596–1650), led to the development of analytic geometry. In his honor, we often refer to this as the Cartesian coordinate system, or simply the Cartesian plane.

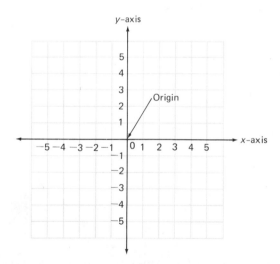

The horizontal line is usually called the **x-axis**, and the vertical line the **y-axis**. The axes divide the plane into four regions called **quadrants**. The quadrants are numbered in a counterclockwise direction as shown in the following figure.

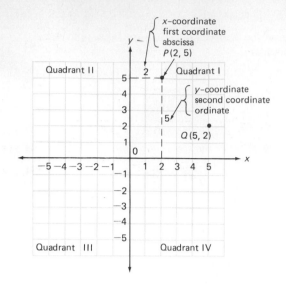

Note that the ordered pair (2, 5) is not the same as the pair (5, 2). Each gives the coordinates of a different point on the plane.

The points in the plane (denoted by the capital letters) are matched with pairs of numbers, referred to as the **coordinates** of these points. For example, starting at the origin, P can be reached by moving 2 units to the right, parallel to the x-axis; then 5 units up, parallel to the y-axis. Thus the first coordinate, 2, of P is called the **x-coordinate** (another name is "abscissa") and the second coordinate, 5, is the **y-coordinate** (also called "ordinate"). We say that the *ordered pair of numbers* (2, 5) is the coordinates of P.

All points in the first quadrant are to the right and above the origin, and therefore have positive coordinates. Any point in quadrant II is to the left and above the origin and therefore has a negative x-coordinate and a positive y-coordinate. In quadrant III both coordinates are negative, and in the fourth quadrant they are positive and negative, respectively.

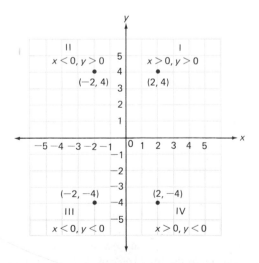

EXAMPLE 1 Find the coordinates of the given points. Also state the quadrant or axis in which each point is located.

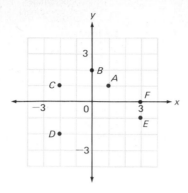

Usually, the points on the axes are labeled with just a single number. In that case it is understood that the missing coordinate is 0. Thus in Example 1, *B* has coordinates (0, 2) and the coordinates of point *F* are (3, 0).

Solution   Point *A* is located at (1, 1), in the first quadrant. Point *B* is at (0, 2), on the *y*-axis. Point *C* is at (−2, 1), in the second quadrant. Point *D* is at (−2, −2), in the third quadrant. Point *E* is at (3, −1), in the fourth quadrant. Point *F* is at (3, 0), on the *x*-axis.

The equality $y = x + 2$ is an equation in two variables. When a specific value for *x* is substituted into this equation, we get a corresponding *y*-value. For example, substituting 3 for *x* gives $y = 3 + 2 = 5$. We therefore say that the ordered pair (3, 5) *satisfies* the equation $y = x + 2$.

In the following table of values there are six more ordered pairs that satisfy this equation. Note that the ordered pairs in the table have been written without the usual parentheses. These ordered pairs have also been *plotted* in a rectangular system.

x	$y = x + 2$
−3	−1
−2	0
−1	1
0	2
1	3
2	4

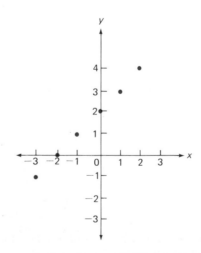

To graph an equation in the variables x and y means to locate all the points in a rectangular system whose coordinates satisfy the given equation. There are an infinite number of ordered pairs that satisfy $y = x + 2$, and all are located on the same straight line. Since a line is endless, we draw a partial graph by joining the specific points previously located.

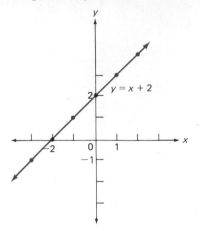

The arrowheads in the figure suggest that the line continues endlessly in both directions.

The straight line contains exactly those points whose ordered pairs (x, y) satisfy the equation $y = x + 2$. Any point not on the line has an ordered pair (x, y) where $y \neq x + 2$. Thus $(1, 5)$ is not on the line, since $5 \neq 1 + 2$.

The graph of $y = x + 2$ is a straight line and the equation is called a *linear equation*. Since two points determine a line, a convenient way to graph a line is to locate its **intercepts**. The **x-intercept** for $y = x + 2$ is -2, the abscissa of the point where the line crosses the x-axis. The **y-intercept** is 2, the ordinate of the point where the line crosses the y-axis.

EXAMPLE 2   Graph the linear equation $y = 2x - 1$ using the intercepts.

Solution   To find the x-intercept, let $y = 0$.

$$2x - 1 = 0$$
$$2x = 1$$
$$x = \tfrac{1}{2} \longleftarrow \text{the } x\text{-intercept}$$

When the line crosses the x-axis, the y-value is 0.

When the line crosses the y-axis, the x-value is 0.

To find the y-intercept, let $x = 0$.

$$y = 2(0) - 1$$
$$y = -1 \longleftarrow \text{the } y\text{-intercept}$$

It is generally wise to locate a third point to verify your work. Thus for $x = 2$, $y = 3$, and the line passes through the point $(2, 3)$.

Plot the points $(\tfrac{1}{2}, 0)$ and $(0, -1)$ and draw the line through them to determine the graph.

Note: If the equation $y = 2x - 1$ were given in the equivalent form $y - 2x = -1$, the intercepts can be found as before. Thus let $y = 0$ to obtain $0 - 2x = -1$ or $x = \tfrac{1}{2}$, the x-intercept. Likewise, if $x = 0$, then $y - 2(0) = -1$ or $y = -1$, the y-intercept.

An equation such as $y = 2x - 1$ defines y as a *linear function* of x. Usually the domain of such a function is the set of all real numbers. However, at times we may wish to limit the domain of a function. For example, the graph of $y = 2x - 1$ for $-2 \leq x \leq 1$ is a line segment with endpoints at $(-2, -5)$ and $(1, 1)$ as in the following figure.

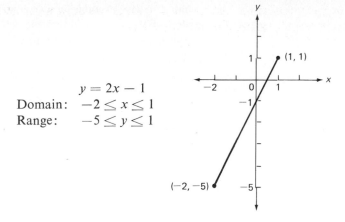

$$y = 2x - 1$$
Domain: $-2 \leq x \leq 1$
Range: $-5 \leq y \leq 1$

The equation $y = 2x - 1$ can also be used to identify two-dimensional regions in the plane. First note that the graph of $y = 2x - 1$ in Example 2 divides the plane into two *half-planes*. These two half-planes represent the graphs for the two statements of inequality, $y < 2x - 1$ (below the line) and $y > 2x - 1$ (above the line). To show these graphs we would use a dashed line for $y = 2x - 1$ and shade the appropriate half-plane, as in the following figures.

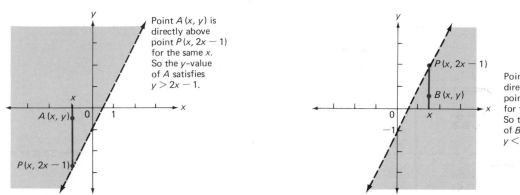

To show a graph for an inequality such as $y \leq 2x - 1$, we would draw both the line and the half-plane.

EXERCISES 3.2

Copy and complete each table of values. Then graph the line given by the equation.

1 $y = x - 2$

x	-3	-2	-1	0	1	2
y						

2 $y = -x + 1$

x	-3	-2	-1	0	1	2	3
y							

3 $y = 2x - 4$

x	-2	-1	0	1	2
y					

4 $y = -2x + 3$

x	-2	-1	0	1	2
y					

Find the x- and y-intercepts and use these to graph each of the following lines.

5 $x + 2y = 4$

6 $2x + y = 4$

7 $x - 2y = 4$

8 $2x - y = 4$

9 $2x - 3y = 6$

10 $3x + y = 6$

11 $y = -3x - 9$

12 $y + 2x = -5$

13 $y = 2x - 1$

14 Sketch the following on the same set of axes.
  (a) $y = x$
  (b) By adding 1 to each y-value (ordinate) in part (a), graph $y = x + 1$. In other words, *shift* each point of $y = x$ one unit up.
  (c) By subtracting 1 from each y-value in part (a), graph $y = x - 1$. That is, shift each point of $y = x$ one unit down.

15 Repeat Exercise 14 for (a) $y = -x$; (b) $y = -x + 1$; (c) $y = -x - 1$.

16 Sketch the following on the same set of axes.
  (a) $y = x$
  (b) By multiplying each y-value in part (a) by 2, graph $y = 2x$. In other words, *stretch* each y-value of $y = x$ to twice its size.
  (c) Graph $y = 2x + 3$ by shifting $y = 2x$ three units upward.

Graph the points that satisfy each equation for the given values of x.

17 $y = \frac{1}{2}x$; $-6 \leq x \leq 6$

18 $y = -2x + 1$; $-2 \leq x \leq 2$

19 $y = 3x - 5$; $1 \leq x \leq 4$

20 $y = x^2$; $x = -3, -2, -1, 0, 1, 2, 3$

21 (a) $y = x^2$; $x = -2, -1, -\frac{1}{2}, 0, \frac{1}{2}, 1, 2$
   (b) $y = x^2$; $-2 \leq x \leq 2$

22 (a) $y = |x|$; $x = -3, -1, 0, 2, 4$
   (b) $y = |x|$; $-3 \leq x \leq 4$

23 (a) $y = \frac{1}{x}$; $x = \frac{1}{2}, 1, \frac{3}{2}, 2, \frac{5}{2}, 3$
   (b) $y = \frac{1}{x}$; $\frac{1}{2} \leq x \leq 3$

24 (a) $y = \sqrt{x}$; $x = 0, \frac{1}{4}, 1, \frac{25}{16}, \frac{9}{4}, 4$
   (b) $y = \sqrt{x}$; $0 \leq x \leq 4$

Graph each inequality.

25 $y > x + 2$

26 $y \leq x + 2$

27 $y \geq x - 1$

28 $y < x - 1$

29 $2x + y - 4 > 0$

30 $x - 2y + 2 \leq 0$

3.3

Slope The adjoining figure shows the graph of the linear equation $y = 2x - 4$, including the coordinates of four specific points. From the diagram you will see that the y-value increases 2 units each time that the x-value increases by 1 unit. The ratio of this change in y compared to the corresponding change in x is $\frac{2}{1} = 2$. Using the coordinates of the points $(3, 2)$ and $(2, 0)$, we have the following:

For convenience, the change in y may be referred to as "Δy" (read "delta y"); the change in x is denoted as "Δx" (read "delta x").

$$\frac{\Delta y}{\Delta x} = \frac{2 - 0}{3 - 2} = \frac{2}{1} = 2$$

$$\frac{\text{change in } y\text{-values}}{\text{change in } x\text{-values}} = \frac{2 - 0}{3 - 2} = \frac{2}{1} = 2$$

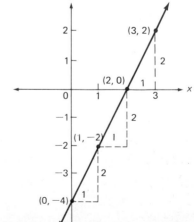

We call this ratio the *slope* of the line, defined as follows.

DEFINITION OF SLOPE

If two points (x_1, y_1) and (x_2, y_2) are on a line ℓ, then the slope m of line ℓ is defined by

Notice that in the definition $x_2 - x_1$ cannot be zero; that is, $x_2 \neq x_1$. The only time that $x_2 = x_1$ is when the line is vertical.

In the following figure the coordinates of two points A and B have been labeled (x_1, y_1) and (x_2, y_2). The change in the y direction from A to B is given by the difference $y_2 - y_1$; the change in the x direction is $x_2 - x_1$. If a different pair of points is chosen, such as P and Q, then the ratio of these differences is still the same because the resulting triangles (ABC and PQR) are similar. That is, since corresponding sides of similar triangles are proportional, we have

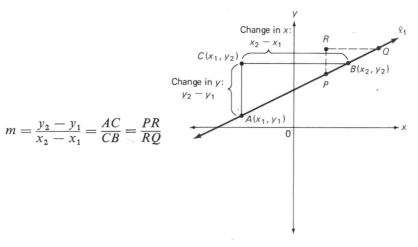

$$m = \frac{y_2 - y_1}{x_2 - x_1} = \frac{AC}{CB} = \frac{PR}{RQ}$$

This discussion shows that there can only be one slope for a given line.

It may be helpful to think of the slope of a line in any of these ways:

$$m = \frac{y_2 - y_1}{x_2 - x_1} = \frac{\text{change in } y}{\text{change in } x} = \frac{\text{vertical change}}{\text{horizontal change}}$$

Another descriptive language for slope is $m = \dfrac{\text{rise}}{\text{run}}$, where *rise* is the vertical change and *run* is the horizontal change.

EXAMPLE 1   Find the slope of line ℓ determined by the points $(-3, 4)$ and $(1, -6)$.

Solution   Use $(x_1, y_1) = (-3, 4)$; $(x_2, y_2) = (1, -6)$. Then

$$m = \frac{-6 - 4}{1 - (-3)} = -\frac{10}{4} = -\frac{5}{2}$$

Note: It makes no difference which of the two points is called (x_1, y_1) or (x_2, y_2) since the ratio will still be the same. If $(x_1, y_1) = (1, -6)$ and $(x_2, y_2) = (-3, 4)$, for example, then $\dfrac{y_2 - y_1}{x_2 - x_1} = \dfrac{4 - (-6)}{-3 - 1} = -\dfrac{5}{2} = m.$

CAUTION: Do not mix up the coordinates like this:

$$\frac{y_2 - y_1}{x_1 - x_2} = \frac{4 - (-6)}{1 - (-3)} = \frac{5}{2}$$

This is the *negative* of the slope.

Reading from left to right, a rising line has a positive slope and a falling line has a negative slope.

EXAMPLE 2 Graph the line with slope 3 that passes through the point $(-2, -2)$.

Solution Write $3 = \dfrac{3}{1} = \dfrac{\text{change in } y}{\text{change in } x}$. Now start at $(-2, -2)$ and move 3 units up and 1 unit to the right. This locates the point $(-1, 1)$. Draw the straight line through these two points.

Alternatively, start at $(-2, -2)$ and move 3 units down and 1 unit to the left to locate $(-3, -5)$.

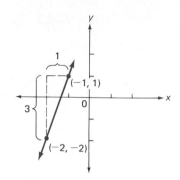

TEST YOUR UNDERSTANDING

Find the slopes of the lines determined by the given pairs of points.

1 $(1, 5)$; $(4, 6)$ **2** $(3, -5)$; $(-3, 3)$

3 $(-2, -3)$; $(-1, 1)$ **4** $(-1, 0)$; $(0, 1)$

Draw the line through the given point and with the given slope.

5 $(0, 0)$; $m = 2$ **6** $(-3, 4)$; $m = -\frac{3}{2}$

In the adjoining figure ℓ is a horizontal line. Since ℓ is parallel to the x-axis, $y_1 = y_2$ or $y_1 - y_2 = 0$, and the slope is therefore 0:

$$m = \frac{y_2 - y_1}{x_2 - x_1} = \frac{0}{x_2 - x_1} = 0$$

CAUTION: Do not confuse a slope of 0 for horizontal lines with no slope for vertical lines.

Now consider a vertical line ℓ. Since ℓ is parallel to the y-axis, $x_1 = x_2$ or $x_1 - x_2 = 0$. Then, since division by 0 is undefined, the formula $m = \dfrac{y_2 - y_1}{x_2 - x_1}$ does not apply. Consequently, it is agreed that *vertical lines do not have slope*, as in the following figure.

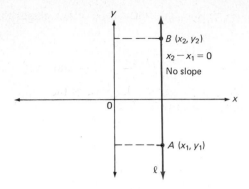

Two nonvertical lines are parallel if and only if they have the same slope. The slope property for perpendicular lines is not as obvious. The adjoining figure suggests the following (see Exercise 35):

Two lines not parallel to the coordinate axes are perpendicular if and only if their slopes are negative reciprocals of one another.

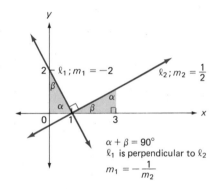

EXAMPLE 3 In the figure, line ℓ_1 has slope $\frac{2}{3}$ and is perpendicular to ℓ_2. If the lines intersect at $P(-1, 4)$, use the slope of ℓ_2 to find the coordinates of another point on ℓ_2.

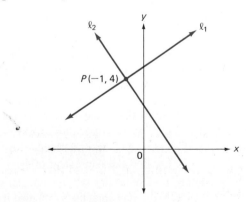

Solution Since the lines are perpendicular, the slope of ℓ_2 is $-\frac{3}{2}$. Now start at P, count 3 units downward and 2 units to the right to reach point $(1, 1)$ on ℓ_2. Other solutions are possible.

EXERCISES 3.3

1 Use the coordinates of each of the following pairs of points to find the slope of ℓ.

(a) A, C (b) B, D
(c) C, D (d) A, E
(e) B, E (f) C, E

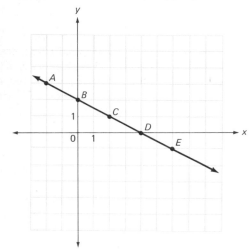

Compute the slope, if it exists, for the line determined by the given pair of points.

2 $(3, 4); (2, -5)$ **3** $(4, 3); (-5, 2)$
4 $(-7, 6); (-7, 106)$ **5** $(6, -7); (106, -7)$
6 $(5\sqrt{2}, 3\sqrt{8}); (\sqrt{2}, \sqrt{8})$
7 $(2, -\frac{3}{4}); (-\frac{1}{3}, \frac{2}{3})$ **8** $(\frac{1}{2}, 0.1); (-9, 0.1)$
9 $(\sqrt{3}, 8); (-1, 6)$ **10** $(-9, \frac{1}{2}); (2, \frac{1}{2})$

In Exercises 11–20, draw the line through the given point having slope m.

11 $(0, 0); m = 2$ **12** $(0, 0); m = -\frac{1}{2}$
13 $(0, 2); m = \frac{3}{4}$ **14** $(-\frac{1}{2}, 0); m = -1$
15 $(-3, 4); m = -\frac{1}{4}$ **16** $(3, -4); m = 4$
17 $(-2, \frac{3}{2}); m = 0$ **18** $(1, 1); m = 2$
19 $(5, -3);$ no slope   **20** $(-\frac{3}{4}, -\frac{1}{2}); m = 1$

21 In the same coordinate system draw five lines, each

with slope -2, through points $(-2, 0)$, $(-1, 0)$, $(0, 0)$, $(\frac{1}{2}, 0)$, and $(1, 1)$, respectively.

22 Follow the instructions of Exercise 21 using $m = \frac{1}{3}$ and $(2, 2)$, $(-2, 2)$, $(-2, -2)$, $(2, -2)$, $(0, 0)$.

23 In the same coordinate system, draw the line:
(a) through $(1, 0)$ with $m = -1$
(b) through $(0, 1)$ with $m = 1$
(c) through $(-1, 0)$ with $m = -1$
(d) through $(0, -1)$ with $m = 1$

24 Use the instructions of Exercise 23 for the following:
(a) $(1, 1)$; slope 0   (b) $(0, \frac{1}{2})$; slope 0
(c) $(1, 1)$; slope $\frac{1}{2}$ (d) $(2, \frac{1}{2})$; slope $\frac{1}{2}$

25 Graph each of the lines with the following slopes through the point $(5, -3)$:
$$m = -2 \quad m = -1 \quad m = 0 \quad m = 1 \quad m = 2$$

26 Line ℓ passes through $(-4, 5)$ and $(8, -2)$.
(a) Draw the line through $(0, 0)$ perpendicular to ℓ.
(b) What is the slope of any line perpendicular to line ℓ?
(c) Draw the four lines, each perpendicular to ℓ, through the points $(-4, 5)$, $(4, \frac{1}{3})$, $(0, \frac{8}{3})$, and $(8, -2)$.

27 Why is the line determined by the points $(6, -5)$ and $(8, -8)$ parallel to the line through $(-3, 12)$ and $(1, 6)$?

28 Verify that the points $A(1, 2)$, $B(4, -1)$, $C(2, -2)$, and $D(-1, 1)$ are the vertices of a parallelogram. Sketch.

29 Consider the four points $P(5, 11)$, $Q(-7, 16)$, $R(-12, 4)$, and $S(0, -1)$. Show that the four angles of the quadrilateral $PQRS$ are right angles. Also show that the diagonals are perpendicular.

30 Lines ℓ_1 and ℓ_2 are perpendicular and intersect at point $(-2, -6)$. ℓ_1 has slope $-\frac{2}{5}$. Use the slope of ℓ_2 to find the y-intercept of ℓ_2.

31 Any horizontal line is perpendicular to any vertical line. Why were such lines excluded from the result, which states that lines are perpendicular if and only if their slopes are negative reciprocals?

32 Find t if the line through $(-1, 1)$ and $(3, 2)$ is parallel to the line through $(0, 6)$ and $(-8, t)$.

33 Find t if the line through $(-1, 1)$ and $(1, \frac{1}{2})$ is perpendicular to the line through $(1, \frac{1}{2})$ and $(7, t)$. Use the fact that two perpendicular lines have slopes that are negative reciprocals of one another.

*34 (a) Prove that nonvertical parallel lines have equal slopes by considering two parallel lines ℓ_1, ℓ_2 as in the figure. On ℓ_1 select points A and B, and choose A' and B' on ℓ_2. Now form the appropriate right triangles ABC and $A'B'C'$ using points C and C' on the x-axis. Prove they are similar and write a proportion to show the slopes of ℓ_1 and ℓ_2 are equal.

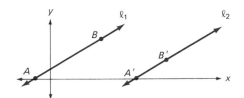

(b) Why is the converse of the fact given in part (a) also true?

*35 This exercise gives a proof that if two lines are perpendicular, then they have slopes that are negative reciprocals of one another.

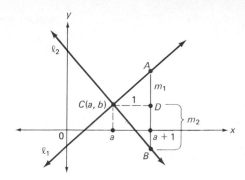

Let line ℓ_1 be perpendicular to line ℓ_2 at the point $C(a, b)$. Use m_1 for the slope of ℓ_1, and m_2 for ℓ_2. We want to show that

$$m_1 m_2 = -1 \qquad \text{or} \qquad m_1 = -\frac{1}{m_2}$$

Add 1 to the x-coordinate a of point C and draw the vertical line through $a + 1$ on the x-axis. This vertical line will meet ℓ_1 at some point A and ℓ_2 at some point B, forming right triangle ABC with right angle at C. Draw the perpendicular from C to AB meeting AB at D. Then CD has length 1.

(a) Using the right triangle CDA, show that $m_1 = DA$.

(b) Show that $m_2 = DB$. Is m_2 positive or negative?

(c) For right triangle ABC, CD is the mean proportional between segments BD and DA on the hypotenuse. Use this fact to conclude that $\frac{m_1}{1} = \frac{1}{-m_2}$, or $m_1 m_2 = -1$.

3.4

Linear functions

Pictured below is a line with slope m and y-intercept k. To find the equation of ℓ we begin by considering any point $P(x, y)$ on ℓ other than $(0, k)$.

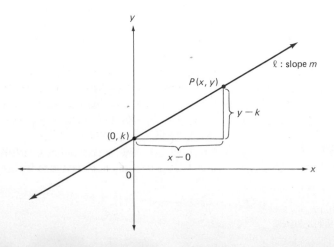

Since the slope of ℓ is given by any two of its points, we may use $(0, k)$ and (x, y) to write

$$m = \frac{y - k}{x - 0} = \frac{y - k}{x}$$

If both sides are multiplied by x, then

$$y - k = mx$$

or

$$y = mx + k \longleftarrow \text{Note that the point } (0, k) \text{ also satisfies this final form.}$$

This leads to the following y-form of the equation of a line.

SLOPE-INTERCEPT FORM OF A LINE

$$y = mx + k$$

where m is the slope and k is the y-intercept.

The equation $y = mx + k$ also defines a function; thus we may think of $y = f(x) = mx + k$ as the *general linear function* with domain consisting of all the real numbers.

EXAMPLE 1   Graph the linear function f defined by $y = f(x) = 2x - 1$ by using the slope and y-intercept. Also indicate the domain and range of f, and display $f(2) = 3$ geometrically; that is, show the point corresponding to $f(2) = 3$.

Solution   The y-intercept is -1. Locate $(0, -1)$ and use $m = 2 = \frac{2}{1}$ to reach $(1, 1)$, another point on the line.

Both the domain and range of f consist of all real numbers.

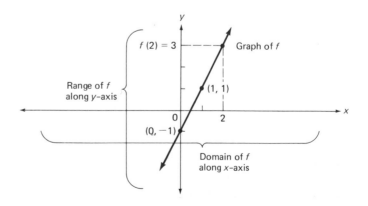

EXAMPLE 2   Find the equation of the line with slope $\frac{2}{3}$ passing through the point $(0, -5)$.

Solution Since $m = \frac{2}{3}$ and $k = -5$, the slope-intercept form gives

$$y = \tfrac{2}{3}x + (-5)$$
$$= \tfrac{2}{3}x - 5$$

A special case of $y = f(x) = mx + k$ is obtained when $m = 0$. Then

$$y = f(x) = k$$

This says that for *each* input x, the output $f(x)$ is always the same value k.

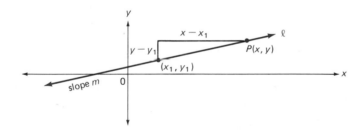

Domain: all reals
Range: the single
         value k

Since $f(x) = k$ is constant for all x, this linear function is also referred to as a *constant function*. Its graph is a horizontal line.

Can a vertical line be the graph of a function where y depends on x? Explain.

Now let ℓ be a line with slope m that passes through (x_1, y_1). We wish to determine the conditions on the coordinates of any point $P(x, y)$ that is on ℓ.

From the figure you can see that $P(x, y)$ will be on ℓ if and only if the ratio $\dfrac{y - y_1}{x - x_1}$ is the same as m. That is, P is on ℓ if and only if

$$m = \frac{y - y_1}{x - x_1}$$

Multiply both sides of this equation by $x - x_1$.

$$m(x - x_1) = y - y_1$$

This step leads to the following form for the equation of a straight line.

This is the form of a line that is most frequently used in calculus.

POINT-SLOPE FORM OF A LINE

$$y - y_1 = m(x - x_1)$$

where m is the slope and (x_1, y_1) is a point on the line.

EXAMPLE 3 Write the point-slope form of the line ℓ with slope $m = 3$ that passes through the point $(-1, 1)$. Verify that $(-2, -2)$ is on the line.

CAUTION: Pay attention to the minus signs on the coordinates when used in the point-slope form. Note the substitution of $x_1 = -1$ in this example.

Solution Since $m = 3$, any (x, y) on ℓ satisfies this equation:

$$y - 1 = 3[x - (-1)]$$
$$y - 1 = 3(x + 1)$$

Let $x = -2$:

$$y - 1 = 3(-2 + 1) = -3$$
$$y = -2$$

Thus $(-2, -2)$ is on the line.

TEST YOUR UNDERSTANDING

Write the slope-intercept form of the line with the given slope and y-intercept.

1 $m = 2$; $k = -2$ **2** $m = -\frac{1}{2}$; $k = 0$ **3** $m = \sqrt{2}$; $k = 1$

Write the point-slope form of the line through the given point with slope m.

4 $(2, 6)$; $m = -3$ **5** $(-1, 4)$; $m = \frac{1}{2}$ **6** $(5, -\frac{2}{3})$; $m = 1$

7 $(0, 0)$; $m = -\frac{1}{4}$ **8** $(-3, -5)$; $m = 0$ **9** $(1, -1)$; $m = -1$

10 Which, if any, of the preceding produce a constant linear function? State its range.

EXAMPLE 4 Write the slope-intercept form of the line through the two points $(6, -4)$ and $(-3, 8)$.

See Exercise 64 for the *two-point form* for the equation of a line. Use that form to complete this example in another way.

Solution First compute the slope.

$$m = \frac{-4 - 8}{6 - (-3)} = \frac{-12}{9} = -\frac{4}{3}$$

Use either point to write the point-slope form, and then convert to the slope-intercept form. Thus, using the point $(6, -4)$,

$$y - (-4) = -\tfrac{4}{3}(x - 6)$$
$$y + 4 = -\tfrac{4}{3}x + 8$$
$$y = -\tfrac{4}{3}x + 4$$

Show that the same final form is obtained using the point $(-3, 8)$.

EXAMPLE 5 Write the equation of the line that is perpendicular to the line $5x - 2y = 2$ and that passes through the point $(-2, -6)$.

Solution First find the slope of the given line by writing it in slope-intercept form.

$$5x - 2y = 2$$
$$-2y = -5x + 2$$
$$y = \tfrac{5}{2}x - 1 \qquad \text{The slope is } \tfrac{5}{2}.$$

The perpendicular line has slope $-\dfrac{1}{\frac{5}{2}} = -\dfrac{2}{5}$. Since this line also goes through $P(-2, -6)$, the point-slope form gives

$$y + 6 = -\tfrac{2}{5}(x + 2)$$
$$y = -\tfrac{2}{5}x - \tfrac{34}{5}$$

Recall that two perpendicular lines have slopes that are negative reciprocals of one another.

A linear equation such as $y = -\tfrac{2}{3}x + 4$ can be converted to other equivalent forms. In particular, when this equation is multiplied by 3, and the variable terms are put on the same side of the equation, we then have $2x + 3y = 12$. This is an illustration of the *general linear equation*.

> **GENERAL LINEAR EQUATION**
>
> $$ax + by = c$$
>
> where a, b, c are constants and a, b are not both 0.

The general linear equation $ax + by = c$ is said to define y as a function of x *implicitly* if $b \neq 0$. In other words, we have these equivalent forms:

$$ax + by = c \qquad \longleftarrow \text{\textit{implicit} form of the linear function}$$

$$by = -ax + c$$

$$y = -\frac{a}{b}x + \frac{c}{b} \longleftarrow \text{\textit{explicit} form of the linear function; slope-intercept form}$$

Note here that the slope is $-\dfrac{a}{b}$ and the y-intercept is $\dfrac{c}{b}$.

EXAMPLE 6 Find the slope and y-intercept of the line $-6x + 2y = 5$.

Solution Convert from the implicit to the explicit form of the linear function.

$$-6x + 2y = 5$$
$$2y = 6x + 5$$
$$y = 3x + \tfrac{5}{2} \longleftarrow \text{slope-intercept form}$$

Thus $m = 3$ and $k = \tfrac{5}{2}$.

WRONG	RIGHT
The slope of the line through (2, 3) and (5, 7) is $$m = \frac{7-3}{2-5} = -\frac{4}{3}$$	The slope of the line through (2, 3) and (5, 7) is $$m = \frac{7-3}{5-2} = \frac{4}{3}$$
The slope of the line $2x - 3y = 7$ is $-\frac{3}{2}$.	The slope is $\frac{2}{3}$.
The line through $(-4, -3)$ with slope 2 is $y - 3 = 2(x - 4)$.	The equation is $y - (-3) = 2[x - (-4)]$ or $y + 3 = 2(x + 4)$.

EXERCISES 3.4

Write the equation of the line with the given slope m and y-intercept k.

1 $m = 2, k = 3$

2 $m = -2, k = 1$

3 $m = 1, k = 1$

4 $m = -1, k = 2$

5 $m = 0, k = 5$

6 $m = 0, k = -5$

7 $m = \frac{1}{2}, k = 3$

8 $m = -\frac{1}{2}, k = 2$

9 $m = \frac{1}{4}, k = -2$

Write the point-slope form of the line through the given point with the indicated slope.

10 $(3, 4); m = 2$

11 $(2, 3); m = 1$

12 $(1, -2); m = 0$

13 $(-2, 3); m = 4$

14 $(-3, 5); m = -2$

15 $(-3, 5); m = 0$

16 $(8, 0); m = -\frac{2}{3}$

17 $(2, 1); m = \frac{1}{2}$

18 $(-6, -3); m = \frac{4}{3}$

19 $(0, 0); m = 5$

20 $(-\frac{3}{4}, \frac{2}{5}); m = 1$

21 $(\sqrt{2}, -\sqrt{2}); m = 10$

22 **(a)** Find the slope of the line determined by the points $A(-3, 5)$ and $B(1, 7)$, and write its equation in point-slope form, using the coordinates of A.

   (b) Do the same as in part (a) using the coordinates of B.

   (c) Verify that the equations obtained in parts (a) and (b) give the same slope-intercept form.

Write each equation in y-form; give the slope and y-intercept.

23 $3x + y = 4$

24 $2x - y = 5$

25 $6x - 3y = 1$

26 $4x + 2y = 10$

27 $3y - 5 = 0$

28 $x = \frac{3}{2}y + 3$

29 $4x - 3y - 7 = 0$

30 $5x - 2y + 10 = 0$

31 $\frac{1}{4}x - \frac{1}{2}y = 1$

Write the equation of the line through the two given points.

32 $(-1, 2), (2, -1)$

33 $(2, 3), (3, 2)$

34 $(1, 1), (-1, -1)$

35 $(3, 0), (0, -3)$

36 $(3, -4), (0, 0)$

37 $(-1, -13), (-8, 1)$

38 $(\frac{1}{2}, 7), (-4, -\frac{3}{2})$

39 $(10, 27), (12, 27)$

40 $(\sqrt{2}, 4\sqrt{2}), (-3\sqrt{2}, -10\sqrt{2})$

41 Two lines, parallel to the coordinate axes, intersect at the point $(5, -7)$. What are their equations?

42 Write the equation of the line that is parallel to $y = -3x - 6$ and with y-intercept 6.

43 Write the equation of the line parallel to $2x + 3y = 6$ that passes through the point $(1, -1)$.

In Exercises 44–47, write the equation of the line that is perpendicular to the given line and passes through the indicated point.

44 $y = -10x; (0, 0)$

45 $y = 3x - 1; (4, 7)$

46 $3x + 2y = 6$; $(6, 7)$ **47** $y - 2x = 5$; $(-5, 1)$

Graph the linear function f by using the slope and y-intercept. Display the point corresponding to $y = f(-2)$ on the graph.

48 $y = f(x) = -2x + 1$

49 $y = f(x) = x + 3$

50 $y = f(x) = 3x - \frac{1}{2}$

51 $y = f(x) = \frac{1}{2}x - 3$

In Exercises 52–55, the domain is given for the function defined by the equation $y = 3x - 7$. Graph each function.

52 All $x \le 4$.   **53** All $x \ge 0$.

54 All x where $-1 \le x \le 3$.

55 $x = -1, 0, 1, 2, 3$

Write the equation for each graph. State the domain and range in case it is the graph of a function.

56
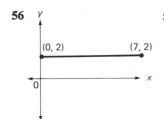

57
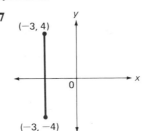

58
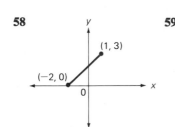

59
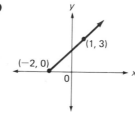

60
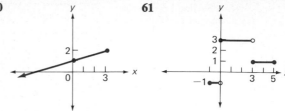

61

62 The sides of the parallelogram with vertices $(-1, 1)$, $(0, 3)$, $(2, 1)$, and $(3, 3)$ are the graphs of four different functions. In each case find the equation that defines the function and state the domain.

*63 Any line having a nonzero slope that does not pass through the origin always has both an x- and a y-intercept. Let ℓ be such a line having equation $ax + by = c$.
   (a) Why is $c \ne 0$?
   (b) What are the x- and y-intercepts?
   (c) Derive the equation

$$\frac{x}{q} + \frac{y}{p} = 1$$

where q and p are the x- and y-intercepts, respectively. This is known as the *intercept form* of a line.
   (d) Use the intercept form to write the equation of the line passing through $(\frac{3}{2}, 0)$ and $(0, -5)$.
   (e) Use the two points in part (d) to find the slope, write the slope-intercept form, and compare with the result in part (d).

*64 Replace m in the point-slope form of a line through points (x_1, y_1) and (x_2, y_2) by $\dfrac{y_2 - y_1}{x_2 - x_1}$. Show that this gives the *two-point form* for the equation of a line:

$$\frac{y - y_1}{y_2 - y_1} = \frac{x - x_1}{x_2 - x_1}$$

65 Use the result of Exercise 64 to find the equation of the line through $(-2, 3)$ and $(5, -2)$. Write the equation in point-slope form.

3.5

Some special functions

We have seen that the graph of a linear function is a straight line. Linear functions can also be used to define other functions which, in themselves, are not linear but may be described as being "partly" or "piecewise" linear. An important example is the **absolute-value function**.

See Section 1.6 to review the meaning of absolute value.

$$f(x) = |x| = \begin{cases} x & \text{if } x \geq 0 \\ -x & \text{if } x < 0 \end{cases}$$

To graph this function, first draw the line $y = -x$ and eliminate all those points on it for which x is positive. Then draw the line $y = x$ and eliminate the part for which x is negative. Now join these two parts to get the graph of $y = |x|$.

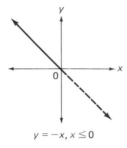

$y = -x, x \leq 0$

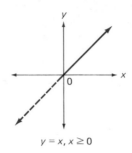

$y = x, x \geq 0$

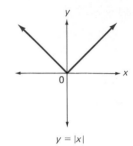

$y = |x|$

The graph of $y = |x|$ consists of two perpendicular rays intersecting at the origin. Now $y = |x|$ is not a linear function, but it is linear in parts; the two halves $y = x$, $y = -x$ are linear.

Note that the graph is symmetric about the y-axis. (If the paper were folded along the y-axis, the two parts would coincide.) This symmetry can be observed by noting that the y-values for x and $-x$ are the same. That is,

$$|x| = |-x| \qquad \text{for all } x$$

EXAMPLE 1 Graph: $y = |x - 2|$.

See Exercise 29 for an alternative method to draw this graph.

Solution For $x \geq 2$, we find that $x - 2 \geq 0$, which implies that $y = |x - 2| = x - 2$. This is the ray through (and to the right of) the point $(2, 0)$, with slope 1. For $x < 2$, we get $x - 2 < 0$, which implies that $y = |x - 2| = -(x - 2) = -x + 2$. This gives the left half of the graph shown.

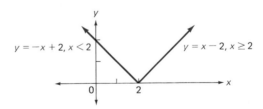

$y = -x + 2, x < 2$ $y = x - 2, x \geq 2$

EXAMPLE 2 Graph the function f defined by the following two equations.

$$y = f(x) = \begin{cases} 2x & \text{if } 0 \leq x \leq 1 \\ -x + 2 & \text{if } 1 < x \end{cases}$$

What are the domain and range of f?

Solution   The domain of f is all $x \geq 0$. From the graph we see that the range consists of all $y \leq 2$.

Note: The open dot at (1, 1) means that this point is not part of the graph; but the point (1, 2) is on the graph since $f(1) = 2 \cdot 1 = 2$.

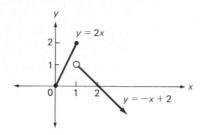

EXAMPLE 3   Graph the function f given by $y = f(x) = \dfrac{|x|}{x}$. What is the domain of f?

Solution   The domain consists of all $x \neq 0$. When $x > 0$, $|x| = x$ and

$$f(x) = \frac{|x|}{x} = \frac{x}{x} = 1$$

Thus $f(x)$ is the constant 1, for all positive x. Similarly, for $x < 0$, $|x| = -x$ and

$$f(x) = \frac{|x|}{x} = \frac{-x}{x} = -1$$

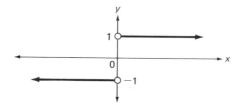

Example 3 is an illustration of a **step function**. Such a function may be described as a function whose graph consists of parts of horizontal lines. Here is another step function defined for $-2 \leq x < 4$. Note that each step is the graph of one of the six equations used to define f.

$$y = f(x) = \begin{cases} -2 & \text{if } -2 \leq x < -1 \\ -1 & \text{if } -1 \leq x < 0 \\ 0 & \text{if } 0 \leq x < 1 \\ 1 & \text{if } 1 \leq x < 2 \\ 2 & \text{if } 2 \leq x < 3 \\ 3 & \text{if } 3 \leq x < 4 \end{cases}$$

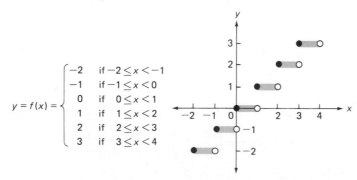

Observe that in each case, say $2 \leq x < 3$, the integer 2 at the left of the inequality is also the corresponding y-value for each x within this inequality. Putting it another way, we say that the y-value 2 is *the greatest integer less than or equal to x.*

For each number x there is an integer n such that $n \leq x < n + 1$. Therefore, the greatest integer less than or equal to x equals n. In other words, the preceding step function may be extended to a step function with domain of *all* real numbers; its graph would consist of an infinite number of steps.

We use the symbol $[x]$ to mean "greatest integer less than or equal to x." Thus

[x] is the greatest integer not exceeding x itself.

$$y = [x] = \text{greatest integer} \leq x$$

Here are a few illustrations:

$[2\frac{1}{2}] = 2$ because 2 is the greatest integer $\leq 2\frac{1}{2}$

$[0.64] = 0$ because zero is the greatest integer ≤ 0.64

$[-2.8] = -3$ because -3 is the greatest integer ≤ -2.8

$[-5] = -5$ because -5 is the greatest integer ≤ -5

TEST YOUR UNDERSTANDING

Evaluate.

1 $[12.3]$	**2** $[12.5]$	**3** $[12.9]$	**4** $[13]$
5 $[-3\frac{3}{4}]$	**6** $[-3\frac{1}{4}]$	**7** $[-3]$	**8** $[0]$
9 $[-0.25]$	**10** $[0.25]$	**11** $[-0.75]$	**12** $[0.75]$

EXERCISES 3.5

Evaluate.

1 $[99.1]$ **2** $[100.1]$

3 $[-99.1]$ **4** $[-100.1]$

5 $[-\frac{7}{2}]$ **6** $[10^3]$

7 $[\sqrt{2}]$ **8** $[\pi]$

Graph each function and state the domain and range.

9 $y = |x - 1|$ **10** $y = |x + 3|$

11 $y = |2x|$ **12** $y = |2x - 1|$

13 $y = |3 - 2x|$ **14** $y = |\frac{1}{2}x + 4|$

15 $y = \begin{cases} 3x & \text{if } -1 \leq x \leq 1 \\ -x & \text{if } 1 < x \end{cases}$

16 $y = \begin{cases} -2x + 3 & \text{if } x < 2 \\ x + 1 & \text{if } x > 2 \end{cases}$

17 $y = \begin{cases} x & \text{if } -2 < x \leq 0 \\ 2x & \text{if } 0 < x \leq 2 \\ -x + 3 & \text{if } 2 < x \leq 3 \end{cases}$

18 $y = \begin{cases} x & \text{if } 0 \leq x < 1 \\ x - 1 & \text{if } 1 \leq x < 2 \\ x - 2 & \text{if } 2 \leq x < 3 \\ x - 3 & \text{if } 3 \leq x \leq 4 \end{cases}$

Graph each step function for its given domain.

19 $y = \dfrac{x}{|x|}$; all $x \neq 0$

20 $y = \dfrac{|x - 2|}{x - 2}$; all $x \neq 2$

21 $y = \dfrac{x + 3}{|x + 3|}$; all $x \neq -3$

22 $y = \begin{cases} -1 & \text{if } -1 \leq x \leq 0 \\ 0 & \text{if } 0 < x \leq 1 \\ 1 & \text{if } 1 < x \leq 2 \\ 2 & \text{if } 2 < x \leq 3 \end{cases}$

23 $y = [x]; -3 \leq x \leq 3$

***24** $y = [2x]; 0 \leq x \leq 2$

***25** $y = 2[x]; 0 \leq x \leq 2$

***26** $y = [3x]; -1 \leq x \leq 1$

***27** $y = [x - 1]; -2 \leq x \leq 3$

***28** (a) The postage for mailing packages depends on the weight and destination. Let the rates for a certain destination be as follows:

x = weight (pounds)	y = postage (cost)
under 1	$0.80
1 or more but under 2	$0.90
2 or more but under 3	$1.00
3 or more but under 4	$1.10
4 or more but under 5	$1.20
5 or more but under 6	$1.30
6 or more but under 7	$1.40
7 or more but under 8	$1.50
8 or more but under 9	$1.60
9 or more but under 10	$1.70

This table defines y to be a function of x. If we use P (for postage) we may write $y = P(x)$, and the table gives $P(x) = 1.20$ for $4 \leq x < 5$. Graph this function on its domain $0 < x < 10$. To achieve clarity, you may want to use a larger unit along the vertical axis then on the x-axis.

(b) A formula for $P(x)$ can be given in terms of the greatest integer function. Find such a formula.

(c) Draw a graph that shows the cost of sending up to 6 ounces of first-class mail at the current postage rate. Can you think of other examples of step functions in daily life situations?

29 The graph of $y = |x - 2|$ was found in Example 1. Here is an alternative procedure. First graph $y = x - 2$ using a dashed line for the part below the x-axis. Now reflect the negative part (the dashed part) through the x-axis to get the final graph of $y = |x - 2|$.

30 Follow the procedure in Exercise 29 to graph $y = |2x + 5|$.

3.6

Any two nonparallel lines intersect in exactly one point. Our objective is to learn how to find the coordinates of this point from the equations of the lines.

Let us consider a linear system of two equations as follows:

$$(1) \quad 2x + 3y = 12$$
$$(2) \quad 3x + 2y = 12$$

We may graph this system by graphing each line on the same axes, using the x- and y-intercepts of each line. For instance, letting $x = 0$ in Equation (1) gives the y-intercept $y = 4$. Similarly, letting $y = 0$ produces the x-intercept $x = 6$. The line through $(0, 4)$ and $(6, 0)$ is the graph of Equation (1). Equation (2) may be graphed similarly. Can you find the point of intersection of the two lines?

Systems of linear equations

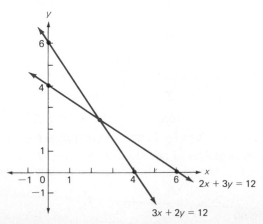

The coordinates of the point of intersection must satisfy *both* equations.

Finding the coordinates of the point of intersection of the two lines is also described as *solving the system*

$$2x + 3y = 12$$
$$3x + 2y = 12$$

Two procedures will now be described to solve such systems. The underlying idea for each of them is that the coordinates of the point of intersection must satisfy each equation. The **substitution method** will be taken up first.

We begin by letting (x, y) be the coordinates of the point of intersection of the preceding system. Then these x- and y-values fit both equations. Hence either equation may be solved for x or y and then substituted into the other equation. For example, solve the second equation for y:

$$y = -\tfrac{3}{2}x + 6$$

Substitute this expression into the first equation and solve for x.

$$2x + 3y = 12$$
$$2x + 3(-\tfrac{3}{2}x + 6) = 12$$
$$2x - \tfrac{9}{2}x + 18 = 12$$
$$-\tfrac{5}{2}x = -6$$
$$x = (-\tfrac{2}{5})(-6) = \tfrac{12}{5}$$

To find the y-value, substitute $x = \tfrac{12}{5}$ into either of the given equations. It is easiest to use the equation that was written in y-form as shown:

$$y = -\tfrac{3}{2}x + 6$$
$$y = -\tfrac{3}{2}(\tfrac{12}{5}) + 6 = \tfrac{12}{5}$$

Check the solution by substituting these values into each of the given equations for this system.

The solution is $(\tfrac{12}{5}, \tfrac{12}{5})$.

TEST YOUR UNDERSTANDING

Use the substitution method to solve each linear system.

1 $y = 3x - 1$
$\quad y = -5x + 7$

2 $y = 4x + 16$
$\quad y = -\tfrac{2}{5}x + \tfrac{14}{5}$

3 $4x - 3y = 11$
$\quad y = 6x - 13$

4 $\quad 2x + 2y = \tfrac{4}{5}$
$\quad -7x + 2y = -1$

5 $\quad x + 7y = 3$
$\quad 5x + 12y = -8$

6 $\quad 4x - 2y = 40$
$\quad -3x + 3y = 45$

Now we will solve the same system as before, this time using the **multiplication–addition (or multiplication–subtraction) method.**

$$2x + 3y = 12$$
$$3x + 2y = 12$$

The idea here is to alter the equations so that the coefficients of one of the variables are either negatives of one another or equal to each other. We may, for example, multiply the first equation by 3 and multiply the second by -2.

The resulting system looks like this:

$$6x + 9y = 36$$
$$-6x - 4y = -24$$

Keep in mind that we are looking for the pair (x, y) that fits both equations. Thus for these x- and y-values we may add equals to equals to eliminate the variable x.

$$5y = 12$$
$$y = \tfrac{12}{5}$$

As before, x is now found by substituting $y = \tfrac{12}{5}$ into one of the given equations.

If in the preceding solution the second equation is multiplied by 2 instead of -2, the system becomes

$$6x + 9y = 36$$
$$6x + 4y = 24$$

Now x can be eliminated by subtracting the equations.

As illustrated in the next example, this method can be condensed into a compact procedure.

EXAMPLE 1 Solve the system by the multiplication–addition method.

$$\tfrac{1}{3}x - \tfrac{2}{5}y = 4$$
$$7x + 3y = 27$$

Solution

$$15(\tfrac{1}{3}x - \tfrac{2}{5}y = 4) \implies 5x - 6y = 60$$
$$2(7x + 3y = 27) \implies 14x + 6y = 54$$
$$\text{Add:} \qquad 19x = 114$$
$$x = 6$$

Multiply both sides of the first equation by 15, and both sides of the second equation by 2.

Substitute to solve for y.

$$7x + 3y = 27 \implies 7(6) + 3y = 27$$
$$3y = -15$$
$$y = -5$$

The solution is $(6, -5)$.

Check: $\tfrac{1}{3}(6) - \tfrac{2}{5}(-5) = 4$; $7(6) + 3(-5) = 27$

TEST YOUR UNDERSTANDING

Use the multiplication–addition (or subtraction) method to solve each linear system.

1 $3x + 4y = 5$
$5x + 6y = 7$

2 $-8x + 5y = -19$
$4x + 2y = -4$

3 $\tfrac{1}{7}x + \tfrac{5}{2}y = 2$
$\tfrac{1}{2}x - 7y = -\tfrac{17}{4}$

4 $10x + 9y = 0$
$\tfrac{2}{3}x = -6y$

There is an important feature that all these procedures have in common. They all begin by eliminating one of the two variables. Thus you soon reach one equation in one unknown. This basic strategy of reducing the number of unknowns can be applied to "larger" linear systems (as well as to systems that are not linear). For instance, here is a system of three linear equations in three variables:

$$
\begin{array}{ll}
(1) & 2x - 5y + z = -10 \\
(2) & x + 2y + 3z = 26 \\
(3) & -3x - 4y + 2z = 5
\end{array}
$$

To solve this system we may begin by eliminating the variable x from the first two equations.

$$
\left. \begin{array}{r}
2x - 5y + z = -10 \\
-2(x + 2y + 3z = 26)
\end{array} \right\} \implies
\begin{array}{r}
2x - 5y + z = -10 \\
-2x - 4y - 6z = -52 \\
\hline
-9y - 5z = -62
\end{array}
$$
$$\text{Add:}$$

Another equation in y and z can be obtained from Equations (2) and (3) by eliminating x:

$$
\left. \begin{array}{r}
3(x + 2y + 3z = 26) \\
-3x - 4y + 2z = 5
\end{array} \right\} \implies
\begin{array}{r}
3x + 6y + 9z = 78 \\
-3x - 4y + 2z = 5 \\
\hline
2y + 11z = 83
\end{array}
$$
$$\text{Add:}$$

Now we have this system in two variables:

$$
\begin{array}{r}
9y + 5z = 62 \\
2y + 11z = 83
\end{array}
$$

You can solve this system as before to find $y = 3$ and $z = 7$. Now substitute these values into an earlier equation, say (2).

$$
\begin{array}{r}
x + 2y + 3z = 26 \\
x + 2(3) + 3(7) = 26 \\
x = -1
\end{array}
$$

The remaining equations can be used for checking:

$$
\begin{array}{ll}
(1) & 2(-1) - 5(3) + 7 = -10 \\
(3) & -3(-1) - 4(3) + 2(7) = 5
\end{array}
$$

The solution is $x = -1$, $y = 3$, $z = 7$.

There are verbal problems that can be solved by using systems of linear equations. In some cases only one equation in one variable can also be used. However, it is worthwhile to learn how to use more than one variable in order to simplify the process of translating from the verbal to the mathematical form. Unfortunately, because of the variety of problems available, as well as the numerous ways in which a problem can be stated in ordinary language, there are no fixed methods of translation that apply to all situations.

EXAMPLE 2 A field goal in basketball is worth 2 points and a free throw is worth 1 point. In a recent game the school basketball team scored 85 points. If there were twice as many field goals as free throws, how many of each were there?

The guidelines given in Section 1.3 to solve verbal problems leading to one equation in one variable can be adjusted and used here. The solution to Example 2 is based on these guidelines.

Solution

(a) Read the problem once or twice.

(b) The quantities involved are numbers of field goals and of free throws.

(c) Let x be the number of field goals and y the number of free throws. Then the points due to field goals is $2x$, and y is the number of points due to free throws.

(d) There were twice as many field goals as free throws, so

$$x = 2y$$

The total points in the game was 85; therefore,

$$2x + y = 85$$

(e) The solution for the system

$$x = 2y$$
$$2x + y = 85$$

is $(34, 17)$.

(f) *Check:* 34 field goals (at 2 points each) gives 68 points; and 17 free throws (1 point each) produces a total of $68 + 17 = 85$ points. Also, there were twice as many field goals as free throws.

Recall that the check for a verbal problem should be done by direct substitution of the answer into the original statement of the problem.

EXAMPLE 3 For her participation in a recent "walk-for-poverty," Kathi collected $2 per mile for a total of $52. She recorded that for a certain time she walked at the rate of 3 miles per hour and the rest at 4 miles per hour. Afterward she mentioned that it was too bad that she did not have the energy to reverse the rates. If she could have walked 4 miles per hour for the same time that she actually walked 3 miles per hour, and vice versa, she would have collected a total of $60. How long did her walk take?

Solution The problem asks for the total time of the walk. This time is broken into two parts: the time she walked at 3 miles per hour and the time at 4 miles per hour.

$$\text{Let} \quad x = \text{time at 3 miles per hour}$$
$$\text{and} \quad y = \text{time at 4 miles per hour}$$

We want to find $x + y$.

Since *distance = rate × time*, $3x$ is the distance at the 3-mile-per-hour rate and $4y$ is the distance at 4 miles per hour; the total distance is the sum $3x + 4y$. This total must equal 26 because she earned $52 at $2 per mile. Thus

$$3x + 4y = 26$$

The $60 she could have earned would have required walking 30 miles, and this 30 miles, she said, would have been possible by reversing the rates for the actual times that she did walk. This says that $4x + 3y = 30$. We now have the system

$$3x + 4y = 26$$
$$4x + 3y = 30$$

The common solution is (6, 2), and therefore the total time for the walk is $6 + 2$, or 8 hours.

Check: She walked $3 \times 6 = 18$ miles at 3 miles per hour, and $4 \times 2 = 8$ miles at miles per hour, for a total of 26 miles. At $2 per mile, she collected $52. Reversing the rates gives $(4 \times 6) + (3 \times 2) = 30$ miles, for which she would have earned $60.

EXERCISES 3.6

Solve each system by the substitution method.

1 $2x + y = -10$
$6x - 3y = 6$

2 $-3x + 6y = 0$
$4x + y = 9$

3 $v - w = 14$
$3v + w = 2$

4 $4x - y = 6$
$2x + 3y = 10$

5 $x + 5y = -9$
$4x - 3y = -13$

6 $s + 2t = 5$
$-3s + 10t = -7$

Solve each system by the multiplication–addition method.

7 $-3x + y = 16$
$2x - y = 10$

8 $2x + 4y = 24$
$-3x + 5y = -25$

9 $3y - 9x = 30$
$8x - 4y = 24$

10 $2u - 6v = -16$
$5u - 3v = 8$

11 $4x - 5y = 3$
$16x + 2y = 3$

12 $\frac{1}{2}x + 3y = 6$
$-x - 8y = 18$

Solve the systems given in Exercises 13–28 by using any method.

13 $x - 2y = 3$
$y - 3x = -14$

14 $2x + y = 6$
$3x - 4y = 12$

15 $-3x + 8y = 16$
$16x - 5y = 103$

16 $3x - 8y = -16$
$7x + 19y = -188$

17 $16x - 5y = 103$
$7x + 19y = -188$

18 $4x = 7y - 6$
$9y = -12x + 12$

19 $3s + t - 3 = 0$
$2s - 3t - 2 = 0$

20 $\frac{1}{2}x - \frac{1}{3}y = 2$
$\frac{3}{4}x + \frac{2}{3}y = -1$

21 $\frac{1}{4}x + \frac{1}{3}y = \frac{5}{12}$
$\frac{1}{2}x + y = 1$

22 $0.1x + 0.2y = 0.7$
$0.01x - 0.01y = 0.04$

23 $\dfrac{x}{2} + \dfrac{y}{6} = \dfrac{1}{2}$
$0.2x - 0.3y = 0.2$

24 $2(x + y) = 4 - 3y$
$\frac{1}{2}x + y = \frac{1}{2}$

25 $2(x - y - 1) = 1 - 2x$
$6(x - y) = 4 - 3(3y - x)$

26 $\dfrac{x - 2}{5} + \dfrac{y + 1}{10} = 1$
$\dfrac{x + 2}{3} - \dfrac{y + 3}{2} = 4$

27 $2x = 7$
$y = 4$

28 $2x - 10c = -y$
$7x - 2y = 2c$
(*c* is constant)

Solve each linear system.

29 $x + y + z = 2$
$x - y + 3z = 12$
$2x + 5y + 2z = -2$

30 $x + 2y + 3z = 5$
$-4x + z = 6$
$3x - y = -3$

31 $-3x + 3y + z = -10$
$4x + y + 5z = 2$
$x - 8y - 2z = 12$

32 $x + 2y + 3z = -4$
$4x + 5y + 6z = -4$
$7x - 15y - 9z = 4$

33 Solve the system

$$ax + by = c$$
$$dx + ey = f$$

for x and y, where a, b, c, d, e, and f are constants with $ae - bd \neq 0$. The solution to this exercise provides a formula for finding the solution of a system of equations where each is written in the standard form shown.

34 Why do we not allow both *a* and *b* to be zero in the linear equation $ax + by = 0$?

Some of the following exercises can be solved by using just one equation with one variable. However, in most cases it is easier to use two equations and two variables.

35 Points $(-8, -16)$, $(0, 10)$, and $(12, 14)$ are three vertices of a parallelogram. Find the coordinates of the fourth vertex if it is located in the third quadrant.

36 Find the point of intersection for the diagonals of the parallelogram in Exercise 35.

37 The total points that a basketball team scored was 96. If there were $2\frac{1}{2}$ times as many field goals as free throws, how many of each were there? (Field goals count 2 points; free throws count 1 point.)

38 During a round of golf a player scored only fours and fives per hole. If he played 18 holes and his total score was 80, how many holes did he play in four strokes and how many in five?

39 The tuition fee at a college plus the room and board comes to $5300 per year. The room and board is $100 less than half the tuition. How much is the tuition, and what does the room and board cost?

40 A college student had a work–study scholarship that paid $3.50 per hour. He also made $1 per hour babysitting. His income one week was $61 for a total of $23\frac{1}{2}$ hours of employment. How many hours did he spend on each of the two jobs?

***41** An airplane, flying with a tail wind, takes 2 hours and 40 minutes to travel 1120 miles. The plane makes the return trip against the wind in 2 hours and 48 minutes. What is the wind velocity and what is the speed of the plane in still air? (Assume that both velocities are constant; add the velocities for the downwind trip, and subtract them for the return trip.)

42 The perimeter of a rectangle is 72 inches. The length is $3\frac{1}{2}$ times as large as the width. Find the dimensions.

***43** A wholesaler has two grades of oil that ordinarily sell for 94¢ per quart and 74¢ per quart. He wants a blend of the two oils to sell at 85¢ per quart. If he antitipates selling 400 quarts of the new blend, how much of each grade should he use? (One of the equations makes use of the fact that the total income will be $400(0.85) = 340.)

44 A store paid $226.19 for a recent mailing. Some of the letters cost 20¢ postage and the rest needed 37¢ postage. How many letters at each rate were mailed if the total number sent out was 887?

45 The annual return on two investments totals $464. One investment gives 8% interest and the other $7\frac{1}{2}$%. How much money is invested at each rate if the total investment is $6000?

***46** A salesman said that it did not matter to him whether he sold one pair of shoes for $21 or two pairs for $35, because he made the same profit on each sale. How much does one pair of shoes cost the salesman, and what is the profit?

***47** To go to work a commuter first averages 36 miles per hour driving his car to the train station and then rides the train, which averages 60 miles per hour. The entire trip takes 1 hour and 22 minutes. It costs the commuter 12¢ per mile to drive the car and 6¢ per mile to ride the train. If the total cost is $5.04, find the distances traveled by car and by train.

***48** A line with equation $y = mx + k$ passes through the points $(-\frac{1}{3}, -6)$ and $(2, 1)$. Find *m* and *k* by substituting the coordinates into the equation and solving the resulting system.

***49** A line with equation $ax + by = 3$ passes through $(6, 3)$ and $(-1, -1)$. Find *a* and *b* without finding the slope.

***50** A student in a chemistry laboratory wants to form a 32-milliliter mixture of two solutions to contain 30% acid. Solution *A* contains 42% acid and solution *B* contains 18% acid. How many milliliters of each solution must be used? (*Hint:* Use the fact that the final mixture will have $0.30(32) = 9.6$ milliliters of acid.)

Can you solve the following system?

$$39x - 91y = -28$$
$$6x - 14y = 7$$

3.7

Classification of linear systems

No matter which technique you use, something unexpected happens. Let us try the substitution method. As usual, assume that there is an (x, y) that satisfies both equations. Solve the second equation for y to get

$$y = \tfrac{3}{7}x - \tfrac{1}{2}$$

Now substitute into the first equation.

$$39x - 91(\tfrac{3}{7}x - \tfrac{1}{2}) = -28$$
$$39x - 39x + \tfrac{91}{2} = -28$$
$$\tfrac{91}{2} = -28$$

*Arriving at a false result, as shown here, is not a wasted effort. As long as there are no computational errors, such a false conclusion tells us that the given system has no solution. That is, **the system has been solved by learning that it has no solution.***

Something went wrong; yet each step appears to be correct. What is the trouble?

Graphing the two lines reveals the difficulty. The lines are parallel and obviously cannot have a point in common. There is no pair (x, y) that satisfies the given system. But we started by assuming that there was a pair (x, y) that fits both equations. It is now clear that this initial assumption is false; therefore, it should not be surprising to get a false conclusion.

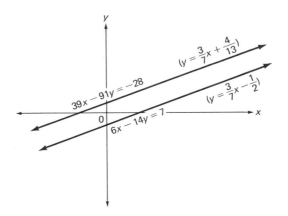

Two lines in the plane either intersect or they are parallel. In the first case the corresponding system of equations has a unique solution, and we say that such a system is **consistent**. When the lines are parallel the corresponding equations do not have a common solution, and such a system is said to be **inconsistent.**

EXAMPLE 1 Decide if each of the systems is consistent or inconsistent.

(a) $-6x + 3y = 9$
      $10x + 5y = -1$

(b) $2x - y = -3$
      $-\tfrac{1}{6}x + \tfrac{1}{12}y = \tfrac{1}{2}$

Solution **(a)** Solve the first equation for y ($y = 2x + 3$) and substitute into the second:

$$10x + 5(2x + 3) = -1$$
$$20x + 15 = -1$$

$$20x = -16$$
$$x = -\tfrac{4}{5}$$

Now solve for y, using $y = 2x + 3$:

$$y = 2(-\tfrac{4}{5}) + 3 = \tfrac{7}{5}$$

The solution is $(-\tfrac{4}{5}, \tfrac{7}{5})$, and thus system (a) is consistent.

(b) Multiply the second equation by 12. Then the system becomes

$$2x - y = -3$$
$$-2x + y = 6$$

By addition we obtain this result:

$$0 = 3$$

This false result tells us that the equations have no common solution; system (b) is inconsistent.

Consistency and inconsistency of a system can also be determined by placing both equations in slope-intercept form. If the slopes are unequal, the lines intersect; that is, there is a common solution, and the system is consistent. In case the slopes are equal and the y-intercepts are different, the lines are parallel; therefore, there is no solution, and the system is inconsistent. This approach is shown in Example 2.

EXAMPLE 2   Decide if the systems in Example 1 are consistent or inconsistent by using the slope-intercept form.

Solution   System (a) is consistent because in slope-intercept form the equations are

$$y = 2x + 3$$
$$y = -2x - \tfrac{1}{5}$$

and the slopes are unequal. For system (b),

$$y = 2x + 3$$
$$y = 2x + 6$$

The slopes are equal but not the y-intercepts; the system is inconsistent.

It might happen that a pair of equations really represents the same straight line. The following system gives two different ways of naming the same straight line. You can see this by changing either equation into the form of the other.

$$y = \tfrac{2}{3}x - 5$$
$$2x - 3y = 15$$

Such systems are said to be **dependent**. The graph for a dependent system, therefore, is always a single line.

In a dependent system each pair (x, y) that satisfies one equation must also satisfy the other. Any attempt at "solving" the system will result in some statement that is always true (an *identity*). For example:

$$3(y = \tfrac{2}{3}x - 5) \Longrightarrow 3y = 2x - 15 \Longrightarrow -2x + 3y = -15$$
$$2x - 3y = 15 \Longrightarrow 2x - 3y = 15 \Longrightarrow \underline{\;2x - 3y = \quad 15\;}$$
$$\text{Add:} \qquad\qquad\qquad\qquad\qquad 0 = \quad\; 0$$

The given system has an infinite number of solutions and it is therefore a dependent system.

TEST YOUR UNDERSTANDING

Decide whether the given systems are consistent, inconsistent, or dependent.

1 $\; x + y = 2$ **2** $\;\; 3x - y = \quad 7$ **3** $\;\; 2x - \quad 3y = \;\; 8$
$\quad\; x + y = 3$ $-9x + 3y = -21$ $-8x + 12y = 33$

4 $\; \tfrac{1}{2}x + 5y = -4$ **5** $\; -6x + 3y = \quad 9$ **6** $\; 20x + 36y = -27$
$\quad\; 7x - 3y = \;\; 17$ $10x + 5y = -1$ $\tfrac{5}{27}x + \tfrac{1}{3}y = \;\; -\tfrac{1}{4}$

See page 91 for graphing a single linear inequality in two variables.

The lines of a linear system, whether the system is consistent, inconsistent, or dependent, separate the plane into regions. Such a region will be the graph of a *system of linear inequalities*. To graph a system of linear inequalities means to locate all points (x, y) that satisfy each inequality in the system. Consider, for example, this system:

$$2x - y + 4 \leq 0$$
$$x + y - 2 \leq 0$$

It is convenient to write each in *y-form* first; that is, express y in terms of x. Verify that the following is correct.

$$y \geq \;\; 2x + 4$$
$$y \leq -x + 2$$

Can you write a system of inequalities whose graph is the unshaded region of the plane, including the boundaries?

Now graph each statement of inequality on the same coordinate system. In the graph that follows, the solution for $y \geq 2x + 4$ is shown with horizontal shading; the solution for $y \leq -x + 2$ is shown with vertical shading. The solution for the given system is the region shaded with *both* horizontal and vertical lines, including the boundaries.

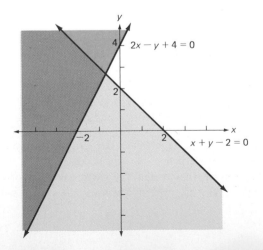

Classify each system by converting the equations into the slope-intercept form.

1 $5x - 3y = 3$
$3y + 5x = 6$

2 $4x + 6y = 30$
$\frac{2}{3}x = 5 - y$

3 $4x + 5y = 6$
$\frac{5}{2}y + 3 = -2x$

4 $\frac{1}{2}x + 3 = \frac{2}{3}y$
$2x + 3y = 15$

5 $\frac{1}{2}x - \frac{2}{3}y = 4$
$3x - 4y = 24$

6 $3x - \frac{1}{2}y = 1$
$2y - 6 = 12x$

In Exercises 7–16, decide if the given system is consistent, inconsistent, or dependent by using any one of the algebraic methods of solving a system of two linear equations. You should arrive at either a common solution (consistent), a false statement (inconsistent), or an identity (dependent).

7 $x + 2y = 3$
$6x + 5y = 4$

8 $x + 2y = 3$
$10x + 20y = 30$

9 $x + 2y = 3$
$-x - 2y = 3$

10 $8x + 4y = 12$
$y = -2x + 3$

11 $4x - 12y = 3$
$x + \frac{1}{3}y = 3$

12 $-7x + y = 2$
$28x - 4y = -2$

13 $2x + 5y = -20$
$x = -\frac{5}{2}y - 10$

14 $x - y = 3$
$-\frac{1}{3}x + \frac{1}{3}y = 1$

15 $x - 5y = 15$
$0.01x - 0.05y = 0.5$

16 $4y = 3x + 2$
$2x = 3y - 3$

Decide whether each of the systems gives parallel or perpendicular lines.

17 $2x - 3y = 4$
$6y = 4x - 30$

18 $2x - 3y - 4$
$3x + 2y = 1$

Graph each system of inequalities.

19 $y > x + 1$
$y < 1 - x$

20 $y > 2x + 2$
$y > -x$

21 $x + 2y - 2 \geq 0$
$x - 2y + 2 \geq 0$

22 $2x - y + 1 \geq 0$
$x - 2y + 2 \leq 0$

23 $y \geq -4x + 1$
$y \leq 4x + 1$

24 $y \leq -4x + 1$
$y \geq 4x + 1$

25 $x - y \leq -1$
$2x + y \geq 7$
$4x - y \leq 11$

26 $x - y \geq -1$
$2x + y \geq 7$
$4x - y \leq 11$

27 $x - y \geq -1$
$2x + y \leq 7$
$4x - y \leq 11$
$x \geq 0$
$y \geq 0$

28 Suppose that someone asked you to find the two numbers in the following puzzle:

The larger of two numbers is 16 more than twice the smaller. The difference between $\frac{1}{4}$ of the larger and $\frac{1}{2}$ the smaller is 2.

Why can you say that there is no answer possible for this puzzle?

29 How many answers are there for the following puzzle?

The difference between two numbers is 3. The larger number decreased by 1 is the same as $\frac{1}{3}$ the sum of the smaller plus twice the larger.

30 How many answers are there to the puzzle in Exercise 29 if the difference between the two numbers is 2?

*31 A bag containing a mixture of 6 oranges and 12 tangerines sold for $2.34. A smaller bag containing 2 oranges and 4 tangerines sold for 77¢. An alert shopper asked the salesclerk if it was a better buy to purchase the larger bag. The clerk was not sure, but said that it really made no difference because the price of each package was based on the same unit price for each kind of fruit. Why was the clerk wrong?

▬ 3.8

Extracting functions from geometric figures

You have recently learned how linear functions correspond to straight lines. This connection and many other interrelationships between algebra and geometry are vital to the study of mathematics. The purpose of this section is to learn how to "extract" algebraic functions from a variety of geometric

▬ The use of this symbol indicates that the material in this section is particularly useful as background for the study of calculus.

A summary of some useful
geometric formulas is given on
the back inside cover of the text.

situations, many of which make use of straight lines and linear functions. This process will prove to be of great value to you when you study applications of calculus.

EXAMPLE 1 In the figure, right triangle ABE is similar to triangle ACD; $CD = 8$ and $BC = 10$; h and x are the measures of the altitude and base of triangle ABE. Express h as a function of x.

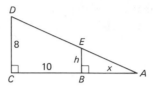

Solution Since corresponding sides of similar triangles are proportional, $\dfrac{BE}{AB} = \dfrac{CD}{AC}$. Substitute as follows:

$$\frac{h}{x} = \frac{8}{x + 10} \qquad AC = AB + BC = x + 10$$

$$h = \frac{8x}{x + 10} \qquad \text{multiply by } x$$

To emphasize that h is a function of x, use the functional notation to write the answer in this form:

$$h(x) = \frac{8x}{x + 10}$$

EXAMPLE 2 A water tank is in the shape of a right circular cone with altitude 30 feet and radius 8 feet. The tank is filled to a depth of h feet. Let x be the radius of the circle at the top of the water level. Solve for h in terms of x and use this to express the volume of water as a function of x.

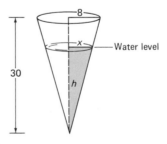

Solution The shaded right triangle is similar to the larger right triangle having base 8 and altitude 30. Therefore,

$$\frac{h}{x} = \frac{30}{8}$$

$$h = \frac{15}{4} x \qquad \text{solve for } h$$

Now substitute for h in the formula for the volume of a right circular cone.

$$V = \tfrac{1}{3}\pi r^2 h \qquad \text{volume of a right circular cone}$$

$$V(x) = \tfrac{1}{3}\pi x^2 (\tfrac{15}{4}x) \qquad \text{substitute for } h \text{ and } r$$

$$= \tfrac{5}{4}\pi x^3$$

EXAMPLE 3 A window is in the shape of a rectangle with a semicircular top as shown. The perimeter of the window is 15 feet. Use r as the radius of the semicircle and express the area of the window as a function of r.

Solution The length of the semicircle is $\tfrac{1}{2}(2\pi r) = \pi r$. Now subtract this from 15 to get

$$15 - \pi r \longleftarrow \text{total length of the three straight sides}$$

The base of the rectangle has length $2r$. Then

$$\frac{(15 - \pi r) - 2r}{2} \qquad \begin{array}{l}\text{length of each} \\ \text{vertical side}\end{array}$$

Using A for the area of the window, we have

$$A(r) = \text{area of semicircle} + \text{area of rectangle}$$

$$= \tfrac{1}{2}\pi r^2 + 2r \left(\frac{15 - \pi r - 2r}{2}\right)$$

$$= \tfrac{1}{2}\pi r^2 + 15r - \pi r^2 - 2r^2$$

$$= 15r - \tfrac{1}{2}\pi r^2 - 2r^2$$

EXAMPLE 4 A 50-inch piece of wire is to be cut into two parts AP and PB as shown. If part AP is to be used to form a square and PB is used to form a circle, express the total area enclosed by these figures as a function of x.

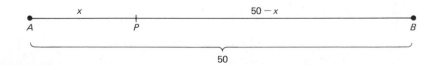

Solution Since the perimeter of the square is x, one of its sides is $\frac{x}{4}$. Then

$$(\tfrac{1}{4}x)(\tfrac{1}{4}x) = \frac{x^2}{16} \qquad \text{area of square}$$

The circumference of the circle is $50 - x$, which can be used to find the radius of the circle.

$$2\pi r = 50 - x$$

$$r = \frac{50 - x}{2\pi}$$

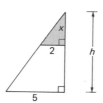

Then

$$\pi r^2 = \pi\left(\frac{50 - x}{2\pi}\right)^2 \qquad \text{area of circle}$$

$$= \frac{(50 - x)^2}{4\pi}$$

Using F to represent the sum of the areas, we have

$$F(x) = \frac{x^2}{16} + \frac{(50 - x)^2}{4\pi}$$

EXERCISES 3.8

1 In the figure, the shaded right triangle, with altitude x, is similar to the larger triangle that has altitude h. Express h as a function of x.

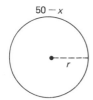

2 Use the result in Exercise 1 to express the area A of the larger triangle as a function of x.

3 In the figure, the shaded triangle is similar to triangle ABC. If $BC = 20$ and the altitude of triangle $ABC = 9$, express w as a function of the altitude h of the shaded triangle.

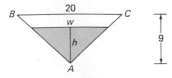

4 In Exercise 3, express the area of the shaded triangle as a function of w.

5 In the figure, s is the length of the shadow cast by a 6-foot person standing x feet from a light source that is 24 feet above the level ground. Express s as a function of x.

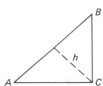

6 Triangle ABC is an isosceles right triangle with right angle at C. h is the measure of the perpendicular from C to side AB. Express the area of triangle ABC as a function of h.

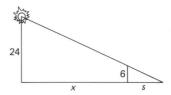

7 Express the area of rectangle $PQRS$ as a function of $x = OP$.

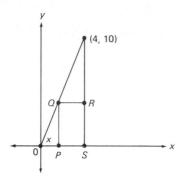

8 Express the area of triangle OPQ in Exercise 7 as a function of x.

9 A square piece of tin is 50 centimeters on a side. Congruent squares are cut from the four corners of the square so that when the sides are folded up a rectangular box (without a top) is formed. If the four congruent squares are x centimeters on a side, what is the volume of the box?

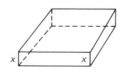

10 Replace the square piece of tin in Exercise 9 by a rectangular piece of tin with dimensions 30 centimeters by 60 centimeters and find the volume of the resulting box in terms of x.

11 An athletic field is semicircular at each end as shown. If the radius of each semicircle is r, and if the total perimeter of the field is 400 meters, express the area of the field in terms of r.

12 A closed tin can with height h and radius r has volume 5 cubic centimeters. Solve for h in terms of r, and express the surface area of the tin can as a function of r.

13 A closed rectangular shaped box is x units wide and it is twice as long. Let h be the altitude of the box. If the total surface area of the box is 120 square units, express the volume of the box as a function of x. (*Hint:* First solve for h in terms of x.)

*14 The vertices of the right triangle are $(0, y)$, $(0, 0)$, and $(x, 0)$. The hypotenuse passes through $(3, 1)$. Express the area of the triangle as a function of x.

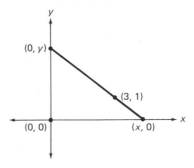

*15 A shaded rectangle is inscribed in an isosceles triangle as shown. Express the area of the rectangle as a function of x.

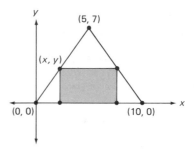

*16 The figure represents a solid with a circular base having radius 2. A plane cutting the solid perpendicular to the xy-plane and to the x-axis, between -2 and 2, forms a cross section in the shape of a square. Express the area of the cross-section in terms of the variable x. (*Hint:* The length of a side of the square is $2y$.)

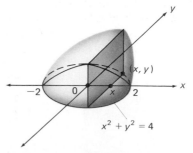

Using matrices and determinants to solve linear systems

We can solve systems of equations by considering the coefficients and constants only. Let us do so for this system:

$$x + 4y + 7z = 10$$
$$2x + 5y + 8z = 11$$
$$3x + 6y + 12z = 15$$

First we consider the rectangular array formed by the coefficients and the constants. This array is an example of a **matrix**; in this case the matrix consists of three rows and four columns.

This matrix is a short-hand way of writing the given system without use of variables.

$$
\begin{array}{c}
\text{Coefficients} \\
\begin{array}{cccc}
\text{of } x & \text{of } y & \text{of } z & \\
\downarrow & \downarrow & \downarrow &
\end{array}
\end{array}
$$

$$
\begin{array}{l}
\text{Row 1} \\
\text{Row 2} \\
\text{Row 3}
\end{array}
\begin{bmatrix}
1 & 4 & 7 & 10 \\
2 & 5 & 8 & 11 \\
3 & 6 & 12 & 15
\end{bmatrix}
$$

Next, we use the same operations we would use with the original set of three equations and attempt to derive a matrix of this form:

$$
\begin{bmatrix}
1 & 0 & 0 & a \\
0 & 1 & 0 & b \\
0 & 0 & 1 & c
\end{bmatrix}
$$

This matrix indicates the solution $x = a$, $y = b$, and $z = c$.

Applying the indicated operations shown in each step to the equations produces these corresponding linear systems.

Our goal is to determine $a, b,$ and c for this system. There is a variety of ways to proceed. Here is one sequence of steps that leads to the desired conclusion.

STEP 1. Multiply Row 1 by -2 and add it to Row 2. Then multiply Row 1 by -3 and add it to Row 3.

$$1x + 4y + 7z = 10$$
$$0x - 3y - 6z = -9$$
$$0x - 6y - 9z = -15$$

$$
\begin{bmatrix}
1 & 4 & 7 & 10 \\
0 & -3 & -6 & -9 \\
0 & -6 & -9 & -15
\end{bmatrix}
$$

STEP 2. Look at the second row of this *derived matrix*. If we multiply by $-\frac{1}{3}$ (or divide by -3) we can obtain a 1 in the second position.

$$1x + 4y + 7z = 10$$
$$0x + 1y + 2z = 3$$
$$0x - 6y - 9z = -15$$

$$
\begin{bmatrix}
1 & 4 & 7 & 10 \\
0 & 1 & 2 & 3 \\
0 & -6 & -9 & -15
\end{bmatrix}
$$

STEP 3. Now multiply the second row by -4 and add this to the first row. Then multiply the second row by 6 and add it to the third row.

$$1x + 0y - 1z = -2$$
$$0x + 1y + 2z = 3$$
$$0x + 0y + 3z = 3$$

$$
\begin{bmatrix}
1 & 0 & -1 & -2 \\
0 & 1 & 2 & 3 \\
0 & 0 & 3 & 3
\end{bmatrix}
$$

STEP 4.   Multiply the third row by $\frac{1}{3}$ (or divide by 3) to obtain 1 in the third position of that row.

$$\begin{bmatrix} 1 & 0 & -1 & -2 \\ 0 & 1 & 2 & 3 \\ 0 & 0 & 1 & 1 \end{bmatrix}$$

$1x + 0y - 1z = -2$
$0x + 1y + 2z = 3$
$0x + 0y + 1z = 1$

STEP 5.   Finally, add the third row to the first row. Then multiply the third row by -2 and add to the second row.

$$\begin{bmatrix} 1 & 0 & 0 & -1 \\ 0 & 1 & 0 & 1 \\ 0 & 0 & 1 & 1 \end{bmatrix}$$

$1x + 0y + 0z = -1$
$0x + 1y + 0z = 1$
$0x + 0y + 1z = 1$

From this last matrix we see that $x = -1$, $y = 1$, and $z = 1$. Check these results by substitution into the original system of equations.

EXAMPLE 1   Use matrices to solve:

$$2x + 4y = 6$$
$$4x + 5y = 6$$

Solution   Begin with this matrix of constants.

$$\begin{bmatrix} 2 & 4 & 6 \\ 4 & 5 & 6 \end{bmatrix}$$

Multiply Row 1 by $\frac{1}{2}$.

$$\begin{bmatrix} 1 & 2 & 3 \\ 4 & 5 & 6 \end{bmatrix}$$

Multiply the first row by -4 and add to the second row.

$$\begin{bmatrix} 1 & 2 & 3 \\ 0 & -3 & -6 \end{bmatrix}$$

Multiply the second row by $-\frac{1}{3}$.

$$\begin{bmatrix} 1 & 2 & 3 \\ 0 & 1 & 2 \end{bmatrix}$$

Multiply the second row by -2 and add to the first row.

$$\begin{bmatrix} 1 & 0 & -1 \\ 0 & 1 & 2 \end{bmatrix}$$

The last form corresponds to this system of equations.

$$1x + 0y = -1$$
$$0x + 1y = 2$$

Thus $x = -1$ and $y = 2$. Check this solution.

Frequently, shortcuts are possible as you solve a system through the use of matrices. Consider, for example, this system of equations and its corresponding matrix of constants.

$$
\begin{aligned}
x + y + z &= 1 \\
2x + y - z &= -3 \\
x - 2y + 2z &= -4
\end{aligned}
\qquad
\begin{bmatrix}
1 & 1 & 1 & 1 \\
2 & 1 & -1 & -3 \\
1 & -2 & 2 & -4
\end{bmatrix}
$$

Now multiply the first row by -2 and add it to the third row. Then add the first row to the second row.

$$
\begin{bmatrix}
1 & 1 & 1 & 1 \\
3 & 2 & 0 & -2 \\
-1 & -4 & 0 & -6
\end{bmatrix}
$$

Search for shortcuts. Whenever we get one row of the matrix to contain exactly two zeros in the first three entries, we are able to find the value of one of the three unknowns. This value can then be used to solve for the other variables.

Multiply the third row by 3 and add to the second row.

$$
\begin{bmatrix}
1 & 1 & 1 & 1 \\
0 & -10 & 0 & -20 \\
-1 & -4 & 0 & -6
\end{bmatrix}
$$

At this point, instead of proceeding with the matrix, note the second row. From this row we deduce that $-10y = -20$, or $y = 2$. Then use this result in the third row:

$$
\begin{aligned}
-x - 4y &= -6 \\
-x - 8 &= -6 \\
x &= -2
\end{aligned}
$$

Finally, in the first row, we have $x + y + z = 1$. That is, $-2 + 2 + z = 1$, so that $z = 1$. Therefore, we have the complete solution: $x = -2$, $y = 2$, and $z = 1$.

A **square matrix** has the same number of rows as columns, such as this one of two rows and two columns.

$$
\begin{bmatrix}
a_1 & b_1 \\
a_2 & b_2
\end{bmatrix}
$$

Associated with this matrix is a **second-order determinant**, a number written and defined as follows.

$$
\begin{vmatrix}
a_1 & b_1 \\
a_2 & b_2
\end{vmatrix} = a_1 b_2 - a_2 b_1
$$

Do not confuse a matrix with a determinant. A determinant is a number; a matrix is a rectangular array of numbers.

The arrows below will help you apply this definition. The arrow from top to bottom gives the product $a_1 b_2$, which is the *first* term in $a_1 b_2 - a_2 b_1$. The arrow from bottom to top gives the *second* product, $a_2 b_1$.

$$
\begin{vmatrix}
a_1 & b_1 \\
a_2 & b_2
\end{vmatrix} = a_1 b_2 - a_2 b_1
$$

EXAMPLE 2 Evaluate:

$$
\begin{vmatrix}
8 & -20 \\
4 & 10
\end{vmatrix}
$$

Solution

$$\begin{vmatrix} 8 & -20 \\ 4 & 10 \end{vmatrix} = 8(10) - (4)(-20) = 160$$

We can use determinants as a convenient way to represent the solution of a system of equations. To see this, first consider a general system of two equations with two unknowns.

$$a_1 x + b_1 y = c_1$$
$$a_2 x + b_2 y = c_2$$

Assuming that this is a consistent system, we can find the unique solution as follows.

Multiply the first equation by b_2 and the second by $-b_1$.

$$a_1 b_2 x + b_1 b_2 y = c_1 b_2$$
$$-a_2 b_1 x - b_1 b_2 y = -c_2 b_1$$

Add to eliminate y.

$$a_1 b_2 x - a_2 b_1 x = c_1 b_2 - c_2 b_1$$

Factor.

$$(a_1 b_2 - a_2 b_1)x = c_1 b_2 - c_2 b_1$$

To solve for x it must be the case that $a_1 b_2 - a_2 b_1 \neq 0$. Then

$$x = \frac{c_1 b_2 - c_2 b_1}{a_1 b_2 - a_2 b_1}$$

Similarly, multiplying the first and second equations by a_2 and $-a_1$, respectively, will produce this solution for y.

$$y = \frac{a_1 c_2 - a_2 c_1}{a_1 b_2 - a_2 b_1}$$

The numerator in the solution for x is $c_1 b_2 - c_2 b_1$. Using our new symbolism, this number is the second-order determinant:

$$\begin{vmatrix} c_1 & b_1 \\ c_2 & b_2 \end{vmatrix} = c_1 b_2 - c_2 b_1$$

Similarly, the numerator for y is

$$\begin{vmatrix} a_1 & c_1 \\ a_2 & c_2 \end{vmatrix} = a_1 c_2 - a_2 c_1$$

Both denominators are

$$\begin{vmatrix} a_1 & b_1 \\ a_2 & b_2 \end{vmatrix} = a_1 b_2 - a_2 b_1$$

In summary, we have the following, known as **Cramer's rule**, for solving a system of linear equations.

Given the consistent system

$$a_1 x + b_1 y = c_1$$
$$a_2 x + b_2 y = c_2$$

the solutions for x and y are

$$x = \frac{\begin{vmatrix} c_1 & b_1 \\ c_2 & b_2 \end{vmatrix}}{\begin{vmatrix} a_1 & b_1 \\ a_2 & b_2 \end{vmatrix}} \quad \text{and} \quad y = \frac{\begin{vmatrix} a_1 & c_1 \\ a_2 & c_2 \end{vmatrix}}{\begin{vmatrix} a_1 & b_1 \\ a_2 & b_2 \end{vmatrix}}$$

EXAMPLE 3 Solve the following system by using determinants.

$$5x - 9y = 7$$
$$-8x + 10y = 2$$

Solution

$$x = \frac{\begin{vmatrix} 7 & -9 \\ 2 & 10 \end{vmatrix}}{\begin{vmatrix} 5 & -9 \\ -8 & 10 \end{vmatrix}} = \frac{70 - (-18)}{50 - 72} = \frac{88}{-22} = -4$$

$$y = \frac{\begin{vmatrix} 5 & 7 \\ -8 & 2 \end{vmatrix}}{\begin{vmatrix} 5 & -9 \\ -8 & 10 \end{vmatrix}} = \frac{10 - (-56)}{-22} = -3$$

The general system

$$a_1 x + b_1 y = c_1$$
$$a_2 x + b_2 y = c_2$$

is either dependent or inconsistent when the determinant of the coefficients is zero, that is, when

$$\begin{vmatrix} a_1 & b_1 \\ a_2 & b_2 \end{vmatrix} = 0$$

For example, consider these two systems:

(1) $\quad 2x - 3y = 5$ $\qquad$ (2) $\quad 2x - 3y = 8$
$\quad -10x + 15y = 8$ $\qquad\qquad\quad -10x + 15y = -40$

In each case we have the following:

$$\begin{vmatrix} a_1 & b_1 \\ a_2 & b_2 \end{vmatrix} = \begin{vmatrix} 2 & -3 \\ -10 & 15 \end{vmatrix} = 0$$

Use the results of Section 3.7 to verify these results. System (1) is inconsistent and (2) is dependent.

We now define a **third-order determinant** as follows.

$$\begin{vmatrix} a_1 & b_1 & c_1 \\ a_2 & b_2 & c_2 \\ a_3 & b_3 & c_3 \end{vmatrix} = a_1 \begin{vmatrix} b_2 & c_2 \\ b_3 & c_3 \end{vmatrix} - a_2 \begin{vmatrix} b_1 & c_1 \\ b_3 & c_3 \end{vmatrix} + a_3 \begin{vmatrix} b_1 & c_1 \\ b_2 & c_2 \end{vmatrix}$$

$$= a_1(b_2 c_3 - b_3 c_2) - a_2(b_1 c_3 - b_3 c_1) + a_3(b_1 c_2 - b_2 c_1)$$

To write the determinant for a_1, cross out the row and column that contains a_1:

$$\begin{vmatrix} \cancel{a_1} & \cancel{b_1} & \cancel{c_1} \\ a_2 & b_2 & c_2 \\ a_3 & b_3 & c_3 \end{vmatrix}$$

Cross out similarly for a_2 and a_3.

Gathering terms, we have

$$a_1 b_2 c_3 + a_2 b_3 c_1 + a_3 b_1 c_2 - a_1 b_3 c_2 - a_2 b_1 c_3 - a_3 b_2 c_1$$

Show that the following alternative definition produces the same result.

$$a_1 \begin{vmatrix} b_2 & c_2 \\ b_3 & c_3 \end{vmatrix} - b_1 \begin{vmatrix} a_2 & c_2 \\ a_3 & c_3 \end{vmatrix} + c_1 \begin{vmatrix} a_2 & b_2 \\ a_3 & b_3 \end{vmatrix}$$

This notation can be used to extend Cramer's rule for the solution of three linear equations in three unknowns. Consider this general system.

$$a_1 x + b_1 y + c_1 z = d_1$$
$$a_2 x + b_2 y + c_2 z = d_2$$
$$a_3 x + b_3 y + c_3 z = d_3$$

By actually completing the tedious computations involved, it can be shown that the solution for this system is the following:

$$x = \frac{\begin{vmatrix} d_1 & b_1 & c_1 \\ d_2 & b_2 & c_2 \\ d_3 & b_3 & c_3 \end{vmatrix}}{D} \qquad y = \frac{\begin{vmatrix} a_1 & d_1 & c_1 \\ a_2 & d_2 & c_2 \\ a_3 & d_3 & c_3 \end{vmatrix}}{D} \qquad z = \frac{\begin{vmatrix} a_1 & b_1 & d_1 \\ a_2 & b_2 & d_2 \\ a_3 & b_3 & d_3 \end{vmatrix}}{D}$$

where $D = \begin{vmatrix} a_1 & b_1 & c_1 \\ a_2 & b_2 & c_2 \\ a_3 & b_3 & c_3 \end{vmatrix}$ and $D \neq 0$.

Note that the determinant D consists of the coefficients of the variables in order. Then the numerators for the solutions for x, y, and z consist of the coefficients, but in each case the constants are used to replace the coefficients of the variable under consideration. Note how this is done in the example that follows.

EXAMPLE 4 Use Cramer's rule to solve this system.

$$x + 2y + z = 3$$
$$2x - y - z = 4$$
$$-x - y + 2z = -5$$

Solution First we find D to be certain that $D \neq 0$.

$$D = \begin{vmatrix} 1 & 2 & 1 \\ 2 & -1 & -1 \\ -1 & -1 & 2 \end{vmatrix} = 1 \begin{vmatrix} -1 & -1 \\ -1 & 2 \end{vmatrix} - 2 \begin{vmatrix} 2 & 1 \\ -1 & 2 \end{vmatrix} + (-1) \begin{vmatrix} 2 & 1 \\ -1 & -1 \end{vmatrix}$$

$$= -12$$

Verify each of the following computations.

$$x = \dfrac{\begin{vmatrix} 3 & 2 & 1 \\ 4 & -1 & -1 \\ -5 & -1 & 2 \end{vmatrix}}{D} = \dfrac{-24}{-12} = 2 \qquad y = \dfrac{\begin{vmatrix} 1 & 3 & 1 \\ 2 & 4 & -1 \\ -1 & -5 & 2 \end{vmatrix}}{D} = \dfrac{-12}{-12} = 1$$

$$z = \dfrac{\begin{vmatrix} 1 & 2 & 3 \\ 2 & -1 & 4 \\ -1 & -1 & -5 \end{vmatrix}}{D} = \dfrac{12}{-12} = -1$$

Thus $x = 2$, $y = 1$, and $z = -1$.

Instead of memorizing the expansion for a third-order determinant, you can use the following scheme. Rewrite the first two columns at the right as shown. Follow the arrows pointing downward to get the three products having a plus sign, and the arrows pointing upward give the three products having a negative sign.

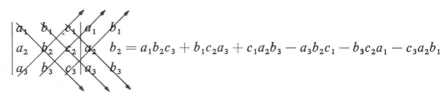

$$b_2 = a_1b_2c_3 + b_1c_2a_3 + c_1a_2b_3 - a_3b_2c_1 - b_3c_2a_1 - c_3a_2b_1$$

Use this procedure to evaluate the determinants in Example 4.

EXERCISES 3.9

Use matrices to solve each system.

1 $x + 5y = -9$
$4x - 3y = -13$

2 $4x - y = 6$
$2x + 3y = 10$

3 $3x + 2y = 18$
$6x + 5y = 45$

4 $2x + 4y = 24$
$-3x + 5y = -25$

5 $4x - 5y = -2$
$16x + 2y = 3$

6 $x = y - 7$
$3y = 2x + 16$

7 $2x = -8y + 2$
$4y = x - 1$

8 $2x + 5y = 4$
$-10x + 25y = 0$

9 $3x + 4y = 7$
$4x + 6y = 8$

10 $-3x + 4y = 2$
$2x - 3y = -3$

11 $3x = 8 - 5y$
$6x + 9y = 14$

12 $-10x + 5y = 8$
$15x - 10y = -4$

13 $x - 2y + 3z = -2$
$-4x + 10y + 2z = -2$
$3x + y + 10z = 7$

14 $2x + 4y + 8z = 14$
$4x - 2y + 2z = 6$
$-5x + 3y - z = -4$

15 $-x + 2y + 3z = 11$
$2x - 3y = -6$
$3x - 3y + 3z = 3$

16 $-2x + y + 2z = 14$
$5x + z = -10$
$x - 2y - 3z = -14$

17 $x - 2z = 5$
$3y + 4z = -2$
$-2x + 3y + 8z = 4$

18 $2x + y = 3$
$4x + 5z = 6$
$-2y + 5z = -4$

Evaluate each determinant.

19 $\begin{vmatrix} 5 & -1 \\ -3 & 4 \end{vmatrix}$

20 $\begin{vmatrix} 1 & 2 \\ 3 & 4 \end{vmatrix}$

21 $\begin{vmatrix} 17 & -3 \\ 20 & 2 \end{vmatrix}$

22 $\begin{vmatrix} -7 & 9 \\ -5 & 5 \end{vmatrix}$

23 $\begin{vmatrix} 10 & 5 \\ 6 & -3 \end{vmatrix}$

25 $\begin{vmatrix} 16 & 0 \\ -9 & 0 \end{vmatrix}$

27 $\begin{vmatrix} 2 & 2 & -1 \\ -1 & 3 & -3 \\ 1 & 2 & 3 \end{vmatrix}$

29 $\begin{vmatrix} 1 & -3 & 2 \\ -5 & 2 & 0 \\ 4 & -1 & 3 \end{vmatrix}$

31 $\begin{vmatrix} 1 & 1 & 1 \\ -1 & 1 & 1 \\ -1 & -1 & 1 \end{vmatrix}$

24 $\begin{vmatrix} 6 & 11 \\ 0 & -9 \end{vmatrix}$

26 $\begin{vmatrix} a & b \\ 3a & 3b \end{vmatrix}$

28 $\begin{vmatrix} 2 & 0 & -1 \\ 3 & -2 & 1 \\ -3 & 0 & 4 \end{vmatrix}$

30 $\begin{vmatrix} 1 & 2 & 3 \\ 4 & 5 & 6 \\ 7 & 8 & 9 \end{vmatrix}$

32 $\begin{vmatrix} 1 & 1 & 4 \\ 2 & 2 & -5 \\ 3 & 3 & 6 \end{vmatrix}$

Solve each system by using determinants.

33 $3x + 9y = 15$
$6x + 12y = 18$

35 $-4x + 10y = 8$
$11x - 9y = 15$

37 $5x + 2y = 3$
$2x + 3y = -1$

39 $x + y + z = 6$
$2x + y - z = 1$
$x - 2y + 2z = 3$

41 $2x + 3y + 2z = 0$
$x - 2y + z = 7$
$3x - 5y - 4z = -2$

34 $x - y = 7$
$-2x + 5y = -8$

36 $7x + 4y = 5$
$-x + 2y = -2$

38 $3x + 3y = 6$
$4x - 2y = -1$

40 $2x + y + 2z = 5$
$x - y - z = -7$
$3x + y - 5z = -3$

42 $3x - y - z = 8$
$x + 2y + z = 3$
$2x + 5y + 3z = 7$

43 When variables are used for some of the entries of a determinant, the determinant itself can be used to state equations. Solve for x.

$$\begin{vmatrix} x & 2 \\ 5 & 3 \end{vmatrix} = 8$$

44 Solve the given system.

$$\begin{vmatrix} x & y \\ 2 & 4 \end{vmatrix} = 5$$

$$\begin{vmatrix} 1 & y \\ -1 & x \end{vmatrix} = -\frac{1}{2}$$

*45 (a) Show that if the rows and columns of a second-order determinant are interchanged, the value of the determinant remains the same.
(b) Do the same for a third-order determinant.

*46 (a) Show that if one of the rows of $\begin{vmatrix} a_1 & b_1 \\ a_2 & b_2 \end{vmatrix}$ is a nonzero multiple of the other, then the determinant is zero.
(b) Use part (a) and Exercise 45 to demonstrate that the determinant is zero if one column is a nonzero multiple of the other.

*47 Answer parts (a) and (b) of Exercise 46 for a third-order determinant.

*48 (a) Show that if each element of a row (or column) of a second-order determinant is multiplied by the same number k, the value of the determinant is multiplied by k.
(b) Do the same for a third-order determinant.

49 Make repeated use of the result in Exercise 48 to show the following.

$$\begin{vmatrix} 27 & 3 \\ 105 & -75 \end{vmatrix} = (45) \begin{vmatrix} 9 & 1 \\ 7 & -5 \end{vmatrix}$$

or

$$\begin{vmatrix} 27 & 3 \\ 105 & -75 \end{vmatrix} = (45) \begin{vmatrix} 3 & 1 \\ 7 & -15 \end{vmatrix}$$

Then evaluate each side to check.

*50 Prove:

$$\begin{vmatrix} a_1 + t_1 & b_1 \\ a_2 + t_2 & b_2 \end{vmatrix} = \begin{vmatrix} a_1 & b_1 \\ a_2 & b_2 \end{vmatrix} + \begin{vmatrix} t_1 & b_1 \\ t_2 & b_2 \end{vmatrix}$$

*51 Prove that if to each element of a row (or column) of a second-order determinant we add k times the corresponding element of the other row (or column), then the value of the new determinant is the same as that of the original determinant.

52 (a) Evaluate $\begin{vmatrix} 3 & 5 \\ -6 & -1 \end{vmatrix}$ by definition.
(b) Evaluate the same determinant using the result of Exercise 51 by adding 2 times row one to row two.
(c) Evaluate the same determinant using the result in Exercise 51 by adding -6 times column two to column one.

Use the results of Exercises 48 and 51 to evaluate the determinants.

53 $\begin{vmatrix} 12 & -42 \\ -6 & 27 \end{vmatrix}$

54 $\begin{vmatrix} 45 & 75 \\ 40 & -25 \end{vmatrix}$

REVIEW EXERCISES FOR CHAPTER 3

The solutions to the following exercises can be found within the text of Chapter 3. Try to answer each question without referring to the text.

Section 3.1

1 State the definition of a function.

2 Explain why the equation $y = \dfrac{1}{\sqrt{x-1}}$ defines y to be a function of x.

3 Decide whether these two equations define y to be a function of x.

$$y = \begin{cases} 3x - 1 & \text{if } x \leq 1 \\ 2x + 1 & \text{if } x \geq 1 \end{cases}$$

Find the domain.

4 $y = \dfrac{2x}{x^2 - 4}$

5 $y = |x|$

6 $y = \sqrt{x}$

7 $y = 6x^4 - 3x^2 + 7x + 1$

8 $y = \sqrt{1 - x^2}$

9 $y = \dfrac{1}{\sqrt{x-1}}$

10 For $g(x) = \dfrac{1}{x}$, find: **(a)** $3g(x)$; **(b)** $g(3x)$; **(c)** $g(3) + g(x)$; **(d)** $g(3 + x)$.

11 For $g(x) = x^2$, evaluate and simplify the difference quotient $\dfrac{g(x) - g(4)}{x - 4}$.

12 For $g(x) = \dfrac{1}{x}$, evaluate and simplify the difference quotient $\dfrac{g(4 + h) - g(4)}{h}$.

Section 3.2

13 Graph the equation $y = x + 2$.

14 Find the x- and y-intercepts for $y = x + 2$.

15 Graph the linear equation $y = 2x - 1$ using the intercepts.

16 Graph $y = 2x - 1$ for $-2 \leq x \leq 1$.

17 Graph: **(a)** $y < 2x - 1$; **(b)** $y > 2x - 1$.

Section 3.3

18 State the definition of the slope of a line.

19 What is the slope of the line through the points (x_1, y_1) and (x_2, y_2)?

20 Find the slope of the line determined by the points $(-3, 4)$ and $(1, -6)$.

21 Graph the line with slope 3 that passes through the point $(-2, -2)$.

22 What is the slope of a horizontal line? Of a vertical line?

23 What is the relationship between the slopes of two perpendicular lines?

Section 3.4

24 Write the slope-intercept form of a line where m is the slope and k is the y-intercept.

25 Write the point-slope form of a line where m is the slope and (x_1, y_1) is a point on the line.

26 Graph the linear function f defined by $y = f(x) = 2x - 1$ by using the slope and y-intercept.

27 Find the equation of the line with slope $\frac{2}{3}$ passing through the point $(0, -5)$.

28 Describe the graph of a constant function.

29 Write the point-slope form of a line with $m = 3$ that passes through the point $(-1, 1)$.

30 Write the slope-intercept form of the line through the points $(6, -4)$ and $(-3, 8)$.

31 Write the equation of the line that is perpendicular to the line $5x - 2y = 2$ and that passes through the point $(-2, -6)$.

32 Find the slope and y-intercept of the line $-6x + 2y = 5$.

Section 3.5

33 Graph $y = |x - 2|$.

34 Graph the function f defined by the following two equations.

$$y = f(x) = \begin{cases} 2x & \text{if } 0 \leq x \leq 1 \\ -x + 2 & \text{if } 1 < x \end{cases}$$

35 Graph the function f given by $y = f(x) = \dfrac{|x|}{x}$. What is the domain of f?

Section 3.6

36 Solve and graph this system:

$$2x + 3y = 12$$
$$3x + 2y = 12$$

Solve each system.

37 $\frac{1}{3}x - \frac{2}{5}y = 4$
$7x + 3y = 27$

38 $2x - 5y + z = -10$
$x + 2y + 3z = 26$
$-3x - 4y + 2z = 5$

39 A field goal in basketball is worth 2 points and a free throw is worth 1 point. In a recent game the school basketball team scored 85 points. If there were twice as many field goals as free throws, how many of each were there?

Section 3.7

Classify each system as consistent, inconsistent, or dependent.

40 $39x - 91y = -28$
$6x - 14y = 7$

41 $-6x + 3y = 9$
$10x + 5y = -1$

42 $y = \frac{2}{3}x - 5$
$2x - 3y = 15$

43 Decide if the system in Exercise 41 is consistent or inconsistent by using the slope-intercept form.

44 Graph this system of inequalities:
$$2x - y + 4 \le 0$$
$$x + y - 2 \le 0$$

Section 3.8

45 A water tank is in the shape of a right circular cone with altitude 30 feet and radius 8 feet. The tank is filled to a depth of h feet. Let x be the radius of the circle at the top of the water level. Solve for h in terms of x and use this to express the volume of water as a function of x.

46 A 50-inch piece of wire is to be cut into two parts. If one part is used to form a square and the other part to form a circle, express the total areas of these figures as a function of one of the parts x.

Section 3.9

47 Use matrices to solve this system:
$$x + 4y + 7z = 10$$
$$2x + 5y + 8z = 11$$
$$3x + 6y + 12z = 15$$

48 Use determinants to solve this system:
$$5x - 9y = 7$$
$$-8x + 10y = 2$$

49 Use Cramer's rule to solve this system:
$$x + 2y + z = 3$$
$$2x - y - z = 4$$
$$-x - y + 2z = -5$$

SAMPLE TEST QUESTIONS FOR CHAPTER 3

Use these questions to test your knowledge of the basic skills and concepts of Chapter 3. Then check your answers with those given at the end of the book.

1 Find the domain of the function given by $y = \sqrt{x^2 - 1}$.

2 Let $g(x) = \frac{3}{x}$. Find **(a)** $g(2 + x)$; **(b)** $g(2) + g(x)$.

3 Let $g(x) = \frac{2}{x}$. Evaluate and simplify:
$\frac{g(3 + h) - g(3)}{h}$.

4 Find the x- and y-intercepts and use these to graph $3x - 2y = 6$.

5 Graph $y = 2 - x$ for $-1 \le x \le 2$.

6 Find the slope of the line determined by the points $(2, -3)$ and $(-1, 4)$.

7 Find the equation of the line with slope $-\frac{3}{4}$ passing through the point $(-2, 3)$.

8 Write the slope-intercept form of the line through the points $(3, -5)$ and $(-2, 4)$.

9 Find the slope and y-intercept of $-3x + 4y = 2$.

10 Write an equation of the line through the point $(2, 8)$ and perpendicular to the line $y = -\frac{2}{5}x + 3$.

11 Graph; state the domain and range for $y = 2x + 1$.

12 Graph the step function $y = \frac{|x + 1|}{x + 1}$.

Solve each system.

13 $2x - y = 7$
$-3x + 2y = -11$

14 $2x + 3y - z = -1$
$3x - y + 2z = 5$
$-3x + 4y - 2z = 1$

15 A firm mailed 40 letters at a total cost of $10.55. Some of the letters cost 20¢ postage and the rest needed 37¢ postage. How many letters were mailed at each of these rates?

In Exercises 16–18, decide whether the system is consistent, inconsistent, or dependent. If it is consistent, find the solution.

16 $4x - 5y = 12$
$-2x + \frac{5}{2}y = -6$

17 $7x + 4y = 1$
$-3x + 2y = -19$

18 $-6x + 4y = -24$
$9x - 6y = 14$

19 Graph this system of inequalities:
$$x + y - 2 \le 0$$
$$2x - y + 2 \ge 0$$

20 A square piece of tin is 40 centimeters on each side. Congruent squares of length x centimeters are cut from the four corners, and the sides are then folded up to form a rectangular box without a top. What is the volume of the box in terms of x?

21 Use matrices to solve this system:
$$x - y + 2z = 5$$
$$2x - z = -6$$
$$-x - 3y + z = -1$$

ANSWERS TO THE TEST YOUR UNDERSTANDING EXERCISES

Page 83

1 Function; all reals.

2 Function; all real $x \neq -2$.

3 Function; all reals.

4 Not a function.

5 Function; $x \geq 2$ or $x \leq -3$.

6 Not a function.

7 Function; all $x \neq 0$.

8 Function; all $x \neq -1$.

Page 94

1 $\dfrac{6-5}{4-1} = \dfrac{1}{3}$

2 $\dfrac{3-(-5)}{-3-3} = -\dfrac{8}{6} = -\dfrac{4}{3}$

3 $\dfrac{1-(-3)}{-1-(-2)} = \dfrac{4}{1} = 4$

4 $\dfrac{1-0}{0-(-1)} = \dfrac{1}{1} = 1$

5

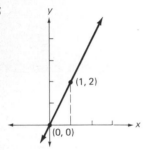

6

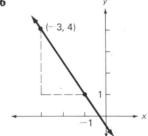

Page 100

1 $y = 2x - 2$

2 $y = -\tfrac{1}{2}x$

3 $y = \sqrt{2}x + 1$

4 $y - 6 = -3(x - 2)$

5 $y - 4 = \tfrac{1}{2}(x + 1)$

6 $y + \tfrac{2}{3} = 1(x - 5)$

7 $y = -\tfrac{1}{4}x$

8 $y + 5 = 0(x + 3)$

9 $y + 1 = -(x - 1)$

10 Exercise 8; $y = -5$ and the range is -5.

Page 106

1 12	**2** 12	**3** 12	**4** 13	**5** −4	**6** −4
7 −3	**8** 0	**9** −1	**10** 0	**11** −1	**12** 0

Page 108

1 $(1, 2)$ **2** $(-3, 4)$ **3** $(2, -1)$ **4** $(\tfrac{1}{5}, \tfrac{1}{5})$ **5** $(-4, 1)$ **6** $(35, 50)$

Page 109

1 $(-1, 2)$ **2** $(\tfrac{1}{2}, -3)$ **3** $(\tfrac{3}{2}, \tfrac{5}{7})$ **4** $(0, 0)$

Page 116

1 Inconsistent.

2 Dependent.

3 Inconsistent.

4 Consistent.

5 Consistent.

6 Dependent.

QUADRATIC FUNCTIONS AND EQUATIONS

4

4.1

Graphing quadratic functions

A function defined by a polynomial expression of degree 2 is referred to as a **quadratic function** in x. Thus the following are all examples of quadratic functions in x:

$$g(x) = 7x^2 - 4$$

$$h(x) = x^2$$

The most general form of such a quadratic function is

$$f(x) = ax^2 + bx + c$$

where a, b, and c represent constants, with $a \neq 0$. If $a = 0$, then the resulting polynomial no longer represents a quadratic function; $f(x) = bx + c$ is a linear function.

The simplest quadratic function is given by $f(x) = x^2$. The graph of this quadratic function will serve as the basis for drawing the graph of any quadratic function $f(x) = ax^2 + bx + c$. We can save some labor by noting the *symmetry* that exists. For example, note the following:

$$f(-3) = f(3) = 9$$

$$f(-1) = f(1) = 1$$

133

$$f(-\tfrac{1}{2}) = f(\tfrac{1}{2}) = \tfrac{1}{4}$$

In general, for this function,

$$f(-x) = (-x)^2 = x^2 = f(x)$$

Note: When $f(-x) = f(x)$, the graph is said to be *symmetric* with respect to the y-axis.

Greater accuracy can be obtained by using more points. But since we can never locate an infinite number of points, we must admit that there is a certain amount of faith involved in connecting the points as we did.

The accompanying table of values gives several ordered pairs of numbers that are coordinates of points on the graph of $y = x^2$. When these points are located on a rectangular system and connected by a smooth curve, the graph of $y = f(x) = x^2$ is obtained.

x	$y = x^2$
-3	9
-2	4
-1	1
0	0
1	1
2	4
3	9

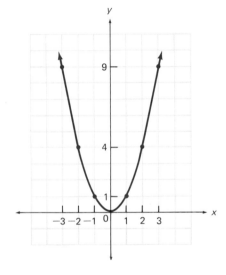

The curve is called a **parabola**, and every quadratic function $y = ax^2 + bx + c$ has such a parabola as its graph. The domain of the function is the set of all real numbers.

An important feature of such a parabola is that it is symmetric about a vertical line called its **axis of symmetry**. The graph of $y = x^2$ is symmetric with respect to the y-axis. This symmetry is due to the fact that $(-x)^2 = x^2$.

The parabola has a *turning point*, called the **vertex**, which is located at the intersection of the parabola with its axis of symmetry. For the preceding graph the coordinates of the vertex are $(0, 0)$.

From the graph you can see that, reading from left to right, the curve is "falling" down to the origin and then is "rising." These features are technically described as f **decreasing** and f **increasing**.

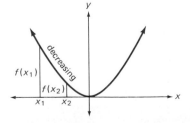

$f(x) = x^2$ is decreasing on $(-\infty, 0]$. because for *each* pair x_1, x_2 in this interval, if $x_1 < x_2$, then $f(x_1) > f(x_2)$.

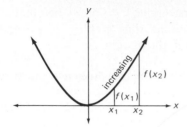

$f(x) = x^2$ is increasing in $[0, \infty)$, because for *each* pair x_1, x_2 in this interval, if $x_1 < x_2$, then $f(x_1) < f(x_2)$.

The graph of $y = -x^2$ may be obtained by multiplying each of the ordinates of $y = x^2$ by -1. This step has the effect of "flipping" the parabola $y = x^2$ downward, a *reflection* in the x-axis. Since the graph of $y = x^2$ bends "upward," we say that the curve is **concave up**. Also, since $y = -x^2$ bends "downward," we say that the curve is **concave down**.

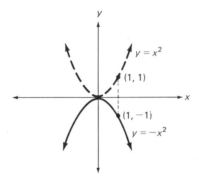

Next consider $y = 2x^2$. It is clear from this equation that the y-values can be obtained by multiplying x^2 by 2. So we may take the graph of $y = x^2$ and double or multiply (stretch) its ordinates by 2 to locate the points on the parabola $y = 2x^2$. Similarly, to obtain the graph of $y = \frac{1}{2}x^2$ we divide (shrink) the y-values of $y = x^2$ by 2.

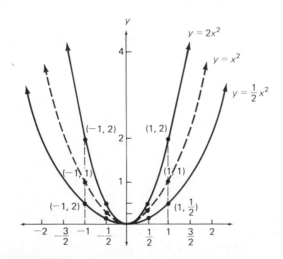

This figure compares the graphs of $y = 2x^2$ and $y = \frac{1}{2}x^2$ to the graph of $y = x^2$.

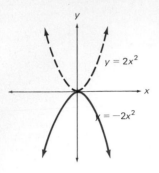

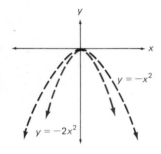

To graph $y = -2x^2$ you may first graph $y = 2x^2$ as before and then draw the reflection in the x-axis, or you may first graph $y = -x^2$ and then multiply by 2, as shown in the figures in the margin.

Now consider the quadratic function $y = g(x) = (x - 1)^2$. If we write x^2 as $(x - 0)^2$, then a useful comparison between these two functions can be made:

$$y = f(x) = (x - 0)^2$$

$$y = g(x) = (x - 1)^2$$

Just as $x = 0$ is the axis of symmetry for the graph of f, so $x = 1$ is the axis of symmetry for g. Similarly, the parabola $y = (x + 1)^2 = [x - (-1)]^2$ has $x = -1$ as an axis of symmetry.

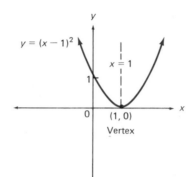

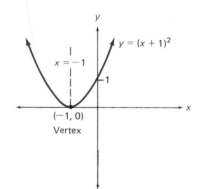

Both of these parabolas are congruent to the basic parabola $y = x^2$. Each may be graphed by *translating* (shifting) the parabola $y = x^2$ by 1 unit, to the right for $y = (x - 1)^2$ and to the left for $y = (x + 1)^2$.

TEST YOUR UNDERSTANDING

Match each graph with one of the given quadratic equations.

1

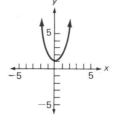

2

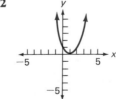

(a) $y = x^2 - 1$
(b) $y = x^2 + 1$
(c) $y = (x - 1)^2$
(d) $y = (x + 1)^2$
(e) $y = -x^2 + 1$
(f) $y = -(x + 1)^2$

3

4

5

6

Let us now put several ideas together and draw the graph of this function:

$$y = f(x) = (x + 2)^2 - 2$$

An effective way to do this is to begin with the graph of $y = x^2$, shift the graph 2 units to the left for $y = (x + 2)^2$, and then 2 units down for the graph of $f(x) = (x + 2)^2 - 2$.

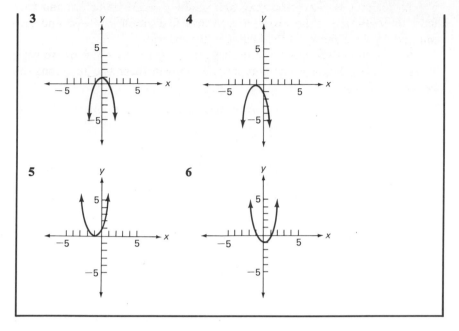

$y = x^2$

$y = (x + 2)^2$

$y = (x + 2)^2 - 2$

Note that the graph of $y = (x + 2)^2 - 2$ is congruent to the graph of $y = x^2$. The vertex of the curve is at $(-2, -2)$, and the axis of symmetry is the line $x = -2$. The minimum value of the function, -2, occurs at the vertex. Also observe that the domain consists of all numbers x, and the range consists of all numbers $y \geq -2$.

We may generalize our results thus far as follows:

> The graph of $y = a(x - h)^2 + k$ is congruent to the graph of $y = ax^2$, but is shifted h units horizontally, and k units vertically.
>
> The horizontal shift is to the right if $h > 0$, and to the left if $h < 0$.
>
> The vertical shift is upward if $k > 0$, and downward if $k < 0$.
>
> The vertex is at (h, k) and the axis of symmetry is the line $x = h$.
>
> If $a < 0$, the parabola opens downward, and k is the maximum value.
>
> If $a > 0$, the parabola opens upward, and k is the minimum value.

EXAMPLE 1 Graph the parabola $y = -2(x - 3)^2 + 4$.

Solution The graph will be a parabola congruent to $y = -2x^2$, with vertex at $(3, 4)$ and with $x = 3$ as axis of symmetry. A brief table of values, together with the graph, is shown.

The function is increasing on $(-\infty, 3]$, decreasing on $[3, \infty)$, and the curve is concave down.

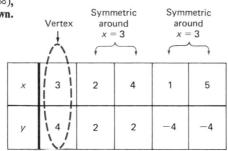

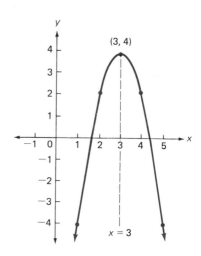

We can extend these ideas to statements of inequality as well. The graph of $y \geq x^2$ is shown below. It consists of all the points where $y = x^2$, as well as the points above the curve where $y > x^2$. (The unshaded region of the plane represents the graph of $y < x^2$.)

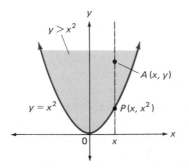

Point $A(x, y)$ is directly above point $P(x, x^2)$ for the same x. So the y-value of A satisfies $y > x^2$.

Draw each set of graphs on the same axes.

1 (a) $y = x^2$ **(b)** $y = (x - 1)^2$
  (c) $y = (x - 1)^2 + 3$

2 (a) $y = x^2$ **(b)** $y = (x + 1)^2$
  (c) $y = (x + 1)^2 - 3$

3 (a) $y = -x^2$ **(b)** $y = -(x - 1)^2$
  (c) $y = -(x - 1)^2 + 3$

4 (a) $y = -x^2$ **(b)** $y = -(x + 1)^2$
  (c) $y = -(x + 1)^2 - 3$

5 (a) $y = x^2$ **(b)** $y = 2x^2$
  (c) $y = 3x^2$

6 (a) $y = -x^2$ **(b)** $y = -\frac{1}{2}x^2$
  (c) $y = -\frac{1}{2}x^2 + 1$

Draw the graph of each function.

7 $y = x^2 + 3$ **8** $y = (x + 3)^2$

9 $y = -x^2 + 3$ **10** $y = -(x + 3)^2$

11 $y = 3x^2$ **12** $y = 3x^2 + 1$

13 $y = \frac{1}{4}x^2$ **14** $y = \frac{1}{4}x^2 - 1$

15 $y = \frac{1}{4}x^2 + 1$ **16** $y = -2x^2$

17 $y = -2x^2 + 2$ **18** $y = -2x^2 - 2$

Graph each of the following functions. Where is the function increasing and decreasing? Discuss concavity.

19 $f(x) = (x - 1)^2 + 2$

20 $f(x) = (x + 1)^2 - 2$

21 $f(x) = -(x + 1)^2 + 2$

22 $f(x) = -(x + 1)^2 - 2$

23 $y = f(x) = 2(x - 3)^2 - 1$

24 $y = f(x) = 2(x + \frac{5}{4})^2 + \frac{5}{4}$

For Exercises 25–30, state (a) the coordinates of the vertex, (b) the equation of the axis of symmetry, (c) the domain, and (d) the range.

25 $y = (x - 3)^2 + 5$ **26** $y = (x + 3)^2 - 5$

27 $y = -(x - 3)^2 + 5$ **28** $y = -(x + 3)^2 - 5$

29 $y = 2(x + 1)^2 - 3$ **30** $y = \frac{1}{2}(x - 4)^2 + 1$

31 Graph the function f where
$$f(x) = \begin{cases} x^2 & \text{if } -2 \le x \le 1 \\ x & \text{if } 1 < x \le 3 \end{cases}$$

*32 Graph f where
$$f(x) = \begin{cases} x^2 - 9 & \text{if } -2 \le x < 4 \\ -3x + 15 & \text{if } 4 \le x < 6 \\ 3 & \text{if } x = 6 \end{cases}$$

33 Graph $x = y^2$. Why is y not a function of x?

34 Compare the graphs of $y = x^2$ and $y = |x|$. In what ways are they alike?

*35 What is the relationship between the graph of $y = x^2 - 4$ on a plane and of $x^2 - 4 > 0$ on a line?

*36 Repeat Exercise 35 for $y = x^2 - 9$ and for $x^2 - 9 < 0$.

*37 The graph of $y = ax^2$ passes through the point $(1, -2)$. Find a.

*38 The graph of $y = ax^2 + c$ has its vertex at $(0, 4)$ and passes through the point $(3, -5)$. Find the values for a and c.

*39 Find the value for k so that the graph of $y = (x - 2)^2 + k$ will pass through the point $(5, 12)$.

*40 Find the value for h so that the graph of $y = (x - h)^2 + 5$ will pass through the point $(3, 6)$.

Graph each of the following inequalities.

41 $y \ge (x + 2)^2$ **42** $y \le (x + 2)^2$

43 $y \le -x^2$ **44** $y \le -(x + 2)^2$

45 $y \ge x^2 - 4$ **46** $y \ge -x^2 + 4$

4.2

Completing the square

When a quadratic function is given in the form $f(x) = ax^2 + bx + c$, the properties of the graph are not evident. However, if this function is converted to the standard form $f(x) = a(x - h)^2 + k$, then the methods of Section 4.1 can be used to sketch the parabola. Our objective here is to learn how to make this algebraic conversion.

Let us begin with the quadratic function given by $y = x^2 + 4x + 3$. First rewrite the equation in this way:

$$y = (x^2 + 4x + \underline{?}) + 3$$

Note that if the question mark is replaced by 4, then we will have a perfect square within the parentheses. However, since this changes the given equation, we must also subtract 4. The completed work looks like this:

$$y = x^2 + 4x + 3$$
$$= (x^2 + 4x + 4) + 3 - 4$$
$$= (x + 2)^2 - 1$$

From this last form you should recognize the graph to be a parabola with vertex at $(-2, -1)$, and $x = -2$ as axis of symmetry.

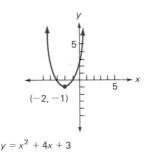

$$y = x^2 + 4x + 3$$

The technique that we have just used is called **completing the square**. Study these illustrations of perfect squares that have been completed. Note that in each case the coefficient of the x^2-term is 1.

The process of completing the square makes use of one of these two identities:

$(x + h)^2 = x^2 + 2hx + h^2$

$(x - h)^2 = x^2 - 2hx + h^2$

In the trinomials, h^2 is the square of one-half the coefficient of the x-term (without regard to sign). That is, the third term $= [\frac{1}{2}(2h)]^2 = h^2$.

$$x^2 + 8x + \underline{?} \longrightarrow x^2 + 8x + \underline{16} = (x + 4)^2$$
$$\frac{1}{2} \cdot 8 = 4$$
$$4^2 = 16$$

$$x^2 - 3x + \underline{?} \longrightarrow x^2 - 3x + \frac{9}{4} = \left(x - \frac{3}{2}\right)^2$$
$$\frac{1}{2}(-3) = -\frac{3}{2}$$
$$\left(-\frac{3}{2}\right)^2 = \frac{9}{4}$$

$$x^2 + \frac{b}{a}x + \underline{?} \longrightarrow x^2 + \frac{b}{a}x + \frac{b^2}{4a^2} = \left(x + \frac{b}{2a}\right)^2$$
$$\frac{1}{2}\left(\frac{b}{a}\right) = \frac{b}{2a}$$
$$\left(\frac{b}{2a}\right)^2 = \frac{b^2}{4a^2}$$

The process of completing the square can be extended to the case where the coefficient of x^2 is a number different than 1. Consider the equation $y = 2x^2 - 12x + 11$. The first step is to factor the coefficient of x^2 from the first two terms only.

$$y = 2x^2 - 12x + 11$$
$$= 2(x^2 - 6x + \underline{\ ?\ }) + 11$$

Next, add 9 within the parentheses to form the square $x^2 - 6x + 9 = (x - 3)^2$. However, because of the coefficient in front of the parentheses, we are really adding $2 \times 9 = 18$; thus 18 must also be subtracted.

$$y = 2(x^2 - 6x + 9) + 11 - 18$$
$$= 2(x - 3)^2 - 7$$

This is a parabola with vertex at $(3, -7)$.

EXAMPLE 1   Convert $-\frac{1}{3}x^2 - 2x + 1$ into the form $a(x - h)^2 + k$.

Solution   First factor $-\frac{1}{3}$ from the first two terms only.

$$-\frac{1}{3}x^2 - 2x + 1 = -\frac{1}{3}(x^2 + 6x) + 1$$

Example 1 illustrates the procedure for completing the square when the coefficient of x^2 is a negative number or a fraction.

Next add 9 inside the parentheses to form the perfect square $x^2 + 6x + 9 = (x + 3)^2$. Because of the coefficient in front of the parentheses, however, we will really be adding $-\frac{1}{3}(9) = -3$. Thus 3 must also be added outside the parentheses.

$$-\frac{1}{3}x^2 - 2x + 1 = -\frac{1}{3}(x^2 + 6x + 9) + 1 + 3$$
$$= -\frac{1}{3}(x + 3)^2 + 4$$

To match the general form $a(x - h)^2 + k$, the answer may be written as

$$-\frac{1}{3}[x - (-3)]^2 + 4$$

The graph of the function $y = -\frac{1}{3}x^2 - 2x + 1$ is a parabola with vertex at $(-3, 4)$ and with $x = -3$ as axis of symmetry.

TEST YOUR UNDERSTANDING

Complete so as to express y as a perfect square trinomial.

1 $y = x^2 + 8x + \underline{\ \ }$ 2 $y = x^2 + 10x + \underline{\ \ }$
3 $y = x^2 - 6x + \underline{\ \ }$ 4 $y = x^2 - 12x + \underline{\ \ }$
5 $y = x^2 + 3x + \underline{\ \ }$ 6 $y = x^2 - 5x + \underline{\ \ }$

Write in standard form: $y = a(x - h)^2 + k$.

7 $y = x^2 + 4x - 3$ 8 $y = x^2 - 6x + 7$
9 $y = x^2 - 2x + 9$ 10 $y = 2x^2 + 8x - 1$
11 $y = -x^2 + x - 2$ 12 $y = \frac{1}{2}x^2 - 3x + 2$

We have seen that any quadratic expression $ax^2 + bx + c$ may be written in the form $a(x - h)^2 + k$. From this form we can identify the vertex, the axis of symmetry, and other information to help us graph the parabola, as illustrated in the next example.

EXAMPLE 2 Write $y = 3x^2 - 4x - 2$ in the form $y = a(x - h)^2 + k$. Find the vertex, axis of symmetry, and graph. On which interval is the function increasing or decreasing? What is the concavity?

Solution First complete the square.

Note: Since the original equation is in the form $y = ax^2 + bx + c$, it is very easy to find the y-intercept by letting $x = 0$. This gives the point $(0, -2)$. Since this point is $\frac{2}{3}$ unit to the left of the axis of symmetry $x = \frac{2}{3}$, we quickly find the *symmetric point* $(\frac{4}{3}, -2)$. Can you locate the x-intercepts?

$$y = 3x^2 - 4x - 2$$
$$= 3(x^2 - \tfrac{4}{3}x) - 2$$
$$= 3(x^2 - \tfrac{4}{3}x + \tfrac{4}{9}) - 2 - \tfrac{4}{3}$$
$$= 3(x - \tfrac{2}{3})^2 - \tfrac{10}{3}$$

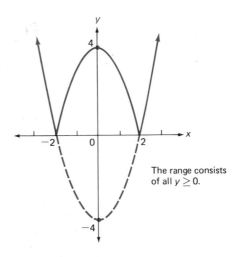

Vertex: $(\frac{2}{3}, -\frac{10}{3})$
Axis of symmetry: $x = \frac{2}{3}$

The function is decreasing on $(-\infty, \frac{2}{3}]$ and increasing on $[\frac{2}{3}, \infty)$, and the curve is concave up.

EXAMPLE 3 Graph the function $y = f(x) = |x^2 - 4|$. Find the range.

Solution First graph the parabola $y = x^2 - 4$. Then take the part of this curve that is below the x-axis (these are the points for which $x^2 - 4$ is negative) and reflect it through the x-axis.

The curve is decreasing on $(-\infty, -2]$ and on $[0, 2]$. It is increasing on $[-2, 0]$ and on $[2, \infty)$. The curve is concave up on $(-\infty, -2]$ and on $[2, \infty)$, and concave down on $[-2, 2]$.

The range consists of all $y \geq 0$.

EXAMPLE 4 State the conditions on the values a and k so that the parabola $y = a(x - h)^2 + k$ opens downward and intersects the x-axis in two points. What are the domain and range of this function?

Solution In order for the parabola to open downward we must have $a < 0$. If $k > 0$, the parabola will intersect the x-axis in two distinct points. The domain is the set of all real numbers and the range consists of $y \leq k$.

Write in standard form: $a(x - h)^2 + k$.

1 $x^2 + 2x - 5$ 2 $x^2 - 2x + 5$

3 $-x^2 - 6x + 2$ 4 $x^2 - 3x + 4$

5 $-x^2 + 3x - 4$ 6 $x^2 - 5x - 2$

7 $x^2 + 5x - 2$ 8 $2x^2 - 4x + 3$

9 $2x^2 + 4x - 3$ 10 $5 - 6x + 3x^2$

11 $-5 + 6x + 3x^2$ 12 $-3x^2 - 6x + 5$

13 $x^2 - \frac{1}{2}x + 1$ 14 $-x^2 - \frac{1}{2}x + 1$

15 $\frac{3}{4}x^2 - x - \frac{1}{3}$ 16 $-\frac{3}{4}x^2 + x - \frac{1}{3}$

17 $-5x^2 - 2x + \frac{4}{5}$ *18 $ax^2 + bx + c$

*19 $(x + 1)^2 - 3(x + 1) - \frac{3}{4}$

*20 $ax^2 - 2ahx + ah^2 + k$

*21 Compare Exercises 18 and 20 and express h and k in terms of a, b, and c.

Write each of the following in standard form. Identify the coordinates of the vertex, the equation of the axis of symmetry, the y-intercept, and check by graphing.

22 $y = x^2 + 2x - 1$ 23 $y = x^2 - 4x + 7$

24 $y = -x^2 + 4x - 1$ 25 $y = x^2 - 6x + 5$

26 $y = 3x^2 + 6x - 3$ 27 $y = 2x^2 - 4x - 4$

28 By Exercise 21, $h = -\dfrac{b}{2a}$ is the first coordinate of the vertex of the parabola $y = ax^2 + bx + c$. Show that $(2h, c)$ is on the parabola and explain why this point is the reflection of $(0, c)$ through the axis of symmetry $x = h$.

In Exercises 29–34, graph the indicated parabola using the three points shown. (Note: $y = ax^2 + bx + c = a(x - h)^2 + k$.)

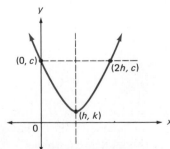

(0, c) ← coordinates of y-intercept

(h, k) ← vertex

($2h$, c) ← reflection of (0, c) through axis of symmetry $x = h$

29 $y = x^2 - 3x + \frac{9}{4}$ 30 $y = -x^2 + 2x$

31 $y = \frac{1}{2}x^2 + \frac{5}{2}x + 5$

32 $y = 3x^2 - 12x + \frac{29}{2}$

33 $y = -2x^2 - 6x - \frac{9}{2}$

34 $y = 3x^2 + 3x + \frac{3}{4}$

35 Graph the function f where $f(x) = |9 - x^2|$.

36 Graph the function f where $f(x) = |x^2 - 1|$.

37 Graph the function f where $f(x) = |x^2 - x - 6|$.

38 Graph the function f where

$$f(x) = \begin{cases} -x^2 + 4 & \text{if } -2 \leq x < 2 \\ x^2 - 10x + 21 & \text{if } \ 2 \leq x \leq 7 \end{cases}$$

39 Graph the function f where

$$f(x) = \begin{cases} 1 & \text{if } -3 \leq x < 0 \\ x^2 - 4x + 1 & \text{if } \ \ 0 \leq x < 5 \\ -2x + 16 & \text{if } \ \ 5 \leq x < 9 \end{cases}$$

In Exercises 40–43, state the conditions on the values a and k so that the parabola $y = a(x - h)^2 + k$ *has the following properties.*

40 Concave down and has range $y \leq 0$.

41 Concave up and has vertex at $(h, 0)$.

42 Concave up and does not intersect the x-axis.

43 Concave up and has range $y \geq 2$.

*44 This exercise supports (but does not prove) the claim that only three points are needed to determine a parabola. Show that points $(-1, 3)$, $(2, 1)$, and $(4, 8)$ determine a unique parabola with equation $y = ax^2 + bx + c$ by proving that the system

$$\begin{aligned} a(-1)^2 + b(-1) + c &= 3 \\ a(2)^2 \ \ \ + b(2) \ \ \ + c &= 1 \\ a(4)^2 \ \ \ + b(4) \ \ \ + c &= 8 \end{aligned}$$

produces a unique solution for a, b, and c.

*45 Follow the procedure in Exercise 44 to find the equation of the parabola that is determined by the points $(-2, -7)$, $(1, 8)$, and $(3, -2)$.

The quadratic The graph of a quadratic function may or may not intersect the x-axis. Here
formula are some typical cases:

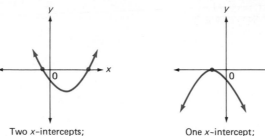

Two x-intercepts;
two solutions for
$y = ax^2 + bx + c = 0$

One x-intercept;
one solution for
$y = ax^2 + bx + c = 0$

No x-intercepts;
no solutions for
$y = ax^2 + bx + c = 0$

It is clear from these figures that if there are x-intercepts, then these values of x are the solutions to the equation $y = ax^2 + bx + c = 0$. If there are no x-intercepts, then the equation will not have any solutions. In this section we learn procedures to handle all cases.

As a first example let us find the x-intercepts of the parabola $y = f(x) = x^2 - x - 6$. This calls for those values x for which $y = 0$. That is, we need to solve the equation $y = f(x) = 0$ for x. This can be done by factoring:

$$x^2 - x - 6 = 0$$
$$(x + 2)(x - 3) = 0$$

To solve a quadratic equation by factoring, we make use of this fact: If $A \cdot B = 0$, then $A = 0$ or $B = 0$ or both $A = 0$ and $B = 0$.

Since the product of two factors is zero only when one or both of them is zero, it follows that

$$x + 2 = 0 \quad \text{or} \quad x - 3 = 0$$
$$x = -2 \quad \text{or} \quad x = 3$$

The x-intercepts are -2 and 3. The x-intercepts of the parabola are also called the *roots* of the equation $f(x) = 0$.

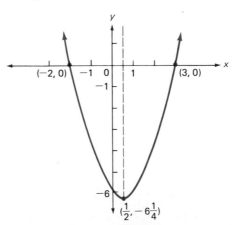

EXAMPLE 1   Find the x-intercepts of $f(x) = 25x^2 + 30x + 9$.

Solution   Let $f(x) = 0$:

$$25x^2 + 30x + 9 = 0$$
$$(5x + 3)(5x + 3) = 0$$
$$5x + 3 = 0$$
$$x = -\tfrac{3}{5}$$

Check: $25(\tfrac{9}{25}) + 30(-\tfrac{3}{5}) + 9 = 9 - 18 + 9 = 0.$

Note: Since there is only *one* answer to this quadratic equation, it follows that the parabola $y = 25x^2 + 30x + 9$ has only one x-intercept; the x-axis is *tangent* to the parabola at its vertex $(-\tfrac{3}{5}, 0)$.

The number $-\tfrac{3}{5}$ is referred to as a *double root* of $25x^2 + 30x + 9 = 0$.

When a quadratic is difficult to factor, the x-intercepts can be found, if there are any, by completing the square. The following illustration shows the procedure for solving $x^2 - 2x - 4 = 0$.

$$x^2 - 2x - 4 = 0$$
$$x^2 - 2x = 4$$
$$x^2 - 2x + 1 = 4 + 1 \qquad \text{(Complete the square by adding 1 to each side.)}$$
$$(x - 1)^2 = 5$$
$$x - 1 = \pm\sqrt{5} \qquad \text{(Take the square root of each side; if } x^2 = a,$$
$$\text{then } x = \pm a.)$$
$$x = 1 \pm \sqrt{5}$$

We use $x = 1 \pm \sqrt{5}$ as an abbreviation for $x = 1 + \sqrt{5}$ or $x = 1 - \sqrt{5}$.

EXAMPLE 2   Find the roots of $2x^2 - 9x - 18 = 0$.

Solution

Try to explain each step in this solution.

$$2x^2 - 9x - 18 = 0$$
$$2x^2 - 9x = 18$$
$$x^2 - \tfrac{9}{2}x = 9$$
$$x^2 - \tfrac{9}{2}x + \tfrac{81}{16} = 9 + \tfrac{81}{16}$$
$$(x - \tfrac{9}{4})^2 = \tfrac{225}{16}$$
$$x - \tfrac{9}{4} = \pm\tfrac{15}{4}$$
$$x = \tfrac{9}{4} \pm \tfrac{15}{4}$$
$$x = 6 \quad \text{or} \quad x = -\tfrac{3}{2}$$

As another check, solve this quadratic equation by factoring.

Check: $2(6)^2 - 9(6) - 18 = 72 - 54 - 18 = 0$
$2(-\tfrac{3}{2})^2 - 9(-\tfrac{3}{2}) - 18 = \tfrac{9}{2} + \tfrac{27}{2} - 18 = 0$

Find the x-intercepts (if any). Use the factoring method or complete the square.

1 $y = f(x) = 2x^2 + 13x - 24$ **2** $y = f(x) = 5x^2 - 3x$

3 $y = f(x) = 4x^2 - 1$ **4** $y = f(x) = -4x^2 + 4x - 1$

5 $y = f(x) = x^2 - 8$ **6** $f(x) = x^2 + 4$

7 $f(x) = x^2 + 2x - 2$ **8** $f(x) = 1 + 4x - 3x^2$

9 $f(x) = x^2 + x + 1$ **10** $f(x) = 9 - 12x + 4x^2$

Another way to solve quadratic equations is by use of a formula. When the general quadratic equation $ax^2 + bx + c = 0$ is solved for x in terms of a, b, and c, we will have a formula that applies to any specific quadratic equation written in this form.

$$ax^2 + bx + c = 0$$

Add $-c$:

$$ax^2 + bx = -c$$

Divide by a $(a \neq 0)$:

$$x^2 + \frac{b}{a}x = -\frac{c}{a}$$

Add $\left[\frac{1}{2}\left(\frac{b}{a}\right)\right]^2 = \frac{b^2}{4a^2}$:

$$x^2 + \frac{b}{a}x + \frac{b^2}{4a^2} = \frac{b^2}{4a^2} - \frac{c}{a}$$

Factor on the left and combine on the right:

$$\left(x + \frac{b}{2a}\right)^2 = \frac{b^2 - 4ac}{4a^2}$$

If $b^2 - 4ac$ is not negative, take square roots and solve for x.

Note:

$$\sqrt{\frac{b^2 - 4ac}{4a^2}} = \frac{\sqrt{b^2 - 4ac}}{\sqrt{4a^2}}$$

$$= \frac{\sqrt{b^2 - 4ac}}{\pm 2a} \begin{cases} +, \text{ if } a > 0 \\ -, \text{ if } a < 0 \end{cases}$$

$$x + \frac{b}{2a} = \pm\sqrt{\frac{b^2 - 4ac}{4a^2}}$$

$$x + \frac{b}{2a} = \pm\frac{\sqrt{b^2 - 4ac}}{2a}$$

$$x = -\frac{b}{2a} \pm \frac{\sqrt{b^2 - 4ac}}{2a}$$

Combine terms to obtain the **quadratic formula**.

QUADRATIC FORMULA

If $ax^2 + bx + c = 0$, $a \neq 0$,

then $x = \dfrac{-b \pm \sqrt{b^2 - 4ac}}{2a}$

The values $x = \dfrac{-b + \sqrt{b^2 - 4ac}}{2a}$ and $x = \dfrac{-b - \sqrt{b^2 - 4ac}}{2a}$ are the **roots** of the quadratic equation. These are also the x-intercepts of the parabola $y = ax^2 + bx + c$.

This formula now allows you to solve any quadratic equation in terms of the constants used. Let us apply it to the equation $2x^2 - 5x + 1 = 0$:

$$2x^2 - 5x + 1 = 0$$

$$a = 2$$

$$b = -5$$

$$c = 1$$

$$x = \frac{-b \pm \sqrt{b^2 - 4ac}}{2a}$$

$$= \frac{-(-5) \pm \sqrt{(-5)^2 - 4(2)(1)}}{2(2)}$$

$$= \frac{5 \pm \sqrt{17}}{4}$$

Thus

$$x = \frac{5 + \sqrt{17}}{4} \quad \text{or} \quad x = \frac{5 - \sqrt{17}}{4}$$

You can use $\sqrt{17} = 4.1$ from the square root table (Appendix Table I) or from a calculator to obtain rational approximations for the solutions.

EXAMPLE 3   Solve for x: $2x^2 = x - 1$.

Solution   First rewrite the equation in the general form $ax^2 + bx + c = 0$.

$$2x^2 - x + 1 = 0$$

Use the quadratic formula with $a = 2$, $b = -1$, and $c = 1$.

$$x = \frac{-(-1) \pm \sqrt{(-1)^2 - 4(2)(1)}}{2(2)}$$

$$= \frac{1 \pm \sqrt{-7}}{4}$$

In Chapter 11 we show that for the set of complex numbers, the solutions can be written as $x = \dfrac{1 \pm i\sqrt{7}}{4}$, where $i = \sqrt{-1}$.

In all cases, unless otherwise stated, assume that all solutions are to be in the set of real numbers. Since $\sqrt{-7}$ is not a real number, there are no real solutions to the given equation.

TEST YOUR UNDERSTANDING

Use the quadratic formula to solve for x.

1 $x^2 + 3x - 10 = 0$ 2 $x^2 - x - 12 = 0$

3 $x^2 - 9 = 0$ 4 $x^2 - 2x - 2 = 0$

5 $x^2 + 6x + 6 = 0$ 6 $x^2 + 6x + 12 = 0$

7 $2x^2 - 2x + 5 = 0$ 8 $2x^2 + x - 4 = 0$

As in Example 3, if $b^2 - 4ac < 0$, then no real square roots are possible. Geometrically, this means that the parabola $y = ax^2 + bx + c$ does not meet the x-axis; there are no real solutions for $ax^2 + bx + c = 0$.

When $b^2 - 4ac = 0$, only the solution $x = -\dfrac{b}{2a}$ is possible; the x-axis is tangent to the parabola. Finally, when $b^2 - 4ac > 0$, we have two solutions that are the x-intercepts of the parabola.

Since $b^2 - 4ac$ tells us how many (if any) solutions $ax^2 + bx + c = 0$ has, it is called the **discriminant**. The use of the discriminant is illustrated in the following table.

Quadratic function	Value of $b^2 - 4ac$	Real solutions of $y = 0$	Number of x-intercepts
$y = x^2 - x - 6$	25	two	two
$y = x^2 - 4x + 4$	0	one	one
$y = x^2 - 4x + 5$	-4	none	none

Note also that when the discriminant $b^2 - 4ac > 0$, then the two solutions of $ax^2 + bx + c = 0$ will be rational numbers if $b^2 - 4ac$ is a perfect square. In case $b^2 - 4ac$ is not a perfect square, then the roots are irrational. We summarize as follows:

USING THE DISCRIMINANT

1 If $b^2 - 4ac > 0$, then $ax^2 + bx + c = 0$ has two real solutions and the graph of $y = ax^2 + bx + c$ crosses the x-axis at two points. If the discriminant is a perfect square, these roots will be rational numbers; if not, they will be irrational.

2 If $b^2 - 4ac = 0$, the solution for $ax^2 + bx + c = 0$ is only one number (a double root), and the graph of $y = ax^2 + bx + c$ touches the x-axis at one point. (The x-axis is said to be *tangent* to the graph.)

3 If $b^2 - 4ac < 0$, $ax^2 + bx + c = 0$ has no real solutions, and the graph of $y = ax^2 + bx + c$ does not cross the x-axis.

The x-intercepts of a parabola can also be used to solve a **quadratic inequality**. Consider, for example, the inequality $x^2 - x - 6 < 0$. To solve this inequality, first examine the graph of $y = x^2 - x - 6$. This is a parabola with x-intercepts at -2 and 3, as can be seen by writing the equation in the factored form $y = (x + 2)(x - 3)$. Note that $y = x^2 - x - 6$ is below the x-axis between the x-intercepts. That is, $x^2 - x - 6 < 0$ for $-2 < x < 3$. Also, $x^2 - x - 6 > 0$ for $x < -2$ or $x > 3$.

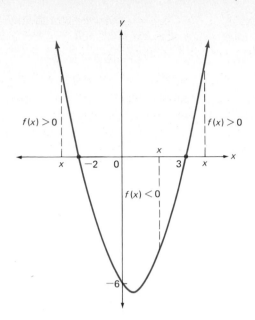

In practice this method can be used without constructing the graph. All you really need to know are the x-intercepts and whether the parabola opens up or down.

Use the quadratic formula to solve for x.

1 $x^2 - 3x - 10 = 0$ **2** $2x^2 + 3x - 2 = 0$

3 $x^2 - 6x + 9 = 0$ **4** $9 - 4x^2 = 0$

5 $3x^2 + 7x + 2 = 0$ **6** $6 - 6x + x^2 = 0$

7 $x^2 = 2x + 4$ **8** $6x - 14 = x^2$

9 $-2x^2 + 3x = -1$

Find the x-*intercepts.*

10 $y = x^2 - 3x - 4$ **11** $y = 2x^2 - 5x - 3$

12 $y = x^2 - 10x + 25$ **13** $y = x^2 - x + 3$

14 $y = 9x^2 - 4$ **15** $y = 2x^2 - 7x + 6$

16 $y = x^2 + 4x + 1$ **17** $y = -x^2 + 4x - 7$

18 $y = 3x^2 + x - 1$

Find the value of $b^2 - 4ac$. *Then state if there are* (a) *no solutions,* (b) *one solution,* (c) *two rational solutions, or* (d) *two irrational solutions.*

19 $x^2 - 8x + 16 = 0$ **20** $x^2 + 3x + 5 = 0$

21 $x^2 + 2x - 8 = 0$ **22** $4x^2 - 4x + 1 = 0$

23 $x^2 + 3x - 1 = 0$ **24** $2x + 15 = x^2$

25 $2x^2 + x = 5$ **26** $6x^2 + 7x = 3$

27 $1 = x - 2x^2$

Use the discriminant to predict how many times, if any, the parabola will cross the x-*axis. Then find* (a) *the vertex,* (b) *the* y-*intercept, and* (c) *the* x-*intercepts.*

28 $y = x^2 - 6x + 13$ **29** $y = 9x^2 - 6x + 1$

30 $y = -x^2 - 4x + 3$

Solve each quadratic inequality.

31 $x^2 - 2x - 3 < 0$ **32** $8 + 2x - x^2 < 0$

33 $x^2 + 3x - 10 \geq 0$ **34** $2x^2 + 3x - 2 \leq 0$

35 $x^2 + 6x + 9 < 0$ **36** $3 - x^2 > 0$

Graph. Show all intercepts.

37 $f(x) = (x - 3)(x + 1)$

38 $f(x) = (x - \frac{1}{2})(5 - x)$

39 $f(x) = 4 - 4x - x^2$

40 $f(x) = x^2 + 1$

41 $f(x) = 3x^2 - 4x + 1$

42 $f(x) = -x^2 + 1$

43 $f(x) = -x^2 + 2x - 4$

44 $f(x) = x^2 + 2x$

In Exercises 45–48 find the values of b *so that the* x-*axis will be tangent to the parabola.*

45 $y = x^2 + bx + 9$ **46** $y = 4x^2 + bx + 25$

47 $y = x^2 - bx + 7$ **48** $y = 9x^2 + bx + 14$

Find the values of k so that equation will have two real roots. (Hint: Let $b^2 - 4ac > 0$.)

49 $-x^2 + 4x + k = 0$ **50** $2x^2 - 3x + k = 0$

51 $kx^2 - x - 1 = 0$ **52** $kx^2 + 3x - 2 = 0$

Find the values of a so that the parabola will not intersect the x-axis.

53 $y = ax^2 - x - 1$ **54** $y = ax^2 + 3x + 7$

*55 Consider the two roots of $ax^2 + bx + c = 0$, where $b^2 - 4ac \geq 0$. Find **(a)** the sum and **(b)** the product of these roots.

In Exercises 56–61, use the results of Exercise 55 to find the sum and product of the roots of the given equation. Then verify your answers by solving for the roots and forming their sum and product.

56 $x^2 - 3x - 10 = 0$ **57** $6x^2 + 5x - 4 = 0$

58 $x^2 = 25$ **59** $3x^2 + 35 = 26x$

60 $x^2 + 2x - 5 = 0$ **61** $2x^2 + 6x - 9 = 0$

*62 Solve for x: $x^4 - 5x^2 + 4 = 0$. (*Hint:* Use $u = x^2$ and solve $u^2 - 5u + 4 = 0$.)

*63 Solve for x: $x^3 + 3x^2 - 4x - 12 = 0$. (*Hint:* Factor by grouping.)

*64 Solve for x: $a^3x^2 - 2ax - 1 = 0$ ($a > 0$).

▪ 4.4

Applications of quadratic functions

The parabola with equation

$$y = ax^2 + bx + c = a(x - h)^2 + k$$

opens upward or downward depending on the sign of a. When $a > 0$, the vertex is the lowest point on the parabola; when $a < 0$, it is the highest point. These special points will be useful in solving certain applied problems.

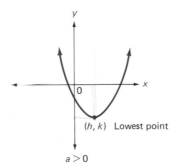

$a > 0$

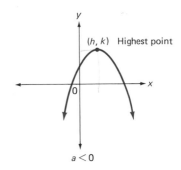

$a < 0$

The conversion to the form $y = a(x - h)^2 + k$ instantly identifies (h, k) as this extreme point. We say that the y-value k is the **minimum value** of f when $a > 0$; it is the **maximum value** of f when $a < 0$.

EXAMPLE 1   Find the maximum value or minimum value of the function $f(x) = 2(x + 3)^2 + 5$.

Solution   Since $2(x + 3)^2 + 5 = 2[x - (-3)]^2 + 5$, we note that $(-3, 5)$ is the turning point. Also since $a = 2 > 0$, the parabola opens upward and $f(-3) = 5$ is the minimum value.

EXAMPLE 2 Find the maximum value of the quadratic function $f(x) = -\frac{1}{3}x^2 + x + 2$. At which value x does f achieve this maximum?

The purpose of converting to the form $a(x - h)^2 + k$ is to find the turning point (h, k).

Solution Convert to the form $a(x - h)^2 + k$:

$$y = f(x) = -\tfrac{1}{3}(x^2 - 3x) + 2$$
$$= -\tfrac{1}{3}(x^2 - 3x + \tfrac{9}{4}) + 2 + \tfrac{3}{4}$$
$$= -\tfrac{1}{3}(x - \tfrac{3}{2})^2 + \tfrac{11}{4}$$

From this form we have $a = -\frac{1}{3}$. Since $a < 0$, $(\frac{3}{2}, \frac{11}{4})$ is the highest point of the parabola. Thus f has a maximum value of $\frac{11}{4}$ when $x = \frac{3}{2}$; $f(\frac{3}{2}) = \frac{11}{4}$ is the maximum.

TEST YOUR UNDERSTANDING

Find the maximum or minimum value of each quadratic function and state the x-value at which this occurs.

1 $f(x) = x^2 - 10x + 21$

2 $f(x) = x^2 + \frac{4}{3}x - \frac{7}{18}$

3 $f(x) = 10x^2 - 20x + \frac{21}{2}$

4 $f(x) = -8x^2 - 64x + 3$

5 $f(x) = -2x^2 - 1$

6 $f(x) = x^2 - 6x + 9$

7 $f(x) = 25x^2 + 70x + 49$

8 $f(x) = (x - 3)(x + 4)$

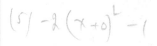

EXAMPLE 3 Suppose that 60 meters of fencing is available to enclose a rectangular garden, one side of which will be against the side of a house. What dimensions of the garden will guarantee a maximum area?

Examples 3, 4, and 5 illustrate how the concepts developed in this section can be used to solve applied problems.

Solution From the sketch you can see that the 60 meters need only be used for three sides, two of which are of the same length x.

For each x between 0 and 30, such a rectangle is possible. Here are a few.

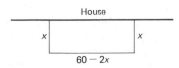

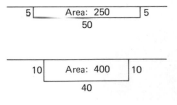

The remaining side has length $60 - 2x$, and the area A is given by

$$A(x) = x(60 - 2x)$$
$$= 60x - 2x^2$$

To "maximize" A, convert to the form $a(x - h)^2 + k$. Thus

$$A(x) = -2(x^2 - 30x)$$
$$= -2(x^2 - 30x + 225) + 450$$
$$= -2(x - 15)^2 + 450$$

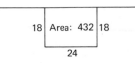

Example 3 shows how to select the rectangle of maximum area from such a vast collection of possibilities. Can you explain why the domain of $A(x)$ is $0 < x < 30$?

Therefore, the maximum area of 450 square meters is obtained when the dimensions are $x = 15$ meters by $60 - 2x = 30$ meters.

EXAMPLE 4 The sum of two numbers is 24. Find the two numbers if their product is to be a maximum.

Solution Let x represent one of the numbers. Since the sum is 24, the other number is $24 - x$. Now let p represent the product of these numbers.

$$p = x(24 - x)$$
$$= -x^2 + 24x$$
$$= -(x^2 - 24x)$$
$$= -(x^2 - 24x + 144) + 144$$
$$= -(x - 12)^2 + 144$$

Try to solve Example 4 if the product is to be a minimum.

Since $a = -1$, the product has a maximum value of 144 when $x = 12$. Hence the numbers are 12 and 12.

EXAMPLE 5 A ball is thrown straight upward from ground level with an initial velocity of 32 feet per second. The formula $s = 32t - 16t^2$ gives its height in feet, s, after t seconds. **(a)** What is the maximum height reached by the ball? **(b)** When does the ball return to the ground?

Solution **(a)** First complete the square in t.

$$s = 32t - 16t^2$$
$$= -16t^2 + 32t$$
$$= -16(t^2 - 2t)$$
$$= -16(t^2 - 2t + 1) + 16$$
$$= -16(t - 1)^2 + 16$$

You should now recognize this as describing a parabola with vertex at $(1, 16)$. Because the coefficient of t^2 is negative, the curve opens downward. The maximum height, 16 feet, is reached after 1 second.

The motion of the ball is straight up and down.

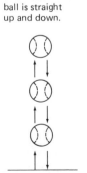

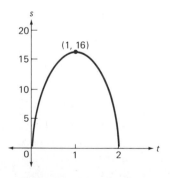

This parabolic arc is the graph of the relation between time t and distance s. It is *not* the path of the ball.

(b) The ball hits the ground when the distance $s = 0$ feet. Thus

$$s = 32t - 16t^2 = 0$$
$$16t(2 - t) = 0$$
$$t = 0 \quad \text{or} \quad t = 2$$

Since time $t = 0$ is the starting time, the ball returns to the ground 2 seconds later, when $t = 2$.

> There is no easy way to become a problem solver. You must continue to solve many problems until they no longer become an object of fear! Do not let the list of problems that follows intimidate you. Try them; you may find that you really enjoy them!

Find the coordinates of the highest or lowest point of the given quadratic and sketch the graph.

1 $y = x^2 - 4x + 7$ **2** $y = 1 - 6x - x^2$

3 $y = 1 - 4x + 4x^2$

4 $y = -2x^2 + 10x - 5$

Find the maximum or minimum value of the quadratic function and state the x-value at which this occurs.

5 $f(x) = -x^2 + 10x - 18$

6 $f(x) = x^2 + 18x + 49$

7 $f(x) = 16x^2 - 64x + 100$

8 $f(x) = -\frac{1}{2}x^2 + 3x - 6$

9 $f(x) = 49 - 28x + 4x^2$

10 $f(x) = x(x - 10)$

11 $f(x) = -x(\frac{2}{3} + x)$

12 $f(x) = (x - 4)(2x - 7)$

13 A manufacturer is in the business of producing small statues called Heros. He finds that the daily cost in dollars, C, of manufacturing n Heros is given by the formula $C = n^2 - 120n + 4200$. How many Heros should be produced per day so that the cost will be minimum? What is the minimal daily cost?

14 A company's daily profit, P, in dollars, is given by $P = -2x^2 + 120x - 800$, where x is the number of articles produced per day. Find x so that the daily profit is a maximum.

15 The sum of two numbers is 12. Find the two numbers if their product is to be a maximum. (*Hint:* Find the maximum value for $y = x(12 - x)$.)

16 The sum of two numbers is n. Find the two numbers such that their product is a maximum.

17 In Exercise 16, are there two numbers that will give a minimum product? Explain.

18 The difference of two numbers is 22. Find the

numbers if their product is to be a minimum and also find this product.

19 A homeowner has 40 feet of wire and wishes to use it to enclose a rectangular garden. What should be the dimensions of the garden so as to enclose the largest possible area?

20 Repeat Exercise 19, but this time assume that the side of the house is to be used as one boundary for the garden. Thus the wire is only needed for the other three sides.

21 The formula $h = 128t - 16t^2$ gives the distance in feet above the ground, h, reached by an object in t seconds. What is the maximum height reached by the object? How long does it take to reach this height?

22 In Exercise 21, how long does it take for the object to return to the ground?

23 In Exercise 21, after how many seconds will the object be at a height of 192 feet? (There are two possible answers.)

24 Suppose it is known that if 65 apple trees are planted in a certain orchard, the average yield per tree will be 1500 apples per year. For each additional tree planted in the same orchard, the annual yield per tree drops by 20 apples. How many trees should be planted in order to produce the maximum crop of apples per year? (*Hint:* If n trees are added to the 65 trees, then the yield per tree is $1500 - 20n$.)

25 It is estimated that 14,000 people will attend a basketball game when the admission price is $7.00. For each 25¢ added to the price, the attendance will decrease by 280. What admission price will produce the largest gate receipts? (*Hint:* If x quarters are added, the attendance will be $14,000 - 280x$.)

26 The sum of the lengths of the two perpendicular sides of a right triangle is 30 centimeters. What are their lengths if the square of the hypotenuse is a minimum?

27 Each point P on the line segment between endpoints $(0, 4)$ and $(2, 0)$ determines a rectangle with dimensions x by y as shown in the figure. Find the coordinates of P that give the rectangle of maximum area.

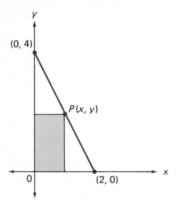

28 (a) Let s be the square of the distance from the origin to point $P(x, y)$ on the line through points $(0, 4)$ and $(2, 0)$. Find the coordinates of P such that s is a minimum value.

(b) The answer to part (a) is also the intersection of the given line with the perpendicular through the origin to this line. Using the result that perpendicular lines have slopes that are negative reciprocals, find this point by solving the appropriate linear system.

29 Find the maximum or minimum value of $y = ax^2 + bx + c$, $a \neq 0$, and state at which x-value this occurs.

From Exercise 29, we have that the vertex of the parabola with equation $y = ax^2 + bx + c$ has coordinates $\left(-\dfrac{b}{2a}, \dfrac{4ac - b^2}{4a}\right)$. Use this general result to find the coordinates of the vertex of each parabola, and decide whether $\dfrac{4ac - b^2}{4a}$ is a maximum or minimum value.

30 $y = 2x^2 - 6x + 9$

31 $y = -3x^2 + 24x - 41$

32 $y = -\frac{1}{2}x^2 - \frac{1}{3}x + 1$

33 $y - x^2 + 5x = 0$

34 $y + \frac{2}{3}x^2 = 9$

35 $y = 10x^2 + 100x + 1000$

Exercises 36–43 call for the solution of a quadratic equation in one variable.

36 The sum of two consecutive positive integers is subtracted from their product to obtain a difference of 71. What are the integers?

37 The measures of the legs of a right triangle are consecutive odd integers. The hypotenuse is $\sqrt{130}$. Find the lengths of the legs. (*Hint:* Use the Pythagorean theorem.)

38 One positive integer is 3 greater than another. The difference of their reciprocals is $\frac{1}{6}$. Find the integers.

39 The sum of a number and twice the square of that number is 3. Find all such numbers.

40 If the length of one pair of opposite sides of a square is increased by 3 centimeters, and the length of the other pair is decreased by 1 centimeter, the area of the new figure will be 7 square centimeters greater than that of the original square. What is the length of the side of the square?

41 If the length of the sides of a square are increased by 2 centimeters, the newly formed square will have an area that is 36 square centimeters greater than the original one. Find the length of a side of the original square.

42 Wendy is 5 years older than Sharon. In 5 years the product of their ages will be $1\frac{1}{2}$ times as great as the product of their present ages. How old is Sharon now? (*Hint:* Let Sharon's age be represented by x and Wendy's age by $x + 5$. Then in 5 years their ages will be $x + 5$ and $x + 10$, respectively.)

43 A square piece of tin is to be used to form a box without a top by cutting off a 2-inch square from each corner, and then folding up the sides. The volume of the box will be 128 cubic inches. Find the length of a side of the original square.

4.5

Circles and their equations

Let $A(x_1, y_1)$ and $B(x_2, y_2)$ be two points in a rectangular system. We will use the symbol AB to represent the distance between the points A and B. Then AB is given by the **distance formula**:

$$AB = \sqrt{(x_1 - x_2)^2 + (y_1 - y_2)^2}$$

You can verify this result by studying this figure:

If A and B are on the same horizontal line, then $y_1 = y_2$ and $AB = \sqrt{(x_1 - x_2)^2} = |x_1 - x_2|$ (see page 28).

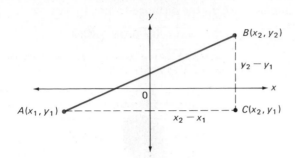

Since AB is the hypotenuse of the right triangle ABC, the Pythagorean theorem gives

$$AB^2 = AC^2 + CB^2$$

But $AC = x_2 - x_1$ and $CB = y_2 - y_1$. Thus

$$AB^2 = (x_2 - x_1)^2 + (y_2 - y_1)^2$$

Taking the positive square root gives the stated result.

Note that the diagram was set up so that $x_2 - x_1 > 0$ and $y_2 - y_1 > 0$. Other situations may have negative values, but it makes no difference because $(x_2 - x_1)^2 = (x_1 - x_2)^2$ and $(y_2 - y_1)^2 = (y_1 - y_2)^2$.

EXAMPLE 1 Find the length of the line segment determined by points $A(-2, 2)$ and $B(6, -4)$.

Solution

$$\begin{aligned}
AB &= \sqrt{(-2 - 6)^2 + [2 - (-4)]^2} \\
&= \sqrt{(-8)^2 + 6^2} \\
&= \sqrt{64 + 36} \\
&= \sqrt{100} \\
&= 10
\end{aligned}$$

The distance formula can be used to obtain the equation of a circle. *A circle consists of all points in the plane, each of which is a fixed distance r from a given point called the **center** of the circle; r is the **radius** of the circle. (r > 0).*

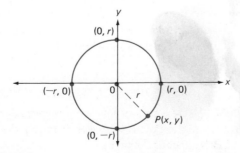

The words "if and only if" here
mean that if P is on the circle,
then $OP = r$ and if $OP = r$
then P is on the circle.

The preceding figure is a circle with center at the origin and radius r. A point will be on this circle if and only if its distance from the origin is equal to r. That is, $P(x, y)$ is on this circle if and only if $OP = r$. Since the origin has coordinates $(0, 0)$, the distance formula gives

$$r = \sqrt{(x - 0)^2 + (y - 0)^2}$$
$$= \sqrt{x^2 + y^2}$$

Squaring produces this result:

$$r^2 = x^2 + y^2$$

We conclude that $P(x, y)$ is on the circle with center O and radius r if and only if the coordinates of P satisfy the preceding equation.

A circle with center at the origin and radius r has the equation

$$x^2 + y^2 = r^2$$

EXAMPLE 2   What is the equation of the circle with center O and radius 3 ?

Solution   Using the equation $x^2 + y^2 = r^2$, we get

$$x^2 + y^2 = 3^2 = 9$$

Now consider any circle of radius r, not necessarily one with the origin as center. Let the center C have coordinates (h, k). Then, using the distance formula, a point $P(x, y)$ is on this circle if and only if

$$CP = r = \sqrt{(x - h)^2 + (y - k)^2}$$

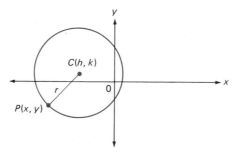

By squaring CP, we obtain the following:

STANDARD FORM FOR THE EQUATION OF A CIRCLE WITH CENTER AT (h, k)
AND RADIUS r

$$(x - h)^2 + (y - k)^2 = r^2$$

EXAMPLE 3 Find the center and radius of the circle with this equation: $(x - 2)^2 + (y + 3)^2 = 4$.

Solution Using $y + 3 = y - (-3)$, rewrite the equation in this form:
$$(x - 2)^2 + [(y - (-3)]^2 = 2^2$$
By comparing to the standard form, we find the radius $r = 2$ and the center at $(2, -3)$.

Circles are not graphs of functions. When $x = 2$ is substituted into the equation of the circle in Example 3, we get two y-values, -1 and -5. This is contrary to the definition of a function that calls for just *one* range value y for each domain value x.

Even though circles are not functions, we include them in this chapter since they tie in nicely with some of our earlier work in this chapter and will prove to be useful in later work as well. Also, their equations are quadratic in two variables.

EXAMPLE 4 Write the equation of the circle with center at $(-3, 5)$ and radius 2.

Solution Use $h = -3$, $k = 5$, and $r = 2$ in the standard form to obtain
$$[x - (-3)]^2 + (y - 5)^2 = 2^2$$
or
$$(x + 3)^2 + (y - 5)^2 = 4$$

TEST YOUR UNDERSTANDING

Find the length of the line segment determined by the two points.

1 $(4, 0); (-8, -5)$ **2** $(9, -1); (2, 3)$ **3** $(-7, -5); (3, -13)$

Find the center and radius of each circle.

4 $x^2 + y^2 = 100$ **5** $x^2 + y^2 = 10$

6 $(x - 1)^2 + (y + 1)^2 - 25$ **7** $(x + \frac{1}{2})^2 + y^2 = 256$

8 $(x + 4)^2 + (y + 4)^2 = 50$

Write the equation of the circle with the given center and radius in standard form.

9 Center at $(0, 4); r = 5$ **10** Center at $(1, -2); r = \sqrt{3}$

The equation in Example 3 can be written in another form.
$$(x - 2)^2 + (y + 3)^2 = 4$$
$$x^2 - 4x + 4 + y^2 + 6y + 9 = 4$$
$$x^2 - 4x + y^2 + 6y = -9$$

This last equation no longer looks like the equation of a circle. Starting with such an equation we can convert it back into the standard form of a circle by completing the square in both variables, if necessary. For example, let us begin with
$$x^2 - 4x + y^2 + 6y = -9$$

Note that the major reason for writing the equation of a circle in standard form is that this form enables us to identify the center and the radius of the circle. This information is sufficient to allow us to draw the circle.

Then complete the squares in x and y:

$$(x^2 - 4x + 4) + (y^2 + 6y + 9) = -9 + 4 + 9$$
$$(x - 2)^2 + (y + 3)^2 = 4$$

EXAMPLE 5 Find the center and radius of the circle with equation $9x^2 + 12x + 9y^2 = 77$.

Solution First divide by 9 so that the x^2 and y^2 terms each has a coefficient of 1.

$$x^2 + \tfrac{4}{3}x + y^2 = \tfrac{77}{9}$$

Complete the square in x; add $\tfrac{4}{9}$ to both sides of the equation.

$$(x^2 + \tfrac{4}{3}x + \tfrac{4}{9}) + y^2 = \tfrac{77}{9} + \tfrac{4}{9}$$
$$(x + \tfrac{2}{3})^2 + y^2 = 9$$

In standard form:

$$[x - (-\tfrac{2}{3})]^2 + (y - 0)^2 = 3^2$$

The center is at $(-\tfrac{2}{3}, 0)$ and $r = 3$.

TEST YOUR UNDERSTANDING

Find the center and radius of each circle.

1 $x^2 - 6x + y^2 - 10y = 2$ 2 $x^2 + y^2 + y = \tfrac{19}{4}$

3 $x^2 - x + y^2 + 2y = \tfrac{23}{4}$ 4 $16x^2 + 16y^2 - 8x + 32y = 127$

A line that is tangent to a circle touches the circle at only one point and is perpendicular to the radius drawn to the point of tangency.

When the equation of a circle is given and the coordinates of a point P on the circle are known, then the equation of the tangent line to the circle at P can be found. For example, the circle $(x + 3)^2 + (y + 1)^2 = 25$ has center $(-3, -1)$ and $r = 5$. The point $P(1, 2)$ is on this circle because its coordinates satisfy the equation of the circle.

$$(1 + 3)^2 + (2 + 1)^2 = 4^2 + 3^2 = 25$$

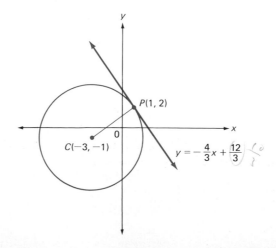

158

The slope of radius CP is $\frac{2-(-1)}{1-(-3)} = \frac{3}{4}$. Then since the tangent at P is

Recall that perpendicular lines have slopes that are negative reciprocals of one another.

perpendicular to the radius CP, its slope is the negative reciprocal of $\frac{3}{4}$, namely $-\frac{4}{3}$. Now using the point-slope form we get this equation of the tangent at P:

$$y - 2 = -\tfrac{4}{3}(x-1)$$

In slope-intercept form this becomes

$$y = -\tfrac{4}{3}x + \tfrac{10}{3}$$

CAUTION: LEARN TO AVOID MISTAKES LIKE THESE

WRONG	RIGHT
The circle $(x+3)^2 + (y-2)^2 = 7$ has center $(3, -2)$ and radius 7.	The circle has center $(-3, 2)$ and radius $\sqrt{7}$.
The equation of the circle with center $(-1, 0)$ and radius 5 has equation $x^2 + (y+1)^2 = 5$.	The circle has equation $(x+1)^2 + y^2 = 25$.

The center of a circle is the midpoint of each of its diameters. So if the endpoints of a diameter are given, the coordinates of the center can be found using the *midpoint formula* shown below. In the figure PQ is a line segment with midpoint M having coordinates (x', y'). Since x_1, x', and x_2 are on the x-axis, $x' = \frac{x_1 + x_2}{2}$. Similarly, $y' = \frac{y_1 + y_2}{2}$.

The midpoint of a segment on a number line is discussed on page 28.

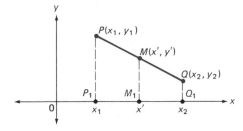

MIDPOINT FORMULA

If (x_1, x_2) and (y_1, y_2) are the endpoints of a line segment, the midpoint of the segment has coordinates

$$\left(\frac{x_1 + x_2}{2}, \; \frac{y_1 + y_2}{2} \right)$$

EXAMPLE 6 Points $P(2, 5)$ and $Q(-4, -3)$ are the endpoints of a diameter of a circle. Find the center, radius, and equation of the circle.

Solution The center is the midpoint of PQ whose coordinates (x', y') are given by

$$x' = \frac{2 + (-4)}{2} = -1, \qquad y' = \frac{5 + (-3)}{2} = 1$$

The center is located at $C(-1, 1)$. To find the radius, use the distance formula between $C(-1, 1)$ and $P(2, 5)$.

$$r = \sqrt{(-1 - 2)^2 + (1 - 5)^2} = \sqrt{25} = 5$$

The equation of the circle is

$$(x + 1)^2 + (y - 1)^2 = 25$$

EXERCISES 4.5

1 Graph these circles in the same coordinate system.
 (a) $x^2 + y^2 = 25$ (b) $x^2 + y^2 = 16$
 (c) $x^2 + y^2 = 4$ (d) $x^2 + y^2 = 2$
 (e) $x^2 + y^2 = 1$

2 Graph these circles in the same coordinate system.
 (a) $(x - 3)^2 + (y - 3)^2 = 9$
 (b) $(x + 3)^2 + (y - 3)^2 = 9$
 (c) $(x + 3)^2 + (y + 3)^2 = 9$
 (d) $(x - 3)^2 + (y + 3)^2 = 9$

Write the equations of each circle in standard form. Find the center and radius for each.

3 $x^2 - 4x + y^2 - 10y = -28$
4 $x^2 - 10x + y^2 - 14y = -25$
5 $x^2 - 8x + y^2 = -14$
6 $x^2 + y^2 + 2y = 7$
7 $x^2 - 20x + y^2 + 20y = -100$
8 $4x^2 - 4x + 4y^2 = 15$
9 $16x^2 + 24x + 16y^2 - 32y = 119$
10 $36x^2 - 48x + 36y^2 + 180y = -160$

Write the equation of each circle in standard form.

11 Center at $(2, 0)$; $r = 2$
12 Center at $(\frac{1}{2}, 1)$; $r = 10$
13 Center at $(-3, 3)$; $r = \sqrt{7}$
14 Center at $(-1, -4)$; $r = 2\sqrt{2}$
15 Draw the circle $x^2 + y^2 = 25$ and the tangent lines at the points $(3, 4)$, $(-3, 4)$, $(3, -4)$, and

$(-3, -4)$. Write the equations of these tangent lines.

16 Where are the tangents to the circle $x^2 + y^2 = 4$ whose slopes equal 0? Write their equations.

17 Write the equations of the tangents to the circle $x^2 + y^2 = 4$ that have no slope.

Draw the given circle and the tangent line at the indicated point for each of the following. Write the equation of the tangent line.

18 $x^2 + y^2 = 80$; $(-8, 4)$
19 $x^2 + y^2 = 9$; $(-2, \sqrt{5})$
20 $(x - 4)^2 + (y + 5)^2 = 45$; $(1, 1)$
21 $x^2 + 4x + y^2 - 6y = 60$; $(6, 0)$
22 $x^2 + 14x + y^2 + 18y = 39$; $(5, -4)$
23 $x^2 - 2x + y^2 - 2y = 8$; $(4, 2)$

Find the coordinates of the midpoint of a line segment with endpoints as given.

24 $P(3, 2)$ and $Q(-2, 1)$
25 $P(-2, 4)$ and $Q(3, -8)$
26 $P(-1, 0)$ and $Q(0, 5)$
27 $P(-8, 7)$ and $Q(3, -6)$
28 Points $P(3, -5)$ and $Q(-1, 3)$ are the endpoints of a diameter of a circle. Find the center, radius, and equation of the circle.

*29 Write the equation of the tangent line to the circle $x^2 + y^2 = 80$ at the point in the first quadrant where $x = 4$.

*30 Write the equation of the tangent line to the circle $x^2 + y^2 = 9$ at the point in the third quadrant where $y = -1$.

*31 Write the equation of the tangent line to the circle $x^2 + 14x + y^2 + 18y = 39$ at the point in the second quadrant where $x = -2$.

▬ 32 Suppose a kite is flying at a height of 300 feet above a point P on the ground. The kite string is anchored in the ground x feet from P.

 (a) If s is the length of the string (assume the string forms a straight line) write s as a function of x.

 (b) Find s when $x = 400$ feet.

▬ 33 A 13-foot-long board is leaning against the wall of a house so that its base is 5 feet from the wall. When the base of the board is pulled y feet further from the wall, the top of the board drops x feet.

 (a) Express y as a function of x.

 (b) Find y when $x = 7$.

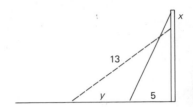

A straight line will intersect a parabola or a circle twice, or once, or not at all. Two parabolas of the form $y = ax^2 + bx + c$ can intersect at most two times; the same is true for two circles. A circle and a parabola can intersect at most four times. These diagrams illustrate some of these possibilities.

Solving nonlinear systems

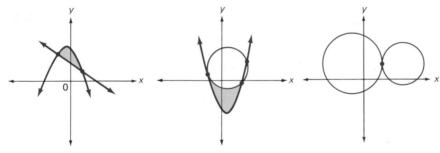

In each of the examples that follow, at least one of the two equations will not be linear. Thus we will be learning how to solve certain types of *nonlinear systems*. The underlying strategy in solving such systems will be the same as it was for linear systems. We first eliminate one of the two variables to obtain an equation in one unknown.

When you study calculus you will learn how to find the areas of the regions between curves. For example, the areas of the shaded regions in the first two diagrams can be found once the coordinates of the points of intersection are known. Here we will address ourselves only to this part of the problem: finding the points of intersection.

EXAMPLE 1 Solve the system and graph:

$$y = x^2$$

$$y = -2x + 8$$

(A parabola and a line.)

Solution Let (x, y) represent the points of intersection. Since these x- and y-values are the same in both equations, we may set the two values for y equal to each other and solve for x.

Various possible cases for nonlinear systems are illustrated by the examples. All the illustrative examples as well as the exercises have been designed so that the solutions are manageable.

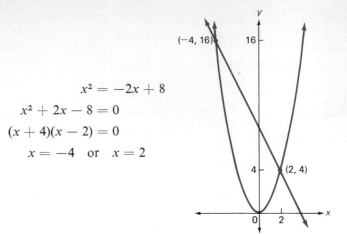

$$x^2 = -2x + 8$$
$$x^2 + 2x - 8 = 0$$
$$(x + 4)(x - 2) = 0$$
$$x = -4 \quad \text{or} \quad x = 2$$

To find the corresponding y-values, either of the original equations may be used. Using $y = -2x + 8$, we have:

For $x = -4$, $y = -2(-4) + 8 = 16$.
For $x = 2$, $y = -2(2) + 8 = 4$.

The solution of the system consists of the two ordered pairs $(-4, 16)$ and $(2, 4)$. The other equation can be used as a check of these results.

(Two parabolas.)   **EXAMPLE 2**   Solve the system and graph:

$$y = x^2 - 2$$
$$y = -2x^2 + 6x + 7$$

Solution   Set the two values for y equal to each other and solve for x.

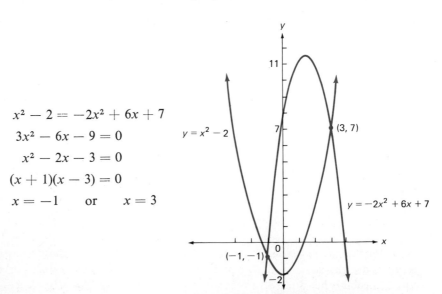

$$x^2 - 2 = -2x^2 + 6x + 7$$
$$3x^2 - 6x - 9 = 0$$
$$x^2 - 2x - 3 = 0$$
$$(x + 1)(x - 3) = 0$$
$$x = -1 \quad \text{or} \quad x = 3$$

Use $y = x^2 - 2$ to solve for y.
$$y = (-1)^2 - 2 = -1 \qquad y = 3^2 - 2 = 7$$
The points of intersection are $(-1, -1)$ and $(3, 7)$.

EXAMPLE 3 Solve the system and graph.

(A circle and a parabola.)

$$x^2 + y^2 - 8y = -7$$
$$y - x^2 = 1$$

Solution Solve the second equation for x^2.
$$x^2 = y - 1$$
Substitute into the first equation and solve for y.

Note: Alternative methods can be used to solve this example (as well as others). Another easy way begins by adding the given equations. Try it. We may also solve $y - x^2 = 1$ for y and substitute into the first equation. You will find that the latter method is more difficult. With practice you will learn how to find the easier methods.

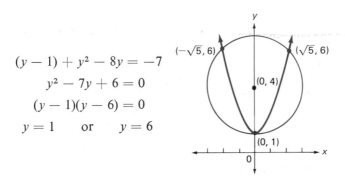

$$(y - 1) + y^2 - 8y = -7$$
$$y^2 - 7y + 6 = 0$$
$$(y - 1)(y - 6) = 0$$
$$y = 1 \quad \text{or} \quad y = 6$$

Use $x^2 = y - 1$ to solve for x.

For $y = 1$: $\quad x^2 = 1 - 1 = 0 \qquad x = 0$

For $y = 6$: $\quad x^2 = 6 - 1 = 5 \qquad x = \pm\sqrt{5}$

The points of intersection are $(0, 1)$, $(\sqrt{5}, 6)$, and $(-\sqrt{5}, 6)$.

EXERCISES 4.6

Solve each system and graph.

1 $y = -x^2 - 4x + 1$
$y - 2x = 10$

2 $3x - 4y = -5$
$(x + 3)^2 + (y + 1)^2 = 25$

3 $(x + 4)^2 + (y - 1)^2 = 16$
$(x + 4)^2 + (y - 3)^2 = 4$

4 $y = x^2 - 6x + 9$
$(x - 3)^2 + (y - 9)^2 = 9$

5 $y = x^2 + 6x + 6$
$y = -x^2 - 6x + 6$

6 $y = \frac{1}{3}(x - 3)^2 - 3$
$(x - 3)^2 + (y + 2)^2 = 1$

Solve each system.

7 $y = (x + 1)^2$
$y = (x - 1)^2$

8 $x^2 + y^2 = 9$
$y = x^2 - 3$

9 $y = x^2$
$y = -x^2 + 8x - 16$

10 $y = x^2$
$y = x^2 - 8x + 24$

11 $7x + 3y = 42$
$y = -3x^2 - 12x - 15$

12 $y + 2x = 1$
$x^2 + 4x = 6 - 2y$

13 $y - x = 0$
 $(x - 2)^2 + (y + 5)^2 = 25$

14 $y - 2x = 0$
 $(x - 2)^2 + (y + 5)^2 = 25$

15 $y = -x^2 + 2x$
 $x^2 - 2x + y^2 - 2y = 0$

16 $x^2 + 4x + y^2 - 4y = -4$
 $(x - 2)^2 + (y - 2)^2 = 4$

*17 $(x - 1)^2 + y^2 = 1$
 $x^2 + (y - 1)^2 = 1$

*18 $4x + 3y = 25$
 $x^2 + y^2 = 25$

*19 $y = \frac{1}{3}(x - 3)^2 - 3$
 $x^2 - 6x + y^2 + 2y = -6$

*20 $y = x^2 - 6x + 9$
 $(x - 3)^2 + (y - 2)^2 = 58$

4.7

The ellipse and the hyperbola

A **conic section** is a curve formed by the intersection of a plane with a double right-circular cone. These curves, also called **conics**, are known as the **circle**, **ellipse**, **parabola**, and **hyperbola**.

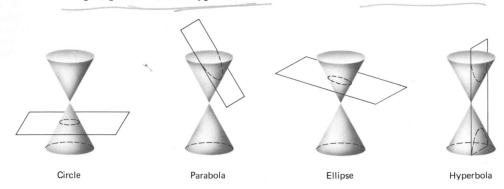

Circle   Parabola   Ellipse   Hyperbola

The figure indicates that the inclination of the plane in relation to the axis of the cone determines the nature of the curve. These four curves have played a vital role in mathematics and its applications from the time of the ancient Greeks until the present day.

Since we have already done some work in this chapter with the parabola and the circle, we now confine our efforts to the study of the ellipse and the hyperbola. Although it is possible to study these curves by using the given geometric interpretations, we will use definitions similar in style to that of a circle as the set of points in a plane equidistant from a fixed point. In the exercises you will also find some work on the parabola along these lines.

By definition, *an ellipse is the set of all points in a plane such that the sum of the distances from two fixed points is a constant.* The two fixed points, F_1 and F_2, are called the **foci** of the ellipse.

We first consider an ellipse whose foci are symmetric about the origin along the x-axis. Thus we let F_1 have coordinates $(-c, 0)$ and F_2 have coordinates $(c, 0)$, where c is some positive number.

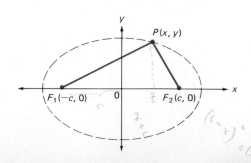

164

Since the sum of the distances PF_1 and PF_2 must be constant, we choose some positive number a and let this constant equal $2a$. (The form $2a$ will prove to be useful to simplify the algebraic computation.) Thus a point $P(x, y)$ is on the ellipse if and only if $PF_1 + PF_2 = 2a$. (Note $a > c$. Why?)

Using the distance formula gives

$$PF_1 = \sqrt{(x + c)^2 + y^2} \quad \text{and} \quad PF_2 = \sqrt{(x - c)^2 + y^2}$$

Thus

$$PF_1 + PF_2 = \sqrt{(x + c)^2 + y^2} + \sqrt{(x - c)^2 + y^2} = 2a$$

which implies the following:

$$\sqrt{(x + c)^2 + y^2} = 2a - \sqrt{(x - c)^2 + y^2}$$

Squaring both sides and collecting terms, we have

$$a\sqrt{(x - c)^2 + y^2} = a^2 - cx$$

Square both sides again and simplify:

$$(a^2 - c^2)x^2 + a^2y^2 = a^2(a^2 - c^2)$$

Since $a^2 - c^2 > 0$ we may let $b = \sqrt{a^2 - c^2}$ so that $b^2 = a^2 - c^2$. Therefore,

$$b^2x^2 + a^2y^2 = a^2b^2$$

Now divide through by a^2b^2 to obtain the following standard form:

ELLIPSE WITH FOCI AT $(-c, 0)$ AND $(c, 0)$

$$\frac{x^2}{a^2} + \frac{y^2}{b^2} = 1, \quad \text{where } b^2 = a^2 - c^2$$

The geometric interpretations of a and b can be found from this last equation. Letting $y = 0$ produces the x-intercepts, $x = \pm a$. The points $V_1(-a, 0)$ and $V_2(a, 0)$ are called the **vertices** of the ellipse. The **major axis** of the ellipse is the chord V_1V_2, which has length $2a$. Letting $x = 0$ produces the y-intercepts, $y = \pm b$. The points $(0, -b)$ and $(0, b)$ are the endpoints of the **minor axis**. The intersection of the major and minor axes is the **center** of the ellipse; in this case the center is the origin.

Note that the minor axis has length $2b$, and $2b < 2a$ since $b = \sqrt{a^2 - c^2} < a$.

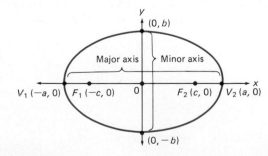

When the foci of the ellipse are on the y-axis, a similar development produces this standard form:

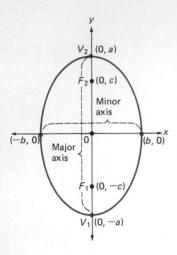

ELLIPSE WITH FOCI AT $(0, -c)$ AND $(0, c)$

$$\frac{x^2}{b^2} + \frac{y^2}{a^2} = 1, \qquad \text{where } b^2 = a^2 - c^2$$

The major axis is on the y-axis, and its endpoints are the vertices $(0, \pm a)$. The minor axis is on the x-axis and has endpoints $(\pm b, 0)$. Center: $(0, 0)$.

EXAMPLE 1   Change $25x^2 + 16y^2 = 400$ into standard form and graph.

Solution   Divide both sides of $25x^2 + 16y^2 = 400$ by 400 to obtain $\frac{x^2}{16} + \frac{y^2}{25} = 1$. Since $a^2 = 25$, $a = 5$ and the major axis is on the y-axis with length $2a = 10$. Similarly, $b^2 = 16$ gives $b = 4$, and the minor axis has length $2b = 8$. Also, $c^2 = a^2 - b^2 = 25 - 16 = 9$, so that $c = 3$, which locates the foci at $(0, \pm 3)$.

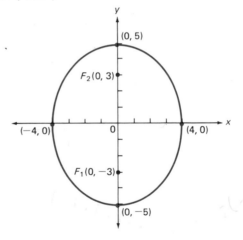

The preceding results can be generalized by allowing the center of the ellipse to be at some point (h, k). If the major axis is horizontal, then the foci have coordinates $(h - c, k)$ and $(h + c, k)$, and it can be shown that the equation has this standard form:

Note: When $a = b$, the standard form produces $(x - h)^2 + (y - k)^2 = a^2$, which is the equation of a circle with center (h, k) and radius a. Thus a circle may be regarded as a special kind of ellipse, one for which the foci and center coincide.

ELLIPSE WITH CENTER (h, k)

$$\frac{(x - h)^2}{a^2} + \frac{(y - k^2)}{b^2} = 1, \qquad \text{where } b^2 = a^2 - c^2$$

What is the equation when the major axis is vertical?

EXAMPLE 2   Write in standard form and graph:

$$4x^2 - 16x + 9y^2 + 18y = 11$$

Solution   We follow a procedure much like that used in Section 4.5 for circles, that is, complete the square in both variables.

$$4x^2 - 16x + 9y^2 + 18y = 11$$

$$4(x^2 - 4x) + 9(y^2 + 2y) = 11$$

$$4(x^2 - 4x + 4) + 9(y^2 + 2y + 1) = 11 + 16 + 9$$

$$4(x - 2)^2 + 9(y + 1)^2 = 36$$

Divide both sides by 36:

$$\frac{(x - 2)^2}{9} + \frac{(y + 1)^2}{4} = 1$$

This is the equation of an ellipse having center at $(2, -1)$, with major axis $2a = 6$ and minor axis $2b = 4$. Since $c^2 = a^2 - b^2 = 5$, $c = \sqrt{5}$, which gives the foci $(2 \pm \sqrt{5}, -1)$.

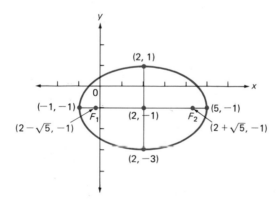

A hyperbola is defined as the set of all points in a plane such that the difference of the distances from two fixed points is constant. The two fixed points, F_1 and F_2, are called the **foci** of the hyperbola, and its **center** is the midpoint of the **transverse axis** F_1F_2. It turns out that a hyperbola consists of two congruent branches which open in opposite directions.

We begin with a hyperbola with foci on the x-axis at $F_1(-c, 0)$ and $F_2(c, 0)$, where $c > 0$. Select a number $a > 0$ so that for any point P on the right branch of the hyperbola we have $PF_1 - PF_2 = 2a$. For any point P on the left branch $PF_2 - PF_1 = 2a$, as in the figure at the top of the following page.

The form $2a$ is used to simplify computations.

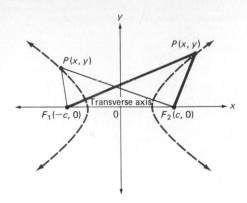

Note that $a < c$, since from triangle F_1PF_2 (P on the right branch) we have $PF_1 < PF_2 + F_1F_2$, which gives $PF_1 - PF_2 < F_1F_2$, or $2a < 2c$.

If we now follow the same type of analysis used to derive the equation of an ellipse, it can be shown that the equation of a hyperbola may be written in this standard form:

HYPERBOLA WITH FOCI AT $(-c, 0)$ AND $(c, 0)$

$$\frac{x^2}{a^2} - \frac{y^2}{b^2} = 1, \quad \text{where } b^2 = c^2 - a^2$$

Letting $y = 0$ gives $x = \pm a$; the points $V_1(-a, 0)$ and $V_2(a, 0)$ are the **vertices** of the hyperbola.

EXAMPLE 3   Write in standard form and identify the foci and vertices: $16x^2 - 25y^2 - 400$.

Solution   Divide through by 400 to place in standard form.

$$\frac{16x^2}{400} - \frac{25y^2}{400} = \frac{400}{400}$$

$$\frac{x^2}{25} - \frac{y^2}{16} = 1$$

Note that $a^2 = 25$ and $b^2 = 16$, so that $a = 5$ and $b = 4$. Then $c^2 = a^2 + b^2 = 25 + 16 = 41$ and $c = \pm\sqrt{41}$. The vertices of the hyperbola are located at $(-5, 0)$ and $(5, 0)$; the foci are at $(-\sqrt{41}, 0)$ and $(\sqrt{41}, 0)$.

Let us return to the standard form for the equation of a hyperbola and solve for y:

$$\frac{x^2}{a^2} - \frac{y^2}{b^2} = 1$$

$$y^2 = \frac{b^2}{a^2}(x^2 - a^2)$$

$$y = \pm\frac{b}{a}\sqrt{x^2 - a^2}$$

Consequently, $|x| \geq a$, which means that there are no points of the hyperbola for $-a < x < a$.

An efficient way to sketch a hyperbola is first to draw the rectangle that is $2a$ units wide and $2b$ units high, as shown in the following figure. Note that the center of the hyperbola is also the center of this rectangle. Draw the diagonals of the rectangle and extend them in both directions; these are the **asymptotes**. Now sketch the hyperbola by beginning at the vertices $(\pm a, 0)$ so that the lines are asymptotes to the curve and the branches are between the asymptotes whose equations are $y = \pm\frac{b}{a}x$.

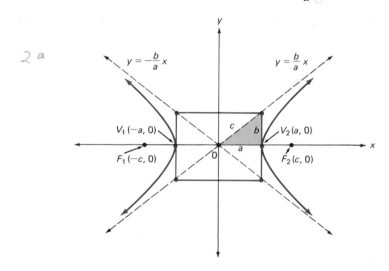

Since $b^2 = c^2 - a^2$, or $a^2 + b^2 = c^2$, it follows that b can be used as a side of a right triangle having hypotenuse c. Thus if we construct a perpendicular at V_2 of length b, the resulting right triangle has hypotenuse c. We also see that this hypotenuse lies on the line $y = \frac{b}{a}x$.

When the foci of a hyperbola are on the y-axis the equation has this standard form:

HYPERBOLA WITH FOCI AT $(0, -c)$ AND $(0, c)$

$$\frac{y^2}{a^2} - \frac{x^2}{b^2} = 1, \qquad \text{where } b^2 = c^2 - a^2$$

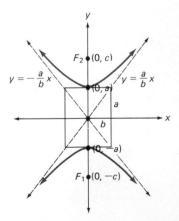

The vertices are $(0, \pm a)$, the transverse axis has length $2a$, and the asymptotes are the lines $y = \pm\frac{a}{b}x$. The branches of this hyperbola open upward and downward.

When the center of the hyperbola is at some point (h, k) and the transverse axis is horizontal, we have the following standard form:

HYPERBOLA WITH CENTER AT (h, k)

$$\frac{(x-h)^2}{a^2} - \frac{(y-k)^2}{b^2} = 1, \qquad \text{where } b^2 = c^2 - a^2$$

EXAMPLE 4 Write in standard form and graph:

$$4x^2 + 16x - 9y^2 + 18y = 29$$

Solution Complete the square in x and y.

$$4(x^2 + 4x) - 9(y^2 - 2y) = 29$$

$$4(x^2 + 4x + 4) - 9(y^2 - 2y + 1) = 29 + 16 - 9$$

$$4(x + 2)^2 - 9(y - 1)^2 = 36$$

Divide both sides by 36:

$$\frac{(x+2)^2}{9} - \frac{(y-1)^2}{4} = 1$$

This is the standard form for a hyperbola with center at $(-2, 1)$. Since
$a^2 = 9$, we have $a = 3$ and the vertices are located 3 units from the center
at $(-5, 1)$ and $(1, 1)$. Since $c^2 = a^2 + b^2 = 13$, the foci are located at
$\sqrt{13}$ units from the center, namely at $(-2 \pm \sqrt{13}, 1)$.

To sketch the hyperbola first draw the 6-by-4 rectangle with center at
$(-2, 1)$ as shown. Draw the asymptotes by extending the diagonals and
sketch the branches.

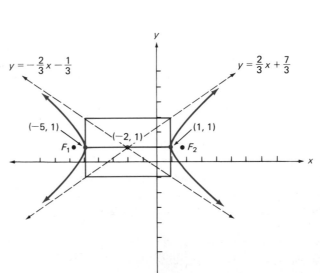

Name the conic section and state the coordinates of the center, vertices, and foci. Give the equations of the asymptotes where applicable.

1 $\dfrac{x^2}{25} + \dfrac{y^2}{16} = 1$ 2 $\dfrac{x^2}{16} + \dfrac{y^2}{25} = 1$

3 $\dfrac{x^2}{36} - \dfrac{y^2}{25} = 1$ 4 $\dfrac{y^2}{36} - \dfrac{x^2}{25} = 1$

5 $25x^2 + 4y^2 = 100$ 6 $x^2 - 2y^2 = 6$

7 $x^2 + \dfrac{(y-1)^2}{4} = 1$

8 $\dfrac{(x+2)^2}{16} + \dfrac{(y+5)^2}{25} = 1$

Name the conic and graph.

9 $\dfrac{x^2}{9} + \dfrac{y^2}{16} = 1$ 10 $\dfrac{x^2}{16} + \dfrac{y^2}{9} = 1$

11 $16y^2 - 9x^2 = 144$ 12 $9x^2 - 16y^2 = 144$

13 $\dfrac{(x-1)^2}{64} + \dfrac{(y-2)^2}{36} = 1$

14 $\dfrac{(y-1)^2}{64} - \dfrac{(x-3)^2}{36} = 1$

15 $16(y-3)^2 - 9(x+2)^2 = -144$

16 $16(y-2)^2 - 9(x+3)^2 = 144$

Write in standard form and identify.

17 $x^2 + y^2 - 2x + 4y + 1 = 0$

18 $x^2 + y^2 + 6x - 4y + 4 = 0$

19 $x^2 + 4y^2 + 2x - 3 = 0$

20 $x^2 - 9y^2 - 2x - 8 = 0$

21 $9x^2 + 18x - 16y^2 + 96y = 279$

22 $4x^2 - 16x + y^2 + 8y = -28$

Write the equation of the ellipse in standard form having the given properties.

23 Center $(0, 0)$; horizontal major axis of length 10; minor axis of length 6.

24 Center $(0, 0)$; foci $(\pm2, 0)$; vertices $(\pm5, 0)$.

25 Vertices $(0, \pm5)$; foci $(0, \pm3)$.

26 Center $(2, 3)$; foci $(-2, 3)$ and $(6, 3)$; minor axis of length 8.

27 Center $(2, -3)$; vertical major axis of length 12; minor axis of length 8.

28 Center $(-5, 0)$; foci $(-5, \pm2)$; $b = 3$.

Write the equation of the hyperbola in standard form having the given properties.

29 Center $(0, 0)$; foci $(\pm6, 0)$; vertices $(\pm4, 0)$.

30 Center $(0, 0)$; foci $(0, \pm4)$; vertices $(0, \pm1)$.

31 Center $(-2, 3)$; vertical transverse axis of length 6; $c = 4$.

32 Center $(4, 4)$; vertex $(4, 7)$; $b = 2$.

*33 Center $(0, 0)$; asymptotes $y = \pm\frac{1}{2}x$; vertices $(\pm4, 0)$.

34 The figure describes an instrument that can be used to draw an ellipse. Put thumbtacks at the points on the paper and place a loop of string around them. Pull the string taut by using a pencil point as indicated. Keeping the string taut, move the pencil around the loop. Why does this motion trace out an ellipse? Draw an ellipse using the construction suggested.

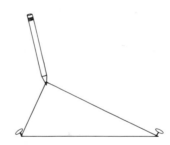

35 A parabola can be defined as the set of all points in a plane equidistant from a given fixed line called the **directrix** and a given fixed point called the **focus**. Let focus F have coordinates $(0, p)$, and let the directrix have equation $y = -p$ as indicated.

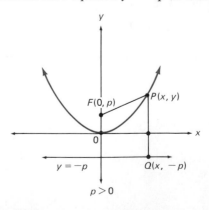

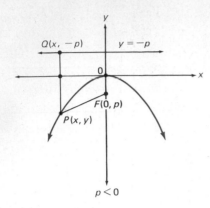

(a) Write the length PF in terms of the coordinates of P and F.

(b) Express the length PQ in terms of y and p.

(c) Equate the results in parts (a) and (b) and derive the form $x^2 = 4py$.

36 Write the equation of the parabola with focus $(0, 3)$ and directrix $y = -3$. Sketch.

37 Write the equation of the parabola with focus $(0, -3)$ and directrix $y = 3$. Sketch.

38 Find the coordinates of the focus and the equation of the directrix for the parabola $y = 2x^2$.

39 Find the coordinates of the focus and the equation of the directrix for the parabola $y = -\frac{1}{4}x^2$.

*40 The origin is the vertex of each parabola having equation $x^2 = 4py$. What is the equation of the parabola with center (h, k) having focus $(h, k + p)$ and directrix $y = k - p$?

*41 A parabola has vertex $(2, -5)$, focus at $(2, -3)$, and directrix $y = -7$. Write its equation in the form of Exercise 40. Then write its equation in the form $y = ax^2 + bx + c$.

*42 Let P be on the right branch of the hyperbola with foci $F_1(-c, 0)$ and $F_2(c, 0)$, and let $PF_1 - PF_2 = 2a$ for $a < c$. Derive the equation $\frac{x^2}{a^2} - \frac{y^2}{b^2} = 1$, where $b^2 = c^2 - a^2$.

REVIEW EXERCISES FOR CHAPTER 4

The solutions to the following exercises can be found within the text of Chapter 4. Try to answer each question without referring to the text.

Section 4.1

Graph each of the following.

1 $y = -x^2$ **2** $y = \frac{1}{2}x^2$

3 $y = (x - 1)^2$ **4** $y = (x + 1)^2$

5 $y = (x + 2)^2 - 2$ **6** $y = -2(x - 3)^2 + 4$

7 For Exercise 6, state the coordinates of the vertex and the equation of the axis of symmetry.

Section 4.2

Write in standard form.

8 $y = x^2 + 4x + 3$ **9** $y = 2x^2 - 12x + 11$

10 $y = -\frac{1}{3}x^2 - 2x + 1$

11 Find the vertex and axis of symmetry of the parabola $y = 3x^2 - 4x - 2$.

12 Graph the function f where $f(x) = |x^2 - 4|$.

13 State the conditions on the values a and k so that the parabola $y = a(x - h)^2 + k$ opens downward and intersects the x-axis in two points.

14 What are the domain and range of the function in Exercise 13?

Section 4.3

15 Find the x-intercepts of $f(x) = 25x^2 + 30x + 9$.

16 Find the roots of $2x^2 - 9x - 18 = 0$.

17 State the quadratic formula.

18 Solve for x: $2x^2 - 5x + 1 = 0$.

19 Solve for x: $2x^2 = x - 1$.

20 Find the value of the discriminant and decide how many x-intercepts there are:

(a) $y = x^2 - x - 6$ (b) $y = x^2 - 4x + 4$

(c) $y = x^2 - 4x + 5$

21 Solve: $x^2 - x - 6 < 0$.

Section 4.4

22 Find the maximum value or minimum value of the function $f(x) = 2(x + 3)^2 + 5$.

23 Find the maximum value of the quadratic function $f(x) = -\frac{1}{3}x^2 + x + 2$. At which value x does f achieve this maximum?

24 Suppose that 60 meters of fencing is available to enclose a rectangular garden, one side of which will be against the side of a house. What dimensions of the garden will guarantee a maximum area?

25 A ball is thrown straight upward from ground level with an initial velocity of 32 feet per second. The formula $s = 32t - 16t^2$ gives its height in feet, s, after t seconds. **(a)** What is the maximum height reached by the ball? **(b)** When does the ball return to the ground?

Section 4.5

26 Find the length of the line segment determined by the points $(-2, 2)$ and $(6, -4)$.

27 Find the center and radius of the circle
$$(x - 2)^2 + (y + 3)^2 = 4$$

28 Find the center and radius of the circle
$$x^2 - 4x + y^2 + 6y = -9$$

29 Find the center and radius of the circle
$$9x^2 + 12x + 9y^2 = 77$$

30 Find the equation of the tangent line to the circle $(x + 3)^2 + (y + 1)^2 = 25$ at the point $(1, 2)$. Sketch.

31 Points $P(2, 5)$ and $Q(-4, -3)$ are the endpoints of a diameter of a circle. Find the center, radius, and equation of the circle.

Section 4.6

Solve each system and graph.

32 $y = x^2$
$y = -2x + 8$

33 $y = x^2 - 2$
$y = -2x^2 + 6x + 7$

34 $x^2 + y^2 - 8y = -7$
$y - x^2 = 1$

Section 4.7

Write in standard form and graph.

35 $4x^2 - 16x + 9y^2 + 18y = 11$

36 $4x^2 + 16x - 9y^2 + 18y = 29$

37 Write in standard form and identify the foci and vertices of $16x^2 - 25y^2 = 400$.

38 Write the standard form for the equation of a hyperbola with center at (h, k) such that the transverse axis is horizontal.

SAMPLE TEST QUESTIONS FOR CHAPTER 4

Use these questions to test your knowledge of the basic skills and concepts of Chapter 4. Then check your answers with those given at the end of the book.

1 Graph $y = (x - 2)^2 + 3$.

2 Graph the function $y = f(x) = x^2 - 9$.

3 Let $y = -5x^2 + 20x - 1$.

   (a) Write the quadratic in the standard form $y = a(x - h)^2 + k$.

   (b) Give the coordinates of the vertex.

   (c) Write the equation of the axis of symmetry.

   (d) State the domain and range of the quadratic function.

4 Solve for x: $3x^2 - 8x - 3 = 0$.

5 Find the x-intercepts of $y = -x^2 + 4x + 7$.

Give the value of the discriminant and use this result to describe the x-intercepts, if any.

6 $y = x^2 + 3x + 1$ **7** $y = 6x^2 + 5x - 6$

8 Find the maximum or minimum value of the quadratic function and state the x-value at which this occurs: $f(x) = -\frac{1}{2}x^2 - 6x + 2$.

9 In the figure the altitude BC of triangle ABC is 4 feet. The part of the perimeter $PQRCB$ is to be a total of 28 feet. How long should x be so that the area of rectangle $PCRQ$ is a maximum?

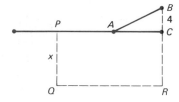

10 The formula $h = 64t - 16t^2$ gives the distance in feet above the ground, h, reached by an object in t seconds. What is the maximum height reached by the object?

11 **(a)** Draw the circle $(x - 3)^2 + (y + 4)^2 = 25$.

   (b) Write the equation of the tangent line to this circle at the point $(6, 0)$.

12 Find the center and radius of the circle $4x^2 + 4x + 4y^2 - 56y = -97$.

13 Find the length of the line segment determined by points $A(-2, 5)$ and $B(3, -4)$.

14 Points $P(1, -5)$ and $Q(-3, 3)$ are the endpoints of a diameter of a circle. Find the center, radius, and equation of the circle.

15 Solve the system

$$y = (x - 2)^2 - 2$$
$$(x - 2)^2 + (y - 2)^2 = 4$$

16 Write in standard form and identify the curve $4x^2 + 16x - y^2 + 6y = -3$. Find the coordinates of the center and the vertices.

17 Write the equation of the ellipse in standard form with center at $(0, 0)$, horizontal major axis of length 8, and minor axis of length 6.

18 Write the equation of the hyperbola in standard form with center at $(0, 0)$, foci at $(\pm 8, 0)$, and vertices at $(\pm 6, 0)$.

ANSWERS TO THE TEST YOUR UNDERSTANDING EXERCISES

Page 136

1 (b)   **2** (c)   **3** (e)   **4** (f)   **5** (d)   **6** (a)

Page 141

1 16   **2** 25   **3** 9

4 36   **5** $\frac{9}{4}$ **6** $\frac{25}{4}$

7 $y = (x + 2)^2 - 7$ **8** $y = (x - 3)^2 - 2$ **9** $y = (x - 1)^2 + 8$

10 $y = 2(x + 2)^2 - 9$ **11** $y = -(x - \frac{1}{2})^2 - \frac{7}{4}$ **12** $y = \frac{1}{2}(x - 3)^2 - \frac{5}{2}$

Page 146

1 $-8, \frac{3}{2}$ **2** $0, \frac{3}{5}$ **3** $\pm\frac{1}{2}$

4 $\frac{1}{2}$ **5** $\pm 2\sqrt{2}$ **6** None.

7 $-1 + \sqrt{3}, -1 - \sqrt{3}$ **8** $\frac{1}{3}(2 + \sqrt{7}), \frac{1}{3}(2 - \sqrt{7})$ **9** None.

10 $\frac{3}{2}$

Page 147

1 $x = -5$ or $x = 2$ **2** $x = -3$ or $x = 4$ **3** $x = -3$ or $x = 3$ **4** $x = 1 \pm \sqrt{3}$

5 $x = -3 \pm \sqrt{3}$ **6** No real solutions.   **7** No real solutions.   **8** $x = \dfrac{-1 \pm \sqrt{33}}{4}$

Page 151

1 Minimum value $= -4$ at $x = 5$.

2 Minimum value $= -\frac{5}{6}$ at $x = -\frac{2}{3}$.

3 Minimum value $= \frac{1}{2}$ at $x = 1$.

4 Maximum value $= 131$ at $x = -4$.

5 Maximum value $= -1$ at $x = 0$.

6 Minimum value $- 0$ at $x = 3$.

7 Minimum value $= 0$ at $x = -\frac{7}{5}$.

8 Minimum value $= -\frac{49}{4}$ at $x = -\frac{1}{2}$.

Page 157

1 13   **2** $\sqrt{65}$ **3** $2\sqrt{41}$

4 $(0, 0)$; 10   **5** $(0, 0)$; $\sqrt{10}$ **6** $(1, -1)$; 5

7 $(-\frac{1}{2}, 0)$; 16   **8** $(-4, -4)$; $5\sqrt{2}$ **9** $x^2 + (y - 4)^2 = 25$

10 $(x - 1)^2 + (y + 2)^2 = 3$

Page 158

1 $(3, 5)$; 6   **2** $(0, -\frac{1}{2})$; $\sqrt{5}$ **3** $(\frac{1}{2}, -1)$; $\sqrt{7}$ **4** $(\frac{1}{4}, -1)$; 3

POLYNOMIAL AND RATIONAL FUNCTIONS

Hints for graphing

The concept of symmetry was used in Chapter 4 when graphing parabolas. Recall that the graph of the function given by $y = f(x) = x^2$ is said to be symmetric about the y-axis. (The y-axis is the axis of symmetry.)

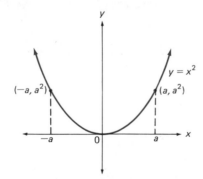

Observe that points such as $(-a, a^2)$ and (a, a^2) are symmetric points about the axis of symmetry. Now we turn our attention to a curve that is symmetric with respect to a point.

As an illustration of a curve that has symmetry through a point we consider the function given by $y = f(x) = x^3$. This function may be referred to as the *cubing function* because for each domain value x, the corresponding range value is the cube of x.

A table of values is a very helpful aid for drawing the graph of a function. Several specific points are located and a smooth curve is drawn through them to show the graph of $y = x^3$.

$y = f(x) = x^3$

x	y
-2	-8
-1	-1
$-\dfrac{1}{2}$	$-\dfrac{1}{8}$
0	0
$\dfrac{1}{2}$	$\dfrac{1}{8}$
1	1
2	8

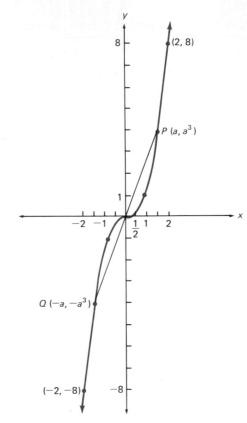

$f(x) = x^3$ is increasing for all x. The curve is concave down on $(-\infty, 0]$ and concave up on $[0, \infty)$.

Domain: all real numbers x
Range: all real numbers y

The table and the graph reveal that the curve is symmetric through the origin. Geometrically this means that whenever a line through the origin intersects the curve at a point P, this line will also intersect the curve in another point Q (on the opposite side of the origin) so that the lengths of OP and OQ are equal. This means that both points (a, a^3) and $(-a, -a^3)$ are on the curve for each value $x = a$. These are said to be **symmetric points** through the origin. In particular, since $(2, 8)$ is on the curve, then $(-2, -8)$ is also on the curve.

In general, the graph of a function $y = f(x)$ is said to be *symmetric through the origin* if for all x in the domain of f, we have

For the function $f(x) = x^3$, we have $f(-x) = (-x)^3 = -x^3 = -f(x)$. Thus $f(-x) = -f(x)$ and we have symmetry with respect to the origin.

$$f(-x) = -f(x)$$

The techniques used for graphing quadratic functions in Chapter 4 can be used for other functions as well. For example, the graph of $y = 2x^3$ can be obtained from the graph of $y = x^3$ by multiplying each of its ordinates by 2. We can also use translations (shifting) as illustrated in the examples that follow.

EXAMPLE 1 Graph $y = g(x) = (x - 3)^3$.

Solution The graph of g is obtained by translating $y = x^3$ by 3 units to the right, as shown below in the left figure.

EXAMPLE 2 Graph $y = f(x) = |(x - 3)^3|$.

Solution First graph $y = (x - 3)^3$ as in Example 1. Then take the part of this curve that is below the x-axis [$(x - 3)^3 < 0$] and reflect it through the x-axis. This is shown below in the figure on the right.

Explain how you can use the graph of g to draw the graph of $y = h(x) = (x - 3)^3 + 2.$

Note: $|(x - 3)^3| = |x - 3|^3.$

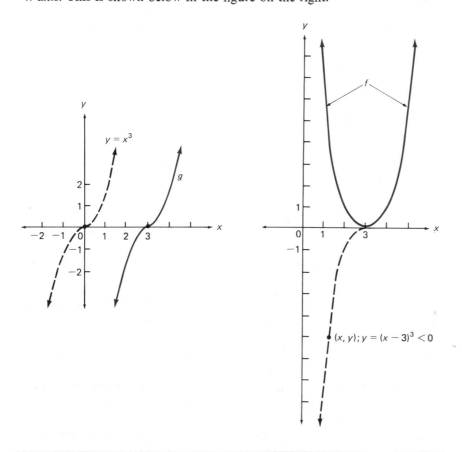

It will be helpful to collect some of the general observations that are useful in graphing functions.

1 If $f(x) = f(-x)$, the curve is symmetric about the y-axis.

2 If $f(-x) = -f(x)$, the curve is symmetric through the origin.

3 The graph of $y = af(x)$ can be obtained by multiplying the ordinates of the curve $y = f(x)$ by the value a. The case $a = -1$ gives $y = -f(x)$, which is the reflection of $y = f(x)$ through the x-axis.

4 The graph of $y = |f(x)|$ can be obtained from the graph of $y = f(x)$ by taking the part of $y = f(x)$ that is below the x-axis and reflecting it through the x-axis.

In each of the following, h is positive.

5 The graph of $y = f(x - h)$ can be obtained by shifting $y = f(x)$ h units to the right.

6 The graph of $y = f(x + h)$ can be obtained by shifting $y = f(x)$ h units to the left.

7 The graph of $y = f(x) + h$ can be obtained by shifting $y = f(x)$ h units upward.

8 The graph of $y = f(x) - h$ can be obtained by shifting $y = f(x)$ h units downward.

Try to supply a specific example that illustrates each of these items.

Note that to shift a curve means the same as to translate a curve.

EXAMPLE 3 In the figure the curve C_1 is obtained by shifting the curve C with equation $y = x^3$ horizontally, and C_2 is obtained by shifting C_1 vertically. What are the equations of C_1 and C_2?

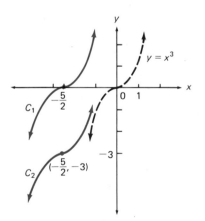

Solution

$$C_1: \quad y = (x + \tfrac{5}{2})^3 \qquad \longleftarrow C \text{ is shifted } \tfrac{5}{2} \text{ units left.}$$

$$C_2: \quad y = (x + \tfrac{5}{2})^3 - 3 \longleftarrow C_1 \text{ is shifted 3 units down.}$$

EXAMPLE 4   Graph: **(a)** $y = f(x) = x^4$;   **(b)** $y = 2x^4$.

Solution

(a) Since $f(-x) = (-x)^4 = x^4 = f(x)$, the graph is symmetric about the y-axis. Use the table of values to locate the right half of the curve; the symmetry gives the rest.

(b) Multiply each of the ordinates of $y = x^4$ by 2 to obtain the graph of $y = 2x^4$.

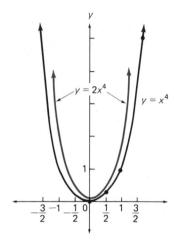

x	y
0	0
$\frac{1}{2}$	$\frac{1}{16}$
1	1
$\frac{3}{2}$	$\frac{81}{16}$
2	16

EXERCISES 5.1

In Exercises 1–8, graph each set of curves in the same coordinate system. For each exercise use a dashed curve for the first equation and a solid curve for each of the others.

1 $y = x^2$, $y = (x - 3)^2$

2 $y = x^3$, $y = (x + 2)^3$

3 $y = x^3$, $y = -x^3$

4 $y = x^4$, $y = (x - 4)^4$

5 $f(x) = x^3$, $g(x) = \frac{1}{2}x^3$, $h(x) = \frac{1}{4}x^3$

6 $f(x) = x^3$, $g(x) = (x - 3)^3 - 3$,
   $h(x) = (x + 3)^3 + 3$

7 $f(x) = x^4$, $g(x) = (x - 1)^4 - 1$,
   $h(x) = (x - 2)^4 - 2$

8 $f(x) = x^4$, $g(x) = -\frac{1}{8}x^4$, $h(x) = -x^4 - 4$

9 Graph $y = |(x + 1)^3|$.

10 Graph $y = 2(x - 1)^3 + 3$.

11 Graph $y = f(x) = |x|$, $y = g(x) = |x - 3|$, and $y = h(x) = |x - 3| + 2$, on the same axes.

Find the equation of the curve C which is obtained from the dashed curve by a horizontal or vertical shift.

12

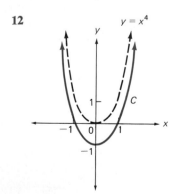

13

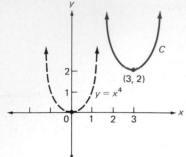

14

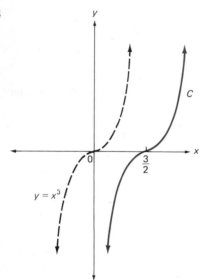

15

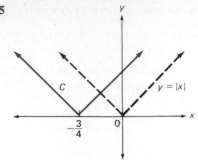

Graph each of the following.

16 $y = |x^4 - 16|$ **17** $y = |x^3 - 1|$

18 $y = |-1 - x^3|$

Graph each of the following. (Hint: Consider the expansion of $(a \pm b)^n$ for appropriate n.)

*19 $y = x^3 + 3x^2 + 3x + 1$

*20 $y = x^3 - 6x^2 + 12x - 8$

*21 $y = -x^3 + 3x^2 - 3x + 1$

*22 $y = x^4 - 4x^3 + 6x^2 - 4x + 1$

■ *Evaluate and simplify the difference quotients.*

23 $\dfrac{f(x) - f(3)}{x - 3}$ where $f(x) = x^3$.

24 $\dfrac{f(-2 + h) - f(-2)}{h}$ where $f(x) = x^3$.

25 $\dfrac{f(1 + h) - f(1)}{h}$ where $f(x) = x^4$.

26 $\dfrac{f(x) - f(-1)}{x + 1}$ where $f(x) = x^4 + 1$.

5.2

Graphing some special rational functions

A *rational expression* is a ratio of polynomials. Such expressions may be used to define rational functions and are considered in more detail in later sections. At this point we introduce the topic by exploring several special rational functions.

Consider the function $y = f(x) = \dfrac{1}{x}$, a rational function whose domain consists of all numbers except zero. The denominator x is a polynomial of degree 1, and the numerator $1 = 1x^0$ is a (constant) polynomial of degree zero.

To draw the graph of this function, first observe that it is symmetric through the origin because

$$f(-x) = \frac{1}{-x} = -\frac{1}{x} = -f(x)$$

Moreover, in $y = \dfrac{1}{x}$ both variables must have the same sign since $xy = 1$, a positive number. That is, x and y must both be positive or both be negative. Thus the graph will only appear in quadrants I and III. Next, we use a table of values to obtain points for the curve in the first quadrant. Finally, use the symmetry with respect to the origin to obtain the remaining portion of the graph in the third quadrant.

The function is decreasing on $(-\infty, 0)$ and on $(0, \infty)$. The curve is concave down on $(-\infty, 0)$ and concave up on $(0, \infty)$.

$y = f(x) = \dfrac{1}{x}$

x	y
$\dfrac{1}{5}$	5
$\dfrac{1}{2}$	2
1	1
2	$\dfrac{1}{2}$
3	$\dfrac{1}{3}$
4	$\dfrac{1}{4}$

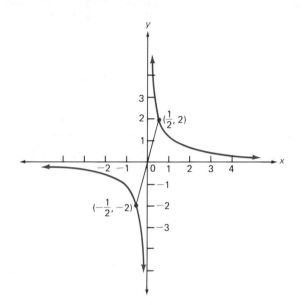

Verify these table entries for $y = \dfrac{1}{x}$.

x	y
10	.1
100	.01
1000	.001
10,000	.0001
$\vdots$	$\vdots$

Getting very large   Getting close to 0

Domain: all $x \neq 0$
Range: all $y \neq 0$

Observe that the curve approaches the x-axis in quadrant I. That is, as the values for x become large, the values for y approach zero. Also, as the values for x approach zero in the first quadrant, the y-values become very large. A similar observation can be made about the curve in the third quadrant. We say that the axes are **asymptotes** for the curve; the curve is *asymptotic* to the axes.

EXAMPLE 1 Sketch the graph of $g(x) = \dfrac{1}{x - 3}$. Find the asymptotes.

Solution Using $f(x) = \dfrac{1}{x}$, we have $f(x - 3) = \dfrac{1}{x - 3} = g(x)$. Therefore, the graph of g can be drawn by shifting the graph of $f(x) = \dfrac{1}{x}$ by 3 units to the right. See the figure at the top of page 182.

The x-axis and the vertical line $x = 3$ are the asymptotes for the graph. The domain is $x \neq 3$, and the range is $y \neq 0$.

Describe the graph of

$$y = h(x) = \frac{1}{x+3}.$$

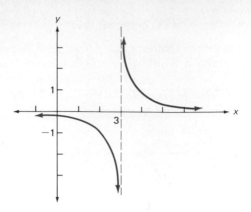

EXAMPLE 2 Graph $y = \frac{1}{x^2}$.

Solution First note that $x \neq 0$. For all other values of x we have $x^2 > 0$, so that the curve will appear in quadrants I and II only. As the values for x become large, the values for $y = \frac{1}{x^2}$ become very small. Moreover, as x approaches zero, y becomes very large. Thus the axes are asymptotes to the curve. Note that the curve is symmetric about the y-axis. That is,

$$f(x) = \frac{1}{x^2} = \frac{1}{(-x)^2} = f(-x)$$

In symbols, we write "As $x \longrightarrow \infty$, $y \longrightarrow 0$." That is, as x becomes larger and larger in value, the value of y becomes very small. Similarly, as $x \longrightarrow 0$, $y \longrightarrow \infty$.

$y = \dfrac{1}{x^2}$

x	y
$\pm\dfrac{1}{2}$	4
$\pm\dfrac{1}{10}$	100
$\pm\dfrac{1}{100}$	10,000

As x is getting close to 0, y is getting very large.

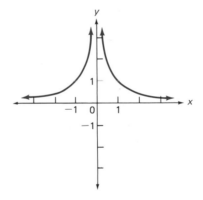

The domain is $x \neq 0$, and the range is $y > 0$.

EXAMPLE 3 Graph $y = \frac{1}{(x+2)^2} - 3$. What are the asymptotes? Find the domain and the range.

Solution Shift the graph of $y = \frac{1}{x^2}$ in Example 2 by 2 units left and then 3 units down.

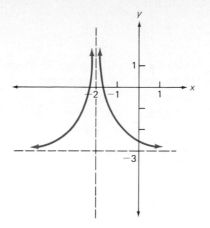

Asymptotes: $x = -2$, $y = -3$ Domain: $x \neq -2$
Range: $y > -3$

The curves studied in this chapter, as well as the parabolas and straight lines discussed in earlier chapters, are very useful in the study of calculus. Having an almost instant recall of the graphs of the following functions will be helpful in future work:

$$y = x \qquad y = |x| \qquad y = x^2 \qquad y = x^3 \qquad y = x^4 \qquad y = \frac{1}{x} \qquad y = \frac{1}{x^2}$$

Not only have you learned what these curves look like, but just as important, you have also learned how to obtain other curves from them by appropriate translations and reflections.

EXERCISES 5.2

In Exercises 1–8, graph each set of curves in the same coordinate system. For each exercise use a dashed curve for the first equation and a solid curve for the other.

1 $y = \dfrac{1}{x}, y = \dfrac{2}{x}$ **2** $y = \dfrac{1}{x}, y = -\dfrac{1}{x}$

3 $y = \dfrac{1}{x}, y = \dfrac{1}{x+2}$ **4** $y = \dfrac{1}{x}, y = \dfrac{1}{x} + 5$

5 $y = \dfrac{1}{x}, y = \dfrac{1}{2x}$ **6** $y = \dfrac{1}{x}, y = \dfrac{1}{x} - 5$

7 $y = \dfrac{1}{x^2}, y = \dfrac{1}{(x-3)^2}$ **8** $y = \dfrac{1}{x^2}, y = -\dfrac{1}{x^2}$

Graph each of the following. Find all asymptotes, if any.

9 $y = \dfrac{1}{x+4} - 2$ **10** $y = \dfrac{1}{(x-2)^2} + 3$

11 $y = \dfrac{1}{|x-2|}$ **12** $y = \dfrac{1}{x^3}$

13 $xy = 3$ **14** $xy = -2$

15 $xy - y = 1$ **16** $xy - 2x = 1$

*17 Graph $y = \left| \dfrac{1}{x} - 1 \right|$.

*18 Graph $x = \dfrac{1}{y^2}$. Why is y not a function of x?

■ *Find the difference quotients and simplify.*

19 $\dfrac{f(x) - f(3)}{x - 3}$ where $f(x) = \dfrac{1}{x}$.

20 $\dfrac{f(1+h) - f(1)}{h}$ where $f(x) = \dfrac{1}{x^2}$.

Polynomial and rational functions

Factoring methods were studied in Chapter 2. We will now use factored forms to determine the signs of polynomial and rational functions, which, in turn, will aid in sketching their graphs.

As a first illustration, consider the polynomial function given by $f(x) = x^3 + 4x^2 - x - 4$. To obtain the factored form, use factoring by grouping.

STEP 1 for graphing polynomial functions. Factor the polynomial and find the x-intercepts.

$$f(x) = x^3 + 4x^2 - x - 4$$
$$= (x + 4)x^2 - (x + 4)$$
$$= (x + 4)(x^2 - 1)$$
$$= (x + 4)(x + 1)(x - 1)$$

Set each factor equal to 0 to get the roots $-4, -1, 1$ of $f(x) = 0$, which are also the x-intercepts of $y = f(x)$. Since there are no other x-intercepts, the curve must stay above or below the x-axis for each of the intervals determined by $-4, -1, 1$.

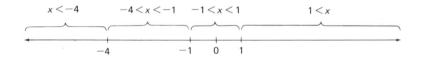

When $f(x) > 0$ the curve is above the x-axis, and it is below for $f(x) < 0$. The following table of signs contains this information, and is used to sketch the graph. (See pages 22–24 for the details in forming such a table.)

STEP 2. Form a table of signs for $f(x)$.

Interval	$(-\infty, -4)$	$(-4, -1)$	$(-1, 1)$	$(1, \infty)$
Sign of $x + 4$	$-$	$+$	$+$	$+$
Sign of $x + 1$	$-$	$-$	$+$	$+$
Sign of $x - 1$	$-$	$-$	$-$	$+$
Sign of $f(x)$	$-$	$+$	$-$	$+$
Position of curve relative to x-axis	below	above	below	above

In general, a polynomial of degree n has at most $n - 1$ turning points and at most n x-intercepts.

Notice that there are two turning points and three x-intercepts. It turns out that for a third-degree polynomial there are at most two turning points and at most three x-intercepts. There may be less of either; for example $y = x^3$ has no turning points and one x-intercept.

$$f(x) = x^3 + 4x^2 - x - 4$$

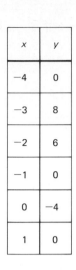

x	y
-4	0
-3	8
-2	6
-1	0
0	-4
1	0

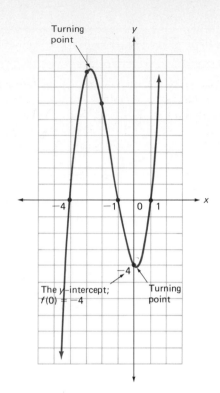

Turning point

The y-intercept; $f(0) = -4$

Turning point

STEP 3. Sketch the graph using the x-intercepts, the signs of $f(x)$, and some additional points including the y-intercept.

To graph rational functions, first locate the asymptotes if there are any. For example, note that $y = \dfrac{1}{x-2}$ has a vertical asymptote at $x = 2$, since as x is taken close to 2, y gets very large in absolute value. It has the horizontal asymptote $y = 0$, because as $|x|$ is taken very large, the y-values get close to 0.

A graph of a rational function has a vertical asymptote at each value a where the denominator is 0, and the numerator is not 0.

The method for finding the horizontal asymptote (if any) for a rational function f can be summarized by referring to the general form of a rational function.

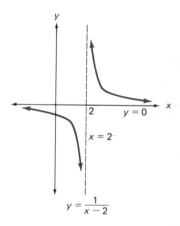

$$y = \frac{1}{x-2}$$

In general, a rational function may have numerous vertical asymptotes, but at most one horizontal asymptote.

$$f(x) = \frac{a_n x^n + a_{n-1}x^{n-1} + \cdots + a_0}{b_m x^m + b_{m-1}x^{m-1} + \cdots + b_0}, \quad a_n \neq 0 \neq b_m$$

The numerator and denominator are polynomials in x of degree n and m respectively (see page 52).

1 If $n < m$, then $y = 0$ is the horizontal asymptote.

2 If $n = m$, then $y = \dfrac{a_n}{b_m}$ is the horizontal asymptote.

3 If $n > m$, there is no horizontal asymptote.

Find the vertical and horizontal asymptotes for each rational function.

1 $y = \dfrac{5}{(x-2)(x-3)}$ **2** $y = \dfrac{x-2}{x+3}$ **3** $y = \dfrac{x^2-1}{x-2}$

4 $y = \dfrac{x}{(x-4)^2}$ **5** $y = \dfrac{2-x}{x^2-x-12}$ **6** $y = \dfrac{2x^3+x}{x^2-x}$

EXAMPLE 1 Graph $y = f(x) = \dfrac{x-2}{x^2-3x-4}$.

Solution

STEP 1 for graphing rational functions. Factor the numerator and denominator.

$$f(x) = \frac{x-2}{(x+1)(x-4)}$$

STEP 2. Find the x-intercepts.

$f(x) = 0$ when the numerator $x - 2 = 0$, so the x-intercept is 2.

STEP 3. Find the vertical asymptotes.

Setting the denominator $(x+1)(x-4)$ equal to 0 gives the vertical asymptotes $x = -1$ and $x = 4$.

STEP 4. Find the horizontal asymptote.

The horizontal asymptote is $y = 0$ since the degree of the numerator is 1, which is less than 2, the degree of the denominator.

The numbers for which the numerator or denominator equals 0 are $-1, 2$, and 4. They determine the four intervals in the table of signs for f.

STEP 5. Form a table of signs for f in the intervals determined by the numbers for which the numerator or denominator equals 0.

Interval	$(-\infty, -1)$	$(-1, 2)$	$(2, 4)$	$(4, \infty)$
Sign of $x + 1$	−	+	+	+
Sign of $x - 2$	−	−	+	+
Sign of $x - 4$	−	−	−	+
Sign of $f(x)$	−	+	−	+
Position of curve relative to x-axis	below	above	below	above

STEP 6. Graph the curve. First draw the asymptotes and locate the intercepts. Use the table of signs and some selected points to complete the graph.

When graphing, remember that the closer the curve is to a vertical asymptote, the steeper it gets. And the larger $|x|$ gets, the closer the curve is to the horizontal asymptote; the curve gets "flatter." Selected points on the curve will help to draw the correct shape.

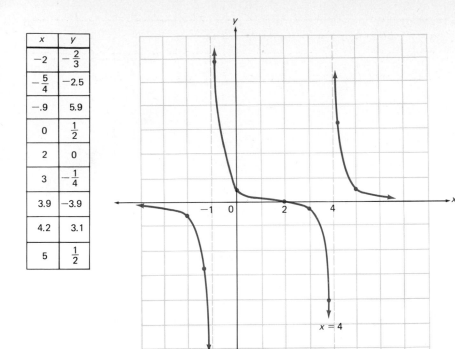

x	y
-2	$-\dfrac{2}{3}$
$-\dfrac{5}{4}$	-2.5
$-.9$	5.9
0	$\dfrac{1}{2}$
2	0
3	$-\dfrac{1}{4}$
3.9	-3.9
4.2	3.1
5	$\dfrac{1}{2}$

This is the graph of

$$f(x) = \frac{x-2}{x^2-3x-4}.$$

The decimals in the table are rounded off to tenths. A calculator can be used. Note that it is easier to substitute into the form $\dfrac{x-2}{(x+1)(x-4)}$ than into $\dfrac{x-2}{x^2-3x-4}.$

Part of our curve sketching is being done on "faith." After all, what is the shape of a curve connecting two points? Here are some possibilities.

Locating more points between P and Q will not really answer the question no matter how close the chosen points are, since the question as to how to connect them still remains. More advanced methods studied in calculus will help answer such questions, and curve sketching can then be done with less ambiguity.

EXERCISES 5.3

Use the table method to determine the signs of f.

1 $f(x) = (x-1)(x-2)(x-3)$

2 $f(x) = x(x+2)(x-2)$

3 $f(x) = \dfrac{(3x-1)(x+4)}{x^2(x-2)}$

4 $f(x) = \dfrac{x(2x+3)}{(x+2)(x-5)}$

Use the table method to solve each inequality.

5 $(x^2 + 2)(x - 4)(x + 1) > 0$

6 $x(x + 1)(x + 2) < 0$

7 $\dfrac{x - 10}{3(x + 1)(5x - 1)} < 0$

8 $\dfrac{3}{(x + 2)(4x + 3)} > 0$

In Exercises 9–22, sketch the graph of the polynomial functions. Indicate all intercepts.

9 $f(x) = (x + 3)(x + 1)(x - 2)$

10 $f(x) = (x - 1)(x - 3)(x - 5)$

11 $f(x) = (x + 3)(x + 1)(x - 1)(x - 3)$

12 $f(x) = -x(x + 4)(x^2 - 4)$

13 $f(x) = x^3 - 4x$

14 $f(x) = 9x - x^3$

15 $f(x) = x^3 + 3x$

16 $f(x) = x^3 + x^2 - 6x$

17 $f(x) = -x^3 - x^2 + 6x$

18 $f(x) = x^3 + 2x^2 - 9x - 18$

19 $f(x) = x^4 - 4x^2$

20 $f(x) = (x - 1)^2(3 + 2x - x^2)$

21 $f(x) = x^4 - 6x^3 + 8x^2$

22 $f(x) = x(x^2 - 1)(x^2 - 4)$

In Exercises 23–36, sketch the graph of the rational function. Indicate the asymptotes and the intercepts.

23 $f(x) = \dfrac{1}{(x - 1)(x + 2)}$

24 $f(x) = \dfrac{1}{x^2 - 4}$

25 $f(x) = \dfrac{1}{4 - x^2}$

26 $f(x) = \dfrac{2}{x^2 - x - 6}$

27 $f(x) = \dfrac{x}{x^2 - 1}$

28 $f(x) = \dfrac{x + 1}{x^2 + x - 2}$

29 $f(x) = \dfrac{3}{x^2 + 1}$

30 $f(x) = \dfrac{2}{x + x^2}$

31 $f(x) = \dfrac{x + 2}{x - 2}$

32 $f(x) = \dfrac{x}{1 - x}$

33 $f(x) = \dfrac{x - 1}{x + 3}$

34 $f(x) = \dfrac{x^2 + x}{x^2 - 4}$

35 $f(x) = \dfrac{x^2 + x - 2}{x^2 + x - 12}$

36 $f(x) = \dfrac{1 - x^2}{x^2 - 9}$

■ *In Exercises 37–42, simplify, obtain factored forms, and determine the signs of f. (The combination of such skills will be needed in the study of calculus.)*

37 $g(x) = 2(2x - 1)(x - 2) + 2(x - 2)^2$

38 $g(x) = 2(x - 3)(x + 2)^2 + 2(x + 2)(x - 3)^2$

39 $g(x) = \dfrac{x^2 - 2x(x + 2)}{x^4}$

40 $g(x) = \dfrac{(x - 3)(2x) - (x^2 - 5)}{(x - 3)^2}$

41 $g(x) = 2\left(\dfrac{x - 5}{x + 2}\right)\dfrac{(x + 2) - (x - 5)}{(x + 2)^2}$

42 $g(x) = \dfrac{5(x + 10)^2 - 10x(x + 10)}{(x + 10)^4}$

5.4

Equations and inequalities with fractions

You already have used properties of equality and inequality to solve equations and inequalities. Now we are ready to extend these ideas to include statements that involve fractions. Consider, for example, this equation:

$$\frac{x - 2}{x} = \frac{3}{4}$$

The first step in finding the solution is to find the least common denominator (LCD) of the two fractions. In this case, the LCD is $4x$. We then use the multiplication property of equality and multiply each member of the equation by $4x$.

Notice that multiplication by the LCD transforms the original equation into one that does not involve any fractions. Thereafter we are able to finish the solution using methods we have previously studied.

$$4x \cdot \left(\frac{x - 2}{x}\right) = 4x \cdot \left(\frac{3}{4}\right)$$

$$4(x - 2) = 3x$$

$$4x - 8 = 3x$$

$$x = 8$$

Check: $\dfrac{8-2}{8} = \dfrac{6}{8} = \dfrac{3}{4}$

The equation that we have just discussed is also called a *proportion*. A proportion is a statement that two ratios are equal, such as the following:

$$\frac{a}{b} = \frac{c}{d}$$

The proportion is in the form of a fractional equation and can be simplified by multiplying both sides by *bd*.

$$\frac{a}{b} = \frac{c}{d}$$

$$(bd)\frac{a}{b} = (bd)\frac{c}{d}$$

$$ad = bc$$

This is often read "*a* is to *b* as *c* is to *d*," and may be written in this form:

$$a:b = c:d$$

PROPORTION PROPERTY

If $\dfrac{a}{b} = \dfrac{c}{d}$, then $ad = bc$.

Using this property, the solution to the earlier equation begins in this way:

If $\dfrac{x-2}{x} = \dfrac{3}{4}$, then $4(x-2) = 3x$.

EXAMPLE 1 Solve for *x*: $\dfrac{2x-5}{x+1} - \dfrac{3}{x^2+x} = 0$.

At times, multiplication by the LCD can give rise to a quadratic equation, as in Example 1. Try to explain each step in the solution.

Solution Factor the denominator in the second fraction.

$$\frac{2x-5}{x+1} - \frac{3}{x(x+1)} = 0$$

Multiply by the LCD which is $x(x+1)$.

$$x(2x-5) - 3 = 0$$
$$2x^2 - 5x - 3 = 0$$
$$(2x+1)(x-3) = 0$$
$$2x+1 = 0 \quad \text{or} \quad x-3 = 0$$
$$x = -\tfrac{1}{2} \quad \text{or} \quad x = 3$$

You can check these answers in the original equation.

It is especially important to check each solution of a fractional equation. The reason for this can best be explained through the use of another example.

EXAMPLE 2 Solve for x: $\dfrac{3}{x-3} + 2 = \dfrac{x}{x-3}$.

Solution The LCD here is $x-3$; thus we multiply each member of the equation by this term.

$$(x-3)\left(\frac{3}{x-3}\right) + (x-3)(2) = (x-3)\left(\frac{x}{x-3}\right)$$

$$3 + 2(x-3) = x$$

$$3 + 2x - 6 = x$$

$$2x - 3 = x$$

$$x = 3$$

In this example we could have noticed at the outset that $x - 3 \neq 0$, and thus $x \neq 3$. In other words, it is wise to notice such restrictions on the variable before starting the solution. These are the values of the variable that would cause division by zero.

The procedure we have just followed *assumed* that there was a solution to the given equation. However, if we replace x by 3 in the original equation, we obtain the following statement:

$$\frac{3}{0} + 2 = \frac{3}{0}$$

Since division by zero is meaningless, we have an impossible equation, and therefore conclude that there are no solutions. That is, there is no replacement for x that will make the original equation true.

TEST YOUR UNDERSTANDING

Solve for x and check your results. Use the proportion property where appropriate.

1. $\dfrac{x}{3} + \dfrac{x}{2} = 10$ 2. $\dfrac{3}{x} + \dfrac{2}{x} = 10$ 3. $\dfrac{x-3}{8} = 4$

4. $\dfrac{8}{x-3} = 4$ 5. $\dfrac{x+3}{x} = \dfrac{2}{3}$ 6. $\dfrac{2}{x+3} = \dfrac{3}{x+3}$

7. $\dfrac{3x}{2} - \dfrac{2x}{3} = \dfrac{1}{4}$ 8. $\dfrac{2}{3x} + \dfrac{3}{2x} = 4$

9. $\dfrac{3x-1}{4} - \dfrac{x-1}{2} = 1$ 10. $\dfrac{x}{x-6} + \dfrac{2}{x} = \dfrac{1}{x-6}$

11. $\dfrac{x}{x-1} - \dfrac{3}{4x} = \dfrac{3}{4} - \dfrac{1}{x-1}$ 12. $\dfrac{2}{x} - \dfrac{3}{2x} = \dfrac{11}{3} - \dfrac{4}{3x}$

Some statements of inequality that involve fractions can be solved very much like equations. First, find the LCD of the fractions. Next, multiply each member of the inequality by this quantity in order to eliminate all fractions. Then solve, using the addition and multiplication properties of inequality.

EXAMPLE 3   Solve: $\dfrac{x}{3} - \dfrac{2x+1}{4} > 1$.

Solution

$$12\left(\dfrac{x}{3}\right) - 12\left(\dfrac{2x+1}{4}\right) > 12(1)$$

$$4x - 3(2x+1) > 12$$

$$4x - 6x - 3 > 12$$

$$-2x > 15$$

$$x < -\dfrac{15}{2} \quad \text{(Why?)}$$

EXAMPLE 4   Solve for x: $\dfrac{x+1}{x} < 3$.

Solution   First rewrite as follows:

$$\dfrac{x+1}{x} - 3 < 0$$

$$\dfrac{1-2x}{x} < 0$$

Now use a table of signs to obtain the solution $x < 0$ or $x > \dfrac{1}{2}$.

An alternative method begins by multiplying through by x. However this is more difficult because it calls for two cases, $x > 0$ and $x < 0$.

The general procedures for solving problems outlined in Section 1.3 apply to problems that involve fractions as well. The reader is advised to review that material at this time. Then study the following illustrative example.

EXAMPLE 5   Working alone Harry can mow a lawn in 3 hours. Elliot can complete the same job in 2 hours. How long will it take them working together?

Solution   To solve work problems of this type, we first consider the part of the job that can be done in 1 hour.

Let $x = $ time (in hours) to do the job together

Then $\dfrac{1}{x} = $ portion of job done in 1 hour working together

Also: $\dfrac{1}{2} = $ portion of job done by Elliot in 1 hour

$\dfrac{1}{3} = $ portion of job done by Harry in 1 hour

Working together should enable the boys to do the job in less time than it would take either of them to do the job alone. If Elliot can do the job alone in 2 hours, together the two boys should take less than this time.

Working together, the part of the job they can do in one hour is $\frac{1}{2} + \frac{1}{3}$. Thus

$$\frac{1}{2} + \frac{1}{3} = \frac{1}{x}$$

$$3x + 2x = 6$$

$$5x = 6$$

$$x = 1\frac{1}{5}$$

Together they need $1\frac{1}{5}$ hours, or 1 hours, 12 minutes.

The final example of this section illustrates how the solution of a rational equation is used in solving a nonlinear system.

EXAMPLE 6 Solve the system

$$y = \frac{2}{x}$$

$$y = -2x + 5$$

Solution Set both values for y equal to each other.

$$\frac{2}{x} = -2x + 5$$

Multiply by x.

$$2 = -2x^2 + 5x$$

Solve for x.

$$2x^2 - 5x + 2 = 0$$

$$(2x - 1)(x - 2) = 0$$

$$x = \tfrac{1}{2} \quad \text{or} \quad x = 2$$

For $x = \frac{1}{2}$, $y = -2(\frac{1}{2}) + 5 = 4$. For $x = 2$, $y = -2(2) + 5 = 1$. The points of intersection are $(\frac{1}{2}, 4)$ and $(2, 1)$. Check these points in the original system.

EXERCISES 5.4

Solve for x and check your results.

1 $\dfrac{x}{2} - \dfrac{x}{5} = 6$

2 $\dfrac{2}{x} - \dfrac{5}{x} = 6$

3 $\dfrac{x-1}{2} = \dfrac{x+2}{4}$

4 $\dfrac{2}{x-1} = \dfrac{4}{x+2}$

5 $\dfrac{5}{x} - \dfrac{3}{4x} = 1$

6 $\dfrac{3x}{4} - \dfrac{3}{2} = \dfrac{x}{6} + \dfrac{4x}{3}$

7 $\dfrac{2x+1}{5} - \dfrac{x-2}{3} = 1$

8 $\dfrac{3x-2}{4} - \dfrac{x-1}{3} = \dfrac{1}{2}$

9 $\dfrac{x+4}{2x-10} = \dfrac{8}{7}$

10 $\dfrac{10}{x} - \dfrac{1}{2} = \dfrac{15}{2x}$

11 $\dfrac{2}{x+6} - \dfrac{2}{x-6} = 0$

12 $\dfrac{1}{3x-1} + \dfrac{1}{3x+1} = 0$

13 $\dfrac{x+1}{x+10} = \dfrac{1}{2x}$

14 $\dfrac{3}{x+1} = \dfrac{9}{x^2 - 3x - 4}$

15 $\dfrac{x^2}{2} - \dfrac{3x}{2} + 1 = 0$

16 $\dfrac{x+1}{x-1} - \dfrac{2}{x(x-1)} = \dfrac{4}{x}$

17 $\dfrac{5}{x^2 - 9} = \dfrac{3}{x+3} - \dfrac{2}{x-3}$

18 $\dfrac{3}{x^2 - 25} = \dfrac{5}{x-5} - \dfrac{5}{x+5}$

19 $\dfrac{1}{x^2 + 4} + \dfrac{1}{x^2 - 4} = \dfrac{18}{x^4 - 16}$

20 $\dfrac{3}{x^3 - 8} = \dfrac{1}{x-2}$

21 $\dfrac{2x-5}{x+1} - \dfrac{3}{x^2 + x} = 0$

22 $\dfrac{2}{x} = -2x + 5$

23 $\dfrac{10 - 5x}{3x} - \dfrac{2}{x+5} = \dfrac{8 - 4x}{x+5}$

24 $\dfrac{2-x}{x+1} + \dfrac{x+8}{x-2} = \dfrac{4-x}{x^2 - x - 2}$

25 $\dfrac{3}{2x^2 - 3x - 2} - \dfrac{x+2}{2x+1} = \dfrac{2x}{10 - 5x}$

26 $\dfrac{2x-2}{x^2 + 2x} - \dfrac{5x-6}{6x} = \dfrac{1-x}{x+5}$

In Exercises 27–34 solve for the indicated variable.

27 $\dfrac{v^2}{K} = \dfrac{2g}{m},$ for m

28 $A = \dfrac{h}{2}(b + B),$ for B

29 $S = \pi(r_1 + r_2)s,$ for r_1

30 $V = \dfrac{1}{3}\pi r^2 h,$ for h

31 $d = \dfrac{s-a}{n-1},$ for s

32 $S = \dfrac{n}{2}[2a + (n-1)d],$ for d

33 $\dfrac{1}{f} = \dfrac{1}{m} + \dfrac{1}{p},$ for m

34 $c = \dfrac{2ab}{a+b},$ for b

Solve the inequalities.

35 $\dfrac{x}{2} - \dfrac{x}{3} \le 5$

36 $\dfrac{x}{3} - \dfrac{x}{2} \le 5$

37 $\dfrac{x+3}{4} - \dfrac{x}{2} > 1$

38 $\dfrac{x}{3} - \dfrac{x-1}{2} < 2$

39 $\frac{1}{2}(x+1) - \frac{2}{3}(x-2) < \frac{1}{6}$

40 $\frac{1}{2}(x-2) - \frac{1}{3}(x-1) > 1$

41 $\dfrac{2x+3}{x} < 1$

42 $\dfrac{x}{x-1} > 2$

43 What number must be subtracted from both the numerator and denominator of the fraction $\frac{11}{23}$ to give a fraction whose value is $\frac{2}{5}$?

44 The denominator of a fraction is 3 more than the numerator. If 5 is added to the numerator and 4 is subtracted from the denominator, the value of the new fraction is 2. Find the original fraction.

45 One pipe can empty a tank in 3 hours. A second pipe takes 4 hours to complete the same job. How long will it take to empty the tank if both pipes are used?

46 Working together Wendy and Julie can paint their room in 3 hours. If it takes Wendy 5 hours to do the job alone, how long would it take Julie to paint the room working by herself?

47 Find two fractions whose sum is $\frac{2}{3}$ if the smaller fraction is $\frac{1}{2}$ the larger one. (*Hint:* Let x represent the larger fraction.)

48 A rope that is 20 feet long is cut into two pieces. The ratio of the smaller piece to the larger piece is $\frac{3}{5}$. Find the length of the shorter piece.

49 The shadow of a tree is 20 feet long at the same time that a 1-foot-high flower casts a 4-inch shadow. How high is the tree?

50 The area A of a triangle is given by $A = \dfrac{bh}{2}$, where b is the length of the base and h is the length of the altitude.
(a) Solve for h in terms of A and b.
(b) Find h when $A = 100$ and $b = 25$.

51 If 561 is divided by a certain number, the quotient is 29 and the remainder is 10. Find the number. (*Hint:* For $N \div D$ we have $\dfrac{N}{D} = Q + \dfrac{R}{D}$, where Q is the quotient and R is the remainder.)

52 A student received grades of 72, 75, and 78 on three tests. What must her score on the next test be for her to have an average grade of 80 for all four tests?

53 The denominator of a certain fraction is 1 more than the numerator. If the numerator is increased by $2\frac{1}{2}$, the value will be equal to the reciprocal of the original fraction. Find the original fraction.

*54 Dan takes twice as long as George to complete a

certain job. Working together they can complete the job in 6 hours. How long will it take Dan to complete the job by himself?

*55 Prove:

$$\text{If } \frac{a}{b} = \frac{c}{d}, \text{ then } \frac{a+b}{b} = \frac{c+d}{d}$$

*56 Prove:

$$\text{If } \frac{a}{b} = \frac{c}{d}, \text{ then } \frac{a}{a+b} = \frac{c}{c+d}$$

*57 A bookstore has a stock of 30 paperback copies of *Algebra*, as well as 50 hardcover copies of the same book. They wish to increase their stock for the new semester. Based on past experience, they want their final numbers of paperback and hard-cover copies to be in the ratio 4 to 3. However, the publisher stipulates that they will only sell the store 2 copies of the paperback edition for each copy of the hardcover edition ordered. Under these conditions, how many of each edition should the store order to achieve the 4:3 ratio?

58 To find out how wide a certain river is, a pole 20 feet high is set straight up on one of the banks. Another pole 4 feet long is also set straight up, on the same side, some distance away from the embankment. The observer waits until the shadow of the 20-foot pole just reaches the other side of the river. At that time he measures the shadow of the 4-foot pole and finds it to be 34 feet. Use this information to determine the width of the river.

*59 A certain college gives 4 points per credit for a grade of A, 3 points per credit for a B, 2 points per credit for a C, 1 point per credit for a D, and 0 for an F. A student is taking 15 credits for the semester. She expects A's in a 4 credit course and in a 3 credit course. She also expects a B in another 3 credit course and a D in a 2 credit course. What grade must she get in the fifth course in order to earn a 3.4 grade point average for the term?

$$\left(\textit{Hint: Grade point average} = \frac{\text{total points}}{\text{total credits}}. \right)$$

*60 Solve $f(x) < 0$, where $f(x) = \dfrac{1}{x^3 + 6x^2 + 12x + 8}$, and graph $y = f(x)$.

Solve each system and graph.

61 $2x + 3y = 7$
$y = \dfrac{1}{x}$

*62 $y = x^2 - 2x - 4$
$y = -\dfrac{8}{x}$

5.5

Variation

If a car is traveling at a constant rate of 40 miles per hour, then the distance d traveled in t hours is given by $d = 40t$. The change in the distance is "directly" affected by the change in the time; as t increases, so does d. We say that d *is directly proportional to t*. This is because $d = 40t$ converts to the proportion $\dfrac{d}{t} = 40$. We also say that d *varies directly as t* and that 40 is the *constant of variation*.

Direct variation is a functional relationship in the sense that $y = kx$ defines y to be a function of x.

DIRECT VARIATION

y varies directly as x if

$$y = kx$$

for some constant of variation k.

EXAMPLE 1
(a) Write the equation that expresses this direct variation: y varies directly as x, and y is 8 when x is 12.
(b) Find y for $x = 30$.

Solution

(a) Since y varies directly as x, we have $y = kx$ for some constant k. To find k, substitute the given values for the variables and solve.

$$8 = k(12)$$
$$\tfrac{2}{3} = k$$

Thus $y = \tfrac{2}{3}x$.

(b) For $x = 30$, $y = \tfrac{2}{3}(30) = 20$.

Numerous examples of direct variation can be found in geometry. Here are some illustrations.

Circumference of a circle of radius r:

$C = 2\pi r$; C varies directly as the radius r;
            2π is the constant of variation.

Area of a circle of radius r:

$A = \pi r^2$; A varies directly as the square of r;
          π is the constant of variation.

Area of an equilateral triangle of side s:

$A = \dfrac{\sqrt{3}}{4}s^2$; A varies directly as s^2;

$\dfrac{\sqrt{3}}{4}$ is the constant of proportionality.

Volume of a cube of side e:

$V = e^3$; V varies directly as the cube of e (as e^3);
        1 is the constant of variation.

EXAMPLE 2 According to Hooke's law, the force F required to stretch a spring x units is directly proportional to the length x. If a force of 20 pounds is needed to stretch a spring 3 inches, how far is the spring stretched by a force of 60 pounds?

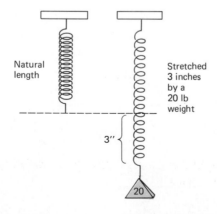

Natural length

Stretched 3 inches by a 20 lb weight

3″

20

Throughout this section the constant of variation k will be a positive number.

Solution Since F varies directly as x, we have $F = kx$. Solve for k by substituting the known values for F and x.

$$20 = k(3)$$

$$\tfrac{20}{3} = k$$

Thus $F = \tfrac{20}{3}x$. Now let $F = 60$ and solve for x.

$$60 = \tfrac{20}{3}x$$

$$60(\tfrac{3}{20}) = x$$

$$9 = x$$

Thus 60 pounds stretches the spring 9 inches.

When y varies directly as x, the variables x and y increase or decrease together. There are other situations where one variable increases as the other decreases. We refer to this as *inverse variation*.

INVERSE VARIATION

y varies inversely as x if

$$y = \frac{k}{x}$$

for some constant of variation k.

EXAMPLE 3 According to Boyle's law, the pressure P of a compressed gas is inversely proportional to the volume V. Suppose that there is a pressure of 25 pounds per square inch when the volume of gas is 400 cubic inches. Find the pressure when the gas is compressed to 200 cubic inches.

Solution Since P varies inversely as V, we have

$$P = \frac{k}{V}$$

Substitute the known values for P and V and solve for k.

$$25 = \frac{k}{400}$$

$$10,000 = k$$

Thus $P = \dfrac{10,000}{V}$, and when $V = 200$ we have

Note that the pressure increases as the volume decreases.

$$P = \frac{10,000}{200} = 50$$

The pressure is 50 pounds per square inch.

The variation of a variable may depend on more than one other variable. Here are some illustrations:

$z = kxy$; z varies *jointly* as x and y.

$z = kx^2y$; z varies *jointly* as x^2 and y.

$z = \dfrac{k}{xy}$; z varies *inversely* as x and y.

$z = \dfrac{kx}{y}$; z varies *directly* as x and *inversely* as y.

$w = \dfrac{kxy^3}{z}$; w varies *jointly* as x and y^3 and *inversely* as z.

EXAMPLE 4 Describe the variation given by these equations:

(a) $z = kx^2y^3$ **(b)** $z = \dfrac{kx^2}{y}$ **(c)** $V = \pi r^2 h$

Solution

(a) z varies jointly as x^2 and y^3.
(b) z varies directly as x^2 and inversely as y.
(c) V varies jointly as r^2 and h.

EXAMPLE 5 Suppose that z varies directly as x and inversely as the square of y. If $z = \frac{1}{3}$ when $x = 4$ and $y = 6$, find z when $x = 12$ and $y = 4$.

Solution

$$z = \frac{kx}{y^2}$$

$$\frac{1}{3} = \frac{k(4)}{6^2}$$

$$\frac{1}{3} = \frac{k}{9}$$

$$3 = k$$

Thus $z = \dfrac{3x}{y^2}$. When $x = 12$ and $y = 4$ we have

$$z = \frac{3(12)}{4^2} = \frac{9}{4}$$

In Exercises 1–4, write the equation for the given variation and identify the constant of variation.

1 The perimeter P of a square varies directly as the side s.

2 The area of a circle varies directly as the square of the radius.

3 The area of a rectangle 5 centimeters wide varies directly as its length.

4 The volume of a rectangular-shaped box 10 centimeters high varies jointly as the length and width.

In Exercises 5–9, write the equation for the given variation using k as the constant of variation.

5 z varies directly as x and y^3.

6 z varies inversely as x and y^3.

7 z varies directly as x and inversely as y^3.

8 w varies directly as x and y and z.

9 w varies directly as x^2 and inversely as y and z.

In Exercises 10–14, find the constant of variation.

10 y varies directly as x; $y = 4$ when $x = \frac{2}{3}$.

11 s varies directly as t^2; $s = 50$ when $t = 10$.

12 y varies inversely as x; $y = 15$ when $x = \frac{1}{3}$.

13 u varies directly as v and w; $u = 2$ when $v = 15$ and $w = \frac{2}{3}$.

14 z varies directly as x and inversely as the square of y; $z = \frac{7}{2}$ when $x = 14$ and $y = 6$.

15 a varies inversely as the square of b and $a = 10$ when $b = 5$. Find a when $b = 25$.

16 z varies jointly as x and y; $z = \frac{3}{2}$ when $x = \frac{5}{6}$ and $y = \frac{9}{20}$. Find z when $x = 2$ and $y = 7$.

17 s varies jointly as l and the square of w; $s = \frac{10}{3}$ when $l = 12$ and $w = \frac{5}{6}$. Find s when $l = 15$ and $w = \frac{9}{4}$.

18 The cost C of producing x number of articles varies directly as x. If it costs \$560 to produce 70 articles, what is C when $x = 400$?

19 If a ball rolls down an inclined plane, the distance traveled varies directly as the square of the time. If the ball rolls 12 feet in 2 seconds, how far will it roll in 3 seconds?

20 The volume V of a right circular cone varies jointly as the square of the radius r of the base, and the altitude h. If $V = 8\pi$ cubic centimeters when $r = 2$ centimeters and $h = 6$ centimeters, find the formula for the volume V.

■ 21 A force of 2.4 kilograms is needed to stretch a spring 1.8 centimeters. Use Hooke's law to determine the force required to stretch the spring 3.0 centimeters.

■ 22 The force required to compress a metal spring from its natural length is directly proportional to the change in the length of the spring. If 235 pounds is required to compress the spring from its natural length of 18 inches to a length of 15 inches, how much force is required to compress it from 18 inches to 12 inches?

23 Fifty kilograms per square centimeter is the pressure exerted by 150 cubic centimeters of a gas.

Use Boyle's law to find the pressure if the gas is compressed to 100 cubic centimeters.

24 The gas in Exercise 23 expands to 500 cubic centimeters. What is the pressure?

■ 25 If we neglect air resistance, the distance that an object will fall from a height near the surface of the earth is directly proportional to the square of the time it falls. If the object falls 256 feet in 4 seconds, how far will it fall in 7 seconds?

26 The volume of a right circular cylinder varies jointly as its height and the square of the radius of the base. The volume is 360π cubic centimeters when the height is 10 centimeters and the radius is 6 centimeters. Find V when $h = 18$ centimeters and $r = 5$ centimeters.

27 If the volume of a sphere varies directly as the cube of its radius and $V = 288\pi$ cubic inches when $r = 6$ inches, find V when $r = 2$ inches.

*28 The resistance to the flow of electricity through a wire depends on the length and thickness of the wire. The resistance R is measured in *ohms* and varies directly as the length l and inversely as the square of the diameter d. If a wire 200 feet long with diameter 0.16 inch has a resistance of 64 ohms, how much resistance will there be if only 50 feet of wire is used?

*29 A wire made of the same material as the wire in Exercise 28 is 100 feet long. Find R if $d = 0.4$ inch. Find R if $d = 0.04$ inch.

*30 If z varies jointly as x and y, how does x vary with respect to y and z?

■ 31 A rectangular shaped beam is to be cut from a round log with a 2.5 foot diameter.

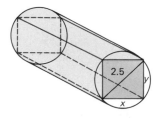

The strength s of the beam varies jointly as its height y and the square of its width x.

(a) Write s as a function of y.

(b) Write s as a function of x.

(c) Use a calculator to find s to two decimal places when $x = y$. Express the answer in terms of the constant of proportionality.

In this and in the following two sections we will learn some methods for finding the x-intercepts of polynomial functions and rational functions. First let us briefly review the process used in division of polynomials; it is very much like the division algorithm in arithmetic. Consider the quotient

$$(x^3 - x^2 - 5x + 6) \div (x - 2)$$

STEP 1. Divide x^3 by x. Place the result in the quotient.

$$\text{Divisor} \overline{\smash{\big)}\, \text{Dividend}}^{\text{Quotient}}$$

$$\begin{array}{r} x^2 \\ x - 2 \overline{\smash{\big)}\, x^3 - x^2 - 5x + 6} \end{array}$$

STEP 2. Multiply $x - 2$ by x^2 and subtract.

$$\begin{array}{r} x^2 \\ x - 2 \overline{\smash{\big)}\, x^3 - x^2 - 5x + 6} \\ x^3 + 2x^2 \\ \hline x^2 \end{array}$$

STEP 3. Bring down the next term, $-5x$, and divide again: $x^2 \div x = x$.

$$\begin{array}{r} x^2 + x \\ x - 2 \overline{\smash{\big)}\, x^3 - x^2 - 5x + 6} \\ x^3 - 2x^2 \\ \hline x^2 - 5x \end{array}$$

STEP 4. Repeat this process until you have used all terms in the dividend. The completed division follows:

$$\begin{array}{r} x^2 + x - 3 \\ x - 2 \overline{\smash{\big)}\, x^3 - x^2 - 5x + 6} \\ x^3 - 2x^2 \\ \hline x^2 - 5x \\ x^2 - 2x \\ \hline -3x + 6 \\ -3x + 6 \\ \hline 0 \end{array}$$

When dividing two polynomials, be sure that both the dividend and the divisor are in descending order of powers of the variable. Also, missing powers of the variable in the dividend should be denoted by using a form of zero as in Example 1.

The remainder is 0. To check, multiply $x^2 + x - 3$ by $x - 2$. The result should be $x^3 - x^2 - 5x + 6$.

EXAMPLE 1 Divide: $(5x + 3x^3 - 8) \div (x + 3)$.

Solution First write the dividend in the form $3x^3 + 0x^2 + 5x - 8$; then divide.

$$\begin{array}{r}
3x^2 - 9x\ + 32 \\
x + 3\overline{\smash{\big)}\,3x^3 + 0x^2 +\ 5x\ -\ \ \ 8} \\
\underline{3x^3 + 9x^2} \\
-\,9x^2 +\ 5x \\
\underline{-\,9x^2 - 27x} \\
32x -\ \ \ 8 \\
\underline{-32x + 96} \\
-\,104
\end{array}$$

The quotient is $3x^3 - 9x + 32$ and the remainder is -104. To check, note that the dividend should be equal to the product of the quotient and the divisor, plus the remainder. Verify that the following is correct.

$$(x + 3)(3x^2 - 9x + 32) + (-104) = 3x^3 + 5x - 8$$

We now develop a special procedure for handling long-division problems with polynomials where the divisor is of the form $x \pm c$. To discover this procedure let us first examine the following long-division problem.

$$\begin{array}{r}
x^2 + 3x - 5 \\
x - 2\overline{\smash{\big)}\,x^3 +\ \ x^2 - 11x + 12} \\
\underline{x^3 - 2x^2} \\
+\,3x^2 - 11x \\
\underline{+\,3x^2 -\ \ 6x} \\
-\ \ 5x + 12 \\
\underline{-\ \ 5x + 10} \\
+2
\end{array}$$

Now it should be clear that all of the work done involved the coefficients of the variables and the constants. Thus we could just as easily complete the division by omitting the variables, as long as we write the coefficients in the proper places. The division problem would then look like this:

$$\begin{array}{r}
1\ +\ 3\ -\ \ 5 \\
1 - 2\overline{\smash{\big)}\,1\ +\ 1\ -\ 11 + 12} \\
\underline{①\ -\ 2} \\
+\ 3\ -\ 11 \\
\underline{+\ ③\ -\ \ 6} \\
-\ 5\ +\ 12 \\
\underline{-\ ⑤\ +\ 10} \\
+\ \ 2
\end{array}$$

Since the circled numerals are repetitions of those immediately above them, this process can be further shortened by deleting them. Moreover, since these circled numbers are the products of the numbers in the quotient by the 1 in the divisor, we may also eliminate this 1. Thus we have the following:

$$\frac{1 + 3 - 5}{-2\overline{\smash{\big)}\,1 + 1 - 11 + 12}}$$
$$\underline{-2}$$
$$+ 3 - 11$$
$$\underline{-6}$$
$$- 5 + 12$$
$$\underline{+10}$$
$$+2$$

It is not necessary to bring down the -11 and 12.

$$\frac{1 + 3 - 5}{-2\overline{\smash{\big)}\,1 + 1 - 11 + 12}}$$
$$\underline{-2}$$
$$+ 3$$
$$\underline{-6}$$
$$- 5$$
$$\underline{+10}$$
$$+2$$

Move the numerals upward.

$$\frac{1 + 3 - 5}{-2\overline{\smash{\big)}\,1 + 1 - 11 + 12}}$$
$$\underline{-2 - 6 + 10}$$
$$+ 3 - 5 + 2$$

When the top numeral 1 is brought down, then the last line contains the coefficients of the quotient and the remainder. So eliminate the line above the dividend.

$$-2\overline{\smash{\big)}\,1 \;+1 \;-11 + 12}$$
$$\underline{-2 \;-\; 6 + 10}$$
$$1 \;+3 \;-\; 5 \;\big|\; +2 \quad \text{remainder}$$

Quotient: $\underbrace{x^2 + 3x - 5}$

We can further simplify this process by changing the sign of the divisor, making it $+2$ instead of -2. This change allows us to add throughout rather than subtract, as follows.

$$+2\overline{\smash{\big)}\,1 \;+1 \;-11 + 12\}} \quad \text{coefficients of dividend}$$
$$\underline{+2 \;+\; 6 - 10}$$
coefficients of quotient: $\;1 \;+3 \;-\; 5 \;\big|\; +2 \quad \text{remainder}$

Quotient: $\underbrace{x^2 + 3x - 5}$

The long-division process has now been condensed to this short form. Doing a division problem by this short form is called **synthetic division**, as illustrated in the examples that follow.

EXAMPLE 2 Use synthetic division to find $(2x^3 - 9x^2 + 10x - 7) \div (x - 3)$.

Solution Write the coefficients of the dividend in descending order. Change the sign of the divisor (change -3 to $+3$).

$$+3\overline{\smash{\big)}\,2 - 9 + 10 - 7}$$

Now bring down the first term, 2, and multiply by $+3$.

$$+3\overline{\smash{\big)}\,2 - 9 + 10 - 7}$$
$$\underline{+6}$$
$$2$$

Add -9 and $+6$ to obtain the sum -3. Multiply this sum by $+3$ and repeat the process to the end. The completed example should look like this:

$$+3\overline{\smash{\big)}\,2 - 9 + 10 - 7}$$
$$\underline{+6 - 9 + 3}$$
$$2 - 3 + 1 \;\big|\; -4$$

Since the original dividend began with x^3 (third degree), the quotient will begin with x^2 (second degree). Thus we read the last line as implying a quotient of $2x^2 - 3x + 1$ and a remainder of -4. Check this result by using the long-division process.

The synthetic division process has been developed for divisors of the form $x - c$. (Thus, in Example 2, $c = 3$.) A minor adjustment also permits divisors by polynomials of the form $x + c$. For example, a divisor of $x + 2$ may be written as $x - (-2)$; $c = -2$.

Note that the quotient in a synthetic division problem is always a polynomial of degree one less than that of the dividend. This is so because the divisor has degree 1. The bottom line in the synthetic division process, except for the last entry on the right, gives the coefficients of the quotient: a polynomial in standard form.

EXAMPLE 3   Use synthetic division to find the quotient and the remainder.

$$(-\tfrac{1}{3}x^4 + \tfrac{1}{6}x^2 - 7x - 4) \div (x + 3)$$

Solution   Write $x + 3$ as $x - (-3)$. Since there is no x^3 term in the dividend, use $0x^3$.

$$
\begin{array}{r}
-3\,\big|\!-\tfrac{1}{3} + 0 + \tfrac{1}{6} - 7 - 4 \\
+1 - 3 + \tfrac{17}{2} - \tfrac{9}{2} \\
\hline
-\tfrac{1}{3} + 1 - \tfrac{17}{6} + \tfrac{3}{2}\,\big|\!-\tfrac{17}{2} = \text{remainder}
\end{array}
$$

Quotient: $-\tfrac{1}{3}x^3 + x^2 - \tfrac{17}{6}x + \tfrac{3}{2}$ Remainder: $-\tfrac{17}{2}$

Check this result.

EXERCISES 5.6

Complete Exercises 1–6 by long division and by synthetic division.

1 $(x^3 - 2x^2 - 5x + 6) \div (x - 3)$
2 $(x^3 - x^2 - 5x + 2) \div (x + 2)$
3 $(2x^3 + x^2 - 3x + 7) \div (x + 1)$
4 $(3x^3 - 2x^2 + x - 1) \div (x - 1)$
5 $(x^3 + 5x^2 - 7x + 8) \div (x - 2)$
6 $(x^3 - 3x^2 + x - 5) \div (x + 3)$

Use synthetic division to find each quotient and check.

7 $(x^4 - 3x^3 + 7x^2 - 2x + 1) \div (x + 2)$
8 $(x^4 + x^3 - 2x^2 + 3x - 1) \div (x - 2)$
9 $(2x^4 - 3x^2 + 4x - 2) \div (x - 1)$
10 $(3x^4 + x^3 - 2x + 3) \div (x + 1)$
11 $(x^3 - 27) \div (x - 3)$
12 $(x^3 - 27) \div (x + 3)$
13 $(x^3 + 27) \div (x + 3)$
14 $(x^3 + 27) \div (x - 3)$
15 $(x^4 - 16) \div (x - 2)$

16 $(x^4 - 16) \div (x + 2)$
17 $(x^4 + 16) \div (x + 2)$
18 $(4x^5 - x^3 + 5x^2 + \tfrac{3}{2}x - \tfrac{1}{2}) \div (x + \tfrac{1}{2})$
19 $(x^4 - \tfrac{1}{2}x^3 + \tfrac{1}{3}x^2 - \tfrac{1}{4}x + \tfrac{1}{5}) \div (x - 1)$

Use long division to find each quotient.

*20 $(2x^3 + 9x^2 - 3x - 1) \div (2x - 1)$
*21 $(x^3 - x^2 - x + 10) \div (x^2 - 3x + 5)$
*22 $(3x^5 + 4x^3 - 12x^2) \div (x^2 - x)$

23 A division problem can be represented in this way:

$$\frac{\text{dividend}}{\text{divisor}} = \text{quotient} + \frac{\text{remainder}}{\text{divisor}}$$

Using N for dividend, D for divisor, Q for quotient, and R for remainder, we can write this relationship as follows:

$$\frac{N}{D} = Q + \frac{R}{D}$$

Multiply each term of this equation by D and explain how this justifies the usual method of checking a division problem by multiplication.

When the polynomial $p(x) = 2x^3 - 9x^2 + 10x - 7$ is divided by $x - 3$, the quotient is the polynomial $q(x) = 2x^2 - 3x + 1$ and the remainder $r = -4$. (See Example 2, page 201.) As a check we see that

The remainder and factor theorems

$$\underbrace{2x^3 - 9x^2 + 10x - 7}_{p(x)} = \underbrace{(2x^2 - 3x + 1)}_{q(x)} \cdot \underbrace{(x - 3)}_{} + \underbrace{(-4)}_{r}$$

In general, whenever a polynomial $p(x)$ is divided by $x - c$ we have

$$p(x) = q(x)(x - c) + r$$

Another form of this is
$$\frac{p(x)}{x - c} = q(x) + \frac{r}{x - c}.$$

where $q(x)$ is the quotient and r is the (constant) remainder. Since this equation holds for all x, we may let $x = c$ and obtain

$$p(c) = q(c)(c - c) + r$$
$$= q(c) \cdot 0 + r$$
$$= r$$

This result may be summarized as follows:

REMAINDER THEOREM

If a polynomial $p(x)$ is divided by $x - c$, the remainder is equal to $p(c)$.

EXAMPLE 1   Find the remainder when $p(x) = 3x^3 - 5x^2 + 7x + 5$ is divided by $x - 2$.

Solution   By the remainder theorem, the answer is $p(2)$.

$$p(x) = 3x^3 - 5x^2 + 7x + 5$$
$$p(2) = 3(2)^3 - 5(2)^2 + 7(2) + 5$$
$$= 23$$

EXAMPLE 2   Let $f(x) = x^3 - 2x^2 + 3x - 1$. Use synthetic division and the remainder theorem to find $f(3)$.

Solution

$$\begin{array}{r} 3 | 1 - 2 + 3 - 1 \\ \underline{+ 3 + 3 + 18} \\ 1 + 1 + 6 \,|\,\underline{+17} = \text{remainder} = f(3) \end{array}$$

Use synthetic division to find the remainder r when $p(x)$ is divided by $x - c$. Verify that $r = p(c)$ by substituting $x = c$ into $p(x)$.

1 $p(x) = x^5 - 7x^4 + 4x^3 + 10x^2 - x - 5;\quad x - 1$
2 $p(x) = x^4 + 11x^3 + 11x^2 + 11x + 10;\quad x + 10$
3 $p(x) = x^4 + 11x^3 + 11x^2 + 11x + 10;\quad x - 10$
4 $p(x) = 6x^3 - 40x^2 + 25;\quad x - 6$

Once again, we are going to consider the division of a polynomial $p(x)$ by a divisor of the form $x - c$. First note that

$$p(x) = q(x)(x - c) + r$$

where $q(x)$ is the quotient and r is the (constant) remainder. Now suppose that $r = 0$. Then the remainder theorem gives $p(c) = r = 0$, and the preceding equation becomes

$$p(x) = q(x)(x - c)$$

It follows that $x - c$ is a *factor* of $p(x)$. Conversely, suppose that $x - c$ is a factor of $p(x)$. This means there is another polynomial, say $q(x)$, so that

$$p(x) = q(x)(x - c)$$

or

$$p(x) = q(x)(x - c) + 0$$

which tells us that when $p(x)$ is divided by $x - c$ the remainder is zero. These observations comprise the following result:

If $p(c) = 0$, then c is a *zero* of the polynomial and is a root of $p(x) = 0$.

FACTOR THEOREM

A polynomial $p(x)$ has a factor $x - c$ if and only if $p(c) = 0$.

EXAMPLE 3   Show that $x - 2$ is a factor of $p(x) = x^3 - 3x^2 + 7x - 10$.

Solution   By the factor theorem we can state that $x - 2$ is a factor of $p(x)$ if $p(2) = 0$.

$$p(2) = 2^3 - 3(2)^2 + 7(2) - 10$$
$$= 0$$

EXAMPLE 4   **(a)** Use the factor theorem to show that $x + 3$ is a factor of $p(x) = x^3 - x^2 - 8x + 12$.   **(b)** Factor $p(x)$ completely.

Solution
(a) First write $x + 3 = x - (-3)$, so that $c = -3$. Then use synthetic division.

$$-3 \underline{|1 - 1 - 8 + 12}$$
$$\underline{-3 + 12 - 12}$$
$$1 - 4 + 4 \boxed{\;+0}$$

Since $p(-3) = 0$, the factor theorem tells us that $x + 3$ is a factor of $p(x)$.

(b) Synthetic division has produced the quotient $x^2 - 4x + 4$. Therefore, since $x + 3$ is a factor of $p(x)$, we get

$$x^3 - x^2 - 8x + 12 = (x^2 - 4x + 4)(x + 3)$$

To get the complete factored form, observe that $x^2 - 4x + 4 = (x - 2)^2$. Thus

$$x^3 - x^2 - 8x + 12 = (x - 2)^2(x + 3)$$

EXERCISES 5.7

In Exercises 1–6, use synthetic division and the remainder theorem.

1 $f(x) = x^3 - x^2 + 3x - 2$; find $f(2)$.

2 $f(x) = 2x^3 + 3x^2 - x - 5$; find $f(-1)$.

3 $f(x) = x^4 - 3x^2 + x + 2$; find $f(3)$.

4 $f(x) = x^4 + 2x^3 - 3x - 1$; find $f(-2)$.

5 $f(x) = x^5 - x^3 + 2x^2 + x - 3$; find $f(1)$.

6 $f(x) = 3x^4 + 2x^3 - 3x^2 - x + 7$; find $f(-3)$.

Find the remainder for each division by substitution, using the remainder theorem. That is, in Exercise 7 (for example) let $f(x) = x^3 - 2x^2 + 3x - 5$ and find $f(2) = r$.

7 $(x^3 - 2x^2 + 3x - 5) \div (x - 2)$

8 $(x^3 - 2x^2 + 3x - 5) \div (x + 2)$

9 $(2x^3 + 3x^2 - 5x + 1) \div (x - 3)$

10 $(3x^4 - x^3 + 2x^2 - x + 1) \div (x + 3)$

11 $(4x^5 - x^3 - 3x^2 + 2) \div (x + 1)$

12 $(3x^5 - 2x^4 + x^3 - 7x + 1) \div (x - 1)$

In Exercises 13–23, show that the given binomial $x - c$ is a factor of $p(x)$, and then factor $p(x)$ completely.

13 $p(x) = x^3 + 6x^2 + 11x + 6$; $x + 1$

14 $p(x) = x^3 - 6x^2 + 11x - 6$; $x - 1$

15 $p(x) = x^3 + 5x^2 - 2x - 24$; $x - 2$

16 $p(x) = -x^3 + 11x^2 - 23x - 35$; $x - 7$

17 $p(x) = -x^3 + 7x + 6$; $x + 2$

18 $p(x) = x^3 + 2x^2 - 13x + 10$; $x + 5$

19 $p(x) = 6x^3 - 25x^2 - 29x + 20$; $x - 5$

20 $p(x) = 12x^3 - 22x^2 - 100x - 16$; $x + 2$

21 $p(x) = x^4 + 4x^3 + 3x^2 - 4x - 4$; $x + 2$

22 $p(x) = x^4 - 8x^3 + 7x^2 + 72x - 144$; $x - 4$

23 $p(x) = x^6 + 6x^5 + 8x^4 - 6x^3 - 9x^2$; $x + 3$

*24 When $x^2 + 5x - 2$ is divided by $x + n$, the remainder is -8. Find all possible values of n and check by division.

*25 Find d so that $x + 6$ is a factor of
$$x^4 + 4x^3 - 21x^2 + dx + 108$$

*26 Find b so that $x - 2$ is a factor of
$$x^3 + bx^2 - 13x + 10$$

*27 Find a so that $x - 10$ is a factor of
$$ax^3 - 25x^2 + 47x + 30$$

5.8

The rational root theorem

Consider the polynomial equation

$$(3x + 2)(5x - 4)(2x - 3) = 0$$

To find the roots, set each factor equal to zero.

$$3x + 2 = 0 \qquad 5x - 4 = 0 \qquad 2x - 3 = 0$$

$$x = -\tfrac{2}{3} \qquad\qquad x = \tfrac{4}{5} \qquad\qquad x = \tfrac{3}{2}$$

Now multiply the original three factors and keep careful note of the details of this multiplication. Your result should be

$$30x^3 - 49x^2 - 10x + 24 = 0$$

which must have the same three rational roots.

As you analyze this multiplication it becomes clear that the constant 24 is the product of the three constants in the binomials, 2, −4, and −3. Also, the leading coefficient, 30, is the product of the three original coefficients of x in the binomials, namely 3, 5, and 2.

Furthermore, 3, 5, and 2 are also the denominators of the roots $-\tfrac{2}{3}, \tfrac{4}{5}$, and $\tfrac{3}{2}$. Therefore, the denominators of the rational roots are all factors of 30, and their numerators are all factors of 24.

These results are not accidental. It turns out that we have been discussing the following general result:

RATIONAL ROOT THEOREM

Let $f(x) = a_n x^n + a_{n-1} x^{n-1} + \cdots + a_1 x + a_0 \ (a_n \neq 0)$ be an nth-degree polynomial with integer coefficients. If $\dfrac{p}{q}$ is a rational root of $f(x) = 0$, where $\dfrac{p}{q}$ is in lowest terms, then p is a factor of a_0 and q is a factor of a_n.

Let us see how this theorem can be applied to find the rational roots of

$$f(x) = 4x^3 - 16x^2 + 11x + 10 = 0$$

Begin by listing all factors of the constant 10 and of the leading coefficient 4.

Factors of 10: $\pm 1, \pm 2, \pm 5, \pm 10$ (possible numerators)

Factors of 4: $\pm 1, \pm 2, \pm 4$ (possible denominators)

Possible rational roots (take each number in the first row and divide by each number in the second row): $\pm 1, \pm\tfrac{1}{2}, \pm\tfrac{1}{4}, \pm 2, \pm 5, \pm\tfrac{5}{2}, \pm\tfrac{5}{4}, \pm 10$

If $f(c) = 0$, then c is a root; if $f(c) \neq 0$, then c is not a root.

To decide which (if any) of these are roots of $f(x) = 0$, we could substitute the values directly into $f(x)$. However, it is easier to use synthetic division because in most cases it leads to easier computations and also makes quotients available. Therefore, we proceed by using synthetic division with divisors c, where c is a possible rational root.

$$\begin{array}{r|rrrr} 1 & 4 & -16 & +11 & +10 \\ & & +4 & -12 & -1 \\ \hline & 4 & -12 & -1 & +9 \end{array}$$

Since $f(1) = 9 \neq 0$, 1 is *not* a root.

$$\begin{array}{r|rrrr} -1 & 4 & -16 & +11 & +10 \\ & & -4 & +20 & -31 \\ \hline & 4 & -20 & +31 & -21 \end{array}$$

Since $f(-1) = -21 \neq 0$, −1 is *not* a root.

$$\tfrac{1}{2}|4 - 16 + 11 + 10$$
$$\underline{+ 2 - 7 + 2}$$
$$4 - 14 + 4\,\big|+12$$

Since $f(\tfrac{1}{2}) = 12 \neq 0$,
$\tfrac{1}{2}$ is *not* a root.

$$-\tfrac{1}{2}|4 - 16 + 11 + 10$$
$$\underline{- 2 + 9 - 10}$$
$$4 - 18 + 20\,\big|+ 0$$

Since $f(-\tfrac{1}{2}) = 0$,
$-\tfrac{1}{2}$ *is* a root.

By the factor theorem it follows that $x - (-\tfrac{1}{2}) = x + \tfrac{1}{2}$ is a factor of $f(x)$, and synthetic division gives the other factor, $4x^2 - 18x + 20$.

$$f(x) = (x + \tfrac{1}{2})(4x^2 - 18x + 20)$$

To find other roots of $f(x) = 0$ we could proceed by using the rational root theorem for $4x^2 - 18x + 20 = 0$. But this is unnecessary because the quadratic expression is factorable.

$$
\begin{aligned}
f(x) &= (x + \tfrac{1}{2})(4x^2 - 18x + 20) \\
&= (x + \tfrac{1}{2})(2)(2x^2 - 9x + 10) \\
&= 2(x + \tfrac{1}{2})(x - 2)(2x - 5)
\end{aligned}
$$

The solution of $f(x) = 0$ can now be found by setting each factor equal to zero. The solutions are $x = -\tfrac{1}{2}$, $x = 2$, and $x = \tfrac{5}{2}$.

EXAMPLE 1 Factor $f(x) = x^3 + 6x^2 + 11x + 6$.

Solution Since the leading coefficient is 1, whose only factors are ± 1, the possible denominators of a rational root of $f(x) = 0$ can only be ± 1. Hence the possible rational roots must all be factors of $+6$, namely ± 1, ± 2, ± 3, and ± 6. Use synthetic division to test these cases.

Whenever a polynomial has 1 as the leading coefficient, then any rational root will be an integer that is a factor of the constant term of the polynomial.

$$1|1 + 6 + 11 + 6$$
$$\underline{+ 1 + 7 + 18}$$
$$1 + 7 + 18\,\big|+24 = r$$

Since $r = f(1) \neq 0$, $x - 1$ is *not* a factor of $f(x)$.

$$-1|1 + 6 + 11 + 6$$
$$\underline{- 1 - 5 - 6}$$
$$1 + 5 + 6\,\big|+0 = r$$

Since $r = f(-1) = 0$, $x - (-1) = x + 1$ *is* a factor of $f(x)$.

$$x^3 + 6x^2 + 11x + 6 = (x + 1)(x^2 + 5x + 6)$$

Now factor the trinomial:

$$x^3 + 6x^2 + 11x + 6 = (x + 1)(x + 2)(x + 3)$$

For each p(x), find (a) the possible rational roots of p(x) = 0, (b) the factored form of p(x), and (c) the roots of p(x) = 0.

1 $p(x) = x^3 - 3x^2 - 10x + 24$

2 $p(x) = x^4 + 6x^3 + x^2 - 24x + 16$

3 $p(x) = 4x^3 + 20x^2 - 23x + 6$

4 $p(x) = 3x^4 - 13x^3 + 7x^2 - 13x + 4$

EXAMPLE 2   Solve for x: $p(x) = 2x^5 + 7x^4 - 18x^2 - 8x + 8 = 0$.

Solution   The possible rational roots are $\pm 1, \pm\frac{1}{2}, \pm 2, \pm 4$, and ± 8. Testing these possibilities (left to right), the first root we find is $\frac{1}{2}$.

$$\frac{1}{2}\underline{|2 + 7 + 0 - 18 - 8 + 8}$$
$$\phantom{\frac{1}{2}|2}\underline{+ 1 + 4 + 2 - 8 - 8}$$
$$\phantom{\frac{1}{2}|}2 + 8 + 4 - 16 - 16\underline{|+0}$$

Therefore, $x - \frac{1}{2}$ is a factor of $p(x)$.

$$p(x) = (x - \tfrac{1}{2})(2x^4 + 8x^3 + 4x^2 - 16x - 16)$$
$$= 2(x - \tfrac{1}{2})(x^4 + 4x^3 + 2x^2 - 8x - 8)$$

To find other roots of $p(x) = 0$ it now becomes necessary to solve

$$x^4 + 4x^3 + 2x^2 - 8x - 8 = 0$$

The possible rational roots for this equation are $\pm 1, \pm 2, \pm 4$, and ± 8. However, values like ± 1 that were tried before need not be tried again. Why? We find that $x = -2$ is a root:

$$-2\underline{|1 + 4 + 2 - 8 - 8}$$
$$\underline{- 2 - 4 + 4 + 8}$$
$$1 + 2 - 2 - 4\underline{|+0}$$

$$x^4 + 4x^3 + 2x^2 - 8x - 8 = (x + 2)(x^3 + 2x^2 - 2x - 4)$$
$$= (x + 2)[x^2(x + 2) - 2(x + 2)]$$
$$= (x + 2)(x^2 - 2)(x + 2)$$
$$= (x + 2)^2(x^2 - 2)$$

This gives

$$p(x) = 2(x - \tfrac{1}{2})(x^4 + 4x^3 + 2x^2 - 8x - 8)$$
$$= 2(x - \tfrac{1}{2})(x + 2)^2(x^2 - 2)$$
$$= 2(x - \tfrac{1}{2})(x + 2)^2(x + \sqrt{2})(x - \sqrt{2})$$

Setting each factor equal to zero produces the solutions of $p(x) = 0$:

$$x = \tfrac{1}{2}, \quad x = -2, \quad x = -\sqrt{2}, \quad x = \sqrt{2}$$

Solve for x.

1 $x^3 + 2x^2 - 29x + 42 = 0$

2 $x^3 + x^2 - 21x - 45 = 0$

3 $2x^3 - 15x^2 + 24x + 16 = 0$

4 $3x^3 + 2x^2 - 75x - 50 = 0$

5 $x^3 + 3x^2 + 3x + 1 = 0$

6 $x^4 + 3x^3 + 3x^2 + x = 0$

7 $x^4 + 6x^3 + 7x^2 - 12x - 18 = 0$

8 $x^4 + 6x^3 + 2x^2 - 18x - 15 = 0$

9 $x^4 - x^3 - 5x^2 - x - 6 = 0$

10 $x^4 + 2x^3 - 7x^2 - 18x - 18 = 0$

11 $x^4 - 5x^3 + 3x^2 + 15x - 18 = 0$

12 $-x^5 + 5x^4 - 3x^3 - 15x^2 + 18x = 0$

13 $x^4 + 4x^3 - 7x^2 - 36x - 18 = 0$

14 $2x^3 - 5x - 3 = 0$

15 $6x^3 - 25x^2 + 21x + 10 = 0$

16 $3x^4 - 11x^3 - 3x^2 - 6x + 8 = 0$

Factor.

17 $x^3 - 3x^2 - 10x + 24$

18 $-x^3 - 3x^2 + 24x + 80$

19 $x^3 - 28x - 48$

20 $6x^4 + 9x^3 + 9x - 6$

Solve the system.

21 $y = x^3 - 3x^2 + 3x - 1$
  $y = 7x - 13$

22 $y = -x^3$
  $y = -3x^2 + 4$

*23 $y = 4x^3 - 7x^2 + 10$
  $y = x^3 + 43x - 5$

*24 $y = x^2 + 4x$
  $(x - 1)^2 + (y - 6)^2 = 37$

*25 Show that $2x^3 - 5x^2 - x + 8 = 0$ has no rational roots.

*26 Solve the system and graph:

$$y = 2x - 5$$

$$y = \frac{1}{x^2 - 2x + 1}$$

5.9

Decomposing rational functions

In Chapter 2 we learned how to combine rational expressions. For example, combining the fractions in

$$(1) \quad \frac{6}{x - 4} + \frac{3}{x - 2} \qquad \text{produces} \qquad (2) \quad \frac{9x - 24}{(x - 4)(x - 2)}$$

It is now our goal to start with a rational expression such as (2) and *decompose* it into the form (1). When this is accomplished we say that $\frac{9x - 24}{(x - 4)(x - 2)}$ has been decomposed into (simpler) **partial fractions**.

$$\frac{9x - 24}{(x - 4)(x - 2)} = \frac{6}{x - 4} + \frac{3}{x - 2}$$

We will only consider examples that involve linear factors in the denominator.

First observe that each factor in the denominator on the left serves as a denominator of a partial fraction on the right. Let us assume, for the moment, that the numerators 6 and 3 are not known. Then it is reasonable to begin by writing

$$\frac{9x - 24}{(x - 4)(x - 2)} = \frac{A}{x - 4} + \frac{B}{x - 2}$$

where A and B are the constants to be found. To find these values, first clear fractions by multiplying both sides by $(x - 4)(x - 2)$.

$$(x - 4)(x - 2) \cdot \frac{9x - 24}{(x - 4)(x - 2)} = (x - 4)(x - 2)\left[\frac{A}{x - 4} + \frac{B}{x - 2}\right]$$

$$9x - 24 = A(x - 2) + B(x - 4)$$

Since we want this equation to hold for all values of x, we may select specific values for x that will produce the constants A and B. Observe that when $x = 4$ the term $B(x - 4)$ will become zero.

$$9(4) - 24 = A(4 - 2) + B(4 - 4)$$

$$12 = 2A + 0$$

$$6 = A$$

Similarly, B can be found by letting $x = 2$.

$$9(2) - 24 = A(2 - 2) + B(2 - 4)$$

$$-6 = 0 - 2B$$

$$3 = B$$

EXAMPLE 1   Decompose $\dfrac{6x^2 + x - 37}{(x - 3)(x + 2)(x - 1)}$ into partial fractions.

Solution   Since there are three linear factors in the denominator we begin with the form

$$\frac{6x^2 + x - 37}{(x - 3)(x + 2)(x - 1)} = \frac{A}{x - 3} + \frac{B}{x + 2} + \frac{C}{x - 1}$$

Multiply by $(x - 3)(x + 2)(x - 1)$ to clear fractions.

$$6x^2 + x - 37 = A(x + 2)(x - 1) + B(x - 3)(x - 1) + C(x - 3)(x + 2)$$

Since the second and third terms on the right have the factor $x - 3$, the value $x = 3$ will make these two terms zero.

$$6(3)^2 + 3 - 37 = A(3 + 2)(3 - 1) + B(3 - 3)(3 - 1) + C(3 - 3)(3 + 2)$$

$$54 + 3 - 37 = A(5)(2) + 0 + 0$$

$$20 = 10A$$

$$2 = A$$

To find B, use $x = -2$.

$$6(-2)^2 + (-2) - 37 = A(-2 + 2)(-2 - 1) + B(-2 - 3)(-2 - 1)$$
$$+ C(-2 - 3)(-2 + 2)$$

$$24 - 2 - 37 = 0 + B(-5)(-3) + 0$$

$$-15 = 15B$$

$$-1 = B$$

To find C, let $x = 1$.

$$6(1)^2 + 1 - 37 = 0 + 0 + C(1-3)(1+2)$$
$$-30 = -6C$$
$$5 = C$$

Substituting the values for A, B, and C into the original form produces the desired decomposition.

$$\frac{6x^2 + x - 37}{(x-3)(x+2)(x-1)} = \frac{2}{x-3} - \frac{1}{x+2} + \frac{5}{x-1}$$

Check this result by combining the fractions on the right side.

TEST YOUR UNDERSTANDING

Decompose into partial fractions.

1 $\dfrac{8x - 19}{(x-2)(x-3)}$

2 $\dfrac{1}{(x+2)(x-4)}$

3 $\dfrac{6x^2 - 22x + 18}{(x-1)(x-2)(x-3)}$

Factor the denominator and decompose into partial fractions.

4 $\dfrac{4x + 6}{x^2 + 5x + 6}$

5 $\dfrac{23x - 1}{6x^2 + x - 1}$

6 $\dfrac{5x^2 - 24x - 173}{x^3 + 4x^2 - 31x - 70}$

Let us look at a somewhat different example.

$$\frac{7}{x+3} - \frac{4}{(x+3)^2} = \frac{7x + 17}{(x+3)^2}$$

Note that the least common denominator is the highest power of the linear factor in either denominator.

Now assume that the specific numerators are not known, and begin the decomposition process in this way:

$$\frac{7x + 17}{(x+3)^2} - \frac{A}{x+3} + \frac{B}{(x+3)^2}$$

Clear fractions:

(1) $7x + 17 = A(x+3) + B$

To find B, let $x = -3$.

$$7(-3) + 17 = A(0) + B$$
$$-4 = B$$

Substitute this value for B into Equation (1).

(2) $7x + 17 = A(x+3) - 4$

Now find A by substituting some easy value for x, say $x = 0$, into (2).

$$7(0) + 17 = A(0+3) - 4$$
$$17 = 3A - 4$$
$$7 = A$$

Note: If the original denominator had been $(x + 3)^3$, then we would have used the additional fraction $\dfrac{C}{(x + 3)^3}$ to start with.

Substituting these values for A and B into our original form produces the decomposition.

$$\frac{7x + 17}{(x + 3)^2} = \frac{7}{x + 3} + \frac{-4}{(x + 3)^2} = \frac{7}{x + 3} - \frac{4}{(x + 3)^2}$$

EXAMPLE 2 Decompose $\dfrac{6 + 26x - x^2}{(2x - 1)(x + 2)^2}$ into partial fractions.

Solution Begin with this form:

$$\frac{6 + 26x - x^2}{(2x - 1)(x + 2)^2} = \frac{A}{2x - 1} + \frac{B}{x + 2} + \frac{C}{(x + 2)^2}$$

Clear fractions.

(1) $6 + 26x - x^2 = A(x + 2)^2 + B(2x - 1)(x + 2) + C(2x - 1)$

Find A by substituting $x = \tfrac{1}{2}$.

$$6 + 13 - \tfrac{1}{4} = A(\tfrac{5}{2})^2 + 0 + 0$$
$$\tfrac{75}{4} = \tfrac{25}{4}A$$
$$3 = A$$

Find C by letting $x = -2$.

$$6 - 52 - 4 = 0 + 0 + C(-5)$$
$$-50 = -5C$$
$$10 = C$$

Substitute $A = 3$ and $C = 10$ into Equation (1).

(2) $6 + 26x - x^2 = 3(x + 2)^2 + B(2x - 1)(x + 2) + 10(2x - 1)$

To find B, use a simple value like $x = 1$ in (2).

$$6 + 26 - 1 = 3(9) + B(1)(3) + 10(1)$$
$$-6 = 3B$$
$$-2 = B$$

Then the decomposition is

$$\frac{6 + 26x - x^2}{(2x - 1)(x + 2)^2} = \frac{3}{2x - 1} - \frac{2}{x + 2} + \frac{10}{(x + 2)^2}$$

You can check this by combining the right side.

An alternative method for finding the unknown constants in a decomposition problem makes use of the techniques of solving linear systems studied in Section 3.6. This method begins the same as before. In Example 2, for instance, we again reach this equation after clearing fractions:

$$6 + 26x - x^2 = A(x + 2)^2 + B(2x - 1)(x + 2) + C(2x - 1)$$

Convert each side to a polynomial in standard form (using decreasing exponents). Thus

$$-x^2 + 26x + 6 = Ax^2 + 4Ax + 4A + 2Bx^2 + 3Bx - 2B + 2Cx - C$$
$$= (A + 2B)x^2 + (4A + 3B + 2C)x + (4A - 2B - C)$$

Now call on the fact that *when two polynomials written in standard form are equal, their coefficients are the same*. According to this criterion we may write:

Coefficients of x^2: $\quad -1 = A + 2B$

Coefficients of x: $\quad\quad 26 = 4A + 3B + 2C$

Constants: $\quad\quad\quad\quad 6 = 4A - 2B - C$

As a working rule *always try to find as many of the unknown constants by the substitution method before you equate coefficients.*

We now have a linear system of three equations in A, B, and C. The solution to this system is $A = 3$, $B = -2$, and $C = 10$.

Thus far, in every decomposition problem the degree of the polynomial in the numerator has been less than the degree in the denominator. Here is an example where this is not the case.

$$\frac{2x^3 + 3x^2 - x + 16}{x^2 + 2x - 3}$$

In such cases the *first* step is to divide.

$$
\begin{array}{r}
2x - 1 \\
x^2 + 2x - 3\,\overline{\smash{\big)}\,2x^3 + 3x^2 - x + 16} \\
\underline{2x^3 + 4x^2 - 6x} \\
-x^2 + 5x \\
\underline{-x^2 - 2x + 3} \\
7x + 13
\end{array}
$$

(remainder has degree *less* than degree of divisor)

Now write

$$\frac{2x^3 + 3x^2 - x + 16}{x^2 + 2x - 3} = \text{quotient} + \frac{\text{remainder}}{\text{divisor}}$$

$$= 2x - 1 + \frac{7x + 13}{x^2 + 2x - 3}$$

The problem will be completed by decomposing $\dfrac{7x + 13}{x^2 + 2x - 3}$. For illustrative purposes we will use the alternative procedure described.

$$\frac{7x + 13}{x^2 + 2x - 3} = \frac{7x + 13}{(x - 1)(x + 3)} = \frac{A}{x - 1} + \frac{B}{x + 3}$$

Clear fractions.

$$7x + 13 = A(x + 3) + B(x - 1)$$
$$= (A + B)x + (3A - B)$$

Equate coefficients and solve for A and B.

$$
\begin{array}{l}
A + B = 7 \\
\underline{3A - B = 13} \quad \text{(add)} \\
4A = 20 \\
A = 5
\end{array}
$$

SEC. 5.9: Decomposing rational functions   213

Substitute into $A + B = 7$ to get $B = 7 - 5 = 2$. Therefore, the final decomposition is

$$\frac{2x^3 + 3x^2 - x + 16}{x^2 + 2x - 3} = 2x - 1 + \frac{5}{x - 1} + \frac{2}{x + 3}$$

Caution: When the degree of the numerator is *not* less than the degree in the denominator, you *must* divide first. If this step is ignored, the resulting decomposition will be wrong. For example, suppose that you started *incorrectly* in this way:

$$\frac{2x^3 + 3x^2 - x + 16}{(x - 1)(x + 2)} = \frac{A}{x - 1} + \frac{B}{x + 3}$$

This approach will produce the following *incorrect* answer:

$$\frac{2x^3 + 3x^2 - x + 16}{(x - 1)(x + 3)} = \frac{5}{x - 1} + \frac{2}{x + 3}$$

EXERCISES 5.9

Decompose into partial fractions.

1 $\dfrac{2x}{(x + 1)(x - 1)}$

2 $\dfrac{x}{x^2 - 4}$

3 $\dfrac{x + 7}{x^2 - x - 6}$

4 $\dfrac{4x^2 + 16x + 4}{(x + 3)(x^2 - 1)}$

5 $\dfrac{5x^2 + 9x - 56}{(x - 4)(x - 2)(x + 1)}$

6 $\dfrac{x}{(x - 3)^2}$

7 $\dfrac{3x - 3}{(x - 2)^2}$

8 $\dfrac{2 - 3x}{x^2 + x}$

9 $\dfrac{3x - 30}{15x^2 - 14x - 8}$

10 $\dfrac{2x + 1}{(2x + 3)^2}$

11 $\dfrac{x^2 - x - 4}{(x - 2)^3}$

12 $\dfrac{x^2 + 5x + 8}{(x - 3)(x + 1)^2}$

In Exercises 13–15, first divide and then complete the decomposition into partial fractions.

13 $\dfrac{x^3 - x + 2}{x^2 - 1}$

14 $\dfrac{4x^2 - 14x + 2}{4x^2 - 1}$

15 $\dfrac{12x^4 - 12x^3 + 7x^2 - 2x - 3}{4x^2 - 4x + 1}$

Decompose into partial fractions.

16 $\dfrac{10x^2 - 16}{x^4 - 5x^2 + 4}$

17 $\dfrac{10x^3 - 15x^2 - 35x}{x^2 - x - 6}$

*18 $\dfrac{25x^3 + 10x^2 + 31x + 5}{25x^2 + 10x + 1}$

*19 $\dfrac{x^5 - 3x^4 + 2x^3 + x^2 + x + 4}{x^3 - 3x^2 + 3x - 1}$

REVIEW EXERCISES FOR CHAPTER 5

The solutions to the following exercises can be found within the text of Chapter 5. Try to answer each question without referring to the text.

Section 5.1

Graph each of the following.

1 $y = f(x) = x^3$

2 $y = f(x) = |(x - 3)^3|$

3 $y = 2x^4$

4 Under what conditions is the graph of a function $y = f(x)$ said to be symmetric through the origin?

5 Under what conditions is the graph of $y = f(x)$ symmetric about the y-axis?

6 Explain how the graph of $y = f(x + h)$ can be obtained from the graph of $y = f(x)$ when $h > 0$, and also when $h < 0$.

7 Explain how the graph of $y = f(x) + h$ can be obtained from the graph of $y = f(x)$ when $h > 0$, and also when $h < 0$.

Section 5.2

8 Draw the graph of the function $y = f(x) = \dfrac{1}{x}$.

On what interval is the curve concave down? Where is it concave up?

Sketch each graph. Find the asymptotes.

9 $g(x) = \dfrac{1}{x - 3}$

10 $y = \dfrac{1}{(x + 2)^2} - 3$

11 Draw the graph of $y = \dfrac{1}{x^2}$ and describe the symmetry of the curve.

Section 5.3

12 Construct a table of signs for the function $f(x) = x^3 + 4x^2 - x - 4$.

13 Graph the function in Exercise 12.

14 What are the conditions needed for the graph of a rational function to have a vertical asymptote?

15 Graph: $y = \dfrac{x - 2}{x^2 - 3x - 4}$.

Section 5.4

Solve for x.

16 $\dfrac{x - 2}{x} = \dfrac{3}{4}$

17 $\dfrac{2x - 5}{x + 1} - \dfrac{3}{x^2 + x} = 0$

18 $\dfrac{3}{x - 3} + 2 = \dfrac{x}{x - 3}$

19 $\dfrac{x}{3} - \dfrac{2x + 1}{4} > 1$

20 State the proportion property.

21 Working alone Harry can mow a lawn in 3 hours. Elliot can complete the same job in 2 hours. How long will it take them working together?

22 Solve the system

$$y = \frac{2}{x}$$

$$y = -2x + 5$$

Section 5.5

23 Write the equation that expresses this direct variation: y varies directly as x, and y is 8 when x is 12. Find y for $x = 30$.

24 According to Hooke's law, the force F required to stretch a spring x units is directly proportional to the length x. If a force of 20 pounds is needed to stretch a spring 3 inches, how far is the spring stretched by a force of 60 pounds?

25 According to Boyle's law, the pressure of a com-pressed gas is inversely proportional to the volume V. Suppose that there is a pressure of 25 pounds per square inch when the volume of gas is 400 cubic inches. Find the pressure when the gas is compressed to 200 cubic inches.

26 Suppose that z varies directly as x and inversely as the square of y. If $z = \frac{1}{3}$ when $x = 4$ and $y = 6$, find z when $x = 12$ and $y = 4$.

Section 5.6

27 Use long division to find the quotient

$$(x^3 - x^2 - 5x + 6) \div (x - 2)$$

28 Use synthetic division to find

$$(2x^3 - 9x^2 + 10x - 7) \div (x - 3)$$

29 Use synthetic division to find the quotient and the remainder:

$$(-\tfrac{1}{3}x^4 + \tfrac{1}{6}x^2 - 7x - 4) \div (x + 3)$$

Section 5.7

30 State the remainder theorem.

31 State the factor theorem.

32 Find the remainder if $p(x) = 3x^3 - 5x^2 + 7x + 5$ is divided by $x - 2$.

33 Let $f(x) = x^3 - 2x^2 + 3x - 1$. Use synthetic division and the remainder theorem to find $f(3)$.

34 Show that $x - 2$ is a factor of $p(x) = x^3 - 3x^2 + 7x - 10$.

35 Use the factor theorem to show that $x + 3$ is a factor of $p(x) = x^3 - x^2 + 8x + 12$. Then factor $p(x)$ completely.

Section 5.8

36 State the rational root theorem.

37 What are the possible rational roots of $p(x) = 4x^3 - 16x^2 + 11x + 10 = 0$?

38 Factor $f(x) = x^3 + 6x^2 + 11x + 6$.

39 Factor $p(x) = 2x^5 + 7x^4 - 18x^2 - 8x + 8$ and find the roots of $p(x) = 0$.

Section 5.9

40 Decompose $\dfrac{6x^2 + x - 37}{(x - 3)(x + 2)(x - 1)}$ into partial fractions.

41 Decompose $\dfrac{6 + 26x - x^2}{(2x - 1)(x + 2)^2}$ into partial fractions.

42 Decompose $\dfrac{2x^3 + 3x^2 - x + 16}{x^2 + 2x - 3}$ into partial fractions.

Use these questions to test your knowledge of the basic skills and concepts of Chapter 5. Then check your answers with those given at the end of the book.

Graph each function and write the equation of the asymptotes if there are any.

1 $f(x) = (x + 2)^3 - \frac{3}{2}$

2 $y = f(x) = x^3$

3 $y = f(x) = -\dfrac{1}{x - 2}$

4 $y = f(x) = \dfrac{x - 1}{x^2 - x - 2}$

5 Graph: $y = x^3 - x^2 - 4x + 4$.

6 Determine the signs of $f(x) = \dfrac{x^2 - 2x}{x + 3}$.

Solve for x.

7 $\dfrac{6}{x} = 2 + \dfrac{3}{x + 1}$ **8** $\dfrac{x}{2} - \dfrac{3x + 1}{3} > 2$

9 A piece of wire that is 10 feet long is cut into two pieces. The ratio of the smaller piece to the larger piece is $\frac{3}{4}$. Find the length of the larger piece.

10 Working alone, Dave can wash his car in 45 minutes. If Ellen helps him, they can do the job together in 30 minutes. How long would it take Ellen to wash the car by herself?

11 z varies directly as x and inversely as y. If $z = \frac{2}{3}$ when $x = 2$ and $y = 15$, find z when $x = 4$ and $y = 10$.

12 If the volume of a sphere varies directly as the cube of its radius and $V = 36\pi$ cubic inches when $r = 3$ inches, find V when $r = 6$ inches.

13 Use synthetic division to divide

$$2x^5 + 5x^4 - x^2 - 21x + 7 \text{ by } x + 3$$

14 (a) Let $p(x) = 27x^4 - 36x^3 + 18x^2 - 4x + 1$.
Use the remainder theorem to evaluate $p(\frac{1}{3})$.
(b) Use the result of part (a) and the factor theorem to determine whether or not $x - \frac{1}{3}$ is a factor of $p(x)$.

15 Show that $x - 2$ is a factor of $p(x) = x^4 - 4x^3 + 7x^2 - 12x + 12$, and factor $p(x)$ completely.

16 Make use of the rational root theorem to factor $f(x) = x^4 + 5x^3 + 4x^2 - 3x + 9$.

17 Solve the system:
$$\begin{aligned} y &= x^3 \\ y - 19x &= -30 \end{aligned}$$

18 Decompose $\dfrac{x - 15}{x^2 - 25}$ into partial fractions.

ANSWERS TO THE TEST YOUR UNDERSTANDING EXERCISES

Page 186

1 Vertical asymptotes: $x = 2$, $x = 3$; horizontal asymptote: $y = 0$

2 Vertical asymptote: $x = -3$; horizontal asymptote: $y = 1$

3 Vertical asymptote: $x = 2$; no horizontal asymptote

4 Vertical asymptote: $x = 4$; horizontal asymptote: $y = 0$

5 Vertical asymptotes: $x = -3$, $x = 4$; horizontal asymptote: $y = 0$

6 Vertical asmptotes: $x = 1$; no horizontal asymptote

Page 190

1 12   **2** $\frac{1}{2}$ **3** 35   **4** 5   **5** -9 **6** No solution.

7 $\frac{3}{10}$ **8** $\frac{13}{24}$ **9** 3   **10** $-4, 3$ **11** $-3, -1$ **12** $\frac{1}{2}$

Page 204

1
$$\begin{array}{r}
1\ \underline{|1 - 7 + 4 + 10 - 1 - 5} \\
+1 - 6 - 2 + 8 + 7 \\
\hline
1 - 6 - 2 + 8 + 7\,\underline{|+2} = r
\end{array}$$
$p(1) = 1 - 7 + 4 + 10 - 1 - 5 = 2$

2
$$\begin{array}{r}
-10\ \underline{|1 + 11 + 11 + 11 + 10} \\
-10 - 10 - 10 - 10 \\
\hline
1 + 1 + 1 + 1\,\underline{|+0} = r
\end{array}$$
$p(-10) = 10{,}000 - 11{,}000 + 1100 - 110 + 10 = 0$

3 10 $\lfloor$ 1 + 11 + $\;$ 11 + $\;\;$ 11 + $\;\;\;$ 10

$\qquad$ + 10 + 210 + 2210 + 22210

$\qquad\overline{1 + 21 + 221 + 2221\,\lfloor + 22220} = r$

$\qquad p(10) = 10{,}000 + 11{,}000 + 1100 + 110 + 10$

$\qquad\qquad = 22{,}220$

4 6 $\lfloor$ 6 − 40 + $\;$ 0 + $\;$ 25

$\qquad$ + 36 − 24 − 144

$\qquad\overline{6 - \;\;4 - 24\,\lfloor - 119} = r$

$\qquad p(6) = 6(6)^3 - 40(6)^2 + 25 = -119$

Page 208

1 (a) $\pm 1, \pm 2, \pm 3, \pm 4, \pm 6, \pm 8, \pm 12, \pm 24$

$\quad$ (b) $(x + 3)(x - 2)(x - 4)$

$\quad$ (c) $-3, 2, 4$

3 (a) $\pm 1, \pm\frac{1}{2}, \pm\frac{1}{4}, \pm 2, \pm 3, \pm\frac{3}{2}, \pm\frac{3}{4}, \pm 6$

$\quad$ (b) $(x + 6)(2x - 1)^2$

$\quad$ (c) $-6, \frac{1}{2}$

2 (a) $\pm 1, \pm 2, \pm 4, \pm 8, \pm 16$

$\quad$ (b) $(x + 4)^2(x - 1)^2$

$\quad$ (c) $-4, 1$

4 (a) $\pm 1, \pm\frac{1}{3}, \pm 2, \pm\frac{2}{3}, \pm 4, \pm\frac{4}{3}$

$\quad$ (b) $(3x - 1)(x - 4)(x^2 + 1)$

$\quad$ (c) $\frac{1}{3}, 4$

Page 211

1 $\dfrac{3}{x - 2} + \dfrac{5}{x - 3}$

2 $-\dfrac{\frac{1}{6}}{x + 2} + \dfrac{\frac{1}{6}}{x - 4}$

3 $\dfrac{1}{x - 1} + \dfrac{2}{x - 2} + \dfrac{3}{x - 3}$

4 $\dfrac{6}{x + 3} - \dfrac{2}{x + 2}$

5 $\dfrac{4}{3x - 1} + \dfrac{5}{2x + 1}$

6 $\dfrac{4}{x + 7} - \dfrac{2}{x - 5} + \dfrac{3}{x + 2}$

RADICAL FUNCTIONS AND EQUATIONS

A radical expression in x, such as $\sqrt{x}$, may be used to define a function f, where $f(x) = \sqrt{x}$, the *square root function*. The domain of f consists of all real numbers $x \geq 0$ since the square root of a negative number is not a real number.

To graph $y = \sqrt{x}$, it is helpful to first square both sides to obtain $y^2 = x$; that is, $x = y^2$. Recall the graph of $y = x^2$ and obtain the graph of $x = y^2$ by reversing the role of the variables.

Graphing some special radical functions

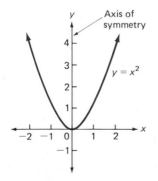

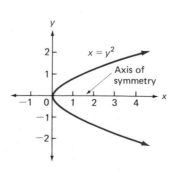

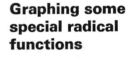

y	$x = y^2$
-2	4
-1	1
0	0
1	1
2	4

The preceding "sideways" parabola is *not* the graph of a function having x as the independent variable because for $x > 0$ there are two corresponding y-values. But if the bottom branch is removed, we have the correct graph of $y = \sqrt{x}$, for $x \geq 0$. (What is the equation for the bottom branch?)

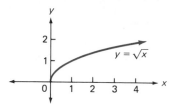

Except for the origin, this graph is in the first quadrant, as could have been predicted by observing that for all $x > 0$, $\sqrt{x} > 0$. You can also verify that the specific points given in the following table are on the graph.

Such a table of values presents us with an alternate method for sketching the graph of $y = \sqrt{x}$; plot the points in the table and connect with a smooth curve.

x	0	$\frac{1}{4}$	$\frac{9}{16}$	1	$\frac{9}{4}$	2	3	4
$y = \sqrt{x}$	0	$\frac{1}{2}$	$\frac{3}{4}$	1	$\frac{3}{2}$	$\sqrt{2}$	$\sqrt{3}$	2

EXAMPLE 1   Find the domain of $y = g(x) = \sqrt{x - 2}$ and graph.

Solution   Since the square root of a negative number is not a real number, the expression $x - 2$ must be nonnegative; therefore, the domain of g consists of all $x \geq 2$. The graph of g may be found by shifting the graph of $y = \sqrt{x}$ by 2 units to the right.

Note: $x - 2 \geq 0$, thus $x \geq 2$.

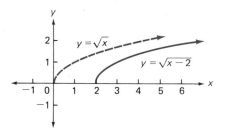

EXAMPLE 2   Find the domain of $y = f(x) = \sqrt{|x|}$ and graph.

Solution   Since $|x| \geq 0$ for all x, the domain of f consists of all real numbers. To graph f, first note that

It is also helpful to locate a few specific points on the curve as an aid to graphing.

$$f(-x) = \sqrt{|-x|} = \sqrt{|x|} = f(x)$$

Therefore, the graph is symmetric about the y-axis. Thus we first find the graph for $x \geq 0$ and use symmetry to obtain the rest. For $x \geq 0$, we get $|x| = x$ and $f(x) = \sqrt{|x|} = \sqrt{x}$.

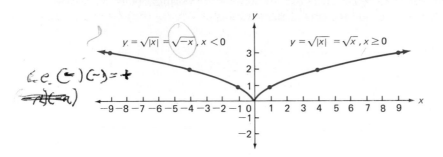

x	y
0	0
1	1
4	2
9	3
−1	1
−4	2
−9	3

EXAMPLE 3   Find the domain of $y = h(x) = x^{-1/2}$ and graph by using a table of values.

Solution   Note that $h(x) = x^{-1/2} = \dfrac{1}{x^{1/2}} = \dfrac{1}{\sqrt{x}}$. Thus the domain consists of all $x > 0$. Furthermore, $\dfrac{1}{\sqrt{x}} > 0$ for all x, so we know that the graph must be in the first quadrant only. Plot the points in the table and connect with a smooth curve.

Explain why $x \neq 0$ in Example 3.

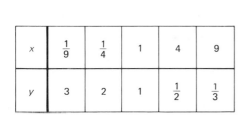

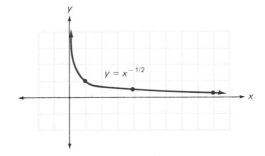

Note that the closer x is to zero, the larger are the corresponding y-values. Also, as the values of x get larger, the corresponding y-values get closer to 0. These observations suggest that the coordinate axes are asymptotes to the curve $y = x^{-1/2}$.

┌───┐
│ **TEST YOUR UNDERSTANDING** │
└───┘

Graph each pair of functions on the same set of axes and state the domain of g.

1 $f(x) = \sqrt{x},\ g(x) = \sqrt{x} - 2$ **2** $f(x) = -\sqrt{x},\ g(x) = -\sqrt{x} - 1$

3 $f(x) = \sqrt{x},\ g(x) = 2\sqrt{x}$ **4** $f(x) = \dfrac{1}{\sqrt{x}},\ g(x) = \dfrac{1}{\sqrt{x+2}}$

The graph of the *cube root function* $y = \sqrt[3]{x}$ can be found by a process similar to that used for $y = \sqrt{x}$. First take $y = \sqrt[3]{x}$ and cube both sides to get $y^3 = x$. Now recall the graph of $y = x^3$ and obtain the graph of $x = y^3$ by reversing the role of the variables.

y	$x = y^3$
-2	-8
-1	-1
0	0
1	1
2	8

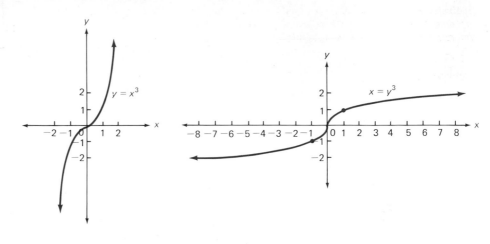

The next example illustrates that a function can be defined by using more than one expression.

EXAMPLE 4   Graph f defined on the domain $-2 \leq x < 5$ as follows:

$$f(x) = \begin{cases} x^2 - 1 & \text{for } -2 \leq x < 2 \\ \sqrt{x - 2} & \text{for } 2 \leq x < 5 \end{cases}$$

Solution   The first part of f is given by $f(x) = x^2 - 1$ for $2 \leq x < 2$. This is an arc of a parabola obtained by shifting the graph of $y = x^2$ downward 1 unit.

The second part of f is given by $f(x) = \sqrt{x - 2}$ for $2 \leq x < 5$. This is an arc of the square root curve obtained by shifting the graph of $y = \sqrt{x}$ two units to the right.

When $x = 2$, the radical part of f is used; $f(2) = \sqrt{2 - 2} = 0$. So there is a solid dot at $(2, 0)$ and an open dot at $(2, 3)$. Also, there is an open dot for $x = 5$ since 5 is not a domain value of f.

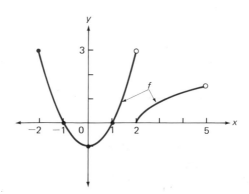

In Exercises 1–4, graph each set of curves on the same coordinate system. Use a dashed curve for the first equation and a solid curve for the second.

1 $f(x) = \sqrt{x}, \quad g(x) = \sqrt{x-1}$

2 $f(x) = -\sqrt{x}, \quad g(x) = -2\sqrt{x}$

3 $f(x) = \sqrt[3]{x}, \quad g(x) = \sqrt[3]{x+2}$

4 $f(x) = -\sqrt[3]{x}, \quad g(x) = -\sqrt[3]{x-3}$

In Exercises 5–16, find the domain of f, sketch the graph, and give the equations of the asymptotic lines if there are any.

5 $f(x) = \sqrt{x+2}$ **6** $f(x) = x^{1/2} + 2$

7 $f(x) = \sqrt{x-3} - 1$ **8** $f(x) = -\sqrt{x}$

9 $f(x) = \sqrt{-x}$ **10** $f(x) = \sqrt{(x-2)^2}$

11 $f(x) = 2\sqrt[3]{x}$ **12** $f(x) = |\sqrt[3]{x}|$

13 $f(x) = -x^{1/3}$ **14** $f(x) = \sqrt[3]{-x}$

15 $f(x) = \dfrac{1}{\sqrt{x}} - 1$ **16** $f(x) = \dfrac{1}{\sqrt{x-2}}$

17 (a) Explain why the graph of $f(x) = \dfrac{1}{\sqrt[3]{x}}$ is symmetric through the origin.

    (b) What is the domain of f?

    (c) Use a table of values to graph f.

    (d) What are the equations of the asymptotes?

18 Find the domain of $f(x) = \dfrac{1}{\sqrt[3]{x}+1}$, sketch the graph, and give the equations of the asymptotes.

*19 Find the graph of the function $y = \sqrt[4]{x}$ by raising both sides of the equation to the fourth power and comparing to the graph of $y = x^4$.

*20 Reflect the graph of $y = x^2$, for $x \geq 0$, through the line $y = x$. Obtain the equation of this new curve by interchanging variables in $y = x^2$ and solving for y.

*21 Follow the instructions of Exercise 20 with $y = x^3$ for all values x.

In Exercises 22 and 23, the function f is defined by using more than one expression. Graph f on its given domain.

22 $f(x) = \begin{cases} \sqrt{x} & \text{for } 0 \leq x \leq 4 \\ 10 - \frac{1}{2}x^2 & \text{for } 4 < x < 6 \end{cases}$

23 $f(x) = \begin{cases} -2x - 1 & \text{for } -3 \leq x < 0 \\ \sqrt[3]{x} - 1 & \text{for } 0 \leq x \leq 2 \end{cases}$

■ In Exercises 24–26, verify the equation involving the difference quotient for the given radical function (see Section 3.1).

24 $\dfrac{f(x) - f(25)}{x - 25} = \dfrac{1}{\sqrt{x}+5}; f(x) = \sqrt{x}$

    (factor $x - 25$ as the difference of squares)

25 $\dfrac{f(4+h) - f(4)}{h} = \dfrac{1}{\sqrt{4+h}+2}; f(x) = \sqrt{x}$

    (rationalize the numerator)

26 $\dfrac{f(x) - f(9)}{x - 9} = -\dfrac{1}{\sqrt{x}+3}; f(x) = -\sqrt{x}$

■ Exercises 27–30 call for the extraction of radical functions from geometric situations (see Section 3.8).

27 A runner starts at point A, goes to point P that is x miles from B, and then runs to D.

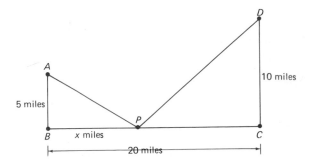

    (a) Write the total distance d traveled as a function of x.

    (b) The runner averages 12 miles per hour from A to P and 10 miles per hour from P to D. Write the time t for the trip as a function of x. (*Hint:* Use time = distance/rate.)

28 In the figure on the next page, AC is along the shoreline of a lake, and the distance from A to C is 12 miles. P represents the starting point of a swimmer who swims at 3 miles per hour along the hypotenuse PB. P is 5 miles from point A on the shore-line. After reaching B he walks at 6 miles per hour to C. Express the total time t of the trip as a function of x, where x is the distance from A to B. (*Hint:* Use time = distance/rate.)

29 Express the distance d from the origin to a point (x, y) on the line $3x + y = 6$ as a function of x.

30 Express the distance d from the point $(2, 5)$ to a point (x, y) on the line $3x + y = 6$ as a function of x.

6.2

Radical equations

To graph $y = f(x) = \sqrt[3]{x + 1} - 2$, it is helpful to know the intercepts. The y-intercept is easy to find:

$$f(0) = \sqrt[3]{0 + 1} - 2 = 1 - 2 = -1$$

Finding the x-intercepts for this graph, as well as for many others, calls for more involved techniques. Since the x-intercepts are values for which $y = f(x) = 0$, we need to solve this equation:

$$\sqrt[3]{x + 1} - 2 = 0$$

First isolate the radical by adding 2 to each side.

$$\sqrt[3]{x + 1} = 2$$

Cube both sides and solve for x.

$$(\sqrt[3]{x + 1})^3 = 2^3$$
$$x + 1 = 8$$
$$x = 7$$

Check this result by substituting into the original equation.

$$\sqrt[3]{7 + 1} - 2 = \sqrt[3]{8} - 2 = 2 - 2 = 0$$

The solution is $x = 7$ and the graph of $y = \sqrt[3]{x + 1} - 2$ crosses the x-axis at $(7, 0)$.

EXAMPLE 1 Find the x-intercepts and the domain of $f(x) = \sqrt{x^2 + x - 6}$.

Solution The x-intercepts occur when $f(x) = 0$. Let $\sqrt{x^2 + x - 6} = 0$ and solve for x.

Check: for $x = -3$, $\sqrt{(-3)^2 + (-3) - 6} = \sqrt{9 - 3 - 6} = \sqrt{0} = 0$; for $x = 2$, $\sqrt{2^2 + 2 - 6} = \sqrt{0} = 0$.

$$(\sqrt{x^2 + x - 6})^2 = (0)^2 \longleftarrow \text{square both sides}$$
$$x^2 + x - 6 = 0$$
$$(x + 3)(x - 2) = 0$$
$$x = -3 \quad \text{or} \quad x = 2$$

You can solve this inequality by forming a table of signs or by noting where the parabola $y = x^2 + x - 6$ is above the x-axis.

Therefore, the x-intercepts are -3 and 2.

The domain of f is the solution of the inequality $(x + 3)(x - 2) \geq 0$, which consists of the intervals $(-\infty, -3]$ and $[2, \infty)$.

For the remainder of this section we focus primarily on the solutions of radical equations in one variable. Keep in mind, however, that the solutions of $f(x) = 0$ can be regarded as the x-intercepts of the graph of the related equation in two variables, $y = f(x)$.

The solution in Example 1 made use of this principle:

$$\text{If } a = b, \text{ then } a^n = b^n$$

This statement says that every solution of $a = b$ will also be a solution of $a^n = b^n$. Sometimes it is convenient to apply this principle after other changes have been made. For instance, to solve the equation

$$\sqrt{x+4} + 2 = x$$

first isolate the radical on one side of the equation.

$$\sqrt{x+4} = x - 2$$

Now square and solve for x.

$$(\sqrt{x+4})^2 = (x-2)^2$$
$$x + 4 = x^2 - 4x + 4$$
$$0 = x^2 - 5x$$
$$0 = x(x-5)$$

Note: If the radical in $\sqrt{x+4} + 2 = x$ is not first isolated, it is still possible to solve the equation, but the work will be more involved. Try it. Also observe that $x = 5$ is the x-intercept of the curve $y = \sqrt{x+4} + 2 - x$.

Thus we get $x = 0$ or $x = 5$. Let us check these values in the given equation.

For $x = 0$: $\sqrt{0+4} + 2 = \sqrt{4} + 2 = 2 + 2 = 4 \neq 0$;
  0 is *not* a solution.
For $x = 5$: $\sqrt{5+4} + 2 = \sqrt{9} + 2 = 3 + 2 = 5$;
  5 is the *only* solution.

How did the *extraneous* solution zero arise? In going from

$$\sqrt{x+4} = x - 2 \qquad \text{to} \qquad (\sqrt{x+4})^2 = (x-2)^2$$

we used the basic principle: If $a = b$, then $a^n = b^n$. Therefore, every solution of the first equation is also a solution for the second. But this principle is not always reversible. In particular, both 0 and 5 are solutions of the second equation, but only 5 is a solution of the first. In summary, the process of raising both sides of an equation in x to the nth power can introduce false solutions. It is therefore vital to check all possible solutions in the original equation.

TEST YOUR UNDERSTANDING

Find the x-intercepts and the domain of f.

1 $f(x) = \sqrt{x} - 5$

2 $f(x) = \dfrac{1}{\sqrt{x+1}} - \dfrac{1}{3}$

3 $f(x) = \sqrt{x^2 - 3x}$

Solve each equation.

4 $\sqrt{x+2} = \sqrt{2x-5}$ 　　　**5** $\sqrt{x^2+9} = -5$

6 $\dfrac{1}{\sqrt{x}} = 3$ 　　　**7** $\dfrac{4}{\sqrt{x-1}} = 2$

8 $\sqrt{x^2-5} = 2$ 　　　**9** $\sqrt[3]{x+3} - 2 = 0$

10 $\sqrt[4]{2x-1} = 3$ 　　　**11** $\sqrt{x+16} - x = 4$

12 $2x = 1 + \sqrt{1-2x}$

Radical equations may contain more than one radical. For such cases it is usually best to transform the equation first into one with as few radicals on each side as possible. For example:

$$\sqrt{x-7} - \sqrt{x} = 1$$
$$\sqrt{x-7} = \sqrt{x} + 1$$

CAUTION:
$(\sqrt{x}+1)^2 \neq x^2+1.$
Use $(a+b)^2 = a^2 + 2ab + b^2$
with $a = \sqrt{x}$ and $b = 1.$

Now square each side.

$$(\sqrt{x-7})^2 = (\sqrt{x}+1)^2$$
$$x - 7 = x + 2\sqrt{x} + 1$$
$$-8 = 2\sqrt{x}$$
$$-4 = \sqrt{x}$$

Square again:

$$16 = x$$

The radical signs may be replaced by appropriate fractional exponents and solved by the same methods; see Example 2.

Check: $\sqrt{16-7} - \sqrt{16} = \sqrt{9} - \sqrt{16} = 3 - 4 = -1 \neq 1.$
Therefore, this equation has no solution, which could have been observed at an earlier stage as well. For example, $-4 = \sqrt{x}$ has no solution. (Why not?)

EXAMPLE 2　Solve for x:

$$\frac{3(2x-1)^{1/2}}{x-3} - \frac{(2x-1)^{3/2}}{(x-3)^2} = 0$$

Solution　Multiply through by $(x-3)^2$ to clear fractions.

$$(x-3)^2\left[\frac{3(2x-1)^{1/2}}{x-3}\right] - (x-3)^2\left[\frac{(2x-1)^{3/2}}{(x-3)^2}\right] = (x-3)^2(0)$$
$$3(x-3)(2x-1)^{1/2} - (2x-1)^{3/2} = 0$$
$$[3(x-3) - (2x-1)](2x-1)^{1/2} = 0$$
$$(x-8)(2x-1)^{1/2} = 0$$

Factor out $(2x-1)^{1/2}$. This is easier to see if we let $a = (2x-1)^{1/2}$ and factor a out of $3(x-3)a - a^3.$

Set each factor equal to zero.

$$x - 8 = 0 \quad \text{or} \quad (2x-1)^{1/2} = 0$$
$$x = 8 \quad \text{or} \quad 2x - 1 = 0$$
$$x = 8 \quad \text{or} \quad x = \tfrac{1}{2}$$

Check in the original equation to show that both $x = \frac{1}{2}$ and $x = 8$ are solutions for Example 2.

As you may have noticed, the algebraic techniques developed earlier involving other kinds of expressions often carry over into this work. Here is an example that uses our knowledge of quadratics in conjunction with radicals.

EXAMPLE 3 Solve for x: $\sqrt[3]{x^2} + \sqrt[3]{x} - 20 = 0$.

Solution First write the equation by using rational exponents.
$$x^{2/3} + x^{1/3} - 20 = 0$$

Then think of $x^{2/3}$ as the square of $x^{1/3}$, $x^{2/3} = (x^{1/3})^2$, and use the substitution $u = x^{1/3}$ as follows:

$$x^{2/3} + x^{1/3} - 20 = 0$$
$$(x^{1/3})^2 + x^{1/3} - 20 = 0$$
$$u^2 + u - 20 = 0$$
$$(u + 5)(u - 4) = 0 \quad \text{(factoring the quadratic)}$$

$u + 5 = 0$	or	$u - 4 = 0$
$u = -5$	or	$u = 4$

> Alternatively, we may keep the radical sign and proceed with $u = \sqrt[3]{x}$.

Now replace u by $x^{1/3}$.
$$x^{1/3} = -5 \quad \text{or} \quad x^{1/3} = 4$$

Cubing gives
$$x = -125 \quad \text{or} \quad x = 64$$

Check to show that both values are solutions of the given equation.

EXAMPLE 4 Solve the system and graph:
$$y = \sqrt[3]{x}$$
$$y = \tfrac{1}{4}x$$

Solution For the points of intersection the x- and y-values are the same in both equations. Thus
$$\tfrac{1}{4}x = \sqrt[3]{x} \quad \longleftarrow \quad x^{1/3} \text{ can be used in place of } \sqrt[3]{x}$$

Cube both sides and solve for x.
$$\tfrac{1}{64}x^3 = x$$
$$x^3 = 64x$$
$$x^3 - 64x = 0$$
$$x(x^2 - 64) = 0 \quad \text{(factoring out } x\text{)}$$
$$x(x + 8)(x - 8) = 0$$
$$x = 0 \quad \text{or} \quad x = -8 \quad \text{or} \quad x = 8$$

> **CAUTION:** A common error is to take $x^3 - 64x = 0$ and divide through by x to get $x^2 - 64 = 0$. This step produces the roots ± 8. The root 0 has been lost because we divided by x, and 0 is the number for which the factor x in $x(x^2 - 64)$ is zero. You may always divide by a nonzero constant and get an equivalent form of the equation. But when you divide by a variable quantity there is the danger of losing some roots, those for which the divisor is 0.

Substitute these values into either of the given equations to obtain the corresponding y-values. The remaining equation can be used for checking. The solutions are $(-8, -2)$, $(0, 0)$, and $(8, 2)$.

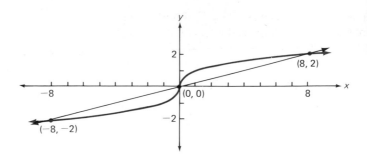

EXERCISES 6.2

In Exercises 1–6, find the x-intercepts of each curve and find the domain of f.

1 $f(x) = \sqrt{x - 1} - 4$

2 $f(x) = \sqrt{3x - 2} - 5$

3 $f(x) = \sqrt{x^2 + 2x}$

4 $f(x) = \sqrt{x - x^2}$

5 $f(x) = \sqrt{x^2 - 5x - 6}$

6 $f(x) = \sqrt{2x^2 - x - 2} - 1$

Solve each equation in Exercises 7–30.

7 $\sqrt{4x + 9} - 7 = 0$

8 $2 + \sqrt{7x - 3} = 7$

9 $(3x + 1)^{1/2} = (2x + 6)^{1/2}$

10 $\sqrt{x - 1} - \sqrt{2x - 11} = 0$

11 $\sqrt{x^2 - 36} = 8$

12 $3x = \sqrt{3 - 5x - 3x^2}$

13 $\sqrt{x^2 + \frac{1}{2}} = \frac{1}{\sqrt{3}}$

14 $3\sqrt{x} = 2\sqrt{3}$

15 $\dfrac{8}{\sqrt{x + 2}} = 4$

16 $\left(\dfrac{5x + 4}{2}\right)^{1/3} = 3$

17 $\dfrac{1}{\sqrt{2x - 1}} = \dfrac{3}{\sqrt{5 - 3x}}$

18 $\sqrt[3]{2x + 7} = 3$

19 $\sqrt[4]{1 - 3x} = \dfrac{1}{2}$

20 $2 + \sqrt[5]{7x - 4} = 0$

21 $\sqrt{x} + \sqrt{x - 5} = 5$

22 $\sqrt{x - 7} = 7 - \sqrt{x}$

23 $x\sqrt{4 - x} - \sqrt{9x - 36} = 0$

24 $2x - 5\sqrt{x} - 3 = 0$

25 $x = 8 - 2\sqrt{x}$

26 $\dfrac{(2x + 2)^{3/2}}{(x + 9)^2} - \dfrac{(2x + 2)^{1/2}}{x + 9} = 0$

27 $\sqrt{x^2 - 6x} = x - \sqrt{2x}$

28 $x^{1/3} - 3x^{1/6} + 2 = 0$

29 $4x^{2/3} - 12x^{1/3} + 9 = 0$

30 $\sqrt[4]{3x^2 + 4} = x$

In Exercises 31 and 32 solve the system and then sketch each graph.

31 $y = \sqrt{x}$

$y = \frac{1}{2}x$

32 $y = \dfrac{2}{\sqrt{x}}$

$x + 3y = 7$

In Exercises 33–36, solve for the indicated variable in terms of the others.

33 $y = \sqrt{16 - x^2}$, for x, $0 < x < 4$

34 $x = \frac{3}{5}\sqrt{25 - y^2}$, for y, $0 < y < 5$

35 $\dfrac{1}{2\sqrt{x}} + \dfrac{f}{2\sqrt{y}} = 0$, for f

36 $\dfrac{1}{\sqrt{xy}}(xf + y) = f$, for f

37 The distance from the point $(3, 0)$ to a point $P(x, y)$ on the curve $y = \sqrt{x}$ is $3\sqrt{5}$. Find the coordinates of P. (*Hint:* Use the formula for the distance between two points.)

38 In the figure, rectangle $ABCD$ is inscribed in a circle of radius 10. Express the area of the rectangle as a function of x.

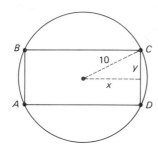

(*Hint:* Solve for y in terms of x.)

39 The volume of a right circular cylinder with altitude h and radius r is 5 cm³. Solve for r in terms of h and express the surface area of the cylinder as a function of h.

40 A right circular cone with height h and radius r is inscribed in a sphere of radius 1 as shown. Solve for r in terms of h and express the volume of the cone as a function of h.

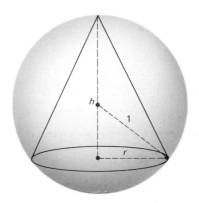

═6.3

The methods used for determining the signs of rational functions are easily modified to determine the signs of functions defined in terms of radical expressions. As a first example, consider this function:

$$f(x) = (x - 5)\sqrt{x - 3}$$

Observe that the factor $\sqrt{x - 3}$ indicates $x \geq 3$. (Why?) Therefore, we do not need to consider any values for $x < 3$. The table shows that $f(x)$ is negative on the interval $(3, 5)$ and positive on the interval $(5, \infty)$.

Determining the signs of radical functions

Interval	$(3, 5)$	$(5, \infty)$
Sign of $\sqrt{x - 3}$	$+$	$+$
Sign of $x - 5$	$-$	$+$
Sign of $f(x)$	$-$	$+$

$(3, 5)$ is the interval consisting of all x where $3 < x < 5$.
$(5, \infty)$ is the interval consisting of all x where $x > 5$.

EXAMPLE 1   Find the domain of $f(x) = \dfrac{x}{\sqrt{4 - x^2}}$ and determine its signs.

Solution   The domain consists of those x for which $4 - x^2 > 0$. To solve this inequality we note that $y = 4 - x^2$ is a parabola that opens downward and crosses the x-axis at ± 2. Hence $4 - x^2 > 0$ on the interval $(-2, 2)$, which is the domain of f. The sign of $f(x)$ depends only on the numerator since the denominator is always positive. Hence $f(x) > 0$ on $(0, 2)$, and $f(x) < 0$ on $(-2, 0)$.

TEST YOUR UNDERSTANDING

Find the domain of each function and determine its signs.

1 $f(x) = \dfrac{x - 4}{\sqrt{x}}$ **2** $f(x) = \dfrac{\sqrt{x + 2}}{x}$ **3** $f(x) = \dfrac{2}{3\sqrt[3]{x}}$

Algebraic procedures developed earlier can be helpful with this type of work. For example, the signs of

$$f(x) = x^{1/2} + \tfrac{1}{2}x^{-1/2}(x - 3)$$

can be determined after combining and simplifying as follows:

$$f(x) = x^{1/2} + \tfrac{1}{2}x^{-1/2}(x - 3)$$

$$= x^{1/2} + \frac{x - 3}{2x^{1/2}}$$

$$= \frac{x^{1/2}(2x^{1/2})}{2x^{1/2}} + \frac{x - 3}{2x^{1/2}} \qquad \text{(the common denominator is } 2x^{1/2}\text{)}$$

$$= \frac{2x + x - 3}{2x^{1/2}}$$

$$= \frac{3x - 3}{2x^{1/2}} = \frac{3(x - 1)}{2\sqrt{x}}$$

$(0, 1)$: $0 < x < 1$
$(1, \infty)$: $x > 1$

Interval	$(0, 1)$	$(1, \infty)$
Sign of $\sqrt{x}$	$+$	$+$
Sign of $x - 1$	$-$	$+$
Sign of $f(x)$	$-$	$+$

Hence $f(x) < 0$ on $(0, 1)$; $f(x) > 0$ on $(1, \infty)$.

EXAMPLE 2   Find the domain of f, the roots of $f(x) = 0$, and determine the signs of f where

$$f(x) = \frac{x^2 - 1}{2\sqrt{x - 1}} + 2x\sqrt{x - 1}$$

Solution The radical in the denominator calls for $x - 1 > 0$. Therefore, the domain consists of all $x > 1$. Now simplify as follows:

$$f(x) = \frac{x^2 - 1}{2\sqrt{x - 1}} + 2x\sqrt{x - 1}$$

$$= \frac{x^2 - 1}{2\sqrt{x - 1}} + \frac{(2x\sqrt{x - 1})(2\sqrt{x - 1})}{2\sqrt{x - 1}}$$

$$= \frac{x^2 - 1 + 4x(x - 1)}{2\sqrt{x - 1}}$$

$$= \frac{5x^2 - 4x - 1}{2\sqrt{x - 1}}$$

$$= \frac{(5x + 1)(x - 1)}{2\sqrt{x - 1}}$$

$$= \frac{5(x + \frac{1}{5})(x - 1)}{2\sqrt{x - 1}}$$

The numerator is zero when $x = -\frac{1}{5}$ or $x = 1$. But these values are *not* in the domain of f. Since a fraction can only be zero when the numerator is zero, it follows that $f(x) = 0$ has no solutions. The signs of $f(x)$ are given in this brief table:

Interval	$(1, \infty)$
Sign of $x + \frac{1}{5}$	$+$
Sign of $x - 1$	$+$
Sign of $\sqrt{x - 1}$	$+$
Sign of $f(x)$	$+$

$(1, \infty): x > 1$

Thus $f(x) > 0$ on its domain $(1, \infty)$.

CAUTION: LEARN TO AVOID MISTAKES LIKE THESE

WRONG	RIGHT
$(9 - x^2)^{1/2}(9 - x^2)^{3/2}$ $= (9 - x^2)^{3/4}$	$(9 - x^2)^{1/2}(9 - x^2)^{3/2}$ $= (9 - x^2)^{(1/2)+(3/2)}$ $= (9 - x^2)^2$
$\dfrac{2}{\sqrt{9 - x^2}} + 3\sqrt{9 - x^2}$ $= \dfrac{2 + 3\sqrt{9 - x^2}}{\sqrt{9 - x^2}}$	$\dfrac{2}{\sqrt{9 - x^2}} + 3\sqrt{9 - x^2}$ $= \dfrac{2}{\sqrt{9 - x^2}} + \dfrac{3(9 - x^2)}{\sqrt{9 - x^2}}$ $= \dfrac{2 + 3(9 - x^2)}{\sqrt{9 - x^2}}$

WRONG	RIGHT
$x^{-1/3} + x^{2/3} = x^{-1/3}(1 + x^{1/3})$	$x^{-1/3} + x^{2/3} = x^{-1/3}(1 + x)$
$x^2\sqrt{1+x} = \sqrt{x^2 + x^3}$	$x^2\sqrt{1+x} = \sqrt{x^4}\sqrt{1+x}$ $= \sqrt{x^4 + x^5}$

EXERCISES 6.3

In Exercises 1–10, (a) find the domain of f, (b) determine the signs of f, and (c) find the roots of $f(x) = 0$.

1 $f(x) = (x + 4)\sqrt{x - 2}$

2 $f(x) = (x + 4)\sqrt[3]{x - 2}$

3 $f(x) = (x - 2)^{2/3}$

4 $f(x) = \frac{2}{3}(x - 2)^{-1/3}$

5 $f(x) = \dfrac{9 + x}{9\sqrt{x}}$

6 $f(x) = \dfrac{9 - x}{9x^{3/2}}$

7 $f(x) = \dfrac{(x + 4)\sqrt[3]{x - 2}}{3\sqrt[3]{x}}$

8 $f(x) = \dfrac{-5x(x - 4)}{2\sqrt{5 - x}}$

9 $f(x) = \dfrac{\sqrt{9 - x^2}}{x}$

10 $f(x) = \dfrac{x}{\sqrt{x^2 - 4}}$

In Exercises 11–18, take the expression at the left and change it into the equivalent form given at the right.

11 $x^{1/2} + (x - 4)\frac{1}{2}x^{-1/2}$; $\dfrac{3x - 4}{2\sqrt{x}}$

12 $x^{1/3} + (x - 1)\frac{1}{3}x^{-2/3}$; $\dfrac{4x - 1}{3\sqrt[3]{x^2}}$

13 $\frac{1}{2}(4 - x^2)^{-1/2}(-2x)$; $-\dfrac{x}{\sqrt{4 - x^2}}$

14 $\dfrac{-\frac{1}{2}(25 - x^2)^{-1/2}(-2x)}{25 - x^2}$; $\dfrac{x}{\sqrt{(25 - x^2)^3}}$

15 $\dfrac{x}{3(x - 1)^{2/3}} + (x - 1)^{1/3}$; $\dfrac{4x - 3}{3(\sqrt[3]{x - 1})^2}$

16 $(x + 1)^{1/2}(2) + (2x + 1)\frac{1}{2}(x + 1)^{-1/2}$; $\dfrac{6x + 5}{2\sqrt{x + 1}}$

17 $\dfrac{x}{(5x - 6)^{4/5}} + (5x - 6)^{1/5}$; $\dfrac{6(x - 1)}{(5x - 6)^{4/5}}$

18 $x^{-3/2} - \frac{1}{9}x^{-1/2}$; $\dfrac{9 - x}{9x^{3/2}}$

Simplify and determine the signs of f.

19 $f(x) = \sqrt{x} - \dfrac{1}{\sqrt{x}}$

20 $f(x) = \frac{3}{2}x^{1/2} - \frac{3}{2}x^{-1/2}$

21 $f(x) = x^{1/2} + \frac{1}{2}x^{-1/2}(x - 9)$

22 $f(x) = x^{2/3} + \frac{2}{3}x^{-1/3}(x - 10)$

23 $f(x) = \dfrac{x^2}{2}(x - 2)^{-1/2} + 2x(x - 2)^{1/2}$

24 $f(x) = \dfrac{\sqrt{x - 1} - \dfrac{x}{2\sqrt{x - 1}}}{x - 1}$

6.4

Combining functions

What does it mean to add two functions f and g? Remember, a function is basically a correspondence; so how do we add correspondences? The answer turns out to be relatively simple.

To illustrate, let us use f and g, where

$$f(x) = \frac{1}{x^3 - 1} \quad \text{and} \quad g(x) = \sqrt{x}$$

The domain of f consists of all $x \neq 1$, and g has domain all $x \geq 0$. The sum of f and g will be symbolized by $f + g$. We will take as the domain of $f + g$ all values x that are in *each* of the domains of f and g simultaneously. Therefore $f + g$ has domain $x \geq 0$ and $x \neq 1$.

Now consider any x in this new domain. What will be the corresponding range value for $f + g$? That is, how should $(f + g)(x)$ be defined? The answer is almost instinctive. For this x, take the two range values $f(x) = \frac{1}{x^3 - 1}$ and $g(x) = \sqrt{x}$, and add them to get $f(x) + g(x)$. Thus

$$(f + g)(x) = f(x) + g(x) = \frac{1}{x^3 - 1} + \sqrt{x}$$

It might be helpful if you momentarily used $f \oplus g$ to emphasize that this plus is not our old familiar addition.

Specifically, for $x = 4$ we have

$$(f + g)(4) = f(4) + g(4) = \frac{1}{64 - 1} + \sqrt{4} = \frac{1}{63} + 2 = \frac{127}{63}$$

Note that the plus sign in $f(x) + g(x)$ is addition of real numbers.

The difference, product, and quotient are found in a similar manner. Using f and g above, we get

$$(f - g)(x) = f(x) - g(x) = \frac{1}{x^3 - 1} - \sqrt{x}$$

$$(f \cdot g)(x) = f(x)g(x) = \frac{1}{x^3 - 1} \cdot \sqrt{x} = \frac{\sqrt{x}}{x^3 - 1}$$

$$\frac{f}{g}(x) = \frac{f(x)}{g(x)} = \frac{\frac{1}{x^3 - 1}}{\sqrt{x}} = \frac{1}{(x^3 - 1)\sqrt{x}}$$

The domains of $f - g$ and $f \cdot g$ are the same as for $f + g$: namely, $x \geq 0$ and $x \neq 1$. The domain of $\frac{f}{g}$ also has those x common to the domains of f and g except those for which $g(x) = 0$; $x > 0$ and $x \neq 1$.

EXAMPLE 1 Let $f(x) = \frac{1}{x^3 - 1}$ and $g(x) = \sqrt{x}$.

(a) Evaluate $f(4)$, and $g(4)$, and compute $f(4) \cdot g(4)$.

(b) Use the expression for $(f \cdot g)(x)$, as in the preceding discussion, to evaluate $(f \cdot g)(4)$.

Solution

(a) $f(4) = \frac{1}{4^3 - 1} = \frac{1}{63}$, $g(4) = \sqrt{4} = 2$, and $f(4) \cdot g(4) = \frac{1}{63} \cdot 2 = \frac{2}{63}$

(b) $(f \cdot g)(x) = \frac{\sqrt{x}}{x^3 - 1}$

$(f \cdot g)(4) = \frac{\sqrt{4}}{4^3 - 1} = \frac{2}{63}$

We are ready to state the general definition for forming the sum, difference, product, and quotient of two functions.

For functions f and g, the functions $f + g$, $f - g$, $f \cdot g$, and $\dfrac{f}{g}$ have range values given by

$$(f + g)(x) = f(x) + g(x)$$
$$(f - g)(x) = f(x) - g(x)$$
$$(f \cdot g)(x) = f(x)g(x)$$
$$\frac{f}{g}(x) = \frac{f(x)}{g(x)}$$

The domains of $f + g, f - g,$ and $f \cdot g$ are all the same and consist of all x common to the domains of f and g. The domain of $\dfrac{f}{g}$ has all x common to the domains of f and g except for those x where $g(x) = 0$.

We will study one more way of forming new functions from given functions. It is referred to as the *composition* of functions. Let f and g be given by

$$f(x) = \frac{1}{x - 2} \quad \text{and} \quad g(x) = \sqrt{x}$$

The output of f becomes the input of g: $f(6) = \frac{1}{4}$ comes out of f and goes into g. Take a specific value in the domain of f, say $x = 6$. Then the corresponding range value is $f(6) = \frac{1}{4}$. Take this range value and use it as a domain value for g to produce $g(\frac{1}{4}) = \sqrt{\frac{1}{4}} = \frac{1}{2}$. This work may be condensed in this way.

$$g(f(6)) = g(\tfrac{1}{4}) = \sqrt{\tfrac{1}{4}} = \tfrac{1}{2}$$

Here are two more illustrations using the condensed notation.

read this as
"g of f of 10" $\longrightarrow$ $g(f(10)) = g\left(\dfrac{1}{10 - 2}\right) = g\left(\dfrac{1}{8}\right) = \sqrt{\dfrac{1}{8}} = \dfrac{1}{2\sqrt{2}}$

$$g\left(f\left(\frac{9}{4}\right)\right) = g\left(\frac{1}{\frac{9}{4} - 2}\right) = g\left(\frac{1}{\frac{1}{4}}\right) = g(4) = \sqrt{4} = 2$$

The roles of f and g may be interchanged. Thus

read this as
"f of g of 10" $\longrightarrow$ $f(g(10)) = f(\sqrt{10}) = \dfrac{1}{\sqrt{10} - 2}$

and

$$f\left(g\left(\frac{9}{4}\right)\right) = f\left(\sqrt{\frac{9}{4}}\right) = f\left(\frac{3}{2}\right) = \frac{1}{\frac{3}{2} - 2} = -2$$

In some cases this process does not work. For instance, if $x = -3$, then $f(-3) = -\frac{1}{5}$; $g(-\frac{1}{5}) = \sqrt{-\frac{1}{5}}$ is not a real number. We therefore say that $g(f(-3))$ is undefined or that it does not exist.

For each pair of functions f and g, evaluate (if possible) each of the following:

(a) $g(f(1))$ **(b)** $f(g(1))$ **(c)** $f(g(0))$ **(d)** $g(f(-2))$

1 $f(x) = 3x - 1; g(x) = x^2 + 4$ **2** $f(x) = \sqrt{x}; g(x) = x^2$

3 $f(x) = \sqrt[3]{3x - 1}; g(x) = 5x$ **4** $f(x) = \dfrac{x + 2}{x - 1}; g(x) = x^3$

The preceding computations for specific values of x can be stated in terms of any allowable x. For instance, using $f(x) = \dfrac{1}{x - 2}$ and $g(x) = \sqrt{x}$, we have

$$g(f(x)) = g\left(\frac{1}{x - 2}\right) = \sqrt{\frac{1}{x - 2}} = \frac{1}{\sqrt{x - 2}}$$

This new correspondence between a domain value x and the range value $\dfrac{1}{\sqrt{x - 2}}$ is referred to as the **composite function of g by f** (or the *composition of g by f*). This composite function is denoted by $g \circ f$. That is, for the given functions f and g, we form the composite of g by f, whose range values $(g \circ f)(x)$ are defined by

$$(g \circ f)(x) = g(f(x)) = \frac{1}{\sqrt{x - 2}}$$

$g(f(x))$ **is read as "g of f of x."**

The domain of $g \circ f$ will consist of all values x in the domain of f such that $f(x)$ is in the domain of g. Since $f(x) = \dfrac{1}{x - 2}$ has domain all $x \neq 2$ and the domain of $g(x) = \sqrt{x}$ is all $x \geq 0$, the domain of $g \circ f$ is all $x \neq 2$ for which $\dfrac{1}{x - 2}$ is positive, that is, all $x > 2$.

Reversing the role of the two functions gives the composite of f by g, where

$$(f \circ g)(x) = f(g(x)) = f(\sqrt{x}) = \frac{1}{\sqrt{x} - 2}$$

$f(g(x))$ **is read as "f of g of x."**

The domain of $f \circ g$ consists of all $x \geq 0$ except $x \neq 4$.

Here is the definition of composite functions.

For functions f and g the composite function g by f, denoted $g \circ f$, has range values defined by

$$(g \circ f)(x) = g(f(x))$$

and domain consisting of all x in the domain of f for which $f(x)$ is in the domain of g.

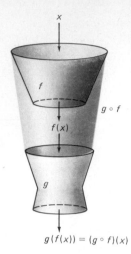

x

f

$g \circ f$

$f(x)$

g

$g(f(x)) = (g \circ f)(x)$

It may help you to remember the construction of composites by looking at the following schematic diagram.

$$x \xrightarrow{\; f \;} f(x) \xrightarrow{\; g \;} g(f(x)) = (g \circ f)(x)$$
$$g \circ f$$

It is also helpful to view the composition $(g \circ f)(x) = g(f(x))$ as consisting of an "inner" function f and an "outer" function g.

EXAMPLE 2   Form the composite functions $f \circ g$ and $g \circ f$ and give their domains, where $f(x) = \dfrac{1}{x^2 - 1}$ and $g(x) = \sqrt{x}$.

Solution   We find that $f \circ g$ is given by

$$(f \circ g)(x) = f(g(x)) = f(\sqrt{x}) = \frac{1}{(\sqrt{x})^2 - 1} = \frac{1}{x - 1}$$

The domain of $f \circ g$ excludes $x < 0$ since such x are not in the domain of g. And it excludes $x = 1$ since $g(1) = 1$, which is not in the domain of f. Therefore, the domain of $f \circ g$ is $x \geq 0$ and $x \neq 1$. Moreover, $g \circ f$ is given by

$$(g \circ f)(x) = g(f(x)) = g\left(\frac{1}{x^2 - 1}\right) = \sqrt{\frac{1}{x^2 - 1}} = \frac{1}{\sqrt{x^2 - 1}}$$

The domain of $g \circ f$ excludes $x = \pm 1$ since these are not in the domain of f. And it excludes $-1 < x < 1$, since negative values of $f(x)$ are not in the domain of g. Therefore, the domain of $g \circ f$ is seen to be $x < -1$ or $x > 1$.

In general, $f(g(x)) \neq g(f(x))$.

From Example 2 it follows that $(f \circ g)(x) \neq (g \circ f)(x)$. We conclude that, in general, the composite of f by g is not equal to the composite of g by f.

The composition of functions may be extended to include more than two functions. For example, if $f(x) = \sqrt{x}$, $g(x) = x^2 + 1$, and $h(x) = \dfrac{1}{x}$, then the composition of f by g by h, denoted $f \circ g \circ h$, is given by

$$(f \circ g \circ h)(x) = f(g(h(x))) \qquad h \text{ is the "inner" function.}$$

$$= f\left(g\left(\frac{1}{x}\right)\right) \qquad g \text{ is the "middle" function.}$$

$$= f\left(\frac{1}{x^2} + 1\right) \qquad f \text{ is the "outer" function.}$$

$$= \sqrt{\frac{1}{x^2} + 1}$$

In Exercises 1–6, let $f(x) = 2x - 3$ and $g(x) = 3x + 2$.

1 (a) Find $f(1)$, $g(1)$, and $f(1) + g(1)$.

(b) Find $(f + g)(x)$ and state the domain of $f + g$.

(c) Use the result in part (b) to evaluate $(f + g)(1)$.

2 (a) Find $g(2)$, $f(2)$, and $g(2) - f(2)$.

(b) Find $(g - f)(x)$ and state the domain of $g - f$.

(c) Use the result in part (b) to evaluate $(g - f)(2)$.

3 (a) Find $f(\frac{1}{2})$, $g(\frac{1}{2})$, and $f(\frac{1}{2}) \cdot g(\frac{1}{2})$.

(b) Find $(f \cdot g)(x)$ and state the domain of $f \cdot g$.

(c) Use the result in part (b) to evaluate $(f \cdot g)(\frac{1}{2})$.

4 (a) Find $g(-2)$, $f(-2)$, and $\dfrac{g(-2)}{f(-2)}$.

(b) Find $\dfrac{g}{f}(x)$ and state the domain of $\dfrac{g}{f}$.

(c) Use the result in part (b) to evaluate $\dfrac{g}{f}(-2)$.

5 (a) Find $g(0)$ and $f(g(0))$.

(b) Find $(f \circ g)(x)$ and state the domain of $f \circ g$.

(c) Use the result in part (b) to evaluate $(f \circ g)(0)$.

6 (a) Find $f(0)$ and $g(f(0))$.

(b) Find $(g \circ f)(x)$ and state the domain of $g \circ f$.

(c) Use the result in part (b) to evaluate $(g \circ f)(0)$.

For each of the functions in Exercises 7–12, find the following:

(a) $(f + g)(x)$; domain of $f + g$.

(b) $\left(\dfrac{f}{g}\right)(x)$; domain $\dfrac{f}{g}$.

(c) $(f \circ g)(x)$; domain $f \circ g$.

7 $f(x) = x^2$, $g(x) = \sqrt{x}$

8 $f(x) = 5x - 1$, $g(x) = \dfrac{5}{1 + 3x}$

9 $f(x) = x^3 - 1$, $g(x) = \dfrac{1}{x}$

10 $f(x) = 3x - 1$, $g(x) = \frac{1}{3}x + \frac{1}{3}$

11 $f(x) = x^2 + 6x + 8$, $g(x) = \sqrt{x - 2}$

12 $f(x) = \sqrt[3]{x}$, $g(x) = x^2$

For each pair of functions in Exercises 13–16, find the following:

(a) $(g - f)(x)$; domain of $g - f$.

(b) $(g \cdot f)(x)$; domain of $g \cdot f$.

(c) $(g \circ f)(x)$; domain of $g \circ f$.

13 $f(x) = -2x + 5$, $g(x) = 4x - 1$

14 $f(x) = |x|$, $g(x) = 3|x|$

15 $f(x) = 2x^2 - 1$, $g(x) = \dfrac{1}{2x}$

16 $f(x) = \sqrt{2x + 3}$, $g(x) = x^2 - 1$

In Exercises 17–24, find $(f \circ g)(x)$ and $(g \circ f)(x)$.

17 $f(x) = x^2$, $g(x) = x - 1$

18 $f(x) = |x - 3|$, $g(x) = 2x + 3$

19 $f(x) = \dfrac{x}{x - 2}$, $g(x) = \dfrac{x + 3}{x}$

20 $f(x) = x^3 - 1$, $g(x) = \dfrac{1}{x^3 + 1}$

21 $f(x) = \sqrt{x + 1}$, $g(x) = x^4 - 1$

22 $f(x) = 2x^3 - 1$, $g(x) = \sqrt[3]{\dfrac{x + 1}{2}}$

23 $f(x) = \sqrt{x}$, $g(x) = 4$

24 $f(x) = \sqrt[3]{1 - x}$, $g(x) = 1 - x^3$

25 Let $f(x) = \dfrac{1}{x}$, $g(x) = 2x - 1$, and $h(x) = x^{1/3}$.

Find the following:

(a) $(f \circ g \circ h)(x)$ **(b)** $(g \circ f \circ h)(x)$

(c) $(h \circ f \circ g)(x)$

26 Let $f(x) = x + 2$, $g(x) = \sqrt{x}$, and $h(x) = x^3$.

Find the following:

(a) $(f \circ g \circ h)(x)$ **(b)** $(f \circ h \circ g)(x)$

(c) $(g \circ f \circ h)(x)$ **(d)** $(g \circ h \circ f)(x)$

(e) $(h \circ f \circ g)(x)$ **(f)** $(h \circ g \circ f)(x)$

27 Let $f(x) = \dfrac{1}{x}$. Find $(f \circ f)(x)$ and $(f \circ f \circ f)(x)$.

28 Let $f(x) = x^2$, $g(x) = \dfrac{1}{x - 1}$, and $h(x) = 1 + \dfrac{1}{x}$.

Find the following:

(a) $(f \circ h \circ g)(x)$ **(b)** $(g \circ h \circ f)(x)$

(c) $(h \circ g \circ f)(x)$

***29** Let $f(x) = x^3$. Find a function g so that $(f \circ g)(x) = x$ and $(g \circ f)(x) = x$.

***30** Let $f(x) = x$. Find $(f \circ g)(x)$ and $(g \circ f)(x)$ for any function g.

***31** If $f(x) = 2x + 1$, find $g(x)$ so that $(f \circ g)(x) = 2x^2 - 4x + 1$.

■ 6.5

Decomposition of composite functions

One of the most useful skills needed in the study of calculus is the ability to recognize that a given function may be viewed as the composition of two or more functions. For instance, let h be given by

$$h(x) = \sqrt{x^2 + 2x + 2}$$

If we let $f(x) = x^2 + 2x + 2$ and $g(x) = \sqrt{x}$, then the composite g by f is

$$(g \circ f)(x) = g(f(x))$$
$$= g(x^2 + 2x + 2)$$
$$= \sqrt{x^2 + 2x + 2} = h(x)$$

Thus the given function h has been *decomposed* into the composition of the two functions f and g. Such decompositions are not unique. More than one decomposition is possible. For h we may also use

$$t(x) = x^2 + 2x \qquad s(x) = \sqrt{x + 2}$$

Then

$$(s \circ t)(x) = s(t(x))$$
$$= s(x^2 + 2x)$$
$$= \sqrt{x^2 + 2x + 2} = h(x)$$

You would most likely agree that the first of these decompositions is more "natural." Just which decomposition one is to choose will, in later work, depend on the situation. For our purposes some additional examples will help to demonstrate the decompositions that are desirable. Other answers for each of these examples are possible.

EXAMPLE 1 Find f and g such that $h = f \circ g$, where $h(x) = \left(\dfrac{1}{3x - 1}\right)^5$ and the inner function g is rational.

Solution Let $g(x) = \dfrac{1}{3x - 1}$ and $f(x) = x^5$.

$$(f \circ g)(x) = f(g(x))$$
$$= f\left(\frac{1}{3x - 1}\right)$$
$$= \left(\frac{1}{3x - 1}\right)^5 = h(x)$$

EXAMPLE 2 Write $h(x) = \dfrac{1}{(3x - 1)^5}$ as the composite of two functions so that the inner function is a binomial.

Solution Let $g(x) = 3x - 1$ and $f(x) = \dfrac{1}{x^5}$.

$$(f \circ g)(x) = f(g(x))$$
$$= f(3x - 1)$$
$$= \frac{1}{(3x - 1)^5} = h(x)$$

EXAMPLE 3 Decompose $h(x) = \sqrt{(x^2 - 3x)^5}$ into two functions so that the inner function is a binomial.

Solution First write $h(x) = (x^2 - 3x)^{5/2}$. Now let $f(x) = x^2 - 3x$ and let $g(x) = x^{5/2}$.

$$(g \circ f)(x) = g(f(x))$$
$$= g(x^2 - 3x)$$
$$= (x^2 - 3x)^{5/2}$$
$$= h(x)$$

EXAMPLE 4 Decompose h in Example 3 so that the outer function is a monomial.

Solution Write $h(x) = (\sqrt{x^2 - 3x})^5$. Let $f(x) = \sqrt{x^2 - 3x}$ and $g(x) = x^5$.

$$(g \circ f)(x) = g(f(x))$$
$$= g(\sqrt{x^2 - 3x})$$
$$= (\sqrt{x^2 - 3x})^5$$
$$= h(x)$$

TEST YOUR UNDERSTANDING

For each function h, find functions f and g so that $h = g \circ f$.

1 $h(x) = (8x - 3)^5$

2 $h(x) = \sqrt[5]{8x - 3}$

3 $h(x) = \sqrt{\dfrac{1}{8x - 3}}$

4 $h(x) = \left(\dfrac{5}{7 + 4x^2}\right)^3$

5 $h(x) = \dfrac{(2x + 1)^4}{(2x - 1)^4}$

6 $h(x) = \sqrt{(x^4 - 2x^2 + 1)^3}$

Examples 3 and 4 showed two different ways of decomposing $h(x) = \sqrt{(x^2 - 3x)^5}$ into the composition of two functions. It is also possible to express h as the composition of three functions. For example, we may use these functions:

$$f(x) = x^2 - 3x \qquad g(x) = x^5 \qquad t(x) = \sqrt{x}$$

Then

$$(t \circ g \circ f)(x) = t(g(f(x))) \qquad \text{f is the "inner" function.}$$
$$= t(g(x^2 - 3x)) \qquad \text{g is the "middle" function.}$$
$$= t((x^2 - 3x)^5) \qquad \text{t is the "outer" function.}$$
$$= \sqrt{(x^2 - 3x)^5}$$
$$= h(x)$$

EXERCISES 6.5

In Exercises 1–14, find functions f and g so that $h(x) = (f \circ g)(x)$. In each case let the inner function g be a polynomial or a rational function.

1 $h(x) = (3x + 1)^2$ **2** $h(x) = (x^2 - 2x)^3$

3 $h(x) = \sqrt{1 - 4x}$ **4** $h(x) = \sqrt[3]{x^2 - 1}$

5 $h(x) = \left(\dfrac{x + 1}{x - 1}\right)^2$ **6** $h(x) = \left(\dfrac{1 - 2x}{1 + 2x}\right)^3$

7 $h(x) = (3x^2 - 1)^{-3}$ **8** $h(x) = \left(1 + \dfrac{1}{x}\right)^{-2}$

9 $h(x) = \sqrt{\dfrac{x}{x - 1}}$ **10** $h(x) = \sqrt[3]{\dfrac{x - 1}{x}}$

11 $h(x) = \sqrt{(x^2 - x - 1)^3}$

12 $h(x) = \sqrt[3]{(1 - x^4)^2}$

13 $h(x) = \dfrac{2}{\sqrt{4 - x^2}}$ **14** $h(x) = -\left(\dfrac{3}{x - 1}\right)^5$

In Exercises 15–24, find three functions f, g, and h such that $k(x) = (h \circ g \circ f)(x)$.

15 $k(x) = (\sqrt{2x + 1})^3$ **16** $k(x) = \sqrt[3]{(2x - 1)^2}$

17 $k(x) = \sqrt{\left(\dfrac{x}{x + 1}\right)^5}$ **18** $k(x) = \left(\sqrt[7]{\dfrac{x^2 - 1}{x^2 + 1}}\right)^4$

19 $k(x) = (x^2 - 9)^{2/3}$ **20** $k(x) = (5 - 3x)^{5/2}$

21 $k(x) = -\sqrt{(x^2 - 4x + 7)^3}$

22 $k(x) = -\left(\dfrac{2x}{1 - x}\right)^{2/5}$

23 $k(x) = (1 + \sqrt{2x - 11})^2$

24 $k(x) = \sqrt[3]{(x^2 - 4)^5} - 1$

25 Find f so that $((x + 1)^2 + 1)^2 = (f \circ f)(x)$.

26 Find f so that
$$\sqrt{1 + \sqrt{1 + \sqrt{1 + x}}} = (f \circ f \circ f)(x).$$

REVIEW EXERCISES FOR CHAPTER 6

The solutions to the following exercises can be found within the text of Chapter 6. Try to answer each question without referring to the text.

Section 6.1

In Exercises 1–3, find the domain and graph.

1 $y = \sqrt{x - 2}$ **2** $y = \sqrt{|x|}$

3 $y = x^{-1/2}$

4 Graph: $f(x) = \begin{cases} x^2 - 1 & \text{if } -2 \le x < 2 \\ \sqrt{x - 2} & \text{if } 2 \le x < 5 \end{cases}$

Section 6.2

5 Find the x-intercepts of $y = \sqrt[3]{x + 1} - 2$.

6 Find the x-intercepts and the domain of $f(x) = \sqrt{x^2 + x - 6}$.

Solve the equations in Exercises 7–9.

7 $\sqrt{x + 4} + 2 = x$ **8** $\sqrt{x - 7} - \sqrt{x} = 1$

9 $\sqrt[3]{x^2} + \sqrt[3]{x} - 20 = 0$

10 Solve the system and graph:
$$y = \sqrt[3]{x}$$
$$y = \tfrac{1}{4}x$$

Section 6.3

11 Find the domain of $f(x) = (x - 5)\sqrt{x - 3}$ and determine the signs of f.

12 Find the domain of $f(x) = \dfrac{x}{\sqrt{4 - x^2}}$ and determine its signs.

13 Determine the signs of $f(x) = x^{1/2} + \tfrac{1}{2}x^{-1/2}(x - 3)$.

14 Find the domain of f, solve $f(x) = 0$, and determine the signs of f, where
$$f(x) = \dfrac{x^2 - 1}{2\sqrt{x - 1}} + 2x\sqrt{x - 1}$$

Section 6.4

15 Determine $(f + g)(x)$, $(f - g)(x)$, $(f \cdot g)(x)$, and $\dfrac{g}{f}(x)$, where $f(x) = \dfrac{1}{x^3 - 1}$ and $g(x) = \sqrt{x}$.

16 What are the domains of $f + g$, $f - g$, and $f \cdot g$ given in Exercise 15?

17 What is the domain of $\dfrac{f}{g}$ given in Exercise 15?

18 Evaluate $g\left(f\left(\dfrac{9}{4}\right)\right)$ and $f\left(g\left(\dfrac{9}{4}\right)\right)$, where $f(x) = \dfrac{1}{x - 2}$ and $g(x) = \sqrt{x}$.

19 Find $(g \circ f)(x)$ for f and g in Exercise 18 and state the domain.

20 Find $(f \circ g)(x)$ for f and g in Exercise 18 and state the domain.

21 Form the composites $g \circ f$ and $f \circ g$ and give their domains, where $f(x) = \dfrac{1}{x^2 - 1}$ and $g(x) = \sqrt{x}$.

22 Find $(f \circ g \circ h)(x)$, where $f(x) = \sqrt{x}$, $g(x) = x^2 + 1$, and $h(x) = \dfrac{1}{x}$.

Section 6.5

23 Find functions f and g so that $h(x) = \sqrt{x^2 + 2x + 2} = (g \circ f)(x)$.

24 Find functions f and g so that $h = f \circ g$, where $h(x) = \left(\dfrac{1}{3x - 1}\right)^5$.

25 Decompose $h(x) = \sqrt{(x^2 - 3x)^5}$ into two functions so that the inner function is a binomial.

26 Decompose h in Exercise 25 so that the outer function is a polynomial.

27 Show that $h(x) = \sqrt{(x^2 - 3x)^5}$ can be written as the composition of three functions.

SAMPLE TEST QUESTIONS FOR CHAPTER 6

Use these questions to test your knowledge of the basic skills and concepts of Chapter 6. Then check your answers with those given at the end of the book.

Graph each function, state its domain, and give the equations of the asymptotes if there are any.

1 $f(x) = -\sqrt[3]{x - 2}$ **2** $g(x) = \dfrac{1}{\sqrt{x}} + 2$

Solve each equation.

3 $\sqrt{18x + 5} - 9x = 1$

4 $6x^{2/3} + 5x^{1/3} - 4 = 0$

5 $\sqrt{x - 7} + \sqrt{x + 9} = 8$

6 Convert $(x + 1)^{1/2}(2x) + (x + 1)^{-1/2}\left(\dfrac{x^2}{2}\right)$ into the equivalent form $\dfrac{x(5x + 4)}{2\sqrt{x + 1}}$. Show your work.

In Questions 7 and 8, determine the signs of f.

7 $f(x) = \dfrac{\sqrt[3]{x - 4}}{x - 2}$

8 $f(x) = x^{1/2} - \frac{1}{2}x^{-1/2}(x + 4)$

9 Let $f(x) = \dfrac{1}{x^2 - 1}$ and $g(x) = \sqrt{x + 2}$. Find

$(f - g)(x)$ and $\dfrac{f}{g}(x)$ and state their domains.

10 For $f(x) = \dfrac{1}{1 - x^2}$ and $g(x) = \sqrt{x}$ find the composites $(f \circ g)(x)$ and $(g \circ f)(x)$ and state their domains.

11 Find functions f and g so that $h(x) = \sqrt[3]{(x - 2)^2} = (f \circ g)(x)$, where g is a binomial.

12 Let $F(x) = \dfrac{1}{(2x - 1)^{3/2}}$. Find functions f, g, and h so that $(f \circ g \circ h)(x) = F(x)$.

13 If y is positive in $\dfrac{x^2}{16} - \dfrac{y^2}{9} = 1$, then $y =$

    (a) $\frac{3}{4}x - 3$ **(b)** $\sqrt{\frac{3}{4}x - 3}$

    (c) $\frac{3}{4}x - 1$ **(d)** $\frac{3}{4}\sqrt{x^2 - 16}$

    (e) $\sqrt{\frac{9}{16}x^2 + 1}$

14 State the domain of $f(x) = \sqrt[3]{3x + 1} - x - 1$ and find the x-intercepts.

15 Solve the system:

$$y = 2\sqrt{x - 1}$$
$$2y - x = 2$$

ANSWERS TO THE TEST YOUR UNDERSTANDING EXERCISES

Page 221

1 Domain of g: $x \geq 0$

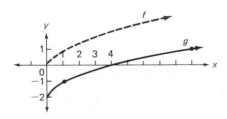

2 Domain of g: $x \geq 1$

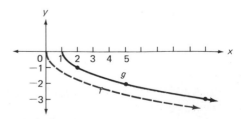

3 Domain of g: $x \geq 0$

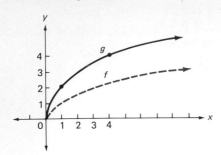

4 Domain of g: $x > -2$

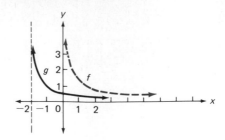

Page 225

1 25; all $x \geq 0$　　**2** 8; all $x > -1$　　**3** 0, 3; all $x \leq 0$ or all $x \geq 3$　　**4** 7

5 No solutions.　　**6** $\frac{1}{9}$　　**7** 5　　**8** $-3, 3$

9 5　　**10** 41　　**11** 0　　**12** $\frac{1}{2}$

Page 230

1 Domain: $x > 0$　　**2** Domain: $x \geq -2$ and $x \neq 0$　　**3** Domain: all $x \neq 0$

　　$f(x) > 0$ on $(4, \infty)$　　　$f(x) > 0$ on $(0, \infty)$　　　$f(x) > 0$ on $(0, \infty)$

　　$f(x) < 0$ on $(0, 4)$　　　$f(x) < 0$ on $(-2, 0)$　　　$f(x) < 0$ on $(-\infty, 0)$

Page 235

1 (a) $g(f(1)) = g(2) = 8$　　　　　　**2** (a) $g(f(1)) = g(1) = 1$

　　(b) $f(g(1)) = f(5) = 14$　　　　　　　(b) $f(g(1)) = f(1) = 1$

　　(c) $f(g(0)) = f(4) = 11$　　　　　　　(c) $f(g(0)) = f(0) = 0$

　　(d) $g(f(-2)) = g(-7) = 53$　　　　　(d) $g(f(-2))$ is undefined.

3 (a) $g(f(1)) = g(\sqrt[3]{2}) = 5\sqrt[3]{2}$　　　**4** (a) $g(f(1))$ is undefined.

　　(b) $f(g(1)) = f(5) = \sqrt[3]{14}$　　　　　(b) $f(g(1))$ is undefined.

　　(c) $f(g(0)) = f(0) = -1$　　　　　　　(c) $f(g(0)) = f(0) = -2$

　　(d) $g(f(-2)) = g(\sqrt[3]{-7}) = -5\sqrt[3]{7}$　　(d) $g(f(-2)) = g(0) - 0$

Page 239

(Other answers are possible.)

1 $f(x) = 8x - 3$; $g(x) = x^5$　　　　**2** $f(x) = 8x - 3$; $g(x) = \sqrt[5]{x}$

3 $f(x) = \dfrac{1}{8x - 3}$; $g(x) = \sqrt{x}$　　　**4** $f(x) = \dfrac{5}{7 + 4x^2}$; $g(x) = x^3$

5 $f(x) = \dfrac{2x + 1}{2x - 1}$; $g(x) = x^4$　　　**6** $f(x) = x^4 - 2x^2 + 1$; $g(x) = \sqrt{x^3}$

EXPONENTIAL AND LOGARITHMIC FUNCTIONS

7

7.1

Inverse functions

By definition, a function has each domain value x corresponding to exactly one range value y. Some (but not all) functions have the additional property that to every range value y there corresponds exactly one domain value x. Such functions are said to be **one-to-one functions**. To understand this concept, consider the functions $y = x^2$ and $y = x^3$.

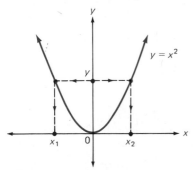

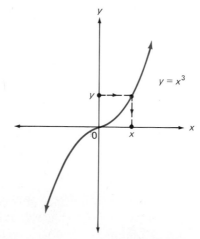

For a one-to-one function you can start at a range value y and trace it back to exactly one domain value x.

243

$y = x^2$ *is not* a one-to-one function. There are two domain values for a range value $y > 0$.

$y = x^3$ *is* a one-to-one function. There is exactly one domain value x for each range value y.

> **DEFINITION**
>
> A function f is a one-to-one function if and only if for each range value there corresponds exactly one domain value.

Once the graph of a function is known, there is a simple visual test for determining the one-to-one property. Consider a horizontal line through each range value y, as in the preceding figures. If the line meets the curve exactly once, then we have a one-to-one function; otherwise, it is not one-to-one.

> **TEST YOUR UNDERSTANDING**
>
> *Use the horizontal line test described above to determine which of the following are one-to-one functions.*
>
> **1** $y = x^2 - 2x + 1$ **2** $y = \sqrt{x}$ **3** $y = \dfrac{1}{x}$
>
> **4** $y = |x|$ **5** $y = 2x + 1$ **6** $y = \sqrt[3]{x}$
>
> **7** $y = -x$ **8** $y = [x]$ **9** $y = \dfrac{1}{x^2}$

If the variables in $y = x^3$ are interchanged, we obtain $x = y^3$. Here are the graphs for these equations, together with the two graphs on the same axes.

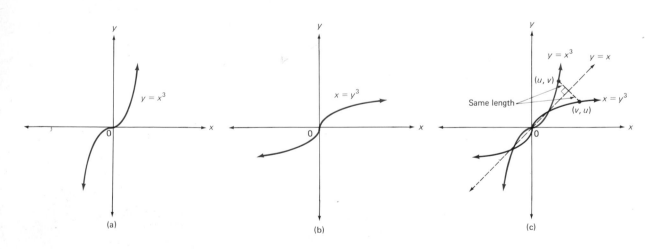

(a)   (b)   (c)

Because of this interchange of coordinates, the two curves are reflections of each other through the line $y = x$, as in part (c) of the figure. Another way to describe this relationship is to say that they are mirror images of one another through the "mirror line" $y = x$.

If the paper were folded along the line $y = x$, the two curves would coincide.

The equation $x = y^3$ may be solved for y by taking the cube root of both sides: $y = \sqrt[3]{x}$. The two equations $x = y^3$ and $y = \sqrt[3]{x}$ are equivalent and therefore define the same function of x. However, since $y = \sqrt[3]{x}$ shows *explicitly* how y depends on x, it is the preferred form.

We began with the one-to-one function $y = f(x) = x^3$ and, by interchanging coordinates, arrived at the new function $y = g(x) = \sqrt[3]{x}$. If the composites $f \circ g$ and $g \circ f$ are formed, something surprising happens.

$$(f \circ g)(x) = f(g(x)) = f(\sqrt[3]{x}) = (\sqrt[3]{x})^3 = x$$

$$(g \circ f)(x) = g(f(x)) = g(x^3) = \sqrt[3]{x^3} = x$$

Function f cubes and function g "uncubes"; f and g are inverse functions.

In each case we obtained the same value x that we started with; whatever one of the functions does to a value x, the other function undoes. Whenever two functions act on each other in such a manner, we say that they are *inverse functions* or that either function is the inverse of the other.

DEFINITION OF INVERSE FUNCTIONS

Two functions f and g are said to be *inverse functions* if and only if:

1 For each x in the domain of g, $g(x)$ is in the domain of f and
$$(f \circ g)(x) = f(g(x)) = x$$
2 For each x in the domain of f, $f(x)$ is in the domain of g and
$$(g \circ f)(x) = g(f(x)) = x$$

The notation f^{-1} is also used to represent the inverse of f. Thus $f(f^{-1}(x)) = x$ and $f^{-1}(f(x)) = x$.

It turns out (as suggested by our work with $y = x^3$) that every one-to-one function f has an inverse g and that their graphs are reflections of each other through the line $y = x$. The technique of interchanging variables, used to obtain $y = \sqrt[3]{x}$ from $y = x^3$, can be applied to many situations, as illustrated in the following examples.

$y = x^2$ is not one-to-one. Its reflection in the line $y = x$ has equation $x = y^2$, or, $y = \pm\sqrt{x}$ which is not a function.

EXAMPLE 1 Find the inverse g of $y = f(x) = 2x + 3$. Then show that $(f \circ g)(x) = x = (g \circ f)(x)$, and graph both on the same axes.

Solution Interchange variables in $y = 2x + 3$ and solve for y.

$$x = 2y + 3$$
$$2y = x - 3$$
$$y = \tfrac{1}{2}x - \tfrac{3}{2}$$

Using $y = g(x) = \tfrac{1}{2}x - \tfrac{3}{2}$, we have

$$(f \circ g)(x) = f(g(x)) = f(\tfrac{1}{2}x - \tfrac{3}{2})$$
$$= 2(\tfrac{1}{2}x - \tfrac{3}{2}) + 3$$
$$= x - 3 + 3$$
$$= x$$

To find the inverse g of f, begin with
$$y = f(x).$$
Then interchange variables
$$x = f(y)$$
and solve for y in terms of x, producing
$$y = g(x).$$

$$(g \circ f)(x) = g(f(x)) = g(2x + 3)$$
$$= \tfrac{1}{2}(2x + 3) - \tfrac{3}{2}$$
$$= x + \tfrac{3}{2} - \tfrac{3}{2}$$
$$= x$$

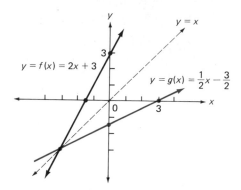

EXAMPLE 2 Follow the instructions in Example 1 for $y = f(x) = \sqrt{x}$.

Solution Interchange variables in $y = \sqrt{x}$ to get $x = \sqrt{y}$. At this point we see that x cannot be negative: $x \geq 0$. Solving for y by squaring produces $y = x^2$. Using the letter g for this inverse function, we have $y = g(x) = x^2$ with domain $x \geq 0$.

$$(f \circ g)(x) = f(g(x)) = f(x^2) = \sqrt{x^2} = |x| = x \qquad \text{(since } x \geq 0)$$
$$(g \circ f)(x) = g(f(x)) = g(\sqrt{x}) = (\sqrt{x})^2 = x$$

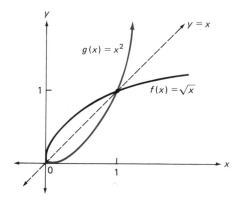

The process of interchanging variables to find the inverse of a function can also be explained in terms of the criterion $f(g(x)) = x$. Begin with a function, say $f(x) = 3x - 2$, and let g be its inverse. Thus $f(g(x)) = x$. Substituting $g(x)$ into the equation for f gives

$$x = f(g(x)) = 3g(x) - 2$$

Solving this last equation for $g(x)$ produces

$$g(x) = \tfrac{1}{3}x + \tfrac{2}{3}$$

Now you can see that in taking $y = f(x) = 3x - 2$ and interchanging the variables to get $x = 3y - 2$, we are really letting y stand for the inverse function g. Thus

$$x = 3y - 2 = 3g(x) - 2 = f(g(x))$$

In many cases you will find it more efficient to use the form $x = 3y - 2$ and solve for y. This procedure is simpler than using $x = 3g(x) - 2$ and solving for $g(x)$. But regardless of which notation is used, this procedure has its limitations. Thus if the defining expression $y = f(x)$ is complicated, it may be algebraically difficult, or even impossible, to do what we did in the special cases above. We will avoid such situations by limiting our work in this section to functions for which the procedure can be applied.

EXERCISES 7.1

In Exercises 1–6, use the horizontal line test to decide if the function is one-to-one.

1 $f(x) = (x - 1)^2$ **2** $f(x) = x^3 - 3x^2$

3 $f(x) = \dfrac{1 - x}{x}$ **4** $f(x) = \dfrac{1}{x - 2}$

5 $f(x) = \sqrt{x} + 3$ **6** $f(x) = \dfrac{1}{x^2 - x - 2}$

In Exercises 7–12, show that f and g are inverse functions according to the criteria $(f \circ g)(x) = x$ and $(g \circ f)(x) = x$. Then graph both functions and the line $y = x$ on the same axes.

7 $f(x) = \tfrac{1}{3}x - 3$; $g(x) = 3x + 9$

8 $f(x) = 2x - 6$; $g(x) = \tfrac{1}{2}x + 3$

9 $f(x) = (x + 1)^3$; $g(x) = \sqrt[3]{x} - 1$

10 $f(x) = -(x + 2)^3$; $g(x) = -\sqrt[3]{x} - 2$

11 $(x) = \dfrac{1}{x - 1}$; $g(x) = \dfrac{1}{x} + 1$

12 $f(x) = x^2 + 2$ for $x \geq 2$; $g(x) = \sqrt{x - 2}$

In Exercises 13–24, find the inverse function g of the given function f.

13 $y = f(x) = (x - 5)^3$

14 $y = f(x) = x^{1/3} - 3$

15 $y = f(x) = \tfrac{2}{3}x - 1$

16 $y = f(x) = -4x + \tfrac{2}{5}$

17 $y = f(x) = (x - 1)^5$

18 $y = f(x) = -x^5$

19 $y = f(x) = x^{3/5}$

20 $y = f(x) = x^{5/3} + 1$

21 $y = f(x) = \dfrac{2}{x - 2}$

22 $y = f(x) = -\dfrac{1}{x} - 1$

23 $y = f(x) = x^{-5}$

24 $y = f(x) = \dfrac{1}{\sqrt[3]{x - 2}}$

In Exercises 25–28, verify that the function is its own inverse by showing that $(f \circ f)(x) = x$.

25 $f(x) = \dfrac{1}{x}$

26 $f(x) = \sqrt{4 - x^2}, 0 \leq x \leq 2$

27 $f(x) = \dfrac{x}{x - 1}$

28 $f(x) = \dfrac{3x - 8}{x - 3}$

In Exercises 29–34, find the inverse g of the given function f, and graph both in the same coordinate system.

29 $y = f(x) = (x + 1)^2$; $x \geq -1$

30 $y = f(x) = x^2 - 4x + 4$; $x \geq 2$

31 $y = f(x) = \dfrac{1}{\sqrt{x}}$

32 $y = f(x) = -\sqrt{x}$

33 $y = f(x) = x^2 - 4$; $x \geq 0$

34 $y = f(x) = 4 - x^2$; $0 \leq x \leq 2$

*35 Aside from the linear function $y = x$, what other

linear functions are their own inverses? (*Hint:* Inverse functions are reflections of one another through the line $y = x$.)

*36 In the figure curve C_1 is the graph of a one-to-one function $y = f(x)$ and curve C_2 is the graph of $y = g(x)$. The points on C_2 have been obtained by interchanging the first and second coordinates of the points on curve C_1. For a specific value x in the domain of f, the point $P(x, f(x))$ on C_1 produces $Q(f(x), x)$ on C_2. How does this figure demonstrate that $(g \circ f)(x) = x$?

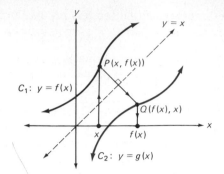

7.2

Exponential functions

$20,000 = (10,000)2^1$
$40,000 = (10,000)2^2$
$80,000 = (10,000)2^3$

Imagine that a bacterial culture is growing at such a rate that after each hour the number of bacteria has doubled. Thus if there were 10,000 bacteria when the culture started to grow, then after 1 hour the number would have grown to 20,000, after 2 hours there would be 40,000, and so on. It becomes reasonable to say that

$$y = (10,000)2^x$$

gives the number y of bacteria present after x hours. This equation defines an **exponential function** with independent variable x and dependent variable y. We call such a function exponential because its exponent is a variable. In this section we study exponential functions of the form $y = b^x$ for $b > 0$. The number b is often referred to as the *base* number.

What does the graph of $y = f(x) = 2^x$ look like? We can get a good idea by forming a table of values, plotting the points, and connecting them with a smooth curve.

The function is increasing and the curve is concave up. The x-axis is a horizontal asymptote.

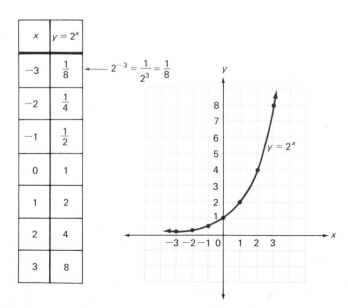

x	$y = 2^x$
-3	$\frac{1}{8}$
-2	$\frac{1}{4}$
-1	$\frac{1}{2}$
0	1
1	2
2	4
3	8

$2^{-3} = \dfrac{1}{2^3} = \dfrac{1}{8}$

The accuracy of this graph can be improved by using more points. Consider rational values of x, such as $\frac{1}{2}$ or $\frac{3}{2}$:

$2^{1/2} = \sqrt{2} = 1.4$ (correct to one decimal place from Appendix Table I)

$2^{3/2} = (\sqrt{2})^3 = (1.4)^3 = 2.7$

Using irrational values for x, such as $\sqrt{2}$ or π, is another matter entirely. (Remember that our development of exponents stopped with the rationals.) To give a precise meaning of such numbers is beyond the scope of this course. It does turn out, however, that the indicated shape of the curve $y = 2^x$ is correct and that the formal definitions of values like $2^{\sqrt{2}}$ are made so that they "fit" the curve.

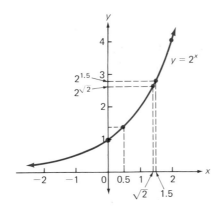

A calculator can be used to better understand such numbers as $2^{\sqrt{2}}$. For example, verify these rational powers of 2 to four decimal places.

$$2^{1.4} = 2.6390$$

$$2^{1.41} = 2.6574$$

$$2^{1.414} = 2.6647$$

$$2^{1.4142} = 2.6651$$

See Ex. 34–35 for similar computations involving irrational powers.

Since the rational exponents are getting closer to the irrational number $\sqrt{2}$, the corresponding powers are getting closer to $2^{\sqrt{2}}$. So the exponential approximations suggest that $2^{\sqrt{2}} = 2.67$ to two decimal places. Now find $2^{\sqrt{2}}$ directly on a calculator and compare.

In advanced work it can be shown that for any positive bases a and b, the following hold for all real numbers r and s.

$$b^r b^s = b^{r+s} \qquad \frac{b^r}{b^s} = b^{r-s} \qquad (b^r)^s = b^{rs}$$

$$a^r b^r = (ab)^r \qquad b^0 = 1 \qquad b^{-r} = \frac{1}{b^r}$$

Our earlier work with the same rules, for rational exponents, can now serve as the basis for accepting these results.

EXAMPLE 1 Graph the curve $y = 8^x$ on the interval $[-1, 1]$ by using a table of values.

Solution

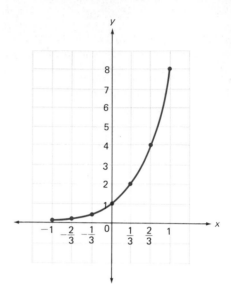

x	y
-1	$\frac{1}{8}$
$-\frac{2}{3}$	$\frac{1}{4}$
$-\frac{1}{3}$	$\frac{1}{2}$
0	1
$\frac{1}{3}$	2
$\frac{2}{3}$	4
1	8

Can you think of reasons why values of $b \leq 0$ are also excluded as bases for exponential functions?

Our attention has been restricted to the exponential functions $y = b^x$, where $b > 1$, all of which have the same general shape as $y = 2^x$. For $b = 1$, we get $y = 1^x = 1$ for all x. Since this is a constant function, we do not use base $b = 1$ in the classification of exponential functions.

The remaining base values for our purposes are those for which $0 < b < 1$. In particular, if $b = \frac{1}{2}$, we get $y = \left(\frac{1}{2}\right)^x = \frac{1}{2^x}$.

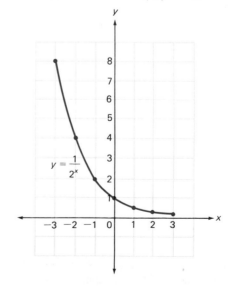

x	$y = 2^{-x}$
-3	8
-2	4
-1	2
0	1
1	$\frac{1}{2}$
2	$\frac{1}{4}$
3	$\frac{1}{8}$

$$y = \frac{1}{2^x}$$

The graph of $y = g(x) = \dfrac{1}{2^x}$ can also be found by comparing it to the graph of $y = f(x) = 2^x$. Since $g(x) = \dfrac{1}{2^x} = 2^{-x} = f(-x)$, the y-values for g are the same as the y-values for f on the opposite side of the y-axis. In other words, the graph of g is the reflection of the graph of f through the y-axis.

All the curves $y = b^x$ for $0 < b < 1$ have this same basic shape. The curve is concave up, the function is decreasing, and $y = 0$ is a horizontal asymptote.

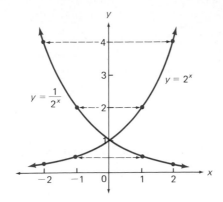

EXAMPLE 2   Use the graph of $y = f(x) = 2^x$ to sketch the curves $y = g(x) = 2^{x-3}$ and $y = h(x) = 2^x - 1$.

Solution   Since $g(x) = f(x - 3)$, the graph of g can be obtained by shifting $y = 2^x$ by 3 units to the right. Moreover, since $h(x) = f(x) - 1$ the graph of h can be found by shifting $y = 2^x$ down 1 unit.

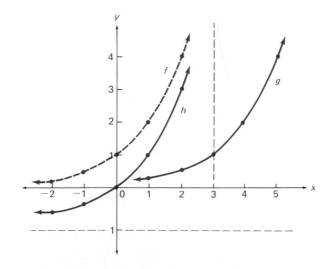

Following are some important properties of the function $y = b^x$, for $b > 0$ and $b \neq 1$.

1 The domain consists of all real numbers x.

2 The range consists of all positive numbers y.

3 The function is increasing (the curve is rising) when $b > 1$, and it is decreasing (the curve is falling) when $0 < b < 1$.

4 The curve is concave up for $b > 1$ and for $0 < b < 1$.

5 It is a one-to-one function.

6 The point $(0, 1)$ is on the curve. There is no x-intercept.

7 The x-axis is a horizontal asymptote to the curve, toward the left for $b > 1$ and toward the right for $0 < b < 1$.

8 $b^{x_1}b^{x_2} = b^{x_1+x_2}$; $b^{x_1}/b^{x_2} = b^{x_1-x_2}$; $(b^{x_1})^{x_2} = b^{x_1x_2}$.

This form of the one-to-one property can sometimes be applied to the solutions of equations.

The one-to-one property of a function f may be stated in this way:

$$\text{If } f(x_1) = f(x_2), \text{ then } x_1 = x_2$$

That is, since $f(x_1)$ and $f(x_2)$ represent the same range value there can only be one corresponding domain value; consequently, $x_1 = x_2$. Using $f(x) = b^x$, this statement means that if $b^{x_1} = b^{x_2}$, then $x_1 = x_2$.

EXAMPLE 3 Use the one-to-one property to solve for t in the exponential equation $5^{t^2} = 625$.

Solution Since $625 = 5^4$ we get

$$5^{t^2} = 5^4$$

Now use the one-to-one property of $f(x) = 5^x$ to equate exponents. Thus

$$t^2 = 4$$
$$t = \pm 2$$

Check: $5^{(\pm 2)^2} = 5^4 = 625$.

EXERCISES 7.2

In Exercises 1–10, graph the exponential function f by making use of a brief table of values. Then use this curve to sketch the graph of g. Indicate the horizontal asymptotes.

1 $f(x) = 2^x$; $g(x) = 2^{x+3}$

2 $f(x) = 3^x$; $g(x) = 3^x - 2$

3 $f(x) = 4^x$; $g(x) = -(4^x)$

4 $f(x) = 5^x$; $g(x) = (\frac{1}{5})^x$

5 $f(x) = (\frac{3}{2})^x$; $g(x) = (\frac{3}{2})^{-x}$

6 $f(x) = 8^x$; $g(x) = 8^{x-2} + 3$

7 $f(x) = 3^x$; $g(x) = 2(3^x)$

8 $f(x) = 3^x$; $g(x) = \frac{1}{2}(3^x)$

9 $f(x) = 2^{x/2}$; $g(x) = 2^{x/2} - 3$

10 $f(x) = 4^x$; $g(x) = 4^{1-x}$

In Exercises 11–14, sketch the curves on the same axes.

11 $y = (\frac{3}{2})^x$, $y = 2^x$, $y = (\frac{5}{2})^x$

12 $y = (\frac{1}{4})^x$, $y = (\frac{1}{3})^x$, $y = (\frac{1}{2})^x$

13 $y = 2^{|x|}$, $y = -(2^{|x|})$

14 $y = 2^x$, $y = 2^{-x}$, $y = 2^x - 2^{-x}$

   (*Hint:* Subtract ordinates.)

In Exercises 15–32, use the one-to-one property of an appropriate exponential function to solve the indicated equation.

15 $2^x = 64$

16 $3^x = 81$

17 $2^{x^2} = 512$

18 $3^{x-1} = 27$

19 $5^{2x+1} = 125$

20 $2^{x^3} = 256$

21 $7^{x^2+x} = 49$

22 $b^{x^2+x} = 1$

23 $\dfrac{1}{2^x} = 32$

24 $\dfrac{1}{10^x} = 10{,}000$

25 $9^x = 3$

26 $64^x = 8$

27 $9^x = 27$

28 $64^x = 16$

29 $(\frac{1}{49})^x = 7$

30 $5^x = \frac{1}{125}$

31 $(\frac{27}{8})^x = \frac{9}{4}$

32 $(0.01)^x = 1000$

33 Graph the functions $y = 2^x$ and $y = x^2$ in the same coordinate system for the interval $[0, 5]$. (Use a larger unit on the x-axis than on the y-axis.) What are the points of intersection?

34 Use a calculator to verify that $\sqrt{3} = 1.732050 \ldots$. Now fill in the powers of 2 in the table, rounding off each entry to four decimal places.

x	1.7	1.73	1.732	1.7320	1.73205
2^x					

On the basis of the results, what is your estimate of $2^{\sqrt{3}}$ to three decimal places? Now find $2^{\sqrt{3}}$ directly on the calculator and compare.

35 Follow the instructions in Exercise 34 for these numbers:

(a) $3^{\sqrt{2}}$ (b) $3^{\sqrt{3}}$

(c) $2^{\sqrt{5}}$ (d) 4^{π}

*36 Solve for x: $(6^{2x})(4^x) = 1728$.

*37 Solve for x: $(5^{2x+1})(7^{2x}) = 175$.

7.3

Logarithmic functions

It was pointed out in the preceding section that $y = f(x) = b^x$, for $b > 0$ and $b \neq 1$, is a one-to-one function. Since every one-to-one function has an inverse, it follows that f has an inverse. The graph of the inverse function g is the reflection of $y = f(x)$ through the line $y = x$. Here are two typical cases for $b > 1$ and for $0 < b < 1$.

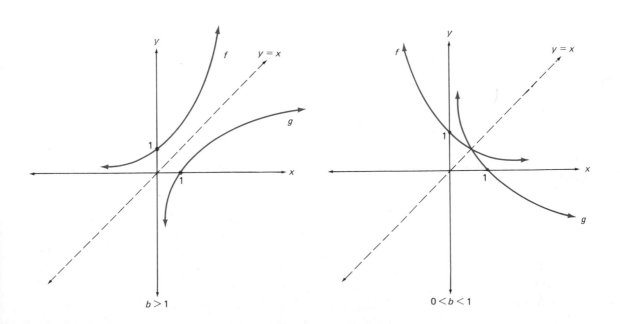

An equation for the inverse function g can be obtained by interchanging the roles of the variables in $y = b^x$. Thus $x = b^y$ is an equation for g. Unfortunately, we have no way of solving $x = b^y$ to get y explicitly in terms of x. To overcome this difficulty we create some new terminology.

The equation $x = b^y$ tells us that *y is the exponent on b that produces x.* In situations like this the word **logarithm** is used in place of *exponent.* A logarithm, then, is an exponent. Now we may say that *y is the logarithm on b that produces x.* This description can be abbreviated to $y = \text{logarithm}_b x$ and abbreviating further we reach the final form

$$y = \log_b x$$

which is read "y equals log x to the base b" or "y equals log x base b."

It is important to realize that we are only defining (not proving) the equation $y = \log_b x$ to have the same meaning as $x = b^y$. In other words, the logarithmic form $y = \log_b x$ and the exponential form $x = b^y$ are equivalent. And since they are equivalent they define the same function g:

$$y = g(x) = \log_b x.$$

Now we know that $y = f(x) = b^x$ and $y = g(x) = \log_b x$ are inverse functions. Consequently,

$$f(g(x)) = f(\log_b x) = b^{\log_b x} = x \quad \text{and} \quad g(f(x)) = g(b^x) = \log_b(b^x) = x$$

Note: $y = b^x$ and $y = \log_b x$ are inverse functions.

EXAMPLE 1 Write the equation of the inverse function g of $y = f(x) = 2^x$ and graph both on the same axes.

Solution The inverse g has equation $y = g(x) = \log_2 x$, and its graph can be obtained by reflecting $y = f(x) = 2^x$ through the line $y = x$.

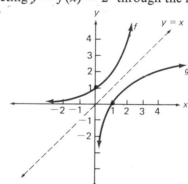

TEST YOUR UNDERSTANDING

1 Find the equation of the inverse of $y = 3^x$ and graph both on the same axes.
2 Find the equation of the inverse of $y = (\frac{1}{3})^x$ and graph both on the same axes.

Let $y = f(x) = \log_5 x$. Describe how the graph of each of the following can be obtained from the graph of f.

3 $g(x) = \log_5(x + 2)$ 　　　　　　　　**4** $g(x) = 2 + \log_5 x$
5 $g(x) = -\log_5 x$ 　　　　　　　　　　**6** $g(x) = 2 \log_5 x$

We found $y = \log_b x$ by interchanging the role of the variables in $y = b^x$. As a consequence of this switching, the domains and ranges of the two functions are also interchanged. Thus

Domain of $y = \log_b x$ is the same as the range of $y = b^x$.

Range of $y = \log_b x$ is the same as the domain of $y = b^x$.

These results are incorporated into the following list of important properties of the function $y = \log_b x$, where $b > 0$ and $b \neq 1$.

PROPERTIES OF $y = f(x) = \log_b x$

1 The domain consists of all positive numbers x.

2 The range consists of all real numbers y.

3 The function increases (the curve is rising) for $b > 1$, and it decreases (the curve is falling) for $0 < b < 1$.

4 The curve is concave down for $b > 1$, and it is concave up for $0 < b < 1$.

5 It is a one-to-one function; if $\log_b(x_1) = \log_b(x_2)$, then $x_1 = x_2$.

6 The point $(1, 0)$ is on the graph. There is no y-intercept.

7 The y-axis is a vertical asymptote to the curve in the downward direction for $b > 1$ and in the upward direction for $0 < b < 1$.

8 $\log_b(b^x) = x$ and $b^{\log_b x} = x$.

EXAMPLE 2 Find the domain for $y = \log_2(x - 3)$.

Solution In $y = \log_2(x - 3)$ the quantity $x - 3$ plays the role that x does in $\log_2 x$. Thus $x - 3 > 0$ and the domain consists of all $x > 3$.

The equation $y = \log_b x$ is equivalent to $x = b^y$ (not to be confused with the inverse $y = b^x$). Studying the following list of special cases will help you to understand this equivalence.

Logarithmic form $\log_b x = y$	Exponential form $b^y = x$
$\log_5 25 = 2$	$5^2 = 25$
$\log_{27} 9 = \frac{2}{3}$	$27^{2/3} = 9$
$\log_6 \frac{1}{36} = -2$	$6^{-2} = \frac{1}{36}$
$\log_b 1 = 0$	$b^0 = 1$

Of the two forms $y = \log_b x$ and $x = b^y$, the exponential form is usually easier to work with. Consequently, when there is a question concerning

$y = \log_b x$ it is often useful to convert to the exponential form. For instance, to evaluate $\log_9 27$ we write

$$y = \log_9 27$$

and convert to exponential form. Thus

$$9^y = 27$$

If you happen to recognize that $9^{3/2} = 27$, you will see that $y = \frac{3}{2}$. Otherwise, try writing each side of $9^y = 27$ with the same base. Since $27 = 3^3$ and $9^y = (3^2)^y = 3^{2y}$, we have

$$3^{2y} = 3^3$$

$$2y = 3 \qquad (f(t) = 3^t \text{ is one-to-one})$$

$$y = \tfrac{3}{2}$$

EXAMPLE 3   Solve for b: $\log_b 8 = \frac{3}{4}$.

Solution   Convert to exponential form.

$$b^{3/4} = 8$$

$8^{4/3} = (\sqrt[3]{8})^4 = 2^4$ Take the $\frac{4}{3}$ power of both sides.

$$(b^{3/4})^{4/3} = 8^{4/3}$$

$$b = 16$$

EXERCISES 7.3

Sketch the graph of the function f. Reflect this curve through the line $y = x$ to obtain the graph of the inverse function g, and write the equation for g.

1 $y = f(x) = 4^x$ **2** $y = f(x) = 5^x$

3 $y = f(x) = (\frac{1}{3})^x$ **4** $y = f(x) = (0.2)^x$

Describe how the graph of h can be obtained from the graph of g. Find the domain of h, and write the equation of the vertical asymptote.

5 $g(x) = \log_3 x$; $h(x) = \log_3(x + 2)$

6 $g(x) = \log_5 x$; $h(x) = \log_5(x - 1)$

7 $g(x) = \log_8 x$; $h(x) = 2 + \log_8 x$

8 $g(x) = \log_{10} x$; $h(x) = 2 \log_{10} x$

Sketch the graph of f and state its domain.

9 $f(x) = \log_{10} x$

10 $f(x) = -\log_{10} x$

11 $f(x) = |\log_{10} x|$

12 $f(x) = \log_{10}(-x)$

13 $f(x) = \log_{10}|x|$

14 $f(x) = \log_{1/10}(x + 1)$

Convert from the exponential to the logarithmic form.

15 $2^8 = 256$ **16** $5^{-3} = \frac{1}{125}$

17 $(\frac{1}{3})^{-1} = 3$ **18** $81^{3/4} = 27$

19 $17^0 = 1$ **20** $(\frac{1}{49})^{-1/2} = 7$

Convert from the logarithmic form to the exponential form.

21 $\log_{10} 0.0001 = -4$ **22** $\log_{64} 4 = \frac{1}{3}$

23 $\log_{\sqrt{2}} 2 = 2$ **24** $\log_{13} 13 = 1$

25 $\log_{12} \frac{1}{1728} = -3$ **26** $\log_{27/8} \frac{9}{4} = \frac{2}{3}$

Solve for the indicated quantity: y, x, or b.

27 $\log_2 16 = y$ **28** $\log_{1/2} 32 = y$

29 $\log_{1/3} 27 = y$ **30** $\log_7 x = -2$

31 $\log_{1/6} x = 3$ **32** $\log_8 x = -\frac{2}{3}$

33 $\log_b 125 = 3$ **34** $\log_b 8 = \frac{3}{2}$

35 $\log_b \frac{1}{8} = -\frac{3}{2}$ **36** $\log_{100} 10 = y$

37 $\log_{27} 3 = y$ **38** $\log_{1/16} x = \frac{1}{4}$

39 $\log_b \frac{16}{81} = 4$ **40** $\log_8 x = -3$

41 $\log_b \frac{1}{27} = -\frac{3}{2}$ **42** $\log_{\sqrt{3}} x = 2$

43 $\log_{\sqrt{8}}\left(\frac{1}{8}\right) = y$ **44** $\log_b \frac{1}{128} = -7$

45 $\log_{0.001} 10 = y$ **46** $\log_{0.2} 5 = y$

47 $\log_9 x = 1$

Evaluate the expressions in Exercises 48–49.

*48 $\log_2(\log_4 256)$ ***49** $\log_{3/4}(\log_{1/27} \frac{1}{81})$

By interchanging the roles of the variables, find the inverse function g. Show that $(f \circ g)(x) = x$ and $(g \circ f)(x) = x$.

*50 $y = f(x) = 2^{x+1}$

*51 $y = f(x) = \log_3(x + 3)$

The laws of logarithms

From the rules of exponents we have

$$2^3 \cdot 2^4 = 2^{3+4} = 2^7$$

Now let us focus on just the exponential part:

$$3 + 4 = 7$$

The three exponents involved here can be expressed as logarithms.

$$3 = \log_2 8 \quad \text{because } 2^3 = 8$$

$$4 = \log_2 16 \quad \text{because } 2^4 = 16$$

$$7 = \log_2 128 \quad \text{because } 2^7 = 128$$

Logarithms are exponents.

Substituting these expressions into $3 + 4 = 7$ gives

$$\log_2 8 + \log_2 16 = \log_2 128$$

Furthermore, since $128 = 8 \cdot 16$, we have

$$\log_2 8 + \log_2 16 = \log_2(8 \cdot 16)$$

This is a special case of the first law of logarithms:

LAWS OF LOGARITHMS

If M and N are positive, $b > 0$ and $b \neq 1$, then

LAW 1. $\log_b MN = \log_b M + \log_b N$

LAW 2. $\log_b \dfrac{M}{N} = \log_b M - \log_b N$

LAW 3. $\log_b(N^k) = k \log_b N$

Law 1 says that the log of a product is the sum of the logs of the factors. Can you give similar interpretations for Laws 2 and 3?

Since logarithms are exponents it is not surprising that these laws can be proved by using the appropriate rules of exponents. Following is a proof of Law 1; the proofs of Laws 2 and 3 are left as exercises.

Let

$$\log_b M = r \quad \text{and} \quad \log_b N = s$$

Convert to exponential form:

$$M = b^r \quad \text{and} \quad N = b^s$$

Multiply the two equations:

$$MN = b^r b^s = b^{r+s}$$

Then convert to logarithmic form:

$$\log_b MN = r + s$$

Substitute for r and s to get the final result:

$$\log_b MN = \log_b M + \log_b N$$

EXAMPLE 1 For positive numbers A, B, and C, show that

$$\log_b \frac{AB^2}{C} = \log_b A + 2 \log_b B - \log_b C$$

Solution

$$\log_b \frac{AB^2}{C} = \log_b(AB^2) - \log_b C \qquad \text{(Law 2)}$$

$$= \log_b A + \log_b B^2 - \log_b C \qquad \text{(Law 1)}$$

$$= \log_b A + 2 \log_b B - \log_b C \qquad \text{(Law 3)}$$

EXAMPLE 2 Express $\frac{1}{2} \log_b x - 3 \log_b(x - 1)$ as the logarithm of a single expression in x.

Solution

Identify the laws of logarithms being used in Examples 2 and 3.

$$\frac{1}{2} \log_b x - 3 \log_b(x - 1) = \log_b x^{1/2} - \log_b(x - 1)^3$$

$$= \log_b \frac{x^{1/2}}{(x - 1)^3}$$

$$= \log_b \frac{\sqrt{x}}{(x - 1)^3}$$

EXAMPLE 3 Given: $\log_b 2 = 0.6931$ and $\log_b 3 = 1.0986$; find $\log_b \sqrt{12}$.

Solution

$$\log_b \sqrt{12} = \log_b 12^{1/2} = \tfrac{1}{2} \log_b 12$$

$$= \tfrac{1}{2} \log_b(3 \cdot 4) = \tfrac{1}{2} [\log_b 3 + \log_b 4]$$

$$= \tfrac{1}{2} [\log_b 3 + \log_b 2^2]$$

$$= \tfrac{1}{2} [\log_b 3 + 2 \log_b 2]$$

$$= \tfrac{1}{2} \log_b 3 + \log_b 2$$

$$= \tfrac{1}{2}(1.0986) + 0.6931$$

$$= 1.2424$$

EXAMPLE 4   Solve for x: $\log_8(x-6) + \log_8(x+6) = 2$.

Examples 4 to 6 illustrate how the laws of logarithms can be used to solve logarithmic equations.

Solution   First note that in $\log_8(x-6)$ we must have $x - 6 > 0$, or $x > 6$. Similarly, $\log_8(x+6)$ calls for $x > -6$. Therefore, the only solutions, if there are any, must satisfy $x > 6$.

$$\log_8(x-6) + \log_8(x+6) = 2$$
$$\log_8(x-6)(x+6) = 2 \qquad \text{(Law 1)}$$
$$\log_8(x^2 - 36) = 2$$
$$x^2 - 36 = 8^2 \qquad \text{(converting to exponential form)}$$
$$x^2 - 100 = 0$$
$$(x+10)(x-10) = 0$$
$$x = -10 \quad \text{or} \quad x = 10$$

The only possible solutions are -10 and 10. Our initial observation that $x > 6$ automatically eliminates -10. (If that initial observation had not been made, -10 could still have been eliminated by checking in the given equation.) The value $x = 10$ can be checked as follows:

$$\log_8(10-6) + \log_8(10+6) = \log_8 4 + \log_8 16$$
$$= \tfrac{2}{3} + \tfrac{4}{3} = 2$$

EXAMPLE 5   Solve: $\log_{10}(x^3 - 1) - \log_{10}(x^2 + x + 1) = 1$.

Solution

$$\log_{10}(x^3 - 1) - \log_{10}(x^2 + x + 1) = 1$$
$$\log_{10}\frac{x^3 - 1}{x^2 + x + 1} = 1 \qquad \text{(Law 2)}$$

$$\log_{10}\frac{(x-1)(x^2+x+1)}{x^2+x+1} = 1 \quad \text{(by factoring)}$$

$$\log_{10}(x-1) = 1$$

$$x - 1 = 10^1 \quad \text{(Why?)}$$

$$x = 11$$

Check: $\log_{10}(11^3 - 1) - \log_{10}(11^2 + 11 + 1) = \log_{10}1330 - \log_{10}133$

$$= \log_{10}\tfrac{1330}{133}$$

$$= \log_{10}10 = 1$$

EXAMPLE 6 Solve: $\log_3 2x - \log_3(x+5) = 0$.

Alternate Solution

Solution

$\log_3 2x - \log_3(x+5) = 0$

$\log_3 2x = \log_3(x+5)$

$2x = x + 5$ (Why?)

$x = 5$

$$\log_3 2x - \log_3(x+5) = 0$$

$$\log_3 \frac{2x}{x+5} = 0$$

$$\frac{2x}{x+5} = 3^0$$

$$\frac{2x}{x+5} = 1$$

$$2x = x + 5$$

$$x = 5$$

Check: $\log_3 2(5) - \log_3(5+5) = \log_3 10 - \log_3 10 = 0$.

CAUTION: LEARN TO AVOID MISTAKES LIKE THESE	
WRONG	RIGHT
$\log_b A + \log_b B = \log_b(A+B)$	$\log_b A + \log_b B = \log_b AB$
$\log_b(x^2-4) = \log_b x^2 - \log_b 4$	$\log_b(x^2-4)$ $= \log_b(x+2)(x-2)$ $= \log_b(x+2) + \log_b(x-2)$
$(\log_b x)^2 = 2\log_b x$	$(\log_b x)^2 = (\log_b x)(\log_b x)$
$\log_b A - \log_b B = \dfrac{\log_b A}{\log_b B}$	$\log_b A - \log_b B = \log_b \dfrac{A}{B}$
If $2\log_b x = \log_b(3x+4)$, then $2x = 3x + 4$	If $2\log_b x = \log_b(3x+4)$, then $\log_b x^2 = \log_b(3x+4)$ and $x^2 = 3x + 4$.

Use the laws of logarithms (as much as possible) to convert the given logarithms into expressions involving sums and differences.

1 $\log_b \dfrac{3x}{x+1}$

2 $\log_b \dfrac{x^2}{x-1}$

3 $\log_b \dfrac{\sqrt{x^2-1}}{x}$

4 $\log_b \dfrac{1}{x}$

5 $\log_b \dfrac{1}{x^2}$

6 $\log_b \sqrt{\dfrac{x+1}{x-1}}$

Convert each expression into the logarithm of a single expression in x.

7 $\log_b(x+1) - \log_b(x+2)$

8 $\log_b x + 2\log_b(x-1)$

9 $\frac{1}{2}\log_b(x^2-1) - \frac{1}{2}\log_b(x^2+1)$

10 $\log_b(x+2) - \log_b(x^2-4)$

11 $3\log_b x - \log_b 2 - \log_b(x+5)$

12 $\frac{1}{3}\log_b(x-1) + \log_b 3 - \frac{1}{3}\log_b(x+1)$

Use the appropriate laws of logarithms to explain why each statement is correct.

13 $\log_b 27 + \log_b 3 = \log_b 243 - \log_b 3$

14 $\log_b 16 + \log_b 4 = \log_b 64$

15 $-2\log_b \frac{4}{9} = \log_b \frac{81}{16}$

16 $\frac{1}{2}\log_b 0.0001 = -\log_b 100$

Find the logarithms in Exercises 17–22 by using the laws of logarithms and the given information that $\log_b 2 = .3010$, $\log_b 3 = 0.4771$, and $\log_b 5 = 0.6990$. Assume that all logs have base b.

17 (a) $\log 4$ (b) $\log 8$ (c) $\log \frac{1}{2}$

18 (a) $\log \sqrt{2}$ (b) $\log 9$ (c) $\log 12$

19 (a) $\log 48$ (b) $\log \frac{2}{3}$ (c) $\log 125$

20 (a) $\log 50$ (b) $\log 10$ (c) $\log \frac{25}{6}$

21 (a) $\log \sqrt[3]{5}$ (b) $\log \sqrt{20^3}$ (c) $\log \sqrt{900}$

22 (a) $\log 0.2$ (b) $\log 0.25$ (c) $\log 2.4$

Solve for x and check.

23 $\log_{10} x + \log_{10} 5 = 2$

24 $\log_{10} x + \log_{10} 5 = 1$

25 $\log_{10} 5 - \log_{10} x = 2$

26 $\log_{10}(x+21) + \log_{10} x = 2$

27 $\log_{12}(x-5) + \log_{12}(x-5) = 2$

28 $\log_3 x + \log_3(2x+51) = 4$

29 $\log_{16} x + \log_{16}(x-4) = \frac{5}{4}$

30 $\log_2(x^2) - \log_2(x-2) = 3$

31 $\log_{10}(3-x) - \log_{10}(12-x) = -1$

32 $\log_{10}(3x^2 - 5x - 2) - \log_{10}(x-2) = 1$

33 $\log_{1/7} x + \log_{1/7}(5x-28) = -2$

34 $\log_{1/3} 12x^2 - \log_{1/3}(20x-9) = -1$

35 $\log_{10}(x^3-1) - \log_{10}(x^2+x+1) = -2$

36 $2\log_{10}(x-2) = 4$

37 $2\log_{25} x - \log_{25}(25-4x) = \frac{1}{2}$

38 $\log_3(8x^3+1) - \log_3(4x^2-2x+1) = 2$

*39 Prove Law 2. (*Hint:* Follow the proof of Law 1 using $\dfrac{b^r}{b^s} = b^{r-s}$.)

*40 Prove Law 3. (*Hint:* Use $(b^r)^k = b^{rk}$.)

*41 Solve for x: $(x+2)\log_b b^x = x$.

*42 Solve for x: $\log_{N^2} N = x$.

*43 Solve for x: $\log_x(2x)^{3x} = 4x$.

*44 (a) Explain why $\log_b b = 1$.
   (b) Show that $(\log_b a)(\log_a b) = 1$.
   (*Hint:* Use Law 3 and the result $b^{\log_b x} = x$.)

*45 Use $B^{\log_B N} = N$ to derive $\log_B N = \dfrac{\log_b N}{\log_b B}$. (*Hint:* Begin by taking the log base b of both sides.)

The base *e*

The graphs of $y = b^x$ for $b > 1$ all have the same basic shape, as shown in the following figure. Notice that the larger the value of b, the faster the curve rises toward the right and the faster it approaches the x-axis toward the left. You can use your imagination to see that as all possible base values $b > 1$ are considered, the corresponding curves will completely fill in the shaded regions.

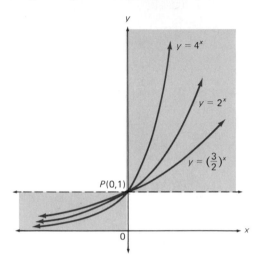

All such curves pass through point $P(0, 1)$. The tangent lines to these curves through P are relatively flat (small positive slope) for values of b close to 1 and very steep for large values of b. The slopes of these tangents consist of all numbers $m > 0$.

These figures show the curves $y = 2^x$ and $y = 3^x$, including the tangent through point $P(0, 1)$.

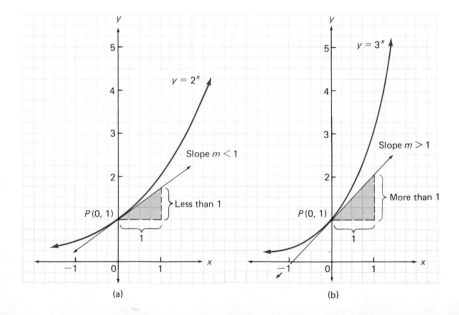

From the grid marks you can observe that the slope of the tangent to $y = 2^x$ is less than 1 because for a horizontal change of 1 unit the vertical change is less than 1 unit. Similarly, you can see that the slope of the tangent to $y = 3^x$ is slightly more than 1. We suspect that there must be a value b so that the slope of the tangent to the corresponding exponential function through point P is exactly equal to 1. In advanced courses it can be shown that such a value does exist. This number plays a very important role in mathematics, and it is designated by the letter e.

e is the real number such that the tangent to the graph of $y = e^x$ at the point $P(0, 1)$ has slope equal to 1.

Since the curve $y = e^x$ is between $y = 2^x$ and $y = 3^x$, we expect that e satisfies $2 < e < 3$. This is correct; in fact, it turns out that e is an irrational number that is closer to 3 than to 2. Carried to five decimal places, $e = 2.71828$.

For theoretical purposes e is the most important base number for exponential and logarithmic functions. The inverse of $y = e^x$ is given by $y = \log_e x$. In place of $\log_e x$ we will now write **ln** x, which is called the **natural log of x**. Thus $x = e^y$ and $y = \ln x$ are equivalent.

The number e is also closely related to the expression $\left(1 + \dfrac{1}{n}\right)^n$. The larger n is taken, the closer $\left(1 + \dfrac{1}{n}\right)^n$ gets to e. For example.

$(1 + \tfrac{1}{10})^{10} \quad = 2.59374$

$(1 + \tfrac{1}{100})^{100} = 2.70481$

$(1 + \tfrac{1}{1000})^{1000} = 2.71692$

See Exercise 57.

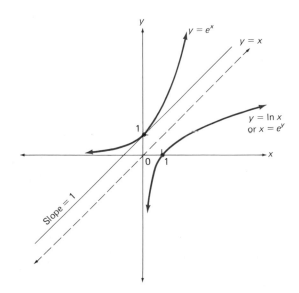

What is the equation of the tangent to $y = e^x$ at $(0, 1)$?

Since $e > 1$, the properties of $y = b^x$ and $y = \log_b x$ $(b > 1)$ carry over to $y = e^x$ and $y = \ln x$. We collect these properties here for easy reference.

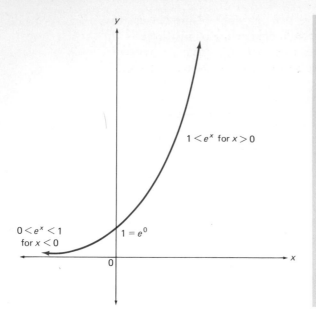

$1 < e^x$ for $x > 0$

$0 < e^x < 1$
for $x < 0$

$1 = e^0$

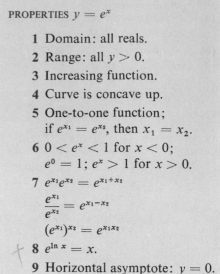

PROPERTIES $y = e^x$

1 Domain: all reals.
2 Range: all $y > 0$.
3 Increasing function.
4 Curve is concave up.
5 One-to-one function;
   if $e^{x_1} = e^{x_2}$, then $x_1 = x_2$.
6 $0 < e^x < 1$ for $x < 0$;
   $e^0 = 1$; $e^x > 1$ for $x > 0$.
7 $e^{x_1} e^{x_2} = e^{x_1 + x_2}$
   $\dfrac{e^{x_1}}{e^{x_2}} = e^{x_1 - x_2}$
   $(e^{x_1})^{x_2} = e^{x_1 x_2}$
8 $e^{\ln x} = x$.
9 Horizontal asymptote: $y = 0$.

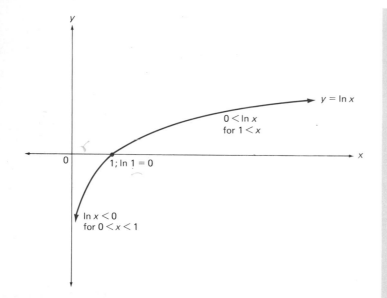

$y = \ln x$

$0 < \ln x$
for $1 < x$

$1; \ln 1 = 0$

$\ln x < 0$
for $0 < x < 1$

PROPERTIES OF $y = \ln x$

1 Domain: all $x > 0$.
2 Range: all reals.
3 Increasing function.
4 Curve is concave down.
5 One-to-one function;
   if $\ln x_1 = \ln x_2$, then $x_1 = x_2$.
6 $\ln x < 0$ for $0 < x < 1$;
   $\ln 1 = 0$; $\ln x > 0$ for $x > 1$.
7 $\ln x_1 x_2 = \ln x_1 + \ln x_2$
   $\ln \dfrac{x_1}{x_2} = \ln x_1 - \ln x_2$
   $\ln x_1{}^{x_2} = x_2 \ln x_1$
8 $\ln e^x = x$.
9 Vertical asymptote; $x = 0$.

The examples that follow utilize the base e and are solved in a manner similar to those done earlier for other bases.

EXAMPLE 1   (a) Find the domain of $y = \ln (x - 2)$; (b) Sketch $y = \ln x^2$ for $x > 0$.

Solution

(a) Since the domain of $y = \ln x$ is all $x > 0$, the domain of $y = \ln(x - 2)$ has all x for which $x - 2 > 0$; all $x > 2$.

(b) Since $y = \ln x^2 = 2 \ln x$, we obtain the graph by multiplying the ordinates of $y = \ln x$ by 2.

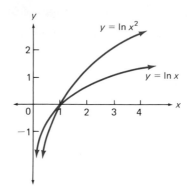

EXAMPLE 2 Solve for t: (a) $e^{\ln(2t-1)} = 5$; (b) $e^{2t-1} = 5$.

Solution

(a) $e^{\ln(2t-1)} = 5$

$\quad 2t - 1 = 5 \quad$ (Property 8
$\quad\quad 2t = 6 \quad$ for $y = e^x$)
$\quad\quad\quad t = 3$

(b) $e^{2t-1} = 5$

$\quad 2t - 1 = \ln 5 \quad$ (Why?)
$\quad\quad 2t = 1 + \ln 5$
$\quad\quad\quad t = \frac{1}{2}(1 + \ln 5)$

Check: for (b): $e^{2[1/2(1+\ln 5)]-1} = e^{1+\ln 5 - 1} = e^{\ln 5} = 5$.

To three decimal places,

$$t = \frac{1}{2}(1 + \ln 5) = 1.305$$

EXAMPLE 3 Solve for x: $\ln(x + 1) = 1 + \ln x$.

Solution

$$\ln(x + 1) - \ln x = 1$$

$$\ln \frac{x + 1}{x} = 1$$

Now convert to exponential form:

$$\frac{x + 1}{x} = e$$

$$ex = x + 1$$

$$(e - 1)x = 1$$

$$x = \frac{1}{e - 1}$$

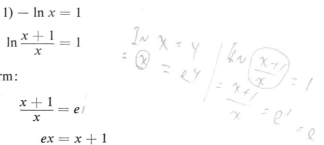

$$\text{Check: } \ln\left(\frac{1}{e-1} + 1\right) = \ln\frac{e}{e-1} = \ln e - \ln(e-1) = 1 + \ln(e-1)^{-1}$$

$$= 1 + \ln\frac{1}{(e-1)}.$$

EXAMPLE 4 **(a)** Show $h(x) = \ln(x^2 + 5)$ as the composite of two functions. **(b)** Show $F(x) = e^{\sqrt{x^2-3x}}$ as the composite of three functions.

Solution

(a) Let $f(x) = \ln x$ and $g(x) = x^2 + 5$. Then

$$(f \circ g)(x) = f(g(x)) = f(x^2 + 5) = \ln(x^2 + 5) = h(x)$$

(b) Let $f(x) = e^x$, $g(x) = \sqrt{x}$, and $h(x) = x^2 - 3x$. Then

$$(f \circ g \circ h)(x) = f(g(h(x))) \qquad h \text{ is the "inner" function.}$$
$$= f(g(x^2 - 3x)) \qquad g \text{ is the "middle" function.}$$
$$= f(\sqrt{x^2 - 3x}) \qquad f \text{ is the "outer" function.}$$
$$= e^{\sqrt{x^2-3x}} = F(x)$$

(Other solutions are possible.)

EXAMPLE 5 Determine the signs of $f(x) = x^2e^x + 2xe^x$.

Solution We find that $f(x) = x^2e^x + 2xe^x = xe^x(x + 2)$ in which $e^x > 0$ for all x, and the other factors are zero when $x = 0$ or $x = -2$.

Interval	$(-\infty, -2)$	$(-2, 0)$	$(0, \infty)$
Sign of $x + 2$	$-$	$+$	$+$
Sign of x	$-$	$-$	$+$
Sign of e^x	$+$	$+$	$+$
Sign of $f(x)$	$+$	$-$	$+$

$f(x) > 0$ on the intervals $(-\infty, -2)$ and $(0, \infty)$

$f(x) < 0$ on the interval $(-2, 0)$

EXERCISES 7.5

Sketch each pair of functions on the same axes.

1 $y = e^x$; $y = e^{x-2}$

2 $y = e^x$; $y = 2e^x$

3 $y = \ln x$; $y = \frac{1}{2}\ln x$

4 $y = \ln x$; $y = \ln(x + 2)$

5 $y = \ln x$; $y = \ln(-x)$

6 $y = e^x$; $y = e^{-x}$

7 $y = e^x$; $y = e^x + 2$

8 $y = \ln x$; $y = \ln |x|$

9 $f(x) = -e^{-x}$, $g(x) = 1 - e^{-x}$

10 $g(x) = 1 - e^{-x}$, $s(x) = 1 - e^{-2x}$

11 $g(x) = 1 - e^{-x}$, $t(x) = 1 - e^{(-1/2)x}$

12 $u(x) = 1 - e^{-3x}$, $v(x) = 1 - e^{(-1/3)x}$

Explain how the graph of f can be obtained from the curve $y = \ln x$. (Hint: First apply the appropriate rules of logarithms.)

13 $f(x) = \ln ex$

14 $f(x) = \ln \dfrac{x}{e}$

15 $f(x) = \ln \sqrt{x}$

16 $f(x) = \ln \dfrac{1}{x}$

17 $f(x) = \ln(x^2 - 1) - \ln(x + 1)$

18 $f(x) = \ln x^{-3}$

Find the domain.

19 $f(x) = \ln(x + 2)$

20 $f(x) = \ln |x|$

21 $f(x) = \ln(2x - 1)$

22 $f(x) = \dfrac{1}{\ln x}$

23 $f(x) = \dfrac{\ln(x - 1)}{x - 2}$

24 $f(x) = \ln(\ln x)$

Use the laws of logarithms (as much as possible) to write $\ln f(x)$ as an expression involving sums and differences.

25 $f(x) = \dfrac{5x}{x^2 - 4}$

26 $f(x) = x\sqrt{x^2 + 1}$

27 $f(x) = \dfrac{(x - 1)(x + 3)^2}{\sqrt{x^2 + 2}}$

28 $f(x) = \sqrt{\dfrac{x + 7}{x - 7}}$

29 $f(x) = \sqrt{x^3(x + 1)}$

30 $f(x) = \dfrac{x}{\sqrt[3]{x^2 - 1}}$

Convert each expression into the logarithm of a single expression.

31 $\frac{1}{2} \ln x + \ln(x^2 + 5)$

32 $\ln 2 + \ln x - \ln(x - 1)$

33 $3 \ln(x + 1) + 3 \ln(x - 1)$

34 $\ln(x^3 - 1) - \ln(x^2 + x + 1)$

35 $\frac{1}{2} \ln x - 2 \ln(x - 1) - \frac{1}{3} \ln(x^2 + 1)$

Simplify.

36 $\ln(e^{3x})$

37 $e^{\ln \sqrt{x}}$

38 $\ln(x^2 e^3)$

39 $e^{-2 \ln x}$

40 $(e^{\ln x})^2$

41 $\ln \left(\dfrac{e^x}{e^{x-1}} \right)$

Solve for x.

42 $e^{3x+5} = 100$

43 $e^{-0.01x} = 27$

44 $e^{x^2} = e^x e^{3/4}$

45 $e^{\ln(1-x)} = 2x$

46 $\ln x + \ln 2 = 1$

47 $\ln(x + 1) = 0$

48 $\ln x = -2$

49 $\ln e^{\sqrt{x+1}} = 3$

50 $e^{\ln(6x^2 - 4)} = 5x$

51 $\ln(x^2 - 4) - \ln(x + 2) = 0$

52 $(e^{x+2} - 1) \ln(1 - 2x) = 0$

53 $\ln x = \frac{1}{2} \ln 4 + \frac{2}{3} \ln 8$

54 $\frac{1}{2} \ln(x + 4) = \ln(x + 2)$

55 $\ln x = 2 + \ln(1 - x)$

56 $\ln(x^2 + x - 2) = \ln x + \ln(x - 1)$

57 Use a calculator to complete the table. Round off the entries to four decimal places.

n	2	10	100	500	1000	5000	10,000
$\left(1 + \dfrac{1}{n}\right)^n$							

■ *Show that each function is the composite of two functions.*

58 $h(x) = e^{2x+3}$

59 $h(x) = e^{-x^2 + x}$

60 $h(x) = \ln(1 - 2x)$

61 $h(x) = \ln \dfrac{x}{x + 1}$

62 $h(x) = (e^x + e^{-x})^2$

63 $h(x) = \sqrt[3]{\ln x}$

■ *Show that each function is the composite of three functions.*

64 $F(x) = e^{\sqrt{x+1}}$

65 $F(x) = e^{(3x-1)^2}$

66 $F(x) = [\ln(x^2 + 1)]^3$

67 $F(x) = \ln \sqrt{e^x + 1}$

■ *Determine the signs of each function.*

68 $f(x) = xe^x + e^x$

69 $f(x) = e^{2x} - 2xe^{2x}$

70 $f(x) = -3x^2 e^{-3x} + 2xe^{-3x}$

71 $f(x) = 1 + \ln x$

72 Show that $(e^x + e^{-x})^2 - (e^x - e^{-x})^2 = 4$.

73 Show that $\ln \left(\dfrac{x}{4} - \dfrac{\sqrt{x^2 - 4}}{4} \right)$
$$= -\ln(x + \sqrt{x^2 - 4}).$$

*74 Solve for x: $\dfrac{e^x + e^{-x}}{2} = 1$.

*75 Solve for x in terms of y if $y = \dfrac{e^x}{2} - \dfrac{1}{2e^x}$. (Hint: Let $u = e^x$ and solve the resulting quadratic in u.)

7.6

Exponential growth and decay

There is a large variety of applied problems dealing with exponential and logarithmic functions. Before considering some of these applications it will be helpful first to learn how to solve for x in an equation such as $2^x = 35$.

$$2^x = 35$$

$$\ln 2^x = \ln 35 \qquad \text{(taking the natural log of both sides)}$$

$$x \ln 2 = \ln 35 \qquad \text{(Why?)}$$

$$x = \frac{\ln 35}{\ln 2}$$

An approximation for x can be found by using Appendix Table III. The entries in this table give values of $\ln x$ to three decimal places. (In most cases $\ln x$ is irrational.) From this table we have $\ln 2 = 0.693$. Even though $\ln 35$ is not given (directly) in the table, it can still be found by applying the second law of logarithms.

Note that the values found in the tables of logarithms are approximations. For the sake of simplicity, however, we will use the equals sign (=).

$$\ln 35 = \ln(3.5)(10) = \ln 3.5 + \ln 10$$

$$= 1.253 + 2.303 \qquad \text{(Table III)}$$

$$= 3.556$$

Now we have

$$x = \frac{\ln 35}{\ln 2} = \frac{3.556}{0.693} = 5.13$$

As a rough check we see that 5.13 is reasonable since $2^5 = 32$.

TEST YOUR UNDERSTANDING

Solve each equation for x in terms of natural logarithms. Approximate the answer by using Table III.

1 $4^x = 5$	2 $4^{-x} = 5$	3 $(\frac{1}{2})^x = 12$
4 $2^{3x} = 10$	5 $4^x = 15$	6 $67^x = 4$

At the beginning of Section 7.2, we developed the formula $y = (10{,}000)2^x$, which gives the number of bacteria present after x hours of growth; 10,000 is the initial number of bacteria. How long will it take for this bacterial culture to grow to 100,000? To answer this question we let $y = 100{,}000$ and solve for x.

$$(10{,}000)2^x = 100{,}000$$

$$2^x = 10 \qquad \text{(divide by 10,000)}$$

$$x \ln 2 = \ln 10$$

$$x = \frac{\ln 10}{\ln 2}$$

$$= \frac{2.303}{0.693} = 3.32$$

It will take about 3.3 hours.

In the preceding illustration the exponential and logarithmic functions were used to solve a problem of "exponential growth." Many problems involving exponential growth, or decay, can be solved by using the general formula

$$y = f(x) = Ae^{kx}$$

which shows how the amount of a substance y depends on the time x. Since $f(0) = A$, A represents the initial amount of the substance and k is a constant. In a given situation $k > 0$ signifies that y is growing (increasing) with time. For $k < 0$ the substance is decreasing. (Compare to the graphs of $y = e^x$ and $y = e^{-x}$.)

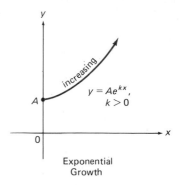

Exponential Growth

The preceding bacterial problem also fits this general form. This can be seen by substituting $2 = e^{\ln 2}$ into $y = (10,000)2^x$:

$$y = (10,000)2^x = (10,000)(e^{\ln 2})^x = 10,000e^{(\ln 2)x}$$

EXAMPLE 1 A radioactive substance is decaying (it is changing into another element) according to the formula $y = Ae^{-0.2x}$, where y is the amount of material remaining after x years.
(a) If the initial amount $A = 80$ grams, how much is left after 3 years?
(b) The **half-life** of a radioactive substance is the time it takes for half of it to decompose. Find the half-life of this substance in which $A = 80$ grams.

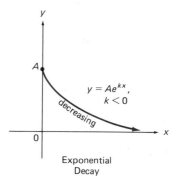

Exponential Decay

Solution
(a) Since $A = 80$, $y = 80e^{-0.2x}$. We need to solve for the amount y when $x = 3$.

$$y = 80e^{-0.2x}$$
$$= 80e^{-0.2(3)}$$
$$= 80e^{-0.6}$$
$$= 80(0.549) \qquad \text{(Table II)}$$
$$= 43.920$$

There will be about 43.9 grams after 3 years.

(b) This question calls for the time x at which only half of the initial amount is left. Consequently, the half-life x is the solution to $40 = 80e^{-0.2x}$. Divide each side by 80:

$$\tfrac{1}{2} = e^{-0.2x}$$

Take the natural log of both sides, or change to logarithmic form, to obtain $-0.2x = \ln \frac{1}{2}$. Since $\ln \frac{1}{2} = \ln 1 - \ln 2 = -\ln 2$, we solve for x as follows.

$$-0.2x = -\ln 2$$

$$x = \frac{\ln 2}{0.2}$$

$$= 3.465$$

The half-life is approximately 3.465 years.

Carbon-14, often written as ^{14}C, is a radioactive isotope of carbon with a half-life of about 5750 years. By finding how much ^{14}C is contained in the remains of a formerly living organism, it becomes possible to determine what percentage this is of the original amount of ^{14}C at the time of death. Once this information is given, the formula $y = Ae^{kx}$ will enable us to date the age of the remains. The dating will be done after we solve for the constant k. Since the amount of ^{14}C after 5750 years will be $\frac{A}{2}$, we have

Explain each step in this solution.

$$\frac{A}{2} = Ae^{5750k}$$

$$\frac{1}{2} = e^{5750k}$$

$$5750k = \ln \frac{1}{2}$$

$$k = \frac{\ln 0.5}{5750}$$

Substitute this value for k in the general formula $y = Ae^{kx}$:

$$y = Ae^{(\ln 0.5/5750)x}$$

EXAMPLE 2 An animal skeleton is found to contain one-fourth of its original amount of ^{14}C. How old is the skeleton?

Solution Let x be the age of the skeleton. Then

$$\frac{1}{4}A = Ae^{(\ln 0.5/5750)x}$$

$$\frac{1}{4} = e^{(\ln 0.5/5750)x}$$

$$\left(\frac{\ln 0.5}{5750}\right)x = \ln \frac{1}{4} = -\ln 4$$

$$x = \frac{(5750)(-\ln 4)}{\ln 0.5}$$

$$= 11,500$$

The skeleton is about 11,500 years old.

EXAMPLE 1 Use scientific notation to compute $\dfrac{1}{800,000}$.

Solution

$$\frac{1}{800,000} = \frac{1}{8 \times 10^5} = \frac{1}{8} \times \frac{1}{10^5} = 0.125 \times 10^{-5}$$

$$= 0.00000125$$

In scientific notation the solution to Example 1 is written **1.25 × 10⁻⁶**.

EXAMPLE 2 Use scientific notation to evaluate

$$\frac{(2,310,000)^2}{(11,200,000)((0.000825)}$$

Solution

$$\frac{(2,310,000)^2}{(11,200,000)(0.000825)} = \frac{(2.31 \times 10^6)^2}{(1.12 \times 10^7)(8.25 \times 10^{-4})}$$

$$= \frac{(2.31)^2 \times (10^6)^2}{(1.12 \times 10^7)(8.25 \times 10^{-4})}$$

$$= \frac{(2.31)^2}{(1.12)(8.25)} \times \frac{10^{12}}{(10^7)(10^{-4})}$$

$$= 0.5775 \times 10^9 = 577,500,000$$

This is a good place to review the rules of exponents given in Section 2.1.

EXERCISES 7.7

Write each number in scientific notation.

1 4680

2 0.0092

3 0.92

4 0.9

5 7,583,000

6 93,000,000

7 25

8 36.09

9 0.000000555

10 0.57721

11 202.4

12 7.93

Write each number in standard form.

13 7.89×10^4

14 7.89×10^{-4}

15 3.0×10^3

16 3.0×10^{-3}

17 1.74×10^{-1}

18 1.74×10^0

19 1.74×10^1

20 2.25×10^5

21 9.06×10^{-2}

Express each of the following as a single power of 10.

22 $\dfrac{10^{-3} \times 10^5}{10}$

23 $\dfrac{10^8 \times 10^4 \times 10^{-5}}{10^2 \times 10^3}$

24 $\dfrac{10^{-3}}{10^{-5}}$

25 $\dfrac{10^1 \times 10^2 \times 10^3 \times 10^4}{10^{10}}$

26 $\dfrac{10^9 \times 10^{-2}}{10^6 \times 10^{-9}}$

27 $\dfrac{(10^2)^3 \times 10^{-1}}{(10^{-3})^4}$

Compute, using scientific notation.

28 $\dfrac{1}{5000}$

29 $\dfrac{1}{0.0005}$

30 $\dfrac{2}{80,000}$

31 $\dfrac{0.0064}{0.000016}$

32 $\dfrac{(6000)(720)}{12,000}$

33 $\dfrac{(0.000025)}{(0.0625)(0.02)}$

34 $\dfrac{(240)(0.000032)}{(0.008)(12,000)}$

35 $\dfrac{4,860,000}{(0.081)(19,200)}$

36 $\dfrac{(0.0111)(66,600)(555)}{(22,200)(0.000333)}$

Perform the indicated operations in Exercises 37–42, using scientific notation.

37 $\sqrt{1,440,000}$

38 $(0.0006)^3$

39 $\dfrac{\sqrt{0.000625}}{3125}$

40 $\dfrac{(40)^4(0.015)^2}{24,000}$

41 $\dfrac{(1{,}728{,}000)^{1/3}}{(0.06)(400)^2}$

42 $[(0.002)(0.2)(200)(20{,}000)]^{1/2}$

43 Light travels at a rate of about 186,000 miles per second. The average distance from the sun to the earth is 93,000,000 miles. Use scientific notation to find how long it takes light to reach the earth from the sun.

*44 Based on information given in Exercise 43, use scientific notation to show that 1 light-year (the distance light travels in 1 year) is approximately $5.87 \times 10^{12} = 5{,}870{,}000{,}000{,}000$ miles.

7.8

Common logarithms

Logarithms were developed about 350 years ago. Since then they have been widely used to simplify involved numerical computations. Much of this work can now be done more efficiently with the aid of computers and calculators. However, logarithmic computations will help us to better understand the theory of logarithms, which plays an important role in many parts of mathematics (including calculus) and in its applications.

For scientific and technical work, numbers are often written in scientific notation and we will therefore be using logarithms to the base 10, called **common logarithms**.

Below is an excerpt of Appendix Table IV, page 449. It contains the common logarithms of three-digit numbers from 1.00 to 9.99. To find a logarithm, say $\log_{10}3.47$, first find the entry 3.4 in the left-hand column under the heading x. Now in the row for 3.4 and in the column headed by the digit 7 you will find the entry .5403. This is the common logarithm of 3.47. We write

Note that the values found in the tables of logarithms are approximations. For the sake of simplicity, however, we will use the equals sign (=).

$$\log_{10}3.47 = 0.5403$$

By reversing this process we can begin with $\log_{10}x = 0.5403$ and find x.

x	0	1	2	3	4	5	6	7	8	9
⋮	⋮	⋮	⋮	⋮	⋮	⋮	⋮	⋮	⋮	⋮
3.3	.5185	.5198	.5211	.5224	.5237	.5250	.5263	.5276	.5289	.5302
3.4	.5315	.5328	.5340	.5353	.5366	.5378	.5391	.5403	.5416	.5428
3.5	.5441	.5453	.5465	.5478	.5490	.5502	.5514	.5527	.5539	.5551
⋮	⋮	⋮	⋮	⋮	⋮	⋮	⋮	⋮	⋮	⋮

The common logarithms in Table IV are four-place decimals between 0 and 1. Except for the case $\log_{10}1 = 0$, they are all approximations. The fact that they are between 0 and 1 will be taken up in the exercises.

Verify these illustrations using Table IV:

$$\log_{10}3.07 = 0.4871 \qquad \log_{10}8.88 = 0.9484$$
$$\text{If } \log_{10}x = 0.7945, \text{ then } x = 6.23$$

To find $\log_{10}N$, where N may not be between 1 and 10, we first write N in scientific notation.

$$N = x10^c$$

where c is an integer and $1 \le x < 10$. For example:

$$62{,}300 = 6.23(10^4) \qquad 0.00623 = 6.23(10^{-3})$$

This form of N, in conjunction with Table IV, will allow us to find $\log_{10}N$. In general,

$$\log_{10}N = \log_{10}(x10^c)$$
$$= \log_{10}x + \log_{10}10^c \qquad \text{(Law 1 for logs)}$$
$$= \log_{10}x + c \qquad \text{(Why?)}$$

The integer c is the **characteristic** of $\log_{10}N$, and the four-place decimal fraction $\log_{10}x$ is its **mantissa**. Using $N = 62{,}300$, we have

$$\log_{10}62{,}300 = \log_{10}6.23(10^4) = \log_{10}6.23 + \log_{10}10^4$$
$$= \log_{10}6.23 + 4$$
$$= 0.7945 + 4 \qquad \text{(Table IV)}$$
$$= 4.7945$$

Since all logarithms considered here are to the base 10, we will simplify the notation and drop the subscript 10 from the logarithmic statements. Thus we write $\log N$ instead of $\log_{10}N$.

Note the distinction:

$\log N \longleftarrow$ **common logarithm, base 10**

$\ln N \longleftarrow$ **natural logarithm, base e**

EXAMPLE 1 Find $\log 0.0419$.

Solution

$$\log 0.0419 = \log 4.19(10^{-2})$$
$$= \log 4.19 + \log 10^{-2}$$
$$= 0.6222 + (-2)$$

Suppose that in Example 1 the mantissa 0.6222 and the negative characteristic are combined:

$$0.6222 + (-2) = -1.3778 = -(1 + 0.3778)$$
$$= -1 + (-0.3778)$$

Since Table IV does not have negative mantissas, like -0.3778, we avoid such combining and preserve the form of $\log 0.0419$ so that its mantissa is positive. For computational purposes there are other useful forms of $0.6222 + (-2)$ in which the mantissa 0.6222 is preserved. Note that $-2 = 8 - 10$, $18 - 20$, and so forth. Thus

$$0.6222 + (-2) = 0.6222 + 8 - 10 = 8.6222 - 10 = 18.6222 - 20$$

Similarly,

$$\log 0.00569 = 7.7551 - 10 = 17.7551 - 20$$
$$\log 0.427 = 9.6304 - 10 = 29.6304 - 30$$

An efficient way to find N, if $\log N = 6.1239$, is to find the three-digit number x from Table IV corresponding to the mantissa 0.1239. Then multiply

x by 10^6. Thus, since log $1.33 = 0.1239$, we have

$$N = 1.33(10^6) = 1,330,000$$

In the following explanation you can discover why this technique works.

$$\log N = 6.1239$$
$$= 6 + 0.1239$$
$$= 6 + \log 1.33$$
$$= \log 10^6 + \log 1.33$$
$$= \log 10^6(1.33)$$
$$= \log 1,330,000$$

Therefore, log $N = $ log $1,330,000$, and we conclude that $N = 1,330,000$.

TEST YOUR UNDERSTANDING

Find the common logarithm.

1 log 267	**2** log 26.7	**3** log 2.67
4 log 0.267	**5** log 0.0267	**6** log 42,000
7 log 0.000813	**8** log 7990	**9** log 0.00111

Find N.

10 log $N = 2.8248$	**11** log $N = 0.8248$
12 log $N = 9.8248 - 10$	**13** log $N = 0.8248 - 3$
14 log $N = 7.7126$	**15** log $N = 18.9987 - 20$

EXAMPLE 2   Estimate $P = (936)(0.00847)$ by using (common) logarithms.

For easy reference:

Law 1. log $MN = $ log $M + $ log N

Law 2. log $\dfrac{M}{N} = $ log $M - $ log N

Law 3. log $N^k = k$ log N

Solution

$$\log P = \log (963)(0.00847)$$
$$= \log 963 + \log 0.00847 \qquad \text{(Law 1)}$$

Now use Table IV.

$$\left.\begin{array}{l} \log 963 = 2.9836 \\ \log 0.00847 = 7.9279 - 10 \end{array}\right\} \text{(add)}$$
$$\log P = 10.9115 - 10 = 0.9115$$
$$P = 8.16(10^0) = 8.16$$

For a more accurate procedure, see Exercise 21. Exercise 20 shows how to find log x when $0 \le x < 1$ and x has more than three digits.

Note: The mantissa 0.9115 is not in Table IV. In this case we use the closest entry, namely 0.9117, corresponding to $x = 8.16$. Such approximations are good enough for our purposes.

EXAMPLE 3   Use logarithms to estimate $Q = \dfrac{0.00439}{0.705}$.

Solution We find $\log Q = \log 0.00439 - \log 0.705$ (by Law 2). Now use the table.

(This form is used to avoid a negative mantissa when subtracting in the next step.)

$$
\begin{aligned}
\log 0.00439 &= 7.6425 - 10 = 17.6425 - 20 \\
\log 0.705\ \ &= 9.8482 - 10 = \ \ 9.8482 - 10
\end{aligned} \Big\} \text{ (subtract)}
$$

$$
\begin{aligned}
\log Q &= \ \ 7.7943 - 10 \\
Q &= 6.23(10^{-3}) \\
&= 0.00623
\end{aligned}
$$

EXAMPLE 4 Use logarithms to estimate $R = \sqrt[3]{0.0918}$.

Solution

$$
\begin{aligned}
\log R &= \log(0.0918)^{1/3} \\
&= \tfrac{1}{3} \log 0.0918 \qquad \text{(Law 3)} \\
&= \tfrac{1}{3}(8.9628 - 10) \\
&= \tfrac{1}{3}(28.9628 - 30) \longleftarrow \text{(We avoid the fractional characteristic } -\tfrac{10}{3} \\
&\qquad\qquad\qquad\qquad\ \text{by changing to } 28.9628 - 30.) \\
&= 9.6543 - 10 \\
R &= 4.51(10^{-1}) = 0.451
\end{aligned}
$$

EXAMPLE 5 To determine how much a paint dealer should charge for a gallon of paint, he needs to find out how much the paint cost him per gallon in the first place. The paint is stored in a cylindrical drum $2\tfrac{1}{2}$ feet in diameter and $3\tfrac{3}{4}$ feet high. If he paid \$400 for this quantity of paint, what did it cost him per gallon? (Use 1 cubic foot = 7.48 gallons.)

Solution The volume of the drum is the area of the base times the height. Thus there are

$$\pi(1.25)^2(3.75)$$

Volume of a cylinder:
$$V = \pi r^2 h$$

cubic feet of paint in the drum. Then the number of gallons is

$$\pi(1.25)^2(3.75)(7.48)$$

Since the total cost was \$400, the cost per gallon is given by

$$C = \frac{400}{\pi(1.25)^2(3.75)(7.48)}$$

We use $\pi = 3.14$ to do the computation, using logarithms:

$$\log C = \log 400 - (\log 3.14 + 2 \log 1.25 + \log 3.75 + \log 7.48)$$

$$\left.\begin{array}{l} \left.\begin{array}{r} \log 1.25 = 0.0969 \longrightarrow 2 \log 1.25 = 0.1938 \\ \log 3.14 = 0.4969 \\ \log 3.75 = 0.5740 \\ \log 7.48 = 0.8739 \end{array}\right\} \text{(add)} \\ \hline 2.1386 \longrightarrow \end{array}\right\}$$

$$\left.\begin{array}{r} \log 400 = 2.6021 \\ \\ \\ \\ 2.1386 \end{array}\right\} \text{(subtract)}$$

$$\log C = 0.4635$$
$$C = 2.91 \times 10^0$$
$$= 2.91$$

The paint cost the dealer approximately $2.91 per gallon.

EXERCISES 7.8

In Exercises 1–12, estimate by using common logarithms.

1 $(512)(84{,}000)$

2 $(906)(2330)(780)$

3 $\dfrac{(927)(818)}{274}$

4 $\dfrac{274}{(927)(818)}$

5 $\dfrac{(0.421)(81.7)}{(368)(750)}$

6 $\dfrac{(579)(28.3)}{\sqrt{621}}$

7 $\dfrac{(28.3)\sqrt{621}}{579}$

8 $\left[\dfrac{28.3}{(579)(621)}\right]^2$

9 $\sqrt{\dfrac{28.3}{(579)(621)}}$

10 $\dfrac{(0.0941)^3(0.83)}{(7.73)^2}$

11 $\dfrac{\sqrt[3]{(186)^2}}{(600)^{1/4}}$

12 $\dfrac{\sqrt[4]{600}}{(186)^{2/3}}$

13 After running out of gasoline, a motorist had her gas tank filled at a cost of $16.93. What was the cost per gallon if the gas tank's capacity is 14 gallons?

14 Suppose that a spaceship takes 3 days, 8 hours, and 20 minutes to travel from the earth to the moon. If the distance traveled was one-quarter of a million miles, what was the average speed of the spaceship in miles per hour?

15 A spaceship, launched from the earth, will travel 432,000,000 miles on its trip to the planet Jupiter. If its average velocity is 21,700 miles per hour, how long will the trip take? Give the answer in years.

16 When P dollars is invested in a bank that pays compound interest at the rate of r percent (expressed as a decimal) per year, the amount A after n years is given by the formula

$$A = P(1 + r)^n$$

(This formula will be derived in Chapter 10.)

(a) Find A for $P = 2500$, $r = 0.09$ (9%), and for $n = 3$.

(b) An investment of $3750 earns compound interest at the rate of 11.2% per year. Find the amount A after 5 years.

17 The formula $P = \dfrac{A}{(1 + r)^n}$ gives the initial investment P in terms of the current amount of money A, the annual compound interest rate r, and the number of years n. How much money was invested at 12.8% if after 6 years there is now $8440 in the bank?

18 If P dollars is invested at an interest rate r and the interest is compounded k times per year, the amount A after n years in given by

$$A = P\left(1 + \frac{r}{k}\right)^{kn}$$

(a) Use this formula to compute A for $P = \$5000$ and $r = 0.08$ if the interest is compounded semiannually for 3 years.

(b) Find A in part (a) with interest compounded quarterly.

(c) Find A in part (a) with $k = 8$.

*19 Explain why the mantissas in Table IV are between 0 and 1. (*Hint:* Take $1 \le x < 10$ and now consider the common logarithms of 1, x, and 10.)

*20 Here is a computation for finding log 6.477. Study this procedure carefully and then find the logarithms below in the same manner.

$$\begin{matrix} & N & & \log N \\ & & & \\ 0.010\left\{0.007\begin{cases}6.470\text{-----------}\to 0.8109\\6.477\text{-----------}\to\ ?\end{cases}\right\}d\right\}0.0007\\ & 6.480\text{-----------}\to 0.8116 \end{matrix}$$

$$\frac{0.007}{0.010} = \frac{d}{0.0007}$$

$$0.7 = \frac{d}{0.0007}$$

$$d = (0.7)(0.0007) = 0.00049$$

$$\log N = 0.8109 + 0.00049$$

$$\quad\quad = 0.8114 \quad\quad \text{(rounded off to four decimal places)}$$

(a) $\log 3.042$ (b) $\log 7.849$

(c) $\log 1.345$ (d) $\log 5.444$

(e) $\log 6.803$ (f) $\log 2.711$

(g) $\log 4.986$ (h) $\log 9.008$

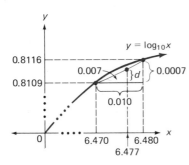

Note that the line segment approximates the curve of the log.

The method used here is called **linear interpolation**. The rationale behind this method is suggested by the accompanying figure.

*21 The method in Exercise 20 can be adapted for finding the number when the given logarithm is not an exact table entry. Study the following procedure for finding N in $\log N = 0.7534$, and then find the numbers N below in the same manner.

$$\begin{matrix} & \log N & & N \\ & & & \\ 0.0008\left\{0.0006\begin{cases}0.7528\text{----------}\to 5.660\\0.7534\text{----------}\to\ ?\end{cases}\right\}d\right\}0.010\\ & 0.7536\text{----------}\to 5.670 \end{matrix}$$

$$\frac{0.0006}{0.0008} = \frac{d}{0.01}$$

$$0.75 = \frac{d}{0.01}$$

$$d = (0.01)(0.75) = 0.0075$$

$$N = 5.660 + 0.0075$$

$$\quad\quad = 5.668 \quad\quad \text{(rounded off to three decimal places)}$$

(a) $\log N = 0.4510$ (b) $\log N = 0.9672$

(c) $\log N = 0.1391$ (d) $\log N = 0.7395$

(e) $\log N = 0.6527$ (f) $\log N = 0.8749$

(g) $\log N = 0.0092$ (h) $\log N = 0.9781$

(i) $\log N = 0.3547$

REVIEW EXERCISES FOR CHAPTER 7

The solutions to the following exercises can be found within the text of Chapter 7. Try to answer each question without referring to the text.

Section 7.1

1 State the definition of a one-to-one function.

2 Describe the horizontal line test for one-to-one functions.

3 Use the horizontal line test to determine which of the following are one-to-one functions.

(a) $y = \sqrt{x}$ (b) $y = \dfrac{1}{x}$

(c) $y = |x|$ (d) $y = x^2 - 2x + 1$

(e) $y = \sqrt[3]{x}$

4 Find the inverse g of $y = f(x) = 2x + 3$ and show that $(f \circ g)(x) = x$ and $(g \circ f)(x) = x$.

5 Find the inverse g of $f(x) = \sqrt{x}$ and show that $(f \circ g)(x) = x$ and $(g \circ f)(x) = x$.

Section 7.2

6 List the important properties of the exponential function $f(x) = b^x$ for $b > 1$, and for $0 < b < 1$.

7 Use a table of values to sketch $y = 8^x$ on the interval $[-1, 1]$.

8 Sketch $y = 2^x$ and $y = (\frac{1}{2})^x$ on the same axes.

9 Explain how to obtain the graphs of $y = 2^{x-3}$ and $y = 2^x - 1$ from $y = 2^x$.

10 If f is a one-to-one function and $f(x_1) = f(x_2)$, then what can you say about x_1 and x_2?

11 Use the one-to-one property of the function $f(x) = 5^x$ to solve the equation $5^{t^2} = 625$ for t.

Section 7.3

12 Which of the following statements are true?

(a) If $0 < b < 1$, the function $f(x) = b^x$ decreases.

(b) The point $(0, 1)$ is on the curve $y = \log_b x$.

(c) $y = \log_b x$, for $b > 1$, increases and the curve is concave down.

(d) The domain of $y = b^x$ is the same as the range of $y = \log_b x$.

(e) The x-axis is an asymptote to $y = \log_b x$ and the y-axis is an asymptote to $y = b^x$.

13 Write the equation of the inverse of $y = 2^x$ and graph both on the same axes.

14 Find the domain for $y = \log_2(x - 3)$.

15 Explain how the graph of $g(x) = \log_5(x + 2)$ can be obtained from $f(x) = \log_5 x$.

16 (a) Change to logarithmic form: $27^{2/3} = 9$.

(b) Change to exponential form: $\log_6 \frac{1}{36} = -2$.

17 Solve for y: $\log_9 27 = y$.

18 Solve for b: $\log_b 8 = \frac{3}{4}$.

Section 7.4

19 Write the three laws of logarithms.

20 Express $\log_b \frac{AB^2}{C}$ in terms of $\log_b A$, $\log_b B$, and $\log_b C$.

21 Given that $\log_b 2 = 0.6931$ and $\log_b 3 = 1.0986$, find $\log_b \sqrt{12}$.

22 Express $\frac{1}{2} \log_b x - 3 \log_b(x - 1)$ as the logarithm of a single expression in x.

23 Solve for x: $\log_8(x - 6) + \log_8(x + 6) = 2$.

24 Solve for x:

$$\log_{10}(x^3 - 1) - \log_{10}(x^2 + x + 1) = 1.$$

25 Solve for x: $\log_3 2x - \log_3(x + 5) = 0$.

Section 7.5

26 Match the columns.

Curve	Slope of tangent to curve through $(0, 1)$ is
(i) $y = 3^x$	(a) less than 1
(ii) $y = 2^x$	(b) equal to 1
(iii) $y = e^x$	(c) more than 1

27 Graph $y = e^x$ and $y = \ln x$ on the same axes.

28 Explain how the curve $y = \ln x^2$ can be obtained from $y = \ln x$.

29 Solve for t: $e^{2t-1} = 5$.

30 Solve for x: $\ln(x + 1) = 1 + \ln x$.

31 Determine the signs of $f(x) = x^2 e^x + 2x e^x$.

32 Match the columns.

(i) $\ln x < 0$	(a) $x < 0$
(ii) $\ln x = 0$	(b) $x = 0$
(iii) $\ln x > 0$	(c) $x > 0$
(iv) $0 < e^x < 1$	(d) $0 < x < 1$
(v) $e^x = 1$	(e) $x = 1$
(vi) $e^x > 1$	(f) $x > 1$

Section 7.6

33 Get an approximate solution for x in $2^x = 35$.

34 A radioactive material is decreasing according to the formula $y = Ae^{-0.2x}$, where y is the amount of material remaining after x years. If the initial amount $A = 80$ grams, how much is left after 3 years?

35 Find the half-life of the radioactive substance in Exercise 34.

36 Solve for k in $\frac{A}{2} = Ae^{5750k}$. Leave your answer in terms of natural logs.

37 Use the formula $y = Ae^{(\ln 0.5/5750)x}$ to estimate the age of a skeleton that is found to contain one-fourth of its original amount of carbon-14.

Section 7.7

38 Convert to scientific notation:

(a) 2,070,000 (b) 0.00000084

39 Convert to standard notation:

(a) 1.21×10^4 (b) 1.21×10^{-2}

40 Evaluate $\frac{1}{800,000}$ using scientific notation.

41 Evaluate $\frac{(2,310,000)^2}{(11,200,000)(0.000825)}$ using scientific notation.

Section 7.8

42 Find $\log 0.0419$.

43 Find N if $\log N = 6.1239$.

44 Use common logarithms to estimate $P = (963)(0.00847)$.

45 Use common logarithms to estimate $Q = \frac{0.00439}{0.705}$.

46 Use common logarithms to estimate $R = \sqrt[3]{0.0918}$.

47 To determine how much a paint dealer should charge for a gallon of paint, he needs to find out how much the paint cost him per gallon in the first place. The paint is stored in a cylindrical drum $2\frac{1}{4}$ feet in diameter and $3\frac{3}{4}$ feet high. If he paid $400 for this quantity of paint, what did it cost him per gallon? (Use 1 cubic foot = 7.48 gallons.)

Use these questions to test your knowledge of the basic skills and concepts of Chapter 7. Then test your answers with those given at the end of the book.

1 Match each curve with one of the given equations listed at the top of the next column.

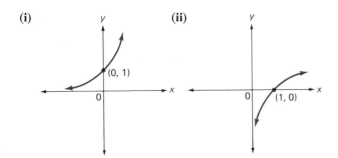

(i)

(ii)

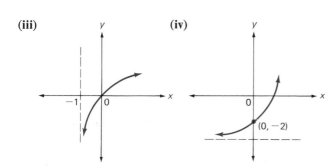

(iii)

(iv)

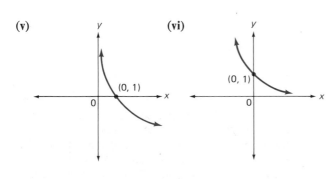

(v)

(vi)

(a) $y = b^x$; $b > 1$

(b) $y = b^x$; $0 < b < 1$

(c) $y = \log_b x$; $b > 1$

(d) $y = \log_b x$; $0 < b < 1$

(e) $y = \log_b(x + 1)$; $b > 1$

(f) $y = \log_b(x - 1)$; $b > 1$

(g) $y = b^{x+2}$; $b > 1$

(h) $y = b^x - 2$; $b > 1$

2 What does it mean to say that a function is one-to-one?

3 Find the inverse g of $y = f(x) = \sqrt[3]{x} - 1$ and show that $(f \circ g)(x) = x$.

4 Solve for x:

(a) $81^x = 9$

(b) $e^{\ln x} = 9$.

5 (a) Solve for b: $\log_b \frac{27}{8} = -3$.

(b) Evaluate $\log_{10} 0.01$.

Find the domain of each function and give the equation of the vertical or horizontal asymptote.

6 $y = f(x) = 2^x - 4$

7 $y = f(x) = \log_3(x + 4)$

8 Solve for x:

$$\log_{25} x^2 - \log_{25}(2x - 5) = \tfrac{1}{2}.$$

9 Sketch the graphs of $y = e^{-x}$ and its inverse on the same axes. Write an equation of the inverse in the form $y = g(x)$.

10 Use the laws of logarithms (as much as possible) to write $\ln \dfrac{x^3}{(x + 1)\sqrt{x^2 + 2}}$ as an expression involving sums and differences.

11 Solve for x in $4^{2x} = 5$ and express the answer in terms of natural logs.

12 A radioactive substance decays according to the formula $y = Ae^{-0.04t}$, where t is the time in years. If the initial amount $A = 50$ grams, find the half-life. Leave the answer in terms of natural logs.

13 Use scientific notation to evaluate $\dfrac{\sqrt{144{,}000{,}000}}{(2000)^2(0.0005)}$.

14 Use common logarithms to estimate

$$N = \frac{(2430)^2}{(0.842)\sqrt{27.9}}.$$

15 Solve for x:

$$\ln 2 - \ln(1 - x) = 1 - \ln(x + 1).$$

ANSWERS TO THE TEST YOUR UNDERSTANDING EXERCISES

Page 244

The functions given in 2, 3, 5, 6, and 7 are one-to-one. The others are not.

Page 254

1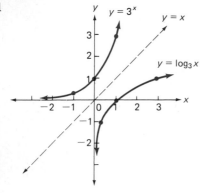

2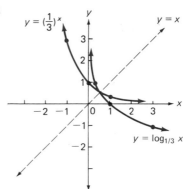

3 Shift 2 units left.

5 Reflect through x-axis.

4 Shift 2 units up.

6 Double the size of each ordinate.

Page 259

1 $\log_b A + \log_b B + \log_b C$

2 $\log_b A - \log_b B - \log_b C$

3 $2\log_b A + 2\log_b B - \log_b C$

4 $\log_b A + 2\log_b B + 3\log_b C$

5 $\log_b A + \frac{1}{2}\log_b B - \log_b C$

6 $\frac{1}{3}\log_b A - 3\log_b B - 3\log_b C$

7 $\log_b 3x^2$

8 $\log_b[\sqrt{x}\,(x-1)^2]$

9 $\log_b \dfrac{2x-1}{(x^2+1)^3}$

10 $\log_b \dfrac{x}{(x-1)(x-2)^2}$

11 2.8903

12 -0.5234

Page 268

(Correct to two decimal places.)

1 $\dfrac{\ln 5}{\ln 4} = \dfrac{1.609}{1.386} = 1.16$

2 $-\dfrac{\ln 5}{\ln 4} = -\dfrac{1.609}{1.386} = -1.16$

3 $\dfrac{\ln 12}{\ln 0.5} = \dfrac{2.485}{-0.693} = -3.59$

4 $\dfrac{\ln 10}{3\ln 2} = \dfrac{2.303}{3(0.693)} = 1.11$

5 $\dfrac{\ln 15}{\ln 4} = \dfrac{2.708}{1.386} = 1.95$

6 $\dfrac{\ln 4}{\ln 67} = \dfrac{1.386}{4.205} = 0.33$

Page 276

1 2.4265	**2** 1.4265	**3** 0.4265	**4** 9.4265 − 10	**5** 8.4265 − 10
6 4.6232	**7** 6.9101 − 10	**8** 3.9025	**9** 7.0453 − 10	**10** 668
11 6.68	**12** 0.668	**13** 0.00668	**14** 51,600,000	**15** 0.0997

TRIGONOMETRY

Trigonometric ratios

The word *trigonometry* is based on the Greek words for triangle (*trigōnon*) and measure (*metron*). This study dates back more than 3000 years and over the centuries has been instrumental in developing knowledge in areas such as architecture, astronomy, navigation, and surveying. Our study of trigonometry will include work with triangles as well as more recent developments that have become important in the modern world. We begin with right triangles.

Our first task is to establish the **trigonometric ratios** for an acute angle. We do this by considering an acute angle within a right triangle. In the figure angle A (also written as $\angle A$ or $\angle BAC$) is an acute angle of both right triangles ABC and $AB'C'$, in which $\angle C$ and $\angle C'$ are right angles. The Greek letter θ (theta) is used to denote the measure of $\angle A$. It is also used to name the angle.

An acute angle has measure between 0° and 90°.

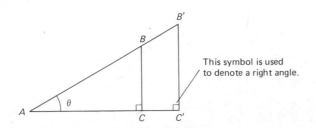

This symbol is used to denote a right angle.

283

Since the two triangles have the measures of their angles respectively equal to one another, the triangles are similar and and we may write

means the measure of the opposite side → $\dfrac{\text{side opposite } \theta}{\text{hypotenuse}} = \dfrac{BC}{AB} = \dfrac{B'C'}{AB'}$ ← corresponding sides of similar triangles are proportional

means the measure of the hypotenuse

SOH CAHTOA

The resulting proportion shows that the ratio of the side opposite θ to the hypotenuse *depends only on the size of the angle and not on the size of the triangle.* This constant ratio is called the sine of the measure of θ. It may be written as *sine of θ*, but we normally use the standard notation *sin θ*.

$$\sin \theta = \frac{\text{side opposite } \theta}{\text{hypotenuse}} = \frac{BC}{AB}$$

Another important ratio is formed by taking the side adjacent to θ and the hypotenuse. We call this ratio the *cosine of θ* and use the notation *cos θ*.

$$\cos \theta = \frac{\text{side adjacent } \theta}{\text{hypotenuse}} = \frac{AC}{AB}$$

You can use similar triangles to verify that cos θ and tan θ depend only on the size of θ, not on the size of the triangle.

When the side opposite θ is compared to the adjacent side, we call the resulting ratio the *tangent of θ* and use the notation *tan θ*.

$$\tan \theta = \frac{\text{side opposite } \theta}{\text{side adjacent } \theta} = \frac{BC}{AC}$$

EXAMPLE 1 Find sin θ, cos θ, and tan θ.

$\dfrac{3}{5}$ $\dfrac{4}{5}$ $\dfrac{3}{4}$

Solution Relative to $\angle A$, BC is the side opposite and AC is the side adjacent.

$$\sin \theta = \frac{\text{side opposite}}{\text{hypotenuse}} = \frac{BC}{AB} = \frac{3}{5}$$

$$\cos \theta = \frac{\text{side adjacent}}{\text{hypotenuse}} = \frac{AC}{AB} = \frac{4}{5}$$

$$\tan \theta = \frac{\text{side opposite}}{\text{side adjacent}} = \frac{BC}{AC} = \frac{3}{4}$$

Three more ratios can be formed from the sides of a triangle by taking the reciprocals of the sine, cosine, and tangent ratios. All six ratios, called the **trigonometric ratios of an angle**, need to be studied carefully and remembered as definitions. Although they are given in the following table in terms of a specific reference triangle, they should be remembered as ratios of sides that can be applied to any acute angle of a right triangle.

Trigonometric ratio	Abbreviation	Definition	
sine of θ	$\sin \theta$	side opposite / hypotenuse	$\dfrac{a}{c}$
cosine of θ	$\cos \theta$	side adjacent / hypotenuse	$\dfrac{b}{c}$
tangent of θ	$\tan \theta$	side opposite / side adjacent	$\dfrac{a}{b}$
cotangent of θ	$\cot \theta$	side adjacent / side opposite	$\dfrac{b}{a}$
secant of θ	$\sec \theta$	hypotenuse / side adjacent	$\dfrac{c}{b}$
cosecant of θ	$\csc \theta$	hypotenuse / side opposite	$\dfrac{c}{a}$

When it is convenient the letter used for the vertex of an angle will also stand for its measure. Thus, in the preceding chart, θ could be replaced by A throughout.

EXAMPLE 2 Use the figure and write the six trigonometric ratios for angle B.

Solution Note that we need to consider sides opposite and adjacent to $\angle B$. The following diagram will help orient you correctly.

$\sin B = \frac{12}{13}$ $\cos B = \frac{5}{13}$

$\tan B = \frac{12}{5}$ $\cot B = \frac{5}{12}$

$\sec B = \frac{13}{5}$ $\csc B = \frac{13}{12}$

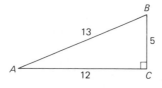

Use the given figure to answer each question.

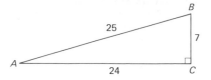

1 Write the six trigonometric ratios for angle A.

2 Write the six trigonometric ratios for angle B.

Note: In later work an expression such as $(\sin A)^2$ is usually written as $\sin^2 A$. Thus $\cos^2 A$ means $(\cos A)^2$, and so on.

3 Find the value of $(\sin A)^2 + (\cos A)^2$.

4 Find the value of $(\sin A)(\csc A)$.

5 Find the value of $(\sec B)^2 - (\tan B)^2$.

6 Find the value of $(\tan B)(\cot B)$.

When only two sides of a right triangle are given, all the trigonometric ratios can still be found by using the Pythagorean theorem to find the third side. This is illustrated in Example 3.

EXAMPLE 3 Triangle ABC is a right triangle with right angle at C. If $\tan A = \frac{3}{2}$, find $\sin B$.

It is common notation to use the same letter, capital and lower case, for an angle and its opposite side such as $\angle A$ and side a.

Solution Since $\tan A = \dfrac{\text{side opposite}}{\text{side adjacent}} = \frac{3}{2}$, label the sides opposite and adjacent to $\angle A$ as shown, and use the Pythagorean theorem to find c.

$$c^2 = a^2 + b^2$$
$$= 9 + 4$$
$$= 13$$

Then

$$c = \sqrt{13} \quad \text{and} \quad \sin B = \frac{AC}{AB} = \frac{2}{\sqrt{13}} \quad \text{or} \quad \frac{2\sqrt{13}}{13}$$

EXAMPLE 4 Use the Pythagorean theorem to solve for AC in terms of x. Then write each of the six trigonometric ratios of $\angle A$ in terms of x.

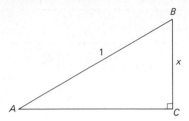

Solution By the Pythagorean theorem, $(AC)^2 + x^2 = 1^2 = 1$. Thus $(AC)^2 = 1 - x^2$ and $AC = \sqrt{1 - x^2}$.

$$\sin A = x \qquad\qquad \cot A = \frac{\sqrt{1 - x^2}}{x}$$

$$\cos A = \sqrt{1 - x^2} \qquad \sec A = \frac{1}{\sqrt{1 - x^2}}$$

$$\tan A = \frac{x}{\sqrt{1 - x^2}} \qquad \csc A = \frac{1}{x}$$

EXAMPLE 5 Use $\triangle ABC$ and show that $(\sin A)(\cos A) = \dfrac{x\sqrt{25 - x^2}}{25}$.

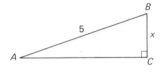

Solution

$$(AC)^2 = 5^2 - x^2 = 25 - x^2$$

$$AC = \sqrt{25 - x^2}$$

$$(\sin A)(\cos A) = \frac{x}{5} \cdot \frac{\sqrt{25 - x^2}}{5} = \frac{x\sqrt{25 - x^2}}{25}$$

Angles of 30°, 45°, and 60° will be of special importance to our work because their trigonometric ratios can be found using basic geometry. The trigonometric ratios of angles of other sizes will be studied in Section 8.4.

Since an isosceles right triangle has acute angles of 45°, it may be referred to as a 45°–45°–90° triangle. Now consider such a triangle whose equal sides are of unit length, solve for the hypotenuse c, and write the ratios.

Remember that the ratios are independent of the length of the sides of the triangle, so the choice of 1 for the equal sides is a matter of convenience.

$$c^2 = 1^2 + 1^2 = 2$$

$$c = \sqrt{2}$$

TRIGONOMETRIC RATIOS OF 45°

$$\sin 45° = \frac{1}{\sqrt{2}} = \frac{\sqrt{2}}{2} \qquad \cot 45° = \frac{1}{1} = 1$$

$$\cos 45° = \frac{1}{\sqrt{2}} = \frac{\sqrt{2}}{2} \qquad \sec 45° = \frac{\sqrt{2}}{1} = \sqrt{2}$$

$$\tan 45° = \frac{1}{1} = 1 \qquad \csc 45° = \frac{\sqrt{2}}{1} = \sqrt{2}$$

Angles of 30° and 60° are complementary since $30° + 60° = 90°$. Consequently, only one triangle is needed to find the ratios for each angle: a 30°–60°–90° triangle. If the side opposite 30° in such a triangle is assigned the unit length 1, then the lengths of the sides can be found as follows:

SAS refers to the side–angle–side congruence theorem from geometry.

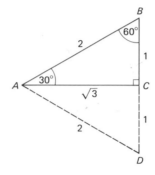

Extend BC to D so that $DC = CB$. Then triangles ABC and ACD are congruent (SAS), so that $AB = 2$. Also, $(AC)^2 = 2^2 - 1^2 = 3$, $AC = \sqrt{3}$.

We may use this right triangle to write the trigonometric ratios of 30° and 60°.

TRIGONOMETRIC RATIOS OF 30° AND 60°

$$\sin 30° = \frac{1}{2} \qquad \cot 30° = \sqrt{3} \qquad \sin 60° = \frac{\sqrt{3}}{2} \qquad \cot 60° = \frac{1}{\sqrt{3}}$$

$$\cos 30° = \frac{\sqrt{3}}{2} \qquad \sec 30° = \frac{2}{\sqrt{3}} \qquad \cos 60° = \frac{1}{2} \qquad \sec 60° = 2$$

$$\tan 30° = \frac{1}{\sqrt{3}} \qquad \csc 30° = 2 \qquad \tan 60° = \sqrt{3} \qquad \csc 60° = \frac{2}{\sqrt{3}}$$

EXERCISES 8.1

In Exercises 1–6, find the six trigonometric ratios of θ.

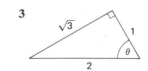

5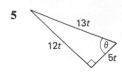

6

In Exercises 7–12, draw an appropriate right triangle and find θ.

7 $\sin \theta = \dfrac{\sqrt{2}}{2}$

8 $\tan \theta = \dfrac{\sqrt{3}}{3}$

9 $\tan \theta = \sqrt{3}$

10 $\cos \theta = \frac{1}{2}$

11 $\csc \theta = 2$

12 $\cot \theta = 1$

In Exercises 13–24, two sides of right $\triangle ABC$ are given in which $\angle C$ is the right angle. Use the Pythagorean theorem to find the third side and then write the six trigonometric ratios of (a) angle A and (b) angle B.

13 $a = 6$; $b = 8$

14 $a = 13$; $b = 5$

15 $a = 4$; $b = 5$

16 $a = 1$; $b = 1$

17 $a = 1$; $b = 2$

18 $a = 4$; $b = 10$

19 $a = 3$; $c = 4$

20 $a = 21$; $c = 29$

21 $b = 2$; $c = 5$

22 $b = 4$; $c = 7$

23 $a = 21$; $c = 29$

24 $a = \frac{1}{3}$; $b = \frac{1}{4}$

Use triangle XYZ to find the value for each of the expressions in Exercises 25–32.

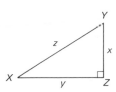

25 $(\tan X)(\cot X)$

26 $(\cos Y)(\sec Y)$

27 $(\sin X)\left(\dfrac{1}{\csc X}\right)$

28 $(\tan Y)\left(\dfrac{1}{\cot Y}\right)$

29 $\sin^2 X + \cos^2 X$

30 $\sin^2 Y + \cos^2 Y$

31 $\sec^2 X - \tan^2 X$

32 $\csc^2 Y - \cot^2 Y$

In Exercises 33–38, angle C is the right angle of right $\triangle ABC$. Use the given information to find the other five ratios of the indicated angle.

33 $\sin A = \frac{3}{4}$

34 $\cos B = \frac{2}{5}$

35 $\tan A = \frac{9}{40}$

36 $\cot A = 1$

37 $\sec B = \dfrac{\sqrt{11}}{\sqrt{2}}$

38 $\csc B = 10$

In Exercises 39–42, use the information given for $\triangle ABC$ and verify the indicated equality.

39 $(\sin A)(\cos A) = x\sqrt{1 - x^2}$

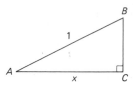

40 $\tan^2 A = \dfrac{x^2}{9 - x^2}$

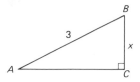

41 $\dfrac{4 \sin^2 A}{\cos A} = \dfrac{x^2}{\sqrt{16 - x^2}}$

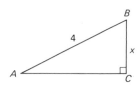

42 $(\sin A)(\cos A) = \dfrac{2x}{4 + x^2}$

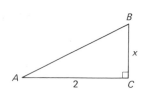

■ In Exercises 43–46, show that the equation is true for an appropriate acute angle θ in a right triangle, having one side equal to x.

43 $(\sin \theta)(\tan \theta) = \dfrac{x^2}{2\sqrt{4 - x^2}}$

44 $\sec^3 \theta = \dfrac{8}{(4 - x^2)^{3/2}}$

45 $(\tan^2 \theta)(\cos^2 \theta) = \dfrac{x^2}{x^2 + 16}$

46 $(\sin^3 \theta)(\cot^3 \theta) = \dfrac{(x^2 - 5)^{3/2}}{x^3}$

47 The side of an equilateral triangle is s centimeters long. Express the area as a function of s.

■ 48 The figure shows an equilateral triangle that is perpendicular to the plane of the circle $x^2 + y^2 = 9$ with one of its sides coinciding with a chord of the circle passing through x. Write the area of the triangle as a function of x. (*Hint: s = 2y.*)

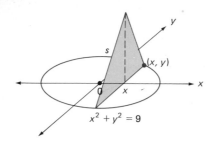

■ 49 Replace the equilateral triangle in Exercise 48 by an isosceles triangle having one of its equal sides coinciding with the chord through x, and find the area of the triangle.

■ 50 Replace the equilateral triangle in Exercise 48 by an isosceles triangle with its hypotenuse coinciding with the chord through x, and find the area of the triangle.

■ 51 The wire AB is 100 inches long and is cut into two pieces at point P as shown. If AP is used to form an equilateral triangle, and PB is used for a circle, express the total area of the two resulting figures in terms of x.

8.2

Angle measure   Angles are often measured in degrees, the traditional method inherited from the Babylonians. They used a numeration system based upon groups of 60 and did much to influence the manner in which we measure. In this system a circle is divided into 360 equal parts, each of which is called a *degree*. Each degree is then divided again into 60 parts, each of which is called a *minute;* each minute is divided into 60 parts, each of which is called a *second*.

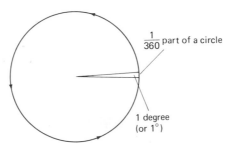

An angle of 40 degrees, 20 minutes, 45 seconds is abbreviated as $40°20'45''$. In much of our work, however, we will consider measures of angles only to the nearest degree or nearest multiple of $10'$ (as in Appendix Table V). Addition and subtraction of these angle measures is accomplished by using the conversions of $1° = 60'$ and $1' = 60''$. For example:

$$40°20'$$
$$+35°50'$$
$$\overline{75°70'} = 76°10'$$

$$40°20' = 39°80'$$
$$-35°50' = 35°50'$$
$$\overline{} \quad \overline{4°30'}$$

Here are illustrations of some angles using degree measure.

The trigonometric ratios of
nonacute angles will be studied
in Section 8.4.

35°

110°

215°

300°

Just as straight-line distances can be measured using different kinds of units (inches, centimeters), there are also different ways to measure angles. The most important of these angular measurements in mathematics is the **radian**.

One *radian* is the measure of a central angle of a circle that is subtended by an arc whose length is equal to the radius of the circle.

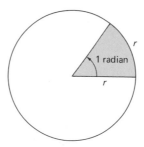

In the following figure $\angle AOB$ has been doubled so that $\angle AOC$ has measure 2 radians, and arc length $AC = 2r$. This demonstrates that

$$\text{Arc length} = \begin{pmatrix} \text{angle measure} \\ \text{in radians} \end{pmatrix} \times (\text{radius})$$

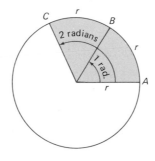

Using s for the arc length, θ for the angle measure, and r for the radius, the preceding can be stated for an angle θ in radians:

Greek letters such as θ are often
used to name an angle and to
indicate the measure. Thus we
write $\theta = 2$ to mean that the
angle θ has measure 2 radians.

$$s = r\theta \qquad \text{or} \qquad \theta = \frac{s}{r}$$

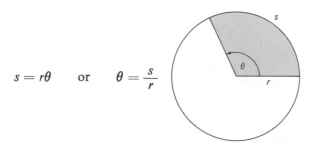

We then say that the measure of the angle θ is given by the quotient $\frac{s}{r}$; that is, angle θ has a measure of $\frac{s}{r}$ radians. Note that the size of the circle does not affect the radian measure of the angle; the measure is the ratio of intercepted arc length to the radius. Thus for $s = 12$ centimeters and $r = 3$ centimeters, $\theta = \frac{12}{3} = 4$ radians. In particular, when $s = r$ then $\theta = \frac{s}{r} = 1$, and the angle has a measure of 1 radian.

From geometry we know that the circumference of a circle is given by the formula $C = 2\pi r$. Thus $\frac{C}{r} = 2\pi$, so there are 2π radians in a complete rotation of 360°. Thus

$$2\pi \text{ radians} = 360°$$

Dividing by 2 produces this fundamental relationship between radians and degrees:

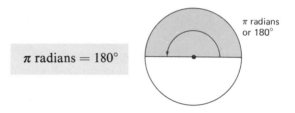

$$\pi \text{ radians} = 180°$$

π radians
or 180°

When both sides of the equation $180° = \pi$ radians are divided by 180, we get this conversion formula:

1° contains $\frac{\pi}{180}$ radians, which is approximately 0.0175 radians. You can verify this using a calculator.

$$1° = \frac{\pi}{180} \text{ radians}$$

Since each degree equals $\frac{\pi}{180}$ radians, degrees can be converted into radians by multiplying the number of degrees by $\frac{\pi}{180}$.

EXAMPLE 1

(a) Convert 30° and 135° degrees into radians. Express the results in terms of π.

(b) Use the conversion factor 0.0175 to change the degree measures in part (a) into approximate radian measure to three decimal places.

Solution

(a) $30° = \left(30 \cdot \dfrac{\pi}{180}\right)$ radians $= \dfrac{\pi}{6}$ radians

$135° = \left(135 \cdot \dfrac{\pi}{180}\right)$ radians $= \dfrac{3\pi}{4}$ radians

(b) $30° = (30)(0.0175)$ radians $= 0.525$ radians
$135° = (135)(0.0175)$ radians $= 2.363$ radians

For the sake of simplicity we use the equals sign and write $30° = 0.525$ radians, even though it is not an exact equality.

From now on radian measures will (in most instances) be stated without using the word "radian." Thus the angle measure 2 automatically means 2 radians unless degree measure is explicitly stated.

EXAMPLE 2   A central angle in a circle of radius 4 centimeters is $75°$. Find the length of the intercepted arc to the nearest tenth of a centimeter.

Solution   First change to radians:

$$75° = \left(75 \cdot \frac{\pi}{180}\right) = \frac{5\pi}{12}$$

Then

$$s = r\theta$$

$$= 4\left(\frac{5\pi}{12}\right)$$

$$= \frac{5\pi}{3} = 5.2 \text{ centimeters}$$
$$\text{(to one decimal place)}$$

The conversion formula to change from radians to degrees is obtained by dividing both sides of the equation π radians $= 180°$ by π.

$$1 \text{ radian} = \frac{180}{\pi} \text{ degrees}$$

A radian contains $\left(\dfrac{180}{\pi}\right)°$, which is approximately $57.296°$.

Since each radian equals $\dfrac{180}{\pi}$ degrees, radians can be converted to degrees by multiplying the number of radians by $\dfrac{180}{\pi}$.

EXAMPLE 3

(a) Express $\dfrac{\pi}{4}$ and $\dfrac{5\pi}{6}$ in degree measure.

(b) Convert $\frac{2}{3}$ radians to degrees. State the result in terms of π and also to the nearest tenth of a degree.

Solution

(a) $\dfrac{\pi}{4} = \left(\dfrac{\pi}{4} \cdot \dfrac{180}{\pi}\right)^{\circ} = 45^{\circ}$

$\dfrac{5\pi}{6} = \left(\dfrac{5\pi}{6} \cdot \dfrac{180}{\pi}\right)^{\circ} = 150^{\circ}$

$\left(\dfrac{180}{\pi}\right)^{\circ} = 57.296^{\circ}$ **(b)** $\dfrac{3}{5} = \left(\dfrac{3}{5} \cdot \dfrac{180}{\pi}\right)^{\circ} = \left(\dfrac{108}{\pi}\right)^{\circ}$

$\dfrac{3}{5} = \left(\dfrac{3}{5}\right)(57.296) = 34.4^{\circ}$ (to the nearest tenth of a degree)

We use radian measure to find the area of a **sector of a circle**. In the figure notice that the area of the shaded sector depends on the central angle θ. That is, $A = k \cdot \theta$, where k is some constant to be determined. To find k, we take the special case where $\theta = 2\pi$. This means that we have the entire circle whose area $A = \pi r^2$. Using this information, we may then proceed as follows:

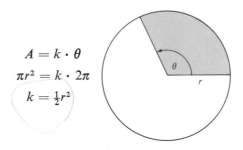

$$A = k \cdot \theta$$
$$\pi r^2 = k \cdot 2\pi$$
$$k = \tfrac{1}{2}r^2$$

Thus the area of a sector of a circle with radius r is given by

$$A = \frac{1}{2}r^2\theta$$

EXAMPLE 4   Find the area of a sector of a circle of radius 6 centimeters if the central angle is 60°.

Solution   First convert 60° to radian measure:

$$60^{\circ} = 60 \times \frac{\pi}{180} = \frac{\pi}{3}$$

Then $A = \dfrac{1}{2}(6)^2\left(\dfrac{\pi}{3}\right) = 6\pi$ square centimeters.

EXERCISES 8.2

Convert the degrees to radians. Leave the answers in terms of π.

1 45° 2 60°

3 90° 4 180°

5 270° 6 360°

7 150° 8 135°

9 225°   **10** 240°

11 210°   **12** 300°

13 330°   **14** 345°

15 75°

Convert the degrees to radians and also use the conversion factor 0.0175 to give the results to two decimal places.

16 10°   **17** 100°

18 220°   **19** 340°

Convert the radians to degrees.

20 $\dfrac{\pi}{2}$ **21** π

22 $\dfrac{3\pi}{2}$ **23** 2π

24 $\dfrac{\pi}{3}$ **25** $\dfrac{5\pi}{9}$

26 $\dfrac{\pi}{6}$ **27** $\dfrac{2\pi}{3}$

28 $\dfrac{3\pi}{4}$ **29** $\dfrac{5\pi}{4}$

30 $\dfrac{7\pi}{6}$ **31** $\dfrac{5\pi}{3}$

32 $\dfrac{\pi}{12}$ **33** $\dfrac{5\pi}{18}$

34 $\dfrac{11\pi}{36}$

Convert the radians to degrees and also use the conversion factor 57.296 to give the results to the nearest tenth of a degree.

35 $\dfrac{\pi}{15}$ **36** $\dfrac{1}{2}$

37 3   **38** 6

Find the trigonometric ratios.

39 $\sin\dfrac{\pi}{4}$ **40** $\cos\dfrac{\pi}{3}$

41 $\tan\dfrac{\pi}{6}$ **42** $\sec\dfrac{\pi}{6}$

Solve for the indicated part s, r, θ (in radians).

43   **44**

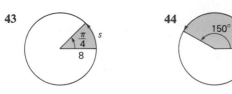

45   **46**

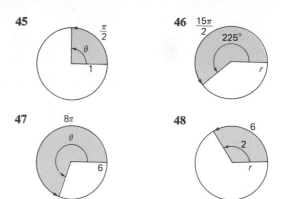

47   **48**

A circle has a radius of 12 centimeters. Find the area of a sector of this circle for each given central angle.

49 30°   **50** 90°

51 135°   **52** 225°

53 315°

54 The area of a sector of a circle with radius 6 centimeters is 15 square centimeters. Find the measure of the central angle of the sector in degrees.

55 Find the area of a sector of a circle whose radius is 2 inches if the length of the intercepted arc is 8 inches.

56 The area of a sector of a circle with radius 4 centimeters is $\dfrac{16\pi}{3}$ square centimeters. Find the measure of the central angle of the sector in degrees.

57 Find the area of a circular sector with central angle 45° if the length of the intercepted arc is $\dfrac{\pi}{2}$ centimeters. Give the exact answer in terms of π, and approximate the area to the nearest tenth of a square centimeter.

58 A flower garden is a 270° sector with a 6-foot radius. Find the exact area of the garden in terms of π, and approximate the area to the nearest tenth of a square foot.

59 A curve along a highway is an arc of a circle with a 250-meter radius. If the curve is 50 meters long, by how many degrees does the highway change its direction? Give the answer to the nearest degree.

60 A 40-inch pendulum swings through an angle of 15°. Find the length of the arc through which the tip of the pendulum swings to the nearest tenth of an inch.

61 A cup is in the shape of a right circular cone made from a circular sector with an 8-inch radius and a central angle of 270°. Find the surface area of the cup to the nearest tenth of a square inch. (Use $\pi = 3.14$.)

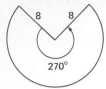

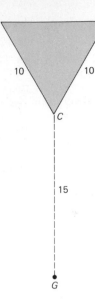

*62 Find the area of the sector inside the square $ABCD$.

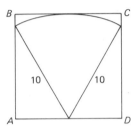

*63 The equilateral triangle ABC represents a wooden platform standing in a lawn. A goat is tied to a corner with a 15-foot rope. What is the maximum amount of grazing area available to the goat?

*64 The shaded region is called a segment of the circle. Show that its area is given by $\frac{1}{2}r^2(\theta - \sin\theta)$.

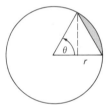

8.3

Right triangle trigonometry

Can you find the distance across the lake between the two cottages at B and C? A surveyor can do this without getting wet. This, and many more problems involving distances that cannot be measured directly, can be solved with the aid of trigonometric ratios.

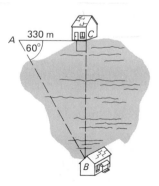

Tan A will be used because this ratio involves the unknown side and the given side. Cot A can also be used.

Here is one way the surveyor can find BC. First locate a point A so that the resulting triangle ABC has a right angle at C and a $60°$ angle at A. From A to C is along flat ground and can be measured directly. Assume that $AC = 330$ meters and solve for BC as follows:

A transit is an instrument that surveyors can use to determine such angles. You may have seen a transit being used in highway or building construction.

$$\tan A = \frac{BC}{AC}$$

$$\sqrt{3} = \frac{BC}{330} \quad \begin{matrix} (\tan 60° = \sqrt{3}, \\ AC = 330) \end{matrix}$$

$$BC = 330\sqrt{3}$$

$$= 571.6 \quad \text{(to one decimal place)}$$

Thus the distance across the lake between the cottages is about 572 meters.

EXAMPLE 1 Solve for x. Give both the exact value and the approximation to the nearest tenth of a unit.

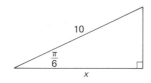

Solution   Both the cosine and secant ratios involve the sides labeled x and 10. The cosine is somewhat easier to use.

$$\cos \frac{\pi}{6} = \frac{x}{10}$$

$$\frac{\sqrt{3}}{2} = \frac{x}{10}$$

$$x = 5\sqrt{3}$$

$$= 8.7$$

Note that $5\sqrt{3}$ is an exact answer, whereas 8.7 is an approximation to one decimal place.

TEST YOUR UNDERSTANDING

Solve for the exact value of x and also give an approximation to one decimal place.

1
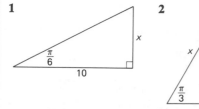

2

3
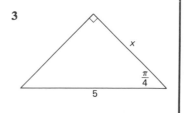

The trigonometric ratios given in Table V are determined using more advanced mathematics. They are really four-place decimal approximations. Rough approximations of some of these ratios can be made by constructing accurate figures and taking careful measurements.

The preceding problems called for trigonometric ratios of the special angles 30°, 45°, and 60°, angles whose ratios had already been determined. However, most practical problems do not involve such special acute angles. In such cases it will become necessary to refer to Appendix Table V. A portion of this table is reproduced here.

Degrees	Radians	sin	cos	tan	cot	sec	csc		Radians	Degrees
27 00'	.4712	.4540	.8910	.5095	1.963	1.122	2.203	1.0996	63 00'
10	741	566	897	132	949	124	190	966	50
20	771	592	884	169	935	126	178	937	40
30	.4800	.4617	.8870	.5206	1.921	1.127	2.166	1.0908	30
40	829	643	857	243	907	129	154	879	20
50	858	669	843	280	894	131	142	850	10
28 00'	.4887	.4695	.8829	.5317	1.881	1.133	2.130	1.0821	62 00'
10	916	720	816	354	868	134	118	792	50
20	945	746	802	392	855	136	107	763	40
30	.4974	.4772	.8788	.5430	1.842	1.138	2.096	1.0734	30
40	.5003	797	774	467	829	140	085	705	20
50	032	823	760	505	816	142	074	676	10
34 00'	.5934	.5592	.8290	.6745	1.483	1.206	1.788	.9774	56 00'
10	963	616	274	787	473	209	731	745	50
20	992	640	258	830	464	211	773	716	40
30	.6021	.5664	.8241	.6873	1.455	1.213	1.766	.9687	30
40	050	688	225	916	446	216	758	657	20
50	080	712	208	959	437	218	751	628	10
35 00'	.6109	.5736	.8192	.7002	1.428	1.221	1.743	.9599	55 00'
10	138	760	175	046	419	223	736	570	50
20	167	783	158	089	411	226	729	541	40
30	.6196	.5807	.8141	.7133	1.402	1.228	1.722	.9512	30
40	225	831	124	177	393	231	715	483	20
50	254	854	107	221	385	233	708	454	10
36 00'	.6283	.5878	.8090	.7265	1.376	1.236	1.701	.9425	54 00'
		cos	sin	cot	tan	csc	sec	Radians	Degrees

First notice that angles are given in both degree and radian measures. The left-hand column of the table gives the measure of angles in units of 10′ from 0° through 45°. The right-hand column, which is read from the bottom of each page to the top, then proceeds from 45° through 90°. Thus to find the ratio of an angle from 0° through 45°, you read the angle at the left and go down the appropriate column according to the headings on top. To find the ratio of an angle between 45° and 90°, read the angle in the column on the right and use the headings that appear at the bottom of the table.

To find tan 35°, for example, we locate 35°00′ (35 degrees and 0 minutes) at the left. Then locate the column headed "tan" at the top. This row and column intersect at the entry that gives the tangent of 35°, namely .7002. Notice that this same entry applies for the cotangent of 55°. Thus locate 55° in the column at the right and the column headed "cot" at the bottom. The intersection here is also .7002, which is what we should expect; that is, tan 35° = cot 55°.

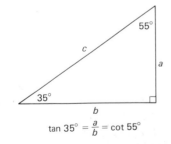

$$\tan 35° = \frac{a}{b} = \cot 55°$$

EXAMPLE 2 Use Table V to find (approximate) each trigonometric ratio.

(a) cos 13° **(b)** cot 26° **(c)** sin 58°10′ **(d)** csc 83°40′

Solution **(a)** .9744 **(b)** 2.050 **(c)** .8496 **(d)** 1.006

EXAMPLE 3 Find θ to the nearest 10′.

(a) $\sin \theta = .4746$ **(b)** $\tan \theta = 2.165$

Solution Since the value of the ratios are given, it is necessary to locate these ratios within the body of the table.

(a) Examine the two columns headed "sin" at the top and bottom of the table. The entry .4746 is found in the column with the "sin" heading at the top, opposite 28°20′. Thus $\theta = 28°20′$.

(b) Examine the columns headed by "tan" at the top and bottom. The closest entry to 2.165 is 2.161 in the column with the "tan" heading at the bottom. Since this entry is opposite 65°10′ at the far right, $\theta = 65°10′$ to the nearest 10′.

When using this table to find an angle measure of a given ratio that is not in the table, we use the angle measure of the closest ratio.

TEST YOUR UNDERSTANDING

Use Table V for these exercises. You may use a calculator to confirm your results. Find each trigonometric ratio.

1 $\sin 27°$ **2** $\cos 38°$ **3** $\tan 72°$ **4** $\cot 58°$

Find each angle θ in both degrees and radians.

5 $\cos \theta = .3907$ **6** $\tan \theta = 1.428$

7 $\sin \theta = .9744$ **8** $\sec \theta = 1.079$

Here are some general guidelines for solving trigonometric problems that involve geometric figures:

1 After carefully reading the problem, draw a figure that matches the given information. Try to draw it as close to scale as possible.

2 Record any given values directly on the corresponding parts, and label the required unknown parts with appropriate letters.

3 Determine the trigonometric ratios and geometric formulas that can be used to solve for an unknown part and solve.

The examples that follow make use of these guidelines.

EXAMPLE 4 The **angle of elevation** of an 80-foot ramp leading to a bridge above a highway is 10°30′. Find the height of the bridge above the highway.

1. After rereading the problem, draw a figure.

2. Label the known angle with its measure, the given side, and the unknown side.

3. Select an appropriate trigonometric ratio to solve for b. The sine or cosecant can be used.

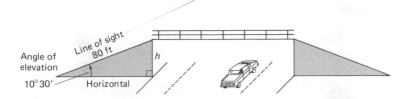

Solution   First note that the angle of elevation is the angle between the horizontal and the line of sight to the top of an object. Since the hypotenuse is given, and the side opposite the 10°30′ angle is the unknown, use the sine ratio.

$$\sin 10°30' = \frac{h}{80}$$

$$h = 80 \sin 10°30'$$

$$= 80(.1822)$$

$$= 14.576$$

$$= 15 \text{ feet to the nearest foot}$$

EXAMPLE 5   From the top of a house the **angle of depression** of a point on the ground is 25°. The point is 45 meters from the base of the building. How high is the building?

Solution   By the **angle of depression** we mean the angle between the horizontal and the line of sight viewed from the top of an object to a point below. As you will note in the figure, this angle of 25° is not within the triangle. However, the complement of the angle, 65°, is the measure of $\angle B$ inside the triangle. Thus we may write this ratio:

If the cotangent ratio had been used, then the quotient $\dfrac{45}{2.145}$ would be replaced by a product, which makes the work easier if you do not have a calculator available.

$$\tan 65° = \frac{45}{x}$$

$$x(\tan 65°) = 45$$

$$x = \frac{45}{\tan 65°}$$

$$= \frac{45}{2.145} \quad \begin{array}{l}(\tan 65° = 2.145;\\ \text{Table V})\end{array}$$

$$= 21 \text{ meters to the nearest meter}$$

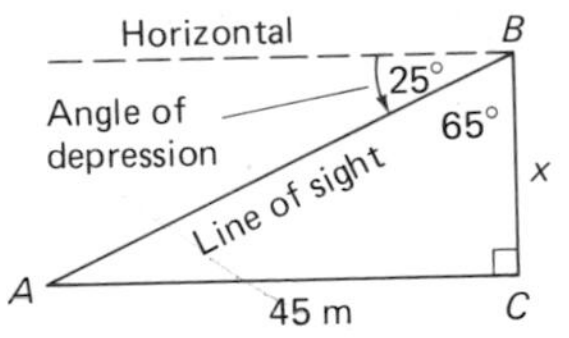

Horizontal

Angle of depression

25°

65°

Line of sight

B

x

A

45 m

C

EXAMPLE 6   The top of a hill is 40 meters higher than a nearby airport, and the horizontal distance from the end of a runway is 325 meters from a point directly below the hilltop. An airplane takes off at the end of the runway in the direction of the hill, at an angle that is to be kept constant until the hill is passed. If the pilot wants to clear the hill by 30 meters, what should be the angle of takeoff?

Solution   Sketch a figure and let the takeoff angle be θ. Since the side opposite θ is 40 + 30, the tangent ratio gives

$$\tan \theta = \frac{70}{325}$$

$$= .2154$$

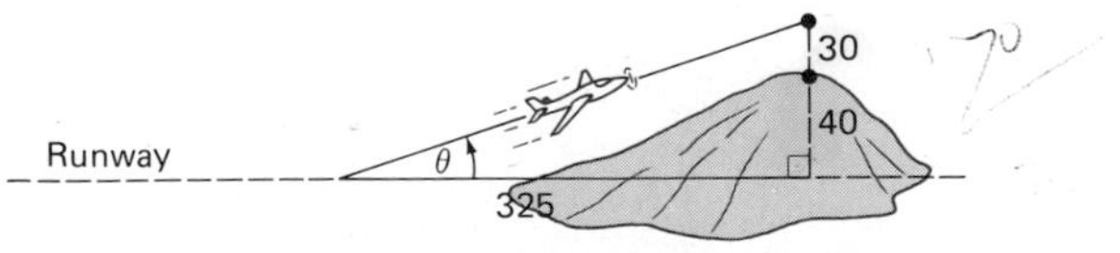

Runway

30

40

θ

325

The closest entry in the tangent column is .2156, which corresponds to 12°10′. Therefore, $\theta = 12°10′$.

Solve for the indicated part of each right triangle without using trigonometric tables or a calculator.

1
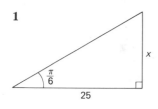

2
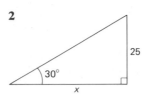

3
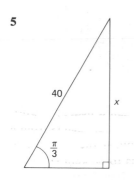

4
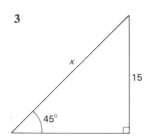

5
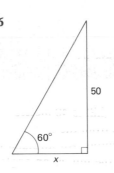

6
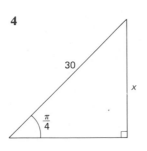

7
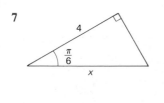

8
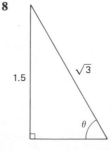

9
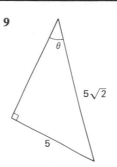

Find the six trigonometric ratios for each θ.

10 $\theta = 78°50′$

11 $\theta = 35°20′$

12 $\theta = 24°40′$

Find the trigonometric ratios.

13 $\sin 42°$	**14** $\cos 48°$
15 $\tan 12°$	**16** $\cot 78°$
17 $\sec 89°$	**18** $\csc 1°$
19 $\sin 2°40′$	**20** $\tan 45°10′$
21 $\cot 44°50′$	**22** $\cos 75°30′$
23 $\sec 19°20′$	**24** $\csc 5°50′$

Find the measure of θ in degrees and minutes (to the nearest 10′) and also use Table V to get the radian measure.

25 $\tan \theta = 6.314$	**26** $\cot \theta = .4592$
27 $\sin \theta = .7214$	**28** $\sec \theta = 14.31$
29 $\cos \theta = .9940$	**30** $\csc \theta = 2.763$

In Exercises 31–38, triangle ABC is a right triangle with $C = 90°$. Solve for the indicated part. Give the sides to the nearest tenth, and the angles to the nearest 10′.

31 $A = 70°$, $a = 35$; find b.

32 $A = 70°$, $a = 35$; find c.

33 $B = 42°20′$, $a = 20$; find b.

34 $B = 42°20′$, $a = 20$; find c.

35 $a = 1$, $b = 3$; find B.

36 $a = 12$, $b = 9.5$; find A.

37 $b = 9$, $c = 25$; find B.

38 $A = 15°30′$, $c = 48$; find a.

39 The angle of elevation to the top of a flagpole is 35° from a point 50 meters from the base of the pole. What is the height of the pole to the nearest meter?

40 How high is a building whose horizontal shadow is 50 meters when the angle of elevation of the sun is 60°20′? Give the answer to the nearest tenth of a foot.

41 At a point 100 feet away from the base of a giant redwood tree a surveyor measures the angle of elevation to the top of the tree to be 70°. How tall is the tree to the nearest tenth of a foot?

42 From the top of a 172-foot-high water tank, the angle of depression to a house is 13°20′. How far away is the house from the water tank to the nearest tenth of a foot?

43 An observation post along a shoreline is 225 feet above sea level. If the angle of depression from this post to a ship at sea is 6°40′, how far is the ship from the shore to the nearest foot?

44 Suppose that a kite string forms a 42°30′ angle with the ground when 740 feet of string are out. What is the altitude of the kite to the nearest foot? (Assume that the string forms a straight line.)

45 One of the cables that helps to stabilize a telephone pole is 82 feet long and is anchored into the ground 14.5 feet from the base of the pole. Find the angle that the cable makes with the ground.

46 One of the equal sides of an isosceles triangle is 18.7 units long and the vertex angle is 33°. Find the length of the base to the nearest tenth of a unit.

47 One side of an inscribed angle of a circle is a diameter of the circle, and the other side is a chord of length 10. If the inscribed angle is 66°, what is the length of the radius to the nearest tenth?

48 From the top of a 250-foot cliff, the angle of depression to the far side of a river is 12°, and the angle of depression to a point directly on the opposite side of the river is 62°. How wide is the river between the two points to the nearest foot?

*49 A surveyor finds that from point A on the ground the angle of elevation to the top of a mountain is 23°. When he is at a point B that is $\frac{1}{4}$ mile closer to the base of the mountain, the angle of elevation is 43°. How high is the mountain? One mile = 5280 feet. (Assume that the base of the mountain and the two observation points are on the same line.) Give the answer to the nearest foot.

*50 A 12-foot flagpole is standing vertically at the edge of the roof of a building. The angle of elevation to the top of the flagpole from a point on the ground that is 64 feet from the building is 78°50′. Find the height of the building to the nearest foot.

8.4

Extending the definitions

An angle with its vertex at the origin and initial side on the positive part of the x-axis is said to be in *standard position*.

The six trigonometric ratios were originally defined only for acute angles: $0 < \theta < \frac{\pi}{2}$. Now we are going to extend these definitions to include all angles. First observe that an acute angle may be placed in a rectangular coordinate system so that its *initial side* lies on the positive part of the x-axis and its *terminal side* is in the first quadrant. Since the trigonometric ratios do not depend on the size of the sides of the right triangle, we may choose the sides so that the length of the terminal side (the hypotenuse) is 1. Conse-

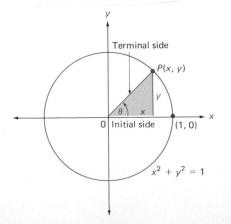

302

quently, the intersection of the terminal side of θ with the unit circle centered at the origin is a point $P(x, y)$ whose coordinates satisfy $x^2 + y^2 = 1$.

From the right triangle we have $\cos \theta = \dfrac{x}{1} = x$ and $\sin \theta = \dfrac{y}{1} = y$.

Therefore, we see that the earlier definitions

$$\sin \theta = \frac{\text{opposite}}{\text{hypotenuse}} \quad \text{and} \quad \cos \theta = \frac{\text{adjacent}}{\text{hypotenuse}}$$

are equivalent to

$$\sin \theta = y \quad \text{and} \quad \cos \theta = x$$

Note that $\sin \theta$ is the second coordinate of point P and $\cos \theta$ is the first coordinate of P.

where (x, y) are the coordinates of the point of intersection of the terminal side of θ with the unit circle whose center is at the origin.

Now look at angles of other sizes. Regardless of the size of θ, its terminal side will always intersect the unit circle at some point $P(x, y)$. For positive angles the terminal side is found by rotating counterclockwise; for negative angles we rotate clockwise. Here are some typical cases.

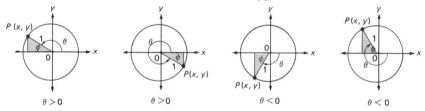

For each case the right triangle formed by drawing the perpendicular from P to the x-axis is called the **reference triangle**, and the acute angle between the terminal side and the x-axis is called the **reference angle**. The reference angle ϕ (phi) is a positive acute angle: $0 < \phi < \dfrac{\pi}{2}$. For example, the reference angle of $\dfrac{2\pi}{3}$ is $\dfrac{\pi}{3}$, and for $-\dfrac{\pi}{4}$ it is $\dfrac{\pi}{4}$. We use the reference triangle to define the trigonometric ratios of θ as follows:

$$\text{vertical side} = y = \sin \theta$$
$$\text{horizontal side} = x = \cos \theta$$

The remaining trigonometric ratios are formed as before; thus

$$\tan \theta = \frac{y}{x} = \frac{\sin \theta}{\cos \theta} \qquad \sec \theta = \frac{1}{x} = \frac{1}{\cos \theta}$$

$$\cot \theta = \frac{x}{y} = \frac{\cos \theta}{\sin \theta} \qquad \csc \theta = \frac{1}{y} = \frac{1}{\sin \theta}$$

The signs of the ratios depend on the quadrant that $P(x, y)$ is in.

See the figure at the top of the next page.

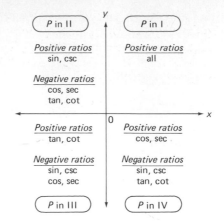

P in II		P in I
Positive ratios sin, csc		*Positive ratios* all
Negative ratios cos, sec tan, cot		
Positive ratios tan, cot		*Positive ratios* cos, sec
Negative ratios sin, csc cos, sec		*Negative ratios* sin, csc tan, cot
P in III		P in IV

EXAMPLE 1   Find the six trigonometric ratios for the obtuse angle $150°$ $\left(\text{or } \dfrac{5\pi}{6}\right)$.

Solution   Construct the $30°$–$60°$–$90°$ reference triangle in quadrant II and find the values of x and y for point P. $y = \frac{1}{2}$ because the side opposite the $30°$ reference angle is one-half the hypotenuse 1. Also, using the Pythagorean theorem,

$$x^2 = 1^2 - (\tfrac{1}{2})^2 = \tfrac{3}{4}$$

$$x = -\frac{\sqrt{3}}{2} \longleftarrow \text{use the negative root since } P \text{ is in quadrant II}$$

Then

$$\sin 150° = y = \frac{1}{2} \qquad\qquad \cot 150° = \frac{x}{y} = -\sqrt{3}$$

$$\cos 150° = x = -\frac{\sqrt{3}}{2} \qquad\qquad \sec 150° = \frac{1}{x} = -\frac{2}{\sqrt{3}}$$

$$\tan 150° = \frac{y}{x} = -\frac{\sqrt{3}}{3} \qquad\qquad \csc 150° = \frac{1}{y} = 2$$

The trigonometric ratios of an angle θ can also be found by making direct use of the reference angle ϕ. This is done by first finding the ratios of the acute angle ϕ, and then using the correct signs by noting the quadrant containing the terminal side of θ. In Example 1, $\phi = 30°$ and the terminal side of $\theta = 150°$ is in quadrant II. For example,

$$\sin 150° = \sin 30° = \frac{1}{2}$$

$$\cos 150° = -\cos 30° = -\frac{\sqrt{3}}{2}$$

$$\tan 150° = -\tan 30° = -\frac{\sqrt{3}}{3}$$

EXAMPLE 2 Find $\tan\left(-\frac{5\pi}{4}\right)$.

Solution (a) For $-\frac{5\pi}{4}$ (or $-225°$) we have a $45°$–$45°$–$90°$– reference triangle in quadrant II. Then the coordinates of P are $\left(-\frac{\sqrt{2}}{2}, \frac{\sqrt{2}}{2}\right)$ and

$$\tan\left(-\frac{5\pi}{4}\right) = \frac{\frac{\sqrt{2}}{2}}{-\frac{\sqrt{2}}{2}} = -1$$

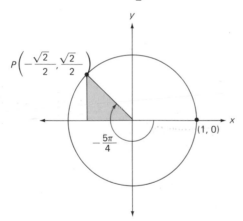

Solution (b) Since $-\frac{5\pi}{4}$ is in quadrant II and the reference angle is $\frac{\pi}{4}$,

$$\tan\left(-\frac{5\pi}{4}\right) = -\tan\frac{\pi}{4} \longleftarrow \text{the tangent is}$$
$$= -1 \qquad \text{negative in the}$$
$$\text{second quadrant}$$

When the reference angle is not one of the special angles, then Appendix Table V can be used, as illustrated next.

EXAMPLE 3 Find cos 200°.

Solution The terminal side of 200° is in quadrant III. Consequently, $x < 0$. Since the reference angle is 20°, we have cos 200° = −cos 20° = −.9397 from Table V.

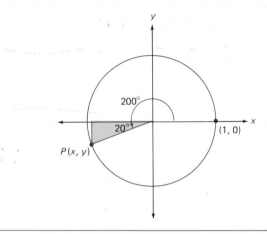

After some practice you will find that such diagrams are not always necessary to find the ratios.

When two angles have the same terminal side, they must have the same ratios. Such angles are said to be **coterminal**. Thus

$$\cos(-160°) = \cos 200° = -.9397$$

because the angles are coterminal.

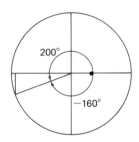

TEST YOUR UNDERSTANDING

Determine each of the following trigonometric ratios. Use Table V whenever the reference angle is not one of the special angles.

1 sin 135°   **2** csc(−135°)   **3** $\tan \dfrac{5\pi}{4}$ **4** sec(−330°)

5 cot 147°   **6** csc 315°   **7** $\sin\left(-\dfrac{4\pi}{3}\right)$ **8** tan(−283°)

An angle that has its terminal side coinciding with one of the coordinate axes is called a **quadrantal angle**. As in the adjoining figures, such angles do not have reference triangles. We take the coordinates of P to define the sine and cosine. Thus $\sin \dfrac{\pi}{2} = 1$, $\cos \dfrac{\pi}{2} = 0$, $\sin(-\pi) = 0$, and $\cos(-\pi) = -1$. The remaining trigonometric ratios are defined by forming the appropriate fractions whenever possible. For example, $\tan \dfrac{\pi}{2}$ is undefined since $\dfrac{1}{0}$ is undefined, and $\cot \dfrac{\pi}{2} = \dfrac{x}{y} = \dfrac{0}{1} = 0$. (Recall that for $P(x, y)$ on the unit circle we have $x = \cos \theta$ and $y = \sin \theta$.)

It is unnecessary to memorize the ratios for quadrantal angles. Visualize the unit circle with the four points on the axes shown in the figure below, and use the coordinates of the appropriate point for the ratios.

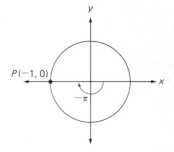

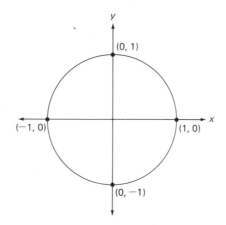

EXAMPLE 4 Determine the ratios of the quadrantal angles $\theta = \dfrac{3\pi}{2}$ and $\theta = -\dfrac{\pi}{2}$.

Solution Since the terminal side of $\dfrac{3\pi}{2}$ coincides with the negative part of the y-axis, use point $(0, -1)$ in the preceding figure as follows:

$$\sin \frac{3\pi}{2} = -1 \qquad\qquad \cot \frac{3\pi}{2} = \frac{0}{-1} = 0$$

$$\cos \frac{3\pi}{2} = 0 \qquad\qquad \sec \frac{3\pi}{2} \text{ is undefined}$$

$$\tan \frac{3\pi}{2} \text{ is undefined} \qquad\qquad \csc \frac{3\pi}{2} = \frac{1}{-1} = -1$$

The ratios for $-\dfrac{\pi}{2}$ are exactly the same as for $\dfrac{3\pi}{2}$ since the angles are coterminal.

To find the trigonometric ratios of angles greater than 2π or less than -2π, we locate the terminal side and then use the coordinates of the point on the unit circle and the terminal side as before. For $\theta > 360°$, first subtract the largest multiple of $360°$ to get the coterminal angle between $0°$ and $360°$. Now the quadrant of the terminal side has been found and the reference angle is used as before. For $\theta < -360°$, the process is similar except that we begin by adding an appropriate multiple of $360°$.

EXAMPLE 5 Find **(a)** sec 932° and **(b)** csc(−383°40′).

Solution

(a) Since $932° - 2(360°) = 212°$, the terminal side is in quadrant III with reference angle 32°.

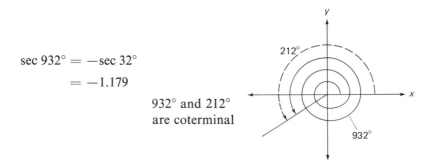

$$\sec 932° = -\sec 32°$$
$$= -1.179$$

932° and 212°
are coterminal

(b) Since $-383°40' + 1(360°) = -23°40'$, the terminal side is in quadrant IV with reference angle 23°40′.

$$\csc(-383°40') = -\csc 23°40'$$
$$= -2.491$$

−383°40′ and −23°40′
are coterminal

CAUTION: LEARN TO AVOID MISTAKES LIKE THESE	
WRONG	RIGHT
$\cos(-50°) = -\cos 50°$	$\cos(-50°) = \cos 50°$
$\cos 125° = \cos 55°$	$\cos 125° = -\cos 55°$

WRONG	RIGHT
$\sin\left(-\dfrac{\pi}{3}\right) = \dfrac{\sqrt{3}}{2}$	$\sin\left(-\dfrac{\pi}{3}\right) = -\sin\dfrac{\pi}{3} = -\dfrac{\sqrt{3}}{2}$
$\sec\dfrac{\pi}{2} = \dfrac{1}{\cos\dfrac{\pi}{2}}$	$\cos\dfrac{\pi}{2} = 0$; $\sec\dfrac{\pi}{2}$ is undefined.

In Exercises 1–6, assume that θ is in standard position.

(a) *Find the quadrant containing the terminal side and find the reference angle ϕ.*

(b) *Find the coterminal angle that is between $-360°$ and $0°$.*

1 $\theta = 73°$ **2** $\theta = 300°$

3 $\theta = 500°$ **4** $\theta = 1110°10'$

5 $\theta = \dfrac{5\pi}{4}$ **6** $\theta = \dfrac{25\pi}{6}$

In Exercises 7–12, assume that θ is in standard position.

(a) *Find the quadrant containing the terminal side and find the reference angle ϕ.*

(b) *Find the coterminal angle that is between $0°$ and $360°$.*

7 $\theta = -73°$ **8** $\theta = -201°$

9 $\theta = -850°$ **10** $\theta = -735°40'$

11 $\theta = -\dfrac{11\pi}{3}$ **12** $\theta = -\dfrac{25\pi}{6}$

In Exercises 13–18, locate θ in a coordinate system, include the reference triangle, and find the reference angle. Then find the coordinates of $P(x, y)$ on the terminal side and on the unit circle, and write the six trigonometric ratios.

13 $\theta = \dfrac{2\pi}{3}$ **14** $\theta = \dfrac{29\pi}{6}$

15 $\theta = -\dfrac{7\pi}{4}$ **16** $\theta = -30°$

17 $\theta = 405°$ **18** $\theta = -930°$

In Exercises 19–21, find the coordinates of $P(x, y)$ on the unit circle and on the terminal side of θ.

19 $\theta = -\dfrac{\pi}{2}$ **20** $\theta = 3\pi$

21 $\theta = -\dfrac{7\pi}{2}$

22 Complete this table of ratios that includes all quadrantal angles.

θ coterminal with	$\sin\theta$	$\cos\theta$	$\tan\theta$	$\cot\theta$	$\sec\theta$	$\csc\theta$
0						
$\dfrac{\pi}{2}$						
π						
$\dfrac{3\pi}{2}$						

Find each trigonometric ratio (if it exists). Use Table V only when necessary.

23 $\tan 220°$ **24** $\sec(-72°)$

25 $\sin 261°$ **26** $\sec(-\pi)$

27 $\csc(-\pi)$ **28** $\tan\dfrac{7\pi}{2}$

29 $\cot\left(\dfrac{7\pi}{2}\right)$ **30** $\tan 0$

31 $\cot 0$ **32** $\cot\left(-\dfrac{5\pi}{2}\right)$

33 $\tan 8\pi$ **34** $\sin\dfrac{9\pi}{2}$

35 $\cos(-275°)$ **36** $\csc(-12°)$

37 $\cot 368°$ **38** $\sin(242°10')$

39 $\cos(-792°30')$ **40** $\tan 120°$

41 $\cot 1200°$ **42** $\sec 420°$

43 $\csc(-80°)$ **44** $\sin(94°20')$

45 $\cos(-200°50')$ **46** $\tan 1°10'$

47 $\cos \dfrac{19\pi}{4}$

48 $\sec\left(-\dfrac{23\pi}{6}\right)$

49 $\csc(-480°)$

50 $\sin 585°$

51 (a) Verify that $P\left(\dfrac{2}{3}, \dfrac{\sqrt{5}}{3}\right)$ is on the unit circle.

    (b) Locate θ, where $0 < \theta < 2\pi$, so that its terminal side intersects the unit circle at P.

    (c) Write the six trigonometric ratios for θ.

    (d) Use Table V to find an approximation for θ.

52 Follow the instructions in Exercise 51 for $P\left(-\dfrac{3}{4}, \dfrac{\sqrt{7}}{4}\right)$.

*53 Find y so that $P\left(\dfrac{\sqrt{3}}{4}, y\right)$ is on the unit circle in the fourth quadrant. Use Table V to find θ, where $-2\pi < \theta < 0$, having OP as its terminal side.

*54 The terminal side of θ coincides with the line $y = -x$ and lies in the second quadrant. Find $\cos \theta$.

*55 In the figure, AB is tangent to the circle at A and meets the terminal side of θ at B. Why is AB equal to $\tan \theta$? Which segment has measure equal to $\sec \theta$?

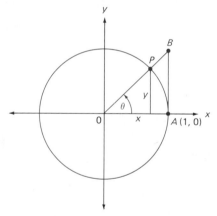

56 Explain why $\sin^2 \theta + \cos^2 \theta = 1$, where θ is any angle.

*57 The terminal side of θ coincides with the line $y = \frac{1}{2}x$ and lies in the third quadrant. Find $\sin \theta$.

*58 Which segment in the figure has length $\cot \theta$? Which has length $\csc \theta$?

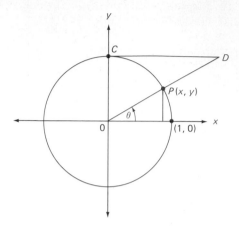

Find all possible values for θ, $0 \le \theta < 2\pi$. Do not use Table V or a calculator.

59 $\sin \theta = 1$ **60** $\cos \theta = -1$

61 $\sin \theta = 0$ **62** $\cos \theta = 0$

63 $\sin \theta = \frac{1}{2}$ **64** $\cos \theta = -\frac{1}{2}$

65 $\cos \theta = -\dfrac{\sqrt{2}}{2}$ **66** $\sin \theta = -\dfrac{\sqrt{3}}{2}$

In Exercises 67–70, use the given information to determine the quadrant containing the terminal side of θ and find the remaining ratios.

67 $\tan \theta = 1$, $\sin \theta = -\dfrac{\sqrt{2}}{2}$

68 $\cos \theta = -\frac{1}{2}$, $\csc \theta = \dfrac{2}{\sqrt{3}}$

69 $\cot \theta = -\sqrt{3}$, $\sin \theta = -\frac{1}{2}$

70 $\sec \theta = \sqrt{2}$, $\cot \theta = 1$

8.5

Identities

Identities will be useful later in solving equations, and eventually they will play an important role in a wide variety of mathematical situations.

Solving the equation $\dfrac{\sin^2 \theta}{\cos^2 \theta} = \dfrac{1}{3}$ for θ is easier to do if $\dfrac{\sin \theta}{\cos \theta}$ is first replaced by the equivalent expression $\tan \theta$ to get $\tan^2 \theta = \frac{1}{3}$. Such equations are discussed in detail in Chapter 9. Our objective here is to learn to recognize and work with **trigonometric identities**, such as $\dfrac{\sin \theta}{\cos \theta} = \tan \theta$. This equation is called an identity because it is a true statement for all values of θ except those when $\cos \theta = 0$.

A trigonometric identity is an equation that is true for all values of the variable for which the expressions in the equation are defined.

The following list of fundamental identities, together with some alternative forms, will be used throughout our work. It is therefore important that you learn to recognize them.

Fundamental identity	Common alternative forms	Restrictions on θ
$\csc \theta = \dfrac{1}{\sin \theta}$	$\sin \theta = \dfrac{1}{\csc \theta}$ $\sin \theta \csc \theta = 1$	Not coterminal with $0, \pi$.
$\sec \theta = \dfrac{1}{\cos \theta}$	$\cos \theta = \dfrac{1}{\sec \theta}$ $\cos \theta \sec \theta = 1$	Not coterminal with $\dfrac{\pi}{2}, \dfrac{3\pi}{2}$.
$\cot \theta = \dfrac{1}{\tan \theta}$	$\tan \theta = \dfrac{1}{\cot \theta}$ $\tan \theta \cot \theta = 1$	Not a quadrantal angle.
$\tan \theta = \dfrac{\sin \theta}{\cos \theta}$		Not coterminal with $\dfrac{\pi}{2}, \dfrac{3\pi}{2}$.
$\cot \theta = \dfrac{\cos \theta}{\sin \theta}$		Not coterminal with $0, \pi$.
$\sin^2 \theta + \cos^2 \theta = 1$	$\sin^2 \theta = 1 - \cos^2 \theta$ $\cos^2 \theta = 1 - \sin^2 \theta$	None.
$\tan^2 \theta + 1 = \sec^2 \theta$	$\tan^2 \theta = \sec^2 \theta - 1$	Not coterminal with $\dfrac{\pi}{2}, \dfrac{3\pi}{2}$.
$1 + \cot^2 \theta = \csc^2 \theta$	$\cot^2 \theta = \csc^2 \theta - 1$	Not coterminal with $0, \pi$.

Each of the preceding identities can be established by using the definitions of the trigonometric ratios on the unit circle $x^2 + y^2 = 1$, as shown on page 312.

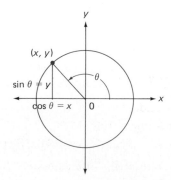

Refer to the unit circle at the bottom of page 311.

$$\csc \theta = \frac{1}{y} = \frac{1}{\sin \theta} \qquad \sec \theta = \frac{1}{x} = \frac{1}{\cos \theta}$$

$$\tan \theta = \frac{y}{x} = \frac{\sin \theta}{\cos \theta} \qquad \cot \theta = \frac{x}{y} = \frac{\cos \theta}{\sin \theta}$$

$$\tan \theta \cot \theta = \frac{y}{x} \cdot \frac{x}{y} = 1$$

$$\sin^2 \theta + \cos^2 \theta = x^2 + y^2 = 1$$

Dividing the last equation by $\cos^2 \theta$ produces

$$\frac{\sin^2 \theta}{\cos^2 \theta} + \frac{\cos^2 \theta}{\cos^2 \theta} = \frac{1}{\cos^2 \theta}$$

$$\left(\frac{\sin \theta}{\cos \theta}\right)^2 + 1 = \left(\frac{1}{\cos \theta}\right)^2$$

$$\tan^2 \theta + 1 = \sec^2 \theta$$

In practice, when working with identities, no special mention is made about the restrictions on the variable. However, you should be able to see what restrictions are necessary. In most cases such restrictions will occur when the denominator of an expression could be equal to 0.

Similarly, when $\sin^2 \theta + \cos^2 \theta = 1$ is divided by $\sin^2 \theta$, we get

$$1 + \cot^2 \theta = \csc^2 \theta$$

EXAMPLE 1 Use fundamental identities to convert $\dfrac{1 - \csc \theta}{\cot \theta}$ into an expression involving only sines and cosines, and simplify.

Solution

$$\frac{1 - \csc \theta}{\cot \theta} = \frac{1 - \dfrac{1}{\sin \theta}}{\dfrac{\cos \theta}{\sin \theta}} \longleftarrow \qquad \begin{cases} \csc \theta = \dfrac{1}{\sin \theta} \\ \cot \theta = \dfrac{\cos \theta}{\sin \theta} \end{cases}$$

Here is another way to simplify the right side.

$$\frac{1 - \dfrac{1}{\sin \theta}}{\dfrac{\cos \theta}{\sin \theta}} = \frac{\sin \theta - 1}{\sin \theta} \cdot \frac{\sin \theta}{\cos \theta}$$

$$= \frac{\sin \theta - 1}{\cos \theta}$$

$$= \frac{1 - \dfrac{1}{\sin \theta}}{\dfrac{\cos \theta}{\sin \theta}} \cdot \frac{\sin \theta}{\sin \theta}$$

$$= \frac{\sin \theta - 1}{\cos \theta} \qquad \text{(multiplying fractions)}$$

The result in Example 1 can be stated as

$$\frac{1 - \csc \theta}{\cot \theta} = \frac{\sin \theta - 1}{\cos \theta}$$

and the solution in Example 1 is the *proof* that this equation is an identity. The solution to Example 1 also suggests the following procedure.

METHOD I FOR VERIFYING IDENTITIES

Use fundamental or previously proven identities to change one side of the equation into the form of the other side.

EXAMPLE 2   Verify this identity:

$$\frac{\tan^2 \theta + 1}{\tan \theta \csc^2 \theta} = \tan \theta$$

Solution   In most cases it is easier to work with the more complicated side. Supply a reason for each step of the proof.

$$\frac{\tan^2 \theta + 1}{\tan \theta \csc^2 \theta} = \frac{\sec^2 \theta}{\tan \theta \csc^2 \theta}$$

$$= \frac{\dfrac{1}{\cos^2 \theta}}{\dfrac{\sin \theta}{\cos \theta} \cdot \dfrac{1}{\sin^2 \theta}}$$

$$= \frac{1}{\cos^2 \theta} \cdot \frac{\cos \theta \sin^2 \theta}{\sin \theta}$$

$$= \frac{\sin \theta}{\cos \theta}$$

$$= \tan \theta$$

> It is often helpful to convert the expression in terms of sines and cosines.

Here is another procedure that can be used to verify an identity.

METHOD II FOR VERIFYING IDENTITIES

Convert each side of the given equation until the same form is obtained on each side.

EXAMPLE 3   Verify the identity: $\dfrac{\csc \theta + 1}{\csc \theta - 1} = (\sec \theta + \tan \theta)^2$.

Solution   When working separately on each side, a vertical line helps to separate the work.

$$\frac{\csc \theta + 1}{\csc \theta - 1} \qquad\qquad (\sec \theta + \tan \theta)^2$$

$$\downarrow \qquad\qquad\qquad \downarrow$$

$\csc \theta = \dfrac{1}{\sin \theta}$ $\dfrac{\dfrac{1}{\sin \theta} + 1}{\dfrac{1}{\sin \theta} - 1} \qquad \left(\dfrac{1}{\cos \theta} + \dfrac{\sin \theta}{\cos \theta}\right)^2$ convert to sines and cosines

$$\downarrow \qquad\qquad\qquad \downarrow$$

$$\frac{\left(\dfrac{1}{\sin \theta} + 1\right) \sin \theta}{\left(\dfrac{1}{\sin \theta} - 1\right) \sin \theta} \qquad \left(\dfrac{1 + \sin \theta}{\cos \theta}\right)^2$$ combine fractions

$$\downarrow \qquad\qquad\qquad \downarrow$$

> Try to complete this solution before turning the page.

simplify	$\dfrac{1+\sin\theta}{1-\sin\theta}$	$\dfrac{(1+\sin\theta)^2}{\cos^2\theta}$ $\qquad \left(\dfrac{a}{b}\right)^2=\dfrac{a^2}{b^2}$

$$\downarrow$$

$$\dfrac{(1+\sin\theta)^2}{1-\sin^2\theta} \qquad \begin{array}{l}\cos^2\theta\\ =1-\sin^2\theta\end{array}$$

$$\downarrow$$

$$\dfrac{(1+\sin\theta)^2}{(1-\sin\theta)(1+\sin\theta)} \qquad \begin{array}{l}a^2-b^2=\\ (a-b)(a+b)\end{array}$$

$$\downarrow$$

$$\dfrac{1+\sin\theta}{1-\sin\theta} \qquad \text{simplify}$$

Since the same form has been obtained for each side, the proof is complete.

It takes practice to become good at verifying identities. You will have to call on a wide variety of algebraic skills to be successful. Example 4 calls on a process similar to the one used earlier in rationalizing denominators.

EXAMPLE 4 Verify the identity: $\dfrac{\sin\theta}{1+\cos\theta}=\dfrac{1-\cos\theta}{\sin\theta}$.

Solution Begin by multiplying the numerator and denominator of the left side by $1-\cos\theta$.

The motivation for this approach is that it gets $1-\cos\theta$ into the numerator.

$$\begin{aligned}
\frac{\sin\theta}{1+\cos\theta} &= \frac{(\sin\theta)(1-\cos\theta)}{(1+\cos\theta)(1-\cos\theta)}\\[2mm]
&= \frac{(\sin\theta)(1-\cos\theta)}{1-\cos^2\theta}\\[2mm]
&= \frac{(\sin\theta)(1-\cos\theta)}{\sin^2\theta}\\[2mm]
&= \frac{1-\cos\theta}{\sin\theta}
\end{aligned}$$

Notice that in all of the preceding solutions we avoided performing the same operations to each side of the given equality at the same time. Doing so could, at times, lead to false results. For example, $\sin\theta=-|\sin\theta|$ is certainly not an identity. Squaring both sides gives $\sin^2\theta=\sin^2\theta$, which might *incorrectly* suggest that the original statement is an identity.

Sometimes a trigonometric equation may have the appearance of an identity but really is not one. A quick way to discover this is to find one value of θ for which the expressions in the equation are defined but for which the equality is false.

To disprove a statement that claims to be true in general, all that is needed is to find one exception; one case for which the statement is false. Such an exception is also called a counterexample.

EXAMPLE 5 Prove that $\sin^2 \theta - \cos^2 \theta = 1$ is *not* an identity.

Solution One counterexample is sufficient. Try $\theta = \dfrac{\pi}{4}$.

$$\sin^2 \frac{\pi}{4} - \cos^2 \frac{\pi}{4} = \left(\frac{1}{\sqrt{2}}\right)^2 - \left(\frac{1}{\sqrt{2}}\right)^2 = 0 \neq 1$$

Since the expressions in the equation are defined for $\dfrac{\pi}{4}$, but the equation is false for $\theta = \dfrac{\pi}{4}$, the equation cannot be an identity.

Complete by using the fundamental identities.

1 $\dfrac{1}{\csc \theta} =$

2 $1 - \sin^2 \theta =$

3 $\csc^2 \theta - \cot^2 \theta =$

4 $\tan \theta \cos \theta =$

5 $\sin \theta \cot \theta =$

6 $-\dfrac{1}{\cos \theta} =$

Without using the trigonometric tables or a calculator, find the value of each of the following.

7 $\sin^2 39° + \cos^2 39°$

8 $\sin(-7°) \csc(-7°)$

9 $\tan^2(3°20') - \sec^2(3°20')$

10 $3 \cos^2 \dfrac{4\pi}{7} \sec^2 \dfrac{4\pi}{7}$

Show that each expression is equal to 1.

11 $(\sin \theta)(\cot \theta)(\sec \theta)$

12 $(\cos \theta)(\tan \theta)(\csc \theta)$

13 $\cos^2 \theta(\tan^2 \theta + 1)$

14 $\tan^2 \theta(\csc^2 \theta - 1)$

In Exercises 15–20, find the values of θ (if any) for which the expressions are defined.

15 $\dfrac{1}{\cos \theta}$

16 $\tan \theta$

17 $\dfrac{1}{\tan \theta}$

18 $\cot \theta$

19 $\dfrac{\cos \theta}{\cot \theta}$

20 $\sec^2 \theta \csc \theta$

In Exercises 21–26, use fundamental identities to convert the expressions into a form involving only sines and cosines of θ, and simplify. Also, find the restrictions on θ, if any.

21 $\dfrac{\tan \theta}{\cot \theta}$

22 $\cot \theta \sec^2 \theta$

23 $\dfrac{1 - \csc \theta}{\cot \theta}$

24 $\dfrac{1 - \cot^2 \theta}{\cot^2 \theta}$

25 $\dfrac{\sec \theta + \csc \theta}{\cos \theta + \sin \theta}$

26 $\dfrac{\sec \theta}{\tan \theta + \cot \theta}$

Express in terms of $\sin \theta$ only.

27 $\cos^2 \theta - \sin^2 \theta$

28 $\tan^2 \theta \csc^2 \theta$

Express in terms of $\cos \theta$ only.

29 $\dfrac{\cot \theta - \sin \theta}{\csc \theta}$

30 $\sec \theta - \sin \theta \tan \theta$

Verify each identity using Method I. Find the restrictions on θ if any.

31 $\dfrac{\cos \theta}{\cot \theta} = \sin \theta$

32 $\cos^2 \theta - \sin^2 \theta = 1 - 2 \sin^2 \theta$

33 $(\tan \theta - 1)^2 = \sec^2 \theta - 2 \tan \theta$

34 $\dfrac{1}{\sec^2 \theta} = 1 - \dfrac{1}{\csc^2 \theta}$

Verify each identity using Method II. Find the restrictions on θ, if any.

35 $\sec \theta - \cos \theta = \sin \theta \tan \theta$

36 $(1 - \sin \theta)(1 + \sin \theta) = \dfrac{1}{1 + \tan^2 \theta}$

37 $\dfrac{\cot \theta - 1}{1 - \tan \theta} = \dfrac{\csc \theta}{\sec \theta}$

38 $\dfrac{1 + \sec \theta}{\csc \theta} = \sin \theta + \tan \theta$

Verify the identities in Exercises 39–72 using either method.

39 $\tan \theta + \cot \theta = \dfrac{1}{(\sin \theta)(\cos \theta)}$

40 $\tan^2 \theta - \sin^2 \theta = \sin^2 \theta \tan^2 \theta$

41 $(\sec \theta + \tan \theta)(1 - \sin \theta) = \cos \theta$

42 $\sec^4 \theta - \tan^4 \theta = 1 + 2 \tan^2 \theta$

43 $(\csc^2 \theta - 1) \sin^2 \theta = \cos^2 \theta$

44 $\sin^4 \theta - \cos^4 \theta + \cos^2 \theta = \sin^2 \theta$

45 $\tan^2 \theta - \sin^2 \theta = \sin^2 \theta \tan^2 \theta$

46 $\dfrac{\cot^2 \theta + 1}{\tan^2 \theta + 1} = \cot^2 \theta$

47 $\dfrac{1 + \sec \theta}{\csc \theta} = \sin \theta + \tan \theta$

48 $\dfrac{\sec^2 \theta}{\sec^2 \theta - 1} = \csc^2 \theta$

49 $\dfrac{1}{1 + \cos \theta} + \dfrac{1}{1 - \cos \theta} = 2 \csc^2 \theta$

50 $\dfrac{\tan \theta \sin \theta}{\sec^2 \theta - 1} = \cos \theta$

51 $\dfrac{1 + \tan^2 \theta}{1 + \cot^2 \theta} = \sec^2 \theta - 1$

52 $\dfrac{\sin \theta + \tan \theta}{1 + \sec \theta} = \sin \theta$

53 $\dfrac{\sin \theta + \cos \theta}{\sin \theta - \cos \theta} = \dfrac{\sec \theta + \csc \theta}{\sec \theta - \csc \theta}$

54 $\tan \theta \sec^2 \theta = \dfrac{\sec \theta}{\csc \theta - \sin \theta}$

55 $\dfrac{1 - \cos \theta}{1 + \cos \theta} = (\csc \theta - \cot \theta)^2$

56 $\dfrac{1 + \tan \theta}{1 - \tan \theta} = \dfrac{\cot \theta + 1}{\cot \theta - 1}$

57 $(\sin^2 \theta + \cos^2 \theta)^5 = 1$

58 $\dfrac{2 + \cot^2 \theta}{\csc^2 \theta} - 1 = \sin^2 \theta$

59 $\dfrac{1}{\cos^2 \theta} + \dfrac{1}{\sin^2 \theta} = \dfrac{1}{\sin^2 \theta - \sin^4 \theta}$

60 $\dfrac{1 + \sin \theta}{\cos \theta} = \dfrac{\cos \theta}{1 - \sin \theta}$

61 $\dfrac{\tan^2 \theta + 1}{\tan^2 \theta} = \csc^2 \theta$

62 $\dfrac{\cot \theta}{\csc \theta + 1} = \sec \theta - \tan \theta$

63 $\dfrac{\tan \theta}{\sec \theta - 1} = \dfrac{\sec \theta + 1}{\tan \theta}$

64 $\dfrac{\cos \theta}{\csc \theta - 2 \sin \theta} = \dfrac{\tan \theta}{1 - \tan^2 \theta}$

*65 $\dfrac{1}{(\csc \theta - \sec \theta)^2} = \dfrac{\sin^2 \theta}{\sec^2 \theta - 2 \tan \theta}$

*66 $\csc \theta - \cot \theta = \dfrac{1}{\csc \theta + \cot \theta}$

*67 $\dfrac{\sec \theta}{\tan \theta - \sin \theta} = \dfrac{1 + \cos \theta}{\sin^3 \theta}$

*68 $\dfrac{1 - \cos \theta}{\sin \theta} + \dfrac{\sin \theta}{1 - \cos \theta} = 2 \csc \theta$

■ **69** $-\ln |\cos x| = \ln |\sec x|$

■ **70** $\ln |\sin x| = -\ln |\csc x|$

■ **71** $-\ln |\sec x - \tan x| = \ln |\sec x + \tan x|$

■ **72** $\ln \left| \dfrac{\sin x}{1 - \cos x} \right| = -\ln \left| \dfrac{\sin x}{1 + \cos x} \right|$

In Exercises 73–78 show that each equation is not an identity by finding one value of θ for which the expressions in the equation are defined but for which the equation is false.

73 $\tan(-x) = \tan x$

74 $\tan \left(x + \dfrac{\pi}{2} \right) = \cot x$

75 $\sin x = -\sqrt{1 - \cos^2 x}$

76 $\tan x = \sqrt{\sec^2 x - 1}$

77 $\dfrac{\cot \theta - 1}{1 - \tan \theta} = \dfrac{\sec \theta}{\csc \theta}$

78 $\dfrac{1 + \sin \theta}{\cos \theta} = \dfrac{\cos \theta}{1 + \sin \theta}$

■ **79** **(a)** Let θ be an acute angle of a triangle where $\tan \theta = \dfrac{x}{3}$. Show that $\ln(\sec \theta + \tan \theta) = \ln \left(\dfrac{\sqrt{x^2 + 9} + x}{3} \right)$.

(b) Let $F(x) = \ln \left(\dfrac{\sqrt{x^2 + 9} + x}{3} \right)$ and evaluate $F(4) - F(0)$.

Prove or disprove that the given equation is an identity.

*80 $\dfrac{\sin x}{\sec x} = \dfrac{1}{\cot x + \tan x}$

*81 $\dfrac{\sin x}{\csc x} - \dfrac{\cos x}{\sec x} = 1$

*82 $\dfrac{1 + \csc x}{\sec x} = \cos x - \tan x$

*83 $\dfrac{\sec^2 x - 2}{(1 + \tan x)^2} = \dfrac{1 - \cot x}{1 + \cot x}$

Suppose that the distance *AB* cannot be measured directly. It cannot be found using the methods in Section 8.3 since that earlier work depended on acute angles within right triangles. But now that trigonometric ratios are available for all size angles, obtuse angles in particular, we will be able to solve this problem (see Exercise 17) after first establishing a new result known as the **Law of Cosines**.

The law of cosines

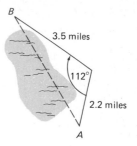

In the following, vertex *A* is placed at the origin ($\angle A$ is in standard position) and side *AC* coincides with the *x*-axis. The measure of $\angle A$ is denoted by the Greek letter α (alpha).

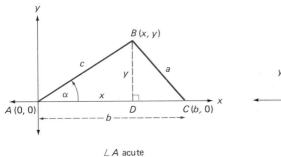

$\angle A$ acute

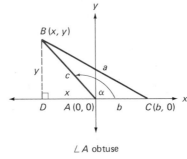

$\angle A$ obtuse

The coordinates of *C* are $(b, 0)$. To find the coordinates of *B*, first construct altitude *BD*. From right $\triangle ABD$ we have

$$\cos \alpha = \frac{AD}{c} \qquad \text{or} \qquad AD = c \cos \alpha \longleftarrow \text{the } x\text{-coordinate of } B$$

Similarly,

$$\sin \alpha = \frac{DB}{c} \qquad \text{or} \qquad DB = c \sin \alpha \longleftarrow \text{the } y\text{-coordinate of } B$$

Apply the distance formula (page 155) to the points $B(c \cos \alpha, c \sin \alpha)$ and $C(b, 0)$.

$$a^2 = (c \cos \alpha - b)^2 + (c \sin \alpha - 0)^2$$
$$= c^2 \cos^2 \alpha - 2bc \cos \alpha + b^2 + c^2 \sin^2 \alpha$$
$$= b^2 + c^2(\cos^2 \alpha + \sin^2 \alpha) - 2bc \cos \alpha$$

Since $\cos^2 \alpha + \sin^2 \alpha = 1$, we have

$$a^2 = b^2 + c^2 - 2bc \cos \alpha$$

If, in turn, $\triangle ABC$ is oriented so that *B* and *C* coincide with the origin, then similar formulas can be derived for b^2 and c^2. These results are summarized in the following. We use the Greek letters α (alpha), β (beta), and

γ (gamma) for the measures of the angles whose vertices are A, B, and C, respectively, in $\triangle ABC$.

> **LAW OF COSINES**
>
> For any $\triangle ABC$ with angle measures α, β, γ, and sides a, b, c,
>
> $$a^2 = b^2 + c^2 - 2bc \cos \alpha$$
> $$b^2 = a^2 + c^2 - 2ac \cos \beta$$
> $$c^2 = a^2 + b^2 - 2ab \cos \gamma$$

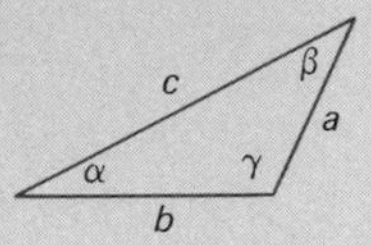

The square of any side of a triangle equals the sum of the squares of the remaining two sides minus twice their product times the cosine of their included angle.

You may find it easier to remember this law by using the verbalized form stated in the margin.

The case side–angle–side: SAS.

The Law of Cosines is used to solve for a side of a triangle when the other two sides and their included angle are given.

EXAMPLE 1   Solve for c in $\triangle ABC$ if $a = 4$, $b = 7$, and $\gamma = 130°$.

Solution

$$
\begin{aligned}
c^2 &= 4^2 + 7^2 - 2(4)(7) \cos 130° \\
&= 65 - 56(-\cos 50°) \\
&= 65 + 56(.6428) \\
&= 100.9968
\end{aligned}
$$

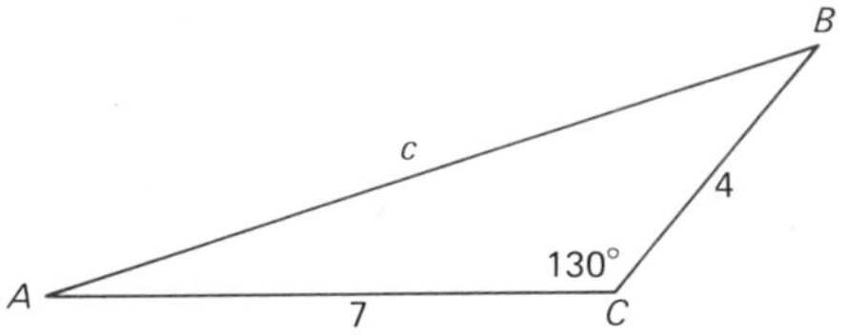

Thus c is approximately 10.

The case side–side–side: SSS.

When the three sides of a triangle are known, the Law of Cosines can be used to find the angles. This is illustrated next.

EXAMPLE 2   Solve for α and β for $\triangle ABC$ in Example 1.

Solution   First solve $a^2 = b^2 + c^2 - 2bc \cos \alpha$ for $\cos \alpha$. Thus

$$\cos \alpha = \frac{b^2 + c^2 - a^2}{2bc}$$

Now substitute $a = 4$, $b = 7$, and $c = 10$,

$$\cos \alpha = \frac{7^2 + 10^2 - 4^2}{2(7)(10)} = .95$$

We use the nearest entry in Table V to find $\alpha = 18°10'$. The solution is completed by noting that

$$
\begin{aligned}
\beta &= 180° - (\alpha + \gamma) \\
&= 180° - (18°10' + 130°) \\
&= 31°50'
\end{aligned}
$$

Use the Law of Cosines, but not Table V or a calculator, to solve for the indicated part of △ABC. Leave the answer in radical form in Exercises 1, 2, and 3.

1 $a = 6$, $b = 4$, $\gamma = 60°$; find c.

2 $b = 15$, $c = 10\sqrt{2}$, $\alpha = \dfrac{\pi}{4}$; find a.

3 $a = 5\sqrt{3}$, $c = 12$, $\beta = 150°$; find b.

4 $a = \sqrt{67}$, $b = 7$, $c = 9$; find α.

5 $a = 8$, $b = \sqrt{34}$, $c = 3\sqrt{2}$; find β.

6 $a = 4$, $b = 6$, $c = \sqrt{76}$; find γ.

When the Law of Cosines is applied to a situation involving an obtuse angle, it is essential that you remember that the cosine of an obtuse angle is negative.

> **An obtuse angle has measure between 90° and 180°.**

EXAMPLE 3   An offshore lighthouse is 2 kilometers from a Coast Guard station C and 2.5 kilometers from a hospital H near the shoreline. If the angle formed by light beams to C and H is 143°, what is the distance CH between the Coast Guard station and the hospital?

Solution   Use the Law of Cosines to solve for CH.

$$(CH)^2 = 2^2 + (2.5)^2 - 2(2)(2.5)(\cos 143°)$$

$$= 4 + 6.25 - 10(-\cos 37°) \qquad \text{(the reference angle is in quadrant II)}$$

$$= 10.25 + 10(.7986)$$

$$= 18.236$$

Taking the square root and rounding off to the nearest tenth, we have

$$CH = 4.3 \text{ kilometers}$$

You may have noticed a similarity between the law of cosines

$$c^2 = a^2 + b^2 - 2ab \cos \alpha$$

and the Pythagorean theorem applied to a right triangle with hypotenuse c

$$a^2 + b^2 = c^2$$

It turns out that the Pythagorean theorem is a special case of the law of cosines. To see this, let △ABC be a right triangle with hypotenuse c and $\alpha = 90°$. Then, by the law of cosines:

$$c^2 = a^2 + b^2 - 2ab \cos \alpha$$

$$= a^2 + b^2 - 2ab \cos 90°$$

$$= a^2 + b^2 - 2ab (0) \qquad (\cos 90° = 0)$$

$$= a^2 + b^2$$

In summary, the law of cosines may be used to solve triangles when you are given the following parts: two sides and an included angle (SAS), and three sides (SSS).

There are two other possibilities for which the law of cosines does not apply: two angles and an included side (ASA), and two sides and an angle opposite one of the sides (SSA). These two cases will be studied in the next section where the *law of sines* will be developed.

EXERCISES 8.6

Use the law of cosines to solve for the indicated parts of △ABC. Do not use Table V or a calculator.

1 Solve for a if $b = 4$, $c = 11$, and $\alpha = 60°$.

2 Solve for b if $a = 20$, $c = 8$, and $\beta = 45°$.

3 Solve for α if $a = 5\sqrt{3}$, $b = 10\sqrt{3}$, and $c = 15$.

4 Solve for β if $a = 9\sqrt{2}$, $b = \sqrt{337}$, and $c = 7$.

Solve for the indicated parts of △ABC. Give the sides to the nearest tenth and the angle to the nearest 10′.

5 $\alpha = 20°$, $b = 8$, $c = 13$; find a and β.

6 $a = 9$, $c = 14$, $\beta = 110°$; find b and γ.

7 $a = 12$, $b = 5$, $c = 13$; find γ and α.

8 $a = b = c = 10$; find α, β, and γ.

9 $a = 18$, $b = 15$, $c = 4$; find β and γ.

10 $\alpha = 65°30′$, $b = 4$, $c = 11$; find a and γ.

11 $a = 18$, $b = 9$, $\gamma = 30°10′$; find c and α.

12 $a = 15$, $c = 5$, $\beta = 157°30′$; find b and α.

13 $b = 2.2$, $c = 6.4$, $\alpha = 42°$; find a and β.

14 $a = 60$, $b = 20$, $c = 75$; find α and β.

15 Two points A and B are on the shoreline of a lake. A surveyor is located at a point C where $AC = 180$ meters and $BC = 120$ meters. He finds the $\angle ACB$ has measure $56°20′$. What is the distance between A and B to the nearest meter?

16 Point C is 2.7 kilometers from a house A and 3 kilometers from house B, where A and B are on opposite sides of a valley. If $\angle ACB$ has measure $130°10′$, find the distance between the houses to the nearest kilometer.

17 Find the distance AB, discussed in the opening to this section, to the nearest tenth of a mile.

18 A diagonal of a parallelogram has length 80 and makes an angle of $20°$ with one of the sides. If this side has length 34, find the length of the other side of the parallelogram to the nearest tenth.

19 The equal sides of an isosceles trapezoid are 10 cm, and the shorter base is 14 cm. If one pair of equal angles has a measure of $40°$ each, find the length of a diagonal to the nearest tenth of a centimeter.

20 The equal sides of an isosceles triangle are each 30 units long and the vertex angle is $27°40′$. Find the base to the nearest tenth of a unit, and the measure of the base angles to the nearest 10′.

21 Solve for AB to the nearest tenth.

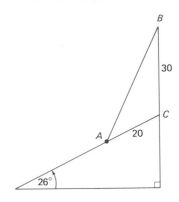

22 The four bases of a baseball diamond form a square 90 feet on a side. The shortstop S is in a position that is 50 feet from second base and forms a $15°$ angle with the base path as shown. Find the distance between the shortstop and first base to the nearest tenth of a foot. (See the following figure.)

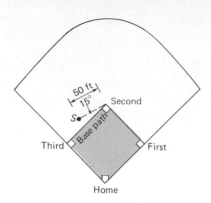

Third

Second

First

Home

Base path

50 ft
15°

S

24 Points A and B are the endpoints of a proposed tunnel through a mountain. From a point P, away from the mountain, a surveyor is able to see both points A and B. The surveyor finds that $PA = 620$ meters, $PB = 450$ meters, and $\angle APB$ has measure $83°20'$. Find the length AB of the tunnel to the nearest meter.

*25 Two trains leave the same station at 11 A.M. and travel in straight lines at speeds of 54 miles per hour and 60 miles per hour, respectively. If the difference in their directions is $124°$, how far apart are they at 11:20 A.M. to the nearest tenth of a mile?

*26 Prove that for any $\triangle ABC$, $c = a \cos \beta + b \cos \alpha$. (*Hint:* Consider the cases where $\angle A$ is acute, obtuse, or a right angle, and put $\angle A$ in standard position.)

23 In Exercise 22, find the distance between the short-stop and home plate to the nearest tenth of a foot.

8.7

The law of sines

Triangular problems in which the given information is either SAS or SSS can be solved using the Law of Cosines. However, if the given information is ASA, AAS, or SSA, then the Law of Cosines is not adequate, and another property of triangles, called the **Law of Sines**, is needed. To establish this new result, first construct altitude DB for $\triangle ABC$ as shown. From right triangles ABD and CBD, we have

See Exercise 28 for the case $\alpha = 90°$.

$$\sin \alpha = \frac{DB}{c} \qquad \text{and} \qquad \sin \gamma = \frac{DB}{a}$$

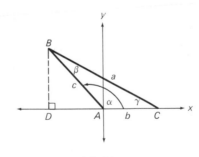

$\angle A$ acute

$\angle A$ obtuse

Then $DB = c \sin \alpha$ and $DB = a \sin \gamma$, which gives

$$a \sin \gamma = c \sin \alpha$$

$$\frac{a}{\sin \alpha} = \frac{c}{\sin \gamma} \qquad \text{(why?)}$$

Similar reasoning produces $\dfrac{a}{\sin \alpha} = \dfrac{b}{\sin \beta}$, which is combined with the first result into the following:

The "double" equality is an abbreviation for these three results:

$$\frac{a}{\sin \alpha} = \frac{b}{\sin \beta}$$

$$\frac{a}{\sin \alpha} = \frac{c}{\sin \gamma}$$

$$\frac{b}{\sin \beta} = \frac{c}{\sin \gamma}$$

THE LAW OF SINES

For any $\triangle ABC$ with angle measures α, β, γ and sides $a, b, c,$

$$\frac{a}{\sin \alpha} = \frac{b}{\sin \beta} = \frac{c}{\sin \gamma}$$

Our first two examples demonstrate the use of the Law of Sines when two angles and one side are given.

The case angle–side–angle: ASA

EXAMPLE 1   Solve $\triangle ABC$ if $\beta = 75°$, $a = 5$, and $\gamma = 41°$.

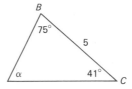

To "solve a triangle" means to solve for each of the unknown parts.

Solution   Since two angles are given, the third is easy to find because the sum of the angles of a triangle is 180°.

$$\alpha = 180° - (\beta + \gamma)$$
$$= 180° - (75° + 41°)$$
$$= 180° - 116°$$
$$= 64°$$

Now use the Law of Sines to solve for b, and substitute the appropriate values. From $\dfrac{a}{\sin \alpha} = \dfrac{b}{\sin \beta}$ we obtain $b = \dfrac{a \sin \beta}{\sin \alpha}$. Thus

$$b = \frac{5 \sin 75°}{\sin 64°} = \frac{5(.9659)}{.8988}$$

$$= 5.4 \qquad \text{(to the nearest tenth using a calculator or logarithms)}$$

We solve for c in a similar manner:

$$c = \frac{a \sin \gamma}{\sin \alpha} = \frac{5 \sin 41°}{\sin 64°}$$

$$= \frac{5(.6561)}{.8988}$$

$$= 3.6 \qquad \text{(to the nearest tenth using a calculator or logarithms)}$$

EXAMPLE 2   Find the distance $AB = c$ to the nearest meter, across the pond if $\beta = 108°$, $\gamma = 39°$, and $AC = 950$ meters.

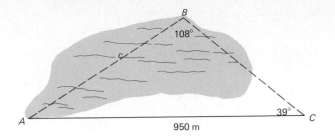

B

108°

c

39° C

A

950 m

Solution $\dfrac{c}{\sin \gamma} = \dfrac{b}{\sin \beta}$ can be used to solve for c since only c is unknown. Thus

$$c = \frac{b \sin \gamma}{\sin \beta}$$

$$= \frac{950 \sin 39°}{\sin 108°} = \frac{950(.6293)}{.9511} = 628.6 \qquad \text{(to one decimal place)}$$

The distance AB is 629 to the nearest meter.

TEST YOUR UNDERSTANDING

Use the Law of Sines to answer the following without using Table V or a calculator.

1 Find a if $\alpha = 30°$, $\beta = 45°$, and $b = 8$.
2 Find c if $\alpha = 30°$, $\gamma = 120°$, and $a = 12$.
3 Find b if $\beta = 60°$, $\gamma = 75°$, and $a = 15$.
4 Find b if $\alpha = 15°$, $\beta = 135°$, and $c = 4$.

When two sides and an angle opposite one of the sides (SSA) are given, there are a number of possibilities. The following figures illustrate the four possible cases when $\angle A$ is acute. It is assumed that parts a, α, and b are given. Note that $h = b \sin \alpha$ is the altitude opposite $\angle A$.

CASE 1.   No solution: $a < b \sin \alpha$

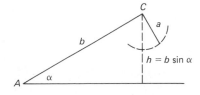

CASE 2.   One solution: $a = b \sin \alpha$

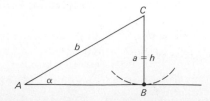

323

CASE 3.   Two solutions: $b \sin \alpha < a < b$

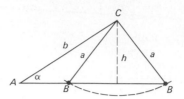

CASE 4.   One solution: $a \geq b$

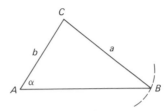

The preceding descriptions are independent of the symbols chosen. Any choice of symbols could be used as long as we have the case SSA.

When $\angle A$ is obtuse, there are only these possibilities:

No solution
$a \leq b$

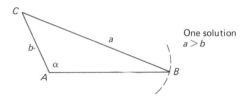

One solution
$a > b$

EXAMPLE 3 Solve $\triangle ABC$ if $a = 50$, $b = 65$, and $\alpha = 57°$.

Solution $b \sin \alpha = 65 \sin 57° = 54.5$. Since $a < 54.5$ we have $a < b \sin \alpha$ and there is no solution possible (case 1).

The next example is an illustration of case 3, in which $b \sin \alpha < a < b$. This is called the *ambiguous* case. The two angles obtained are supplementary, and therefore have the same sine value.

EXAMPLE 4 Approximate the remaining parts of $\triangle ABC$ if $a = 10$, $b = 13$, and $\alpha = 25°$.

Solution $b \sin \alpha = 13 \sin 25° = 5.5$. Since $5.5 < 10 < 13$, we have $b \sin \alpha < a < b$ (case 3) and there are two solutions for β. From the Law of Sines,

$$\sin \beta = \frac{b \sin \alpha}{a} = \frac{13(\sin 25°)}{10} = .5494$$

Using Table V, we find the closest entry to be .5495 and therefore use $\beta = 33°20'$. The other solution is $\beta = 180 - 33°20' = 146°40'$. If $\beta = 33°20'$, then $\gamma = 180° - (\alpha + \beta) = 121°40'$, and

$$c = \frac{a \sin \gamma}{\sin \alpha} = \frac{10 \sin(121°40')}{\sin 25°}$$

$$= \frac{10 \sin(58°20')}{\sin 25°} = 20.1$$

If $\beta = 146°40'$, we get $\gamma = 8°20'$ and $c = 3.4$.

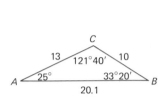 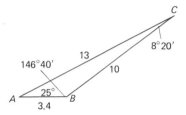

Use the Law of Sines to solve for the indicated parts of $\triangle ABC$. *Do not use Table V or a calculator.*

1 Solve for a and c if $\alpha = 30°$, $\beta = 120°$, and $b = 54$

2 Solve for c if $\gamma = 30°$, $\alpha = 135°$, and $a = 100$.

3 Solve for γ if $a = 12$, $c = 4\sqrt{3}$, and $\alpha = \frac{2\pi}{3}$.

4 Solve for β if $a = 5\sqrt{2}$, $b = 10$, and $\alpha = \frac{\pi}{6}$.

In Exercises 5–8, use the Law of Sines to solve $\triangle ABC$.

5 $\alpha = 25°$, $\gamma = 55°$, $b = 12$

6 $\gamma = 110°$, $\beta = 28°$, $a = 8$

7 $\alpha = 62°20'$, $\beta = 50°$, $b = 5$

8 $\alpha = 155°$, $\beta = 15°30'$, $c = 20$

In Exercises 9–14, determine the number of triangles possible with the given parts.

9 $\alpha = 32°$, $a = 5.1$, $b = 10$

10 $\alpha = 32°$, $a = 6$, $b = 10$

11 $\alpha = 30°$, $a = 9.5$, $b = 19$

12 $\alpha = 50°$, $a = 15$, $b = 14.3$

13 $\alpha = 126°$, $a = 20$, $b = 25$

14 $\alpha = 77°$, $a = 49$, $b = 50$

Use the Law of Sines to solve for the indicated parts of $\triangle ABC$ *whenever possible.*

15 Solve for β and c if $\alpha = 53°$, $a = 12$, and $b = 15$.

16 Solve for γ and a if $\beta = 122°$, $b = 20$, and $c = 8$.

17 Solve for β if $b = 25$, $a = 7$, and $\alpha = 75°$.

18 Solve for β if $\alpha = 44°$, $a = 9$, and $b = 12$.

19 Solve for γ if $\beta = 22°40'$, $b = 25$, and $c = 30$.

20 Solve for γ if $\beta = 22°40'$, $b = 8$, and $c = 30$.

21 Solve for the larger angle of the given parallelogram.

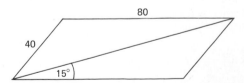

22 Two guy wires support a telephone pole. They are attached to the top of the pole and are anchored into the ground on opposite sides of the pole at points A and B. If $AB = 120$ feet and the angles of elevation at A and B are $72°$ and $56°$, respectively, find the length of the wires to the nearest tenth of a foot.

23 An airplane is flying in a straight line toward an airfield at a fixed altitude. At one point the angle of depression to the airfield is 32°. After flying 2 more miles the angle of depression is 74°. What is the distance between the airplane and the airfield when the angle of depression is 74°? Give your answer to the nearest tenth of a mile.

24 Use the Law of Sines to find AD to the nearest tenth.

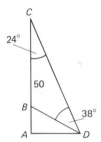

25 From the top of a 250-foot hill, the angles of depression of two cottages A and B on the shore of a lake are 15°30′ and 29°10′, respectively. If the cottages are due north of the observation point, find the distance between them to the nearest foot.

*26 A 45-foot tower standing vertically on a hillside casts a shadow down the hillside that is 72 feet long. The angle at the tip of the shadow S, subtended by the tower, is 28°. Find the angle of elevation of the sun at S.

27 In $\triangle ABC$ let D be a point between A and C such that $\angle BDA = 58°$. If $\angle A = 110°$, $\angle C = 43°$, and $DC = 20$ cm, find AD to the nearest tenth of a centimeter.

28 (a) Use the law of sines to prove that any two sides of a triangle are in the same ratio as the sines of their opposite angles.

(b) Two of the angles of a triangles are 105° and 45°. The side opposite the smallest angle of the triangle has length 10. Use the result in (a) to find the length of the side opposite the 45° angle without using Table V or a calculator.

*29 In the figure $AB = 12$, $BC = 4$, $AD = 10$, and the measure of $\angle B$ is 20°. Solve for CD to the nearest unit. (*Hint*: Begin with the Law of Cosines.)

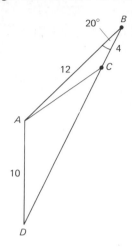

*30 Show that if $\alpha = 90°$, the Law of Sines is consistent with the definition of the sine of an acute angle.

*31 In the figure, A and B are two points on one side of a canyon with $AB = 300$ meters. Use a calculator to find the distance between the points C and D on the opposite side of the canyon.

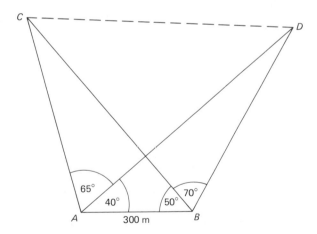

*32 (a) Prove that the area of a triangle equals one-half the product of two of its sides times the sine of the included angle.

(b) Find the area of $\triangle ABC$ if $\alpha = 82°$, $b = 14$, and $c = 31$.

The solutions to the following exercises can be found within the text of Chapter 8. Try to answer each question without referring to the text.

Section 8.1

1 For a right triangle having sides of length 3, 4, and 5, find the sine and cosine of each of the acute angles.

2 For a right triangle having sides 5, 12, and 13, find the six trigonometric ratios of the angle opposite the side of length 12.

3 Triangle ABC has a right angle at C. If $a = 3$ and $b = 2$, find $\sin B$.

4 Find the six trigonometric ratios for angle A in terms of x, where x is the side opposite acute angle A in a right triangle with hypotenuse 1.

5 Show that $(\sin A)(\cos A) = \dfrac{x\sqrt{25 - x^2}}{25}$ where x is the side opposite acute angle A in a right triangle with hypotenuse 5.

6 Write the six trigonometric ratios of $45°$.

7 Write the six trigonometric ratios of $30°$.

8 Write the six trigonometric ratios of $60°$.

Section 8.2

9 Convert $30°$ and $135°$ into radians.

10 Use the conversion factor 0.0175 to change the degree measures in Exercise 9 into approximate radian measure.

11 Convert $\dfrac{\pi}{4}$ and $\dfrac{5\pi}{6}$ into degree measure.

12 Convert $\frac{3}{5}$ radians into degrees and state the answer in terms of π. Also, use the conversion factor 57.296 to express $\frac{3}{5}$ radians to the nearest tenth of a degree.

13 If an arc length $s = 12$ subtends a central angle θ in a circle of radius 3, find the measure of θ in terms of radians.

14 A central angle in a circle of radius 4 centimeters is $75°$; find the length of the intercepted arc to the nearest tenth of a centimeter.

15 Find the area of a sector of a circle of radius 6 centimeters if the central angle is $60°$.

Section 8.3

16 Solve for the adjacent side of a $30°$ angle in a right triangle with hypotenuse 10. Give the exact answer and the approximation to the nearest tenth.

17 Use Table V to find these values:
 (a) $\cos 13°$ (b) $\cot 26°$
 (c) $\sin 58°10'$ (d) $\csc 83°40'$

18 Use Table V to solve for θ to the nearest 10 minutes:
 (a) $\sin \theta = .4746$ (b) $\tan \theta = 2.165$

19 The angle of elevation of an 80-foot ramp leading to a bridge above a highway is $10°31'$. Find the height of the bridge above the highway.

20 From the top of a house the angle of depression of a point on the ground is $25°$. The point is 45 meters from the base of the building. How high is the building?

21 The top of a hill is 40 meters higher than a nearby airport, and the horizontal distance from the end of a runway is 325 meters from a point directly below the hilltop. An airplane takes off at the end of the runway in the direction of the hill, at an angle that is to be kept constant until the hill is passed. If the pilot wants to clear the hill by 30 meters, what should be the angle of takeoff?

Section 8.4

22 Find the six trigonometric ratios for $\dfrac{5\pi}{6}$.

23 Find $\tan\left(-\dfrac{5\pi}{4}\right)$.

24 Use Table V to find $\cos 200°$.

25 Determine the trigonometric ratios of $\dfrac{3\pi}{2}$ and $-\dfrac{\pi}{2}$.

26 Find $\sec 932°$ and $\csc(-383°40')$.

Section 8.5

27 Write two equivalent forms of $\sin \theta \csc \theta = 1$ and state the restrictions on θ.

28 Use the unit circle to explain why $\cos^2 \theta + \sin^2 \theta = 1$ is true for all θ.

29 Use the identity in Exercise 28 to derive $1 + \tan^2 \theta = \sec^2 \theta$ and state the restrictions on θ.

30 Convert $\dfrac{1 - \csc \theta}{\cot \theta}$ into an expression involving only $\sin \theta$ and $\cos \theta$.

In Exercises 31–33, verify the identity.

31 $\dfrac{\tan^2 \theta + 1}{\tan \theta \csc^2 \theta} = \tan \theta$

32 $(\sec \theta + \tan \theta)^2 = \dfrac{\csc \theta + 1}{\csc \theta - 1}$

33 $\dfrac{\sin \theta}{1 + \cos \theta} = \dfrac{1 - \cos \theta}{\sin \theta}$

34 Prove that $\sin^2 \theta - \cos^2 \theta = 1$ is not an identity.

Section 8.6

35 Write the Law of Cosines for a triangle with sides a, b, c and angle measures α, β, γ.

36 Solve for c in $\triangle ABC$ if $a = 4$, $b = 7$, and $\gamma = 130°$.

37 Solve for α and β in $\triangle ABC$ given in Exercise 36.

38 An offshore lighthouse is 2 kilometers from a Coast Guard station C and 2.5 kilometers from a hospital H near the shoreline. If the angle formed by light beams to C and H is 143°, what is the distance CH between the Coast Guard station and the hospital?

Section 8.7

39 State the Law of Sines for a triangle with sides a, b, c and angle measures α, β, γ.

40 Solve $\triangle ABC$ if $\beta = 75°$, $a = 5$, and $\gamma = 41°$.

41 Solve for c in $\triangle ABC$ in which $\beta = 108°$, $\gamma = 39°$, and $b = 950$ meters.

42 Solve $\triangle ABC$ if $a = 50$, $b = 65$, and $\alpha = 57°$.

43 Approximate the remaining parts of the triangle if $a = 10$, $b = 13$, and $\alpha = 25°$.

SAMPLE TEST QUESTIONS FOR CHAPTER 8

Use these questions to test your knowledge of the basic skills and concepts of Chapter 8. Then test your answers with those given at the end of the book.

1 Use the given figure to write the following trigonometric ratios:

(a) $\tan A$ (b) $\sin B$

(c) $\sec A$

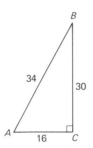

2 If $\angle A$ is an acute angle such that $\sec A = \frac{3}{2}$, find $\sin A$, $\cos A$, and $\tan A$.

3 Use the given triangle to show that

$$3(\sin^2 A)(\sec A) = \dfrac{x^2}{\sqrt{x^2 + 9}}$$

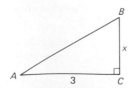

4 A sector of a circle with radius 10 inches has a central angle of 120°. Find the arc length of the sector.

5 Find each ratio (if it exists):

(a) $\sin \dfrac{\pi}{3}$ (b) $\cot \dfrac{3\pi}{2}$

(c) $\sin(-135°)$

6 Find each ratio (if it exists):

(a) $\tan 510°$ (b) $\cos 3\pi$

(c) $\csc\left(-\dfrac{7\pi}{6}\right)$

7 Solve for the hypotenuse of an isosceles right triangle, one of whose legs has length 20.

8 A building casts a shadow of 100 feet. The angle of elevation from the tip of the shadow to the top of the building is 75°. Find the height of the building correct to the nearest foot.

In Questions 9–11, verify the identities.

9 $\cot^2 \theta - \cos^2 \theta = \cos^2 \theta \cot^2 \theta$

10 $\dfrac{1 - \sin \theta}{1 + \sin \theta} = (\sec \theta - \tan \theta)^2$

11 $\dfrac{\tan \theta - \sin \theta}{\csc \theta - \cot \theta} = \sec \theta - \cos \theta$

12 The terminal side of θ coincides with the line $y = 2x$ and lies in the first quadrant. Find $\cos \theta$.

13 A sector is inscribed in a 30°–60°–90° triangle as in the following figure. The side opposite the 30° angle is 2 units. Find the area of the shaded part.

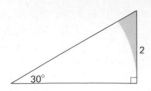

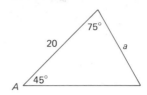

(a) $\alpha = 30°$, $a = 5.8$, $b = 12$

(b) $\alpha = 30°$, $a = 4.1$, $b = 8$

16 Solve for a in the figure.

14 (a) Solve for a if $\angle A = 60°$, $b = 8$, and $c = 12$. Give $\angle A$ in radians.

(b) Write an expression for sin B in terms of other known parts of triangle ABC given in part (a).

15 Determine the number of triangles possible with the given parts.

ANSWERS TO THE TEST YOUR UNDERSTANDING EXERCISES

Page 286

1 and 2

$$\sin A = \tfrac{7}{25} = \cos B \qquad \cot A = \tfrac{24}{7} = \tan B$$
$$\cos A = \tfrac{24}{25} = \sin B \qquad \sec A = \tfrac{25}{24} = \csc B$$
$$\tan A = \tfrac{7}{24} = \cot B \qquad \csc A = \tfrac{25}{7} = \sec B$$

3 $\tfrac{49}{625} + \tfrac{576}{625} = \tfrac{625}{625} = 1$ **4** $(\tfrac{7}{25})(\tfrac{25}{7}) = 1$ **5** $\tfrac{625}{49} - \tfrac{576}{49} = \tfrac{49}{49} = 1$ **6** $(\tfrac{24}{7})(\tfrac{7}{24}) = 1$

Page 297

1 $\dfrac{10\sqrt{3}}{3}$; 5.8 **2** $10\sqrt{3}$; 17.3 **3** $\dfrac{5\sqrt{2}}{2}$; 3.5

Page 299

1 .4540 **2** .7880 **3** 3.078 **4** .6249

5 $67° = 1.1694$ radians **6** $55° = .9599$ radians **7** $77° = 1.3439$ radians **8** $22° = .3840$ radians

Page 306

1 $\dfrac{\sqrt{2}}{2}$ **2** $-\sqrt{2}$ **3** 1 **4** $\dfrac{2\sqrt{3}}{3}$

5 -1.540 **6** $-\sqrt{2}$ **7** $\dfrac{\sqrt{3}}{2}$ **8** 4.331

Page 319

1 $2\sqrt{7}$ **2** $5\sqrt{5}$ **3** $\sqrt{399}$ **4** $\dfrac{\pi}{3}$ **5** $\dfrac{\pi}{4}$ **6** $\dfrac{2\pi}{3}$

Page 323

1 $4\sqrt{2}$ **2** $12\sqrt{3}$ **3** $\tfrac{15}{2}\sqrt{6}$ **4** $4\sqrt{2}$

THE CIRCULAR FUNCTIONS

On the unit circle, arc length is numerically the same as the radian measure of the central angle subtended by the arc.

The sine and cosine functions

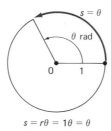

$$s = r\theta = 1\theta = \theta$$

Remember that for a circle of radius r, $s = r\theta$ is the length of an arc with a central angle of θ radians (see page 291).

Therefore, the sine of θ radians, $\sin \theta$, may also be thought of as the sine of the arc length θ. But arc lengths may be regarded as real numbers, just as the lengths on a number line are given by real numbers. Consequently, $\sin \theta$ can be interpreted as the sine of the *number* θ.

Since $\sin \theta$ is a unique value for any real number (radian), it is now correct to say that the equation $y = \sin \theta$ defines y to be a function of θ, with domain all real numbers. Also, since $y = \sin \theta$ is the second coordinate of the point on the terminal side of θ and on the unit circle, the range consists of all y such that $-1 \le y \le 1$.

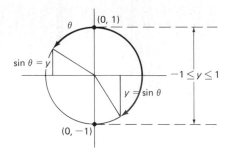

One way to graph $y = \sin \theta$ in a rectangular system is to use the θ values on the horizontal axis with the corresponding $y = \sin \theta$ becoming the ordinates.

You may think of the circle as being "unrolled" to get the θ values on the horizontal.

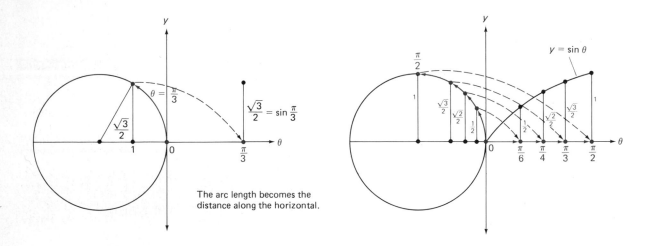

The arc length becomes the distance along the horizontal.

Now that you see the connection between $y = \sin \theta$, defined on the unit circle, and its graph in a rectangular system, we will obtain a more accurate graph using a table of values. First recall that $\sin \theta$ is positive for θ in quadrants I and II; $0 < \theta < \pi$. Also, $\sin \theta$ is negative for $\pi < \theta < 2\pi$. Let us

Additional points may be found by using Table V or a calculator.

form a table of values by using intervals of $\frac{\pi}{6}$ for $0 \le \theta \le 2\pi$.

θ	0	$\frac{\pi}{6}$	$\frac{\pi}{3}$	$\frac{\pi}{2}$	$\frac{2\pi}{3}$	$\frac{5\pi}{6}$	π	$\frac{7\pi}{6}$	$\frac{4\pi}{3}$	$\frac{3\pi}{2}$	$\frac{5\pi}{3}$	$\frac{11\pi}{6}$	2π
$y = \sin \theta$	0	$\frac{1}{2}$	$\frac{\sqrt{3}}{2}$	1	$\frac{\sqrt{3}}{2}$	$\frac{1}{2}$	0	$-\frac{1}{2}$	$-\frac{\sqrt{3}}{2}$	-1	$-\frac{\sqrt{3}}{2}$	$-\frac{1}{2}$	0

We plot these points (using the approximation $\frac{\sqrt{3}}{2} = 0.87$) and connect the points with a smooth curve to find the graph of $y = \sin\theta$ for $0 \leq \theta \leq 2\pi$. The segment from zero to 2π on the horizontal axis may be viewed as the circumference of the unit circle after it has been "unrolled."

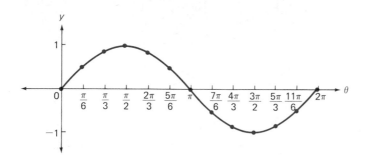

The sine function increases on the intervals $\left[0, \frac{\pi}{2}\right]$ and $\left[\frac{3\pi}{2}, 2\pi\right]$ and decreases on $\left[\frac{\pi}{2}, \frac{3\pi}{2}\right]$. The curve is concave down on $[0, \pi]$ and concave up on $[\pi, 2\pi]$.

For values of θ, where $2\pi \leq \theta \leq 4\pi$, we know that the terminal sides of θ (in the unit circle) are the same as for those angles from 0 to 2π. Hence everything repeats. Similarly for $-2\pi \leq \theta \leq 0$, and so on. Thus we say that the sine function is *periodic*, with **period** 2π; $\sin(\theta + 2\pi) = \sin\theta$. That is, the sine curve repeats itself to the right and left as shown in the figure on the top of page 334.

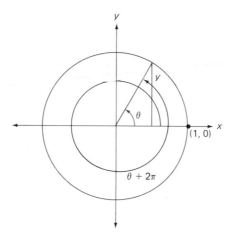

A function f is said to be periodic with period p in case p is the smallest positive constant, if any, such that $f(x + p) = f(x)$ for all x in the domain of f.

Even though $\sin(\theta + 4\pi) = \sin\theta$, the period is not 4π because 4π is not the smallest positive number having this property.

THE SINE FUNCTION

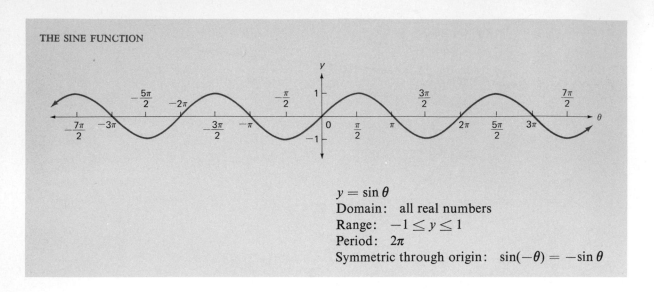

$y = \sin \theta$
Domain: all real numbers
Range: $-1 \leq y \leq 1$
Period: 2π
Symmetric through origin: $\sin(-\theta) = -\sin \theta$

The graph of $y = \sin \theta$ indicates that the sine function is symmetric through the origin. This symmetry can be verified by returning to the unit circle.

Letting $f(\theta) = \sin \theta$, we have

$$f(-\theta) = \sin(-\theta) = -\sin(\theta) = -f(\theta)$$
$$f(-\theta) = -f(\theta)$$

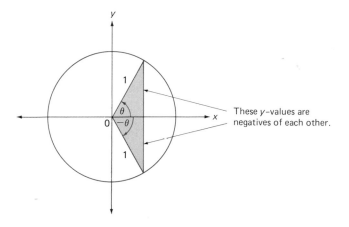

These y-values are negatives of each other.

The graph of the cosine function can be obtained from the graph of $y = \sin \theta$ by observing that $\cos \theta = \sin \left(\theta + \dfrac{\pi}{2}\right)$. To see why this is true, consider these two typical situations:

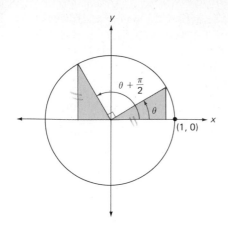 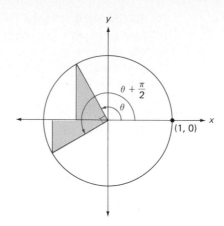

In each case the reference triangles for θ and $\theta + \dfrac{\pi}{2}$ are congruent. Consequently, the side adjacent to the reference angle for θ has the same measure as the side opposite the reference angle for $\theta + \dfrac{\pi}{2}$. It follows that $\cos \theta = \sin\left(\theta + \dfrac{\pi}{2}\right)$.

The graph of $y = \sin\left(\theta + \dfrac{\pi}{2}\right)$ can be obtained by shifting the graph of $y = \sin \theta$ by $\dfrac{\pi}{2}$ units to the left. Thus the cosine curve can be obtained by shifting the sine curve $\dfrac{\pi}{2}$ units to the left.

Due to the relationship of the sine and cosine to the unit circle, as well as to right triangles, we refer to them as *circular* or *trigonometric* functions.

THE COSINE FUNCTION

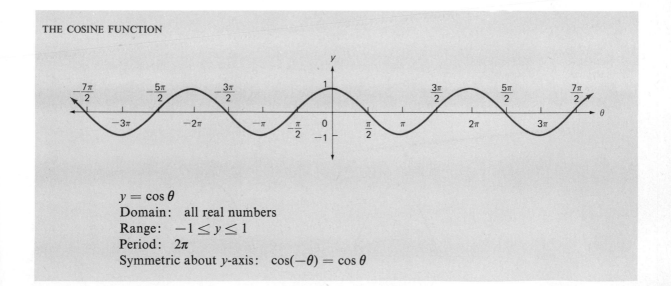

$y = \cos \theta$
Domain: all real numbers
Range: $-1 \le y \le 1$
Period: 2π
Symmetric about y-axis: $\cos(-\theta) = \cos \theta$

In Chapter 8 we used the unit circle to arrive at $\cos \theta = x$. However, to be consistent with the usual labeling of the vertical axis in a rectangular system, we have written the equation in the form $y = \cos \theta$. Furthermore, from now on we will use x instead of θ for the horizontal axis. We use the letter θ when making direct reference to the unit circle.

The cosine curve may be regarded as being $\dfrac{\pi}{2}$ units ahead (or behind) the sine curve, and vice versa. Both functions have the same period, 2π. The symmetry about the y-axis can be verified by studying the following unit circle diagram.

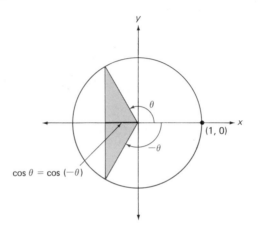

The sine function has a maximum value of $M = 1$ and a minimum value of $m = -1$. One-half of the difference is called the **amplitude**.

$$\text{Amplitude} = \frac{M - m}{2}$$

For $y = \sin x$, amplitude $= \dfrac{1 - (-1)}{2} = 1$. Thus for $y = 2 \sin x$, $M = 2$,

Note that $-1 \le \sin x \le 1$ is equivalent to $-2 \le 2 \sin x \le 2$.

$m = -2$, and the amplitude is $\dfrac{2 - (-2)}{2} = 2$. In general, the amplitude of $y = a \sin x$ or of $y = a \cos x$ is equal to $|a|$.

In the next figure the idea of amplitude is illustrated for a few cases. Notice that each of these functions has period 2π.

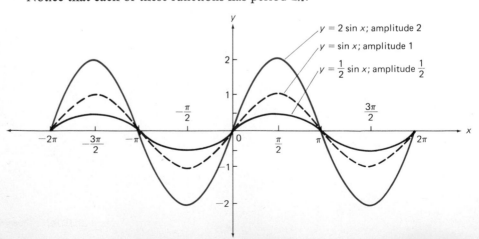

$y = 2 \sin x$; amplitude 2
$y = \sin x$; amplitude 1
$y = \dfrac{1}{2} \sin x$; amplitude $\dfrac{1}{2}$

Graph the curve for the values $-2\pi \leq x \leq 2\pi$.

1 $y = -\sin x$ **2** $y = 3 \cos x$ **3** $y = \sin(-x)$

Find the amplitude.

4 $y = 10 \sin x$ **5** $y = -\frac{2}{3} \cos x$ **6** $y = \frac{1}{2} - \cos x$

Explain how the graph of g can be obtained from the graph of f.

7 $f(x) = \sin x$; $g(x) = \sin(x - 2)$ **8** $f(x) = \cos x$; $g(x) = 2 + \cos x$

For $y = \sin x$, the coefficient of x is 1. By changing the coefficient, we alter the period of the function. Consider, for example, the graph of $y = \sin 2x$. As x assumes values from 0 through π, $2x$ takes on values from 0 through 2π. That is, $0 \leq 2x \leq 2\pi$ is equivalent to $0 \leq x \leq \pi$. Thus the graph goes through a complete cycle for $0 \leq x \leq \pi$ and has period π. This information is shown in the following table of values and graph. Note that the graph completes two full cycles in the interval $0 \leq x \leq 2\pi$.

x	0	$\frac{\pi}{4}$	$\frac{\pi}{2}$	$\frac{3\pi}{4}$	π
$2x$	0	$\frac{\pi}{2}$	π	$\frac{3\pi}{2}$	2π
$y = \sin 2x$	0	1	0	-1	0

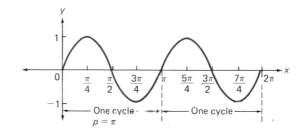

The equivalence of $0 \leq 2x \leq 2\pi$ and $\frac{0}{2} \leq \frac{2x}{2} \leq \frac{2\pi}{2}$ gave the period $p = \pi$ for $y = \sin 2x$. In a similar manner you can show that both $y = a \sin bx$ and $y = a \cos bx$ have period $p = \dfrac{2\pi}{|b|}$

GUIDELINES FOR GRAPHING $y = a \sin bx$, $y = a \cos bx$

1. Find the period $p = \dfrac{2\pi}{|b|}$ and the amplitude $|a|$.

2. Divide the segment $[0, p]$ into four equal parts:

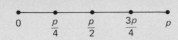

Use the guidelines here and on the next page to help you graph the sine and cosine functions.

3. For $y = a \sin bx$, $y = 0$ at $x = 0, \frac{p}{2}, p$ and $y = \pm a$ at $x = \frac{p}{4}, \frac{3p}{4}$, depending on the sign of a.

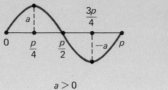

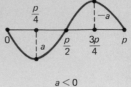

$a > 0$ $a < 0$

4. For $y = a \cos bx$, $y = 0$ at $x = \frac{p}{4}, \frac{3p}{4}$, and $y = \pm a$ at $x = 0, \frac{p}{2}$, p, depending on the sign of a.

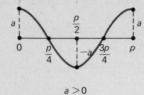

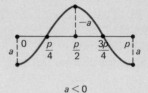

$a > 0$ $a < 0$

5. Connect the five points as shown and repeat the basic cycle as required in either direction.

EXAMPLE 1 Graph $y = 2 \cos \frac{x}{2}$ on the interval $[-p, p]$, where p is the period, and compare to the graph of $y = \cos x$.

Solution The amplitude is $|a| = |2| = 2$, and $p = \frac{2\pi}{|b|} = \frac{2\pi}{\frac{1}{2}} = 4\pi$. Now divide $[0, 4\pi]$ into four equal parts and note that $a = 2$ is positive to get the following:

$$y = 0 \text{ at } x = \pi, 3\pi$$
$$y = 2 \text{ at } x = 0, 4\pi$$
$$y = -2 \text{ at } x = 2\pi$$

Connect the five points as shown.

Complete the problem by repeating the cycle to -4π at the left and include the graph of $y = \cos x$.

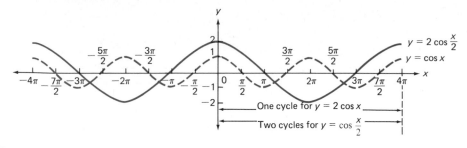

The next example demonstrates how to graph the sum of two circular functions by adding the ordinates.

EXAMPLE 2 Graph $y = \sin x + \cos x$ on $[-2\pi, 2\pi]$.

Solution First graph $y = \sin x$ and $y = \cos x$ on the same set of axes.

With practice you can learn to locate points, like those marked with the crosses, by visual inspection and avoid using a table of values.

x	$\sin x$	$\cos x$	$\sin x + \cos x$	
0	0	1	1	
$\dfrac{\pi}{4}$	$\dfrac{\sqrt{2}}{2}$	$\dfrac{\sqrt{2}}{2}$	$\sqrt{2}$	
$\dfrac{\pi}{2}$	1	0	1	
$\dfrac{3\pi}{4}$	$\dfrac{\sqrt{2}}{2}$	$-\dfrac{\sqrt{2}}{2}$	0	
π	0	-1	-1	
$\dfrac{5\pi}{4}$	$\dfrac{\sqrt{2}}{2}$	$-\dfrac{\sqrt{2}}{2}$	$-\sqrt{2}$	
$\dfrac{3\pi}{2}$	-1	0	-1	
$\dfrac{7\pi}{4}$	$-\dfrac{\sqrt{2}}{2}$	$\dfrac{\sqrt{2}}{2}$	0	$\dfrac{7\pi}{4}$
2π	0	1	1	

Select specific values of x in $[0, 2\pi]$ for which $\sin x$ and $\cos x$ are easy to find and add these ordinates. The adjoining table contains such values, and the resulting points have been indicated by the crosses. After connecting the crosses by a smooth curve, the graph is completed either by repeating the process described on $[-2\pi, 0]$ or by copying the cycle obtained on $[0, 2\pi]$ onto $[-2\pi, 0]$.

EXERCISES 9.1

1 Complete the table and use these points and the symmetry through the origin to graph $y = \sin x$ for $-\pi \le x \le \pi$.

x	$-\pi$	$-\dfrac{5\pi}{6}$	$-\dfrac{2\pi}{3}$	$-\dfrac{\pi}{2}$	$-\dfrac{\pi}{3}$	$-\dfrac{\pi}{6}$	0
$y = \sin x$							

2 (a) Complete the table and use these points and the symmetry about the y-axis to graph $y = \cos x$ for $-\pi \le x \le \pi$.

x	0	$\dfrac{\pi}{4}$	$\dfrac{\pi}{2}$	$\dfrac{3\pi}{4}$	π
$y = \cos x$					

(b) On which intervals is the cosine increasing? decreasing? On which intervals is the graph of the cosine concave up? down?

In Exercises 3–8, explain how the graph of g can be obtained from the graph of f. Graph both functions on the same axes for $0 \le x \le 2\pi$.

3 $f(x) = \sin x,\ g(x) = \sin\left(x - \dfrac{\pi}{2}\right)$

4 $f(x) = \sin x,\ g(x) = \sin\left(x + \dfrac{\pi}{4}\right)$

5 $f(x) = \cos x,\ g(x) = \cos\left(x - \dfrac{\pi}{3}\right)$

6 $f(x) = \cos x,\ g(x) = \cos\left(x + \dfrac{\pi}{3}\right)$

7 $f(x) = \sin x,\ g(x) = 2\sin(x + \pi)$

8 $f(x) = \cos x,\ g(x) = -\cos(x - \pi)$

In Exercises 9 and 10, graph for $-2\pi \le x \le 2\pi$.

9 $y = |\sin x|$ **10** $y = -|\cos x|$

11 Graph $y = 3\sin x$, $y = \frac{1}{3}\sin x$, and $y = -3\sin x$ on the same axes for $0 \le x \le 2\pi$. Find the amplitudes.

12 Graph $y = 2\cos x$, $y = \frac{1}{2}\cos x$, and $y = -2\cos x$ on the same axes for $-\pi \le x \le \pi$. Find the amplitudes.

Sketch the curve on the interval $0 \le x \le 2\pi$. Find the amplitude and period.

13 $y = \cos 2x$ **14** $y = -\sin 2x$

15 $y = -\frac{3}{2}\sin 4x$ **16** $y = \cos 4x$

17 $y = -\cos \frac{1}{2}x$ **18** $y = -2\sin \frac{1}{2}x$

19 Find the period p of $y = \frac{1}{2}\cos \frac{1}{4}x$. Graph this curve and the curve $y = \cos x$ for $-p \le x \le p$ on the same axes.

20 Find the period p of $y = 3\sin \frac{1}{3}x$. Graph this curve and the curve $y = \sin x$ for $-p \le x \le p$ on the same axes.

21 Find the period p of $y = 2\sin \pi x$ and sketch the curve for $0 \le x \le p$.

22 Find the period p of $y = -\dfrac{3}{4}\cos \dfrac{\pi}{2}x$ and sketch the curve for $0 \le x \le p$.

In Exercises 23–26, the curve has equation of the form $y = a\sin bx$ or $y = a\cos bx$. Find a and b and write the equation.

23

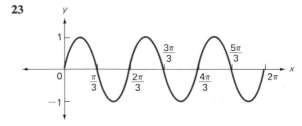

24

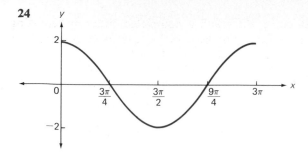

25

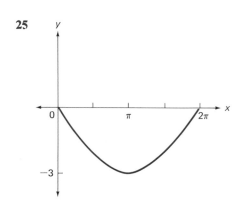

26

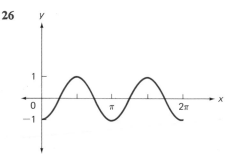

27 How can the graph of $y = \sin(2x - 1)$ be obtained from the graph of $y = \sin 2x$? (*Hint:* $2x - 1 = 2(x - \frac{1}{2})$.)

*28 Generalize the observation made in Exercise 27 and describe how the graph of $y = a \sin(bx - c)$ for $b > 0$ can be obtained from the graph of $y = \sin bx$ when $c > 0$ and when $c < 0$. Answer the same question for $y = a \cos(bx - c)$ using $y = a \cos bx$.

In Exercises 29–32, use the results of Exercise 28 to sketch the graph of the equation.

29 $y = \sin(4x - \pi)$

30 $y = \sin\left(2x + \dfrac{\pi}{2}\right)$

31 $y = 2\cos\left(2x - \dfrac{\pi}{2}\right)$

32 $y = \frac{1}{2}\cos(3x + \pi)$

Sketch the graphs of the functions for $0 \le x \le 2\pi$.

33 $f(x) = \sin x - \cos x$

34 $f(x) = 2\sin x + \cos x$

*35 $f(x) = \cos x + \cos 2x$

*36 $f(x) = \sin 2x + \frac{1}{2}\cos x$

*37 $f(x) = |\sin x| + |\cos x|$

*38 $f(x) = x + \sin x$

39 Let $f(x) = 2x + 5$ and $g(x) = \cos x$. Form the composites $f \circ g$ and $g \circ f$.

40 Let $f(x) = \sqrt{x^2 + 1}$ and $g(x) = \sin x$. Form the composites $f \circ g$ and $g \circ f$.

■ **41** Let $h(x) = \cos(5x^2)$. Find f and g so that $h = f \circ g$, where the inner function g is quadratic.

■ **42** Let $h(x) = \sin(\ln x)$. Find f and g so that $h = f \circ g$, where the outer function is trigonometric.

■ **43** Let $F(x) = \cos \sqrt[3]{1 - 2x}$. Find $f, g,$ and h so that $F = f \circ g \circ h$, where h is linear.

■ **44** Let $F(x) = \ln(\sin(x^2 - 1))$. Find $f, g,$ and h so that $F = f \circ g \circ h$, where h is a binomial.

*45 Prove that if p is the period of the function f, then $f(x + 2p) = f(x)$ for x in the domain of f.

9.2

Graphing other circular functions

Since $\tan x = \dfrac{\sin x}{\cos x}$, the properties of the tangent function depend on the sine and cosine functions. First observe that $\cos x = 0$ for $x = \pm\dfrac{\pi}{2}, \pm\dfrac{3\pi}{2},$ $\pm\dfrac{5\pi}{2}, \dots$. Therefore, the domain of $\tan x = \dfrac{\sin x}{\cos x}$ consists of all real numbers x except those of the form $x = \dfrac{\pi}{2} + k\pi$, where k is any integer.

The graph of $y = \tan x$ is symmetric through the origin since for any x in the domain, we have

$$\tan(-x) = \frac{\sin(-x)}{\cos(-x)} = \frac{-\sin x}{\cos x} = -\frac{\sin x}{\cos x} = -\tan x$$

The period of $y = \tan x$ is π, as can be observed by returning to the unit circle. Consider, for example, the case where the terminal side of an angle θ is in quadrant I; in particular, we assume that $0 < \theta < \frac{\pi}{2}$. Adding π to

It is also true that $\tan(\theta + 2\pi) = \tan\theta$. Why, then, is the period not 2π?

θ gives the angle $\theta + \pi$, whose terminal side is in quadrant III. Since the two terminal sides are on the same line, the reference triangles are congruent, and $\frac{\text{opposite}}{\text{adjacent}}$ is positive in each case. Therefore, $\tan(\theta + \pi) = \tan\theta$.

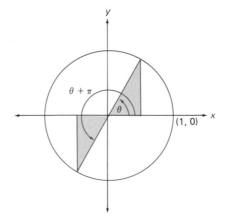

It is possible to construct the graph of $y = \tan x$ after considering the geometric interpretation of the tangent ratio as suggested in the following figure. (See also Exercise 55, page 310.)

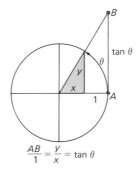

$$\frac{AB}{1} = \frac{y}{x} = \tan\theta$$

For $0 \le \theta < \frac{\pi}{2}$ put θ on the horizontal axis and place the corresponding tangent segment vertically at the end of θ. As the θ-values "unroll" along the horizontal axis, the tangent line to the circle at 0 is "stretched" and "curved" to become the tangent curve in a rectangular system.

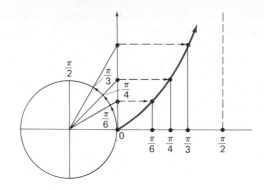

Now reflect this branch of the curve through the origin to get one full cycle on $\left(-\dfrac{\pi}{2}, \dfrac{\pi}{2}\right)$. In doing so, the variable θ has been replaced by x.

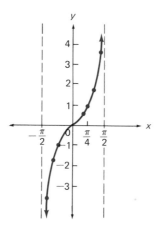

x	$\tan x$
0	0
$\dfrac{\pi}{6}$	$\dfrac{\sqrt{3}}{3}$
$\dfrac{\pi}{4}$	1
$\dfrac{\pi}{3}$	$\sqrt{3}$
1.3	3.6

←—Table V

The tangent function is increasing on $\left(-\dfrac{\pi}{2}, \dfrac{\pi}{2}\right)$. It is concave down on $\left(-\dfrac{\pi}{2}, 0\right)$ and concave up on $\left(0, \dfrac{\pi}{2}\right)$. There is no amplitude.

Notice that the vertical lines $x = \pm\dfrac{\pi}{2}$ are asymptotes to the curve. You can observe this "growth" of $y = \tan x$ by noting that as x gets close to $\dfrac{\pi}{2}$, the sine gets close to 1 and the cosine gets close to 0. Hence the fraction $\dfrac{\sin x}{\cos x}$ gets very large. This is also demonstrated by the following values taken from Table V.

θ	1.3963	1.4835	1.5533	$-\,-\,\blacktriangleright$ getting close to $\dfrac{\pi}{2} = 1.5707$.
$\sin \theta$	.9848	.9962	.9998	$-\,-\,\blacktriangleright$ getting close to 1
$\cos \theta$	.1736	.0875	.0175	$-\,-\,\blacktriangleright$ getting close to 0
$\tan \theta$	5.671	11.43	57.29	$-\,-\,\blacktriangleright$ getting very large

You can also observe this on a calculator. Enter either degree measures getting closer to 90° or radians getting closer to $\dfrac{\pi}{2}$ and watch the growth of $\tan \theta$.

Since the period of tan x is π, the preceding figure shows one cycle of the tangent function, which repeats to the left and right. The range of $y = \tan x$ consists of all real numbers.

THE TANGENT FUNCTION

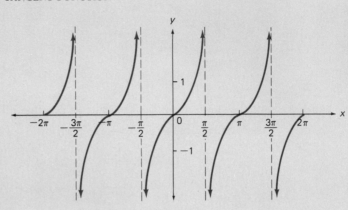

$y = \tan x$

Domain: all $x \neq \dfrac{\pi}{2} + k\pi$ where k is any integer

Range: all real numbers y

Period: π

Asymptotes: $y = \dfrac{\pi}{2} + k\pi$, k any integer

Symmetric through origin: $\tan(-x) = -\tan x$

EXAMPLE 1 Graph $y = -\tan 3x$.

Solution Since $0 \le 3x < \pi$ is equivalent to $0 \le x < \dfrac{\pi}{3}$, the period is $\dfrac{\pi}{3}$.
To graph $y = -\tan 3x$, first graph $y = \tan 3x$ and then reflect through the x-axis.

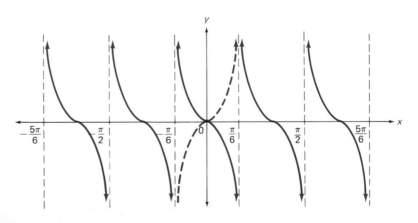

A similar analysis leads to the graph of $y = \cot x = \dfrac{\cos x}{\sin x}$.

THE COTANGENT FUNCTION

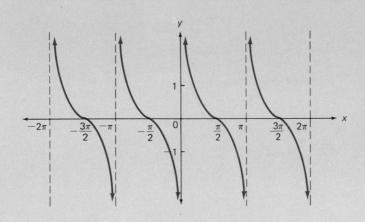

$y = \cot x$
Domain: all $x \neq k\pi$ where k is any integer
Range: all real numbers y
Period: π
Asymptotes: $x = k\pi$, k any integer
Symmetric through origin: $\cot(-x) = -\cot x$

The secant function can be graphed by making use of the cosine because $\sec x = \dfrac{1}{\cos x}$ for $\cos x \neq 0$. We need only consider $x \geq 0$ since

$$\sec(-x) = \frac{1}{\cos(-x)} = \frac{1}{\cos x} = \sec x$$

shows that the secant is symmetric with respect to the y-axis. Now consider $0 \leq x < \dfrac{\pi}{2}$. For such x take the reciprocal of $\cos x$ to get $y = \dfrac{1}{\cos x} = \sec x$. Below are some specific cases to help graph the curve.

x	0	$\dfrac{\pi}{6}$	$\dfrac{\pi}{4}$	$\dfrac{\pi}{3}$
$\cos x$	1	$\dfrac{\sqrt{3}}{2}$	$\dfrac{1}{\sqrt{2}}$	$\dfrac{1}{2}$
$\sec x$	1	$\dfrac{2}{\sqrt{3}}$	$\sqrt{2}$	2

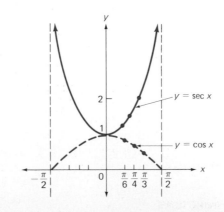

Using a calculator in the radian
mode $\left(\frac{\pi}{2} = 1.570796\ldots\right)$,
we obtain
sec 1.5 = 14
sec 1.57 = 1256
sec 1.5707 = 10381
rounded to the nearest unit.

You can see that as x gets close to $\frac{\pi}{2}$, $\cos x$ gets close to 0, and therefore the reciprocals get very large. It follows that $x = \frac{\pi}{2}$ is a vertical asymptote and, by symmetry, so is $x = -\frac{\pi}{2}$. By similar analysis the graph of $y = \sec x$ can be found for $\frac{\pi}{2} < x < \frac{3\pi}{2}$. Then the periodicity gives the rest. Note that for all x in the domain of the secant, we have

$$\sec(x + 2\pi) = \frac{1}{\cos(x + 2\pi)} = \frac{1}{\cos x} = \sec x$$

THE SECANT FUNCTION

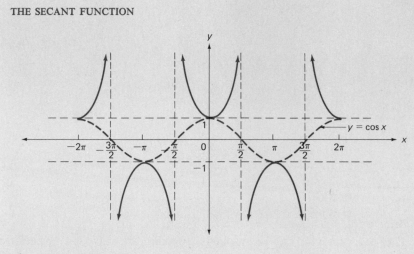

$y = \sec x$

Domain: all $x \neq \frac{\pi}{2} + k\pi$, k any integer

Range: all $y \geq 1$ and all $y \leq -1$

Period: 2π

Asymptotes: $x = \frac{\pi}{2} + k\pi$, k any integer

Symmetric about y-axis: $\sec(-x) = \sec x$

For what parts of $\left(-\frac{\pi}{2}, \frac{3\pi}{2}\right)$ is the secant increasing or decreasing? Where is the curve concave up or down? Is there an amplitude?

The properties of $y = \csc x = \dfrac{1}{\sin x}$ can be obtained from $y = \sin x$, just as the properties of the cosine were used for the secant.

THE COSECANT FUNCTION

$y = \csc x$
Domain: all $x \neq k\pi$, k any integer
Range: all $y \geq 1$ and all $y \leq -1$

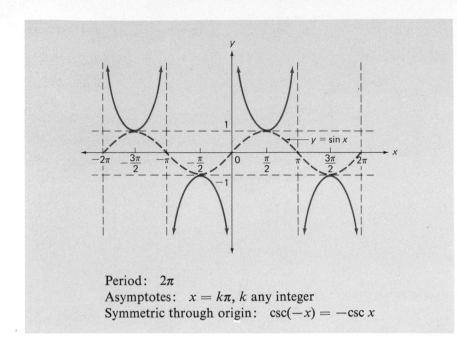

Period: 2π
Asymptotes: $x = k\pi$, k any integer
Symmetric through origin: $\csc(-x) = -\csc x$

1 Complete the following table (using Appendix Table V only if necessary) and sketch the curve $y = \tan x$ for $-\dfrac{\pi}{2} < x \le 0$. Then use the symmetry through the origin to obtain the graph for $-\dfrac{\pi}{2} < x < \dfrac{\pi}{2}$.

x	-1.4	-1.3	$-\dfrac{\pi}{3}$	$-\dfrac{\pi}{4}$	$-\dfrac{\pi}{6}$	0
$y = \tan x$						

2 (a) Verify that $\cot(x + \pi) = \cot x$ for a typical value x in quadrants I or II, using a unit circle diagram.
  (b) Complete the table of values and sketch the graph of $y = \cot x$ for $0 < x < \pi$.

x	$\dfrac{\pi}{6}$	$\dfrac{\pi}{4}$	$\dfrac{\pi}{3}$	$\dfrac{\pi}{2}$	$\dfrac{2\pi}{3}$	$\dfrac{3\pi}{4}$	$\dfrac{5\pi}{6}$
$y = \cot x$							

Use the result in part (a) to extend the graph for $\pi < x < 2\pi$.
  (c) Refer to part (b) and discuss when the cotangent is increasing or decreasing, and where the curve is concave up or down.

3 (a) Show that the cotangent is symmetric through the origin by verifying that $\cot(-x) = -\cot x$.
  (b) Repeat part (a) for the cosecant.
  (c) Verify that $\csc(x + 2\pi) = \csc x$.

In Exercises 4–7, sketch the graph of f by making an appropriate shift of the graph of g.

4 $f(x) = \tan\left(x - \dfrac{\pi}{2}\right)$; $g(x) = \tan x$

5 $f(x) = \cot\left(x + \dfrac{\pi}{2}\right)$; $g(x) = \cot x$

6 $f(x) = \sec\left(x + \dfrac{\pi}{4}\right)$; $g(x) = \sec x$

7 $f(x) = \csc\left(x - \dfrac{\pi}{3}\right)$; $g(x) = \csc x$

8 Compare the graph of the tangent and cotangent and decide which of the following equations are identities.
  (a) $\cot x = -\tan x$

(b) $\tan x = \cot\left(x + \dfrac{\pi}{2}\right)$

(c) $\cot x = -\tan\left(x - \dfrac{\pi}{2}\right)$

In Exercises 9–17, sketch the graph of the equation, including at least two cycles. Indicate the period and vertical asymptotes.

9 $y = \cot 3x$

10 $y = \tan 2x$

11 $y = -2 \cot \dfrac{x}{2}$

12 $y = \dfrac{1}{2} \tan \dfrac{x}{2}$

13 $y = \sec 4x$

14 $y = -\sec x$

15 $y = -\csc \frac{1}{3}x$

16 $y = \csc 2x$

17 $y = 2 \sec \dfrac{3x}{2}$

Sketch the graph of the equations.

18 $y = |\sec x|$

19 $y = |\tan x|$

20 $y = -|\cot x|$

21 Let $f(x) = x^2$ and $g(x) = \tan x$. Form the composites $f \circ g$ and $g \circ f$.

22 Let $f(x) = \dfrac{x}{x + 1}$ and $g(x) = \sec x$. Form the composites $f \circ g$ and $g \circ f$.

23 Let $f(x) = e^x$, $g(x) = \sqrt{x}$, and $h(x) = \sec x$. Form the composites $f \circ g \circ h$, $g \circ f \circ h$, and $h \circ g \circ f$.

■ **24** Let $h(x) = \cot^3 x$. Find f and g so that $h = f \circ g$, where the outer function f is a polynomial.

■ **25** Let $F(x) = \sqrt{\tan(2x + 1)}$. Find f, g, and h so that $F = f \circ g \circ h$ and g is trigonometric.

■ **26** Let $F(x) = \tan^2\left(\dfrac{x + 1}{x - 1}\right)$. Find f, g, and h so that $F = f \circ g \circ h$, where h is rational and f is quadratic.

■ **27** Refer to the figure and explain why $0 < \dfrac{\sin \theta}{\theta} < 1$ for $0 < \theta < \dfrac{\pi}{2}$. (*Hint:* In a unit circle the central angle in radians is the same as the length of the intercepted arc.)

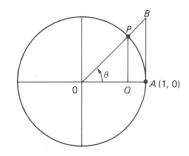

■ **28** Refer to the figure in Exercise 27 and prove that $\cos \theta < \dfrac{\sin \theta}{\theta} < \dfrac{1}{\cos \theta}$ for $0 < \theta < \dfrac{\pi}{2}$. (*Hint:* Use the areas of the two right triangles and the sector of the circle.)

9.3

The addition and subtraction formulas

Is it true that $\cos(30° + 60°) = \cos 30° + \cos 60°$? Some quick calculations show that it is not.

$$\cos(30° + 60°) = \cos 90° = 0 \qquad \text{but} \qquad \cos 30° + \cos 60° = \frac{\sqrt{3}}{2} + \frac{1}{2}$$

To write $\cos(\theta_1 + \theta_2) = \cos \theta_1 + \cos \theta_2$ would be to assume, incorrectly, that the cosine function obeys the distributive property. We emphasize that cos is the *name* of a function; it is not a number.

The cosine of the sum of two angles is correctly evaluated by using Formula (3) as follows; it is one of several important trigonometric identities in *two* variables that give the trigonometric values of sums and differences.

ADDITION AND SUBTRACTION FORMULAS

(1) $\qquad\qquad \sin(\alpha + \beta) = \sin \alpha \cos \beta + \cos \alpha \sin \beta$

(2) $\qquad\qquad \sin(\alpha - \beta) = \sin \alpha \cos \beta - \cos \alpha \sin \beta$

(3)	$\cos(\alpha + \beta) = \cos\alpha\cos\beta - \sin\alpha\sin\beta$	$\cos(30° + 60°)$
(4)	$\cos(\alpha - \beta) = \cos\alpha\cos\beta + \sin\alpha\sin\beta$	$= \cos 30° \cos 60°$ $\quad - \sin 30° \sin 60°$
(5)	$\tan(\alpha + \beta) = \dfrac{\tan\alpha + \tan\beta}{1 - \tan\alpha\tan\beta}$	$= \dfrac{\sqrt{3}}{2} \cdot \dfrac{1}{2} - \dfrac{1}{2} \cdot \dfrac{\sqrt{3}}{2}$ $= 0 = \cos 90°$
(6)	$\tan(\alpha - \beta) = \dfrac{\tan\alpha - \tan\beta}{1 + \tan\alpha\tan\beta}$	

These formulas are stated in terms of the variables α and β, which can represent angles measured in either degrees or radians (real numbers.) We now prove Formula (4) by making use of the unit circle.

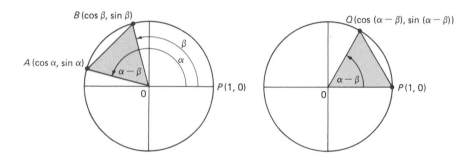

The unit circle at the left contains a typical situation in which $\alpha > \beta$. Since point A is on the unit circle, we find that the coordinates of A are $(\cos\alpha, \sin\alpha)$. Similarly, B has coordinates $(\cos\beta, \sin\beta)$. Then, by the distance formula applied to points A and B,

$$(AB)^2 = (\cos\alpha - \cos\beta)^2 + (\sin\alpha - \sin\beta)^2$$
$$= (\cos^2\alpha - 2\cos\alpha\cos\beta + \cos^2\beta) + (\sin^2\alpha - 2\sin\alpha\sin\beta + \sin^2\beta)$$
$$= (\cos^2\alpha + \sin^2\alpha) + (\cos^2\beta + \sin^2\beta) - 2(\cos\alpha\cos\beta + \sin\alpha\sin\beta)$$
$$= 2 - 2(\cos\alpha\cos\beta + \sin\alpha\sin\beta)$$

In the unit circle at the right the central angle $\alpha - \beta$ is in standard position. Therefore, the coordinates of Q are $(\cos(\alpha - \beta), \sin(\alpha - \beta))$. Using the distance formula for points P and Q, we have

$$(PQ)^2 = [\cos(\alpha - \beta) - 1]^2 + [\sin(\alpha - \beta) - 0]^2$$
$$= \cos^2(\alpha - \beta) - 2\cos(\alpha - \beta) + 1 + \sin^2(\alpha - \beta)$$
$$= 2 - 2\cos(\alpha - \beta)$$

Triangles AOB and QOP are congruent. (SAS) Then $AB = PQ$ and this implies $(AB)^2 = (PQ)^2$. We may therefore equate the preceding results and then simplify.

$$2 - 2\cos(\alpha - \beta) = 2 - 2(\cos\alpha\cos\beta + \sin\alpha\sin\beta)$$
$$\cos(\alpha - \beta) = \cos\alpha\cos\beta + \sin\alpha\sin\beta$$

Formula (3) is now easy to prove by using Formula (4). The trick is to write $\alpha + \beta = \alpha - (-\beta)$.

$$\cos(\alpha + \beta) = \cos(\alpha - (-\beta))$$
$$= \cos\alpha\cos(-\beta) + \sin\alpha\sin(-\beta) \qquad \text{(by (4))}$$
$$= \cos\alpha\cos\beta + (\sin\alpha)(-\sin\beta) \qquad (\cos(-\theta) = \cos\theta,$$
$$\sin(-\theta) = -\sin\theta)$$
$$= \cos\alpha\cos\beta - \sin\alpha\sin\beta$$

The proofs of Formulas (1) and (2) will be called for in the exercises.

EXAMPLE 1 Evaluate $\sin\dfrac{7\pi}{12}$ and $\tan\dfrac{7\pi}{12}$ by using $\dfrac{7\pi}{12} = \dfrac{\pi}{4} + \dfrac{\pi}{3}$. State the answers in radical form.

Solution Use Formulas (1) and (5) with $\alpha = \dfrac{\pi}{4},\ \beta = \dfrac{\pi}{3}$.

$$\sin\frac{7}{12}\pi = \sin\left(\frac{\pi}{4} + \frac{\pi}{3}\right)$$
$$= \sin\frac{\pi}{4}\cos\frac{\pi}{3} + \cos\frac{\pi}{4}\sin\frac{\pi}{3}$$
$$= \frac{\sqrt{2}}{2}\cdot\frac{1}{2} + \frac{\sqrt{2}}{2}\cdot\frac{\sqrt{3}}{2}$$
$$= \frac{1}{4}(\sqrt{2} + \sqrt{6})$$

$$\tan\frac{7}{12}\pi = \tan\left(\frac{\pi}{4} + \frac{\pi}{3}\right)$$
$$= \frac{\tan\dfrac{\pi}{4} + \tan\dfrac{\pi}{3}}{1 - \tan\dfrac{\pi}{4}\tan\dfrac{\pi}{3}}$$
$$= \frac{1 + \sqrt{3}}{1 - \sqrt{3}}$$

TEST YOUR UNDERSTANDING

Complete each equation to get a specific case of an addition or subtraction formula.

1 $\sin 5°\cos 12° + \cos 5°\sin 12° = \ ?$

2 $\cos\dfrac{3\pi}{10}\cos\dfrac{\pi}{5} + \sin\dfrac{3\pi}{10}\sin\dfrac{\pi}{5} = \ ?$

3 $\dfrac{\tan(-15°) - \tan(-20°)}{1 + \tan(-15°)\tan(-20°)} = \ ?$

4 $\sin(\theta + 5°) \cos(\theta - 5°) - \cos(\theta + 5°) \sin(\theta - 5°) = ?$

State the answers to these exercises in radical form.

5 Use $15° = 45° - 30°$ and appropriate subtraction formulas to evaluate $\sin 15°$, $\cos 15°$, and $\tan 15°$.

6 Repeat Exercise 5 with $15° = 60° - 45°$.

7 Use $\dfrac{11\pi}{12} = \dfrac{\pi}{6} + \dfrac{3\pi}{4}$ and appropriate addition formulas to evaluate $\sin \dfrac{11\pi}{12}$, $\cos \dfrac{11\pi}{12}$, and $\tan \dfrac{11\pi}{12}$.

8 Repeat Exercise 7 with $\dfrac{11\pi}{12} = \dfrac{7\pi}{6} - \dfrac{\pi}{4}$ using subtraction formulas.

9 Use an addition or subtraction formula to evaluate $\sin 195°$.

10 Use an addition or subtraction formula to evaluate $\cos \dfrac{5\pi}{12}$.

Formulas (1) and (3) can be used to verify the addition formula for the tangent function.

$$\tan(\alpha + \beta) = \frac{\sin(\alpha + \beta)}{\cos(\alpha + \beta)} = \frac{\sin \alpha \cos \beta + \cos \alpha \sin \beta}{\cos \alpha \cos \beta - \sin \alpha \sin \beta}$$

Divide the numerator and denominator by $\cos \alpha \cos \beta$.

$$\tan(\alpha + \beta) = \frac{\dfrac{\sin \alpha \cos \beta}{\cos \alpha \cos \beta} + \dfrac{\cos \alpha \sin \beta}{\cos \alpha \cos \beta}}{\dfrac{\cos \alpha \cos \beta}{\cos \alpha \cos \beta} - \dfrac{\sin \alpha \sin \beta}{\cos \alpha \cos \beta}}$$

Thus

(5)
$$\tan(\alpha + \beta) = \frac{\tan \alpha + \tan \beta}{1 - \tan \alpha \tan \beta}$$

A similar analysis will verify Formula (6).

With the aid of the addition and subtraction formulas, we will be able to derive other useful formulas, some of which have already been encountered. For example, the result $\cos \theta = \sin\left(\theta + \dfrac{\pi}{2}\right)$ was derived in Section 9.1 by using the unit circle. This formula can be described as a *reduction formula* in the sense that a trigonometric function of $\theta + \dfrac{\pi}{2}$ is "reduced" to a trigonometric function of just θ.

REDUCTION FORMULAS

$\sin(\theta - 2\pi) =$	$\sin \theta$	$\sin(\theta + 2\pi) =$	$\sin \theta$
$\cos(\theta - 2\pi) =$	$\cos \theta$	$\cos(\theta + 2\pi) =$	$\cos \theta$
$\tan(\theta - \pi) =$	$\tan \theta$	$\tan(\theta + \pi) =$	$\tan \theta$

Each of these results may be restated in degrees; for example, $\cos(180° - \theta) = -\cos \theta$. They are collected here and on the top of the next page for easy reference.

$$\sin(\pi - \theta) = \sin\theta \qquad \sin(\pi + \theta) = -\sin\theta$$
$$\cos(\pi - \theta) = -\cos\theta \qquad \cos(\pi + \theta) = -\cos\theta$$
$$\tan(\pi - \theta) = -\tan\theta \qquad \tan(\pi + \theta) = \tan\theta$$
$$\sin\left(\frac{\pi}{2} - \theta\right) = \cos\theta \qquad \sin\left(\frac{\pi}{2} + \theta\right) = \cos\theta$$
$$\cos\left(\frac{\pi}{2} - \theta\right) = \sin\theta \qquad \cos\left(\frac{\pi}{2} + \theta\right) = -\sin\theta$$
$$\tan\left(\frac{\pi}{2} - \theta\right) = \cot\theta \qquad \tan\left(\frac{\pi}{2} + \theta\right) = -\cot\theta$$

Formulas (3) and (4) can be used to prove two of the preceding reduction formulas. Others will be taken up in the exercises.

$$\cos\left(\frac{\pi}{2} - \theta\right) = \cos\frac{\pi}{2}\cos\theta + \sin\frac{\pi}{2}\sin\theta \qquad \text{(by Formula (4))}$$
$$= 0\cdot\cos\theta + (1)\sin\theta$$
$$= \sin\theta$$
$$\cos(\pi + \theta) = \cos\pi\cos\theta - \sin\pi\sin\theta \qquad \text{(by Formula (3))}$$
$$= (-1)\cos\theta - 0\cdot\sin\theta$$
$$= -\cos\theta$$

The reduction formulas involving the tangent can be obtained from the results for the sine and cosine. Thus

Why can't the formula for $\tan(\alpha - \beta)$ be used here?

$$\tan\left(\frac{\pi}{2} - \theta\right) = \frac{\sin\left(\dfrac{\pi}{2} - \theta\right)}{\cos\left(\dfrac{\pi}{2} - \theta\right)} = \frac{\cos\theta}{\sin\theta} = \cot\theta$$

From the reduction formulas we see that the function of an acute angle θ is equal to the co-named function of its complement, $\frac{\pi}{2} - \theta$. For example:

$$\sin 30° = \cos 60°$$
$$\tan 52° = \cot 38°$$
$$\sec 17° = \csc 73°$$

EXAMPLE 2   Verify the identity $\sin\left(\theta + \frac{\pi}{3}\right) = \frac{1}{2}(\sin\theta + \sqrt{3}\cos\theta)$.

Solution   Use Formula (1).

$$\sin\left(\theta + \frac{\pi}{3}\right) = \sin\theta\cos\frac{\pi}{3} + \cos\theta\sin\frac{\pi}{3}$$
$$= \frac{1}{2}\sin\theta + \frac{\sqrt{3}}{2}\cos\theta$$
$$= \frac{1}{2}(\sin\theta + \sqrt{3}\cos\theta)$$

EXAMPLE 3 Let $\cos \alpha = -\frac{4}{5}$ and $\cos \beta = -\frac{12}{13}$ where α and β have terminal sides in quadrants II and III, respectively. Find $\cos(\alpha - \beta)$.

Solution Place α and β in standard position and draw reference triangles. Since $\cos \alpha = \dfrac{-4}{5} = \dfrac{\text{adjacent}}{\text{hypotenuse}}$, the triangle for α has hypotenuse 5 and adjacent side -4. The third side is 3 by the Pythagorean theorem. Similarly, the triangle for β has sides 13, -12, -5.

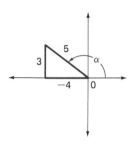
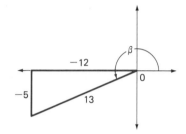

Although a unit circle is not used here, triangles such as these may be used since the ratios do not depend on the size of the triangle.

$$\cos(\alpha - \beta) = \cos \alpha \cos \beta + \sin \alpha \sin \beta$$
$$= (-\tfrac{4}{5})(-\tfrac{12}{13}) + (\tfrac{3}{5})(-\tfrac{5}{13})$$
$$= \tfrac{48}{65} - \tfrac{15}{65}$$
$$= \tfrac{33}{65}$$

EXERCISES 9.3

In Exercises 1–4, use an addition or subtraction formula to evaluate the expression. Do not use Table V or a calculator.

1 $\cos 22° \cos 38° - \sin 22° \sin 38°$

2 $\sin 52° \cos 7° - \cos 52° \sin 7°$

3 $\dfrac{\tan 25° - \tan 55°}{1 + \tan 25° \tan 55°}$

4 $\cos \dfrac{5\pi}{12} \cos \dfrac{7\pi}{12} + \sin \dfrac{5\pi}{12} \sin \dfrac{7\pi}{12}$

In Exercises 5–12, use the addition or subtraction formulas to evaluate $\sin \theta$, $\cos \theta$, and $\tan \theta$ for the specified value of θ.

5 $\theta = 75°$

6 $\theta = 105°$

7 $\theta = \dfrac{\pi}{12}$

8 $\theta = \dfrac{19\pi}{12}$

9 $\theta = 165°$

10 $\theta = 345°$

11 $\theta = \dfrac{17\pi}{12}$

12 $\theta = \dfrac{7\pi}{3}$

For Exercises 13–16, prove the reduction formula by using an appropriate addition or subtration formula.

13 $\sin(\pi - \theta) = \sin \theta$

14 $\cos\left(\dfrac{\pi}{2} + \theta\right) = -\sin \theta$

15 $\tan(\pi - \theta) = -\tan \theta$

16 $\cos(\theta - 2\pi) = \cos \theta$

17 If α and β are acute angles having $\sin \alpha = \frac{3}{5}$ and $\cos \beta = \frac{12}{13}$, find $\sin(\alpha - \beta)$ and $\tan(\alpha + \beta)$.

18 Suppose that $\sin \alpha$ and $\cos \beta$ are the same as in Exercise 17, but α is in quadrant II and β is in quandrant IV. Find $\sin(\alpha - \beta)$ and $\tan(\alpha + \beta)$.

19 Find $\sin(\alpha + \beta)$ and $\cos(\alpha + \beta)$ for α in quadrant III and β in quadrant IV, where $\sin \alpha = -\frac{1}{3}$ and $\cos \beta = \frac{2}{3}$.

20 Let $\cos \alpha = \frac{24}{25}$ with α in quadrant I, and $\tan \beta = -\frac{15}{8}$ with β in quadrant II. Find $\cos(\alpha - \beta)$ and $\tan(\alpha - \beta)$.

21 Evaluate the following ratios by using a reduction formula that calls for a ratio of an acute angle. Thus $\cos 155° = \cos(180° - 25°) = -\cos 25° = -.9063$, from Table V.

(a) $\cos 191°$ **(b)** $\sin 132°$

(c) $\tan 200°$ **(d)** $\cos \dfrac{17\pi}{30}$

In Exercises 22–36, use addition or subtraction formulas to verify the identity.

22 $\tan\left(\dfrac{\pi}{4} + \theta\right) = \dfrac{1 + \tan\theta}{1 - \tan\theta}$

23 $\cos\left(\theta - \dfrac{\pi}{4}\right) = \dfrac{\sqrt{2}}{2}(\cos\theta + \sin\theta)$

24 $\sin\left(\dfrac{\pi}{6} - \theta\right) = \dfrac{1}{2}(\cos\theta - \sqrt{3}\sin\theta)$

25 $\cos(\theta + 30°) + \cos(\theta - 30°) = \sqrt{3}\cos\theta$

26 $\cos\left(\theta + \dfrac{\pi}{6}\right) + \sin\left(\theta - \dfrac{\pi}{3}\right) = 0$

27 $\dfrac{\sin\left(\theta + \dfrac{\pi}{2}\right)}{\cos\left(\theta + \dfrac{\pi}{2}\right)} = -\cot\theta$

28 $\sec\left(\dfrac{\pi}{2} - \theta\right) = \csc\theta$

29 $\csc(\pi - \theta) = \csc\theta$

30 $\cos(\alpha + \beta) + \cos(\alpha - \beta) = 2\cos\alpha\cos\beta$

31 $\sin(\alpha + \beta) - \sin(\alpha - \beta) = 2\cos\alpha\sin\beta$

32 $\dfrac{\sin(\alpha - \beta)}{\cos(\alpha + \beta)} = \dfrac{\cot\beta - \cot\alpha}{\cot\alpha\cot\beta - 1}$

33 $\dfrac{\sin(\alpha + \beta)}{\sin(\alpha - \beta)} = \dfrac{\tan\alpha + \tan\beta}{\tan\alpha - \tan\beta}$

*34 $\cos(\alpha + \beta)\cos(\alpha - \beta) = \cos^2\alpha - \sin^2\beta$

*35 $2\sin\left(\dfrac{\pi}{4} - \theta\right)\sin\left(\dfrac{\pi}{4} + \theta\right) = \cos^2\theta - \sin^2\theta$

*36 $\cos\alpha\cos(\alpha - \beta) + \sin\alpha\sin(\alpha - \beta) = \cos\beta$

37 Let $x = \dfrac{\pi}{2} - \theta$ in the equation $\cos\left(\dfrac{\pi}{2} - x\right) = \sin x$. Then prove that $\sin\left(\dfrac{\pi}{2} - \theta\right) = \cos\theta$.

38 Prove addition formula (1). $\left(\textit{Hint: Begin with} \right.$ $\sin(\alpha + \beta) = \cos\left[\dfrac{\pi}{2} - (\alpha + \beta)\right]$ and note that $\dfrac{\pi}{2} - (\alpha + \beta) = \left(\dfrac{\pi}{2} - \alpha\right) - \beta.\left.\right)$

39 Use addition formula (1) to prove (2). (*Hint:* Use $\alpha - \beta = \alpha + (-\beta)$.)

40 Use addition formula (5) to prove (6). (*Hint:* Use $\alpha - \beta = \alpha + (-\beta)$.)

41 Derive $\cot(\alpha + \beta) = \dfrac{\cot\alpha\cot\beta - 1}{\cot\alpha + \cot\beta}$ by forming $\dfrac{\cos(\alpha + \beta)}{\sin(\alpha + \beta)}$ and using Formulas (1) and (3).

42 Derive the formula in Exercise 41 by forming $\dfrac{1}{\tan(\alpha + \beta)}$ and using Formula (5).

43 Explain how the graph of the sine can be obtained from the cosine curve by using the reduction formula $\cos\left(\dfrac{\pi}{2} + \theta\right) = -\sin\theta$.

44 Explain how the graph of the sine can be obtained from the cosine curve by using the reduction formula $\cos\left(\dfrac{\pi}{2} - \theta\right) = \sin\theta$.

■ 45 Let $f(x) = \sin x$. Prove:
$$\dfrac{f(x + h) - f(x)}{h}$$
$$= \left(\dfrac{\cos h - 1}{h}\right)\sin x + \left(\dfrac{\sin h}{h}\right)\cos x$$

46 Let α, β be acute angles such that $\tan\alpha = \dfrac{3}{5}$ and $\tan\beta = \dfrac{1}{4}$. Find $\alpha + \beta$.

*47 Find $\tan\beta$ for β in the given figure. (*Hint:* Use the formula for $\tan(\alpha + \beta)$.)

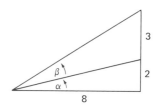

■ 48 Use a calculator to complete this table where h is given in radians.

h	1	0.5	0.25	0.1	0.01
$\dfrac{\sin h}{h}$					

As h approaches 0 in value, what appears to be happening to the ratio $\dfrac{\sin h}{h}$?

The formula $\sin(\alpha + \beta) = \sin \alpha \cos \beta + \cos \alpha \sin \beta$ is true for all values of α and β. If, in particular, we let $\beta = \alpha$, then

$$\sin 2\alpha = \sin(\alpha + \alpha) = \sin \alpha \cos \alpha + \cos \alpha \sin \alpha$$

Consequently, we have the following *double-angle formula*:

(7) $$\sin 2\alpha = 2 \sin \alpha \cos \alpha$$

Next use $\alpha = \beta$ in the formula for $\cos(\alpha + \beta)$:

$$\cos(\alpha + \beta) = \cos \alpha \cos \beta - \sin \alpha \sin \beta$$
$$\cos 2\alpha = \cos(\alpha + \alpha) = \cos \alpha \cos \alpha - \sin \alpha \sin \alpha$$

Thus a double-angle formula for the cosine is

(8) $$\cos 2\alpha = \cos^2 \alpha - \sin^2 \alpha$$

Since $\cos^2 \alpha = 1 - \sin^2 \alpha$, Formula (8) may be written as

(9) $$\cos 2\alpha = 1 - 2 \sin^2 \alpha$$

Similarly, using $\sin^2 \alpha = 1 - \cos^2 \alpha$, we have

(10) $$\cos 2\alpha = 2 \cos^2 \alpha - 1$$

Substituting $\alpha = \beta$ in $\tan(\alpha + \beta) = \dfrac{\tan \alpha + \tan \beta}{1 - \tan \alpha \tan \beta}$ gives

(11) $$\tan 2\alpha = \frac{2 \tan \alpha}{1 - \tan^2\alpha}$$

Here is a summary of the double-angle formulas stated in terms of the variable θ.

DOUBLE-ANGLE FORMULAS

(7) $$\sin 2\theta = 2 \sin \theta \cos \theta$$

(8) $$\cos 2\theta = \cos^2\theta - \sin^2\theta$$

(9) $$\cos 2\theta = 1 - 2 \sin^2\theta$$

(10) $$\cos 2\theta = 2 \cos^2\theta - 1$$

(11) $$\tan 2\theta = \frac{2 \tan \theta}{1 - \tan^2\theta}$$

EXAMPLE 1   Evaluate $\sin 15° \cos 15°$ using a double-angle formula.

Solution   Rewrite $2 \sin \theta \cos \theta = \sin 2\theta$ in the equivalent form

$$\sin \theta \cos \theta = \tfrac{1}{2} \sin 2\theta$$

Then

$$\sin 15° \cos 15° = \tfrac{1}{2} \sin 2(15°)$$
$$= \tfrac{1}{2} \sin 30°$$
$$= \tfrac{1}{2}(\tfrac{1}{2})$$
$$= \tfrac{1}{4}$$

TEST YOUR UNDERSTANDING

Complete each equation to obtain a special case of a double-angle formula.

1 $2 \sin 5° \cos 5° = ?$

2 $\dfrac{2 \tan \dfrac{\theta}{2}}{1 - \tan^2 \dfrac{\theta}{2}} = ?$

3 $2 \cos^2 3\theta - 1 = ?$

4 $\cos^2 \dfrac{\alpha}{6} - \sin^2 \dfrac{\alpha}{6} = ?$

Evaluate the following using the double-angle formulas.

5 $\cos^2 15° - \sin^2 15°$

6 $2 \sin \dfrac{\pi}{8} \cos \dfrac{\pi}{8}$

7 $\dfrac{4 \tan(22°30')}{1 - \tan^2(22°30')}$

8 $2 \sin^2 \dfrac{\pi}{12} - 1$

EXAMPLE 2   If θ is obtuse such that $\sin \theta = \frac{5}{13}$, find $\sin 2\theta$, $\cos 2\theta$, and $\tan 2\theta$.

Solution   Since θ is in quadrant II, and $\sin \theta = \frac{5}{13} = \dfrac{\text{opposite}}{\text{hypotenuse}}$, the third side of the reference triangle is found using the Pythagorean theorem; $-\sqrt{13^2 - 5^2} = -12$.

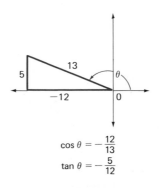

$$\cos \theta = -\frac{12}{13}$$
$$\tan \theta = -\frac{5}{12}$$

Then, from the reference triangle,

$$\sin 2\theta = 2(\tfrac{5}{13})(-\tfrac{12}{13}) \qquad \text{Formula (7)}$$

$$= -\tfrac{120}{169}$$

$$\cos 2\theta = 2(-\tfrac{12}{13})^2 - 1 \qquad \text{Formula (10)}$$

$$= \tfrac{119}{169}$$

$$\tan 2\theta = \frac{2(-\tfrac{5}{12})}{1 - (-\tfrac{5}{12})^2} \qquad \text{Formula (11)}$$

$$= -\tfrac{120}{119}$$

Note: $\cos \theta$ and $\tan \theta$ can also be found without using a reference triangle. Thus

$$\cos \theta = -\sqrt{1 - \sin^2 \theta}$$
$$= -\sqrt{1 - \tfrac{25}{169}}$$
$$= -\tfrac{12}{13}$$

$$\tan \theta = \frac{\sin \theta}{\cos \theta} = \frac{\tfrac{5}{13}}{-\tfrac{12}{13}}$$
$$= -\tfrac{5}{12}$$

EXAMPLE 3 Let θ be an acute angle of a right triangle where $\sin \theta = \frac{x}{2}$. Show that $\sin 2\theta = \frac{x\sqrt{4 - x^2}}{2}$

Solution Since $\sin \theta = \frac{x}{2}$, use x as the side opposite θ and 2 as the hypotenuse. The Pythagorean theorem gives the third side. Now use Formula (7) to solve for $\sin 2\theta$.

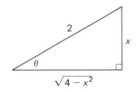

$$\sin 2\theta = 2 \sin \theta \cos \theta$$

$$= 2\left(\frac{x}{2}\right)\left(\frac{\sqrt{4 - x^2}}{2}\right)$$

$$= \frac{x\sqrt{4 - x^2}}{2}$$

EXAMPLE 4 Show that $\cos 3\theta = 4 \cos^3 \theta - 3 \cos \theta$.

Solution

$$\cos 3\theta = \cos(2\theta + \theta)$$

$$= \cos 2\theta \cos \theta - \sin 2\theta \sin \theta \qquad \text{by (3)}$$

$$= (2 \cos^2 \theta - 1) \cos \theta - (2 \sin \theta \cos \theta) \sin \theta \qquad \text{by (10) and (7)}$$

$$= 2 \cos^3 \theta - \cos \theta - 2 \cos \theta \sin^2 \theta$$

$$= 2 \cos^3 \theta - \cos \theta - 2 \cos \theta(1 - \cos^2 \theta)$$

$$= 4 \cos^3 \theta - 3 \cos \theta$$

Formula (9) may be solved for $\sin^2 \alpha$ as follows:

$$\cos 2\alpha = 1 - 2\sin^2 \alpha$$

$$2\sin^2 \alpha = 1 - \cos 2\alpha$$

(12)
$$\sin^2 \alpha = \frac{1 - \cos 2\alpha}{2}$$

Similarly, Formula (10) produces a formula for $\cos^2 \alpha$ and the result for $\tan^2 \alpha$ is found using $\dfrac{\sin^2 \alpha}{\cos^2 \alpha}$.

(12)
$$\sin^2 \theta = \frac{1 - \cos 2\theta}{2}$$

(13)
$$\cos^2 \theta = \frac{1 + \cos 2\theta}{2}$$

(14)
$$\tan^2 \theta = \frac{1 - \cos 2\theta}{1 + \cos 2\theta}$$

Notice that these identities convert the second power of a trigonometric function into an expression involving only the first power. This type of reduction makes these identities useful when it is necessary to reduce the powers within a given trigonometric expression.

EXAMPLE 5 Convert $\sin^4 \theta$ to an expression involving only the first power of the cosine.

Solution
$$\sin^4 \theta = (\sin^2 \theta)^2$$

$$= \left(\frac{1 - \cos 2\theta}{2} \right)^2 \qquad \text{by (12)}$$

$$= \frac{1 - 2\cos 2\theta + \cos^2 2\theta}{4}$$

$$= \tfrac{1}{4} - \tfrac{1}{2}\cos 2\theta + \tfrac{1}{4}\cos^2 2\theta$$

$$= \tfrac{1}{4} - \tfrac{1}{2}\cos 2\theta + \tfrac{1}{4}\left(\frac{1 + \cos 4\theta}{2} \right) \qquad \text{by (13)}$$

$$= \tfrac{1}{4} - \tfrac{1}{2}\cos 2\theta + \tfrac{1}{8} + \tfrac{1}{8}\cos 4\theta$$

$$= \tfrac{3}{8} - \tfrac{1}{2}\cos 2\theta + \tfrac{1}{8}\cos 4\theta$$

Since (12) is an identity for all values of θ, we may change the form of θ by writing $\theta = \dfrac{\phi}{2}$ and substitute to obtain the half-angle formula for the sine function.

$$\sin^2 \frac{\phi}{2} = \frac{1 - \cos \phi}{2}$$

(15) $\sin\dfrac{\phi}{2} = \pm\sqrt{\dfrac{1-\cos\phi}{2}}$ (if $x^2 = a$, then $x = \pm\sqrt{a}$)

When using this formula, the appropriate sign will depend on the location of the terminal side of $\dfrac{\phi}{2}$.

EXAMPLE 6   Evaluate $\sin 15°$ by using the half-angle formula.

Solution   Note that $15° = \dfrac{30°}{2}$ is in quadrant I. Therefore, we use the plus sign in the half-angle formula for $\sin\dfrac{\phi}{2}$:

$$\sin 15° = \sqrt{\frac{1-\cos 30°}{2}} = \sqrt{\frac{1-\dfrac{\sqrt{3}}{2}}{2}} = \frac{\sqrt{2-\sqrt{3}}}{2}$$

Following the procedure used to get the formula for $\sin\dfrac{\phi}{2}$ from (12), half-angle formulas for the cosine and tangent are obtained from (13) and (14), respectively. These results are summarized in terms of the variable θ.

HALF-ANGLE FORMULAS

(15) $\sin\dfrac{\theta}{2} = \pm\sqrt{\dfrac{1-\cos\theta}{2}}$

(16) $\cos\dfrac{\theta}{2} = \pm\sqrt{\dfrac{1+\cos\theta}{2}}$

(17) $\tan\dfrac{\theta}{2} = \pm\sqrt{\dfrac{1-\cos\theta}{1+\cos\theta}}$

The plus or minus sign depends on the location of the terminal side of $\dfrac{\theta}{2}$.

In Exercises 45 and 46, you will find the following equivalent forms for $\tan\dfrac{\theta}{2}$.

(18) $\tan\dfrac{\theta}{2} = \dfrac{1-\cos\theta}{\sin\theta} = \dfrac{\sin\theta}{1+\cos\theta}$

EXAMPLE 7   Solve for b without using Table V or a calculator.

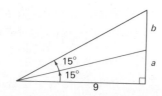

Show that the same result is
obtained by using the form
$$\tan 15° = \frac{\sin 30°}{1 + \cos 30°}$$

Solution   From the preceding figure $\tan 15° = \dfrac{a}{9}$. Also, using (18),

$$\tan 15° = \tan \frac{30°}{2} = \frac{1 - \cos 30°}{\sin 30°}$$

$$= \frac{1 - \dfrac{\sqrt{3}}{2}}{\dfrac{1}{2}}$$

$$= 2 - \sqrt{3}$$

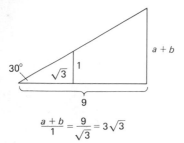

$$\frac{a+b}{1} = \frac{9}{\sqrt{3}} = 3\sqrt{3}$$

Then

$$\frac{a}{9} = 2 - \sqrt{3} \qquad \text{or} \qquad a = 18 - 9\sqrt{3}$$

But $a + b = 3\sqrt{3}$, since $a + b$ is opposite 30° in a 30°–60°–90° triangle where the adjacent side is 9. Therefore,

$$b = 3\sqrt{3} - a = 3\sqrt{3} - (18 - 9\sqrt{3})$$

$$= 12\sqrt{3} - 18$$

CAUTION: LEARN TO AVOID MISTAKES LIKE THESE

WRONG	RIGHT
$\sin 4x = 4 \sin x$	$\sin 4x = \sin 2(2x) = 2 \sin 2x \cos 2x$
$\cos^4 x = \dfrac{1 + \cos^2 2x}{2}$	$\cos^4 x = \left(\dfrac{1 + \cos 2x}{2}\right)^2$

EXERCISES 9.4

In Exercises 1–4, evaluate the expression using an appropriate double-angle formula. Do not use Table V or a calculator.

1 $1 - 2 \sin^2 \dfrac{7\pi}{12}$

2 $\sin 105° \cos 105°$

3 $\dfrac{6 \tan 75°}{1 - \tan^2 75°}$

4 $\dfrac{1}{4}\left(\cos^2 \dfrac{3\pi}{8} - \sin^2 \dfrac{3\pi}{8}\right)$

In Exercises 5–8, use half-angle formulas to verify the equation.

5 $\cos 75° = \dfrac{1}{2}\sqrt{2 - \sqrt{3}}$

6 $\sin\left(-\dfrac{\pi}{8}\right) = -\dfrac{1}{2}\sqrt{2 - \sqrt{2}}$

7 $\tan \dfrac{3\pi}{8} = \dfrac{\sqrt{\sqrt{2} + 1}}{\sqrt{\sqrt{2} - 1}}$

8 $\sin \dfrac{\pi}{12} = \dfrac{1}{2}\sqrt{2 - \sqrt{3}}$

9 (a) Show that the half-angle formulas in (18) give $\tan 15° = 2 - \sqrt{3}$.

  (b) Use Tables I and V or a calculator to verify that $2 - \sqrt{3}$ and $\tan 15°$ are the same.

10 (a) Show that $\cos^2 \dfrac{\pi}{8} = \dfrac{2 + \sqrt{2}}{4}$.

  (b) From part (a) show that $\cos \dfrac{\pi}{8} = \dfrac{1}{2}\sqrt{2 + \sqrt{2}}$.

  (c) Use Tables I and V or a calculator to verify that $\dfrac{1}{2}\sqrt{2 + \sqrt{2}}$ and $\cos \dfrac{\pi}{8}$ are the same.

11 (a) Show that $\tan^2(22°30') = \dfrac{(2 - \sqrt{2})^2}{2}$.

(b) Use the result in part (a) to show that $\tan(22°30') = \sqrt{2} - 1$.

(c) Use Tables I and V or a calculator to show that $\sqrt{2} - 1$ and $\tan(22°30')$ are the same.

12 If $\cos\theta = \frac{12}{13}$ and θ is in the first quadrant, use double-angle formulas to find:

(a) $\sin 2\theta$ **(b)** $\cos 2\theta$
(c) $\tan 2\theta$

13 If θ is obtuse and $\tan\theta = -\frac{15}{8}$, use double-angle formulas to find:

(a) $\sin 2\theta$ **(b)** $\cos 2\theta$
(c) $\tan 2\theta$

14 If $\sin\theta = -\frac{24}{25}$ and $\tan\theta > 0$, find $\cos 2\theta$.

15 If $\tan\theta = -\frac{2}{3}$ and $\cos\theta > 0$, find $\sin 2\theta$.

■ 16 Use the information from the triangle to derive $\cos 2\theta = 1 - \frac{2}{9}x^2$.

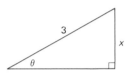

■ 17 Use the information in Exercise 16 to derive $9\sin 2\theta = 2x\sqrt{9 - x^2}$.

■ 18 Let θ be an acute angle of a right triangle so that $\tan\theta = x$. Find expressions for $\sin 2\theta$, $\cos 2\theta$, and $\tan 2\theta$ in terms of x.

Verify the identities in Exercises 19–40.

19 $\cot x \sin 2x = 2\cos^2 x$

20 $\dfrac{\sin 2x}{1 + \cos 2x} = \tan x$

21 $\sec^2 \dfrac{x}{2} = \dfrac{2}{1 + \cos x}$

22 $\sin^2 \dfrac{x}{2} = \dfrac{\sec x - 1}{2\sec x}$

23 $\cos^2 \dfrac{x}{2} = \dfrac{\tan x + \sin x}{2\tan x}$

24 $\tan^2 \dfrac{x}{2} = \dfrac{\sec x - 1}{\sec x + 1}$

25 $\cot \dfrac{x}{2} = \csc x + \cot x$

26 $\dfrac{1}{2}\tan 2x = \dfrac{1}{\cot x - \tan x}$

27 $(\sin x + \cos x)^2 = 1 + \sin 2x$

28 $\sin 3x = 3\sin x - 4\sin^3 x$

29 $\tan 3x = \dfrac{3\tan x - \tan^3 x}{1 - 3\tan^2 x}$

30 $\sin 2x = \dfrac{2\tan x}{\sec^2 x}$

31 $\cot 2x = \dfrac{\cot^2 x - 1}{2\cot x}$

32 $\csc 2x = \frac{1}{2}\csc x \sec x$

33 $\csc 2x - \cot 2x = \tan x$

34 $\sec 2\theta = \dfrac{\sec^2\theta}{2 - \sec^2\theta}$

35 $\cos 2x = \cos^4 x - \sin^4 x$

36 $\sin 4x = 8\sin x \cos^3 x - 4\sin x \cos x$

37 $\cos 4x = 8\cos^4 x - 8\cos^2 x + 1$

38 $\sin^4 \dfrac{x}{2} = \dfrac{1}{4} - \dfrac{1}{2}\cos x + \dfrac{1}{4}\cos^2 x$

39 $\cos^4 x = \frac{1}{8}\cos 4x + \frac{1}{2}\cos 2x + \frac{3}{8}$

40 $\tan \dfrac{x}{2} + \cot \dfrac{x}{2} = 2\csc x$

*41 (a) Add the formulas for $\cos(\alpha + \beta)$ and $\cos(\alpha - \beta)$ to derive this *product formula:*
$$\cos\alpha\cos\beta = \tfrac{1}{2}[\cos(\alpha + \beta) + \cos(\alpha - \beta)]$$

(b) Use a similar analysis to prove these product formulas:
$$\sin\alpha\sin\beta = \tfrac{1}{2}[\cos(\alpha - \beta) - \cos(\alpha + \beta)]$$
$$\sin\alpha\cos\beta = \tfrac{1}{2}[\sin(\alpha + \beta) + \sin(\alpha - \beta)]$$
$$\cos\alpha\sin\beta = \tfrac{1}{2}[\sin(\alpha + \beta) - \sin(\alpha - \beta)]$$

42 Use the results of Exercise 41 to express each of the following as a sum or difference:

(a) $\sin 6x \sin 2x$ **(b)** $2\cos x \cos 4x$

(c) $3\cos 5x \sin(-2x)$ **(d)** $4\sin x \cos \dfrac{x}{2}$

*43 Substitute $\alpha = \dfrac{u + v}{2}$ and $\beta = \dfrac{u - v}{2}$ into the formulas in Exercise 41 and derive these *sum formulas:*
$$\cos u + \cos v = 2\cos\dfrac{u + v}{2}\cos\dfrac{u - v}{2}$$
$$\cos v - \cos u = 2\sin\dfrac{u + v}{2}\sin\dfrac{u - v}{2}$$
$$\sin u + \sin v = 2\sin\dfrac{u + v}{2}\cos\dfrac{u - v}{2}$$
$$\sin u - \sin v = 2\cos\dfrac{u + v}{2}\sin\dfrac{u - v}{2}$$

44 Use the results of Exercise 43 to express each of the following as a product:

(a) $\sin 4x + \sin 2x$ **(b)** $\cos 6x - \cos 3x$
(c) $2\sin 5x - 2\sin x$

(d) $\dfrac{1}{2}\cos \dfrac{x}{2} + \dfrac{1}{2}\cos \dfrac{5x}{2}$

*45 (a) The sign of $\tan \dfrac{\theta}{2}$ and $\sin \theta$ is the same. Verify this for these cases: (i) $\dfrac{\pi}{2} < \theta < \pi$;

(ii) $\pi < \theta < \dfrac{3\pi}{2}$; (iii) $\dfrac{3\pi}{2} < \theta < 2\pi$.

(b) Show that $\tan^2 \dfrac{\theta}{2} = \dfrac{\sin^2 \theta}{(1 + \cos \theta)^2}$ and deduce that $\tan \dfrac{\theta}{2} = \dfrac{\sin \theta}{1 + \cos \theta}$ (*Hint:* Note that $1 + \cos \theta > 0$ and use part (a).)

(c) Explain how $\tan \dfrac{\theta}{2} = \dfrac{\sin \theta}{1 + \cos \theta}$ is demonstrated in the figure.

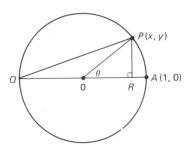

*46 (a) Verify the identity $\dfrac{\sin \theta}{1 + \cos \theta} = \dfrac{1 - \cos \theta}{\sin \theta}$.

(b) Find a geometric interpretation of $\tan \dfrac{\theta}{2} = \dfrac{1 - \cos \theta}{\sin \theta}$. (*Hint:* consider $\triangle PAR$ above.)

In Exercises 47 and 48, solve for b without using Table V or a calculator.

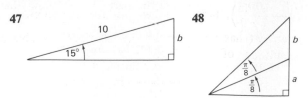

*49 At a point A that is 50 meters from the base of a tower, the angle of elevation to the top of the tower is twice as large as is the angle of elevation from a point B that is 150 meters from the tower. Assuming that the base of the tower and the points A and B are in the same line on level ground, find the height of the tower h.

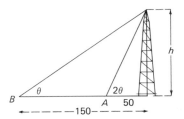

9.5

Trigonometric equations   Can you find the points of intersection of the sine and cosine curves?

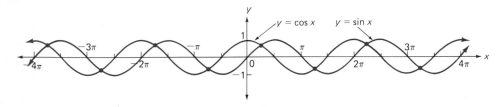

A trigonometric equation that is not an identity is a **conditional equation.**   Answering this question amounts to finding all values x for which $\sin x = \cos x$. To solve this **trigonometric equation** for x, first divide by $\cos x$.

$$\sin x = \cos x$$

$$\frac{\sin x}{\cos x} = 1$$

Now use $\dfrac{\sin x}{\cos x} = \tan x$ and solve $\tan x = 1$. For x in the interval $\left(-\dfrac{\pi}{2}, \dfrac{\pi}{2}\right)$, $\tan x = 1$ has only the one solution, $x = \dfrac{\pi}{4}$. Then, since the tangent has period π, all the solutions are obtained by adding on all the multiples of π:

$$x = \frac{\pi}{4} + k\pi, \qquad \text{where } k \text{ is any integer}$$

$x = \dfrac{\pi}{4} + k\pi,\ k$ **any integer, is the general solution of** $\sin x = \cos x.$

For $k = -2, -1, 0, 1, 2$, the following specific solutions are produced:

$$-\frac{7\pi}{4},\quad -\frac{3\pi}{4},\quad \frac{\pi}{4},\quad \frac{5\pi}{4},\quad \frac{9\pi}{4}$$

or

$$-315°,\quad -135°,\quad 45°,\quad 225°,\quad 405°$$

EXAMPLE 1 Find the general solution: $\sqrt{3}\ \csc x - 2 = 0$.

Solution Begin by isolating $\csc x$ on one side.

$$\sqrt{3}\ \csc x - 2 = 0$$
$$\sqrt{3}\ \csc x = 2$$
$$\csc x = \frac{2}{\sqrt{3}} \qquad \left(\text{or } \sin x = \frac{\sqrt{3}}{2}\right)$$

Thus, in the interval $(0, 2\pi)$, $x = \dfrac{\pi}{3}$ or $x = \dfrac{2\pi}{3}$. Since the cosecant has period 2π, we obtain the general solution by adding on the multiples of 2π.

$$x = \begin{cases} \dfrac{\pi}{3} + 2k\pi \\[2mm] \dfrac{2\pi}{3} + 2k\pi \end{cases} \qquad k \text{ any integer}$$

or, using degrees,

$$x = \begin{cases} 60° + k(360°) \\ 120° + k(360°) \end{cases} \qquad k \text{ any integer}$$

EXAMPLE 2 Find the general solution: $\sin 2x = 1$.

Solution Let $\theta = 2x$ and solve $\sin \theta = 1$. In $[0, 2\pi)$ the only solution is $\theta = \dfrac{\pi}{2}$. Now add the multiples $k(2\pi)$, where k is any integer.

$$\theta = \frac{\pi}{2} + 2k\pi$$

or, replacing θ by $2x$,

$$2x = \frac{\pi}{2} + 2k\pi$$

CAUTION: Be sure to add $2k\pi$ *before* **dividing by 2.**

Divide by 2 to obtain

$$x = \frac{\pi}{4} + k\pi, \qquad k \text{ any integer}$$

which is the general solution of $\sin 2x = 1$. You can check this solution by substituting into the original equation as follows:

$$\sin 2x = \sin\left[2\left(\frac{\pi}{4} + k\pi\right)\right]$$

$$= \sin\left(\frac{\pi}{2} + 2k\pi\right)$$

$$= \sin\frac{\pi}{2} \qquad \left(\frac{\pi}{2} \text{ and } \frac{\pi}{2} + 2k\pi \text{ are coterminal}\right)$$

$$= 1$$

EXAMPLE 3   Find the general solution: $\cos^2 x = \cos x$.

Solution   Since the cosine has period 2π, first solve for x in the interval $0 \le x < 2\pi$. Begin by subtracting $\cos x$ from both sides. Thus

$$\cos^2 x - \cos x = 0$$

Factor out $\cos x$.

$$\cos x(\cos x - 1) = 0$$

Then

$$\cos x = 0 \qquad \text{or} \qquad \cos x - 1 = 0$$

CAUTION: Do not begin by dividing $\cos^2 x = \cos x$ by $\cos x$. This step would produce $\cos x = 1$ and we would have lost all the roots of $\cos x = 0$. (This error is comparable to solving the equation $x^2 = x$ by first dividing each side by x.)

Hence $\cos x = 0$ for $x = \frac{\pi}{2}$ or $\frac{3\pi}{2}$ and $\cos x = 1$ for $x = 0$. Since the period of the cosine is 2π, we obtain all the solutions by taking each solution in $[0, 2\pi)$ and adding all multiples of 2π. The general solution may be presented in these forms, where k is any integer.

$$x = \begin{cases} \dfrac{\pi}{2} + 2k\pi \\[2mm] \dfrac{3\pi}{2} + 2k\pi \\[2mm] 2k\pi \end{cases} \qquad \text{or} \qquad x = \begin{cases} 90° + k(360°) \\ 270° + k(360°) \\ k(360°) \end{cases}$$

Numerous situations in trigonometry only call for the solutions of an equation in the interval $[0, 2\pi)$. This is illustrated in the next example.

EXAMPLE 4   Solve $\sin 2x = \sin x$ for $0 \le x < 2\pi$.

Solution   Using the double-angle formula for $\sin 2x$, we may write

$$2 \sin x \cos x = \sin x$$

or

$$2 \sin x \cos x - \sin x = 0$$

Factor the left side.

$$(\sin x)(2 \cos x - 1) = 0$$

Then

$$\sin x = 0 \quad \text{or} \quad 2 \cos x = 1$$

$$\sin x = 0 \quad \text{or} \quad \cos x = \tfrac{1}{2}$$

Now $\sin x = 0$ for $x = 0$ and π; $\cos x = \tfrac{1}{2}$ for $x = \dfrac{\pi}{3}$ and $\dfrac{5\pi}{3}$. The

solutions in $[0, 2\pi)$ are 0, $\dfrac{\pi}{3}$, π, and $\dfrac{5\pi}{3}$.

EXAMPLE 5   Solve: $\dfrac{\sec x}{\cos x} - \dfrac{1}{2} \sec x = 0$.

Solution

$$\frac{\sec x}{\cos x} - \frac{1}{2} \sec x = 0$$

$$(\sec x)\left(\frac{1}{\cos x} - \frac{1}{2}\right) = 0$$

$$\sec x = 0 \quad \text{or} \quad \frac{1}{\cos x} - \frac{1}{2} = 0$$

$$\sec x = 0 \quad \text{or} \quad \frac{1}{\cos x} = \frac{1}{2}$$

$$\sec x = 0 \quad \text{or} \quad \cos x = 2$$

Since $\sec x \geq 1$ or $\sec x \leq -1$ for all x, $\sec x = 0$ has no roots. Also, since $|\cos x| \leq 1$, $\cos x = 2$ has no roots. Thus the given equation has no solutions.

Some trigonometric equations have no solutions. This is comparable to an algebraic equation such as $x^2 + 1 = 0$, which has no real solutions.

EXAMPLE 6   Solve: $\cos^2 x + \tfrac{1}{2} \sin x - \tfrac{1}{2} = 0$ for $0 \leq x < 2\pi$.

Solution   Multiply by 2 to clear fractions.

$$2(\cos^2 x + \tfrac{1}{2} \sin x - \tfrac{1}{2}) = 2 \cdot 0$$

$$2 \cos^2 x + \sin x - 1 = 0$$

Convert to an equivalent form involving only $\sin x$ by using $\cos^2 x = 1 - \sin^2 x$.

$$2(1 - \sin^2 x) + \sin x - 1 = 0$$

$$2 \sin^2 x - \sin x - 1 = 0$$

The left side is quadratic in $\sin x$, which is factorable.

$$(2 \sin x + 1)(\sin x - 1) = 0$$

$$2 \sin x + 1 = 0 \quad \text{or} \quad \sin x - 1 = 0$$

$$\sin x = -\tfrac{1}{2} \quad \text{or} \quad \sin x = 1$$

Think of $u = \sin x$ and factor $2u^2 - u - 1$ as $(2u + 1)(u - 1)$.

Now $\sin x = -\tfrac{1}{2}$ for $x = \dfrac{7\pi}{6}$ and $\dfrac{11\pi}{6}$; $\sin x = 1$ for $x = \dfrac{\pi}{2}$. The solutions

in $[0, 2\pi)$ are $\dfrac{\pi}{2}$, $\dfrac{7\pi}{6}$, and $\dfrac{11\pi}{6}$.

EXAMPLE 7 Use Table V to approximate the solutions of $3 \tan x - 7 = 0$ in degree measure, where $0° \leq x < 360°$.

Solution Since $3 \tan x - 7 = 0$, we get $\tan x = \frac{7}{3} = 2.3333$ (four decimal places). We use the closest entry in Table V to obtain $x = 66°50'$. Adding $180°$ produces the second answer, $246°50'$, which is in the third quadrant.

EXERCISES 9.5

In Exercises 1–15, find the general solution and check.

1 $\cos x = 1$ 2 $\sin x = 1$

3 $\sin x = \frac{1}{2}$ 4 $\cos^2 x = \frac{1}{2}$

5 $\sec x = -1$ 6 $\csc x = 2$

7 $\sin 2x = 1$ 8 $2 \cos \frac{x}{3} = 1$

9 $\frac{1}{2} \sin^2 x = 1$ 10 $\tan x = \sqrt{3}$

11 $\tan 2x = \sqrt{3}$ 12 $2 \sin(x - 1) = \sqrt{2}$

13 $2 \cos(x + 1) = -2$ 14 $\dfrac{1}{\sec x} = 2$

15 $\dfrac{1}{\cos x} = 0$

In Exercises 16–27, solve the equation for θ in the interval $[0°, 360°)$ and check.

16 $2 \sin \theta = 1$ 17 $\sqrt{3} \csc \theta = 2$

18 $2 \cos \theta + 3 = 0$ 19 $2 \sec \theta - 2\sqrt{2} = 0$

20 $\tan^2 \theta - 3 = 0$ 21 $\sin^2 \theta - \cos^2 \theta = 1$

22 $2 \csc^2 \theta - 1 = 0$ 23 $2 \sin \dfrac{\theta}{2} - 1 = 0$

24 $1 + \sqrt{2} \sin 4\theta = 0$ 25 $-1 + \tan \dfrac{3\theta}{2} = 0$

26 $\sin^2 \theta - \cos^2 \theta = 0$ 27 $2 \tan \theta \cos^2 \theta = 1$

In Exercises 28–57, solve the equation for x in the interval $0 \leq x < 2\pi$.

28 $\sin x(\cos x + 1) = 0$

29 $(\cos x - 1)(2 \sin x + 1) = 0$

30 $\sin x + \cos x = 0$

31 $\sin x - \sqrt{3} \cos x = 0$

32 $\sec x + \tan x = 0$

33 $2 \cos^2 x - \sqrt{3} \cos x = 0$

34 $2 \tan x = \sin x$

35 $\sin^2 x + \sin x - 2 = 0$

36 $2(\cos^2 x - \sin^2 x) = \sqrt{2}$

37 $\sin 2x = \cos x$

38 $\sin^2 x + 2 \cos^2 x = 2$

39 $\sin^2 x + \cos^2 x = 1.5$

40 $\sec^2 x = 2 \tan x$

41 $2 \cos^2 x + 9 \cos x - 5 = 0$

42 $\cos 2x - \cos x = 0$

43 $\cos^2 2x = \cos 2x$

44 $3 \cos^4 x + 4 \cos^2 x = 0$

45 $2 \sin^4 x - 3 \sin^2 x + 1 = 0$

46 $2 \sin^2 x - 1 = \sin x$

47 $2 \tan x - 1 = \tan^2 x$

48 $\sin x \cot^2 x - 3 \sin x = 0$

49 $3 \tan^2 x = 7 \sec x - 5$

50 $\sin^3 2x - \sin 2x = 0$

51 $\cos^2 x - \sin^2 x + \sin x = 1$

52 $2 \cos x - 2 \sec x - 3 = 0$

53 $3 \cos 2x + 2 \sin^2 x = 2$

54 $\cos 4x = \sin 2x$

55 $\sin 2x + \sin 4x = 0$

*56 $\sec x + \tan x = 1$ (*Hint:* Square both sides.)

*57 $\sin x + \cos x = 1$ (*Hint:* Square both sides.)

Use Table V to approximate the solutions of each equation to the nearest multiple of 10 minutes for x in the interval $[0°, 360°)$.

58 $3 \sin x = 2$ 59 $7 \sec x - 15 = 0$

60 $\cos 2x = .9038$ 61 $\sin \dfrac{x}{2} = .8258$

62 $12 \cos^2 x + 5 \cos x - 3 = 0$

63 $4 \cot^2 x - 12 \cot x + 9 = 0$

64 $\tan^2 x + \tan x - 1 = 0$ (*Hint:* Use the quadratic formula.)

65 $\cos^2 x - \sin^2 x = -\frac{3}{4}$

66 $4 \sin x - 5 \cos x = 0$

*67 In the figure α and β are acute angles.

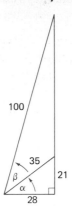

100

35

21

β

α

28

(a) Show that $\alpha < \dfrac{\pi}{4}$ by comparing cos α and $\cos \dfrac{\pi}{4}$.

(b) Without using Table V or a calculator, prove that $\alpha = \beta$. (*Hint:* Apply a double-angle formula to 2α.)

In Exercises 68–70, find the coordinates of the points of intersection of the two curves for the interval $[0, 2\pi]$.

68 $y = \tan x$
$y = \cot x$

69 $y = \sin x$
$y = -\cos x$

70 $y = \sin x$
$y = \cos 2x$

9.6

The sine function is not one-to-one. This fact is apparent from its graph, since a horizontal line through a range value y intersects the curve more than once; more than one x corresponds to y.

Inverse circular functions

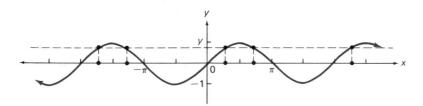

If we restrict the domain to $\left[-\dfrac{\pi}{2}, \dfrac{\pi}{2} \right]$, then $y = \sin x$ is one-to-one because for each range value there corresponds exactly one domain value.

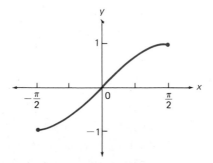

Notice that the range of this restricted function is the same as for the original function: $-1 \leq y \leq 1$.

Since $y = \sin x$ for $-\dfrac{\pi}{2} \leq x \leq \dfrac{\pi}{2}$ is one-to-one, we know that there is an inverse function. The graph of the inverse is obtained by reflecting the graph of $y = \sin x$ through the line $y = x$, and the equation of the inverse

See Section 7.1. is obtained by interchanging the variables in $y = \sin x$. We also know that the domain and range of the restricted function $y = \sin x$ become the range and domain of the inverse, respectively.

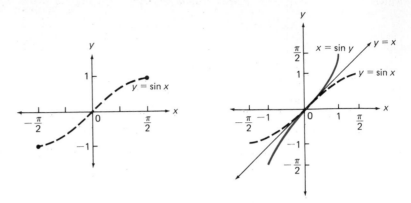

$$\left(\begin{array}{c}\text{Begin with } y = \sin x \text{ for}\\ -\dfrac{\pi}{2} \leq x \leq \dfrac{\pi}{2} \leq \text{ and } -1 \leq y \leq 1\end{array}\right) \rightarrow \left(\begin{array}{c}\text{Reflect}\\ \text{through } y = x\end{array}\right) \rightarrow \left(\begin{array}{c}\text{To get the inverse } x = \sin y\\ \text{for } -1 \leq x \leq 1 \text{ and } -\dfrac{\pi}{2} \leq y \leq \dfrac{\pi}{2}\end{array}\right)$$

The equation of the inverse, $x = \sin y$, does not express y explicitly as a function of x. To do this we create some new terminology. First observe that $x = \sin y$ means that y is the angle whose sine is x, or

y is the arc on the unit circle whose sine is x

To shorten this, we replace "arc on the unit circle whose sine is x" by "arc sin of x," and this phrase is further abbreviated to "arcsin x." Thus $y = \textbf{arcsin } x$ is, by definition, equivalent to $x = \sin y$. To sum up, here is the basic information about this new function.

THE INVERSE SINE FUNCTION

$y = \text{arcsin } x$
  (equivalent to $x = \sin y$)
Domain: $-1 \leq x \leq 1$

Range: $-\dfrac{\pi}{2} \leq y \leq \dfrac{\pi}{2}$

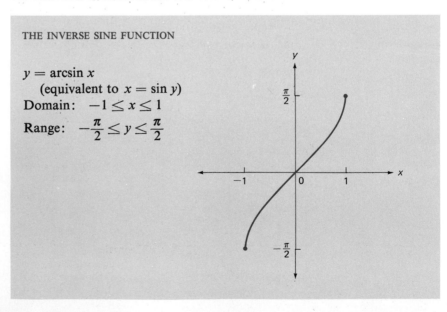

Another common notation for the inverse sine function is $y = \sin^{-1} x$, in which the -1 is not an exponent; it does *not* represent $\dfrac{1}{\sin x}$.

Since we are dealing with inverse functions, the following are true:

$$\arcsin (\sin x) = x \qquad \text{if } -\frac{\pi}{2} \le x \le \frac{\pi}{2}$$

$$\sin (\arcsin x) = x \qquad \text{if } -1 \le x \le 1$$

EXAMPLE 1 Evaluate $\arcsin \frac{1}{2}$.

Solution Let $y = \arcsin \frac{1}{2}$. Then y is the angle whose sine is equal to $\frac{1}{2}$. Thus $y = \dfrac{\pi}{6}$ (or 30°). To check this we use the fact that $y = \arcsin x$ is equivalent to $x = \sin y$. Hence

$$\sin y = \sin \frac{\pi}{6} = \frac{1}{2} = x$$

CAUTION: Even though $\sin \dfrac{5\pi}{6} = \dfrac{1}{2}$, we do not have $\arcsin \dfrac{1}{2} = \dfrac{5\pi}{6}$ because the range of the arcsin function consists of the numbers in the interval $\left[-\dfrac{\pi}{2}, \dfrac{\pi}{2}\right]$.

You will find it helpful in finding values like $\arcsin \frac{1}{2}$ to remember that $y = \arcsin x$ is negative for $-1 \le x < 0$ and positive for $0 < x \le 1$. You can see this from its graph.

EXAMPLE 2 Use Table V to approximate $\arcsin(-.3960)$.

Solution The closest entry in the sine column is .3961 that corresponds to .4072 radians or 23°20′. Then, since $x = -.3960 < 0$, we find that $\arcsin(-.3960) = -.4072$ or $-23°20′$.

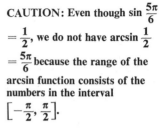

To define the inverse cosine function, known as *arccos*, we begin by restricting $y = \cos x$ to $0 \le x \le \pi$. Next, reflect the curve for $0 \le x \le \pi$ through the line $y = x$ to obtain the graph of the inverse whose equation is $x = \cos y$.

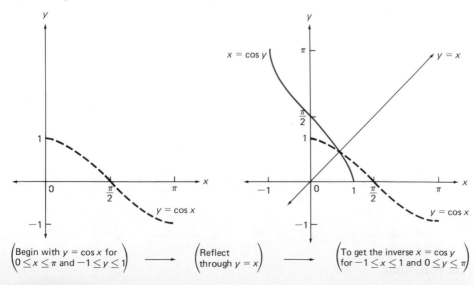

$\begin{pmatrix} \text{Begin with } y = \cos x \text{ for} \\ 0 \le x \le \pi \text{ and } -1 \le y \le 1 \end{pmatrix}$ $\longrightarrow$ $\begin{pmatrix} \text{Reflect} \\ \text{through } y = x \end{pmatrix}$ $\longrightarrow$ $\begin{pmatrix} \text{To get the inverse } x = \cos y \\ \text{for } -1 \le x \le 1 \text{ and } 0 \le y \le \pi \end{pmatrix}$

369

Now define $y = \textbf{arccos } x$ to mean $x = \cos y$ and call it the *inverse cosine function*. (This function is also written in the form $y = \cos^{-1} x$.)

$$\arccos(\cos x) = x \qquad \text{if } 0 \leq x \leq \pi$$
$$\cos(\arccos x) = x \qquad \text{if } -1 \leq x \leq 1$$

THE INVERSE COSINE FUNCTION

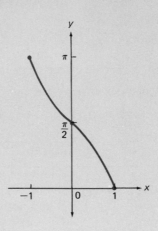

$y = \arccos x$ (equivalent to $x = \cos y$)
Domain: $-1 \leq x \leq 1$
Range: $0 \leq y \leq \pi$

EXAMPLE 3 Find $\arccos(-\tfrac{1}{2})$.

Solution Since $\cos 120° = -\tfrac{1}{2}$ we have $\arccos(-\tfrac{1}{2}) = 120°$.

EXAMPLE 4 Find $\sin(\arccos \tfrac{1}{2})$.

Solution Since $\arccos \dfrac{1}{2} = \dfrac{\pi}{3}$, we have

$$\sin\left(\arccos \frac{1}{2}\right) = \sin \frac{\pi}{3} = \frac{\sqrt{3}}{2}$$

CAUTION: Do not confuse $(\sin x)(\arccos x)$ with $\sin(\arccos x)$. The first represents the product of the two numbers $\sin x$ and $\arccos x$. The second represents the composite of the inner function arccos with the outer function sin.

EXAMPLE 5 Find the exact value of $\cos(\arcsin \tfrac{2}{3})$.

Solution We know that $y = \arcsin \tfrac{2}{3}$ is an acute angle. (Why?) Now construct a right triangle with y an acute angle and $\sin y = \tfrac{2}{3}$. Then, from the triangle,

$$\cos\left(\arcsin \frac{2}{3}\right) = \cos y = \frac{\sqrt{5}}{3}$$

Adjacent side $= \sqrt{9-4} = \sqrt{5}$

The sine and cosine functions are "connected" through a variety of identities. The most fundamental of these identities is $\sin^2 \theta + \cos^2 \theta = 1$; another is $\cos\left(\frac{\pi}{2} - x\right) = \sin x$. We almost expect the inverse sine and cosine functions to be connected by some identity. Such an identity does exist, as is illustrated in the next example.

EXAMPLE 6 Show that $\arcsin x + \arccos x = \frac{\pi}{2}$ for all x in the common domain $-1 \le x \le 1$.

Solution Let $\arcsin x = y$; $-\frac{\pi}{2} \le y \le \frac{\pi}{2}$. Then $x = \sin y$. Now for any y value we have $\cos\left(\frac{\pi}{2} - y\right) = \sin y$. Therefore,

$$x = \sin y = \cos\left(\frac{\pi}{2} - y\right)$$

However, $x = \cos\left(\frac{\pi}{2} - y\right)$ is equivalent to $\frac{\pi}{2} - y = \arccos x$ because $0 \le \frac{\pi}{2} - y \le \pi$. Then, adding y yields

$$\frac{\pi}{2} = y + \arccos x$$

and substituting for y gives

$$\frac{\pi}{2} = \arcsin x + \arccos x$$

Note that the identity $\arcsin x + \arccos x = \frac{\pi}{2}$ says that the angle whose sine is x and the angle whose cosine is x must be complementary.

TEST YOUR UNDERSTANDING

Evaluate the following where possible.

1 $\arcsin(-1)$ **2** $\arccos\left(\frac{\sqrt{3}}{2}\right)$ **3** $\arcsin 2$

4 $\arccos(-\frac{1}{2})$ **5** $\cos(\arcsin 0)$ **6** $\cos\left[\arcsin\left(-\frac{\sqrt{3}}{2}\right)\right]$

7 $\sin(\arcsin 1)$ **8** $\cos(\arccos x)$ **9** $\sin(\arccos \frac{3}{5})$

Use Table V to approximate the following.

10 $\arccos(-.4436)$ **11** $\arcsin(.7314)$ **12** $\cos(\arcsin .0872)$

The tangent function has period π and completes a full cycle on the interval $\left(-\frac{\pi}{2}, \frac{\pi}{2}\right)$. Thus when $y = \tan x$ is restricted to $-\frac{\pi}{2} < x < \frac{\pi}{2}$ we have a one-to-one function whose range consists of all real numbers.

$y = \tan x$

Domain: $-\dfrac{\pi}{2} < x < \dfrac{\pi}{2}$

Range: all real numbers

Asymptotes: $x = \pm\dfrac{\pi}{2}$

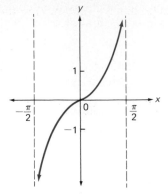

We define the inverse by $y = $ **arctan** x, which means that $x = \tan y$. Its graph is obtained by reflecting the curve in the figure through the line $y = x$. (The inverse tangent function is also written in the form $y = \tan^{-1} x$.)

$$\arctan(\tan x) = x \qquad \text{if } -\dfrac{\pi}{2} < x < \dfrac{\pi}{2}$$

$$\tan(\arctan x) = x \qquad \text{for all } x$$

THE INVERSE TANGENT FUNCTION

$y = \arctan x$
  (equivalent to $x = \tan y$)
Domain: all real numbers

Range: $-\dfrac{\pi}{2} < y < \dfrac{\pi}{2}$

Asymptotes: $y = \dfrac{\pi}{2}, y = -\dfrac{\pi}{2}$

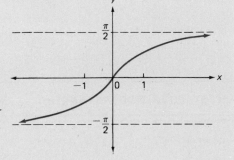

EXAMPLE 7   Evaluate arctan $\sqrt{3}$.

Solution   Let $y = \arctan \sqrt{3}$. Then y is the angle whose tangent is $\sqrt{3}$. Therefore, since $-\dfrac{\pi}{2} < y < \dfrac{\pi}{2}$, we have $y = \dfrac{\pi}{3}$ (or 60°).

EXAMPLE 8   Evaluate tan(arctan 3 — arctan 2).

Solution   Let $\alpha = \arctan 3$ and $\beta = \arctan 2$. Now use the formula for $\tan(\alpha - \beta)$ on page 349.

$$\tan(\arctan 3 - \arctan 2) = \tan(\alpha - \beta)$$
$$= \frac{\tan \alpha - \tan \beta}{1 + \tan \alpha \tan \beta}$$
$$= \frac{3 - 2}{1 + 3 \cdot 2}$$
$$= \frac{1}{7}$$

EXERCISES 9.6

Evaluate. Use Table V only when necessary.

1 arcsin 0

2 arccos 0

3 arcsin(−1)

4 arccos(−1)

5 arctan(−1)

6 $\arcsin \frac{\sqrt{2}}{2}$

7 $\arccos\left(-\frac{\sqrt{2}}{2}\right)$

8 $\arctan \frac{\sqrt{3}}{3}$

9 arctan 115

10 $\arcsin \frac{3}{2}$

11 arcsin(.5592)

12 arccos(−2)

13 arccos(.1475)

14 arctan(.6128)

15 $\sin(\arctan \frac{1}{12})$

16 $\tan(\arcsin \frac{1}{2})$

17 cos[arcsin(−1)]

18 $\tan(\arccos \frac{4}{5})$

19 $\sin\left(\arcsin \frac{\sqrt{3}}{2}\right)$

20 cos(arctan 2.35)

21 $\sin(\arccos \frac{12}{13})$

22 $\arcsin\left(\cos \frac{\pi}{3}\right)$

23 arccos(tan 45°)

24 arctan(tan 30°)

25 Explain why sin(arcsin x) = x for $-1 \le x \le 1$.

26 Explain why tan(arctan x) = x for all x.

Graph the curves in Exercises 27–34. State the domain and range.

27 $y = 2 \arcsin x$

28 $y = \arcsin(x - 2)$

29 $y = 2 + \arctan x$

30 $y = -\arcsin x$

31 $y = \frac{1}{2} \arcsin 2x$

32 $y = 2 \arccos \frac{x}{2}$

33 $y = \sin(\arcsin x)$

34 $y = \arcsin x + \arccos x$

In Exercises 35–40, use the formulas in Sections 9.3 and 9.4 to evaluate the expression.

35 tan(arctan 3 + arctan 4)

36 $\sin(\arcsin \frac{2}{3} + \arctan \frac{4}{5})$

37 $\cos(\arcsin \frac{8}{17} - \arccos \frac{12}{13})$

38 $\tan(2 \arctan \frac{4}{5})$

39 $\cos(2 \arcsin \frac{1}{3})$

40 $\sin(\frac{1}{2} \arccos \frac{3}{5})$

In Exercises 41–44, solve for x and check.

41 $\arcsin(x + 2) = \frac{\pi}{6}$

42 $\arctan \frac{x}{3} = \frac{\pi}{4}$

43 $\arctan(x^2 + 4x + 3) = -\frac{\pi}{4}$

44 $\arccos(2x - 1) = \frac{2\pi}{3}$

45 Verify that tan(π + arctan x) = x.

46 Verify that $\sin\left(\frac{\pi}{2} - \arccos x\right) = x$.

*47 Prove that arcsin(−x) = −arcsin x.

*48 Prove that cos(arcsin x) = $\sqrt{1 - x^2}$.

In Exercises 49–51, solve the equation and express the solutions using inverse function notation. Approximate those solutions that are not exact by using Table V or a calculator.

49 $\tan^2 x = 4 \tan x - 4$

50 $15 \sin^2 x - 7 \sin x - 2 = 0$

51 $2 \sin 2x + \cos x = 0$

52 Let $f(x) = \arctan x$ and $g(x) = x^2$ and form the composites $f \circ g$ and $g \circ f$.

53 Let $f(x) = \arcsin x$ and $g(x) = 3x + 2$ and form the composites $f \circ g$ and $g \circ f$.

*54 In the figure, θ represents the angle subtended by a 5-foot picture when viewed from point P that is 7 feet below the picture and 14 feet away from the wall on which the picture hangs. Solve for θ and express the answer using the arctan notation, and then approximate θ using Table V or a calculator.

■ 55 Let $h(x) = \ln(\arccos x)$. Find f and g so that $h = f \circ g$.

■ 56 Let $k(x) = \arctan \sqrt{x^2 - 1}$. Find f, g, and h so that $k = f \circ g \circ h$.

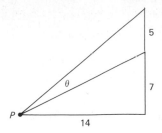

REVIEW EXERCISES FOR CHAPTER 9

The solutions to the following exercises can be found within the text of Chapter 9. Try to answer each question without referring to the text.

Section 9.1

1 Graph the curves $y = \sin x$, $y = \frac{1}{2} \sin x$, and $y = 2 \sin x$ on the same set of axes for $-2\pi \leq x \leq 2\pi$ and find the amplitudes.

2 For which subintervals of $[0, 2\pi]$ is the sine increasing? decreasing?

3 Find the period of $y = \sin 2x$ and graph for $0 \leq x \leq 2\pi$

4 Find the period and amplitude of $y = 2 \cos \frac{1}{2} x$ and graph for $0 \leq x \leq 4\pi$.

5 Graph $y = \sin x + \cos x$ on $[-2\pi, 2\pi]$.

Section 9.2

6 Graph $y = \tan x$ for $\dfrac{-3\pi}{2} < x < \dfrac{3\pi}{2}$.

7 Prove that $y = \tan x$ is symmetric through the origin.

8 What is the domain of the tangent function? What is the range? Write the equations of the asymptotes.

9 For which subintervals of $\left(-\dfrac{\pi}{2}, \dfrac{\pi}{2}\right)$ is the tangent increasing? decreasing? For which subintervals is the curve concave up? down?

10 Graph $y = \cot x$ for $-\pi < x < \pi$.

11 Graph $y = -\tan 3x$ for $\dfrac{-\pi}{2} < x < \dfrac{\pi}{2}$.

12 Graph $y = \sec x$ for one full cycle.

13 What are the domain and range of the cosecant? Write the equations of the asymptotes.

Section 9.3

14 Complete these addition or subtraction formulas:

$$\sin(\alpha - \beta) = \qquad \cos(\alpha + \beta) = \qquad \tan(\alpha - \beta) =$$

15 Use an addition formula to evaluate $\sin \dfrac{7\pi}{12}$.

16 Verify the identity

$$\sin\left(\theta + \frac{\pi}{3}\right) = \tfrac{1}{2}(\sin \theta + \sqrt{3} \cos \theta)$$

17 Derive the addition formula for $\tan(\alpha + \beta)$ using the addition formula for the sine and cosine.

18 Find $\cos(\alpha - \beta)$ for α in quadrant II with $\cos \alpha = -\frac{4}{5}$, and β in quadrant III with $\cos \beta = -\frac{12}{13}$.

Section 9.4

19 Complete these double-angle formulas:

$$\sin 2\theta = \qquad \cos 2\theta = \qquad \tan 2\theta =$$

20 Evaluate $\sin 15° \cos 15°$ using a double-angle formula.

21 If θ is obtuse such that $\sin \theta = \frac{5}{13}$, find $\sin 2\theta$, $\cos 2\theta$, and $\tan 2\theta$.

22 Let $\sin \theta = \dfrac{x}{2}$ for $0 < \theta < \dfrac{\pi}{2}$. Show that $\sin 2\theta = \dfrac{x\sqrt{4 - x^2}}{2}$.

23 Complete these half-angle formulas:

$$\sin \frac{\theta}{2} = \qquad \cos \frac{\theta}{2} = \qquad \tan \frac{\theta}{2} =$$

24 Use a half-angle formula to evaluate $\sin 15°$.

25 Verify the identity $\cos 3\theta = 4 \cos^3 \theta - 3 \cos \theta$.

26 Verify the identity

$$\sin^4 \theta = \tfrac{3}{8} - \tfrac{1}{2} \cos 2\theta + \tfrac{1}{8} \cos 4\theta$$

Section 9.5

In Exercises 27–29, find the general solution.

27 $\sqrt{3} \cos x - 2 = 0$

28 $\sin 2x = 1$

29 $\cos^2 x = \cos x$

30 Solve $\sin 2x = \sin x$ for $0 \leq x < 2\pi$.

31 Solve $\cos^2 x + \frac{1}{2} \sin x - \frac{1}{2} = 0$ for $0 \le x < 2\pi$.

32 Solve $\dfrac{\sec x}{\cos x} - \dfrac{1}{2} \sec x = 0$.

33 Approximate the solutions of $3 \tan x - 7 = 0$ for $0° \le x < 360°$ using Table V.

Section 9.6

34 State the domain and range of $y = \arcsin x$ and graph.

35 State the domain and range of $y = \arccos x$ and graph.

36 State the domain and range of $y = \arctan x$ and graph.

In Exercises 37–41, find the exact value of the expression.

37 $\arcsin \frac{1}{2}$

38 $\arccos(-\frac{1}{2})$

39 $\arctan \sqrt{3}$

40 $\sin(\arccos \frac{1}{2})$

41 $\cos(\arcsin \frac{2}{3})$

42 Approximate $\arcsin(-.3960)$ using Table V.

43 Prove: $\arcsin x + \arccos x = \dfrac{\pi}{2}$.

44 Find the exact value of $\tan(\arctan 3 - \arctan 2)$.

SAMPLE TEST QUESTIONS FOR CHAPTER 9

10 Find the general solution of $\cos 2x = 2 \sin^2 x - 2$.

11 (a) State the domain and range of $y = \arctan x$ and graph.

(b) Evaluate $\arctan\left(-\dfrac{\sqrt{3}}{3}\right)$.

12 Evaluate each of the following:

(a) $\arcsin \dfrac{\sqrt{2}}{2}$

(b) $\sin\left(\arccos \dfrac{3}{7}\right)$

(c) $\cos\left(2 \arcsin \dfrac{1}{2}\right)$

13 The given curve has equation $y = a \cos bx$ or $y = a \sin bx$. Find a and b and write the equation of the curve.

Use these questions to test your knowledge of the basic skills and concepts of Chapter 9. Then check your answers with those given at the end of the book.

1 Find the amplitude and period of $y = 2 \sin 2x$ and graph for x in the interval $0 \le x \le 2\pi$.

2 State the domain and range of $y = \sec x$ and graph for x in the interval $-\dfrac{\pi}{2} < x < \dfrac{\pi}{2}$.

3 Use $165° = 135° + 30°$ and an appropriate addition formula to evaluate $\cos 165°$.

4 Use a half-angle formula to evaluate $\sin\left(-\dfrac{\pi}{12}\right)$.

5 If $\sin \theta = \frac{1}{3}$ and θ is acute, find $\sin 2\theta$.

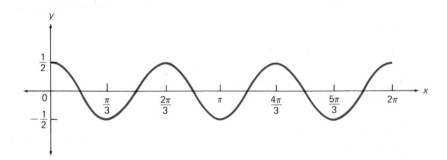

In Questions 6–8, verify the identities.

6 $\sin\left(\dfrac{\pi}{4} - \theta\right) = \dfrac{\sqrt{2}}{2}(\cos \theta - \sin \theta)$.

7 $\csc 4x = \frac{1}{4}(\csc x)(\sec x)(\sec 2x)$.

8 $\sin^2 \dfrac{x}{2} = \dfrac{\tan x - \sin x}{2 \tan x}$.

9 Solve $\sin^2 x - \cos^2 x + \sin x = 0$ for x in the interval $0 \le x < 2\pi$.

14 Find the period of $y = \tan 2x$ and write the equation of each asymptote that occurs on the interval $[0, \pi]$.

15 Find $\cos(\alpha + \beta)$ if α is in quadrant II with $\sin \alpha = \frac{3}{5}$, and β is in quadrant III with $\tan \beta = \frac{12}{5}$.

16 $\triangle ABC$ has $\angle C = 90°$, $\angle A = 15°$, and $a = 8$. Find the exact value of b using a half angle formula.

ANSWERS TO THE TEST YOUR UNDERSTANDING EXERCISES

Page 337

1

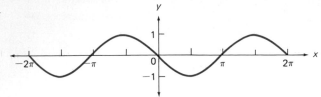

2

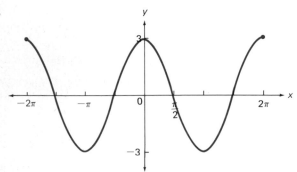

3 Same as in Exercise 1.   **4** 10   **5** $\frac{2}{3}$

6 1   **7** Shift 2 units right.   **8** Shift 2 units upward.

Page 350

1 $\sin 17°$ **2** $\cos \dfrac{\pi}{10}$ **3** $\tan 5°$

4 $\sin 10°$ **5** $\frac{1}{4}(\sqrt{6} - \sqrt{2})$; $\frac{1}{4}(\sqrt{6} + \sqrt{2})$; $\dfrac{3 - \sqrt{3}}{3 + \sqrt{3}} = 2 - \sqrt{3}$

6 Same as Exercise 5. $\left(Note:\ \dfrac{\sqrt{3} - 1}{1 + \sqrt{3}} \cdot \dfrac{\sqrt{3}}{\sqrt{3}} = \dfrac{3 - \sqrt{3}}{3 + \sqrt{3}} = 2 - \sqrt{3}\right)$

7 $\frac{1}{4}(\sqrt{6} - \sqrt{2})$; $-\frac{1}{4}(\sqrt{6} + \sqrt{2})$; $\dfrac{1 - \sqrt{3}}{1 + \sqrt{3}} = -2 + \sqrt{3}$ **8** Same as Exercise 7.

9 $\frac{1}{4}(\sqrt{2} - \sqrt{6})$ **10** $\frac{1}{4}(\sqrt{6} - \sqrt{2})$

Page 356

1 $\sin 10°$ **2** $\tan \theta$ **3** $\cos 6\theta$ **4** $\cos \dfrac{\alpha}{3}$

5 $\dfrac{\sqrt{3}}{2}$ **6** $\dfrac{\sqrt{2}}{2}$ **7** 2   **8** $-\dfrac{\sqrt{3}}{2}$

Page 371

1 $-\dfrac{\pi}{2}$ **2** $\dfrac{\pi}{6}$ **3** Undefined.   **4** $\dfrac{2\pi}{3}$ **5** 1   **6** $\frac{1}{2}$

7 1   **8** x **9** $\frac{4}{5}$ **10** 116°20′   **11** 47°   **12** .9962

SEQUENCES AND SERIES

10.1

Sequences

The same equation can be used to define a variety of functions by changing the domain. For example, below are the graphs of three functions all of whose range values are given by the equation $y = x^2$ for the indicated domains.

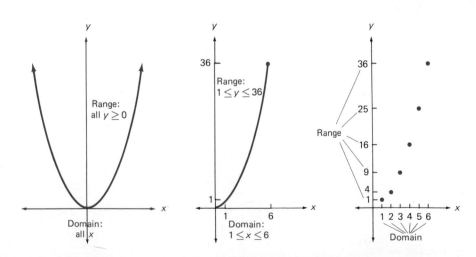

The type of function that is studied in this chapter is illustrated by the preceding graph at the right, where the domain consists of the consecutive integers 1, 2, 3, 4, 5, 6. This kind of function is called a **sequence**.

> A sequence is a function whose domain is a set of consecutive integers, usually a set of positive consecutive integers beginning with 1.

s_n is read "s-sub-n" and has the same meaning as the functional notation $s(n)$, that is, "s of n."

Instead of using the variable x, letters, such as n, k, i are normally used for the domain variable of a sequence. Frequently, sequences (functions) will be denoted by the lowercase letter s and the range values by s_n, which are also called the **terms** of the sequence.

Sequences are often given by stating their **general** or **nth terms**. Thus the general term of the sequence, previously given by $y = x^2$, becomes $s_n = n^2$.

EXAMPLE 1   Find the range values of the sequence given by $s_n = \dfrac{1}{n}$ for the domain {1, 2, 3, 4, 5} and graph.

Solution   The range values and graph are as follows.

This is an example of a *finite* sequence since the domain is finite. That is, the domain is a set of integers having a last element.

$$s_1 = 1$$
$$s_2 = \tfrac{1}{2}$$
$$s_3 = \tfrac{1}{3}$$
$$s_4 = \tfrac{1}{4}$$
$$s_5 = \tfrac{1}{5}$$

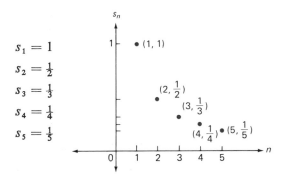

EXAMPLE 2   List the first seven terms of the sequence given by $s_k = \dfrac{(-1)^k}{k^2}$.

Solution

$$s_1 = \frac{(-1)^1}{1^2} = -1$$

$$s_2 = \frac{(-1)^2}{2^2} = \frac{1}{4}$$

$$s_3 = \frac{(-1)^3}{3^2} = -\frac{1}{9}$$

$$s_4 = \frac{(-1)^4}{4^2} = \frac{1}{16}$$

$$s_5 = \frac{(-1)^5}{5^2} = -\frac{1}{25}$$

$$s_6 = \frac{(-1)^6}{6^2} = \frac{1}{36}$$

$$s_7 = \frac{(-1)^7}{7^2} = -\frac{1}{49}$$

Sometimes a sequence is given by a verbal description. If, for example, we ask for the increasing sequence of odd integers beginning with -3, then this implies the infinite sequence whose first few terms are

$$-3, -1, 1, \ldots$$

A sequence can also be given by presenting a listing of its first few terms, possibly including the general term. Thus the preceding sequence is

$$-3, -1, 1, \ldots, 2n - 5, \ldots$$

EXAMPLE 3 Find the tenth term of the sequence

$$-3, 4, \frac{5}{3}, \ldots, \frac{n+2}{2n-3}, \ldots$$

This is an example of an *infinite* sequence since the domain is infinite. That is, the domain consists of an endless collection of integers.

Solution Since the first term -3 is obtained by letting $n = 1$ in the general term $\dfrac{n+2}{2n-3}$, the tenth term is

$$s_{10} = \frac{10 + 2}{2(10) - 3} = \frac{12}{17}$$

EXAMPLE 4 Write the first four terms of the sequence given by $s_n = \left(1 + \dfrac{1}{n}\right)^n$. Round off to two decimal places when appropriate.

Solution

$$s_1 = (1 + \tfrac{1}{1})^1 = 2$$
$$s_2 = (1 + \tfrac{1}{2})^2 = (\tfrac{3}{2})^2 = \tfrac{9}{4} = 2.25$$
$$s_3 = (1 + \tfrac{1}{3})^3 = (\tfrac{4}{3})^3 = \tfrac{64}{27} = 2.37$$
$$s_4 = (1 + \tfrac{1}{4})^4 = (\tfrac{5}{4})^4 = \tfrac{625}{256} = 2.44$$

The terms of the sequence in Example 4 are getting successively larger. But the increase from term to term is getting smaller. That is, the differences between successive terms are decreasing:

$$s_2 - s_1 = 0.25$$
$$s_3 - s_2 = 0.12$$
$$s_4 - s_3 = 0.07$$

Use a calculator to verify these table entries to four decimal places.

n	$s_n = \left(1 + \dfrac{1}{n}\right)^n$
10	2.5937
50	2.6916
100	2.7048
500	2.7156
1000	2.7169
5000	2.7180
10,000	2.7181

If more terms of $s_n = \left(1 + \dfrac{1}{n}\right)^n$ were computed, you would see that while the terms keep on increasing, the amount by which each new term increases keeps getting smaller.

It turns out that no matter how large n is, the value of $\left(1 + \dfrac{1}{n}\right)^n$ is never more than 2.72. In fact, the larger the n that is taken, the closer $\left(1 + \dfrac{1}{n}\right)^n$ gets to the irrational value $e = 2.71828 \ldots$. This is the number that was introduced in Chapter 7 in reference to natural logarithms and exponential functions.

EXERCISES 10.1

The domain of each sequence in Exercises 1–6 consists of the integers 1, 2, 3, 4, 5. Write the corresponding range values and graph the sequence.

1 $s_n = 2n - 1$

2 $s_n = 10 - n^2$

3 $s_n = (-1)^n$

4 $s_k = -\dfrac{6}{k}$

5 $s_i = 8(-\tfrac{1}{2})^i$

6 $s_i = (\tfrac{1}{2})^{i-3}$

Write the first four terms of the sequence given by the formula in each of Exercises 7–30.

7 $s_k = (-1)^k k^2$

8 $s_j = 3(\tfrac{1}{10})^{j-1}$

9 $s_j = 3(\tfrac{1}{10})^j$

10 $s_j = 3(\tfrac{1}{10})^{j+1}$

11 $s_j = 3(\tfrac{1}{10})^{2j}$

12 $s_n = \dfrac{(-1)^{n+1}}{n+3}$

13 $s_n = \dfrac{1}{n} - \dfrac{1}{n+1}$

14 $s_n = \dfrac{n^2 - 4}{n+2}$

15 $s_k = (2k - 10)^2$

16 $s_k = 1 + (-1)^k$

17 $s_n = -2 + (n-1)(3)$

18 $s_n = a + (n-1)(d)$

19 $s_i = \dfrac{i-1}{i+1}$

20 $s_i = 64^{1/i}$

21 $s_n = \left(1 + \dfrac{1}{n}\right)^{n-1}$

22 $s_n = \dfrac{1}{2^n}$

23 $s_n = -2(\tfrac{3}{4})^{n-1}$

24 $s_k = ar^{k-1}$

25 $s_k = \dfrac{k}{2^k}$

26 $s_n = \dfrac{(-1)^n}{n} + n$

27 $s_k = \dfrac{k}{k+1} - \dfrac{k+1}{k}$

28 $s_n = \left(1 + \dfrac{1}{n+1}\right)^n$

29 $s_n = 4$

30 $s_n = \dfrac{n}{(n+1)(n+2)}$

31 Find the sixth term of $1, 2, 5, \ldots, \tfrac{1}{2}(1 + 3^{n-1}), \ldots$.

32 Find the ninth and tenth terms of $0, 4, 0, \ldots$, $\dfrac{2^n + (-2)^n}{n}, \ldots$.

33 Find the seventh term of $s_k = 3(0.1)^{k-1}$.

34 Find the twentieth term of $s_n = (-1)^{n-1}$.

35 Find the twelfth term of $s_i = i$.

36 Find the twelfth term of $s_i = (i - 1)^2$.

37 Find the twelfth term of $s_i = (1 - i)^3$.

38 Find the hundredth term of $s_n = \dfrac{n+1}{n^2 + 5n + 4}$.

39 Write the first four terms of the sequence of even increasing integers beginning with 4.

40 Write the first four terms of the sequence of decreasing odd integers beginning with 3.

41 Write the first five positive multiples of 5 and find the formula for the nth term.

42 Write the first five powers of 5 and find the formula for the nth term.

43 Write the first five powers of -5 and find the formula for the nth term.

44 Write the first five terms of the sequence of reciprocals of the negative integers and find the formula for the nth term.

45 The numbers 1, 3, 6, and 10 are called **triangular numbers** because they correspond to the number of dots in the triangular arrays.

Find the next three triangular numbers.

46 Write the first eight terms of $s_n = \sin \dfrac{n\pi}{2}$.

47 Write the first five terms of $s_n = \dfrac{3^n}{2^n + 1}$.

48 Write the first seven terms of $s_n = n!$ ($n!$ is read as "n factorial" and is defined by
$$n! = n(n-1) \cdot (n-2) \cdots 3 \cdot 2 \cdot 1)$$

49 Write the first four terms of
$$s_n = \frac{(2n+1)(2n-1) \cdots 5 \cdot 3}{(2n)(2n-2) \cdots 4 \cdot 2}.$$

*50 When an investment earns **simple interest** it means the interest is earned only on the original investment. For example, if P dollars are invested in a bank that pays simple interest at the annual rate of r percent, then the interest for the first year is Pr, and the amount in the bank at the end of the year is $P + Pr$. For the second year, the interest is again Pr; the amount now would be $(P + Pr) + Pr = P + 2Pr$.

(a) What is the amount after n years?

(b) What is the amount in the bank if an investment of \$750 has been earning simple interest for 5 years at the annual rate of 12%?

(c) If the amount in the bank is \$5395 after 12 years, what was the original investment P if it has been earning simple interest at the annual rate of $12\frac{1}{2}\%$?

10.2
Sums of finite sequences

How long would it take you to add up the integers from 1 to 1000? Here is a quick way. List the sequence displaying the first few and last few terms.

$$1, 2, 3, \ldots, 998, 999, 1000$$

Add them in pairs, the first and last, the second and second from last, and so on.

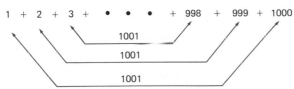

Since there are 500 such pairs to be added, the total is

$$500(1001) = 500{,}500$$

It is told that Carl Friedrich Gauss (1777–1855) discovered how to compute such sums when he was 10 years old. He became one of the greatest mathematicians of all time.

For any finite sequence we can add up all its terms and say that we have found the *sum of the sequence*. The sum of a sequence is called a **series**. For example, the sequence

$$1, 3, 5, 7, 9, 11$$

can be associated with the series

$$1 + 3 + 5 + 7 + 9 + 11$$

The sum of the terms in this series can easily be found, by adding, to be 36.

As another example, the sequence $s_n = \dfrac{1}{n}$ for $n = 1, 2, 3, 4, 5$ has the sum

$$1 + \frac{1}{2} + \frac{1}{3} + \frac{1}{4} + \frac{1}{5} = \frac{60 + 30 + 20 + 15 + 12}{60} = \frac{137}{60}$$

EXAMPLE 1   Find the sum of the first seven terms of $s_k = 2k$.

Solution

$$s_1 + s_2 + s_3 + s_4 + s_5 + s_6 + s_7 = 2 + 4 + 6 + 8 + 10 + 12 + 14 = 56$$

There is a very handy notational device available for expressing the sum of a sequence. The Greek letter $\sum$ (capital sigma) is used for this purpose. Referring to Example 1, the sum of the seven terms is expressed by the symbol $\sum_{k=1}^{7} s_k$; that is,

Just think of the sigma as the command to add.

$$\sum_{k=1}^{7} s_k = s_1 + s_2 + s_3 + s_4 + s_5 + s_6 + s_7$$

Add the terms s_k for consecutive values of k, starting with $k = 1$ up to and including $k = 7$. With this symbolism, the question in Example 1 can now be stated by asking for the value of $\sum_{k=1}^{7} s_k$, where $s_k = 2k$, or by asking for the value of $\sum_{k=1}^{7} 2k$.

EXAMPLE 2   Find $\sum_{n=1}^{5} s_n$, where $s_n = \dfrac{2}{n}$.

Solution

$$\sum_{n=1}^{5} s_n = s_1 + s_2 + s_3 + s_4 + s_5$$

$$= \frac{2}{1} + \frac{2}{2} + \frac{2}{3} + \frac{2}{4} + \frac{2}{5}$$

$$= \frac{120 + 60 + 40 + 30 + 24}{60}$$

$$= \frac{274}{60} = \frac{137}{30}$$

EXAMPLE 3   Find $\sum_{k=1}^{4} (2k + 1)$.

Solution   It is understood here that we are to find the sum of the first four terms of the sequence whose general term is $s_k = 2k + 1$.

$$\sum_{k=1}^{4} (2k + 1) = (2 \cdot 1 + 1) + (2 \cdot 2 + 1) + (2 \cdot 3 + 1) + (2 \cdot 4 + 1)$$

$$= 3 + 5 + 7 + 9$$

$$= 24$$

EXAMPLE 4 Find $\sum_{k=1}^{5} s_i$, where $s_i = (-1)^i(i + 1)$.

Solution

$$\sum_{i=1}^{5} s_i = s_1 + s_2 + s_3 + s_4 + s_5$$

$$= (-1)^1(1 + 1) + (-1)^2(2 + 1) + (-1)^3(3 + 1)$$
$$+ (-1)^4(4 + 1) + (-1)^5(5 + 1)$$

$$= -2 + 3 - 4 + 5 - 6$$

$$= -4$$

EXERCISES 10.2

Find the sum of the first five terms of the sequence given by the formula in each of Exercises 1–6.

1 $s_n = 3n$

2 $s_k = (-1)^k \dfrac{1}{k}$

3 $s_i = i^2$

4 $s_i = i^3$

5 $s_k = \dfrac{3}{10^k}$

6 $s_n = -6 + 2(n - 1)$

7 Find $\sum_{n=1}^{8} s_n$ where $s_n = 2^n$.

8 Find $\sum_{n=0}^{8} s_n$ where $s_n = \dfrac{1}{2^n}$.

9 Find $\sum_{k=1}^{20} s_k$ where $s_k = 3$.

Find each of the following sums for n = 7.

10 $2 + 4 + \ldots + 2n$

11 $2 + 4 + \ldots + 2^n$

12 $-7 + 2 + \ldots + (9n - 16)$

13 $3 + \frac{3}{2} + \ldots + 3(\frac{1}{2})^{n-1}$

Compute each of the following.

14 $\sum_{k=1}^{6} (5k)$

15 $5\left(\sum_{k=1}^{6} k\right)$

16 $\sum_{n=1}^{4} (n^2 + n)$

17 $\sum_{n=1}^{4} n^2 + \sum_{n=1}^{4} n$

18 $\sum_{i=1}^{8} (i - 2i^2)$

19 $\sum_{k=1}^{4} \dfrac{k}{2^k}$

20 $\sum_{k=1}^{7} (-1)^k$

21 $\sum_{k=1}^{8} (-1)^k$

22 $\sum_{k=3}^{7} (2k - 5)$

23 $\sum_{j=1}^{6} [-3 + (j - 1)5]$

24 $\sum_{k=-3}^{3} 10^k$

25 $\sum_{k=-3}^{3} \dfrac{1}{10^k}$

26 $\sum_{k=1}^{5} 4(-\frac{1}{2})^{k-1}$

27 $\sum_{i=1}^{4} (-1)^i 3^i$

28 $\sum_{n=1}^{3} \left(\dfrac{n+1}{n} - \dfrac{n}{n+1}\right)$

29 $\sum_{n=1}^{3} \dfrac{n+1}{n} - \sum_{n=1}^{3} \dfrac{n}{n+1}$

30 $\sum_{k=1}^{8} \dfrac{1 + (-1)^k}{2}$

31 $\sum_{k=1}^{3} (0.1)^{2k}$

32 Read the discussion at the beginning of this section, where we found the sum of the first 1000 positive integers, and find a formula for the sum of the first n positive integers for n even.

33 (a) Find $\sum_{k=1}^{n} (2k - 1)$ for each of the following values of n: 2, 3, 4, 5, 6.

(b) On the basis of the results in part (a), find a formula for the sum of the first n odd numbers.

34 The sequence 1, 1, 2, 3, 5, 8, 13, ... is called the *Fibonacci sequence*. Its first two terms are ones, and each term thereafter is computed by adding the preceding two terms.

(a) Write the next seven terms of this sequence.

(b) Let $u_1, u_2, u_3, \ldots, u_n, \ldots$ be the Fibonacci sequence. Evaluate $S_n = \sum_{k=1}^{n} u_k$ for these values of n: 1, 2, 3, 4, 5, 6, 7, 8.

*(c) Note that $u_1 = u_3 - u_2$, $u_2 = u_4 - u_3$, $u_3 = u_5 - u_4$, and so on. Use this form for the first n numbers to derive a formula for the sum of the first n Fibonacci numbers.

*35 Let s_n be a sequence with $s_1 = 2$ and $s_m + s_n = s_{m+n}$, where m and n are any positive integers. Show that $s_n = 2n$ for any n.

*36 Show that $\sum_{k=1}^{9} \log \dfrac{k+1}{k} = 1$.

$\left(Hint:\ \log \dfrac{a}{b} = \log a - \log b. \right)$

*37 Prove: $\sum_{k=1}^{n} s_k + \sum_{k=1}^{n} t_k = \sum_{k=1}^{n} (s_k + t_k)$.

*38 Prove: $\sum_{k=1}^{n} cs_k = c \sum_{k=1}^{n} s_k$, c a constant.

*39 Prove: $\sum_{k=1}^{n} (s_k + c) = \left(\sum_{k=1}^{n} s_k \right) + nc$, c a constant.

*40 Evaluate $\sum_{k=1}^{10} \dfrac{1}{k(k+1)}$ using the result

$$\dfrac{1}{k(k+1)} = \dfrac{1}{k} - \dfrac{1}{k+1}$$

10.3

Arithmetic sequences and series

Here are the first five terms of the sequence whose general term is $s_k = 7k - 2$:

$$5,\ 12,\ 19,\ 26,\ 33$$

Do you notice any special pattern? It does not take long to observe that each term, after the first, is 7 more than the preceding term. This sequence is an example of an *arithmetic sequence*.

An arithmetic sequence is also referred to as an *arithmetic progression*.

ARITHMETIC SEQUENCE

A sequence is said to be *arithmetic* if each term, after the first, is obtained from the preceding term by adding a common value.

Let us consider the first four terms of three different arithmetic sequences:

$$2, 4, 6, 8, \ldots$$
$$-\tfrac{1}{2}, -1, -\tfrac{3}{2}, -2, \ldots$$
$$11, 2, -7, -16, \ldots$$

For the first sequence, the common value (or difference) that is added to each term to get the next is 2. Thus it is easy to see that 10, 12, and 14 are the next three terms. You might guess that the nth term is $s_n = 2n$.

The second sequence has the common difference $-\tfrac{1}{2}$. This can be found by subtracting the first term from the second, or the second from the third, and so forth. The nth term is $s_n = -\tfrac{1}{2}n$.

The third sequence has -9 as its common difference, but it is not so easy to see what the general term is. Rather than employ a hit-or-miss process in trying to find the general term of this sequence, we will instead consider arithmetic sequences in general, thus making it possible to write the general term of any such sequence.

Let s_n be the nth term of an arithmetic sequence. Denote its first term by the letter a; that is, $s_1 = a$. Also, let d be the common difference. Then the first four terms are

$$s_1 = a$$
$$s_2 = s_1 + d = a + d$$
$$s_3 = s_2 + d = (a + d) + d = a + 2d$$
$$s_4 = s_3 + d = (a + 2d) + d = a + 3d$$

The pattern is clear. Without further computation we see that
$$s_5 = a + 4d$$
$$s_6 = a + 5d$$

Since the coefficient of d is always 1 less than the number of the term, the nth term is given as follows.

The nth term of an arithmetic sequence is
$$s_n = a + (n - 1)d$$
where a is the first term and d is common difference.

This formula says that the nth term of an arithmetic sequence is completely identified by its first term a and its common difference d.

By substituting the values $n = 1, 2, 3, 4, 5, 6$, you can check that this formula gives the preceding terms s_1 through s_6.

Let us return to the sequence given earlier: $11, 2, -7, -16, \ldots$. It is now easy to find its nth term, with $a = 11$ and $d = -9$:
$$s_n = 11 + (n - 1)(-9)$$
$$= -9n + 20$$

TEST YOUR UNDERSTANDING

Each of the following gives the first few terms of an arithmetic sequence. Find the nth term in each case.

1 $5, 10, 15, \ldots$

2 $6, 2, -2, \ldots$

3 $\frac{1}{10}, \frac{1}{5}, \frac{3}{10}, \ldots$

4 $-5, -13, -21, \ldots$

5 $1, 2, 3, \ldots$

6 $-3, -2, -1, \ldots$

Find the nth term s_n of the arithmetic sequence with the given values for the first term and the common difference.

7 $a = \frac{2}{3}; d = \frac{2}{3}$

8 $a = 53; d = -12$

9 $a = 0; d = \frac{1}{5}$

10 $a = 2; d = 1$

Adding the terms of a finite sequence may not be much work when the number of terms to be added is small. When many terms are to be added, however, the amount of time and effort needed can be overwhelming. For example, to add the first 10,000 terms of the arithmetic sequence beginning with

$$246, 261, 276, \ldots$$

The sum of an arithmetic
sequence is called an *arithmetic
series*.

would call for an enormous effort, unless some shortcut could be found. Fortunately, there is an easy way available to find such sums. This method (in disguise) was already used in the question at the start of Section 10.2. Let us look at the general situation. Let S_n denote the sum of the first n terms of the arithmetic sequence given by $s_k = a + (k - 1)d$:

$$S_n = \sum_{k=1}^{n} [a + (k - 1)d]$$

$$= a + [a + d] + [a + 2d] + \cdots + [a + (n - 1)d]$$

Put this sum in reverse order and write the two equalities together as follows:

$$S_n = \quad a \quad + \quad [a+d] \quad + \cdots + [a+(n-2)d] + [a+(n-1)d]$$

$$\updownarrow \qquad\qquad \updownarrow \qquad\qquad\qquad \updownarrow \qquad\qquad \updownarrow$$

$$S_n = [a+(n-1)d] + [a+(n-2)d] + \cdots + \quad [a+d] \quad + \quad a$$

Now add to get

$$2S_n = [2a+(n-1)d] + [2a+(n-1)d] + \cdots + [2a+(n-1)d] + [2a+(n-1)d]$$

On the right-hand side of this equation there are n terms of the form $2a + (n - 1)d$. Therefore,

$$2S_n = n[2a + (n - 1)d]$$

Divide by 2 to solve for S_n:

$$S_n = \frac{n}{2}[2a + (n - 1)d]$$

Returning to the sigma notation, we can summarize our results this way:

ARITHMETIC SERIES

$$\sum_{k=1}^{n} [a + (k - 1)d] = \frac{n}{2}[2a + (n - 1)d]$$

EXAMPLE 1 Find S_{20} for the arithmetic sequence whose first term is $a = 3$ and whose common difference is $d = 5$.

Solution Substituting $a = 3$, $d = 5$, and $n = 20$ into the formula for S_n, we have

$$S_{20} = \frac{20}{2}[2(3) + (20 - 1)5]$$

$$= 10(6 + 95)$$

$$= 1010$$

EXAMPLE 2 Find the sum of the first 10,000 terms of the arithmetic sequence beginning with 246, 261, 276, ...

Solution Since $a = 246$ and $d = 15$,

$$S_{10,000} = \frac{10,000}{2}[2(246) + (10,000 - 1)15]$$

$$= 5000(150,477)$$

$$= 752,385,000$$

EXAMPLE 3 Find the sum of the first n positive integers.

Solution First observe that the problem calls for the sum of the sequence $s_k = k$ for $k = 1, 2, \ldots, n$. This is an arithmetic sequence with $a = 1$ and $d = 1$. Therefore,

$$\sum_{k=1}^{n} k = \frac{n}{2}[2 + (n - 1)1] = \frac{n(n + 1)}{2}$$

With the result of Example 3 we are able to check the answer for the sum of the first 1000 positive integers, found at the beginning of Section 10.2, as follows:

$$\sum_{k=1}^{1000} k = \frac{1000(1001)}{2} = 500,500$$

The form $s_k = a + (k - 1)d$ for the general term of an arithmetic sequence easily converts to

$$s_k = dk + (a - d)$$

It is this latter form that is ordinarily used when the general term of a *specific* arithmetic sequence is given. For example, we would usually begin with the form

$$s_k = 3k + 5$$

instead of

$$s_k = 8 + (k - 1)3$$

The important thing to notice in the form $s_k = dk + (a - d)$ is that the common difference is the coefficient of k.

EXAMPLE 4 Find: $\sum_{k=1}^{50} (-6k + 10)$.

Solution First note that $s_k = -6k + 10$ is an arithmetic sequence with $d = -6$ and with $a = s_1 = 4$.

$$\sum_{k=1}^{50} (-6k + 10) = \frac{50}{2}[2(4) + (50 - 1)(-6)]$$

$$= -7150$$

EXERCISES 10.3

Each of the following gives the first two terms of an arithmetic sequence. Write the next three terms; find the nth term; and find the sum of the first 20 terms.

1 $1, 3, \ldots$ 2 $2, 4, \ldots$

3 $2, -4, \ldots$ 4 $1, -3, \ldots$

5 $\frac{15}{2}, 8, \ldots$ 6 $-\frac{4}{3}, -\frac{11}{3}, \ldots$

7 $\frac{2}{5}, -\frac{1}{5}, \ldots$ 8 $-\frac{1}{2}, \frac{1}{4}, \ldots$

9 $50, 100, \ldots$ 10 $-27, -2, \ldots$

11 $-10, 10, \ldots$ 12 $225, 163, \ldots$

Find the indicated sum by using ordinary addition; also find the sum by using the formula for the sum of an arithmetic sequence.

13 $5 + 10 + 15 + 20 + 25 + 30 + 35 + 40 + 45 + 50 + 55 + 60 + 65$

14 $-33 - 25 - 17 - 9 - 1 + 7 + 15 + 23 + 31 + 39$

15 $\frac{3}{4} + 1 + \frac{5}{4} + \frac{3}{2} + \frac{7}{4} + 2 + \frac{9}{4} + \frac{5}{2} + \frac{11}{4}$

16 $128 + 71 + 14 - 43 - 100 - 157$

In Exercises 17–24, find S_{100} for the arithmetic sequence with the given values for a and d.

17 $a = 3; d = 3$ 18 $a = 1; d = 8$

19 $a = -91; d = 21$ 20 $a = -7; d = -10$

21 $a = \frac{1}{7}; d = 5$ 22 $a = \frac{2}{5}; d = -4$

23 $a = 725; d = 100$ 24 $a = 0.1; d = 10$

25 Find S_{28} for the sequence $-8, 8, \ldots, 16n - 24,$ $\ldots$

26 Find S_{25} for the sequence $96, 100, \ldots, 4n + 92,$ $\ldots$

27 Find the sum of the first 50 positive multiples of 12.

28 (a) Find the sum of the first 100 positive even numbers.

     (b) Find the sum of the first n positive even numbers.

29 (a) Find the sum of the first 100 positive odd numbers.

     (b) Find the sum of the first n positive odd numbers.

Evaluate the series in each of Exercises 30–37.

30 $\sum\limits_{k=1}^{12} [3 + (k - 1)9]$ 31 $\sum\limits_{k=1}^{9} [-6 + (k - 1)\frac{1}{2}]$

32 $\sum\limits_{k=1}^{20} (4k - 15)$ 33 $\sum\limits_{k=1}^{30} (10k - 1)$

34 $\sum\limits_{k=1}^{40} (-\frac{1}{3}k + 2)$ 35 $\sum\limits_{k=1}^{49} (\frac{3}{4}k - \frac{1}{2})$

36 $\sum\limits_{k=1}^{20} 5k$ 37 $\sum\limits_{k=1}^{n} 5k$

38 Find u such that $7, u, 19$ is an arithmetic sequence.

39 Find u such that $-7, u, \frac{5}{2}$ is an arithmetic sequence.

40 Find the twenty-third term of the arithmetic sequence $6, -4, \ldots$.

41 Find the thirty-fifth term of the arithmetic sequence $-\frac{2}{3}, -\frac{1}{3}, \ldots$.

42 An object is dropped from an airplane and falls 32 feet during the first second. During each successive second it falls 48 feet more than in the preceding second. How many feet does it travel during the first 10 seconds? How far does it fall during the tenth second?

43 Suppose you save $10 one week and that each week thereafter you save 50¢ more than the preceding week. How much will you have saved by the end of 1 year?

44 A pyramid of blocks has 26 blocks in the bottom row and 2 fewer blocks in each successive row thereafter. How many blocks are there in the pyramid?

*45 Find $\sum\limits_{n=6}^{20} (5n - 3)$.

*46 Find the sum of all the even numbers between 33 and 427.

*47 If $\sum\limits_{k=1}^{30} [a + (k - 1)d] = -5865$ and

$\sum\limits_{k=1}^{20} [a + (k - 1)d] = -2610$, find a and d.

48 Listing the first few terms of a sequence like 2, 4, 6, . . . , without stating its general term or describing just what kind of sequence it is makes it impossible to predict the next term. Show that both $t_n = 2n$ and $s_n = 2n + (n - 1)(n - 2)(n - 3)$ produce these first three terms but that their fourth terms are different.

*49 Find u and v such that $3, u, v, 10$ is an arithmetic sequence.

*50 Show that the sum of an arithmetic sequence of n terms is n times the average of the first and last terms.

Use the result in Exercise 50 to find S_{80} for the given arithmetic sequences.

51 $s_k = 3k - 8$

52 $s_k = \frac{1}{2}k + 10$

53 $s_k = -5k$

54 What is the connection between arithmetic sequences and linear functions?

*55 The function f defined by $f(x) = 3x + 7$ is a linear function. Evaluate the series $\sum\limits_{k=1}^{16} f_k$, where $f_k = f(k)$ is the arithmetic sequence associated with f.

10.4

Suppose that a ball is dropped from a height of 4 feet and bounces straight up and down, always bouncing up exactly one-half the distance it just came down. How far will the ball have traveled if you catch it after it reaches the top of the fifth bounce? The following figure will help you to answer this question. For the sake of clarity, the bounces have been separated in the figure.

Geometric sequences and series

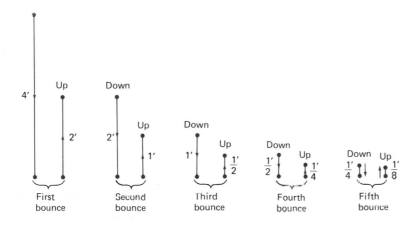

From this diagram we can determine how far the ball has traveled on each bounce. On the first bounce it goes 4 feet down and 2 feet up, for a total of 6 feet; on the second bounce the total distance is $2 + 1 = 3$ feet; and so on. These distances form the following sequence of five terms (one for each bounce):

$$6, \ 3, \ \tfrac{3}{2}, \ \tfrac{3}{4}, \ \tfrac{3}{8}$$

This sequence has the special property that, after the first term, each successive term can be obtained by multiplying the preceding term by $\frac{1}{2}$; that is, the second term, 3, is half the first, 6, and so on. This is an example of a *geometric sequence*. Later we will develop a formula for finding the sum of such a sequence; in the meantime, we can find the total distance the ball has traveled during the five bounces by adding the five terms as follows:

$$6 + 3 + \frac{3}{2} + \frac{3}{4} + \frac{3}{8} = \frac{48 + 24 + 12 + 6 + 3}{8} = 11\frac{5}{8}$$

A geometric sequence is also referred to as a *geometric progression.*

GEOMETRIC SEQUENCE

A sequence is said to be *geometric* if each term, after the first, is obtained by multiplying the preceding term by a common value.

Here are the first four terms of three different geometric sequences.

$$2, -4, 8, -16, \ldots$$
$$1, \tfrac{1}{3}, \tfrac{1}{9}, \tfrac{1}{27}, \ldots$$
$$5, -5, 5, -5, \ldots$$

By inspection you can determine that the common multipliers for these sequences are -2, $\tfrac{1}{3}$, and -1, respectively. We will find their nth terms by deriving the formula for the nth term of any geometric sequence.

Let s_n be the nth term of a geometric sequence, and let a be its first term. The common multiplier, which is also called the **common ratio**, is denoted by r. Here are the first five terms:

$$s_1 = a$$
$$s_2 = ar$$
$$s_3 = ar^2$$
$$s_4 = ar^3$$
$$s_5 = ar^4$$

Notice that the exponent of r is 1 less than the number of the term. This observation allows us to write the nth term as follows:

This formula says that the nth term of a geometric sequence is completely determined by its first term a and common ratio r.

The nth term of a geometric sequence is

$$s_n = ar^{n-1}$$

where a is the first term and r is the common ratio.

With this result, the first four terms and the nth terms of the three given geometric sequences are as follows:

$$2, -4, 8, -16, \ldots, 2(-2)^{n-1}$$
$$1, \tfrac{1}{3}, \tfrac{1}{9}, \tfrac{1}{27}, \ldots, 1(\tfrac{1}{3})^{n-1}$$
$$5, -5, 5, -5, \ldots, 5(-1)^{n-1}$$

You can substitute the values $n = 1, 2, 3,$ and 4 into the forms for the nth terms and see that the given first four terms are obtained in each case.

EXAMPLE 1 Find the hundredth term of the geometric sequence having $r = \tfrac{1}{2}$ and $a = \tfrac{1}{2}$.

Solution The nth term of this sequence is given by

$$s_n = \frac{1}{2}\left(\frac{1}{2}\right)^{n-1}$$

$$= \frac{1}{2}\left(\frac{1}{2^{n-1}}\right)$$

$$= \frac{1}{2^n}$$

Thus

$$s_{100} = \frac{1}{2^{100}}$$

The reason r is called the common ratio of a geometric sequence $s_n = ar^{n-1}$ is that for each n the ratio of the $(n+1)$st term to the nth term equals r. Thus

$$\frac{s_{n+1}}{s_n} = \frac{ar^n}{ar^{n-1}} = r$$

EXAMPLE 2 Find the nth term of the geometric sequence beginning with

$$6, 9, \tfrac{27}{2}, \ldots$$

and find the seventh term.

Solution First find r.

$$r = \frac{s_2}{s_1} = \frac{9}{6} = \frac{3}{2}$$

Then the nth term is

$$s_n = 6\left(\frac{3}{2}\right)^{n-1}$$

Let $n = 7$ to get

$$s_7 = 6\left(\frac{3}{2}\right)^{7-1} = 6\left(\frac{3}{2}\right)^6$$

$$= (3 \cdot 2) \cdot \frac{3^6}{2^6} = \frac{3^7}{2^5} = \frac{2187}{32}$$

r can also be found using s_2 and s_3.

$$\frac{s_3}{s_2} = \frac{\frac{27}{2}}{9} = \frac{27}{2 \cdot 9} = \frac{3}{2}$$

EXAMPLE 3 Write the kth term of the geometric sequence $s_k = (\tfrac{1}{2})^{2k}$ in the form ar^{k-1} and find the value of a and r.

Solution

$$s_k = (\tfrac{1}{2})^{2k} = [(\tfrac{1}{2})^2]^k = (\tfrac{1}{4})^k$$

$$= \tfrac{1}{4}(\tfrac{1}{4})^{k-1} \quad \leftarrow \quad \text{this is now in the form } ar^{n-1}$$

Then $a = \tfrac{1}{4}$ and $r = \tfrac{1}{4}$.

Note: The first term a can *also* be found by simply computing s_1 in the given formula for s_k; the value of r, however, is not so obvious in this original form.

Write the first five terms of the geometric sequences with the given general term. Also write the nth term in the form ar^{n-1} and find r.

1 $s_n = (\frac{1}{2})^{n-1}$ **2** $s_n = (\frac{1}{2})^{n+1}$

3 $s_n = (-\frac{1}{2})^n$ **4** $s_n = (-\frac{1}{3})^{3n}$

Find r and the nth term of the geometric sequence with the given first two terms.

5 $\frac{1}{5}, 2$ **6** $27, -12$

Let us return to the original problem of this section. We found that the total distance the ball traveled was $11\frac{5}{8}$ feet. This is the sum of the first five terms of the geometric sequence whose nth term is $6(\frac{1}{2})^{n-1}$. Adding these five terms was easy. But what about adding the first 100 terms? There is a formula for the sum of a geometric sequence that will enable us to find such answers efficiently.

The sum of a geometric sequence is called a **geometric series**. Just as with arithmetic series, there is a formula for finding such sums. To discover this formula, let $s_k = ar^{k-1}$ be a geometric sequence and denote the sum of the first n terms by $S_n = \sum_{k=1}^{n} ar^{k-1}$. Then

$$S_n = a + ar + ar^2 + \cdots + ar^{n-2} + ar^{n-1}$$

Multiplying this equation by r gives

$$rS_n = ar + ar^2 + \cdots + ar^{n-1} + ar^n$$

Now consider these two equations:

$$S_n = a + ar + ar^2 + \cdots + ar^{n-2} + ar^{n-1}$$
$$rS_n = \quad\quad ar + ar^2 + \cdots + ar^{n-2} + ar^{n-1} + ar^n$$

Subtract and factor:

$$S_n - rS_n = a - ar^n$$
$$(1 - r)S_n = a(1 - r^n)$$

Divide by $1 - r$ to solve for S_n:

$$S_n = \frac{a(1 - r^n)}{1 - r}$$

Here $r \neq 1$. However, when $r = 1$, $s_k = ar^{k-1} = a$, which is an arithmetic sequence having $d = 0$.

Returning to sigma notation, we can summarize our results this way:

GEOMETRIC SERIES

$$\sum_{k=1}^{n} ar^{k-1} = \frac{a(1 - r^n)}{1 - r}$$

This formula can be used to verify the earlier result for the bouncing ball:

$$\sum_{k=1}^{5} 6\left(\frac{1}{2}\right)^{k-1} = \frac{6[1 - (\frac{1}{2})^5]}{1 - \frac{1}{2}}$$

$$= \frac{6(1 - \frac{1}{32})}{\frac{1}{2}}$$

$$= \frac{93}{8}$$

$$= 11\frac{5}{8}$$

EXAMPLE 4 Find the sum of the first 100 terms of the geometric sequence given by $s_k = 6(\frac{1}{2})^{k-1}$ and show that the answer is very close to 12.

Solution

$$S_{100} = \frac{6\left(1 - \frac{1}{2^{100}}\right)}{1 - \frac{1}{2}}$$

$$= 12\left(1 - \frac{1}{2^{100}}\right)$$

Next observe that the fraction $\frac{1}{2^{100}}$ is so small that $1 - \frac{1}{2^{100}}$ is very nearly equal to 1, and therefore S_{100} is very close to 12.

EXAMPLE 5 Evaluate $\sum_{k=1}^{8} 3(\frac{1}{10})^{k+1}$.

Solution We get $3(\frac{1}{10})^{k+1} = \frac{3}{100}(\frac{1}{10})^{k-1}$. Then $a = 0.03$, $r = 0.1$, and

$$S_8 = \frac{0.03[1 - (0.1)^8]}{1 - 0.1}$$

$$= \frac{0.03(1 - 0.00000001)}{0.9}$$

$$= 0.033333333$$

Geometric sequences have many applications, as illustrated in the next example. You will find others in the exercises at the end of this section.

EXAMPLE 6 Suppose that you save $128 in January and that each month thereafter you only manage to save half of what you saved the previous month. How much do you save in the tenth month, and what are your total savings after 10 months?

Solution The amounts saved each month form a geometric sequence with $a = 128$ and $r = \frac{1}{2}$. Then $s_n = 128(\frac{1}{2})^{n-1}$ and

$$s_{10} = 128\left(\frac{1}{2}\right)^9 = \frac{2^7}{2^9} = \frac{1}{4} = 0.25$$

This means that you saved 25¢ in the tenth month. Your total savings is given by

$$S_{10} = \frac{128\left(1 - \dfrac{1}{2^{10}}\right)}{1 - \frac{1}{2}}$$

$$= 256\left(1 - \frac{1}{2^{10}}\right)$$

$$= 256 - \frac{256}{2^{10}}$$

$$= 256 - \frac{2^8}{2^{10}}$$

$$= 255.75$$

EXERCISES 10.4

The first three terms of a geometric sequence are given in Exercises 1–12. Write the next three terms and also find the formula for the nth term.

1 $2, 4, 8, \ldots$

2 $2, -4, 8, \ldots$

3 $1, 3, 9, \ldots$

4 $2, -2, 2, \ldots$

5 $-3, 1, -\frac{1}{3}, \ldots$

6 $100, 10, 1, \ldots$

7 $-1, -5, -25, \ldots$

8 $12, -6, 3, \ldots$

9 $-6, -4, -\frac{8}{3}, \ldots$

10 $-64, 16, -4, \ldots$

11 $\frac{1}{1000}, \frac{1}{10}, 10, \ldots$

12 $\frac{27}{8}, \frac{3}{2}, \frac{2}{3}, \ldots$

In Exercises 13–15, find the sum of the first six terms of the indicated sequence by using ordinary addition and also by using the formula for a geometric series.

13 The sequence in Exercise 1.

14 The sequence in Exercise 5.

15 The sequence in Exercise 9.

16 Find the tenth term of the geometric sequence $2, 4, 8, \ldots$.

17 Find the fourteenth term of the geometric sequence $\frac{1}{8}, \frac{1}{4}, \frac{1}{2}, \ldots$.

18 Find the fifteenth term of the geometric sequence
$$\frac{1}{100,000}, \frac{1}{10,000}, \frac{1}{1000}, \ldots.$$

19 What is the one-hundred-first term of the geometric sequence having $a = 3$ and $r = -1$?

20 For the geometric sequence with $a = 100$ and $r = \frac{1}{10}$, use the formula $s_n = ar^{n-1}$ to find which term is equal to $\frac{1}{10^{10}}$.

Evaluate the series in Exercises 21–29.

21 $\sum\limits_{k=1}^{10} 2^{k-1}$

22 $\sum\limits_{j=1}^{10} 2^{j+2}$

23 $\sum\limits_{k=1}^{n} 2^{k-1}$

24 $\sum\limits_{k=1}^{8} 3(\frac{1}{10})^{k-1}$

25 $\sum\limits_{k=1}^{5} 3^{k-4}$

26 $\sum\limits_{k=1}^{6} (-3)^{k-2}$

27 $\sum\limits_{j=1}^{5} (\frac{2}{3})^{j-2}$

28 $\sum\limits_{k=1}^{8} 16(\frac{1}{2})^{k+2}$

29 $\sum\limits_{k=1}^{8} 16(-\frac{1}{2})^{k+2}$

30 Find $u > 0$ such that $2, u, 98$ forms a geometric sequence.

31 Find $u < 0$ such that $\frac{1}{7}, u, \frac{25}{63}$ forms a geometric sequence.

32 Suppose that the amount you save in any given month is twice the amount you saved in the previous months. How much will you have saved at the end of 1 year if you save \$1 in January? How much if you saved 25¢ in January?

33 A certain bacterial culture doubles in number

every day. If there were 1000 bacteria at the end of the first day, how many will there be after 10 days? How many after n days?

*34 A radioactive substance is decaying so that at the end of each month there is only one-third as much as there was at the beginning of the month. If there were 75 grams of the substance at the beginning of the year, how much is left at midyear?

*35 Suppose that an automobile depreciates 10% in value each year for the first 5 years. What is it worth after 5 years if its original cost was $5280? (*Hint:* Use $a = 5280$ and $n = 6$.)

*36 Compound-interest problems can be explained in terms of geometric sequences. The basic idea is that an investment P will earn i percent interest for the first year. Then the new total, consisting of the original investment P plus the interest Pi, will earn i percent interest for the second year, and so on. In such a situation we say that P earns i percent interest **compounded annually**.

(a) If $1000 is invested in a bank paying 6% interest compounded annually, the amount at the end of the first year is

$$1000 + 1000(0.06) = 1000(1.06) = 1060$$

After 2 years the amount becomes

$$1060 + 1060(0.06) = 1060(1.06) = 1123.60$$

What is the amount after 3 years?

(b) Let A_1 be the amount after 1 year on an investment of P dollars at i percent interest compounded annually. Then

$$A_1 = P + Pi = P(1 + i)$$

After the second year:

$$\begin{aligned} A_2 &= P(1 + i) + P(1 + i)i \\ &= P(1 + i)(1 + i) \\ &= P(1 + i)^2 \end{aligned}$$

Find A_3.

(c) Referring to part (b), find the formula for A_n, the amount after n years, and show that this is the nth term of a geometric sequence having ratio $r = 1 + i$.

*37 A sum of $800 is invested at 11% interest compounded annually.

(a) What is the amount after n years?

(b) What is the amount after 5 years? (Use common logarithms to get an approximation.)

*38 How much money must be invested at the interest rate of 12%, compounded annually, so that after 3 years the amount is $1000?

*39 Use a calculator to find the amount of money that an investment of $1500 earns at the interest rate of 8% compounded annually for 5 years.

10.5

Infinite geometric series

In decimal form the fraction $\frac{3}{4}$ becomes 0.75, which means $\frac{75}{100}$. This can also be written as $\frac{7}{10} + \frac{5}{100}$. What about $\frac{1}{3}$? As a decimal we can write

$$\tfrac{1}{3} = 0.333 \ldots$$

where the dots mean that the 3 repeats endlessly. We can express this decimal as the sum of fractions whose denominators are powers of 10:

$$\tfrac{1}{3} = \tfrac{3}{10} + \tfrac{3}{100} + \tfrac{3}{1000} + \cdots$$

The numbers being added here are the terms of the *infinite geometric sequence* with first term $a = \frac{3}{10}$ and common ratio $r = \frac{1}{10}$. Thus the nth term is

The sum of an infinite sequence is an infinite series.

$$\begin{aligned} ar^{n-1} &= \frac{3}{10}\left(\frac{1}{10}\right)^{n-1} = 3\left(\frac{1}{10}\right)\left(\frac{1}{10}\right)^{n-1} \\ &= 3\left(\frac{1}{10}\right)^{n} \\ &= \frac{3}{10^{n}} \end{aligned}$$

The sum of the first n terms is found by using the formula

$$S_n = \sum_{k=1}^{n} ar^{k-1} = \frac{a(1 - r^n)}{1 - r}$$

Here are some cases:

$$S_1 = \frac{\frac{3}{10}\left(1 - \frac{1}{10}\right)}{1 - \frac{1}{10}} = \frac{1}{3}\left(1 - \frac{1}{10}\right) = 0.3$$

$$S_2 = \frac{\frac{3}{10}\left(1 - \frac{1}{10^2}\right)}{1 - \frac{1}{10}} = \frac{1}{3}\left(1 - \frac{1}{10^2}\right) = 0.33$$

$$S_3 = \frac{\frac{3}{10}\left(1 - \frac{1}{10^3}\right)}{1 - \frac{1}{10}} = \frac{1}{3}\left(1 - \frac{1}{10^3}\right) = 0.333$$

$$S_{10} = \frac{\frac{3}{10}\left(1 - \frac{1}{10^{10}}\right)}{1 - \frac{1}{10}} = \frac{1}{3}\left(1 - \frac{1}{10^{10}}\right) = 0.3333333333$$

$$S_n = \frac{\frac{3}{10}\left(1 - \frac{1}{10^n}\right)}{1 - \frac{1}{10}} = \frac{1}{3}\left(1 - \frac{1}{10^n}\right) = 0.\underbrace{333\ldots3}_{n \text{ places}}$$

You can see that as more and more terms are added, the closer and closer the answer gets to $\frac{1}{3}$. This can be seen by studying the form for the sum of the first n terms:

$$S_n = \frac{1}{3}\left(1 - \frac{1}{10^n}\right)$$

It is clear that the bigger n is, the closer $\frac{1}{10^n}$ is to zero, the closer $1 - \frac{1}{10^n}$ is to 1 and, finally, the closer S_n is to $\frac{1}{3}$. Although it is true that S_n is never exactly equal to $\frac{1}{3}$, for very large n the difference between S_n and $\frac{1}{3}$ is very small. Saying this another way:

By taking n large enough, S_n can be made as close to $\frac{1}{3}$ as we like.

This is what we mean when we say that the sum of all the terms is $\frac{1}{3}$. In symbols:

$$\frac{3}{10} + \frac{3}{10^2} + \frac{3}{10^3} + \cdots + \frac{3}{10^n} + \cdots = \frac{1}{3}$$

The summation symbol, $\sum$, can also be used here after an adjustment in notation is made. Traditionally, the symbol ∞ has been used to suggest an infinite number of objects. So we use this and make the transition from the sum of a finite number of terms

$$S_n = \sum_{k=1}^{n} \frac{3}{10^k} = \frac{3}{10} + \frac{3}{10^2} + \cdots + \frac{3}{10^n} = \frac{1}{3}\left(1 - \frac{3}{10^n}\right)$$

to the sum of an infinite number of terms:

$$S_\infty = \sum_{k=1}^{\infty} \frac{3}{10^k} = \frac{3}{10} + \frac{3}{10^2} + \cdots + \frac{3}{10^n} + \cdots = \frac{1}{3}$$

In calculus the symbol S_∞ is replaced by $\lim_{n \to \infty} S_n = \frac{1}{3}$, which is read as "the limit of S_n as n gets arbitrarily large is $\frac{1}{3}$."

Not every geometric sequence produces an infinite geometric series that has a finite sum. For instance, the sequence

$$2, 4, 8, \ldots, 2^n, \ldots$$

is geometric, but the corresponding geometric series

$$2 + 4 + 8 + \cdots + 2^n + \cdots$$

cannot have a finite sum.

By now you might suspect that the common ratio r determines whether or not an infinite geometric sequence can be added. This turns out to be true. To see how this works, the general case will be considered next.

Let

$$a, ar, ar^2, \ldots, ar^{n-1}, \ldots$$

be an infinite geometric sequence. The sum of the first n terms is

$$S_n = \frac{a(1 - r^n)}{1 - r}$$

Rewrite in this form:

$$S_n = \frac{a}{1 - r}(1 - r^n)$$

At this point the importance of r^n becomes clear. If, as n gets larger, r^n gets very large, then the infinite geometric series will not have a finite sum. But when r^n gets arbitrarily close to zero as n gets larger, then S_n gets closer and closer to $\frac{a}{1 - r}$.

The values of r for which r^n gets arbitrarily close to zero are precisely those values between -1 and 1; that is, $|r| < 1$. For instance, $\frac{3}{5}$, $-\frac{1}{10}$, and 0.09 are values of r for which r^n gets close to zero; and 1.01, -2, and $\frac{3}{2}$ are values for which r^n does not get close to zero.

To sum up, we have the following useful result:

Use a calculator to verify the powers of $r = 0.9$ and $r = 1.1$ to the indicated decimal places.

$(0.9)^1$	$= 0.9$
$(0.9)^{10}$	$= 0.35$
$(0.9)^{20}$	$= 0.12$
$(0.9)^{40}$	$= 0.015$
$(0.9)^{80}$	$= 0.0002$
$(0.9)^{100}$	$= 0.00003$

getting close to 0

SUM OF AN INFINITE GEOMETRIC SERIES

If $|r| < 1$, then $\sum_{k=1}^{\infty} ar^{k-1} = \frac{a}{1 - r}$. For other values of r the series has no finite sum.

$(1.1)^1$	$= 1.1$
$(1.1)^5$	$= 1.6$
$(1.1)^{10}$	$= 2.6$
$(1.1)^{20}$	$= 6.7$
$(1.1)^{50}$	$= 117.4$
$(1.1)^{100}$	$= 13780.6$

getting very large

EXAMPLE 1   Find the sum of the infinite geometric series

$$27 + 3 + \frac{1}{3} + \cdots$$

Solution Since $r = \frac{3}{27} = \frac{1}{9}$ and $a = 27$, the preceding result gives

$$27 + 3 + \frac{1}{3} + \cdots = \frac{27}{1 - \frac{1}{9}} = \frac{27}{\frac{8}{9}}$$

$$= \frac{243}{8}$$

EXAMPLE 2 Why does the infinite geometric series $\sum\limits_{k=1}^{\infty} 5(\frac{4}{3})^{k-1}$ have no finite sum?

Solution The series has no finite sum because the common ratio $r = \frac{4}{3}$ is not between -1 and 1.

EXAMPLE 3 Find: $\sum\limits_{k=1}^{\infty} \frac{7}{10^{k+1}}$.

Solution Since $\frac{7}{10^{k+1}} = 7\left(\frac{1}{10^{k+1}}\right) = 7\left(\frac{1}{10^2}\right)\left(\frac{1}{10^{k-1}}\right) = \frac{7}{100}\left(\frac{1}{10}\right)^{k-1}$, it follows that $a = \frac{7}{100}$ and $r = \frac{1}{10}$. Therefore, by the formula for the sum of an infinite geometric series we have

$$S_\infty = \sum_{k=1}^{\infty} \frac{7}{10^{k+1}} = \frac{\frac{7}{100}}{1 - \frac{1}{10}} = \frac{7}{100 - 10}$$

$$= \frac{7}{90}$$

TEST YOUR UNDERSTANDING

Find the common ratio r, and then find the sum if the given infinite geometric series has one.

1 $10 + 1 + \frac{1}{10} + \cdots$ 2 $\frac{1}{64} + \frac{1}{16} + \frac{1}{4} + \cdots$

3 $36 - 6 + \frac{1}{6} - \cdots$ 4 $-16 - 4 - 1 - \cdots$

5 $\sum\limits_{k=1}^{\infty} (\frac{4}{3})^{k-1}$ 6 $\sum\limits_{k=1}^{\infty} 3(0.01)^k$

7 $\sum\limits_{i=1}^{\infty} (-1)^i 3^i$ 8 $\sum\limits_{n=1}^{\infty} 100(-\frac{9}{10})^{n+1}$

9 $101 - 102.01 + 103.0301 - \cdots$

The introduction to this section indicated how the endless repeating decimal 0.333. . . can be regarded as an infinite geometric series. The next example illustrates how such decimal fractions can be written in the rational form $\frac{a}{b}$ (the ratio of two integers) by using the formula for the sum of an infinite geometric series.

EXAMPLE 4 Express the repeating decimal 0.242424. . . in rational form.

Solution First write

$$0.242424\ldots = \frac{24}{100} + \frac{24}{10,000} + \frac{24}{1,000,000} + \cdots$$

$$= \frac{24}{10^2} + \frac{24}{10^4} + \frac{24}{10^6} + \cdots + \frac{24}{10^{2k}} + \cdots$$

$$= \sum_{k=1}^{\infty} \frac{24}{10^{2k}}$$

Next observe that

$$\frac{24}{10^{2k}} = 24\left(\frac{1}{10^{2k}}\right) = 24\left(\frac{1}{10^2}\right)^k$$

$$= 24\left(\frac{1}{100}\right)^k = \frac{24}{100}\left(\frac{1}{100}\right)^{k-1}$$

Then $a = \frac{24}{100}$, $r = \frac{1}{100}$, and

$$0.242424\ldots = \sum_{k=1}^{\infty} \frac{24}{10^{2k}}$$

$$= \frac{\frac{24}{100}}{1 - \frac{1}{100}}$$

$$= \frac{24}{99} = \frac{8}{33}$$

Compare the method shown in Example 4 with that developed in Exercise 45 of Section 1.2.

You can check this answer by dividing 33 into 8.

EXAMPLE 5 A racehorse running at the constant rate of 30 miles per hour will finish a 1-mile race in 2 minutes. Now consider the race broken down into the following parts: before the racehorse can finish the 1-mile race it must first reach the halfway mark; having done that, the horse must next reach the quarter pole; then it must reach the eighth pole; and so on. That is, it must always cover half the distance remaining before it can cover the whole distance. Show that the sum of the infinite number of time intervals is also 2 minutes.

It seems as if the horse cannot finish the race this way. But read on to see that there is really no contradiction with this interpretation.

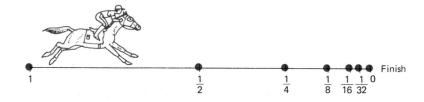

Solution For the first $\frac{1}{2}$ mile the time will be $\dfrac{\frac{1}{2}}{\frac{1}{2}} = 1$ minute; for the next

$\frac{1}{4}$ mile the time will be $\dfrac{\frac{1}{4}}{\frac{1}{2}} = \frac{1}{2}$ minute; for the next $\frac{1}{8}$ mile the time will be

$T = \dfrac{D}{R}\left(\text{time} = \dfrac{\text{distance}}{\text{rate}}\right)$

$\frac{\frac{1}{8}}{\frac{1}{2}} = \frac{1}{4}$ minute; and for the nth distance, which is $\frac{1}{2^n}$ miles, the time will be $\frac{\frac{1}{2^n}}{\frac{1}{2}} = \frac{1}{2^{n-1}}$.

Thus the total time is given by this series:

$$\sum_{k=1}^{\infty} \frac{1}{2^{k-1}} = 1 + \frac{1}{2} + \frac{1}{4} + \cdots + \frac{1}{2^{n-1}} + \cdots$$

This is an infinite geometric series having $a = 1$ and $r = \frac{1}{2}$. Thus

$$\sum_{k=1}^{\infty} 1\left(\frac{1}{2}\right)^{k-1} = \frac{1}{1 - \frac{1}{2}} = 2$$

which is the same result as before.

CAUTION: LEARN TO AVOID MISTAKES LIKE THESE

WRONG	RIGHT
$\sum_{k=1}^{\infty} \left(\frac{1}{2}\right)^{n+1} = \dfrac{1}{1 - \frac{1}{2}}$	$\sum_{n=1}^{\infty} \left(\frac{1}{2}\right)^{n+1} = \sum_{n=1}^{\infty} \frac{1}{4}\left(\frac{1}{2}\right)^{n-1}$ $= \dfrac{\frac{1}{4}}{1 - \frac{1}{2}}$
$\sum_{n=1}^{\infty} \left(-\frac{1}{3}\right)^{n-1} = \dfrac{1}{1 - \frac{1}{3}}$	$\sum_{n=1}^{\infty} \left(-\frac{1}{3}\right)^{n-1} = \dfrac{1}{1 - \left(-\frac{1}{3}\right)}$
$\sum_{n=1}^{\infty} 3(1.02)^{n-1} = \dfrac{3}{1 - 1.02}$	$\sum_{n=1}^{\infty} 3(1.02)^{n-1}$ is not a finite sum since $r = 1.02 > 1$

EXERCISES 10.5

Find the sum, if it exists, of each infinite geometric series.

1 $2 + 1 + \frac{1}{2} + \cdots$

2 $8 + 4 + 2 + \cdots$

3 $25 + 5 + 1 + \cdots$

4 $1 + \frac{4}{3} + \frac{16}{9} + \cdots$

5 $1 - \frac{1}{2} + \frac{1}{4} - \cdots$

6 $100 - 1 + \frac{1}{100} - \cdots$

7 $1 + 0.1 + 0.01 + \cdots$

8 $52 + 0.52 + 0.0052 + \cdots$

9 $-2 - \frac{1}{4} - \frac{1}{32} - \cdots$

10 $-729 + 81 - 9 + \cdots$

Decide whether or not the given infinite geometric series has a sum. If it does, find it using $S_\infty = \dfrac{a}{1 - r}$.

11 $\sum_{k=1}^{\infty} (\frac{1}{3})^{k-1}$

12 $\sum_{k=1}^{\infty} (\frac{4}{3})^{k}$

13 $\sum_{k=1}^{\infty} (\frac{1}{3})^{k+1}$

14 $\sum_{n=1}^{\infty} \frac{1}{2^{n+1}}$

15 $\displaystyle\sum_{n=1}^{\infty} \frac{1}{2^{n-2}}$ 16 $\displaystyle\sum_{k=1}^{\infty} (\tfrac{1}{10})^{k-1}$

17 $\displaystyle\sum_{k=1}^{\infty} 2(0.1)^{k-1}$ 18 $\displaystyle\sum_{k=1}^{\infty} (-\tfrac{1}{2})^{k-1}$

19 $\displaystyle\sum_{n=1}^{\infty} (\tfrac{3}{2})^{n-1}$ 20 $\displaystyle\sum_{n=1}^{\infty} (-\tfrac{1}{3})^{n+2}$

21 $\displaystyle\sum_{k=1}^{\infty} (0.7)^{k-1}$ 22 $\displaystyle\sum_{k=1}^{\infty} 5(0.7)^{k}$

23 $\displaystyle\sum_{k=1}^{\infty} 5(1.01)^{k}$ 24 $\displaystyle\sum_{k=1}^{\infty} (\tfrac{1}{10})^{k-4}$

25 $\displaystyle\sum_{k=1}^{\infty} 10(\tfrac{2}{3})^{k-1}$ 26 $\displaystyle\sum_{k=1}^{\infty} (-1)^{k}$

27 $\displaystyle\sum_{k=1}^{\infty} (0.45)^{k-1}$ 28 $\displaystyle\sum_{k=1}^{\infty} (-0.9)^{k+1}$

29 $\displaystyle\sum_{n=1}^{\infty} 7(-\tfrac{3}{4})^{n-1}$ 30 $\displaystyle\sum_{k=1}^{\infty} (0.1)^{2k}$

31 $\displaystyle\sum_{k=1}^{\infty} (-\tfrac{2}{5})^{2k}$

Find a rational form for each of the following repeating decimals in a manner similar to that in Example 4. Check your answers.

32 $0.444\ldots$ 33 $0.777\ldots$

34 $7.777\ldots$ 35 $0.131313\ldots$

36 $13.131313\ldots$ 37 $0.0131313\ldots$

38 $0.050505\ldots$ 39 $0.999\ldots$

40 $0.125125125\ldots$

*41 Suppose that a 1-mile distance a racehorse must run is divided into an infinite number of parts, obtained by always considering $\frac{2}{3}$ of the remaining distance to be covered. Then the lengths of these parts form the sequence $\frac{2}{3}, \frac{2}{9}, \frac{2}{27}, \ldots, \frac{2}{3^n}, \ldots$.

(a) Find the sequence of times corresponding to these distances. (Assume that the horse is moving at a rate of $\frac{1}{2}$ mile per minute.)

(b) Show that the sum of the times in part (a) is 2 minutes.

*42 A certain ball always rebounds $\frac{1}{3}$ the distance it falls. If the ball is dropped from a height of 9 feet, how far does it travel before coming to rest? (See the similar situation at the beginning of Section 10.4)

*43 A substance initially weighing 64 grams is decaying at a rate such that after 4 hours there are only 32 grams left. In another 2 hours only 16 grams remain; in another 1 hour after that only 8 grams remain; and so on. How long does it take altogether until nothing of the substance is left?

*44 After it is set in motion, each swing in either direction of a particular pendulum is 40% as long as the preceding swing. What is the total distance that the end of the pendulum travels before coming to rest if the first swing is 30 inches long?

*45 Assume that a racehorse takes 1 minute to go the first $\frac{1}{2}$ mile of a 1-mile race. After that, the horse's speed is no longer constant: for the next $\frac{1}{4}$ mile it takes $\frac{2}{3}$ minute; for the next $\frac{1}{8}$ mile it takes $\frac{4}{9}$ minute; for the next $\frac{1}{16}$ mile it takes $\frac{40}{81}$ minute; and so on, so that the time intervals form a geometric sequence. Why can't the horse finish the race?

10.6

Mathematical induction

Study these statements:

$$1 = 1^2$$
$$1 + 3 = 2^2$$
$$1 + 3 + 5 = 3^2$$
$$1 + 3 + 5 + 7 = 4^2$$
$$1 + 3 + 5 + 7 + 9 = 5^2$$

Do you see the pattern? The last statement shows that the sum of the first five positive odd integers is 5^2. What about the sum of the first six positive odd integers? The pattern is the same:

$$1 + 3 + 5 + 7 + 9 + 11 = 6^2$$

It would be reasonable to guess that the sum of the first *n* positive odd integers is n^2. That is,

$$1 + 3 + 5 + \cdots + (2n - 1) = n^2$$

But a guess is not a proof. It is our objective in this section to learn how to prove a statement that involves an infinite number of cases.

Let us refer to the *n*th statement above by S_n. Thus $S_1, S_2, S_3, S_4, S_5,$ and S_6 are the first six cases of S_n that we know are true.

Does the truth of the first six cases allow us to conclude that S_n is true for all positive integer *n*? No! We cannot assume that a few special cases guarantee an infinite number of cases. If we allowed "proving by a finite number of cases," then the following example is such a "proof" that all positive even integers are less than 100.

The first positive even integer is 2, and we know that $2 < 100$. The second is 4, and we know that $4 < 100$. The third is 6, and $6 < 100$. Therefore, since $2n < 100$ for a finite number of cases, we might conclude that $2n < 100$ for all *n*.

This false result should convince you that in trying to prove a collection of statements S_n for all positive integers $n = 1, 2, 3, \ldots$, we need to do more than just check it out for a finite number of cases. We need to call on a type of proof known as **mathematical induction**.

Suppose that we had a long (endless) row of dominoes each 2 inches long all standing up in a straight row so that the distance between any two of them is $1\frac{1}{2}$ inches. How can you make them all fall down with the least effort?

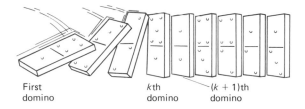

First
domino

*k*th
domino

(*k* + 1)th
domino

The answer is obvious. Push the first domino down toward the second. Since the first one must fall, and because the space between each pair is less than the length of a domino, they will all (eventually) fall down. The first knocks down the second, the second knocks down the third, and, in general, the *k*th domino knocks down the (*k* + 1)st. Two things guaranteed this "chain reaction":

1 The first domino will fall.

2 If any domino falls, then so will the next.

These two conditions are guidelines in forming the **principle of mathematical induction**.

THE PRINCIPLE OF MATHEMATICAL INDUCTION

Let S_n be a statement for each positive integer n. Suppose that the following two conditions hold:

1 S_1 is true.
2 If S_k is true, then S_{k+1} is true, where k is any positive integer.

Then S_n is a true statement for all n.

Condition 1 starts the "chain reaction" and condition 2 keeps it going.

Note that we are not proving this principle; rather, it is a basic principle that we accept and use to construct proofs. It is very important to realize that in condition 2 we are not proving S_k to be true; rather, we must prove this proposition:

$$\text{If } S_k \text{ is true, then } S_{k+1} \text{ is true}$$

Consequently, a proof by mathematical induction *includes* a proof of the proposition that S_k implies S_{k+1}, a proof within a proof. Within that inner proof, we are allowed to *assume* and use S_k.

At the beginning of this section, we guessed at the formula for the sum of the squares of the first n odd integers. Now, using mathematical induction, this formula is proved in Example 1.

EXAMPLE 1 Prove by mathematical induction that S_n is true for all positive integers n, where S_n is the statement

$$1 + 3 + 5 + \cdots + (2n - 1) = n^2$$

Proof Both conditions 1 and 2 of the principle of mathematical induction must be satisfied. We begin with the first.

1 S_1 is true because $1 = 1^2$.
2 Suppose that S_k is true, where k is a positive integer. That is, we assume

$$1 + 3 + 5 + \cdots + (2k - 1) = k^2$$

Proving S_1 starts the chain. The first domino has fallen.

We assume S_k to be true to see what effect it has on the next case, S_{k+1}. This is comparable to considering what happens when the kth domino falls.

The next odd number after $2k - 1$ is $2(k + 1) - 1 = 2k + 1$, which is added to the preceding equation:

$$
\begin{array}{r}
1 + 3 + 5 + \cdots + (2k - 1) \qquad\quad = k^2 \\
2k + 1 = 2k + 1 \\
\hline
1 + 3 + 5 + \cdots + (2k - 1) + (2k + 1) = k^2 + 2k + 1
\end{array}
$$

Factor the right side.

$$1 + 3 + 5 + \cdots + (2k + 1) = (k + 1)^2$$

This is the statement S_{k+1}. Therefore, we have shown that if S_k is given, then S_{k+1} must follow. This, together with the fact that S_1 is true, allows us to say that S_n is true for all n by the principle of mathematical induction.

Now that S_k implies S_{k+1}; the chain reaction keeps going.

EXAMPLE 2   Prove that the sum of the squares of the first n consecutive positive integers is given by $\dfrac{n(n+1)(2n+1)}{6}$.

Proof   Let S_n be the statement

$$\underbrace{1^2 + 2^2 + 3^2 + \cdots + n^2}_{\text{(sum of first } n \text{ squares)}} = \frac{n(n+1)(2n+1)}{6}.$$

for any positive integer n.

(1) S_k is true because $1^2 = \dfrac{1(1+1)(2 \cdot 1 + 1)}{6}$.

(2) Suppose that S_k is true for any k. That is, we assume

$$1^2 + 2^2 + 3^2 + \cdots + k^2 = \frac{k(k+1)(2k+1)}{6}$$

Add the next square $(k+1)^2$ to both sides.

(A) $1^2 + 2^2 + 3^2 + \cdots + k^2 + (k+1)^2 = \dfrac{k(k+1)(2k+1)}{6} + (k+1)^2$

Combine the right side.

$$\frac{k(k+1)(2k+1)}{6} + (k+1)^2 = \frac{k(k+1)(2k+1) + 6(k+1)^2}{6}$$

$$= \frac{2k^3 + 9k^2 + 13k + 6}{6}$$

$$= \frac{(k+1)(k+2)(2k+3)}{6}$$

Substitute back into Equation (A).

$$1^2 + 2^2 + 3^2 + \cdots + (k+1)^2 = \frac{(k+1)(k+2)(2k+3)}{6}$$

To see that this is S_{k+1}, rewrite the right side:

$$1^2 + 2^2 + 3^2 + \cdots + (k+1)^2 = \frac{(k+1)[(k+1)+1][2(k+1)+1]}{6}$$

Now both conditions of the principle of mathematical induction have been satisfied, and it follows that

$$1^2 + 2^2 + 3^2 + \cdots + n^2 = \frac{n(n+1)(2n+1)}{6}$$

is true for all integers $n \geq 1$.

Examples 1 and 2 involved equations that were established by mathematical induction. However, this principle is also used for other types of mathematical situations. The next example demonstrates the application of this principle when an inequality is involved.

EXAMPLE 3 Let $t > 0$ and use mathematical induction to prove that $(1 + t)^n > 1 + nt$ for all positive integers $n \geq 2$.

Try a few specific cases. Use a calculator to verify these:

$$(1.02)^2 > 1 + 2(0.02)$$
$$(1.001)^2 > 1 + 2(0.001)$$
$$(1.00054)^2 > 1 + 2(0.00054)$$

Proof Let S_n be the statement $(1 + t)^n > 1 + nt$, where $t > 0$ and n is any integer where $n \geq 2$.

(1) For $n = 2$, $(1 + t)^2 = 1 + 2t + t^2$. Since $t^2 > 0$, we get

$$1 + 2t + t^2 > 1 + 2t$$

because

$$(1 + 2t + t^2) - (1 + 2t) = t^2 > 0.$$

Recall that $a > b$ if and only if $a - b > 0$.

(2) Suppose that for $k \geq 2$ we have $(1 + t)^k > 1 + kt$. Multiply both sides by $(1 + t)$.

$$(1 + t)^k(1 + t) > (1 + kt)(1 + t)$$

Then

$$(1 + t)^{k+1} > 1 + (k + 1)t + kt^2$$

But $1 + (k + 1)t + kt^2 > 1 + (k + 1)t$. Therefore, by transitivity of $>$,

$$(1 + t)^{k+1} > 1 + (k + 1)t$$

By (1) and (2) above, the principle of mathematical induction implies that $(1 + t)^n > 1 + nt$ for all integers $n \geq 2$.

EXERCISES 10.6

Use mathematical induction to prove the following statements for all positive integers n.

1 $1 + 2 + 3 + \cdots + n = \dfrac{n(n + 1)}{2}$

2 $2 + 4 + 6 + \cdots + 2n = n(n + 1)$

3 $\displaystyle\sum_{i=1}^{n} 3i = \dfrac{3n(n + 1)}{2}$

4 $1 + 4 + 7 + \cdots + (3n - 2) = \dfrac{n(3n - 1)}{2}$

5 $\dfrac{5}{3} + \dfrac{4}{3} + 1 + \cdots + \left(-\dfrac{1}{3}n + 2\right) = \dfrac{n(11 - n)}{6}$

6 $1 \cdot 2 + 2 \cdot 3 + 3 \cdot 4 + \cdots + n(n + 1)$
$$= \dfrac{n(n + 1)(n + 2)}{3}$$

7 $\dfrac{1}{1 \cdot 2} + \dfrac{1}{2 \cdot 3} + \dfrac{1}{3 \cdot 4} + \cdots + \dfrac{1}{n(n + 1)} = \dfrac{n}{n + 1}$

8 $3 + 3^2 + 3^3 + \cdots + 3^n = \dfrac{3^{n+1} - 3}{2}$

9 $-2 - 4 - 6 - \cdots - 2n = -n - n^2$

10 $1 + \dfrac{1}{2} + \dfrac{1}{2^2} + \cdots + \dfrac{1}{2^{n-1}} = 2\left(1 - \dfrac{1}{2^n}\right)$

11 $1 + \dfrac{2}{5} + \dfrac{4}{25} + \cdots + \left(\dfrac{2}{5}\right)^{n-1} = \dfrac{5}{3}[1 - \left(\dfrac{2}{5}\right)^n]$

12 $1 - \dfrac{1}{3} + \dfrac{1}{9} - \cdots + \left(-\dfrac{1}{3}\right)^{n-1} = \dfrac{3}{4}[1 - \left(-\dfrac{1}{3}\right)^n]$

13 $1^3 + 2^3 + 3^3 + \cdots + n^3 = \dfrac{n^2(n + 1)^2}{4}$

14 Which of Exercises 1–13 can also be proved using the formula for an arithmetic series? Which ones can be proved using the formula for a geometric series?

Use mathematical induction to prove the following for all positive integers $n \geq 1$.

15 $\displaystyle\sum_{i=1}^{n} ar^{i-1} = \dfrac{a(1 - r^n)}{1 - r}, r \neq 1$

16 $\displaystyle\sum_{i=1}^{n} [a + (i - 1)d] = \dfrac{n}{2}[2a + (n - 1)d]$

17 $a^n < 1$, where $0 < a < 1$.

18 Let $0 < a < 1$. Use mathematical induction to prove that $a^n < a$ for all integers $n \geq 2$.

19 Let a and b be real numbers. Then use mathematical induction to prove that $(ab)^n = a^n b^n$ for all positive integers n.

20 Use mathematical induction to prove the generalized distributive property
$$a(b_0 + b_1 + \cdots + b_n) = ab_0 + ab_1 + \cdots + ab_n$$
for all positive integers n, where a and b_i are real numbers. (Assume that parentheses may be inserted into or extracted from an indicated sum of real numbers.)

*21 Give an inductive proof of
$$|a_0 + a_1 + \cdots + a_n| \le |a_0| + |a_1| + \cdots + |a_n|$$
for all positive integers n, where the a_i are real numbers.

*22 Use induction to prove that if $a_0 a_1 \cdots a_n = 0$, then at least one of the factors is zero for all positive integers n. (Assume that parentheses may be inserted into or extracted from an indicated product of real numbers.)

*23 (a) Prove by induction that
$$\frac{a^n - b^n}{a - b} = a^{n-1} + a^{n-2}b + \cdots + ab^{n-2} + b^{n-1}$$
for all integers $n \ge 2$.
$$\left(Hint: \text{Consider } \frac{a^{n+1} - b^{n+1}}{a - b} = \frac{a^n a - b^n b}{a - b} \right.$$
$$\left. = \frac{a^n a - b^n a + b^n a - b^n b}{a - b} \right)$$

(b) How does the result in part (a) give the factorization of the difference of two nth powers?

*24 Let u_n be the sequence such that $u_1 = 1$, $u_2 = 1$, and $u_{n+1} = u_{n-1} + u_n$ for $n \ge 2$. (This is the Fibonacci sequence; see Exercise 34, page 383.) Use mathematical induction to prove that for any positive integer n, $\sum_{i=1}^{n} u_i = u_{n+2} - 1$.

In Exercises 25 and 26, you are first asked to investigate a pattern leading to a formula and then asked to prove the formula by mathematical induction.

REVIEW EXERCISES FOR CHAPTER 10

The solutions to the following exercises can be found within the text of Chapter 10. Try to answer each question without referring to the text.

Section 10.1

1 Find the range values of the sequence $s_n = \dfrac{1}{n}$ for the domain $\{1, 2, 3, 4, 5,\}$ and graph.

25 (a) Complete the statements.
$$1 \qquad\qquad =$$
$$1 + 2 + 1 \qquad\qquad =$$
$$1 + 2 + 3 + 2 + 1 \qquad\qquad =$$
$$1 + 2 + 3 + 4 + 3 + 2 + 1 \qquad =$$
$$1 + 2 + 3 + 4 + 5 + 4 + 3 + 2 + 1 =$$

(b) Use the results in part (a) to *guess* the sum in the general case.
$$1 + 2 + 3 + \cdots + (n - 1) + n + (n - 1)$$
$$+ \cdots + 3 + 2 + 1 =$$

(c) Prove part (b) by mathematical induction.

26 (a) The left-hand column contains a number of points in a plane, no three of which are collinear. The right-hand column contains the number of distinct lines that the points determine. Complete this information for the last three cases.

Number of Points	Number of Lines
2	1
3	3
4	
5	
6	

(b) Observe that when there are 4 points, there are $6 = \dfrac{4(3)}{2}$ lines. Write similar statements when there are 2, 3, 5, or 6 points.

(c) Conjecture (guess) what the number of distinct lines is for n points, no three of which are collinear. Prove the conjecture by mathematical induction.

2 List the first seven terms of the sequence $s_k = \dfrac{(-1)^k}{k^2}$.

3 Find the tenth term of the sequence $s_n = \dfrac{n + 2}{2n - 3}$.

4 Write the first four terms of the sequence $s_n = \left(1 + \dfrac{1}{n}\right)^n$ and round off the terms to two decimal places.

Section 10.2

5 Find the sum of the first seven terms of $s_k = 2k$.

6 Find $\sum_{n=1}^{5} s_n$, where $s_n = \frac{2}{n}$.

7 Find $\sum_{k=1}^{4} (2k + 1)$.

8 Find $\sum_{i=1}^{5} (-1)^i(i + 1)$.

Section 10.3

9 What is the nth term of an arithmetic sequence whose first term is a and whose common difference is d?

10 Find the nth term of the arithmetic sequence 11, 2, $-7, \ldots$.

11 Write the formula for the sum S_n of the arithmetic sequence $s_k = a + (k - 1)d$.

12 Find S_{20} for the arithmetic sequence with $a = 3$ and $d = 5$.

13 Find the sum of the first 10,000 terms of the arithmetic sequence 246, 261, 276, ...

14 Find the sum of the first n positive integers.

15 Find $\sum_{k=1}^{50} (-6k + 10)$.

Section 10.4

16 What is a geometric sequence?

In Exercises 17–19, write the nth term of the geometric sequence.

17 2, -4, 8, . . .

18 5, -5, 5, . . .

19 6, 9, $\frac{27}{2}$, . . .

20 Find the hundredth term of the geometric sequence having $r = \frac{1}{2}$ and $a = \frac{1}{2}$.

21 Write the kth term of the geometric sequence $s_k = (\frac{1}{2})^{2k}$ in the form ar^{k-1} and find the values of a and r.

22 Write the formula for the sum S_n of a geometric sequence $s_k = ar^{k-1}$.

23 Find the sum of the first 100 terms of the geometric sequence $s_k = 6(\frac{1}{2})^{k-1}$.

24 Evaluate $\sum_{k=1}^{8} 3\left(\frac{1}{10}\right)^{k+1}$.

Use these questions to test your knowledge of the basic skills and concepts of Chapter 10. Then check your answers with those given at the end of the book.

25 Suppose that you save \$128 in January and that each month thereafter you only manage to save half of what you saved the previous month. How much do you save in the tenth month? What are your total savings after 10 months?

Section 10.5

26 For which values of r does $\sum_{k=1}^{\infty} ar^{k-1} = \frac{a}{1 - r}$?

27 Find the sum of the infinite geometric series $27 + 3 + \frac{1}{3} + \ldots$.

28 Why does the infinite series $\sum_{k=1}^{\infty} 5(\frac{4}{3})^{k-1}$ have no finite sum?

29 Evaluate $\sum_{k=1}^{\infty} \frac{7}{10^{k+1}}$.

30 Express the repeating decimal 0.242424 . . . in rational form (the ratio of two integers).

31 A racehorse running at the constant rate of 30 miles per hour will finish a 1-mile race in 2 minutes. Now consider the race broken down into the following parts. Before the racehorse can finish the 1-mile race it must first reach the halfway mark; having done that, the horse must next reach the quarter pole; then it must reach the eighth pole; and so on. That is, it must always cover half the distance before it can cover the whole distance. Show that the sum of the infinite number of time intervals is also 2 minutes.

Section 10.6

32 To prove that a statement S_n is true for each positive integer n, what two conditions must be established according to the principle of mathematical induction?

33 Prove by mathematical induction:
$$1 + 3 + 5 + \cdots + (2n - 1) = n^2$$

34 Use mathematical induction to prove:
$$1^2 + 2^2 + 3^2 + \cdots + n^2 = \frac{n(n + 1)(2n + 1)}{6}$$

35 Let $t > 0$ and use mathematical induction to prove that $(1 + t)^n > 1 + nt$ for all positive integers $n \geq 2$.

SAMPLE TEST QUESTIONS FOR CHAPTER 10

1 Find the first four terms of the sequence given by
$$s_n = \frac{n^2}{6 - 5n}.$$

2 Find the tenth term of the sequence in Question 1.

In questions 3 and 4, an arithmetic sequence has $a = -3$ and $d = \frac{1}{2}$.

3 Find the forty-ninth term.

4 What is the sum of the first 20 terms?

5 Write the next three terms of the geometric sequence beginning $-768, 192, -48, \ldots$.

6 Write the nth term of the sequence in Question 5.

7 Use the formula for the sum of a finite geometric sequence to show that

$$\sum_{k=1}^{4} 8(\tfrac{1}{2})^k = \tfrac{15}{2}$$

8 Find $\sum_{j=1}^{101} (4j - 50)$.

Decide whether each of the given infinite geometric series in Exercises 9–11 has a sum. Find the sum if it exists; otherwise, give a reason why there is no sum.

9 $\sum_{k=1}^{\infty} 8(\tfrac{3}{4})^{k+1}$

10 $1 + \tfrac{3}{2} + \tfrac{9}{4} + \cdots$

11 $0.06 - 0.009 + 0.00135 - \cdots$

12 Change the repeating decimal $0.363636\ldots$ into rational form.

13 Suppose you save \$10 one week and that each week thereafter you save 10¢ more than the week before. How much will you have saved after 1 year?

14 An object is moving along a straight line such that each minute it travels one-third as far as it did during the preceding minute. How far will the object have moved before coming to rest if it moves 24 feet during the first minute?

15 Prove by mathematical induction:

$$5 + 10 + 15 + \cdots + 5n = \frac{5n(n+1)}{2}$$

16 Prove by mathematical induction:

$$\frac{1}{1 \cdot 3} + \frac{1}{3 \cdot 5} + \frac{1}{5 \cdot 7} + \cdots$$
$$+ \frac{1}{(2n-1)(2n+1)} = \frac{n}{2n+1}$$

ANSWERS TO THE TEST YOUR UNDERSTANDING EXERCISES

Page 385

1 $5n$ **2** $-4n + 10$ **3** $\tfrac{1}{10}n$ **4** $-8n + 3$ **5** n

6 $n - 4$ **7** $\tfrac{2}{3}n$ **8** $-12n + 65$ **9** $\tfrac{1}{3}n - \tfrac{1}{5}$ **10** $n + 1$

Page 392

1 $1, \tfrac{1}{2}, \tfrac{1}{4}, \tfrac{1}{8}, \tfrac{1}{16}; 1(\tfrac{1}{2})^{n-1}; r = \tfrac{1}{2}$ **2** $\tfrac{1}{4}, \tfrac{1}{8}, \tfrac{1}{16}, \tfrac{1}{32}, \tfrac{1}{64}; \tfrac{1}{4}(\tfrac{1}{2})^{n-1}; r = \tfrac{1}{2}$

3 $-\tfrac{1}{2}, \tfrac{1}{4}, -\tfrac{1}{8}, \tfrac{1}{16}, -\tfrac{1}{32}; -\tfrac{1}{2}(-\tfrac{1}{2})^{n-1}; r = -\tfrac{1}{2}$

4 $-\frac{1}{27}, \frac{1}{27^2}, -\frac{1}{27^3}, \frac{1}{27^4}, -\frac{1}{27^5}; -\frac{1}{27}\left(-\frac{1}{27}\right)^{n-1}; r = -\frac{1}{27}$

5 $r = 10; \tfrac{1}{5}(10)^{n-1}$ **6** $r = -\tfrac{4}{9}; 27(-\tfrac{4}{9})^{n-1}$

Page 398

1 $r = \tfrac{1}{10}; S_\infty = 11\tfrac{1}{9}$ **2** $r = 4$; no finite sum. **3** $r = -\tfrac{1}{6}; S_\infty = 30\tfrac{6}{7}$

4 $r = \tfrac{1}{4}; S_\infty = -21\tfrac{1}{3}$ **5** $r = \tfrac{4}{3}$; no finite sum. **6** $r = 0.01; S_\infty = \tfrac{1}{33}$

7 $r = -3$; no finite sum. **8** $r = -\tfrac{9}{10}; S_\infty = \tfrac{810}{19}$ **9** $r = -1.01$; no finite sum.

COMPLEX NUMBERS AND POLAR COORDINATES

Complex numbers

In the definition of a radical, care was taken to avoid the even root of a negative number, such as $\sqrt{-4}$. This was necessary because there is no real number x whose square is -4. Consequently, there can be no real number that satisfies the equation $x^2 + 4 = 0$. Suppose, for the moment, that we could solve $x^2 + 4 = 0$ using our algebraic methods. Then we might write the following:

See Section 2.2 for a review of radicals.

$$x^2 + 4 = 0$$
$$x^2 = -4$$
$$x = \pm\sqrt{-4}$$
$$= \pm\sqrt{4(-1)}$$
$$= \pm\sqrt{4}\sqrt{-1}$$
$$= \pm 2\sqrt{-1}$$

It could now be claimed that $2\sqrt{-1}$ is a solution of $x^2 + 4 = 0$. But it is certainly not a *real* solution. What we now do is to introduce formally $\sqrt{-1}$ as a new kind of number; it will be the unit for a new set of numbers, the *imaginary numbers*. The symbol i is used to stand for this number and is defined as follows.

409

$$i = \sqrt{-1} \quad \text{and} \quad i^2 = -1$$

Using i, the square root of a negative real number is now defined:

$$\sqrt{-x} = \sqrt{-1}\sqrt{x} = i\sqrt{x} \qquad \text{for } x > 0$$

EXAMPLE 1 Simplify: **(a)** $\sqrt{-16} + \sqrt{-25}$ **(b)** $\sqrt{-16} \cdot \sqrt{-25}$

Solution

(a) $\sqrt{-16} = \sqrt{-1} \cdot \sqrt{16} = i \cdot 4 = 4i$

$\qquad \sqrt{-25} = \sqrt{-1} \cdot \sqrt{25} = i \cdot 5 = 5i$

In the example, *4i* and *5i* are combined by using the usual rules of algebra. You will see later that such procedures apply for this new kind of number.

Thus

$$\sqrt{-16} + \sqrt{-25} = 4i + 5i = 9i$$

(b) $\sqrt{-16} \cdot \sqrt{-25} = (4i)(5i) = 20i^2 = 20(-1) = -20$

TEST YOUR UNDERSTANDING

Express as the product of a real number and i.

1 $\sqrt{-9}$ **2** $\sqrt{-49}$ **3** $\sqrt{-5}$ **4** $-2\sqrt{-1}$ **5** $\sqrt{-\dfrac{4}{9}}$

Simplify.

6 $\sqrt{-16} \cdot \sqrt{-25}$ **7** $\sqrt{9} \cdot \sqrt{-49}$

8 $\sqrt{-50} + \sqrt{-32} - \sqrt{-8}$ **9** $3\sqrt{-20} + 2\sqrt{-45}$

An indicated product of a real number times the imaginary unit i, such as $7i$ or $\sqrt{2}\,i$, is called a **pure imaginary number**. The sum of a real number and a pure imaginary number is called a **complex number**.

A complex number has the form $a + bi$, where a and b are real numbers and $i = \sqrt{-1}$.

We say that the real number a is the **real part** of $a + bi$ and the real number b is called the **imaginary part** of $a + bi$. In general, two complex numbers are equal only when both their real parts and their imaginary parts are equal. Thus

$$a + bi = c + di \quad \text{if and only if} \quad a = c \text{ and } b = d$$

The collection of complex numbers contains all the real numbers, since

any real number a can also be written as $a = a + 0i$. Similarly, if b is real, $bi = 0 + bi$, so that the complex numbers also contain the pure imaginaries.

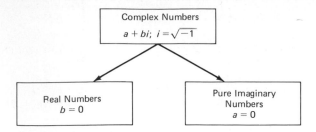

EXAMPLE 2 Name the sets of numbers to which each of the following belongs: **(a)** $\sqrt{\frac{4}{9}}$ **(b)** $\sqrt{-10}$ **(c)** $-4 + \sqrt{-12}$

Various sets of numbers are described in Section 1.2.

Solution

(a) $\sqrt{\frac{4}{9}} = \frac{2}{3} = \frac{2}{3} + 0i$ is complex, real, and rational.

(b) $\sqrt{-10} = i\sqrt{10}$ is complex and pure imaginary.

(c) $-4 + \sqrt{-12} = -4 + i\sqrt{12} = -4 + 2i\sqrt{3}$ is complex.

How should complex numbers be added, subtracted, multiplied, or divided? In answering this question, it must be kept in mind that the real numbers are included in the collection of complex numbers and the definitions we construct for the complex numbers must preserve the established operations for the reals. We do not want, for example, to add complex numbers in such a way that would produce inconsistent results for the addition of real numbers.

We add and subtract complex numbers by combining their real and their imaginary parts separately, according to these definitions.

SUM AND DIFFERENCE OF COMPLEX NUMBERS

$$(a + bi) + (c + di) = (a + c) + (b + d)i$$
$$(a + bi) - (c + di) = (a - c) + (b - d)i$$

Actually, these procedures are quite similar to those used for combining polynomials. For example, compare these two sums:

$$(2 + 3x) + (5 + 7x) = (2 + 5) + (3 + 7)x = 7 + 10x$$
$$(2 + 3i) + (5 + 7i) = (2 + 5) + (3 + 7)i = 7 + 10i$$

Similarly, compare these subtraction problems:

$$(8 + 5x) - (3 + 2x) = (8 - 3) + (5 - 2)x = 5 + 3x$$
$$(8 + 5i) - (3 + 2i) = (8 - 3) + (5 - 2)i = 5 + 3i$$

To decide how to multiply two complex numbers we go back to the set of real numbers and extend the multiplication process. Recall the procedure for multiplying two binomials:

$$(a + b)(c + d) = ac + bc + ad + bd$$

Now compare these two products:

$$(3 + 2x)(5 + 3x) = 15 + 10x + 9x + 6x^2$$

$$(3 + 2i)(5 + 3i) = 15 + 10i + 9i + 6i^2$$

This last expression can be simplified by noting that $10i + 9i = 19i$ and $6i^2 = -6$. The final result is $9 + 19i$.

In general, we can develop a rule for multiplication of two complex numbers by finding the product of $a + bi$ and $c + di$ as follows:

$$(a + bi)(c + di) = ac + adi + bci + bdi^2$$

$$= ac + (ad + bc)i + bd(-1)$$

$$= (ac - bd) + (ad + bc)i$$

PRODUCT OF COMPLEX NUMBERS

$$(a + bi)(c + di) = (ac - bd) + (ad + bc)i$$

Note: In practice, it is easier to find the product by using the procedure for multiplying binomials rather than by memorizing the formal definition.

EXAMPLE 3   Multiply: $(5 - 2i)(3 + 4i)$.

Solution

$$(5 - 2i)(3 + 4i) = 15 - 6i + 20i - 8i^2$$

$$= 15 - 6i + 20i + 8$$

$$= 23 + 14i$$

Now consider the quotient of two complex numbers such as

$$\frac{2 + 3i}{3 + i}$$

The term imaginary is said to have been first applied to these numbers precisely because they seem mysteriously to vanish under certain multiplications.

Our objective is to express this quotient in the form $a + bi$. To do so, we use a method similar to rationalizing the denominator. Note what happens when $3 + i$ is multiplied by its **conjugate**, $3 - i$:

$$(3 + i)(3 - i) = 9 + 3i - 3i - i^2 = 9 - i^2 = 9 + 1 = 10$$

We are now ready to complete the division problem.

$$\frac{2 + 3i}{3 + i} = \frac{2 + 3i}{3 + i} \cdot \frac{3 - i}{3 - i}$$

$$= \frac{6 + 9i - 2i - 3i^2}{9 - i^2}$$

$$= \frac{6 + 9i - 2i + 3}{9 + 1}$$

$$= \frac{9 + 7i}{10}$$

$$= \frac{9}{10} + \frac{7}{10}i$$

In general, multiplying the numerator and denominator of $\frac{a + bi}{c + di}$ by the conjugate of $c + di$ leads to the following definition for division (see Exercise 71).

QUOTIENT OF COMPLEX NUMBERS

$$\frac{a + bi}{c + di} = \frac{ac + bd}{c^2 + d^2} + \frac{bc - ad}{c^2 + d^2}i; \qquad c + di \neq 0$$

Rather than memorize this definition, simply find quotients as in the preceding illustration.

The conjugate of a complex number $z = a + bi$ is sometimes denoted as $\bar{z}$, so that $\bar{z} = \overline{a + bi} = a - bi$. In the exercises you will be asked to prove that the conjugate of a sum is equal to the sum of the conjugates; $\overline{z + w} = \bar{z} + \bar{w}$; and similarly for differences, products, and quotients.

EXAMPLE 4 For $z = -2 + 5i$ and $w = 4 - 7i$, verify that (a) $\overline{z + w} = \bar{z} + \bar{w}$ and (b) $\overline{zw} = \bar{z} \cdot \bar{w}$.

Solution

(a) $\overline{z + w} = \overline{(-2 + 5i) + (4 - 7i)}$ $\qquad$ $\bar{z} + \bar{w} = \overline{-2 + 5i} + \overline{4 - 7i}$

$\qquad\quad = \overline{2 - 2i}$ $\qquad\qquad\qquad\qquad = (-2 - 5i) + (4 + 7i)$

$\qquad\quad = 2 + 2i$ $\qquad\qquad\qquad\qquad\quad = 2 + 2i$

(b) $\overline{zw} = \overline{(-2 + 5i)(4 - 7i)}$ $\qquad\qquad$ $\bar{z}\bar{w} = \overline{(-2 + 5i)}\ \overline{(4 - 7i)}$

$\qquad\quad = \overline{27 + 34i}$ $\qquad\qquad\qquad\qquad = (-2 - 5i)(4 + 7i)$

$\qquad\quad = 27 - 34i$ $\qquad\qquad\qquad\qquad\quad = 27 - 34i$

Although we will not go into the details here, it can be shown that some of the basic algebraic rules apply for the complex numbers. For example, the commutative, associative, and distributive laws hold, whereas the rules of order do not apply.

It is also true that the rules for integer exponents apply for complex numbers. For example, $(2 - 3i)^0 = 1$ and $(2 - 3i)^{-1} = \frac{1}{2 - 3i}$. In particular, the integral powers of i are easily evaluated. Following are the first four powers of i.

$$i = \sqrt{-1}$$
$$i^2 = -1$$
$$i^3 = i^2 \cdot i = -1 \cdot i = -i$$
$$i^4 = i^2 \cdot i^2 = (-1)(-1) = 1$$

After the first four powers of i a repeating pattern exists, as can be seen from the next four powers of i:

$$i^5 = i^4 \cdot i = 1 \cdot i = i$$
$$i^6 = i^4 \cdot i^2 = 1 \cdot i^2 = -1$$
$$i^7 = i^4 \cdot i^3 = 1 \cdot i^3 = -i$$
$$i^8 = i^4 \cdot i^4 = 1 \cdot i^4 = 1$$

The cycle for consecutive powers of i is: $i, -1, -i, 1$.

To simplify i^n when $n > 4$, begin by finding the largest multiple of 4 in the integer n as in the next example.

EXAMPLE 5 Simplify (a) i^{22} (b) i^{39}

$20 = 5(4)$ is the largest multiple of 4 in 22
$36 = 9(4)$ is the largest multiple of 4 in 39

Solution
(a) $i^{22} = i^{20} \cdot i^2 = (i^4)^5 \cdot i^2 = 1^5 \cdot i^2 = i^2 = -1$
(b) $i^{39} = i^{36} \cdot i^3 = (i^4)^9 \cdot i^3 = 1^9 \cdot i^3 = i^3 = -i$

The following example illustrates how to operate with a negative integral power of i.

EXAMPLE 6 Express $2i^{-3}$ as the indicated product of a real number and i.

The general results for rational exponents of complex numbers will not be studied here, although the nth roots will be considered in Section 11.3.

Solution First note that $2i^{-3} = \dfrac{2}{i^3}$. Next multiply numerator and denominator by i to obtain a real number in the denominator.

$$2i^{-3} = \frac{2}{i^3} \cdot \frac{i}{i} = \frac{2i}{i^4} = \frac{2i}{1} = 2i$$

Alternative Solution

$$2i^{-3} = \frac{2}{i^3} = \frac{2}{-i}$$
$$= \frac{2}{-i} \cdot \frac{i}{i} \qquad (i \text{ is the conjugate of } -i)$$
$$= \frac{2i}{-i^2} = \frac{2i}{-(-1)}$$
$$= 2i$$

Many algebraic procedures studied earlier can be extended to complex numbers. For example, the factoring formula for the difference of squares,

$$a^2 - b^2 = (a + b)(a - b)$$

can now be used to factor the sum of squares such as $x^2 + 1$ that was not factorable using real coefficients. This becomes possible after first writing $x^2 + 1$ as $x^2 - (-1)$ and letting $-1 = i^2$. Thus

$$x^2 + 1 = x^2 - (-1)$$
$$= x^2 - i^2$$
$$= (x + i)(x - i)$$

The quadratic formula used to find the roots of $ax^2 + bx + c = 0$ is also applicable when complex numbers are involved. In fact, the situation in which there are no real roots, because the discriminant is negative, now produces complex roots.

This is a good place to review the quadratic formula developed in Section 4.3.

Assume $b^2 - 4ac < 0$:

$$x = \frac{-b \pm \sqrt{b^2 - 4ac}}{2a} = \frac{-b \pm \sqrt{-(4ac - b^2)}}{2a}$$
$$= \frac{-b \pm i\sqrt{4ac - b^2}}{2a}$$
$$= -\frac{b}{2a} \pm \frac{i\sqrt{4ac - b^2}}{2a}$$

Since $b^2 - 4ac < 0$, then $4ac - b^2 > 0$.

EXAMPLE 7 Solve $x^2 + x + 1 = 0$.

Solution $b^2 - 4ac = 1 - 4 = -3 < 0$ shows that there are no real roots. However, there are these complex roots:

$$x = \frac{-1 \pm \sqrt{-3}}{2} = \frac{-1 \pm i\sqrt{3}}{2}$$
$$= -\frac{1}{2} \pm \frac{\sqrt{3}}{2}i$$

EXERCISES 11.1

Classify each statement as true or false.

1 Every real number is a complex number.
2 Every complex number is a real number.
3 Every irrational number is a complex number.
4 Every integer can be written in the form $a + bi$.
5 Every complex number may be expressed as an irrational number.
6 Every negative integer may be written as a pure imaginary number.

Express each of the following numbers in the form $a + bi$.

7 $5 + \sqrt{-4}$
8 $7 - \sqrt{-7}$
9 -5
10 $\sqrt{25}$

Express in the form bi.

11 $\sqrt{-16}$
12 $\sqrt{-81}$

13 $\sqrt{-144}$
14 $-\sqrt{-9}$
15 $\sqrt{-\frac{9}{16}}$
16 $\sqrt{-3}$
17 $-\sqrt{-5}$
18 $-\sqrt{-8}$

Simplify.

19 $\sqrt{-9} \cdot \sqrt{-81}$
20 $\sqrt{4} \cdot \sqrt{-25}$
21 $\sqrt{-3} \cdot \sqrt{-2}$
22 $(2i)(3i)$
23 $(-3i^2)(5i)$
24 $(i^2)(i^2)$
25 $\sqrt{-9} + \sqrt{-81}$
26 $\sqrt{-12} + \sqrt{-75}$
27 $\sqrt{-8} + \sqrt{-18}$
28 $2\sqrt{-72} - 3\sqrt{-32}$
29 $\sqrt{-9} - \sqrt{-3}$
30 $3\sqrt{-80} - 2\sqrt{-20}$

Complete the indicated operation. Express all answers in the form $a + bi$.

31 $(7 + 5i) + (3 + 2i)$
32 $(8 + 7i) + (9 - i)$

33 $(8 + 2i) - (3 + 5i)$ **34** $(7 + 2i) - (4 - 3i)$

35 $(7 + \sqrt{-16}) + (3 - \sqrt{-4})$

36 $(8 + \sqrt{-49}) - (2 - \sqrt{-25})$

37 $2i(3 + 5i)$ **38** $3i(5i - 2)$

39 $(3 + 2i)(2 + 3i)$

40 $(\sqrt{5} + 3i)(\sqrt{5} - 3i)$

41 $(5 - 2i)(3 + 4i)$ **42** $(\sqrt{3} + 2i)^2$

43 $\dfrac{3 + 5i}{i}$ **44** $\dfrac{5 - i}{i}$

45 $\dfrac{5 + 3i}{2 + i}$ **46** $\dfrac{7 - 2i}{2 - i}$

47 $\dfrac{3 - i}{3 + i}$ **48** $\dfrac{8 + 3i}{3 - 2i}$

Use $z = -6 + 8i$ *and* $w = \frac{1}{2} + \frac{1}{2}i$ *to verify the following.*

49 $\overline{z + w} = \bar{z} + \bar{w}$

50 $\overline{z - w} = \bar{z} - \bar{w}$

51 $\overline{zw} = \bar{z} \cdot \bar{w}$

52 $\overline{\left(\dfrac{z}{w}\right)} = \dfrac{\bar{z}}{\bar{w}}$

Express in the form bi.

53 $3i^3$ **54** $-5i^5$

55 $2i^7$ **56** $3i^{-3}$

57 $-4i^{18}$ **58** i^{-32}

Simplify and express each answer in the form a + bi.

59 $(3 + 2i)^{-1}$ **60** $(3 + 2i)^{-2}$

61 One of the basic rules for operating with radicals is that $\sqrt{ab} = \sqrt{a} \cdot \sqrt{b}$, where a and b are nonnegative real numbers. Prove that this rule does not work when both a and b are negative by showing that $\sqrt{(-4)(-9)} \neq \sqrt{-4} \cdot \sqrt{-9}$.

62 Use the definition $\sqrt{-x} = i\sqrt{x}$ $(x \geq 0)$ to prove that $\sqrt{ab} = \sqrt{a} \cdot \sqrt{b}$ when $a < 0$ and $b \geq 0$.

63 Use complex numbers to factor each binomial.

  (a) $x^2 + 4$

  (b) $3x^2 + 27$

  (c) $x^2 + 2$

  (d) $5x^2 + 15$

Solve each quadratic equation for real or complex roots using the quadratic formula or by factoring when possible.

64 $x^2 + 7 = 0$

65 $x^2 + 6x + 25 = 0$

66 $x^3 + 9x = 0$

67 $2x^2 + x = -5$

68 $6x^2 = 7x - 3$

69 $\frac{1}{2}x^2 - 3x + 7 = 1$

70 Find the value of $x^2 + 3x + 5$ when $x = \dfrac{-3 + \sqrt{11}i}{2}$.

71 Write $\dfrac{a + bi}{c + di}$ in the form $x + yi$. (*Hint:* Multiply the numerator and denominator by the conjugate of $c + di$.)

72 The set of complex numbers satisfies the associative property for addition. Verify this by completing this problem in two different ways.

$$(3 + 5i) + (2 + 3i) + (7 + 4i)$$

73 Repeat Exercise 72 for multiplication, using $(3 + i)(3 - i)(4 + 3i)$.

74 We say that $0 = 0 + 0i$ is the additive identity for the complex numbers since $0 + z = z$ for any $z = a + bi$. Find the additive inverse (negative) of z.

Perform the indicated operations and express the answers in the form a + bi.

75 $(5 + 4i) + 2(2 - 3i) - i(1 - 5i)$

76 $2i(3 - 4i)(3 - 6i) - 7i$

77 $\dfrac{(2 + i)^2(3 - i)}{2 + 3i}$

78 $\dfrac{1 - 2i}{3 + 4i} - \dfrac{2i - 3}{4 - 2i}$

Find all real and complex roots of each equation. (The rational root theorem can be used in Exercises 81 and 82.)

79 $x^4 - 81 = 0$

80 $x^3 - 1 = 0$

*81 $3x^3 - 5x^2 + 2x - 8$

*82 $2x^4 - 5x^3 + x^2 + 4x - 4 = 0$

Use $z = a + bi$ *and* $w = c + di$ *to prove the following.*

83 $\overline{z + w} = \bar{z} + \bar{w}$

84 $\overline{z - w} = \bar{z} - \bar{w}$

*85 $\overline{\left(\dfrac{z}{w}\right)} = \dfrac{\bar{z}}{\bar{w}}$

*86 $\overline{zw} = \bar{z}\bar{w}$

An ordered pair of real numbers (x, y) determines the unique complex number $x + yi$, and vice versa. This correspondence between the complex numbers and the ordered pairs of real numbers allows us to give a geometric interpretation of the complex numbers by using the **complex plane**. This plane is a rectangular coordinate system in which the horizontal axis is called the **real axis** and the vertical axis is the **imaginary axis**. The following figure illustrates how complex numbers are plotted (graphed) in the complex plane.

Trigonometric form and the complex plane

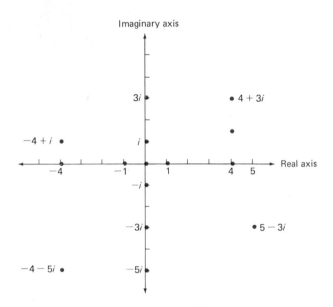

There is a geometric interpretation for the sum of two complex numbers. First locate $z = a + bi$ and $w = c + di$ and use line segments to connect these points to the origin. Then complete the parallelogram as shown. The tip of the diagonal of the parallelogram that passes through the origin will represent the sum $z + w$ (see Exercise 10). This graphic procedure for finding sums is known as the **parallelogram rule**.

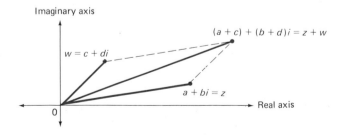

EXAMPLE 1 Find the sum $(3 + 2i) + (2 - 4i)$ using the parallelogram rule, and verify using the definition for addition of complex numbers.

Solution

$$(3 + 2i) + (2 - 4i)$$
$$= (3 + 2) + (2 - 4)i$$
$$= 5 - 2i$$

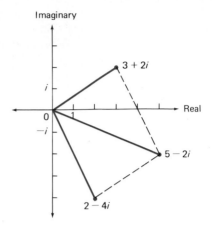

EXAMPLE 2 Describe the diagonal formed when finding the sum of $3 + 2i$ and $3 - 2i$ by use of the parallelogram rule.

Solution The diagonal is six units in length on the x-axis, from $(0, 0)$ to $(6, 0)$. The sum is $6 + 0i = 6$.

Complex numbers can also be subtracted graphically. This is done in Example 3 using a parallelogram after changing the difference $z - w$ into the sum $z + (-w)$.

EXAMPLE 3 Use a parallelogram to find $(3 + 2i) - (2 - 4i)$.

Solution First locate $3 + 2i$ and $-(2 - 4i) = -2 + 4i$. Then add using the parallelogram rule to get the difference, $1 + 6i$.

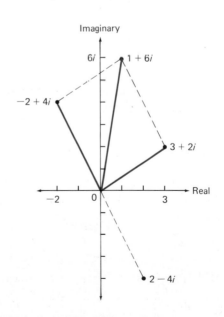

Any complex number z determines a unique point in the plane. Its distance from the origin, $r \geq 0$, is called the **modulus** or **absolute value** of z, and is also denoted by $|z|$.

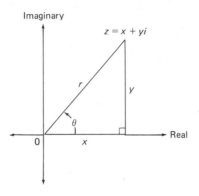

Imaginary

$z = x + yi$

r

y

θ

0 x

Real

$$r = |x + yi| = \sqrt{x^2 + y^2}$$

For z not on an axis the triangle indicates why $r = \sqrt{x^2 + y^2}$. You can verify that this definition also applies for z on an axis. On the x-axis this is consistent with our earlier definition of absolute value.

The line segment connecting z to the origin and the positive part of the real axis determine an angle θ where $0 \leq \theta < 360°$ (or $0 \leq \theta < 2\pi$). θ is called the **principal argument** of z, which is also referred to simply as the argument of z. (The choice of principal argument can vary. Another interval that is used for this is $-180° \leq \theta < 180°$.) From the triangle we have

$$x = r \cos \theta \qquad \text{and} \qquad y = r \sin \theta$$

Consequently,

$$z = x + iy = r \cos \theta + i(r \sin \theta)$$

You can verify that these formulas also apply when z is on an axis.

or, when factored, produces the **trigonometric form**

$$z = r(\cos \theta + i \sin \theta)$$

Any angle coterminal with θ will give the same result and may also be referred to as an argument of z. However, we will work primarily with the principal argument.

For $z = 0 + 0i = 0$, $r = 0$ and any θ can be used.

EXAMPLE 4 Convert $\sqrt{3} + i$ and $-1 - i$ into trigonometric form.

Solution Graph the points and observe that $\sqrt{3} + i$ determines a $30°$–$60°$–$90°$ triangle and $-1 - i$ determines a $45°$–$45°$–$90°$ triangle.

$$r = \sqrt{(\sqrt{3})^2 + 1^2} = 2$$

$$\theta = 30° = \frac{\pi}{6}$$

$$\sqrt{3} + i = 2(\cos 30° + i \sin 30°)$$

$$= 2\left(\cos \frac{\pi}{6} + i \sin \frac{\pi}{6}\right)$$

r is the modulus and θ is the argument.

Imaginary

$\sqrt{3} + i$

$30°$ 1

0   $\sqrt{3}$ Real

$$r = \sqrt{(-1)^2 + (-1)^2} = \sqrt{2}$$

$$\theta = 225° = \frac{5\pi}{4}$$

$$-1 - i = \sqrt{2}(\cos 225° + i \sin 225°)$$

$$= \sqrt{2}\left(\cos \frac{5\pi}{4} + i \sin \frac{5\pi}{4}\right)$$

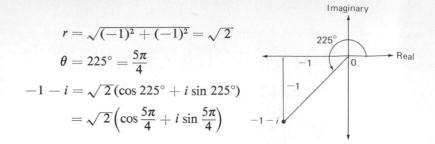

In constrast to the trigonometric form $z = r(\cos \theta + i \sin \theta)$, we call $z = x + yi$ the **rectangular form** of z.

EXAMPLE 5 Use Table V to convert $3(\cos 50° + i \sin 50°)$ into rectangular form $x + yi$.

Solution

$$3(\cos 50° + i \sin 50°) = 3(.6428 + .7660i)$$

$$= 1.9284 + 2.2980i$$

The multiplication and division of complex numbers is sometimes simpler to do using the trigonometric forms. To see how this is done, we begin with

$$z_1 = r_1(\cos \theta_1 + i \sin \theta_1) \quad \text{and} \quad z_2 = r_2(\cos \theta_2 + i \sin \theta_2)$$

and multiply.

$$z_1 z_2 = [r_1(\cos \theta_1 + i \sin \theta_1)][r_2(\cos \theta_2 + i \sin \theta_2)]$$

$$= r_1 r_2[(\cos \theta_1 \cos \theta_2 - \sin \theta_1 \sin \theta_2) + i(\sin \theta_1 \cos \theta_2 + \cos \theta_1 \sin \theta_2)]$$

Now use addition formulas (3) and (1), page 348, to obtain

> If $\theta_1 + \theta_2$ is not in $[0, 2\pi)$, replace it with the principal argument, which is the smallest nonnegative coterminal angle.

$$z_1 z_2 = r_1 r_2[\cos(\theta_1 + \theta_2) + i \sin (\theta_1 + \theta_2)]$$

EXAMPLE 6 Let $z_1 = 2 + 2\sqrt{3}i$ and $z_2 = -1 - \sqrt{3}i$.

(a) Evaluate $z_1 z_2$ by using the rectangular forms.
(b) Evaluate $z_1 z_2$ by using trigonometric forms and verify that the result is the same as in part (a).

Solution

(a) $z_1 z_2 = (2 + 2\sqrt{3}i)(-1 - \sqrt{3}i)$

$$= (-2 + 6) + (-2\sqrt{3} - 2\sqrt{3})i = 4 - 4\sqrt{3}i$$

(b) Converting z_1 and z_2 to trigonometric form, we get

$$z_1 = 4\left(\cos \frac{\pi}{3} + i \sin \frac{\pi}{3}\right) \text{ and } z_2 = 2\left(\cos \frac{4\pi}{3} + i \sin \frac{4\pi}{3}\right)$$

Then

$$z_1 z_2 = \left[4\left(\cos\frac{\pi}{3} + i\sin\frac{4\pi}{3}\right)\right]\left[2\left(\cos\frac{4\pi}{3} + i\sin\frac{4\pi}{3}\right)\right]$$

$$= 4 \cdot 2\left[\cos\left(\frac{\pi}{3} + \frac{4\pi}{3}\right) + i\sin\left(\frac{\pi}{3} + \frac{4\pi}{3}\right)\right]$$

$$= 8\left(\cos\frac{5\pi}{3} + i\sin\frac{5\pi}{3}\right)$$

$$= 8\left[\frac{1}{2} + i\left(-\frac{\sqrt{3}}{2}\right)\right]$$

$$= 4 - 4\sqrt{3}\,i$$

TEST YOUR UNDERSTANDING

Let $z_1 = -2 + 2i$ and $z_2 = 3\sqrt{3} - 3i$. Convert to trigonometric form; evaluate $z_1 z_2$.

By similar reasoning as for the product (see Exercise 46), the result for division is

$$\frac{z_1}{z_2} = \frac{r_1}{r_2}[\cos(\theta_1 - \theta_2) + i\sin(\theta_1 - \theta_2)] \qquad z_2 \neq 0$$

If $\theta_1 - \theta_2$ is not in $[0, 2\pi)$, replace it with the principal argument, which is the smallest nonnegative coterminal angle.

EXAMPLE 7 For z_1, z_2 in Example 6, find:

(a) $\frac{z_1}{z_2}$ using rectangular forms.

(b) $\frac{z_1}{z_2}$ using trigonometric forms and verify that the result is the same as in part (a).

Solution

(a) $\dfrac{2 + 2\sqrt{3}\,i}{-1 - \sqrt{3}\,i} = \dfrac{2 + 2\sqrt{3}\,i}{-1 - \sqrt{3}\,i} \cdot \dfrac{-1 + \sqrt{3}\,i}{-1 + \sqrt{3}\,i}$

$$= \frac{(-2 - 6) + (2\sqrt{3} - 2\sqrt{3})i}{1 + 3}$$

$$= \frac{-8}{4} = -2$$

(b) $\dfrac{4\left(\cos\dfrac{\pi}{3} + i\sin\dfrac{\pi}{3}\right)}{2\left(\cos\dfrac{4\pi}{3} + i\sin\dfrac{4\pi}{3}\right)} = 2\left[\cos\left(\frac{\pi}{3} - \frac{4\pi}{3}\right) + i\sin\left(\frac{\pi}{3} - \frac{4\pi}{3}\right)\right]$

$$= 2[\cos(-\pi) + i\sin(-\pi)]$$

$$= 2(\cos\pi + i\sin\pi) \qquad (\pi \text{ is the principal}$$

$$= 2(-1 + 0) \qquad\qquad \text{argument})$$

$$= -2$$

EXERCISES 11.2

Find $z + w$ using the parallelogram rule and verify using the definition of addition for complex numbers.

1 $z = 3 + 4i$, $w = 4 + 3i$

2 $z = 3 - 4i$, $w = 4 - 3i$

3 $z = -3 + 2i$, $w = -2 - 3i$

4 $z = 1 + 3i$, $w = -3 - i$

Find $z - w$ using parallelograms and verify using the definition of subtraction for complex numbers.

5 $z = 3 + 4i$, $w = 4 + 3i$

6 $z = 3 - 4i$, $w = 4 - 3i$

7 $z = -3 + 2i$, $w = -2 - 3i$

8 $z = 1 + 3i$, $w = -3 - i$

9 Find the sum graphically on a complex plane.

$$[(2 + 5i) + (2 - 2i)] + (3 - 5i)$$

*10 Verify the parallelogram rule by showing that $x = a + c$ and $y = b + d$.

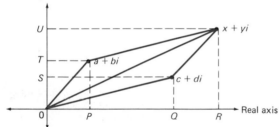

11 Use the parallelogram rule to show that the sum of a complex number and its conjugate is a real number.

12 Let $z = a + bi$ and $w = c + di$. What must be true if $z + w$ is purely imaginary?

Convert each of the following into trigonometric form and plot each point in a coordinate plane.

13 $1 + i$

14 $3 + 3i$

15 $-1 + \sqrt{3}i$

16 $-2 + 2\sqrt{3}i$

17 $\frac{\sqrt{3}}{2} - \frac{1}{2}i$

18 5

19 -10

20 $-4i$

21 $-10 - 10i$

Express each of the following complex numbers in the rectangular form $x + yi$. Use Table V only if necessary.

22 $2(\cos 30° + i \sin 30°)$

23 $3(\cos 120° + i \sin 120°)$

24 $\frac{1}{2}\left(\cos \frac{\pi}{2} + i \sin \frac{\pi}{2}\right)$

25 $5\left(\cos \frac{3\pi}{2} + i \sin \frac{3\pi}{2}\right)$

26 $9(\cos 0° + i \sin 0°)$

27 $\sqrt{2}(\cos 60° + i \sin 60°)$

28 $1(\cos \pi + i \sin \pi)$

29 $4(\cos 315° + i \sin 315°)$

30 $3(\cos 65° + i \sin 65°)$

31 $\cos 350° + i \sin 350°$

Find zw, $\dfrac{z}{w}$, and $\dfrac{w}{z}$. Give the answers in trigonometric form, and convert to rectangular form.

32 $z = 3(\cos 41° + i \sin 41°)$
$\quad w = 2(\cos 20° + i \sin 20°)$

33 $z = \frac{1}{2}(\cos 100° + i \sin 100°)$
$\quad w = 10(\cos 50° + i \sin 50°)$

34 $z = \cos \frac{\pi}{3} + i \sin \frac{\pi}{3}$
$\quad w = 6\left(\cos \frac{\pi}{4} + i \sin \frac{\pi}{4}\right)$

35 $z = \sqrt{2}\left(\cos \frac{5\pi}{4} + i \sin \frac{5\pi}{4}\right)$
$\quad w = 8\left(\cos \frac{7\pi}{4} + i \sin \frac{7\pi}{4}\right)$

Evaluate zw and $\dfrac{z}{w}$ using trigonometric forms and convert the answers to rectangular form.

36 $z = 1 + i$
$\quad w = -2 - 2i$

37 $z = 7i$
$\quad w = \sqrt{3} + i$

38 $z = -5i$
$\quad w = 7$

39 $z = -2 + 2\sqrt{3}i$
$\quad w = -2\sqrt{3} - 2i$

40 $z = 10 - 10i$
$\quad w = -4\sqrt{2} + 4\sqrt{2}i$

41 $z = -1 + i$
$\quad w = 1 - i$

Multiply as indicated and express the answer in rectangular form. Use Table V only if necessary.

42 $[4(\cos 23° + i \sin 23°)][2(\cos 37° + i \sin 37°)]$

43 $[\frac{1}{2}(\cos 20° + i \sin 20°)][\sqrt{2}(\cos 70° + i \sin 70°)]$

44 $[15(\cos 25° + i \sin 25°)][3(\cos 205° + i \sin 205°)]$

45 $[\frac{2}{3}(\cos 122° + i \sin 122°)][\frac{9}{4}(\cos 77° + i \sin 77°)]$

*46 Derive the formula for quotients in trigonometric

form on page 421. (*Hint:* Use the conjugate of $\cos \theta_2 + i \sin \theta_2$ and Formulas (2) and (4) on page 348.)

*47 Use $z = a + bi$ and $w = c + di$ to prove that $|zw| = |z||w|$.

11.3

The formula for the product of two complex numbers in trigonometric form can be used to derive a special formula for the nth power of a complex number z. We begin with the case $n = 2$. First, let

De Moivre's theorem

$$z_1 = z_2 = z = r(\cos \theta + i \sin \theta)$$

Now substitute into

$$z_1 z_2 = r_1 r_2 [\cos(\theta_1 + \theta_2) + i \sin (\theta_1 + \theta_2)]$$

Thus

$$z^2 = r^2[\cos 2\theta + i \sin 2\theta]$$

For $n = 3$, write $z^3 = z^2 z$ and let $z_1 = z^2$ and $z_2 = z$ in the formula for $z_1 z_2$ to obtain

$$z^3 = z^2 z = [r^2(\cos 2\theta + i \sin 2\theta)][r(\cos \theta + i \sin \theta)]$$
$$= r^3(\cos 3\theta + i \sin 3\theta)$$

In this manner it can be shown that $z^n = r^n(\cos n\theta + i \sin n\theta)$ for each positive integer n. Since $z = r(\cos \theta + i \sin \theta)$, we get the following result:

DE MOIVRE'S THEOREM

$$[r(\cos \theta + i \sin \theta)]^n = r^n(\cos n\theta + i \sin n\theta)$$

for any positive integer n.

Try to prove this formula using mathematical induction (see Section 10.6).

EXAMPLE 1 Use De Moivre's theorem to evaluate $(1 - i)^8$.

Solution Converting $z = 1 - i$ to trigonometric form, we obtain

$$z = 2^{1/2}\left(\cos \frac{7\pi}{4} + i \sin \frac{7\pi}{4}\right)$$

Now use De Moivre's theorem.

$$z^8 = (2^{1/2})^8\left[\cos \left(8 \cdot \frac{7\pi}{4}\right) + i \sin \left(8 \cdot \frac{7\pi}{4}\right)\right]$$
$$= 2^4(\cos 14\pi + i \sin 14\pi)$$
$$= 16(\cos 0 + i \sin 0) \qquad \text{(0 is the principal argument)}$$
$$= 16(1 + 0)$$
$$= 16$$

Use De Moivre's theorem to evaluate the following powers.

1 $(\cos 15° + i \sin 15°)^3$

2 $[\frac{1}{2}(\cos 15° + i \sin 15°)]^6$

3 $(-\frac{1}{2} + \frac{1}{2}i)^4$

4 $(-\sqrt{3} + i)^{10}$

Example 1 shows that $(1 - i)^8 = 16$. This says that $1 - i$ is an 8th root of 16. There are seven more 8th roots of 16. For the integers $n \geq 2$ every complex number has n distinct nth roots. De Moivre's theorem can be used to derive the following formula, which enables us to find such roots.

THE nTH-ROOT FORMULA

The formula can be restated for θ in degree measure. In this case, replace 2π by $360°$.

If n is a positive integer and if $z = r(\cos \theta + i \sin \theta)$ is a nonzero complex number, the nth roots of z are given by

$$r^{1/n}\left(\cos \frac{\theta + 2k\pi}{n} + i \sin \frac{\theta + 2k\pi}{n}\right) \qquad \text{for } k = 0, 1, 2, \ldots, n - 1$$

When $k = 0, 1, 2, \ldots, n - 1$ the nth-root formula produces the n distinct roots. For larger values of k, say $k = n, n + 1, \ldots, 2n - 1$, the periodicity of sin and cos will produce the same roots. This is discussed in Exercise 33 at the end of this section, and also in Example 2, which is presented after the following verification of the nth-root formula.

One way to justify the nth-root formula is to take an nth root of z, raise it to the nth power, and obtain z. Thus, if $k = 0, 1, 2, \ldots, n - 1$,

$$\left[r^{1/n}\left(\cos \frac{\theta + 2k\pi}{n} + i \sin \frac{\theta + 2k\pi}{n}\right)\right]^n$$

$$= (r^{1/n})^n\left[\cos\left(n \cdot \frac{\theta + 2k\pi}{n}\right) + i \sin \left(n \cdot \frac{\theta + 2k\pi}{n}\right)\right] \quad \text{(by De Moivre's theorem)}$$

$$= r[\cos(\theta + 2k\pi) + i \sin(\theta + 2k\pi)]$$

$$= r[\cos \theta + i \sin \theta] \qquad \text{(by the addition formulas for sin and cos, page 348)}$$

$$= z$$

EXAMPLE 2 Find the three cube roots of $z = 8i$.

Solution First convert z into trigonometric form.

$$z = 8i = 0 + 8i = 8\left(\cos \frac{\pi}{2} + i \sin \frac{\pi}{2}\right)$$

Now use the nth-root formula with $n = 3$, $r = 8$, and $\theta = \frac{\pi}{2}$. The values $k = 0, 1, 2$ product the cube roots as follows:

$$k = 0: \quad 8^{1/3}\left(\cos\frac{\dfrac{\pi}{2}+0}{3} + i\sin\frac{\dfrac{\pi}{2}+0}{3}\right) = 2\left(\cos\frac{\pi}{6} + i\sin\frac{\pi}{6}\right)$$

$$= \sqrt{3} + i$$

Substitute $k = 3, 4, 5$ into the nth-root formula to see that the same three cube roots are obtained.

$$k = 1: \quad 8^{1/3}\left(\cos\frac{\dfrac{\pi}{2}+2\pi}{3} + i\sin\frac{\dfrac{\pi}{2}+2\pi}{3}\right) = 2\left(\cos\frac{5\pi}{6} + i\sin\frac{5\pi}{6}\right)$$

$$= -\sqrt{3} + i$$

$$k = 2: \quad 8^{1/3}\left(\cos\frac{\dfrac{\pi}{2}+4\pi}{3} + i\sin\frac{\dfrac{\pi}{2}+4\pi}{3}\right) = 2\left(\cos\frac{3\pi}{2} + i\sin\frac{3\pi}{2}\right)$$

$$= -2i$$

The roots found in **Example 2** can be checked by showing that their cubes equal $8i$. For example, here is a check for $\sqrt{3} + i$ using rectangular forms.

You can also check this root by applying De Moivre's theorem to the trigonometric form of $\sqrt{3} + i$.

$$(\sqrt{3} + i)^3 = (\sqrt{3} + i)^2(\sqrt{3} + i) = (3 - 1 + 2\sqrt{3}\,i)(\sqrt{3} + i)$$
$$= (2 + 2\sqrt{3}\,i)(\sqrt{3} + i) = 2\sqrt{3} - 2\sqrt{3} + 2i + 6i$$
$$= 8i$$

The nth-root formula shows that each root has modulus $r^{1/n}$. Therefore, since the modulus of a complex number is its distance from the origin, the nth roots are on a circle with center at the origin having radius $r^{1/n}$. Furthermore, the arguments of a pair of successive roots differ by $\dfrac{2\pi}{n}$ For instance,

$$\left.\begin{array}{l} \text{argument for } k = 3: \quad \dfrac{\theta + 6\pi}{n} = \dfrac{\theta}{n} + \dfrac{6\pi}{n} \\[2mm] \text{argument for } k = 2: \quad \dfrac{\theta + 4\pi}{n} = \dfrac{\theta}{n} + \dfrac{4\pi}{n} \end{array}\right\} \quad \text{difference} = \dfrac{2\pi}{n}$$

This means that the nth roots are equally spaced around the circle. Here is the diagram for the cube roots of $8i$.

$$\frac{2\pi}{n} = \frac{360°}{3} = 120°$$

$$\text{radius} = 2$$

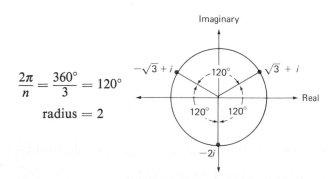

The trigonometric form of $z = 1$ is $1 = 1(\cos 0 + i \sin 0)$. Then, using $r = 1$ and $\theta = 0$ in the nth-root formula, we obtain the following:

nth ROOTS OF UNITY

$$\cos \frac{2k\pi}{n} + i \sin \frac{2k\pi}{n} \qquad \text{for } k = 0, 1, 2, \ldots, n-1$$

These roots are uniformly spaced on the unit circle and determine a regular polygon.

EXAMPLE 3 Find the 6th roots of unity and sketch the regular hexagon.

Solution Use $n = 6$ in the preceding formula.

k	$\cos \frac{k\pi}{3} + i \sin \frac{k\pi}{3} = x + yi$
0	$\cos 0 + i \sin 0 = 1$
1	$\cos \frac{\pi}{3} + i \sin \frac{\pi}{3} = \frac{1}{2} + \frac{\sqrt{3}}{2}i$
2	$\cos \frac{2\pi}{3} + i \sin \frac{2\pi}{3} = -\frac{1}{2} + \frac{\sqrt{3}}{2}i$
3	$\cos \pi + i \sin \pi = -1$
4	$\cos \frac{4\pi}{3} + i \sin \frac{4\pi}{3} = -\frac{1}{2} - \frac{\sqrt{3}}{2}i$
5	$\cos \frac{5\pi}{3} + i \sin \frac{5\pi}{3} = \frac{1}{2} - \frac{\sqrt{3}}{2}i$

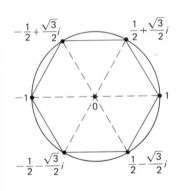

EXERCISES 11.3

Use De Moivre's theorem to evaluate the given powers and express the answers in the rectangular form $x + yi$. Use Appendix Table V only when necessary.

1 $(\cos 6° + i \sin 6°)^{10}$

2 $\left(\cos \frac{\pi}{5} + i \sin \frac{\pi}{5}\right)^{15}$

3 $(\cos 40° + i \sin 40°)^8$

4 $\left[2\left(\cos \frac{\pi}{9} + i \sin \frac{\pi}{9}\right)\right]^6$

5 $\left[\frac{1}{2}\left(\cos \frac{\pi}{8} + i \sin \frac{\pi}{8}\right)\right]^6$

6 $[3(\cos 15° + i \sin 15°)]^5$

7 $(-1 - i)^4$

8 $(1 - \sqrt{3}\,i)^8$

9 $(-\sqrt{3} + \sqrt{3}\,i)^6$

10 $\left(\frac{1}{2} + \frac{\sqrt{3}}{2}i\right)^6$

11 $\left(\frac{\sqrt{2}}{2} - \frac{\sqrt{2}}{2}i\right)^{10}$

12 $(2 - 2i)^4$

13 $\left(-\frac{\sqrt{3}}{2} + \frac{1}{2}i\right)^{12}$

14 $(2^{1/4} + 2^{1/4}i)^{12}$

In Exercises 15–18, find the indicated roots and express them in trigonometric form.

15 The cube roots of $27\left(\cos \frac{\pi}{15} + i \sin \frac{\pi}{15}\right)$.

16 The cube roots of $-4\sqrt{2} - 4\sqrt{2}i$.

17 The 5th roots of $32\left(\cos\dfrac{\pi}{8} + i\sin\dfrac{\pi}{8}\right)$.

18 The 4th roots of $4 - 4\sqrt{3}\,i$.

In Exercises 19–22, write the roots in rectangular form and graph them on the appropriate circle.

19 The 4th roots of 16.

20 The cube roots of 27.

21 The cube roots of -1.

22 The 6th roots of -1.

Find the following nth roots of unity for the given n, and sketch the regular polygon determined by the roots.

23 $n = 3$ **24** $n = 4$

25 $n = 5$ **26** $n = 8$

In Exercises 27–32, solve the given equation.

27 $z^3 = -27$ **28** $z^4 + 81 = 0$

29 $z^3 + 8i = 0$ **30** $z^4 - \tfrac{1}{16}i = 0$

31 $z^3 + i = -1$ **32** $z^4 + 1 - \sqrt{3}\,i = 0$

*33 (a) Show that $k = 0$ and $k = n$ give the same nth roots in the nth-root formula.

(b) Repeat part (a) for $k = 1$ and $k = n + 1$.

(c) Repeat part (a) for k and $k + n$.

*34 Prove De Moivre's theorem by mathematical induction.

*35 (a) Let n be a positive integer. Prove that
$$[r(\cos\theta + i\sin\theta)]^{-n} = r^{-n}(\cos n\theta - i\sin n\theta)$$
(Hint: $(\cos\theta + i\sin\theta)^{-1} = \cos\theta - i\sin\theta.)$

(b) Explain why
$$[r(\cos\theta + i\sin\theta)]^n = r^n(\cos n\theta + i\sin n\theta)$$
holds for all integers n.

*36 (a) Two complex numbers $a + bi$ and $c + di$ are equal if and only if $a = c$ and $b = d$. Use this criterion of equality in conjunction with De Moivre's theorem to derive the double-angle formulas for the sine and cosine. *(Hint:* Expand the right side of $\cos 2\theta + i\sin 2\theta = (\cos\theta + i\sin\theta)^2$.)

(b) Follow the procedure that is described in part (a) to derive the formulas $\cos 3\theta = 4\cos^3\theta - 3\cos\theta$ and $\sin 3\theta = 3\sin\theta - 4\sin^3\theta$.

Polar coordinates

When a complex number is given in trigonometric form, it can be located in the complex plane using its argument θ and modulus r. A similar method, using **polar coordinates**, can be used for locating points in the plane without using complex numbers. In a **polar coordinate system** a point in the plane is located in reference to a fixed point 0, called the **pole**, and a fixed ray called the **polar axis**. The pole is the endpoint of the polar axis which is usually horizontal and extends endlessly to the right.

Any point $P \neq 0$ is on some ray that forms an angle θ with the polar axis as its initial side, and is some distance r from the pole. The ordered pair (r, θ) are the polar coordinates of P. Consequently, when the polar coordinates (r, θ) of a point P are given, P can be located as follows:

1 Start at the polar axis and rotate through an angle θ to determine the ray.

2 On the ray θ move r units from the pole 0 to locate P.

The terminal side of θ is also referred to as the ray θ. The pole 0 is the initial point of ray θ.

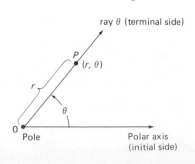

ray θ (terminal side)

P

(r, θ)

r

θ

0
Pole

Polar axis
(initial side)

EXAMPLE 1 Plot the points with these polar coordinates:

$$\left(1, \frac{\pi}{6}\right), \quad \left(2, \frac{2\pi}{3}\right), \quad \left(\frac{3}{2}, 225°\right), \quad \left(\frac{2}{3}, 330°\right)$$

Observe that for positive angles we rotate counterclockwise.

Solution

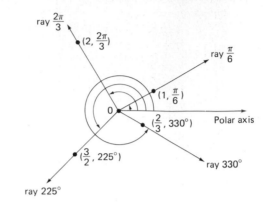

A ray for an angle θ may be extended through the pole 0 in the opposite or backward direction. Points on this opposite side have polar coordinates (r, θ), where $r < 0$.

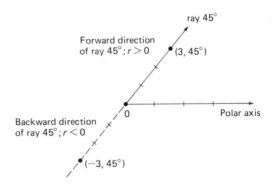

The opposite or backward extension of a ray θ is the same as the ray $\theta + \pi$. Therefore, (r, θ) and $(-r, \theta + \pi)$ are polar coordinates of the same point.

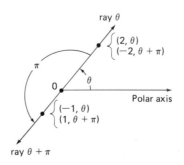

The angle θ may also be negative. In this case we rotate clockwise from the polar axis to determine the ray θ.

EXAMPLE 2   Plot the points with these polar coordinates:

$$\left(2, -\frac{\pi}{3}\right), \quad \left(-2, -\frac{\pi}{3}\right)$$

Solution

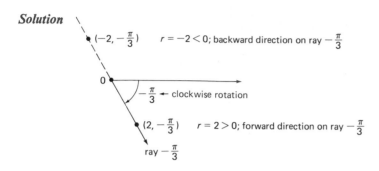

A pair of polar coordinates (r, θ) determine exactly one point. However, a point in the plane has more than one set of polar coordinates. For example, the point P with coordinates $(2, 60°)$ also has these polar coordinates:

$$(2, 420°), \quad (2, -300°), \quad (-2, 240°), \quad (-2, -120°)$$

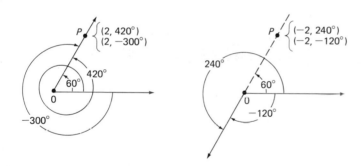

In fact, a point has an infinite number of polar coordinates. If (r, θ) are polar coordinates of point P, then $(r, \theta + 2k\pi)$ and $(-r, \theta + (2k + 1)\pi)$, for all integers k, give all the polar coordinates of P. The pole 0 is assigned the polar coordinates $(0, \theta)$ for any angle θ.

EXAMPLE 3   Let $\left(3, \frac{\pi}{6}\right)$ be polar coordinates of point P. Find polar coordinates (r, θ) of P subject to these conditions:

(a) $r > 0,$ $-2\pi < \theta < 0$ **(b)** $r < 0,$ $0 < \theta < 2\pi$

Solution

(a)

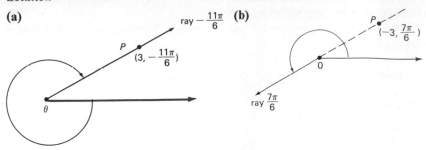

(b)

TEST YOUR UNDERSTANDING

In Exercises 1 and 2, plot the points having the given polar coordinates.

1 $(2, 45°)$, $(-2, 45°)$, $(2, -45°)$, $(-2, -45°)$

2 $\left(-2, \dfrac{3\pi}{4}\right)$, $\left(0, \dfrac{3\pi}{4}\right)$, $\left(1, \dfrac{3\pi}{4}\right)$, $\left(3, \dfrac{3\pi}{4}\right)$

3 If $\left(5, \dfrac{\pi}{12}\right)$ are polar coordinates of P, find the polar coordinates (r, θ) of P
such that:

(a) $r > 0$, $2\pi < \theta < 4\pi$ (b) $r < 0$, $0 < \theta < 2\pi$
(c) $r > 0$, $-2\pi < \theta < 0$ (d) $r < 0$, $-2\pi < \theta < 0$

To see the relationship between polar and rectangular coordinates, we superimpose a rectangular system onto a polar system so that the pole coincides with the origin, the polar axis coincides with the positive part of the x-axis, and the ray $\dfrac{\pi}{2}$ coincides with the positive part of the y-axis.

$r^2 = x^2 + y^2$ **is equivalent to**
$r = \pm\sqrt{x^2 + y^2}$. **The usual**
restrictions apply to $\tan \theta = \dfrac{y}{x}$.

$$x = r \cos \theta$$
$$y = r \sin \theta$$
$$x^2 + y^2 = r^2$$
$$\tan \theta = \frac{y}{x}$$

The equations listed next to the figure are easy to derive using the given triangle, which assumes that (x, y) is not on an axis, and $r > 0$. Furthermore, it can be shown that these equations hold when $r \leq 0$ or when (x, y) is on an axis (see Exercises 35, 36 and 37).

The preceding equations are used to change from one type of coordinates into the other.

EXAMPLE 4 Convert from polar to rectangular coordinates.

(a) $\left(4, \dfrac{3\pi}{4}\right)$ (b) $\left(\dfrac{1}{2}, -\dfrac{\pi}{3}\right)$

Solution

(a) $x = r \cos \theta = 4 \cos\left(\dfrac{3\pi}{4}\right) = 4\left(-\dfrac{\sqrt{2}}{2}\right) = -2\sqrt{2}$

$y = r \sin \theta = 4 \sin\left(\dfrac{3\pi}{4}\right) = 4\left(\dfrac{\sqrt{2}}{2}\right) = 2\sqrt{2}$

$(x, y) = (-2\sqrt{2}, 2\sqrt{2})$

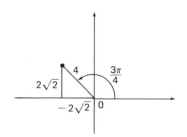

(b) $x = r \cos \theta = \dfrac{1}{2} \cos\left(-\dfrac{\pi}{3}\right) = \dfrac{1}{2} \cos \dfrac{\pi}{3} = \dfrac{1}{2}\left(\dfrac{1}{2}\right) = \dfrac{1}{4}$

$y = r \sin \theta = \dfrac{1}{2} \sin\left(-\dfrac{\pi}{3}\right) = -\dfrac{1}{2} \sin \dfrac{\pi}{3} = -\dfrac{1}{2}\left(\dfrac{\sqrt{3}}{2}\right) = -\dfrac{\sqrt{3}}{4}$

$(x, y) = \left(\dfrac{1}{4}, -\dfrac{\sqrt{3}}{4}\right)$

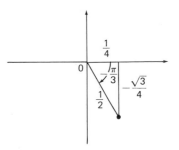

EXAMPLE 5 Convert from rectangular to polar coordinate (r, θ) so that $r \geq 0$ and $0 \leq \theta < 2\pi$.

(a) $(3\sqrt{3}, -3)$ (b) $(-5, -5)$

Solution

(a) $r = \sqrt{x^2 + y^2} = \sqrt{(3\sqrt{3})^2 + (-3)^2}$

$\qquad = \sqrt{27 + 9}$

$\qquad = 6$

$\tan \theta = \dfrac{-3}{3\sqrt{3}} = -\dfrac{\sqrt{3}}{3}$. Then $\theta = \dfrac{11\pi}{6}$ since (x, y) is in quadrant IV.

Therefore,

$$(r, \theta) = \left(6, \dfrac{11\pi}{6}\right)$$

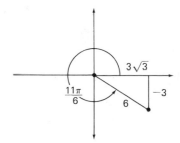

(b) $r = \sqrt{(-5)^2 + (-5)^2} = \sqrt{50} = 5\sqrt{2}$

$\tan \theta = \dfrac{-5}{-5} = 1$. Then $\theta = \dfrac{5\pi}{4}$, since (x, y) is in quadrant III.

Therefore,

$$(r, \theta) = \left(5\sqrt{2}, \dfrac{5\pi}{4}\right)$$

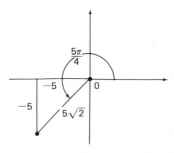

In Exercises 1–6, plot the points in the same polar coordinate system.

1 $(1, 30°), (-1, 30°), (1, -30°), (-1, -30°)$

2 $(2, 90°), (-2, 90°), (2, -90°), (-2, -90°)$

3 $(4, 0°), (-4, 0°)$

4 $\left(3, \frac{\pi}{4}\right), \left(3, -\frac{\pi}{4}\right), \left(-3, \frac{\pi}{4}\right), \left(-3, -\frac{\pi}{4}\right)$

5 $(\frac{1}{2}, \pi), (-\frac{1}{2}, \pi), (\frac{1}{2}, -\pi), (-\frac{1}{2}, -\pi)$

6 $\left(5, \frac{4\pi}{3}\right), \left(-5, \frac{4\pi}{3}\right), \left(5, -\frac{4\pi}{3}\right), \left(-5, -\frac{4\pi}{3}\right)$

In Exercises 7–10, the polar coordinates of a point P are given. Find the polar coordinates (r, θ) of P subject to each of the following:

(a) $r > 0$ and $2\pi < \theta < 4\pi$
(b) $r > 0$ and $-2\pi < \theta < 0$
(c) $r < 0$ and $0 < \theta < 2\pi$
(d) $r < 0$ and $-2\pi < \theta < 0$

7 $(1, 45°)$

8 $(\frac{1}{2}, 200°)$

9 $\left(-3, \frac{\pi}{6}\right)$

10 $\left(-\frac{3}{4}, \frac{5\pi}{4}\right)$

Convert the following polar coordinates into rectangular coordinates.

11 $\left(7, -\frac{5\pi}{2}\right)$

12 $\left(-8, \frac{13\pi}{6}\right)$

13 $\left(-\frac{3}{2}, \frac{5\pi}{2}\right)$

14 $(-1, -540°)$

15 $\left(\frac{4}{5}, 405°\right)$

16 $(-10, -420°)$

Convert the following rectangular coordinates into polar coordinates (r, θ) so that $r \geq 0$ and $0 \leq \theta < 2\pi$.

17 $(2, 0)$

18 $(0, 2)$

19 $(-2, 0)$

20 $(0, -2)$

21 $(-6, -6)$

22 $(3, -3\sqrt{3})$

23 $(2\sqrt{2}, 2\sqrt{2})$

24 $(-2\sqrt{2}, 2\sqrt{2})$

25 $(\sqrt{3}, -1)$

Convert the following rectangular coordinates into polar coordinates (r, θ) so that $r < 0$ and $0 \leq \theta < 2\pi$.

26 $(0, 7)$

27 $(7, 0)$

28 $(2, 2)$

29 $(-\sqrt{3}, 1)$

30 $(4, -4\sqrt{3})$

31 $(\sqrt{3}, \sqrt{3})$

Convert the following rectangular coordinates into polar coordinates (r, θ) so that $r > 0$ and $-180° \leq \theta < 180°$.

32 $(-1, -1)$

33 $(0, -10)$

34 $(4, -4\sqrt{3})$

Exercises 35–37 call for the verification of the formulas $x = r \cos \theta$ and $y = r \sin \theta$ in various cases. Assume that they hold when $r > 0$.

35 Verify the formulas for the origin whose polar coordinates are $(0, \theta)$, where θ is any angle.

36 Verify the formulas for a point whose rectangular coordinates are $(x, 0)$ with $x < 0$.

*37 Verify the formulas for a point P with rectangular coordinates (x, y) and polar coordinates (r, θ) with $r < 0$. (*Hint:* Since P also has polar coordinates $(-r, \theta + \pi)$, you may apply the formulas since $-r > 0$.)

11.5

Graphing polar equations

The ray $\frac{\pi}{4}$ and its opposite ray form a straight line through the pole 0. This line contains all points with polar coordinates $\left(r, \frac{\pi}{4}\right)$ regardless of the value of r. Thus the graph of the equation $\theta = \frac{\pi}{4}$ (for all r) is the line as shown.

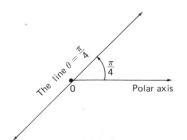

In general,

$$\theta = \theta_0$$

is the equation of a line through the pole at an angle θ_0 with the polar axis.

θ_0 designates a constant angle.

EXAMPLE 1 Write a polar equation of the line ℓ through the points with rectangular coordinates $(-2, 2)$ and $(3, -3)$.

Solution ℓ has equation $\theta = 135°$, since ℓ bisects quadrants II and IV.

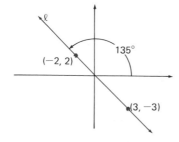

All points of the form $(4, \theta)$ for any value θ are four units from the pole and therefore determine a circle with center 0 and radius 4. Thus the graph of the polar equation $r = 4$ (for all θ) is the circle as shown. Note that the points $(-4, \theta)$ are also on this circle. However, these are the same points as before, since $(-4, \theta)$ and $(4, \theta + \pi)$ represent the same point.

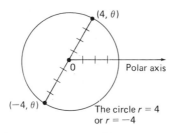

In general,

$$r = r_0$$

is the equation of the circle with center 0 and radius $|r_0|$.

r_0 designates a nonzero constant.

Equations written in terms of polar coordinates are called **polar equations**, and equations using rectangular coordinates may be referred to as **rectangular equations**. When you first learned to graph using rectangular equations, you became accustomed to locating points by moving horizontally for the x coordinate, and vertically for y. With polar coordinates you need to become accustomed to moving in a circular direction for the θ coordinate and forward or backward from the pole for the r coordinate.

EXAMPLE 2 Graph the polar equation $r = 2 \cos \theta$.

Solution As the values of θ increase from 0 to $\dfrac{\pi}{2}$ the corresponding values of r decrease from 2 to 0.

θ	0	$\dfrac{\pi}{6}$	$\dfrac{\pi}{4}$	$\dfrac{\pi}{3}$	$\dfrac{\pi}{2}$
$\cos \theta$	1	$\dfrac{\sqrt{3}}{2}$	$\dfrac{\sqrt{2}}{2}$	$\dfrac{1}{2}$	0
$r = 2 \cos \theta$	2	$\sqrt{3}$	$\sqrt{2}$	1	0

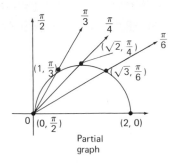

Partial
graph

As the values of θ increase from $\dfrac{\pi}{2}$ to π, the values of r decrease from 0 to -2. Since the rays θ for $\dfrac{\pi}{2} < \theta < \pi$ are in quadrant II, and the r values are negative, the points are in quadrant IV.

θ	$\dfrac{\pi}{2}$	$\dfrac{2\pi}{3}$	$\dfrac{3\pi}{4}$	$\dfrac{5\pi}{6}$	π
$\cos \theta$	0	$-\dfrac{1}{2}$	$-\dfrac{\sqrt{2}}{2}$	$-\dfrac{\sqrt{3}}{2}$	-1
$r = 2 \cos \theta$	0	-1	$-\sqrt{2}$	$-\sqrt{3}$	-2

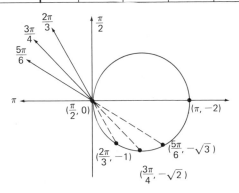

The curve is traced out twice from $\theta = 0$ to $\theta = 2\pi$. For values of $\theta = \pi$ to 2π the same points as before are obtained. For example, the pair $\left(\dfrac{5\pi}{4}, -\sqrt{2}\right)$ and $\left(\dfrac{\pi}{4}, \sqrt{2}\right)$ represent one point, as do the pair $\left(\frac{5\pi}{3}, 1\right)$ and $\left(\frac{2\pi}{3}, -1\right)$. Furthermore, the periodicity of the cosine will produce the same points for $\theta < 0$ or $\theta > 2\pi$. Therefore, the complete graph of $r = 2\cos\theta$ is obtained for $\theta = 0$ to $\theta = \pi$, as shown.

The graph in Example 2 is a circle, as are the graphs of the polar equations $r = 2a\cos\theta$, for $a > 0$. To prove this, consider the circle with radius a, center $(a, 0)$, and let P be a point on this circle with polar coordinates (r, θ). Now recall that an angle inscribed in a semicircle is a right angle. Then, from the right triangle, $\cos\theta = \dfrac{\text{adjacent}}{\text{hypotenuse}} = \dfrac{r}{2a}$, or $r = 2a\cos\theta$.

Repeat the argument for P on the lower semicircle.

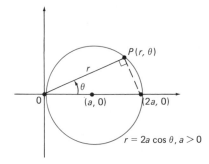

Similarly, the graph of $r = -2a\cos\theta$, $a > 0$, is the circle with radius a whose center has polar coordinates (a, π).

In the exercises you will be asked to verify that

$$\left.\begin{array}{l} r = 2a\sin\theta \\[2mm] r = -2a\sin\theta \end{array}\right\} \quad a > 0$$

are the polar equations of circles with radius a and centers with polar coordinates $\left(a, \frac{\pi}{2}\right)$ and $\left(a, \frac{3\pi}{2}\right)$, respectively.

EXAMPLE 3 Graph the polar equations.

(a) $r = -4\cos\theta$ (b) $r = \frac{1}{2}\sin\theta$

Solution

(a) $r = -4\cos\theta$

    $= -2(2)\cos\theta$

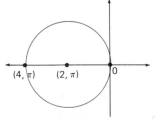

This is the form $-2a\cos\theta$, $a = 2$.

(b) $r = \frac{1}{2} \sin \theta$

$\qquad = 2(\frac{1}{4}) \sin \theta$

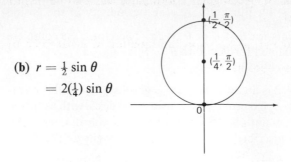

This is the form $2a \sin \theta$, $a = \frac{1}{4}$.

TEST YOUR UNDERSTANDING

Write a polar equation of the line through the points with the given polar coordinates.

1 $(0, 0°)$, $(2, 30°)$ **2** $(0, 0°)$, $(-1, 140°)$ **3** $\left(3, \frac{\pi}{2}\right)$, $\left(-3, \frac{\pi}{2}\right)$

Write a polar equation of the line through the points with the given rectangular coordinates.

4 $(1, 1)$, $(5, 5)$ **5** $(0, 2)$, $(0, 4)$ **6** $(0, 0)$, $(-\sqrt{3}, 1)$

7 Write a polar equation of the circle with center at the pole containing the given point.

  (a) $(4, 72°)$ **(b)** $(-5, 5°)$

  (c) $(1, 1)$; rectangular coordinates

Write the polar equation of the circle with the given radius a and center in polar coordinates.

8 $a = 2$, $(2, 0)$ **9** $a = \frac{3}{2}$, $\left(\frac{3}{2}, \pi\right)$ **10** $a = \frac{2}{3}$, $\left(\frac{2}{3}, \frac{3\pi}{2}\right)$

Another way to show that the graph of $r = 2a \cos \theta$ is a circle is to convert the equation into rectangular form. To do this, begin by multiplying the equation by r.

$$r = 2a \cos \theta$$

$$r^2 = 2a(r \cos \theta) \qquad \text{(multiplying by } r\text{)}$$

Since $r^2 = x^2 + y^2$ and $r \cos \theta = x$, we get

$$x^2 + y^2 = 2ax$$

Now complete the square in x.

$$x^2 - 2ax + y^2 = 0$$

$$x^2 - 2ax + a^2 + y^2 = a^2$$

$$(x - a)^2 + y^2 = a^2 \quad \longleftarrow \quad \text{a circle with radius } a \text{ and center } (a, 0)$$

Converting from polar to rectangular coordinates can also be helpful in identifying polar graphs.

EXAMPLE 4 Show that $r = \dfrac{2}{1 - \sin \theta}$ is the equation of a parabola by converting to rectangular coordinates.

Solution

$$r = \frac{2}{1 - \sin \theta}$$

$$r - r \sin \theta = 2$$

$$r = r \sin \theta + 2$$

$$\pm\sqrt{x^2 + y^2} = y + 2 \qquad \begin{cases} r = \pm\sqrt{x^2 + y^2} \\ y = r \sin \theta \end{cases}$$

$$x^2 + y^2 = y^2 + 4y + 4 \qquad \text{(squaring both sides)}$$

$$4y = x^2 - 4$$

$$y = \tfrac{1}{4}x^2 - 1 \qquad \longleftarrow \qquad \text{a parabola with vertex } (0, -1), \text{ opening upward}$$

EXAMPLE 5 Graph the polar curve $r = 2(1 + \sin \theta)$.

Solution Since the sine has period 2π, it is only necessary to consider values of θ from 0 to 2π. We form a table of selected values for θ (in intervals of 30°), plot the points on a *polar grid system*, and connect the points with a smooth curve.

θ	0°	30°	60°	90°	120°	150°	180°	210°	240°	270°	300°	330°	360°
$\sin \theta$	0	.5	.87	1	.87	.5	0	−.5	−.87	−1	−.87	−.5	0
$r = 2(1 + \sin \theta)$	2	3	3.7	4	3.7	3	2	1	.3	0	.3	1	2

This heart-shaped curve is a *cardioid*. Cardioids are given by these polar equations:

$$r = a(1 \pm \sin \theta)$$
$$r = a(1 \pm \cos \theta)$$

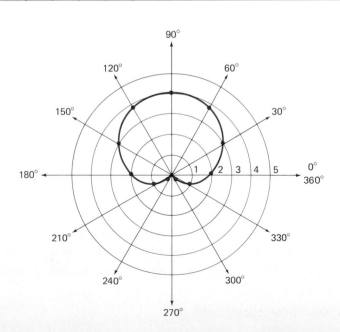

437

EXAMPLE 6 Sketch the polar curve $r = \sin 2\theta$.

Solution As θ increases from 0 to $\frac{\pi}{4}$, 2θ increases from 0 to $\frac{\pi}{2}$, and therefore $r = \sin 2\theta$ increases from 0 to 1. Also, as θ increases from $\frac{\pi}{4}$ to $\frac{\pi}{2}$, 2θ increases from $\frac{\pi}{2}$ to π, and therefore r decreases from 1 to 0. This produces the curve for $\theta = 0$ to $\theta = \frac{\pi}{2}$.

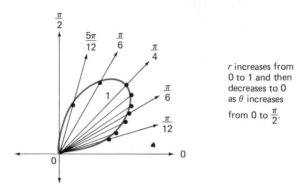

r increases from
0 to 1 and then
decreases to 0
as θ increases

from 0 to $\frac{\pi}{2}$.

As θ increases from $\frac{\pi}{2}$ to $\frac{3\pi}{4}$, 2θ increases from π to $\frac{3\pi}{2}$ and r decreases from 0 to -1. These negative r-values produce points in the fourth quadrant, since the rays are in the second quadrant. Similarly, as θ increases from $\frac{3\pi}{4}$ to π, r increases from -1 to 0. This completes the loop for $\theta = \frac{\pi}{2}$ to $\theta = \pi$.

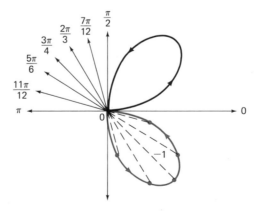

By similar analysis we find that there is such a loop in each of the remaining quadrants. The complete graph has four loops as shown in the following figure.

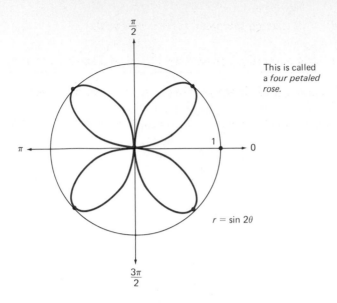

This is called a *four petaled rose.*

$r = \sin 2\theta$

EXAMPLE 7 Graph the polar curve $r = \theta$ for $\theta > 0$.

Solution Form a table of values and note that as θ increases, so does r.

θ	0	$\frac{\pi}{4}$	$\frac{\pi}{2}$	π	$\frac{3\pi}{2}$	2π	$\frac{9\pi}{4}$
$r = \theta$	0	$\frac{\pi}{4}$	$\frac{\pi}{2}$	π	$\frac{3\pi}{2}$	2π	$\frac{9\pi}{4}$
(approximations)		.8	1.6	3.1	4.7	6.3	7.1

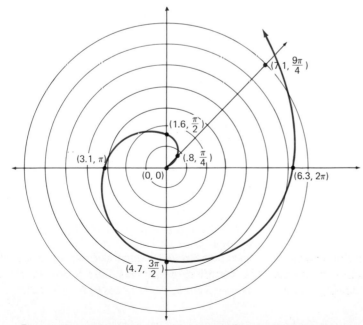

The curve is an endless, ever widening spiral called the **spiral of Archimedes**.

EXERCISES 11.5

In Exercises 1–5, sketch the graphs of the given polar equations in the same polar system.

1 $\theta = 30°, \theta = 210°, \theta = -150°, \theta = -30°$

2 $\theta = \frac{2\pi}{3}, \theta = \frac{5\pi}{3}, \theta = -\frac{\pi}{4}, \theta = \frac{15\pi}{4}$

3 $\theta = 0, \theta = \frac{\pi}{2}, \theta = \pi, \theta = -\frac{\pi}{2}$

4 $r = 1, r = \frac{3}{2}, r = 3$

5 $r = -2, r = 4, r = -4$

Write a polar equation of the line through the given points.

6 $(3, 150°), (2, -30°)$ **7** $(0, 0°), (10, -6°)$

8 $(1, -1), (-1, 1);$ (rectangular coordinates)

9 $(\sqrt{3}, 1), (-\sqrt{6}, -\sqrt{2});$ (rectangular coordinates)

In Exercises 10–15, graph the polar equation and convert it into rectangular form.

10 $r = \cos\theta$ **11** $r = \sin\theta$

12 $r = -3\cos\theta$ **13** $r = 5\sin\theta$

14 $r = -5\sin\theta$ **15** $r = -\frac{1}{3}\cos\theta$

16 Convert the polar equations into rectangular equations.

   (a) $\theta = 45°$ **(b)** $\theta = \frac{\pi}{3}$ **(c)** $\theta = \frac{2\pi}{3}$

17 Convert the polar equations into rectangular equations.

   (a) $r = 2$ **(b)** $r = -2$ **(c)** $r = \sqrt{5}$

Sketch each cardioid.

18 $r = 1 + \cos\theta$ **19** $r = 3 + 3\cos\theta$

20 $r = 4 - 4\sin\theta$ **21** $r = 2(1 - \cos\theta)$

Graph the polar curves.

22 $r\cos\theta = 2$ **23** $r\sin\theta = -2$

24 $\tan\theta = 3$ **25** $\cot\theta = -3$

26 $r = \frac{1}{2}\theta, \theta \geq 0$ **27** $r = \theta, \theta \leq 0$

28 $r = 2\sin 2\theta$ **29** $r = \cos 2\theta$
   (four-petal rose)   (four-petal rose)

30 $r = \cos 3\theta$ **31** $r = 2\sin 3\theta$
   (three-petal rose)   (three-petal rose)

32 $r^2 = \sin 2\theta$
   (lemniscate; two loops)

33 $r^2 = 4\cos 2\theta$
   (lemniscate; two loops)

34 $r = 1 + 2\sin\theta$
   (limaçon; like a cardioid but with an inner loop)

35 $r = 1 - 2\cos\theta$
   (limaçon; like a cardioid but with an inner loop)

Convert the polar equation into rectangular form and identify the curve.

36 $r = \dfrac{1}{1 - \sin\theta}$ **37** $r = \dfrac{4}{1 + \cos\theta}$

38 $r = 2\csc\theta$ **39** $r = -5\sec\theta$

40 $r = 2\cos\theta + 2\sin\theta$

41 $r = 6\cos\theta + 8\sin\theta$

42 $r^2 = \dfrac{2}{\sin 2\theta}$

43 $r(2\cos\theta + 3\sin\theta) = 3$

44 $r(8\cos\theta - 4\sin\theta) = 20$

45 $r\cos\left(\theta - \dfrac{\pi}{3}\right) = \sqrt{3}$

46 (a) Show that the polar equation of the given circle is $r = 2a\sin\theta, a > 0$.

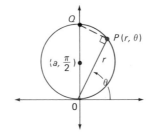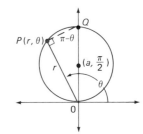

   (b) Repeat part (a) for the case $r = -2a\sin\theta$, $a > 0$.

***47** Show that the vertical line $x = c$ has polar form $r\cos\theta = c$.

***48** Show that the horizontal line $y = c$ has polar form $r\sin\theta = c$.

Find the polar coordinates of the points of intersection of the given curves for the indicated interval of θ. (Note: A point of intersection must have the same polar coordinates for each curve.)

49 $r = 3\cos\theta, r = 1 + \cos\theta; 0 \leq \theta < 2\pi$

50 $r = 1, r = 1 - \sin \theta; 0 \le \theta < 2\pi$

52 $r = \sin \theta, r = \cos \theta; 0 \le \theta \le \dfrac{\pi}{2}$

*51 $r = \sin 2\theta, r = \cos \theta; 0 \le \theta \le \pi$

53 $r \cos \theta = \frac{1}{2}, 2r \sin \theta = -\sqrt{3}; -\dfrac{\pi}{2} \le \theta \le 0$

REVIEW EXERCISES FOR CHAPTER 11

The solutions to the following exercises can be found within the text of Chapter 11. Try to answer each question without referring to the text.

Section 11.1

1 Multiply: $(5 - 2i)(3 + 4i)$.

2 Divide: $\dfrac{2 + 3i}{3 + i}$.

3 Simplify: **(a)** i^{22}; **(b)** i^{39}.

4 For $z = -2 + 5i$ and $w = 4 - 7i$, evaluate $\overline{z + w}$ and $\overline{z \cdot w}$.

5 Write $2i^{-3}$ in the form bi.

6 Solve $x^2 + x + 1 = 0$.

Section 11.2

7 Use the parallelogram rule to evaluate the sum $(3 + 2i) + (2 - 4i)$.

8 Use a parallelogram to evaluate the difference $(3 + 2i) - (2 - 4i)$.

Convert the complex numbers into trigonometric form.

9 $\sqrt{3} + i$

10 $-1 - i$

11 Use Table V to convert $3(\cos 50° + i \sin 50°)$ into rectangular form.

12 Use trigonometric forms to evaluate the product $(2 + 2\sqrt{3}\,i)(-1 - \sqrt{3}\,i)$. State the answer in both trigonometric and rectangular forms.

13 Use trigonometric forms to evaluate the quotient $\dfrac{2 + 2\sqrt{3}\,i}{-1 - \sqrt{3}\,i}$. State the answer in both trigonometric and rectangular forms.

Section 11.3

14 Complete this formula for De Moivre's theorem: $[r(\cos \theta + i \sin \theta)]^n =$

15 Use De Moivre's theorem to evaluate $(1 - i)^8$.

16 If $z = r(\cos \theta + i \sin \theta)$ is a nonzero complex number, write the form of the nth roots of z for $k = 0, 1, 2, \ldots, n - 1$.

17 Find the three cube roots of $8i$ and display them as points on an appropriate circle.

18 Write the form of the nth roots of unity for $k = 0, 1, 2, \ldots, n - 1$.

19 Find the 6th roots of unity and display them as points on an appropriate circle.

Section 11.4

20 Plot the points with these polar coordinates:

$$\left(1, \frac{\pi}{6}\right), \left(2, \frac{2\pi}{3}\right), \left(\frac{3}{2}, 225°\right), \left(\frac{2}{3}, 330°\right)$$

21 Plot the points with these polar coordinates:

$$\left(2, -\frac{\pi}{3}\right), \left(-2, -\frac{\pi}{3}\right)$$

22 Let P have polar coordinates $(2, 60°)$. Find the value of r in each case so that the resulting pair becomes a set of polar coordinates for P.

$$(r, 420°), (r, -300°), (r, 240°), (r, -120°)$$

23 Let P have polar coordinates $\left(3, \dfrac{\pi}{6}\right)$. Find polar coordinates of (r, θ) subject to these conditions:
(a) $r > 0, -2\pi < \theta < 0$
(b) $r < 0, 0 < \theta < 2\pi$

24 Convert $\left(4, \dfrac{3\pi}{4}\right)$ and $\left(\dfrac{1}{2}, -\dfrac{\pi}{3}\right)$ into rectangular coordinates.

25 Convert the rectangular coordinates $(3\sqrt{3}, -3)$ and $(-5, -5)$ into polar coordinates so that $r \ge 0$ and $0 \le \theta < 2\pi$.

Section 11.5

Sketch the graphs of the polar equation.

26 $r = 2 \cos \theta$

27 $r = -4 \cos \theta$

28 $r = \frac{1}{2} \sin \theta$

29 How many times is the complete graph of $r = 2 \cos \theta$ traced out as θ varies from $\theta = 0$ to $\theta = 2\pi$?

30 Convert the polar equation $r = 2a \cos \theta$ into a rectangular equation.

31 Show that $r = \dfrac{2}{1 - \sin \theta}$ is the equation of a parabola by converting to rectangular coordinates.

Sketch the graphs of the polar equations.

32 $r = 2(1 + \sin \theta)$

33 $r = \sin 2\theta$

34 $r = \theta$ for $\theta > 0$

SAMPLE TEST QUESTIONS FOR CHAPTER 11

Use these questions to test your knowledge of the basic skills and concepts of Chapter 11. Then test your answers with those given at the end of the book.

1 Simplify and express the answer in the form $a + bi$.

$$2(3 - 4i) - 4i^7 + (-2 + 5i)i$$

2 Multiply the complex numbers $3 + 7i$ and $5 - 4i$ and express the result in the form $a + bi$.

3 Divide $3 + 7i$ by $5 - 4i$ and express the result in the form $a + bi$.

4 Simplify $(2 - i)^{-2}$ and express the result in the form $a + bi$.

5 Solve for x: $2x^2 - 5x + 4 = 0$.

For Questions 6 and 7, let $z = \dfrac{\sqrt{3}}{4} + \dfrac{1}{4}i$ *and* $w = -1 + \sqrt{3}\,i$.

6 Convert z and w into trigonometric form and evaluate the quotient $\dfrac{z}{w}$.

7 Use De Moivre's theorem to evaluate z^5 and express the answer in rectangular form.

8 Find the three cube roots of 8 and locate them graphically.

9 Find the four fourth roots of $z = -8\sqrt{2} + 8\sqrt{2}i$ and express them in trigonometric form.

10 Point P has polar coordinates $(-3, 60°)$. Find the polar coordinates (r, θ) of P so that
(a) $r < 0$ and $-360° < \theta < 0°$
(b) $r > 0$ and $0 < \theta < 360°$

11 (a) Convert the polar coordinates $\left(\dfrac{1}{3}, -\dfrac{\pi}{6}\right)$ into rectangular coordinates.

(b) Convert the rectangular coordinates $(-7\sqrt{2}, 7\sqrt{2})$ into polar coordinates.

12 Convert the polar equation $r = 2\sin\theta$ into a rectangular equation and identify the curve.

Sketch the graphs of the polar equations.

13 $2r\sin\theta = 6$ **14** $r = 2 + 2\cos\theta$

15 $r = 4\sin 2\theta$

ANSWERS TO THE TEST YOUR UNDERSTANDING EXERCISES

Page 410

1 $3i$ **2** $7i$ **3** $\sqrt{5}\,i$ **4** $-2i$ **5** $\tfrac{2}{3}i$ **6** -20

7 $21i$ **8** $7\sqrt{2}\,i$ **9** $12\sqrt{5}\,i$

Page 421

$z_1 = 2\sqrt{2}\left(\cos\dfrac{3\pi}{4} + i\sin\dfrac{3\pi}{4}\right)$

$z_2 = 6\left(\cos\dfrac{11\pi}{6} + i\sin\dfrac{11\pi}{6}\right)$

$z_1z_2 = 12\sqrt{2}\left(\cos\dfrac{31\pi}{12} + i\sin\dfrac{31\pi}{12}\right)$

$\quad\;\; = 12\sqrt{2}\left(\cos\dfrac{7\pi}{12} + i\sin\dfrac{7\pi}{12}\right)$

Page 424

1 $\dfrac{\sqrt{2}}{2} + \dfrac{\sqrt{2}}{2}i$ **2** $\dfrac{1}{64}i$ **3** $-\dfrac{1}{4}$ **4** $512 + 512\sqrt{3}\,i$

Page 430

1

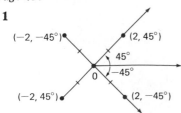

2

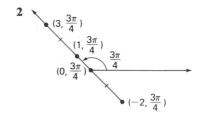

3 (a) $\left(5, \frac{25\pi}{12}\right)$ (b) $\left(-5, \frac{13\pi}{12}\right)$ (c) $\left(5, -\frac{23\pi}{12}\right)$ (d) $\left(-5, -\frac{11\pi}{12}\right)$

Page 436

1 $\theta = 30°$ **2** $\theta = 140°$ **3** $\theta = \frac{\pi}{2}$ **4** $\theta = \frac{\pi}{4}$ **5** $\theta = \frac{\pi}{2}$ **6** $\theta = \frac{5\pi}{6}$

7 (a) $r = 4$ (b) $r = 5$ (c) $r = \sqrt{2}$

8 $r = 4\cos\theta$ **9** $r = -3\cos\theta$ **10** $r = -\frac{4}{3}\sin\theta$

TABLES

445

Table I: Square Roots and Cube Roots

N	$\sqrt{N}$	$\sqrt[3]{N}$	N	$\sqrt{N}$	$\sqrt[3]{N}$	N	$\sqrt{N}$	$\sqrt[3]{N}$	N	$\sqrt{N}$	$\sqrt[3]{N}$
1	1.000	1.000	51	7.141	3.708	101	10.050	4.657	151	12.288	5.325
2	1.414	1.260	52	7.211	3.733	102	10.100	4.672	152	12.329	5.337
3	1.732	1.442	53	7.280	3.756	103	10.149	4.688	153	12.369	5.348
4	2.000	1.587	54	7.348	3.780	104	10.198	4.703	154	12.410	5.360
5	2.236	1.710	55	7.416	3.803	105	10.247	4.718	155	12.450	5.372
6	2.449	1.817	56	7.483	3.826	106	10.296	4.733	156	12.490	5.383
7	2.646	1.913	57	7.550	3.849	107	10.344	4.747	157	12.530	5.395
8	2.828	2.000	58	7.616	3.871	108	10.392	4.762	158	12.570	5.406
9	3.000	2.080	59	7.681	3.893	109	10.440	4.777	159	12.610	5.418
10	3.162	2.154	60	7.746	3.915	110	10.488	4.791	160	12.649	5.429
11	3.317	2.224	61	7.810	3.936	111	10.536	4.806	161	12.689	5.440
12	3.464	2.289	62	7.874	3.958	112	10.583	4.820	162	12.728	5.451
13	3.606	2.351	63	7.937	3.979	113	10.630	4.835	163	12.767	5.463
14	3.742	2.410	64	8.000	4.000	114	10.677	4.849	164	12.806	5.474
15	3.873	2.466	65	8.062	4.021	115	10.724	4.863	165	12.845	5.485
16	4.000	2.520	66	8.124	4.041	116	10.770	4.877	166	12.884	5.496
17	4.123	2.571	67	8.185	4.062	117	10.817	4.891	167	12.923	5.507
18	4.243	2.621	68	8.246	4.082	118	10.863	4.905	168	12.961	5.518
19	4.359	2.668	69	8.307	4.102	119	10.909	4.919	169	13.000	5.529
20	4.472	2.714	70	8.367	4.121	120	10.954	4.932	170	13.038	5.540
21	4.583	2.759	71	8.426	4.141	121	11.000	4.946	171	13.077	5.550
22	4.690	2.802	72	8.485	4.160	122	11.045	4.960	172	13.115	5.561
23	4.796	2.844	73	8.544	4.179	123	11.091	4.973	173	13.153	5.572
24	4.899	2.884	74	8.602	4.198	124	11.136	4.987	174	13.191	5.583
25	5.000	2.924	75	8.660	4.217	125	11.180	5.000	175	13.229	5.593
26	5.099	2.962	76	8.718	4.236	126	11.225	5.013	176	13.267	5.604
27	5.196	3.000	77	8.775	4.254	127	11.269	5.027	177	13.304	5.615
28	5.292	3.037	78	8.832	4.273	128	11.314	5.040	178	13.342	5.625
29	5.385	3.072	79	8.888	4.291	129	11.358	5.053	179	13.379	5.636
30	5.477	3.107	80	8.944	4.309	130	11.402	5.066	180	13.416	5.646
31	5.568	3.141	81	9.000	4.327	131	11.446	5.079	181	13.454	5.657
32	5.657	3.175	82	9.055	4.344	132	11.489	5.092	182	13.491	5.667
33	5.745	3.208	83	9.110	4.362	133	11.533	5.104	183	13.528	5.677
34	5.831	3.240	84	9.165	4.380	134	11.576	5.117	184	13.565	5.688
35	5.916	3.271	85	9.220	4.397	135	11.619	5.130	185	13.601	5.698
36	6.000	3.302	86	9.274	4.414	136	11.662	5.143	186	13.638	5.708
37	6.083	3.332	87	9.327	4.431	137	11.705	5.155	187	13.675	5.718
38	6.164	3.362	88	9.381	4.448	138	11.747	5.168	188	13.711	5.729
39	6.245	3.391	89	9.434	4.465	139	11.790	5.180	189	13.748	5.739
40	6.325	3.420	90	9.487	4.481	140	11.832	5.192	190	13.784	5.749
41	6.403	3.448	91	9.539	4.498	141	11.874	5.205	191	13.820	5.759
42	6.481	3.476	92	9.592	4.514	142	11.916	5.217	192	13.856	5.769
43	6.557	3.503	93	9.644	4.531	143	11.958	5.229	193	13.892	5.779
44	6.633	3.530	94	9.695	4.547	144	12.000	5.241	194	13.928	5.789
45	6.708	3.557	95	9.747	4.563	145	12.042	5.254	195	13.964	5.799
46	6.782	3.583	96	9.798	4.579	146	12.083	5.266	196	14.000	5.809
47	6.856	3.609	97	9.849	4.595	147	12.124	5.278	197	14.036	5.819
48	6.928	3.634	98	9.899	4.610	148	12.166	5.290	198	14.071	5.828
49	7.000	3.659	99	9.950	4.626	149	12.207	5.301	199	14.107	5.838
50	7.071	3.684	100	10.000	4.642	150	12.247	5.313	200	14.142	5.848

Table II: Exponential Functions

x	e^x	e^{-x}	x	e^x	e^{-x}
0.0	1.00	1.000	3.1	22.2	0.045
0.1	1.11	0.905	3.2	24.5	0.041
0.2	1.22	0.819	3.3	27.1	0.037
0.3	1.35	0.741	3.4	30.0	0.033
0.4	1.49	0.670	3.5	33.1	0.030
0.5	1.65	0.607	3.6	36.6	0.027
0.6	1.82	0.549	3.7	40.4	0.025
0.7	2.01	0.497	3.8	44.7	0.022
0.8	2.23	0.449	3.9	49.4	0.020
0.9	2.46	0.407	4.0	54.6	0.018
1.0	2.72	0.368	4.1	60.3	0.017
1.1	3.00	0.333	4.2	66.7	0.015
1.2	3.32	0.301	4.3	73.7	0.014
1.3	3.67	0.273	4.4	81.5	0.012
1.4	4.06	0.247	4.5	90.0	0.011
1.5	4.48	0.223	4.6	99.5	0.010
1.6	4.95	0.202	4.7	110	0.0091
1.7	5.47	0.183	4.8	122	0.0082
1.8	6.05	0.165	4.9	134	0.0074
1.9	6.69	0.150	5.0	148	0.0067
2.0	7.39	0.135	5.5	245	0.0041
2.1	8.17	0.122	6.0	403	0.0025
2.2	9.02	0.111	6.5	665	0.0015
2.3	9.97	0.100	7.0	1097	0.00091
2.4	11.0	0.091	7.5	1808	0.00055
2.5	12.2	0.082	8.0	2981	0.00034
2.6	13.5	0.074	8.5	4915	0.00020
2.7	14.9	0.067	9.0	8103	0.00012
2.8	16.4	0.061	9.5	13360	0.00075
2.9	18.2	0.055	10.0	22026	0.000045
3.0	20.1	0.050			

Table III: Natural Logarithms (Base *e*)

x	$\ln x$	x	$\ln x$	x	$\ln x$
0.0		3.4	1.224	6.8	1.917
0.1	−2.303	3.5	1.253	6.9	1.932
0.2	−1.609	3.6	1.281	7.0	1.946
0.3	−1.204	3.7	1.308	7.1	1.960
0.4	−0.916	3.8	1.335	7.2	1.974
0.5	−0.693	3.9	1.361	7.3	1.988
0.6	−0.511	4.0	1.386	7.4	2.001
0.7	−0.357	4.1	1.411	7.5	2.015
0.8	−0.223	4.2	1.435	7.6	2.028
0.9	−0.105	4.3	1.459	7.7	2.041
1.0	0.000	4.4	1.482	7.8	2.054
1.1	0.095	4.5	1.504	7.9	2.067
1.2	0.182	4.6	1.526	8.0	2.079
1.3	0.262	4.7	1.548	8.1	2.092
1.4	0.336	4.8	1.569	8.2	2.104
1.5	0.405	4.9	1.589	8.3	2.116
1.6	0.470	5.0	1.609	8.4	2.128
1.7	0.531	5.1	1.629	8.5	2.140
1.8	0.588	5.2	1.649	8.6	2.152
1.9	0.642	5.3	1.668	8.7	2.163
2.0	0.693	5.4	1.686	8.8	2.175
2.1	0.742	5.5	1.705	8.9	2.186
2.2	0.788	5.6	1.723	9.0	2.197
2.3	0.833	5.7	1.740	9.1	2.208
2.4	0.875	5.8	1.758	9.2	2.219
2.5	0.916	5.9	1.775	9.3	2.230
2.6	0.956	6.0	1.792	9.4	2.241
2.7	0.993	6.1	1.808	9.5	2.251
2.8	1.030	6.2	1.825	9.6	2.262
2.9	1.065	6.3	1.841	9.7	2.272
3.0	1.099	6.4	1.856	9.8	2.282
3.1	1.131	6.5	1.872	9.9	2.293
3.2	1.163	6.6	1.887	10.0	2.303
3.3	1.194	6.7	1.902		

Table IV: Four-Place Common Logarithms (Base 10)

x	0	1	2	3	4	5	6	7	8	9
1.0	.0000	.0043	.0086	.0128	.0170	.0212	.0253	.0294	.0334	.0374
1.1	.0414	.0453	.0492	.0531	.0569	.0607	.0645	.0682	.0719	.0755
1.2	.0792	.0828	.0864	.0899	.0934	.0969	.1004	.1038	.1072	.1106
1.3	.1139	.1173	.1206	.1239	.1271	.1303	.1335	.1367	.1399	.1430
1.4	.1461	.1492	.1523	.1553	.1584	.1614	.1644	.1673	.1703	.1732
1.5	.1761	.1790	.1818	.1847	.1875	.1903	.1931	.1959	.1987	.2014
1.6	.2041	.2068	.2095	.2122	.2148	.2175	.2201	.2227	.2253	.2279
1.7	.2304	.2330	.2355	.2380	.2405	.2430	.2455	.2480	.2504	.2529
1.8	.2553	.2577	.2601	.2625	.2648	.2672	.2695	.2718	.2742	.2765
1.9	.2788	.2810	.2833	.2856	.2878	.2900	.2923	.2945	.2967	.2989
2.0	.3010	.3032	.3054	.3075	.3096	.3118	.3139	.3160	.3181	.3201
2.1	.3222	.3243	.3263	.3284	.3304	.3324	.3345	.3365	.3385	.3404
2.2	.3424	.3444	.3464	.3483	.3502	.3522	.3541	.3560	.3579	.3598
2.3	.3617	.3636	.3655	.3674	.3692	.3711	.3729	.3747	.3766	.3784
2.4	.3802	.3820	.3838	.3856	.3874	.3892	.3909	.3927	.3945	.3962
2.5	.3979	.3997	.4014	.4031	.4048	.4065	.4082	.4099	.4116	.4133
2.6	.4150	.4166	.4183	.4200	.4216	.4232	.4249	.4265	.4281	.4298
2.7	.4314	.4330	.4346	.4362	.4378	.4393	.4409	.4425	.4440	.4456
2.8	.4472	.4487	.4502	.4518	.4533	.4548	.4564	.4579	.4594	.4609
2.9	.4624	.4639	.4654	.4669	.4683	.4698	.4713	.4728	.4742	.4757
3.0	.4771	.4786	.4800	.4814	.4829	.4843	.4857	.4871	.4886	.4900
3.1	.4914	.4928	.4942	.4955	.4969	.4983	.4997	.5011	.5024	.5038
3.2	.5051	.5065	.5079	.5092	.5105	.5119	.5132	.5145	.5159	.5172
3.3	.5185	.5198	.5211	.5224	.5237	.5250	.5263	.5276	.5289	.5302
3.4	.5315	.5328	.5340	.5353	.5366	.5378	.5391	.5403	.5416	.5428
3.5	.5441	.5453	.5465	.5478	.5490	.5502	.5514	.5527	.5539	.5551
3.6	.5563	.5575	.5587	.5599	.5611	.5623	.5635	.5647	.5658	.5670
3.7	.5682	.5694	.5705	.5717	.5729	.5740	.5752	.5763	.5775	.5786
3.8	.5798	.5809	.5821	.5832	.5843	.5855	.5866	.5877	.5888	.5899
3.9	.5911	.5922	.5933	.5944	.5955	.5966	.5977	.5988	.5999	.6010
4.0	.6021	.6031	.6042	.6053	.6064	.6075	.6085	.6096	.6107	.6117
4.1	.6128	.6138	.6149	.6160	.6170	.6180	.6191	.6201	.6212	.6222
4.2	.6232	.6243	.6253	.6263	.6274	.6284	.6294	.6304	.6314	.6325
4.3	.6335	.6345	.6355	.6365	.6375	.6385	.6395	.6405	.6415	.6425
4.4	.6435	.6444	.6454	.6464	.6474	.6484	.6493	.6503	.6513	.6522
4.5	.6532	.6542	.6551	.6561	.6571	.6580	.6590	.6599	.6609	.6618
4.6	.6628	.6637	.6646	.6656	.6665	.6675	.6684	.6693	.6702	.6712
4.7	.6721	.6730	.6739	.6749	.6758	.6767	.6776	.6785	.6794	.6803
4.8	.6812	.6821	.6830	.6839	.6848	.6857	.6866	.6875	.6884	.6893
4.9	.6902	.6911	.6920	.6928	.6937	.6946	.6955	.6964	.6972	.6981
5.0	.6990	.6998	.7007	.7016	.7024	.7033	.7042	.7050	.7059	.7067
5.1	.7076	.7084	.7093	.7101	.7110	.7118	.7126	.7135	.7143	.7152
5.2	.7160	.7168	.7177	.7185	.7193	.7202	.7210	.7218	.7226	.7235
5.3	.7243	.7251	.7259	.7267	.7275	.7284	.7292	.7300	.7308	.7316
5.4	.7324	.7332	.7340	.7348	.7356	.7364	.7372	.7380	.7388	.7396
N	0	1	2	3	4	5	6	7	8	9

x	0	1	2	3	4	5	6	7	8	9
5.5	.7404	.7412	.7419	.7427	.7435	.7443	.7451	.7459	.7466	.7474
5.6	.7482	.7490	.7497	.7505	.7513	.7520	.7528	.7536	.7543	.7551
5.7	.7559	.7566	.7574	.7582	.7589	.7597	.7604	.7612	.7619	.7627
5.8	.7634	.7642	.7649	.7657	.7664	.7672	.7679	.7686	.7694	.7701
5.9	.7709	.7716	.7723	.7731	.7738	.7745	.7752	.7760	.7767	.7774
6.0	.7782	.7789	.7796	.7803	.7810	.7818	.7825	.7832	.7839	.7846
6.1	.7853	.7860	.7868	.7875	.7882	.7889	.7896	.7903	.7910	.7917
6.2	.7924	.7931	.7938	.7945	.7952	.7959	.7966	.7973	.7980	.7987
6.3	.7993	.8000	.8007	.8014	.8021	.8028	.8035	.8041	.8048	.8055
6.4	.8062	.8069	.8075	.8082	.8089	.8096	.8102	.8109	.8116	.8122
6.5	.8129	.8136	.8142	.8149	.8156	.8162	.8169	.8176	.8182	.8189
6.6	.8195	.8202	.8209	.8215	.8222	.8228	.8235	.8241	.8248	.8254
6.7	.8261	.8267	.8274	.8280	.8287	.8293	.8299	.8306	.8312	.8319
6.8	.8325	.8331	.8338	.8344	.8351	.8357	.8363	.8370	.8376	.8382
6.9	.8388	.8395	.8401	.8407	.8414	.8420	.8426	.8432	.8439	.8445
7.0	.8451	.8457	.8463	.8470	.8476	.8482	.8488	.8494	.8500	.8506
7.1	.8513	.8519	.8525	.8531	.8537	.8543	.8549	.8555	.8561	.8567
7.2	.8573	.8579	.8585	.8591	.8597	.8603	.8609	.8615	.8621	.8627
7.3	.8633	.8639	.8645	.8651	.8657	.8663	.8669	.8675	.8681	.8686
7.4	.8692	.8698	.8704	.8710	.8716	.8722	.8727	.8733	.8739	.8745
7.5	.8751	.8756	.8762	.8768	.8774	.8779	.8785	.8791	.8797	.8802
7.6	.8808	.8814	.8820	.8825	.8831	.8837	.8842	.8848	.8854	.8859
7.7	.8865	.8871	.8876	.8882	.8887	.8893	.8899	.8904	.8910	.8915
7.8	.8921	.8927	.8932	.8938	.8943	.8949	.8954	.8960	.8965	.8971
7.9	.8976	.8982	.8987	.8993	.8998	.9004	.9009	.9015	.9020	.9025
8.0	.9031	.9036	.9042	.9047	.9053	.9058	.9063	.9069	.9074	.9079
8.1	.9085	.9090	.9096	.9101	.9106	.9112	.9117	.9122	.9128	.9133
8.2	.9138	.9143	.9149	.9154	.9159	.9165	.9170	.9175	.9180	.9186
8.3	.9191	.9196	.9201	.9206	.9212	.9217	.9222	.9227	.9232	.9238
8.4	.9243	.9248	.9253	.9258	.9263	.9269	.9274	.9279	.9284	.9289
8.5	.9294	.9299	.9304	.9309	.9315	.9320	.9325	.9330	.9335	.9340
8.6	.9345	.9350	.9355	.9360	.9365	.9370	.9375	.9380	.9385	.9390
8.7	.9395	.9400	.9405	.9410	.9415	.9420	.9425	.9430	.9435	.9440
8.8	.9445	.9450	.9455	.9460	.9465	.9469	.9474	.9479	.9484	.9489
8.9	.9494	.9499	.9504	.9509	.9513	.9518	.9523	.9528	.9533	.9538
9.0	.9542	.9547	.9552	.9557	.9562	.9566	.9571	.9576	.9581	.9586
9.1	.9590	.9595	.9600	.9605	.9609	.9614	.9619	.9624	.9628	.9633
9.2	.9638	.9643	.9647	.9652	.9657	.9661	.9666	.9671	.9675	.9680
9.3	.9685	.9689	.9694	.9699	.9703	.9708	.9713	.9717	.9722	.9727
9.4	.9731	.9736	.9741	.9745	.9750	.9754	.9759	.9763	.9768	.9773
9.5	.9777	.9782	.9786	.9791	.9795	.9800	.9805	.9809	.9814	.9818
9.6	.9823	.9827	.9832	.9836	.9841	.9845	.9850	.9854	.9859	.9863
9.7	.9868	.9872	.9877	.9881	.9886	.9890	.9894	.9899	.9903	.9908
9.8	.9912	.9917	.9921	.9926	.9930	.9934	.9939	.9943	.9948	.9952
9.9	.9956	.9961	.9965	.9969	.9974	.9978	.9983	.9987	.9991	.9996
N	0	1	2	3	4	5	6	7	8	9

Table V: Trigonometric Functions

Degrees	Radians	sin	cos	tan	cot	sec	csc		
0° 00′	.0000	.0000	1.0000	.0000	——	1.000	——	1.5708	90° 00′
10	029	029	000	029	343.8	000	343.8	679	50
20	058	058	000	058	171.9	000	171.9	650	40
30	.0087	.0087	1.0000	.0087	114.6	1.000	114.6	1.5621	30
40	116	116	.9999	116	85.94	000	85.95	592	20
50	145	145	999	145	68.75	000	68.76	563	10
1° 00′	.0175	.0175	.9998	.0175	57.29	1.000	57.30	1.5533	89° 00′
10	204	204	998	204	49.10	000	49.11	504	50
20	233	233	997	233	42.96	000	42.98	475	40
30	.0262	.0262	.9997	.0262	38.19	1.000	38.20	1.5446	30
40	291	291	996	291	34.37	000	34.38	417	20
50	320	320	995	320	31.24	001	31.26	388	10
2° 00′	.0349	.0349	.9994	.0349	28.64	1.001	28.65	1.5359	88° 00′
10	378	378	993	378	26.43	001	26.45	330	50
20	407	407	992	407	24.54	001	24.56	301	40
30	.0436	.0436	.9990	.0437	22.90	1.001	22.93	1.5272	30
40	465	465	989	466	21.47	001	21.49	243	20
50	495	494	988	495	20.21	001	20.23	213	10
3° 00′	.0524	.0523	.9986	.0524	19.08	1.001	19.11	1.5184	87° 00′
10	553	552	985	553	18.07	002	18.10	155	50
20	582	581	983	582	17.17	002	17.20	126	40
30	.0611	.0610	.9981	.0612	16.35	1.002	16.38	1.5097	30
40	640	640	980	641	15.60	002	15.64	068	20
50	669	669	978	670	14.92	002	14.96	039	10
4° 00′	.0698	.0698	.9976	.0699	14.30	1.002	14.34	1.5010	86° 00′
10	727	727	974	729	13.73	003	13.76	981	50
20	756	756	971	758	13.20	003	13.23	952	40
30	.0785	.0785	.9969	.0787	12.71	1.003	12.75	1.4923	30
40	814	814	967	816	12.25	003	12.29	893	20
50	844	843	964	846	11.83	004	11.87	864	10
5° 00′	.0873	.0872	.9962	.0875	11.43	1.004	11.47	1.4835	85° 00′
10	902	901	959	904	11.06	004	11.10	806	50
20	931	929	957	934	10.71	004	10.76	777	40
30	.0960	.0958	.9954	.0963	10.39	1.005	10.43	1.4748	30
40	989	987	951	992	10.08	005	10.13	719	20
50	.1018	.1016	948	.1022	9.788	005	9.839	690	10
6° 00′	.1047	.1045	.9945	.1051	9.514	1.006	9.567	1.4661	84° 00′
10	076	074	942	080	9.255	006	9.309	632	50
20	105	103	939	110	9.010	006	9.065	603	40
30	.1134	.1132	.9936	.1139	8.777	1.006	8.834	1.4573	30
40	164	161	932	169	8.556	007	8.614	544	20
50	193	190	929	198	8.345	007	8.405	515	10
7° 00′	.1222	.1219	.9925	.1228	3.144	1.008	8.206	1.4486	83° 00′
10	251	248	922	257	7.953	008	8.016	457	50
20	280	276	918	287	7.770	008	7.834	428	40
30	.1309	.1305	.9914	.1317	7.596	1.009	7.661	1.4399	30
40	338	334	911	346	7.429	009	7.496	370	20
50	367	363	907	376	7.269	009	7.337	341	10
8° 00′	.1396	.1392	.9903	.1405	7.115	1.010	7.185	1.4312	82° 00′
10	425	421	899	435	6.968	010	7.040	283	50
20	454	449	894	465	6.827	011	6.900	254	40
30	.1484	.1478	.9890	.1495	6.691	1.011	6.765	1.4224	30
40	513	507	886	524	6.561	012	6.636	195	20
50	542	536	881	554	6.435	012	6.512	166	10
9° 00′	.1571	.1564	.9877	.1584	6.314	1.012	6.392	1.4137	81° 00′
		cos	sin	cot	tan	csc	sec	Radians	Degrees

Degrees	Radians	sin	cos	tan	cot	sec	csc		
9° 00′	.1571	.1564	.9877	.1584	6.314	1.012	6.392	1.4137	81° 00′
10	600	593	872	614	197	013	277	108	50
20	629	622	868	644	084	013	166	079	40
30	.1658	.1650	.9863	.1673	5.976	1.014	6.059	1.4050	30
40	687	679	858	703	871	014	5.955	1.4021	20
50	716	708	853	733	769	015	855	992	10
10° 00′	.1745	.1736	.9848	.1763	5.671	1.015	5.759	1.3963	80° 00′
10	774	765	843	793	576	016	665	934	50
20	804	794	838	823	485	016	575	904	40
30	.1833	.1822	.9833	.1853	5.396	1.017	5.487	1.3875	30
40	862	851	827	883	309	018	403	846	20
50	891	880	822	914	226	018	320	817	10
11° 00′	.1920	.1908	.9816	.1944	5.145	1.019	5.241	1.3788	79° 00′
10	949	937	811	974	066	019	164	759	50
20	978	965	805	.2004	4.989	020	089	730	40
30	.2007	.1994	.9799	.2035	4.915	1.020	5.016	1.3701	30
40	036	.2022	793	065	843	021	4.945	672	20
50	065	051	787	095	773	022	876	643	10
12° 00′	.2094	.2079	.9781	.2126	4.705	1.022	4.810	1.3614	78° 00′
10	123	108	775	156	638	023	745	584	50
20	153	136	769	186	574	024	682	555	40
30	.2182	.2164	.9763	.2217	4.511	1.024	4.620	1.3526	30
40	211	193	757	247	449	025	560	497	20
50	240	221	750	278	390	026	502	468	10
13° 00′	.2269	.2250	.9744	.2309	4.331	1.026	4.445	1.3439	77° 00′
10	298	278	737	339	275	027	390	410	50
20	327	306	730	370	219	028	336	381	40
30	.2356	.2334	.9724	.2401	4.165	1.028	4.284	1.3352	30
40	385	363	717	432	113	029	232	323	20
50	414	391	710	462	061	030	182	294	10
14° 00′	.2443	.2419	.9703	.2493	4.011	1.031	4.134	1.3265	76° 00′
10	473	447	696	524	3.962	031	086	235	50
20	502	476	689	555	914	032	039	206	40
30	.2531	.2504	.9681	.2586	3.867	1.033	3.994	1.3177	30
40	560	532	674	617	821	034	950	148	20
50	589	560	667	648	776	034	906	119	10
15° 00′	.2618	.2588	.9659	.2679	3.732	1.035	3.864	1.3090	75° 00′
10	647	616	652	711	689	036	822	061	50
20	676	644	644	742	647	037	782	032	40
30	.2705	.2672	.9636	.2773	3.606	1.038	3.742	1.3003	30
40	734	700	628	805	566	039	703	974	20
50	763	728	621	836	526	039	665	945	10
16° 00′	.2793	.2756	.9613	.2867	3.487	1.040	3.628	1.2915	74° 00′
10	822	784	605	899	450	041	592	886	50
20	851	812	596	931	412	042	556	857	40
30	.2880	.2840	.9588	.2962	3.376	1.043	3.521	1.2828	30
40	909	868	580	994	340	044	487	799	20
50	938	896	572	.3026	305	045	453	770	10
17° 00′	.2967	.2924	.9563	.3057	3.271	1.046	3.420	1.2741	73° 00′
10	996	952	555	089	237	047	388	712	50
20	.3025	979	546	121	204	048	356	683	40
30	.3054	.3007	.9537	.3153	3.172	1.049	3.326	1.2654	30
40	083	035	528	185	140	049	295	625	20
50	113	062	520	217	108	050	265	595	10
18° 00′	.3142	.3090	.9511	.3249	3.078	1.051	3.236	1.2566	72° 00′
		cos	sin	cot	tan	csc	sec	Radians	Degrees

Degrees	Radians	sin	cos	tan	cot	sec	csc		
18° 00′	.3142	.3090	.9511	.3249	3.078	1.051	3.236	1.2566	**72° 00′**
10	171	118	502	281	047	052	207	537	50
20	200	145	492	314	018	053	179	508	40
30	.3229	.3173	.9483	.3346	2.989	1.054	3.152	1.2479	30
40	258	201	474	378	960	056	124	450	20
50	287	228	465	411	932	057	098	421	10
19° 00′	.3316	.3256	.9455	.3443	2.904	1.058	3.072	1.2392	**71° 00′**
10	345	283	446	476	877	059	046	363	50
20	374	311	436	508	850	060	021	334	40
30	.3403	.3338	.9426	.3541	2.824	1.061	2.996	1.2305	30
40	432	365	417	574	798	062	971	275	20
50	462	393	407	607	773	063	947	246	10
20° 00′	.3491	.3420	.9397	.3640	2.747	1.064	2.924	1.2217	**70° 00′**
10	520	449	387	673	723	065	901	188	50
20	549	475	377	706	699	066	878	159	40
30	.3578	.3502	.9367	.3739	2.675	1.068	2.855	1.2130	30
40	607	529	356	772	651	069	833	101	20
50	636	557	346	805	628	070	812	072	10
21°00′	.3665	.3584	.9336	.3839	2.605	1.071	2.790	1.2043	**69° 00′**
10	694	611	325	872	583	072	769	1.2014	50
20	723	638	315	906	560	074	749	985	40
30	.3752	.3665	.9304	.3939	2.539	1.075	2.729	1.1956	30
40	782	692	293	973	517	076	709	926	20
50	811	719	283	.4006	496	077	689	897	10
22° 00′	.3840	.3746	.9272	.4040	2.475	1.079	2.669	1.1868	**68° 00′**
10	869	773	261	074	455	080	650	839	50
20	898	800	250	108	434	081	632	810	40
30	.3927	.3827	.9239	.4142	2.414	1.082	2.613	1.1781	30
40	956	854	228	176	394	084	595	752	20
50	985	881	216	210	375	085	577	723	10
23° 00′	.4014	.3907	.9205	.4245	2.356	1.086	2.559	1.1694	**67° 00′**
10	043	934	194	279	337	088	542	665	50
20	072	961	182	314	318	089	525	636	40
30	.4102	.3987	.9171	.4348	2.300	1.090	2.508	1.1606	30
40	131	.4014	159	383	282	092	491	577	20
50	160	041	147	417	264	093	475	548	10
24° 00′	.4189	.4067	.9135	.4452	2.246	1.095	2.459	1.1519	**66° 00′**
10	218	094	124	487	229	096	443	490	50
20	247	120	112	522	211	097	427	461	40
30	.4276	.4147	.9100	.4557	2.194	1.099	2.411	1.1432	30
40	305	173	088	592	177	100	396	403	20
50	334	200	075	628	161	102	381	374	10
25° 00′	.4363	.4226	.9063	.4663	2.145	1.103	2.366	1.1345	**65° 00′**
10	392	253	051	699	128	105	352	316	50
20	422	279	038	734	112	106	337	286	40
30	.4451	.4305	.9026	.4770	2.097	1.108	2.323	1.1257	30
40	480	331	013	806	081	109	309	228	20
50	509	358	001	841	066	111	295	199	10
26° 00′	.4538	.4384	.8988	.4877	2.050	1.113	2.281	1.1170	**64° 00′**
10	567	410	975	913	035	114	268	141	50
20	596	436	962	950	020	116	254	112	40
30	.4625	.4462	.8949	.4986	2.006	1.117	2.241	1.1083	30
40	654	488	936	.5022	1.991	119	228	054	20
50	683	514	923	059	977	121	215	1.1025	10
27° 00′	.4712	.4540	.8910	.5095	1.963	1.122	2.203	1.0996	**63° 00′**
		cos	sin	cot	tan	csc	sec	Radians	Degrees

Degrees	Radians	sin	cos	tan	cot	sec	csc		Degrees
27° 00′	.4712	.4540	.8910	.5095	1.963	1.122	2.203	1.0996	63° 00′
10	741	566	897	132	949	124	190	966	50
20	771	592	884	169	935	126	178	937	40
30	.4800	.4617	.8870	.5206	1.921	1.127	2.166	1.0908	30
40	829	643	857	243	907	129	154	879	20
50	858	669	843	280	894	131	142	850	10
28° 00′	.4887	.4695	.8829	.5317	1.881	1.133	2.130	1.0821	62° 00′
10	916	720	816	354	868	134	118	792	50
20	945	746	802	392	855	136	107	763	40
30	.4974	.4772	.8788	.5430	1.842	1.138	2.096	1.0734	30
40	.5003	797	774	467	829	140	085	705	20
50	032	823	760	505	816	142	074	676	10
29° 00′	.5061	.4848	.8746	.5543	1.804	1.143	2.063	1.0647	61° 00′
10	091	874	732	581	792	145	052	617	50
20	120	899	718	619	780	147	041	588	40
30	.5149	.4924	.8704	.5658	1.767	1.149	2.031	1.0559	30
40	178	950	689	696	756	151	020	530	20
50	207	975	675	735	744	153	010	501	10
30° 00′	.5236	.5000	.8660	.5774	1.732	1.155	2.000	1.0472	60° 00′
10	265	025	646	812	720	157	1.990	443	50
20	294	050	631	851	709	159	980	414	40
30	.5323	.5075	.8616	.5890	1.698	1.161	1.970	1.0385	30
40	352	100	601	930	686	163	961	356	20
50	381	125	587	969	675	165	951	327	10
31° 00′	.5411	.5150	.8572	.6009	1.664	1.167	1.942	1.0297	59° 00′
10	440	175	557	048	653	169	932	268	50
20	469	200	542	088	643	171	923	239	40
30	.5498	.5225	.8526	.6128	1.632	1.173	1.914	1.0210	30
40	527	250	511	168	621	175	905	181	20
50	556	275	496	208	611	177	896	152	10
32° 00′	.5585	.5299	.8480	.6249	1.600	1.179	1.887	1.0123	58° 00′
10	614	324	465	289	590	181	878	094	50
20	643	348	450	330	580	184	870	065	40
30	.5672	.5373	.8434	.6371	.1570	1.186	1.861	1.0036	30
40	701	398	418	412	560	188	853	1.0007	20
50	730	422	403	453	550	190	844	977	10
33° 00′	.5760	.5446	.8387	.6494	1.540	1.192	1.836	.9948	57° 00′
10	789	471	371	536	530	195	828	919	50
20	818	495	355	577	520	197	820	890	40
30	.5847	.5519	.8339	.6619	1.511	1.199	1.812	.9861	30
40	876	544	323	661	501	202	804	832	20
50	905	568	307	703	1.492	204	796	803	10
34° 00′	.5934	.5592	.8290	.6745	1.483	1.206	1.788	.9774	56° 00′
10	963	616	274	787	473	209	731	745	50
20	992	640	258	830	464	211	773	716	40
30	.6021	.5664	.8241	.6873	1.455	1.213	1.766	.9687	30
40	050	688	225	916	446	216	758	657	20
50	080	712	208	959	437	218	751	628	10
35° 00	.6109	.5736	.8192	.7002	1.428	1.221	1.743	.9599	55° 00′
10	138	760	175	046	419	223	736	570	50
20	167	783	158	089	411	226	729	541	40
30	6196	.5807	.8141	.7133	1.402	1.228	1.722	.9512	30
40	225	831	124	177	393	231	715	483	20
50	254	854	107	221	385	233	708	454	10
36° 00′	.6283	.5878	.8090	.7265	1.376	1.236	1.701	.9425	54° 00′
		cos	sin	cot	tan	csc	sec	Radians	Degrees

Degrees	Radians	sin	cos	tan	cot	sec	csc		
36° 00′	.6283	.5878	.8090	.7265	1.376	1.236	1.701	.9425	**54° 00′**
10	312	901	073	310	368	239	695	396	50
20	341	925	056	355	360	241	688	367	40
30	.6370	.5948	.8039	.7400	1.351	1.244	1.681	.9338	30
40	400	972	021	445	343	247	675	308	20
50	429	995	004	490	335	249	668	279	10
37° 00′	.6458	.6018	.7986	.7536	1.327	1.252	1.662	.9250	**53° 00′**
10	487	041	969	581	319	255	655	221	50
20	516	065	951	627	311	258	649	192	40
30	.6545	.6088	.7934	.7673	1.303	1.260	1.643	.9163	30
40	574	111	916	720	295	263	636	134	20
50	603	134	898	766	288	266	630	105	10
38° 00′	.5632	.6157	.7880	.7813	1.280	1.269	1.624	.9076	**52° 00′**
10	661	180	862	860	272	272	618	047	50
20	690	202	844	907	265	275	612	.9018	40
30	.6720	.6225	.7826	.7954	1.257	1.278	1.606	.8988	30
40	749	248	808	.8002	250	281	601	959	20
50	778	271	790	050	242	284	595	930	10
39° 00′	.6807	.6293	.7771	.8098	1.235	1.287	1.589	.8901	**51° 00′**
10	836	316	753	146	228	290	583	872	50
20	865	338	735	195	220	293	578	843	40
30	.6894	.6361	.7716	.8243	1.213	1.296	1.572	.8814	30
40	923	383	698	292	206	299	567	785	20
50	952	406	679	342	199	302	561	756	10
40° 00′	.6981	.6428	.7660	.8391	1.192	1.305	1.556	.8727	**50° 00′**
10	.7010	450	642	441	185	309	550	698	50
20	039	472	623	491	178	312	545	668	40
30	.7069	.6494	.7604	.8541	1.171	1.315	1.540	.8639	30
40	098	517	585	591	164	318	535	610	20
50	127	539	566	642	157	322	529	581	10
41° 00′	.7156	.6561	.7547	.8693	1.150	1.325	1.524	.8552	**49° 00′**
10	185	583	528	744	144	328	519	523	50
20	214	604	509	796	137	332	514	494	40
30	.7243	.6626	.7490	.8847	1.130	1.335	1.509	.8465	30
40	272	648	470	899	124	339	504	436	20
50	301	670	451	952	117	342	499	407	10
42° 00′	.7330	.6691	.7431	.9004	1.111	1.346	1.494	.8378	**48° 00′**
10	359	713	412	057	104	349	490	348	50
20	389	734	392	110	098	353	485	319	40
30	.7418	.6756	.7373	.9163	1.091	1.356	1.480	.8290	30
40	447	777	353	217	085	360	476	261	20
50	476	799	333	271	079	364	471	232	10
43° 00′	.7505	.6820	.7314	.9325	1.072	1.367	1.466	.8203	**47° 00′**
10	534	841	294	380	066	371	462	174	50
20	563	862	274	435	060	375	457	145	40
30	.7592	.6884	.7254	.9490	1.054	1.379	1.453	.8116	30
40	621	905	234	545	048	382	448	087	20
50	650	926	214	601	042	386	444	058	10
44° 00′	.7679	.6947	.7193	.9657	1.036	1.390	1.440	.8029	**46° 00′**
10	709	967	173	713	030	394	435	999	50
20	738	988	153	770	024	398	431	970	40
30	.7767	.7009	.7133	.9827	1.018	1.402	1.427	.7941	30
40	796	030	112	884	012	406	423	912	20
50	825	050	092	942	006	410	418	883	10
45° 00′	.7854	.7071	.7071	1.000	1.000	1.414	1.414	.7854	**45° 00′**
		cos	sin	cot	tan	csc	sec	Radians	Degrees

ANSWERS TO ODD-NUMBERED EXERCISES AND SAMPLE TEST QUESTIONS

1.1   REAL NUMBERS AND THEIR PROPERTIES (*Page 6*)

1 Closure property for addition.   **3** Inverse property for addition.   **5** Commutative property for multiplication.

7 Commutative property for addition.   **9** Identity property for addition.   **11** Additive inverse.

13 Multiplication property of zero.   **15** Distributive property.   **17** 3   **19** 5   **21** 7

23 If $ab = 0$, then at least one of a or b is zero. Since $5 \neq 0$, $x - 2 = 0$ which implies $x = 2$.

25 (i) $a(-b) = -(ab)$; (ii) Definition of $\div$; (iii) associative of $\times$.

27 (i) Distributive; (ii) distributive; (iii) associative for $+$; (iv) commutative for $\times$; (v) commutative for $+$; (vi) distributive; (vii) commutative for $+$.

29 No; as a counterexample $2^3 \neq 3^2$.

31 If $10 - x = 7$, then $7 + x = 10$; if $7 + x = 10$, then $10 - x = 7$.

33 If n is an even integer, then n^2 is an even integer; if n^2 is an even integer, then n is an even integer.

35 If $\triangle ABC$ is congruent to $\triangle DEF$, then the three sides of one triangle are congruent to the three sides of the other triangle; if three sides of $\triangle ABC$ are congruent to the three sides of $\triangle DEF$, then $\triangle ABC$ is congruent to $\triangle DEF$.

37 n is a multiple of 3 if and only if n^2 is a multiple of 3.

39 Let $\frac{0}{0} = x$, where x is some number. Then the definition of division gives $0 \cdot x = 0$. Since any number x will work, the answer to $\frac{0}{0}$ is not unique; therefore, $\frac{0}{0}$ is undefined.

1.2 SETS OF NUMBERS (*Page 10*)

1 0, 1, 2 **3** 3, 4, 5, 6 **5** −2, −1 **7** . . . , −3, −2, −1, 0 **9** There are none. **11** True. **13** True. **15** False.
17 False. **19** True. **21** b, c, e **23** d, e **25** a, b, c, e **27** a, b, c, e **29** d, e **31** c, e **33**

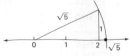

35 π; circumference $= 2\pi(\frac{1}{2}) = \pi$ **37** 0.8 **39** $0.\overline{285714}$ **41** $3.\overline{461538}$ **43** $0.01\overline{4}$ **45** (a) $\frac{5}{11}$; (b) $\frac{37}{99}$; (c) $\frac{26}{111}$; (d) 1

1.3 INTRODUCTION TO EQUATIONS AND PROBLEM SOLVING (*Page 16*)

1 $x = 4$ **3** $x = -4$ **5** $x = -4$ **7** $x = -8$ **9** $x = \frac{9}{2}$ **11** $x = -9$ **13** $x = \frac{20}{3}$ **15** $x = 15$ **17** $x = -10$
19 $x = -\frac{22}{3}$ **21** $x = 5$ **23** $x = 3$ **25** $x = 90$ **27** $\dfrac{P - 2\ell}{2}$ **29** $\dfrac{N - u}{10}$ **31** $\dfrac{C}{2\pi}$ **33** $\dfrac{w - 7}{4}$ **35** 50°F **37** 0°C
39 $w = 7, l = 21$ **41** 10 at 10¢, 13 at 20¢, 5 at 18¢. **43** $3\frac{1}{2}$ hours.
45 Let $x + (x + 2) + (x + 4) = 180$. Then $3x = 174$ and $x = 58$. Therefore, the integers must be even.
47 $w = 5, l = 14$ **49** 77, 79, 81

1.4 PROPERTIES OF ORDER (*Page 20*)

1 < **3** < **5** < **7** = **9** (a) $x < 1$; (b) $x > -\frac{2}{3}$; (c) $x \geq 5$; (d) $-10 < x \leq 7$ **11** True.
13 False; $-10 < 5$ and $-4 < 6$, but $(-10)(-4) = 40 > 30$ **15** True. **17** True.

19  **21**  **23**
25  **27** $[-5, 2]$ **29** $[-6, 0)$ **31** $(-10, 10)$ **33** $(-\infty, 5)$ **35** $[-2, \infty)$

37 $(-\infty, -1]$ **39** (a) $b - a$ is positive; (b) $(b - a)c$; (c) $bc - ac$; (d) $bc - ac$; (e) $ac < bc$
41 We are given that $1 < a$. Since $0 < 1$ the transitive property gives $0 < a$. Now use Rule 3 to get $a \cdot 1 < a \cdot a$, or $a < a^2$.

1.5 CONDITIONAL INEQUALITIES (*Page 25*)

1 $x < -4$:  **3** $x \geq 5$:

5 $x \leq \frac{4}{3}$:  **7** $x \leq -\frac{1}{4}$:

9 $x > 2$:  **11** $x < -3$:

13 $x \leq 2$:  **15** $x < -1$:

17 (a) Negative; (b) negative. **19** (a) Positive; (b) positive; (c) negative; (d) negative.

21 $x \leq 2$:  **23** $x \neq 13$:

25 $x \leq 3$:  **27** $x \leq -8$:

29

Interval	$x < -1$	$-1 < x < 1$	$1 < x$
Sign of $x + 1$	$-$	$+$	$+$
Sign of $x - 1$	$-$	$-$	$+$
Sign of $(x+1)(x-1)$	$+$	$-$	$+$

Solution: $-1 < x < 1$

31

Interval	$x < -5$	$-5 < x < \frac{1}{2}$	$\frac{1}{2} < x$
Sign of $x + 5$	$-$	$+$	$+$
Sign of $2x - 1$	$-$	$-$	$+$
Sign of $(x+5)(2x-1)$	$+$	$-$	$+$

Solution: $-5 \leq x \leq \frac{1}{2}$

33

Interval	$x < -1$	$-1 < x < 0$	$0 < x$
Sign of $x + 1$	$-$	$+$	$+$
Sign of x	$-$	$-$	$+$
Sign of $\dfrac{x}{x+1}$	$+$	$-$	$+$

Solution: $x < -1$ or $x > 0$

35

Interval	$x < -5$	$-5 < x < 2$	$2 < x$
Sign of $x + 5$	$-$	$+$	$+$
Sign of $2 - x$	$+$	$+$	$-$
Sign of $\dfrac{x+5}{2-x}$	$-$	$+$	$-$

Solution: $x < -5$ or $x > 2$

37

Interval	$x < -3$	$-3 < x < 1$	$1 < x < 2$	$2 < x$
Sign of $x + 3$	−	+	+	+
Sign of $x - 1$	−	−	+	+
Sign of $x - 2$	−	−	−	+
Sign of $(x + 3)(x - 1)(x - 2)$	−	+	−	+

Solution: $-3 \leq x \leq 1$ or $x \geq 2$

39 $x < 2$ or $x > 5$

1.6 ABSOLUTE VALUE (*Page 30*)

1 False. **3** False. **5** True. **7** True. **9** False. **11** $x = \pm\frac{1}{2}$ **13** $x = -2, x = 4$ **15** $x = -2, x = 5$
17 $x = 1, x = 7$ **19** $x = -\frac{20}{3}, x = 4$ **21** $x > 0$

23 $x = -4$ or $x = 2$:

25 $x \leq -2$ or $x \geq 4$:

27 $-5 \leq x \leq 1$:

29 $x = -5$ or $x = 5$:

31 $x \leq -5$ or $x \geq 5$:

33 $2 \leq x \leq 8$:

35 $2.9 < x < 3.1$:

37 $-3 < x < 4$:

39 $2 < x < 6$:

41 $3 \leq x \leq 5$:

43 All $x \neq 3$:

45 -5 **47** $\frac{11}{2}$ **49** 0

51 $|5 - 2| \geq ||5| - |2||; 3 \geq 3$
$|5 - (-2)| \geq ||5| - |-2||; 7 \geq 3$
$|-5 - 2| \geq ||-5| - |2||; 7 \geq 3$
$|-5 - (-2)| \geq ||-5| - |-2||; 3 \geq 3$

53 $\left|\dfrac{x}{y}\right| = -\dfrac{x}{y}$ since $\dfrac{x}{y} < 0$

$= \dfrac{-x}{y}$

$= \dfrac{|x|}{|y|}$ since $x < 0$ and $y > 0$

55 (a) $|x| < 3$; (b) $|2x| < \frac{1}{2}$; (c) $|x - 2| < 3$; (d) $|x - \frac{1}{2}| < 1$
57 (a) $\frac{9}{10} < x < \frac{11}{10}$; (b) $\frac{27}{10} < 3x < \frac{33}{10}$; (c) $-\frac{3}{10} < 3x - 3 < \frac{3}{10}$; (d) $-\frac{3}{10} < y - 8 < \frac{3}{10}$; (e) $|y - 8| < \frac{3}{10}$

SAMPLE TEST QUESTIONS FOR CHAPTER 1 (*Page 32*)

1

	Whole numbers	Integers	Rational numbers	Irrational numbers	Negative integers
$\dfrac{-6}{3}$		✓	✓		
0.231					
$\sqrt{12}$				✓	
$\sqrt{\frac{9}{4}}$			✓		
1983	✓	✓	✓		

2 Construct a perpendicular of unit length at the point with coordinate 3. The hypotenuse of the resulting right triangle has length $\sqrt{3^2 + 1^2} = \sqrt{10}$. Now use a compass with this hypotenuse as radius and the origin as center to locate $\sqrt{10}$ on the number line.

3 (a) False; (b) true; (c) false; (d) true; (e) false; (f) false; (g) true; (h) false.

4 (a) Distributive property; (b) identity property for addition; (c) identity property for multiplication; (d) definition of subtraction; (e) associative property for multiplication; (f) definition of $a < b$.

5 (a) If $a \doteq b$, then $a + c = b + c$; (b) if $a = b$, then $ac = bc$. **6** (a) 1; (b) 3 **7** $x = 16$ **8** $x = -11$

9 $x = -\frac{9}{2}$ **10** Width = 7 inches; length = 19 inches. **11** 2:27 P.M.

12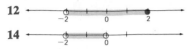

13

14

15

16 $x = \frac{5}{4}, x = \frac{1}{4}$ **17** $x < -2$ **18** $x > 2$

19 $x < \frac{2}{9}$:

20 $x \le -1$ or $x \ge 2$:

21 $x > 2$:

22 $-5 < x < \frac{1}{2}$:

CHAPTER 2: FUNDAMENTALS OF ALGEBRA

2.1 INTEGRAL EXPONENTS (*Page 41*)

1 False; 3^6. **3** False; 2^7. **5** True. **7** True. **9** False; $2 \cdot 3^4$. **11** False; 1. **13** False; 2^3. **15** False; 2^{-8}.

17 7 **19** $\frac{5}{3}$ **21** 1 **23** 4 **25** 24 **27** 4 **29** $\frac{15}{4}$ **31** $\frac{1}{x^6}$ **33** x^{12} **35** $72a^5$ **37** $16a^8$ **39** $x^6 y^2$ **41** $\frac{x^8}{y^6}$ **43** $\frac{y^7}{x^5}$

45 $5x$ **47** $\frac{b^2}{9}$ **49** $(a + b)^6$ **51** $-3x^3 y^3$ **53** $\frac{1}{(a + 3b)^{22}}$ **55** $\frac{1}{x^2} + \frac{1}{y^2}$ **57** $x^2 y^3$ **59** $\frac{10}{(4 - 5x)^3}$ **61** 9 **63** 8

65 -3 **67** $\frac{ab}{a + b}$ **69** $\frac{1}{a^{-n}} = \frac{1}{\frac{1}{a^n}} = 1 \cdot \frac{a^n}{1} = a^n$

2.2 RADICALS AND RATIONAL EXPONENTS (*Page 47*)

1 $11^{1/2}$ **3** $9^{1/4}$ **5** $6^{2/3}$ **7** $(-\frac{1}{3})^{3/5}$ **9** $\sqrt{3}$ **11** $\sqrt[3]{-19}$ **13** $\frac{1}{\sqrt{2}}$ **15** $\frac{1}{\sqrt[4]{\frac{3}{4}}}$ **17** True. **19** True.

21 False; -2. **23** False; 1.2. **25** True. **27** 5 **29** $\frac{1}{9}$ **31** $\frac{1}{16}$ **33** -3 **35** $\frac{1}{2}$ **37** 9 **39** 50 **41** $\frac{1}{32}$ **43** 5

45 13 **47** $\frac{\sqrt[3]{35}}{6}$ **49** $\frac{148}{135}$ **51** $-\frac{11}{4}$ **53** $\frac{4a^2}{b^6}$ **55** $\frac{1}{a^3 b^6}$ **57** 1 **59** $16a^4 b^6$ **61** $\frac{a^2}{b}$ **63** $\frac{3x}{(3x^2 + 2)^{1/2}}$

65 $\frac{x + 2}{(x^3 + 4x)^{1/2}}$ **67** x **69** $\frac{1}{xy^n}$

71 Let $x = \sqrt[n]{a}$, $y = \sqrt[n]{b}$. Then $x^n = a$ and $y^n = b$. Now we get $\frac{a}{b} = \frac{x^n}{y^n} = \left(\frac{x}{y}\right)^n$. Thus, by definition, $\sqrt[n]{\frac{a}{b}} = \frac{x}{y}$. But $x = \sqrt[n]{a}$ and $y = \sqrt[n]{b}$. Therefore, $\sqrt[n]{\frac{a}{b}} = \frac{\sqrt[n]{a}}{\sqrt[n]{b}}$.

2.3 SIMPLIFYING RADICALS (*Page 51*)

1 $4\sqrt{2}$ **3** 12 **5** $-\sqrt{3}$ **7** $10\sqrt{2}$ **9** $17\sqrt{5}$ **11** $10\sqrt{2}$ **13** $6\sqrt[3]{2}$ **15** $7\sqrt{2}$ **17** $14\sqrt{2}$ **19** $3\sqrt[3]{7x}$

21 $|x|\sqrt{2}$ **23** $5\sqrt[4]{2}$ **25** $5\sqrt{10}$ **27** $\frac{33\sqrt{2}}{2}$ **29** $5\sqrt{6} - 3\sqrt{2}$ **31** $7\sqrt{2x}$ **33** $12|x|$

35 $|x|\sqrt{y} + 12|x|\sqrt{2y}$ **37** $7a\sqrt{5a}$ **39** $4\sqrt{5}$ **41** $4x\sqrt{2}$ **43** $2\sqrt{2} + 2\sqrt{3}$ **45** $\dfrac{\sqrt{2}}{6}$ **47** $\dfrac{8\sqrt{3}}{|x|}$ **49** $4\sqrt[3]{4}$

51 $|xy| = \sqrt{(xy)^2} = \sqrt{x^2y^2} = \sqrt{x^2}\sqrt{y^2} = |x||y|$

2.4 FUNDAMENTAL OPERATIONS WITH POLYNOMIALS (*Page 56*)

1 $8x^2 - 2x + 7$ **3** $4x^3 - 9x^2 + 3$ **5** $2x^3 + x^2 + 11x - 28$ **7** $x^3 - 7x^2 - 10x + 8$ **9** $4x^3 - x^2 - 5x - 22$
11 $3x + 1$ **13** $6y + 6$ **15** $x^3 + 2x^2 + x$ **17** $7y + 8$ **19** $-4x^2 - 5x + 3$ **21** $-20x^4 + 4x^3 + 2x^2$
23 $x^2 + 2x + 1$ **25** $4x^2 + 26x - 14$ **27** $20x^2 - 42x + 18$ **29** $x^2 + \frac{1}{4}x - \frac{1}{8}$ **31** $-6x^2 - 3x + 18$
33 $-6x^2 + 3x + 18$ **35** $\frac{4}{9}x^2 + 8x + 36$ **37** $-63 + 55x - 12x^2$ **39** $a^2x^2 - b^2$ **41** $x^2 - 0.01$
43 $\frac{1}{25}x^2 - \frac{1}{10}x + \frac{1}{16}$ **45** $x - 100$ **47** $x - 2$ **49** 1 **51** $x^4 - 2x^3 + 2x^2 - 31x - 36$
53 $8x^4 + 12x^3 + 6x^2 - 18x - 27$ **55** $x^3 - 8$ **57** $x^5 - 32$ **59** $x^{4n} - x^{2n} - 2$ **61** $3x - 6x^2 + 3x^3$
63 $-6x^3 + 19x^2 - x - 6$ **65** $5x^4 - 12x^2 + 2x + 4$ **67** $6x^5 + 15x^4 - 12x^3 - 27x^2 + 10x + 15$
69 $x^3 - 3x^2 + 3x - 1$ **71** $a^4 + 4a^3b + 6a^2b^2 + 4ab^3 + b^4$ **73** $8x^3 + 36x^2 + 54x + 27$

75 $\frac{1}{27}x^3 + x^2 + 9x + 27$ **77** $6(\sqrt{5} + \sqrt{3})$ **79** $-2(\sqrt{2} + 3)$ **81** $\dfrac{x + 2\sqrt{xy} + y}{x - y}$ **83** $\dfrac{-4}{5 - 3\sqrt{5}}$

85 $\dfrac{x - y}{x - 2\sqrt{xy} + y}$ **87** Multiply numerator and denominator of the first fraction by $\sqrt{4 + h} + 2$ and simplify.

2.5 FACTORING POLYNOMIALS (*Page 62*)

1 $5(x - 1)$ **3** $2x(8x^3 + 4x^2 + 2x + 1)$ **5** $2ab(2a - 3)$ **7** $2x(y + 2x + 4x^3)$ **9** $5(a - b)(2x + y)$
11 $(9 + x)(9 - x)$ **13** $(2x + 3)(2x - 3)$ **15** $(a + 11b)(a - 11b)$ **17** $(x + 4)(x^2 - 4x + 16)$
19 $(5x - 4)(25x^2 + 20x + 16)$ **21** $(2x + 7y)(4x^2 - 14xy + 49y^2)$ **23** $(\sqrt{3} + 2x)(\sqrt{3} - 2x)$
25 $(\sqrt{x} + 6)(\sqrt{x} - 6)$ **27** $(2\sqrt{2} + \sqrt{3x})(2\sqrt{2} - \sqrt{3x})$ **29** $(\sqrt[3]{7} + a)[(\sqrt[3]{7})^2 - a\sqrt[3]{7} + a^2]$
31 $(3\sqrt[3]{x} + 1)(9\sqrt[3]{x^2} - 3\sqrt[3]{x} + 1)$ **33** $(\sqrt[3]{3x} - \sqrt[3]{4})(\sqrt[3]{9x^2} + \sqrt[3]{12x} + \sqrt[3]{16})$ **35** $(x - 1)(x + y)$
37 $(x - 1)(y - 1)$ **39** $(2 - y^2)(1 + x)$ **41** $7(x + h)(x^2 - hx + h^2)$ **43** $xy(x + y)(x - y)$
45 $(x^2 + y^2)(x + y)(x - y)$ **47** $(a^4 + b^4)(a^2 + b^2)(a + b)(a - b)$
49 $(a - 2)(a^4 + 2a^3 + 4a^2 + 8a + 16)$ **51** $(1 - h)(1 + h + h^2 + h^3 + h^4 + h^5 + h^6)$
53 $3(a + 1)(x + 2)(x^2 - 2x + 4)$ **55** $(x - y)(a + b)(a^2 - ab + b^2)$ **57** $(x^2 + 4y^2)(x + 2y)(x - 2y)^2$
59 $(x + 2)^2(8x + 7)$ **61** $x(x^3 + 1)^2(11x^3 - 9x + 2)$ or $x(x + 1)^2(x^2 - x + 1)^2(11x^3 - 9x + 2)$
63 (a) $(x + 2)(x^4 - 2x^3 + 4x^2 - 8x + 16)$; (b) $x(2x + y)(64x^6 - 32x^5y + 16x^4y^2 - 8x^3y^3 + 4x^2y^4 - 2xy^5 + y^6)$.

2.6 FACTORING TRINOMIALS (*Page 66*)

1 $(x + 2)^2$ **3** $(a - 7)^2$ **5** $(1 + b)^2$ **7** $4(a + 1)^2$ **9** $9(x - y)^2$ **11** $(3x + 2y)^2$ **13** $(x + 2)(x + 3)$
15 $(x + 17)(x + 3)$ **17** $(5a - 1)(4a - 1)$ **19** $(x + 2)(x + 18)$ **21** $(3x + 1)^2$ **23** $(5a - 1)^2$
25 $(3x + 2)(x + 6)$ **27** $(7x + 1)(2x + 5)$ **29** $(8x - 1)(x - 1)$ **31** $(2a + 5)^2$ **33** $(b + 15)(b + 3)$
35 $2(2x - 3)(2x - 1)$ **37** $(4a - 3)(3a - 4)$ **39** $(5x + 1)(3x - 2)$ **41** $(3a + 7)(2a - 3)$ **43** $(2x - 1)(2x + 3)$
45 $(8a + 3b)(3a + 2b)$ **47** $5(x + 1)(x + 4)$ **49** $a(2x + 1)^2$ **51** Not factorable. **53** $2(3x - 5)(x + 2)$
55 Not factorable. **57** $2(x - 8)(x + 7)$ **59** $2(b + 2)(b + 4)$ **61** $ab(a - b)^2$ **63** $8(2x - 1)(x - 1)$
65 $25(a + b)^2$ **67** $(a - 1)^2(a^2 + a + 1)^2$ **69** $3xy(x^2 + 2y)(2x^2 - 5y)$ **71** $(a - b)^2(a^2 + ab + b^2)^2$

2.7 FUNDAMENTAL OPERATIONS WITH RATIONAL EXPRESSIONS (*Page 72*)

1 False; $\frac{1}{21}$. **3** False; $\dfrac{ax}{2} - \dfrac{5b}{6}$. **5** True. **7** $\dfrac{2x}{3z}$ **9** $-x$ **11** $\dfrac{n + 1}{n^2 + 1}$ **13** $\dfrac{3(x - 1)}{2(x + 1)}$ **15** $\dfrac{2x + 3}{2x - 3}$

17 $\dfrac{a - 4b}{a^2 - 4ab + 16b^2}$ **19** $\dfrac{2y}{x}$ **21** $\dfrac{2}{a^2}$ **23** $\dfrac{x}{y}$ **25** $\dfrac{-3a - 8b}{6}$ **27** $\dfrac{x^2 + 1}{3(x + 1)}$ **29** 1 **31** $\dfrac{2 - xy}{x}$ **33** $\dfrac{5y^2 - y}{y^2 - 1}$

35 $\dfrac{3x}{x + 1}$ **37** $\dfrac{8 - x}{x^2 - 4}$ **39** $\dfrac{3(x + 9)}{(x - 3)(x + 3)^2}$ **41** $x - 3$ **43** $\dfrac{2(n^2 + 4)}{n + 2}$ **45** $\dfrac{1}{2(x + 2)}$ **47** $-\dfrac{1}{4x}$ **49** $-\dfrac{1}{4(4 + h)}$

51 $-\dfrac{1}{3(x+3)}$ **53** $\dfrac{4-x}{16x^2}$ **55** $\dfrac{xy}{y+x}$ **57** $\dfrac{-4x}{(1+x^2)^2}$ **59** $-\dfrac{4}{x^2}$ **61** $-\dfrac{1}{ab}$ **63** $\dfrac{y^2-x^2}{x^3y^3}$

65 (a) $\dfrac{\dfrac{AD}{B}+C}{D}=\dfrac{AD+BC}{BD}=\dfrac{AD}{BD}+\dfrac{BC}{BD}=\dfrac{A}{B}+\dfrac{C}{D}$

(b) $\left[\dfrac{\left(\dfrac{AB}{D}+C\right)D}{F}+E\right]\cdot F=\left[\dfrac{AB+CD}{F}+E\right]\cdot F=AB+CD+EF$

67 $\dfrac{2xy^2-2x^2y\left(\dfrac{x^2}{y^2}\right)}{y^4}=\dfrac{2xy^2-\dfrac{2x^4}{y}}{y^4}=\dfrac{2xy^3-2x^4}{y^5}=\dfrac{2x(x^3+8)-2x^4}{y^5}=\dfrac{16x}{y^5}$

2.8   THE BINOMIAL EXPANSION (*Page 76*)

1 $x^5+5x^4+10x^3+10x^2+5x+1$ **3** $x^7+7x^6+21x^5+35x^4+35x^3+21x^2+7x+1$
5 $a^4-4a^3b+6a^2b^2-4ab^3+b^4$ **7** $243x^5-405x^4y+270x^3y^2-90x^2y^3+15xy^4-y^5$
9 $a^{10}+5a^8+10a^6+10a^4+5a^2+1$
11 $1-10h+45h^2-120h^3+210h^4-252h^5+210h^6-120h^7+45h^8-10h^9+h^{10}$ **13** $3+3h+h^2$
15 $3c^2+3ch+h^2$ **17** $2(5x^4+10x^3h+10x^2h^2+5xh^3+h^4)$
19 $(1+1)^{10}=1+10+45+120+210+252+210+120+45+10+1=1024$
21 $c^{20}+20c^{19}h+190c^{18}h^2+1140c^{17}h^3+4845c^{16}h^4+\cdots+4845c^4h^{16}+1140c^3h^{17}+190c^2h^{18}+20ch^{19}$
$+h^{20}$
23 The nth row of the triangle contains the coefficients in the expansion of $(a+b)^n$.
25   1   7   21   35   35   21   7   1
          1   8   28   56   70   56   28   8   1
        1   9   36   84   126   126   84   36   9   1
      1   10   45   120   210   252   210   120   45   10   1
27 $x^{10}-10x^9h+45x^8h^2-120x^7h^3+210x^6h^4-252x^5h^5+210x^4h^6-120x^3h^7+45x^2h^8-10xh^9+h^{10}$

SAMPLE TEST QUESTIONS FOR CHAPTER 2 (*Page 78*)

1 False.   **2** True.   **3** False.   **4** False.   **5** True.   **6** False.   **7** (b)   **8** (a)   **9** (b)   **10** $7cd-6a^2$
11 $11x^2-14x-21$ **12** $5x^4+12x^3-2x-3$ **13** $(4-3b)(16+12b+9b^2)$ **14** $3x(x-2)(x+2)(x^2+4)$
15 $(2x-3)(3x+1)$ **16** $(x-2)(x^4+2x^3+4x^2+8x+16)$ **17** $(2x+y^2)(x-3y)$ **18** $(x+3)(ax-2)$
19 $\dfrac{2(x+3)}{(x+2)(x+5)}$ **20** x **21** $-\dfrac{7+x}{49x^2}$ **22** $\dfrac{1}{x+1}$ **23** $\dfrac{3x^2-18x+25}{(x-3)(x+3)(2x-5)}$
24 $a^{20}-40a^{19}+760a^{18}-9120a^{17}$ **25** $x^4-12x^3y+54x^2y^2-108xy^3+81y^4$

CHAPTER 3: LINEAR FUNCTIONS AND EQUATIONS

3.1   INTRODUCTION TO THE FUNCTION CONCEPT (*Page 86*)

1 Function: all reals.   **3** Function: all $x>0$.   **5** Not a function.   **7** Function: all $x\neq-1$.   **9** Not a function.
11 Function: $x<-2$ or $x>2$.   **13** Not a function; for $x=3$, $y=4$ or $y=1$.   **15** True.   **17** False; -3.
19 True.   **21** False: $-x^2+16$.   **23** True.   **25** (a) -3; (b) -1; (c) 0.   **27** (a) 1; (b) 0; (c) $\frac{1}{4}$.
29 (a) -2; (b) -1; (c) $-\frac{7}{8}$.   **31** (a) 2; (b) 0; (c) $\frac{5}{16}$.   **33** (a) $-\frac{1}{2}$; (b) -1; (c) -2.
35 (a) -1; (b) does not exist; (c) $\sqrt[3]{2}$.   **37** (a) 81; (b) 5; (c) $\frac{25}{36}$; (d) $\frac{1}{36}$.   **39** $3h(2)=24\neq48=h(6)$
41 $x+3$ **43** $-\dfrac{1}{3x}$ **45** 2   **47** 1   **49** $-4-h$ **51** $-\dfrac{4+h}{4(2+h)^2}$

1

x	-3	-2	-1	0	1	2
y	-5	-4	-3	-2	-1	0

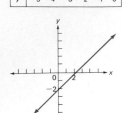

3

x	-2	-1	0	1	2
y	-8	-6	-4	-2	0

5

7

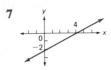

9

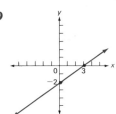

11

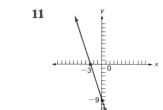

13

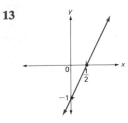

15

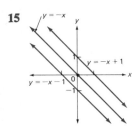

17

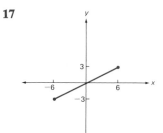

19

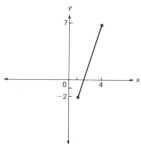

21 (a)

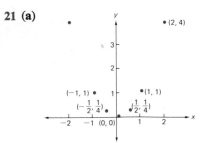

(b)

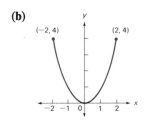

23 (a)

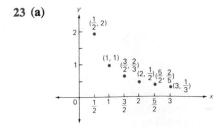

(b)

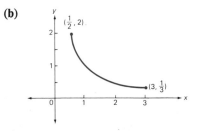

25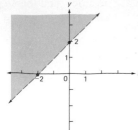

27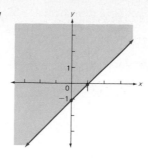

29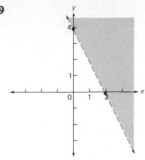

1 Each quotient gives the same slope, $-\frac{1}{2}$. **(a)** $\dfrac{3-1}{-2-2}$; **(b)** $\dfrac{2-0}{0-4}$; **(c)** $\dfrac{1-0}{2-4}$; **(d)** $\dfrac{3-(-1)}{-2-6}$; **(e)** $\dfrac{2-(-1)}{0-6}$;

(f) $\dfrac{1-(-1)}{2-6}$

3 $\frac{1}{9}$ **5** 0   **7** $-\frac{17}{28}$ **9** $\dfrac{2}{\sqrt{3}+1} = \sqrt{3}-1$

11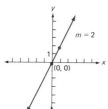

13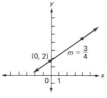

15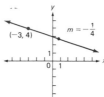

17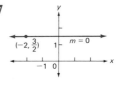

19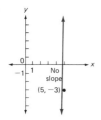

21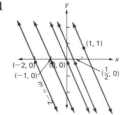

23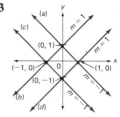

25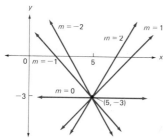

27 Both have the same slope of $-\frac{3}{2}$.

29 The slopes of *PQ* and *RS* are each $-\frac{5}{12}$; the slopes of *PS* and *QR* are each $\frac{12}{5}$. Thus the sides of the figure are perpendicular to each other and form right angles. Also, the diagonals are perpendicular because the slope of *PR* is $\frac{7}{17}$ and the slope of *QS* is the negative reciprocal, $-\frac{17}{7}$.

31 Horizontal lines have slope 0, which does not have a reciprocal. Also, vertical lines have no slope, and therefore a slope comparison cannot be made.

33 $\frac{49}{2}$

35 (a) Slope $\ell_1 = m_1 = \dfrac{DA}{CD} = \dfrac{DA}{1} = DA$; (b) slope $\ell_2 = m_2 = \dfrac{DB}{CD} = \dfrac{DB}{1} = DB$; $m_2 < 0$;

(c) $\dfrac{DA}{CD} = \dfrac{CD}{BD}$ or $\dfrac{m_1}{1} = \dfrac{1}{-m_2}$, since $BD = -DB = -m_2$.

3.4 LINEAR FUNCTIONS (*Page 102*)

1 $y = 2x + 3$ **3** $y = x + 1$ **5** $y = 5$ **7** $y = \frac{1}{2}x + 3$ **9** $y = \frac{1}{4}x - 2$ **11** $y - 3 = x - 2$
13 $y - 3 = 4(x + 2)$ **15** $y - 5 = 0$ **17** $y - 1 = \frac{1}{2}(x - 2)$ **19** $y = 5x$ **21** $y + \sqrt{2} = 10(x - \sqrt{2})$
23 $y = -3x + 4$; $m = -3$; $k = 4$ **25** $y = 2x - \frac{1}{3}$; $m = 2$; $k = -\frac{1}{3}$ **27** $y = \frac{5}{3}$; $m = 0$; $k = \frac{5}{3}$
29 $y = \frac{4}{3}x - \frac{7}{3}$; $m = \frac{4}{3}$; $k = -\frac{7}{3}$ **31** $y = \frac{1}{2}x - 2$; $m = \frac{1}{2}$; $k = -2$ **33** $y = -x + 5$ **35** $y = x - 3$
37 $y = -2x - 15$ **39** $y = 27$ **41** $x = 5, y = -7$ **43** $y = -\frac{2}{3}x - \frac{1}{3}$ **45** $y - 7 = -\frac{1}{3}(x - 4)$

47 $y - 1 = -\frac{1}{2}(x + 5)$ **49**  **51**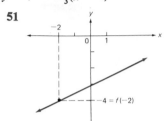

53 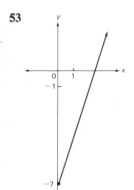 **55**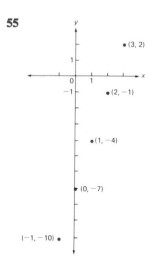

57 $x = -3$; not a function **59** $y = x + 2$; $-2 \le x$; $0 \le y$
61 $y = -1$ for $-1 \le x < 0$; $y = 3$ for $0 \le x < 3$; $y = 1$ for $3 \le x \le 5$
63 (a) If $c = 0$ then $(0, 0)$ fits the equation and the line would then pass through the origin.

(b) $\dfrac{c}{b} = y$-intercept; $\dfrac{c}{a} = x$-intercept.

(c) $ax + by = c$; $\dfrac{ax}{c} + \dfrac{by}{c} = 1$; $\dfrac{x}{\left(\dfrac{c}{a}\right)} + \dfrac{y}{\left(\dfrac{c}{b}\right)} = 1$; $\dfrac{x}{q} + \dfrac{y}{p} = 1$ (d) $\dfrac{x}{\frac{3}{2}} + \dfrac{y}{-5} = 1$ or $10x - 3y = 15$

(e) $m = \dfrac{0 - (-5)}{\frac{3}{2} - (0)} = \dfrac{5}{\frac{3}{2}} = \dfrac{10}{3}$; $y = \dfrac{10}{3}x - 5$ **65** $y - 3 = -\frac{5}{7}(x + 2)$

1 99 **3** −100 **5** −4 **7** 1

9 Domain: all reals.
Range: $y \geq 0$.

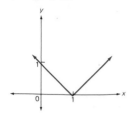

11 Domain: all reals.
Range: $y \geq 0$.

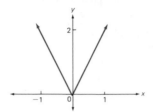

13 Domain: all reals.
Range: $y \geq 0$.

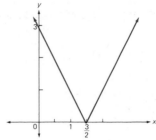

15 Domain: $x \geq -1$.
Range: $y \leq 3$.

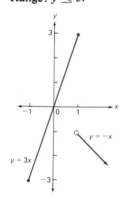

17 Domain: $-2 < x \leq 3$.
Range: $-2 < y \leq 4$.

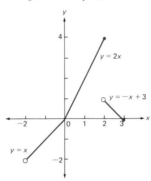

19

21

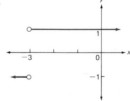

23

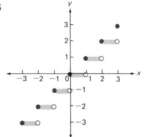

25

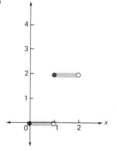

27

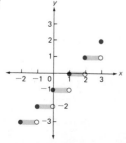

29

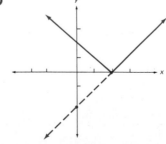

3.6 SYSTEMS OF LINEAR EQUATIONS (*Page 112*)

1 $(-2, -6)$ **3** $(4, -10)$ **5** $(-4, -1)$ **7** $(-26, -62)$ **9** $(-16, -38)$ **11** $(\frac{21}{88}, -\frac{9}{22})$ **13** $(5, 1)$ **15** $(8, 5)$
17 $(3, -11)$ **19** $(1, 0)$ **21** $(1, \frac{1}{2})$ **23** $(1, 0)$ **25** $(\frac{17}{18}, \frac{7}{18})$ **27** $(\frac{7}{2}, 4)$ **29** $(1, -2, 3)$ **31** $(2, -1, -1)$
33 $\left(\dfrac{ce - bf}{ae - bd}, \dfrac{af - cd}{ae - bd}\right)$ **35** $(-20, -20)$ **37** 40 field goals; 16 free throws.
39 \$1700 room and board; \$3600 tuition.
41 Speed of plane $= 410$ miles per hour; wind velocity $= 10$ miles per hour.
43 180 quarts of 74¢ oil; 220 quarts of 94¢ oil.   **45** \$2800 at 8%; \$3200 at $7\frac{1}{2}\%$.
47 6 miles by car; 72 miles by train.   **49** $a = 4$, $b = -7$

3.7 CLASSIFICATION OF LINEAR SYSTEMS (*Page 117*)

1 Consistent.   **3** Inconsistent.   **5** Dependent.   **7** Consistent.   **9** Inconsistent.   **11** Consistent.   **13** Dependent.
15 Inconsistent.   **17** Parallel.

19

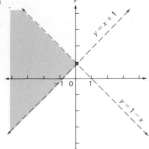

21

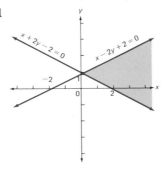

23

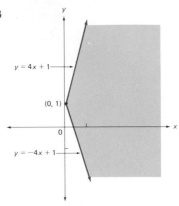

25

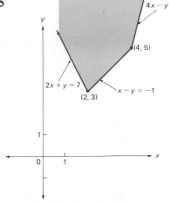

27

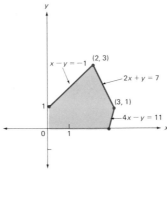

29 An infinite number of answers.

31 Yes, the clerk was wrong. If there were common unit prices, say $x =$ cost per orange and $y =$ cost per tangerine, then

$$6x + 12y = 234$$
$$2x + 4y = 77$$

which is an inconsistent system. (*Note:* The smaller bag is a better buy since 2 (oranges) + 4 (tangerines) = $\frac{1}{3}$(6 oranges + 12 tangerines) = $\frac{1}{3}$(2.34) = 0.78, and 77¢ is cheaper.)

1 $h(x) = \frac{5}{2}x$ **3** $w(h) = \frac{20}{9}h$ **5** $s(x) = \frac{1}{3}x$ **7** $A(x) = \frac{5}{2}x(4 - x)$ **9** $V(x) = x(50 - 2x)^2$
11 $A(x) = \pi r^2 + 2r(200 - \pi r)$ **13** $V(x) = \frac{4}{3}x(30 - x^2)$ **15** $\frac{7}{3}x(10 - 2x)$

3.9 USING MATRICES AND DETERMINANTS TO SOLVE LINEAR SYSTEMS (*Page 128*)

1 $(-4, -1)$ **3** $(0, 9)$ **5** $(\frac{1}{8}, \frac{1}{2})$ **7** $(1, 0)$ **9** $(5, -2)$ **11** $(-\frac{2}{3}, 2)$ **13** $(5, 2, -1)$ **15** $(3, 4, 2)$ **17** No solutions.
19 17 **21** 94 **23** -60 **25** 0 **27** 35 **29** -45 **31** 4 **33** $(-1, 2)$ **35** $(3, 2)$ **37** $(1, -1)$ **39** $(1, 2, 3)$
41 $(0, -2, 3)$ **43** 6

45 (a) $\begin{vmatrix} a_1 & b_1 \\ a_2 & b_2 \end{vmatrix} = a_1b_2 - a_2b_1 = a_1b_2 - b_1a_2 = \begin{vmatrix} a_1 & a_2 \\ b_1 & b_2 \end{vmatrix}$

(b) $\begin{vmatrix} a_1 & b_1 & c_1 \\ a_2 & b_2 & c_2 \\ a_3 & b_3 & c_3 \end{vmatrix} = a_1b_2c_3 + a_2b_3c_1 + a_3b_1c_2 - a_1b_3c_2 - a_2b_1c_3 - a_3b_2c_1 = \begin{vmatrix} a_1 & a_2 & a_3 \\ b_1 & b_2 & b_3 \\ c_1 & c_2 & c_3 \end{vmatrix}$

47 (a) $a_2 = ka_1, b_2 = kb_1, c_2 = kc_1$, so

$\begin{vmatrix} a_1 & b_1 & c_1 \\ a_2 & b_2 & c_2 \\ a_3 & b_3 & c_3 \end{vmatrix} = \begin{vmatrix} a_1 & b_1 & c_1 \\ ka_1 & kb_1 & kc_1 \\ a_3 & b_3 & c_3 \end{vmatrix} = ka_1b_1c_3 + ka_1b_3c_1 + ka_3b_1c_1 - ka_1b_3c_1 - ka_1b_1c_3 - ka_3b_1c_1 = 0$

(Similarly for the other rows.)

(b) Let $b_1 = ka_1, b_2 = ka_2, b_3 = ka_3$. Then

$\begin{vmatrix} a_1 & b_1 & c_1 \\ a_2 & b_2 & c_2 \\ a_3 & b_3 & c_3 \end{vmatrix} = \begin{vmatrix} a_1 & ka_1 & c_1 \\ a_2 & ka_2 & c_2 \\ a_3 & ka_3 & c_3 \end{vmatrix} = \begin{vmatrix} a_1 & a_2 & a_3 \\ ka_1 & ka_2 & ka_3 \\ c_1 & c_2 & c_3 \end{vmatrix} = 0$ (by part (a))

(by Exercise 45)

(Similarly for the other columns.)

49 $\begin{vmatrix} 27 & 3 \\ 105 & -75 \end{vmatrix} = 3 \begin{vmatrix} 9 & 1 \\ 105 & -75 \end{vmatrix} = 45 \begin{vmatrix} 9 & 1 \\ 7 & -5 \end{vmatrix} = -2340$

$\begin{vmatrix} 27 & 3 \\ 105 & -75 \end{vmatrix} = 3 \begin{vmatrix} 9 & 1 \\ 105 & -75 \end{vmatrix} = 9 \begin{vmatrix} 3 & 1 \\ 35 & -75 \end{vmatrix} = 45 \begin{vmatrix} 3 & 1 \\ 7 & -15 \end{vmatrix} = -2340$

51 $\begin{vmatrix} a_1 + kb_1 & b_1 \\ a_2 + kb_2 & b_2 \end{vmatrix} = \begin{vmatrix} a_1 & b_1 \\ a_2 & b_2 \end{vmatrix} + \begin{vmatrix} kb_1 & b_1 \\ kb_2 & b_2 \end{vmatrix} = \begin{vmatrix} a_1 & b_1 \\ a_2 & b_2 \end{vmatrix} + 0 = \begin{vmatrix} a_1 & b_2 \\ a_2 & b_2 \end{vmatrix}$

(by Exercise 50)　　　(by Exercise 46)

53 (Sample Solution)

$\begin{vmatrix} 12 & -42 \\ -6 & 27 \end{vmatrix} = 6 \begin{vmatrix} 2 & -42 \\ -1 & 27 \end{vmatrix} = 12 \begin{vmatrix} 1 & -21 \\ -1 & 27 \end{vmatrix} = 12 \begin{vmatrix} 1 & -21 \\ 0 & 6 \end{vmatrix} = 12(6) = 72$

　　Ex. 48　　　　　　Ex. 48　　　　　　Ex. 51

SAMPLE TEST QUESTIONS FOR CHAPTER 3 (*Page 131*)

1 $x \le -1$ or $x \ge 1$ **2 (a)** $\dfrac{3}{2 + x}$; **(b)** $\dfrac{3}{2} + \dfrac{3}{x} = \dfrac{3x + 6}{2x}$ **3** $-\dfrac{2}{3(3 + h)}$ **4**

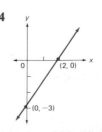

5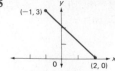
(−1, 3)

(2, 0)

6 $-\frac{7}{3}$ **7** $y - 3 = -\frac{3}{4}(x + 2)$ **8** $y = -\frac{9}{5}x + \frac{2}{5}$ **9** $\frac{3}{4}; \frac{1}{2}$

10 $y - 8 = \frac{5}{2}(x - 2)$

11 Domain: all x.
Range: all y.

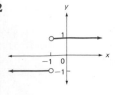

12

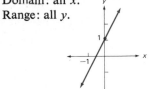

13 $x = 3, y = -1$ **14** $x = -1, y = 2, z = 5$ **15** 25 at 20¢; 15 at 37¢ **16** Dependent. **17** Consistent; (3, −5).

18 Inconsistent. **19**

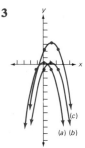

20 $V(x) = x(40 - 2x)^2$ **21** $x = -1, y = 2, z = 4$

CHAPTER 4: QUADRATIC FUNCTIONS AND EQUATIONS

4.1 GRAPHING QUADRATIC FUNCTIONS (*Page 139*)

1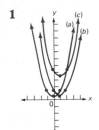

3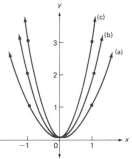

5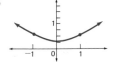

7

9

11

13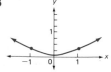

15

17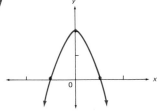

19 Decreasing on $(-\infty, 1]$; increasing on $[1, \infty)$; concave up.

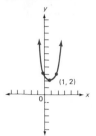

(1, 2)

21 Increasing on $(-\infty, -1]$; decreasing on $[-1, \infty)$; concave down.

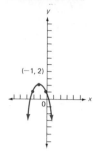

(−1, 2)

23 Decreasing on $(-\infty, 3]$; increasing on $[3, \infty)$; concave up.

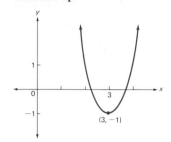

(3, −1)

25 (a) $(3, 5)$; (b) $x = 3$; (c) Set of real numbers; (d) $y \geq 5$

27 (a) $(3, 5)$; (b) $x = 3$; (c) Set of real numbers; (d) $y \leq 5$

29 (a) $(-1, -3)$; (b) $x = -1$; (c) Set of real numbers; (d) $y \geq -3$

31

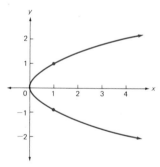

33 Not a function because for $x > 0$ there are two corresponding y-values.

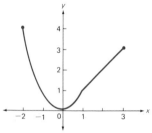

35 The graph of $x^2 - 4 > 0$ consists of all points on the number line where $x < -2$ or where $x > 2$. On the coordinate plane, the graph of $y = x^2 - 4$ is positive (above the x-axis) for $x < -2$ or $x > 2$.

37 $a = -2$

39 $k = 3$

41

43

45

4.2 COMPLETING THE SQUARE (*Page 143*)

1 $(x + 1)^2 - 6$ **3** $-(x + 3)^2 + 11$ **5** $-(x - \frac{3}{2})^2 - \frac{7}{4}$ **7** $(x + \frac{5}{2})^2 - \frac{33}{4}$ **9** $2(x + 1)^2 - 5$
11 $3(x + 1)^2 - 8$ **13** $(x - \frac{1}{4})^2 + \frac{15}{16}$ **15** $\frac{3}{4}(x - \frac{2}{3})^2 - \frac{2}{3}$ **17** $-5(x + \frac{1}{5})^2 + 1$ **19** $(x - \frac{1}{2})^2 - 3$
21 $h = -\frac{b}{2a}; k = \frac{4ac - b^2}{4a}$ **23** $y = (x - 2)^2 + 3; (2, 3); x = 2; y = 7$
25 $y = (x - 3)^2 - 4; (3, -4); x = 3; y = 5$ **27** $y = 2(x - 1)^2 - 6; (1, -6); x = 1; y = -4$

29

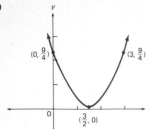

31

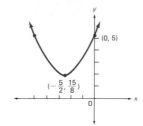

33

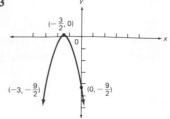

35

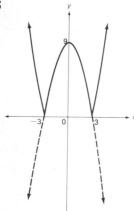

37

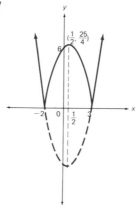

39

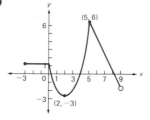

41 $a > 0; k = 0.$ **43** $a > 0; k = 2.$ **45** $y = -2x^2 + 3x + 7$

4.3 THE QUADRATIC FORMULA (*Page 149*)

1 $x = -2; x = 5$ **3** $x = 3$ **5** $x = -2; x = -\frac{1}{3}$ **7** $x = 1 - \sqrt{5}; x = 1 + \sqrt{5}$
9 $x = \frac{3 - \sqrt{17}}{4}; x = \frac{3 + \sqrt{17}}{4}$ **11** $3; -\frac{1}{2}$ **13** None. **15** $\frac{3}{2}; 2$ **17** None. **19** $0;$ (b) **21** $36;$ (c) **23** $13;$ (d)
25 $41;$ (d) **27** $-7;$ (a) **29** Once; (a) $(\frac{1}{3}, 0)$; (b) 1; (c) $\frac{1}{3}$ **31** $-1 < x < 3$ **33** $x \leq -5$ or $x \geq 2$
35 No solution. **37**

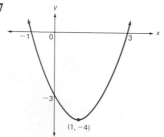

39

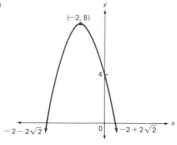

41

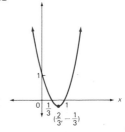

472 ANSWERS TO ODD-NUMBERED EXERCISES AND SAMPLE TEST QUESTIONS

43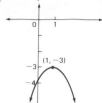

45 -6 or 6 **47** $\pm 2\sqrt{7}$ **49** $k > -4$ **51** $k > -\frac{1}{4}$ **53** $a < -\frac{1}{4}$ **55** (a) $-\frac{b}{a}$; (b) $\frac{c}{a}$

57 sum $= -\frac{5}{6}$ **59** sum $= \frac{26}{3}$ **61** sum $= -3$ **63** $x = -3$; $x = -2$; $x = 2$
product $= -\frac{2}{3}$ product $= \frac{35}{3}$ product $= -\frac{9}{2}$

4.4 APPLICATIONS OF QUADRATIC FUNCTIONS (*Page 153*)

1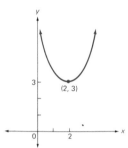

3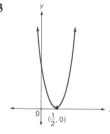

5 Maximum $= 7$ at $x = 5$.

7 Minimum $= 36$ at $x = 2$. **9** Minimum $= 0$ at $x = \frac{7}{2}$. **11** Maximum $= \frac{1}{9}$ at $x = -\frac{1}{3}$. **13** 60; $600 **15** 6, 6
17 No; the product $y = x(n - x) = -x^2 + nx$ gets arbitrarily small as x becomes very large or very small since the graph of this quadratic opens downward.
19 10 feet by 10 feet. **21** 256 feet; 4 seconds. **23** 2, 6 **25** $9.75 **27** (1, 2)
29 Maximum or minimum $= \dfrac{4ac - b^2}{4a}$ at $x = -\dfrac{b}{2a}$. **31** (4, 7); 7 is maximum.
33 $(\frac{5}{2}, -\frac{25}{4})$; $-\frac{25}{4}$ is minimum. **35** $(-5, 750)$; 750 is minimum. **37** 7, 9 **39** $-\frac{3}{2}$ or 1 **41** 8 centimeters.
43 12 inches.

4.5 CIRCLES AND THEIR EQUATIONS (*Page 160*)

1

3 $(x - 2)^2 + (y - 5)^2 = 1$; $C(2, 5)$, $r = 1$

5 $(x - 4)^2 + (y - 0)^2 = 2$; $C(4, 0)$, $r = \sqrt{2}$ **7** $(x - 10)^2 + (y + 10)^2 = 100$; $C(10, -10)$, $r = 10$
9 $(x + \frac{3}{4})^2 + (y - 1)^2 = 9$; $C(-\frac{3}{4}, 1)$, $r = 3$ **11** $(x - 2)^2 + y^2 = 4$ **13** $(x + 3)^2 + (y - 3)^2 = 7$

15

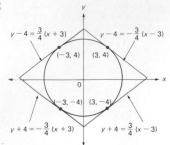

$y - 4 = \frac{3}{4}(x + 3)$ $y - 4 = -\frac{3}{4}(x - 3)$

$(-3, 4)$ $(3, 4)$

$(-3, -4)$ $(3, -4)$

$y + 4 = -\frac{3}{4}(x + 3)$ $y + 4 = \frac{3}{4}(x - 3)$

17 $x = 2; x = -2$

19

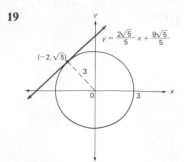

$y = \frac{2\sqrt{5}}{5}x + \frac{9\sqrt{5}}{5}$

$(-2, \sqrt{5})$ 3

21

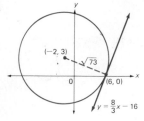

$(-2, 3)$ $\sqrt{73}$

$(6, 0)$

$y = \frac{8}{3}x - 16$

23

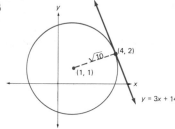

$\sqrt{10}$ $(4, 2)$

$(1, 1)$

$y = 3x + 14$

25 $(\frac{1}{2}, -2)$ **27** $(-\frac{5}{2}, \frac{1}{2})$

29 $y = -\frac{1}{2}x + 10$ **31** $5x + 12y = 26$ **33** (a) $y(x) = \sqrt{25 + 24x - x^2} - 5$; (b) $y(7) = 7$

4.6   SOLVING NONLINEAR SYSTEMS (*Page 163*)

1

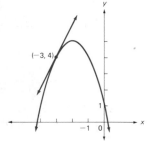

$(-3, 4)$

3

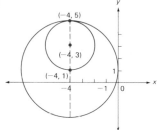

$(-4, 5)$

$(-4, 3)$

$(-4, 1)$

5

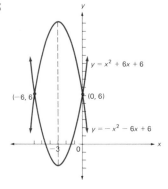

$y = x^2 + 6x + 6$

$(-6, 6)$ $(0, 6)$

$y = -x^2 - 6x + 6$

7 $(0, 1)$ **9** No solutions.   **11** No solutions.   **13** $(-1, -1); (-2, -2)$.   **15** $(0, 0); (2, 0)$.   **17** $(0, 0); (1, 1)$.
19 $(3, -3); (3 + \sqrt{3}, -2); (3 - \sqrt{3}, -2)$.

4.7   THE ELLIPSE AND THE HYPERBOLA (*Page 171*)

1 Ellipse; center $(0, 0)$, vertices $(\pm 5, 0)$, foci $(\pm 3, 0)$.
3 Hyperbola; center $(0, 0)$, vertices $(\pm 6, 0)$, foci $(\pm\sqrt{61}, 0)$, asymptotes $y = \pm\frac{5}{6}x$.
5 Ellipse; center $(0, 0)$, vertices $(0, \pm 5)$, foci $(0, \pm\sqrt{21})$.
7 Ellipse; center $(0, 1)$, vertices $(0, -1)$ and $(0, 3)$, foci $(0, 1 - \sqrt{3})$ and $(0, 1 + \sqrt{3})$.

9 Ellipse:

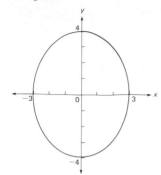

11 Hyperbola:

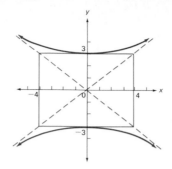

13 Ellipse:

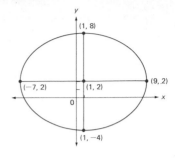

15 Hyperbola:

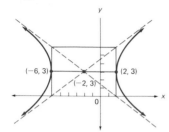

17 $(x - 1)^2 + (y + 2)^2 = 4$; circle; center $(1, -2)$; $r = 2$.

19 $\dfrac{(x + 1)^2}{4} + \dfrac{y^2}{1} = 1$; ellipse; center $(-1, 0)$; vertices $(-3, 0)$ and $(1, 0)$; foci $(-1 - \sqrt{3}, 0)$ and $(-1 + \sqrt{3}, 0)$.

21 $\dfrac{(x + 1)^2}{16} - \dfrac{(y - 3)^2}{9} = 1$; hyperbola; center $(-1, 3)$; vertices $(-5, 3)$ and $(3, 3)$; foci $(-6, 3)$ and $(4, 3)$.

23 $\dfrac{x^2}{25} + \dfrac{y^2}{9} = 1$ **25** $\dfrac{x^2}{16} + \dfrac{y^2}{25} = 1$ **27** $\dfrac{(x - 2)^2}{16} + \dfrac{(y + 3)^2}{36} = 1$ **29** $\dfrac{x^2}{16} - \dfrac{y^2}{20} = 1$ **31** $\dfrac{(y - 3)^2}{9} - \dfrac{(x + 2)^2}{7} = 1$

33 $\dfrac{x^2}{16} - \dfrac{y^2}{4} = 1$ **35** (a) $\sqrt{x^2 + (y - p)^2}$; (b) $y + p$. (c) $\sqrt{x^2 + (y - p)^2} = y + p$

$$x^2 + (y - p)^2 = (y + p)^2$$
$$x^2 = 4py$$

37 $x^2 = -12y$

39 $(0, -1)$; $y = 1$ **41** $(x - 2)^2 = 8(y + 5)$; $y = \frac{1}{8}x^2 - \frac{1}{2}x - \frac{9}{2}$

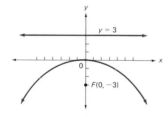

1

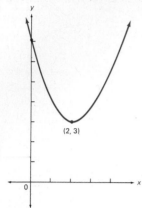

2

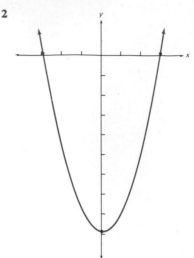

3 (a) $y = -5(x - 2)^2 + 19$; (b) $(2, 19)$; (c) $x = 2$; (d) domain: all real numbers; range: all $y \leq 19$.
4 $x = -\frac{1}{3}$, $x = 3$ **5** $2 - \sqrt{11}$, $2 + \sqrt{11}$ **6** 5; two irrational numbers.   **7** 169; two rational numbers.

8 Maximum $= 20$ at $x = -6$.   **9** 6 feet.   **10** 64 feet.   **11** (a)

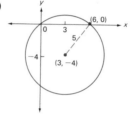

(b) $y = -\frac{3}{4}x + \frac{9}{2}$

12 $C(-\frac{1}{2}, 7)$; $r = 5$ **13** $\sqrt{106}$ **14** $(-1, -1)$; $\sqrt{20}$; $(x + 1)^2 + (y + 1)^2 = 20$
15 $(0, 2)$; $(4, 2)$; $(2 + \sqrt{3}, 1)$; $(2 - \sqrt{3}, 1)$
16 $\frac{(x + 2)^2}{1} - \frac{(y - 3)^2}{4} = 1$; a hyperbola with center at $(-2, 3)$, and vertices at $(-3, 3)$, and $(-1, 3)$.
17 $\frac{x^2}{16} + \frac{y^2}{9} = 1$ **18** $\frac{x^2}{36} - \frac{y^2}{28} = 1$

5.1   HINTS FOR GRAPHING (*Page 179*)

1
$y = (x - 3)^2$

3
$y = -x^3$

5
f g h

7
f g h
$(0, 0)$
$(1, -1)$
$(2, -2)$

9
$y = |(x + 1)^3|$

11
h
$(3, 2)$
f g

13 $y = (x - 3)^4 + 2$ **15** $y = |x + \frac{3}{4}|$ **17**

19
$y = (x + 1)^3$

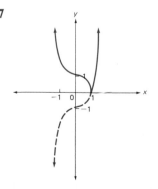

21

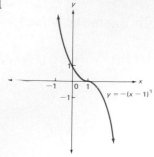

$y = -(x-1)^3$

23 $x^2 + 3x + 9$ **25** $4 + 6h + 4h^2 + h^3$

5.2   GRAPHING SOME SPECIAL RATIONAL FUNCTIONS (*Page 183*)

1

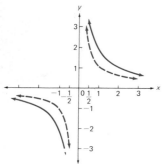

3

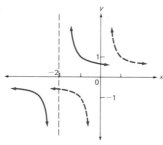

5

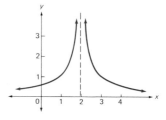

7

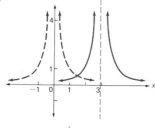

9 Asymptotes: $x = -4$, $y = -2$.

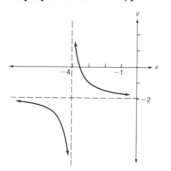

11 Asymptotes: $x = 2$, $y = 0$.

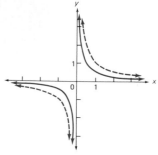

13 Asymptotes: $y = 0$; $x = 0$.

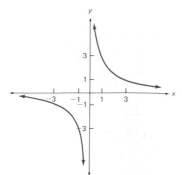

15 Asymptotes: $y = 0$; $x = 1$.

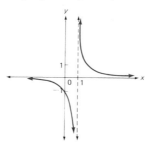

17

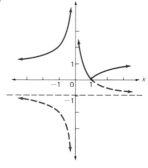

19 $-\dfrac{1}{3x}$

1 $f(x) < 0$ on both $(-\infty, 1)$ and $(2, 3)$; $f(x) > 0$ on both $(1, 2)$ and $(3, \infty)$.
3 $f(x) < 0$ on $(-\infty, -4)$ and $(\frac{1}{3}, 2)$; $f(x) > 0$ on $(-4, 0)$, $(0, \frac{1}{3})$, and $(2, \infty)$.   **5** $x < -1$ or $x > 4$
7 $x < -1$ or $\frac{1}{5} < x < 10$

9

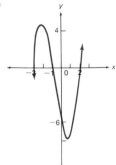

11

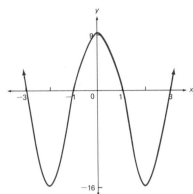

13

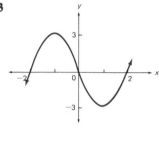

15

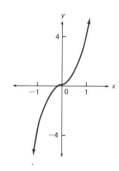

17

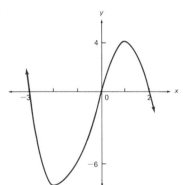

19

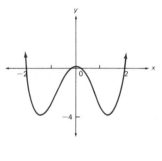

21

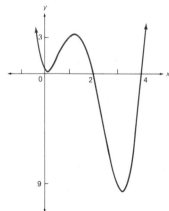

23 Asymptotes: $x = -2$; $x = 1$; $y = 0$.

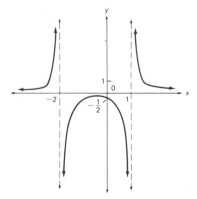

25 Asymptotes: $x = -2$; $x = 2$; $y = 0$.

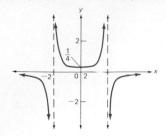

27 Asymptotes: $x = -1$; $x = 1$; $y = 0$.

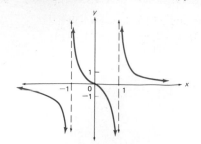

29 Asymptote: $y = 0$.

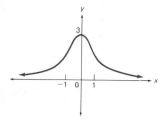

31 Asymptotes: $x = 2$; $y = 1$.

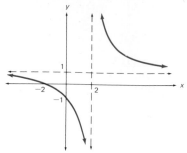

33 Asymptotes: $x = -3$; $y = 1$.

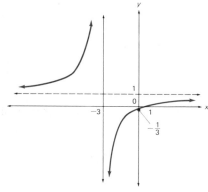

35 Asymptotes: $x = -4$; $x = 3$; $y = 1$.

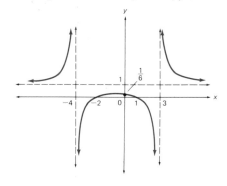

37 $g(x) = 6(x - 2)(x - 1)$; $g(x) > 0$ on both $(-\infty, 1)$ and $(2, \infty)$; $g(x) < 0$ on $(1, 2)$.

39 $g(x) = -\dfrac{x + 4}{x^3}$; $g(x) > 0$ on $(-4, 0)$; $g(x) < 0$ on both $(-\infty, -4)$ and $(0, \infty)$.

41 $g(x) = \dfrac{14(x - 5)}{(x + 2)^3}$; $g(x) > 0$ on both $(-\infty, -2)$ and $(5, \infty)$; $g(x) < 0$ on $(-2, 5)$.

5.4 EQUATIONS AND INEQUALITIES WITH FRACTIONS (*Page 192*)

1 $x = 20$ **3** $x = 4$ **5** $x = \frac{17}{4}$ **7** $x = 2$ **9** $x = 12$ **11** No solutions. **13** $x = -\frac{5}{2}$; $x = 2$ **15** $x = 1$; $x = 2$

17 $x = 20$ **19** $x = -3$; $x = 3$ **21** $x = -\frac{1}{2}$; $x = 3$ **23** $x = 5$; $x = \frac{10}{7}$ **25** $x = 7$; $x = -5$ **27** $m = \dfrac{2gK}{v^2}$

29 $r_1 = \dfrac{S}{\pi s} - r_2$ **31** $s = a + (n - 1)d$ **33** $m = \dfrac{fp}{p - f}$ **35** $x \le 30$ **37** $x < -1$ **39** $x > 10$ **41** $-3 < x < 0$

43 3 **45** $1\frac{5}{7}$ hours. **47** $\frac{2}{9}, \frac{4}{9}$ **49** 60 feet. **51** 19 **53** $\frac{2}{3}$

55 $\frac{a}{b} = \frac{c}{d}$ implies $ad = bc$. Then, $ad + bd = bc + bd$; $d(a + b) = b(c + d)$; therefore $\frac{a + b}{b} = \frac{c + d}{d}$.

57 110 paperbacks and 55 hardcover copies.

59 Use $\dfrac{4(4) + 4(3) + 3(3) + 1(2) + x(3)}{15} = 3.4$ to get $x = 4$; grade must be A. **61**

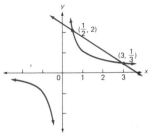

5.5 VARIATION (*Page 197*)

1 $P = 4s$; $k = 4$ **3** $A = 5l$; $k = 5$ **5** $z = kxy^3$ **7** $z = \dfrac{kx}{y^3}$ **9** $w = \dfrac{kx^2}{yz}$ **11** $\frac{1}{2}$ **13** $\frac{1}{5}$ **15** $\frac{2}{5}$ **17** $\frac{243}{8}$

19 27 feet. **21** 4 kilograms. **23** 75 kilograms. **25** 784 feet. **27** $\dfrac{32\pi}{3}$ cubic inches. **29** 5.12 ohms; 512 ohms.

31 (a) $s(y) = ky(\frac{25}{4} - y^2)$; (b) $s(x) = \frac{1}{2}kx^2\sqrt{25 - 4x^2}$; (c) $s\left(\dfrac{2.5}{\sqrt{2}}\right) = 5.52k$

5.6 SYNTHETIC DIVISION (*Page 202*)

1 $x^2 + x - 2$; $r = 0$ **3** $2x^2 - x - 2$; $r = 9$ **5** $x^2 + 7x + 7$; $r = 22$ **7** $x^3 - 5x^2 + 17x - 36$; $r = 73$
9 $2x^3 + 2x^2 - x + 3$; $r = 1$ **11** $x^2 + 3x + 9$; $r = 0$ **13** $x^2 - 3x + 9$; $r = 0$ **15** $x^3 + 2x^2 + 4x + 8$; $r = 0$
17 $x^3 - 2x^2 + 4x - 8$; $r = 32$ **19** $x^3 + \frac{1}{2}x^2 + \frac{5}{6}x + \frac{7}{12}$; $r = \frac{47}{60}$ **21** $x + 2$; $r = 0$
23 $N = Q \cdot D + R$; to obtain the dividend, multiply the quotient by the divisor and add the remainder.

5.7 THE REMAINDER AND FACTOR THEOREMS (*Page 205*)

1 8 **3** 59 **5** 0 **7** 1 **9** 67 **11** −4

For Exercises 13–23, use synthetic division to obtain $p(c) = 0$, showing $x - c$ to be a factor of $p(x)$. The remaining factors of $p(x)$ are obtained by factoring the quotient obtained in the synthetic division.
13 $(x + 1)(x + 2)(x + 3)$ **15** $(x - 2)(x + 3)(x + 4)$ **17** $-(x + 2)(x - 3)(x + 1)$
19 $(x - 5)(3x + 4)(2x - 1)$ **21** $(x + 2)^2(x + 1)(x - 1)$ **23** $x^2(x + 3)^2(x + 1)(x - 1)$ **25** −36 **27** 2

5.8 THE RATIONAL ROOT THEOREM (*Page 209*)

1 2; 3; −7 **3** $-\frac{1}{2}$; 4 **5** −1 **7** −3; $-\sqrt{2}$; $\sqrt{2}$ **9** −2; 3 **11** $-\sqrt{3}$; $\sqrt{3}$; 2; 3
13 −3; 3; $-2 - \sqrt{2}$; $-2 + \sqrt{2}$ **15** $-\frac{1}{3}$; 2; $\frac{5}{2}$ **17** $(x - 2)(x - 4)(x + 3)$ **19** $(x + 2)(x + 4)(x - 6)$
21 $(-2, -27)$; $(2, 1)$; $(3, 8)$ **23** $(-3, -161)$; $(5, 335)$; $(\frac{1}{3}, \frac{253}{27})$
25 By the rational root theorem, the only possible rational roots are: ± 1, $\pm\frac{1}{2}$, ± 2, ± 4, ± 8. Using synthetic division, we see that none of these are roots.

5.9 DECOMPOSING RATIONAL FUNCTIONS (*Page 214*)

1 $\dfrac{1}{x + 1} + \dfrac{1}{x - 1}$ **3** $\dfrac{2}{x - 3} - \dfrac{1}{x + 2}$ **5** $\dfrac{6}{x - 4} + \dfrac{3}{x - 2} - \dfrac{4}{x + 1}$ **7** $\dfrac{3}{x - 2} + \dfrac{3}{(x - 2)^2}$ **9** $\dfrac{6}{5x + 2} - \dfrac{3}{3x - 4}$

11 $\dfrac{1}{x - 2} + \dfrac{3}{(x - 2)^2} - \dfrac{2}{(x - 2)^3}$ **13** $x + \dfrac{1}{x - 1} - \dfrac{1}{x + 1}$ **15** $3x^2 + 1 + \dfrac{1}{2x - 1} - \dfrac{3}{(2x - 1)^2}$

17 $10x - 5 + \dfrac{6}{x - 3} + \dfrac{14}{x + 2}$ **19** $x^2 - 1 - \dfrac{1}{x - 1} + \dfrac{2}{(x - 1)^2} + \dfrac{6}{(x - 1)^3}$

1 No asymptotes.

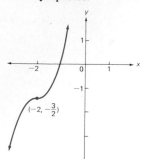

2 No asymptotes.

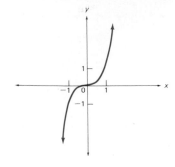

3 Asymptotes: $x = 2$, $y = 0$.

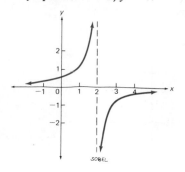

4 Asymptotes: $x = -1$, $x = 2$, $y = 0$.

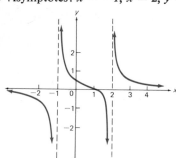

5

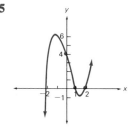

6 $f(x) < 0$ on both $(-\infty, -3)$ and $(0, 2)$;
$f(x) > 0$ on both $(-3, 0)$ and $(2, \infty)$.

7 $-\frac{3}{2}$; 2   **8** $x < -\frac{14}{3}$ **9** $5\frac{5}{7}$ feet.   **10** 90 minutes.   **11** $z = 2$ **12** $V = 288\pi$ cubic inches.

13 $-3\,\big|\,2 + 5 + 0 -\ \ 1 - 21 + \ 7$ \qquad quotient: $2x^4 - x^3 + 3x^2 - 10x + 9$
$\underline{\hphantom{-3\,\big|\,} -6 + 3 -\ \ 9 + 30 - 27}$ \qquad remainder: -20
$\hphantom{-3\,\big|\,} 2 - 1 + 3 - 10 + \ 9\,\big|\,{-20}$

14 **(a)** When $p(x)$ is divided by $x - \frac{1}{3}$, the remainder is $\frac{2}{3}$. Then, by the remainder theorem, we have $p(\frac{1}{3}) = \frac{2}{3}$.
(b) Since $p(\frac{1}{3}) \neq 0$, the factor theorem says that $x - \frac{1}{3}$ is not a factor of $p(x)$.

15 $2\,\big|\,1 - 4 + 7 - 12 + 12$
$\underline{\hphantom{2\,\big|\,} +2 - 4 + \ \ 6 - 12}$
$\hphantom{2\,\big|\,} 1 - 2 + 3 - \ \ 6\,\big|\,{+ \ \ 0} = r$
Since $r = 0$, $x - 2$ is a factor of $p(x)$, and we get
$$p(x) = (x - 2)(x^3 - 2x^2 + 3x - 6) = (x - 2)[x^2(x - 2) + 3(x - 2)] = (x - 2)(x^2 + 3)(x - 2)$$
$$= (x - 2)^2(x^2 + 3)$$

16 $(x + 3)^2(x^2 - x + 1)$ **17** $(2, 8)$; $(3, 27)$; $(-5, -125)$ **18** $\dfrac{2}{x + 5} - \dfrac{1}{x - 5}$

6.1   GRAPHING SOME SPECIAL RADICAL FUNCTIONS (*Page 223*)

1

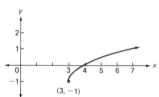

3

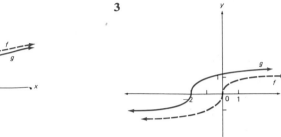

5

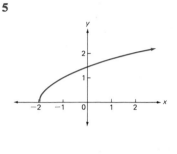

7 Domain: $x \geq 3$.

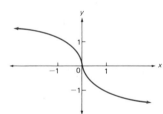

9 Domain: $x \leq 0$.

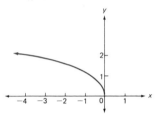

11 Domain: all real x.

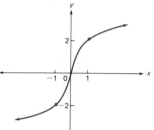

13 Domain: all real x.

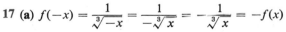

15 Domain: $x > 0$.
Asymptotes: $x = 0, y = -1$.

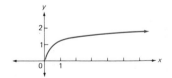

17 (a) $f(-x) = \dfrac{1}{\sqrt[3]{-x}} = \dfrac{1}{-\sqrt[3]{x}} = -\dfrac{1}{\sqrt[3]{x}} = -f(x)$

(b) All $x \neq 0$.

(c)

x	$\frac{1}{27}$	$\frac{1}{8}$	1	8
y	3	2	1	$\frac{1}{2}$

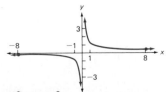

(d) $x = 0; y = 0$

19 $y = \sqrt[4]{x}$ is equivalent to $y^4 = x$ for $x \geq 0$.

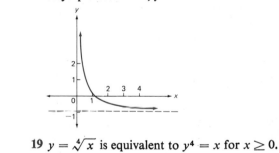

21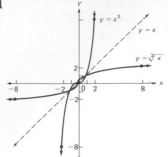

23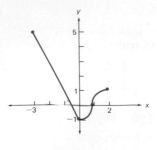

25 $\dfrac{\sqrt{4+h}-2}{h} = \dfrac{(\sqrt{4+h}-2)(\sqrt{4+h}+2)}{h(\sqrt{4+h}+2)} = \dfrac{4+h-4}{h(\sqrt{4+h}+2)} = \dfrac{1}{\sqrt{4+h}+2}$

27 (a) $d(x) = \sqrt{25+x^2} + \sqrt{100+(20-x)^2}$; (b) $t(x) = \dfrac{\sqrt{25+x^2}}{12} + \dfrac{\sqrt{100+(20-x)^2}}{10}$

29 $d(x) = \sqrt{x^2 + (6-3x)^2}$

6.2 RADICAL EQUATIONS (*Page 228*)

1 17; domain: $x \geq 1$. **3** $-2, 0$; domain: $x \leq -2$ or $x \geq 0$. **5** $-1, 6$; domain: $x \leq -1$ or $x \geq 6$. **7** $x = 10$
9 $x = 5$ **11** $x = \pm 10$ **13** No solution. **15** $x = 2$ **17** $x = \frac{2}{3}$ **19** $x = \frac{5}{16}$ **21** $x = 9$ **23** $x = 4$ **25** $x = 4$

27 $x = 0, x = 8$ **29** $x = \frac{27}{8}$ **31**

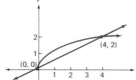

33 $x = \sqrt{16 - y^2}$ **35** $f = -\dfrac{\sqrt{y}}{\sqrt{x}}$

37 $(9, 3)$ **39** $S = \dfrac{10}{h} + 2\sqrt{5\pi h}$

6.3 DETERMINING THE SIGNS OF RADICAL FUNCTIONS (*Page 232*)

1 (a) $x \geq 2$; (b) $f(x) > 0$ for all $x > 2$; (c) 2. **3** (a) All real x; (b) $f(x) > 0$ for all $x \neq 2$; (c) 2.
5 (a) All $x > 0$; (b) $f(x) > 0$ for $x > 0$; (c) none.
7 (a) All $x \neq 0$; (b) $f(x) < 0$ on both $(-\infty, -4)$, $(0, 2)$; $f(x) > 0$ on both $(-4, 0)$ $(2, \infty)$; (c) $-4, 2$.
9 (a) $-3 \leq x \leq 3, x \neq 0$; (b) $f(x) < 0$ on $(-3, 0)$; $f(x) > 0$ on $(0, 3)$; (c) $-3, 3$.

11 $x^{1/2} + (x-4)\dfrac{1}{2}x^{-1/2} = x^{1/2} + \dfrac{x-4}{2x^{1/2}} = \dfrac{2x+x-4}{2\sqrt{x}} = \dfrac{3x-4}{2\sqrt{x}}$

13 $\dfrac{1}{2}(4-x^2)^{-1/2}(-2x) = \dfrac{-2x}{2(4-x^2)^{1/2}} = -\dfrac{x}{\sqrt{4-x^2}}$

15 $\dfrac{x}{3(x-1)^{2/3}} + (x-1)^{1/3} = \dfrac{x+3(x-1)}{3(x-1)^{2/3}} = \dfrac{4x-3}{3(\sqrt[3]{x-1})^2}$

17 $\dfrac{x}{(5x-6)^{4/5}} + (5x-6)^{1/5} = \dfrac{x+(5x-6)}{(5x-6)^{4/5}} = \dfrac{6(x-1)}{(5x-6)^{4/5}}$

19 $f(x) = \dfrac{x-1}{\sqrt{x}}$; $f(x) < 0$ on $(0, 1)$, $f(x) > 0$ on $(1, \infty)$.

21 $f(x) = \dfrac{3(x-3)}{2\sqrt{x}}$; $f(x) < 0$ on $(0, 3)$, $f(x) > 0$ on $(3, \infty)$. **23** $f(x) = \dfrac{x(5x-8)}{2\sqrt{x-2}}$; $f(x) > 0$ on $(2, \infty)$.

1 (a) $-1, 5, 4$; (b) $5x - 1$, all reals; (c) 4.   **3** (a) $-2, \frac{7}{2}, -7$; (b) $6x^2 - 5x - 6$, all reals; (c) -7.

5 (a) 2, 1; (b) $6x + 1$, all reals; (c) 1.   **7** (a) $x^2 + \sqrt{x}$; $x \geq 0$; (b) $x^{3/2}$; $x > 0$; (c) x; $x \geq 0$.

9 (a) $x^3 - 1 + \frac{1}{x}$; all $x \neq 0$; (b) $x^4 - x$; all $x \neq 0$; (c) $\frac{1}{x^3} - 1$; all $x \neq 0$.

11 (a) $x^2 + 6x + 8 + \sqrt{x - 2}$; $x \geq 2$; (b) $\frac{x^2 + 6x + 8}{\sqrt{x - 2}}$; $x > 2$; (c) $x + 6 + 6\sqrt{x - 2}$; $x \geq 2$

13 (a) $6x - 6$, all reals; (b) $-8x^2 + 22x - 5$, all reals; (c) $-8x + 19$, all reals.

15 (a) $\frac{1}{2x} - 2x^2 + 1$, all $x \neq 0$; (b) $x - \frac{1}{2x}$, all $x \neq 0$; (c) $\frac{1}{4x^2 - 2}$, all $x \neq \pm \frac{1}{\sqrt{2}}$.

17 $(f \circ g)(x) = (x - 1)^2$; $(g \circ f)(x) = x^2 - 1$ **19** $(f \circ g)(x) = \frac{x + 3}{3 - x}$; $(g \circ f)(x) = 4 - \frac{6}{x}$

21 $(f \circ g)(x) = x^2$; $(g \circ f)x = x^2 + 2x$ **23** $(f \circ g)(x) = 2$; $(g \circ f)(x) = 4$

25 (a) $\frac{1}{2\sqrt[3]{x} - 1}$; (b) $\frac{2}{\sqrt[3]{x}} - 1$; (c) $\frac{1}{\sqrt[3]{2x - 1}}$ **27** $(f \circ f)(x) = x$; $(f \circ f \circ f)(x) = \frac{1}{x}$ **29** $g(x) = \sqrt[3]{x}$

31 $x^2 - 2x$

(Other answers are possible for Exercises 1–23.)

1 $g(x) = 3x + 1$; $f(x) = x^2$ **3** $g(x) = 1 - 4x$; $f(x) = \sqrt{x}$ **5** $g(x) = \frac{x + 1}{x - 1}$; $f(x) = x^2$

7 $g(x) = 3x^2 - 1$; $f(x) = x^{-3}$ **9** $g(x) = \frac{x}{x - 1}$; $f(x) = \sqrt{x}$ **11** $g(x) = (x^2 - x - 1)^3$; $f(x) = \sqrt{x}$

13 $g(x) = 4 - x^2$; $f(x) = \frac{2}{\sqrt{x}}$ **15** $f(x) = 2x + 1$; $g(x) = x^{1/2}$; $h(x) = x^3$

17 $f(x) = \frac{x}{x + 1}$; $g(x) = x^5$; $h(x) = x^{1/2}$ **19** $f(x) = x^2 - 9$; $g(x) = x^2$; $h(x) = x^{1/3}$

21 $f(x) = x^2 - 4x + 7$; $g(x) = x^3$; $h(x) = -\sqrt{x}$ **23** $f(x) = 2x - 11$; $g(x) = 1 + \sqrt{x}$; $h(x) = x^2$

25 $f(x) = (x + 1)^2$

1 Domain: all reals.

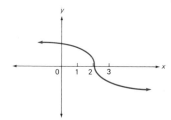

2 Domain: $x > 0$.

Asymptotes: $y = 2$, $x = 0$.

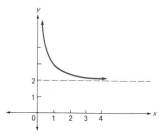

3 $\frac{2}{9}$ **4** $-\frac{64}{27}$; $\frac{1}{8}$.   **5** $x = 16$

6 $(x + 1)^{1/2}(2x) + (x + 1)^{-1/2}\left(\frac{x^2}{2}\right) = 2x(x + 1)^{1/2} + \frac{x^2}{2(x + 1)^{1/2}} = \frac{4x(x + 1) + x^2}{2\sqrt{x + 1}} = \frac{5x^2 + 4x}{2\sqrt{x + 1}} = \frac{x(5x + 4)}{2\sqrt{x + 1}}$

7 $f(x) < 0$ on $(2, 4)$; $f(x) > 0$ on $(-\infty, 2)$ and $(4, \infty)$.   **8** $f(x) < 0$ on $(0, 4)$; $f(x) > 0$ on $(4, \infty)$.

9 $(f - g)(x) = \frac{1}{x^2 - 1} - \sqrt{x + 2}$; all $x \geq -2$ and $x \neq \pm 1$. $\frac{f}{g}(x) = \frac{1}{(x^2 - 1)\sqrt{x + 2}}$; all $x > -2$ and $x \neq \pm 1$.

10 $(f \circ g)(x) = \dfrac{1}{1-x}$; all $x > 0$ and $x \neq 1$. $(g \circ f)(x) = \dfrac{1}{\sqrt{1-x^2}}$; $-1 < x < 1$.

(Other answers are possible for Exercises 11 and 12.)

11 $g(x) = x - 2$; $f(x) = x^{2/3}$ **12** $h(x) = 2x - 1$; $g(x) = x^{3/2}$; $f(x) = \dfrac{1}{x}$ **13** (d)

14 All real numbers; $x = -3$, $x = 0$.   **15** $(2, 2), (10, 6)$

CHAPTER 7: EXPONENTIAL AND LOGARITHMIC FUNCTIONS

7.1 INVERSE FUNCTIONS (*Page 247*)

1 Not one-to-one.   **3** One-to-one.   **5** One-to-one.

7 $(f \circ g)(x) = \frac{1}{3}(3x + 9) - 3 = x$ **9** $(f \circ g)(x) = (\sqrt[3]{x} - 1 + 1)^3 = x$ **11** $(f \circ g)(x) = \dfrac{1}{\dfrac{1}{x} + 1 - 1} = x$
  $(g \circ f)(x) = 3(\frac{1}{3}x - 3) + 9 = x$ $(g \circ f)(x) = \sqrt[3]{(x + 1)^3} - 1 = x$

$$(g \circ f)(x) = \dfrac{1}{\dfrac{1}{x-1}} + 1 = x$$

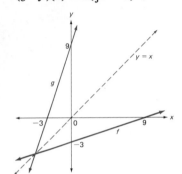
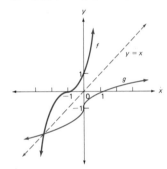
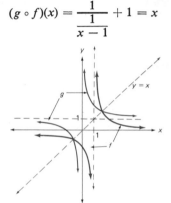

13 $g(x) = \sqrt[3]{x} + 5$ **15** $g(x) = \frac{3}{2}x + \frac{3}{2}$ **17** $g(x) = \sqrt[5]{x} + 1$ **19** $g(x) = x^{5/3}$ **21** $g(x) = 2 + \dfrac{2}{x}$

23 $g(x) = \dfrac{1}{\sqrt[5]{x}}$ **25** $(f \circ f)(x) = f(f(x)) = f\left(\dfrac{1}{x}\right) = \dfrac{1}{\dfrac{1}{x}} = x$

27 $(f \circ f)(x) = f(f(x)) = f\left(\dfrac{x}{x-1}\right) = \dfrac{\dfrac{x}{x-1}}{\dfrac{x}{x-1} - 1} = \dfrac{x}{x - (x-1)} = x$

29 $g(x) = \sqrt{x} - 1$ **31** $g(x) = \dfrac{1}{x^2}$ **33** $g(x) = \sqrt{x + 4}$

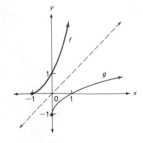
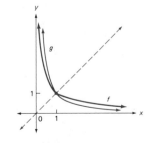
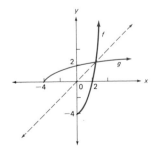

35 $y = mx + k$, where $m = -1$.

7.2 EXPONENTIAL FUNCTIONS (*Page 252*)

1
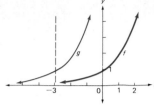

3
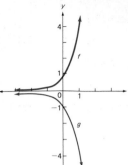

5
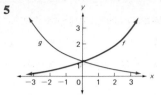

7
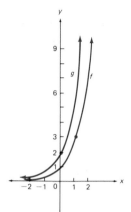

9
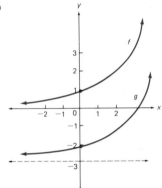

11
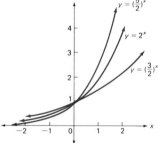

13
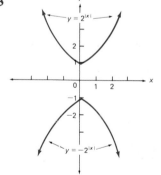

15 6 **17** ±3 **19** 1 **21** −2; 1 **23** −5 **25** $\frac{1}{2}$ **27** $\frac{3}{2}$ **29** $-\frac{1}{2}$ **31** $\frac{2}{3}$ **33**

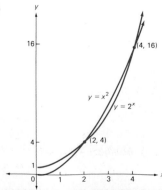

35 (a) $\sqrt{2} = 1.414213\ldots$

x	1.4	1.41	1.414	1.4142	1.41421
3^x	4.6555	4.7070	4.7277	4.7287	4.7288

(b) $\sqrt{3} = 1.732050\ldots$

x	1.7	1.73	1.732	1.7320	1.73205
3^x	6.4730	6.6899	6.7046	6.7046	6.7050

(c) $\sqrt{5} = 2.236068\ldots$

x	2.2	2.23	2.236	2.2360	2.23606
2^x	4.5948	4.6913	4.7109	4.7109	4.71109

(d) $\pi = 3.141592\ldots$

x	3.1	3.14	3.141	3.1415	3.14159
4^x	73.5167	77.7085	77.8163	77.8702	77.8799

37 $x = \frac{1}{2}$

7.3 LOGARITHMIC FUNCTIONS (*Page 256*)

1 $g(x) = \log_4 x$

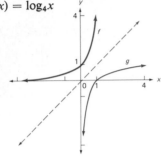

3 $g(x) = \log_{1/3} x$

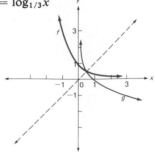

5 Shift 2 units left; $x > -2$; $x = -2$.   **7** Shift 2 units upward; $x > 0$; $x = 0$.

9

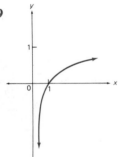

11

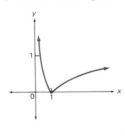

13

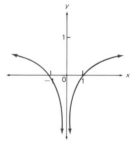

15 $\log_2 256 = 8$ **17** $\log_{1/3} 3 = -1$ **19** $\log_{17} 1 = 0$ **21** $10^{-4} = 0.0001$ **23** $(\sqrt{2})^2 = 2$ **25** $12^{-3} = \frac{1}{1728}$
27 4   **29** -3 **31** $\frac{1}{216}$ **33** 5   **35** 4   **37** $\frac{1}{3}$ **39** $\frac{2}{3}$ **41** 9   **43** -2 **45** $-\frac{1}{3}$ **47** 9   **49** -1
51 $g(x) = 3^x - 3$, $(f \circ g)(x) = \log_3(3^x - 3 + 3) = \log_3 3^x = x$; $(g \circ f)(x) = 3^{\log_3(x+3)} - 3 = (x + 3) - 3 = x$

7.4 THE LAWS OF LOGARITHMS (*Page 261*)

1 $\log_b 3 + \log_b x - \log_b(x + 1)$ **3** $\frac{1}{2}\log_b(x^2 - 1) - \log_b x = \frac{1}{2}\log_b(x + 1) + \frac{1}{2}\log_b(x - 1) - \log_b x$
5 $-2\log_b x$ **7** $\log_b \dfrac{x + 1}{x + 2}$ **9** $\log_b \sqrt{\dfrac{x^2 - 1}{x^2 + 1}}$ **11** $\log_b \dfrac{x^3}{2(x + 5)}$

13 $\log_b 27 + \log_b 3 = \log_b 81$ (Law 1)
   $\log_b 243 - \log_b 3 = \log_b 81$ (Law 2)

15 $-2\log_b \frac{4}{9} = \log_b(\frac{4}{9})^{-2}$ (Law 3)
   $= \log_b \frac{81}{16}$

17 (a) 0.6020; (b) 0.9030; (c) -0.3010 **19** (a) 1.6811; (b) -0.1761; (c) 2.0970
21 (a) 0.2330; (b) 1.9515; (c) 1.4771   **23** 20   **25** $\frac{1}{20}$ **27** 17   **29** 8   **31** 2   **33** 7   **35** 1.01   **37** 5

39 Let $r = \log_b M$ and $s = \log_b N$. Then $b^r = M$ and $b^s = N$. Divide:

$$\frac{M}{N} = \frac{b^r}{b^s} = b^{r-s}$$

Convert to log form and substitute:

$$\log_b \frac{M}{N} = r - s = \log_b M - \log_b N$$

41 $-1; 0$.   **43** 8

45 $B^{\log_B N} = N$

$$\log_b B^{\log_B N} = \log_b N \qquad \text{(take log base } b)$$

$$(\log_B N)(\log_b B) = \log_b N \qquad \text{(Law 3)}$$

$$\log_B N = \frac{\log_b N}{\log_b B} \qquad \text{(divide by } \log_b B)$$

7.5   THE BASE e (Page 266)

1
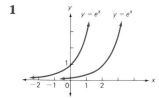

3
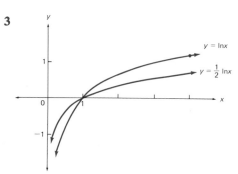

5
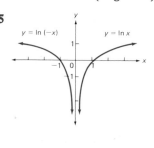

7
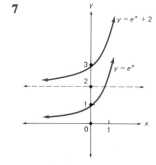

9
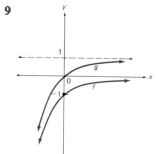

11
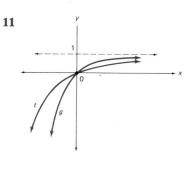

13 Since $f(x) = 1 + \ln x$, shift one unit upward.   **15** Since $f(x) = \frac{1}{2} \ln x$, multiply the ordinates by $\frac{1}{2}$.
17 Since $f(x) = \ln(x - 1)$, shift one unit to the right.   **19** $x > -2$ **21** $x > \frac{1}{2}$ **23** All $x > 1$ except for $x = 2$.
25 $\ln 5 + \ln x - \ln(x^2 - 4) = \ln 5 + \ln x - \ln(x + 2) - \ln(x - 2)$
27 $\ln(x - 1) + 2\ln(x + 3) - \frac{1}{2}\ln(x^2 + 2)$ **29** $\frac{3}{2}\ln x + \frac{1}{2}\ln(x + 1)$ **31** $\ln \sqrt{x}\,(x^2 + 5)$ **33** $\ln(x^2 - 1)^3$
35 $\ln \dfrac{\sqrt{x}}{(x - 1)^2 \sqrt[3]{x^2 + 1}}$ **37** $\sqrt{x}$ **39** $\dfrac{1}{x^2}$ **41** 1   **43** $x = -100 \ln 27$ **45** $x = \frac{1}{3}$ **47** $x = 0$ **49** $x = 8$
51 $x = 3$ **53** $x = 8$ **55** $x = \dfrac{e^2}{1 + e^2}$

57

n	2	10	100	500	1000	5000	10000
$\left(1 + \frac{1}{n}\right)^n$	2.2500	2.5937	2.7048	2.7156	2.7169	2.7181	2.7181

(Other answers are possible for Exercises 59–67.)

59 Let $g(x) = -x^2 + x$ and $f(x) = e^x$. Then $(f \circ g)(x) = f(g(x)) = f(-x^2 + x) = e^{-x^2+x} = h(x)$.

61 Let $g(x) = \dfrac{x}{x+1}$ and $f(x) = \ln x$. Then $(f \circ g)(x) = f(g(x)) = f\left(\dfrac{x}{x+1}\right) = \ln \dfrac{x}{x+1} = h(x)$.

63 Let $g(x) = \ln x$ and $f(x) = \sqrt[3]{x}$. Then $(f \circ g)(x) = f(g(x)) = f(\ln x) = \sqrt[3]{\ln x} = h(x)$.

65 Let $h(x) = 3x - 1$, $g(x) = x^2$, and $f(x) = e^x$. Then
$$(f \circ g \circ h)(x) = f(g(h(x))) = f(g(3x - 1)) = f((3x - 1)^2) = e^{(3x-1)^2} = F(x)$$

67 Let $h(x) = e^x + 1$, $g(x) = \sqrt{x}$, and $f(x) = \ln x$. Then
$$(f \circ g \circ h)(x) = f(g(h(x))) = f(g(e^x + 1)) = f(\sqrt{e^x + 1}) = \ln \sqrt{e^x + 1} = F(x)$$

69 $f(x) > 0$ on the interval $(-\infty, \frac{1}{2})$; $f(x) < 0$ on the interval $(\frac{1}{2}, \infty)$.

71 $f(x) > 0$ on the interval $\left(\frac{1}{e}, \infty\right)$; $f(x) < 0$ on the interval $\left(0, \frac{1}{e}\right)$.

73 $\ln\left(\dfrac{x}{4} - \dfrac{\sqrt{x^2 - 4}}{4}\right) = \ln\left(\dfrac{x - \sqrt{x^2 - 4}}{4}\right) = \ln\left(\dfrac{x - \sqrt{x^2 - 4}}{4} \cdot \dfrac{x + \sqrt{x^2 - 4}}{x + \sqrt{x^2 - 4}}\right)$

$\qquad = \ln\left(\dfrac{x^2 - (x^2 - 4)}{4(x + \sqrt{x^2 - 4})}\right) = \ln\left(\dfrac{1}{x + \sqrt{x^2 - 4}}\right) = -\ln(x + \sqrt{x^2 - 4})$

75 $x = \ln(y + \sqrt{y^2 + 1})$

7.6 EXPONENTIAL GROWTH AND DECAY (*Page 271*)

(These answers were found using Tables II and III. Using a calculator may result in slightly different answers in some cases.)

1 2010 **3** 27 **5** $\frac{1}{2} \ln 100$ **7** $\frac{1}{4} \ln \frac{1}{3}$ **9** 667,000 **11** 1.83 days. **13** 17.31 years.
15 (a) $\frac{1}{5} \ln \frac{4}{3}$; (b) 6.4 grams; (c) 15.5 years. **17** 93.2 seconds. **19** 18.47 years. **21** 4200 years. **23** 114,000 years.

7.7 SCIENTIFIC NOTATION (*Page 273*)

1 4.68×10^3 **3** 9.2×10^{-1} **5** 7.583×10^6 **7** 2.5×10^1 **9** 5.55×10^{-7} **11** 2.024×10^2 **13** 78,900
15 3000 **17** 0.174 **19** 17.4 **21** 0.0906 **23** 10^2 **25** 10^0 **27** 10^{17} **29** 2000 **31** 400 **33** 0.02 **35** 3125
37 1200 **39** 0.000008 **41** 0.0125 **43** 500 seconds.

7.8 COMMON LOGARITHMS (*Page 278*)

(These answers were found using Table IV. If a calculator is used for the common logarithms, then some of these answers will be slightly different.)

1 43,000,000 **3** 2770 **5** 0.000125 **7** 1.22 **9** 0.00887 **11** 6.58 **13** \$1.21 per gallon. **15** 2.27 years.
17 \$4050
19 For $1 \le x < 10$ we get $\log 1 \le \log x < \log 10$ because $f(x) = \log x$ is an increasing function. Substituting $0 = \log 1$ and $1 = \log 10$ into the preceding inequality gives $0 \le \log x < 1$.
21 (a) 2.825; (b) 9.273; (c) 1.378; (d) 5.489; (e) 4.495; (f) 7.497; (g) 1.021; (h) 9.508; (i) 2.263.

SAMPLE TEST QUESTIONS FOR CHAPTER 7 (*Page 281*)

1 (i) a; (ii) c; (iii) e; (iv) h; (v) d; (vi) b. **2** Each range value corresponds to exactly one domain value.
3 $g(x) = (x + 1)^3$; $(f \circ g)(x) = f(g(x)) = f((x + 1)^3) = \sqrt[3]{(x + 1)^3} - 1 = x$ **4** (a) $\frac{1}{2}$; (b) 9 **5** (a) $\frac{2}{3}$; (b) -2.
6 All real values x; $y = -4$. **7** All $x > -4$; $x = -4$. **8** 5 **9**

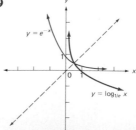

10 $3 \ln x - \ln(x + 1) - \frac{1}{2} \ln(x^2 + 2)$ **11** $\dfrac{\ln 5}{2 \ln 4}$ **12** $25 \ln 2$ **13** 6   **14** 1,330,000   **15** $x = \dfrac{e - 2}{e + 2}$

CHAPTER 8: TRIGONOMETRY

8.1   TRIGONOMETRIC RATIOS (*Page 288*)

	$\sin \theta$	$\cos \theta$	$\tan \theta$	$\cot \theta$	$\sec \theta$	$\csc \theta$
1	$\dfrac{8}{17}$	$\dfrac{15}{17}$	$\dfrac{8}{15}$	$\dfrac{15}{8}$	$\dfrac{17}{15}$	$\dfrac{17}{8}$
3	$\dfrac{\sqrt{3}}{2}$	$\dfrac{1}{2}$	$\sqrt{3}$	$\dfrac{1}{\sqrt{3}}$	2	$\dfrac{2}{\sqrt{3}}$
5	$\dfrac{12}{13}$	$\dfrac{5}{13}$	$\dfrac{12}{5}$	$\dfrac{5}{12}$	$\dfrac{13}{5}$	$\dfrac{13}{12}$

7

9

11

	$\sin A$	$\cos A$	$\tan A$	$\cot A$	$\sec A$	$\csc A$
13	$\dfrac{3}{5}$	$\dfrac{4}{5}$	$\dfrac{3}{4}$	$\dfrac{4}{3}$	$\dfrac{5}{4}$	$\dfrac{5}{3}$
15	$\dfrac{4}{\sqrt{41}}$	$\dfrac{5}{\sqrt{41}}$	$\dfrac{4}{5}$	$\dfrac{5}{4}$	$\dfrac{\sqrt{41}}{5}$	$\dfrac{\sqrt{41}}{4}$
17	$\dfrac{1}{\sqrt{5}}$	$\dfrac{2}{\sqrt{5}}$	$\dfrac{1}{2}$	2	$\dfrac{\sqrt{5}}{2}$	$\sqrt{5}$
19	$\dfrac{3}{4}$	$\dfrac{\sqrt{7}}{4}$	$\dfrac{3}{\sqrt{7}}$	$\dfrac{\sqrt{7}}{3}$	$\dfrac{4}{\sqrt{7}}$	$\dfrac{4}{3}$
21	$\dfrac{\sqrt{21}}{5}$	$\dfrac{2}{5}$	$\dfrac{\sqrt{21}}{2}$	$\dfrac{2}{\sqrt{21}}$	$\dfrac{5}{2}$	$\dfrac{5}{\sqrt{21}}$
23	$\dfrac{21}{29}$	$\dfrac{20}{29}$	$\dfrac{21}{20}$	$\dfrac{20}{21}$	$\dfrac{29}{20}$	$\dfrac{29}{21}$
	$\cos B$	$\sin B$	$\cot B$	$\tan B$	$\csc B$	$\sec B$

25 1   **27** $\dfrac{x^2}{z^2}$ **29** 1   **31** 1

33 $\cos A = \dfrac{\sqrt{7}}{4}$; $\tan A = \dfrac{3}{\sqrt{7}}$; $\cot A = \dfrac{\sqrt{7}}{3}$; $\sec A = \dfrac{4}{\sqrt{7}}$; $\csc A = \dfrac{4}{3}$

35 $\sin A = \dfrac{9}{41}$; $\cos A = \dfrac{40}{41}$; $\cot A = \dfrac{40}{9}$; $\sec A = \dfrac{41}{40}$; $\csc A = \dfrac{41}{9}$

37 $\sin B = \dfrac{3}{\sqrt{11}}$; $\cos B = \dfrac{\sqrt{2}}{\sqrt{11}}$; $\tan A = \dfrac{3}{\sqrt{2}}$; $\cot A = \dfrac{\sqrt{2}}{3}$; $\csc A = \dfrac{\sqrt{11}}{3}$

39 $(\sin A)(\cos A) = (\sqrt{1 - x^2})(x) = x\sqrt{1 - x^2}$ **41** $\dfrac{4\sin^2 A}{\cos A} = \dfrac{4\left(\dfrac{x}{4}\right)^2}{\dfrac{\sqrt{16 - x^2}}{4}} = \dfrac{x^2}{\sqrt{16 - x^2}}$

43 $(\sin\theta)(\tan\theta) = \left(\dfrac{x}{2}\right)\left(\dfrac{x}{\sqrt{4 - x^2}}\right) = \dfrac{x^2}{2\sqrt{4 - x^2}}$ **45** $(\tan^2\theta)(\cos^2\theta) = \left(\dfrac{x}{4}\right)^2\left(\dfrac{4}{\sqrt{x^2 + 16}}\right)^2 = \dfrac{x^2}{x^2 + 16}$

47 $A(s) = \dfrac{\sqrt{3}}{4}s^2$ **49** $A(x) = 2(9 - x^2)$ **51** $A(x) = \dfrac{\sqrt{3}}{36}x^2 + \dfrac{(100 - x)^2}{4\pi}$

8.2   ANGLE MEASURE (*Page 294*)

1 $\dfrac{\pi}{4}$ **3** $\dfrac{\pi}{2}$ **5** $\dfrac{3\pi}{2}$ **7** $\dfrac{5\pi}{6}$ **9** $\dfrac{5\pi}{4}$ **11** $\dfrac{7\pi}{6}$ **13** $\dfrac{11\pi}{6}$ **15** $\dfrac{5\pi}{12}$ **17** $\dfrac{5\pi}{9}$; 1.75 **19** $\dfrac{17\pi}{9}$; 5.95 **21** 180° **23** 360°

25 100° **27** 120° **29** 225° **31** 300° **33** 50° **35** 12°; 12.0° **37** $\left(\dfrac{540}{\pi}\right)°$; 171.9° **39** $\dfrac{\sqrt{2}}{2}$ **41** $\dfrac{\sqrt{3}}{3}$

43 $s = 2\pi$ **45** $\theta = \dfrac{\pi}{2}$ **47** $r = 6$ **49** 12π square centimeters. **51** 54π square centimeters.

53 126π square centimeters. **55** 8 square inches. **57** $\dfrac{\pi}{2}$; 1.6 **59** 11° **61** 150.7 **63** $\dfrac{1225\pi}{6}$ square feet.

8.3   RIGHT TRIANGLE TRIGONOMETRY (*Page 301*)

1 $x = \dfrac{25}{\sqrt{3}}$ **3** $x = 15\sqrt{2}$ **5** $x = 20\sqrt{3}$ **7** $x = \dfrac{8}{\sqrt{3}}$ **9** $\theta = \dfrac{\pi}{4}$

11 $\sin\theta = .5783$; $\cos\theta = .8158$; $\tan\theta = .7089$; $\cot\theta = 1.411$; $\sec\theta = 1.226$; $\csc\theta = 1.729$ **13** .6691

15 .2126 **17** 57.30 **19** .0465 **21** 1.006 **23** 1.060 **25** 81°00′ = 1.4137 radians. **27** 46°10′ = .8058 radians.
29 6°20′ = .1105 radians. **31** 12.7 **33** 18.2 **35** 71°30′ **37** 21°10′ **39** 35 meters. **41** 274.7 feet. **43** 1925 feet.
45 79°50′ **47** 12.3 **49** 1028 feet using the cotangent ratio; 1029 feet using the tangent ratio.

8.4   EXTENDING THE DEFINITIONS (*Page 309*)

1 (a) I; $\phi = 73°$; (b) −287° **3** (a) II; $\phi = 40°$; (b) −220° **5** (a) III; $\phi = \dfrac{\pi}{4}$; (b) $-\dfrac{3\pi}{4}$

7 (a) IV; $\phi = 73°$; (b) 287° **9** (a) III; $\phi = 49°50′$; (b) 229° 50′ **11** (a) I; $\phi = \dfrac{\pi}{3}$; (b) $\dfrac{\pi}{3}$

13 $\sin\dfrac{2\pi}{3} = \dfrac{\sqrt{3}}{2}$; $\cot\dfrac{2\pi}{3} = -\dfrac{\sqrt{3}}{3}$ **15** $\sin\left(-\dfrac{7\pi}{4}\right) = \dfrac{\sqrt{2}}{2}$; $\cot\left(-\dfrac{7\pi}{4}\right) = 1$ **17** Ratios are the same as in Exercise 15.

$\cos\dfrac{2\pi}{3} = -\dfrac{1}{2}$; $\sec\dfrac{2\pi}{3} = -2$ $\cos\left(-\dfrac{7\pi}{4}\right) = \dfrac{\sqrt{2}}{2}$; $\sec\left(-\dfrac{7\pi}{4}\right) = \sqrt{2}$

$\tan\dfrac{2\pi}{3} = -\sqrt{3}$; $\csc\dfrac{2\pi}{3} = \dfrac{2\sqrt{3}}{3}$ $\tan\left(-\dfrac{7\pi}{4}\right) = 1$; $\csc\left(-\dfrac{7\pi}{4}\right) = \sqrt{2}$

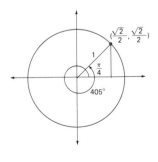

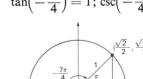

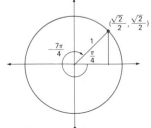

19 $(0, -1)$ **21** $(0, 1)$ **23** .8391   **25** $-.9877$ **27** Undefined.   **29** 0   **31** Undefined.   **33** 0   **35** .0872

37 7.115   **39** .3007   **41** $-\dfrac{\sqrt{3}}{3}$ **43** -1.015 **45** $-.9346$ **47** $-\dfrac{\sqrt{2}}{2}$ **49** $-\dfrac{2\sqrt{3}}{3}$

51 (a) $\left(\dfrac{2}{3}\right)^2 + \left(\dfrac{\sqrt{5}}{3}\right)^2 = \dfrac{4}{9} + \dfrac{5}{9} = \dfrac{9}{9} = 1$

(b)

(c) $\sin \theta = \dfrac{\sqrt{5}}{3}$; $\cos \theta = \dfrac{2}{3}$; $\tan \theta = \dfrac{\sqrt{5}}{2}$;

$\cot \theta = \dfrac{2\sqrt{5}}{5}$; $\sec \theta = \dfrac{3}{2}$; $\csc \theta = \dfrac{3\sqrt{5}}{5}$

(d) $48°10'$

53 $y = -\dfrac{\sqrt{13}}{4} = -.9014$; $\theta = -64°20'$

55 $AB = \dfrac{AB}{1} = \dfrac{AB}{OA} = \dfrac{y}{x} = \tan \theta$; OB

57 $-\dfrac{\sqrt{5}}{5}$

59 $\dfrac{\pi}{2}$

61 $0; \pi$

63 $\dfrac{\pi}{6}; \dfrac{5\pi}{6}$

65 $\dfrac{3\pi}{4}; \dfrac{5\pi}{4}$

67 III; $\cos \theta = -\dfrac{\sqrt{2}}{2}$; $\cot \theta = 1$; $\sec \theta = -\sqrt{2}$; $\csc \theta = -\sqrt{2}$

69 IV; $\cos \theta = \dfrac{\sqrt{3}}{2}$; $\tan \theta = -\dfrac{\sqrt{3}}{3}$; $\sec \theta = \dfrac{2\sqrt{3}}{3}$; $\csc \theta = -2$

8.5   IDENTITIES (*Page 315*)

1 $\sin \theta$ **3** 1   **5** $\cos \theta$ **7** 1   **9** -1 **11** $(\sin \theta)(\cot \theta)(\sec \theta) = (\sin \theta)\left(\dfrac{\cos \theta}{\sin \theta}\right)\left(\dfrac{1}{\cos \theta}\right) = 1$

13 $\cos^2 \theta(\tan^2 \theta + 1) = \cos^2 \theta\left(\dfrac{\sin^2 \theta}{\cos^2 \theta} + 1\right) = \sin^2 \theta + \cos^2 \theta = 1$ **15** θ not coterminal with $\dfrac{\pi}{2}, \dfrac{3\pi}{2}$.

17 θ not a quadrantal angle.   **19** Same as Exercise 17.   **21** $\dfrac{\sin^2 \theta}{\cos^2 \theta}$, θ not a quadrantal angle.

23 $\dfrac{\sin \theta - 1}{\cos \theta}$; θ not a quadrantal angle.   **25** $\dfrac{1}{\sin \theta \cos \theta}$; θ not a quadrantal angle.   **27** $1 - 2 \sin^2 \theta$

29 $\cos^2 \theta + \cos \theta - 1$ **31** $\dfrac{\cos \theta}{\cot \theta} = (\cos \theta)\dfrac{\sin \theta}{\cos \theta} = \sin \theta$; θ not a quadrantal angle.

33 $(\tan \theta - 1)^2 = \tan^2 \theta - 2 \tan \theta + 1 = \sec^2 \theta - 2 \tan \theta$; θ not coterminal with $\dfrac{\pi}{2}, \dfrac{3\pi}{2}$.

35

$\sec \theta - \cos \theta$	$\sin \theta \tan \theta$
$\dfrac{1}{\cos \theta} - \cos \theta$	$\sin \theta \dfrac{\sin \theta}{\cos \theta}$
$\dfrac{1 - \cos^2 \theta}{\cos \theta}$	$\dfrac{\sin^2 \theta}{\cos \theta}$
$\dfrac{\sin^2 \theta}{\cos \theta}$	

θ not coterminal with $\dfrac{\pi}{2}$ or $\dfrac{3\pi}{2}$.

37

$\dfrac{\cot \theta - 1}{1 - \tan \theta}$	$\dfrac{\csc \theta}{\sec \theta}$
$\dfrac{\dfrac{\cos \theta}{\sin \theta} - 1}{1 - \dfrac{\sin \theta}{\cos \theta}}$	$\dfrac{\dfrac{1}{\sin \theta}}{\dfrac{1}{\cos \theta}}$
$\dfrac{\cos^2 \theta - \sin \theta \cos \theta}{\sin \theta \cos \theta - \sin^2 \theta}$	$\dfrac{\cos \theta}{\sin \theta}$
$\dfrac{\cos \theta(\cos \theta - \sin \theta)}{\sin \theta(\cos \theta - \sin \theta)}$	
$\dfrac{\cos \theta}{\sin \theta}$	

θ not a quadrantal angle or not coterminal with $\dfrac{\pi}{4}, \dfrac{5\pi}{4}$.

39 $\tan \theta + \cot \theta = \dfrac{\sin \theta}{\cos \theta} + \dfrac{\cos \theta}{\sin \theta} = \dfrac{\sin^2 \theta + \cos^2 \theta}{\sin \theta \cos \theta} = \dfrac{1}{\sin \theta \cos \theta}$

41 $(\sec \theta + \tan \theta)(1 - \sin \theta) = \sec \theta + \tan \theta - \sec \theta \sin \theta - \tan \theta \sin \theta = \sec \theta + \tan \theta - \dfrac{\sin \theta}{\cos \theta} - \dfrac{\sin^2 \theta}{\cos \theta}$

$$= \sec \theta - \dfrac{\sin^2 \theta}{\cos \theta} = \dfrac{1}{\cos \theta} - \dfrac{\sin^2 \theta}{\cos \theta} = \dfrac{1 - \sin^2 \theta}{\cos \theta} = \dfrac{\cos^2 \theta}{\cos \theta} = \cos \theta$$

43 $(\csc^2 \theta - 1) \sin^2 \theta = \cot^2 \theta \sin^2 \theta = \dfrac{\cos^2 \theta}{\sin^2 \theta} \sin^2 \theta = \cos^2 \theta$

45 $\tan^2 \theta - \sin^2 \theta = \dfrac{\sin^2 \theta}{\cos^2 \theta} - \sin^2 \theta = \sin^2 \theta\left(\dfrac{1}{\cos^2 \theta} - 1\right) = \sin^2 \theta\left(\dfrac{1 - \cos^2 \theta}{\cos^2 \theta}\right) = \sin^2 \theta\left(\dfrac{\sin^2 \theta}{\cos^2 \theta}\right)$

$$= \sin^2 \theta \tan^2 \theta$$

47 $\dfrac{1 + \sec \theta}{\csc \theta} = \dfrac{1 + \dfrac{1}{\cos \theta}}{\dfrac{1}{\sin \theta}} = \sin \theta + \dfrac{\sin \theta}{\cos \theta} = \sin \theta + \tan \theta$

49 $\dfrac{1}{1 + \cos \theta} + \dfrac{1}{1 - \cos \theta} = \dfrac{1 - \cos \theta + 1 + \cos \theta}{(1 + \cos \theta)(1 - \cos \theta)} = \dfrac{2}{1 - \cos^2 \theta} = \dfrac{2}{\sin^2 \theta} = 2 \csc^2 \theta$

51 $\dfrac{1 + \tan^2 \theta}{1 + \cot^2 \theta} = \dfrac{\sec^2 \theta}{\csc^2 \theta} = \dfrac{\dfrac{1}{\cos^2 \theta}}{\dfrac{1}{\sin^2 \theta}} = \dfrac{\sin^2 \theta}{\cos^2 \theta}$

$$= \tan^2 \theta = \sec^2 \theta - 1$$

53 $\dfrac{\sec \theta + \csc \theta}{\sec \theta - \csc \theta} = \dfrac{\dfrac{1}{\cos \theta} + \dfrac{1}{\sin \theta}}{\dfrac{1}{\cos \theta} - \dfrac{1}{\sin \theta}} = \dfrac{\sin \theta + \cos \theta}{\sin \theta - \cos \theta}$

55 $(\csc \theta - \cot \theta)^2 = \left(\dfrac{1}{\sin \theta} - \dfrac{\cos \theta}{\sin \theta}\right)^2$

$$= \dfrac{(1 - \cos \theta)^2}{\sin^2 \theta} = \dfrac{(1 - \cos \theta)^2}{1 - \cos^2 \theta}$$

$$= \dfrac{(1 - \cos \theta)^2}{(1 - \cos \theta)(1 + \cos \theta)} = \dfrac{1 - \cos \theta}{1 + \cos \theta}$$

57 $(\sin^2 \theta + \cos^2 \theta)^5 = 1^5 = 1$

59 $\dfrac{1}{\cos^2 \theta} + \dfrac{1}{\sin^2 \theta} = \dfrac{\sin^2 \theta + \cos^2 \theta}{\cos^2 \theta \sin^2 \theta} = \dfrac{1}{(1 - \sin^2 \theta) \sin^2 \theta} = \dfrac{1}{\sin^2 \theta - \sin^4 \theta}$

61 $\dfrac{\tan^2 \theta + 1}{\tan^2 \theta} = 1 + \dfrac{1}{\tan^2 \theta} = 1 + \cot^2 \theta = \csc^2 \theta$

63 $\dfrac{\tan \theta}{\sec \theta - 1} = \dfrac{\tan \theta (\sec \theta + 1)}{(\sec \theta - 1)(\sec \theta + 1)}$

$$= \dfrac{\tan \theta (\sec \theta + 1)}{\sec^2 \theta - 1} = \dfrac{\tan \theta (\sec \theta + 1)}{\tan^2 \theta}$$

$$= \dfrac{\sec \theta + 1}{\tan \theta}$$

65 $\dfrac{1}{(\csc \theta - \sec \theta)^2} = \dfrac{1}{\left(\dfrac{1}{\sin \theta} - \dfrac{1}{\cos \theta}\right)^2} = \dfrac{1}{\left(\dfrac{\cos \theta - \sin \theta}{\sin \theta \cos \theta}\right)^2}$

$$= \dfrac{\sin^2 \theta \cos^2 \theta}{(\cos \theta - \sin \theta)^2} = \dfrac{\sin^2 \theta \cos^2 \theta}{\cos^2 \theta - 2 \cos \theta \sin \theta + \sin^2 \theta}$$

$$= \dfrac{\sin^2 \theta \cos^2 \theta}{1 - 2 \cos \theta \sin \theta} = \dfrac{\sin^2 \theta}{\dfrac{1}{\cos^2 \theta} - 2\dfrac{\sin \theta}{\cos \theta}} = \dfrac{\sin^2 \theta}{\sec^2 \theta - 2 \tan \theta}$$

67 $\dfrac{\sec\theta}{\tan\theta - \sin\theta} = \dfrac{\dfrac{1}{\cos\theta}}{\dfrac{\sin\theta}{\cos\theta} - \sin\theta} = \dfrac{1}{\sin\theta - \sin\theta\cos\theta} = \dfrac{1}{\sin\theta\,(1 - \cos\theta)}$

$$= \dfrac{1 + \cos\theta}{\sin\theta\,(1 - \cos^2\theta)} = \dfrac{1 + \cos\theta}{\sin\theta\sin^2\theta} = \dfrac{1 + \cos\theta}{\sin^3\theta}$$

69 $-\ln|\cos x| = \ln|\cos x|^{-1} = \ln\dfrac{1}{|\cos x|}$

$$= \ln\left|\dfrac{1}{\cos x}\right| = \ln|\sec x|$$

71 $-\ln|\sec x - \tan x| = \ln|\sec x - \tan x|^{-1} = \ln\dfrac{1}{|\sec x - \tan x|}$

$$= \ln\left|\dfrac{1}{\sec x - \tan x}\right| = \ln\left|\dfrac{\sec x + \tan x}{\sec^2 x - \tan^2 x}\right|$$

$$= \ln|\sec x + \tan x|$$

73 $\tan\left(-\dfrac{\pi}{4}\right) = -1 \neq 1 = \tan\dfrac{\pi}{4}$

75 $\sin\dfrac{\pi}{2} = 1 \neq -1 = -\sqrt{1 - \cos^2\dfrac{\pi}{2}}$

77 $\dfrac{\cot\dfrac{\pi}{3} - 1}{1 - \tan\dfrac{\pi}{3}} = \dfrac{\dfrac{1}{\sqrt{3}} - 1}{1 - \sqrt{3}} = \dfrac{1}{\sqrt{3}} \neq \sqrt{3} = \dfrac{2}{\dfrac{2}{\sqrt{3}}} = \dfrac{\sec\dfrac{\pi}{3}}{\csc\dfrac{\pi}{3}}$

79 (a) $\sqrt{9 + x^2}$

$\ln(\sec\theta + \tan\theta) = \ln\left(\dfrac{\sqrt{9 + x^2}}{3} + \dfrac{x}{3}\right)$

$$= \ln\left(\dfrac{\sqrt{9 + x^2} + x}{3}\right)$$

(b) $\ln 3$

81 Not an identity since $\dfrac{\sin 45°}{\csc 45°} - \dfrac{\cos 45°}{\sec 45°} = \dfrac{\dfrac{1}{\sqrt{2}}}{\sqrt{2}} - \dfrac{\dfrac{1}{\sqrt{2}}}{\sqrt{2}} = 0 \neq 1.$

83 Identity since $\dfrac{\sec^2 x - 2}{(1 + \tan x)^2} = \dfrac{\tan^2 x + 1 - 2}{(\tan x + 1)^2} = \dfrac{\tan^2 x - 1}{(\tan x + 1)^2}$

$$= \dfrac{(\tan x + 1)(\tan x - 1)}{(\tan x + 1)^2} = \dfrac{\tan x - 1}{\tan x + 1}$$

$$= \dfrac{1 - \dfrac{1}{\tan x}}{1 + \dfrac{1}{\tan x}} = \dfrac{1 - \cot x}{1 + \cot x}$$

8.6 THE LAW OF COSINES (*Page 320*)

(These answers were found using Table V. If a calculator is used for the trigonometric ratios then some of these answers will be slightly different.)

1 $a = \sqrt{93}$ **3** $\alpha = 30°$ **5** $a = 6.1$; $\beta = 26°20'$ **7** $\gamma = 90°$; $\alpha = 67°20'$ **9** $\beta = 37°$; $\gamma = 9°10'$
11 $c = 11.2$; $\alpha = 125°40'$ **13** $a = 5.0$; $\beta = 17°20'$ **15** 151 meters. **17** 4.8 miles. **19** 22.6 centimeters.
21 42.7 **23** 111.1 feet. **25** 33.6 miles.

8.7 THE LAW OF SINES (*Page 325*)

(These answers were found using Table V. If a calculator is used for the trigonometric ratios then some of these answers will be slightly different.)

1 $a = c = 18\sqrt{3}$ **3** $\gamma = \dfrac{\pi}{6}$ **5** $\beta = 100°$; $a = 5.1$; $c = 10.0$ **7** $\gamma = 67°40,$; $a = 5.8$; $c = 6.0$ **9** No solution.

11 One solution. **13** No solution. **15** $\beta = 86°40,$; $c = 9.7$ or $\beta = 93°20'$; $c = 8.3$ **17** No solution.
19 $\gamma = 27°30'$ or $\gamma = 152°30'$ **21** $133°50'$ **23** 1.6 miles. **25** 454 feet. **27** 11.7 centimeters. **29** 16
31 724 meters.

SAMPLE TEST QUESTIONS FOR CHAPTER 8 (*Page 328*)

1 (a) $\dfrac{15}{8}$; (b) $\dfrac{8}{17}$; (c) $\dfrac{17}{8}$ **2** $\sin A = \dfrac{\sqrt{5}}{3}$; $\cos A = \dfrac{2}{3}$; $\tan A = \dfrac{\sqrt{5}}{2}$.

3 $AB = \sqrt{9 + x^2}$; $3(\sin^2 A)(\sec A)$

$$= 3\left(\frac{x^2}{x^2 + 9}\right)\left(\frac{\sqrt{x^2 + 9}}{3}\right) = \frac{x^2}{\sqrt{x^2 + 9}}$$ **4** $\dfrac{20\pi}{3}$

5 (a) $\dfrac{\sqrt{3}}{2}$; (b) 0; (c) $-\dfrac{\sqrt{2}}{2}$ **6** (a) $-\dfrac{\sqrt{3}}{3}$; (b) -1; (c) 2 **7** $20\sqrt{2}$ **8** 373 feet.

9 $\cot^2 \theta - \cos^2 \theta = \dfrac{\cos^2 \theta}{\sin^2 \theta} - \cos^2 \theta$

$$= \cos^2 \theta \left(\frac{1}{\sin^2 \theta} - 1\right) = \cos^2 \theta \left(\frac{1 - \sin^2 \theta}{\sin^2 \theta}\right)$$

$$= \cos^2 \theta \left(\frac{\cos^2 \theta}{\sin^2 \theta}\right) = \cos^2 \theta \cot^2 \theta$$

10 $(\sec \theta - \tan \theta)^2 = \left(\dfrac{1}{\cos \theta} - \dfrac{\sin \theta}{\cos \theta}\right)^2$

$$= \frac{(1 - \sin \theta)^2}{\cos^2 \theta} = \frac{(1 - \sin \theta)^2}{1 - \sin^2 \theta}$$

$$= \frac{(1 - \sin \theta)^2}{(1 - \sin \theta)(1 + \sin \theta)} = \frac{1 - \sin \theta}{1 + \sin \theta}$$

11 $\dfrac{\tan \theta - \sin \theta}{\csc \theta - \cot \theta} = \dfrac{\dfrac{\sin \theta}{\cos \theta} - \sin \theta}{\dfrac{1}{\sin \theta} - \dfrac{\cos \theta}{\sin \theta}} = \dfrac{\sin^2 \theta - \sin^2 \theta \cos \theta}{\cos \theta - \cos^2 \theta}$

$$= \frac{\sin^2 \theta (1 - \cos \theta)}{\cos \theta (1 - \cos \theta)} = \frac{\sin^2 \theta}{\cos \theta} = \frac{1 - \cos^2 \theta}{\cos \theta}$$

$$= \frac{1}{\cos \theta} - \cos \theta = \sec \theta - \cos \theta$$

12 $\dfrac{\sqrt{5}}{5}$ **13** $2\sqrt{3} - \pi$ square units. **14** (a) $4\sqrt{7}, \dfrac{\pi}{3}$; (b) $\sin B = \dfrac{8 \sin 60°}{4\sqrt{7}} = \dfrac{\sqrt{21}}{7}$. **15** (a) None; (b) two.

16 $\dfrac{20\sqrt{6}}{3}$

9.1   THE SINE AND COSINE FUNCTIONS (*Page 340*)

1

x	$-\pi$	$-\dfrac{5\pi}{6}$	$-\dfrac{2\pi}{3}$	$-\dfrac{\pi}{2}$	$-\dfrac{\pi}{3}$	$-\dfrac{\pi}{6}$	0
$y = \sin x$	0	$-\dfrac{1}{2}$	$-\dfrac{\sqrt{3}}{2}$	-1	$-\dfrac{\sqrt{3}}{2}$	$-\dfrac{1}{2}$	0

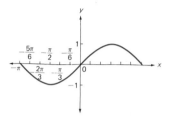

3 Shift the graph of f $\dfrac{\pi}{2}$ units to the right.

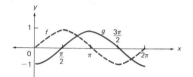

5 Shift the graph of f $\dfrac{\pi}{3}$ units to the right.

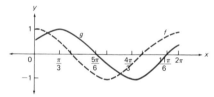

7 Shift the graph of f π units to the left and multiply the ordinates by 2.

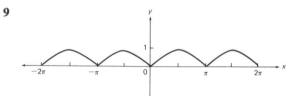

9

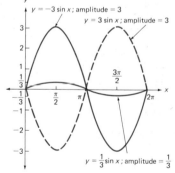

11

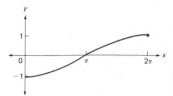

13 Amplitude $= 1$; period $= \pi$.

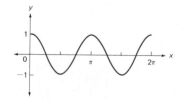

15 Amplitude $= \dfrac{3}{2}$; period $= \dfrac{\pi}{2}$.

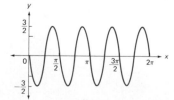

17 Amplitude $= 1$; period $= 4\pi$.

19 $p = 8\pi$

 21 $p = 2$

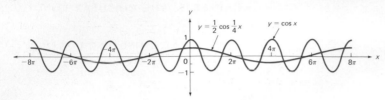

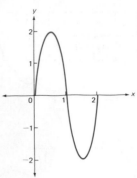

23 $a = 1, b = 3; y = \sin 3x$ **25** $a = 2, b = \dfrac{2}{3}; y = 2\cos\dfrac{2x}{3}$ **27** Shift $y = \sin 2x$ by $\frac{1}{2}$ unit to the right.

29

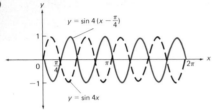

FIG. C-14

31

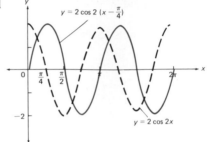

33

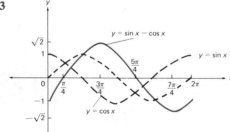

35

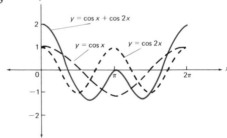

37

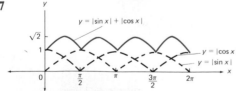

39 $(f \circ g)(x) = 2\cos x + 5; (g \circ f)(x) = \cos(2x + 5)$ **41** $g(x) = 5x^2; f(x) = \cos x$

43 $h(x) = 1 - 2x; g(x) = \sqrt[3]{x}; f(x) = \cos x$ **45** $f(x + 2p) = f((x + p) + p) = f(x + p) = f(x)$

1

x	-1.4	-1.3	$-\dfrac{\pi}{3}$	$-\dfrac{\pi}{4}$	$-\dfrac{\pi}{6}$	0
$y = \tan x$	-5.8	-3.6	$-\sqrt{3}$	-1	$-\dfrac{\sqrt{3}}{3}$	0

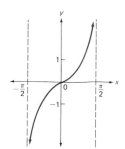

3 (a) $\cot(-x) = \dfrac{\cos(-x)}{\sin(-x)} = \dfrac{\cos x}{-\sin x} = -\dfrac{\cos x}{\sin x} = -\cot x$

(b) $\csc(-x) = \dfrac{1}{\sin(-x)} = \dfrac{1}{-\sin x} = -\dfrac{1}{\sin x} = -\csc x$

(c) $\csc(x + 2\pi) = \dfrac{1}{\sin(x + 2\pi)} = \dfrac{1}{\sin x} = \csc x$

5 Shift the graph of g $\dfrac{\pi}{2}$ units to the left.

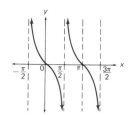

7 Shift the graph of g $\dfrac{\pi}{3}$ units to the right.

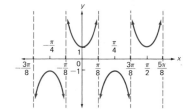

9 $p = \dfrac{\pi}{3}$

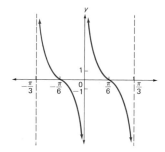

11 $p = 2\pi$

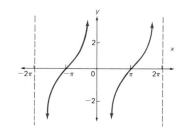

13 $p = \dfrac{\pi}{2}$

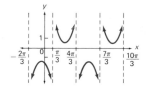

15 $p = 6\pi$

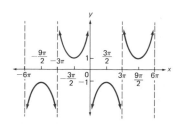

17 $p = \dfrac{4\pi}{3}$

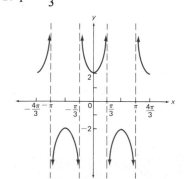

19

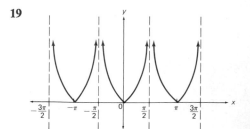

21 $(f \circ g)(x) = \tan^2 x$; $(g \circ f)(x) = \tan x^2$

23 $(f \circ g \circ h)(x) = e^{\sqrt{\sec x}}$; $(g \circ f \circ h)(x) = \sqrt{e^{\sec x}}$; $(h \circ g \circ f)(x) = \sec \sqrt{e^x}$

25 $h(x) = 2x + 1$, $g(x) = \tan x$; $f(x) = \sqrt{x}$ **27** $0 < QP = \sin \theta < \overset{\frown}{AP} = \theta$; divide by θ to get $0 < \dfrac{\sin \theta}{\theta} < 1$

9.3 THE ADDITION AND SUBTRACTION FORMULAS (*Page 353*)

1 $\cos 60° = \frac{1}{2}$ **3** $\tan(-30°) = -\dfrac{1}{\sqrt{3}}$

5 $\sin 75° = \sin(45° + 30°)$
$$= \sin 45° \cos 30° + \cos 45° \sin 30° = \tfrac{1}{4}(\sqrt{6} + \sqrt{2})$$
$\cos 75° = \cos(45° + 30°)$
$$= \cos 45° \cos 30° - \sin 45° \sin 30° = \tfrac{1}{4}(\sqrt{6} - \sqrt{2})$$
$\tan 75° = \tan(45° + 30°)$
$$= \frac{\tan 45° + \tan 30°}{1 - \tan 45° \tan 30°} = \frac{\sqrt{3} + 1}{\sqrt{3} - 1}$$

7 $\sin \dfrac{\pi}{12} = \sin\left(\dfrac{\pi}{3} - \dfrac{\pi}{4}\right)$
$$= \sin \frac{\pi}{3} \cos \frac{\pi}{4} - \cos \frac{\pi}{3} \sin \frac{\pi}{4} = \frac{1}{4}(\sqrt{6} - \sqrt{2})$$
$\cos \dfrac{\pi}{12} = \cos\left(\dfrac{\pi}{3} - \dfrac{\pi}{4}\right)$
$$= \cos \frac{\pi}{3} \cos \frac{\pi}{4} + \sin \frac{\pi}{3} \sin \frac{\pi}{4} = \frac{1}{4}(\sqrt{2} + \sqrt{6})$$
$$\tan \frac{\pi}{12} = \tan\left(\frac{\pi}{3} - \frac{\pi}{4}\right) = \frac{\tan \dfrac{\pi}{3} - \tan \dfrac{\pi}{4}}{1 + \tan\dfrac{\pi}{3} \tan \dfrac{\pi}{4}} = \frac{\sqrt{3} - 1}{1 + \sqrt{3}}$$

9 $\sin 165° = \sin(135° + 30°) = \sin 135° \cos 30° + \cos 135° \sin 30° = \tfrac{1}{4}(\sqrt{6} - \sqrt{2})$
$\cos 165° = \cos(135° + 30°) = \cos 135° \cos 30° - \sin 135° \sin 30° = -\tfrac{1}{4}(\sqrt{6} + \sqrt{2})$
$$\tan 165° = \tan(135° + 30°) = \frac{\tan 135° + \tan 30°}{1 - \tan 135° \tan 30°} = \frac{-\sqrt{3} + 1}{\sqrt{3} + 1}$$

11 $\sin \dfrac{17\pi}{12} = \sin\left(\dfrac{7\pi}{6} + \dfrac{\pi}{4}\right) = \sin \dfrac{7\pi}{6} \cos \dfrac{\pi}{4} + \cos \dfrac{7\pi}{6} \sin \dfrac{\pi}{4} = -\dfrac{1}{4}(\sqrt{2} + \sqrt{6})$
$\cos \dfrac{17\pi}{12} = \cos\left(\dfrac{7\pi}{6} + \dfrac{\pi}{4}\right) = \cos \dfrac{7\pi}{6} \cos \dfrac{\pi}{4} - \sin \dfrac{7\pi}{6} \sin \dfrac{\pi}{4} = \dfrac{1}{4}(\sqrt{2} - \sqrt{6})$
$$\tan \frac{17\pi}{12} = \tan\left(\frac{7\pi}{6} + \frac{\pi}{4}\right) = \frac{\tan \dfrac{7\pi}{6} + \tan \dfrac{\pi}{4}}{1 - \tan \dfrac{7\pi}{6} \tan \dfrac{\pi}{4}} = \frac{\sqrt{3} + 1}{\sqrt{3} - 1}$$

13 $\sin(\pi - \theta) = \sin \pi \cos \theta - \cos \pi \sin \theta = -(-1)\sin \theta = \sin \theta$

15 $\tan(\pi - \theta) = \dfrac{\tan \pi - \tan \theta}{1 + \tan \pi \tan \theta} = \dfrac{0 - \tan \theta}{1 + 0} = -\tan \theta$

17 $\sin(\alpha - \beta) = \frac{16}{65}$; $\tan(\alpha + \beta) = \frac{56}{33}$

19 $\sin(\alpha + \beta) = \frac{2}{15}(\sqrt{42} - 1)$; $\cos(\alpha + \beta) = \frac{1}{15}(\sqrt{21} - 4\sqrt{2})$

21 (a) $\cos 191° = \cos(180° + 11°) = -\cos 11° = -.9816$;
   (b) $\sin 132° = \sin(90° + 42°) = \cos 42° = .7431$;
   (c) $\tan 200° = \tan(180° + 20°) = \tan 20° = .3640$;
   (d) $\cos \dfrac{17\pi}{30} = \cos\left(\dfrac{\pi}{2} + \dfrac{\pi}{15}\right) = -\sin \dfrac{\pi}{15} = -\sin 12° = -.2079$

23 $\cos\left(\theta - \dfrac{\pi}{4}\right) = \cos \theta \cos \dfrac{\pi}{4} + \sin \theta \sin \dfrac{\pi}{4} = \dfrac{\sqrt{2}}{2}(\cos \theta + \sin \theta)$

25 $\cos(\theta + 30°) + \cos(\theta - 30°) = \cos\theta\cos 30° - \sin\theta\sin 30° + \cos\theta\cos 30° + \sin\theta\sin 30°$
$$= 2\cos\theta\cos 30°$$
$$= \sqrt{3}\,\cos\theta$$

27 $\dfrac{\sin\left(\theta + \dfrac{\pi}{2}\right)}{\cos\left(\theta + \dfrac{\pi}{2}\right)} = \dfrac{\cos\theta}{-\sin\theta} = -\cot\theta$

29 $\csc(\pi - \theta) = \dfrac{1}{\sin(\pi - \theta)} = \dfrac{1}{\sin\theta} = \csc\theta$

31 $\sin(\alpha + \beta) - \sin(\alpha - \beta) = \sin\alpha\cos\beta + \cos\alpha\sin\beta - \sin\alpha\cos\beta + \cos\alpha\sin\beta$
$$= 2\cos\alpha\sin\beta$$

33 $\dfrac{\sin(\alpha + \beta)}{\sin(\alpha - \beta)} = \dfrac{\sin\alpha\cos\beta + \cos\alpha\sin\beta}{\sin\alpha\cos\beta - \cos\alpha\sin\beta} = \dfrac{\dfrac{\sin\alpha\cos\beta}{\cos\alpha\cos\beta} + \dfrac{\cos\alpha\sin\beta}{\cos\alpha\cos\beta}}{\dfrac{\sin\alpha\cos\beta}{\cos\alpha\cos\beta} - \dfrac{\cos\alpha\sin\beta}{\cos\alpha\cos\beta}} = \dfrac{\tan\alpha + \tan\beta}{\tan\alpha - \tan\beta}$

35 $2\sin\left(\dfrac{\pi}{4} - \theta\right)\sin\left(\dfrac{\pi}{4} + \theta\right) = 2\left[\sin\dfrac{\pi}{4}\cos\theta - \cos\dfrac{\pi}{4}\sin\theta\right]\left[\sin\dfrac{\pi}{4}\cos\theta + \cos\dfrac{\pi}{4}\sin\theta\right]$
$$= 2\left[\dfrac{\cos\theta}{\sqrt{2}} - \dfrac{\sin\theta}{\sqrt{2}}\right]\left[\dfrac{\cos\theta}{\sqrt{2}} + \dfrac{\sin\theta}{\sqrt{2}}\right]$$
$$= 2\left[\dfrac{\cos^2\theta}{2} - \dfrac{\sin^2\theta}{2}\right] = \cos^2\theta - \sin^2\theta$$

37 $\cos\left(\dfrac{\pi}{2} - x\right) = \sin x;$
$$\cos\left[\dfrac{\pi}{2} - \left(\dfrac{\pi}{2} - \theta\right)\right] = \sin\left(\dfrac{\pi}{2} - \theta\right);$$
$$\cos\theta = \sin\left(\dfrac{\pi}{2} - \theta\right)$$

39 $\sin(\alpha - \beta) = \sin[\alpha + (-\beta)]$
$$= \sin\alpha\cos(-\beta) + \cos\alpha\sin(-\beta)$$
$$= \sin\alpha\cos\beta - \cos\alpha\sin\beta$$

41 $\cot(\alpha + \beta) = \dfrac{\cos(\alpha + \beta)}{\sin(\alpha + \beta)}$
$$= \dfrac{\cos\alpha\cos\beta - \sin\alpha\sin\beta}{\sin\alpha\cos\beta + \cos\alpha\sin\beta}$$
$$= \dfrac{\dfrac{\cos\alpha\cos\beta}{\sin\alpha\sin\beta} - \dfrac{\sin\alpha\sin\beta}{\sin\alpha\sin\beta}}{\dfrac{\sin\alpha\cos\beta}{\sin\alpha\sin\beta} + \dfrac{\cos\alpha\sin\beta}{\sin\alpha\sin\beta}} = \dfrac{\cot\alpha\cot\beta - 1}{\cot\beta + \cot\alpha}$$

43 Since $\sin\theta = -\cos\left(\theta + \dfrac{\pi}{2}\right)$, shift $y = \cos\theta$ by $\dfrac{\pi}{2}$ units to the left and reflect through the θ-axis.

45 $\dfrac{f(x + h) - f(x)}{h} = \dfrac{\sin(x + h) - \sin x}{h}$
$$= \dfrac{\sin x\cos h + \cos x\sin h - \sin x}{h}$$
$$= \dfrac{\sin x(\cos h - 1)}{h} + \dfrac{\cos x\sin h}{h}$$
$$= \left(\dfrac{\cos h - 1}{h}\right)\sin x + \left(\dfrac{\sin h}{h}\right)\cos x$$

47 $\dfrac{12}{37}$

1 $\cos \dfrac{7\pi}{6} = -\dfrac{\sqrt{3}}{2}$ **3** $3 \tan 150° = -\sqrt{3}$ **5** $\cos 75° = \cos \dfrac{150°}{2} = \sqrt{\dfrac{1 + \cos 150°}{2}}$

$$= \sqrt{\dfrac{1 - \dfrac{\sqrt{3}}{2}}{2}} = \dfrac{1}{2}\sqrt{2 - \sqrt{3}}$$

7 $\tan \dfrac{3\pi}{8} = \sqrt{\dfrac{1 - \cos \dfrac{3\pi}{4}}{1 + \cos \dfrac{3\pi}{4}}} = \sqrt{\dfrac{1 + \dfrac{1}{\sqrt{2}}}{1 - \dfrac{1}{\sqrt{2}}}} = \sqrt{\dfrac{\sqrt{2} + 1}{\sqrt{2} - 1}} = \dfrac{\sqrt{\sqrt{2} + 1}}{\sqrt{\sqrt{2} - 1}}$

9 (a) $\tan 15° = \tan \dfrac{30°}{2} = \dfrac{1 - \cos 30°}{\sin 30°} = \dfrac{1 - \dfrac{\sqrt{3}}{2}}{\dfrac{1}{2}} = 2 - \sqrt{3}$

$\tan 15° = \tan \dfrac{30°}{2} = \dfrac{\sin 30°}{1 + \cos 30°} = \dfrac{\dfrac{1}{2}}{1 + \dfrac{\sqrt{3}}{2}} = \dfrac{1}{2 + \sqrt{3}}$

$$= \dfrac{1}{2 + \sqrt{3}} \cdot \dfrac{2 - \sqrt{3}}{2 - \sqrt{3}} = \dfrac{2 - \sqrt{3}}{4 - 3} = 2 - \sqrt{3}$$

(b) $\tan 15° = 0.2679$ to four decimal places from Table V or a calculator.
$2 - \sqrt{3} = 0.2679$ to four decimal places using a calculator.
$2 - \sqrt{3} = 0.268$ using Table I.

11 (a) $\tan^2 (22°30') = \tan^2 \dfrac{45°}{2} = \dfrac{1 - \cos 45°}{1 + \cos 45°}$

$$= \dfrac{1 - \dfrac{\sqrt{2}}{2}}{1 + \dfrac{\sqrt{2}}{2}} = \dfrac{2 - \sqrt{2}}{2 + \sqrt{2}}$$

$$= \dfrac{2 - \sqrt{2}}{2 + \sqrt{2}} \cdot \dfrac{2 - \sqrt{2}}{2 - \sqrt{2}} = \dfrac{(2 - \sqrt{2})^2}{2}$$

(b) $\tan 22°30' = \sqrt{\dfrac{(2 - \sqrt{2})^2}{2}} = \dfrac{2 - \sqrt{2}}{\sqrt{2}}$

$$= \dfrac{(2 - \sqrt{2})\sqrt{2}}{2} = \dfrac{2\sqrt{2} - 2}{2}$$

$$= \dfrac{2(\sqrt{2} - 1)}{2} = \sqrt{2} - 1$$

(c) $\tan 22°30' = 0.4142$ to four decimal places from Table V or a calculator.
$\sqrt{2} - 1 = 0.4142$ to four decimal places using a calculator.
$\sqrt{2} - 1 = 0.414$ using Table I.

13 (a) $-\tfrac{240}{289}$; **(b)** $-\tfrac{161}{289}$; **(c)** $\tfrac{240}{161}$ **15** $-\tfrac{12}{13}$ **17** $9 \sin 2\theta = 18 \sin \theta \cos \theta = 18\left(\dfrac{x}{3}\right)\left(\dfrac{\sqrt{9 - x^2}}{3}\right) = 2x\sqrt{9 - x^2}$

19 $\cot x \sin 2x = \dfrac{\cos x}{\sin x} \cdot 2 \sin x \cos x = 2 \cos^2 x$ **21** $\sec^2 \dfrac{x}{2} = \dfrac{1}{\cos^2 \dfrac{x}{2}} = \dfrac{1}{\dfrac{1 + \cos x}{2}} = \dfrac{2}{1 + \cos x}$

23 $\cos^2 \dfrac{x}{2} = \dfrac{1 + \cos x}{2} = \dfrac{\tan x + \tan x \cos x}{2 \tan x} = \dfrac{\tan x + \sin x}{2 \tan x}$

25 $\cot \dfrac{x}{2} = \dfrac{1}{\tan \dfrac{x}{2}} = \dfrac{1}{\dfrac{\sin x}{1 + \cos x}} = \dfrac{1 + \cos x}{\sin x} = \dfrac{1}{\sin x} + \dfrac{\cos x}{\sin x} = \csc x + \cot x$

27 $(\sin x + \cos x)^2 = \sin^2 x + 2 \sin x \cos x + \cos^2 x = 1 + 2 \sin x \cos x = 1 + \sin 2x$

29 $\tan 3x = \tan(2x + x) = \dfrac{\tan 2x + \tan x}{1 - \tan 2x \tan x}$

$$= \frac{\dfrac{2 \tan x}{1 - \tan^2 x} + \tan x}{1 - \dfrac{2 \tan x}{1 - \tan^2 x} \cdot \tan x}$$

$$= \frac{2 \tan x + \tan x - \tan^3 x}{1 - \tan^2 x - 2 \tan^2 x} = \frac{3 \tan x - \tan^3 x}{1 - 3 \tan^2 x}$$

31 $\cot 2x = \dfrac{1}{\tan 2x} = \dfrac{1}{\dfrac{2 \tan x}{1 - \tan^2 x}} = \dfrac{1 - \tan^2 x}{2 \tan x}$

$$= \frac{\dfrac{1}{\tan^2 x} - \dfrac{\tan^2 x}{\tan^2 x}}{\dfrac{2 \tan x}{\tan^2 x}} = \frac{\cot^2 x - 1}{2 \cot x}$$

33 $\csc 2x - \cot 2x = \dfrac{1}{\sin 2x} - \dfrac{\cos 2x}{\sin 2x} = \dfrac{1 - \cos 2x}{\sin 2x} = \tan \dfrac{2x}{2} = \tan x$

35 $\cos^4 x - \sin^4 x = (\cos^2 x - \sin^2 x)(\cos^2 x + \sin^2 x) = (\cos^2 x - \sin^2 x) = \cos 2x$

37 $\cos 4x = \cos 2(2x) = 2 \cos^2 2x - 1$
$\qquad = 2(2 \cos^2 x - 1)^2 - 1$
$\qquad = 2(4 \cos^4 x - 4 \cos^2 x + 1) - 1$
$\qquad = 8 \cos^4 x - 8 \cos^2 x + 1$

39 $\cos^4 x = (\cos^2 x)^2 = \left(\dfrac{1 + \cos 2x}{2}\right)^2$

$$= \frac{1}{4}(1 + 2 \cos 2x + \cos^2 2x)$$

$$= \frac{1}{4}\left(1 + 2 \cos 2x + \frac{1 + \cos 4x}{2}\right)$$

$$= \frac{1}{8} \cos 4x + \frac{1}{2}\cos 2x + \frac{3}{8}$$

41 (a) $\cos \alpha \cos \beta - \sin \alpha \sin \beta = \cos(\alpha + \beta)$
$\qquad \dfrac{\cos \alpha \cos \beta + \sin \alpha \sin \beta = \cos(\alpha - \beta)}{}$
$\qquad 2 \cos \alpha \cos \beta = \cos(\alpha + \beta) + \cos(\alpha - \beta)$
$\qquad \cos \alpha \cos \beta = \frac{1}{2}[\cos(\alpha + \beta) + \cos(\alpha - \beta)]$

(b) $\cos \alpha \cos \beta + \sin \alpha \sin \beta = \cos(\alpha - \beta)$
$\qquad \dfrac{\cos \alpha \cos \beta - \sin \alpha \sin \beta = \cos(\alpha + \beta)}{}$
$\qquad 2 \sin \alpha \sin \beta = \cos(\alpha - \beta) - \cos(\alpha + \beta)$
$\qquad \sin \alpha \sin \beta = \frac{1}{2}[\cos(\alpha - \beta) - \cos(\alpha + \beta)]$

$\qquad \sin \alpha \cos \beta + \cos \alpha \sin \beta = \sin(\alpha + \beta)$
$\qquad \dfrac{\sin \alpha \cos \beta - \cos \alpha \sin \beta = \sin(\alpha - \beta)}{}$
$\qquad 2 \sin \alpha \cos \beta = \sin(\alpha + \beta) + \sin(\alpha - \beta)$
$\qquad \sin \alpha \cos \beta = \frac{1}{2}[\sin(\alpha + \beta) + \sin(\alpha - \beta)]$

$\qquad \sin \alpha \cos \beta + \cos \alpha \sin \beta = \sin(\alpha + \beta)$
$\qquad \dfrac{\sin \alpha \cos \beta - \cos \alpha \sin \beta = \sin(\alpha - \beta)}{}$
$\qquad 2 \cos \alpha \sin \beta = \sin(\alpha + \beta) - \sin(\alpha - \beta)$
$\qquad \cos \alpha \sin \beta = \frac{1}{2}[\sin(\alpha + \beta) - \sin(\alpha - \beta)]$

43 $2 \cos \dfrac{u + v}{2} \cos \dfrac{u - v}{2} = \cos\left(\dfrac{u + v}{2} - \dfrac{u - v}{2}\right) + \cos\left(\dfrac{u + v}{2} + \dfrac{u - v}{2}\right) = \cos v + \cos u$

Similarly for the other formulas.

45 (a) **(i)** $\dfrac{\pi}{2} < \theta < \pi$ implies $\dfrac{\pi}{4} < \dfrac{\theta}{2} < \dfrac{\pi}{2}$. Then $\dfrac{\theta}{2}$ is in quadrant I, so $\tan \dfrac{\theta}{2}$ and $\sin \theta$ are both positive.

(ii) $\pi < \theta < \frac{3\pi}{2}$ implies $\frac{\pi}{2} < \frac{\theta}{2} < \frac{3\pi}{4}$. Then $\frac{\theta}{2}$ is in quadrant II, so $\tan \frac{\theta}{2}$ and $\sin \theta$ are both negative.

(iii) Similar to part (ii).

(b) $\tan^2 \frac{\theta}{2} = \frac{1 - \cos \theta}{1 + \cos \theta} = \frac{1 - \cos^2 \theta}{(1 + \cos \theta)^2} = \frac{\sin^2 \theta}{(1 + \cos \theta)^2}$. Then $\tan \frac{\theta}{2} = \pm \frac{\sin \theta}{1 + \cos \theta}$. Since $\tan \frac{\theta}{2}$ and $\sin \theta$ have the same sign, and since $1 + \cos \theta > 0$, we get $\tan \frac{\theta}{2} = \frac{\sin \theta}{1 + \cos \theta}$.

(c) Since $\angle Q$ is an inscribed angle of a circle, its measure is $\frac{1}{2}(\text{arc } AP) = \frac{\theta}{2}$. Then $\tan Q = \tan \frac{\theta}{2} = \frac{RP}{QR}$

$= \frac{RP}{1 + OR} = \frac{\sin \theta}{1 + \cos \theta}$.

47 $\frac{b}{10} = \sin 15° = \sin \frac{30°}{2} = \sqrt{\frac{1 - \cos 30°}{2}} = \frac{\sqrt{2 - \sqrt{3}}}{2}$; $b = 5\sqrt{2 - \sqrt{3}}$

49 Use $\tan 2\theta = \frac{2 \tan \theta}{1 - \tan^2 \theta}$, where $\tan 2\theta = \frac{h}{50}$ and $\tan \theta = \frac{h}{150}$ to find that $h = 50\sqrt{3}$.

9.5 TRIGONOMETRIC EQUATIONS (*Page 366*)

In the following answers k represents any integer.

1 $2k\pi$ **3** $\frac{\pi}{6} + 2k\pi$; $\frac{5\pi}{6} + 2k\pi$ **5** $\pi + 2k\pi$ **7** $\frac{\pi}{4} + k\pi$ **9** No solutions. **11** $\frac{\pi}{6} + \frac{k\pi}{2}$; $\frac{2\pi}{3} + \frac{k\pi}{2}$

13 $\pi + 2k\pi - 1$ **15** No solutions. **17** $60°, 120°$ **19** $45°; 315°$ **21** $90°; 270°$ **23** $60°; 300°$ **25** $30°; 150°$

27 $45°; 225°$ **29** $0; \frac{7\pi}{6}; \frac{11\pi}{6}$ **31** $\frac{\pi}{3}; \frac{4\pi}{3}$ **33** $\frac{\pi}{2}; \frac{3\pi}{2}; \frac{\pi}{6}; \frac{11\pi}{6}$ **35** $\frac{\pi}{2}$ **37** $\frac{\pi}{6}; \frac{5\pi}{6}; \frac{\pi}{2}; \frac{3\pi}{2}$ **39** No solutions.

41 $\frac{\pi}{3}; \frac{5\pi}{3}$ **43** $0; \frac{\pi}{4}; \frac{3\pi}{4}; \frac{5\pi}{4}; \frac{7\pi}{4}; \pi$ **45** $\frac{\pi}{4}; \frac{\pi}{2}; \frac{3\pi}{4}; \frac{5\pi}{4}; \frac{3\pi}{2}; \frac{7\pi}{4}$ **47** $\frac{\pi}{4}; \frac{5\pi}{4}$ **49** $\frac{\pi}{3}; \frac{5\pi}{3}$ **51** $0; \frac{\pi}{6}; \frac{5\pi}{6}; \pi$

53 $\frac{\pi}{6}; \frac{5\pi}{6}; \frac{7\pi}{6}; \frac{11\pi}{6}$ **55** $0; \frac{\pi}{3}; \frac{\pi}{2}; \frac{2\pi}{3}; \pi; \frac{4\pi}{3}; \frac{3\pi}{2}; \frac{5\pi}{3}$ **57** $0; \frac{\pi}{2}$ **59** $62°10'; 297°50'$ **61** $111°20'; 248°40'$

63 $33°40'; 213°40'$ **65** $69°20'; 290°40'; 110°40'; 249°20'$

67 (a) $\cos \frac{\pi}{4} = \frac{\sqrt{2}}{2} = .7071 \ldots$; $\cos \alpha = \frac{28}{35} = .8 > .7071 \ldots$. Then $\alpha < \frac{\pi}{4}$ since the cosine is decreasing for $0 \le x \le \frac{\pi}{2}$.

(b) $\cos 2\alpha = 2 \cos^2 \alpha - 1 = 2\left(\frac{4}{5}\right)^2 - 1 = \frac{7}{25} = \frac{28}{100} = \cos(\alpha + \beta)$. Then, since the cosine is one-to-one for $0 \le x \le \frac{\pi}{2}$, $2\alpha = \alpha + \beta$, or $\alpha = \beta$.

69 $\left(\frac{3\pi}{4}, \frac{\sqrt{2}}{2}\right), \left(\frac{7\pi}{4}, -\frac{\sqrt{2}}{2}\right)$

9.6 INVERSE CIRCULAR FUNCTIONS (*Page 373*)

1 0 **3** $-\frac{\pi}{2}$ **5** $-\frac{\pi}{4}$ **7** $\frac{3\pi}{4}$ **9** 1.5621 (89°30') **11** .5934 (34°) **13** 1.4224 (81°30') **15** $\frac{\sqrt{145}}{145}$ **17** 0 **19** $\frac{\sqrt{3}}{2}$

21 $\frac{5}{13}$ **23** 0 **25** Sin and arcsin are inverse functions. **27** Domain: $-1 \le x \le 1$. Range: $-\pi \le y \le \pi$.

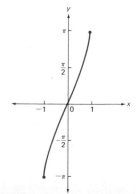

29 Domain: all real x.

Range: $2 - \dfrac{\pi}{2} < y < 2 + \dfrac{\pi}{2}$.

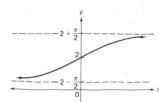

31 Domain: $-\dfrac{1}{2} \le x \le \dfrac{1}{2}$.

Range: $-\dfrac{\pi}{4} \le y \le \dfrac{\pi}{4}$.

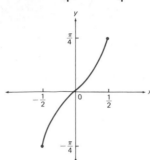

33 Domain: $-1 \le x \le 1$.

Range: $-1 \le y \le 1$.

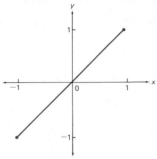

35 $-\dfrac{7}{11}$ **37** $\dfrac{220}{221}$ **39** $\dfrac{7}{9}$ **41** $-\dfrac{3}{2}$ **43** -2

45 $\tan(\pi + \arctan x) = \dfrac{\tan \pi + \tan(\arctan x)}{1 - (\tan \pi)\tan(\arctan x)} = \dfrac{0 + x}{1 - 0 \cdot x} = x$

47 Let $y = \arcsin x$. Then $x = \sin y$;
$-x = -\sin y = \sin(-y)$; $-y = \arcsin(-x)$;
$-\arcsin x = \arcsin(-x)$.

49 $x = \arctan 2 = 63°30'$ to the nearest $10'$,
or 1.1083 radians (Table V).

51 $x = \arccos 0 = \dfrac{\pi}{2}$; $x = \arcsin(-.25) = -14°30'$ to the nearest $10'$, or $-.2531$ radians (Table V).

53 $(f \circ g)(x) = \arcsin(3x + 2)$; $(g \circ f)(x) = 3 \arcsin x + 2$ **55** $g(x) = \arccos x$; $f(x) = \ln x$

SAMPLE TEST QUESTIONS FOR CHAPTER 9 (*Page 375*)

1 Amplitude $= 2$;

period $= \pi$.

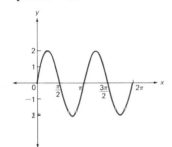

2 Domain: all $x \ne \dfrac{\pi}{2} + k\pi$.

Range: all $y \ge 1$ or $y \le -1$.

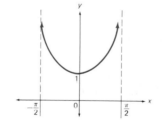

3 $-\dfrac{1}{4}(\sqrt{6} + \sqrt{2})$ **4** $-\dfrac{1}{2}\sqrt{2 - \sqrt{3}}$ **5** $\dfrac{2\sqrt{8}}{9} = \dfrac{4\sqrt{2}}{9}$

6 $\sin\left(\dfrac{\pi}{4} - \theta\right) = \sin \dfrac{\pi}{4} \cos \theta - \cos \dfrac{\pi}{4} \sin \theta$

$= \dfrac{\sqrt{2}}{2} \cos \theta - \dfrac{\sqrt{2}}{2} \sin \theta = \dfrac{\sqrt{2}}{2}(\cos\theta - \sin\theta)$

7 $\csc 4x = \dfrac{1}{\sin 4x} = \dfrac{1}{2 \sin 2x \cos 2x}$

$= \dfrac{1}{4 \sin x \cos x \cos 2x} = \dfrac{1}{4} \csc x \sec x \sec 2x$

8 $\sin^2 \dfrac{x}{2} = \dfrac{1 - \cos x}{2} = \dfrac{\tan x - \tan x \cos x}{2 \tan x} = \dfrac{\tan x - \sin x}{2 \tan x}$

9 $\dfrac{\pi}{6}$; $\dfrac{5\pi}{6}$; $\dfrac{3\pi}{2}$

10

$x = \begin{cases} -\dfrac{\pi}{3} + k\pi \\[2mm] \dfrac{\pi}{3} + k\pi \end{cases}$, k any integer

11 (a) Domain: all reals.

Range: $-\dfrac{\pi}{2} < y < \dfrac{\pi}{2}$.

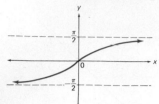

(b) $-\dfrac{\pi}{6}$

12 (a) $\dfrac{\pi}{4}$; **(b)** $\dfrac{2}{7}\sqrt{10}$; **(c)** $\dfrac{1}{2}$

13 $a = \dfrac{1}{2}$, $b = 3$, $y = \dfrac{1}{2}\cos 3x$

14 $p = \dfrac{\pi}{2}$; $x = \dfrac{\pi}{4}$; $x = \dfrac{3\pi}{4}$

15 $\dfrac{56}{65}$ **16** $8(2 + \sqrt{3})$

CHAPTER 10: SEQUENCES AND SERIES

10.1   SEQUENCES (*Page 380*)

1 $s_1 = 1, s_2 = 3, s_3 = 5, s_4 = 7, s_5 = 9$

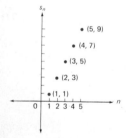

3 $s_1 = -1, s_2 = 1, s_3 = -1, s_4 = 1, s_5 = -1$

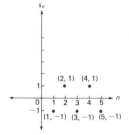

5 $s_1 = -4, s_2 = 2, s_3 = -1, s_4 = \dfrac{1}{2}, s_5 = -\dfrac{1}{4}$

7 $-1, 4, -9, 16$

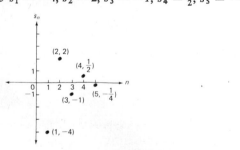

9 $\dfrac{3}{10}, \dfrac{3}{100}, \dfrac{3}{1000}, \dfrac{3}{10,000}$ **11** $\dfrac{3}{100}, \dfrac{3}{10,000}, \dfrac{3}{1,000,000}, \dfrac{3}{100,000,000}$

13 $\dfrac{1}{2}, \dfrac{1}{6}, \dfrac{1}{12}, \dfrac{1}{20}$ **15** $64, 36, 16, 4$ **17** $-2, 1, 4, 7$ **19** $0, \dfrac{1}{3}, \dfrac{1}{2}, \dfrac{3}{5}$ **21** $1, \dfrac{3}{2}, \dfrac{16}{9}, \dfrac{125}{64}$ **23** $-2, -\dfrac{3}{2}, -\dfrac{9}{8}, -\dfrac{27}{32}$

25 $\dfrac{1}{2}, \dfrac{1}{2}, \dfrac{3}{8}, \dfrac{1}{4}$ **27** $-\dfrac{3}{2}, -\dfrac{5}{6}, -\dfrac{7}{12}, -\dfrac{9}{20}$ **29** $4, 4, 4, 4$ **31** 122 **33** 0.000003 **35** 12 **37** -1331 **39** $4, 6, 8, 10$

41 $5, 10, 15, 20, 25$; $s_n = 5n$ **43** $-5, 25, -125, 625, -3125$; $s_n = (-5)^n$ **45** $15, 21, 28$ **47** $1, \dfrac{9}{5}, 3, \dfrac{81}{17}, \dfrac{81}{11}$

49 $\dfrac{3}{2}, \dfrac{15}{8}, \dfrac{35}{16}, \dfrac{315}{128}$

1 45 **3** 55 **5** 0.33333 **7** 510 **9** 60 **11** 254 **13** $\frac{381}{64}$ **15** 105 **17** 40 **19** $1\frac{3}{8}$ **21** 0 **23** 57 **25** 1111.111
27 60 **29** $\frac{35}{12}$ **31** 0.010101 **33** (a) 4, 9, 16, 25, 36; (b) n^2.

$$\overbrace{}^{n \text{ terms}}$$

35 $s_n = s_1 + s_{n-1} = s_1 + (s_1 + s_{n-2}) = \cdots = s_1 + s_1 + s_1 + \cdots + s_1 = 2 + 2 + 2 + \cdots + 2 = 2n$

37 $\sum_{k=1}^{n} s_k + \sum_{k=1}^{n} t_k = (s_1 + s_2 + \cdots + s_n) + (t_1 + t_2 + \cdots + t_n) = (s_1 + t_1) + (s_2 + t_2) + \cdots + (s_n + t_n)$

$$= \sum_{k=1}^{n} (s_k + t_k)$$

39 $\sum_{k=1}^{n} (s_k + c) = (s_1 + c) + (s_2 + c) + \cdots + (s_n + c) = (s_1 + s_2 + \cdots + s_n) + (c + c + \cdots + c)$

$$= \left(\sum_{k=1}^{n} s_k \right) + nc$$

1 5, 7, 9; $2n - 1$; 400 **3** $-10, -16, -22$; $-6n + 8$; -1100 **5** $\frac{17}{2}, 9, \frac{19}{2}$; $\frac{1}{2}n + 7$; 245
7 $-\frac{4}{5}, -\frac{7}{5}, -2$; $-\frac{3}{5}n + 1$; -106 **9** 150, 200, 250; $50n$; 10,500 **11** 30, 50, 70; $20n - 30$; 3600 **13** 455 **15** $\frac{63}{4}$
17 15,150 **19** 94,850 **21** $\dfrac{173,350}{7}$ **23** 567,500 **25** 5824 **27** 15,300 **29** (a) 10,000; (b) n^2 **31** -36
33 4620 **35** $\frac{3577}{4}$ **37** $\frac{5}{2}n(n + 1)$ **39** $-\frac{9}{4}$ **41** $\frac{228}{15} = \frac{76}{5}$ **43** $1183 **45** 930 **47** $a = -7; d = -13$
49 $u = \frac{16}{3}, v = 2\frac{2}{3}$ **51** 9080 **53** $-16,200$ **55** 520

1 16, 32, 64; 2^n **3** 27, 81, 243; 3^{n-1} **5** $\frac{1}{9}, -\frac{1}{27}, \frac{1}{81}$; $-3(-\frac{1}{3})^{n-1}$ **7** $-125, -625, -3125$; -5^{n-1}
9 $-\frac{16}{9}, -\frac{32}{27}, -\frac{64}{81}$; $-6(\frac{2}{3})^{n-1}$ **11** 1000, 100,000, 10,000,000; $\frac{1}{1000}(100)^{n-1}$ **13** 126 **15** $-\frac{1330}{81}$ **17** 1024 **19** 3
21 1023 **23** $2^n - 1$ **25** $\frac{121}{27}$ **27** $\frac{211}{54}$ **29** $-\frac{85}{64}$ **31** $-\frac{5}{21}$ **33** 512,000; $1000(2^{n-1})$ **35** $3117.79
37 (a) $800(1.11)^n$; (b) $1350 **39** $703.99

1 4 **3** $\frac{125}{4}$ **5** $\frac{2}{3}$ **7** $\frac{10}{9}$ **9** $-\frac{16}{7}$ **11** $\frac{3}{2}$ **13** $\frac{1}{6}$ **15** 4 **17** $\frac{20}{9}$ **19** No finite sum. **21** $\frac{10}{3}$ **23** No finite sum.
25 30 **27** $\frac{20}{11}$ **29** 4 **31** $\frac{4}{21}$ **33** $\frac{7}{9}$ **35** $\frac{13}{99}$ **37** $\frac{13}{990}$ **39** 1 **41** (a) $\frac{4}{3}, \frac{4}{9}, \frac{4}{27}, \ldots, \frac{4}{3^n}, \ldots$; (b) $\sum_{n=1}^{\infty} \frac{4}{3^n} = \dfrac{\frac{4}{3}}{1 - \frac{1}{3}} = 2.$

43 8 hours. **45** The time for the last $\frac{1}{2}$ mile would have to be $\sum_{n=1}^{\infty} \frac{2}{5}(\frac{10}{9})^{n-1}$, which is not a finite sum, since $\frac{10}{9} > 1$.

For these exercises, $\mathcal{S}_n$ represents the given statement where n is an integer ≥ 1 ($n \geq 2$ when appropriate). The second part of each proof begins with the hypothesis $\mathcal{S}_k$, where k is an arbitrary positive integer.

1 Since $1 = \dfrac{1(1 + 1)}{2}$, $\mathcal{S}_1$ is true. Assume $\mathcal{S}_k$ and add $k + 1$ to obtain

$$1 + 2 + 3 + \cdots + k + (k + 1) = \frac{k(k + 1)}{2} + (k + 1) = \frac{k^2 + 3k + 2}{2} = \frac{(k + 1)(k + 2)}{2} = \frac{(k + 1)[(k + 1) + 1]}{2}$$

Therefore, $\mathcal{S}_{k+1}$ holds. Since $\mathcal{S}_1$ is true and $\mathcal{S}_k$ implies $\mathcal{S}_{k+1}$, the principle of mathematical induction makes $\mathcal{S}_n$ true for all integers $n \geq 1$. *Note:* The preceding sentence is an appropriate final statement for the remaining proofs. For the sake of brevity, however, it will not be repeated.

3 Since $\sum_{i=1}^{1} 3i = 3 = \frac{3(1+1)}{2}$, S_1 is true. Assume S_k and add $3(k+1)$ to obtain the following. $\sum_{i=1}^{k+1} 3i = \left(\sum_{i=1}^{k} 3i\right)$ $+ 3(k+1) = \frac{3k(k+1)}{2} + 3(k+1)$; $\sum_{i=1}^{k+1} 3i = \frac{3(k^2+3k+2)}{2} = \frac{3(k+1)(k+2)}{2} = \frac{3(k+1)[(k+1)+1]}{2}$.

Therefore, S_{k+1} holds.

5 Since $\frac{5}{3} = \frac{1(11-1)}{6}$, S_1 is true. Assume S_k and add $-\frac{1}{3}(k+1) + 2$ to obtain $\frac{5}{3} + \frac{4}{3} + 1 + \cdots +$ $\left(-\frac{1}{3}k + 2\right) + \left[-\frac{1}{3}(k+1) + 2\right] = \frac{k(11-k)}{6} + \left[-\frac{1}{3}(k+1) + 2\right] = \frac{10+9k-k^2}{6} = \frac{(k+1)(10-k)}{6}$ $= \frac{(k+1)[11-(k+1)]}{6}$. Therefore, S_{k+1} holds.

7 Since $\frac{1}{1 \cdot 2} = \frac{1}{1+1}$, S_1 is true. Assume S_k and add $\frac{1}{(k+1)[(k+1)+1]}$ to obtain $\frac{1}{1 \cdot 2} + \frac{1}{2 \cdot 3} + \cdots + \frac{1}{k(k+1)}$ $+ \frac{1}{(k+1)(k+2)} = \frac{k}{k+1} + \frac{1}{(k+1)(k+2)} = \frac{k^2+2k+1}{(k+1)(k+2)} = \frac{(k+1)^2}{(k+1)(k+2)} = \frac{k+1}{k+2} = \frac{k+1}{(k+1)+1}$

Therefore, S_{k+1} holds.

9 S_1 is true since $-2 = -1 - (1^2)$. Assume S_k and add $-2(k+1)$ to obtain
$$-2 - 4 - 6 - \cdots - 2k - 2(k+1) = -k - k^2 - 2(k+1) = -(k+1) - (k^2 + 2k + 1)$$
$$= -(k+1) - (k+1)^2$$

Therefore, S_{k+1} holds.

11 S_1 is true since $1 = \frac{5}{3}[1 - (\frac{2}{5})^1]$. Assume S_k and add $(\frac{2}{5})^k$ to obtain
$$1 + \frac{2}{5} + \frac{4}{25} + \cdots + (\tfrac{2}{5})^{k-1} + (\tfrac{2}{5})^k = \tfrac{5}{3}[1 - (\tfrac{2}{5})^k] + (\tfrac{2}{5})^k$$
$$= \tfrac{5}{3}[1 - (\tfrac{2}{5})^k + \tfrac{3}{5}(\tfrac{2}{5})^k]$$
$$= \tfrac{5}{3}[1 - (\tfrac{2}{5})^k(1 - \tfrac{3}{5})]$$
$$= \tfrac{5}{3}[1 - (\tfrac{2}{5})^k(\tfrac{2}{5})]$$
$$= \tfrac{5}{3}[1 - (\tfrac{2}{5})^{k+1}]$$

Therefore, S_{k+1} holds.

13 S_1 is true since $1^3 = 1 = \frac{1^2(1+1)^2}{4}$. Assume S_k and add $(k+1)^3$ to obtain

$$1^3 + 2^3 + 3^3 + \cdots + k^3 + (k+1)^3 = \frac{k^2(k+1)^2}{4} + (k+1)^3$$
$$= \frac{k^2(k+1)^2 + 4(k+1)^3}{4}$$
$$= \frac{(k+1)^2[k^2 + 4k + 4]}{4}$$
$$= \frac{(k+1)^2[k+2]^2}{4}$$
$$= \frac{(k+1)^2[(k+1)+1]^2}{4}$$

Therefore, S_{k+1} holds.

15 S_1 is true since $\sum_{i=1}^{1} ar^{i-1} = a = \frac{a(1-r^1)}{1-r}$. Assume S_k and add $ar^{(k+1)-1}$ to obtain

$$\sum_{i=1}^{k} ar^{i-1} + ar^k = \frac{a(1-r^k)}{1-r} + ar^k \quad -$$
$$\sum_{i=1}^{k+1} ar^{i-1} = \frac{a(1-r^k)}{1-r} + ar^k$$
$$= \frac{a(1-r^k) + ar^k - ar^{k+1}}{1-r}$$
$$= \frac{a - ar^{k+1}}{1-r}$$
$$= \frac{a(1-r^{k+1})}{1-r}$$

Therefore, S_{k+1} holds.

17 Since $a^1 < 1$, $\mathcal{S}_1$ is true. Assume $\mathcal{S}_k$ and multiply by a to obtain $a \cdot a^k < a \cdot 1$ or $a^{k+1} < a$. But $a < 1$; hence $a^{k+1} < 1$ and, therefore, $\mathcal{S}_{k+1}$ holds.

19 $\mathcal{S}_1$ is true since $(ab)^1 = a^1 b^1$. Assume that $(ab)^k = a^k b^k$ and multiply by ab to obtain

$$(ab)^k(ab) = (a^k b^k)ab$$
$$(ab)^{k+1} = (a^k a)(b^k b)$$
$$(ab)^{k+1} = a^{k+1} b^{k+1}$$

Therefore, $\mathcal{S}_{k+1}$ holds.

21 $\mathcal{S}_1$ is true since $|a_0 + a_1| \le |a_0| + |a_1|$. Assume $\mathcal{S}_k$. Then

$$\begin{aligned}
|a_0 + a_1 + \cdots + a_k + a_{k+1}| &= |(a_0 + a_1 + \cdots + a_k) + a_{k+1}| \\
&\le |a_0 + a_1 + \cdots + a_k| + |a_{k+1}| \quad \text{(by } \mathcal{S}_1) \\
&\le (|a_0| + |a_1| + \cdots + |a_k|) + |a_{k+1}| \quad \text{(by } \mathcal{S}_k) \\
&= |a_0| + |a_1| + \cdots + |a_{k+1}|
\end{aligned}$$

Therefore, $\mathcal{S}_{k+1}$ holds.

23 (a) Since $\dfrac{a^2 - b^2}{a - b} = a + b = a^{2-1} + b^{2-1}$, $\mathcal{S}_2$ is true. Assume $\mathcal{S}_k$. Then

$$\begin{aligned}
\frac{a^{k+1} - b^{k+1}}{a - b} &= \frac{a^k a - b^k b}{a - b} \\
&= \frac{a^k a - b^k a + b^k a - b^k b}{a - b} \\
&= \frac{a(a^k - b^k) + b^k(a - b)}{a - b} = \frac{a(a^k - b^k)}{a - b} + b^k \\
&= a[a^{k-1} + a^{k-2}b + \cdots + ab^{k-2} + b^{k-1}] + b^k \quad \text{(by } \mathcal{S}_k) \\
&= a^k + a^{k-1}b + \cdots + a^2 b^{k-1} + ab^{k-1} + b^k
\end{aligned}$$

Therefore, $\mathcal{S}_{k+1}$ holds.

(b) Since $\dfrac{a^n - b^n}{a - b} = a^{n-1} + a^{n-2}b + \cdots + ab^{n-2} + b^{n-1}$, multiplying by $a - b$ gives

$$a^n - b^n = (a - b)(a^{n-1} + a^{n-2}b + \cdots + ab^{n-2} + b^{n-1})$$

25 (a) 1; 4; 9; 16; 25;   **(b)** n^2

(c) $\mathcal{S}_1$ is true since $1 = 1^2$. Assume $\mathcal{S}_k$ and add $k + (k + 1)$ to obtain

$$\begin{aligned}
1 + 2 + 3 + \cdots + (k - 1) + k + (k + 1) + k + (k - 1) + \cdots + 3 + 2 + 1 &= k^2 + k + (k + 1) \\
&= k^2 + 2k + 1 \\
&= (k + 1)^2
\end{aligned}$$

Therefore, $\mathcal{S}_{k+1}$ holds.

SAMPLE TEST QUESTIONS FOR CHAPTER 10 (*Page 407*)

1 1, −1, −1, −$\frac{8}{7}$ **2** −$\frac{25}{11}$ **3** 21   **4** 35   **5** 12, −3, $\frac{3}{4}$ **6** −768$(-\frac{1}{4})^{n-1}$ **7** $\sum\limits_{k=1}^{4} 8\left(\dfrac{1}{2}\right)^k = \dfrac{4\left(1 - \dfrac{1}{2^4}\right)}{1 - \frac{1}{2}} = \dfrac{15}{2}$

8 15,554   **9** 18   **10** No finite sum since $r = \frac{3}{2} > 1$.   **11** $\frac{6}{115}$ **12** $\frac{4}{11}$ **13** \$652.60   **14** 36 feet.

15 For $n = 1$, we have $5 = \dfrac{5 \cdot 1(1 + 1)}{2}$. If $5 + 10 + \cdots + 5k = \dfrac{5k(k + 1)}{2}$, then $5 + 10 + \cdots + 5k + 5(k + 1)$

$$= \frac{5k(k + 1)}{2} + 5(k + 1) = \frac{5k(k + 1) + 10(k + 1)}{2} = \frac{5(k + 1)(k + 2)}{2} = \frac{5(k + 1)[(k + 1) + 1]}{2}$$

Thus the statement holds for the $k + 1$ case, and by the principle of mathematical induction the statement is true for all $n \ge 1$.

16 For $n = 1$, $\dfrac{1}{1 \cdot 3} = \dfrac{1}{2 \cdot 1 + 1}$. For $n = k$, assume that

$$\frac{1}{1 \cdot 3} + \frac{1}{3 \cdot 5} + \cdots + \frac{1}{(2k - 1)(2k + 1)} = \frac{k}{2k + 1}$$

Add $\dfrac{1}{(2k+1)(2k+3)}$ to get

$$\frac{1}{1\cdot 3}+\frac{1}{3\cdot 5}+\cdots+\frac{1}{(2k-1)(2k+1)}+\frac{1}{(2k+1)(2k+3)}$$

$$=\frac{k}{2k+1}+\frac{1}{(2k+1)(2k+3)}$$

$$=\frac{k(2k+3)+1}{(2k+1)(2k+3)}$$

$$=\frac{2k^2+3k+1}{(2k+1)(2k+3)}$$

$$=\frac{(2k+1)(k+1)}{(2k+1)(2k+3)}$$

$$=\frac{k+1}{2(k+1)+1}$$

Thus the statement holds for $n=k+1$, and by the principle of mathematical induction the statement is true for all $n \geq 1$.

CHAPTER 11: COMPLEX NUMBERS AND POLAR COORDINATES

11.1   COMPLEX NUMBERS (*Page 415*)

1 True. **3** True. **5** False. **7** $5+2i$ **9** $-5+0i$ **11** $4i$ **13** $12i$ **15** $\frac{3}{4}i$ **17** $-\sqrt{5}i$ **19** -27 **21** $-\sqrt{6}$
23 $15i$ **25** $12i$ **27** $5i\sqrt{2}$ **29** $(3-\sqrt{3})i$ **31** $10+7i$ **33** $5-3i$ **35** $10+2i$ **37** $-10+6i$ **39** $13i$
41 $23+14i$ **43** $5-3i$ **45** $\frac{13}{5}+\frac{1}{5}i$ **47** $\frac{4}{5}-\frac{3}{5}i$
49 $\overline{z+w}=\overline{(-6+8i)+(\frac{1}{2}+\frac{1}{2}i)}=\overline{-\frac{11}{2}+\frac{17}{2}i}=-\frac{11}{2}-\frac{17}{2}i$
  $\bar{z}+\bar{w}=\overline{-6+8i}+\overline{\frac{1}{2}+\frac{1}{2}i}=(-6-8i)+(\frac{1}{2}-\frac{1}{2}i)=-\frac{11}{2}-\frac{17}{2}i$
51 $\overline{zw}=\overline{(-6+8i)(\frac{1}{2}+\frac{1}{2}i)}=\overline{-7+i}=-7-i$; $\bar{z}\bar{w}=\overline{(-6+8i)}(\overline{\frac{1}{2}+\frac{1}{2}i})=(-6-8i)(\frac{1}{2}-\frac{1}{2}i)=-7-i$
53 $-3i$ **55** $-2i$ **57** 4 **59** $\frac{3}{13}-\frac{2}{13}i$
61 $\sqrt{(-4)(-9)}=\sqrt{36}=6$; $\sqrt{-4}\sqrt{-9}=(2i)(3i)=6i^2=-6$
63 (a) $(x+2i)(x-2i)$; (b) $3(x+3i)(x-3i)$; (c) $(x+i\sqrt{2})(x-i\sqrt{2})$; (d) $5(x+i\sqrt{3})(x-i\sqrt{3})$
65 $-3\pm 4i$ **67** $-\dfrac{1}{4}\pm\dfrac{\sqrt{39}}{4}i$ **69** $3\pm\sqrt{3}i$ **71** $\dfrac{ac+bd}{c^2+d^2}+\dfrac{bc-ad}{c^2+d^2}i$
73 $[(3+i)(3-i)](4+3i)=(9-i^2)(4+3i)=10(4+3i)=40+30i$
  $(3+i)[(3-i)(4+3i)]=(3+i)(15+5i)=40+30i$
75 $4-3i$ **77** $\frac{53}{13}-\frac{21}{13}i$ **79** $\pm 3,\ \pm 3i$ **81** $2,\ -\dfrac{1}{6}\pm\dfrac{\sqrt{47}}{6}i$
83 $\overline{z+w}=\overline{(a+bi)+(c+di)}=\overline{(a+c)+(b+d)i}=(a+c)-(b+d)i$
  $\bar{z}+\bar{w}=\overline{a+bi}+\overline{c+di}=(a-bi)+(c-di)=(a+c)-(b+d)i$
85 $\overline{\left(\dfrac{z}{w}\right)}=\overline{\left(\dfrac{a+bi}{c+di}\right)}=\overline{\dfrac{ac+bd}{c^2+d^2}+\dfrac{bc-ad}{c^2+d^2}i}=\dfrac{ac+bd}{c^2+d^2}-\dfrac{bc-ad}{c^2+d^2}i$
  $\dfrac{\bar{z}}{\bar{w}}=\dfrac{\overline{a+bi}}{\overline{c+di}}=\dfrac{a-bi}{c-di}=\dfrac{a-bi}{c-di}\cdot\dfrac{c+di}{c+di}=\dfrac{ac+bd}{c^2+d^2}-\dfrac{bc-ad}{c^2+d^2}i$

11.2   TRIGONOMETRIC FORM AND THE COMPLEX PLANE (*Page 422*)

1

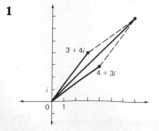

3

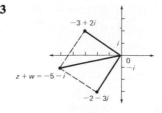

5

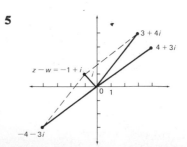

7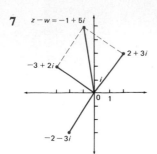

$z - w = -1 + 5i$

9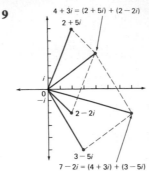

$4 + 3i = (2 + 5i) + (2 - 2i)$
$7 - 2i = (4 + 3i) + (3 - 5i)$

11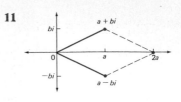

13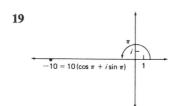

$\sqrt{2}\left(\cos\frac{\pi}{4} + i\sin\frac{\pi}{4}\right)$

15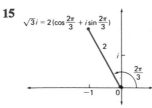

$\sqrt{3}i = 2\left(\cos\frac{2\pi}{3} + i\sin\frac{2\pi}{3}\right)$

17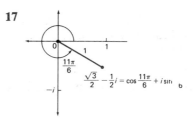

$\frac{\sqrt{3}}{2} - \frac{1}{2}i = \cos\frac{11\pi}{6} + i\sin\frac{11\pi}{6}$

19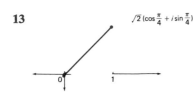

$-10 = 10(\cos\pi + i\sin\pi)$

21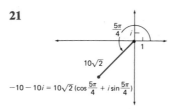

$-10 - 10i = 10\sqrt{2}\left(\cos\frac{5\pi}{4} + i\sin\frac{5\pi}{4}\right)$

23 $-\dfrac{3}{2} + \dfrac{3\sqrt{3}}{2}i$ **25** $-5i$ **27** $\dfrac{\sqrt{2}}{2} + \dfrac{\sqrt{6}}{2}i$ **29** $2\sqrt{2} - 2\sqrt{2}i$ **31** $.9848 - .1736i$

33 $zw = 5(\cos 150° + i\sin 150°) = -\dfrac{5\sqrt{3}}{2} + \dfrac{5}{2}i$

$\dfrac{z}{w} = \dfrac{1}{20}(\cos 50° + i\sin 50°) = .0321 + .0383i$

$\dfrac{w}{z} = 20(\cos 310° + i\sin 310°) = 12.856 - 15.32i$

35 $zw = 8\sqrt{2}(\cos\pi + i\sin\pi) = -8\sqrt{2}$

$\dfrac{z}{w} = \dfrac{\sqrt{2}}{8}\left(\cos\dfrac{3\pi}{2} + i\sin\dfrac{3\pi}{2}\right) = -\dfrac{\sqrt{2}}{8}i$

$\dfrac{w}{z} = 4\sqrt{2}\left(\cos\dfrac{\pi}{2} + i\sin\dfrac{\pi}{2}\right) = 4\sqrt{2}i$

37 $zw = \left[7\left(\cos\dfrac{\pi}{2} + i\sin\dfrac{\pi}{2}\right)\right]\left[2\cos\left(\dfrac{\pi}{6} + i\sin\dfrac{\pi}{6}\right)\right] = 14\left(\cos\dfrac{2\pi}{3} + i\sin\dfrac{2\pi}{3}\right) = -7 + 7\sqrt{3}i$

$\dfrac{z}{w} = \dfrac{7}{2}\left(\cos\dfrac{\pi}{3} + i\sin\dfrac{\pi}{3}\right) = \dfrac{7}{4} + \dfrac{7\sqrt{3}}{4}i$

39 $zw = \left[4\left(\cos\dfrac{2\pi}{3} + i\sin\dfrac{2\pi}{3}\right)\right]\left[4\left(\cos\dfrac{7\pi}{6} + i\sin\dfrac{7\pi}{6}\right)\right] = 16\left(\cos\dfrac{11\pi}{6} + i\sin\dfrac{11\pi}{6}\right) = 8\sqrt{3} - 8i$

$\dfrac{z}{w} = \cos\dfrac{3\pi}{2} + i\sin\dfrac{3\pi}{2} = -i$

41 $zw = \left[\sqrt{2}\left(\cos\dfrac{3\pi}{4} + i\sin\dfrac{3\pi}{4}\right)\right]\left[\sqrt{2}\left(\cos\dfrac{7\pi}{4} + i\sin\dfrac{7\pi}{4}\right)\right] = 2\left(\cos\dfrac{\pi}{2} + i\sin\dfrac{\pi}{2}\right) = 2i$

$\dfrac{z}{w} = \cos\pi + i\sin\pi = -1$

43 $\dfrac{\sqrt{2}}{2}(\cos 90° + i\sin 90°) = \dfrac{\sqrt{2}}{2}i$ **45** $\dfrac{3}{2}(\cos 199° + i\sin 199°) = -1.4183 - .4884i$

47 $|zw| = |(a + bi)(c + di)| = |(ac - bd) + (bc + ad)i|$

$\qquad = \sqrt{(ac - bd)^2 + (bc + ad)^2} = \sqrt{a^2c^2 + b^2d^2 + b^2c^2 + a^2d^2}$

$|z||w| = |a + bi||c + di| = \sqrt{a^2 + b^2}\sqrt{c^2 + d^2}$

$\qquad = \sqrt{(a^2 + b^2)(c^2 + d^2)} = \sqrt{a^2c^2 + b^2d^2 + b^2c^2 + a^2d^2}$

11.3   DE MOIVRE'S THEOREM (*Page 426*)

1 $\cos 60° + i\sin 60° = \dfrac{1}{2} + \dfrac{\sqrt{3}}{2}i$ **3** $\cos 320° + i\sin 320° = .7660 - .6428i$

5 $\dfrac{1}{64}\left(\cos\dfrac{3\pi}{4} + i\sin\dfrac{3\pi}{4}\right) = -\dfrac{\sqrt{2}}{128} + \dfrac{\sqrt{2}}{128}i$ **7** $4(\cos 5\pi + i\sin 5\pi) = -4$ **9** $216\left(\cos\dfrac{9\pi}{2} + i\sin\dfrac{9\pi}{2}\right) = 216i$

11 $\cos\dfrac{35\pi}{2} + i\sin\dfrac{35\pi}{2} = -i$ **13** $\cos 10\pi + i\sin 10\pi = 1$

15 $3\left(\cos\dfrac{\pi}{45} + i\sin\dfrac{\pi}{45}\right),\ 3\left(\cos\dfrac{31\pi}{45} + i\sin\dfrac{31\pi}{45}\right),\ 3\left(\cos\dfrac{61\pi}{45} + i\sin\dfrac{61\pi}{45}\right)$

17 $2\left(\cos\dfrac{\pi}{40} + i\sin\dfrac{\pi}{40}\right),\ 2\left(\cos\dfrac{17\pi}{40} + i\sin\dfrac{17\pi}{40}\right),\ 2\left(\cos\dfrac{33\pi}{40} + i\sin\dfrac{33\pi}{40}\right),\ 2\left(\cos\dfrac{49\pi}{40} + i\sin\dfrac{49\pi}{40}\right),$

$\quad 2\left(\cos\dfrac{65\pi}{40} + i\sin\dfrac{65\pi}{40}\right)$

19 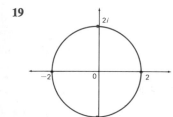   **21** 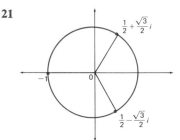   **23**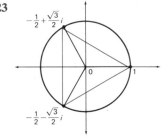

25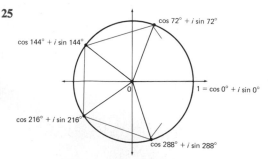

27 $\dfrac{3}{2} + \dfrac{3\sqrt{3}}{2}i,\ -3,\ \dfrac{3}{2} - \dfrac{3\sqrt{3}}{2}i$ **29** $2i,\ -\sqrt{3} - i,\ \sqrt{3} - i$

31 $2^{\frac{1}{6}}\left(\cos\dfrac{5\pi}{12} + i\sin\dfrac{5\pi}{12}\right),\ 2^{\frac{1}{6}}\left(\cos\dfrac{13\pi}{12} + i\sin\dfrac{13\pi}{12}\right),\ 2^{\frac{1}{6}}\left(\cos\dfrac{21\pi}{12} + i\sin\dfrac{21\pi}{12}\right)$

33 (**a**) For $k = 0$, the formula gives $r^{1/n}\left(\cos\dfrac{\theta}{n} + i\sin\dfrac{\theta}{n}\right)$

For $k = n$, the formula gives

$$r^{1/n}\left(\cos\frac{\theta + 2n\pi}{n} + i\sin\frac{\theta + 2n\pi}{n}\right) = r^{1/n}\left[\cos\left(\frac{\theta}{n} + 2\pi\right) + i\sin\left(\frac{\theta}{n} + 2\pi\right)\right] = r^{1/n}\left(\cos\frac{\theta}{n} + i\sin\frac{\theta}{n}\right)$$

(b) For $k = 1$, the formula gives $r^{1/n}\left(\cos\dfrac{\theta + 2\pi}{n} + i\sin\dfrac{\theta + 2\pi}{n}\right)$

For $k = n + 1$, the formula gives

$$r^{1/n}\left(\cos\frac{\theta + 2(n+1)\pi}{n} + i\sin\frac{\theta + 2(n+1)\pi}{n}\right) = r^{1/n}\left[\cos\left(\frac{\theta + 2\pi}{n} + 2\pi\right) + i\sin\left(\frac{\theta + 2\pi}{n} + 2\pi\right)\right]$$

$$= r^{1/n}\left(\cos\frac{\theta + 2\pi}{n} + i\sin\frac{\theta + 2\pi}{n}\right)$$

(c) Use k in the formula to get $r^{1/n}\left(\cos\dfrac{\theta + 2k\pi}{n} + i\sin\dfrac{\theta + 2k\pi}{n}\right)$

Use $k + n$ in the formula to get

$$r^{1/n}\left(\cos\frac{\theta + 2(n+k)\pi}{n} + i\sin\frac{\theta + 2(n+k)\pi}{n}\right) = r^{1/n}\left[\cos\left(\frac{\theta + 2k\pi}{n} + 2\pi\right) + i\sin\left(\frac{\theta + 2k\pi}{n} + 2\pi\right)\right]$$

$$= r^{1/n}\left(\cos\frac{\theta + 2k\pi}{n} + i\sin\frac{\theta + 2k\pi}{n}\right)$$

35 (a) $[r(\cos\theta + i\sin\theta)]^{-n} = r^{-n}(\cos\theta + i\sin\theta)^{-n} = r^{-n}[(\cos\theta + i\sin\theta)^{-1}]^n$
$\phantom{[r(\cos\theta + i\sin\theta)]^{-n}} = r^{-n}[(\cos\theta - i\sin\theta)]^n$ (see the hint)
$\phantom{[r(\cos\theta + i\sin\theta)]^{-n}} = r^{-n}[\cos(-\theta) + i\sin(-\theta)]^n$
$\phantom{[r(\cos\theta + i\sin\theta)]^{-n}} = r^{-n}[\cos(-n\theta) + i\sin(-n\theta)]$ (since $n > 0$)
$\phantom{[r(\cos\theta + i\sin\theta)]^{-n}} = r^{-n}(\cos n\theta - i\sin n\theta)$

(b) Assuming the rule $z^0 = 1$, the formula holds for $n = 0$. The formula is given in Section 11.3 for positive integers n. If in part (a) we let $m = -n$, where m is a negative integer, then

$$[r(\cos\theta + i\sin\theta)]^m = [r(\cos\theta + i\sin\theta)]^{-n} = r^{-n}(\cos n\theta - i\sin n\theta) \qquad \text{(by part (a))}$$

$$= r^{-n}[\cos(-n\theta) + i\sin(-n\theta)]$$

$$= r^m[\cos(m\theta) + i\sin(m\theta)]$$

which shows that the formula holds for negative integers.

11.4   POLAR COORDINATES (*Page 432*)

1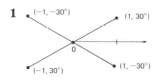

3

5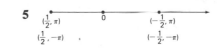

7 (a) $(1, 405°)$; **(b)** $(1, -315°)$; **(c)** $(-1, 225°)$; **(d)** $(-1, -135°)$

9 (a) $\left(3, \dfrac{19\pi}{6}\right)$; **(b)** $\left(3, -\dfrac{5\pi}{6}\right)$; **(c)** $\left(-3, \dfrac{\pi}{6}\right)$; **(d)** $\left(-3, -\dfrac{11\pi}{6}\right)$ **11** $(0, -7)$ **13** $\left(0, -\dfrac{3}{2}\right)$ **15** $\left(\dfrac{2\sqrt{2}}{5}, \dfrac{2\sqrt{2}}{5}\right)$

17 $(2, 0)$ **19** $(2, \pi)$ **21** $\left(6\sqrt{2}, \dfrac{5\pi}{4}\right)$ **23** $\left(4, \dfrac{\pi}{4}\right)$ **25** $\left(2, \dfrac{11\pi}{6}\right)$ **27** $(-7, \pi)$ **29** $\left(-2, \dfrac{11\pi}{6}\right)$ **31** $\left(-\sqrt{6}, \dfrac{5\pi}{4}\right)$

33 $(10, -90°)$ **35** $r\cos\theta = 0 \cos\theta = 0 = x$; $r\sin\theta = 0\sin\theta = 0 = y$

37 Using the polar coordinates $(-r, \theta + \pi)$, $x = -r\cos(\theta + \pi)$ and $y = -r\sin(\theta + \pi)$ since $-r > 0$. Then

$$x = -r(\cos\theta\cos\pi - \sin\theta\sin\pi) = -r(-\cos\theta) = r\cos\theta$$

$$y = -r(\sin\theta\cos\pi + \cos\theta\sin\pi) = -r(-\sin\theta) = r\sin\theta$$

11.5 GRAPHING POLAR EQUATIONS (*Page 440*)

1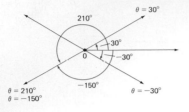

3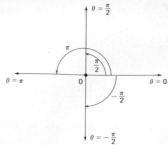

5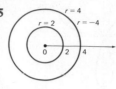

7 $\theta = -6°$ **9** $\theta = \dfrac{\pi}{6}$

11 $x^2 + (y - \frac{1}{2})^2 = \frac{1}{4}$

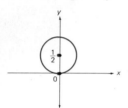

13 $x^2 + (y - \frac{5}{2})^2 = \frac{25}{4}$

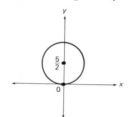

15 $(x + \frac{1}{6})^2 + y^2 = \frac{1}{36}$

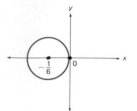

17 (a) $x^2 + y^2 = 4$; (b) $x^2 + y^2 = 4$; (c) $x^2 + y^2 = 5$

19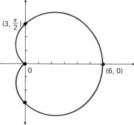

21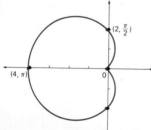

23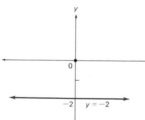

25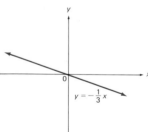

27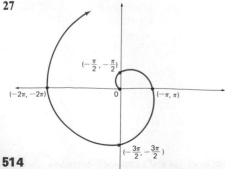

29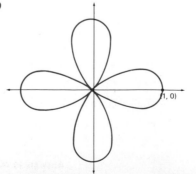

514

31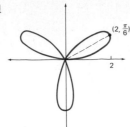

33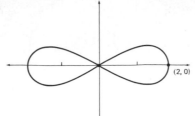

35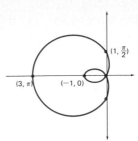

37 $y^2 = 16 - 8x$ (parabola) **39** $x = -5$ (vertical line) **41** $(x - 3)^2 + (y - 4)^2 = 25$ (circle)

43 $2x + 3y = 3$ (line) **45** $x + \sqrt{3}\,y = 2\sqrt{3}$ (line) **47** $\cos\theta = \dfrac{c}{r}$ or $r\cos\theta = c$.

49 $\left(\dfrac{3}{2}, \dfrac{\pi}{3}\right), \left(\dfrac{3}{2}, \dfrac{5\pi}{3}\right)$ **51** $\left(0, \dfrac{\pi}{2}\right), \left(\dfrac{\sqrt{3}}{2}, \dfrac{\pi}{6}\right), \left(-\dfrac{\sqrt{3}}{2}, \dfrac{5\pi}{6}\right)$ **53** $\left(1, -\dfrac{\pi}{3}\right)$

SAMPLE TEST QUESTIONS FOR CHAPTER 11 (*Page 442*)

1 $1 - 6i$ **2** $43 + 23i$ **3** $-\dfrac{13}{41} + \dfrac{47}{41}i$ **4** $\dfrac{3}{25} + \dfrac{4}{25}i$ **5** $x = \dfrac{5}{4} \pm \dfrac{\sqrt{7}}{4}i$

6 $z = \dfrac{1}{2}\left(\cos\dfrac{\pi}{6} + i\sin\dfrac{\pi}{6}\right), w = 2\left(\cos\dfrac{2\pi}{3} + i\sin\dfrac{2\pi}{3}\right), \dfrac{z}{w} = \dfrac{1}{4}\cos\left(\dfrac{3\pi}{2} + i\sin\dfrac{3\pi}{2}\right)$

7 $\dfrac{1}{32}\left(\cos\dfrac{5\pi}{6} + i\sin\dfrac{5\pi}{6}\right) = -\dfrac{\sqrt{3}}{64} + \dfrac{1}{64}i$

8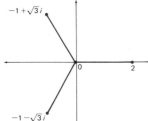

9 $2\left(\cos\dfrac{3\pi}{16} + i\sin\dfrac{3\pi}{16}\right), 2\left(\cos\dfrac{11\pi}{16} + i\sin\dfrac{3\pi}{16}\right), 2\left(\cos\dfrac{19\pi}{16} + i\sin\dfrac{19\pi}{16}\right), 2\left(\cos\dfrac{27\pi}{16} + i\sin\dfrac{27\pi}{16}\right)$

10 (a) $(-3, -300°)$; (b) $(3, 240°)$. **11** (a) $\left(\dfrac{\sqrt{3}}{6}, \dfrac{1}{6}\right)$, (b) $\left(14, \dfrac{5\pi}{4}\right)$.

12 $x^2 + (y - 1)^2 = 1$; a circle with radius 1 and center $(0, 1)$ in rectangular coordinates.

13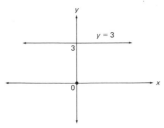

14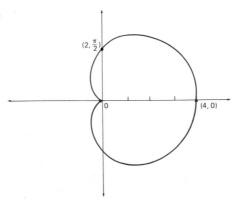

15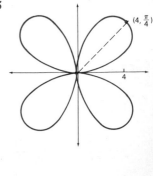

INDEX

Numbers:
  complex, 409
  counting, 7
  imaginary, 409
  irrational, 9
  natural, 7
  ordered pair, 88, 427
  pure imaginary, 410
  rational, 8, 206
  real, 1, 9, 410
  triangular, 381

O

One-to-one:
  correspondence, 1
  function, 243, 252
Order:
  properties, 17
  rules of, 18
  transitive property, 18
Ordered pair of numbers, 88, 427
Ordinate, 88
Origin, 87

P

Parabola, 134
  axis of symmetry, 134
  directrix, 171
  focus, 171
  maximum value, 150
  minimum value, 150
  vertex, 134
  x-intercepts, 144, 147, 148
Parallel lines, 95, 97
Parallelogram rule, 417, 422
Partial fractions, 209
Pascal's triangle, 76
Perfect trinomial square, 63
Period, 333
  of cosecant function, 347
  of cosine function, 335
  of cotangent function, 345
  of secant function, 346
  of sine function, 333
  of tangent function, 344
Perpendicular lines, slope of, 95, 97
Pi (π), 9
Point-slope form of a line, 100
Polar axis, 427
Polar coordinates, 427
Polar coordinate system, 427
Polar equations, 433
Polar grid system, 437
Pole, 427
Polynomial:
  coefficients, 52
  degree, 52
  equation, 205
  factored form, 57

function, 184
fundamental operations, 52
standard form, 52
terms, 52
Positive integers, 8
Principal argument, 419
Principal nth root, 42
Principle of mathematical induction, 403
Problem solving, 14–16, 111, 151–153,
    191–192, 194–196, 269–270, 277,
    299–300, 319–320, 393–394
Problem solving, guidelines for, 15, 299
Product formulas, 361
Properties:
  of absolute value, 26–30
  of addition, 12
  of b^x, 252
  of e^x, 264
  of $\ln_x$, 264
  of $\log_b x$, 255
  of multiplication, 12
  of order, 17
  of real numbers, 1–5
Proportion property, 189
Pure imaginary numbers, 410
Pythagorean theorem, 9

Q

Quadrantal angle, 307
Quadrants, 87
Quadratic equation, 146
Quadratic formula, 146
Quadratic functions, 133
  application, 150
Quadratic inequality, 148
Quotient(s), 199
  of complex numbers, 413, 421
  difference, 85
  of functions, 233
  of integers, 8

R

Radian, 291
Radical(s), 42
  rules for, 43
  simplifying, 48
Radical equation, 224
Radical function(s), 219
  graphing, 219–222
  signs, 229
Radical sign, 42
Radicand, 43
Radius, 155
Range, 82
Ratio, common, 390
Rational exponents, 45
Rational expression, 67, 180
  fundamental operations, 67